1 MONTH OF
FREE
READING

at

www.ForgottenBooks.com

By purchasing this book you are eligible for one month membership to ForgottenBooks.com, giving you unlimited access to our entire collection of over 1,000,000 titles via our web site and mobile apps.

To claim your free month visit:

www.forgottenbooks.com/free148175

ISBN 978-1-5281-8493-9
PIBN 10148175

For support please visit www.forgottenbooks.com

REPORTS

OF

CASES ARGUED AND DETERMINED

IN THE

High Court of Chancery,

FROM THE YEAR M DCC LXXXIX TO M DCCC XVII.

WITH A DIGESTED INDEX.

BY FRANCIS VESEY, JUN. ESQ.

OF LINCOLN'S INN, BARRISTER AT LAW.

In Twenty Volumes.

VOL. VI.

COMMENCING IN THE SITTINGS BEFORE EASTER TERM, XLI GEO. III, ENDING IN
THE SITTINGS BEFORE EASTER TERM, XLII GEO. III.

FROM THE LAST LONDON EDITION, WITH THE NOTES OF FRANCIS VESEY, JUN. ESQ.
AND THE EXTENSIVE ANNOTATIONS OF JOHN E. HOVENDEN, ESQ.
OF GRAY'S INN, BARRISTER AT LAW.

THE WHOLE EDITED,

WITH NOTES AND REFERENCES TO AMERICAN LAW,

AND SUBSEQUENT ENGLISH DECISIONS,

BY

CHARLES SUMNER, ESQ.

Omne jus, quod est certum, aut scripto, aut moribus constat. Dubium æquitatis regula examinandum est. Quæ scripta sunt, aut posita in more civitatis, nullam habent difficultatem: cognitionis sunt enim, non inventionis. At quæ consultorum responsis explicantur, aut in verborum interpretatione sunt posita, aut in recti pravique discrimine............ Quintilian, de Jure Civili.

BOSTON:

CHARLES C. LITTLE AND JAMES BROWN.

M DCCC XLIV.

BOSTON:
C. HICKLING'S STEAM-POWER PRESS,
DEVONSHIRE STREET.

TABLE

OF

THE CASES REPORTED IN VOLUME SIX.

DOUBLY ARRANGED.

N. B.—" VERSUS" ALWAYS FOLLOWS THE NAME OF THE PLAINTIFF.

TABLE

OF

CASES CITED IN VOLUME SIX.

MANUSCRIPT, AND THOSE IN PRINT, IMPEACHED, CORRECTED, OR OTHERWISE
PARTICULARLY NOTICED.

———

THIS TABLE DOES NOT EMBRACE THE CASES CITED BY THE EDITORS.

———

STATUTES CITED IN VOLUME SIX.

CASES IN CHANCERY, ETC.

THE SITTINGS AFTER EASTER TERM.

[41 Geo. III. 1801.]

Lord Chancellor, Lord ELDON. *Master of the Rolls*, Sir RICHARD
PEPPER ARDEN ; Sir WILLIAM GRANT—*appointed in the Vacation after Easter Term. Attorney General*, Sir EDWARD LAW.
Solicitor General, Sir WILLIAM GRANT ; The Hon. SPENCER
PERCEVAL.

IN BANKRUPTCY.

[1801.]

THE Lord CHANCELLOR [ELDON] took the first occasion of expressing strong indignation at the frauds committed under cover of the Bankrupt laws, and his determination to repress such practices. Upon this subject his Lordship observed, that the abuse of the Bankrupt law is a disgrace to the country ; and it would be better at once to repeal all the statutes than to suffer them to be applied to such purposes. There is no mercy to the estate. Nothing is less thought of than the object of the commission. As they are frequently conducted in the country, they are little more than stock in trade for the commissioners, the assignees, and the solicitor. Instead of solicitors attending to their duty as ministers of the Court, for they are so, commissions of bankruptcy are treated as matter of traffic: A. taking out the commission ; B. and C. to be his commissioners. They are considered as stock in trade ; and calculations are made, how many commissions can be brought into the partnership. Unless the Court holds a * strong hand over bank-   [* 2] ruptcy, particularly as administered in the country, it is itself accessary to as great a nuisance as any known in the land ; and known to pass under the forms of its law. The punishment of the solicitor by striking him off the roll is rendered merely nominal, by the common practice of others lending their names. It is too hastily taken for granted, that the solicitor is entitled to his bill. In one Court of Westminster Hall it was held, that if a solicitor undertakes to bring an action, or do any business, part of the undertaking is, that he shall faithfully and honestly bring that business to a conclusion; and if he fails in that, he cannot bring an action for any thing (1).

His Lordship added, that he was determined to make the officers of this Court responsible to the justice of the country for their dealings in this Court; and declared, with reference to the practice of lending a name to a person forbid by the Court to take out a commission, that he would not hesitate to strike a solicitor off the roll, who dares to lend his name to a person under such an interdict; and for that reason alone: but he would go farther; and whenever a case of this nature should be brought forward, would direct the Attorney General to prosecute for conspiracy; for no worse conspiracy can be than that, the object of which is to make what the Legislature intended as a lenient process against the bankrupt a mode of defrauding the creditors and the bankrupt (2).

The paper of petitions in bankruptcy afforded too much foundation for these remarks. In *Ex parte Stevens* (3), and *Ex parte Kirshaw* (4), the object of the petitions was to supersede commissions of the description alluded to by the Lord Chancellor. In the latter the commission was taken out after a general assignment for the benefit of all the creditors; the effects were not above 80 or 90*l.*; and the petitioning creditor at first swore to a debt for goods sold and delivered, and afterwards stated it to be money lent. The Lord Chancellor ordered, that the petition should stand over, and that the solicitor, who sued out the commission, should, if he thought fit, state by affidavit, how he came to permit the petitioning creditor to make that mistake in swearing to his debt; and what object he had in suing out the commission. A similar order was made in
[* 3]   the other petition; and * his Lordship declared, that upon
a commission so suspicious in its circumstances, he should always expect the solicitor to give an account of his conduct. The solicitors in these commissions having accordingly made affidavits in some degree exculpating themselves, the commissions were superseded at the expense of the respective petitioning creditors; and it was ordered, that the proceedings should be kept in the office, and the bonds assigned.

In *Ex parte Blackmore*(5), the bankrupt was a Lieutenant-Colo-

---

(1) *Post, Merryweather* v. *Mellish,* vol. xiii. 161, and the note, 162; *Cresswell* v. *Byron,* xiv. 273; 1 Sid. 31; 1 Tidd's Pract. 112; Beames on Costs, 281, 2.
(2) *Ex parte Cawthorne, post,* vol. xix. 260.
(3) April 25th, June 6th, 1801; *Ex parte Thorpe, ante,* vol. i. 304.
(4) May 4th, 9th, 1801.
(5) June 6th, 1801.

nel of the Fencible Cavalry, and the petitioning creditor a Clergy-man; and the trading was by dealing in horses. The Lord Chancellor reprobated the commission, as the result of a most dishonest transaction, effected by procuring poor, ignorant, marksmen to swear to the trading, &c.; and refused to permit the petitioning creditor to try the bankruptcy, unless he or the solicitor would previously satisfy the Court by affidavit, that they had made due inquiry with regard to the effects, the nature of the trading, and the other circumstances.

With respect to the trading his Lordship said, that if they could bring it to the case of the inn-keeper (1), that a jury could infer from some acts of selling, that he meant to sell more, so as to constitute a general dealing, neither his situation in the army nor any other would prevent the effect of the bankrupt laws: but it could not be maintained, that if he bought a horse, and sent him to Tattersal's with the hope of getting a guinea or two more, that would make him a trader; or his buying horses for his regiment, to make it look well. The laws were never meant to attach upon such occasional transactions; and the affidavit, upon which the bankruptcy was found, could not for an instant stand an examination at *nisi prius.*

In *Ex parte Edwards* (2) also the circumstances called forth the strong animadversion of the Court. The commission was taken out in the country. One of the commissioners, who was a barrister, resident in the country, and two of the assignees, one of whom was also, the solicitor, who sued out the commission, were partners in a country * bank; into which the money received under   [*4] the bankruptcy was paid; and an account was opened with the solicitor, as assignee, commencing in 1795, and continuing down to 1801; at which period the firm of the bank was reduced to the gentleman acting as commissioner; all of the other partners having retired. The third assignee was a customer of the bank. The solicitor was in October 1797, under an order of the Lord Chancellor, discharged from the situation of assignee; but the balances were afterwards carried to his account. The petition was presented by the new assignees; praying, that the solicitor and the other partners in the bank may be ordered to pay the respective balances due to the estate, and the costs.

The Lord CHANCELLOR [ELDON] expressed strong disapprobation of the manner, in which this commission was conducted, and especially of the union of the characters of banker, commissioner, solicitor, and assignee; observing, that it is a most unwholesome practice to permit an assignee to be removed as upon his own consent, when the Court ought to remove him by its own act, upon motives of a different and a higher nature; and referring to the rule of Courts of

(1) *Saunderson* v. *Rowles*, 4 Burr. 2064; *Buscall* v. *Hogg*, 3 Wils. 146; *Patman* v. *Vaughan*, 1 Term Rep. B. R. 572.
(2) June 22d, July 3d, 1801. See *post*, *Ex parte Lacey*, 625; *Ex parte Bennett*, vol. x. 381.

law, founded upon very good sense, that an attorney shall not have his name struck off the roll upon his own application without an affidavit, that he does not apply under an apprehension, that an application will be made against him for that purpose (1). His Lordship farther declared, that assignees are chargeable with interest, upon all the principles of the Court, if they do not actively bring forward their accounts for the inspection of the commissioners, without waiting for an application.

The petition was ordered to stand over, for the purpose of giving to the commissioner and the solicitor an opportunity of showing cause by affidavit, why an order should not be made, that no future commission should be directed to the former, and that the latter should never be permitted to take out another commission. Afterwards upon their affidavits that order was made against the solicitor only. The commissioner was ordered to pay costs (2).

[* 5]   * In Michaelmas Term the Lord Chancellor took notice, that the order (3), requiring two barristers in every country commission, had been evaded by putting in the names of two barristers residing in town, who cannot attend ; and directed, that when the name of any barrister residing in town shall be put into a country commission, it shall be attended with a certificate to the Great Seal, that he proposes to act in that commission.

In *Ex parte Gibson* (4) the bankrupt was an attorney : but the commission was taken out against him by the description of a cheesemonger. The object of the petition was to stay the certificate ; suggesting, that the creditors of the bankrupt might not know him by the character, under which he was described. Afterwards, on the bankrupt's paying a sum of money, the petition was withdrawn.

The Lord CHANCELLOR expressed strong disapprobation of the conduct of the solicitors for the petition : and ordered the petition to stand over, and advertisements to be inserted for the creditors. When the petition came on again, his Lordship directed, as a general order, that no petition presented to stay a certificate shall ever be withdrawn without the leave of the Court ; adding, that the parties should swear, there were none of these transactions. His Lordship farther intimated, that though there is no authority, that a sum of money given to withdraw an opposition to a certificate will vitiate the certificate in the same manner as money given to obtain it, that should be considered ; and also how the money paid by the bankrupt should be restored to him ; which certainly ought in some way to be effected. The petition was therefore ordered again to stand over. On the 11th of February, the order was made, that the

---

(1) That practice has been adopted by the Lord Chancellor in the case of a solicitor. *Post, Ex parte Owen*, 11 ; *Ex parte Foley*, vol. viii. 33.

(2) Commissioners of bankruptcy, though not generally charged with costs, may be ordered to pay costs in respect of conduct out of the course of their duty as commissioners. *Ex parte Searth, post,* vol. xiv. 204 ; xv. 293.

(3) See the order, *ante*, at the beginning of the 5th volume.

(4) January 25th, 1802.

bankrupt should have his certificate, without prejudice to any application as to the money so paid by him.

That assignees under a commission of bankruptcy, or agents concerned in the sale, cannot purchase for their own benefit either any part of the estate of the bankrupt or a creditor's rights to the dividends, see *Ex parte Reynolds, ante* Vol. V. 707 ; *post, Ex parte Hughes, Ex parte Lyon, Ex parte Lacey,* 617, 625.

SEE, *ante,* the note to *Ex parte Thorpe,* 1 V. 394. Many ameliorations of the bankrupt code, both as to principle and practice, have been effected by the statute 6 Geo. IV. c. 15, which consolidates nearly the whole of the previous enactments on the subject : but it is understood, the act cited is about to receive amendments. With a view to prevent improper petitions in bankruptcy, a general order, bearing date August the 12th, 1809, has been issued, directing that "the signature of each person signing as a petitioner shall be attested by the solicitor actually presenting the petition, or by some person who shall state himself in his attestation to be the attorney, solicitor, or agent of the party signing, *in the matter of the petition.*" This order obviously contains provisions applicable to two distinct cases ; and it has been determined, that where the signature of the petitioner is attested by the solicitor actually presenting the petition, there no particular form of attestation is required, provided distinct proof be given that the petition is in fact presented by the same solicitor who attested it : but where the signature is attested by some other person than the solicitor who presents it, the attestation should describe the attesting party as being the agent of the party signing, in the matter of the petition. *Ex parte Wilkinson,* 1 Glyn & Jameson, 354 ; *Ex parte Rawlinson,* 1 Glyn & Jameson, 19. A declaration, made on the 6th of February, 1816, by Lord Eldon, has been stuck up in the office of the secretary of bankrupts, announcing that the attestation of the signature of petitioners was to be strictly according to the directions of the order above cited. This declaration was subsequent to the occasion upon which his Lordship said, that as the object was to have the pledge and responsibility of a solicitor of the Court to the propriety of the application, he thought the spirit of the order was sufficiently complied with, when the signature of the petitioner purported to be "authenticated," not "attested," by his solicitor, who had not witnessed the signing, but put his name to the instrument from his knowledge of the petitioner's hand-writing. *Ex parte Titley,* 4 Rose, 84. This authority, (notwithstanding the subsequent declaration above stated,) Sir Thomas Plumer held to be decisive, that a petition might be attested by the agent of the petitioner's attorney, and would be valid if the hand-writing of the petitioner were "authenticated" by the attorney employed by the petitioner. *Ex parte Bellott,* 2 Mad. 261. But Sir John Leach expressed, in *Ex parte Bury,* Buck, 394, and in *Ex parte Dumbell,* 2 Glyn & Jameson, 121, acted upon an opinion, that as *attestation* is a legal expression, and has in Courts of law a certain definite meaning attached to it, whilst *authentication* has not the same meaning, and is not a technical definite word, the intention of the Lord Chancellor, in *Ex parte Titley,* must have been to relieve against the mistake in that particular case, and not to establish, as a general rule, that authentication is equivalent to attestation. And clearly the attestation of the *solicitor's agent* alone, if the signature to the petition be not authenticated by the solicitor employed by the petitioner, is not a compliance with the general order. *Ex parte Weston,* 1 Mad. 75 ; *Ex parte Hirst,* 1 Glyn & Jameson, 77. A solicitor who presents an improper petition in bankruptcy may be made to pay the costs attending it ; it is not, however, to be understood that, the solicitor is answerable for the success of a petition ; for the facts may have been misrepresented to him, or the law of the case may not have been clear : the order is directed only against solicitors who present petitions with fraudulent or interested views. *Ex parte Cuthbert,* 1 Mad. 79. Of course, where a solicitor presents a petition on his own account, he cannot attest his own signature, and the order does not apply. *Ex parte Kingdon,* 1 Mad. 446.

LORD ASHBURTON *v.* LADY ASHBURTON.

[1801, APRIL 20.]

PERSONAL property of an infant ordered to be laid out in the purchase of land; though there was no authority in the will for changing the nature of the property: but it was ordered, that the estate purchased should be conveyed in trust for the infant, his executors and administrators, till he should attain twenty-one, and afterwards for him and his heirs (*a*).

LORD ASHBURTON by his will, dated the 4th of April, 1780, taking notice, that he had engaged to settle 1000*l.* a-year by way of jointure on Lady Ashburton, directed an investment in the funds or other securities for that purpose ; and not then having any issue he declared, that he left his real property to descend to his sister ; and his personal estate he gave to his father, in case he should survive him (the testator) ; if not, then to his sister.

By a codicil, dated the 31st of October, 1781, taking notice of the death of his father and the birth of a son, the testator gave directions for the maintenance and education of his son ; and as to his real estate, which would descend to his son, desired it might be under the care and management of his executors and guardians of his son ; and, after giving 5000*l.* to his sister in addition to his note for that sum, he gave all the residue of his personal estate to his executors, in trust to place out the same and the rents and profits of his real estate in real or government securities, as they should from time to time judge best, during his son's minority ; and out of the produce thereof or of any real estate to pay what they should judge proper for his maintenance and education ; the whole surplus to accumulate during his minority ; and upon his attaining the age of twenty-one to pay, assign, and transfer, the whole principal and interest to him or his order : but in case he should die under age, and the testator should have no other child, who should attain that age, he gave his wife, if then living, 20,000*l*, in lieu of her annuity, or 10,000*l.* in addition, at her option, and the whole residue with the accumulations to his sister.

By another codicil, dated the 1st of June, 1783, the testator taking notice of the death of his eldest son, and having a second, substituted him for the other with the same disposition over.

The testator died soon afterwards, possessed of very large property in the funds ; leaving issue the present Lord Ashburton, the son mentioned in the second codicil ; who when of the age of

---

(*a*) Guardians will not ordinarily be permitted to change the personal property of the infant into real property, or the real into personalty ; since it may not only affect the rights of the infant himself, but also of his representatives, if he should die under age. It is common for them to ask the positive sanction of the Court to any acts of this sort. And when the Court directs any such change of property, it directs the new investment to be in trust for the benefit of those, who would be entitled to it, if it had remained. in its original state. 2 Story, Eq. Jur. § 1357. In this respect the Court acts differently in cases of infancy, from what it does in lunacy.

eighteen, presented a petition, suggesting an opportunity of laying out a considerable part of the said sums in the purchase of lands in the county of Devon, where all the rest of the petitioner's landed property lies; and praying, that he may be at liberty, when and as convenient purchases may offer, to lay proposals before the Master for investing the funds in land.

Mr. *Romilly*, in support of the Petition.

The Lord CHANCELLOR [ELDON] asked, whether there was any instance in which the Court took upon itself to change the nature of the property in such a case, where there was no clause in the will authorising it.

Mr. *Alexander* (*amicus curiæ*) said, he had known orders upon this subject at the Rolls; and mentioned one case; in which the land purchased was directed to be conveyed to a trustee, in trust for the person interested, his executors and administrators, until he should attain the age of 21, and afterwards for him and his heirs.

The Lord CHANCELLOR approved that qualification: and made the order accordingly (1).

SEE note 2 to *Lord Compton* v. *Oxenden*, 2 V. 265.

LYTTLETON, *Ex parte.*

[1801, APRIL 20.]

ACCESS to a lunatic by a person entitled upon the death of the lunatic in default of appointment by her, to see, whether she was in a state to exercise the power, refused.

ONE object of this petition in lunacy was, that the petitioner, who was entitled upon the death of the lunatic, in case she should not exercise a power of appointment, might have access to the lunatic, either personally or by physicians, for the purpose of seeing, whether she was in a state to make an appointment,

Mr *Agar*, in support of the Petition.

The Lord CHANCELLOR [ELDON] asked whether there was any instance of an order for access to the lunatic upon the principle of *quia timet*; and, no instance being produced, his Lordship refused the *application; observing, that such a visit may [*8] be very dangerous, and have a very bad effect in irritating the mind of the lunatic from the mere purpose of the visit without any intention of producing that effect.

SEE the concluding part of note 5 to *Ex parte Wragg*, 5 V. 452.

(1) *Post*, vol. xi. 278; 2 Atk. 413; *Gibson* v. *Scudamore*, 1 Dick. 45.

application for this purpose is too late. The bond contained a submission to have the award made a rule of Court.

Mr. *Stanley,* in support of the motion, admitted, that the words of the act (1) are future; but said, this objection had not been taken.

Mr. *Pemberton,* for the Defendant, consented to the motion.

Lord CHANCELLOR [ELDON].—The constant practice of both Courts of Law for years has been against this objection: but I am afraid, a decision of that kind is not sufficient to overrule a decision of the Court, where the objection was made. I will look into this case. My present inclination is this: the Court can take no jurisdiction but in the cases, in which the act gives it jurisdiction: but I have always understood, that if the submission bears date before the award, the Court will act upon that submission. The consent cannot give the Court a jurisdiction, the Act of Parliament does not give it.

April 22d. Lord CHANCELLOR.—It seems to me, that this submission may be made a rule of the Court: 1st, it is not inconsistent with the words of the statute; 2dly, I think, the case in Peere Williams does not necessarily decide the point supposed to be decided; and in *Alardes* v. *Campbell* (2) the objection was taken, that the submission was made a rule of Court after the award; and the Court treated *it as a point of no difficulty; considering it as no objection within the statute, and according to the constant practice; and in *Chicot* v. *Lequesne* (3) it is considered by Lord Hardwicke as the constant practice. Independent of that, I think, by the consent of the parties this might be made a rule of the Court; to bě enforced, not perhaps by the process under the statute, but by the common process of the Court.

[* 11]

———

IT is quite settled, in accordance with the principal case, that a submission to arbitration may be made a rule of *Court,* after the award has been completed. *Fetherstone* v. *Cooper,* 9 Ves. 67; *Smith* v. *Symes,* 5 Mad. 75.

———

(1) 9 & 10 Will. III. c. 15.
(2) 1 Barnard Rep. K. B. 152.
(3) 2 Ves. 315; *Fetherstone* v. *Cooper, post,* vol. ix. 67; *Smith* v. *Symes,* 5 Madd. 75.

OWEN, *Ex parte.*

[1801, April 24.]

THE Court will not strike a solicitor off the roll at his own request without an affidavit, that there is no other reason for the application.

MR. OWEN moved, as of course, that a solicitor may be struck off the roll at his own request.

Lord CHANCELLOR [ELDON].—That will not do without an affidavit, that there is no other reason for it; for a solicitor apprehending, that an application will be made against him, may desire to be struck off the roll. Therefore the Courts of Law have required ˙ upon an application by an attorney to be struck off the roll, that they shall be satisfied, there is no other reason; and I shall accordingly require an affidavit, that he does not apply under an apprehension that somebody else will.

 Mr. *Owen* said, there was not the least ground for such an apprehension in this instance: this gentleman had not practised for two years; and made the application with a view to be called to the Bar.

Lord CHANCELLOR said, for that reason he should the more require the affidavit; for, when it is insisted on in such a case, no objection can be made in any other (1).

———

THE rule laid down in the principal case, was followed in *Ex parte Foley*, 8 Ves. 33; and see the " Regulations in Bankruptcy," 6 Ves. 4.

---

(1) *Ex parte Foley, post*, vol. viii. 33; *ante*, 4.

COOTH v. JACKSON.

[1800, Jan. 29.   1801, April 28, 29.]

To a bill for specific performance of an agreement a plea of the statute of frauds, being coupled with another defence, was ordered to stand till the hearing.

Bill for specific performance of an agreement, originating in communications by the commissioners, who took the depositions in a cause, and by the witnesses, to the Defendant as to the nature and effect of the evidence. Though the Plaintiff was not implicated in the transaction, the bill was dismissed on grounds of public policy (a).

Lord Loughborough's opinion, that upon a bill for specific performance of a parol agreement within the statute of frauds, the Defendant, though admitting the agreement by his answer, may, if he insists upon the statute, have the benefit of it at the hearing (b), [p. 17.]

Whether bonds of arbitration are sufficient to take the case of an agreement out of the Statute of Frauds, Quære (c), [p. 17.]

The execution of the commission in a cause is the act of the Court, carried on by its ministers, [p. 30.]

Witnesses ought not to disclose their evidence to parties, [p. 33.]

Upon a reference to arbitration, if the award is not made in the time and manner stipulated, no case at law or in equity, that the Court has substituted itself for the arbitrators, and made the award; even where the substantial thing to be done is agreed between the parties: still less, where any thing substantial is to be settled by the arbitrators, [p. 34.]

Lord Eldon's opinion, that a specific performance of a parol agreement cannot be decreed, though the agreement is admitted by the answer; if the Defendant insists upon the Statute of Frauds: if he does not, he must be taken to renounce the benefit of it, [p. 37.]

Distinction in the administration of law and equity in this country by different Courts; and consequences of that distinction, [p. 39.]

In Equity the denial of a parol agreement within the Statute of Frauds by the answer is conclusive, [p. 39.]

In Equity against the answer there can be no decree upon the testimony of a single witness, unless supported by special circumstances (d), [p. 40.]

Upon a parol agreement for a compromise and a division of the estate by arbitration acts done by arbitrators towards the execution of their duty, as surveying, &c. cannot be considered acts of part-performance to sustain the agreement (e), [p. 41.]

(a) Agreements founded upon violations of public trust, or of the rules adopted by Courts in furtherance of the administration of justice, are held void. 1 Story, Eq. Jur. § 294.

(b) There has been on this question a great conflict of judicial opinion; but the doctrine seems to be firmly established, that even where the answer confesses the parol agreement, if it insists, by way of defence, upon the protection of the statute, the defence must prevail as a competent bar. See ante, note (a), Moore v. Edwards, 4 V. 23.

As to the effect of admission of a parol agreement, see ante, note (a) to Hare v. Shearwood, 1 V. 241; to Brodie v. St. Paul, 1 V. 326.

(c) See 2 Stephens, Nisi Prius, 1985.

(d) For the reason of this rule, and its recognition in the United States, see ante, note (b), Mortimer v. Orchard, 2 V. 243.

(e) In order to make the acts such as a Court of Equity will deem part-performance of an agreement within the statute, it is essential, that they should clearly appear to be done solely with a view to the agreement being performed. If they are acts, which might have been done with other views, they will not take the case out of the statute, since they cannot properly be said to be done by way of part-performance of the agreement. On this account, acts merely introductory or ancillary to an agreement, are not considered as a part-performance thereof, although

THE bill stated, that in 1795 a bill was filed by the Plaintiff Edmund Cooth against the Reverend Richard Jackson and the Reverend Gilbert Jackson, the latter being the only son and heir of Gilbert Jackson, the surviving trustee in a marriage settlement, under which the Plaintiff claimed premises, called Lye Farm and Burnthouse Farm, by virtue of a limitation in remainder, subject to the life estate of Richard Jackson, and in default of issue of him and his wife, for the benefit of John Cooth, the Plaintiff's father, deceased, and the heirs of his body.   That bill stated, that all the children of Richard Jackson died in their infancy without issue, and then his wife died without leaving any issue; and Richard Jackson continued in possession.   He and his wife soon after their marriage levied a fine; and declared the uses in failure of issue of them to the survivor.

The bill farther stated, that Gilbert Jackson acknowledged to the Plaintiff, that such settlement was in his possession; and Richard Jackson, after the decease of his wife, wrote several letters acknowledging that he was entitled only for life; and that after his death Cooth would be entitled; and he also acknowledged, that he had accepted from Charles Cooth, the Plaintiff's elder brother, who died without issue, a mortgage of the reversion for money lent.   The bill also stated, that Richard Jackson endeavored to get Charles Cooth to execute a will in his favor; and never suggested, that any settlement was in existence, or that any fine had been levied to bar the limitations thereof; and he never set up any claim under the fine until after the death of the trustees in the settlement, and until after Richard and Gilbert Jackson had got both parts of the said marriage settlement into their hands, and suppressed the same.   The bill prayed a discovery; and that the defendant might be decreed to leave the settlement in the hands of the Master; and that the right of the Plaintiff might be declared.

The bill farther stated, that to that bill the Defendant put in an answer; and afterwards, upon the 19th of September, 1796, Richard Jackson died; having devised the estate to Gilbert Jackson; who *was also his nephew and heir at law.   A bill   [* 13] of revivor and supplement was filed; stating the above matters; and that Gilbert Jackson possessed himself of the settlement; and prayed accordingly.   An answer was put in to that bill; and a commission issued, directed to Thomas Bartlett and Thomas Gould Reade, commissioners named on the part of the Plaintiff, and to James Still and Joseph Charles Still, commissioners named on the part of the Defendant.   The three commissioners first mentioned met and executed the commission upon the 30th and 31st of October, 1798; and the examination was made up and closed, but never returned.   After all the witnesses were examined, the Defendant proposed a compromise by dividing the said farms and lands; the Plaintiff accepted the proposal; and it was thereupon agreed, that the

_____

they should be attended with expense.   2 Story, Eq. Jur. § 762; *Phillips* v. *Thompson*, 1 Johns. Ch. 149; *Parkhurst* v. *Van Cortlandt*, 1 Johns. Ch. 283.   See *ante*, note (a) to *Willes* v. *Stradling*, 3 V., 378.

Plaintiff should take the whole Burnthouse farm and so much of the Lye farm as should make up an equivalent to a moiety of the whole, and that the Defendant should retain the remainder ; and it was farther agreed that the commissioners should not return the commission ; and that all proceedings in the suit should cease. Upon the said agreement being concluded the Defendant and Plaintiff named Bartlett, Reade, and James Still, to divide and allot the said farms and lands between Jackson and the Plaintiff in manner afore- said, and to arbitrate and settle all matters between them incident to such division and allotment. Bartlett, Reade, and Still accepted the appointment of arbitrators, and undertook to divide and allot said farms and lands, as aforesaid ; and mutual bonds of arbitration were executed to abide by and perform the award and final determi- nation of the said arbitrators.

The bill farther stated, that though the bonds purported to be to submit to the award of the arbitrators to be made of all matters in difference, yet they were intended to relate to their division of the said farms, &c. between the Plaintiff and Jackson ; all other matters, which had been in difference between them, being at that time ended by the aforesaid agreement; and the bonds were executed for no other purpose than to bind them to abide by the allotment and division of the said farms, &c. in pursuance and part-performance of the said agreement, the said commission so made up and closed by the said commissioners hath never been returned ; and in farther pursuance of the said agreement the 14th of November, 1798, was appointed for a meeting of Bartlett, Reade, and Still,
[* 14]   * to proceed to make the allotment, &c. of the said premises as aforesaid, and to make their award upon said arbitration : and in the mean time Still, Bartlett, and Reade, but particularly Still, went over the whole of the premises ; and formed an estimate of the value; and marked out part of the Lye farm, to be allotted and added to the Burnthouse farm, &c. ; but Bartlett and Reade mistook the day ; and in consequence did not attend the meeting: but it was attended by Still and the Plaintiff. The meeting was adjourned to the 22d of December, 1798; and in the mean time Still, Bartlett, and Reade, caused the lands to be surveyed and val- ued, for the purpose of making their award and concluding said business upon the said 22d of December, 1798. They did meet ac- cordingly ; the Plaintiff was present: but Jackson did not come ; and they were ready to settle the allotment and division, and make their award ; but Jackson caused his solicitor to write to the arbitra- tors, that he should not abide by their award; which letters they received a few days before the 22d of December. The meeting was therefore adjourned to the 31st of December. Notice in writing, signed by the arbitrators, was given to Jackson ; but before that day he prevailed upon Still to refuse joining in the award ; and he in- formed the other arbitrators he would not join, and should not attend. The other two arbitrators met on that day, but as Still did not attend, no award was made.

The bill then stating, that the plaintiff was always ready to perform his part, prayed, that the Defendant may be decreed to perform the agreement: and that the said two farms may be divided into two equal parts; and that the Burnthouse farm, with so much of the other farm as shall render the same of equal value with the remainder of the latter, may be decreed to the Plaintiff; with the necessary directions, and a production of all title-deeds.

To this bill the Defendant put in the following plea and answer.

As to so much of the bill as seeks, that the Defendant may be decreed to perform the agreement alleged, &c., and that the said two farms may be divided into two equal parts, and that the Burnthouse farm, and so much of the Lye farm as shall together be equal to the remainder of the Lye farm, may be decreed to belong to the Plaintiff and his heirs, and a * commission for   [* 15] making such division, with the necessary directions for that purpose, and that the title deeds and writings relating to the said estates may be produced and left with the Master, or any other relief founded upon the said agreement, the Defendant pleaded in bar the statute of Frauds (1); with an averment that there was no contract in writing concerning any division of the said two farms, &c.

The Defendant admitted the proceedings in the former suit; and stated, that being advised, that it was not necessary for him to produce witnesses at the execution of the commission, he attended unaccompanied by his solicitor, with James Still, one of the commissioners, named by or on behalf of the defendant. The two commissioners named by or on behalf of the Plaintiff, met them; and examined witnesses; and the commission was closed. In October, 1798, on the last day of executing the commission, after the commission was made up and closed, Smith, who had been examined as a witness for the Plaintiff, came to the Defendant, and proposed, and pressed him, as he had frequently done, to compromise the cause; intimating, that, if the cause proceeded to a hearing, such a string of evidence would be brought forward, as would ruin his uncle's (Richard Jackson) character for ever; and that a settlement of the estates in dispute had been made, which was in favor of the Plaintiff's father; and that the Defendant's said uncle and his wife had upon some occasion, made an affidavit thereof. The Defendant saying, he must take the advice of his solicitor, Smith intimated, that, if the cause was not immediately settled, the Plaintiff would probably afterwards refuse to settle it. James Still shortly afterwards called the Defendant into his room; and also recommended to him to settle the cause on account of the evidence, which he intimated to the Defendant, had been adduced on the part of the Plaintiff; and Still not having prevailed upon the Defendant to agree to settle it, Smith came again, and brought Rideout, another witness for the Plaintiff; and they pressed the Defendant with the same arguments;

---

(1) 29 Car. II. c. 3.

and particularly, that his late uncle had written several letters (which had been proved under the commission), which were in contradiction to his answer in the *cause; and that if the cause proceeded, and the letters were brought into Court, his character would be ruined.

[* 16]

During the execution of the commission Bartlett and Reade severally recommended the Defendant to compromise the suit; and the Defendant being greatly alarmed at such representations, and believing them true, though he now believes them unfounded, and being very anxious, that nothing should be brought forward, which might affect the character of his uncle, and believing, that Smith was his friend, and well acquainted with the facts urged by him, he did at length, and for such reasons, (and which otherwise he would not have done), propose to the Plaintiff and verbally agree to settle said suit, by dividing the estate in dispute between them; to which the Plaintiff acceded; and thereupon such bonds of arbitration were entered into. It was understood by the Defendant, and, as he believes, by the Plaintiff, that the basis upon which the arbitrators would proceed to settle the differences referred to them, was by making an equal division of the property in question between the Plaintiff and the Defendant; and that said bonds were intended to relate only to such division, and to bind the Defendant and the Plaintiff by such allotment and division, as said arbitrators should make between them; all other matters being then agreed to be settled between them. The Defendant did not attend the adjourned meeting. He admits the notice of the last adjournment; and that Still did not attend, and would not join in the award, in consequence of the representations made to him by and on behalf of the Defendant, and of his conviction of the impropriety of so doing; having declared to the Defendant, that he was ignorant of some important facts, when he recommended to the Defendant the compromise. It may be true, that between the time of entering the bonds and the 14th of November, 1798, the day first appointed for making the arbitration, the arbitrators, and particularly Still, did go over the premises, and value the same, and mark out great part of so much of the great farm, called Lye, as was (as is pretended by the bill) to be allotted and added to the Burnthouse farm; in order that the premises might be divided into moieties equivalent in quantity and value between the Defendant and the Plaintiff; and that between the 14th of November and the 22d of December they caused the lands to be surveyed and valued for the purpose of making the award.

The answer then insisted, that the not returning the commission and the circumstances aforesaid are not to be considered us done *in performance of the said agreement, especially as the Defendant was led to compromise the suit by such unfounded representations, so as to take the case out of the statute.

[* 17]

1800 *Jan, 29th.* This cause was set down upon the plea, which was supported by Mr. *Mansfield* and Mr. *Stratford.* The *Attorney General* [Sir *John Mitford*] and Mr. *Hart* for the Plaintiff insisted, that the agreement being admitted by the answer, and being in part performed by the Plaintiff, as far as he could perform it, by not proceeding to the examination of witnesses, the commissioners proceeding no farther, and the depositions taken not being returned, the case was not within the statute; and if the Defendant was improperly induced to come to the agreement, that is a distinct defence, and waives the benefit of the plea. The bonds of arbitration are certainly in their terms general, for all matters in dispute; but nothing remained between them but the division of the land; for it was expressly agreed the suit should be put an end to; that there should be no farther proceedings; and the land should be equally divided between them.

Lord CHANCELLOR [LOUGHBOROUGH].—This is a double defence. I cannot allow the plea of the statute, where it is coupled with another defence. There is no purpose in pleading it. He may have the benefit of the statute at the hearing. He says distinctly, he was drawn in by misrepresentation. It struck me at first, he would have done better to have demurred; for I do not conceive, how the bill can be sustained. The consequence of there being no award is, that the suit must go on. Upon the case made by this bill the strict decree would be to order another reference; for upon the state of the case there is a division to be made of the estate by giving one farm to one, another to the other, and making up the difference in value. The reference being abortive, the suit must go on.

I should not wish to decide it now: but I have great doubt, whether the executing the bonds of arbitration is not a writing. Suppose a bond of reference to a surveyor, the price to depend upon his valuation, only to ascertain, how much an acre the purchaser was to pay for the land: that I should conceive not within *the statute. There is a writing, and a solemn writ-   [* 18] ing, a deed between the parties. Then the only question is as to the object of it. It is to settle the price and terms upon an agreement concluded between the parties. I do not wish at the moment to decide it; as there is a complicated defence here; and reserving the benefit of the plea to the hearing I keep the question entire.

The plea was ordered to stand over till the hearing of the cause; and the parties went into evidence.

Reade, one of the arbitrators, by his depositions stated, that the proposal for a compromise was made by the Defendant to the Plaintiff voluntarily; and it did not appear to the deponent, that the Defendant was in any manner forced or constrained to make the same. It having been suggested by some of the friends of the Plaintiff and Defendant, after the commission was closed, that it would be for the interest of both to put an end to the dispute, it was at last proposed by the Defendant, and agreed to by the Plaintiff, that an equal division of the estate should be made; viz. that the Plaintiff should take the Burnthouse farm and so much of the Lye as should make up an equivalent to a moiety of the whole; and that the Defendant should take the remainder; and it was also agreed, that the commission should not be returned; that all proceedings should cease; and the deponent, Bartlett, and Still, were requested by the Plaintiff and the Defendant to take the charge of dividing and allotting the land in equal moieties, pursuant to the agreement; and for that purpose bonds were entered into for leaving all matters and things in dispute between the parties to their arbitration; and Still living near the spot agreed to look over the estate and make a valuation. The Defendant was neither forced nor surprised into the agreement; and next day expressed himself much satisfied at it. The purpose of executing the bonds was, that the estate should be equally divided according to the said agreement. The deponent does not know of any other matter in difference but the division and allotment of the estate.

This witness also stated the adjournment, the reason for not making the award, viz. that Still would not join, and the
[* 19]   *other circumstances, which were also proved by the other witnesses.

Charles Bowles gave the same account as Reade of the proposal for the compromise, the terms of division, &c. and that the Defendant was not forced into it. He stated, that Still proposed, that, though it might be too much trouble to make special bonds, stating all the circumstances, yet it would be better to fill up the common printed bonds to bind them to the agreement; which were provided, and filled up accordingly. It was proposed, that all the papers and pleadings in the cause should at this meeting be destroyed: but it was afterwards agreed, that they should remain, till after the division should be finally adjusted. No subject of difference remained but the allotment and division.

Bartlett stated, that, whether the proposal of the Defendant and the agreement were made freely and voluntarily, or in consequence of any recommendation to him for that purpose, or, whether he was forced or constrained, or surprised or imposed upon, in it, the deponent does not know. The next day he expressed himself satisfied with it. The deponent does not know of any thing else in dispute between the parties.

James Still, being produced as a witness for the Defendant, stated, that he and the other commissioners during the execution of the commission had frequent conversations respecting the contents of some of the late Dr. Jackson's letters; and they agreed, that, if it could be brought about it was a cause very proper to go to a reference; and he undertook to speak to the Defendant upon the subject: and accordingly went to the Defendant in a room at the inn, where the commission was executing; and mentioned to him, that it would be a very disagreeable thing for the cause to come to a hearing on account of Dr. Jackson's letters, and his answer to the bill; and upon that account advised him to consent to a reference; but used no persuasion; but recommended to him to consult his friends before he decided. The deponent believes, he did consult

Smith and Rideout; and that in consequence of the conversation with them he was induced to agree to an amicable adjustment, and make such proposal.

* Rideout deposed, that the deponent having been exam-   [* 20]
ined as a witness under the commission on the part of the
Plaintiff had divers conversations with the Defendant respecting the matters in question in the cause ; and, a compromise having been talked of, the deponent at the desire of the Defendant walked out into the town ; and the Defendant asking his opinion, he asked, whether the Defendant had consulted his commissioner, as the most proper judge.   The Defendant said, he had ; and his commissioner advised him to the compromise ; and asking the deponent, what he would do in such a case, the deponent said, he would agree to the compromise ; and in a subsequent conversation said, he should agree to the compromise, if it was only for the sake of his uncle's memory.

Smith deposed, that, the Defendant asking his advice, he repeated the same arguments and advice he often had given before, when consulted, viz. to compromise.   Upon the second day of the commission the Defendant informed him, that his commissioner Still said, he advised him to put an end to the suit; but added, "Remember, I do not persuade you."   The Defendant requested the deponent to ask Still, what he meant by the word "persuade."   Still replied, "Would he have me force him to do it?   Tell him it is my decided opinion, that he should make it up."

April 28*th*.—Upon this evidence the cause came on before Lord Eldon.

Mr. *Romilly* and Mr. *Hart*, for the Plaintiff.

This bill stands upon three points : 1st, Though the Defendant insists upon the statute by the answer, yet the admission of the parol argeement takes the case out of the statute (1): 2dly, The agreement is in part performed : 3dly, There is a sufficient agreement in writing.

The first point has been frequently discussed in this Court; but never decided.   The doubts Lord Thurlow entertained, and the declarations of Lord Hardwicke, are in opposition, to what is now supposed the Law of the Court; that a Defendant admitting a parol agreement by his answer can insist upon the statute.   The case, that approaches nearest to this point, is *Moore* v. *Edwards* (2).   The late Lord Chancellor there did not consider himself as
* deciding the point : but he stated, that it was not decid-   [* 21]
ed the other way.   The point was not expressly decided
by Lord Hardwicke : but he has said in many cases, particularly (3) in the *Attorney General* v. *Day*, that where the party admits the agreement, he shall be compelled to perform it, because there is no danger of perjury.   The same thing is stated by Sir John Strange (4)

(1) *Child* v. *Godolphin*, 1 Dick. 39.
(2) *Ante*, vol. iv. 23.
(3) 1 Ves. 221.
(4) 1 Ves. 441.

in *Potter* v. *Potter.* In *Symondson* v. *Tweed* (1) a parol agreement admitted was performed by the Court. In *Whitchurch* v. *Bevis* (2), and *Whitbread* v. *Brockhurst* (3) Lord Thurlow expressed great doubt upon this subject. The question in those cases was, whether the Defendant could be compelled to answer. Upon that his Lordship entertained great doubt. The difficulty however perhaps is not so great; for if the agreement is in part performed, then it is clear, the Court will perform it: but if the Defendant can deny the part performance in pursuance of the supposed or any other agreement, then he need not be under the necessity of answering. It is not however necessary to enter into that; for this Defendant has answered; and admitted a parol agreement. It is of very great importance, that this question upon the statute, as to the effect of such admission, should be decided. Great doubt has at different times been entertained upon it. Mr. Fonblánque in a note (4) has collected the cases upon this subject; and it does not appear there, or in another note (5) upon the same subject several years afterwards, that this point has been decided. Upon the several *dicta* of Lord Hardwicke and Sir John Strange, that, where the Defendant admits the agreement, the case is entirely out of the statute, it will be said that is confined to the case, where, admitting the agreement, he does not insist on the statute. What is the ground of that distinction? The statute is a public statute. A decision upon such grounds would create a strictness in pleading, that certainly has not prevailed, at least as to answers. The Defendant cannot be precluded from insisting upon the statute, merely because he has not stated it in his answer. The statute of limitations bears a very strict analogy to this. All a Defendant has occasion to aver is, that he has not promised within the last six years, without taking notice of the statute.

[* 22]   * This question depends upon the fourth section of the statute. That section and the seventh are of the same nature, very different from other sections requiring instruments to be executed with certain ceremonies, and destroying the instrument, if the statute in those respects is not complied with. But the fourth and seventh sections are manifestly a law of evidence. The latter has the expression "manifested and proved." Agreements have been repeatedly carried into execution, where there has been no contract in writing, but evidence in writing; as in *Tawney* v. *Crowther* (6). *Seagood* v. *Meale* (7) is the case of a letter, not to the party with whom the Defendant contracted, but to his own agent. Unquestionably that could not be more than evidence of an agreement; and Lord Hardwicke so states it. So, in the case of part perform-

(1) Pre. Ch. 374; Gilb. 35.
(2) 2 Bro. C. C. 559.
(3) 1 Bro. C. C. 404.
(4) 1 Fonbl. Treat. Eq. 1st. ed. 163, note (*d*), 171, note (*e*); 2d ed. 178, note (*d*), 182, note (*e*).
(5) *Ante,* vol. iii. 38.
(6) 3 Bro. C. C. 161, 318; *Forster* v. *Hale, ante,* vol. iii. 696; v. 308.
(7) Pre. Ch. 560.

ance; upon which the other acts. I do not find any case upon the fourth section of the statute, where the party admitted the agreement, but insisted on the statute. In *Cottington* v. *Fletcher* (1) that very point was decided upon the other section as to declarations of trust. It may be said, that if he ought to be compelled to perform the agreement, if confessed, it would be absurd not to compel him to answer to the fact of an agreement: but where is the absurdity of compelling him to answer that fact? This has been put with great force by Mr. Fonblanque; that the statute was made to prevent perjury; and as the answer cannot be falsified, there is a strong temptation to perjury; and that has been adopted in *Rondeau* v. *Wyatt* (2). The statute was certainly made to prevent perjury: but it was also made to prevent fraud by the means of perjury. The argument on the ground of avoiding the temptation to perjury would put an end to all discovery in this Court. The temptation to perjury in putting in an answer is infinitely stronger in many cases than in that of a parol agreement; as where a gross fraud is imputed to the Defendant. An answer in Chancery is in this respect just the same as a plea at law, except in the circumstance, that the former is put in on oath. It is quite clear, that, if he had denied this agreement by his answer, the Plaintiff might have produced a letter, for instance, to his agent. Suppose, in that letter he had said, he would not perform the agreement on account of the statute; can there be a doubt, that would be sufficient evidence, upon which the Court * would compel him to execute it? If   [* 23] that is so, is it not infinitely stronger, when the Defendant in his answer upon oath admits the agreement; talking however about the statute? It is supposed, that great inconvenience might follow from this; which was also said in *Whitchurch* v. *Bevis*, and *Whitbread* v. *Brockhurst:* but there is no inconvenience, even if the Plaintiff states a fictitious agreement. He must know, that he must prove, not only the circumstances of part performance, but likewise the agreement; and he could not complain, if his bill was dismissed, because he could not prove the essential part of his case. If there were a part performance, it would be clearly competent to prove the agreement.

This depends very much upon principle and general reasoning. A very high authority, Pothier, in his treatise upon Obligations, puts this case. By the French law an agreement was not binding for any sum exceeding 100 livres, unless it was in writing. Pothier says, that does not apply, where the party admits the agreement; and the other has a right to make him give his oath, whether he did enter into such agreement; this being a law of evidence. But there is an agrement in writing; and that opinion was intimated by the late Lord Chancellor [Loughborough] upon the former occasion. The answer admits, that there was no matter in dispute but the division of the estate. It has never been decided, that, where there

(1) 3 Atk. 155.
(2) 2 Hen. Black. 63.

is an ambiguity upon the face of the written agreement, which must be cleared up by evidence, you may not put questions to the Defendant as to that ambiguity. In *Brodie* v. *St. Paul* (1) it was not suggested, that, if the Defendant had admitted, that certain covenants were read, and there was no dispute about the terms, the Court would not have executed it. Suppose an ambiguity occasioned by a chasm left for the price, to be afterwards agreed upon, or to be fixed by some third person, as in a late case (2) at the Rolls; some evidence is necessary.

The circumstances of part performance are the delay, the not publishing the depositions, and not hearing the cause ; next, the executing of the bonds : the attendance of the arbitrators ; and all the trouble and expense arising from the bonds of arbitration. It is extremely difficult to say, upon what ground the cases of [*24] *part-performance have proceeded ; and it is much to be lamented, that the Court has not given the same relief in those as in other cases of fraud. But certainly they have not proceeded upon the ground of compensation, where there might be complete compensation. There can be no difference between this case and those, where upon the circumstance of possession delivered the Court has performed the whole agreement. No specific acts have been pointed out. Either acts or omissions will be sufficient to bind the conscience of the Defendant. How can the Court know the prejudice to the Plaintiff?

Lord CHANCELLOR [ELDON].—Which agreement am I to execute? The agreement proved and the agreement admitted are very different in their terms; the one leaves it to the arbitrators to divide, as they please ; the other compels them to form particular lots. Do you remember any case, in which the bill states one agreement, the answer states a different agreement, and the Plaintiff proves another agreement different from either, and that has been performed? There has been a case, in which the answer having admitted an agreement different from that stated by the bill, that has been taken up by the bill by amendment, and a performance decreed.

For the Plaintiff.—In *Mortimer* v. *Orchard* (3) one agreement was stated, another admitted, and another proved by a single witness; and the Lord Chancellor bound the Defendants by the admission.

The impropriety of commissioners disclosing the evidence must be admitted : but the Plaintiff is clear of all suspicion with respect to that. The Defendant acted under apprehensions raised by knowledge improperly obtained : but that cannot excuse him ; the Plaintiff being innocent, and not implicated in the transaction. Upon this part of the cause, in *Mortimer* v. *Capper* (4) there is a case

---

(1) *Ante,* vol. i. 326.
(2) *Emery* v. *Wase, ante,* vol. v. 846.
(3) *Ante,* vol. ii. 243.
(4) 1 Bro. C. C. 156.

cited (1) by Lord Thurlow; which, as stated in the Report, is not very intelligible; but by a manuscript note of *Mortimer* v. *Capper*, Lord Thurlow appears to have stated it thus. A common was to be enclosed. One man, having a right of common, agreed, before the commissioners had made any allotment, or any one could *know, what it was to be, to sell his allotment for   [* 25] 20*l.* Afterwards it turned out to be worth 200*l.* Sir Joseph Jekyll said, the contract ought to be enforced; as no one could know, what the allotment would be; and both parties were equally in the dark: but it might be very different, if the circumstances had been known to the Plaintiff. That case applies strongly to this. So do *Beckley* v. *Newland* (2) and *Jones* v. *Randall* (3); and if the circumstance, that the latter is the case of a wager, makes any difference, it is in favor of this Plaintiff; who having a considerable property at stake, and desirous by taking half of the estate to reduce what was uncertain to a certainty, enters into this agreement without any advantage over the other party; who, particularly when his conduct in obtaining that information from the commissioner's witnesses is considered, cannot say, this agreement was improper. It must be presumed, that he now refuses to perform it upon some farther information obtained.

Mr. *Mansfield* and Mr. *Stratford*, for the Defendant.—The most important question is, whether this agreement can be sustained by the Court; considering the manner, in which it was obtained; whether the Court will suffer its own officer in the exercise of the authority delegated to him by the Court, availing himself of the information derived thereby, to go to either party, and recommend him from what passes in the cause to settle it. The policy of the law will never permit an agreement made under such impressions to stand. The opinion and advice, under which the Defendant acted, comes from a commissioner, bound to keep it secret. He happens to be the commissioner named by the Defendant: but he is the commissioner of the Court. If commissioners can do this, what an opening for fraud and bribery! The Defendant was forced into this agreement. What stronger argument could they use? The commissioner gave his decided opinion; knowing all the evidence: this Defendant a clergyman; and no solicitor attending on his part. What imputation can there be upon the Defendant from his talking to the commissioner and the witnesses? He could not know, that it was improper. It is enough, that such attempts at subornation, &c. may be made; though no evidence of that exists in this case. The cases of wagers, &c. have no application to this. * Suppose, the arbitrators had proceeded under the   [* 26] bonds: could this parol agreement have been set up against the arbitration? The parties have appointed judges for themselves,

(1) 1 Bro. C. C. 158.
(2) 2 P. Will. 182.
(3) Cowp. 37.

and have fixed the time for making their decision. Is there any instance, where the Court has said, that, the arbitrators not having done it within the time, the Court will do it? The time is material. The Court cannot assume a jurisdiction, which the parties have given to others. The real agreement is, that it shall be referred to these persons to make the division between them. The only decree could be, that the arbitrators, though they have not proceeded to make their award within the time, shall now proceed. That would be a novel case.

With respect to the question upon the statute, there is nothing to authorise the Court to carry this agreement into execution. The reservation of the plea to the hearing furnishes a pretty strong intimation of the opinion of the Court, that this admission of a parol promise by the answer could not possibly avail against the statute. The point certainly received a very short discussion. It is said, this is only a law of evidence: but the law is positive; that no action, which must include suits in equity, shall be brought. It has been lately decided in that very strong case, *Rondeau* v. *Wyatt*, that no agreement, but one in writing, will do at law. It is said, there is no danger of perjury. There is just as little danger upon an action at law as in equity: the agreement being once admitted upon oath here. It is enough to say, the point does not appear to have been decided; and your Lordship will not make a precedent liable to such objections. But in two cases in the Court of Exchequer in 1785, *Eyre* v. *Iveson*, and *Steward* v. *Careless*, cited (1) in *Whitchurch* v. *Bevis*, that Court was of opinion, that if the Defendant insisted upon the statute by his answer, though he confessed the agreement, a specific performance could not be decreed. Observe, how this has grown to the law, as it is said. The case of *Croyston* v. *Banes* (2) makes it the indispensable ground, that the statute is not insisted on, though it is said to be a public law, &c. Such are the confused ideas entertained upon this subject. *Symondson* v. *Tweed* admits, that there never was a case upon the mere admission of a parol agreement; they all amount to nothing but declarations [* 27] of the effect of such admission: and they *are general; never stating the circumstances. These two cases show, how extremely loose the ideas of those, who took the notes, were upon this subject. It is impossible to collect any clear, plain, ground, authorising the Court to dispose of the statute in that way. In *Whitchurch* v. *Bevis* and *Whitbread* v. *Brockhurst* it is evident, the strong inclination of Lord Thurlow's opinion was, that there was no ground for those *dicta*, that the mere admission of a parol agreement without other circumstances would authorise the Court to compel a performance. Since that period the question seems to have been at rest; and it appears to have been understood, that the mere admission of a parol agreement, unless accompanied with part-perform-

---

(1) 2 Bro. C. C. 563, 564.
(2) Pre. Ch. 208.

ance, is of no more avail than at law. The cases of part-performance go upon this plain ground ; that, where the party acting under the agreement has been put to great expense, as by repairing, rebuilding, manuring, &c., improving the property of the other, the Court interposes upon the ground of gross fraud : the statute being made the engine of fraud.

The section relating to trusts does not depend upon the same ground as the 4th section. There is a remarkable difference of expression. *Cottington* v. *Fletcher* was upon the same principle as the cases of part-performance ; that it was a gross fraud in the trustee, taking the estate for his own benefit. The cases of resulting trusts fall within the same rule. None of the cases prove, that a parol contract will do, where it is admitted ; and *Rondeau* v. *Wyatt* goes the whole length of deciding, that it shall have no effect in equity ; for that case was equally clear of the danger of perjury. But all this argument is not necessary in this case ; for at least the agreement must be admitted in *totidem verbis,* and in the same manner as stated. Here the admission is not of an agreement in the terms of that contained in the bill. The circumstances, very shortly alluded to, as amounting to a part-performance, the arbitration bonds, the delay in returning the commission, and the attendance of the arbitrators, have no sort of similitude to part-performance ; of which there is not the least pretence. The circumstance, whether the commission was or was not returned, is of no consequence ; and it seems singular to state as an act the desisting from doing a thing. The agreement is to put an end to the suit. The commission may be returned at any time. The agreement itself put an end to the suit. Then as to executing the * bonds, that was   [* 28] no part of the agreement. Upon the pleadings these bonds are general bonds of reference. They contain nothing of the agreement. How do they help the proof of the agreement ? How does the admission, that the division of this estate was the only object of the bonds, though general in their expression, help the agreement ? The admission of that circumstance is much weaker than the admission of a parol agreement. Then as to the attendance of the arbitrators at the distance of a few miles, what effect has that : the suit, the estate, all remaining in the same condition ? Going to view the estate has been held not to be an act for this purpose, even, if by the parties themselves : *Clerk* v. *Wright* (1.) *Mortimer* v. *Orchard* is a singular case ; but has no relation to this. The ground of that was part-performance in the strict sense, by building ; and the Lord Chancellor took it the most favorable way to the Defendants, according to their admission. This resembles a plea of the statute of limitations ; which is pleaded thus ; that no cause of action has accrued within six years (2). Though in this case there is a plea of the

(1) 1 Atk. 12.
(2) *Bayley* v. *Adams, post,* 586.

the consideration of the Statute of Frauds; whether, attending to the state of the record in this cause, by which I mean the bill, answer, and evidence, the case is according to the rules and principles acted upon in this Court a case, in which the Defendant has not a right to insist, the statute has said, no action, which duly interpreted embraces every suit in equity, shall be maintained against him under such circumstances.

As to the actual circumstances, that led to the compromise, I state them pretty correctly thus. Two commissioners, called in a proper sense the Plaintiff's commissioners, when that is understood to mean, that they are nominated by him, another commissioner, properly called the Defendant's commissioner in the same sense, met to execute part of the duty of this Court. They met under as solemn an obligation as an oath can impose, that, by whatever party named, they are at least in this sense to consider themselves as neither the Plaintiff's nor the Defendant's commissioners, that they are sworn not to disclose what passes before them; and it is not an unwholesome or a strained interpretation of that obligation to say, that he violates it equally, who discloses the particulars of the evidence to either the Plaintiff or the Defendant, and he, who gives an intimation to either, that cannot but lead the mind to form a reasonably sound conjecture upon the general effect of that evidence, the particulars of which are not disclosed. I observe, and it was truly stated for the Plaintiff, that the Defendant, whether ignorant or not, that this was the state of these commissioners as to their public duty, had certainly conceived an idea of a compromise, before any communication passed with the commissioners: but it is equally clear, that, whatever intention he had of a compromise, that intention was not so much matured as to induce him to propose a compromise, until it was strengthened and confirmed by the circumstances I am about to mention. These three commissioners, if I am to believe Mr. Still, having gone through that part of their duty that relates to the mere execution of the commission, agree that it is fit, that a communication should be made to the Defendant, in substance, that it would be for the interest of that Defendant, that he [* 32] should compromise the suit. I am * bound to say, these commissioners acted ill. They acted in violation of the duty they owe to the Court, and the justice due to the Plaintiff. Either they did or did not disclose the general effect of the evidence to the Plaintiff. If they did not, they did him this gross injustice: they concealed from him, that a case was made out entitling him probably to the relief prayed by the bill; and they communicated to the Defendant, that it would be for his advantage to make a good compromise, if he could. If they communicated it to one only, they were guilty of manifest injustice to one; and if they communicated it to both, of which, I must observe, there is no evidence, they acted most unjustly to the Court. The Defendant having received this intimation, that it would be for his interest to compromise the suit, notwithstanding there had been floating in his mind a wish to compromise before any such communication, and notwithstanding that communication, which, though made in the dryest terms, yet coming from that quarter must be considered as a strong hint to a party, even then was not inclined to come to a determination to compromise the suit ; and according to the evidence of one witness a communication took place with the arbitrator Still ; who was distinctly asked as to the meaning of the word " persuade." Of his answer to that inquiry it may be said, "*qui tacet clamat.*" What is the meaning of those very few, but comprehensive words, but, that independent of force he meant the strongest persuasion that could be offered to the Defendant's mind ?

In considering the agreement I shall take it from the prayer of the bill ; and am anxious so to take it : for, whatever may be the case, where different agreements are stated in the bill and the answer, this case in its circumstances shows, that if the Court is at liberty to indulge any inclination, that will be the most sound construction, which leaves the Court at liberty not to go one iota farther than the cases ; which have already gone so far as nearly to cancel the statute. Upon the conduct of the witnesses, as disclosed by this answer, I must observe, not for the sake of animadverting upon the conduct of the witnesses in this case, but to prevent similar errors in other cases, that it is not altogether without blame. They probably did not know the habit of the Court and the reason of that habit, that the effect of their depositions should not be disclosed : * but it is my duty to observe, that the Court does expect   [* 33] from witnesses, that they should not disclose their evidence to parties. These gentlemen certainly do not by any means admit, and I take them as denying by their depositions, that circumstance, that the agreement arose out of the communication with them. Between the credit due to their depositions and the answer I must interpose the credit due to Still ; who says, it was in consequence of the communication with them ; and I must fairly say also, after reading their evidence with the greatest attention, I cannot discharge from my mind the full conviction, that they do know, the Defendant made the agreement in consequence of some communication by some person. It is fair to observe, that much may arise from the manner, in which in this Court the questions are put to the witnesses : but it is impossible to doubt, that upon a *viva voce* examination the result of their evidence would be very different from what it now is.

The agreement, according to the prayer of the bill, is, that the Plaintiff was to take the smaller farm, the Defendant the larger farm ; and that for equality of partition, a portion was to be taken from the latter, so as to make the value equal. That agreement the Defendant certainly does not admit ; if it be part of the substance of the agreement, that the one farm should be allotted to the Plaintiff, the other to the Defendant. If that is not part of the substance of the agreement, then the consideration occurs, whether it may not be said, the Defendant has admitted the agreement. The bonds of arbitration upon the face of them are general, to settle all matters in difference.   The subsequent part of the answer, it has been fairly and convincingly argued, provided the rules of the Court will allow you to attend to it, reduces the matters in dispute to that one mentioned in the subsequent part of the answer, to divide the estate equally.   But it is to be remembered, that, when the subsequent part of the answer puts that interpretation upon the generality of the terms of the agreement, it attributes a duty to the arbitrators different from that, which the Plaintiff says he expected from them ; if there is any substantial difference between an agreement to give one farm to one, the other to the other, making up the difference in value out of the larger, and an agreement to divide the aggregate property, as they should think proper.   A proposition *being made for a compromise, it was of necessity a part of that compromise, whether the division was precisely in the terms of the agreement, as stated by the Plaintiff, or generally, according to the agreement admitted, that the commission should not be returned ; that all such steps should be taken as were necessary to enable them to make the award ; that the estate should be viewed and surveyed, &c.   Those were necessary acts in the execution of the duty the arbitrators had taken upon them to discharge.   This compromise was in the course of the cause ; and I will now suppose, the bond had expressed upon the face of it, that nothing was in difference between them but an equal division of the estate.   Suppose, instead of taking place at the execution of the commission, on the day the cause was to be heard the parties had agreed not to abide the judgment of the Court, but to make an equal division of the estate, provided that was made by the two persons in whose judgment they confided, and on or before a particular day, is that more or less than referring the cause upon particular terms to the award of individuals ; and removing the cause out of Court forever after that day, and in the interim, until that day ; but leaving the cause in Court, as it was before, if the award is not make on that day ?   I am not aware of any case even at law, nor that a Court of Equity has ever entertained this jurisdiction, that, where a reference has been made to arbitration, and the judgment of the arbitrators is not given in the time and manner, according to the agreement, the Court have substituted themselves for the arbitrators, and made the award.   I am not aware, that has been done, even in a case, where the substantial thing to be done is agreed between the parties, but the time and manner, in which it is to be done, is that, which they have put upon others to execute (1).

[*34]

But there is another circumstance in this case ; which appears to render it more difficult to do that in this particular instance than in the ordinary cases ; that here we are upon a parol agreement. What right has the Court to say, there is no substantial difference in

---

(1) *Post,* vol. xvii. 242.   The Lord Chancellor, referring to this passage, says, he should rather have used the word " prescribe " than " execute."   See *Milnes* v. *Gery,* xiv. 400; *Blundell* v. *Brettargh,* xvii. 232; *ante,* vol. v. 849, and the note.

an agreement composed of these different terms? The person suing alleging, that the whole estate belongs to him, a proposal is made to him to divide the estate equally. He says, he has no objection; but he bargains, that a particular part of the estate shall be allotted to him. That agreement, he alleges, and proves by some of the witnesses, is acceded to. Other witnesses leave it as large as the answer states it. The Defendant says that is not the agreement He says, it was a general power to the *arbi-   [*35] trators to divide; and he was to have his chance, what particular part of the estate was to be his. The question, which was the real agreement, resting in doubt upon the parol evidence, the reference upon the bonds being general, of all matters in difference, it would be very strong to say, if the very terms are in dispute between the parties, that the arbitrators have it not within their authority to say, what the agreement was as to its terms: if not, how are they to execute the authority delegated to them? If the Plaintiff could make out, that it was part of his bargain, that he was to have the one farm, the court has no authority to inquire, whether the ground of that is *pretium affectionis*, or not. It is part of his contract; and he would have a right to quarrel with the award, if it did not give him that part. If so, is it of no consequence to parties in such a situation, who are the individuals to settle the dispute between them, and within what time it is to be settled. The *res gsetæ* point out, that it was of some importance to the Defendant; for concealment of the disgrace attaching upon the character of his relation was the very motive that induced him to enter into the agreement. On the other hand, it was a circumstance essential, that, as the award was only to be put an end to, if not made in due time, some time should be mentioned. The arbitrators might die. They might refuse to act. If the award was not made in due time, it does not appear to me that there was any thing to preclude them from going on with the suit. Putting it simply upon this ground, it is very difficult to find any thing either of principle or authority, that an agreement to enjoy according to an award can be executed by the Court, by compelling a division of the estate, not according to the judgment of the persons, in whose judgment the parties confided, and within the time stipulated, but according to the judgment of the Court, with regard to the value of these estates.

Upon the evidence in this cause, I am impressed, if not to conviction, nearly to conviction, that it is so dangerous to justice to execute this contract under all its circumstances, that no individual has a right to ask the relief, if it cannot be given but at the expense of general rules, formed for the protection of the general justice due to suitors, even if it is a case of particular hardship to him. I lay out of the case the conduct of the Plaintiff. It justifies this observation. He had proceeded with the *suit, claiming   [*36] the whole estate, to a particular period; as I must suppose, thinking he had a reasonable chance of success. It is left totally unexplained why he immediately acceded to the proposal to give up half the estate, Upon that I cannot found any thing against him; for it was competent to the Defendant, to ask him by a cross bill, what he knew from the Commissioners. The Defendant not having done so, I should act unjustly towards the Plaintiff, if I considered his conduct as evincing any thing but that upon the uncertainty of all suits he thought it more for his advantage to enjoy half the property, than to go through a litigation for the whole of it. With respect to the Defendant, without inquiring as to the propriety of his conduct, I must consider it upon this fact; whether the Defendant moved in the treaty he entered into, and acted in it, under a persuasion generated in his mind by the conduct of the commissioner, that it was for his interest, and therefore probably against the interest of the Plaintiff, when he entered into this contract; in other words whether the contract is generated out of a gross breach of the duty of the commissioner. If it is, the next question is, Whether the policy of justice will permit the Plaintiff to come here; saying, the evidence satisfied the Court, that the defendant entered into the contract in consequence of communications, which the policy of the law will not permit, which are a breach of the duty of the commissioner, and desiring me to give him a pecuniary advantage arising from such a contract. As to the fact, I have no doubt, the Defendant entered into the contract under what I may state as a species of duress, with a full conviction that these commissioners stating the distinction to him between persuasion and force meant to tell him, persuasion was force; and if he did not take the proposition immediately, he would get nothing. How can it be consistent with the security of the administration of justice, that the Court can act upon that, if it is the fact? There is no reason upon the evidence to say, that representation is false. The Court, in the nature of things, have no evidence, that it is true; for it depends upon the substance of that evidence not yet disclosed to the Court. Supposing it false, how is it possible for the Court to grant a specific performance of an agreement founded upon such a transaction? Can I say, even if true, it can be founded upon such a fact? But how is the Court to

[*37] act, if it cannot know, whether it is true or false? Suppose, after I have dismissed this bill, I * should hear the other cause to-morrow; it would not be a satisfactory reflection, that the day before the Court was in any hazard of giving .relief founded upon a gross breach of duty in the officer of the Court. If therefore it happens, that the Plaintiff without any fault of his, should fail, he stands, as many other Plaintiffs have stood, in a situation, in which the Court, though inclined to give relief to the individual, have, upon general principles of policy, been obliged to refuse it. Upon these grounds, therefore, I am inclined to dismiss the bill.

Upon the other question, if I am well founded in the reasons I have assigned for dismissing the bill, I should feel gratified in declining to give a decisive opinion. It is impossible for me to look without great apprehension upon the decision of any question involving so much doubt in the minds of those, to whose authority I am bound to look with respect and veneration. If I am to state what rather seems to me the better result of all the cases, I should be disposed to say, the statute would stand in the way of the relief. I feel all' the disinclination, which has been lately expressed, and strongly expressed, in many cases to carry what may be called the struggles of Courts of Justice to take cases out of the reach of that statute farther than they have been carried; and I am free to say, the very circumstance, admitted in the argument, that there is no case, in which a Defendant admitting a parol agreement, but insisting upon the benefit of the statute, has been decreed to perform the agreement, would weigh much with me: so much, that I am not disposed at this moment to think, that any judgment I could form upon the simple question, upon which side the better reasoning could be arranged, would shake me from the purpose, which I think a salutary one, of not forming a new head of cases out of the statute. At the same time I must say, and this subject I have thought of very anxiously, while I have practiced in this Court, I have not been able to deliver my mind from the embarrassment as to the cases, which have been stated to be taken out of the statute upon part-performance; if it be the doctrine of this Court, that the admission of an agreement, though accompanied by a prayer for the benefit of the Statute, shall oust the Defendant of the benefit of the statute. The way, in which it has struck my mind, is this. If the party has a right to relief in this Court, he has a right to an answer from the Defendant to every * allegation of his bill, the admission of the truth   [* 38] of which, or the proof of the truth of which, is necessary to entitle him to that relief. If his title to relief therefore stands both upon the fact of a parol agreement and part-performance of that parol agreement, there must in some stage of the cause be proof that there was a parol agreement and a part-performance of that parol agreement; by which I mean some parol agreement certain and definite in its terms, and to which those acts of part-performance can be clearly and certainly referred. If the Defendant answers in the first instance, admitting the agreement, and saying nothing about the statute, I suppose, if he says nothing about the circumstances of part-performance, though not craving the benefit of the statute, the Plaintiff would not think it material to prove the circumstances of part-performance, but would proceed upon that admission; for upon this supposition the Court would decree it. Suppose, he prays the benefit of the statute. He must go on to state the acts of part-performance. Why? If it is the doctrine of this Court, that a parol agreement, notwithstanding the Defendant craves the benefit of the statute, is to be executed, why does the Court do such an unnecessary thing as to make him answer as to the part-performance; for if there is no difference, whether he says any thing about the statute, or not, why is not the Plaintiff to have a decree in the former case as well as the latter? Therefore it would be a necessary consequence in that case, that the Court should not put the party to the expense of going on to answer as to the part-performance. On the other hand, suppose, he was to answer as to the part-performance, and not to the fact of the agreement; denying the acts of part-performance. Then the Plaintiff goes on to proof with regard to all those acts. It may happen, that they may be of such a nature as to be themselves pregnant evidence of some agreement, containing terms incapable of being misunderstood: but in ninety-nine cases out of one hundred that cannot be expected upon the mere acts of part-performance. Nothing of them is known, till the depositions are published. The Court knows nothing of them till the hearing. Then the Court is to see, if there is any thing in the answer about a parol agreement, and so connected with the acts of part-performance as to make one whole; upon which the Court will decree. But as there is no admission or denial of the agreement in the answer, the justice of the case requires, that there should be some method of examining, whether there was a [*39] *parol agreement, or not. I wish to know, whether there is any instance: has the Court ever adopted any means of satisfying itself as to that? Then the most rational way seems to me to be, that, if the Defendant admits the agreement, but insists upon the benefit of the statute, the statute protects him: if he does not say any thing about the statute, then he must be taken to renounce the benefit of it; and there is no occasion to inquire about the part-performance. This leads me to the conclusion, which appears in those two cases in the Court of Exchequer, and the inclination of Lord Thurlow's opinion in *Whitchurch* v. *Bevis* and *Whitbread* v. *Brockhurst*, and also more than an inclination of Lord Loughborough in *Rondeau* v. *Wyatt*; which I have reason to think would induce him with much greater experience to state himself more strongly in the same way upon this part of the case.

I take notice of the distinction observed (1) in *Rondeau* v. *Wyatt* as to Courts of Equity, in order to make an observation upon *Brodie* v. *St. Paul*, the case, in which Mr. Justice Buller sitting here said (2), there is no difference whatsoever between Courts of Law and Equity as to the doctrine of part-performance. I have had occasion, while sitting in the Court of Common Pleas, to think, the character of the Law of this country, dividing itself into distinct Courts of Law and Equity, has suffered more by the circumstance of Courts of Law acting upon what they conceive to be the rules of equity than by any other circumstance. If you address yourself to the question, how Courts of Law are to execute the equitable jurisdiction upon this question, it is absolutely impossible that they can exercise it. All the doctrine of this Court upon this subject attributes great weight to the oath of the Defendant. It seems to have been forgotten in Courts of Law, that here the testimony of witnesses is appreciated, not only by the intrinsic credit due to that testimony, but also by the consideration, what the Defendant, against

(1) 2 H. Black. 68.
(2) *Ante*, vol. i. 333; *post*, 163, 333.

whom it is produced, has said by his answer. If the Defendant denies, that any parol agreement ever took place, a Court of Equity will not inquire into the truth of that denial. Then can the doctrine of a Court of Law and a Court of Equity with regard to part-performance be the same? In every case, where the parties go to issue, a Court of Law must understand, that the Defendant does deny it; and a single witness would according to * that   [* 40] doctrine fix upon the Defendant at law the whole effect of the equitable jurisdiction; whereas, if the Plaintiff comes here, the moment the Defendant in the form, in which issue is here joined, by his answer says, there was no agreement, the witness could not be heard; or, if he was heard, unless supported by special circumstances, giving his testimony greater weight than the denial by the answer, the Court would not make the decree (1).

I have taken the liberty of saying more upon this, because I am seriously apprehensive, that Courts of Law, supposing, they are administering the rules of this Court, have totally misunderstood them. There is another class of cases, with which you are all familiar; where a person treating for his daughter's marriage, asks a question as to the circumstances of the intended husband. A favorable account is given to him; as the Plaintiff states. There are other cases; in which a man acts upon character given to him by one person of another (2). It has happened to me to try causes of this nature, while sitting in the Court of Common Pleas; and the Defendant positively denying, that any such conversation ever passed, and a single witness proving the effect of the conversation, large damages were given upon that testimony; and the argument in those cases has constantly been, that it must prevail; because the rules of law and equity ought to be the same; when in those very cases without special circumstances, making the single testimony of the witness preponderate over the denial by the answer, in equity the Plaintiff must have failed. What is this but saying, courts of law can administer equity, where courts of equity would not dare to move?

Without entering into the question upon the statute, farther than to say, I am strongly inclined to think, the safest construction, and that, which, if I were obliged to decide the question, I must adopt, would be, that I must dismiss the bill, because this case is within the statute of frauds, adding only, that this case affords another striking instance of the danger of departing from the statute, because the parties differ as to the species of the agreement; and the witnesses differ as much as the parties do, I think I can rely safely in dismissing this bill upon the ground I stated in the outset.

* With respect to the costs, if I dismiss the bill, I cannot   [* 41] give the Plaintiff his costs. Certainly I shall not give the Defendant his costs, though I do dismiss the bill; for, to say nothing more of his conduct, a party making such an inquiry from commission-

---

(1) See the notes, *post*, 185; *ante*, vol. ii. 244.
(2) See *Haycraft* v. *Creasy*, 2 East, 92.

ers, whether he knows or is ignorant that it is improper to do so, falls either wilfully or inadvertently into a gross impropriety of conduct. In consequence of that impropriety he is implicated in this suit. No principle of justice therefore calls upon me to give him costs. Taking the Plaintiff to have acted without any impropriety, the consideration, how he is to be reimbursed that expense, into which he has been, I will say innocently led, remains with himself. Whether in the suit, in which he stands a party, in which the depositions have now been published, or in any other mode, he shall make an application to this Court, founded upon the conduct of the commissioners, that they should pay the whole or any part of that expense, it is unfit to intimate, what the determination upon that question ought to be: but upon my view of the conduct of the commissioners, I should not do my duty, if I did not say, the question, whether they should not pay that expense, is a question, that would be very properly addressed to the Court; for if the Court can find itself able to give the Plaintiff, if not involved in the thing, the expense of his being involved in this suit, the Court would find satisfaction in doing it.

With respect to these circumstances as part-performance, I think, they do not fall within that character. They are nothing more or less than acts done by arbitrators towards the execution of the duty, which it was their business to complete; from completing which, no representations of the parties should have restrained them. These circumstances have therefore no more weight than circumstances of conduct of the arbitrators would have in any other case; where the arbitrators do not finally proceed to execute the whole of the duty they have undertaken.

Bill dismissed (1). ____

1. THAT admission of a verbal agreement, respecting lands, does not preclude a defendant from insisting at the hearing of the cause, on the Statute of Frauds; although he may not have prayed the benefit of the statute by his answer; see, *ante*, note 3 to *Moore* v. *Edwards*, 4 V. 23.

2. A mere agreement to a reference is not binding; not only a parol submission to arbitration, but even a submission by deed, may be revoked at any time before the award is made; see note 3 to *Mitchell* v. *Harris*, 2 V. 129.

3. Unless part-performance has taken the case out of the statute, Courts of Equity, it seems, will not decree specific execution of an agreement different from that which the plaintiff has alleged by his bill; notwithstanding such different agreement may be established by proofs, in the progress of the cause; see note 3 to *Mortimer* v. *Orchard*, 2 V. 243.

4. Allotments made under an act for inclosure, may be capable of disposition before the award is completed; if, therefore, the party contracting to purchase, have full notice of the existing circumstances, he must perform his contract; notwithstanding any possible variations, which he must have known were inherent in the nature of property so situated: *Kingsley* v. *Young*, 17 Ves. 473; *S. C.* on appeal, 18 Ves. 208; but this decision went, (partly, at all events,) upon the ground, that the legislature had, by the local inclosure act affecting the lands in question, given the seisin and legal estate upon the allotment only; under the general inclosure act, (41 Geo. III. c. 109,) the legal title to an allotment is not acquired

(1) The original cause was afterwards heard, and upon the 12th of March, 1803, the following issue was directed; whether by the settlement of 1743 any estate was limited to Cooth.

before the proclamation of the award. *Farrer* v. *Billing*, 2 Barn. & Ald. 175, 178.

5. That, where a matter has been referred to arbitration, but the arbitrators have made no award, or have not made one within the time and manner prescribed; a Court of Equity will not assume their office, but will leave the party desirous of enforcing the agreement to make the most of it at law; see note 2 to *Emery* v. *Wase*, 5 V. 846; but, of course, if one of the parties has been himself the cause of preventing the award from being made in due time; he cannot, in Equity, set up a legal defence growing out of his own misconduct. *Morse* v. *Merest*, 6 Mad. 27.

6. The right of Courts of Equity to enforce, or to refuse enforcing, specific performance of an agreement, is a discretionary jurisdiction; not, indeed, to be exercised arbitrarily, or capriciously, but according to a sound and temperate consideration of the circumstances of each particular case: see note 1 to *Brodie* v. *St. Paul*, 1 V. 326.

7. That circumstances not amounting to legal duress, may afford sufficient grounds, not merely for refusing to enforce an agreement, but even for setting aside a formally executed instrument, extorted by such means; see note 2 to *The Countess of Strathmore* v. *Bowes*, 1 V. 22.

8. Lord Eldon has frequently expressed a strong opinion that the attempt of some judges to act in Courts of Common Law, upon supposed analogy to the practice and principles of Courts of Equity, is much to be lamented; see note 3 to *Brodie* v. *St. Paul*, 1 V. 326, note 2 to *Toulmin* v. *Price*, 5 V. 235, and note 3 to *Lyster* v. *Dolland*, 1 V. 431.

9. The oath of a single witness, if supported by collateral circumstances, may prevail against the oath of a defendant; so as to enable a plaintiff, after part performance of a parol agreement, to obtain a decree for specific execution. *Morphett* v. *Jones*, 1 Swanst. 182; *Toole* v. *Medlicott*, 1 Ball & Bea. 402; *Savage* v. *Brocksop*, 18 Ves. 338.

10. As to the question of costs in the principal case; see *Lewis* v. *Loxham*, 3 Meriv. 430; *Jones* v. *Lewis*, 1 Cox, 199; *Bennet College* v. *Carey*, 3 Brown, 390.

SMITH *v.* CONEY.   [* 42]

[ROLLS.—1801, MAY 2.]

THOUGH the christian name of the legatee was mistaken in the will, the legacy was established upon the description and evidence, notwithstanding great delay in filing the bill (a).

THE Will of the testatrix contained the following clause : " I give to the Reverend Charles Smith of Stapleford Tawney in the county of Essex, clerk, the sum of 500*l.*"

This bill was filed by the Reverend Richard Smith, claiming the legacy, upon evidence, that there was no person answering the description of the legatee according to the will; and that the Plaintiff was at the date of the Will incumbent of Stapleford Tawney, and well known to the testatrix; who had a great regard for him.

The Defendant, the executor and trustee for infant residuary legatees, by his answer suggested, that the person intended was Charles

---

(a) See *ante*, note (a), *Abbot* v. *Massie*, 3 V. 148. Parol evidence is admissible to explain latent ambiguities, and to apply an instrument to its subject. See *ante*, note (a) to *Baugh* v. *Read*, 1 V. 257.

Smith an officer in the army ; who lived at Romford in Essex ; and died in the life of the testatrix; and therefore the legacy lapsed.

In opposition to the claim set up by the answer, it was proved by the widow of Charles Smith, that her husband died, before the testatrix made her Will; and that she was informed of that circumstance by the deponent, before the Will was made. The bill was not filed until many years after the death of the testatrix, and six years after the death of a lady, who lived with her in great intimacy ; and who, it was suggested, knew her intentions.

Mr. *Cooke*, for the Plaintiff.

The Master of the Rolls called on the Counsel for the Defendant ; observing, it was hardly possible to raise a doubt ; and asking how Captain Smith could answer this description.

Mr. *Romilly*, for the Defendant, observed upon the delay in setting up this claim.

The MASTER OF THE ROLLS [Sir RICHARD PEPPER ARDEN].—

[*43] There must be some farther inquiry. But it will be very difficult to oppose this, and to suppose, the *testatrix made such a mistake, with so particular description and such evidence. This sort of question is settled now. There are many instances of children going by wrong names. My only difficulty is, that the legacy was not called for during so long a time.

The Defendant then gave up the point ; and consented to a decree for the legacy, with interest, and without costs (1).

See note 3 to *Parsons* v. *Parsons*, 1 V. 266.

(1) *Ante*, vol. i. 259 ; *Parsons* v. *Parsons*, 260 ; *Rylott* v. *Walter*, at the Rolls, 17th Feb. 1802, stated in the note, 267 ; *Garth* v. *Meyrick*, 1 Bro. C. C. 30. So evidence is admitted to explain initials ; not a blank : *ante*, *Abbot* v. *Massie*, vol. iii. 148 ; *Price* v. *Page*, iv. 680. See 3 Woodd. 328 ; *Hunt* v. *Hort*, 3 Bro. C. C. 311.

GODFREY *v.* DAVIS.

[1801, MAY 2, 5.]

AN illegitimate child not entitled under the description of a child in a will; though the testator knew the state of the family, viz. several illegitimate and no legitimate children (*a*).

 A bequest to a particular description of persons at a particular time vests in persons answering the description at that time exclusively (*b*).

Therefore an annuity being bequeathed over upon the death of the annuitant to the eldest child of A.. there being at the death no child, an after-born child is not entitled.

JOHN CREE by his Will required, that all his estates, real and personal, should be converted into money after his decease, and placed at interest upon solid land security (mortgage) ; and the issue and profits thereof annually to be disposed of in manner following: *Imprimis*, To his daughter Eleanor Cree (afterwards Eleanor Davis) the annual sum of 300*l.* during her life, to be paid half yearly ; to James Cree 100*l.* per annum, for his life, payable half yearly ; to James M'Mahon 200*l.* per annum, for his life, payable half yearly ; and in case of his death, his widow Ann M'Mahon to receive during her life 100*l.* per annum half yearly. The testator then gave the following annuities, also payable half yearly ; to Miss Elizabeth Francis 300*l.* per annum for life ; to John Godfrey, Esq. 100*l.* per annum for life ; to John Byrn 100*l.* per annum for life ; with remainder to his daughter Caroline Byrn for life ; to Jane Harris 60*l.* per annum ; to John Parsons 40*l.* per annum ; to revert to his daughter after his death ; to James Archdekin 100*l.* per annum ; and 100*l.* per annum to David Godfrey. The will then proceeded thus :

 " And the first annuity of the great ones that drops in, I will and desire may devolve upon the eldest child male or female for

* life and in two half yearly payments of William Harwood ; [*44]
and in case the interest of my property produces a sum more than sufficient to answer the payment of the several annuities herein specified, then the proportion of the annuities to increase ; but if less, to diminish in the like due proportion excepting the annuities of Miss Jane Harris and my butler John Parsons. And I hereby will and require, that as the said annuities drop in, their amount is to go to the increase of the annuities of the survivors, so to increase to the last survivor who shall hold the same during life : Jane Harris and John Parsons excepted. And when the said annuitants are all dead the whole and sole property devolve without any condition upon the heirs male of Philip Francis, Esq. of St. James's Square, and in default of issue, to female branch of the said family of Philip Francis, Esq. taking the name and arms of Cree."

 The testator died in 1791 soon after the execution of the will.

 (*a*) See *ante,* note (*a*) *Cartwright* v. *Vawdry,* 5 V. 530.
 (*b*) See *ante,* note (*b*), *Hill* v. *Chapman,* 1 V. 405 ; note (*a*), *Clarke* v. *Blake* 2 V. 673.

David Godfrey died upon the 15th of May, and Eleanor Davis upon
the 24th of June, 1798. The eldest daughter of William Harwood
claimed the annuity of 300*l.* a-year; which claim was disallowed on
the ground, that she was a natural daughter. An exception was
taken on her part to the report. It was proved, that the testator was
very intimate with Harwood and his family; and knew, he had no
legitimate child; and that this daughter and all his other children
were treated by him as his children (1). The parents of these
children married several years after the testator's death. That exception was disallowed.

Another claim was afterwards set up to the same annuity by
Clara Elizabeth Harwood, as the only legitimate child; having been
born after the marriage. Her claim being also disallowed by the
Master, she took an exception to the report; which came on to be
argued. Another question was made at the bar, but not determined:
supposing her claim well founded, whether she was entitled
to the annuity of 300*l.* a-year or 100*l.* a-year.

[*45]   *Mr. *Romilly* and Mr. *Benyon* in support of the exception.—The cases of *Baldwin* v. *Karver* (2), *Heathe* v.
Heathe (3), and others of that class, are distinguished from this;
as in those there were two classes of children; and then there
can be no doubt the intention is in favor of all those children, who shall be alive at the time the contingency happens;
for if the distribution is not confined to some particular period, it cannot be ascertained, who are to take, until after the
deaths of the parents of all the persons to take: which leads to this
inconvenience; that none of the persons, for whom the fund is intended, may receive any benefit from it. But this is confined to one
person. The testator knowing, the parent was unmarried, must have
had in contemplation the birth of a child in future. He had in contemplation the suvivorship of these annuitants, until the last of
them should be dead. In that event only he gives it over. *Weld*
v. *Bradbury* (4) is an authority in support of this exception; though
certainly different in its circumstances. There are no words in this
will requiring the object of this bequest to be alive at the death of
the testator, or of the annuitant; who dropt. If she had been alive
at the death of the annuitant, she would have been entitled within
many modern cases; the last of which is *Middleton* v. *Messenger* (5). This is not like those cases, where the distribution is to be
among all the children *in esse* at the death of the tenant for life.
This is not confined to the period of any life; but might last during
several lives. In that respect it differs from *Congreve* v. *Congreve* (6).

(1) *Cartwright* v. *Vawdry, ante,* vol. v. 530. See the note.
(2) Cowp. 309.
(3) 2 Atk. 121. See cases collected in Mr. Sanders's note, 122.
(4) 2 Vern. 705.
(5) *Ante,* vol. v. 136.
(6) 3 Bro. C. C. 531.

Mr. *Alexander* and Mr. *Cox*, for the surviving Annuitants.
—The claim of the illegitimate child was rejected; because no intention was sufficiently expressed in her favor. Phrases occur in this will, singularly denoting, that the testator intended the person to take to be alive at the death of the annuitant. Upon the whole will there can be no doubt, that if this child had not been born for ten years, the existing annuitants would have enjoyed the annuities dropping in increase of their own annuities. It must be contended, in order to maintain this exception, that, even if the ultimate limitation had taken effect, the whole interest should go back upon the birth of a child, after all these events were past. Upon the old cases no one could take, who was not in existence * at the   [* 46] date of the will (1). The construction that afterwards prevailed was, that those must be intended, who came into existence before the death of the testator. Afterwards every one was let in, who answered the description, before the fund became disposable in some way. In the ordinary case, a disposition to the children at the age of 21, all, who are *in esse*, before the eldest attains 21, are let in (2): in the case of a tenant for life, all, who are *in esse* before the death of the tenant in life (3). That is the general rule; and in order to extend it a distinct intention to suspend the vesting must be shown. *Ellison* v. *Airey* (4) has been recognized in almost every subsequent case. In substance there must be a legatee in being; unless an intention to the contrary is clearly shown; in order to avoid suspending. The direction for the devolution of the annuity implies, that there is a person in being, upon whom it is to devolve; and is not applicable to a suspension for 15 or 20 years. The most explicit declaration is necessary to produce the effect of calling it back. The great difference upon this question as to marriage settlements is, that all the children are the objects of those provisions. The case cited from Vernon is a loose note upon very different circumstances, and inconsistent with the subsequent authorities. With respect to the distinction from the other cases, a dispute between two different classes of persons, that is the case upon this will: 1st, there is a particular class of persons described: 2dly, there are the other annuitants. Upon what principle can *Ellison* v. *Airey* and the other cases be distinguished from this? If all the children were intended, the construction of the Court confining it was directly against the intention. The question must rest entirely upon the principle originally laid down in that case, and invariably acted upon since. It is said, upon this construction no person might take the benefit of this: but this is a case, in which there might or might not be a child of Harwood existing at the time the annuity falls in.

---

(1) *Northey* v. *Strange*, 1 P. Will. 340.
(2) *Andrews* v. *Partington*, 3 Bro. C. C. 401; *ante, Prescott* v. *Long*, vol. ii. 690; *Hoste* v. *Pratt*, iii. 730.
(3) *Spencer* v. *Bullock, ante,* vol. ii. 687.
(4) 1 Ves. 111. In *Hill* v. *Chapman, ante,* vol. i. 405, Lord Thurlow says, that case went upon a refinement, but cannot now be shaken. See 408, and the note.

Can the construction be determined by the event? There certainly
might be a person existing at the time; which clearly dis-
[47 *]   tinguishes it from *those cases, in which of necessity there
could be no person existing at the time. The express disposition of the annuity at the moment it falls in to the surviving
annuitants negatives all idea of suspension. But the general rule,
admitted to be the result of the authorities, is sufficient to over-
rule this exception.

Mr. *Romilly*, in reply. .

This case does not fall within the general rule; and no case is
produced in circumstances like it. Taking the will and the facts as
to the state of the family together, well known to the testator, he
must have had the intention maintained by this exception. He
must have intended a legitimate child, according to the decision
upon the former exception. He was aware of the probability, that
one of the annuities might soon fall in: so many annuities being
given, and not to young people. It is impossible upon the will not
to see the intention. He must have had in contemplation a period,
that might be distant, and some person, of whom he knew nothing;
which distinguishes this case from *Congreve* v. *Congreve*; where, if
not confined, it must have extended to a time, when all the objects
of bounty might be dead. Such a limitation as this clearly means
only, that there shall be a person standing as the representative of
that family at some distant period; having no view to particular persons. The argument would apply to every case of executory devise.
In the famous case of *Hopkins* v. *Hopkins* (1) it might be said, it
was unnatural to suppose, the testator intended it to devolve to the
heir-at-law, until some person should come *in esse:* but no such argument prevailed; and what stronger reason is there against the
suspension in this case? We do not argue from the event; but it
appears clearly, the testator must have known, if one of the annuitants had died the day after the execution of the will, there was no
one to answer the description; and then there is nothing to show
he meant to confine it to the death of the annuitant, except the
word "devolve:" but why is the devolution to be immediate in this
instance more than in *Hopkins* v. *Hopkins*, or any other case? *Ellison* v. *Airey* is relied on only for the general doctrine. The case
in Vernon is the only case, that has any resemblance in circumstances; the disposition being to the children of persons, who
[* 48]   had none at the time: whereas in the others the *dispute
was between two classes of children: there being some
at the date of the will. Who are the annuitants meant in the
clause of survivorship? Not the persons named as such only, but
those expressly named and the person described as the child of Harwood; and then there is no inconsistency in supposing that a child
born at any time might take the annuity. It is not material to con-

---

(1) 1 Vern. 268; For. 44; 1 Atk. 581; 1 Ves. 268. Mr. Butler's note, 231;
Co Lit. 271 *b.*

tend, whether it was disposed of in the mean time. I think not: but it would fall into the residue.

May 5th. The MASTER OF THE ROLLS [Sir RICHARD PEPPER ARDEN] (after stating the case.)—Upon the former exception by the eldest of the illegitimate children of Harwood, a daughter, who claimed as the person intended by the description of "the eldest child," it was contended, that though by the determinations, that have taken place, no one can claim under the description of a child but such as can claim as a legitimate child (1), yet upon the circumstances appearing in evidence, the situation of Harwood's family not unknown to the testator, a family of illegitimate children, recognised by their father as his children, that daughter was entitled to the annuity falling in, as *persona designata* in this will. Upon that exception I was of opinion, there was not sufficient to entitle an illegitimate child to claim; for, whatever the real intention of the testator might be, and though it could hardly be supposed, he had not some children then existing in his contemplation, yet as the words are "the eldest child," such persons only could be intended, who could entitle themselves as children by the strict rule of law ; and no illegitimate child can claim under such a description, unless particularly pointed out by the testator, and manifestly and incontrovertibly intended, though in point of law not standing in that character. Notwithstanding the evidence of the testator's knowledge of the situation of this family, I did not think, that entitled these children to claim under this description (2). Therefore I over-rule that exception.

Another claim is now brought forward by another daughter of Harwood by the same mother ; who being born after the marriage of her parents has certainly a right to claim as the eldest child ; provided, the testator did not intend upon this will a disposition at a given period. With respect to this the first consideration is, whether upon this will enough appears to prove, the testator intended, * that immediately upon his death these annuities　　[* 49] should take place : whether the whole produce of his property, though portioned out into annuities, was not manifestly intended to be divided among all these annuitants in different proportions, according to the degree of their annuities; and I am of opinion, that it is neither more nor less than a division of the whole interest of his fortune, that might arise during the lives of any of the persons there named, be it more or less, in proportion to their annuities, except the two given to Harris and Parsons, which I lay totally out of the case upon this question ; with the qualification, that if any die, there should be a substitution in the room of the first dying. I am not under the necessity of saying, which are to be considered the great annuities. I consider all as the great annuities for the purpose of entitling the child of Harwood to the first, that might fall in. In

---

(1) *Cartwright* v. *Vawdry, ante,* vol. v. 530, and the note, 534.
(2) *Ratcliffe* v. *Buckley, post,* vol. x. 195.

the view I have of this will it makes no difference, whether the right
of survivorship and of substitution in favor of the person described
as the eldest child of Harwood attached upon the first or the second
of the annuities now vacant.

The next question is, whether, as upon the death of the first annuitant there was no person answering that description living, that
annuity was to be divided among the survivors, or to be suspended,
and the profits to accumulate, to see, whether any such person should
come *in esse.* It is clearly established by *De Visme* v. *Mello* (1),
and many other cases, that, where the testator gives any legacy or
benefit to any person, not as *persona designata,* but under a qualification and description at any particular time, the person answering
that description at that time, is the person to claim; and if there
are any persons answering the description, they are not to wait to
see, whether any other persons shall come *in esse:* but it is to be
divided among those capable of taking, when by the tenor of the
will the testator intended the property to vest in possession (2).
That case was much considered by Lord Thurlow; and seems to
have settled the law upon the subject. The first question is, whether it is clear, the testator meant, any given set of persons should take
at any given time: if so, it is clear, all persons answering
[* 50]   that description, whether born before or afterwards, *shall
take: but if there are no such persons, it shall not suspend
the rights of others: but they shall take; as if no such persons were
substituted. Before that case this point was not quite so clear:
Singleton v. *Singleton* and *Ayton* v. *Ayton* (3). Where the gift is
to all the children of A. at twenty-one, if there is no estate for life, it
will vest in all the children coming into existence, until one attains
the age of twenty-one. Then that one has a right to claim a share;
admitting into participation all the children then existing: so, if it is
to a person for life, and after the death of that person then to the
children of A. the intention is marked; that until the death of the
person entitled for life no interest vests. When that person dies, the
question arises, whether there are then any persons answering that
description: if so, they take, without waiting to see, whether any
others will come *in esse,* answering the description. If it is given
over, in the event that there are no children, and there are no children at that period, the person, to whom it is given over, takes. It
is clear, this testator meant these annuities to commence at his
death: and that each annuitant should receive a proportionable
share of his fortune, with benefit of survivorship and right of accru-
er, subject upon the death of the first annuitant to the substitution
of the eldest child of Harwood. Upon the death therefore of the
first annuitant, unless there was some one, who had a right of substitution in the room of that person, (and there was no such person),
it was to go among the survivors. The person substituted, viz. the

---

(1) 1 Bro. C. C. 537.
(2) See *Hutcheson* v. *Jones,* 2 Madd. 124.
(3) 1 Bro. C. C. 542, note.

eldest child of Harwood, not having been then in existence, cannot now claim. That construction is much fortified by the manner, in which it is given over ; for it is perfectly clear, he meant the persons, to whom it is given over under the description of the heirs of Francis, to take upon the death of the persons, to whom it was first given over. If the construction contended for is to prevail, those persons, supposing all the other annuitants, claiming by survivorship, were dead, must wait not only the death of the survivor, but also the death of Harwood ; for during his life there would be a possibility, that a child might be born : who upon that construction might say, he was the survivor. That would be quite contrary to the words and what must be supposed the intention. Much stress was laid upon the event of the former exception ; that not having in his contemplation the illegitimate children, or at least not having described them sufficiently, he *might mean a child here-   [* 51] after to be born. But that does not follow : that, because by incorrect words he had not described his intention, so as to enable the Court to determine in favor of an illegitimate child, I am on that account to make a different determination on this point. It appears, he must have intended a person existing at the time any of these annuitants dropt ; or to borrow an expression from the case of *Thellusson* v. *Woodford* (1), of which we have heard so much lately, all the candles must be burning together. That must be the intention ; and he could not mean, that there might be a person in embryo, to come out after the deaths of all the annuitants.

Upon these grounds and upon the construction of the will being of opinion, that the interest in these annuities was intended to vest in possession, and unless there was some person to claim under the substitution, the whole interest would survive to the others until the death of the last survivor, and that there was no person to answer that description at the time the event took place, I think, the Master was right in rejecting this claim ; and the exception must be overruled.

I shall not decide the question, which of these are to be considered the great annuities.

___

1. THAT, notwithstanding legitimate and illegitimate children cannot both take under the same description in a will ; yet, where there are no legitimate children, illegitimate offspring may take under a bequest to "children," provided they are distinctly shown to have been the intended objects of the testator's bounty, by a clear *designatio personarum* ; see, *ante*, note 3 to *Standen* v. *Standen*, 2 V. 589. But, it was held in *Radcliffe* v. *Buckley*, 10 Ves. 303, as well as in the principal case, that the proper construction of the word "children" will not be altered, merely because the testator knew, that at the time he made his will, there were no legitimate children of the family in favor of which his bequest was made. And that, under a gift by will to "children," even grand-children can never claim, except in cases where the will must be inoperative, if they are not let in ; or where the context plainly shows, that the word "children," was not used in its strict sense ; see note 5 to *Bristow* v. *Warde*, 2 V. 336.

2. That when a bequest is made to a class who may happen to answer tho testator's description, at a particular time ; those who are *in esse* at the time fixed

for distribution of the fund must take the whole ; notwithstanding other individuals, who, had they been born in time, might have been equally entitled, may afterwards come *in esse ;* see note 3 to *Hill* v. *Chapman,* 1 V. 405.

3. A child in *ventre sa mere* is, generally, to be considered as in existence ; but, the possibility that, at some future period, an embryo may make its appearance, must not alter the construction of a will, when the testator appears to have had no such event in his contemplation ; see note 2 to *Clarke* v. *Blake,* 2 V. 673.

PILLSWORTH *v.* HOPTON.

[1801, MAY 6.]

INJUNCTION to restrain waste not granted against Defendant in possession, claiming by an adverse title.

MR. THOMSON, for the Plaintiff, moved for an injunction to restrain the Defendant from committing waste.   The Defendant was in possession : the tenants had attorned ; and the Plaintiff having brought an ejectment, had failed in it ; but, as the bill alleged, not upon the merits.

Lord CHANCELLOR [ELDON].—I do not recollect, that the Court has ever granted an injunction against waste under any [* 52] such circumstances (a) : the Defendant in * possession ; the tenants having attorned : the Plaintiff having failed in his ejectment : both setting up pretences of title.   I remember perfectly being told from the Bench very early in my life, that if the Plaintiff filed a bill for an account, and an injunction to restrain waste, stating, that the Defendant claimed by a title adverse to his, he stated himself out of Court as to the injunction.

His Lordship having inquired, if the bar knew any instance, and none being produced, would not make the order (1).

SEE the note to *Price* v. *Williams,* 1 V. 401.

(a) See *Shubrick* v. *Guerrand,* 2 Desaus. 616, where an injunction was granted ; but the grounds of the decision do not appear.   On the subject of injunctions to prevent waste, see 2 Story, Eq. Jur. § 909 to § 921.

(1) *Post, Davies* v. *Leo,* 784.   See *Hanson* v. *Gardiner,* vol. vii. 305 ; *Smith* v. *Collyer,* viii. 89 ; xix. 154 ; *Jones* v. *Jones,* 3 Mer. 161.

MUCKLESTON v. BROWN.

[1801, MAY 6, 8.]

BILL by the heir at law against residuary devisees, legatees, and executors; suggesting a secret trust, undertaken at the request of the testator, either not legally
declared, or, if so, void as to the real estate, and written acknowledgments by
the Defendants of an intended trust for charitable purposes: the will also by
equal legacies to them, and some particular expressions, importing a trust. A
general demurrer to the discovery and relief was overruled (a).
The interrogating part of a bill is to be construed by the alleging part; and not
to be considered more extensive (b), [p. 62.]
If the Plaintiff is not entitled to the relief, though he is entitled to discovery, a
general demurrer is good (c), [p. 63.]
Equal legacies to two executors make them trustees of the residue undisposed of;
notwithstanding inequality as to the real estate. So, though the legacies are
given by a subsequent instrument (d), [p. 64.]

THE Bill stated, that the Plaintiffs were co-heirs at law of Isaac
Hawkins; who being seised of the manor and estates of Overseal in
the county of Leicester, applied to the Defendants Isaac Hawkins
Brown, and the Reverend Thomas Gisborne, and to the Reverend
John Hepworth, to act as trustees in the execution of certain trusts;
upon which he had devised or bequeathed, or proposed to devise or
bequeath, all the rest and residue of his real and personal estate not
otherwise disposed of; and that they or some or one of them having
agreed to take upon themselves or himself, the execution of the
trusts, as Hawkins did then or should duly declare, he made his will,
dated the 9th of August, 1793; reciting, that the Plaintiffs were his
co-heirs; and specifically devising certain estates to each of them
and to another person respectively in fee; and giving several legacies: and as to all and every other his real estates whatsoever and

---

(a) Courts of Equity will set aside agreements and acts in fraud of the policy of
the law. If a devise is made upon a secret trust for charity, in evasion of the
statute of mortmain, it will be set aside. 1 Story, Eq. Jur. § 297.

(b) This rule is indispensable for the preservation of due form and order in the
pleadings and particularly to keep the answer to the matters in the Bill. Story,
Eq. Pl. § 36; *Wilkes* v. *Rogers*, 6 Johns. 565. If a plea is put in, its validity will
be heard with reference to the stating and charging part, and not with reference
to the interrogating part, if they differ. *Clayton* v. *Winchelsea*, 3 Younge & C.
683. See, also, *Mechanics' Bank* v. *Levy*, 3 Paige, 605; *James* v. *McKernon*,
6 Johns. 543; *Woodcock* v. *Bennett*, 11 Cowen, 734.

(c) A bill of discovery, properly so called, never prays any relief. If a bill,
therefore, which is maintainable in Equity solely as a bill of discovery, should
contain a prayer for relief also, it will, in England, although not in the United
States, be open to a demurrer to the whole bill; and the party will not be allowed
to maintain his bill for the discovery only; for he is bound to shape his bill, according to what he has a right to pray. Story, Eq. Pl. § 312, and English cases
cited. The rule formerly adopted in England was different. In the United States
the old English rule is adhered to. *Livingston* v. *Story*, 9 Peters, 632, 658. See
ante, note (a), *Renison* v. *Ashley*, 2 V. 459; note (b), *Brandon* v. *Sands*, 2 V. 514.

(d) This turns upon the presumption of a gift of the unbequeathed residue of
the estate to the executor; but this is of little practical consequence in the United
States, where the residue is by law generally distributed among the next of kin,
in the absence of all contrary expressions of intention by the testator. See *ante*,
note (a) to *Barnet* v. *Batchelor*, 1 V. 68.

wheresoever not before disposed of and the residue of his personal estate, subject to the payment of his debts and legacies, he gave and devised the said real and personal estates unto his good friend and relation Isaac Hawkins Brown, Esq. also to his kinsman the Reverend Thomas Gisborne, of, &c. and John Hepworth, Rector of Eggington in the county of Derby, and their heirs; and he appointed them to be executors of that his will.

By a codicil, dated the 29th of November, 1796, the testator reciting, that since the making his will he had purchased two [* 53] * small farms, one at Overseal, the other at Hilton in the county of Derby, gave and devised such farm and all his lands and estates at Hilton aforesaid to the Reverend Thomas Gisborne and his heirs for ever; and as to the farm at Overseal he devised the same to Gisborne and Brown and to their heirs; "upon trust for the like uses and purposes as my manor and estate at Overseal now stand limited." He then gave several legacies; concluding with legacies to Brown and Gisborne of 1000*l.* each; all which legacies or sums of money he directed to be paid to the several legatees by the executors named in his will within twelve months after his decease.

The bill farther stated, that Hepworth died in the life of the testator in 1795; and the testator died upon the 6th of February, 1800; that the Defendants entered upon and took possession of the residue of the testator's real and personal estates; that the manor of Overseal was not specifically devised; but was included in and passed by the general devise of all the residue of his real estates; that no use or purpose was by the will or otherwise declared of the same; and it appears by the codicil, that the said manor and estates at Overseal should be held by Brown, Gisborne, and Hepworth, upon certain trusts. The bill then stated applications to the Defendants, and their pretences, that the Plaintiffs are not entitled as co-heirs to the residue of the real estates, the same being by the will and codicil devised to the Defendants absolutely; and charged, that it is manifest from the codicil, that the devise was to them as trustees; and that the testator did not intend them to take any beneficial interest in the residue of his real and personal estates; and that they were so fully convinced, that such was the purpose and intention, that they have repeatedly acknowledged the same; particularly Gisborne in a letter to Brown; which the bill stated; and which, as far as it was material, was in the following terms:

"It was as early as the spring of 1789, and probably earlier, that the testator explained his intentions and wishes upon the subject in question to me. To the best of my recollection the testator stated, that he proposed to bequeath to his heirs at law in certain proportions the estates he had inherited; and, after providing for [* 54] Miss Wilkinson, and, I presume, for any specific * legacies, to bequeath the whole residuum of his estates real and personal to his executors, not however for their private emoluments, but in full confidence, that conformably to his intentions they

would have laid out the whole of it in charity or for charitable uses:
I think, those were the precise terms: and am certain, they fully
explain his meaning. He then mentioned the other executors; and
proposed to me to be a third; to which I assented; and assured
him, I would faithfully perform according to his intentions my share
of the trusts (for so I considered it), if it should ever devolve upon
me. He said, we must repay ourselves out of the residuum all expenses incurred in executing his intentions. I understood him also
to mean, that we were not to have any specific legacies. I have a
faint recollection, that he said, we might keep what we thought fit
for our trouble: but I did not hear him say any thing, that would
have authorized me, even supposing he had left me no specific legacy, to retain for my own use, had I been so disposed, any thing
material; and I have no idea, I should have thought it right to have
taken any thing. I understood him to have had public charities,
primarily at least, in his own view; though I do not say, exclusively.
Though I cannot absolutely recollect his using the word 'private,' I
am particularly sure, that appropriating to private charity whatever
we might find ourselves legally excluded from assigning to public
charities would fulfil the spirit of his intention. I expressed my
wishes to him, that his will should specify, that the bequest was not
intended for our private emolument, but for charity: but he intimated decidedly, that it would not be done without invalidating the bequest. Whether he distinctly named the mortmain (1) or other
statutes, as those, which in that case would destroy the bequest, I
cannot say positively. I asked him to give me some information as
to the particular kind of charity, to which he would have his executors appropriate part or the whole of his bequest: but he always replied, that we should be the best judges, or to that import. I
requested written directions. His answer did not excite in me any
hope, that he would give any. He once said, it would be very
large: approaching 200,000l. Many years after the original disclosure of his intentions he expressed a wish, that a farm
he had * purchased should go to the benefit of the des-   [* 55]
cendants of the family, from which he purchased; and
said he must do something for the poor of Barton; talking of settling
12l. a year or some such sum. His conversation afterwards threw
no farther light upon his intention."

The Bill then set forth a statement, drawn out by the Defendant
Brown, of his conversations with the testator, and his opinion of the
intention; the material parts of which are, as follows:

"February 10th, 1800. The first time I saw him after Mrs.
Hawkins's death he said, he intended to leave the residue of his real
and personal estate to me and Gisborne; giving reason to suppose,
we should have discretionary powers as to the application; unless
we received particular directions; which I expected. I considered

---

(1) 9 Geo. II. c. 36.

it to be his intention, that a considerable part was to be disposed to charitable uses, and another part, perhaps considerable, was to be given in private donations, not only to those, who were objects of charity, but to persons, who had claims upon his generosity ; one of whom he described; and all of whom I hoped he would have mentioned in some papers of his own writing; and that a third part I might legally reserve to my own use; though it was never my intention to do so; because he said, I might keep what I pleased to myself. The impression upon my mind was not altered by subsequent conversations, except in the following particulars. He told me, he had made another will; but had not made any alterations (except as to executors). He told me, he intended to leave me a specific legacy; which I guessed to be 1000*l*. In one conversation I said to him, the real estate might be affected by the Mortmain Act. He said, it was impossible; because I and Gisborne or the other executors (for I do not recollect, whether it was after the alteration in the trusts) would have the full and legal right to the whole residue: the distribution would be our own act and deed; or to that purport."

The Bill farther stated, that the Defendants pretend, the testator has by some writing or otherwise declared the trusts, upon which they and Hepworth were intended to take the residue of the real estate; and that they are willing to hold the said estate to and for *the objects of such trusts; and charging, that the said testator hath not legally or in any effective manner declared the trusts, and, that if he hath declared the same, they are as to the real estate of the testator, of which he was seised at the time of his death, null and void, prayed a discovery; and that the Plaintiffs may be declared entitled as co-heirs to the residue of the testator's real estates, on account of the residue of the real estates, and the rents and profits received by the Defendants, and general relief.

[* 56]

The Defendants put in a general demurrer to the discovery and relief.

The *Solicitor General* [Sir *William Grant*], Mr. *Romilly*, and Mr. *Cox*, in support of the Demurrer.—If this case stood upon the will alone, it would be without question a devise of the whole beneficial as well as legal estate to the Defendants: but upon the codicil it will be said, a trust is declared of the estates at Overseal; or, if not declared, the intention of the testator, that they should not be taken beneficially by the executors, is manifest. The trust does not appear. It is not sufficient for the Plaintiff to show, that there might be a disposition for some person by some other instrument. It might be in trust for the heir or a stranger: but that person coming for relief must show, that he is entitled to it. It is not however to be admitted, that this is the interpretation of the codicil. Though awkwardly expressed, it may be referred to the payment of the debts and legacies; to which by the will the residue of the real and personal estate is subject. There is therefore a plain and obvious sense to be attributed to these words in the codicil without referring to any other trust. From the legacies given to the executors by the codicil, 1000*l.* to each, it might be contended, that it is impossible they should take the beneficial interest in the whole of this property: but in all they receive under the will they have a joint estate; and these legacies are distinct: the intention therefore is perfectly inconsistent; to give them a joint interest in the general residue and a separate interest in these legacies.

The next consideration is as to the circumstance stated by the bill. There is no suggestion of any fraud by the executors, intimating to the testator, that he need not declare the trusts in writing; but they would execute his objects. The whole moved from *him of his own accord. In those cases also the bill   [* 57] is filed by the person, against whom the fraud is directed; viz. the legatee. The Plaintiffs endeavor to show, a trust was declared, not to give effect to it, but to disappoint the intention. That circumstance distinguishes this case from *Cottington* v. *Fletcher* (1); where the admission of the trust was required by the person claiming under it. With respect to the application of that case to this it is farther to be observed, that it turned upon the admission; and Lord Hardwicke says, it might have been different, if the Defendant had demurred. This bill represents, that no trust was declared: but upon the will there is a trust; viz. the payment of the debts and legacies. The effect of the papers stated in the bill is an admission by the executors, that they do not consider themselves entitled as to the whole or part of the property to take it to their own use. But how is the Court entitled to look at those papers, as evidence of a declaration of trust either by the testator or by themselves? Considered in the former light they can be only evidence of a parol declaration, such as by the Statute of Frauds (2) cannot have effect. These letters cannot have more effect than they would have had, if written by the testator as directions for his executors to follow; and even in that case according to the statute the Court could not have looked at them. This is an attempt to make use of a parol declaration of the testator, evidenced in this manner; which by the statute cannot prevail. But consider, what these papers are. One of the Defendants says, he does not recollect, that the testator used the word "private:" but a disposition to private charities would fulfil the spirit of his intention. Suppose, this had been incorporated in the will; and he had said, his leading wish was to dispose of the whole in public charities: but if that could not be, he gave them power to dispose in private charities in any way they could: it would have been competent to him to give that direction, and to them to execute it: and the Court would not interfere.

All the questions, that can arise upon this state of the case, were before the Court in *Adlington* v. *Cann* (3). How could the Court draw the line as to the proportion to be given to charity; as Lord

(1) 2 Atk. 155.
(2) 29 Car. II. c. 3.
(3) 3 Atk. 141.

Hardwicke states the distinction there? These Defendants give
very contrary accounts of the intention. Your Lordship
[* 58]   will be *under the same difficulty, that Lord Hardwicke
felt upon that occasion; and the uncertainty here is much
greater. If this is considered as a declaration of trust by the Defendants, that cannot avail the heir. They may dispose of it in
charity; and if they do it by an invalid instrument, that disposition
would be void; and the estate would remain in them; as if that instrument had not been executed. The Statute of Mortmain does
not apply to a devise to a trustee; in whom the devisor has a confidence, that he will dispose of it: as the devisor himself might have
done in his life. That discretion may be exercised so that it will
not interfere with the statute.

As to the discovery, having prayed relief, to which they are not
entitled, a general demurrer holds, according to the late cases (1);
though formerly otherwise.

Mr. *Mansfield*, Mr. *Lloyd*, and Mr. *Fonblanque*, for the Plaintiffs.—It is clear, an express trustee, if no trust is declared, cannot
take for his own benefit. *The Bishop of Cloyne* v. *Young* (2), and
Lord Guildford's Case (3). Those are cases of personal estate;
but the law is stronger as to real. So, if in any way it legally and
sufficiently appears, that the testator intended to give the estate for
purposes forbidden by the Mortmain Act; or it fails for want of any
requisite. Has not the heir a right to a discovery, to make them
admit or deny, that the estate was devised to them in trust; and
that they agreed to take it upon that trust? Either no trust was
declared: or, if any, it is by parol. In either case the beneficial
interest results to the heir; who does not require an intention in his
favor. Are not the Defendants to answer, whether the trusts are
forbidden by the Statute of Mortmain? If these papers are contradictory, yet they expressly show, there were trusts: which is enough
for the heir. It would be a gross evasion of the Mortmain Act to
say, that though the trustees admit, the estate is devised to them
upon trusts prohibited by that act, yet it is not void; as there is no
obligation upon them but that of honor; and they may dispose of
it in a manner not prohibited. That would be a gift,
[* 59]   not by the trustees, but by the testator; who had *by
binding them in honor compelled them to comply with his
intention. Whatever argument there might be at the hearing, if
the devise is void at law, what reason is that for refusing to answer?
The construction, that the words in the codicil "upon trust for the
like uses and purposes as my manor and estate at Overseal now
stand limited," can refer to that part of the will, which subjects the
real estate to the debts, is impossible. Why would not *Thynn* v.
Thynn (4) and the other cases of that class apply, where the bill is

(1) See the notes, *ante*, vol. iii. 371; ii. 461.
(2) 2 V. 91.
(3) *Lord North and Guildford* v. *Purdon*, 2 Ves. 495; *Nisbett* v. *Murray*, *ante*,
vol. v. 149, and the references in note, 158.
(4) 1 Vern. 296. Other cases of that nature are collected in the note, *ante*,
vol. iii. 38, 39, to *Pym* v. *Blackburn*.

filed by the heir? If the trust is not sufficiently declared, why is
not he to-avail himself of it. Shall these Defendants, having agreed
to take the estate upon trust, take it discharged of the trust? In
this sense it is a fraud upon the heir; a secret trust; which, if inserted in the will, would be void; and the heir would take. *Cot-*
tington v. *Fletcher* goes the whole length of deciding. this cause for
the Plaintiffs; though Lord Hardwicke appears to rely on the admission in the answer; for it is perfectly incomprehensible, that, if the
Court will decide upon the answer, they will not compel an answer.
In *Adlington* v. *Cann* there was no charge, that the estate was given
to them in trust; and that they agreed to take it upon trust; and it
cannot be concluded, that the Court would not have compelled
them to answer as to that. Neither is it there stated, that they had
acknowledged, the estate was devised to them in trust. The discovery, to which the plea was put in, was, whether by some parol
declaration the testator had not said, he gave them the estate in
trust. Lord Hardwicke's argument is, that it is dangerous to say,
the statute of Mortmain had over-ruled the statute of Frauds, and to
admit parol evidence in such cases. In this case there is no such
question. The whole goes upon the ground, that they accepted as
trustees; and have clearly expressed that by writing under their
hands. As to the personal estate upon the codicil they are clearly
trustees by their legacies. If there is any thing in the bill, which,
if admitted, the Court would execute, as a trust or an agreement, it
follows of course, they must answer; and *Cottington* v. *Fletcher* is
in point to that. Lord Hardwicke determined *Adlington* v. *Cann*
upon the uncertainty of the paper: the Defendants denying, that
there was any trust, except what appeared upon that paper: but if
the fact had been admitted, that the Defendants were trustees for * charity, there would have been no occasion for   [* 60]
parol evidence. The ground, upon which the *Bishop of*
Cloyne v. *Young* proceeded, was, that it was clear, the executors
were not to take beneficially: which was all that was necessary.
In *Loder* v. *Loder* there cited (1) even as to what was not exhausted by the particular purposes of the trust there was a resulting
trust for the heir. The burthen is not upon him. The law gives it
to him; if the trustees cannot show a disposition of it for their benefit.
In the *Attorney General* v. *Duplessis* (2) the words of Chief Baron
Parker upon *Adlington* v. *Cann* are—"But Lord Chancellor was of
opinion, that they should answer. And yet there would have been
a disability and loss of the estate by the Mortmain Act 1736; if it
had come out, that it had been formally devised upon a trust for
charitable uses (3)." That decides this case; for in 1740 they had
pleaded: but Lord Hardwicke said, they should answer. They did
answer; and produced that paper unattested; and said, there was

---

(1) 2 Ves. 96.
(2) Park. 144.
(3) Park. 160.

no other trust. The reason, upon which they were compelled to answer, was, that there was no penalty, forfeiture, &c.: but the disbility to take arose from the policy of the law.

The case of *Bishop* v. *Talbot* (1), cannot be distinguished from *Adlington* v. *Cann*. George Bishop by his will, after some legacies, reciting, that he was possessed of a certain estate as to four tenths, as to his own share, he gave the same to Thomas Talbot and his nephew Bishop, their heirs and assigns for ever in trust; and he gave his personal estate to hold to the use of them, their executors, administrators, and assigns, for ever, upon condition to pay his debts, funeral expenses, &c.: and the residue of his personal estate he gave to them. The bill was filed, stating a secret trust. Exceptions were taken to the answer. By the second answer the Defendants stated, that they had a memorandum in writing; which they believed to be that of the testator, with no witnesses; reciting the will, &c. ; and declaring to them, the executors, the true intent and meaning, that he had given the real and personal estate in trust for charitable purposes specified ; and they stated, that they believed, the premises were not devised upon any secret trust for charitable uses, or to be disposed of otherwise than in the will.

[* 61]   It * came before Sir Thomas Sewell; who said, he did not think, the principal matter would be the validity of the paper writing: the question was, what would be the effect of the answer; supposing, there was no paper; admitting, there was no trust for charitable purposes, except what was mentioned in the answer, this is a sort of disclaimer upon their part ; and the question is, who shall have it ?   The accounts were decreed ; and afterwards upon farther directions it was declared, that the devise of the real estate, subject to the debts and legacies, and the costs, was to be considered as a resulting trust for the heir at law.

In *Boyle* v. *Edwards* (2) a secret trust for a charity was held void ; and there was another case, *Martin* v. *Hutton* (3).   In this case upon the distinct engagement alleged in the bill, to undertake such trust as the testator should declare, the Plaintiffs are entitled to discovery.   The circumstances in *Cottington* v. *Fletcher* did not call for what Lord Hardwicke is represented to have said : it was so palpable, that the Plaintiff could not entitle himself to the estate, that it was immaterial to give him the discovery.   That case was in March 1740 ; and *Adlington* v. *Cann* in July in that year.   The Defendants did there rely on the plea only ; and no notice is taken in Atkyns of what passed upon the discussion of the plea : but it is stated in Barnardiston (4).   That case is very different from this upon the previous engagement by these Defendants, binding the conscience, and the privity between them and the testator as to his

(1) Mss. at the Rolls, 6th February, 1772, referred to, *post*, vol. ix. 520.
(2) In Chancery before Lord Northington, 1769: perhaps *Edwards* v. *Pike*, 1 Eden, 267.
(3) In Chancery before Lord Camden, Nov. 1766.
(4) 3 Barnard. 130.

purpose; but there the devise being perfect by the will was to be affected by something *dehors* the will; to which the devisees were strangers; and resting upon the production of a paper not executed according to the statute of frauds.

As to the right to discovery, certainly in some late instances, where there has been a clear demand at law, and a bill has been filed for discovery, also praying relief, a general demurrer has been allowed: but the contrary practice formerly prevailed. In this case however the Court has a concurrent, and in some respects, a peculiar, jurisdiction. There is no trust whatsoever in writing; *and it is doubtful, whether a Court of Law   [* 62] would suffer the answer admitting the trust to be read: *Rondeau* v. *Wyatt* (1).

The *Solicitor General* [Sir *William Grant*], in reply.—Can the true construction of the statute be, that a declaration of trust not according to the statute shall be obtained by compulsion from the Defendants? Sir Thomas Sewell in the case before him considered the answer as a disclaimer: but if they had by a demurrer protected themselves from answering, the jurisdiction of the Court would not apply. The result of *Adlington* v. *Cann* is, that all the material points arising in this case upon the statute of frauds were before Lord Hardwicke in that; who decided, that he would not give the relief prayed. The plea was ordered to stand for an answer with liberty to except: then all the benefit of the plea was saved to the hearing.

With respect to the discovery, in *Collis* v. *Swayne* (2) the former practice was overturned; and that has been followed ever since.

Lord CHANCELLOR [ELDON], stating the case with great particularity, delivered his opinion.

The bill is filed both for discovery and relief. It is far from my meaning to state, that it does not involve many very important considerations: but upon the whole I shall do better by delivering the opinion I entertain at this moment, with the reasons, upon which it is formed, and giving an immediate opportunity of rehearing the argument, in case that opinion should be wrong, than by withholding the judgment, which at least upon the ground of any argument my own mind at present suggests I do not hope to alter, delay the parties in the opportunity they have by a rehearing to offer better information to the Court than it can suggest to itself.

It is observable upon the interrogating part of the bill, that part does not in the terms of it connect itself with any trust necessarily confined to a secret trust for charitable purposes. I agree, if all the allegations of the bill are necessarily confined to such trust, the interrogating part must be construed according to the alleging part; *and is not to be considered more extensive   [* 63] than the propositions, out of which those interrogatories arise. But it will be seen, whether the allegations do not substantially embrace cases of trust far beyond the purpose to devise on

_____
(1) 2 Hen. Black. 63.
(2) 4 Bro. C. C. 480.

one hand, and carry into execution on the other, a mere trust for
charitable uses; for stating declarations of trust effectual or ineffectual, the bill states a case, in which the heir may be clearly entitled; for there is no doubt, if the trust was ineffectually declared in
its origin, or being effectual, becomes ineffectual, the *Cestuys que
trust*, or a part of them having died in the life of the testator, independent of all questions as to the statutes of fraud or mortmain,. the
trustees would take upon trusts ineffectual in part or the whole.
The bill prays a discovery; and that the Plaintiffs may be declared
entitled as coheirs at law to the residue of the real estate, and an
account; and the general prayer, which frequently has been said to
involve every thing, might be taken as a prayer, that the title-deeds
might be delivered up: but in my view of the case, and admitting
the rule, which I should be sorry to find altered, since I left this
Court, that where you pray both discovery and relief, if not entitled
to the relief, you are not to the discovery (1). I do not examine,
whether the general part of the prayer, understood as asking a general discovery of deeds, &c. would or would not support the bill, if
the other part could not; for independent of that, in my view of the
case this demurrer cannot be maintained; and in cases, which this
bill might possibly bring forth, relief might be due, even if it should
turn out, that the Defendants do not recollect, that any thing relative to charitable uses was in the purpose of the testator. I have
not any conception, that any answer they ever will put in will vary
the case: but I must suppose, that it is possible, these Defendants
may upon their oath give a different account from that, which the
bill alleges they have given. It is not immaterial, that the suggestion of the bill, that the testator applied to them to act as trustees,
is much fortified in Gisborne's letter; for he admits, he had communication with the testator as early as 1789. The allegation is, that he applied to them to act as trustees in the
execution of certain trusts; upon which he had devised or bequeathed, or proposed to devise or bequeath, the residue of his
real and personal estate; and that they agreed to take upon them
the execution of the trusts; as he did then or should duly declare;
which, I admit, means "effectually declare." But still, if
[* 64]   * it is necessary to put the case upon that ground, that
they had agreed to accept the devise upon such trusts as
he should duly declare, I am not quite prepared to say, it is clear,
that, if he made the devise, meaning at the time thereafter duly to
declare trusts, and it happened, that he did not declare any, that
sort of case would not be within the equity of this Court; and
whether, if they admitted, his will was made upon an undertaking,
that they would execute such trusts, the heir would not have a right
to say, no trust was duly declared: the purpose therefore failed;
and the trust results by law to him, not upon the intention, but upon
the ground, that there is no intention; and he is entitled to avail
himself of that. Upon that ground therefore the bill must be answered.

(1) See the references, *ante*, vol. ii. 461; iii. 347.

Strong as the testator's purpose appears upon Gisborne's letter, he did not feel himself quite equal to disappointing his heirs; and therefore he specifically devises some estates to them. If the case stood simply upon the will, the Defendants are as to the personal estate trustees, not merely by virtue of the office, but by express bequest. The legacies of 1000*l.* to each of them in the codicil being equal legacies, the inequality in the amount of the testator's bounty as to the real estate would not alter the inference, that they were to have only the office of executors; and the equality of the legacies would make them trustees of the residue of the personal estate (1). I do not know a case, in which a legacy by a subsequent instrument has attached a trust upon the residue under a prior instrument: but I do not know a case to the contrary; and a strong inference arises, that they should not have the whole, of which the legacies of 1000*l.* were a part; and that is very material here; for it gives countenance to the first allegation in the bill; that, before the will was made the testator applied to them to know, whether they would take the estates upon trusts, which he would or would not declare; and it raises upon just grounds and principles a supposition, that even between the dates of the will and codicil there might have been some uses and trusts, either effectually or ineffectually declared, which attaching themselves upon the gift of the residue of the personal estate by the will would explain, why the testator gave the legacies of 1000*l.* by the codicil to them, to whom by the will he had given the whole residue of his personal estate.

Though it must necessarily * be admitted, that if there   [* 65] were nothing more than the will and codicil, I must put this construction upon the latter, that all these words " uses, trusts," &c. would be satisfied by that, which is really not, strictly speaking, a use or a trust, but a mere charge upon the real estate; if it should be necessary to have resort to it in case of a deficiency of the personal estate, yet upon the will and the codicil, attending to the particular nature of the expressions, and connecting the particularity of the expressions and the inference to be thence deduced, with the allegation, that the Defendants did undertake to take by a devise expressive of some uses, intents, and purposes, the Court is authorised to hold, that though this might have been the construction of the will and codicil alone, it may not be the construction, the whole case being taken together.

In the allegation, that no use or purpose was by the will or otherwise declared, I construe the expression " use or purpose," as contradistinguished from " trust." Though in one sense a trust is a use or purpose, it is capable of being used in a distinct sense; as I think it was by the person, who drew this bill. The latter part of that passage admits of two interpretations; that in fact the testator has not declared any use or purpose; or, that in law he has ineffectually declared; or, that the effectual declaration made has

---

(1) See the note, *ante,* vol. i. 362.

failed.   The question as to that must be answered by looking at the
whole context.   I do not think the Defendants bound to answer the
question, whether it is not manifest by the will and codicil, that they
are trustees.· That must be tried by the contents of the will and
codicil.   The letter of Gisborne discloses communications between
him and the testator from the spring of 1789 to the execution of the
will and codicil; and Gisborne appears to have enjoyed a great deal
of his confidence.   It is most distinctly disclosed in that letter, that
the testator projected an evasion of the law.   Whether he looked to
private donation or public charity, whatever was the nature of the
charity he meant to establish, a distinct communication appears in
this letter, that he dared not put his purpose in writing on account
of the statute of mortmain.   That is a purpose, in aiding which I
can go no farther than the law obliges me either on the part of him,
who projects it, or of him, who promotes it by adopting the execution of it.   On the other hand I can go no farther in
[* 66]   * destroying that purpose than the law furnishes the means.
      But the policy of the law requires, that Courts of justice
should distinctly state, that it is incorrect conduct in both parties, both
him, who projects such a purpose, and him, who carries it into execution.   Though there is great weight in the argument upon *Adlington v. Cann*, that if a trust is declared, yet if it is so loose and
uncertain, how much is for charity, how much for private disposition, that the Court cannot see specifically, what is the subject, upon
which the trust is to attach, it is very difficult, I agree, to attach any ·
trust, I am not prepared to say, upon this letter alone the Court
would be at much loss; or would feel much difficulty upon the
statement of Brown.   An intention is disclosed in that letter not altogether consistent with the other : but it is not to be denied, that
each of those papers leaves a great deal to be disposed of in charity,
according to the declarations of the testator himself; and if the declaration of trust reserved to the Defendants a power of disposing of
such charities as they should think proper, I am not quite sure, the
heir has not a right to call upon them to say, whether they have
done so ; or mean to do so ; and how much they mean to dispose
of, and to give him the rest.   It is a fair subject of argument, whether
Gisborne's apprehension of the testator's meaning would bind the
Court; or whether the Court would not say from the apprehension
of the testator as to the statute of mortmain, the purpose would apply to the whole of the property.
      A very material part of this bill is, the allegation, that the Defend-
ants pretend, the testator has by some writing or otherwise declared
the trusts, upon which they were intended to take the residue of the
real estate ; and that they are willing to hold upon such trusts : and
charging, that the testator has not legally or in any effective manner
declared the trusts; and if he has declared them, they are as to the
real estate, of which the testator was seized at the time of his death,
null and void.   They might be void at his death, but good at the
time they were created.   Surely the heir has a right to know, wheth-

er the trusts were legally declared, and continued effectual to the
testator's death. If bound to answer those questions, they may say,
there was a trust, a writing ; and that, if effectual, they must act according to it. The heir may say, the trust was not well
declared, or has become * ineffectual in the whole or in   [*67]
part. In this view of the case beyond all question the Defendants must answer this bill ; and if they must answer as to any of
the allegations, it is very unnecessary to say at present, whether they
must answer as to the other part. I will not prejudice that part of
the case farther than by saying, that upon an allegation of this kind,
a trust against the policy of the law, the Court does insist, they shall
answer it.

In *Adlington* v. *Cann* there was no trust upon the face of the
will : but a paper was written afterwards, which clearly demonstrates, that the testator's intention was to devote the benefit to charitable purposes. If it rested there, it is clear, a man cannot by an
unexecuted instrument attach a trust upon real estate. But they
pleaded the statute. That must have been allowed to be a good
plea ; unless the Lord Chancellor could have said, though they plead
the statute, yet, if they answer, admitting the trust, it would be fit to
discuss at the hearing, whether he would give the heir the benefit of
the resulting trust. Otherwise he would have allowed the plea at
once ; for they would except ; because there was no answer to the
charge, that the Defendants knew the secret trust, &c. They must
have answered those exceptions, I think, upon the subsequent cases.
When the cause came on again, the plea, the benefit of which was
saved to the hearing, was certainly beneficial ; for it alleged, that,
if there was nothing more in the case than a will expressing no trust,
and a paper that could not be read, and no admission of the trust by
the Defendants, there was nothing in the cause applying to the conscience of the Defendants, or raising the argument upon the policy
of the law, or in favor of the heir ; that if the intention cannot be
effectuated according to law, he shall take the estate upon the
ground, that it is not effectually disposed of. In a subsequent case (1),
Sir Thomas Parker, who must have known *Adlington* v. *Cann*,
took upon himself to examine it ; and when it was very material to
be accurate upon it ; and he says (2) expressly, Lord Hardwicke
compelled the Defendants to answer. If so, we see in a subsequent
case, how Sir Thomas Sewell, no mean authority, a Judge very able
and conversant in equity cases, understood it ; and this appears also
to be the history of *Adlington* v. *Cann* by a note of Serjeant Hill.
In the case before Sir Thomas Sewell the original answer simply
stated the will. A farther answer was required ; and by
the farther answer the Defendants * stated, that there was   [*68]
a memorandum, not duly executed according to the
statute of Frauds : and that memorandum did certainly point to a

(1) *The Attorney General* v. *Duplessis*, Park. 144.
(2) Park. 160.

disposition of the real estate to charitable purposes. Sir Thomas Sewell went a great length upon that, I confess. If he had said, the law would authorize him to hold that a sufficient denotation of an intention, that the devisees should be trustees, the difficulty would be, how he came to read that memorandum. But he took it in another way; that, as they set forth the memorandum, they admitted the purpose of the testator, and put it, not upon the effect of the memorandum *vi suâ*, if I may so express it, but as taken as their admission. I doubt, whether that is quite correct reasoning: but still it furnishes an authority; for Sir Thomas Sewell might be wrong in the fact, that that was an admission: but his opinion is an authority in point of law, that, if there was an admission, he would execute the trust. Then it comes to this; that the doctrine of the Court is, that the Defendant shall answer in such a case; and if he answers in the affirmative, there is a resulting trust for the heir.

Cottington v. *Fletcher* does not affect this case. That case was upon the grant of an advowson contrary to the policy of the law, by a Roman Catholic in trust for himself. Afterwards he turns Protestant; and desires a discovery as to his own act. The Defendant put in a plea of the statute of Frauds; but by answer admitted the trust. Lord Hardwicke is made to say, that upon the admission he would act (1). I do not know, whether he did act upon it; but it is questionable, whether he should; for there is a great difference between the case of an heir coming to be relieved against the act of his ancestor in fraud of the law, and of a man coming upon his own act under such circumstances. It is there said, it might be different, if it had come on upon demurrer. The reason given is, that as this assignment was done in fraud of the law, and merely in order to evade the statutes, it was doubtful whether at the hearing the Plaintiff could be relieved. Lord Hardwicke means to say, that, if the Defendant admits the trust, though against the policy of the law, he would relieve; but if he does not admit the trust, but demurs, [*69] he would do, what does *not apply in the least to this case; the Plaintiff stating, he had been guilty of a fraud upon the law, to evade, to disappoint, the provision of the Legislature, to which he is bound to submit, and coming to equity to be relieved against his own act, and the defence being dishonest, between the two species of dishonesty the Court would not act; but would say, "Let the estate lie, where it falls." That is not this case.

Then as to the principle: why should it not be so? Surely the law will not permit secret agreements to evade what upon grounds of public policy is established? Is the Court to feel for individuals, and to oblige persons to discover in particular cases, and not to feel for the whole of its own system and compel a discovery of frauds, that go to the roots of its whole system? Suppose, the trust was to pay 100*l*. out of the estate; and the devisee undertakes to pay it, if it is not inserted in the will: this Court would have compelled an

---

(1) *Cooth* v. *Jackson, ante,* 12; *post,* vol. ix. 520.

answer, on the ground, that the testator would not have devised the estate to him, unless he had undertaken to pay that sum (1).   The principle is, that the statute shall not be used to cover a fraud.   If that is so between individuals, and upon an individual claim, there is surely a stronger call upon the justice of the Court to say, upon a private bargain between the testator and those, who are to take apparently under his will, which is to defeat the whole of the provisions and policy of the law; that they shall be called on to say, whether they took the estate, as they legally may not do, for charitable purposes.   It is very difficult to say, that, if the justice due to individuals obliges them to disclose in the one case, the justice due to the public shall not oblige them in the other.   I am very glad to find upon the authorities, that they are to make the disclosure.   It is difficult to say in sound argument, that the principle of policy is not sufficient : but I do not mean to decide upon this.   The other grounds, that I first stated, are quite sufficient.   If I am bound to say, whether the bill stating the letters does or does not make a difference, I can find no authority, that the defendants shall not answer, whether they put the declaration of trust in writing.

Upon the former of these grounds therefore I over-rule this demurrer (2).

1. A GENERAL charge in a bill brought in Equity, enables the plaintiff to put all incidental questions, necessary or material, to the proof of the fact charged: *Faulder* v. *Stuart*, 11 Ves. 302: but he cannot interrogate as to substantive distinct facts, not noticed in the allegations of his bill: *Bullock* v. *Richardson*, 11 Ves. 376; and see, *post*, the note to *Clarke* v. *Turton*, 11 V. 240: for the plaintiff's equity should appear in the stating or charging part of his bill; otherwise a demurrer will hold: *Flint* v. *Field*, 2 Anstr. 543; *Hovenden* v. *Lord Annesley*, 2 Sch. & Lef. 638: though if the defendant answer interrogatories not founded on the allegations of the bill, he thereby cures the informality of the bill; since the facts may be put in issue by the answer and replication thereto, as well as by the bill; and either party may thereupon proceed to examine witnesses. *Attorney General* v. *Whorwood*, 1 Ves. Sen. 539.

2. As to the extent to which relief may be given under the general prayer of a bill; see note 5 to *Weymouth* v. *Bowyer*, 1 V. 416.

3. With respect to the general doctrine, that a plaintiff who asks relief to which he is not entitled, cannot insist on a discovery, to which if he had asked no more, he would have been entitled; see note 1 to *Renison* v. *Ashley*, 2 V. 459.

4. That *equal* legacies to all a testator's executors, exclude them from a beneficial interest in the residue of his property; see note 2 to *Nisbett* v. *Murray*, 5 V. 149.

5. Not only when, as in the principal case, a defendant's answer admits a secret trust for charitable purposes; but also whenever any written declaration of the testator corroborates the suggestion of a secret trust of the kind, affecting real estate, as alleged by the bill of the testator's heir; the devisee must at least answer.   By such answer, however, he may insist on his title under a will duly executed, and (when he was not privy to the writing creating an honorary trust,) that he ought not to be prevented from retaining the devised estate for *his own* use : *Stickland* v. *Aldridge*, 9 Ves. 516; *Boson* v. *Statham*, 1 Cox, 19: and if the heir produce no evidence, either of a trust expressed, or of such an engagement, (by

(1) See cases of that kind referred to in the note, *ante*, vol. iii. 38.
(2) This case was afterwards argued upon the answer, admitting the trust; and, after standing some time for judgment, was compromised. See *post, Stickland* v. *Aldridge*, vol. ix. 516; *Paine* v. *Hall*, xviii. 475.

words, or by silence,) as would authorize the Court to say, the devisee undertook
to do that which prevented the devisor from imposing upon him an express trust; ·
the bill must be dismissed with costs, unless the heir ask for an issue *devisavit vel
non*; to that he is entitled: *Paine v. Hall*, 18 Ves. 475; for every heir has a
right to be satisfied whether he is effectually disinherited: *White* v. *Wilson*, 13 Ves.
91; *Berney* v. *Eyre*, 3 Atk. 387: but if, at the hearing of the cause, he refuse an
issue, the Court will establish the will against him. *Jackson* v. *Barry*, 2 Cox, 225.

6. That the Statute of Frauds may be insisted on, by a defendant who has
admitted a verbal agreement; see note 3 to *Moore* v. *Edwards*, 4 V. 23.

7. An undertaking, express or implied, by which the formal insertion of a provision in a will is prevented, raises a trust against the party who entered into such
engagement, see the note to *Barrow* v. *Greenough*, 3 V. 152.

[* 70]   WALKER *v.* FROBISHER.

[1801, MAY 7.]

AWARD set aside: the arbitrator having received evidence after notice to the parties, that he would receive no more; in which they acquiesced (a).
Under a reference to settle the matter in difference, and award such alterations in
the Defendant's works as to the arbitrator should seem necessary, regard being
had to their state at a particular period, an award, directing no other alteration
than that parts of the machinery, which were made of wood, should be made
of cast iron, was held a due execution of the authority.

THE object of the bill in this cause, was to quiet the Plaintiff in
the possession of his mill; after he had recovered damages in two
actions against the Defendant for using his mill in a manner, that
impeded the use and enjoyment of that belonging to the Plaintiff.
When the cause came on before Lord Rosslyn, his Lordship with
the consent of the parties, directed a reference to Mr. Busfield to
settle the matter in difference between the parties, and award such
alterations to be made in the Defendant's works as to him (Mr.
Busfield) should seem necessary; regard being had to their state
previous to June 1794.

The arbitrator by his award found, that the working of the Plaintiffs's mill had not been impeded to any material extent, if at all, by
the alterations of the Defendant's; regard being had to their state
previous to June 1794; and he directed, that the Defendant's works
should be continued in the same state, as they were; but that, as
they were made of wood, and easily alterable, certain parts of the

(a) If an arbitrator examine one of the parties, or his witnesses, without notice
to the opposite party, the award will be set aside. *In re Hick*, 8 Taunt. 694;
Pepper v. *Gorham*, 4 J. B. Moore, 148; *Watson* v. *Trower*, 1 R. & M. 18. Notwithstanding an oath from the arbitrator that such examination did not influence
his judgment. *Featherstone* v. *Cooper, post*, 9 V. 69; *Harcourt* v. *Ramsbottom*,
1 Jac. & W. 512; *contra, Atkinson* v. *Abraham*, 1 Bos. & P. 175; 1 Stephens,
Nisi P. 87. As to awards, and particularly the impeachment thereof, see *ante*,
note (a), *Price* v. *Williams*, 1 V. 365; note (a), *Knox* v. *Symmonds*, 1 V. 369;
note (a), *Morgan* v. *Mather*, 2 V. 15; note (a), *Emery* v. *Wase*, 5 V. 847.

machinery should be made of cast iron. The award did not direct any other alteration.

A motion was made to set aside this award upon the following facts disclosed by two affidavits.

At one of the meetings, the arbitrator expressed his opinion, that the inlets to the Defendant's mill were too deep ; but not so much too deep as the Plaintiff insisted they were ; and that the truth lay between them. After several witnesses had been examined on both sides in the presence of the parties or their attorneys, the arbitrator advised the parties to produce no more witnesses ; declaring his determination to examine no more witnesses in the cause ; but on the day which he had settled for finally arranging his award, and on which he had directed the surveyors to attend, whom he was authorised to call in, and had called in, for the purpose of assisting him, three persons attended on the part of the Defendant ; and the arbitrator examined those three persons ; and took minutes of what they said: although no person attended on *be- [*71] half of the Plaintiff; and the arbitrator then made his award as above stated.

The arbitrator by his affidavit stated, that he had examined all the witnesses produced before him on either side at different meetings for that purpose ; and having fully made up his mind on the subject on the 3d of February he appointed the surveyors to meet him on the 10th for the purpose of preparing the award : but, one being unable to attend, he had adjourned to a future day to make his award. On the 10th of February, several persons came into the room, where the deponent and the surveyors were, unattended by the solicitors on either side ; and did mention some circumstances relative to the matters in dispute ; of which the deponent believes he made some minutes : but they were at the same time told by him, that he had previously satisfied his mind on the subject, and he should proceed to make his award.

The affidavit farther stated, that nothing, which passed, had the least weight with him ; and that the award contains his decided opinion before the 10th of February, and since ; and he denied, to the best of his recollection having said at any meeting, that the Defendants inlets were too deep, or having expressed any opinion whatsoever on the subject.

(1) Mr. *Sutton* and Mr. *Heald,* in support of the motion, referred to *Morgan* v. *Mather* (2) ; as stating the grounds on which awards might be set aside ; within which they insisted the facts disclosed by the affidavits, brought this case. They contended farther that the arbitrator had not pursued his authority ; and the answer admitting, that the mills were not in the same state as they were previously to June 1794, was conclusive against the Defendant ; and the arbitrator was bound to award such alteration as would bring them to that state.

(1) *Ex relatione.*
(2) *Ante,* vol. ii. 15.

Mr. *Lloyd* and Mr. *King*, in support of the award, urged, that the parties had produced all the evidence in their power on either side, and the affidavits do not insinuate, that any new evidence was or could have been pronounced. They insisted that [* 72]   * the award was consonant to the order of reference, to award such alterations, as to the arbitrator should seem necessary ; and there was no necessity for him to award any alteration ; if he did not think it requisite.

Upon the last point they were stopped by the Lord Chancellor ; who said, in that respect, the arbitrator had properly exercised his power.

(1) Lord CHANCELLOR [ELDON].—This award cannot be supported. The arbitrator, having been named by the late Lord Chancellor [Loughborough], is, I am well assured, a most respectable man : but he has been surprised into a conduct, which upon general principles must be fatal to the award. It does not appear to me, that he has by the award improperly exercised the authority given by the order of reference : but on account of the transaction that took place on the 10th of February, the award cannot stand. He had examined different witnesses at different times in the presence of the parties. He recommended to them not to produce any more witnesses. To that recommendation they accede ; and in effect say, "Upon the view of what is disclosed to you do what is right between us." After this he hears these other persons ; and he admits, he took minutes of what was said. It did not pass as mere conversation. It does not appear, that he afterwards held any communication with the other party ; or disclosed what passed to him : but the arbitrator swears it had no effect upon his award. I believe him. He is a most respectable man. But I cannot from respect for any man do that, which I cannot reconcile to general principles. A Judge must not take upon himself to say, whether evidence improperly admitted had or had not an effect upon his mind. The award may have done perfect justice : but upon general principles it cannot be supported (2).

———

SEE note 4 to *Knox* v. *Symmonds*, 1 V. 369.

———

(1) *Ex relatione.*
(2) See *post*, vol. ix. 68 ; *Atkinson* v. *Abraham*, 1 Bos. & Pul. 175.

PULTENEY *v.* WARREN.

[1801, April 22, 24; May 11.]

Account of *mesne* profits, since the title accrued, decreed against executors upon the special ground, that the Plaintiff was prevented from recovering in ejectment by a rule of the Court of law and by an injunction at the instance of the occupier; who ultimately failed both at law and in equity (a).

No action of trespass for *mesne* profits against the executor (b), [p. 86.]

The simple case of the death of the occupier will not sustain a bill for an account of the *mesne* profits under the head of accident (c), [p. 88.]

Upon such a bill by an infant the ground is infancy, and the character of the Defendant, as bailiff or receiver (d), [p. 89.]

No such bill by an heir, merely as such, unless some impediment at law; as possession of the deeds by the Defendant, terms, &c. [p. 89.]

The case of the dowress has turned upon the difficulty arising from her want of information and the possession of it by the Defendant (e), [p. 89.]

Ground of the case of mines; which is in nature of a trade: as to timber, the account depends upon the jurisdiction for an injunction, [p. 89.]

The case of tithes turns upon the property in the tithes (f), [p. 90.]

There must be either a difficulty to recover at law, or fraud, concealment, &c. [p. 90.]

Upon a motion for a new trial for excessive damages, the Court of law would take care, that the right of the Plaintiff should not be prejudiced by the death of the Defendant, [p. 90.]

Whether action for *mesne* profits can be maintained before judgment in ejectment, *Quære* (g), [p. 91.]

No relief, where the interest goes beyond the penalty of a bond, if occasioned by the delay of the Plaintiff, the obligor (h), [p. 92.]

A creditor prevented by the act of the Court from obtaining judgment put in the same situation, as if he had it, [p. 93.]

Account of rents and profits confined to the filing of the bill, filed upon grounds of equitable relief against a mere adverse possession, without fraud, &c. [p. 93.]

(a) As to the jurisdiction of Equity in regard to rents and profits, see 1 Story, Eq. Jur. § 508 to § 519. In the ordinary cases of *mesne* profits, where a clear remedy exists at law, Equity will not interfere, but will leave the party to his remedy at law. Some special circumstances are necessary to draw into activity the remedial interference of a Court of Equity; and when they exist, it will interfere, not only in cases arising under contract, but in cases arising under direct or constructive *torts.* Ibid, § 511.

(b) At common law an action for trespass of *mesne* profits cannot be maintained against an executor or administrator. 2 Williams, Exec. 1232. Yet he is liable in an action for use and occupation for the rent up to the day of the demise in the action of ejectment. Ibid.

(c) See 1 Story, Eq. Jur. § 513.

(d) See 1 Story, Eq. Jur. § 511.

(e) See *ante*, note (a), *Mundy* v. *Mundy*, 2 V. 122; 1 Story, Eq. Jur. § 627.

(f) 2 Williams, Exec. 1234.

(g) Where the term of the plaintiff in ejectment expires before the trial, although the possession of the property cannot be recovered, yet he may proceed for damages for the trespass, and for the *mesne* profits. *Brown* v. *Galloway*, 1 Peters, C. C. 292.

(h) As to the computation of interest beyond the penalty of a bond. See *ante*, note (a), *Mackworth* v. *Thomas*, 5 V. 330. Courts of Equity will decree the obligee of a bond interest beyond the penalty of the bond, where, by unfounded and protracted litigation, the obligor has prevented the obligee from prosecuting his claim at law for a length of time, which has deprived the latter of his legal rights, when they might otherwise have been made available at law. In such

THIS cause arose in consequence of the final decision of the causes of *Lady Cavan* v. *Pulteney*, and *Lord Darlington* v. *Pulteney* (1), concerning the validity of the leases granted by the late General Pulteney of several houses in Sackville Street, Piccadilly. The result of those suits being against the leases, this bill was filed against the executors of the late Dr. Warren, one of the tenants, for an account of the mesne profits in respect of the house occupied by him from July, 1791, when the possession was required by the Plaintiff, to July 1797.

The circumstances and dates were these. Upon the 2d of July, 1790, Dr. Warren and the other tenants received notices to quit. Upon the 5th of July, 1791, a formal demand to quit was served upon them. In Trinity Term 1791 an ejectment was brought in the Court of King's Bench by Sir William Pulteney against Spottiswood, an under-tenant of Lady Cavan, one of the lessees; who by a rule of the Court was admitted to defend the action in the room of Spottiswood. The demise in that ejectment was dated the 6th of July. Issue was joined upon a plea of the general issue; and at the trial after Michaelmas Term 1791, a special verdict was found; which was argued in Easter Term 1794; and a final judgment was obtained by the Plaintiff upon the 24th of May, 1794. Soon afterwards Lady Cavan sued out a writ of error returnable in the House of Lords. In Easter Term 1794 other ejectments were brought by Sir William Pulteney against Dr. Warren and all the other occupiers; who pleaded the general issue; and in Trinity Term following upon their application to the Court of King's Bench an order was made in each of these actions, that the proceedings should be stayed; the Defendants undertaking to abide the event of the special verdict in the cause against Lady Cavan, and not to bring any writ of error for delay. Upon the 7th of May, 1795, the judgment obtained against Lady Cavan was affirmed in the House of Lords. The bill of Lady Cavan, Dr. Warren, and the other tenants, was then filed;

[*74]   and the bill of *Lord Darlington; and upon the 1st of May, 1795, the order for the injunction was obtained in those causes; with liberty to move to dissolve it, in case the Plaintiffs should not set down their causes for hearing in Michaelmas Term ensuing. Under that order the injunction issued upon the 29th of July; and, the causes not being set down pursuant to the order, a motion to dissolve the injunction was made in Michaelmas Term. 1795. That motion was refused. Upon the 3d of June, 1797, Lord Darlington's bill was dismissed; and upon the 3d and 19th of June the order was made in the other cause, retaining the bill for twelve months; the Plaintiffs to be at liberty to bring actions in con-

---

cases Courts of Equity do no more than supply and administer, within their own jurisdiction, a substitute for the original legal rights of the obligee, of which he has been unjustifiably deprived by the misconduct of the obligor. *East India Co.* v. *Campion*, 11 Bligh, 159; 2 Story, Eq. Jur. § 1316a. See, also, *Moneypenny* v. *Bristow*, 2 Russ. & M. 117.

(1) *Ante*, vol. ii. 544; iii. 384.

sequence of their eviction; and an inquiry was directed, how the assets of General Pulteney were disposed of; and the injunction was dissolved. Upon the 16th of December, 1797, the minutes of that order were varied by inserting a direction, that the Plaintiffs should not take out execution in those actions till farther order. Upon the 17th of June, 1797, Sir William Pulteney moved the Court of King's Bench for leave to enter up judgment against Dr. Warren; which was ordered in Trinity Term. Upon the 22d of June, 1797, Dr. Warren died. Upon the 19th of July following possession was delivered by his executors.

The bill represented, that the Plaintiff was prevented by the order made by the Court of King's Bench for staying the proceedings from entering up judgment against Dr. Warren; and that before the necessary application could be made to that Court for leave to enter up judgment, the bill was filed by the tenants; upon which the injunction was obtained.

The Defendants by their answer insisted, that they ought not to account for the mesne profits demanded by the Plaintiff; the same not being recoverable at law or in equity; and suggested, that the Plaintiff stood by; and allowed Dr. Warren to lay out considerable sums in improvements. They also filed a bill against Sir William Pulteney: praying a discovery as to that among other things; and whether Sir William Pulteney did not know previously, that the lease was void. The answer to that bill stated, that most of the expensive alterations were made before the decision of the point; that the Defendant never concealed, but avowed, his intention to break the lease if he could; that he did not know, in 1794 or *1796, that Dr. Warren had laid out large sums; and that [*75] the estate was managed by his agent.

A treaty had been entered into for ascertaining the mesne profits, and making an allowance in respect of the improvements: but they could not agree.

Mr. *Alexander*, Mr. *Romilly*, and Mr. *Dowdeswell*, for the Plaintiff.—This Plaintiff stands in a situation very different from the abstract case of a person seeking relief in respect of the mesne profits merely upon the death of the Defendant. The application for equity raises a very different case. The question however is so considerable to the jurisdiction of the Court, that it is proper to argue it as an abstract question; as if the circumstance of the injunction did not occur. The great objection will be, that there is no authority for such a demand. Certainly there is no particular case to be found; but it stands upon principle; and relief of the same nature is granted in cases, where the claims of justice are not so strong. The nature of this claim at law and of the obstruction is to be first ascertained. The difficulty arises from the axiom "*actio personalis moritur cum persona*." That is not universally, or even generally, true. It holds generally in the case of a tort: but trover and many other actions, though in the form of a tort are really claims of property. There is a great distinction even at law as to the action not surviving against an executor in respect of the cause of action and in respect of the form of action. Instances of the former are actions of assault, battery, &c. But where the form of the action is a tort, but it is in substance a claim of property and a duty demanded from the assets of the testator, in respect of his having enjoyed a benefit, as in the action for mesne profits, the action would survive; either an action for money had and received, or for use and occupation; according to the circumstance of possession either by the Defendant himself or by a tenant. In *Hambly* v. *Trott* (1) Lord Mansfield fully discusses this distinction.

Next, what is the particular nature of the impediment at law? The case of *Birch* v. *Wright* (2) shows, that Courts of law have said, by perhaps too narrow a construction, that having [* 76]   once * treated the Defendant as a trespasser, the Plaintiff shall not bring an action for use and occupation. But in this case that arises from an accidental and collateral circumstance, his obstinacy in refusing to deliver possession, and putting the Plaintiff to an action of trespass. There can be no question, the legal duty survives on account of the benefit to the estate. Is it not also the invariable rule of this Court to act in aid of a legal duty, where the objection is only of form? Though no direct, precise, authority upon the abstract question can be produced, it is said by the *Solicitor General* in *Dormer* v. *Fortescue* (3), and not denied at the bar or by the Court,'that there are many such cases. The only denial of it is in the argument of the late Attorney General (4) in *Curtis* v. *Curtis* (5): and upon principle and cases bearing the closest analogy the question must be determined with the Plaintiff. In *The Bishop of Winchester* v. *Knight* (6) the Lord Chancellor in granting the account of the ore and timber points evidently at the distinction; which is more developed by Lord Mansfield in the case in Cowper. The principle is precisely the same upon the possession of an esta e and the profit arising from digging ore or cutting timber. There is no distinction between waste and any other case. The action of waste dies with the person, as the action of trespass for mesne profits : but in both the duty is imposed upon the assets in respect of the benefit received. It may be said, the habit of the Court to grant accounts of this nature is founded on the difficulty of ascertaining the quantum of damages. But what difference arises upon that? The Court acts only in aid of the legal remedy; and where that legal right against the executor does exist, the Court will act in support of it; and will not suffer the right to be without a remedy. In *Taylor* v. *Crompton* (7), a difficulty was stated in recovering at law; and upon ex-

(1) Cowp. 371.
(2) 1 Term Rep. B. R. 378.
(3) 3 Atk. 124.
(4) Lord Redesdale.
(5) 2 Bro. C. C. 620.
(6) 1 P. Will. 406. See *Lord Hardwicke* v. *Vernon, ante,* vol. iv. 411.
(7) Bunb. 95.

amining the record it appears, the bill was retained, with liberty to .
the Plaintiff to proceed at law. In *Curtis* v. *Curtis* nothing turned
upon the circumstance, that the bill was retained ; and the account of
the mesne profits was decreed.   Consider the nature of the title to
mesne profits in the action of dower ; which is very analogous.   At
common law the widow was not entitled to mesne profits.   That
right was given by the Statute of Merton (1) ; and Lord
*Coke observes (2), was only recoverable in one form of   [*77]
action, the writ of dower, *unde nihil habet.*   Upon what
principle then was the account decreed in *Curtis* v. *Curtis*, but that,
wherever a debt is fixed upon the assets as to the mesne profits, this
Court will enforce it, though the remedy should be entirely gone at
law ?   That is the first case, in which the remedy was given for the
mesne profits : all the others being merely cases as to setting out
dower.   The inference, there is no such limitation of the power of
this Court as will be contended, appears even from the cases, in
which relief was refused : and the objection, that will be stated, is
not to be found in those cases ; but they are put upon other grounds,
intelligible, analogous to the principle of law, and not affecting the
principle, upon which the relief is sought.   It is clear, that even at
law, the title to mesne profits does not accrue before entry, or some
act analogous, as that of bringing an ejectment ; and in those cases
the objection is, that for want of that there is no duty at law.   In
Hutton v. *Simpson* (3) it was put upon that ground : but no idea
was entertained of this objection.   In *Norton* v. *Frecker* (4) also it
was put upon the same point ; and no such objection was made,
that the action for mesne profits cannot be maintained against an executor.   Both classes of cases therefore establish the proposition,
that, wherever there is a legal duty, and a defect of remedy, the
Court will give relief according to the circumstances.

With respect to the right of tenants in common against each other
as to the mesne profits the history of the law is singular.   It appears, there is no remedy by the one against the other for mesne
profits, unless the other was bailiff (5).   Littleton (6) says, if the
one occupy all, and put the other out of possession and occupation,
the latter shall have against the former a writ of *ejectione firmæ* of
the moiety, &c.   Lord Coke says upon that, the words " and put
the other out of possession and occupation " are materially added ; for
though one take the whole profits, the other has no remedy by law
against him ; for the taking the whole profits is no ejectment.   This
mischief was not remedied until the act for the amendment of
the law (7) gave an action of account by one tenant in com-

(1) 20 Hen. III. c. 1.
(2) Co. Lit. 32 *b.*
(3) 2 Vern. 722 ; the 6th resolution.
(4) 1 Atk. 524.
(5) Co. Lit. 199 *b.* ; 200 *b.*
(6) Sect. 322.
(7) Stat 4, Ann. c. 16, s. 27.

mon against the other.   Before that period the habit of this
Court was to grant relief upon the legal title in respect of the
want of a legal remedy. *Drury* v. *Drury* (1). *Dean* v. *Wade* (2).
The last case upon looking into the record appears to be precisely like the other.   A trial at law was ordered; in which
there was a recovery by the Plaintiff of one moiety.   The Court
was disposed to direct an account; but no Counsel appearing for
the Defendant, it was to be argued on his behalf on a subsequent
day.   There is no doubt upon that case, that this was the habit of
the Court; though there was no legal remedy.   In modern times
the same point has been determined: *The Duke of Leeds* v. *Powell* (3).   *The Duke of Leeds* v. *The Corporation of New Radnor* (4); and the same principle is laid down by Lord Hardwicke in
Benson v. *Baldwyn* (5).   The whole jurisdiction of the Court is a
comment upon, and establishes, this principle; that wherever a legal
duty is disappointed by accident, this Court will support it; and
there is not a dictum to the contrary, except what is said at the bar
in *Curtis* v. *Curtis*.

   Next, as to the particular circumstances in this case; the dates
show, the Plaintiff was prevented from recovering by the application of the Defendants and the interposition of the Court in consequence.   *Dormer* v. *Fortescue* and many other cases ascertain, that
this Court will give this account, where it is not essential; as, where
the Plaintiff has occasion to come to this Court for a discovery of a
deed. All those instances of such relief upon the legal title are founded in convenience: this is upon the stronger ground of necessity.
They come under a pretence of equity sufficiently plausible to induce the Court to assist them for a time; but which ultimately fails.
The Plaintiff, if not so prevented, might have executed his writ of
possession immediately; and then have commenced the action, 2
Chan. Cas. 217.   *Tilly* v. *Bridges* (6).   It is admitted, that from
July 1791 to the death of Dr. Warren, he was wrongfully in possession; that there is no legal remedy; that the Plaintiff was prevented from availing himself of the legal remedy he once had by the
                 interposition of this Court upon the unfounded claim of
[*79]   the Defendants. The institution of Courts of *Equity as
                 Lord Mansfield has expressed it, is to prevent substan-
tial justice from being entangled in the net of form.   Is the Court
by a form, instituted by itself, to prevent a party having a legal
remedy from availing himself of it?   The injustice is manifest. Suppose an unquestionable legal right to a sum of money: and from negligence or indolence nearly six years are suffered to elapse; and then
the creditor intimates, that he means to bring an action, and the

(1) Rep. Ch. 26.
(2) Rep. Ch. 26.
(3) 1 Ves. 171.
(4) 2 Bro. C. C. 338, 518.
(5) 1 Atk. 598.
(6) Pre. Ch. 252; 2 Vern. 519; 2 Eq. Ca. Ab. 588.

other should file a bill for an injunction; stating a great number of circumstances, founded in fiction, and so entangled, that it is impossible to put in an answer in time; and afterwards it appears upon oath, that the Court was imposed upon by the Plaintiff: could the Court suffer itself to be made the instrument of iniquity? The case (1) in 2 Chancery Cases is exactly of that kind.

Lord CHANCELLOR [ELDON].—There is a case in Shower's Parliamentary Cases (2): where a decree for principal and interest beyond the penalty of the bond was affirmed upon the very ground, that the party was prevented from going on at law, while the demand was under the penalty.

For the Plaintiff.—That strongly fortifies the argument. The Plaintiff could not bring the action for mesne profits, until the judgment was affirmed in the House of Lords: but if he could, it would not have been proper to do so.

Mr. *Mansfield* and Mr. *Fonblanque*, for the Defendants.—The question can only be upon the particular circumstances, whether the bill brought by the lessees gives Sir William Pulteney a right to sue here for mesne profits; for as to any other equity the claim is against all principle, and the rules, that have long prevailed in this Court. If a legal demand has existed, which is gone by the death of the person, against whom it existed, this Court has never upon the ground of accident enforced that demand against the representative. Death is not the sort of accident, that gives such a jurisdiction. In *Hambly* v. *Trott* it was determined, that trover does not lie against the executor, because the plea is "not guilty." It was never imagined, that because the action of trover is gone this Court has a jurisdiction. With respect to the timber, no principle will support *The Bishop of * Winchester* v. *Knight*;   [80] though certainly this Court has entertained bills *inter vivos*: *Lee* v. *Alston* (3); probably on account of the difficulty and inadequacy of the remedy at law; and that it was necessary to come for a discovery. The case in Bunbury is very obscure. Those cases stand by themselves. In the old books a bill for mesne profits is talked of in a very obscure way; as if this Court had a concurrent jurisdiction with the law: but that has long ceased to be the law of this Court; which in later times has never assumed any jurisdiction as to mesne profits. In *Jesus College* v. *Bloom* (4) it was held, that a bill does not lie for an account of waste after the determination of the estate of the tenant. The true grounds for coming here for an account of mesne profits are stated by Lord Hardwicke in the judgment (5) upon *Dormer* v. *Fortescue*. The result is, that where

---

(1) *Anonymous*, 2 Ch. Ca. 217.
(2) *Duvall* v. *Terry*, Show. P. C. 15. By mistake it is stated, that the Respondents were arrested. The Appellant Elizabeth Duvall was the obligor. See the note, *ante*, vol. i. 452; 1 Sch. & Lef. 434.
(3) 3 Bro. C. C. 37; *ante*, vol. i. 78.
(4) 3 Atk. 262.
(5) 3 Atk. 129.

the Plaintiff is obliged on account of a trust term standing out, or fraud, misrepresentation, or concealment, to sue here, and not at law, this Court will give the mesne profits; but never, where there is a remedy at law; and Lord Hardwicke expressly disclaims the jurisdiction; and does not admit the latitude of the case in Vernon (1). There is no sense in what is said in *Hutton* v. *Simpson* as to there being no entry. In the other case cited from the same book the circumstances do not appear. The case of tenants in common has no relation to any suit like this. Certainly the old law in not permitting an account between them was extraordinary; but before the statute there was no legal remedy; as there is in this case. The case as to rents proceeds upon this ground; that it was not known, what rent was due: *The Duke of Leeds* v. *The Corporation of New Radnor* (2); which is the common case : the rent being inconsiderable; and the landlord not knowing upon what part of the land to distrain; and therefore the legal remedy is gone. Those cases will not sustain this jurisdiction, where there is a plain legal remedy. It is contrary to all experience, that the single circumstance, that a party has by death lost his legal remedy, raises this jurisdiction, except upon mere personal injuries. It is admitted, there is no authority; but it is contended upon the principle. In *Curtis* v. *Curtis* all this doctrine was considered. The whole case proceeds upon the equitable right the widow had originally to come into this Court. In *The Duke of Bolton* v. *Deane* (3) [*81]   *there was the clear ground of concealment and misrepresentation.

The only real question therefore is upon the circumstances of this case; whether what passed in consequence of the bills filed in this Court gives this jurisdiction : the Plaintiff being by the injunction prevented from pursuing his legal remedy. That cannot be maintained. He was stopped by the Court of King's Bench till 1795. The moment the judgment was affirmed in the House of Lords, if he had applied here, he might have had leave to obtain judgment in the Court of King's Bench. Instead of that he took no step to enable himself to proceed in his ejectment. He ought to have applied to the Court; stating, that the party might die, and he might be prejudiced. Therefore he is himself guilty of laches; having rested for two years longer. The answer to the cases put of the Statute of Limitations is, that if a party is apprehensive of being injured by any such accident, the constant course of the Court is to order the party not to set up the Statute of Limitations, or, that five years have elapsed since a fine, &c.; but that is done upon an application in the suit, in which the injunction is granted by the party in danger from the delay, for an order to prevent that advantage being gained by the other. If he does not make the application, that cannot be the subject of a new suit. To found the jurisdiction there must

---

(1) *Anon.* 1 Vern. 105.
(2) 2 Bro. C. C. 338, 518.
(3) Pre. Ch. 516.

be an original equity drawing with it as a consequence the account
of mesne profits. It is an established rule, that, where one party
has obtained a legal advantage, he shall not be deprived of it, unless
by an equity prior to that, which he can connect with· his legal advantage. They must at least make out a case of higher equity ; for
if the equities are equal, the Court will not interpose against the legal
right. The material point is, whether the Defendants can with a
safe conscience retain what is demanded. From the absence of
precedent the presumption, that there is no such principle, is not unfair. Many instances must have occurred, if such a principle, that
wherever the legal remedy is gone, the Court will take jurisdiction,
exists. In all the cases, the relief has been founded upon special
circumstances, excluding the notion of any general principle. In
Bouverie v. *Prentice* (1) Lord Thurlow held, that this Court
will not relieve in the case of a quit-rent, where the *party   [* 82]
has a remedy at law. The case of the dowress is really
an anomalous case ; and is so treated in *Mundy* v. *Mundy* (2), subsequent to *Curtis* v. *Curtis.*

If the Plaintiff had laid the demise more recently, he might have
brought his action for use and occupation, instead of trespass : but
he has converted the occupier into a trespasser in a Court of Law
from the time his title accrued by laying the demise so far back ; and
now wishes to treat him as tenant in equity. Having the choice of
treating him as tenant or trespasser he chose the latter. The impediment to proceeding at law is created by their own act. That
cannot constitute a ground for coming here. A jury would have
had to determine, not merely as to the rents and profits, but the
quantum of damages. It would have been competent to the Defendant to have shown, that the Plaintiff was benefited by an expenditure upon the premises far exceeding the rents and profits ;
and therefore, that it was a case for nominal damages. This bill
does not take in that consideration. It seeks dryly an account of
rents and profits, without offering any allowance in respect of repairs
and improvements ; which would have been taken into consideration
at law ; the gist of the action being the extent of the damage. But
whatever may be the rule at law, in this Court a case may arise so
strong, that the Defendants would be entitled to an allowance even
beyond substantial improvements ; though in general the reference
is confined to substantial improvements, to prevent it from being
entangled.

However harsh it may appear, that a party should suffer loss by the
act of the Court, it would be more inconvenient to lay down, that the
Court is bound to repair the defect of every judicial act. The Court
cannot do wrong to the party, according to the maxim *"actus legis
nemini facit injuriam."* Suppose, the order made by the Court was
wrong: it does not follow, that the party, at whose instance it was

(1) 1 Bro. C. C. 200.
(2) *Ante*, vol. ii. 122.

made, is to forfeit any right, or repair the mischief occasioned by
that erroneous order.   In the case put of a creditor restrained, as it
turns out, without any ground from suing within six years, in the
event of the debtor's death before judgment would the Court, in respect of the suspension of the action by the injunction and the loss
occasioned by that interference of the Court, consider the Plaintiff as
a judgment creditor, having a lien upon the real assets?   There is no
authority to support that.   The cases coming nearest to it
[* 83]   are those referred to by your Lordship; where by * the
effect of an injunction, restraining the obligee in a bond
from proceeding at law, the amount of the principal and interest ex-
ceeds the penalty.   *Duvall* v. *Terry* (1) perfectly establishes that;
which is also supported by *Godfrey* v. *Watson* (2).   The reason is,
that the Plaintiff restraining the legal right by the very terms of his
bill offers to do right.   In those. cases he must have prayed an account, and of course must have offered to pay the balance.   The
terms of the bill therefore gave jurisdiction.   *Audeley* v. *Ward* (3).
Supposing the abstract rule true, it will not apply to a case, where
the interposition of the Court is made necessary by the act of the
party.   In *Taylor* v. *Compton* (4) the Court made no order; but
in *Geast* v. *Barber* (5), a case exactly similar to that, Lord Kenyon,
though he retained the bill, said, he would dismiss it rather than decree an account: the remedy being at law.

The principle, upon which this relief is sought, is plausible; but
would be attended with infinite inconvenience.   If it is a principle
of universal justice, it must apply to every Court.   Suppose a personal action brought at law; and from the pressure of business at
the Assizes it could not be tried; and stood with a *remanet* to the
next Assizes; and in the interval the Defendant dies: or suppose,
the delay proceeded from the application of the party on account of
the absence of a material witness: though the act of the Court prevents the remedy from being available, the action cannot be sustained against the executor; and the remedy is gone.   In fact this
Plaintiff might have brought an action for mesne profits.   It is clear,
the action of ejectment, as now prevailing, originated in the time of
King Henry VII.   In Reeves (6) the history of this action is very
full and accurate; and agrees with what is stated by Lord Chief
Justice Wilmot in *Goodtitle* v. *Tombs* (7).   Previously to the reign
of Henry VII. the mesne profits were usually recovered before the
recovery of actual possession; and if the action for mesne profits is
now the substitute for the " *Quare ejecit infra terminum*,"
[* 84]   it is to be considered entitled to the * same effects, and is

(1) Show. P. C. 15.
(2) 3 Atk. 517.
(3) Hardr. 136.
(4) Bunb. 95.
(5) 2 Bro. C. C. 61.
(6) History of the Common Law, vol. iv. 165.
(7) 3 Wils. 118.

to have the same course of operation. But whatever doubt there may be upon that, it is settled, that trespass for mesne profits may be brought pending a writ of error: *Donford* v. *Ellys* (1) ; and it follows, that it might be brought before the writ of possession ; which is suspended by the writ of error. The difficulty is, that to support trespass for mesne profits there must have been actual entry (2) ; and it may be objected, that this Plaintiff could not consistently with that order have complied with that by entering. But by the usual course of ejectments now the Defendant by entering into the usual rule is estopped from availing himself of that objection ; and in *Bell* v. *Clarke* (3) a delivery of a declaration was held a sufficient entry. Entry therefore is not of the essence of the action of trespass for mesne profits. The only use now made of the judgment in ejectment, where the party brings trespass for mesne profits, is, that the Plaintiff is relieved from the necessity of showing his title by producing that judgment, and asking damages only in respect of possession from the time of the demise. He may ask the mesne profits from the time his title accrued, though the demise is laid within that time : but then his judgment will not avail him : but he must prove his title (4). The former practice has obtained from convenience : but the Plaintiff is not estopped, if he chooses to go for the profits anterior to the demise. It is not necessary therefore in an action for mesne profits to show the judgment in the ejectment. The Plaintiff may now, as he might before the time of King Henry VII. treat the Defendant as a trespasser ; recovering damages from time to time, without proceeding to recover the land itself.

Mr. *Alexander*, in reply.—The reason, that no authorities are to be found in support of this equity, is that such applications are not frequent. In all other cases, where the claim of the Plaintiff is a debt, the law does supply a remedy ; as in the case of trover. It is peculiar to the combination of the two remedies, the action of ejectment, and the action for mesne profits, that this disappointment of the Plaintiff arises. In the case of a specific chattel, where the *pretium affectionis* has influence, the Plaintiff at law can only have damages : but this Court compels a delivery of the specific chattel (5). So, before a Court of Law exercised jurisdiction upon a *lost deed for want of *profert* (6), this Court inter-   [*85] posed. There is no reason, founded in substantial justice, why a tenant should for six years have the profits of the Plaintiff's estates without accounting for them. *The Duke of Bolton* v. *Deane* (7) is a strong authority for the Plaintiff. It was a case not of concealment or fraud, but of innocent mistake. If eject-

---

(1) 12 Mod. 138.
(2) *Stanynought* v. *Cosins*, 2 Barnes, 367 ; 3d edit. 456.
(3) Comb. 453.
(4) *De Costa* v. *Atkyns*, Bul. Ni. Pri. 87 ; 2 Bur. 668.
(5) *Fells* v. *Read, ante*, vol. iii. 70.
(6) *Read* v. *Brookman*, 3 Term Rep. B. R. 151. See the note, *ante*, vol. v. 238 ; *post*, 812 ; 1 Fonblanque's Treat. on Eq. 16, 2d edit.
(7) Pre. Ch. 516.

ments had been brought against all the tenants, before it was absolutely necessary, that would have been considered oppression. The order restrained any farther proceedings against the tenants generally, without any limitation as to proceeding to judgment. After the judgment was affirmed, nothing but the injunction prevented the Plaintiff from proceeding against Dr. Warren ; who lived about two years afterwards ; and the injunction was got rid of only three days before his death. The opportunity of proceeding according to the ordinary form was therefore lost by the interposition of this Court upon his application. This case is therefore very different from the case put of a *remanet* at the assizes, or the question whether, as a general proposition, the Court will relieve against the consequence of its own act; this injunction being obtained, and the dissolution of it resisted, by the act of the party. The case in Shower goes upon the same principle. The answer to the argument from the rule not to go beyond the penalty always is, that the delay was occasioned by the application of the party. The remedy in such a case as this must be the same ; though the party does not remain before the Court. Though the practice in bills for tithes is to waive the penalties, it has been lately held in the Court of Exchequer, that if the discovery has been obtained by a bill not containing that offer, and the Plaintiff afterwards files another bill for an account of the tithes, and sues for the penalties, he will be enjoined. The justice of the Court would be a mockery, if, because he had dismissed his bill, and was not before the Court, he could not be restrained from such a proceeding.

The supposed possibility of proceeding in an action for mesne profits without obtaining judgment in ejectment, proceeds upon error. In every case, in which there is no actual entry but only the ordinary proceeding in ejectment, it is necessary in the action for mesne profits not only to have the judgment but [*86] the * writ of possession. Even where the judgment is against the casual ejector, the writ of possession has been given in evidence: *Aslin* v. *Parkin* (1). The principle is, that where there is no actual entry, as the injury is to the possession, it is necessary in support of that action to show the possession executed.

With respect to the repairs, which the Defendants make a sort of set-off, that point was at issue in the bill filed by the tenants ; and it was in evidence, that Sir William Pulteney long before the formal notice to quit gave a general notice to all parties, that as soon as the existing leases should be determined, he would proceed to set aside the farther leases; and these repairs were made after that time. The Defendants have produced no evidence in support of their allegation : and there is a complete answer on the records of the Court.

· *May* 11*th.* Lord CHANCELLOR [ELDON] stating the case, and observing, that the Court of King's Bench in making the rule for stay-

---

(1) 2 Burr. 665.

ing the proceedings in the several actions of ejectment for some reason, not apparent, and perhaps, because they might think, there was a question fit to be agitated in equity, did not add as a term, that the Defendants should bring no suit in equity, and that it was clear, that, if there is any mode of recovery at law, it cannot be by an action of Trespass for mesne profits, delivered his judgment.

The Plaintiff insists, that he has a remedy for these mesne profits in equity ; more especially as he was by the act of the Court of King's Bench and the subsequent act of this Court upon the application of Dr. Warren, restrained from proceeding during his life ; and that the Plaintiff ought not to be injured by the consequences of that act, preventing him from pursuing his legal remedy. In the argument at the bar it was considered, 1st, With regard to the claim, in case the Plaintiff had not been restrained from proceeding by the acts of Dr. Warren in the Court of King's Bench and in this Court ; and it was said, that, though it is true, a personal action dies with the person as to the injury committed in the fact constituting the cause of that action, yet if the personal injury has been committed with a profit to the party doing that injury * there is   [* 87] both in law and equity a remedy sufficient to extract out of his pocket that profit, which he has reaped by his injurious act, and, that this bill may be sustained upon the general ground. It was argued, that this is a principle, which may be demonstrated by the reasoning in *Hambly* v. *Trott,* as far as the doctrine of law is to be looked to ; and it is said very truly, that all natural justice is with the Plaintiff; who is now clearly to be taken to be entitled both in law and equity to the possession from the moment he made the demand ; and if so, the mesne profits are consequential upon his obtaining possession ; and therefore it is at least according to natural justice, that he should now be placed in the same situation, as if there had not been an adverse possession at law against him and these adverse proceedings in equity. It was farther insisted, that merely from the circumstance of his having brought actions of ejectment, which action is founded in trespass, he cannot now maintain, upon *Hambly* v. *Trott* and other cases, at least for the mesne profits accrued since the ejectment, an action for use and occupation. With regard to that *Birch* v. *Wright* was cited. All, which that case decides, is, that in the ordinary case of a tenant, if you bring an ejectment, you cannot afterwards bring an action for use and occupation for the rent subsequent to the demise ; because, having treated his holding as founded in trespass you shall not treat it as founded in contract. That case establishes this distinction ; that that rule will not apply to the time previous to the ejectment. Therefore, if that doctrine is to be applied to this case, that authority does not preclude the Plaintiff from trying, what he can make of the action for use and occupation for the time between 1791 and 1794 ; though it would preclude him from the time of bringing the ejectment down to the recovery under it. If I was satisfied, I ought not to interpose upon the special grounds in this case, I should yield so far to the ar-

gument for the Plaintiff as to that, that, finding it admitted, as it must be, that this is an application new, as far as it stands upon general principles, if it could be maintained, that an action for use and occupation would lie, that action being founded upon contract, it would' follow, that they might be considered as indebted to him, and he might have a remedy against the assets. But I feel so much doubt upon that point, whether an action for use and occupation could be maintained, that I should not think myself authorized to make the decree upon the ground, that could maintain that action, without
[*88]   first permitting an action to be brought * upon the terms of not setting up the ejectment, the statute of limitations, or any other legal bar, against that action; but that it should be considered simply upon the Plaintiff's title, as it stood in 1791, without embarrassment from the subsequent proceedings. The difficulty I have in supposing, that action could be maintained, turns upon this; that these parties claim under a title neither adverse, nor altogether otherwise. Taking it to be adverse, as tenants claiming under a lease, which is contended to be effectual to bind the plaintiff, that lease determines the terms of their holding: and the recovery must be upon the foot of those terms. If they do not hold under that lease, they are not in the same relation to the Plaintiff as the tenant stood in *Birch* v. *Wright*; for he had the character of tenant; but if you say, the lease was not binding upon the Plaintiff, you destroy the relation of landlord and tenant; and then there is an adverse title; and it is difficult to say, they hold under that contract; which is the foundation of the action for use and occupation.

If it cannot be put upon that ground, or if it is not thought prudent so to put it, the next question is, if in no form of action, that can be devised, this question can be tried at law, has the Court· upon the general case, without adverting to the circumstances of this case, a jurisdiction to say, these executors shall account for the mesne rents and profits? To put that question correctly, I must for the present lay out of the case the fact, that Dr. Warren was with a variety of other persons a Defendant in a Court of Law, and a complainant with those persons in this Court; and I must look at him as being alone and individually a Defendant in an ejectment; under which the Plaintiff has not been able to obtain possession, until it happened, that by the accident, as it is called, of his death the Plaintiff cannot proceed in an action for mesne profits. I agree, it is impossible to consider the mere circumstance of his death as that species of accident, against which this Court would relieve. It is admitted, this case is new in its kind. It is contended however, that the demand upon the general principle can be supported by analogy to other cases. Upon the best consideration on that head they have not been able to state any case, strictly speaking, analogous. I feel very strongly, that this claim is founded in natural and moral justice; and
[*89]   if it could be sustained upon the general principle, the Court would be very strongly inclined to *support it: but if it is to be determined upon the general principle, it must

be decisively put upon that ground, and not upon an analogy, which will not hold. With respect to the analogy, the bills by infants have gone upon the ground of infancy, and the character, in which the other party was considered to stand, as a bailiff or receiver. As to the case of the heir, without going through *Dormer* v. *Fortescue*, and the other cases, which were all discussed in *Pincke* v. *Thornycroft* (1), I do not know a case, in which the heir has claimed merely as heir an account, not stating any impediment to his recovering at law; that the Defendant has the title-deeds necessary to maintain his title; that terms are in the way of his recovery at law; or other legal impediments, which do, or which may probably, prevent it; upon which probability or upon the fact the Court founds its jurisdiction.

The case of the dowress is upon a principle, somewhat, and not entirely, analogous to that of the heir. An indulgence has been allowed to her case upon the great difficulty of determining *a priori*, whether she could recover at law, ignorant of all the circumstances; and the person, against whom she seeks relief, as was strongly observed by the Master of the Rolls in *Curtis* v. *Curtis*, having in his possession all the information necessary to enable her to establish her rights. Therefore it is considered unconscientious in him to expose her to all that difficulty, to which, if that information was fairly imparted, as conscience and justice require, she could not possibly be exposed.

The case of mines is very different upon another ground. There the bill will originally lie against the party himself; if not, I do not know, that originally it could be brought against the personal representative. The case of timber is also upon a very different principle. Lord Hardwicke says the case of the mines is in the nature of a trade; and as to the timber, the equitable jurisdiction is put by him upon this, to prevent a multiplicity of suits; and the Court having jurisdiction with regard to the waste, takes the whole together; but he states expressly, that if there is not a ground for an injunction to restrain waste, the party must go to law (2).

The case of tithes is also very different. When sev-   [90] ered they belong to the tithe-owner. It is an acquisition of property, as stated in *Hambly* v. *Trott*, put into the possession of a party; who ought to give it to another,

Upon *The Bishop of Winchester* v. *Knight* therefore and all these cases, there must be either a difficulty to recover at law, or fraud, concealment, &c. which enables the party to say otherwise than that if he had gone to law he would have recovered. There is therefore no analogy, arising from these cases. If I was obliged to decide, whether this claim could be supported upon the general principle, I should wish to hear the case farther argued, before I should venture

(1) 1 Bro. C. C. 289.
(2) *Jesus College* v. *Bloom*, 3 Atk. 262. See *post*, 701, n. 705; vol. ix. 346. Distinction upon equitable waste, *Marquis of Lansdown* v. *Marchioness of Lansdown*, 1 Madd. 116.

to introduce a new decision upon this subject. But I am relieved
from that by the special circumstances of this case; which make it
unnecessary to decide upon the general principle. The Plaintiff
must now be taken in this Court to have had a clear legal right to
the possession as early as 1791. In that year he brings an ejectment
against one occupier. The bill does not inform me, why he abstained from bringing ejectments against the others till 1794. In
that year he brought ejectments against all the tenants; and then
they in a mass feel the justice of his acting against one only; and
they make an application, a very proper application, to the Court of
King's Bench to restrain him from proceeding against them upon
this ground, distinctly stated, that they hold by the same title as
Lady Cavan; and that it was equitable, that action should decide
the question between the Plaintiff and all of them; praying, that the
Plaintiff should not be at liberty to proceed one step farther against
them; undertaking that the recovery against Lady Cavan should
bind them, as far as the law was to deal between them; asserting
therefore, that the Plaintiff acted with great propriety in forbearing
to bring actions against them till 1794. In law therefore they iden-
tify their case with Lady Cavan's. It was not adverted to in the
Court of King's Bench, that there was a manifest call of justice upon
them to have done more; and I am entitled to say so upon their
ordinary practice; taking care that inquiries shall not prejudice the
ultimate rights of parties by the effect of their rules, operating as injunctions. If a verdict had been obtained in an action for damages,
which that Court might think excessive, they would hardly grant a
new trial without taking care, that the Plaintiff in the inter-
[*91]   im should not lose all benefit of the verdict by *the
death of the Defendant. I allude now to the rule with
great propriety adopted in the case of Lord Dorchester (1) and a
gentleman in the west of England. It would have been perfectly
just in this case to have said, the Defendants should put the Plaintiff in the situation, in which he would have been, if they had not
interposed. That however was not added. I do not stay to examine, whether it was necessary, that the judgment in the ejectment
should precede the action for mesne profits : but if it was necessary,
the Plaintiff could not avail himself of the judgment, affirmed in
1795, on account of the bill filed in this Court; insisting, that notwithstanding the recovery at law still it was against conscience, that
the Plaintiff should have the possession on account of the circumstances, making it equitable, that he should not avail himself of his
legal rights. Upon that ground the injunction was obtained. If
that injunction was not capable of being maintained at the hearing,
and it was not suggested to the Court to provide against accident
as to the mesne profits, I cannot agree, that it is the Plaintiff's fault;
because he does not ask enough. It is the duty of the Counsel to
inform the Court : and if they do not, and the Court happens not

---

(1) *Pleydell* v. *The Earl of Dorchester*, 7 Term Rep. B. R. 529.

to have acted upon its information up to the point, which it ought to have reached, it is bound to relieve the party, as far as it can, from the injustice, to which the shortness of .its proceedings may have exposed them. If upon the application for the injunction, the question had been put, whether the Court would expose the Defendant in that cause to the hazard of losing the rents and profits of the premises by the death or insolvency of the Plaintiffs, and the Court had been reminded of the justice due to the Defendant in its full extent, it is impossible that injunction should have been granted without the terms, that a fair rent for the premises should be brought into Court from time to time, that the Court might be in possession of a fund, that would enable it to do justice, whatever accident might happen during the time necessary for the consideration of the question, whether he, who had recovered at law, could sustain the benefit of that judgment.

It has been said by Mr. *Fonblanque*, the action for mesne profits may be maintained, though no judgment has been obtained in *ejectment. I will not trust myself with the [* 92] decision of that question in this cause. In *Norton* v. · *Frecker* (1) Lord Hardwicke says, trespass will not lie for mesne profits, till the possession is recovered by ejectment. I will not say, there can be no action founded upon the old learning: but under these circumstances I am not bound to determine that; for, if in the ordinary action for mesne profits the Plaintiff might have recovered what he now seeks in equity, and if under the circumstances of this case he has been restrained from proceeding in that action, and all conscientious views of the case require me to say, he would have been restrained in any other action from receiving them, it would be very hard, that, because he did not make the experiment, whether that other species of action could be maintained, the Court will give him no relief. If there be a principle, upon which Courts of justice ought to act without scruple, it is this; to relieve parties against that injustice occasioned by its own acts or oversights, at the instance of the party, against whom the relief is sought. That proposition is broadly laid down in some of the cases. The case, in which the Court would not relieve, though the interest went beyond the penalty of a bond (2) still strikes me as a very strong case. If the Plaintiff submitted to nothing, by the mere circumstance of filing the bill he would be taken to submit to every thing conscience and justice require. Upon that principle he would be held to do that, which is just :- and the Court duly acting with him would compel him to pay the principal, interest, and costs, occasioned by his delay. It may be said, that is a relief, given against a Plaintiff, coming for relief. I consider these persons as Plaintiffs, asking an injunction, and impliedly saying, they ask it upon the terms of putting this Plaintiff in exactly the same situation, as if it had been de-

---

(1) 1 Atk. 524.
(2) *Ante*, 79. See the note, vol. i. 452.

termined, they were not entitled : for otherwise there is no color of justice calling upon the Court to discuss the question, whether they are entitled to equitable relief. The case of a *remanet* at *nisi prius* was put. If the application is founded in fraud, or concealment, or misrepresentation, I am not prepared to say, a Court of Equity might not find the means of relief in that sort of case ; but it is very different, where the party applies, not upon his notion of what the law is, but upon the fact ; to the existence of which he does not
[* 93] administer by his conduct. Upon that it seems there * can be no relief in equity ; for it is not the act of the parties ; but a necessity arising out of the act of third persons, affecting their rights ; not done at the instance of either of them: the occasion not furnished by their acts. The case was also put of a creditor prevented from obtaining judgment by the act of this Court ; and the question, whether he ought to be considered as a judgment creditor. I will not say, what the answer might be to the case, put so generally. A Court of law always takes care, that a creditor so prevented shall be put in the same situation, as if he had his judgment, and no such application had been made ; and I rather think, in every instance of an application for an injunction it is the duty of the Court to consider, whether the party ought not to have the benefit of his judgment ; and if the Court decides wrong, I should be sorry, if the Court had not the means of reinstating him.

The ground therefore, upon which this case is decided, is, that the *res gestæ* show, that Dr. Warren has amalgamated and mixed himself with the other tenants. The equity as to all of them arises from their joint act, operating to prevent the Plaintiff from having that redress at law, which in all moral probability he would have had, if this Court had not interfered ; and which in all moral justice he ought to have had. I had considerable doubt how far back the account ought to go. It ought to go back as far as natural justice requires. Where there has been an adverse possession, and upon an application to this Court upon grounds of equitable relief the Plaintiff appears entitled to an account of the rents and profits, if there has been a mere adverse possession without fraud, concealment, or an adverse possession of some instrument, without which the Plaintiff could not proceed, the Court has said, the account shall be taken only from the time of filing the bill (1) ; for it is his own fault not to file it sooner. But the question here is, not, what relief is due to the Plaintiff with regard to the period at which this bill was filed, but attending to the circumstances stated by this bill, forming the facts of the prior causes in this Court. Attending to those circumstances, the question is, if it had not been for what passed in those prior causes, would not this Plaintiff have recovered from 1791 : and do not the circumstances of those causes demonstrate, that he was substantially and in conscience proceeding ad-

(1) *Ante, Drummond v. The Duke of St. Albans*, vol. v. 433, and the note, 439, as to the limitation of accounts.

versely from that period, until he was restrained from farther proceedings; giving notice to quit, and making a formal demand of the possession; abstaining, as, they say themselves, it was fit he should abstain forever, from bringing any other action except that against Lady Cavan. He has therefore demanded the rents and profits from 1791 down to the decree in the other causes. If he had brought an action for mesne profits, as soon as he could upon the ejectment, the production of the record would have entitled him from the day of the demise. But it is equally clear on the other hand, that would not necessarily have prevented him from recovering from the time his title accrued; provided he gave them an opportunity of questioning that title; for I take it to be clear, he is not bound to demand no more than from the day of the demise. He may, if he pleases to put the title in hazard, insist upon the mesne profits from the time the title accrued; saving only the benefit of the statute of limitations: but then he must prove his title. He would therefore have been entitled to the rents and profits from 1791. If so, upon what ground is he not entitled in equity from the same period?

The decree must therefore be according to the prayer of the bill. As to the mode of estimating the mesne profits, it will be better, that they should settle that among themselves (1).

SEE, *ante*, the notes to *S. C.* 2 V. 544.

HUNTER, *Ex parte.*

[1801, MAY 16.]

THOUGH unliquidated damages cannot be proved under a commission of bankruptcy, yet, if the demand is partly of that nature, and partly liquidated, as the difference of price upon a re-sale, the creditor, having a security, may apply it first to the former, then to the latter, and may prove the residue.

Lien under the usual condition at an auction, that, if the vendee should fail to complete his purchase, the vendor should be at liberty to re-sell, and the vendee pay the expenses and make good the deficiency, &c.

BY articles, dated the 23d of November, 1795, between Smith, an auctioneer, as agent for the petitioners, trustees in a marriage settlement, and Jenkins and Aubrey, in consideration of 200*l.* paid to Smith by Jenkins in part of 4670*l.* it was agreed, that upon payment of 4470*l.* upon the 23d of September next certain estates should be conveyed to Jenkins in fee; and it was provided, that if the purchaser should fail to complete his purchase according to the agreement, the said sum of 200*l.* should be forfeited to the * vendors; who should be at liberty to resell the estate: [* 95]

(1) *Bond* v. *Hopkins*, 1 Sch. & Lef. 413; *O'Donel* v. *Browne*, 1 Ball & Beat. 262.

and Jenkins should pay all the expenses attending the same; and make good all deficiency of price, and loss of interest of the purchase money.

Jenkins failed in completing the purchase; and upon the 1st of August, 1797, the estate was put up to auction at Swansea; at which auction Jenkins again was the purchaser at the same price, 4670*l.*; and Smith received a joint note of Williams and Aubrey, for 470*l.* in part. This sale took place upon the usual terms; a deposit of 10*l.* per cent.; and if the purchaser should fail to comply with the conditions the deposit to be forfeited; and the proprietors to be at liberty to sell; and the deficiency, if any, by such sale, together with all charges attending the same, to be made good by the defaulter.

Jenkins again failed in completing his purchase; and upon the 9th of February, 1798, the estate was sold at Garraway's for 2950*l.* Upon the 14th of July, 1798, a commission of bankruptcy issued against Jenkins. The petitioners attempted to prove a debt of 1349*l.* 11*s.* 4*d.* in respect of the difference upon the re-sale and the expenses; including the following articles:

Auctioneer's charges upon the re-sale	£70	11	0
Interest	99	11	7
Auctioneer's charge . . .	44	10	0
Moiety of auction duty . .	36	17	6
Solicitor's charges . . .	30	18	6

The amount of the deposits, and 200*l.* paid by Jenkins on account, were deducted from the proof. The Commissioners rejecting the proof, the prayer of the petition was, that they might be ordered to receive it.

Mr. *Cooke,* in support of the Petition.—In *Bowles* v. *Rogers* (1) a similar case, Lord Rosslyn having directed a re-sale upon [* 96] farther directions, ordered * the deficiency upon the re-sale to be proved; saying, the whole purchase-money was the debt. It was taken, as if it was a mortgage. This is a contract to pay a certain sum of money at a given day; and falls exactly within the statute (2), providing, that debts payable at a future day may be proved.

---

(1) *In Chancery,* 31st July, 1800. The bill was filed by a person claiming title under the will of Sir Richard Bampfielde, dated the 17th of March, 1775, against the assignees of a bankrupt; *inter alia,* to compel a specific performance of an agreement made by the bankrupt with the plaintiff, as trustee, for the purchase of estates of Sir Richard Bampfielde; or, if the defendants should be unable or unwilling to perform the contract, that the estates might be re-sold; and if the purchase-money arising by the re-sale, together with the deposit, should not amount to 37,240*l.* the original purchase-money, that the plaintiff might be admitted a creditor under the commission for the amount of the deficiency.

Upon the 17th of November, 1797, a decree was made for a re-sale. The deficiency upon that re-sale was 5016*l.*; and the cause coming on for farther directions, the Lord Chancellor directed that sum to be proved under the commission; saying, the whole purchase-money was the debt; and the vendor had a lien upon the estate; which proving by the re-sale deficient, the residue was to be proved under the commission.

(2) Stat. 7 Geo. I. c. 31, s. 1.

Mr. *Lloyd*, for the Assignees.—Attending to the circumstances and the nature of this demand, the case cited is not applicable ; that going merely upon the difference of value, a mere matter of calculation. The demand under this commission is, not the purchase-money or any other certain sum ; but the difference in value between the sales, and the interest and expenses. They were not liquidated at the time of issuing the commission ; and could be recovered only in an action for damages. It is impossible therefore, that they could be within the statute referred to. Beside the difference between the two sums, deducting the deposits, there are the interest, the charges of the auctioneer, a subject for evidence before a jury, a moiety of the auction duty, and the solicitor's charge. These items are perfectly uncertain ; and clearly take this case out of the statute ; which relates to future debts having no contingency in them. What Lord Kenyon says in *Utterson* v. *Vernon* (1) is very applicable. In the other case nothing was to be done but to calculate the difference between the two sums ; and that was going a great way. But great part of this demand was wholly unascertained, when the commission issued ; and was only capable of being ascertained by a jury.

Mr. *Cooke*, in reply.—By this contract it was agreed, that the purchaser, if he should not perform his contract, should be at the expense of the re-sale. The petitioners not having conveyed the *estate, had a pledge, the title-deeds ; and therefore   [*97] are entitled to apply the produce of the property, when sold, to that debt, which they could not prove under the commission, viz. the interest and expenses, in the first instance, and then in reduction of the debt. Where a creditor by a debt arising partly previous and partly subsequent, to the act of bankruptcy has a pledge, he may apply the pledge to the latter first ; which was determined by Lord Thurlow, *Ex parte Havard* (2). This is very like the case of a pledge. If the estate had turned out to be of greater value than 4670*l.* the assignees could not have redeemed, and insisted upon performing the contract, without giving the petitioners the interest and expenses.

The Lord CHANCELLOR [ELDON].—Nothing is more clear, than that unliquidated damages cannot be proved ; that was determined in *Utterson* v. *Vernon*. That was a contract to replace stock upon demand. A bankruptcy happened ; and no demand was made before the bankruptcy. The majority of the Court of King's Bench at first thought, it could be proved : afterwards the Court were unanimously of opinion, that it could not ; and that clearly was Lord Thurlow's opinion. But this is very different. This is a sale under a contract for the purchase of an estate ; by which the purchaser became owner of the estate and the seller parted with it. The condition, in case the purchaser should fail to complete his contract, that

(1) 3 Term Rep. B. R. 539 ; 4 Term Rep. B. R. 570.
(2) 1 Cooke's Bank. Law, 120, 4th edit. ; 8th edit. by Mr. Roots, 147.

there shall be a re-sale, and the purchaser shall make good the loss
and answer the expenses, forms a lien upon the estate for the purchase-money.   It is in some respects like a mortgaged estate, sold to
pay the mortgage-money : and the residue is the debt to be proved :
but, strictly speaking, it is not in the nature of a mortgage ; for if
the second sale produced more than the original purchase-money,
the purchaser, who had violated his agreement, could not call for an
account of the surplus; or if he was really a mortgagor : but the
vendor contracts for this ; that if the second sale produces less, he
shall be considered as a mortgagee ; and shall be a creditor for the
rest.   With respect to the objection to this proof, the difference between the sums produced by these sales is a clear liquidated debt.   As
to some items of the account, I agree, they could not be
[* 98]   proved : but, * considering the equity of the vendors, they
may have the effect by a circuitous mode.   I remember an
instance of a mortgage made as an indemnity against acceptances of
cash advanced by the mortgagee.   Some of the bills had been paid
before the bankruptcy : but he was under acceptances of bills floating at the time of the bankruptcy, which were not capable of being
proved : but he had a right to model his security ; applying it first to
those bills, which he could not prove.

Upon the authority of those cases then the vendors in this case
have a right to apply the sum, produced by the last sale, first in payment of those articles, which it is just they should receive, but which
they could not prove under the bankruptcy ; and those articles being
taken out of that sum will leave the sum capable of being proved.
In that circuitous way therefore they are entitled to prove.

Let the commissioners inquire into those articles: they are to be
first satisfied out of the 2950l. ; deduct the residue from the original
purchase-money ; and let the balance be proved.

---

1. DEBTS not payable at the time when the debtor became bankrupt, may be
proved under the commission against him, deducting a rebate of interest; see the
51st section of the statute 6 Geo. IV. c. 16; and, by the 52d section of the same
statute, any person liable for acceptances in favor of a bankrupt, or any other debt
which is substantially the bankrupt's, may, after paying the same, come in under
his commission; see, *ante*, the note to *Wright* v. *Hunter*, 5 V. 792.

2. Every vendor has a *lien* upon the estate he has sold, to the amount of the
purchase money, unless he has, by his own act, waived this right ; *Ex parte Gyde*,
1 Glyn & Jameson, 325; *Hughes* v. *Kearney*, 1 Sch. & Lef. 135; *Austen* v. *Halsey*, 6 Ves. 483; and the lien will be available as against third persons, who had
notice; *Mackreth* v. *Symmons*, 15 Ves. 345; *Hughes* v. *Kearney, ubi supra ;* a
bond taken, and a receipt given for the purchase money, will not discharge the
lien if the money is not paid.   *Saunder* v. *Leslie*, 2 Ball & Bea. 514.   Nor will
the fact, that the vendor has taken bills for the amount of the purchase money, be
a waiver of his *lien* on the estate sold; bills of exchange are not, in such a case, to
be considered, *prima facie*, as a substitution for the *lien*, but merely as a mode of
payment ; and it will rest on the purchaser to show, that the vendor consented to
rest on the collateral security alone.   *Grant* v. *Mills*, 2 V. & B. 309, *Ex parte
Peake*, 1 Mad. 356.   Lord Eldon, it is true, (admitting himself to be bound by the
decided cases, to the extent which those decisions have gone,) has expressed a
wish, that this species of *lien* had never been admitted where the vendor had
accepted a different security ; *Ex parte Loaring*, 2 Rose, 81 ; and it is not to be
understood, that an acceptance of no security will be a waiver of the *lien :* if the

security be totally distinct and independent, circumstances *may* show this to have been intended as a substitution for the *lien*, instead of a credit given in reliance upon such *lien; Nairn* v. *Prowse*, 6 Ves. 759. *Winter* v. *Lord Anson*, 1 Sim. & Stu. 445: no universal rule seems to be laid down on this head, but each case must be determined upon its own circumstances. *Mackreth* v. *Symmons*, 15 Ves. 349. *Cood* v. *Pollard*, 10 Price, 112.

THE AMICABLE SOCIETY OF LANCASTER, *Ex parte.*

[ROLLS.—1801, MAY 19.]

THE statute 33 Geo. III. c. 54, giving preference to Friendly Societies, having money due to them from their officers, dying or becoming bankrupt or insolvent, does not extend to debts due from them individually, and not in their official characters.

Whether the preference to Friendly Societies under the st. 33 Geo. III.' would prevail against the Crown; *Quære*, [p. 99.]

THE petition, presented by John Corless, stated, that previously to February 1792, James Parkinson, a member and treasurer of the Amicable Society of Lancaster for that year, having as such treasurer got into his hands the sum of 70*l*. belonging to the society, and the society being also possessed of the farther sum of 30*l*., such sum was in February 1792 paid into his hands as treasurer; and thereupon he executed a bond, dated the 13th of February, 1792, to the petitioner, also a member of the society, and appointed co-treasurer with him, in the penal sum of 200*l*.; with a condition to be void upon payment by Parkinson, his heirs, executors, or administrators, to the petitioner, his executors, or assigns, in trust for the society, of 100*l*., with interest at 4*l*. 15s. per cent. upon the 13th of February next.

* In October 1797, Parkinson died intestate; and his   [* 99] widow took out administration. The petition was presented under the act of Parliament (1); alleging notice, before the administratrix had fully administered: the affidavit in support of it stating, that she knew of this debt before her husband's death; and that, except the sum of 35*l*. which was lent to Parkinson by the society, the money came to his hands as treasurer, while he was in office.

The administratrix by her affidavit stated, that her husband died indebted to the Crown as postmaster, to his landlord for rent, and

---

(1) Stat. 33 Geo. III. c. 54, s. 10, enacting, that if any person appointed to any office by any such society, and entrusted with, or having in his hands or possession, any moneys or effects belonging to such society, or any securities relating to the same, shall die, or become a bankrupt, or insolvent, his executors, or administrators, or assignees, shall deliver over all things belonging to such society, and shall p-y out of the assets or effects all sums of money remaining due, which such person received by virtue of his said office, before any of his other debts are paid or satisfied; and all such assets and effects shall be bound to the payment and discharge thereof accordingly.

by bond and mortgage, to an amount exceeding the real and personal estate; and that soon after his death she gave warrants of attorney; being threatened by the creditors. She denied, that any application was made to her, or, that she had any notice of this debt, till eight months after his death. She also stated, that this money, or the greater part of it, had been lent to him under a vote of the society; and consisted of money called in for that purpose; and was not in his hands as treasurer.

(1) MASTER OF THE ROLLS [Sir RICHARD PEPPER ARDEN].— The words of the act are very large; sufficient, as it seems, to give this preference against debts due to the Crown; though perhaps it would not be so construed. The debts to be preferred are, not generally all debts due to the society, but only debts due from an officer or trustee of the society: but if the society trusts any person upon his private security, those debts have no preference. The question therefore is, whether this money came to the hands of Parkinson as trustee of the society. Upon the whole I am of opinion, this money was not left in his hands as a member of the society, but was voluntarily left in his hands, after he ceased to be trustee, upon his security. It is really incumbent upon these societies to give early notice to the personal representatives, and not [* 100] to lie by and let * them administer the assets. The act does not limit any time for making the demand upon the administrator.

The ground, upon which I dismiss this petition is, that this money was not received by him as an officer of the society (2).

———

THE preference which the 10th section of the statute 33 Geo. 3. c. 54, gives to Friendly Societies, over other creditors, is confined to debts due to them in respect of money received or retained by their officers by virtue of their offices, and independent of contract, and must not be extended to the debts of individuals not charged with special duties and trusts as the officers of such societies. *Ex parte Ashley,* 6 Ver. 444. *Ex parte Ross,* 6 Ves. 804. *Ex parte The Stamford Friendly Society,* 15 Ves. 280. Nor has the Court any jurisdiction, on petition, in the matter of Friendly Societies, which have ceased to act in strict pursuance of the statute. *Ex parte Norrish,* Jacob's Rep. 162. *Ex parte Ross,* 6 Ves. 804. And it should be observed, that by the bill now pending in Parlia-   [1827] ment for the regulation of the practice in Chancery, it is proposed, that the jurisdiction of the Court of Chancery, in regard to Friendly Societies, shall cease, except as to any proceedings relating to any such Friendly Society which may have been commenced before the said act shall take effect.

———

(1) *Ex relatione.*
(2) *Post, Ex parte Ashley & Corser,* 441; *Ex parte Ross,* 802; *Ex parte Stamford Friendly Society,* vol. xv. 280; *Ex parte Buckland,* Buck, 214.

CONSTANTINE *v.* CONSTANTINE.

[Rolls.—1801, May 29.]

Rules of construction of wills:
Every word to have effect, if not inconsistent with the general intention; which is to control (a):
If two parts are totally inconsistent, the latter prevails (b):
If a meaning can be collected, but it is wholly doubtful, in what manner it is to take effect, it is void for uncertainty.

THIS bill was filed by executors to have the rights of the parties under the following obscure will of John Constantine, a goldsmith, ascertained. After directing his debts, funeral expenses, &c. to be paid out of his estate and effects by his executors, and appointing his nephews Richard and Jonathan Constantine to be his executors, he proceeded thus:

" I give and bequeath all my household furniture of every description, plate and linen, china, watches, rings, diamonds, pier glasses, images, pictures, and all the books, and my meaning is that she shall have all my clothes at her own disposal, and every thing within the house, unto my dearly beloved wife Margaret Constantine, for her own use. I also give and bequeath unto my dearly beloved wife Margaret Constantine upon trust during her life the interest of sundry funds now standing in my name at the Bank of England, that is to say, New 5 per cents. 4 per cents. 3 per cent. consols, 3 per cent. Reduced Annuities, 3 per cent. Annuities 1726, 3 per cent. Imperial Annuities, Short Annuities, Long Annuities, Imperial Annuities, and New South Sea Annuities and it is my will and desire that my executors grant a power of attorney to my said wife or to whom she shall appoint to receive her dividends. My will is that my executors sell stock if wanted but what remains unsold to be kept in my name until after the death of my dear wife. I give my said wife 1000*l.* 3 per cent. consols, to be paid her immediately after my decease, provided there is not money sufficient to pay her out of monies in hand. I give unto my niece Jane Constantine daughter of my brother Henry Constantine deceased *3000*l. reduced annuities after the death of my dear   [* 101] wife I leave my brother John Constantine of Settle York-shire 30*l.* per annum from my death during his life allowing now 20*l.* a year from the rent of the houses I have upon mortgage and after my brother's death I give to his son Richard Constantine my executor forever   The chariot and every thing belonging thereto I give to my dear wife and the provision I have made for her will I hope be enabled to keep it   To each of my executors I give 50*l.* each as they will be benefited hereafter when the stock comes to be transferred after the death of their aunt Margaret Constantine   I

(a) See *ante*, notes (a) and (b), *Collet* v. *Lawrence*, 1 V. 268.
(b) See *ante*, note (d), *Sims* v. *Doughty*, 5 V. 243, and generally, as to the construction of wills, see the latter part of note (a), *Thellusson* v. *Woodford*, 4 V. 227.

leave to Jane Constantine my niece's mother 10*l.* a year during her life and Jane Constantine's brother Henry Constantine 20*l.* a year for his life to. commence at my decease and his share of the stock that will fall to him hereafter shall be tied up that he shall only have the interest during 'his life and then to come to sister Jane along with her share she have with him which is my will and desire to be tied up for the issue of Jane Constantine after her decease but every one's share to be transferred in stock   The issue of my brother John Constantine children share and share alike the issue sister Alice Woodhead the same and brother William Constantine children the same   And this is my last will and testament set my hand and seal this 25 day of January 1799."

The testator died on the 26th of January, 1799, without issue ; leaving his widow and several nephews and nieces surviving. His stock consisted of 1200*l.* New 5 per cents.: 1000*l.* 4 per cents.: 7000*l.* 3 per cent. Consolidated Annuities : 3000*l.* 3 per cent. Reduced Annuities: 5100*l.* 3 per cents. 1726: 5000*l.* 3 per cent. Imperial Annuities : 100*l.* per annum Short Annuity: 20*l.* per annum Long Annuity : 20*l.* per annum Imperial Annuity : 1008*l.* 6*s.* 8*d.* New South Sea Annuities : 1100*l.* Exchequer bills. The testator was also possessed of leasehold premises at Settle in Yorkshire, household furniture, ready money, and other personal estate.

By articles executed upon the marriage of the testator and his wife Margaret, dated the 13th of January, 1769, he covenanted, that, if she should survive him, she should have for her [* 102]   own use * all the rings, jewels, plate, and wearing apparel whatsoever, which she then had, or which should be given to her during the coverture, with all the plate, linen, household goods and furniture, belonging to him at the time of his death ; and in case there should be no issue of the marriage living at such time, then she should have to her own use three fourths of all such other personal estate as he, or any person in trust for him, should be possessed of, interested in, or entitled to, at his decease, after payment of his debts and funeral expenses, and dower or thirds of his lands.

The cause stood for judgment.

The MASTER OF THE ROLLS [Sir RICHARD PEPPER ARDEN.]— I am at last under the very disagreeable necessity of giving judgment upon a case, on which the judgment cannot be satisfactory to the Court, and by which I must be sure I am not performing the intention. This testator, it appears, must have totally forgotten the whole state of his property. The will itself states circumstances plainly showing, that if he was competent to make a will, as I must now suppose, he had not about him that degree of recollection, which a testator disposing of his property ought to have. I know no rule I can adopt more safely than that, which I did adopt in *Sims* v. *Doughty* (1), and upon which I have always acted, viz. to

(1) *Ante*, vol. v. 243. See the note, 247.

give effect to every word of the will; provided an effect can be given to it not inconsistent with the general intent of the whole will, taken together; for if the general intention can be collected, it is the duty of the Court to adapt every regulation to that general intent. If two parts of a will are totally inconsistent, and cannot possibly be reconciled, the proper rule, as I thought upon that occasion, and still think, is, that the latter shall prevail. Doubts have been entertained, where the same thing has been given to two persons, whether they should not be joint tenants: but the case, to which I allude, is, where two parts of the will are totally inconsistent; so that it is impossible for them to coincide. Another rule is this: if a meaning can be collected, but it is left wholly doubtful, in what manner that is to take effect, though I must to a certain degree run counter to the will, I know no other means than by declaring, as I must in this instance with regard to a very considerable part of the property, that the will is totally void for uncertainty.

This testator appears to have totally forgot the cove-   [103] nant entered into upon his marriage, It is plain, the legacy to his wife of 1000*l.* 3 per cent. consols is not a specific legacy of the stock, of which she was to have the dividends for her life; for he gives it, provided there is not money sufficient to pay her out of the moneys in hand. Upon her legacy there is no question. Upon the next legacy of 3000*l.* annuities reduced, for a long time I thought it a specific legacy (*a*); and I should have been of that opinion, if it had not been for the preceding legacy of 1000*l.*; which it is clear he did not mean to be a specific legacy, by the effect of that proviso, if there should not be sufficient money in hand to pay her the value of that 1000*l.* stock; leaving her in that case the dividends of the 1000*l.* stock afterwards. I am forced to put some such construction upon it. Therefore I must hold that legacy of 3000*l.* reduced annuities not specific (1) but a legacy of quantity. Then, as to the bequest of an annuity of 30*l.* to his brother John, and what immediately follows that, I defy any man to tell, what he could mean. I shall only give to his brother that, which I am sure the testator must have meant; that is, the annuity of 30*l.*: and not finding that charged, so as to be sure, he meant it to be a charge upon the mortgage, I shall determine, that it must come out of the general personal estate. As to Richard Constantine, I once thought it a gift to him of the mortgaged premises: but I am not sure the testator did mean that; and I must see, that Richard Constantine is entitled to take for ever that, which his father was to take for life. After the death of John Constantine therefore

(*a*) As to specific legacies, and the inclination of the Court against them, see *ante*, note (*a*), *Coleman* v. *Coleman*, 2 V. 639; as to the distinctions between specific and pecuniary legacies, particularly with regard to stock, see note (*a*), *Kirby* v. *Potter*, 4 V. 748; as to legacies of debts, see note (*a*), *Chaworth* v. *Beech*, 4 V. 555.

(1) *Ante, Coleman* v. *Coleman*, vol. ii. 639, and the note, 641; *Chaworth* v. *Beech, Innes* v. *Johnson, Kirby* v. *Potter*, iv. 555, 568, 748; *Raymond* v. *Brodbelt, Barton* v. *Cooke*, v. 199, 461.

Richard is entitled to a perpetual annuity of 30*l.*, but not charged upon the mortgages. He gives 50*l.* each to his executors ; stating, that they will be benefited hereafter, when the stock comes to be transferred after the death of their aunt Margaret Constantine : but there is no mention of any share or proportion, in which his executors should take ; which might be expected to follow. Adhering to the rules, that prevailed in *Sims* v. *Doughty,* I must declarè, that the legacy of 3000*l.* reduced annuities is not specific, but a legacy of quantity ; that John Constantine is entitled to an annuity of 30*l.*

[* 104]   for his life ; and after his death Richard Constantine is entitled to an annuity of 30*l.* for ever out * of the general personal estate, including the houses ; and declare, the disposition of the stock after the death of the testator's wife, is void for uncertainty ; and the residue is undisposed of, and divisible among the next of kin of the testator.

———

1. WITH respect to some of the leading rules as to the construction of testamentary dispositions, and the qualifications which those general rules may, occasionally, admit, or even require, see *ante,* note 4, to *Blake* v. *Bunbury,* 1 V. 194; and as to the doctrine, that, where two parts of a will are totally inconsistent, the latter must be understood as the expression of the testator's final intention, see note 2, to *Sims* v. *Doughty,* 5. V. 243.

2. The criterion marking the distinctions between general, specific, and demonstrative legacies, are stated in the notes to *Coleman* v. *Coleman,* 2 V. 639. That courts of Equity are always desirous of holding a legacy to be pecuniary, rather than specific, where the testator's intent is ambiguous, see note 2 to *Chaworth* v. *Beech,* 4 V. 555; and, as to legacies of stock, see note 2 to *Baugh* v. *Read,* 1 V. 25; and the notes to *Kirby* v. *Potter,* 4 V. 748.

———

BARRET *v.* BLAGRAVE.

[1801, MAY 7, 15.—ANTE, VOL. V. 555.]

THE injunction, obtained upon a breach of covenant, in nature of a specific performance, dissolved upon the answer, contradicting the affidavits, and showing consent for several years (*a*).

THE *Solicitor General* [Sir *William Grant*] and Mr. *Grimwood* showed cause against dissolving the injunction, that had been obtained in this cause (1).

The answer stated, that the Defendant had for a considerable time kept a tap-house in Kennington Lane ; and had applied to the proprietors of Vauxhall Gardens for a lease of that ground, for the purpose of building a house ; which they refused : but they agreed, that Digby and Sandbank should take the ground to build on, which they did ; and let the house to the Defendant. The proprietors of Vauxhall knew the purpose, for which the house was intended ;

———

(*a*) See *ante,* note (*a*), *S. C.* 5 V. 555.
(1) See the report, *ante,* vol. v. 555.

went over it with their surveyor; recommended, that tables should
be put up for the accommodation of the customers; and consented
to round off some of the paling of the gardens, to make the house
more public.   After the house was opened, the lease not having
been executed, Sandbank refused to execute the lease with that
covenant, unless they would consent, that this trade should not be
considered a breach of the covenant; and a memorandum, dated
the 31st of July, 1790, in which year the house was opened, was
prepared by the surveyor and signed: stating, that Mr. Blagrave's
present mode of using the house is not any injury to the proprietors
of Vauxhall, nor contrary to the lease; upon which the lease was
executed.   The business was carried on from the 22d of May, 1790,
until the injunction was obtained, precisely in the same way without
objection.   The Defendant denies, that he retails liquors; and that
he fitted up any room to accommodate persons coming from Vauxhall; only one small box with deal tables being placed there, with
the consent of the proprietors; and the persons resorting
to the house consist of hackney-coach men, * mechanics,   [* 105]
&c.; and the business is confined to the sale of meat, as
a cook's shop.   The Defendant denies, that any persons resort to
this house from the public gardens for the purpose of refreshment,
and return afterwards. '

In support of the injunction the case of *Gibbs* v. *Cole* (1) was
cited, as an authority for reading affidavits against the answer: but
the Counsel for the Defendant did not object to reading the affidavits produced on the former occasion.

For the Plaintiff.—This injunction is in nature of a specific performance.   The application was made upon the ground, that this
Court would have enjoined the Plaintiff from proceeding at law:
the penalty being *in terrorem*, and not in the nature of specific
damages.   There is certainly a considerable evidence of consent;
but the question is, whether this sort of evidence can be admitted to
enable them to get rid of a covenant under seal.

Mr. *Pemberton*, for the Defendant.—Under these circumstances
there is no pretence for this injunction; which was granted upon
the ground, that above 100 persons of a night have quitted the gardens, and gone to the Defendant's house for refreshment, and returned to the gardens: but the affidavits do not bear that out;
amounting only to this; that 100 persons of an evening have been
seen in that house; whereby an injury is stated to have been sustained by the proprietors of the gardens; and the other fact is denied.

The *Solicitor General* [Sir *William Grant*], in reply.—The two
questions are, 1st, whether this business is within the covenant;
and if so, 2dly, whether the evidence referred to in the answer shall
get rid of it.

The Lord CHANCELLOR [ELDON].—May not a very different question be made; whether, if you have permitted this to go on for eleven

(1) 3 P. Will. 254.

years, you must not take your chance at law? I have not the least
doubt, that what is stated in the affidavits is within the terms of the
covenant: but the question is, whether you can have a specific performance under such circumstances: the parties having from the
execution of the lease eleven years ago permitted that covenant
to stand an ineffective part of the lease. I rather doubt,
[* 106] *whether, so far from the Court's interfering at your instance, a bill might not be filed to prevent your suing at
law upon that covenant. If there are equitable circumstances to
prevent your taking your legal remedy, surely they will prevent your
having a specific performance.

The injunction was dissolved.

———

On the 22d of May, 1801, Sir RICHARD PEPPER ARDEN, having
resigned the office of Master of the Rolls, was called to the degree
of Serjeant at Law in Lincoln's-Inn Hall, under the late act of Parliament (1), and appointed Chief Justice of the Court of Common
Pleas, on the resignation of that office by the Lord Chancellor; and
was created a Peer, by the title of Baron ALVANLEY, of Alvanley, in
the County Palatine of Chester (a).

Sir WILLIAM GRANT was appointed Master of the Rolls; and
was sworn a Member of His Majesty's most Honorable Privy Council (b).

———

SEE, *ante,* the notes to S. C. 5 V. 555.

———

(1) *Ante,* the beginning of the 4th Volume.
(a) For a sketch of Lord Alvanley's life and character, see *ante* note (a), 1 V. 86.
(b) One of the brightest ornaments of English Courts. He was born in Scotland, in 1755, and after studying at the college of Aberdeen, passed two years at
Leyden, which had not yet wholly lost its ancient renown, that he might perfect his
studies in the Roman law. It is not improbable that to these studies we are indebted
for something of the peculiar juridical tone which marked his judgments. In the
autumn of 1775, he went to Canada to practice law, and arriving at Quebec shortly
before its siege by General Montgomery, for a while divested himself of the
forensic character, and commanded a body of volunteers. At the early age of
twenty-five, he was appointed Attorney General of Canada; but finding this field
too limited, soon afterwards returned to England, and in 1787, in his thirty-third
year, was regularly called to the bar. In 1790, he was returned to Parliament,
where he distinguished himself by his aptness in debate, and his peculiar powers
of argumentation, in which pure reason seemed to triumph. In 1799, on the promotion of Sir John Scott, to the seat of Chief Justice of the Common Pleas, he
became Solicitor General, while Sir John Mitford was Attorney General. It fell
to their lot to conduct the important State trial of Hatfield, for shooting at the
king. And when Sir Richard Pepper Arden was transferred to the Common
Pleas, Sir William Grant received the vacant post of Master of the Rolls. Of
all judicial stations this is the only one, that is not inconsistent with a seat in the
House of Commons, where he continued till the dissolution of Parliament in 1812.
On the 23d of December, 1817, at the age of sixty-three, and in the full possession
of his remarkable powers, he voluntarily descended from the bench, which he
illustrated by his transcendant judicial qualities, amidst the affectionate regrets of
the bar. The remainder of his long life was passed in literary leisure. He died
May 25th, 1832, in his seventy-eighth year. It is said that more than once the
Great Seal was within his reach. His modesty and contentment, within the range

LORD GREY DE WILTON v. SAXON.

[1801, MAY 22.]

INJUNCTION on affidavit to restrain the tenant of a farm from breaking up meadow, contrary to express covenant, for the purpose of building (a).
Whether, if no express covenant, it would do upon the ground of waste, *Quære.*

THE *Solicitor General,* supported by Mr. *Romilly,* moved upon affidavits for an injunction to restrain the Defendant, a tenant to the Plaintiff, from breaking up meadow for the purpose of building, contrary to the covenants of his lease.

The lease contained covenants not to convert any meadow land, and all the other usual covenants in a lease of a farm, similar to those in *Pulteney* v. *Shelton* (1) ; showing clearly the nature of the lease, for the purpose of tillage, as a farm.

Lord CHANCELLOR [ELDON] granted the injunction till   [107] appearance and farther order; observing, that he did so upon the ground of the covenant not to convert any meadow; otherwise he should doubt, whether it would do upon the ground of waste without any affidavit, that it was ancient meadow.

---

of his duties, are not the least of his exalted merits. There are judges, who have left a stronger impression on the jurisprudence of their country, but not one who has drawn from such various quarters such glowing tributes to his judicial excellence. Mr. Charles Butler and Lord Brougham seem to vie with each other in eulogy of his genius and character. We can only quote from Mr. Butler. " The most perfect model," he says, " of judicial eloquence, which has come under the observation of the reminiscent, is that of Sir William Grant. In hearing him it was impossible not to think of the character given of Menelaus by Homer, or rather by Pope. 'He spoke no more than just the thing he ought.' But Sir William did much more; in decompounding and analysing an immense mass of confused and contradictory matter, and forming clear and unquestionable results, the sight of his mind was infinite. His exposition of acts, and of the consequences deducible from them, his discussion of former decisions, and showing their legitimate weight and authority, and their real bearings upon the point in question, were above praise; but the whole was done with such admirable ease and simplicity, that, while real judges felt its supreme excellence, the herd of hearers believed that they could have done the same. Never was the merit of Dr. Johnson's definition of a perfect style, 'proper words in proper places,' more sensibly felt than it was by those who listened to Sir William Grant. The charm of it was indescribable; its effect on the hearers was that which Milton describes, when he paints Adam listening to the angel after the angel had ceased to speak. Often and often has the reminiscent beheld the bar listening at the close of a judgment given by Sir William with the same feeling of admiration at what they had heard, and the same regret that it was heard no more." See 8 London Law Mag. 283, 285 ; 28 Ib. 53, 89.

(a) A Court of Equity will frequently grant injunctions in the nature of a specific performance to restrain the violation by a tenant of covenants contained in his lease. Although many of them have been granted solely on the equity of restraining a *breach of covenant,* it is impossible not to observe, that in the greater part of the cases injunctions might have been supported, on the ground of waste. Eden, Injunctions, 237 (2d Am. ed.) A distinction has been taken as to enforcing by injunction the specific performance of *express covenants* and *implied agreements.* Ibid. See *ante* note (a) *Lathrop* v. *Marsh,* 5 V. 259.

(1) *Ante,* vol. v. 147, 260, 261 ; *post, Onslow* v. ———, xvi. 173.

Mr. *Romilly* said, that question was much discussed in *Brydges* v. *Kilburne* (1), a case upon the conversion of a mill of one species to a mill of another species. ____

Sᴇᴇ note 2, to *Pulteney* v. *Shelton*, 5 V. 147.

THE MARQUIS OF DOWNSHIRE *v.* LADY SANDYS.

[1801, Mᴀʏ 13, 22.]

Iɴᴊᴜɴᴄᴛɪᴏɴ restraining tenant for life without impeachment of waste from cutting timber growing for ornament or shelter, extended to clumps of firs on a common two miles from the house, having been planted for ornament (*a*).

The power of tenant for life under the general words "without impeachment of waste," not enlarged by implication from more extensive powers given to trustees for special purposes after her death.

Tenant for life without impeachment of waste restrained by injunction from cutting timber planted or left standing for ornament or shelter by an absolute owner of the estate; whether ornamental, or the reverse: the protection extended beyond the mansion house to rides or avenues through a wood at a considerable distance: but not to the whole wood, to prevent cutting other parts for repairs and sale, [p. 110, note.]

Security, to reimburse the tenant for life, if wrongfully restrained, to be ascertained by the Master; and issues directed, whether the timber, or any part, was planted or left standing for ornament or shelter by any former owner, of what estate and interest to be indorsed on the *postea*; and whether consistently with such purpose any and what part may be cut for repairs or sale, [p. 110, note.]

Legal right of tenant for life without impeachment of waste to cut timber and apply the produce to his own use, [p. 110*a*, note.]

Difference between the powers of tenant for life without impeachment of waste and trustees under the same words; the latter are bound to a provident execution of their powers, [p. 115.]

Uɴᴅᴇʀ indentures of settlement, dated the 2d of August, 1798, Lady Sandys was seised of the manor of Ombersley, and the mansion-house, called Ombersley Court, and other hereditaments in the county of Worcester, as tenant for life, without impeachment of waste; remainder to trustees to preserve contingent remainders; remainder to the Marquis of Downshire for life, and, after payment of the sums to be raised by the terms after created, without impeachment of waste; with similar remainder to the Marchioness of Downshire, and remainders over, subject to the said terms, to Lord Hilsborough for life, without impeachment of waste, and to his first and other sons, and other remainders over.

The trust of the terms was to raise money to discharge mortgages, and 3000*l.* for the executors of Lady Sandys; and the deed contained a proviso, that till the said sums should be paid, it should be lawful for the trustees at such time or times after the decease of Lady

----

(1) Stated *ante*, vol. v. 689, 691, in *Jackson* v. *Cator.*
(*a*) Jeremy, Eq. Jur. 335, 336.

Sandys and in such manner as they thought proper to enter into
and upon all or any part or parts of the manors, &c. by the said indenture limited in strict settlement, and to fell and cut down such
timber and other trees as should from time to time be wanted for
building and other necessary purposes therein mentioned ;
and also to *fell, cut down, and sell any timber or other   [* 108]
trees, which were at the time of the said indenture standing or growing, and which should from time to time thereafter stand
or grow upon the manors, &c. thereby limited in strict settlement or
any part or parts thereof ; provided that such falls of timber or other
trees be made in due course, and at proper times of the year for felling
such timber or other trees ; and so that the same do not in any wise
injure the beauty of the said capital messuage or mansion-house,
called Ombersley Court.

In this cause an injunction was obtained to restrain the Defendant
from cutting down or felling any trees or timber standing or growing for ornament, shade or shelter, of the mansion-house and buildings at Ombersley Court, or any other houses or, buildings on the
settled estates, or which grow for ornament in any of the vistas, avenues, walks, pleasure grounds or plantations, belonging to Ombersley
Court, or to any part of the estates, hereditaments, and premises,
late belonging to Edwin Lord Sandys deceased, settled and conveyed by the indenture of settlement to the use of the Plaintiffs, and
from cutting down or felling saplings growing on any part of the said
estates not proper to be felled.

This injunction was continued till answer ; and afterwards in November 1799 upon a motion to dissolve the injunction an order was
pronounced, continuing it till the hearing ; but it was varied by leaving out the word "shade."

A motion was made for a sequestration against the Defendant for
breach of the injunction by felling trees on Lineal common in the
parish and manor of Ombersley, part of the settled estate.   The affidavits in support of the motion stated, that the trees felled were fir
trees ; which were planted with order and regularity in rows and
clumps for ornament to the said common : and which were highly
ornamental, not only to the common, but to the surrounding country
from the manner and very elevated situation, in which they were
planted.   They represented the distance of the nearest plantation
from the mansion-house to be two miles.

The affidavits in opposition to the motion stated, that Lineal common is about three miles from the mansion-house and
grounds of Ombersley Court ; and is separated therefrom   [109]
by land of other persons, not the property of the Defendant, as tenant for life ; and is not even in sight, from the said mansion-house or any part of the grounds ; and the common is open
and uninclosed ; upon which the copyholders have a right of common : which they enjoy ; that the trees, that were on the common,
were not planted for the ornament of, and were not an ornament
to, any part of the estate ; and though the trees were planted in

clumps and rows, none of them were planted in vistas, avenues, and walks.

The farther affidavits, filed in reply, stated, that the common may be seen from many parts of the grounds; and that parts of the estate are contiguous to the common.

Mr. *Mansfield*, Mr. *Trower*, and Mr. *Thomson*, in support of the motion—Mr. *Richards*, Mr. *Sutton*, Mr. *Romilly*, and Mr. *Stratford*, against it.

Lord CHANCELLOR [ELDON].—When this Court took upon itself to depart from the rule of law as to waste, and interpose its restraining power, upon what is called equitable waste, beyond the rule of law, one duty at least was imposed upon the Court; to define with precision and accuracy, in what cases the Court would interpose, and to take great care, that in the terms of its injunctions a language should be adopted, that might be clearly understood by the parties, whose rights were to be bound at such a peril as that of disobeying an injunction of this Court. But the Court has in all times upon this subject adopted language exceedingly difficult to be understood. In arguing cases of this sort I have been asked from this place, what I meant by "thriving timber, timber-like trees, and ornamental timber"; and I have not been able to give any farther answer than by referring to the language of the Court in former instances.

Upon this question I cannot admit the argument, that my mind is to be influenced in any degree by the propriety of the injunction.

[* 110]   If it goes beyond the terms, in which other injunctions have been granted, or the reach of the principle, *and I think this injunction does not, the true line of conduct would have been to have applied to the Court to alter the terms of the injunction, and not to have-risked a disobedience to it. A party disobeying an injunction is not at liberty to shelter himself by saying, the Court was wrong in granting the injunction in such terms. The case stands before me upon this dry question; whether the Defendant is within the meaning of this injunction prohibited from cutting the trees upon Lineal common. By the terms used in this injunction I understand trees very distinguishable from trees, to which the word "ornamental" only can be applied. Many trees may be ornamental, and yet not within the meaning of the words in a process of this kind "standing or growing for ornament." It is difficult to comprehend these trees under the words "vistas, avenues," &c. The parties certainly have been always left by the language of the Court at great hazard, to determine, what is or is not timber growing for ornament. In *Chamberlayne v. Dummer* (1), the case of Mr. Johnes (2) and his mother, and a great variety of

(1) 1 Bro. C. C. 166. Other orders, June 1789, and 3 Bro. C. C. 549.
(2) *Johnes* v. *Johnes*, Hilary, 1797. Other orders of Injunction against cutting ornamental timber were made in *Lord Castlemain* v. *Lord Craven*, December, 1733; *Leighton* v. *Leighton*, March, 1747-8; *O'Brien* v. *O'Brien*, May, 1751; *Jebb* v. *Jebb*, April, 1792; *Post, Lord Tamworth* v. *Ferrers*, 419; *Williams* v. *M'Namara*, vol. viii. 70; *Day* v. *Merry*, xvi. 375. See also 132, and *The Attor-*

others, persons of taste upon this subject have differed; and the taste of Mr. Brown has been set up against the taste of former systems. The principle, upon which the Court has gone, seems to be, that, if the testator or the author of the interest by deed had gratified his own taste by planting for ornament, though he had adopted

---

ney General v. *The Duke of Marlborough,* 3 Madd. 498; but this has not been extended beyond trees planted or growing for ornament, as in avenues or vistas, to timber merely ornamental, viz. an extensive wood: *post, Burges* v. *Lamb,* vol. xvi. 174; *Wombwell* v. *Lady Belasyse*; nor to timber, too young to be felled in a course of husband-like management: *Smythe* v. *Smythe,* 2 Swanst. 251; nor to trees protecting premises from the effects of the sea: *Coffin* v. *Coffin,* 1 Jac. 70.

WOMBWELL v. BELASYSE: (*From a Short-hand Writer's Note*). *In Chancery, April 22, 23, 1825.*—The Lord CHANCELLOR [ELDON].—The doctrine of the Court is extremely well settled. If the object in planting timber, or in leaving timber standing, is ornament, whether that object is affected, whether the effect is truly ornamental, or the most absurd exhibition that ever was produced, this Court will protect that timber; and the protection is not confined to trees planted, or left standing, as ornamental to a house or park: nor does it depend on the distance from the mansion; but I do not recollect, that it has gone to this extent; that, if a ride is made through a wood, in which wood the proprietor has been in the habit of cutting timber for the use and repair of the mansion, that ride shall protect the whole wood from being cut at the time of making the ride, and in all future times: as, if the purposes of that ride can be as well consulted by leaving a tenth part of the wood standing, it would be most absurd to require, that the whole should be left. Neither do I recollect any issue ever directed upon this; and in directing an issue attention must be had to the interests of all parties; that, if the injunction restrains the legal right to cut timber, security shall be given, that in case of the death of him, whose enjoyment of that legal right may have been restrained improperly, his estate shall, to the extent of the benefit he would have derived from the exercise of that right, be reimbursed hy those, who restrained him. I think also, that two issues would be necessary; not only whether the timber was planted, or left standing, for ornament, but also, how far consistently with that object, trees might be cut; as I cannot hold, that the effect of making a ride through a wood is to be, that an axe shall not be laid to the root of a tree in that wood; which would be carrying this doctrine to an extent, to which it has never yet gone.

In framing the issue another thing also must be attended to; by whom the trees were planted or left standing for ornament: as, if they had been planted by tenant for life without impeachment of waste, unless afterwards left standing with that view by some person having the inheritance, they would not be entitled to this protection.

April 23d. The Lord CHANCELLOR.—This is an application to discharge an order of the Vice Chancellor, directing an issue to try, whether certain trees in a wood, called Prestwood, part of the Newburgh estate, were planted or left standing for ornament to the mansion house, park, grounds, &c. an order formed upon the equitable doctrine of this Court, with reference to waste. I do not apprehend, that there are any particular circumstances requiring attention: but the question turns simply upon this; whether Lady Charlotte Belasyse, being now tenant for life without impeachment of waste, can, consistently with that equitable doctrine, exercise the legal right she unquestionably has. First, I may state, as established doctrine, that the question is not, whether the timber is, or is not, ornamental: but the fact to be determined is, that it was planted for ornament; or, if not originally planted for ornament, was, as we express it, left standing for ornament by some person, having the absolute power of disposition. If such a proprietor had even the bad taste to plant or leave standing, a couple of yew trees cut in the shape of peacocks on the road side, I do not shrink from what I laid down in *The Marquis of Downshire* v. *Lady Sandys,* (*ante,* 107) that they must be protected, until some person, having the same absolute power of disposition with more correct taste, comes into possession; and this doctrine applies in the same manner to the species the most disgusting to the tenant for life, and the most agreeable to the tenant in tail, and upon the competition between those parties the Court should see, that the tenant for life was right, and the other wrong, in point of taste, yet the taste of the testator, like his will, binds them; and it is not competent to them to sub-

---

a pleasant ride, although at the distance of two miles from the mansion house; but I do not agree, that a mere tenant for life, coming into possession, can vary the estate. That can be done only by some person having the absolute dominion over it.

A farther subject of consideration is, how far this protection can be applied to an avenue or ride through a wood, which had previously supplied timber for the purpose both of repairs and sale; how far the act of making that ride is to be considered as a consecration of the wood to this purpose of ornament. It seems to me rather a strong proposition, that, if tenant in tail or in fee, whose predecessors had supplied all the exigencies of the estate and all their own exigencies by an appropriation of the timber and sale of part of it, forms a ride or avenue, all the withered arms and branches must remain for ever in that state, which one of the affidavits, on which this injunction has been granted, and this issue directed, represents as most ornamental on a Yorkshire estate. I have known instances on an application for an injunction of an inquiry directed before the Master to ascertain, whether trees were planted or left standing for ornament: a course which I can easily conceive may lead to a great length of unnecessary proceeding, and prove extremely prejudicial. A tenant for life without impeachment of waste has the right by law to cut timber, and apply the produce to his own use; and if this Court restrains the exercise of that legal right without making the party, at whose instance the injunction is granted, give ample security to insure justice being done, in case it should turn out, that the restraint ought not to have been imposed, it may happen, that after the death of that tenant for life his estate may lose the value of that timber, which he had a legal right to cut. In a case of this sort it is extremely difficult to ascertain, whether this timber was planted or left standing for ornament by a person having such an interest in the estate, that his will was to control those, who were to take after him; and, when the affidavits leave the question excessively doubtful, the Court cannot possibly send it to a farther inquiry, unless the person calling for it will give such security, that, if it shall appear, that this lady had the right to cut, and ought not to have been restrained, she, or those who take after her, shall be reimbursed the whole value.

Although I do not recollect an instance of sending such a question to a jury, I think there may be cases, in which that course ought to be taken; admitting both a more speedy and a better decision than in the Master's office: but it would be extremely dangerous to send it to a jury without very special directions, not only for ample security, but also confining the issue to these questions; whether the timber was planted or left standing for ornament, and by whom; and what estate that person had: otherwise we shall be left just where we were, with a verdict upon evidence such as these affidavits afford; amounting to no more than that, which no man can doubt, that these woods are ornamental to this estate. Another inquiry must be added; (for this does appear to me to go considerably beyond what has been the doctrine of this Court) whether the act of cutting rides through a wood, certainly a circumstance of evidence, that the wood was in some measure appropriated, and intended to be appropriated, to the purpose of ornament, is inconsistent with cutting a great part of that wood, leaving sufficient to answer that purpose of ornament; and upon this the acts of the owner, who made those rides, will be extremely material; as, if that owner, after those rides were made, had been in the habit of cutting in that wood for the purpose of repairs and sale, it cannot be represented as his intention, that, not a sufficient part, but the whole wood, should be consecrated to that purpose of ornament, so that a Court of Equity must say, it shall stand until it shall be entirely decayed.

Let the Plaintiff go before the Master, and give such security as will in the Master's judgment secure to the Defendants the value of all the trees, which the Defendants shall be prevented from cutting by the injunction of this Court, in case it shall finally turn out in the judgment of this Court, that they ought not to

stitute another species of ornament for that, which the testator designed. The question, which is the most fit method of clothing an estate with timber for the purpose of ornament, cannot be safely trusted to the Court. The principle has been extended from ornament of the house to out-houses and grounds, then to plantations, vistas, avenues, to all the rides about the estate for ten miles round. If that principle has been rightly applied, it is very difficult in argument to say, it cannot be applied to a common as well as in-field lands; and that the contiguity or remoteness, if *de facto* it was planted for ornament, can alter the principle, upon which * the rule of the Court is to be applied. As to its   [* 111] being, not part of the estate, but the property of the Lord, with common rights, suppose a manor-house at one side of the extremity of a very large estate ; and a common is on the east side of the house, and upon that common the Lord has planted ornamental trees in the same form as in the in-field lands upon the west side of the house : those trees being admitted to have been planted for ornament, will the injunction be confined to the west side, and not extended to the common? If contiguity, which exists in the case I now put, is necessary, can it be said, that if there is a very small slip of land, a single field, and the owner of the estate has been exerting all the providence of his life in endeavoring to purchase that slip, and in the hope of succeeding has planted the common, that circumstance will alter the rule of the Court, and prevent the injunction from going to the plantation, admitted to be planted for ornament? Is contiguity necessary for the whole of the land, or for a small part? Will the greater or less degree of remoteness alter it? I am of opinion, it will not? I agree, the facts of contiguity, remoteness, &c. are very fit to be considered, when the fact, whether the common was planted for ornament, is under discussion : but if the true conclusion is, that it was for ornament, why is not that common to be considered as much a part of this estate to be protected as any other part of the estate?

My construction therefore of this order is, that it·will embrace trees or timber planted upon the common in question as part of the

have been enjoined in Equity; and let the Master proceed *de die in diem.* Declare, that in the issue hereinafter directed it is intended by this Court, that the jury shall try, and determine, not whether the timber in question, or any part of it, is ornamental, but whether the timber in Prestwood, or any part thereof, ornamental or not, was planted or left standing for ornament or the purpose of shelter by any former owner of the estate: 2dly, whether consistently with the purposes, for which such trees were planted or left standing, if planted or left standing for ornament or shelter, any and what part thereof may be cut for the purposes of repairs or sale; and let the jury, in case they shall find, that such wood, or any part thereof, was planted or left standing for ornament or shelter by any former owner, indorse upon the *Postea* what estate and interest in the lands such former owner had.

I do not confine the directions to the mansion-house; declaring my opinion, that consistently with this doctrine, which, I admit, has taken great liberties with the rights of mankind, I must abide by what has been laid down in such cases; and therefore not only the mansion-house, but these rides and shelter to the park also, must be protected.

estate : and I think, the injunction ought to go thus far; for it is evident, the views of the author of the ornament of this estate will be wholly disappointed, if the protection is not afforded in the extent of this injunction. Looking at all the estates in the north of England, where the country is not in so high a state of cultivation, and in part of Nottinghamshire, can any man decline saying, that these clumps of firs upon the surrounding and adjoining commons, severed in many instances, the lands being divided in ownership, ought not to be protected? If the in-field lands and plantations-are protected, is it not fit also to protect that, which is scattered round, and is really part of the same plan of improvement? It is impossible, that a principle for general application can depend upon the circumstance, whether a little slip of land connects the estate with the [* 112] common, or is interposed between *them; or, whether the common is in sight. Suppose, it is situated on a different side of a hill from the house: if the system of plantation for the ornament of the estate embraced the- whole circuit of the hill, will it be said, that is not to be protected, because it is on the other side of the hill? So, if it is at the distance of two miles: it is a very material circumstance upon the question of the fact; whether it was planted for ornament, or not: but, if it could be seen from the grounds, or, if it was the ride of the family for pleasure, that is evidence, that it was planted for ornament; and the distance is only a circumstance of fact, material as evidence to decide the fact, whether the trees are growing for ornament, or not.

Upon the affidavits, the expression "afford ornament" is equivocal; whether they were planted for ornament; or, whether the effect is ornament. That affidavit alone would be much too loose for granting the process of injunction. But the next affidavit states, they were planted in this manner for ornament; and adds, that they were highly ornamental, not only to the common, but to the surrounding country. That I must lay out of the question; for there is no instance of arguing, that an injunction is to be granted upon that ground, that the trees are ornamental, not to the estate, upon which they grow, but to the surrounding country. These affidavits, which go to.the fact, that these trees were planted for ornament to the common, grounded on the notion, that the common is part of the estate within the meaning of the injunction, are met by an affidavit; which proves, that this Court decides at great hazard as to facts upon written depositions; for the facts are not fairly stated by it. The original affidavits, which were confined to the question of ornament to the common, left the matter exceedingly short, whether the trees could be seen from the grounds, forming part of the estate, which might or might not be connected, not by contiguity, but by approach. They would have laid a material fact before the Court by stating, to what extent and in what degree the common could be seen 'from the estate, and was ornamental to it. The farther affidavits disclose the fact; that the common may be seen from many parts of the grounds; and is with these plantations a very ornamental object;

that there are estates, part of this estate, contiguous to the common; and upon the argument I find, it is not distinguishable from two other heaths, planted in this way; as to which an injunction has been granted.   Upon what ground am I to refuse this injunction but the simple fact, that this common was at a considerable distance, and that single affidavit, contradicted by a great number of others, asserting, that these trees were planted for ornament; and if so, I shall not inquire, whether they are ornamental; which is not an inquiry for me. I must hold therefore, that this injunction has been violated. If my mind could by the affidavits be brought into doubt, whether these trees were really planted for ornament, or not, I should be disposed to relieve myself from deciding such a question by directing an issue; taking care, that if in the result of such a direction the Defendant should be prejudiced by not being permitted to cut in the mean time, the Plaintiff should undertake to pay the value, if the decision should be against him: but, attending to the value of the property, and the contrast between the affidavits, and the circumstance, that it is impossible to conceive, why these trees were planted, unless for ornament, without attending to the question, whether they are more or less ornamental, I think, the preponderance of evidence is in the Plaintiff's favor; and the single affidavit in opposition to it is too short even to obtain an issue. The value of the trees cut must therefore be accounted for by the Defendant; or the process of sequestration must go; unless you can bring that fact into more doubt.

May 22d.   After this decision a motion was made on the part of the Defendant to discharge all the orders upon a new and distinct ground; viz. the particular expression of the deed of August 1798, in the proviso contained in the power to the trustees to fell timber; which, it was contended, showed, that the protection was intended by the parties to be confined to the trees, the fall of which would injure the beauty of the mansion-house; and that intention being expressly stated by the parties, the injunction ought not to go beyond it.

The case was argued upon this ground; the Plaintiffs insisting that the intention of the parties could not have been so restrained; * and that the mansion-house was particu-   [* 114] larly mentioned only as the principal part of the estate.

Lord CHANCELLOR [ELDON].—With regard to the conduct of the parties at the time they entered into this agreement, I do not say a word; having endeavored to cultivate a habit not to weigh the motives, which induced parties to enter into a contract, when I am to decide upon the legal effect of that contract.   The question is a dry question of law, whether these parties, either in a strict sense claiming under Lord Sandys, or those, under whom he claimed, or in an accurate sense, though not so strict a sense, claiming under him, that is, holding the estate between them according to some limitation under him, can be said by this deed to have imposed

upon the Court the necessity of declaring, that in this contract the words "without impeachment of waste" cannot admit of the construction given to them by this injunction, as it now stands.   In deciding that question the difficulty I have is of this sort; that I am obliged to impute to parties in the construction of this deed an intention to use terms according to their legal import; though I am perfectly satisfied, none of the parties understood the terms of the deed; and I doubt, whether even those, whose business it was to frame the deed, correctly understood the effect of it.   This at least is clear; that Lady Sandys claiming an estate for life without impeachment of waste, upon the deed in general, must be understood upon the deed to claim that estate with such powers as the law of the land, administered in a Court of law, subject to such restraints, to which that law is subject, as administered in a Court of equity, gives her, as to felling timber; and neither party can allege surprise in finding their legal rights affected by those restraints.   With respect to the question, whether there is context enough in this deed to authorize me to say, the Defendant can do those acts, which in general a tenant for life expressly without impeachment of waste is not entitled to do, because some other persons are authorized after her death to cut timber under the particular terms specified in the power of the trustees, I do not know, that it is a necessary inference, that one party shall have a power to-day, because another party has a power capable of being exercised to-morrow.   The whole must be taken together.   The consideration, upon which the Plaintiff may be taken to give this power to the Defend-
[* 115]   ant, may be this very condition; * that the power in this general language, *ultra* what a tenant for life without impeachment of waste has, shall not be exercised against him until the death of that tenant for life.   I cannot weigh the consideration: but I am not at liberty to say, it is of no value.   It is not to be denied, that the terms "without impeachment of waste," as applied to trustees of a term for special purposes, have a very different sense from that of the same words annexed to a tenancy for life: and in the ordinary case I do not apprehend the Court would have permitted the trustees to execute their trust by cutting timber, merely, because they were trustees without impeachment of waste; though they might at law.   This Court would say, that having a discretion they must act in their trust, as the Court itself would act.   There is no pretence therefore to say, that limitation would in the ordinary case enable them to cut timber; much less that species of timber, which a tenant for life unquestionably might have cut.   But, whatever may be the extent of that power, it is a power vested in trustees; and it is a new argument, that because powers larger in terms are given to trustees, it necessarily follows, that persons, who are not trustees, are to have rights as extensive, though given in less liberal terms.   The principal object of the trust was to make the estate of Lord and Lady Downshire exonerate the inheritance from those debts.   I am very far from being sure, that this Court would

allow them unnecessarily to execute their powers, even when the right to exercise them arises, otherwise than this Court thinks a provident execution, and far from admitting, that it would be in the breast of the trustees at the instance of the Plaintiff to cut ornamental timber and leave the other. The Court would, I think, direct them to cut that, which was not ornamental. But there is more in this; for it is absolutely in the discretion of the trustees as to the times and manner of cutting. They stand between the takers of the inheritance and the tenants for life. I do not say, if a provident and husband-like mode of treating the estate was proposed, they would not have a right to call upon the trustees: but the Court would at least hear them upon the point, whether they were discreetly called upon under this contract; and it would be very strong to say, that, because these trustees, to accelerate the payment, have this large power after the death of the Defendant, therefore she has the same power in her life, to whose discretion that power is not entrusted. * The question results to this; whether   [* 116] I am reasonably sure, that, because this power is given to the trustees after the death of the Defendant, the parties, using language with respect to her power which has now by authority had this restrictive sense put upon it, meant all, which in clear and ample language they have described in the powers given after her death. I cannot so enlarge the expression as to the power given to the Defendant; and therefore I cannot vary the injunction upon this special ground.

The motion was refused. ____

See notes 4, 5, and 6, to *Piggott* v. *Bullock*, 1 V. 479.

BENNET, *Ex parte.*
DOLMAN, *Ex parte.*

[1801, June 3.]

UNDER the st. 39 & 40 Geo. III. c. 56, authorising payment of money, to be laid out in land to be settled, to the tenant in tail, the order was thus qualified; in case he should be living on the second day of the ensuing Term; and an inquiry as to incumbrances was directed.

THESE petitions were presented under the late act of Parliament (1), authorising the Court to order money in trust to be laid out in land to be settled, to be paid to the person, who as tenant in tail of the land could bar the remainders by a recovery.

Lord CHANCELLOR [ELDON] referred to, and adopted, the con-

(1) Stat. 39 & 40 Geo. III. c. 56.

struction put upon the Statute by Lord Rosslyn [Loughborough] in *Lowton* v. *Lowton* (1), to prevent the party from getting the money unless he should be living on the second day of the ensuing Term.

In the second petition the prayer was for an absolute transfer of Bank Annuities arising from the sale of estates, of which the petitioner was tenant in tail, with remainders over; which had been sold under an act of Parliament, directing the money produced by the sale to be invested in other lands, to be settled to the same uses.

Upon the 3d of March Lord ALVANLEY [Sir RICHARD PEPPER ARDEN], then MASTER OF THE ROLLS, made an order, directing an inquiry, whether there were any incumbrances affecting the residue of the Bank Annuities; and declaring, that in case the Master should find, that there was no incumbrances, the peti- [* 117] tioner would be entitled to a transfer: but * that this order as to the petitioner should not take effect, or be of any force, unless the petitioner should be living on the second day of Easter Term then next.

The petition coming on upon the Report, that there were no incumbrances, the Lord Chancellor declared his approbation of that inquiry.

Orders were made upon both petitions accordingly.

SEE the note to *Binford* v. *Bawden*, 1 V. 512.

RIGBY v. M'NAMARA.

[1801, JUNE 5.]

BIDDINGS opened by a person, who was present at the sale (a).

MR. TROWER had moved to open the biddings of a lot, which had been bought before the Master for 1000*l.*, upon an advance of 300*l.*; and·offered to pay in half of the money.

Mr. *Piggott*, for the purchaser, opposed the motion, on the ground, that the person making this offer had been present at the sale.

Lord CHANCELLOR [ELDON] inclined to discourage a person, present at the sale, and lying by, speculating upon the event; and afterwards coming forward with an advance; but Mr. *Trower* observing, that there was only one case (2), before Lord Rosslyn, [Lough-

---

(1) *Ante*, vol. v. 12, note. See the note, vol. i. 512.
(a) When biddings shall be opened in the United States, see *ante*, note (a), *Anonymous*, 1.V. 453; note (a), *Chetham* v. *Grugeon*, 5 V. 86.
(2) *Sumner* v. *Charlton*, cited in *Tait* v. *Lord Northwick*, *ante*, vol. v. 655. See *M'Culloch* v. *Cotbach*, 3 Madd. 314; *Thornhill* v. *Thornhill*, 2 Jac. & Walk. 347.

borough] in which this objection had prevailed, and the distinction upon that was, that the person coming to open the bidding, having been present at the sale, was a party in the cause, it stood over.

The motion being renewed, and the party offering 400*l.* advance and to pay in 700*l.*, the Lord Chancellor said, he had mentioned that case to Lord Rosslyn; who did not consider himself as laying that down as a general rule; and what is now offered would have abundantly satisfied him.

The order was made on paying in 700*l.* and paying the purchaser all costs and expenses (1).

[This note relates also to *S. C. post*, 466 and 515.]

1. THE opinion of the Court, as to allowing a person who has been present at a sale before the Master to open the biddings, has fluctuated; *M'Culloch* v. *Colbach*, 3 Mad. 314. *Preston* v. *Barker*, 16 Ves. 140; and it rather appears, that there is no invariable rule upon the subject, but each case must be governed by its special circumstances; *Williams* v. *Attenborough*, 1 Turn. 76; *Tyndale* v. *Warre*, Jacob's Rep. 526; *Thornhill* v. *Thornhill*, 2 Jac. & Walk. 348; the Court, however, will always be cautious as to opening biddings after a report confirmed, see the note to the *Anonymous case*, 1 V. 543.

2. Though it is a general rule, as laid down in the principal case, and also in *The Earl of Macclesfield* v. *Blake*, 8 Ves. 214, and *Trefusis* v. *Clinton*, 1 V. & B. 362, not to allow the costs of a person who has opened the biddings, unless he become the purchaser, notwithstanding any increase of price which may have been obtained by the resale; still, it is in the discretion of the Court to allow the costs of a party who has opened the biddings, not with any view to his own advantage, but solely and expressly for the benefit of the parties concerned; *Owen* v. *Foulkes*, 9 Ves. 348; *West* v. *Vincent*, 12 Ves. 6. The return of the deposit seems to be of course, when the resale has been made at an advanced price; *Trefusis* v. *Clinton, ubi supra; Williams* v. *Attenborough*, 1 Turn. 77.

3. As to the caution which the Court uses, in allowing one purchaser to be substituted for another, see *Vale* v. *Davenport*, 6 Ves. 615; *Blackbeard* v. *Lindigren*, 1 Cox, 205; though where all the parties interested consent, such an *affidavit* as was required in the principal case may, perhaps, be dispensed with; *Matthews* v. *Stubbs*, 2 Brown, 391.

CHALLNOR *v.* MURHALL.   [* 118]

[1801, JUNE 5, 6.]

The Court cannot dispense with a prerogative administration.

AN order had been made in this cause upon a bill by creditors, that the residue of money to arise by a sale of estates of the testator, which had been directed, should be applied in payment to the several creditors named in the Report, or to the personal representatives of such of them as were or might be dead, of what had been, or should be, reported due. The report stated, that the sev-

(1) *Watson* v. *Birch, ante,* vol. ii. 51; and the note, 55.

eral sums mentioned were due to the several creditors, or the personal representatives of such as were dead.

Mr. *Pemberton* moved, that the Master might alter his report by inserting in the schedule the names of the personal representatives of the creditors, who were dead, from the provincial administration, granted to such personal representatives.

The object of the motion was, that the prerogative administration might be dispensed with: the sums being small; and it was said the practice of late had been so.

Lord CHANCELLOR [ELDON].—Upon what principle does the practice proceed? If those persons are the proper representatives, the Master should have done it without a special authority; if they are not, I will not direct him to annex the names of persons, who are not the representatives. I have no objection to order him to annex the names of the personal representatives of such creditors as are dead.

June 6th. The order was so made; which, it was said, would answer the purpose: but the next day the motion was repeated; Mr. *Pemberton* observing, that the order, as it stood, might be a surprise on the Master and the Court; and referring to *Sweet* v. *Partridge* (1); and *Upton* v. *Lord Ferrers* (2). In the latter several small sums were reported due to a number of creditors, who had ob-
[119]   tained provincial administration; and * upon an application, that the whole amount of their debts might be paid to the Solicitor, who was one of the executors of the debtor, he undertaking to distribute, it was so ordered. Another case was mentioned, which was first before Lord Alvanley, when Master of the Rolls; who wished to consult the Lord Chancellor; and the order was made by his Lordship at the seal after last Hilary term. The Lord Chancellor applied to the Bar; and it was said, the practice had been established to the extent of the sum of 40*l.*: but Lord Thurlow being desired to go beyond that sum refused to dispense with the prerogative administration, wherever it was necessary from the circumstances. It was also said, that in *Upton* v. *Lord Ferrers*, the receiver made the distribution at his peril; there was no indemnity.

Lord CHANCELLOR.—Upon what ground can the Court dispense with the proper administration? Suppose, in *Upton* v. *Lord Ferrers* after the distribution it turned out, that the effects were more than had been expected by the recovery of a debt supposed to be bad, and a prerogative administration had been taken out: would not an action lie by that administrator against the person who had received the money? Is the Court to make an order directly in opposition to the law. Where am I to stop? It may be said here-

_____

(1) *Ante,* vol. v. 148. See the note, 149.
(2) At the Rolls, Feb. 23d, March 2d, 4th, 1801.

after, that a provincial administration is too great an expense; and therefore the money ought to be paid to the next of kin without any administration.

The order was not made. ____

See the note to *Sweet* v. *Partridge*, 5. V. 148.

RUFFIN, *Ex parte*.

[1801, June 6.]

A FAIR dissolution of partnership between two: one retiring; and assigning the partnership property to the other; and taking a bond for the value and a covenant of indemnity against the debts: the other continued the trade separately a year and a half; and then became a bankrupt. The Lord Chancellor was of opinion, the joint creditors had no equity attaching upon partnership effects remaining in specie; and at all events such a claim ought to be by a bill, not a petition (a).

Various modes of dissolution of partnership; and the consequences, [p. 126.]
Debts within the statute 21 James I. c. 19, s. 10, 11, [p. 128.]

In June 1797 Thomas Cooper of Epsom, brewer, took James Cooper into partnership. That partnership was dissolved by articles, dated the 3d of November, 1798; under which the buildings,

---

(a) This is an important and leading case in the law of partnership.
Upon a dissolution of the partnership each partner has a *lien* upon the partnership effects, as well for his indemnity as for his proportion of the surplus. But creditors have no *lien* upon the partnership effects for their debts. Their equity is the equity of the partners assenting to the payment of the partnership debts. 3 Kent, Comm. 65; *Campbell* v. *Mullett*, 2 Swanst. 608, 610; *Ex parte Harris*, 1 Maddock, 583; *Murray* v. *Murray*, 5 Johns. Ch. 60; *Woodrop* v. *Ward*, 3 Desaus. 203; *Bell* v. *Newman*, 5 S. & R. 78; *Douer* v. *Stauffer*, 1 Penn. 198; *White* v. *Union Ins. Co.* 1 Nott and McC. 557; *Ridgeley* v. *Carey*, 4 Har. & Mc. 167; *M'Culloch* v. *Dashiell*, 1 Harr. & G.; *Hoxie* v. *Carr*, 1 Sumner, 181. See also Story, Partnership, § 97, 326, where the case *Ex parte Ruffin*, is much considered. The *lien* of partners upon the whole funds of the partnership, for the balance finally due to them respectively, seems incapable of being enforced in any other manner, than by a Court of Equity, through the instrumentality of a sale. The creditors of the partnership have a preference to have their debts paid out of the partnership funds, before the private creditors of either of the partners. But this preference is, at law, generally disregarded; in Equity it is worked out through the Equity of the partners over the whole funds. 1 Story, Eq. Jur. § 675; *Commercial Bank* v. *Wilkins*, 9 Greenl. 28.

It is now the established doctrine, that a partnership contract is several, as well as joint, 1 Story Eq. Jur. § 976, note; *Hammersley* v. *Lambert*, 2 Johns. Ch. 509; *Wilkinson* v. *Henderson*, 1 Mylne & K. 582; *Thorpe* v. *Jackson*, 2 Y. & C. 553.

The partnership property may be taken in execution upon a separate judgment against one partner; but the sheriff can only seize and sell the interest and right of the partner therein, subject to the prior rights and liens of the other partners, and the joint creditors therein. For the illustrations of this principle, and the authorities, see *ante*, note (b), *Hankey* v. *Garratt*, 1 V. 239; note (b), *Taylor* v. *Fields*, 4 .V. 396; *Moody* v. *Payne*, 2 Johns. Ch. 548.

premises, stock in trade, debts, and effects, were assigned to James Cooper by Thomas Cooper; who retired from the trade. Upon the 2d of April, 1800, a commission of bankruptcy issued against James Cooper; under which the joint creditors attempted to prove their debts; but the Commissioners refused to permit them; upon which a petition was presented to Lord Rosslyn; who made an order, that the joint creditors should be at liberty to prove; with the usual directions for keeping distinct accounts, and an application of the joint estate to the joint debts, and of the separate estate to the separate debts. At a meeting for the purpose of declaring a dividend the Commissioners postponed the dividend, in order to give an opportunity of applying to the Lord Chancellor; in consequence of which this petition was presented; praying, that the partnership effects remaining in specie, and possessed by the assignees, may be sold; and that the outstanding debts may be accounted joint estate.

By the articles of dissolution the parties covenanted to abide by a valuation to be made of the partnership property; and James Cooper covenanted to pay the partnership debts then due, and to indemnify Thomas Cooper against them; and Thomas Cooper covenanted not to carry on the trade of a brewer for twenty years within twenty miles of Epsom. A bond for 3000l., the calculated value of the partnership property assigned, was given to Thomas Cooper by James Cooper and his father, as surety. In pursuance of the covenant the partnership property consisting of leases, the premises, where the trade had been carried on, stock, implements, outstanding debts, and other effects, were valued by arbitrators at 2030l. after charging all the partnership debts then due. James Cooper by his affidavit stated, that all the joint creditors knew of the dissolution and the assignment of the property; that advertisements were published; and the deponent after the dissolution received many debts due to the partnership; but paid more on account of the partnership. His father by affidavit stated, that he paid the interest of the bond regularly; and intended to pay the principal, when due.

Mr. *Romilly* and Mr. *Cullen* for the joint Creditors, and Mr. *Bell* for *Thomas Cooper.*—If one partner can by assigning all his interest in the effects prevent the joint creditors from going against those effects, fraud must be the consequence. The partners may *agree to divide the effects, and carry on business separately. By this agreement between the partners the whole fund of the joint creditors is taken away. Upon the principles, upon which the effects, joint at the date of the bankruptcy, are applied to the joint debts, effects, joint at the dissolution of the partnership, and remaining the same in specie at the time the commission issues, should be considered joint property. The ground is, that credit has been given upon the faith of the joint property; and it is a fraud upon the persons giving that credit to apply that fund to the separate creditors, trusting only to the individual and to the separate effects; and that ground applies equally to this case. Until the partnership accounts are taken, there is no separate prop-

[* 121]

erty but in the surplus after paying the partnership debts (1) : the
creditors standing in the place of the bankrupt. The joint creditors therefore have a mediate, if not a direct, lien upon the whole of.
the partnership effects.   At law, the partnership creditors have more
advantage than under a commission ; taking the partnership effects
exclusively, and the separate effects with the separate creditors.
What difference arises from the circumstance, that the partnership
did not exist at the time of the bankruptcy?   That is not sufficient
to take the case out of the common rule.   In *West* v. *Skip* (2) it is
laid down, that upon a dissolution by agreement or by time the
partner out of possession is not divested of his property in and lien
upon the partnership effects.   The same right remains to an account of the partnership effects; in which the first item always is
the payment of the partnership debts.   The position, that partners
can as between themselves by any act or agreement alter the partnership stock, so as to affect the rights of third persons, cannot be
maintained,   Why have they not an equal right in the same manner to discharge their persons by such act or agreement ; especially,
if with the knowledge of the joint creditors ; but *Heath* v. *Percival* (3) shows, that circumstance will not bind them ; the transaction being *res inter alias acta*.   That an actual assignment and
divesting partnership property out of one partner will not defeat the
right against the partnership effects, is proved by *Ex parte Burnaby* (4).   No evidence is produced to show, that the separate creditors * thought, this was separate property ; and   [* 122]
gave credit accordingly : it must therefore be taken, that
they knew, it was not.   The assignment is made upon condition,
and subject to the payment of the partnership debts.   A considerable part of the property consisted of debts ; which are not assignable.

But this question has been decided by the order made by the late
Lord Chancellor.

Mr. *Mansfield*, and Mr. *Cooke*, for the assignees.—No such attempt was ever made before under such circumstances : a fair dissolution ; and an assignment by one partner of all the effects to the
other ; and trade carried on by that other ; and at this distance of
time.   Upon the petition before the late Lord Chancellor there was
no debate ; and the separate creditors not appearing, and Thomas
Cooper consenting, the usual order was made.   The circumstance,
that part of the property consisted of debts, makes no difference.
Thomas Cooper, is a solvent partner, endeavoring to get what he
can through the medium of the joint creditors.   It is perfectly immaterial to them ; for he is solvent ; and able to pay them.   The
petition is in truth his.   If this was not a complete assignment, it
will be impossible to draw the line.   Why may not joint creditors

(1) *Taylor* v. *Fields, ante,* vol. iv. 396 ; *post,* xv. 559, n.
(2) 1 Ves. 239, 456.
(3) 1 P. Will. 682.
(4) 1 Cooke's Bank. Law, 253, 4th edit. ; 8th edit. by Mr. Roots, 269.

as well at the end of twenty years fix upon a house or any specific article, once partnership property ? Certainly, fraud will vitiate transactions of all sorts: but this would be a singular fraud; for if the bankruptcy does not follow soon enough to prevent the joint creditors from enforcing their remedy at law, the object cannot be attained; and it is only in bankruptcy that the question can ever arise; for at law the joint creditors take joint as well as separate property; and the distribution takes place in bankruptcy only. The object of such a plan must be to serve the separate creditors, not the partners themselves; and the bankruptcy must follow so immediately, as to prevent the creditors from pursuing their remedies at law. There is no pretence of fraud. The consideration was a bond; but the question is precisely the same, as if it was paid in money. The trade was carried on a year and a half; and there is nothing to show that any one looked on Thomas as a partner. The effect would be, that until all the joint debts are paid, there never could be a complete assignment from one partner to [* 123]   another. Consider, how separate * creditors may be defrauded, giving credit to what they see as separate property. Cases infinitely stronger occur in daily practice; as the case of *Shakeshaft, Stirrup,* and *Salisbury* (1). One of three partners, by arrangement between them, happens in the course of trade, he living in London, and the others in the country, to get into his possession a quantity of goods. A commission of bankruptcy issued. Lord Thurlow said, he could not take accounts between the respective partners: but finding the effects in the hands of one, whatever might be the demands of the others, or the consequences to the joint creditors, the goods were the separate property of that one, and must be applied to his separate debts. There it happened by accident, that a considerable part of the partnership stock was transferred to one of the partners: not by an actual assignment for consideration, as in this instance; which is in effect a purchase. There is no sound distinction between this transaction and the sale of partnership effects to any other person, a stranger. After the assignment Thomas Cooper, in whose right the petitioners claim, had no interest whatsoever. None of the cases cited, apply. The joint creditors have no lien; though in the arrangement in bankruptcy the joint effects are applied to the joint debts. The doctrine of *West* v. *Skip* is not disputed; that a partner put out of possession, whether by agreement or effluxion of time, does not lose his right: what were partnership effects at that time still remain so: but Lord Hardwicke never said, that notwithstanding a sale of the partnership effects, and a separate trade carried on with them for years afterwards by the person who bought them, they remain joint. The agreement of partners can neither discharge goods nor the person: but it may change the property in the goods. *Heath* v. *Percival* has not the least relation to this case. There was no agreement to give up the

---

(1) *Post,* vol. xi. 414.

joint bond. The party therefore had a right to enforce it, notwithstanding his giving time to Sir Stephen Evans. In *Ex parte Burnaby* it does not appear, that any one of the partners had gone out ; nor, when *Crispe* committed the act of bankruptcy ; which might have been prior to the assignment. That assignment was merely of the share of one to the other, not attended with any dissolution of the partnership ; which in this case was actually dissolved ; and the share legally assigned. The partnership subsisting up to that time, there was a right to insist, that the partnership debts should be paid.

* With respect to the lien, in the case of *Lodge and*　　[*124]
Fendal, to which your Lordship has referred, Dr. Fendal
had paid 10,000*l.* into a banker's hands ; and immediately afterwards Lodge stopped payment. The utmost contended for there was, that the assignees of the separate estate might be at liberty to prove that sum, not to take it out. Lord Thurlow there established the rule, that unless there was a transmutation of the estate by fraud, the creditors must take it, as it happened at the time of the bankruptcy. That rule has been since acted upon in other cases, and the law is established, that the date of the act of bankruptcy is the commencement of the lien ; and until then there is no lien. At law there is no lien upon the effects of the debtor, until the execution is delivered to the sheriff. At the date of this deed there was neither act of bankruptcy nor execution. There being no lien therefore at law, what objection is there to this deed, public, attended with possession, and upon *bonâ fide* consideration ? The intent of the deed was to convey all the property to James Cooper. He was to use his capital in the continuing trade. For that purpose the assignment was necessary. It is not necessary in such a case to prove, that the separate creditors trusted to the apparent separate stock. To what else could they trust ? James Cooper swears, no idea was entertained of his having any partnership property : that he contracted debts to the amount of 5000*l.* ; and that he laid out considerable sums upon this very property ; and that he paid partnership debts to the whole amount of what he received. But the case is not to be decided upon such circumstances, but on the legal right of the creditors. The joint property was liable to their execution, but in common with any other property. But suppose, a separate creditor had obtained a prior judgment and execution : could that have been superseded by the subsequent execution of a joint creditor ?

In *Hankey v. Garratt* (1), also referred to by your Lordship, the question was the same as in *Ex parte Burnaby ;* whether under the separate bankruptcy there was a right to distribute the joint property among the joint creditors : Lord Thurlow's doubt being, whether the solvent partner had not a right to appear. That doubt has
been of late got over : the Court having been in the * habit　　[*125]
of disposing of joint property under a separate commission

---

(1) *Ante*, vol. i. 236.

without a bill, or the appearance of the other partner. But in those cases the question was not, what is or is not joint property ; but as to the jurisdiction.

Mr. *Romilly,* in reply.—Though this order was not made by Lord Rosslyn [Loughborough] upon argument, it certainly did not pass as a mere matter of course. This must be decided as a general case. There is one very important fact ; that there were outstanding debts to a very considerable amount. None of those debts could be collected but by action in the joint names of the two partners until the bankruptcy, and now, of the assignees. The effect therefore was not to make James Cooper the legal owner : an equitable interest only could be transferred, subject to all equities, and therefore to the equitable lien upon the covenant to pay all the debts ; to which these outstanding debts, as well as the other property, were liable. The joint creditors claim, not by way of lien, but as having by the rules established in this Court an equitable claim upon the joint property, in preference to the separate creditors, until the former are paid twenty shillings in the pound. There is an analogy to the case of a partner dying ; in which case all survives at law to the other: but this Court either in a suit or in bankruptcy would direct an account of all the debts at the dissolution. So, where an executor becomes bankrupt : all the effects would belong to the assignees: but the Court considers them trustees ; as he was. So in this case the bankrupt was a trustee for the joint creditors after the dissolution of the partnership ; as both were before. The case of *Lodge and Fendal* is materially distinguishable. In this the whole fund of the joint creditors is done away. In that also the question was not as to specific effects, but a sum of money paid in by one partner. These petitioners only say those specific effects subsisting in the hands of this partner, ought to be applied. *Ex parte Burnaby* is an express decision upon the point. The ground of this claim is upon the assignment, not the dissolution ; which is immaterial: but how can one partner assign all his property to the other without a dissolution ? As to the fraud, suppose, the person going out is insolvent : a case extremely likely to happen.

[* 126]   * Lord CHANCELLOR [ELDON].—This case is admitted, unless *Ex parte Burnaby* applies to it, to be new in its circumstances. Therefore, if I was of opinion, that the petition could be supported, I should be very unwilling to express that in bankruptcy ; where my opinion would not be subject to review. If the case I have mentioned has decided the point, there is the authority of Lord Hardwicke upon it ; which would weigh down the most considerable doubt, that I could be disposed to entertain. I feel great difficulty in complying with the prayer of the petition ; and, when I read it, was struck with it, as a new case ; and as one, upon which I do not clearly see my way to the relief prayed. It is the case of two partners ; who owed several joint debts ; and had joint effects. Under these circumstances their creditors, who had a demand upon them in respect of those debts, had clearly no lien whatsoever upon

the partnership effects. They had power of suing, and by process creating a demand, that would directly attach upon the partnership effects. But they had no lien upon or interest in them in point of law or equity. If any creditor had brought an action, the action would be joint : his execution might be either joint or several. He might have taken in execution both joint and separate effects. It is also true, that the separate creditors of each by bringing actions might acquire a certain interest even in the partnership effects ; taking them in execution in the way, in which separate creditors can affect such property. But there was no lien in either.

The partnership might dissolve in various ways: first by death (1) : secondly, by the act of the parties : that act extending to nothing more than mere dissolution ; without any special agreement as to the disposition of the property, the satisfaction of the debts, much less any agreement for an assignment from either of the partners to the others. The partnership might also be dissolved by the bankruptcy of one (2) or of both, and by effluxion of time. If it dissolved by death, referring to the law of merchants and the well known doctrine of this Court, the death being the act of God, the legal title in some respects, in all the equitable title, would remain notwithstanding the survivorship (3) ; and the executor would have a right to insist, that the property should be applied to the partnership debts. I do not know, that the partnership creditors would have that right, supposing both remained solvent. So, upon the bankruptcy of one of them there would be an equity to say, the assignees stand in the place of the bankrupt; and can take * no more than he could ; and consequently nothing, until [* 127] the partnership debts are paid. So, upon a mere dissolution, without a special agreement, or a dissolution by effluxion of time: to wind up the accounts the debts must be paid ; and the surplus be distributed in proportion to the different interests. In all these ways the equity is not that of the joint creditors, but that of the partners with regard to each other, that operates to the payment of the partnership debts. The joint creditors must of necessity be paid in order to the administration of justice to the partners themselves. When the bankruptcy of both takes place, it puts an end to the partnership certainly : but still it is very possible, and it often happens in fact, that the partners may have different interests in the surplus ; and out of that a necessity arises, that the partnership debts must be paid : otherwise the surplus cannot be distributed according to equity, and no distinction has been made with reference to their interests, whether in different proportions, or equally. Many cases have occurred upon the distribution between the separate and joint estates ; and the principle in all of them, from the great case of *Mr. Fordyce*, has been, that if the Court should say, that what has

(1) *Post*, vol. xi. 5; xv. 227; 3 Mer. 614; 1 Swanst. 509; *Gillespie* v. *Hamilton*, 3 Madd. 251.
(2) *Post, Crawshay* v. *Collins*, vol. xv. 218; 3 Mer. 614.
(3) *Ante*, vol. i. 434, 435; *post*, vol. ix. 596, 7, and the notes.

ever been joint or separate property shall always remain so, the consequence would be, that no partnership could ever arrange their affairs. Therefore a *bona fide* transmutation of the property is understood to be the act of men acting fairly, winding up the concern ; and binds the creditors ; and therefore the Court always let the arrangement be, as they stand, not at the time of the commission, but of the act of bankruptcy.

Thomas Cooper is admitted to be solvent. He certainly has no such equity, as if the partnership had been dissolved by bankruptcy, death, effluxion of time, or any other circumstance, not his own act. But he dissolves the partnership a year and a half ago ; and, instead of calling upon these effects according to his equity at the dissolution to pay the partnership debts, he assigns his interest to the other, to deal as he thinks fit with the property, to act with the world respecting it ; desiring only a bond to pay a given value in three or four years. Therefore he or his executors could not sue. If it was necessary for the creditors to operate their relief through [* 128] his equity, he has no equity. It is then said, * and the circumstance had struck me, that all the property is not assignable at law : for instance the debts : but as between the two Coopers they were the property of the bankrupt ; for debts are within the statute of King James (1) ; and if left in the order and disposal of the bankrupt, he is proprietor of the debt. Therefore Thomas Cooper could never set up the insufficiency of the legal operation of the assignment against his own deed. The assignment was not made subject to the payment of the debts, but in consideration of a covenant, leaving no duty upon the property, but attaching a personal obligation upon the assignee to pay the debts. The creditors therefore cannot rest upon the equity of the partner going out. I was struck with the argument of inconvenience : the inconvenience on all sides is great. To say this seems to me a monstrous proposition : that, which at any time during the partnership has been part of the partnership effects, shall in all future time remain part of the partnership effects ; notwithstanding a *bona fide* act. Suppose, an improbable case, that the partners in Child's house chose to shift their shop from Temple Bar to the west end of the town ; and that house, now the property of the partnership, was *bona fide* bought by one of the partners ; and the money was invested in the purchase of the new house, in which they were going to reside : suppose a still more improbable case, that a year and a half or ten years afterwards they became bankrupt : would that house be part of the partnership effects ? It would be so, if it remained without the legal interest being passed, or without any equitable claim, taking it out of the reach of a legal execution : but where the effect is a *bona fide* transaction of this sort, if it were held at any time afterwards to be partnership property, not for the purpose of satisfying demands of the

(1) Stat. 21 Jam. I. c. 19, s. 10, 11 ; *post, Jones* v. *Gibbons,* vol. ix. 407, and the notes, 409 ; xix. 494.

partners, or of any creditor, who cannot otherwise be satisfied, but to
enable them to undo all the intermediate equities, commercial transactions could not go on at all.   It would be much less inconvenience
to examine the *bona fides* of each transaction than to say, such transactions shall never take place.

The case of *West* v. *Skip* falls within some of the observations I
have made.   *Heath* v. *Percival* does not apply at all.   The bond in
that case was not given up; and therefore the creditor
keeping * the best security, and refusing to part with it,   [* 129]
no inference can be made against the conclusion arising
from that.   *Hankey* v. *Garratt* is also very different.   There the
partnership was dissolved by bankruptcy or by death: and there was
no actual transfer of the property to take it out of the reach of legal
execution.   I am unwilling to make any observation upon *Burnaby's
Case.*   I do not know how to understand it.   Whether there was
any thing special in the assignment, I cannot find out from the report.   I shall endeavor to find the papers.   It looks very like this
case ; if it is in specie this case, as an authority I should think myself bound to submit to it.   But if it is not in specie this case, there
is so much doubt, whether this relief can be given, that I am satisfied, it ought to be given, if at all, in a jurisdiction, where my
opinion would be subject to review.   My present inclination is that
the creditors have not this equity.   I have considerable doubt also,
whether, if they have it, Thomas Cooper would be benefited by it;
and a farther subject of grave and serious doubt is, whether, if the
joint creditors disturb the arrangement, the separate creditors would
not have a right to set the arrangement right at his expense.

I now think, there is a circumstance that distinguishes *Burnaby's
Case.*   The assignment was not by one to the other two, but by
one to one of the other two ; which may be very different.   I think,
that circumstance distinguishes the case so much, that I shall consult the interest of the parties better by saying, they may file a bill,
if they think proper, than by farther delay.

The Petition was dismissed (1).

———

1. The opinion expressed by Lord Eldon in the principal case, that joint creditors have no *lien* upon partnership effects, until such effects are taken into the
custody of the law by due process, and that the equity for distribution of such
effects, in discharge of joint debts, is worked out through the rights of the partners, as against each other, was firmly adhered to by his Lordship in *Ex parte
Williams*, 11 Ves. 4; *Ex parte Rowlandson*, 2 V. & B. 173, and on various other

———

(1) *Post, Ex parte Fell*, vol. x. 347 ; *Ex parte Williams*, xi. 3 ; *Ex parte Rowlandson*, 2 Ves. & Bea. 172.   In *Ex parte Freeman*, Buck, 471, both partners became bankrupts five months after the assignment to one of them ; and the joint
creditors were not permitted to elect to go against his separate estate.   *Ex parte
Peake*, 1 Madd. 346, 589.   In *Ex parte Fry*, 1 Glyn & Jam. 96, the Vice Chancellor, upon a representation, that his decision in *Ex parte Freeman* had been over-
ruled upon appeal, by some misunderstanding without argument, made a similar
order.   The interval between the assignment and bankruptcy in *Ex parte Fry* was
near three years.

occasions; the doctrine, therefore, may be considered as perfectly established; see *Campbell* v. *Mullett*, 2 Swanst. 575, the notes 3 and 4 to *Hankey* v. *Garratt*, 1 V. 236, and note 6 to *Curtis* v. *Perry*, 6 V. 739.

2. The death of a partner works a dissolution of the partnership; (*Crawshay* v. *Maule*, 1 Swanst. 569;) and want of notice of a dissolution, so effected, does not render the deceased partner's estate liable to the subsequent debts of the continuing partners; (*Vulliamy* v. *Noble*, 3 Meriv. 614:) as a general rule, however, the estate of a deceased partner remains liable to the debts which affected him at the time of his death; (*S. C.* p. 619; *Sleech's case*, in *Devaynes* v. *Noble*, 1 Meriv. 566;) though, even from this liability, it may be exonerated, if the subsequent dealings of the creditors with the surviving partners have been of such a nature as to show, that they have consented to shift the obligation to pay from the estate of the deceased partner, and to accept the surviving partners for their sole debtors: *Ex parte Kendall*, 17 Ves. 519, 526: but this inference will not be lightly made, and certainly not from the mere circumstance, that the creditor has continued to carry on an account with the surviving partners. *Palmer's case*, in *Devaynes* v. *Noble*, 1 Meriv. 624.

3. In the absence of express contract, any partner may dissolve the connexion whenever he thinks proper, as amongst the partners themselves, the existence of still depending partnership engagements cannot prevent a dissolution; (*Featherstonhaugh* v. *Fenwick*, 17 Ves. 308;) but, of course, all the engagements subsisting at the time must be wound up, and, to that extent, they will remain jointly interested. *Crawshay* v. *Collins*, 15 Ves. 227; *Peacock* v. *Peacock*, 16 Ves. 57. From this rule, that an indefinite partnership may be dissolved whenever any partner pleases, it follows, as a regular consequence, that, under ordinary circumstances, no bill will hold for a specific execution of an agreement to enter into a partnership, which (unless the contract was for a partnership of certain duration) the defendant might dissolve immediately; (*Hercy* v. *Birch*, 9 Ves. 360;) but, in particular cases, it may be right to enforce performance even of such short-lived agreement. *Buxton* v. *Lister*, 3 Atk. 385; *Anonymous case*, 2 Ves. Sen. 629.

4. Although a partnership was entered into for a term of years, it will (unless there were express stipulations to the contrary) be dissolved by the death of a partner previously to the time fixed for the expiration of the partnership. *Crawford* v. *Hamilton*, 3 Mad. 254.

5. As the death of a partner dissolves a partnership, so the bankruptcy of one partner equally causes a dissolution; but if the solvent partners continue to trade with the partnership capital, as they are thus exposing to responsibility and loss, not only their own property, but the share of the bankrupt, there would be no mutuality if it were not held, that they must account to his assignees for any profit which they have made by such an application of the funds. *Crawshay* v. *Collins*, 15 Ves. 218; *S. C.* 1 Jac. & Walk. 279; *Featherstonhaugh* v. *Fenwick*, 17 Ves. 310; *Brown* v. *De Tastet*, Jacob's Rep. 296. A similar rule, founded on the same obviously equitable principle, prevails, when a partnership has been dissolved by death; if the surviving partners continue to trade with the capital of the deceased partner, any profits will belong to the joint estate; (*Hammond* v. *Douglas*, 5 Ves. 539;) for, though the representatives of a deceased partner, or the assignees of a bankrupt partner, are not strictly partners with the surviving, or the solvent partners, still, a community of interest remains, until the affairs in which the joint property is interested are finally wound up. *Ex parte Williams*, 11 Ves. 5.

6. Although the common law has not adopted the *lex mercatoria* throughout, in all that relates to partnership in trade, so fully as Courts of Equity have done, yet all Courts agree in holding, that, notwithstanding partners are in the nature of joint tenants, there shall be no survivorship between them in point of interest. *Devaynes* v. *Noble*, 1 Meriv. 564.

7. *Debts* due to a partnership, and assigned, upon a dissolution, by the retiring partners to a continuing partner, without notice to the debtors, will be held, in case of the bankruptcy of the continuing partner, to have remained within the order and disposition of the joint partnership; see, *post*, note 1 to *Jones* v. *Gibbons*, 9 V. 407; for until the debtors receive notice of the assignment, they might properly have paid their debts to any of the retired partners, whose receipt would have been a good discharge. *Ex parte Monro*, Buck, 303; *Ex parte Burton*, 1 Glyn & Jameson, 209; *Ex parte Usborne*, 1 Glyn & Jameson, 360.

8. A contract between two partners, merely to enable one of them to withdraw funds out of the reach of the joint creditors, is fraudulent; (*Anderson* v. *Maltby*, 2 Ves. Jun. 255;) but a contract that a retiring partner shall receive a premium for relinquishing his share, even in what at the time is not a solvent firm, is not necessarily fraudulent; (*Ex parte Peake*, 1 Mad. 354;) so with respect to an agreement, upon a dissolution of partnership, that the continuing partner shall take the whole stock and effects, and pay all the joint debts, if such continuing partner becomes bankrupt, the right of joint creditors to the joint property, then remaining in specie, will depend entirely on the *bona fides* of the transaction; the mode of conveyance or assignment; and the nature of their stipulations. *Ex parte William*, 11 Ves. 5; *Ex parte Fry*, 1 Glyn & Jameson, 96; *Ex parte Freeman*, Buck, 412; *Ex parte Fell*, 10 Ves. 348; *Ex parte Rowlandson*, 2 V. & B. 174; *Duff* v. *The East India Company*, 15 Ves. 215, 217.

WHITMORE v. TRELAWNY.

[1801, June 9.]

GENERAL words controlled, in order to make the whole will consistent (*a*).
Survivorship by words in a will creating a joint interest: the intention of severance not being sufficiently clear (*b*).

OWEN SALISBURY BRERETON by his will, dated the 15th of December, 1795, gave and devised all his lands, tenements and hereditaments, in Cheshire, Chester, Flintshire, Denbighshire, and Middlesex, to the Plaintiff and Charles Potts, their heirs and assigns; in trust to and for the use of the testator's wife during her
* life ; and after her decease he devised all the said lands,   [* 130]
in Cheshire and Chester and Middlesex, in trust to the
same trustees, to and for the use and benefit of Charles Trelawny during his natural life; remainder to his eldest and every other son in tail male; remainder to his heirs for ever. He devised to the same trustees his lands, &c. in Flintshire and Denbighshire, for the use of William Trelawny for life; remainder to the next and every other son in succession of Sir Harry Trelawny in tail male; remainder to his, the said William Trelawny's heirs for ever. The will directed the devisees to take the name of Brereton; and after several other dispositions proceeded thus :

"I give to my dear wife the interest of all my 3 per cent. consolidated stock at the Bank during her natural life (except of what I hereinafter bequeath) with power by her last will to devise 5000*l.* consols between her and my nieces. After my wife's decease I give two thirds of the above interest of the Consols to General Trelawny,

---

(*a*) As to the controlling effect of general words, see *ante*, notes (*a*) and (*b*), *Collett* v. *Lawrence*, 1 V. 268; and generally as to the construction of wills, note (*d*), *Sims* v. *Doughty*, 5 V. 243; note (*a*), *Thellusson* v. *Woodford*, 4 V. 227.

(*b*) Where a legacy is given to two or more persons, they will take a joint tenancy, unless the will contains words to show that the testator intended a severance of the interest, and to take away the right of survivorship. See *ante*, note (*a*), *Morley* v. *Bird*, 3 V. 628.

and his brother Thomas of Odiam, Esq. for their lives; and after their deaths I give the same to the two persons in possession of my said several land estates."

The testator then gave his wife several specific legacies of his said Bank 3 per cent. Annuities, amounting in the whole to 8000l. of such Annuities; and he appointed his wife and the Plaintiff executors; and made his wife residuary legatee.

The testator died soon after the execution of his will. After paying the legacies the fund of 3 per cent. consolidated Bank annuities was reduced from 30,000l. to 22,000l. The widow received the dividends until her death in May 1800. By her will, dated the 11th of January, 1800, after giving specific legacies to a large amount of 3 per cent. consolidated Bank Annuities and other legacies, and in part reciting the will of her husband, and stating the power given to her by that will, she therefore did in pursuance of such power vested in her by her said late husband's will devise and bequeath the said sum of 5000l. Consols in manner following. She then directed 2500l., one moiety of the said sum, to be divided between four nieces; and as to the other 2500l. she willed, devised and bequeathed, the same to six other nieces; viz. 2400l. among [* 131] five, and 100l. to another; and she gave the * residue of the money in the funds not therein disposed of and the remainder of her estate and effects of what nature and kind soever to the Plaintiff; and appointed him executor.

After the deaths of the testatrix and of General Harry Trelawny the bill was filed; stating, that the 5000l. ought to be taken by the Plaintiff, as executor of the widow, out of the 22,000l. stock; and that after that deduction two thirds of the residue ought to be appropriated and applied between Thomas Trelawny and the persons, who shall successively become entitled to the testator's real estates; and praying, that the rights of the parties may be ascertained.

The Defendants by their answers submitted, whether the 5000l. stock ought to be taken out of the 22,000l. and two thirds of the remaining 17,000l. only to be applied for the benefit of the Defendants, according to the suggestion of the bill, or, whether the 5000l. was not to be taken out of the general residue.

The Defendants Charles Trelawny Brereton and William Trelawny Brereton farther submitted, whether the Defendant Thomas Trelawny did or did not upon the death of General Harry Trelawny become entitled to receive all the dividends and interest of the two third parts of the residue of the 3 per cent. annuities for life; or, whether upon the death of General Trelawny a moiety of the two thirds of the dividends, &c. to which he was entitled for life, did not immediately become vested in the Defendants Charles Trelawny Brereton and William Trelawny Brereton. The Defendant Thomas Trelawny claimed the whole of the two thirds of the dividends by survivorship.

The *Solicitor General* [Hon. *Spencer Perceval*] and Mr. *Hart*, for the Plaintiff.—The sum of 5000l. 3 per cent. Bank annuities was a specific bequest for the benefit of the nieces of the testator and his wife ; and her authority extended no farther than to apportion that sum. As to that only a discretion was to be exercised: but the nieces took substantial interests under his will. Therefore the interest given to General Trelawny and his brother was in nature of a specific bequest of the residue. The construction, that the 5000*l.* is to come out of the aggregate fund, is the rational construction.

* Mr. *Richards* and Mr. *Grimwood*, for the Defendant	[* 132] Thomas Trelawny.—Upon the general question this Defendant agrees with the other Defendants against the Plaintiff; but contends, that this is a joint bequest to the two persons in remainder : the other Defendants insisting, it is several. Upon the first question, it is upon them to show, that these words, "the above interest," importing by reference to the former words the interest of all the consols, mean only a part of them. The decision of *Brown* v. *Higgs* (1), as it now stands, is an authority, that the words of the power operate as a bequest to the nieces : but that case is a subject of appeal. Upon the Defendant's construction every part of the will has effect without absurdity : upon the other, words must be supplied.

With respect to the question between the Defendants, this is a joint bequest plainly ; and therefore survives.

Mr. *Stanley*, for the Defendant Charles Trelawny Brereton and William Trelawny Brereton upon the first question concurred with the other Defendants. Upon the point between the Defendants he contended from the manner, in which the real estate was disposed of, that the testator did not mean survivorship as to the money fund ; and that upon the whole will there was an intention of severance as to that.

The *Solicitor General*, in reply.—The construction, that the whole interest without any deduction in any shape is intended, is impossible. A different modification of the interest is distinctly introduced ; showing a diminution of the fund by the previous disposition of the 5000*l.* The power is only to apportion ; and presumes the thing given, before that power commences.

Lord CHANCELLOR [ELDON].—It is impossible in the construction of such a will as this to be quite sure, I am right in the opinion I have formed ; and yet I confess an inclination of opinion, rising almost to confidence, that the claims of the Defendants must be restrained to two thirds of the dividends of 17,000*l.* Bank annuities only, and not of 22,000*l.* The testator had at the date of the * will about 30,000*l.* 3 per cent. consolidated Bank	[* 133] annuities ; but in construing a will the Court must consider, what would be the construction in all the given changes of property, that might have taken place between the date of the will and the death of the testator ; and though in this instance there was

(1) *Ante,* vol. iv. 708; v. 495; *post,* viii. 561.

no such change, regard must be had to what would have been the
construction, if the state of the property had been charged by act in
his life.   Upon the clause respecting the 5000*l.* it is contended, that
there was a mere power to the testator's wife, independent of the
exercise of which power the nieces would take nothing.   On the
other hand it was insisted, that there was a vested interest in the
nieces; the proportions to be regulated by the exercise of that power upon the property ; to go equally among them, if the power should
not be exercised.   In my view of this case it is not necessary to
say, what is the true effect of the will upon that point ; and I am
happy to deliver myself from the necessity of considering upon this
day the authority of that case, which is to come before me by appeal ; for, taking this either as a power, or as a vested interest, my
mind comes to the same conclusion.   If it was a power, and was
executed by the wife, it is clear, under the execution of the power
the nieces would take the 5000*l.* at the death of the wife.   If an interest vested in them independent of the execution of the power, it
is equally clear, they would take it at the death of the wife.   From
that sum of 5000*l.* therefore it is impossible, that the Defendants
could have either two thirds of the interest or any other part.   That
sum therefore being to be subtracted from the bulk of this fund, the
testator goes on to make the disposition of two thirds of the above
interest of the Consols after his wife's decease ; which words may
undoubtedly mean, and more naturally mean in ordinary language,
all the Consols than a part.   But terms so inaccurate as these must
be construed not merely with regard to their ordinary meaning : but
that construction must be adopted, that will make the whole will
consistent and capable of being executed ; and in that view the
question is, whether the testator meant two thirds of that, of which
he had not before disposed, or of 22,000*l.*, having left to dispose of
only 17,000*l.*

But there may be another view of this case.   Suppose, the testator's wife had died in his life.   In that case the nieces take their interests at his own decease.   He had authorised 5000*l.* to
[* 134]   be *subtracted from the bulk of the fund for their benefit ;
and if that was subtracted at his death, it is utterly impossible, that under the subsequent words the Defendants could receive
more than two thirds of what remained.   But a much stronger case
might be put.   Suppose, he had in his life sold 25,000*l.* of the
stock : upon the construction of the Defendants this consequence
would follow ; that, though the wife might have given 5000*l.* by the
execution of the power, or the testator had given that sum independent of the power, to the nieces, the Defendants might have received
two thirds of the dividends of the remaining 5000*l.*   It is impossible he could have meant that ; and if not, the consequence follows,
that under the present circumstances of the fund he meant, that
after that sum of 5000*l.* subtracted the remaining 17,000*l.* should be
the fund, two thirds of the interest of which the Defendants are to
receive.   It is a circumstance, not affording a very solid ground of

argument, that the power extends over the whole property ; and the disposition in favor of the nieces, either by virtue of the power extending over the whole or by the bequest of the testator out of the whole, must have been satisfied, however he diminished the property, if sufficient was left to satisfy it.   The wife as residuary legatee had·an interest ; by virtue of which without the power she might dispose to the nieces : but if they are to take under the act of the wife, they are to take by her authority, not her interest, and not only out of a fund, in which she had an interest, but out of the whole ; in which she had partly a power and partly an interest. Upon the whole the Defendants are to take only two thirds of the dividends of 17,000*l.* Bank annuities.

As to the other question it is exceedingly probable, the testator did not mean survivorship : but he has actually given in words creating a joint tenancy ; which is not severed ; and therefore the whole must go to him, who survived.

Direct two thirds of the 17,000*l.* Bank annuities to be transferred to the Accountant-General : the dividends to be paid to the Defendant Thomas Trelawny for his life ; with liberty to apply : the costs to be paid out of the general residue by the Plaintiff.

As to the general rules laid down for the construction of wills, see, *ante,* note 4 to *Blake* v. *Bunbury,* 1 V. 194 ; and that, where there are no words of express or implied severance in the will by which the bequest is made, legatees must take as joint tenants, although the leaning of Courts is in favor of tenancy in common ; see the note to *Morley* v. *Bird,* 3 V. 628.

HODSON *v.* ———.   [* 135]

[1801, June 3, 13.]

ORDER upon the Register of the Consistory Court, that an original will may be produced for the hearing upon giving security.

MR. STANLEY for the Plaintiff moved for an order upon the Register of the Consistory Court of Durham, that an original will might be produced for the hearing of the cause upon giving security.

Lord CHANCELLOR asking, what was the foundation of the jurisdiction, Mr. *Stanley* said, there had been many such orders.   His Lordship however expressing considerable doubt upon it, no order was made.   Afterwards Mr. *Stanley* repeated the motion ; and cited *Forder* v. *Wade* (1) ; referring to former orders ; and *Ross* v. *Cropper* ; in which Lord Rosslyn made an order upon the officer of the Ecclesiastical Court in Chester.

Lord CHANCELLOR asked, what was the nature of the security ; and, who was to settle it.

---

(1) 4 Bro. C. C. 476.

Mr. *Stanley* said, the Master, if necessary.

Lord CHANCELLOR [ELDON].—How is his judgment to be regulated upon it? Suppose a will giving legacies to the amount of 5000*l*. This is possible: if all parties interested in the will are before the Court, all those parties might call for an order upon the Register to deliver the will; for if it should be lost or cancelled by their having called on him, he would not be answerable to any one.

Mr. *Stanley* said, the object of this bill was to have an estate sold for payment of debts.

Mr. *Hart* (*Amicus Curiæ*) said that in *Baron* v. *Baron*, upon a bill to prove a will, he had obtained such an order.

Lord CHANCELLOR.—What authority has the Ecclesiastical Court to enforce the Chancellor's order? Would this Court order the officer of the Court of King's Bench to produce any of the documents of that Court? However upon the ground of the practice [*136] tice * you may take the order. I do not know, upon what it stands: but I cannot renounce the authority of so many of my predecessors (1).

THOUGH the jurisdiction of the Court of Chancery to order the original of a will to be delivered out by the officer of the Ecclesiastical Court in which it is lodged, for a special purpose, has been thought doubtful; (*Fauquier* v. *Tynte*, 7 Ves. 292;) still, upon the ground of long practice, an application for that purpose seems, as in the present case, to be pretty sure of success. *Ford* v. ———, 6 Ves. 802; *Frederick* v. *Aynscombe*, 1 Atk. 628; *Morse* v. *Roach*, 2 Str. 961.

BROWNE, *Ex parte.*

[1801, JUNE 13.]

UPON a separate commission of bankruptcy the benefit of an insurance, effected by the bankrupt upon his own account upon joint property, is not liable to the joint creditors.

THE ships Maria and Betsey the joint property of Cullen, Buddicombe and Martin, were insured by Cullen only; and having been captured, the money recovered from the underwriters was applied in payment of his separate creditors under the bankruptcy. The object of the petition of creditors in respect of the outfit and cargoes of the ships was to prove against the separate estate of Cullen.

The Lord CHANCELLOR [ELDON] expressed on a former day a clear opinion against the petition: but it stood over upon the suggestion of Mr. *Richards*, that there was some case in favor of it.

---

(1) *Post, Fauquier* v. *Tynte*, vol. vii. 292; *Anon.* i. 152, and the notes; *Qualey* v. *Qualey*, 4 Madd. 213.

Mr. *Richards,* now referring to *Ex parte Parry* (1), gave up the point; and said, the order in the bankruptcy of *Fitzhenry and Rogers* arose from a slip.

The petition was dismissed. ____

As the estate of a bankrupt could have no contribution from the other joint owners, in respect of the premium he paid out of his own funds for an insurance which he made upon his separate account, there would be no equal justice in hold-. ing that any sums he recovered from the underwriters should become joint prop-. erty. *Ex parte Parry,* 5 Ves. 576.

DINWIDDIE *v.* BAILEY.

[1801, June 10, 17.]

BILL by an insurance broker for a discovery and account of money paid and received by him in that capacity on account of the Defendants, and money due to him for commission, &c. and for promissory notes indorsed to him, and to restrain an action, as brought contrary to the universal custom of the business. Demurrer allowed: the subject being matter of set-off, and capable of proof at law (*a*).

To sustain a bill for an account there must be mutual demands. The case of dower stands upon its own specialties: so the case of a steward (*b*), [p. 141.]

THE bill stated, that the Plaintiff carried on the business of insurance broker at Manchester; and was employed by the Defendants from time to time to effect insurances upon ships, goods, wares, and merchandize; and paid divers sums of money on account thereof;' and became entitled as such insurance broker to divers sums of money for his commission upon effecting such insurances, and otherwise respecting the same, and the money received on account thereof, and for postage of letters, and upon sums

---

(1) *Ante,* vol. v. 575.

(*a*) Courts of Equity will maintain jurisdiction where there are mutual accounts. 1 Story, Eq. Jur. §457, 458, 459; *Armstrong* v. *Gilchrist,* 2 Johns. Cas. 424; *Rathbone* v. *Warren,* 10 Johns. 587; *King* v. *Baldwin,* 17 Johns. 384; *Ludlow* v. *Simond,* 2 Caines, Err. 1, 38, 52; *Post* v. *Kemberly,* 9 Johns. 493; *Hawley* v. *Cramer,* 4 Cowen, 727; 2 Parl. Rep. of Common Law Commissioners, 1830, p. 26; *Porter* v. *Spencer,* 2 Johns. Ch. 171, where the principal case is cited. Also where the accounts are on one side only, and a discovery is wanted in aid of the account, and is obtained. 1 Story, Eq. Jur. §458, note. But in the latter case, if no discovery is asked, or required by the form of the bill, the jurisdiction will not be maintainable. Ibid.; *Frietas* v. *Don Santos,* 1 Y. & Jer. 574; *King* v. *Rossett,* 2 Y. & Jer. 33; but see, *Mackenzie* v. *Johnston,* 4 Madd, 374; *Massey* v. *Banner,* 4 Madd. 416.

In the present case the interposition of Equity was regarded as unnecessary; for upon the allegations of the bill, the relief at law was perfect. Story, Eq. Pl. § 482; *Moses* v. *Lewis,* 12 Price, 502.

(*b*) As to the case of dower, see *ante,* p. 73, note (*b*) to *Pulteney* v. *Warren*; also note (*a*), *Mundy* v. *Mundy,* 2 V. 122. In general a bill will not lie by an agent against his principal, for an account, unless some special ground is laid; as the incapacity to get proof, except by discovery. 1 Story, Eq. Jur. § 462, note.

of money paid, laid out, and expended, on account of the Defendants in effecting the insurances, &c. ; and that the Defendants
were also indebted in divers sums of money upon promissory notes
indorsed to the Plaintiff in the usual course of business.

The bill farther stated, that the Plaintiff received some money
from the underwriters in respect of losses upon some ships ; but that
it hath constantly been the universal custom of persons, who carry
on the business of insurance brokers at Lloyd's Coffee House, at
Liverpool, and for all other persons, who carry on the trade of insurance brokers, in the business, which they transact for merchants at
Liverpool or in any other part of the county of Lancaster, to be allowed one month from the day, upon which the loss upon ships or
goods, which are insured, is ascertained, and the documents respecting such loss found to be satisfactory, to obtain the signatures of the
underwriters to the adjustment of the policy, and to apply to such
underwriters for payment of their proportions ; and at the end of
that month, and not before, to accept bills, drawn upon them by the
persons, for whom they effected such insurances, for the amount of
such loss, until the end of four months from the day, upon which
the loss was ascertained, and the documents found satisfactory ;
and such custom has been always adopted, and acted upon, by the
Plaintiff in all his dealings with the Defendants; and they have
constantly allowed the Plaintiff the said space of four months for the
payment of the amount of the losses until the commencement of
the action.

The bill then stated losses upon ships under insurances effected
by the Plaintiff for the Defendants ; one settled upon the 7th,
another, upon the 11th of October, 1800; which according to the
said custom would be payable three months from the 7th and 11th
of November ; that no account of the said dealing was stated between the Plaintiff and Defendants ; but an action was brought by
the Defendants in December ; in which they held the Plaintiff to
bail for 1192*l.* 5*s.* 11*d.* ; though the money due in respect of the
said losses was not due until February ; and the Defendants had not
drawn upon the Plaintiff; and the Defendants at the time of the action brought were, and now are, indebted to the Plaintiff in a much
larger sum on the accounts before mentioned and also by
[*138] virtue of three promissory notes; one, dated the 19th * of
October, 1799, at twelve months after date for 600*l.* ;
another of the same date and for the same time for 650*l.* ; another
dated the 18th of November, 1799, at fifteen months after date, for
1440*l.* 16*s.* ; all indorsed to the Plaintiff; and on account a large
balance would be found due to the Plaintiff. The bill then stated
applications for the sums paid for premiums, commission, &c. ; that
the Defendants threaten to proceed to trial ; well knowing, that the
Plaintiff cannot obtain adequate justice in the said action without an
account, and cannot recover therein the balance due to him from
them, as aforesaid ; and prayed an account of the sums of money
paid by the Plaintiff for and on account of the Defendants in respect

of the insurances effected, also the money due to him for commission, and otherwise respecting the same, and the money received on account thereof, postage of letters, and the other sums of money, paid, laid out and expended, by him on their account about the same, and also an account of the money due to him in respect of the promissory notes, of the several sums of money he received from the under-writers or others on account of the losses, and all other sums due to them from him; and a decree for payment; offering to pay what shall be due from him; and an injunction to restrain proceedings at law.

The Defendants put in a general demurrer to the discovery and relief.

Mr. *Mansfield* and Mr. *Pemberton*, in support of the Demurrer.—This bill seeks a discovery and account, not of money the Defendants have received, or with the receipt of which they are acquainted, but of money paid and received by the Plaintiff on account of the Defendants for premiums of insurances effected by him for them, also of money due to him in respect of promissory notes, also money received by him from under-writers on account of losses, and money due to him for commission, and paid by him for postage of letters or otherwise on their account. With respect to the custom alleged, it is impossible for this Court to decide. All these matters must be tried upon notice of set-off.

Lord CHANCELLOR [ELDON].—The fact as to the promissory notes he could prove without discovery. He states the custom; and that in fact such has been your habit of dealing with him. He does * not want discovery for that. What he has paid   [* 139] for premiums of insurance, and what for postage, is rather in his mind than yours. I do not recollect any such bill.

Mr. *Romilly* and Mr. *W. Agar*, in support of the bill.—The Defendants admit the custom by the demurrer, and that all the facts alleged are true. The question therefore is, whether all this account must be gone through before a jury. There have been many bills of this nature, by stewards for an account between them and their employers, as to receiving rents and paying sums of money. The Defendants must make out, that the Court will not maintain a bill for an account at the suit of an accounting party. There is one instance, in which this question was much discussed; and an opinion given upon it by a very great authority, in a case much more unfavorable to the Plaintiff: *Wells* v. *Cooper* (1). The bill was filed by the executor of a builder against a person, who had employed him for many years, and from time to time paid him money; stating that upon the account a balance was due to the testator: and charging, that the Defendant agreed to account with the executor. The answer admitted, that applications had been made; and the Defendant had said, that if the Plaintiff would produce the account, he would settle it in an amicable way; but insisted then, that the

(1) In the Court of Exchequer, 1791, MSS.

Plaintiff had no right to such an account ; and claimed the same benefit as if he had demurred.   Lord Chief Baron Eyre said, it was a very unfavorable case, reviving a dormant claim ; that, if it was only one matter, it could not be the subject of a bill : but, where there had been a series of transactions on the one side, and of payments on the other, he was not satisfied, that it was not matter of account.   He dismissed the bill however upon the ground of the length of time, that had elapsed.

This is not a very positive opinion, that such a bill may be entertained : but that opinion was expressed ; and there is no case or opinion to the contrary.   If any doubt arises, whether the custom exists, that may be ascertained hereafter by an issue.   The Plaintiff has a right to a discovery on oath, what commission he was entitled to have from them.   He states, that at the time of

[* 140]   * the action brought no sum was due from him to the Defendants ; on the contrary, that a large sum was due from them.   *Mundy* v. *Mundy* (1) bears some analogy to this case.   A balance must be taken to be due to the Plaintiff : therefore, as it is said there, nothing is left to try at law.

Mr. *Mansfield*, in reply.—I can easily conceive such a case as that in the Court of Exchequer; mutual transactions between two persons, money paid from time to time, &c. especially in the case of a builder.   But here no account is required from the Defendants, that can be had.   There is no allegation of any money paid or received by them.   This is an abuse of the term "account;" which supposes something mutual.   All these charges are payments and business done and money received by the Plaintiff.   I admit the case where books or papers are wanted, or, where there are mutual demands : but what books and papers are sought here : or what mutual demands are there, except as to those promissory notes indorsed by the Defendants?   The Plaintiff can prove the handwriting.   If he wanted evidence as to his legal demand for commission, that is not a ground for such a bill as this.   He does not suggest the least difficulty in proving, what is due to him for commission, or as to the custom, either general, or as in fact that, upon which they settled.   As to the supposed confession of a balance due to the Plaintiff, that is *pro hâc vice*, for the purpose of arguing the demurrer : but that would turn every action into a bill ; for the demurrer would be a confession.   The case of the Steward is clearly a case of mutual accounts.

Lord CHANCELLOR [ELDON].—I should feel infinite reluctance in supporting such a bill.   It contains rather a statement of facts, the effect of which it is a little difficult to collect.   With regard to all these allegations, some of which import, that he has received, some, that he has paid, money, he does not go on to allege, that upon the effect of the whole, taken together, they are indebted to him.   The only allegation of debt that I can find, is with regard to the money

due upon the promissory notes.   With respect to the allegation of
a universal custom if the fact is true, there can be no manner
of difficulty in the proof: so that, if an action was
* brought before the end of the four months, it would be   [* 141]
a complete defence to say, according to this general, notorious, custom, very capable of proof, that it was brought too soon.
With respect to this particular fact, it does not proceed upon any
alleged special agreement, the proof, and therefore the discovery, of
which might be necessary to sustain the defence to an action.   The
bill applies itself, not to a special agreement, but to a fact, capable
of proof; out of which it might be for a jury to infer, that there
was a special agreement conformable to the custom.   The allegation
is, that taking the whole together, this custom does exist at Lloyd's
Coffee House, at Liverpool, and in every part of Lancashire; and
that conformably to that custom the Plaintiff was constantly allowed
four month's credit; which is a fact to be evidenced by some transaction; and the gravamen of the bill is, that the action was brought
too soon: the four months not being expired.   He alleges farther,
that these promissory notes form a counter-demand; and upon the
whole alleges, that a considerable sum of money is due to him; and
in the sense in which such words are used, the bill must be taken to
be true.

It is clear, this case might be disposed of altogether at law.   It is
another question, whether the jurisdiction of this Court might not attach upon it: but it is beyond all doubt, it might be disposed of at
law; for every fact alleged is a fact, with regard to which it is impossible, that the Plaintiff must not be in possession of proof.   He
must know, what he paid for premiums of insurance, for postage;
what was due to him for commission; which is settled by the law
and usage of merchants; unless there is a special agreement; which
is not alleged.   All these particulars are known to himself.   If an
action was brought therefore, he would have had only to prove what
is here stated; which would be easy.   He has a set-off; the ordinary
case of set-off, of a sum of money, which he says is not only equal to
their demand, but gives him a right to sustain himself as a Plaintiff
for the balance due to him.   It is not to be said, that in every case,
where the Defendant owes more to the Plaintiff, that is a ground for
a bill.   There must be mutual demands, forming the ground.   The
case of dower is always considered a case standing upon its own
specialties.   So is the case of the steward (1).   The nature
of his dealing is, that money is paid in confidence, * with-   [* 142]
out vouchers; embracing a great variety of accounts with
the tenants; and nine times in ten it is impossible that justice can be
done to the steward.   If I sustain this bill, there never would be an
action in the city against a broker without a bill in equity.   I hesitate excessively in permitting such a bill; and the strong inclination

---

(1) This has been extended to the case of principal and agent generally;
Mackenzie v. *Johnston*, *Massey* v. *Banner*, 4 Madd. 373, 413.   See *ante*, *Lord
Hardwicke* v. *Vernon*, vol. iv. 411, and the note, 418.

of my opinion is, that the demurrer ought to be allowed. I feel great sanction for the doubt I entertain from the opinion of Lord Chief Justice Eyre in the case cited : a Judge, whose habit was not to express doubts, where he had a clear opinion. That case is very different, as being the case of an executor upon payments made to his testator, not of the party himself coming for relief. The executor can only go upon conjecture as to the amount of the money paid ; and therefore would go to law completely at his peril. There is hardly a case of set-off, in which a bill might not be sustained, if this may.

June 17*th.* The cause having stood over for the purpose of searching for precedents, Mr. Agar said, there were numerous cases of accounts sought by a principal against a factor, and one upon the bill of the factor against the principal, *Chapman* v. *Derby* (1) ; which was disposed of upon another point : but he could not find any case of an insurance broker.

Lord CHANCELLOR [ELDON] said, it was impossible to sustain the bill, without laying down, that wherever a person is entitled to a set-off, he may come into this Court.

The demurrer was afterwards allowed.

---

1. To what extent, and for what purposes only, a demurrer admits the allegations made by the plaintiff's bill, see, *ante*, note 3 to *Ford* v. *Peering*, 1 V. 72.

2. That the right of a dowress to come into a Court of Equity for an account, is a case standing on its own specialties, see note 8 to *Pulteney* v. *Warren*, 6 V. 73 ; but that the case of a steward may, without any special circumstances, come within the general rule, that every principal may file a bill for an account against any one who has been employed as his agent, see note 1 to *Lord Hardwicke* v. *Vernon*, 4 V. 411.

M'NAMARA *v.* WILLIAMS.

[1801, JUNE 17.]

To a bill against a vendor for a specific performance his stewards and receivers ought not to be made parties (*a*).

A specific performance being decreed, the bill as against them was dismissed with costs.

THE bill was filed to obtain a specific performance of an agreement to sell an estate to the Plaintiff ; which was decreed upon the

---

(1) 2 Vern. 117.

(*a*) A person is not properly a party to a suit, between whom and the plaintiff there is no privity or common interest. Story, Eq. Pl. §227. Nor should a person be made a party, who has no interest in the suit, and against whom, no decree can be had ; Ibid. §231, Mitford, Eq. Pl. by Jeremy, 160 ; *West* v. *Randall*, 2 Mason, 192 ; *Trecothick* v. *Austin*, 4 Mason, 42 ; *Petch* v. *Dalton*, 8 Price, 12. On this ground a person, who is a mere agent in a transaction, ought not to be made a party to a bill ; as, for example, an auctioneer, who has sold an estate, the sale being the matter in controversy. Cooper, Eq. Pl. 41, 42.

submission in the answer of the vendor ; with the usual directions for an account of the arrear of rents, and the delivery of the title-deeds, &c.   But a question arose as to the propriety of making two persons of the name of Allen parties, as receivers and stewards of the estate and in possession of the Court-rolls and title-deeds ; one of whom by his answer stated, that he had ceased to be steward in 1795.

Lord CHANCELLOR [ELDON].—With regard to this bill, as against the Allens, it is the case of a vendor having his Court-rolls, &c. in the possession of a steward.   The arrears of rent are assigned in this instance : but that does not differ this case from that of an agreement to be executed in six months : if not then executed, so that it became necessary for the vendor to file a bill, he would be as much entitled to the arrears of the rents, as in this case under the express stipulation.   In such a case I never heard of loading the suit by making the receivers and stewards of the vendor parties.   To permit it would be most dangerous.   In some cases the vendor may be wrong, in others it may be perfectly consistent with justice to refuse to perform the agreement: is the vendee, filing the bill, to go to the steward of the vendor, in the one case rightly contending, that he is not bound to perform the agreement, and to desire, pending the suit, that the steward shall not pay the rents to his master, but hand them over to him ; for if he has a right to maintain the suit, when the cause comes to a hearing, it is founded upon the right to call for the rents at that moment.   There is no such right.   The ordinary decree was made for the vendor to account for the arrear of rent.   How can this be consistent with the usual language of the decree, to account for the rent received by him or by any other person or persons by his order or for his use ?   The decree must be against him for an account of the rents accrued due and received by his stewards since the time, at which the title was to be made ; and according to my view it would be a most dangerous thing, if an agreement was to be considered by *a Court of Equity as changing   [* 144] the character of the steward ; making him no longer the steward of the vendor, but the steward of the purchaser, receiving the rents for him, and not for the vendor, while contending in a suit with the purchaser against the performance.

So with respect to the title-deeds : can the agreement be stated to have this effect ; that, while the contest respecting the execution of the contract is going on, it gives the purchaser a right to call upon the steward for the title-deeds ?   That cannot be.   He has a right to come here, calling on the vendor to deliver up all the deeds in his custody, power, or possession : but these deeds, in the hands of the steward, are in the view of the Court physically in the custody, power or possession, of the vendor ; and the jurisdiction of the Court is satisfied by the order upon him to hand them over to the purchaser. By the effect of the decree he is bound to get them out of the hands of those persons ; and it is less inconvenient to have him attached for not bringing them here, than to permit persons of this description to be made parties pending the suit.

In order to prevent the necessity of loading causes with unnecessary parties, this bill as against the Allens must be dismissed with costs.

THAT, as a general rule, no one ought to be made a party defendant to a bill in Equity, against whom no decree can be made, see, *ante,* note 3 to *Cartwright* v. *Hately,* 1 V. 292; where the exceptions to the rule are also stated.

GREGOR *v.* LORD ARUNDEL.

[1801, JUNE 18.]

AFTER two answers reported insufficient the Defendant is not entitled to six weeks time to answer (a).

MR. STEELE for the Plaintiff moved to discharge an order obtained for six weeks' time to answer, after two answers reported insufficient upon exceptions; referring to the general order (1).

The motion, having stood over, was granted; and the former order discharged with costs.

SEE the note to the *Anonymous case,* 2 V. 270.

[* 145]   LLOYD *v.* MAKEAM.

[1801, JUNE 13, 18.]

ORDER to strike out the names of two of the Plaintiffs on giving security for costs made without consent (b).

MR. COOPER for the Plaintiff moved to amend the bill by striking out the names of two of four Plaintiffs upon giving security for costs. They had executed releases to the other Plaintiffs. The object was to obtain their evidence. Notice had been given; but the Defendants did not appear.

Lord CHANCELLOR [ELDON] refused the motion; saying, it must be upon a positive consent; and on its being then desired, that

(a) As to the time for putting in an original answer, and the proceedings for a better answer, and when it should be filed, see *ante,* note (a), *Anonymous,* 2 V. 270.

(1) January 23d, 1794; 4 Bro. C. C. 544; *ante,* vol. ii. 270, and the note.

(b) See *ante,* note (a), *Motteaux* v. *Mackreth,* 1 V. 142.

they might be made Defendants, said, that would not do; as they would then get rid of their liability to costs (1).

The motion was afterwards repeated, as originally made, upon the authority of *Motteaux* v. *Mackreth* (2) ; in which Lord Thurlow at first thought, a consent was necessary for an order to make a Plaintiff Defendant ; but afterwards made the order without consent. It was said, that the practice had been according to this case; and *Pullen's Case* was mentioned ; in which the Lord Chancellor had been Counsel: the property was very considerable ; and Shaw, a principal Plaintiff, was struck out, not only without consent, but without the knowledge of the Defendant.

Mr. *Pemberton (Amicus Curiæ)* mentioned *The Attorney General* v. *The Haberdashers' Company*, the case of Newport School; in which an application to strike out the names of some of the relators, with a view to make them witnesses, was opposed by the Lord Chancellor, then at the bar ; but was finally ordered upon giving security for the costs to that time; and said, there had been several orders of the same kind.

Lord CHANCELLOR said, it seemed to him, Lord Thurlow's first thoughts in *Motteaux* v. *Mackreth* were right: and he had had an idea, that Lord Thurlow had always refused it : but upon the authority of that case and the practice his Lordship granted the motion.

SEE the note to *Motteaux* v. *Mackreth*, 1 V. 142, and the farther references there given.

MAXWELL *v.* PHILLIPS.   [* 146]

[1801, JUNE 19, 22.]

NOTICE of motion on Saturday must be given for Tuesday, not Monday.

MR. WYATT for the Plaintiff moved, that an order, that the bill should be dismissed for want of prosecution should be discharged for irregularity ; the notice of motion being given on Saturday for Monday.

Lord CHANCELLOR [ELDON] said, that on inquiry at the Register's Office, it appeared that notice on Saturday is not good, unless it is given for Tuesday.

The order was discharged. ____

By the Bill now [1827] before Parliament for the regulation of the practice of the Court of Chancery, it is proposed, that every notice of motion, or petition, notice of which is necessary, shall be served at least two clear days before the hearing of such motion or petition. And that every order *nisi* for dissolving an injunction, shall be served at least two clear days before the day on which the plaintiff shall be required to show cause against the same.

(1) *Post*, 613.
(2) *Ante*, vol. i. 142; *Tappen* v. *Norman, post*, vol. ix. 563.

SLATER, *Ex parte.*

[1801, June 22.]

Proof under the bankruptcy of one joint debtor after receiving a composition from the other expunged: the release to one being a release to both (a).

Pashley and Dennis commenced business in partnership as liquor merchants in January, 1795; which was dissolved in May, 1796; Pashley retiring; and assigning to Dennis all his share of the partnership stock, debts, &c.; being indemnified by Dennis. Pashley commenced the same business on his own account. Upon the 13th of October 1796 Dennis compounded with his creditors for 10s. in the pound. Popplewell and Jansen, two of the creditors of the partnership of Pashley and Dennis for 141l. 6s. executed the agreement for Dennis's composition. Upon the 25th of November a commission of bankruptcy issued against Pashley; under which Popplewell and Jansen were permitted to prove their debt; and afterwards they received the composition.

The petition was presented by the assignees under the commission; praying, that the proof of the debt of Popplewell and Jansen might be expunged.

Mr. *Piggott,* in support of the Petition, cited *Bower* v. *Swadlin* (1).

[* 147]   * Mr. *Romilly,* against the Petition.—Without doubt a release to one of two joint debtors is a release to both, according to the case cited: but that is upon technical reasons; and courts of equity have always lamented the necessity of following the law in that. It is impossible to suppose any intention to discharge this man upon receiving 10s. in the pound from the other.

Lord Chancellor [Eldon] made the order according to the prayer of the petition.

See note 2 to *Rees* v. *Berrington,* 2 V. 540.

(a) Story, Partnership, § 168; Co. Litt, 232a; Bac. Abr. *Release* (g); *Rowley* v. *Stoddart,* 7 Johns. 207.
(1) 1 Atk. 294.

MITCHELL *v.* DORS.

[1801, June 23.]

INJUNCTION where the Defendant having begun to take coal in his own land had worked into that of the Plaintiff (a).

MR. MANSFIELD and Mr. *Bell* moved for an injunction against the Defendant; who having begun to get coal in his own ground had worked into that of the Plaintiff.

Lord CHANCELLOR.—That is trespass, not waste. But I will grant the injunction upon the authority of a case before Lord Thurlow (1): a person, landlord of two closes, had let one to a tenant, who took coal out of that close, and also out of the other, which was not demised; and the difficulty was, whether the injunction should go as to both; and it was ordered as to both.

The order was made.

See, *ante*, note 3 to *The Mayor of London v. Bolt*, 5 V. 129, and, *post*, the note to *Smith v. Collyer*, 8 V. 89.

DAVIES, *Ex parte.*

[ROLLS.—1801, June 26.]

DEVISE and bequest until a certain period from the nature of the purpose and circumstances not transmissible to representatives.

EDWARD COTTREL by his will gave and bequeathed to his dear wife all his estate and effects, both real and personal, of whatsoever kind, which he then enjoyed, or might by virtue of any will or wills then made or hereafter to be made in his favor; to be fully enjoyed, by her during the minority of his son and heir Henry Cottrel;

(a) Courts of Equity will interfere in cases of trespasses, to prevent irreparable mischiefs, or to suppress multiplicity of suits and oppressive litigation. 2 Story, Eq. Jur. § 928, 929; *New York Printing and Dying Establishment v. Fitch*, 1 Paige, 97; *Livingston v. Livingston*, 6 Johns. Ch. 497: *Attaquin v. Fish*, 5 Metcalf, 148. In *Frost v. Beekman*, 1 Johns. Ch. 318, the injunction was refused, the case being that of an ordinary trespass. See *Hawley v. Clowes*, 2 Johns. Ch. 122.

The authority given in Massachusetts to the Supreme Court, by the Rev. St. c. 81, § 8 and c. 105, § 44, to hear and determine in equity all suits and matters concerning waste, where there is not an adequate remedy at law, extends to cases of technical waste only, and not to those trespasses which courts that have full chancery powers, restrain by injunction; *Attaquin v. Fish*, 5 Metcalf, 140.

(1) *Post, Flamang's Case*, cited by the Lord Chancellor, vol. vii. 308, in *Hanson v. Gardener*; viii. 90; *Grey v. The Duke of Northumberland*, xiii. 236; xvii. 281, and the note, 282; *Crockford v. Alexander*, xv. 138; *Kinder v. Jones*, *Earl Cowper v. Baker*, xvii. 110, 128; *Thomas v. Oakley*, xviii. 184; *Norway v. Rowe*, xix. 144; *De Salis v. Crosson*, 1 Ball & Beat. 188; 1 Swanst. 208.

which minority he directed should cease and determine on the
first day of November, 1805: his said wife until that period finding him with suitable education, maintenance, and cloth-
[* 148]   ing; *and he declared his will, that from the said period
his said son should have a moiety of the said income ; and
that his said wife should enjoy and have to her use during her life
all the clothes, jewels, plate, trinkets, linen and furniture, of every
kind he then had or hereafter might be possessed of : at her decease
then every thing, as aforesaid, should totally belong to and centre
in his said son, his heirs, executors, administrators, and assigns, for
ever: if his son should die, before the period of his minority expired, then the whole to rest with his said wife during her life.

The testator then declaring, that he bound his estate and effects
to pay all his lawful debts and funeral expenses, constituted and appointed his said dear wife sole executrix of his will; resting in
the full hope and desire, that if his wife should want any advice or
assistance, his friends Colonel Preston and William Barton Berwick,
Esquire, would give it to her ; and for which boon he begged each
of them to accept of a mourning ring. Then he gave a ring to
John Cottrel; and declared, that, if his said wife die, before
his said son attains the aforesaid age, he hoped that all or any of
these three aforesaid gentlemen would be kind and good enough to
act as guardians and trustees for him during his said minority ; and
that as such he did thereby nominate and appoint them ; and he declared his will, that if his son should die in his minority or afterwards without devising the aforesaid estate and effects to his heirs,
executors, administrators, or assigns, he then bequeathed the said
estate and effects unto John Cottrel ; but he desired, that notwithstanding that if his son should attain the said age, he should have
full power and authority to sell, give, assign, or bequeath, the said
estate and effects in as full and ample a manner as possible notwithstanding this clause.

The testator died in 1788.   His widow married the petitioner ;
and died on the 3d of June, 1800.   The petition prayed, that the
interest, until the son should attain the age of twenty-one, should
be paid to the petitioner, as administrator to his wife.   The period,
at which the son would attain twenty-one, would be two or three
months before November 1805.

[* 149]   *Mr. *King*, in support of the Petition.—This is an absolute interest for a certain period, and transmissible.
The period of minority is extended by the will for two or three
months beyond the age of twenty-one ; if it had been prolonged for
ten years, that would have increased the interest of the wife.   A
devise during a certain period, or until a certain event, is good.
It is not merely personal to the wife, notwithstanding the addition
as to finding maintenance, &c.   That must be found by the representative.

Mr. *Cox*, for the Infant.—Considering the nature and purpose of
the disposition, this construction is impossible. The proposition as

to a devise till a certain time cannot be disputed, as a general proposition, in the case of a stranger ; but this is a disposition of the interest of the infant's fortune to his own mother until the period
specified, she in the mean time maintaining and educating him.
The testator might mean some benefit to her in the mean time : but
is that to go, not only to that near relation, but to any person, who
may be her personal representative ?   The period is evidently calculated with a view to this particular age, and treated as a period of
minority.   Nothing is said about the executors or administrators of
the wife ; but in another part of the will he provides for the event
of her death before the son attains that age ; expressing his hope,
that in that event the three persons named will act as guardians and
trustees.   The petitioner contends, that he is to do that.   The dry,
general proposition cannot apply to such a case as this.   This is a
residue.   Therefore what is not disposed of accumulates ; and no
difficulty of that kind can arise.

Mr. *King*, in reply.—That clause does not make a difference ;
for he meant to distinguish the situation, in which those persons
were to stand, from the interest vested in his wife.   He cannot be
supposed to intend them to take all the benefit and interest he had
given to her, and which vested absolutely in her by the first part of
the will, in very strong words.   May not they be guardians and trustees of the person of the infant, as to his education, without being
entitled to the property, clearly disposed of during a certain period?

The MASTER OF THE ROLLS (a) [Sir WILLIAM GRANT].—The
question is, whether this is an absolute bequest of the interest until the 1st of November 1805 : * the disposition being   [* 150]
general of all real and personal estate.   No doubt, he
might have made that bequest, and, if so, it would pass to the representative of the wife.   At the same time that would be a very extraordinary intention against his own son; giving the interest of his
fortune to any stranger, who might happen to be the executor or
administrator of the widow.   It is quite clear upon the whole, that
he meant this interest to go to her, only provided she should live so
long, and should be in a situation to find her son with suitable education, maintenance, and clothing.   The expression there is, "my
said wife."   He does not trust that to any one else.   He appears
here not to have attended to the possibility, that she might die before that period.   Then afterwards, if she dies during the minority,
he appoints guardians and trustees.   As it has been observed, there
is no use for them ; for there would be nothing to manage.   He
would have been at the mercy of the wife to find him with education
and maintenance ; and that burthen, it is admitted, would have
passed to her representatives.   He supposes, there would in that
event be occasion for guardians and trustees.   But this farther provision occurs: If the son dies during the minority, the whole is to

(a) This is the first judgment which we find from the distinguished Master of
the Rolls, see *ante*, p. 106.

rest with his said wife during her life, not until 1805. The construction therefore is, that though as against strangers he meant it only to her for life, yet as against his son he meant to give it to her representatives: putting strangers in a better situation than his son. The meaning upon the whole is quite clear; and the petitioner can take nothing.

The petition was dismissed. ____

See note 4 to *Blake v. Bunbury*, 1 V. 194.

WALTON *v.* LAW.

[ROLLS.—1801, JUNE 26.]

THE cases, where the bill is retained, that there may be a trial at law, are, where it is necessary to establish the legal right, in order to found the equitable relief(a); but, where the subject appeared to be matter of law, the bill was dismissed.

THE bill was filed by the executor of a person, who died on his passage to England from the East Indies, for an account of the money received by the Defendants under a policy of insurance upon a ship; which was captured.

[* 151]   *Mr. *Romilly* for the Defendants, objected, that this was merely the subject of an action.

Mr. *Piggott*, for the Plaintiff said, then they ought to have demurred; but they answered; and went into evidence. He pressed, that the bill should be retained, in order to try it at law.

Mr. Romilly said, the only cases of that sort are, where it is necessary to establish the right at law in order to found the equitable relief,; but not to try, whether they have any claim at law; and if they fail there, to come into this court, and try to raise an equity. The Defendants may have the same benefit at the hearing, as if they had demurred.

The MASTER OF THE ROLLS, [Sir WILLIAM GRANT] acknowledged the rule, as stated by the Defendants; and dismissed the bill.

WHERE the legal claim is doubtful, and the title to equitable relief depends on the previous establishment of the legal claim, there, although it may be necessary to come back to a Court of Equity in order to obtain access to the fund in question, the plaintiff must first establish his right at law. *Duke of Bolton v. Williams*, 2 Ves. Jun. 142; *Mundy v. Mundy*, 2 Ves. Jun. 128.

(a) If the legal title is doubtful, the course is to send the complainant to a Court of Law to have his title first established; *Cox v. Smith*, 4 Johns. Ch. 271; *Phelps v. Green*, 3 Id. 302; *Phillips v. Thompson*, 1 Id. 132.

ASTON *v* GREGORY.

[ROLLS.—1801, JUNE 27.]

DEVISE in trust to sell, and apply the money to and among such persons as the trustees in their discretion should think had or have any just or indisputable demand upon A. at his death, to each in equal degree and proportion according to the principal sum, as far as the money would extend; the securities to be delivered up: but the money to be given and received in no other manner than as voluntary bounty. The fund, being more than sufficient, is liable to interest of bonds to the extent of the penalties (a).

RICHARD HAWKINS by his will, made in 1785, devised to Barnard Gregory and Walter Marsh, their heirs and assigns, freehold estates: in trust to sell; and to give and apply the moneys, which might arise by the sale or sales thereof, to and among such persons, or the legal representatives of such persons, as the said Barnard Gregory and Walter Marsh, or the survivor or the heirs of such survivor, in their or his discretion shall think had or have any just or indisputable demand upon Mr. William Horton the elder, deceased, at the time of his death ; and giving to each such person in equal degree and proportion according to the principal sum, which may appear to be due to them severally and respectively, as far as the money arising by such sale or sales will extend ; and upon receipt of such money the person or persons giving the same shall deliver up to be cancelled any security in his or their custody or power, which had been given by the said * William Horton to them, or to his,   [* 152] her or their, testator or intestate: but whatever sum or sums of money may be given to any such person or persons by virtue of this my will, those sums are to be given and received in no other manner than as free and voluntary gifts made by his will to them in testimony of the regard he had for William Horton.

The bill was filed after the testator's death by the creditors of Horton; praying a sale under this will. Horton died many years ago insolvent. A sale was decreed : and the sum produced by the sale amounted to 2928*l*. ; and there was a fund arising from the rents in the hands of the Defendants of 617*l*. 1*s.* 8*d*. The only debts carrying interest were two old bonds for 200*l*. and 77*l*. ; and the debts not carrying interest amounted to 626*l*.

The cause coming on for farther directions, the residuary legatees resisted the demand of interest upon the bonds up to the penalty.

Mr. *Piggott* and Mr. *Hart*, for the Plaintiffs, insisted, that the penalty of the bond being the debt would cover interest as well as principal.

Mr. *Lloyd* and Mr. *Wooddeson*, for the Defendants.—The penalty of a bond is not the just debt in equity. This question depends upon the construction of the Will, the meaning of which is, that all the

---

(a) This case seems to stand on its peculiar circumstances. When interest will be avoided, see *ante*, notes (a) and (c), *Creuze* v. *Hunter*, 2 V. 157.

creditors shall be upon an equal footing, and that no person should have interest upon his debt. They claim only under the voluntary bounty of the testator; and this would contradict his intention by giving the bond creditors more than the others.

Mr. *Piggott*, in reply, was stopped by the Court.

The MASTER OF THE ROLLS [Sir WILLIAM GRANT].—It is certainly true, that these creditors must be contented to take what this testator thought fit to give them; if he had said, they should have only the principal without interest, they must have been contented with that. But the question is, what he meant to give them. He leaves it to trustees to determine, what are just and indisputable debts. Those debts he meant to pay. Then the interest of the debt is just as much a part of the debt as the principal [*153] sum. I do not agree, * that if he had said, only the principal should be paid, that would extend to the penalty of the bond. In that case there would be a clear distinction between principal and interest. But these words "the principal sum" are introduced for a very different purpose. He means, that the debts shall be paid; but in case of deficiency to pay all he directs them to be paid in equal degrees and proportions according to the principal sum. He does not say, "the principal sum," or "only the principal sum;" but if it is necessary to resort to degrees and proportions, that is to regulate the proportions, so far as the money arising from the sale will extend; and he expresses an apprehension, that the money might not extend far enough to pay all, that was due. But if there should be no necessity to make an apportionment, then what he meant to be paid was the debt; and the question is, whether the interest is not a part of the debt. The interest therefore must be included to the extent of the penalty.

———

THE debt due upon a bond is the principal and interest, up to the extent of the penalty; under a devise, therefore, for payment of debts, interest must be paid upon a bond as being part of the debt; but, with respect to debts not carrying interest by contract, or in their own nature, interest can be claimed (under such a devise) only from the date at which payment of such debts (as liquidated by the Master's report) is ordered by the Court; see, *ante,* note 2 to *Creuze* v. *Hunter,* 2 V. 157.

ROACH v. HAYNES.

[ROLLS.—1801, JUNE 29.]

TESTATRIX gave a fund, over which she had a power of appointment, and some specific articles to trustees, in trust for her residuary legatee after named; and gave the general residue to A. By a codicil she revoked the bequest of the residue; and gave it to A. and B.
A. was held solely entitled to the fund under the appointment.

CATHARINE HAYNES by her will, reciting the will of David Franco (1), and that he had given to Ann Roach an annuity of 300l. for life, and two other annuities of 100l. and 50l. and 30l. a-year to each of his servants, who had lived with him five years, and for securing the payment of the said annuities directed his executors to purchase Long Annuities in the names of Tomkyns Dew and Albany Wallis, sufficient to answer them, in trust, among other things, to pay the annuities,; and as to so much of the annuities to be purchased as should be appropriated to the annuities of Ann Roach, Jane Kensey, and John Roach, when and as they should respectively die, all arrears of their annuities being paid, that the trustees should stand possessed thereof to and for the separate use of Catharine Haynes notwithstanding present or future coverture; and to be paid, applied and disposed of in such manner as she should in writing under her hand and seal or by her last will and testament direct or appoint; and in case of no such will, direction, or appointment, the same Long Annuities should become part of the residue of his personal estate; and as to the annuities purchased * to   [* 154] answer the other annuities, as those annuities fall in, to become part of the residue of his personal estate; in farther execution of the powers and authorities in her vested gave, bequeathed, directed, limited, and appointed, the said Long Annuities so purchased or to be purchased for securing unto Ann Roach, &c. the said several annuities during their respective lives, and given to her after the several deceases, as aforesaid, and also all her plate, linen, china, household furniture, stock of cattle, and other stock, goods, and chattels whatsoever at Lonesome or elsewhere at the time of her decease, unto the said Tomkyns Dew and Albany Wallis; in trust, that they and the survivor of them and the executors and administrators of such survivor shall stand possessed thereof for the use and benefit of her residuary legatee hereinafter named. All her other estate and effects not hereinbefore disposed, and which she had in possession, or was in any way entitled to, and had power to dispose of, she did thereby give and bequeath, direct, limit, or appoint, the same unto her son David Haynes, his executors, &c.; and she appointed Dew and Wallis her executors.

The testatrix afterwards in 1796 made the following codicil : " I

---

(1) See these wills, which appeared imperfectly on the pleadings, more fully stated upon the appeal, post, vol. viii. 584.

Catharine Haynes, having by my will, dated the 19th of September, 1788, given my son William 1000l. and the residue of my estate to my son David, and having also given legacies to my own maid servant and other domestic servants, I do hereby revoke all the above bequests; and give the residue of my estate and effects unto my sons William and David Haynes equally between them."

Then, after giving several pecuniary legacies and her wearing apparel to her maid servants, equally to be divided among them, as should be living with her at her death, she added, that with these alterations she confirmed her will; revoking all other codicils; and declaring this to be the only codicil to her said will.

The bill was filed by the annuitants. The only question was between the Defendants: David Haynes claiming solely under the appointment: William Haynes claiming jointly with him: and the residuary legatees of Franco claiming the fund as undisposed of.

[* 155]   * Mr. *Hart*, for the Defendant David Haynes.—The testatrix has sufficiently executed the power of appointment, and done no act to invalidate it. The power is general, not limited either to time or objects. The gift to Dew and Wallis is a complete execution of the power; and the testatrix has directed the application. She has certainly added a designation of the person to have the benefit; viz. her residuary legatee hereinafter named. The question then is, whether by a codicil, depriving that person of the description of sole residuary legatee, she shall be considered as substituting another person, who is thereby joined with him in that character. But the codicil has no reference to the execution of this power. It is merely a residuary disposition to two persons jointly. This fund is not given as part of the residue. The codicil is not the will itself; though it is part of the will, as to the residue, upon which it treats, and to which it is confined; and being directed to operate as a revocation of distinct parts of her will it cannot operate beyond that.

Mr. *Stanley*, for the Defendant William Haynes.—The Defendant is under the codicil entitled to one moiety of all the residue, including the fund appropriated to answer these annuities. The object of the testator Franco was only, that the fund should not be in the disposition of the husband of Catharine Haynes, but that she should have the separate disposition of it. The true construction of her will is to unite that property to her general personal estate; and giving the whole to David Haynes she does not mean to distinguish between this fund and her general personal estate. Then she revokes the residuary bequest to David; and gives the residue to both of them.

Mr. *Trower*, for the residuary legatees under the will of Franco claimed this fund; insisting, that the residuary bequest in the will of Catharine Haynes was entirely revoked; and the codicil was confined to the residuary personal estate, without reference to this fund.

The MASTER OF THE ROLLS [Sir WILLIAM GRANT].—There is no doubt in this case, and it is admitted, that there would be a good appointment, if it stood merely upon the will. Then what does the will do? It gives the capital set apart to answer the annuities and some specific articles, plate, linen, china, &c., to trustees in trust for her residuary legatee therein-after named. So she separates from her residue the capital of the annuities and these specific effects; and vests them in trustees. The will then goes on to give the residue directly, and without the interposition of trustees, to her son David Haynes. There is therefore an appointment for the benefit of the person, to whom she shall give the residue; who turns out to be David Haynes. Then does the codicil, revoking the bequest of the residue, extend to the specific articles she had given to the trustees? That would be contrary to the intention; which was to separate them and take them from the residue. Then if David is to have these specific articles, is he not to have the capital of this fund; which is equally separated from the residue? The conclusion is, that the codicil does not in the least affect this fund. A nice argument is used for the residuary legatees of Franco; that the codicil does affect it for one purpose, viz. to revoke the disposition, but not for the other. If the effect was to throw the whole into the residue, then the codicil would affect it.

Declare David Haynes solely entitled (1).

1. THAT an interest, with respect to which a testator had a power of disposition, will not (except in rare and peculiar cases) pass under a mere general devise by him, and never by a mere general bequest, when the subject is personalty, see, *ante,* note 5 to *Blake* v. *Bunbury,* 1 V. 194.

2. With respect to testamentary dispositions by a *feme coverte* of her separate property, see note 1 to *Fettiplace* v. *Gorges,* 1 V. 46; and notes 3, 10, and 12 to *Pybus* v. *Smith,* 1 V. 189.

3. For a statement of some of the leading rules as to the construction of testamentary instruments, see note 4 to *Blake* v. *Bunbury, ubi supra;* see also notes 4 and 5 to *Thellusson* v. *Woodford,* 4 V. 227.

4. As to the exclusion of an executor, who has not acted under the testator's will, from a legacy bequeathed to him *qua* executor, see note 2 to *Abbot* v. *Massie,* 3 V. 148.

(1) This decree was affirmed upon appeal to the Lord Chancellor, *post,* vol. viii. 584.

STERNE, *Ex parte*.

[ROLLS.—1801, JUNE 30.]

THE Court refused upon an *ex parte* petition to order money to be paid under the statute 39 & 40 Geo. III. c. 56; the subject involving a doubtful question, viz. the construction of a trust of an estate for lives, to permit two sisters to receive the rents for their lives; remainder to the heirs of their bodies; and in case they should die without issue, from and after their deceases, over.
An interest in an estate *pur auter vie*, that would be an estate tail, if applied to freehold lands of inheritance, may be disposed of by deed, [p. 258.]
An estate *pur auter vie* be limited in tail, [p. 158.]
A limitation, which would create an estate tail as to freehold property, would give the absolute interest as to personal estate (*a*), [p. 168.]

By indentures, dated the 3d of July, 1757, the Archbishop of York demised certain premises to William Sterne; to hold to him, his heirs and assigns, for the lives of himself and two other persons.

William Sterne by his will, dated the 24th of March, 1770, gave to trustees and their heirs the lands comprised in the lease; to hold the same to them and their heirs; upon trust to permit his two daughters to take and receive the rents, issues, and profits thereof for and during their natural lives; with remainder to the heirs of their bodies lawfully begotten; and in case they should die without
[* 157]   issue, from and after their deceases upon trust to convey *and assign the same to and for the use of his son William Sterne and the heirs of his body lawfully to be begotten; and in case he should die without issue, and the testator's wife should survive his said children, he gave the said leasehold lands to the use of his said wife, her heirs, executors, administrators, and assigns, for ever.

The testator died; leaving his wife surviving, and all the children mentioned in the will, infants. In December 1775 articles were executed for the sale of the estate, as soon as an act of Parliament could be procured, to Hodgkinson, his heirs and assigns, during the remaining lives, for 1200*l*.

By the Act of Parliament, which was obtained, it was enacted, that the residue of the purchase-money, after paying the costs, should be laid out by the trustees in the purchase of lands and hereditaments, to be settled and conveyed to such and the same uses, and upon and to the same trusts and purposes, as the premises stood limited under the will; and that the money should be paid into the Bank and laid out, till a proper purchase could be procured: the dividends in the mean time to be paid to such person or persons as would for the time being be entitled to receive the yearly rents and profits.

(*a*) Whether there can be an estate tail in a chattel interest; see *ante*, note (*a*), *Douglas* v. *Chalmer*, 2 V. 501; note (*a*), *Fordyce* v. *Ford*, 2 V. 536; note (*a*), *Rawlins* v. *Goldfrap*, 5 V. 440.

The clear produce of the sale was 1190*l*. 14*s*. 10*d*. 3 per cent. Consolidated Bank Annuities, and 17*l*. 17*s*. cash. The petition was presented by the testator's two daughters, who had attained the age of twenty-one ; praying a transfer under the late Act of Parliament (1). When the petition was opened, the Master of the Rolls expressed considerable doubt, whether it could be granted ; and it stood for judgment.

(2) MASTER OF THE ROLLS [Sir WILLIAM GRANT] (after stating the case).—I apprehend, the act for the relief of tenants in tail only applies to cases, where the right is clear and indisputable ; and, that, where there is any question, the Court in an *ex parte* petition is not to enter into the question in the absence of all the parties entitled. But, if a *question occurs, whether the party   [* 158] applying be tenant for life or tenant in tail, I apprehend, the Court upon an *ex parte* petition would not under the statute, (notwithstanding the inclination of the Court might be, when the question came to be discussed, to hold the party to be tenant in tail) decide the right.

The question therefore is, whether there is in this case a fair doubt.

It appears to me, that there is in this case a fair doubt. The Act of Parliament has gone no farther than to allow the money to be laid out in freehold lands of inheritance.

Where a person has an interest in an estate *pur auter vie*, which would be an estate tail, if applied to freehold lands of inheritance, he may dispose of such estate *pur auter vie* by deed. But it may be a question, whether the blending of estates in freehold lands of inheritance does or does not necessarily apply to estates *pur auter vie*.

In respect of freehold lands it is said sometimes, that the freehold cannot be in abeyance : but here is no fee. Sometimes it has been held, that the estates shall unite, the better to effectuate the general intent: but that is not necessary in an estate *pur auter vie ;* for there is no descent: the heir takes as special occupant: therefore there is no necessity, that the estate for life and the estate in remainder should unite. *Forster* v. *Forster* (3). *Williams* v. *Jekyl* (4).

It has been settled, that an estate *pur auter vie* may be limited in tail: *Low* v. *Burron* (5) ; which was a limitation of a freehold lease for life with remainder to the heirs of the body in tail.

But supposing it as a general rule quite clear, that the two estates would unite together, there is still upon this will a question, whether by the particular wording of the will the testator's intention was not

---

(1) Stat. 39 & 40 Geo. III. c. 56. Upon this Act of Parliament see *ante*, *Ex parte Bennet*, *Ex parte Dolman*, 116, and the notes, *ante*, vol. v. 12 ; i. 512.

(2) *Ex relatione.*

(3) 2 Atk. 259.

(4) 2 Ves. 681.

(5) 3 P. Will. 262.

to confine the first taker to an estate for life, and that in this particular case the two estates should not unite.

[* 159]   * With respect to personal estate it has been held, that
where there is a limitation, which, if it were freehold property, would create an estate tail, it shall give the absolute interest in
personalty : *Hodgeson* v. *Bussey* (1). *Read* v. *Snell* (2). *Sabbarton* v. *Sabbarton* (3). But this is the case of a trust, and there is
strong ground for the issue or remainder-men to contend, that, taking the whole of this will together, it was the intention, that the
daughters should only take for life. I do not say, how it would be
determined. It is sufficient to say, that it creates doubt enough for
me not to decide it in this summary way, and therefore I must refuse the prayer of the petition.

The Petition was dismissed. ____

1. SEE, *ante*, the note to *Binford* v. *Bawden*, 1 V. 512, with respect to the
course of proceedings under the statute of 7 Geo. IV. c. 45.
2. That the *quasi* tenant in tail of a lease held for lives may, by surrendering
the lease, bar the remainders over, see note 2 to *Fletcher* v. *Tollet*, 5 V. 3; and
that an estate tail in a copyhold may be barred by surrender in the lord's court,
see the notes to *Challoner* v. *Murhall*, 2 V. 524.
3. The very same words of limitation may operate very differently upon freehold and upon personal property. *Walker* v. *Denne*, 2 Ves. Jun. 173.

GASKELL v. HARMAN.

[ROLLS.—1801, JUNE 23, 27, 30.]

A RESIDUARY bequest upon the whole will vested only as the property was received ;
one of the residuary legatees therefore being dead, his representatives were entitled only to that part, which was got in before his death (a).
Bequest of a debt, as it stood on a certain day, good, [p. 170.]

JOHN STRETTELL by his will, dated the 3d of March, 1786, confirming his marriage settlement, by a bond, previous to his marriage,
the condition of which he stated that he had performed by a devise

---

(1) 2 Atk. 89.
(2) 2 Atk. 642.
(3) For. 245. See *Rawlins* v. *Goldfrap*, *ante*, vol. v. 440, and the references in
the note, 444.
(a) Although the payment of legacies be expressly postponed till the testator's
debts be discharged, or till the sale of an estate be effected, or till after the residue
of personal estate shall be laid out in the purchase of lands, yet the general rule
that the gift is immediate and the payment alone is postponed, will operate; and
the legacy will be transmissible, though the legatee die before the discharge of
debts, or other event until which the payment is expressly postponed, 2 Williams
Exec. 883. But the general rule is always subservient to the intention of the
testator, See *ante*, note (a), *Mackell* v. *Winter*, 3 V. 236; note (a), *Hutcheon* v.
Mannington, 1 V. 366.

of his house at Croydon and a transfer of 11,000*l.* 3 per cent. Consolidated Bank Annuities, in addition gave to his wife an annuity of 395*l.* ; to be paid out of the best security he should die possessed of, except his estate, called Gotwick ; and directed, that such security should afterwards be considered as part of the fortune bequeathed to his son Amos, and should be estimated at 16,00'*l.* He gave to his wife the house at Croydon, the use of his furniture, plate, and the choice of the furniture of one of his houses ; and made several other bequests in her favor ; and directed, that after her decease the said several particulars, or such as shall be existing, shall be either kept for the use of his son, or be sold, and that the produce should fall into the residue of his personal estate, according as his wife shall by will appoint; and for want of appointment that the same shall be sold for the purpose aforesaid. All the remainder of his goods, chattels, furniture, &c. after his wife should have made such choice, he directed should be sold * by his executors ;   [* 160] and that Joseph Brickwood, hereinafter named, should have the preference of purchasing the lease of his house in Riche's Court, with the furniture.

The testator then gave to his friends Daniel Mildred, John Harman, Alexander Forbes, and his brother-in-law Joseph Hayling, describing them as his executors hereinafter named, freehold estates, describing them, and all other his freehold estates; to hold to them, their heirs and assigns, for ever ; as to the house at Croydon to the use of his wife for life in part of the provision by her marriage settlement ; and after her decease to other uses : and as to Gotwick and other premises, in case his son should attain the age of twenty-one, in trust to convey to the use of his son for life, without impeachment of waste ; remainder to his issue in tail ; and for want of such issue, or, in case there should be none, who should attain twenty-one, over ; and he gave all the other estates to other uses. He gave his son 30,000*l.* to be paid him when he shall attain the age of twenty-one, or as soon after as he can be put in possession thereof, according to the direction after mentioned: that is to say ; he directed, that the several funds or securities, which should be appropriated for the securing the aforesaid annuity of 800*l.* to his wife, (made up of the interest and rents provided by him in performance of his marriage settlement and the additional annuity of 395*l.*) which altogether should be considered of the value of 16,000*l.* and no more, should be computed as part of the 30,000*l.* ; the remaining 14,000*l.* to make up the same to be appropriated or set apart and invested by his executors at interest : the estate at Gotwick to be considered as part of the 14,000*l.* and valued at 1000*l.*: such other of his real estates as his executors should not find it necessary to mortgage or sell for the purposes after mentioned, to be considered as a farther part, and be conveyed to him in fee ; to be valued at twenty years' purchase upon the improved rent. He empowered his executors and trustees to advance and pay out of his estate any sum, not exceeding 1500*l.* to be laid out in educating his son. He gave his son an

annuity of 150*l.* purchased by him for the lives of himself and his
son ; to be kept insured upon his son's life until his age 'of twenty-
one : the surplus income to be applied to maintenance and education ; with full power to his executors, as his son should
[161]   advance in years, to make any farther allowance * out of
his estate for the purpose aforesaid : the residue of the income of his son's fortune beyond maintenance and education to be
applied in or towards payment of the several annuities after mentioned and bequeathed.

The testator then appointed his wife sole guardian of his son until
his age of twenty-one ; and in case of her decease he appointed his
executors and Brickwood ; expressing particular confidence in the
latter ; that he will exert himself for his (the testator's) son's interest ; and reciting, that he had made his will under the fullest conviction, that his fortune would ultimately amount to the sum of
45,000*l.* or upwards, he proceeds to make the following bequests :

To his wife 2000*l.* to be at her disposal by will : the interest during her life to be applied to the other purposes of his will ; empowering her to apply it or any part during her life for the advantage
of their son : to Forbes 100*l.* and several other pecuniary legacies ;
and he recommended to his executors, if the same could conveniently be done, to discharge all these last-mentioned legacies at one
payment, without waiting for the general distribution herein after
mentioned and provided : to Hayling 500*l.*, and several other legacies ; some, subject to conditions. The will then proceeded thus :

" I give to my very worthy and kind friends Daniel Mildred and
John Harmon two of my executors hereinafter named the sum of
500*l.* each ; with my most grateful acknowledgments for that last
essential proof of their affection and regard. I also give to my friend
Alexander Forbes, one other of my executors, the sum of 400*l.* ;
and to my brother-in-law Joseph Hayling, my other executor, 250*l.* ;
but these four legacies to my said executors are not to be paid in
preference to any other of the legacies herein last before given ; and
I give to Mr. John Brickwood, who will be assisting to my executors in collecting my effects and settling my affairs, the sum of 500*l.*"

He then gave several annuities, among them 50*l.* a-year to Forbes
for life ; and if they find occasion for the extension of the annuities,
authorizes his executors, in case the circumstances of
[* 162]   * his fortune will admit it, 'to extend the annuities to any
sum not exceeding 100*l. per annum* ; and he directed his
executors at the beginning of the annuities for securing the payment
thereof to invest a sufficient part of his personal estate in the funds
or mortgages at their discretion : distinguishing in their accounts the
capital for each annuitant ; that at their decease the same may be
applied in manner hereinafter directed. He then proceeds thus :

" And whereas by reason of the agreement I have lately entered
into with Mr. John Brickwood before named, and Mr. Thomas Pattle, junior, for their taking to themselves my debts owing in America,
and paying me the same by instalments, to be secured by their bond

or bonds, I cannot fix any period for the payment of the pecuniary legacies or the annuities hereinbefore given, which are not already particularly directed as to time, I must leave it to the discretion of my executors to make a first dividend upon the said legacies, so soon after the receipt of the said Messrs. Brickwood and Pattle's first payment as they shall have sufficient to divide 5s. in the pound or any greater sum among my said legatees : and at the same time invest or set apart for the said annuitants a sufficient sum or sums to produce and bring in one quarter part of their annuities ; and the like proportions to be continued, until the whole are discharged or provided for : my said son's fortune in every such division being considered a creditor for 14,000l. ;" and for the more speedy payment of the said legacies and annuities "my said executors" to mortgage or sell all or any part of his real estate before devised, except the houses at Croydon and Gotwick ; and to cut timber and underwood upon the latter, when of sufficient growth : the annuities to Forbes and some others to be paid quarterly, and to commence three months after his decease. · He gave three other annuities, payable quarterly ; directing the first payment thereof to be made, when his executors shall have sufficient effects in their hands to invest one quarter part of the capital producing the same, and from thence to continue payable, as aforesaid ; and he submitted the settlement of accounts with his late brother to his executors ; and gave directions for the adjustment of other accounts ; and declared, it was not his intention to extinguish debts from legatees ; but such debts to be first paid. The will then proceeded thus :

* "And whereas the long minority of my son will most　　[* 163] probably create a considerable addition to my fortune, and it is my earnest wish and intention, that my residuary legatees shall each of them receive 500l. at the least over and above their respective legacies, I therefore direct, that, when that sum can clearly be ascertained to them, after provision for the payment of my son's fortune and the several legacies and annuities herein before contained, then what farther shall be received or accumulated of my estate shall be disposed of as follows : to wit, to my son Amos the sum of 2500l. in addition to his fortune, and payable at the same time therewith : to the several pecuniary legatees, whose legacies are to be gradually discharged by way of dividend, as herein before is directed, the farther sum of 25l. per cent. or one quarter part more upon the capitals of their respective legacies ; and if any farther surplus shall be made or arise, be it more or less, the same to go and be equally divided among my residuary legatees or such of them as shall be then living : but in case my son shall happen to depart this life, before he attains the age of twenty-one years, his fortune being then in the hands of my executors, I give and bequeath to my several annuitants herein-after named the several annuities herein-after mentioned : with such conditions, and the capital producing the same to go and be applied in like manner, as herein before is mentioned and appointed respecting the annuities herein before given to them ;" then after

giving his wife 300*l.* a year, Forbes 100*l.* a year, and two other annuities, " but in case my said son's fortune shall not be then all in hand, then such smaller equally proportioned augmentation of the said annuities as the part of my son's fortune in hand will admit ;" and after the decease of his wife and provision being made for his then surviving annuitants he bequeaths the money then in the hands of his executors, in ninths ; and after the disposition of eight ninths concludes thus :

"And the remaining ninth part thereof in equal shares to such of my residuary legatees as shall be then living ; and as the then re- maining annuitants shall from time to time depart this life, the fund for payment of their annuities, which is not herein before specifically disposed of, shall go to and be equally divided among such [* 164] of my residuary legatees as shall be living * at the decease of each separate annuitant ; and as to all the rest, residue and remainder, of my estate and effects, whatsoever and wheresoever, after payment of my debts, funeral expenses, and the legacies and annuities herein before given, I give and bequeath the same and every part thereof equally to be divided among my good friends and executors, Daniel Mildred, John Harman. Alexander Forbes, and Joseph Hayling, and Mr. John Brickwood, herein before named ; in whose zeal respecting the assisting my executors in collecting my effects and settling my affairs, and in whose attachment to the inter- est and welfare of my dear wife and child I place the most unreserv- ed confidence."

The testator then, after some farther expressions of confidence in Brickwood declared, that he should not be entitled to receive any part of the residue of his estate herein before bequeathed to him, until the bonds given to the testator by him and Pattle shall be fully paid and discharged ; and he then appointed Mildred, Harman, Forbes, and Hayling, executors ; and directed, that in case of the death of the trustees the survivors from time to time should appoint new trustees ; and that a legacy of 250*l.* should be paid to each new trustee upon his appointment ; and gave powers to the trustees to compound debts and submit to arbitration ; with the common clause of indemnity.

The testator died upon the 28th of July 1786. Mildred died in February 1788; Forbes in October 1790 ; and Hayling in January 1796. Forbes bequeathed all his estate and effects to his sister; whose residuary legatee and administrator with the will annexed filed the bill ; claiming a fifth of the residue under Strettell's will, as vested at his death in Forbes. That claim was resisted, except as to so much as was got in during the life of Forbes.

Mr. *Lloyd,* Mr. *Romilly,* and Mr. *Ainge,* for the Plaintiffs—Mr. *Alexander* and Mr. *Toller,* for the representatives of Mildred—Mr. *Stanley,* for the representatives of Hayling.—The question is, what interest these residuary legatees had in the residue ; and at what particular times such residue vested in them : the surviving trustees insisting, there was no vested interest in the surplus at the death of

the testator; but, that it was to be divided at the time of
* making or arising of such surplus. The part of the will   [* 165]
upon which that is contended, expressing an intention,
that each of his residuary legatees shall receive 500*l.* at least in addition, when that sum can clearly be ascertained to them, applies
only to his son's fortune : and will not control the subsequent general residuary clause : which no doubt vests the residue in them as
tenants in common ; for no particular period is expressed there.
His property being abroad, he could not ascertain, when the whole
of the legacies would be paid ; and therefore he adopts the mode of
an addition of 25 per cent. In the case of two contradictory
clauses in a will the latter must control (1). The inclination of the
Court is always to vest a residue; and there is a great difference in
that respect between a residue and a pecuniary legacy ; where in
any event the residue is given to a person, who survives the testator, the strongest ground is necessary to make out an intestacy. The
construction of the Defendants is, that as every shilling was received,
so it was to vest; a construction never before attempted. The survivors of these residuary legatees by the accident of their surviving,
claim so much as had not been got in. Suppose, they also had
died ; could it be said, with that clause in the will, there was a
general intestacy ? He cannot be understood to mean, that
he gives that addition only, when that sum arises: but if ever
that sum can be clearly ascertained, these additions shall be paid.
It is very uncertain, to what the words, " or such of them as shall
be then living," in that part of the will, shall be referred. It will
be said, they refer to the time, when the surplus shall be made or
arise. Nothing can be more vague. It may be said to arise, when
it is ascertained, as well as when it is paid to the executors. There
is nothing in favor of the latter inference. Then comes the
general, residuary disposition ; and then only he names his residuary legatee.

But suppose there was no such obscurity, and the intention was
clear to confine it to the time of actual receipt, the Court cannot
carry that intention into execution. That point was decided in
Hutcheon v. *Mannington* (2). Lord Thurlow thought, there
would be great danger in leaving it to the executor to
determine, who * would be entitled, by delaying the pay-   [* 166]
ment. That objection is of greater weight in this case ;
for there the executors were to determine against strangers ; and
had no interest to delay it ; but all these residuary legatees except
one are also executors. It might be their interest to delay it and
speculate upon the chance of surviving any one residuary legatee ;
and Brickwood as one of the purchasers of the debts in America
had the means of influencing the payment of the residue, and by
protracting the payment of determining, to whom the residue should

<hr />

(1) *Ante, Constantine* v. *Constantine,* 100 ; *Sims* v. *Doughty,* vol. v. 243 ; see
the note, 247.
(2) *Ante,* vol. i. 366. See the notes, 367 ; *post, Sitwell* v. *Bernard,* 520.

go.   The possibility of such management will determine the Court
to adopt the general rule established in that case, and since cited
and acted upon in *Stapleton* v. *Palmer* (1), and *Kirkpatrick* v. *Kirkpatrick* (2).

Mr. *Piggott*, Mr. *Richards*, and Mr. *Winthrop*, for the two surviving residuary legatees, Defendants.—This will makes a complete
disposition of all the testator's property in the preceding part ; and
the only object of the general clause at the close of it is to name
the residuary legatees, no where named before.   The testator had
already given the residue.   At the close of the will he only repeats
the gift for that particular purpose.   Is that to efface all, that was
before done ?   This was a gift upon the ground of personal exer-
tion in the settlement of his affairs ; as the best mode of securing
this fortune to his son.   Upon the Plaintiffs' construction they are
entitled, without regard to the principal object, their exertions, or
the time of their deaths.   Upon such a will the intention is clear.
No difficulty can arise upon it.   What part of the residue was got
in in 1788, when one died, what part in 1790, when another died,
these are facts, that can be ascertained ; and so much can be divided, if the preceding charges are paid.   As to the alleged danger of enabling some executors to defraud others, if fraud is shown,
the Court would not let it have effect : but that is not pretended in
this case.   In a very late case, *Innes* v. *Mitchell* (3), a debt was bequeathed at a particular day ; whatsoever it might be ; and then it
was ascertained ; and this may be as easily ascertained.   Such a
disposition is far from being unwise or impolitic ; uniting interest
with duty   *Hutcheon* v. *Mannington* is no authority upon this
case.   It is clearly distinguishable.   There was first a gift to the
legatees, not accompanied by any condition, but absolute.
[* 167]   Death before * receipt was a bare naked fact, upon which
it was to divest.   No time was fixed for the payment : if
it had been so given, it is plain from Lord Thurlow's reasoning, he
would have referred the receipt to that time, upon the common
principle, that executors are to be supposed to perform their duty.
His difficulty was, to what time he was to refer the bare naked fact
of the receipt : was it to depend upon the caprice of the executor ?
There might have been infants or married women ; which might
have prevented the receipt.   The present Lord Chancellor seems to
have felt the nature of that opinion as very doubtful ; and finally the
parties stood upon the agreement.   Is that like a gift of this sort, to
residuary legatees ; and no uncertainty as to the time, or the fund ;
which is what is left after the legacies, &c. are paid ?   This is a
condition precedent to the gift, not to divest it.   If they are not
living, nothing is given to them.   The general plan of the will is
founded upon the circumstance, that the testator had a considerable
property outstanding ; that might be made more or less available

(1) 4 Bro. C. C. 490.
(2) At the Rolls.
(3) *Post*, 461.

according to the exertions or negligence of his executors; and the intention is clearly such of these residuary legatees as should be living, when the surplus should be received and actually in hand. Lord Rosslyn certainly did not confirm *Hutcheon* v. *Mannington* in *Stapleton* v. *Palmer*, which was decided upon the fact, that they all concurred in the direction as to the sale: but it is not necessary to dispute the former case. No two cases can be more dissimilar.

Mr. *Lloyd*, in reply.—The argument for these Defendants goes upon minute observation upon a very inaccurate will.. The testator had in effect named his residuary legatees in the will by giving them particular legacies; and then his naming them in the latter part is not material. It does not appear, that this was given to them for their exertions and in that character. It is extraordinary, that it is not expressed to be given to them for their care and trouble: nor is the word "survivors" inserted. That their exertions were the consideration is mere conjecture. He must have had a considerable regard for each of them, not in the character of executors; and must have intended a benefit to their families. No act or negligence of executors can vary the rights of the parties. In *Booth* v. *Booth* (1) and many other cases the Court has strained against an intestacy; where the residue is given. So absurd a construction as that they * are to take vested interests in every   [* 168] sum of 20*l.*, as it arises, for it cannot be confined to any particular sum, requires an express direction. Every thing is against survivorship. It is given to them as tenants in common. *Hutcheon* v. *Mannington* is a much stronger case than this. The principle decided by it is, that where a legacy is given at an indefinite period, the Court will not go upon a nice construction; but will say, it vested at the death of the testator. In that case the executor could not get any thing by the delay; in this there is a strong temptation to them. The death there could have been ascertained as well as here; and that will was not confused, as this is. Suppose, the period extended beyond all the lives, the objects upon this construction would have no benefit. There is great convenience in Lord Thurlow's rule; and a certain rule or principle is much safer to property than conjecturing upon words.

June 30th.   The MASTER OF THE ROLLS [Sir WILLIAM GRANT] (2).—This bill claims one fifth part of the clear residue and surplus of the testator's estate. It is contended on the part of the two Defendants, who are the surviving residuary legatees, that the Plaintiffs are only entitled to a fifth of so much of the residue as accrued during Forbes's life. The doubt arises from the testator's having in effect made two residuary bequests. There are two questions:

---

(1) *Ante*, vol. iv. 399.
(2) The judgment *ex relatione*.

1st, What was the intention.

2dly, Whether that intention can be carried into execution: whether it is legal and practicable.

From the whole frame of the will the testator appears to have been sensible, that a considerable time must elapse, before his personal estate could be got in; and that, until it was collected, which he seems to suppose could not be completely done until his son would be of age, the residue could not be estimated. Making his will under that impression he directs a few legacies to be paid immediately: as to the rest the distribution was to be made, as the property was realized; that is, as it got into the hands of his executors. He gives his residuary legatees 500*l.* each in addition to the pecuniary legacies he had before given them. But when [* 169] he gives them * the legacies of 500*l.*, he does not name or describe, who they are. But they are to have 500*l.* a-piece at any rate. Afterwards, having made a farther disposition for his son and legatees out of what farther shall be received or accumulated, he declares, that if any farther surplus shall be made or arise, be it more or less, the same to go and be equally divided among his residuary legatees, or such of them as shall be then living. Then he gives away his son's legacy in case of his death before the age of twenty-one; and of that, subject to an additional provision for his annuitants, he gives one ninth part to such of his residuary legatees as shall be then living.

It seems to have been his intention therefore, that they, that is, such of them as should be then living, should take whatever was indefinite surplus. As to that there is no doubt or ambiguity. He intended, they should take only the first pecuniary legacies and the legacies of 500*l.* a-piece absolutely. The rest was contingent; and only vested in them, if living at the time, when the surplus arose.

That being the intention, it is objected, that though distinct and explicit, that intention is not practicable. It is said, the surplus arises from day to day; and that such a bequest is too vague and indefinite to be carried into execution; and for this the case of *Hutcheon* v. *Mannington* is cited. In that case there was nothing, to which the receipt was to be applied. It was to be a bare possibility. Lord Thurlow said, the testator had given no standard, to which the Court was to apply the event, on which the testator had given over those legacies; and the claimants there came to devest a legacy absolutely given. They were to make out a case, in which it was given over to them. It was, as the Lord Chancellor expressed it, an immeasurable purpose. When it might have been received, it was impossible to determine. Nothing could be more indefinite. That case therefore is clearly distinguishable; and *Stapleton* v. *Palmer* went off upon another point. Here nothing vests in the residuary legatees, unless they are living, when the existence of that surplus in their hands is ascertained: when it is received and accumulated. There can be no difficulty in ascertaining, when the surplus is made; and it might just as well have arisen on a claim of one of the pecuniary legatees; for their dividends are made payable, when there is a fund collected by the executors; and if a pecuniary legatee had claimed such dividends on a given day, he must have shown, that there was a fund capable of paying that dividend at the time of the claim; and there could be no difficulty in taking that account. In this case the account is not to be taken day by day: but all, that is to be done, is to see, how the accounts of the executors stand on the day of the death of any one of the deceased residuary legatees. There is nothing impracticable in that. It is as easily done as the account of the debt given in the case of *Innes* v. *Mitchell* (1); where a debt was given, as it stood on a certain day. In the instance of the annuitants under this will, that part of the estate appropriated to secure the annuities vests in such only of the residuary legatees as shall be living at the death of the annuitants.

It is said, this would make it arbitrary; as the executors might regulate their conduct in collecting the testator's debts upon a speculation as to the state of some among themselves. But the whole frame of this will shows, that the state of the testator's property did not admit of an immediate distribution; and the necessity of that power arose out of the situation of his affairs. Is it not to be permitted to a testator to postpone the vesting of his property, till his funds shall be collected? He supposes, the Court must suppose, till the contrary is shown, that the executors act *bona fide*. But had not the testator a right to say so? If the executor might by possibility act improperly or arbitrarily, it was the business of the testator to contemplate that possibility, and to provide against it. But there never was a case, in which there was less temptation to executors to act improperly: for their own legacies of 500l., vested absolutely, would not be paid, till the funds were collected; and they could take no surplus, till there was a surplus; and it is not here alleged, that there was any unfair conduct of the executors.

Then it is said, the last residuary clause has no effect. That is not so; for in the first place it names, who are the residuary legatees; who are not before named. Next, if they all had died, perhaps the last residuary clause would have * given   [* 171] the residue to the representatives of all of them. But two residuary legatees being now living, to take whatever surplus arises, no such question as that last now occurs.

I am therefore of opinion, the Plaintiffs are not entitled to one fifth part of the clear residue, which has arisen; but are entitled only to a fifth of so much as had arisen and was ascertained at the time of Forbes's death (2).

1. THAT, notwithstanding the inconvenience of making the vesting of a legacy depend upon the collection of the testator's assets into the hands of his executor,

(1) At the Rolls, Trin. Term, 1801; *post*, 461.
(2) See this decree, as erroneously drawn up, varied, *post*, vol. xi. 489, by Lord Eldon, suspending the declaration, and directing preliminary inquiries.

still, where a will clearly denotes that intention, it must be carried into execution, see, *ante*, note 3 to *Hutcheon* v. *Mannington*, 1 V. 366; but that a Court of Equity will not be disposed to make such a construction, if the context of the will authorizes a different one, see note 2 to the same, just cited, case.

2. Courts of Equity hold, that a testator's personal estate must be considered as reduced into possession within a year after his death, and although it may be so circumstanced as to make its actual receipt within that time impossible, still, the constructive receipt imputed by law will entitle the legatees to interest. See note 4 to *Hutcheon* v. *Mannington*, *ubi supra*.

3. That, generally speaking, trustees are bound to press on *all* the remedies for recovery of a debt to the trust estate, and that, if such peremptory measures appear likely to be prejudicial to the interests of the *cestuis que trusts*, the Court must be applied to, as being alone competent to exercise a discretion in such cases, see the note to *Powell* v. *Evans*, 5 V. 839.

4. No fraudulent or unnecessary delay on the part of trustees will be allowed to benefit themselves, or to affect the interests of third persons. See note 6 to *Hutcheon* v. *Mannington*, *ubi supra*.

5. The original decree in this cause, pronounced at the Rolls, was not drawn up according to Sir William Grant's meaning, and, consequently, the argument on the appeal took quite a different course from that which was held before the Master of the Rolls, who never had occasion to deliver any opinion upon the points ascertained by the Lord Chancellor, whose reversal of part of the original decree (as that was improperly drawn up) was directed to points which constituted no part of the judgment at the Rolls upon the question at issue. See Sir William Grant's own explanations in *Wood* v. *Penoyre*, 13 Ves. 329, and in *Bernark* v. *Montague*, 1 Meriv. 432.

GELEDNEKI v. CHARNOCK.

[1801, July 2.]

ORDER, that service of subpœna to answer the amended bill upon the Clerk in Court or Solicitor may be good service, upon the special circumstances; that, though the Defendant had not been served with a subpœna, he had appeared on two motions; that his answer would be very important; that he lived abroad out of the jurisdiction; and would not appear, to answer.

Mr. STANLEY for the Plaintiff moved, that the service of a subpœna to answer the amended bill upon the Clerk in Court or the Solicitor of the Defendant Thompson may be deemed good service under these circumstances: the Defendant had never been served with a subpœna; but had appeared upon two motions; that his answer would be very important; that he lived abroad, out of the jurisdiction, and would not appear to answer.

Lord CHANCELLOR [ELDON] asked, whether it should be absolute in the first instance: but upon the allegation, that he could not be served with the order *nisi*, his Lordship granted the motion.

HAD the plaintiff, in the principal case, been once served with a *subpœna*, as he had never answered the original bill, no new *subpœna* would have been necessary when the bill was amended. See, *ante*, note 2 to *Lord Abingdon* v. *Butler and Benson*, 1 V. 206. A plaintiff is entitled to so much assistance from the Court as may be necessary to bring in a party who is abroad, or to put him in default for not coming in; and for this purpose service upon his attorney may be allowed to be good service, but not for the purpose of issuing a special injunction in the first instance. *Anderson* v. *Darcy*, 18 Ves. 448. For some of the cases in which substitution of service is permitted, see, *ante*, the note to *Jackson* v. ———, 2 V. 417, note 1 to *Pulteney* v. *Shelton*, 5 V. 147, and the note to *Ellison* v. *Pickering*, 8 V. 319.

——— v. LAKE.

[1801 (1), JUNE 25; JULY 2.]

UNDER special circumstances and by consent the Six Clerk was directed to receive the answer to a bill of foreclosure, though not signed by the Defendant (*a*).

UPON a bill of foreclosure Mr. *Bell* for the Defendant, moved, that the Defendant might be at liberty to put in his answer without oath; and that the Six Clerk may receive it, though not signed by him; upon the circumstances, that the Defendant, who was an officer in the army, had sailed for India under orders *im-   [* 172] mediately after service of the subpœna and appearance, and before he had time to put in his answer.

Lord CHANCELLOR [ELDON] would not make the order; observing, that he had a right in such a case to a commission; and that upon a bill of foreclosure the delay is an advantage to the Defendant.

Afterwards a motion was made in the alternative; either that a commission might issue; or, that the Six Clerk may be at liberty to take the answer without oath, though not signed by the Defendant.

Mr. *Richards*, for the Plaintiff, said, he was very desirous, that the answer might be put in this way. The Plaintiff was anxious to obtain a decree for a foreclosure; the money being considerable and the security small: but it was of great consequence to the Defendant to keep the estate. He certainly does not go abroad to avoid the process.

Lord CHANCELLOR [ELDON].—Then in this particular case upon the consent of the Plaintiff the Six Clerk must be directed to receive the answer without being signed by the Defendant (2).

———

UNDER special circumstances, as in the principal case, an answer may certainly be allowed to be put in without oath or signature: ——— v. *Gwillim*, 6 Ves. 285;

———

(1) The last day of term being Midsummer Day, the motions were heard at Westminster Hall on the following day.

(*a*) The answer must be actually signed by the defendant putting it in, although an answer on oath is waived, unless an order has been obtained allowing it to be taken without signature. 1 Barb. Ch. Pr. 141; *Denison* v. *Bassford*, 7 Paige, 370. The Court has, sometimes, under special circumstances, directed the clerk to receive an answer, though it has not been signed by the defendant. *Dumond* v. *Magee*, 2 Johns. Ch. 240. Where the signature is waived by the plaintiff, the answer may be filed without it. *Fulton Bank* v. *Beach*, 2 Paige, 307; S. C. 6 Wend. 36.

(2) *Post*, ——— v. *Gwillim*, 285; *Bayley* v. *De Walkiers*, vol. x. 441; *Harding*.

Bayley v. *De Walkiers*, 10 Ves. 442; *Harding* v. *Harding*, 12 Ves. 159: it even
seems that this order is of course, upon motion to that effect by the *plaintiff*, when
the defendant is in this country; but when the defendant is abroad, the Court
requires some authority to show that he is willing an answer should be put in for
him. *Codner* v. *Hersey*, 18 Ves. 469.

KING *v.* KING.

[1801, JULY 2.]

INJUNCTION, restraining a transfer, and a receiver appointed, to preserve the property during a litigation in the Ecclesiastical Court upon the will (*a*).

OPPOSITE claims had been set up in the Ecclesiastical Court under different wills; and a decision had been made that one will was
not sufficiently proved.

Mr. *Benyon*, for the Plaintiff, moved, that the property might be
paid into the Bank, and transferred to the Accountant General; and
a receiver appointed to collect the outstanding property.   The motion was made on the authority of Mitford (1); that during a suit
in the Ecclesiastical Court for administration of the effects a Court
of Equity will entertain a suit for the mere preservation
[*173]   *of the property, till the litigation is determined.   It was
said, that Lord Thurlow had directed, that the party should
be examined upon interrogatories.

Mr. *Mansfield*, for the Defendant, objected, that it did not appear
the property was in danger; observing, that the decision was not
satisfactory; and the Ecclesiastical Court might receive farther evidence; and the proper course would be, that an administrator *pendente lite* should be appointed by the Ecclesiastical Court.

Lord CHANCELLOR [ELDON].—This is almost a motion of course.
There is no doubt, this Court has appointed a Receiver, when it has
been in dispute, who was the personal representative; where the
matter is in controversy in the Spiritual Court; as whether there is
an intestacy, or not.   The Court goes upon this; that it will do its
best to collect the effects.   The property is in danger in this sense;
that it may get into the hands of persons, who have nothing to do
with it.   That he may be examined upon interrogatories is not part
of the motion.   Let him transfer the funds to the Accountant Gen-

---

v. *Harding*, xii. 159.   In *Codner* v. *Hersey*, xviii. 468, this practice was extended
to a Defendant in this country without any special circumstances: but the order,
being obtained on the Plaintiff's motion, was thus qualified, that the Defendant
shall be at liberty to put in his answer without oath or signature.

(*a*) Where there is a controversy respecting the title to stock under different
wills, an injunction will be granted to restrain any transfer *pendente lite*. 2 Story,
See Eq. Jur. § 907.   *Osborn* v. *Bank of United States*, 9 Wheaton, 845; *Spendlove*
v. *Spendlove*, Cam. & Norw. 36.

(1) Mitf. 122, 123.

eral according to the notice of motion ; and a Receiver must be appointed (1).

Mr. *Piggott* (*Amicus Curiæ*) observing, that no one could transfer, the order made was, that the Defendant should be restrained from transferring any stock or dividends standing in the name of the testator, or standing in his own name, that belonged to the testator ; and that a Receiver should be appointed.

IT is well settled that a Court of Equity has jurisdiction to protect the property of a testator, or intestate, by appointing a receiver pending a litigation in the Ecclesiastical Court for probate or administration, notwithstanding the power of such Court to grant an administration *pendente lite* ; (*Atkinson* v. *Henshaw*, 2 Ves. & Bea. 85 ; *Ball* v. *Oliver*, 2 Ves. & Bea. 96 ;) for there are many cases in which an administration *pendente lite* would not secure the property. *Edmunds* v. *Bird*, 1 Ves. & Bea. 543.

---

(1) This decision, though not adopted in its full extent by Lord Erskine in *Richards* v. *Chave*, *post*, vol. xii. 462, is confirmed by subsequent cases. See *Edmunds* v. *Bird*, 1 Ves. & Bea. 542 ; *Atkinson* v. *Henshaw*, *Ball* v. *Oliver*, 2 Ves. & Bea. 85, 96 ; *Rutherford* v. *Douglas*, 1 Sim. & Stu. 111, *n.* ; establishing the jurisdiction, even though an administrator *pendente lite* might be obtained in the Ecclesiastical Court ; as before probate. It is not exercised for the preservation of real estate *pendente lite* between devisee and heir ; *Smith* v. *Collyer*, *post*, vol. viii. 89. See the observations of Sir William Grant, 3 Mer. 173.

EVANS *v.* BICKNELL.

[1801, MAY 8; JUNE 9; JULY 6.]

BILL to charge a trustee, as having by delivering the title-deeds to the tenant for life enabled him to make a mortgage of a settled estate as tenant in fee, dismissed; the fraudulent purpose of enabling him to mortgage resting upon the evidence of a single witness, and being positively denied by the answer, as far as the allegations of the bill gave an oportunity of answering; but without costs, on the ground of negligence; and without prejudice to an action; and with an option to the Plaintiff to take an issue (a).

An old head of Equity, that if a representation is made to a man, going to deal on the faith of it in a matter of interest, the person making the representation, knowing it false, shall make it good (b); and the jurisdiction assumed by Courts of Law in such cases will not prevent relief in Equity, [p. 183.]

Not a general rule in equity, that a second mortgagee, who has the title-deeds, without notice of a prior incumbrance, shall be preferred: negligence alone will not postpone the first: it must amount to fraud (c), [p. 183.]

A rule of property in equity is not therefore to be adopted at law: the Courts in some respects proceeding upon different principles: Courts of Equity, for in-

---

(a) In many cases fraud is effectually remediable at law. *Jackson* v. *Burgott,* 457, 462; 1 Story, Eq. Jur. § 201. There are some cases of fraud, in which Equity does not ordinarily grant relief, as in warranties, misrepresentations, and frauds, on the sale of personal property; but leaves the parties to their remedy at law. The Supreme Court of the United States has said that no case is recollected where a Court of Equity has afforded relief for an injury sustained by the fraud of a person, who is no party to a contract induced by that fraud. It is true that, if certain facts, essential to the merits of a claim purely legal, be exclusively within the knowledge of the party against whom that claim is asserted, he may be required, in a Court of Chancery, to disclose those facts; and the Court, being thus rightly in possession of the cause, will proceed to determine the whole matter in controversy. If the answer of the defendant discloses nothing, and the plaintiff supports his claim by evidence in his own possession, unaided by the confessions of the defendant, the established rules, limiting the jurisdiction of Courts, require that he should be dismissed from the Court of Chancery, and permitted to assert his rights in a Court of law. *Russell* v. *Clark,* 7 Cranch, 69. But see *Bacon* v. *Bronson,* 7 Johns. Ch. 201. It has been declared in Kentucky, that wherever a matter respects personal chattels, and lies merely in damages, the remedy is at law only and for these reasons; 1st, because Courts of law are as adequate as a Court of Chancery, to grant complete and effectual reparation to the party injured; 2d, because the ascertainment of damages is peculiarly the province of a jury. *Hardwick* v. *Forbes,* 1 Bibb, 212; *Waters* v. *Mattinglay,* 1 Id. 244.'

The deposit of title-deeds in England may have many important consequences. In the United States the general system of Registration will defeat many of these consequences. See note (a), *Ford* v. *Peering,* 1 V. 72; 2 Story, Eq. Jur. § 1020; *Keys* v. *Williams,* 3 Y. & C. 55.

(b) One of the largest classes of cases, in which Courts of Equity are accustomed to grant relief, is where there has been a misrepresentation, or *suggestio falsi.* 1 Story, Eq. Jur. § 191; 2 Kent, Comm. 484; *Atwood* v. *Small,* 6; *Clark* v. *Finelly,* 232. But the misrepresentation must be of something material, constituting an inducement or motive to the other party, and on which he placed trust, so as to be misled to his injury. Ib. See, also, *The People* v. *Kendall,* 25 Wendell, 399; *Cary* v. *Hotailing,* 1 Hill, N. Y. 311.

It will be a fraud, if the party intentionally misrepresents a material fact, or produces a false impression, in order to mislead another. *Laidlaw* v. *Organ,* 2 Wheaton, 178, 195; *Pidlock* v. *Bishop,* 3 B. & C. 605; *Smith* v. *The Bank of Scotland,* 1 Dow. Parl. 272; 1 Story, Eq. Jur. § 192, 197.

(c) *Qui tacet, consentire videtur; qui potest et debet vetare, jubet, si non vetal.*

stance, not allowing a single witness, unless supported by circumstances, to prevail against a positive denial by the answer (*a*), [p. 183*a*.]

In equity a second mortgagee without notice, getting in a satisfied term, may protect himself: the conscience being equal (*b*), [p. 184.]

The Lord Chancellor of opinion, that at law an assignment of such term is not to be presumed without some dealing upon it. Consequences of the late doctrine of Courts of Law on this subject, [p. 184.]

Consequences of permitting an action for an injury sustained by giving credit upon a false representation by the Defendant (*c*), [p. 186.]

If the intention is fraudulent, though not pointing exactly to the object accomplished, yet the party is bound (*d*), [p. 191.]

By indentures of lease and release, dated the 8th and 9th of September, 1792, William Stansell, a biscuit baker at Bristol, conveyed to Elizabeth Reed, also of Bristol, her heirs, executors, administrators, and assigns, respectively, certain freehold and leasehold estates, by way of mortgage for the sum of 300*l.*; and it was provided, that Hawkins, an attorney, was to receive the rents and profits, and to apply them in the first instance to the interest, and then to accumulate them for the discharge of the principal. At the date of the mortgage the only interest Stansell had in these estates was under a settlement, executed in November 1785, previous to his marriage with Elizabeth Bicknell; by which all the said leasehold and freehold estates were assigned and conveyed to John Bicknell and John Taylor, their executors and administrators, and heirs and assigns, respectively; upon trust for the separate use of Elizabeth Bicknell for life; remainder to the use of Stansell for life; remainder to the

---

See *Wendell* v. *Van Rensselaer*, 1 Johns. Ch. 354; *Storrs* v. *Barker*, 6 Johns. Ch. 166; *Bright* v. *Boyd*, 1 Story, 478. A person having an incumbrance or security upon an estate, who suffers the owner to procure additional money upon the estate by way of lien or mortgage, concealing his prior incumbrance or security, will be postponed to the second incumbrancer; for it would be inequitable to allow him to profit by his own wrong in concealing his claim, and thus lending encouragement to the new loan. 1 Story, Eq. Jur. § 390. If a prior mortgagee, whose mortgage is not registered, should be a witness to a subsequent mortgage or conveyance of the same property, knowing the contents of the deed, and should not disclose his prior incumbrance, he would be postponed or barred of his title. *Brinckerhoff* v. *Lansing*, 4 Johns. Ch. 65; *Lee* v. *Munroe*, 7 Cranch, 366.

Such cases as the above stand on the ground of constructive fraud, or of gross negligence, which in effect implies fraud. 1 Story, Eq. Jur. § 391, 393; *Berry* v. *Mutual Ins. Co.* 2 Johns. Ch. 603.

(*a*) For the reason of this rule as to evidence, see *ante*, note (*a*), *Mortimer* v. *Orchard*, 2 V. 243.

(*b*) As to the doctrine of tacking, see *ante*, note (*a*), *Hamerton* v. *Rogers*, 1 V. 513; note (*c*) *Jones* v. *Smith*, 2 V. 372.

(*c*) The doctrine of the case of *Pasley* v. *Freeman*, which is questioned by Lord Eldon, is now well settled both in the English and American jurisprudence. The principle is, that fraud, accompanied with damage, is a good cause of action. 2 Kent, Comm. 489; *Eyre* v. *Dunsford*, 1 East, 318; *Haycraft* v. *Creasy*, 2 Ib. 92; *Wise* v. *Wilcox*, 1 Day, 22; *Hart* v. *Tallmadge*, 2 ib. 381; *Russell* v. *Clark*, 7 Cranch, 92; *Patten* v. *Gurney*, 17 Mass. 182; *Upton* v. *Vail*, 6 Johns. 181; *Gallagher* v. *Brunel*, 6 Cowen, 346; *Benton* v. *Pratt*, 2 Wendell, 385; *Allen* v. *Addington*, 7 Wendell, 1; *S. C.* 1 ib. 374; *Russell* v. *Clark*, 7 Cranch, 69. See *post*, p. 187, note (*a*).

(*d*) 1 Story, Eq. Jur. § 392.

children, as he should appoint, and, in default of appointment, equally; with a reversionary interest to Stansell in default of children. They had issue two children. Afterwards, two or three years before the mortgage, Stansell became insolvent; and separated from his wife.

Elizabeth Reed having married Evans, the bill was filed by them; stating these circumstances; and that the real title of Stansell had been discovered since the mortgage; that all the title-deeds had been upon the marriage delivered to Bicknell, the trustee: and charging a design to raise money upon the credit of the premises; and that Bicknell delivered the deeds out of his custody for the purpose of enabling Stansell to represent himself to the Plaintiff to be the owner of the premises; that he has admitted or declared upon different occasions and in the hearing of different persons, and that Stansell at the time of the application informed him, he wanted them for the purpose of obtaining credit; and he made such declaration or admission in the presence of the Plaintiff and Hawkins, the Solicitor, and the Defendant Taylor. The bill prayed, that the estates may be sold to satisfy the mortgage; and [* 175] *that the Defendant Bicknell should be decreed to answer the deficiency, or the whole, if the Court should be of opinion, that the estate should not be sold.

The Defendant Bicknell by his answer stated, that Stansell some years after the execution of the settlement, and prior to the execution of the mortgage, became insolvent: and assigned all his estate for the benefit of his creditors; which was a matter of notoriety in Bristol; and advertisements were inserted in the Bristol newspapers. The title-deeds were soon after the execution and previous to the marriage delivered by Stansell to the Defendant Bicknell; and remained in his custody, till they were delivered by him to Stansell a short time previous to the mortgage: when all the title-deeds except the said settlement were delivered at the desire and with the approbation of Elizabeth Stansell to the Defendant William Stansell; who promised to re-deliver them in a few hours, or next morning at the farthest. Upon the Defendant's application afterwards Elizabeth Stansell admitted, she had them; but refused to part with them. He denied, that the delivery was to enable him to obtain a mortgage from the Plaintiff or any one; and stated, that he never did admit or declare, in the presence of Hawkins, Taylor, or any other person, nor did Stansell, when he applied for the deeds, or at any time, inform him, that he wanted to obtain money by way of mortgage or otherwise: but he admitted, Stansell did inform him, he wanted the use of the title-deeds merely to show or convince some person or persons, with whom he was in the habit of taking credit in the way of trade, that he and his wife were legally in possession of the rents and profits of the freehold and leasehold estates.

The Defendant John Taylor, after the answer of Bicknell was put in, was examined by the Plaintiffs; and by his depositions he stated, that upon the 29th of January, 1794, Elizabeth Evans and Hawkins, the attorney, came to him about the mortgage; and they and the deponent went to Bicknell; who strenuously denied, that he had delivered the deeds for the purpose of a mortgage; but at length, after much altercation and abusive language between him and Hawkins, informed them, that Stansell had desired him to lend him the title-deeds, belonging to the marriage settlement, to show to some person; who would credit him with *goods in   [*176] his trade to the amount of 40*l.* or 50*l.* upon seeing them; and the person to lend the money was to receive two years' rents; that he had promised to return them in an hour; that he (Bicknell) had lent them; and had often sent, but never could get them; and he denied, that he knew of the mortgage.

Hawkins died, before the cause went to issue.

The Lord CHANCELLOR [ELDON] early in the argument put it to the Plaintiffs' Counsel, whether they could not bring an action.

Mr. *Romilly* and Mr. *Hart*, for the Plaintiffs.—With respect to your Lordship's question, whether the Plaintiffs may not bring an action, they are not entitled to relief at law, upon the principles upon which *Pasley* v. *Freeman*, (1) and *Scott* v. *Lara* (2) were determined. In this case there is no privity between Bicknell and the Plaintiff; no assumpsit or contract.

It is unnecessary to say, what the Court has done in the case of a first mortgagee, leaving the deeds in the hands of a mortgagor. Bicknell had in himself the fee-simple in the freehold estate and the absolute interest in the terms for years. Giving the deeds to Stansell, enabling him to act as absolute owner, Bicknell must be answerable for all the consequences, as much as if they had followed from his own act. He knew, Stansell intended to gain a credit upon these deeds; as he thought, only to the extent of 50*l.*, according to the witness; but his answer does not state the extent. The Plaintiff is entitled to the whole of the money advanced, not merely the 50*l.*; supposing that sum the extent of the fraud intended. The principle of law upon that is stated by Lord Bacon (3), that a party enabling another to commit a fraud must be answerable for all the consequences. Mr. Justice Foster (4), treating upon accomplices, puts several cases upon it. In the cases of marriage agreements, where the husband has been represented to be in good circumstances, the party making that false representation has been held answerable out of his own property. In one case, *Arnot* v. *Biscoe* (5), which is not to be distinguished from this, a perfect stranger was compelled to pay the loss out of *his own pocket.   [*177] The circumstance, that the Defendant in that case was an attorney, cannot make any difference. This Defendant is a trustee; and his duty was not to let those deeds go out of his hands. There

(1) 3 Term Rep. B. R. 51.
(2) Peake, N. P. 226.
(3) Maxim, 16, fol. 82.
(4) Fost. C. L. 370.
(5) 1 Ves. 95.

is no material contradiction between the answer and the evidence. The rule (I), that there can be no decree upon the 'evidence of a single witness against the answer, prevails only, where the denial by the answer is positive: but in this case the answer alone would be a sufficient foundation for the decree. The only instance, in which a decree has not been made against the Defendant to such a bill, is the case of the *Thatched House Tavern* (2): the representation being, that the object being to build, the mortgagee by parting with the deeds for an hour would improve his security; and he would not trust the deeds with the mortgagor; but went with him; and stayed in his house, while they were in his possession. The jurisdiction of this Court would be very defective, if it cannot from the acts of parties, infer a fraud; not relying only upon the admission. This trustee had the deeds in his possession for a double purpose; to protect the title; and for the general purpose of protecting the public from frauds, that might be committed by means of them. Supposing, as the Court has intimated, that the cases do not go the length of postponing a first mortgagee, who has parted with the deeds, upon mere negligence, this is more than negligence. In *Beckett* v. *Cordley* (3) the Lord Chancellor lays it down (4), that though there is no case in the books, but where the party, to whom the fraud is imputed, was conusant of the treaty, in which it was practised, yet, if it appeared, the parties were confederating together to cheat some one, though the particular person was not known, the case would fall within the same principle; and must receive· the same determination. What possible purpose could there be in this· transaction, but the purpose supposed, and admitted by the Defendant, to convince some innocent person, that Stansell and his wife were in the legal possession of the rents and profits of these estates, and to induce that person to give him a credit, which he would not otherwise have given? Though there is no case exactly

[* 178]   in point, yet upon the principles, on ✻ which *Arnot* v. *Biscoe* and the other cases were determined the Plaintiffs are entitled to a decree.

Mr. *Richards* and Mr. *Horne,* for the Defendant Bicknell.—The bill as against Bicknell is merely an action for 300*l.* It is impossible upon this bill to arrange any equity as against Stansell. It is merely an action on the case, in the nature of an action of deceit. Where is the equity any more· than against an obligee in a bond suing the surety in this Court; the principal being insolvent? It is said, there must be relief somewhere; and if it cannot be had at law, upon *Pasley* v. *Freeman,* it must be in this Court: but Courts of law do take notice of personal frauds; and if they will not give relief upon this case, it is only because upon sound principles they

(1) *Walton* v. *Hobbs,* 2 Atk. 19, and the references; *Mortimer* v. *Orchard, ante,* vol. ii. 243, and the note, 244.
(2) *Peter* v. *Russel,* 1 Eq. Ca. Ab. 321.
(3) 1 Bro. C. C. 353.
(4) 1 Bro. C. C. 357.

will not act upon such a loose ground. This would bring every action of a personal nature founded in fraud into this Court.

But, supposing the case was at law, there is no pretence for sustaining an action. They in truth admit, they have no remedy at
law. *Arnot* v. *Biscoe* and the other cases referred to are quite different; and that of the *Thatched House Tavern* is very strong; the
deed being given up by the mortgagee, he ought to have seen, what
use was to be made of it; yet the Court seeing no intention to defraud would not affect him. *Mocatta* v. *Murgatroyd* (1) was determined upon the implied consent of the mortgagee to be postponed. *Ibbotson* v. *Rhodes* (2) was a case of fraud. *Berrisford* v.
Milward (3) was a case, either of clear fraud, or, in which the party
was bound by his own undertaking not to look to the mortgaged
estate, but to look upon the father as his personal debtor. *Head* v.
Egerton (4) proceeds upon the ground, that the first mortgagee had
beyond all doubt a right to keep his mortgage. Those cases therefore afford no ground for saying, the mere absence of the title-deeds
affects the mortgagee; unless fraud is imputed to him. The case
of the remainder-man, cited (5) in *Arnot* v. *Biscoe*, is a strong case
of fraud; the representation being, that a person, in fact only tenant
in tail, had a title to make a mortgage in fee. In *Plumb*
v. *Fluitt* (6), the general * purpose of deceiving the world   [* 179]
is stated. As to the cases of a felonious intention to mur-
der one person, in pursuance of which by accident another is killed,
they cannot be applied to a transaction of this sort, having nothing
in it felonious or criminal. According to an accurate note of *Beck-*
ett v. *Cordley* Lord Thurlow says, *Hobbs.* v. *Norton* (7) was a very
strong case: but the Defendant treated with the very party, to whom
fraud was imputed: and there is no case, in which the Court has
gone upon any other ground, than the party's being conusant of
the transaction: to be sure if parties enter into a confederacy together, and are conusant of the general purpose, it is not necessary
to show an intent to cheat a particular person: but if they are conusant of the general purpose, it is brought to the same point.

There is nothing in this case to show such a general purpose of
fraud. There was only one person willing to advance money, if
Stansell was entitled to the possession of the premises. He was entitled sufficiently for that purpose. Notwithstanding the artifice of
endeavoring in a conversation to draw something from the Defendant by irritating him, an attorney being brought, to take advantage
of any thing, that could be drawn from him, they are forced to admit, that he strenuously denied the purpose imputed to him. His

---

(1) 1 P. Will. 393.
(2) 2 Vern. 554.
(3) 2 Atk. 49.
(4) 3 P. Will. 280.
(5) 1 Ves. 96.
(6) 2 Anst. 432.
(7) 1 Vern. 136.

retaining the settlement affords no inference, that he meant fraud: Stansell and his wife having another part. This case is admitted to be new in principle. The maxim of Lord Bacon referred to amounts only to this; that a man shall not take advantage of his own wrong, as a general proposition: but they must prove an unlawful intention. If the Defendant denies the charge, the Plaintiff cannot have a decree upon the evidence of one witness; unless there are unequivocal circumstances corroborating the evidence; and in this case the circumstances, instead of corroborating, afford an inference the other way. They all lived in Bristol; and therefore notice must be presumed.

Lord CHANCELLOR [ELDON].—It is still for the consideration of the Plaintiff's Counsel, whether an action may not be maintained at law; for if upon their state of the case this Court can interfere, [*180]   I doubt very much, whether an action might not be maintained. * Then this is in truth a suit in a Court of Equity for damages. This Defendant has got the legal estate in the freehold and leasehold; but in both upon a trust for persons, whom you do not affect. If one *cestuy que trust* has acted honestly, can the Court take away the estate, because the other has acted dishonestly? I do not mean at present to say, that if an action can be maintained, therefore this Court will not maintain its jurisdiction, executed perhaps upon much more correct principles; for Courts of law have taken very strong steps.

Mr. *Romilly*, in reply.—The relief sought is a compensation in money; as in *Arnot* v. *Biscoe*. If they rely upon notice of the settlement by the Plaintiff, they ought to have put that in issue: not having done so, they can neither give direct evidence of it, nor raise an inference. The bill does not even suggest notice. But that fact was in issue in a cause instituted by Mrs. Stansell against this Plaintiff and the two trustees; expressly charging, that the Plaintiff had notice; which was denied by the answer. Some of your Lordship's predecessors have lamented, that the Court had gone so far in affecting a principal by notice to an agent. Can the Court now say, for what fair purpose the Defendant gave up these deeds to this insolvent debtor? The maxim from Lord Bacon was referred to only to show, that the purpose being illegal, the party could not say, he was not to answer; because the other had exceeded the intention; and various instances of that nature are put. How can all the world be supposed to have had notice of the insolvency of an obscure tradesman in Bristol?

With respect to the supposed relief at law, there is no instance of such an action: nor can it be supported upon any principle. *Pasley* v. *Freeman* and *Eyre* v. *Dunford* (1) are the only cases, that have the least analogy; and it is very doubtful, whether they would bear out this case. Courts of law have carried the principle farther than Courts of Equity. No form of action is provided; and that is

(1) 1 East, 318.

an objection to our going to law. The objection, that relief might be had at law was of much more force in *Arnot* v. *Biscoe*. But at least there is a concurrent jurisdiction ; and a Court of Equity ought to interfere upon a case of gross fraud ; in which it is im-
* possible to assign a good motive. The ground in this　　[* 181]
Court is, that this man having the legal estate and a de-
posit of the title-deeds, enables another person to deal with the estate, as he himself might have done ; to make a mortgage ; which, if done by himself, would have made him clearly answerable.

Lord CHANCELLOR.—Though the sum, which is the subject in question, is small, a cause of more consequence to the public has very seldom been heard.

July 6*th*. The Lord CHANCELLOR [ELDON] stated the case ; and delivered his judgment.—There is a peculiarity in this mortgage from the circumstance, that Hawkins, the attorney, was appointed to receive the rents and profits ; and to apply them in the first instance to the interest, and then to accumulate them for the discharge of the principal : so that it is in fact a mortgage aiming at the delivery of possession immediately to the mortgagee ; to the intent to repay the money lent by the rents and profits, as soon as possible. Though that circumstance is a peculiarity, it is not a circumstance pressing at all upon the application of any principle, that ought otherwise to dispose of the case. The question in this cause is, whether upon the doctrine of this Court the Defendant Bicknell is liable to make good the deficiency to the Plaintiff upon this transaction beyond the value of Stansell's interest under the settlement ; which would be the first to be applied. The bill contended at first, that this was a gross fraud on the part of the wife ; that she was privy to all the circumstances, under which her husband obtained the loan ; and gave positive encouragement to the party lending ; an allegation, which, if made out, would be sufficient to postpone her to the mortgagee ; for coverture is no excuse for fraud. Upon her answer, however, and the evidence, it is not now, nor can it be contended, that there was upon her part either distinct fraud, or that gross degree of negligence, which this Court looks at
* as fraud with regard to the consequences attaching to it.　　[* 182]
Therefore her estate, so far as it depends upon her own
act, appears secure to her. The bill then fails altogether as a bill requiring a conveyance from any of the Defendants to make good the Plaintiff's title. From her there can be no conveyance : her estate being settled to her separate use, and protected by the legal estate of Taylor and Bicknell : the former so little implicated in the fraud or negligence, that he was examined as a witness ; and therefore it is impossible to affect his estate, protecting her's ; and if Bicknell was the sole trustee, it is much too strong to say, this married woman, *cestuy que trust*, should be deprived of her interest, though an innocent party ; because there might have been fraud or

negligence in Bicknell; in whom the legal estate was. Her equity to be protected would be as strong as the Plaintiffs' to have their estate made good. The Court, if it stood indifferent upon such a case, would have acted upon its usual principles.

The question then is, supposing the husband's interest insufficient to satisfy the mortgage, whether there is a personal demand against Bicknell upon the circumstances of his conduct; and whether, if there is, it can be enforced in a Court of Equity. I shall dispose of the last consideration first. If there is a jurisdiction at law in such cases, there is also a jurisdiction in equity; and then, if there is a concurrent jurisdiction, there can be reason for dismissing the bill. Attending to the cases decided at law, there can be very little doubt; that a declaration might be framed upon the circumstances of this case, so that an·action might be maintained, if there be fraud in the conduct of Bicknell: but it will not follow, that this Court cannot give relief. *Pasley* v. *Freeman*, which is the first case of its kind, proceeded upon this ground; that the Defendant was averred by the declaration to have falsely, deceitfully, and fraudulently, asserted, that Falch was safely to be trusted. The action was maintained upon the ground of fraud and deceit in the Defendant and damage to the Plaintiff; circumstances, which were held by a majority of the Judges sufficient to maintain the action. It has oc-[* 183] curred to me, that that case * upon the principles of many decisions in this Court might have been maintained here; for it is a very old head of equity, that if a representation is made to another person, going to deal in a matter of interest upon the faith of that representation, the former shall make that representation good, if he knows it to be false (1); and in that case and some others there appears a disposition to hold, that if there was relief to be administered in equity, there ought to be relief at law: a proposition, that seems to me excessively questionable; and I doubt, whether it is not founded in pure ignorance of the constitution and doctrine of this Court. I allude to it the rather on account of a case frequently mentioned, *Goodtitle* v. *Morgan* (2), in which Mr. Justice Buller expresses himself in this manner (3):

"It is an established rule in a Court of Equity, that a second mortgagee, who has the title-deeds, without notice of any prior incumbrance, shall be preferred; because, if a mortgagee lends money upon mortgage without taking the title-deeds, he enables the mortgagor to commit a fraud. If this has become a rule of property in a Court of Equity, it ought to be adopted in a Court of Law. Here the Defendants took mortgages without inquiring after the title-deeds: the subsequent mortgagee is a purchaser without notice; and as he has taken the title-deeds, he has the better title."

The first of these propositions is certainly upon the late decisions not true. I do not wonder, that Mr. Justice Buller stated the doc-

(1) *Burrowes* v. *Lock*, *post*, vol. x. 470.
(2) 1 Term Rep. B. R. 755.
(3) 1 Term Rep. B. R. 762.

trine, as he did; for in *Ryall* v. *Rowles* (1) it is so stated by Mr. Justice Burnet (2), and without observation by the Lord Chancellor, or the other learned persons, by whom his Lordship was assisted, as being contrary to the law of this Court; and in *Beckett* v. *Cordley*, in which I was Counsel with Mr. Ambler, who had a good memory of that time, he certainly was impressed with a full conviction, that such was the doctrine of this Court (3).

With regard to the second proposition of Mr. Justice Buller, that, if this had become a rule of property in equity, therefore, it *ought to be adopted in a Court of Law, with great   [*184] deference to the learning and memory of that Judge, that appears to me a very hasty proposition; and the converse undoubtedly will not hold; for it is impossible for this Court upon the principles, upon which it acts, to say, that whatever is a rule of proceeding at Law is of course a rule of proceeding in Equity. It may be asserted, that it should be the case: but it is impossible it can. For instance: in the case of the mortgagee, put in *Pasley* v. *Freeman*, if the man makes a false declaration, and an action can be maintained upon that, and the principle, upon which it can be maintained, is, that a Court of Equity will relieve, the converse ought to hold; that, where an action can be maintained, Equity should give relief. But is that so? A Defendant in this Court has the protection arising from his own conscience in a degree, in which the law does not affect to give him protection. If he positively, plainly, and precisely, denies the assertion, and one witness only proves it as positively, clearly, and precisely, as it is denied, and there is no circumstance, attaching credit to the assertion overbalancing the credit due to the denial, as a positive denial, a Court of Equity will not act upon the testimony of that witness. Not so at law. There the Defendant is not heard. One witness proves the case; and, however strongly the Defendant may be inclined to deny it upon oath, there must be a recovery against him (4).

It seems to me rather surprising, if I may presume to say so, that Lord Mansfield, who concurred with Mr. Justice Buller in a great many of these equitable principles in a Court of Law, should not have attended to these distinctions; which perhaps will be found in the very principles, upon which this Court exists. Titles to property may possibly be found to be very considerably shaken by the doctrine of the Court of King's Bench as to satisfied terms (5). The law as to that here is, that a second mortgagee having no notice of the first mortgage, if he can get in a satisfied term, would do that, which is the true ground of the decision, *though   [*185]

---

(1) 1 Ves. 348, 375; 1 Atk. 165.
(2) 1 Ves. 360; 1 Atk. 168.
(3) See *Barnett* v. *Weston*, *post*, vol. xii. 130; *Harper* v. *Faulder*, 4 Madd. 129.
(4) See 2 Ves. & Bea. 110; 2 Madd. 217.
(5) See Doe on the demise of *Bristowe* v. *Pegge*, 1 Term Rep. B. R. 758, n.; Doe on the demise of *Hodsden* v. *Staple*, 2 Term Rep. B. R. 684; *Goodtitle* v. *Jones*, 7 Term Rep. 47; Doe on the demise of *Da Costa* v. *Wharton*, 8 Term Rep. B. R. 2.

it is not put upon that by Mr. Justice Buller: he would, as
in conscience he might, get the legal estate ; and by virtue of that
protect his estate against the first mortgagee, having got a prior
title ; the conscience being equal between the parties.   When once
it is said at law, that a satisfied term should not be set up in an
ejectment, the whole security of that title is destroyed ; and therefore even with the modern correction that doctrine has received in
the late cases, which is, that you may set up the term, though satisfied, and put it as a question to the Jury, whether an assignment is
to be presumed, it seems to me very dangerous between purchasers ;
and the leaning of the Court ought to be, that it was not assigned ;
and I fully concur with Lord Kenyon, that it is not fit for a Judge
to tell a Jury, they are to presume a term assigned, because it is satisfied ; but there ought to be some dealing upon it : or you take
from a purchaser the effect of his diligence in having got in the legal
estate ; to the benefit of which he is entitled.   Then, suppose, the
law takes upon itself to decide the question between purchasers upon
this subject : can it decide upon the same rule as Courts of Equity,
as upon the question of notice?   It will be said upon this doctrine,
a Court of Equity does inquire into this ; and it is a rule of property
in Equity ; and therefore ought to be a rule of property at Law.
But, how has it become a rule of property in Equity?   In Equity the
first mortgagee may ask the second, whether he had notice.   If that
Defendant positively denies notice, and one witness only is produced
to the fact of notice, if the denial is as positive as the assertion, and
there is nothing more in the case, a Court of Equity will not take the
benefit of the term from the second mortgagee :- placing as much reliance on the conscience of the Defendant as on the testi-
[* 186]   mony of a single witness ; without some * circumstances
attaching a superior degree of credit to the latter (1).   It
is impossible therefore, that the rule of property can be said to be
the same at law ; and as if it stands upon different principles, in fact
it is perfectly different.

So, as to the case of *Pasley* v. *Freeman*.   It is almost improper at
this day to say any thing, having a tendency to shake it : but I know
Mr. Justice Grose very lately held the same opinion as he did at the

(1) *Ante*, 40 ; vol. ii. 244, and the note.   This rule, considered simply as a general rule of evidence, seems open to observation, 1st, as preferring the evidence of
a party ; 2dly, upon the obvious defect of written, compared with oral, testimony.
It is difficult to determine the balance of inconvenience and danger, on the one
hand from permitting in a commercial country the Defendant to avail himself of
his own oath to a degree in some respects beyond the old wager of Law ; and on
the other, from deciding upon the evidence of a single witness, in cases even requiring the utmost accuracy and precision in the proof.
   In *Haycraft* v. *Creasy*, 2 East, 92, an attempt was made to extend the doctrine
of *Pasley* v. *Freeman* to a case, in which the Defendant could not be affected with
fraud ; having given the character under a false impression ; in consequence of
which he had sustained a considerable loss : but three Judges of the Court of
King's Bench decided, against the opinion of Lord Kenyon, that fraud is the
ground of this action.   *Ex parte Carr*, 3 Ves. & Bea. 108.   See Lord Erskine's
opinion in favor of the case of *Pasley* v. *Freeman*. considered as a case of fraud,
post, vol. xiii. 133, *Clifford* v. *Brooke*.

time of the judgment. The doctrine laid down in that case is in practice and experience most dangerous. I state that upon my own experience; and if the action is to be maintained in opposition to the positive denial of the Defendant against the stout assertion of a single witness, where the least deviation in the account of the conversation varies the whole, it will become necessary, in order to protect men from the consequences, that the Statute of Frauds (1) should be applied to that case. Suppose, a man asked, whether a third person may be trusted, answers, " You may trust him; and if he does not pay you, I will." Upon that the Plaintiff cannot recover; because it is a verbal undertaking for the debt of another. But if he does not undertake, but simply answers, " You may trust him: he is a very honest man, and worthy of trust," &c. then an action will lie. Whether it is fit the law should remain with such distinctions, it is not for me to determine. - Upon the case of *Pasley* v. *Freeman*, I have always said, when I was Chief Justice, that I so far doubted the principles of it, as to make it not unfit to offer, as I always did, to the Counsel, that a special verdict should be taken: but that offer was so uniformly rejected, that I suppose I was in some error upon this subject. I could therefore only point out to the Jury the danger of finding verdicts upon such principles; and I succeeded in impressing them with a sense of that danger so far, that the Plaintiffs in such actions very seldom obtained verdicts. It appears to me a very extraordinary state of the law, that if the Plaintiff in the case of *Pasley* v. *Freeman* had come into equity, insisting, that the Defendant should make good the consequence of his representation, and the Defendant positively denied, that he had made that representation, and only one witness was produced to prove it, the Court of Equity would give the Defendant so much protection, that they would refuse the relief; and yet upon the very same circumstances the law would enable the Plaintiff to * recover.		[* 187] Whether that is following equity, or not quite outstripping equity, is not a question for discussion now: but it leads to the absolute necessity of affording protection by a statute, requiring, that these undertakings shall be in writing (*a*).

With regard to the circumstances of this case, this is an amended bill; and I do not know, but I rather suspect from the frame of the bill and the nature of the answer, that this was an after-thought: but still the Plaintiff must have the relief, if it is founded. The bill at first must have gone upon the ground of fraud in the wife. Her answer removes all possibility of charging her estate with the mortgage; and then the bill suggesting pretences by Bicknell, that he was a stranger to the application of Stansell to the Plaintiff to

(1) 29 Ch. II. c. 3.
(*a*) This was finally done by the statute of 6 Geo. IV. ch. 14, commonly called Lord Tenterden's Act, which extends the Statute of Frauds, by requiring a memorandum in writing signed by the party to be charged, of representations of another's character and ability, with a view to give credit to him. The same provision may be found in the Revised Statutes of Massachusetts, cap. 74, § 3.

lend him the money, and did not know, what use Stansell intended
to make of the deeds, charged, that Bicknell delivered the deeds for
the express purpose of enabling Stansell to represent himself to the
Plaintiff to be the owner of the premises; and that Bicknell has
admitted or declared upon different occasions and in the hearing of
different persons, that Stansell at the time of the application informed him, that he wanted them for the purpose of obtaining credit:
and made such declaration or admission in the presence of the
Plaintiff and Hawkins, the solicitor, and the Defendant Taylor; and
insists, that Bicknell having enabled Stansell to practice such fraud
he ought to pay the Plaintiff whatever sum she may lose by those
means. If the purpose imputed by this charge was proved, it would '
be sufficient to maintain the bill.

Next, the admission, that he said he wanted them to enable him
to obtain credit from some person or persons, admits a variety of
constructions. First, if he was about to borrow the money, the
person, to whom he applied, might have consented to lend it; if
satisfied, that the estate was in his family. On the other hand it
might be, that he wanted by means of the title-deeds to obtain credit
by representing himself as owner of the premises. It is necessary
therefore to consider very accurately what it must be taken to mean;
regard being had to what the Defendant says in his answer: who in
this Court has the benefit of his own conscience, and to what it
proved in evidence. Having in his first answer stated,
. [* 188] that he knew nothing of the purpose to make a *mortgage, by his second answer he positively denies, that the
delivery to Stansell was to enable him to obtain a mortgage. The
result of the answer is, that he knew, Stansell was covered with insolvency; which was notorious in] Bristol; and that Stansell suggested to him, that for the purpose of his trade he could obtain a
credit in the way of his trade, if he could show, that he and his wife
had a title to that property; and for that reason Bicknell parted
with the deeds. It is to be remembered, he retained the settlement:
but-I take the fact now to be, that the counterpart was in the hands
of the husband or the wife (1). Therefore he delivered the deeds to
those, who had the settlement; and retained that part, I presume, as
evidence of his claim to have back the title-deeds. It is not the
case therefore of a person delivering them to another; who had not
in his hands, that, which would show the real nature of the title;
but to one, who acting honestly would produce that settlement. It
was to a certain degree trusting to his honesty as to that: but it varies
the state of the case; where a party is to be charged upon the ground
of fraud, or negligence so gross as to be evidence of an intention of
fraud. If Hawkins was living, he might have given an account, that
would have removed all doubt: but it might have been favorable to
the Defendant; and if there is a doubt upon the result, that is a circumstance the Court must deal with as well as they can. I am a

---

(1) It was said at the bar, that upon inquiry the fact turned out to be so.

little struck with the circumstance, first, that in the mortgage of the freehold estate the wife was not made a party with regard to her dower; also, with the peculiarity, that the person lending the money by Hawkins, the attorney, bargains for the possession of the estate; to the intent, that by perception of the rents and profits not only the interest, but the principal also, should be paid; and when the state of the title is recollected, that upon the wife's death the property would go to the children, a strong ground of prudence appears for taking the mortgage in that way.   If so, the Defendant has a right to the benefit of that circumstance; which would naturally have occurred in the dealing of persons, providing for repayment by the application of a partial interest; which proving ineffectual, the money itself would be in danger.   These circumstances must not be forgot.

* Then Taylor, a trustee, entirely without interest, and   [* 189] therefore though a Defendant, examined as a witness, is the only witness, upon whose testimony the decree is to be made. The bill being amended, and this being a case, in which the Court ought to be particularly sure of the ground, on which it decides upon a fact equivocal, or a declaration, more or less according to the recollection of the precise terms by the witness, it is not unfair to observe, that probably before the amendment the Plaintiff must have collected the account of it from Taylor; if he was the only person, from whom she could have got the account; and the bill was then amended, in order to introduce the allegation as to Stansell's representation to Bicknell.   Taylor does not recollect half as much in his answer as in his evidence; and that is a very material circumstance, when the Defendant is to be charged upon this ground, that more credit is to be given to the Defendant's denial than to the assertion of one witness.   It ought to be with reasonable certainty, put in issue by the allegations of the bill.   Taylor's account is not necessarily inconsistent, I do not say it is necessarily consistent, with Bicknell's: but it must be necessarily inconsistent, and more credible than the denial by the answer, before the decree can be made.   He says, the purpose, as represented by Bicknell, was to show the deeds to some person, who would let him have credit in the way of his trade; and in the same conversation they were to be brought back in an hour.   That negatives the very idea, that the estate was to be pledged.   That mode of representing the conversation, instead of opposing, confirms Bicknell's answer.   Upon his answer therefore and Taylor's evidence, there is not that sort of contradiction, that entitles the Plaintiff to a decree against Bicknell on the ground of fraud.   The circumstance of Taylor's examination shows the danger; for Bicknell had no opportunity of answering the farther evidence of express charge.   It is very extraordinary to say, this Court will not act upon the evidence of one witness contradicting the answer, and yet it will act upon that evidence, in order to charge the Defendant in a circumstance, to which he has had no

opportunity of stating himself. That therefore could only be a ground for inquiry.

But, even taking the whole of Taylor's evidence, I still entertain great doubt, whether upon such a transaction a party should be charged personally ; for even upon that it amounts to no [*190] more *than that a trustee delivers the deeds into the hands of a party, who has the settlement. I do not say, it is not negligence ; but it is too dangerous upon such loose evidence to hold, that it is that gross negligence, that amounts to evidence of fraud. The conversation, that the re-payment was to be by the application of two years' rents, does not look like the suggestion of a mortgage ; and it is remarkable, that. there is a provision for re-payment out of the rents. The question therefore will be, whether Taylor's evidence is to be taken, as constituting evidence rising as high as fraud ; so as to support a personal decree against Bicknell; and to the extent of excluding Bicknell from an inquiry, and an opportunity of giving his own account; and upon the principle of this Court I think it cannot.

I conceive, it is now very well settled, that the doctrine of Mr. Justice Buller, that I have just stated, is founded upon error. It would be an idle waste of time to go through all the cases ; which will be found in *Plumb* v. *Fluitt* (1), and admirably well stated by Mr. Fonblanque (2). The doctrine at last is, that the mere circumstance of parting with the title-deeds, unless there is fraud, concealment, or some such purpose, or some concurrence in such purpose, or that gross negligence, that amounts to evidence of a fraudulent intention, is not of itself a sufficient ground to postpone the first mortgagee (*a*). I agree with Chief Justice Eyre, I should have been glad to have found the rule established in the Court the other way. At the same time allowance must be made for the cases put by Mr. Fonblanque of joint-tenants, and tenants in common ; cases of necessary exception : all cannot have the deeds. Therefore, if the rule could be pressed to the extent to which Mr. Justice Buller carried it, those cases must be excepted, in which, from the nature of the title the deeds may be honestly out of the possession. With that exception, such a rule would avoid a great deal of fraud in mortgage titles; upon which this observation arises : that no man can tell, when he is perfectly secure. But there is not such a rule.

Then, as to concealment ; as the case of persons standing by, as witnesses to deeds : if it is to be taken as a fact, that the witness knows the contents of the instrument, to which he is a [*191] witness ; *the engrossment of the mortgage by a person entitled under a prior entail; no recovery having been suffered : all these cases, either of positive representation contrary to the truth, or concealment of what ought to have been represented,

---

(1) 2 Anst. 432; *Barnett* v. *Weston, post,* vol. xii. 130 ; *Harper* v. *Faulder,* 4 Madd. 127.

(2) 1 Fonb. Treat. Eq. 262, note (*n*).

(*a*) 1 Story, Eq. Jur. § 393 ; *Berry* v. *Mutual Ins. Co.* 2 Johns. Ch. 603, 608.

are intelligible; but it is not to be denied, that, where there has been meer negligence, though it may have very mischievous consequences, the Court has not charged the party, unless it has been so gross as to amount to evidence of fraud. The case of the *Thatched House Tavern* was very strong. The mortgagor, desiring to have the deeds, represented to the mortgagee, that he was about to make additional buildings; which would improve his security. The purpose of delivering the deeds was innocent: but it gave the other the complete power of executing the fraudulent purpose. Having got the title-deeds he makes a mortgage; and then contrived to get the lease back from the second mortgagee and restored it to the first. But the negligence did not rest upon that only. The mortgagor applied a second time to the first mortgagee, and under another pretence got the deeds again; which enabled him a second time to cheat third persons: and he made a third mortgage. The circumstance of his parting with them again was strong. Then the question arose upon these mortgages; whether the first should not be postponed to the second and third : but the Court thought, there must be some concurrence in a fraudulent purpose; and the purpose held out disclosed nothing of fraud. If negligence alone was sufficient, it ought to have had the effect in that case: but the Court said, the first mortgagee had done nothing unconscientious; and did not conceive themselves entitled to relieve the subsequent mortgagees. If he had not got back the lease again, perhaps by consequence he would have been postponed; but not upon the ground, that he had parted with it, but upon *Head* v. *Egerton* (1); for it would have been impossible to have taken it from the second mortgagee; and notwithstanding any decree, that may be made, the case is open to these Plaintiffs, if they can make any thing of it upon that.

If then the cases go to this only, that there must be positive fraud or concealment, or negligence so gross as to amount to fraud, is there in this case evidence, resting upon that high degree of probability, upon which the Court, guided by its conscience must * act, that this trustee had a fraudulent purpose :   [* 192] if not, is there negligence so gross as to amount to constructive fraud; as Chief Justice Eyre expresses it in *Plumb* v. *Fluitt*; such evidence of fraud, that he shall not be heard in a Court of justice to say, there was not fraud? I agree, if the intention is fraudulent in any respect, though not pointing exactly to the object accomplished, yet he will be bound. That was Lord Thurlow's doctrine in *Beckett* v. *Cordley* (2); and was the doctrine in much older cases; as, where a bond was given upon a marriage; and the marriage with that person went off, and took place with another: the party could not say, the bond was not intended as to the marriage, which took effect. The Court would say, it was a fraudulent act;

(1) 3 P. Will. 279.
(2) See 1 Glyn & Jam. 243.

and though not precisely that intended by the parties, yet a use was
made of it, to which the delivery of that bond naturally led ; and
therefore he should be bound. If therefore in this case I could be
perfectly satisfied, that the intention was, according to the allegations
in this bill, taken altogether, that he might represent himself as entitled to credit as owner of the premises, and obtain credit in his trade
by representing himself. as owner of the premises, and that Bicknell
acceded to that purpose, so understood, I should be strongly disposed to hold Bicknell liable to the extent, in which Stansell's holding himself out as owner, had involved a third party. But I cannot
say, it is clear, that at the time of the application to Bicknell Stansell had this design. It is not clear, that it did not occur to him,
after he had obtained possession of the deeds; and it is far from
being clear upon the evidence, that Bicknell knew, that such was the
intention ; for the transaction was not unnatural. I cannot expect
them to reason upon the niceties of title. When we consider the
title of the wife, as her separate interest, it is an argument; but it
would be very hard to press it as an evidence of fraud ; and a fraud,
of the nature of which such a trustee must be sensible : so that I
must collect a fraudulent purpose. I hesitate also in giving Taylor
credit for his evidence, carried in the depositions so much farther than
the answer ; and the bill containing no allegation to give Bicknell
the benefit of his answer (1) ; with the conversation, that the money
was to be repaid by two years' rents ; and the circumstance, that in
the security the rents are really devoted to the principal as well as
the interest.   Then, if there is no express declaration or concealment
by the trustee, it results to this ; whether under all the
[* 193]   circumstances and the *answer and evidence together
the mere parting with the deeds for the purpose stated and
on condition to return them in a few hours to a man, having the settlement in his possession, is a circumstance of so gross negligence,
and because it may possibly lead to mischief, that it is conclusive
evidence of fraud. I am very sorry the Court acts upon a rule so
loose and dangerous to property: but if such is the rule, I cannot
under all the circumstances upon this state of the record charge
Bicknell with this sum of 300*l.*

The only remaining question is, whether there ought to be farther
inquiry upon the subject. That may be by dismissing this bill without prejudice to an action ; and probably in that way the Plaintiffs
may meet with more favorable equity than I should give them by directing an issue ; for I should not direct that without giving Bicknell
the same benefit, that might result from the honesty or dishonesty
of his conscience, as he would have in equity. The issue
ought to be upon this question ; whether the deeds were fradulently
delivered to enable Stansell to obtain money of other persons ; for
that general direction would be consistent with the principle I
adopt ; that, if the intention was fraudulent, it is not material, wheth-

_____

(1) *Hall* v. *Maltby*, 6 Pri. 240.

er it was to obtain money of other persons in the way of his trade
by representing himself as owner of the premises, or by a mortgage.
I am not so perfectly satisfied, that Bicknell meant well, as to refuse
that issue, if the Plaintiffs choose to take it; but unless I am satisfied by a Jury, that there was such fraudulent intent, I shall dismiss
the bill without costs; for there is negligence enough for me to say,
he shall not have his costs.

The case of *Arnot* v. *Biscoe* which was relied upon, is very distinguishable. The Defendant declared the title to be in every respect good; a fact very materially discriminating that case from this;
for Lord Hardwicke very properly puts the attorney in the situation
of the vendor himself; and then the Plaintiff's money was advanced
upon the express declaration of that attorney, that the title was
clear. Lord Hardwicke lays down the principle of equity, that,
wherever the buyer is drawn in by misrepresentation or concealment of a material fact or circumstance, so as to be injured thereby,
and that done with intention and fraud, he is entitled to satisfaction
here. In that passage and others Lord Hardwicke
* lays so much stress upon the title to relief here (1), that   [* 194]
I think it very questionable, whether he foresaw the relief,
that has been given upon the principle these cases furnish so liberally at law; and there seems something like a declaration by him,
that if a first mortgagee does not take the title-deeds, he shall be
postponed. That appears to have been the old notion of the Court.

The decree was made against Stansell for the sale of his interest
in the estate, and payment of the deficiency: as against Bicknell
the bill to be dismissed without costs; unless the Plaintiff would
take the issue; in which case Bicknell was to be examined; and if
they chose to have the bill dismissed, it was to be without prejudice to an action.

---

1. A BILL which prays relief merely in the nature of damages, and where the
complaint is properly the subject of an action, will be dismissed, with costs; but
in cases where the law cannot give an equally effectual remedy, Courts of Equity
have a concurrent jurisdiction. *Clifford* v. *Brooke*, 13 Ves. 133; and see, *ante*,
note 2 to *Toulmin* v. *Price*, 5 V. 235, with the farther references there given.

2. Neither coverture nor infancy will excuse fraud: *Savage* v. *Foster*, 9 Mod.
Rep. 37; *Cory* v. *Gertcken*, 2 Mad. 51; *Evroy* v. *Nicholas*, 2 Eq. Ca. Ab. 489:
and any mortgagee who has collusively left the title deeds with the mortgagor,
with a view to enable him to commit frauds on third persons, may be postponed to
incumbrancers who have been so deluded into lending their money; but the mere
circumstance of not taking, or keeping, possession of the title deeds of an estate
upon which he holds a mortgage, is not of itself a sufficient ground for postponing
the first mortgagee. *Barnett* v. *Weston*, 12 Ves. 133; *Bailey* v. *Fermor*, 9 Price,
267; *Peter* v. *Russell*, Gilb. Eq. Rep. 123. And, of course, a prior incumbrancer,
to whose charge on the mortgaged estate possession of the title deeds is not a
necessary incident, cannot be postponed to subsequent incumbrancers because he
is not in possession of the title deeds. *Harper* v. *Faulder*, 4 Mad. 138; *Tourle* v.
Rand, 2 Brown, 652.

3. With respect to the case of *Pasley* v. *Freeman*, 3 T. R. 51, (cited in the prin-

---

(1) *Burrowes* v. *Lock*, *post*, vol. x. 470.

194EVANS *V.* BICKNELL.[1801.

cipal case,) and the difference of judicial opinions as to the propriety of that decision, see *Clifford* v. *Brooke*, 13 Ves. 133.

4. That in cases of wilful and fraudulent misrepresentation Courts of Equity have, at all events, concurrent jurisdiction, see *Burrowes* v. *Locke*, 10 Ves. 475; *De Manneville* v. *Crompton*, 1 Ves. & Bea. 356; *Ex parte Carr*, 3 Ves. & Bea. 111; *Neville* v. *Wilkinson*, 1 Brown, 546; *Mereweather* v. *Shaw*, 2 Cox, 135; *Ainslie* v. *Medlycott*, 9 Ves. 21: and see notes 2 and 3 to that case, *post*.

5. A decree may be made on the testimony of a single witness, if supported by circumstances against the positive denial contained in the defendant's answer. See, *ante*, note 2 to *Mortimer* v. *Orchard*, 2 V. 243.

6. Lord Kenyon, though disinclined to permit ejectments to be maintained upon equitable titles, always admitted that it might be left to the jury to presume a conveyance of the legal estate, (see *Emera* v. *Grocock*, 6 Mad. 58; *Cooke* v. *Soltau*, 2 Sim. & Stu. 163,) though he dissented from those cases in which a legal estate, clearly outstanding, was held to be no impediment to a recovery at law by the party beneficially entitled: *Hillary* v. *Waller*, 12 Ves. 251; *White* v. *Foljambe*, 11 Ves. 351: that class of cases, and the doctrine therein held as to the satisfied terms, (which doctrine Lord Eldon has declared went to shake all titles,) is now got rid of, and it is established, that if a purchaser (or a mortgagee, who is a purchaser *pro tanto*) can get in a satisfied term, he will not be prevented from making use of it to protect himself, by the legal title against prior equities. *Barnett* v. *Weston*, 12 Ves. 135; *Wallwyn* v. *Lee*, 9 Ves. 31. To give him this advantage, however, he must (in all cases except one, to be presently noticed) have a clear conscience, and as good a right as any other claimant: *Bond* v. *Hopkins*, 1 Sch. & Lef. 430; and he cannot protect himself, by a *satisfied* term, against a prior incumbrancer, unless the term be in some sense got in—either by an assignment to his use, or by making the trustee of the term a party to the instrument of conveyance to himself, or at least, by taking possession of the deed creating the term. It is also essential that, when he advanced his money, he should not have had notice of any mesne incumbrance or charge, (with one exception, resting on no principle, but become inveterate in practice,) to the prejudice of a dowress, whose right of dower a purchaser, with full notice thereof, may exclude, by buying in an outstanding term. *Maundrell* v. *Maundrell*, 10 Ves. 260, 271; *Wynn* v. *Williams*, 5 Ves. 134. The doctrine deduced from Lord Hardwicke's judgment in *Willoughby* v. *Willoughby*, 1 T. R. 772, and already alluded to, namely, that a *puisne* incumbrancer may protect himself by bare possession of the deed creating an outstanding term, seems to have been much disliked, but not expressly repudiated, by Lord Eldon: see *Maundrell* v. *Maundrell, ubi supra; Ex parte Knott*, 11 Ves. 613. It appears, however, to be pretty plainly intimated by all the cases just cited, (by that before Lord Hardwicke as well as those before Lord Eldon,) that bare possession of the deed creating a term will not entitle an incumbrancer to call for an assignment of the term, when another incumbrancer has a better equity to call for such assignment; and where the legal estate is not to be considered as actually got in, and none of the claimants have any thing more than an equity to insist on, a purchaser without notice will never be annoyed in Equity when he has a better right to call for the legal estate than another who holds an incumbrance prior to his title; (*Wilks* v. *Boddington*, 2 Vern. 599; *Medlicott* v. *O'Donnel*, 1 Ball & Bea. 171; *Cholmondeley* v. *Clinton*, 2 Jac. & Walk. 159;) for, in such cases, an exception must be made to the general rule that, *qui prior est tempore, portior est jure: Earl of Pomfret* v. *Lord Windsor*, 2 Ves. Sen. 466: the distinction, as to the application of this maxim, arises out of the different rights in estates which parties may have in law and in equity in this country, where the two branches of jurisdiction are administered in different Courts: *Wortley* v. *Birkhead*, 2 Ves. Sen. 574: even an actual assignment of the legal estate, if it be not got in before a decree is made, will not avail the party to whom such assignment has been made, but he must come in under the decree according to the date of his own incumbrance. *Earl of Bristol* v. *Hungerford*, 2 Vern. 525.

TOWNLEY *v.* BEDWELL.

[1801, July 6.]

Trust of real and personal estate by will, for the purpose of establishing a perpetual Botanical Garden, declared void upon the expression of the testator, that he trusted it would be a public benefit.

Benjamin Robertson by his will, dated the first of September, 1800, gave to Mary Smalt an annuity of 30*l.*; to.her daughter Charlotte Smalt 200*l.* a-year; to his sister Esther Moore and to a sister-in-law 20*l.* a-year each; and to each of the children of his deceased sister Mary Bedwell a legacy of 100*l.*; not to be vested before the age of twenty-one. He devised to Charlotte Smalt the house he dwelt in at Stockwell with the kitchen-garden and appurtenances, for her life; with the household furniture, beds, linen, &c. and other articles, belonging to the house; to be used and enjoyed by her for life, or as long as she lives in the house; and after some other legacies and annuities he proceeded in the following manner:

"And whereas I have after many years' labor, and at a very great expense, raised a freehold botanic garden at Stockwell aforesaid, with several buildings for the purpose of containing a very large collection of plants and other things, and not having any family or very near relations (other than those before mentioned) I am desirous of devising and bequeathing all my freehold estates and the reversion of my said house *and kitchen garden at Stock-   [* 195] well with the appurtenances thereunto belonging, herein-before devised to Charlotte Smalt for life, or so long as she shall think fit to reside in the said premises; and all the residue of my stock, funds, personal estate, and other property, unto trustees, to maintain and improve the said collection of plants and other things either in my new botanic garden at Stockwell, or in such other garden as they shall think proper, as far as the property I mean to devise to the said trustees will admit of, for ever, and under however the inspection of my executors herein named during their lives and the life of the survivor of them; and I also wish (if occasion require and the property devised will admit of it) that my said botanic garden may be enlarged (by taking in a part of my ground adjoining) and the collection of plants increased, in such a manner as my trustees shall think proper, and find convenient: as I trust it will be a public benefit: and do wish and desire, that my present botanic garden, with any enlargement thereof, or any other botanic garden to be purchased or formed and established under and by virtue of this my will by my trustees (wheresoever situated) should be called ' Stockwell Botanic Garden, founded by Benjamin Robertson, Esquire;' and an inscription accordingly placed and preserved over the principal gate or door of such garden for the time being; now for the purpose of carrying this my intention into execution I do give, devise, and bequeath, my said bo-

tanic garden at Stockwell, and all other my lands and grounds near
or adjoining thereto, and the reversion of my house and kitchen garden at Stockwell, with the appurtenances after the death of Charlotte Smalt, or when and so soon as she shall cease to reside in the
said premises, and all other my real estates whatsoever and wheresoever situated, and all the rest, residue, and remainder of my money
in the public funds, and of all other my personal estate and effects
of whatsoever nature or kind the same is or may be at the time of
my decease, and wheresoever the same is or may be, and every part
and parcel thereof, with their and every of their rights, members,
and appurtenants (the botanic books before mentioned al-
[* 196]   ways to * accompany and belong to the botanic garden for
the time being) unto Edward William Townley, one of my
executors, Robert Barclay, of Clapham, Esquire, Adrian Hardy Ha-
worth, of Chelsea, Esquire, William Acton, of Kew, Esquire, Alexander M'Leay, Secretary to the Linnean Society, Mr. Thomas Goode,
one of my executors, and Alexander Malcolm, of Stockwell, nursery-
man, and their heirs, executors, administrators, and assigns, according to the respective natures of the several and respective estates by
me hereby given, devised, and bequeathed, to them for ever ; (the
real estates not to be unalienable but saleable and assignable at the
will and with the consent of all my trustees for the time being),
upon trust, that they do and shall with the produce and profits thereof keep, preserve, and for ever hereafter maintain and support, my
botanic garden at Stockwell aforesaid, or some other garden to be
purchased, formed, and established, under and by virtue of this my
will (no such garden to be unalienable but saleable and assignable
in manner and form aforesaid and as herein expressed) at the discretion of all and not less than all of my trustees for the time being;
and it is my will, and I recommend to my trustees for the time being
to consult with and call in my executors herein named, during their
lives in and about the management and keeping up the said garden,
or any other garden, all (but not less or fewer in number than all)
my trustees for the time being may think fit to purchase, form, and
establish, under and by virtue of this my will, and all things apper-
taining to such garden for the time being.   But my will and desire
is, that, if any new garden should be purchased, formed, and established, the same should be freehold ; and be situated (if possible) at
Stockwell, or as near thereto as can be ; and I direct, that such garden for the time being shall for ever hereafter be called and known
by the name of 'Stockwell Botanic Garden founded by Benjamin
Robertson, Esquire ; ' and that such inscription be put up, and preserved, as aforesaid ; and I will and direct, that my trustees for the
time being shall each be answerable for his own acts only and not
one for another ; and they shall not be liable (otherwise than as
hereafter mentioned) to account for any surplus or residue of the
rents, interest, income, or produce of my estate and effects, which
may at any time accrue or happen, after answering the purposes
aforesaid, to any person whomsoever ; it being my express wish

and desire, that such garden for the time being may be from time to time kept up and improved and extended in as ample a manner as the income of my estate will admit of; and my will and mind is, that it shall and may at all times hereafter be lawful to and for my trustees for the time being to sell and dispose of my present botanic garden, with the buildings and appurtenances thereto belonging, whenever all and not fewer than all of them shall think fit, for the best price, that can be procured and got for the same; and with the money to arise from the sale thereof to purchase other freehold ground and buildings, or erect buildings, and form and establish another botanic garden, premises, and appurtenances, of equal value at least with the premises sold: the same to be situated in the county of Surrey, and as near to Stockwell as may be; and it shall in like manner be lawful for all but not less or fewer in number than all my trustees for the time being to sell the botanic garden and buildings with the appurtenances for the time being, and make the like purchase, and form and establish such other freehold botanic garden with buildings and appurtenances of equal value in manner and form aforesaid, in or as near to Stockwell as may be: And it is my will, that my trustees for the time being (if they should be all desirous of selling my present botanic garden) do before the sale remove as many of the plants and other things growing and being therein as they conveniently can; and re-plant and place the same in the new purchased ground, garden, buildings and premises, and keep possession of my present garden until removal of such plants and other things; and so *toties quoties*, whenever they shall sell one garden, and purchase, form and establish, another; and I will and desire, that whenever any sale is in contemplation the trustees for the time being, if less than seven in number, do before entering into any contract for sale fill up the number of trustees to the number of seven in manner herein after mentioned."

The testator then gave directions for keeping up the number of trustees by the appointment of the majority upon death or declining to act. The testator died upon the 7th of December, 1800. The bill was filed by the executors against the next of kin according to the Statute; viz. Esther Moore, the only surviving sister of the testator, the son and three daughters of his sister Mary Bedwell, who died in his life, and against the other trustees and the * Attorney General, for the purpose of having the will es- [* 198] tablished, and the trusts carried into execution.

The Defendants Esther Moore and John Bedwell, the infant nephew of the testator, claimed the real estate, either upon the ground, that the devise was void, or, if not, as a resulting trust; no use being declared for any one. They also claimed the personal estate directed to be laid out in land. The real estate produced a rent of 1200*l.* a-year; and the personal property consisted of above 23,000*l.*

Lord CHANCELLOR [ELDON] asked, for whose benefit all this was to be.

The *Solicitor General* [Mr. *Spencer Perceval*] and Mr. *Romilly,*

BY a settlement executed in 1743, previous to the marriage of Abraham Weekes, certain fee-farm rents, of which he was seised in tail, were settled to the use of himself for life; remainder to trustees to preserve contingent remainders; remainder to his intended wife for life; remainder for a term of years for raising portions for younger children; remainder to his first and other sons in tail male; remainder to trustees for another term, for raising portions for daughters in failure of issue male; remainder to the heirs and assigns of Abraham Weekes.

In 1749 a recovery was suffered; but no uses were declared (1).

Abraham Weekes by his will, dated the 24th of May, 1750, directed, that his debts and funeral expenses should be first paid; and charged all his estates in possession, reversion, remainder or expectancy, with the payment thereof; and subject thereto he devised all his real estates to his wife for life; and after her death he devised a part of his estate, called Canefield, to his sister Elizabeth Weekes for life; and after her death he devised such estate, and devised the rest of his real estate immediately after the death of his wife, to his sister Mellicent Crop and to her heirs for ever; and he directed, that, as soon after his death as conveniently might be, [* 200] * part of his real estate, except the said part, called Canefield, should be sold for payment of all his debts; and that his wife, and his sister Crop and her husband, and all other proper parties, should join in the sale.

In November 1750 the testator borrowed the sum of 5500*l.* of Mellicent Neate upon mortgage of part of his real estate by indentures, executed on the 16th of November, for 1000 years; and by indentures of lease and release, dated the 15th and 16th of November, 1750, for the farther and better securing the re-payment of the said sum of 5500*l.* with interest, and for barring all estates tail and all reversions and remainders thereupon expectant in said fee-farm rents, and for limiting and assuring the same for such uses, upon such trusts, and to and for such intents and purposes, as herein after expressed concerning the same, Abraham Weekes and his wife conveyed the fee-farm rents to Charles Lawrence, his heirs and assigns, to hold to him, his heirs and assigns, to the intent that a recovery might be suffered; and it was declared, that such recovery should enure to Mellicent Neate for the term of 1000 years, subject to the proviso of redemption, &c.; and from and after the determination of the term, to the use of Abraham Weekes and his assigns for life, without impeachment of waste; remainder to Frances, his wife, and her assigns for life: remainder to Abraham Weekes, his heirs and assigns.

---

with *Williams* v. *Owens*, 2 V. 595. In the present case the Master of the Rolls seems to labor hard to vindicate his judgment in *Williams* v. *Owens*.

Courts of Equity will not encourage stale demands. See *ante*, note (a), 2 V. 13.

(1) The pleadings represented, that the use was declared to Weekes in fee. See that and other errors and omissions in this cause, as it was heard at the Rolls, corrected and supplied upon the appeal, *post*, vol. viii. 106.

Some proceedings were had towards suffering a recovery : but it was never completed.   In May 1755 the testator died, without issue ; leaving three sisters, his co-heiresses at law : Elizabeth Weekes, Mellicent Crop, and Mary Harmood.   His widow married James O'Donnell ; and a bill was filed by them ; under which the will was established ; part of the real estates sold ; and the debts, including the mortgage to Mellicent Neate, paid.   In June 1764 Mellicent Crop died ; and Mrs. O'Donnell in December following.

This bill was filed in April 1796 by the heirs at law of Mary Harmood ; who was also dead ; praying an account from the heirs of Mellicent Crop and the representatives of Elizabeth * Weekes, and a conveyance of one third from the heirs   [* 201] of Lawrence, the trustee, on the ground, that the will was revoked.

The Defendants by their answers insisted, that the will was not revoked ; relying also on the laches of the Plaintiffs.   Letters from the principal Defendant, dated in 1786, and 1787, were produced ; suggesting, that he had heard, the Plaintiffs had some pretension ; desiring them to put it in a course of discussion ; and proposing to leave a proportion of the rents, until it should be settled ; and it was admitted by the answers, that a claim was at different times set up ; but never asserted by any suit.

The questions upon the pleadings were 1st, whether the devise was revoked : 2dly, as to the effect of the length of time.   A third question was suggested by the Court ; whether, supposing the devise revoked, the fee-farm rents descending to the heir at law would not be primarily applicable to the debts, as descended estates, before estates devised (1).

Mr. *Cox* and Mr. *Fonblanque,* for the Plaintiffs.—The principal question is, whether the settlement subsequent to the will disposing of the fee-farm rents, though not perfected, had not the effect of revoking the devise.   Though no Recovery was suffered at the execution of the settlement of 1743, it is rightly insisted, that the recovery suffered in 1749, the uses of which were declared to Abraham Weekes in fee (2), enured to the uses of the settlement.

The question of revocation has been discussed so much at length within the last few years (3), that it is unnecessary to go through all

(1) See Mr. Cox's note, 3 P. Will. 294 ; *ante, Manning* v. *Spooner,* vol. iii. 114, and the notes, 117, 119.
(2) This is a mistake : see *ante,* 199, and the note.
(3) *Ante, Brydges* v. *The Duchess of Chandos,* vol. ii. 417 ; iii. 761 ; *Williams* v. *Owens,* ii. 595 ; *Cave* v. *Holford, Goodtitle* v. *Otway,* ii. 604, note ; iii. 650 ; iv. 850 ; 1 Bos. & Pul. 576 ; 7 Term Rep. B. R. 399 ; *Earl Temple* v. *The Duchess of Chandos,* iii. 685 ; *Baxter* v. *Dyer,* v. 656 ; *Knollys* v. *Alcock,* v. 648 ; *post,* vii. 558 ; *Attorney General* v. *Vigor,* viii. 256 ; *Reid* v. *Shergold,* x. 370 ; *Charman* v. *Charman,* xiv. 580 ; *Vawser* v. *Jeffrey,* xvi. 519 ; xvii. 133, 134 ; *Rawlins* v. *Burges,* 2 Ves. & Bea. 382.
As to revocation by marriage and the birth of a child, see *ante, Gibbons* v. *Caunt,* vol. iv. 480, and the note, 848 ; and *Kenebel* v. *Scrafton,* stated, vol. v. 663 ; 2 East, 530 ; and for the distinction upon a devise of real estate to the children of a former marriage, and the clashing decisions in the Ecclesiastical Court as to personal estate, *Sheath* v. *York,* 1 Ves. & Bea. 390.

the cases. The whole of the law upon this subject originates in the principle laid down by Lord Hardwicke in *Sparrow* v.

[* 202]   *Hardcastle* (1), and afterwards, more at length, in that very elaborate judgment of the Lord Chancellor in *Brydges* v. *The Duchess of Chandos*; that the devisor must not only have the estate at the conception of the will, but it must continue in him: otherwise there is a revocation. That is the word constantly used: but "ademption" is the more proper expression: the devisor not having the estate in him any longer for the will to operate upon. This rule is universal. The cases spoken of as exceptions are improperly called so. They fall in with the rule, and the principle, upon which it is established. The rule applies equally to equitable and real estates. In *Brydges* v. *The Duchess of Chandos* the Lord Chancellor takes great pains to prevent being misunderstood; and his opinion is clear; that there is no case in equity of revocation as to equitable estates, that would not upon legal principles be a revocation; and your Honor in the subsequent case (2) takes notice of that. The intention is not material. It proceeds upon the rule of law. Nothing shows that more clearly than the case of the Recovery suffered on purpose to substantiate the will: but the effect is to take back a new estate. The act of a devisor seised in fee conveying and taking back an estate in fee was long ago held a revocation. It is not material, that he takes back the same quantity of interest. It must be the same estate he had in him at the execution of the will. Nor, as the Lord Chancellor observes in the same case, is the particular purpose of any consequence; and he puts the instance of *Lord Lincoln's Case* (3), than which nothing more particular could be.

The cases of mortgages and charges for payment of debts do not impeach the rule; and can hardly be considered as exceptions. A mortgage here is a mere charge; and is considered as personal estate of the mortgagee. The estate therefore is that of the mortgagor. This doctrine applies, notwithstanding the estate passes at law: equity considering a mortgage in that point of view, the estate is still in the mortgagor, subject only to the mortgage; never having been parted with; but continuing in him unaltered, except only in respect of that mortgage.

[* 203]   * Another class of cases is, where the devisor having only an equitable estate in him at the date of the will devises that; and then takes the legal estate; which has been determined to be no revocation (4). That is not inconsistent with the general rule. The equitable estate devised is not destroyed; though for some purposes it may be considered as a merger (5). The devisor has it in him; and therefore it is within the rule, which may be

(1) 3 Atk. 798; Amb. 224; Lord Ashburton's note, 7 Term Rep. 416.
(2) *Williams* v. *Owens, ante,* vol. ii. 595.
(3) 1 Eq. Ca. Ab. 411; Show. P. C. 154.
(4) *Watts* v. *Fullarton*; cited Dougl. 691; *ante,* vol. ii. 602.
(5) *Philips* v. *Brydges, ante,* vol. iii. 120.

stated generally: that the act always operates a revocation, where the devisor has not the same estate in him, that he had at the time he made his will.   The deed in this case was made with a view to a Recovery; which in fact was never suffered: but it is decided, that a deed for the purpose of making a tenant to the *Præcipe* is a revocation.   As far as the intention can be material, the devisor had more in view by this deed than merely making a security.   That was to be done only by the term of 1000 years: but beyond that these fee-farm rents are limited and assured to the devisor for life; then to his wife for life; then to him, his heirs and assigns.   If there had been no mortgage, and the devisor had made such a conveyance, can it be doubted, that it would be a revocation?   How could it be otherwise, if that would be the effect, as it certainly would, of a conveyance by a devisor, seised in fee, taking back an estate in fee, or a fine levied by tenant in tail, having the reversion in fee, the uses of which are declared to him in fee?   This case has no difference but this term to make a security.   If he had confined himself to that purpose, it would be very different: but he has gone much farther.   The object was, subject to that term, to take back a new estate; which must have the effect of a revocation.   It is not the estate, that was in him, when he made his will; and that is all, that is necessary for this purpose.   It is only necessary to show the inconsistency of the two instruments.   It is clearly not a question of intention; but, in the emphatical language of the Civil Law, *presumptio,* or rather, *conclusio juris et de jure;* for there can be no averment against it.   The question is only, whether that seisin, which the testator had, was or was not broken in upon by the subsequent indentures.   If the purpose had stopped at providing for the debt, that even at law would have been a revocation.   If he had made a mortgage in fee, this Court would have considered the seisin to continue, certainly * not upon any rule of its   [* 204] own, but following legal principles; and the Court would have found a strong authority for that in the Statute of Wills (1); the language of which is not "seised," but "having."   Observe the manner, in which the Lord Chancellor in *Brydges* v. *The Duchess of Chandos* felt himself obliged to treat the subsequent settlement, made in pursuance of the articles, at least in part, with every disposition to support the will.   In *Williams* v. *Owens* your Honor founded your judgment, that the will was not revoked, very much upon the authority of that case.   If the conveyance had been merely a fulfilment of the articles, clothing the equitable interest with the legal estate, the seisin necessary for the purpose of the will could not have been said to be disturbed.   The Lord Chancellor found himself under the necessity of declaring the rule.

The case of partition certainly is the most doubtful, and the most difficult, to be reconciled with the seisin; but the Lord Chancellor in *Brydges* v. *The Duchess of Chandos* adopted the rule established

---

(1) 32 Hen. VIII. c. 1; 34 Hen. VIII. c. 5.

in *Tickner* v. *Tickner*, and followed by Lord Hardwicke ; that, where the object of the deed went farther than a mere partition, and beyond dividing it was even the mere act of conveying the estate to such uses as the party should appoint, it was a revocation (1) ; and your Honor's reasoning in *Williams* v. *Owens* is the same.   In *Cave* v. *Holford* (2) the principles are fully recognised; and the difference of opinion arose only upon the application of the principles and authorities to that case.   Lord Chief Justice Eyre upon the case of partition felt himself pressed with the same difficulty, that had embarrassed Lord Hardwicke and Lord Loughborough.   The conclusion is, that wherever there is an *ultra* purpose, that makes a revocation; though perhaps directly against the avowed intention.

But upon this occasion all this is unnecessary ; for it is impossible, that these two instruments can be reconciled.   It will be said, the reversion is reserved ; and the Will can operate upon that: [* 205]   * but all the authorities are against that.   Among Mr. Melmoth's collection of manuscripts is a case of *James'* v. *Philips*, the 20th of April 1733.   A. made his will ; and devised to the Plaintiff.   Afterwards the devisor marries; and settles this interest, which he had devised, to the use of himself for life, then to his wife for life ; remainder to the issue of the marriage: remainder to his own right heirs: and dies without issue.   The Plaintiff insisted, the Will was not revoked ; and might operate upon the reversion in fee ; but the Master of the Rolls would not suffer it to be spoken to; and said, the *Earl of Lincoln's Case* was much stronger.

No case is more favorable than that special purpose to provide for the issue of the marriage.

As to the objection from the length of time, that also has been often before your Honor ; and the result of the authorities is, that length of time can operate only in three ways : either by analogy to some legal bar, established by positive law : or, 2dly, where it affords a presumption, that something has been done ; which, if done, would *per se* be a bar to the demand ; or, 3dly, where the claim is of such a nature, that after great length of time such inconvenience would arise, that the Court would not enforce it (3).   The principal question in *Smith* v. *Clay* (4) belongs to the first of these heads: though certainly Lord Camden went rather beside the question upon the point of laches.   In *Pickering* v. *Lord Stamford* (5) your Honor after great consideration laid down, that length of time *per se* is no bar to a claim in this Court.   The result of that case, *Hercy* v. *Dinwoody* (6), and the others of that class, is, that it can have effect only in the above three cases.   The legislative provisions and the pre-

---

(1) See also *Kenyon* v. *Sutton*, cited *ante*, vol. ii. 601 ; and *Nott* v. *Shirley*, stated *ante*, ii. 604, in the note to *Williams* v. *Owens*.
(2) *Ante*, vol. ii. 604, *n.*; iii. 650; iv. 850; 1 Bos. & Pul. 576; 7 Term Rep. B. R. 399.
(3) *Pearson* v. *Belchier*, *ante*, vol. iv. 627 ; *Fletcher* v. *Tollet*, v. 3.
(4) Amb. 645; 3 Bro. C. C. 639, in a note to *Lord Deloraine* v. *Browne*.
(5) *Ante*, vol. ii. 272, 581 ; iii. 332, 492.
(6) *Ante*, vol. ii. 87. See the note, 15.

sumptions of Courts of Justice proceed upon the same principle, an anxiety to quiet rights and preserve evidence. In the former the effect is a bar, but not in the latter. The rule " *Stabit prcsumptio, donec probeter in contrarium,*" is a wise rule, and ought not to be strained too far. The Plaintiffs are therefore entitled to the account. There is no analogy to any legal bar. If * we [* 206] are to recur to legal proceedings, we must recur to the remedy by assize ; in which the rents and profits will be the measure of the damages under the statute of Gloucester (1). The letters show, this claim was made many years ago; and continued down to 1787. They must have been aware, that it was a serious claim. Several eminent opinions were taken. There is no such inconvenience therefore as in *Hercy* v. *Dinwoody*, and the other cases.

With respect to the difficulty thrown out by the Court, a mere charge upon a particular estate will not exempt the descended estate : but it is as clearly established by *Donne* v. *Lewis* (2), that, where a real fund is created expressly for the purpose of discharging the debts, and the other part of the estate is permitted to descend, the fund created for that purpose must be primarily applied. That case underwent great consideration; as it was thought to break in upon *Galton* v. *Hancock* (3) ; and Lord Thurlow did not pronounce that decree lightly. It was made upon the inconsistency between *Powis* v. *Corbet* (4) and *Galton* v. *Hancock*. Here this part is not made a fund merely auxiliary to the personal estate ; not that it would extend to exempt the personal estate (5), but it would be the next fund in the order after that.

Mr. *Lloyd*, Mr. *Richards*, Mr. *Thomson*, and Mr. *E. Morris*, for the Defendants.—This is not a favorable case for the Plaintiffs. If they succeed, they get an estate by mere accident ; guilty also of uncommon laches. Upon the last point there could be no decision without an inquiry: but it shows the extreme difficulty arising from bringing forward these stale demands. This devisor thought, no part of his estate would descend to his heir.

The question now before the Court is, what was the transaction between these parties in 1750 : whether any thing more in substance than to make a security for a sum of money to Mrs. Neate ; for it must be admitted, that if these instruments do substantially go beyond that, and extend to vary their interests, it is impossible * upon the late cases to dispute what is now become [* 207] law certainly. The devisor certainly must have the same quantity of dominion and the same mode of disposition. That must be admitted upon *Tickner* v. *Tickner* and *Kenyon* v. *Sutton ;* the latter decided by your Honor with great reluctance on account merely

(1) 6 Edw. I. c. 1.
(2) 2 Bro. C. C. 257.
(3) 2 Atk. 424.
(4) 3 Atk. 556, stated from the Register's Book, *ante*, vol. iii. 116, in a note to *Manning* v. *Spooner.*
(5) See *Hartley* v. *Hurle, ante*, vol. v. 540, and the references.

of the introduction of the power of appointment. If it can be shown, that no estate was displaced, but the object was merely to let in the incumbrance, it is within the exception. We are to look to the intention. Admitting, many of the cases have nothing to do with the intention, many depend upon the intention. Instances of the latter species are the case of the bargain and sale without enrolment, the grant of a reversion without attornment, &c. In all those cases though the act is void, there is a revocation upon the intention. After all, these reasons are perhaps more nice than intelligible, and more technical than sensible : but such is the rule. Here there is no dominion ; and no exercise of dominion, otherwise than the devisor had it before. This is precisely within the principle of the cases of revocation *pro tanto.* No intention appears, and the instruments have no operation beyond letting in that mortgage ; which over-rides all the limitations. Suppose the deed of 1750, instead of those three limitations to the devisor for life, then to his wife, with remainder to him, his heirs and assigns, had copied the uses of the deed of 1743 exactly : that would clearly not have been a revocation ; being only a reservation of the equity of redemption in the very same manner, in which it would have resulted, if there had been no declaration of uses. So, if it had merely expressed the use to him and her for their lives, and said nothing as to the reversion, that would not have been a revocation ; for the equity of redemption would have resulted exactly in the same manner. It is the same, whether it results, or is reserved ; and the reason is, it does not carry the estate farther than it before extended. Why then should the omission of the estate to the first and other sons and the term for portions make it a revocation ? There is no instance of an omission producing that effect. All the cases are, where the deed has gone farther ; and it must be admitted, that, if the deed went any farther, or if the devisor's interest was different in any respect from what it was before, it would be a revocation. The object of this deed being confined to [*208]   making a security distinguishes this * case from *Lord Lincoln's Case* and all the rest. There was no estate tail, to make a recovery necessary. They did not copy the limitations of the former deed, or introduce a provision for children, because it was probable, there would not be any children. The devisor was supposed to be tenant in tail ; and that occasioned the recovery. These deeds are founded wholly in mistake ; but the single object, to secure this debt, is clear. There is no deed, declaring the uses of a recovery, that does not contain the general words, " for limiting and assuring," &c.; which are relied upon. All beyond the mortgage operates nothing. Though the three excepted cases are commonly said to be mortgages, conveyances for payment of debts, and partition, yet there are other cases ; as, if the deed had been obtained by fraud ; or executed under a mistake, a misapprehension of the devisor's rights, upon a consideration, that did not exist, under a misrepresentation, appearing upon the face of the deed. In those cases the Court would relieve against the deed : and upon the same principle would not hold it a revocation. Another consideration is whether, as no recovery ever was suffered, any of these uses ever sprang. It is doubtful even, whether the legal estate is in Lawrence, the trustee. There is however some difficulty in maintaining that: but clearly none of the uses arose; and he took as a trustee for the devisor. Then he had only the estate under the settlement, accompanied with the reversion in fee. No uses arose therefore, that could produce any effect. In *Luther* v. *Kidby* (1), the partition being effected by deed and fine, the estate could not continue to be in the testator to the time of his death. The form of the conveyance in that case did produce an alteration in the seisin; and yet the suspension of the seisin did not produce a revocation. The material distinction between that case and *Tickner* v. *Tickner* (2) is the introduction of the power of appointment in the latter. That will must have been revoked upon a solid ground, not a technical form. The devise was to the wife and her heirs: in the deed the limitation was to the husband in fee: therefore there was a manifest inconsistency between the will and the deed; and a revocation upon other grounds than that set up in *Luther* v. *Kidby.* The form must be considered immaterial. In construction of law * there can   [* 209] be no difference between a partition by deed and fine and a partition by writ. So in this case there is nothing but the particular form of the conveyance; and no substantial alteration. The devisor after the execution of the deed was seised as to the substantial interest of precisely the same estate, The remainder to the wife is no new limitation; but existed antecedently. Whether it was introduced into the deed, or not, was immaterial. As far as any interest was conferred upon her, she derived that interest, not under this deed, but under the marriage settlement. As the effect of imperfect, inoperative, conveyances for this purpose, all the Judges, from the old case in Roll. (3) to *Cave* v. *Holford,* state, that the reason is, that no other intention could be presumed under which the party could have made that conveyance. Then it becomes a question of intention. The case has been put of a recovery suffered by tenant in tail with the reversion in fee in him for the purpose of authenticating his Will. That must proceed upon this ground; that the effect is a most important alteration in the estate. The estates of the devisor previous and subsequent to the recovery are very different. The former is subject to all the incumbrances of his ancestors: the latter is a new purchase, discharged of all those incumbrances. If the estate is in its nature altered, the previous will cannot operate upon it. If the intention is to make a security to the mortgagee, the form of the conveyance is nothing. What other intention can be presumed in this instance? This deed considered with that view is valid and effectual: with a view to barring estates tail, remainders and reversions, it is futile and nugatory.

(1) 3 P. Will. 170, n.; 2 Eq. Ca. Ab. 774; 8 Vin. 148.
(2) Stated in *Parsons* v. *Freeman,* 3 Atk. 741; Amb. 116; 1 Wils. 308.
(3) 1 Roll. Ab. 616.

Supposing this deed a revocation, the second point, upon the length of time, is not now to be determined: but the parties ought to be sent to law. It would be very unjust to decide that question, when the Defendants have entered into no case, have stated no circumstances; and it does not appear, whether any thing has been done, amounting to an actual ouster. Certainly the possession of one tenant in common is *prima facie* the possession of both; but not, if an actual ouster can be made out. The only evidence consists of these letters; which certainly amount to a knowledge of the claim of the others, and a wish, that it should be as-
[* 210]   serted. But how can that bind the parties entitled to * the inheritance? There is nothing else to mark any thing like a claim made. The answers to these letters were merely in general terms, acknowledging the receipt of them. A long period had elapsed antecedent to the date of these letters, from 1764 to 1786, respecting which there is not the least evidence of any assertion of the Plaintiff's claim. The letters amount to nothing more than a knowledge, that there was such a claim in the minds of the Plaintiffs; but are nothing like an acknowledgment of the justice of that claim; inviting them to have their claim legally discussed and decided: not by any means acquiescing in it. It was not competent to the author of them, nor did he intend to bind the inheritance. It would be very improper to get rid of the objection from the length of time by any loose communication. Some step ought to have been taken for the purpose of agitating the question. Is it just for the Court to interpose to devest these rents, in the enjoyment of which the Defendants and their ancestors have been since 1764 without one application? They have been counting upon this property as their own. The consequence of that in forming connections in life is very material; and, without proving settlements, &c. shows the fallacy of saying, there is no injury. Though length of time alone is not a bar in this Court, as at law, yet there is a strict analogy in this Court to the Statute of Limitations; the principles of which were in truth derived out of this Court, and only adopted in Courts of Law. In cases of debt or legacy the admission of the party is very decisive evidence; but that is upon this ground; that being matter of privity between the parties, the remedy is barred only by the presumption of payment. In this case, upon the assertion of a legal claim, no such presumption can be raised. The only question then is, whether upon grounds of public policy the Court will allow a party at this distance of time to set up a claim, in which he had not sufficient confidence to make it the subject of inquiry in a Court of Justice. It would shake the security of all the property of the country. Possession for twenty years by the mortgagee would have barred the mortgagor. It is therefore only by the act of the Defendants that there is any subject of claim. The decree, that was made in this cause, is decisive evidence, that the attention of the parties was drawn to this will at that time: but this point of revocation did not enter into the imagination

of any one concerned for the family. The Defendants therefore are entitled to say, that there was some good reason, inducing them not to dispute this will then; and therefore they should be precluded from raising the question now. Republication may be presumed. Lord Kenyon has directed a surrender to be presumed within twenty years. Why should not these Defendants have the benefit of any legal defence they may have? Upon a pure legal question, where· there is any probability, that there may be a legal defence, the Court will not determine it. Therefore, if the Court is with the Plaintiffs upon the point of revocation, the trustee Lawrence ought to be directed to convey to the uses of the deed, generally; in order that the Defendants may not be deprived of any defence they may have at law from the statute of limitations, or otherwise.

Upon the third point, supposing the rents in question were subject to the payment of the debts, or liable to contribution, in consequence of the silence of these parties it may be impossible to have justice done on that account. *Donne* v. *Lewis* is nothing like this case. That was a purchase subsequent to the will, and a question between volunteers. Here an estate, that ought to be charged in proportion at least, has slipped out of the will by accident. The consequence of the laches of the Plaintiffs is, that the Defendants are without the means of enforcing their right in this respect with the least prospect of justice.

Reply.—The principle as to revocation is not to be disputed; that the intention is of no consequence: if a plain unequivocal act has been done, taking out of the devisor the estate he had in him, the will cannot operate, notwithstanding an express declaration, that what he was about was not intended to be a revocation; and the reason is, that he had not in him at his death the estate he meant to devise. Creating a security for the mortgage upon these fee-farm rents by a term, having on the same day executed another deed, merely creating a term for the same purpose upon another part of his estate, does he stop there as to these fee-farm rents? No; he declares other estates beyond that, and quite beside that purpose. If he has done any thing beyond that, if he has taken a new estate, his intention is of no consequence. What is meant by saying, the equity of redemption was reserved? A mortgage in fee is at law a conveyance upon condition. Nothing * is   [*212] reserved. The equity of redemption is the creature of this Court. The Plaintiff's case rests upon the distinction of going beyond the purpose of making a security. In *Lord Lincoln's Case* it was not attempted to argue, that if he had the legal estate in him, it would not have been a revocation: but it was contended, thàt there was no revocation; as, having made a previous mortgage he had only the equitable estate. It was however decided otherwise. The deed had its effect; conveying the equitable estate ;· that, which he had in him. No purpose could be more particular. How does that apply to this case? This conveyance was for the purpose of suffering a recovery; which never was suffered. They must go farther, beyond the conveyance to Lawrence, and look to the purpose. It was said, the deed was executed under a mistake; and therefore ought not to operate. There is no authority, that, if a will is revoked at law by a misapprehension of the devisor, this Court would set it up as between volunteers, or rectify it for the devisee against the heir at law, the favorite of the Court. If the estates are the same in point of interest and quantity of estate, still this is a new estate; and if so, the effect is a revocation, whatever the quantity or interest may be. For the purpose of the argument, admitting, he acted under a mistake, it is a revocation, upon the principles contained in Lord Hardwicke's notes, stated by the Lord Chancellor (1) in *Brydges* v. *The Duchess of Chandos;* if in fact he has gone beyond what was necessary for the mortgage.

As to the objection from the length of time, *prima facie* the Plaintiffs are entitled; and it lies on the Defendants to show, why they are not. No analogy to a legal bar has been shown. It is said, a republication of the will may be presumed. Has that ever been done? Why was not that suggested in 1787? If it had been mentioned, could it have been countenanced a moment? Such a presumption would be most extraordinary; and has never been made. in the case of a purchase subsequent to the will; upon which Judges have been so much embarrassed, and obliged to decide in all probability against the intention. *Bunker* v. *Cooke* (2) and those cases would not have arisen upon this hypothesis. The Statute of
     Frauds (3) might be got rid of in the same way. Lord
[* 213] * Mansfield endeavored to go as far as any one in presuming; and your Honor is also liberal in that respect. Lord Mansfield 'said, he would presume even an Act of Parliament: but it is impossible to presume a clause in an Act of Parliament; which act is produced; and this is an attempt to raise a presumption with regard to a will, which will is produced, and in opposition to their own decree. Upon a writ of right by an heir at law could the Jury without any ground, in the absence of all evidence, merely in respect of the possession of the Defendant, presume, that a will was duly attested, which will was produced, attested by two witnesses only? The Court is required *per saltum* to conclude, this was an adverse possession. In *Doe* v. *Prosser* (4) the Court of King's Bench certainly presumed upon 36 years' possession by one tenant in common an ouster of his companion. Lord Mansfield there says, "So, in the case of tenants in common; the possession of one tenant in common, *eo nomine*, as tenant in common, can never bar his companion; because such a possession is not adverse to the right of his companion, but in support of their common title; and by paying him his share he acknowledges him co-tenant. Nor indeed is a refusal to pay of itself sufficient without denying his title."

---

(1) *Ante,* vol. ii. 431, 432.
(2) Fitzg. 225; Holt, 236, 746.
(3) 29 Cha. II. c. 3.
(4) Cowp. 217.

Apply that position to this case.   From 1764, as the Plaintiffs contend, these parties were entitled to possess in thirds.   The property does not admit of actual entry : but an agent was receiving from 1764 to 1788.   Where is the adverse possession?   The doubt was merely as to the right of the Plaintiffs from the circumstance of their ancestor being out of possession.   *Eldridge* v. *Knott* (1) is to the same effect.   This case has circumstances to explain the apparent acquiescence.   They were closely connected in blood and friendship.   The decree only directed the will to be established; which without doubt was to be established.   The devise is not of these fee-farm rents specifically, but generally, of his estates.   If there had been a Report, that these rents passed, and the question of revocation had arisen upon farther directions or Exceptions, there would have been something of *res judicata ;* which might be operative.

Next as to the account of the rents and profits de-   [214] manded, a trustee is bound to account from any period.

So in the old action of Assize the party is bound to account for any period for rents by-gone, received by him wrongfully.   By the Statute of Ann (2) a tenant in common may sue out a Writ of Account.   Before that they were under the necessity of coming into Equity ; and the usual decree was an account.   But the Statute has not taken away the equitable jurisdiction.   Neither has it taken away the Writ of Assize, and in that certainly you may recover in damages beyond the six years the whole wrongfully received.   No Statute of Limitations applies to it; Bro. Abridg. (3) referring to 33 Hen. VI., and the Statute of Gloucester.   In any other action certainly you cannot recover beyond the six years.   The form of the action gives the extraordinary right.   The assurance in this case, that the rents should be held for the right owners, and the proposal in the letter, that they shall be laid out and produce interest, naturally produced a suspension of the claim.   If ever there was a case, in which the Court would recur to its old doctrine of making a Receiver account strictly as trustee, this is the case.   As to the inconvenience, it is not to be supposed after admissions of the claim from time to time.   No such fact, as that there was any settlement, is alleged or proved in the cause: nor is there any ground for such a supposition.   This claim was set up by the father of the Plaintiff.   That is admitted by the answers.   It does not therefore rest upon the letters.   They knew, Mr. Fearne and another eminent Counsel had given opinions in favor of it.

As to the effect of the decree, that this is a revocation, to obtain even an inquiry as to that there must be some foundation laid, to show, that a descended estate is applicable before the remainder of the devisor's estates ; which in fact have borne the burthen of the debts.   The reasoning in *Donne* v. *Lewis* is completely in point.   Lord Thurlow took a considerable time and great pains in endeavoring to

---

(1) Cowp. 214.
(2) 4 Ann. c. 16.
(3) 1 Bro. Abr. 50, tit. Assize, pl. 10.

reconcile the previous cases; which are not easily to be reconciled. Your Honor followed that case exactly in *Manning* v. *Spooner* (1). This is very different from a mere charge. Stronger words cannot be used. They are stronger than *Manning* v. *Spooner;* [* 215] in which the charge covered the whole * estate: but here is an exception of a particular part; which shows, he was forming a judgment between one part of his estate and another; making a destination of one part to his debts before another. The effect is leaving the whole of the debts upon that part.

The Court during the argument admitting, that the parties were aware of the claim, expressed a strong opinion against granting the account, at least farther back than six years (2).

The Master of the Rolls also observed upon the point of revocation; that as to a deed executed by mistake he did not admit that to be a revocation; and as to a deed obtained by fraud, though certainly Lord Thurlow reversed the decree in *Hawes* v. *Wyatt* (3), (and his Honor said, he would not set his judgment in competition with the high authority of that noble Lord) yet the case of *Hick* v. *Mors* (4) was a strong corroboration of the decree at the Rolls; which proceeded upon this; that though the son was induced by his father to execute the deed, it was a revocation; as the son intended, the will should not operate: it would be different if it was such a fraud as making him execute one deed, when he thought he was executing another.

March 21*st.*   The MASTER OF THE ROLLS [Sir RICHARD PEPPER ARDEN].—This case is attended with very peculiar circumstances. The bill is filed in 1796 for an account of fee-farm rents; which became due to the present Plaintiffs, or those, under whom they claim, in 1764. After a possession from 1764 to 1796 this bill is brought. Upon such a bill, and when, as it is said, no less than three descents have been cast, and those persons have been receiving and acting upon the property, the Court undoubtedly will not do any thing to farther such a claim: but if by the rules of equity, as well as of law, for a question of law has been raised, they are entitled, they must prevail: to what extent, will be matter of future consideration, when the cause comes back; for I do not think myself at liberty to decide it entirely at present.

[* 216]   * Abraham Weekes being seised under this settlement, with the reversion in fee. to himself, upon the 24th of May, 1750, makes his will; upon which the question arises.

In November 1750 he takes it into his head, for what reason I

(1) *Ante,* vol. iii. 114.
(2) As to the limitation of accounts, see *Drummond* v. *The Duke of St. Albans, Acherley* v. *Roe, Bromley* v. *Holland, Reade* v. *Reade, Chambers* v. *Goldwin, ante,* vol. v. 433, and the note, 539, 565, 610, 744, 834; *Pettiward* v. *Prescott, post,* vii. 541; *Domer* v. *Fortescue,* 3 Atk. 124.
(3) 3 Bro. C. C. 156. See *post,* vol. vii. 373; viii. 283.
(4) Amb. 215.

cannot tell, to make this deed; thinking another recovery necessary; and he begins with making a mortgage to Mellicent Neate for
1000 years; and for the farther and better securing the payment of
said sum of 5500l. with interest, and for the barring all estates tail
and all reversions and remainders thereupon expectant in said fee-
farm rents, and for limiting and assuring the same for such uses,
upon such trusts, and for such intents and purposes, as hereinafter
expressed, Abraham Weekes and his wife convey these fee-farm
rents, being part of the estates comprised in the will, to Charles
Lawrence, his heirs and assigns, to make a tenant to the *praecipe*,
that a recovery might be suffered; to enure to Mellicent Neate for
securing the mortgage; and, after the determination of the term, to
the use of Abraham Weekes for life; remainder to his wife for life;
remainder to Abraham Weekes, his heirs and assigns.

He seems to have very much perplexed himself with respect to
his interest in these estates; for in truth he had no right to suffer
a recovery. He was a mere tenant for life of the estates; and had
no right to bar the estates of his first and other sons. I suppose,
he took it for granted, he should have no children. It is said, and, I
believe, his object was merely to give effect to the mortgage. The
first thing to be considered is, what passed under his will; as it
stood before the recovery. Unquestionably, only the remainder in
fee expectant upon the deaths of himself and his wife without issue,
charged with the payment of his debts. It must not be forgot, that
by this deed, if it is to have any operation, the will would to a certain degree be altered; for nothing is said in it about the debts;
which by the will are first charged upon all his estates.

The testator died in 1755; leaving his three sisters his co-heiresses
at law. His widow married James O'Donnell. She had both under
her marriage settlement and under this farther settlement in 1750 an
estate for life; and she filed a bill against Mellicent Crop
and Mary Harmood and their *husbands; praying, that	[*217]
the will might be established, the debts paid, &c.; which
was done under a decree.

Mrs. O'Donnell died in 1764; and then arose the claim of the
present Plaintiffs; insisting, that the will was revoked by the subsequent deed. From that time the Plaintiffs' title accrued. But it is
said, it is not barred; for it is an equitable title; the legal estate
having passed by the deed to Lawrence; and that it was a revocation of the will both at law and in equity; and the legal estate remained in Lawrence, (the recovery never having been suffered) as
a trustee for the heirs at law of the testator; and therefore that, if
ever entitled, they are entitled from the year 1764.

Unquestionably it cannot be denied, that some idea of this claim
was entertained; and letters were produced from Dr. Taunton, entitled in right of his wife, which show, they had an idea of this claim
of the Plaintiffs to these rents: but it is equally clear, that the Plaintiffs did not receive them. They permitted them to be received by
persons in opposition to their claim; which was never asserted by

any suit, till this bill was filed in 1796; insisting, that as these are fee-farm rents, and the legal estate in Lawrence, as trustee for them, they are not barred by any length of time; but have a right to the account. I should have been extremely glad to have dismissed the bill now; for I should be very sorry to have it understood to be the rule of this Court, that there is no limitation whatsoever to trust estates; and that, let the legal estate once get into a trustee, the *Cestuy que trust* may permit others to enjoy the property; and come to this Court at any distance of time for an account. I do not know, that this Court will ever act upon so very broad a principle.

But several objections were taken to this claim. First, it was insisted, that under all the circumstances this deed was not a revocation of the will either at law, or at least not in equity.

[* 218] * First, to consider, whether it is a revocation of the will at law. I do not think, much doubt can be entertained of that. I, for one, have no difficulty in saying, that, wherever the whole legal estate is conveyed, whether for a partial or a general purpose, with the single exception of the case of *Luther* v. *Kidby*, which I shall have occasion to consider hereafter, a Court of Law has nothing to do with the purpose; but is to see, whether the interest remains the same in the devisor, as it did at the date of the will; and if not, without question, whether the purpose is partial or general, whether it is by way of charge, or not, it is a revocation at law.

But then it is insisted, that the Court may under the circumstances presume a republication of the will. I will not take away from the Defendants any advantage they may have from such a presumption: but it must be remembered, that is a mere question at law; with which this Court can have nothing to do.

The question therefore is, whether this is a revocation in equity. It was said, if the deed is for a partial purpose, if the mere purpose was to secure this mortgage, its being done by recovery will not make any difference; that, if the object of the conveyance is merely to effectuate the mortgage, it is no more a revocation in equity than a simple mortgage would be.

This brings before the Court a question, that has of late been so much agitated, and upon which so much argument has been used; and, as I believe my opinion in the case of *Williams* v. *Owens* (1) has been in some degree misunderstood, I am very anxious to explain it; and it bears such an analogy to the present case, that in stating my opinion of that case, and comparing it with the present case, I shall show the ground of my opinion upon this case also. I observe, in the report of *Cave* v. *Holford* (2) it is said by the then

(1) *Ante*, vol. ii. 595.
(2) *Ante*, vol. iii. 684. This opinion was repeated by the Lord Chancellor, arguing *Brydges* v. *The Duchess of Chandos*, and *Cave* v. *Holford*, at the bar of the House of Lords, and in the judgment on the appeal in this case. See *post*, vol. viii. 127.

Attorney-General, that it is impossible to reconcile *Williams* v. *Owens* with *Brydges* v. *The Duchess of Chandos.*   There is this distinction between them : *Williams* v. *Owens* is, I take it, a strict literal execution of the articles, by which the party was bound, and nothing more : the deed in the *other case differs from   [* 219] them.   In the former, it is true, as the legal estate was never out of the devisor, he cannot be said to have acquired it after making the will ; and the distinction was marked by Mr. Romilly in the argument ; but I consider, that the testator having modelled his legal interest in the estate in conformity to the articles makes no difference.

It is unnecessary to go over the doctrine of revocation ; as it has been ably stated by the Judges of the Court of Common Pleas in *Goodtitle* v. *Otway.*   I entirely agree with the three Judges, who held the deed of revocation of the will as to all the estates : but I think with Mr. Justice Buller, the articles ought not to have formed any part of the special verdict.   The question in a Court of Law is simply, whether the legal devise is revoked by the deed.   All other questions, as to the partial purpose, &c. are merely equitable questions.   I perfectly agree with all the determinations, that have taken place in Courts of Law on questions of revocation, except *Luther* v. *Kidby ;* which with great deference to the authority, by which it was decided, I cannot but consider as anomalous ; and I perceive from the report of *Goodtitle* v. *Otway,* that Mr. Justice Heath looks upon that case in the same light that I do.   The question then is, in what cases a Court of Equity has determined, that a deed clearly revoking a will at law is not in equity a revocation, or is only a partial revocation ; and I take it to be fully established now, that, if the deed is only for the partial purpose of introducing a particular charge or incumbrance, and does not affect the interest of the testator beyond that purpose, it is only a partial revocation in equity ; and though the devisees under the will take no estate, and the estate is vested in the mortgagee or a trustee for a particular purpose, and, after that purpose shall be answered, the use is declared to be for the testator and his heirs, yet a Court of Equity being satisfied, that there was no other object *but the partial one,   [* 220] will hold the party a trustee, not for the heir, but for the devisees.   Lord Hardwicke expressly laid it down, that, if a man devises an equitable estate, and afterwards takes a conveyance of the legal estate to him and his heirs, though the consequence will be, that the estate will descend upon the heir, the heir will be only a trustee for the devisees.

Now, to apply these principles to the case of *Williams* v. *Owens* and to this case.   In *Williams* v. *Owens* it is admitted, that if the testator had died without having conveyed according to the articles, his heir at law, to whom the legal estate would have descended, would have been a trustee for the uses of the articles, and, after they were satisfied, for the devisees.   It is likewise admitted, that the testator would have been liable to be called upon to convey accord-

ing to the articles. What did he convey by the will? At Law,
the whole legal estate : in Equity, only the remainder in fee. In
Equity he remained seised as before ; and the conveyance being
only for a particular purpose, and in conformity to the obligation he
was under, when he must be supposed to act under the articles, it
would be a perversion of the principles, upon which these cases are
determined, to consider it a revocation in Equity.

This is upon the supposition, that Lord Hardwicke is right in
holding, that, if a man devises an equitable estate, and afterwards
takes a conveyance to him and his heirs, he does not revoke the
will. It is admitted, that if the testator, instead of covenanting,
that he would convey according to the articles, had before the date
of the will conveyed to a trustee upon those trusts, and after the
will had called upon the trustee to convey upon the trusts, the will
would not have been revoked : yet without question the legal estate
would have descended to the heir. The Court would have controlled the law ; and would have held the heir to be a trustee for the
devisees. What distinction in common sense can there be between
the two cases? In *Williams* v. *Owens* the testator, instead of conveying according to the articles before the will, gave the estate subject to the articles by the will, and then, as he was bound to do,
          conveyed the legal estate so as to leave himself at law,
[* 221]   what he had before in equity, the remainder * in fee. It
          is said, that the legal estate passed by the will ; and that a
conveyance of the legal estate after a devise is a revocation at law ;
and why should equity control the law? The reason, why a deed
revokes a will, is, that a Court of Law cannot look at the articles.
But a Court of Equity attends to both : considers the interest at the
date of the will and of the deed ; and upon all the circumstances
determines, whether that, which without the intervention of circumstances, (by which the interest in equity is distinct from the legal
interest) must be held a revocation of the beneficial as well as the
legal interest, shall in equity be no revocation of the will, so far as
it affects the actual interest in a Court of Equity.

To give some examples. *A.* seised in fee, devises to *B.* in fee,
charged with the payment of debts : then makes a mortgage in fee ;
then pays that off: and takes back the estate from the mortgagee to
himself and his heirs. This would fall directly within Lord Hardwicke's rule ; that taking the legal estate from a trustee is not a revocation. By the mortgage there is a complete revocation at law :
but a Court of Equity says, he still remains possessed of the estate in
equity, subject to the debt secured by the mortgage. Therefore the
mortgagee shall be a trustee for the devisee : the mode taken for
the security of the debt not being regarded in equity ; and the devisor being complete owner, as before, in equity, subject only to the
mortgage. Put the case, not of a mortgage ; for it may be said,
that in equity is only a chattel interest ; and that he is seised of his
former estate : suppose, after the devise, a conveyance of the whole
fee, upon trust to sell and pay debts ; the surplus, if any, for the tes-

tator and his executors; and the remainder of the lands unsold, for him and his heirs. It has been determined by Lord Thurlow and other great Judges to be no revocation in equity. Suppose afterwards, the debts being fully paid, the trustee is called upon by the testator, and conveys to the testator and his heirs: that would be clearly no revocation. Now in this case Equity takes upon it to make the heir, upon whom the estate descends by virtue of a conveyance, by which his ancestor acquired an entirely new estate, a trustee for the devisee under a will made prior to his acquisition of that legal estate. That, I admit, is a strong case; and perhaps it would have been as well for a Court of Equity to have refused to assist the devisee against the heir in such a case; and yet unquestionably the principle is settled and established, that the heir is a trustee for the devisee. I admit the difference in the
case of a will and a conveyance afterwards for a partial   [222]
purpose, the testator then dying without taking back the
legal estate; for a Court of Equity has only to decide, to whom the beneficial interest belongs. A Court of Equity declares, he did not mean to revoke; and therefore holds him a trustee for the devisee, and not for the heir; and directs a conveyance.

Consider then, what circumstances make a revocation, which is clearly a revocation at law, no revocation in-equity. What is a revocation in equity? They are fully stated in *Cave* v. *Holford*, and in the note of Mr. Serjeant Williams in his very valuable edition of Saunders's Reports (1). He there expresses a doubt as to what was said by me as to the operation of a fine (2); where there is no deed to declare their uses; and I think, he is justified in that doubt. The result of these cases is, that any alteration of the estate, or a new estate taken, is at law a revocation; whether for a partial or a general purpose; to which circumstance a Court of Law cannot advert: neither ought they to take any notice of articles, or covenants, charging the estate in equity. They have only to look at the will and the subsequent deed; and say, whether at law the old estate is changed and a new estate acquired.

Consider, in what cases Courts of Equity have controlled the law; not upon the ground of a partial purpose only, nor upon the act being done without an intention to revoke; for that will not authorise a Court of Equity to interfere. A Court of Equity has never interfered with the operation of a will and a subsequent deed, where the testator at the time of the will had the same estate at law and in equity. But where his beneficial interest is different from his legal one, or, where the equitable interest is devised, and the legal estate is not affected, and the testator calls upon the trustee for his legal estate, though the legal estate descends to the heir, yet a Court of Equity says, as the whole beneficial interest passed by the devise, and the trustee, if the devisor had died without calling for the legal es-

---

(1) Vol. i. 277, note 4.
(2) *Ante,* vol. ii. 600, in the note.

tate, would have been a trustee for the devisee (1), the mere circumstance of the devisor's clothing himself with the legal estate shall not
operate as a revocation of the devise of the beneficial interest.
    Therefore they hold the heir a trustee for the uses of the
[*223]   will. This is expressly laid down *in *Parsons* v. *Freeman,*
    and is not denied in any case, that I am aware of. In
that case, it is to be observed the testator had no estate at all at law,
upon which his will could operate. Therefore the conveyance from
the trustees was a completely new estate. Suppose, a man seised in
fee makes his will, and then conveys his estate to a trustee for the
payment of debts : the law has nothing to do with the purpose of the
deed ; but can only judge of the legal operation of the deed. But
equity says, the estate is not taken out of the testator substantially :
he has the same estate in equity as before; and though the mode
amounts to a revocation, yet subject to those debts he remains in
equity master of the estate, as before ; and the will continued to operate upon his interest. In fact they consider him still owner in equity ;
and therefore, if he calls for the legal estate, by which at law he becomes the purchaser of a new estate, not affected by the will, yet
equity holds the heir to be a trustee for the devisees, just as if the
legal estate had remained in the trustee.
    This doctrine is applicable also to this case. The principles are,
first, that equity will never control the law ; except, where the testator has at the date of the will a different interest in equity from that,
which he has at law ; and devises that beneficial interest ; and then
only takes the legal estate, without any new modification or alteration : secondly, where he has the complete legal and beneficial estate
at the date of the will ; and afterwards devests himself of the legal estate ; but still remains owner of the equitable interest ; as in the case
of a mortgage or a conveyance for payment of debts : if he dies without taking a conveyance of the legal estate, his equitable interest still
continues; and if he has taken back the legal estate, that alone will
not revoke the devise of the equitable interest. These rules are
clearly deducible from the series of determinations of great Judges
in equity. To apply them to *Williams* v. *Owens.* If, instead of
articles, the testator had before marriage conveyed to a trustee, in
trust for himself till the marriage, then for himself for life; remainder to the issue in tail ; remainder to himself in fee ; then made the
will ; and then had called upon the trustee to convey ; and he had conveyed, it is admitted, that would be a complete revocation at law ;
but as clearly it would not be a revocation in equity ; and the heir
    must convey to the uses of the will. In principle that does
[*224]   not differ *from the case of *Williams* v. *Owens.* The de-
    visor was bound by the articles ; and he might have been
compelled to convey accordingly. That would not revoke his will.
Then it is strange to say, if the conveyance was taken from a trustee it would be no revocation, but, if according to his obligation he

(1) *Post*, vol. ix. 510, and the note.

himself conveyed to the same uses, it would be a revocation. No one can deny, that articles are in equity equal to a conveyance. No one can deny, that he remained a trustee to the uses of the articles ; and must have conveyed accordingly, if he had been called upon. Having the whole legal estate in himself, for the legal estate was entirely unaffected, instead of being under the necessity of calling upon a trustee to convey, he conveys himself according to the articles. Is that to be a revocation, when, if he had happened to have conveyed to a trustee, instead of entering into articles, a conveyance from the trustee would not have had that effect? Such a determination, if it does not reverse the determinations, which have hitherto prevailed in equity, will in my opinion overturn every principle, upon which they have been decided.

I have entered much at large into this question ; as I am anxious, that the grounds of opinion upon revocation in equity should not be misunderstood ; and as they apply to the present case, I thought this a proper opportunity to state them at large.

To apply them to this case. It was contended, that this deed was for a partial purpose, and no revocation : but I am of opinion, the mode he took was clearly a revocation at law, provided any estate passed : and there was no republication. If the devisor conveys for the purpose of suffering a recovery and thereby taking back to himself a new estate, it is clearly a revocation at law as well as in equity. It is said, and I think it is probable, that the only object of the intended recovery was to give effect to the mortgage. That circumstance alone will not do, if he does it by way of recovery and taking back a new estate. Equity will not interpose, except in the cases I have so fully enlarged upon. I am of opinion, this deed is a revocation both at law and in equity ; whatever was the intention of the recovery intended to be suffered. The consequence is, unless there was a republication, the will is revoked. Consequently the right to · the fee-farm rents descended * upon the heirs ; and they   [*225] have forborne their claim all this time. I shall not assist the Plaintiffs. The other side, one would think, would have come here to restrain them from proceeding at law. I do not mean to debar them from any right they may have to resist any decree whatsoever being made, after these questions shall be determined at law ; for it was determined by Lord Kenyon in *Barber* v. *Geast* (1), that it is not a necessary consequence that the Court will not ultimately determine against the Plaintiffs in Equity, because the bill has been retained ; and, if I am not mistaken, Lord Kenyon dismissed that bill. At present I do not think myself at liberty to dismiss this bill. At the same time I am not at liberty to assist the Plaintiffs. The utmost I can do is to retain the bill, with liberty for the Plaintiffs to bring an action in the name of Lawrence (2), to whom the estate was conveyed for the particular purpose. Then they will have the opportunity of taking the opinion of a Court of Law, whether there

(1) 2 Bro. C. C. 61.
(2) 2 Mer. 360.

is a revocation at law, or, whether a Court of Law will presume a republication from this long possession. That is the only decree I shall make; leaving open the other point, whether under the circumstances the Plaintiffs are entitled to any account, or to what length of time they may go back; for it was strongly pressed for the Plaintiffs, that they have a right to recover in a Court of Equity these rents from the very first. That is perfectly alarming, if a man having a trust estate may lie by for any length of time, permitting others to retain the whole profit, and then come for an account. There must be some limitation.

I am of opinion, that, if this is a revocation at law, and I have very little difficulty at present in saying it is, it is also a revocation in equity: but I by no means wish to have it understood, that after so long an acquiescence the Plaintiffs are entitled to relief in a Court of Equity. Retain the bill; with liberty for the Plaintiffs to bring such action or suit as they may be advised (1).

1. For a statement of the general doctrines with respect to revocations of testamentary instruments, see, *ante*, the notes to *Brydges* v. *The Duchess of Chandos,* 2 V. 417.

2. That Courts of Equity are never disposed to encourage stale demands, see note 2 to *Jones* v. *Turberville,* 2 V. 11.

3. A mere general charge upon a devised estate will still leave descended estates previously applicable to the discharge of the testator's debts, see the note to *Manning* v. *Spooner,* 3 V. 114.

[* 226]   ADAMS *v.* CLAXTON.

[Rolls.—1801, July 3, 6.]

No tacking against creditors or assignees for valuable consideration (a).
Trustee not charged with a loss by the failure of the banker to the agent; in whose hands the money was deposited pending a transaction for the change of a. trustee (b).
No lien under the circumstances.
Upon farther directions a question decided by the Master was opened, without any exception: all the circumstances appearing on the report (c).

THE bill was filed by creditors of William Wood, for the purpose of obtaining the benefit of a deed, conveying all his estate to Adams and Claxton, two of his creditors, in trust for the benefit of

(1) See the decree, and the Lord Chancellor's judgment on the appeal, affirming the revocation in equity as well as at law, *post,* vol. viii. 106.

(a) As to the doctrine of tacking in cases of mortgages, see *ante,* note (a), *Hamerton* v. *Rogers,* 1 V. 513; note (c), *Jones* v. *Smith,* 2 V. 372.

(b) Where a trustee acts by other hands, either from necessity, or conformably to the usage of mankind, he is not to be made answerable for losses. See *ante,* note (a), *Rowth* v. *Howell,* 3 V. 565.

(c) Errors apparent in the schedules have been corrected, even after enrolment, on a summary application. *Weston* v. *Haggerston,* Coop. 134; 2 Dan. Pr. 963; 1 Barbour, Ch. Pr. 557. Upon the allowance of an exception to a report as to the

his creditors. The accounts were directed; and the Master by his Report stated, that the late Defendant William Claxton under an assignment made to him by the testator Wood of a policy of insurance upon his life for 1386*l.* 10*s.* for securing 1000*l.* advanced by Claxton, received the money from the Insurance Office upon the death of Wood; and he claimed to retain out of the surplus 319*l.* 10*s.* 7*d.* for principal and interest, due upon a subsequent promissory note for 300*l.* payable a year after date. That question was submitted by the Master to the Court.

Another question arose on the following circumstances, appearing on the Report. Adams desiring to be discharged from the trust, pending the transaction for the change of trustees the agent for the trust in April 1796 received three payments on account of the trust, to the amount of 252*l.* 15*s.* 8*d.*; which sum was deposited with Nightingale, the agent's banker, until another trustee should be appointed, or some banker should be agreed on to receive the trust money. This money was paid in in the agent's name as a temporary matter only. Nightingale stopped payment. The deed contained no covenant or condition for depositing the money received under the trust in any bank, until it should be distributed. Wood died a few days after the execution of the deed. The question was, whether the trustee was personally liable to that loss.

The third question arose upon the following facts. The testator Wood effected an insurance for 1000*l.* upon his own life on the 6th of January, 1790. Upon that policy the following indorsement appeared in the hand-writing of the testator Wood:

"No. 9964. 6. January 1790. Policy upon the life of William Wood for 1000*l.* annual premium 30*l.* 13*s.* payable 5th January. R. B."

*The Report stated, that it was alleged before the [*227] Master, that the two last letters of that indorsement, were intended to signify the initial letters of the name of Richard Boyfield; under whose will the testator Wood was principal acting, as well as surviving executor; and to whose estate he had as executor become considerably indebted. The Policy was discovered among Wood's papers, delivered up by him in February 1796, upon his making the assignment of his effects to trustees for his creditors; and annexed to the Policy was found the following paper, all in Wood's handwriting: "The annexed Policy of insurance, from the Equitable Insurance Office Blackfriar's Bridge for securing to my executors, administrators, or assigns, the payment of 1000*l.* upon the event of my death, is hereby agreed and intended by me to be vested in Mary Woodyear, of Camberwell, Surrey, widow; in trust to lay out the same and apply the principal together with the produce of 2500*l.* 3 per cent. Consols, now in the Bank in my name, but bought by me as executor for the use and benefit of the Boyfield family, and to-

---

amount of damages sustained, the Court can modify the report, and settle the amount, without referring it back to the Master. *Taylor* v. *Reed,* 4 Paige, 561.

gether with the rents of the late Richard Boyfield's estate for the benefit of Mrs. Boyfield and said Mrs. Woodyear for their respective lives, and then to be applied for the use of Mary Woodyear's child or children according to the will of the said Richard Boyfield ; and I do farther agree, that the said Mary Woodyear shall have a lien upon the said Policy of assurance for the said sum of one thousand pounds to be applied for the purposes accordingly ; and which Policy so hereby assigned or agreed or intended so to be vested in the said Mary Woodyear as aforesaid is No. 9964 and bears date the 6th day of January 1790 : as witness my hand this 18th day of April, 1790.   Wm. Wood."

Upon the 25th of January, 1797, Claxton received the money in respect of that Policy : which he invested in stock ; and he transferred the stock to the Accountant General ; and invested the dividends. The Master stated, that he conceived, the testator Wood did by the said paper so appropriate the benefit of the Policy, that the persons interested under the will of Boyfield have a right to the benefit of the moneys arising therefrom.

The cause came on for farther directions.

[* 228]   * Mr. *Romilly* and Mr. *Steele*, for the Defendant Claxton, the personal representative of the trustee, upon the second question insisted, the trustee was not to be charged with the money paid into the bank of Nightingale : the trustee having dealt with this money, till the appointment of another trustee, just as he would with his own property, and for the benefit of the parties. *Knight* v. *Lord Plymouth* (1), *Ex parte Belchier* (2).

Mr. *Piggott*, Mr. *Richards*, and Mr. *Hart*, for the Plaintiffs, upon an intimation from the MASTER OF THE ROLLS [Sir WILLIAM GRANT], that it would be impossible to charge the trustee, gave up that point.

Upon the third question they contended, that under these circumstances Wood could not give one creditor this preference. Without delivery of the instrument it could not be an assignment. He never mentions it : keeps it for two or three years, until, executing the deed of trust, he delivers it with his other papers to the trustee. As against creditors it cannot possibly prevail. A lien springs from contract. Here the persons, who claim this lien, knew nothing of it.   •

Mr. *Sutton* and Mr. *Raithby*, for the personal representatives of Boyfield, insisted, that a preference might be given, if not with a fraudulent view, or in contemplation of bankruptcy ; and that this was an appropriation : the money being marked out.

The MASTER OF THE ROLLS asked, how it was to operate ; being admitted not to be an assignment. He must give them or some

---

(1) 3 Atk. 480.
(2) Amb. 218 ; *Bacon* v. *Bacon, Powell* v. *Evans, ante,* vol. v. 331, 839 ; *Rowth* v. *Howell,* iii. 565 ; *Balchen* v. *Scott,* ii. 678 ; see the note, 679.

one on their behalf power over it. If any thing, it seemed to be of a legatory nature, to take effect after his death.

July 6th. The MASTER OF THE ROLLS.—Upon the first question, the claim of the representative of Claxton to retain beyond the 1000*l.* so much of the money as will pay him the subsequent debt upon a note of hand, under the circumstances I am of opinion, that claim cannot * be allowed. At the time,   [* 229] when the assignment was made to the trustees for the benefit of Wood's creditors, Claxton had an assignment of this Policy to secure the sum of 1000*l.* and no more. By that assignment every thing, which it was competent to Wood to assign, passed from him to his trustee; and consequently the equity of redemption of the Policy so pledged. Claxton had not at that time received the money upon the Policy. That might have raised a different consideration; if he had the money in his hands: but he was merely a mortgagee for 1000*l.* It is clearly settled, that, in the case of a mortgage the right to attach a subsequent debt to the mortgage cannot be made available against an assignee of the equity of redemption. That has been repeatedly determined in the case of real estate. *Troughton* v. *Troughton* (1). The anonymous case, (2) 2 Ves. 662. *Heams* v. *Bance* (3) is a still stronger case; where a trust for the benefit of creditors was raised by the will of the mortgagor.

With respect to pledges of personal estate, *Demainbray* v. *Metcalfe* (4) arose upon a pledge of jewels. The party afterwards borrowed other sums upon a general account; and he insisted upon his right of redeeming the jewels upon payment of the first sum only. It was held, that he must pay the whole: but it was admitted, that if there had been bond creditors, or in case of a bankruptcy, the pledge could have been retained only for the first sum; and the creditor in the case of a bankruptcy must have come in under the commission for the remainder. In *Vanderzee* v. *Willis* (5) there was an assignment of bonds to secure 1000*l.* borrowed by the testator from his bankers. At that time he was indebted to them in more; and he continued indebted in more to his death. His executrix filed a bill to redeem. The bankers insisted upon the right to tack; and so standing the case, it would, I think, have been held, that they must be paid the whole:. but it was insisted, that a bill had been filed by creditors, and a decree made. Lord Thurlow seems to have held, that * would have made it a   [* 230] question with creditors, not with the executrix simply;

---

(1) 1 Ves. 86.
(2) The name of that case is *Jackson* v. *Langford*, July 21st, 1755, Reg. Lib. A. 1754.
(3) 3 Atk. 630.
(4) Pre. Ch. 419; 2 Vern. 691. See *Jones* v. *Smith*, *ante*, vol. ii. 372. The decree in that case was reversed by the House of Lords.
(5) 3 Bro. C. C. 21.

stating the principle; that, where the equity has passed to an assignee, you cannot insist upon retaining against the assignee. In
this case the equity of redemption passed by the assignment for the
benefit of Wood's creditors; and therefore Claxton cannot insist on
paying himself the additional sum.

The other question arises in consequence of a reference to the
Master to inquire, to whom a Policy of insurance upon Wood's life,
or the money, that may be received thereon, belongs. The Report
states all the circumstances; and concludes, that the Master conceives, the testator Wood did by that paper writing so appropriate
the benefit of the Policy, that the persons interested under the will
of Boyfield have a right to the benefit of the money. No exception
is taken to the Report: but the whole matter appears upon the face
of it; and therefore it is contended, that it is open to inquire,
whether the Master's conclusion is right; and I apprehend, it is so
open (1). The date of this paper must be false; for Boyfield was
not at that time dead. The Report does not state, whether Wood
at the time he made this writing was or was not indebted to the
persons, for whose benefit he professes to make this species of appropriation: but it turns out, and appears by the schedule to the
Report, that the Representatives of Boyfield were creditors of Wood
to the extent of 4000*l*. It is contended, that this was such an appropriation as gives these persons, the representatives of Boyfield, a
lien against the creditors. It is admitted, this Policy, when first
made, was entirely Wood's own property. It could not have been
procured in trust for them; for then Boyfield was not dead; and
they had not become his representatives. Being Wood's own property, how did it cease to be so? Has it been transferred? How
has any other person acquired a lien; so as to prevent the effect of
any general or special assignment? This paper is quite insufficient
for that purpose. I do not very well know, what is meant by an
appropriation of the Policy to a debt: how a man, sitting in his
closet, could by writing a paper, declaring, that certain bonds, or
part of his stock, should be applied to a particular debt, appropriate
that property. That is not an assignment; a lien, giving that creditor a right to a specific application in his favor, to the prejudice of
[* 231]   creditors: who might in any other way have obtained a
    right to * the general effects. If he had given an order
upon a particular fund to a creditor, that would have been
an appropriation of so much of that fund to the debt; and the creditor would have a right upon that. But in this case there was no
communication between the creditor and the debtor; there is nothing but a mere piece of paper. It is not even written upon the Policy, but a detached slip of paper; which he pins to it; keeping it
in his own possession; and not even communicating the fact, that he
had written it. He might have destroyed, or detached, it. He
keeps it some years; and at last delivers it up to the trustees, to

_____

(1) *Brodie* v. *Barry*. 1 Jac. & Walk. 470.

whom he had assigned the whole of his effects for the benefit of his creditors. But there is no statement upon the paper, that it is in satisfaction of any debt ; or, that he owes any debt. The words, as far as they relate to the Policy are purely words of gift. Perhaps they might have operated as legatory words ; as a bequest after his death. There is no mention, that it is in satisfaction of any debt, or that any debt was due. I only collect from another part of the paper, that there was stock, standing in his name, purchased with the assets of Boyfield : but that goes only to that stock. I do not collect, that any satisfaction of that debt was intended. It is said, that though this is an undelivered instrument, a kind of contract with himself, and in his own power, yet it was all he could do, all the delivery, that could take place ; for he had embezzled part of the assets ; and this was meant as a satisfaction for that embezzlement : but it is not true, that this was all he could have done. He might have assigned it immediately to a trustee upon the trusts of Boyfield's will ; and he professes to intend to do that. This does not purport to be a final instrument. But it rests as mere declaration of intention ; which can in my apprehension produce no effect whatsoever.

Therefore upon this question the Master has drawn a wrong conclusion ; and this Policy must be considered as constituting part of the general effects for the benefit of the creditors (1). Upon the only remaining question declare, that the Defendant Claxton is not to be charged with the money deposited in Nightingale's bank.

---

1. As to the responsibility of agents for the safety of their employer's money, when the agents have lodged such money in the hands of their own bankers, to their own individual account, see, *ante*, the note to *Rowth* v. *Howell*, 3 V. 565.

2. Where an estate is mortgaged, and afterwards money is taken up on bond by the mortgagor, who then sells the equity of redemption, the purchaser may redeem on payment of the mortgage debt only ; he is no more bound to pay the bond debt than he would be bound to discharge the simple contract debts of the mortgagor ; for the bond can give no *lien* on the lands in the hands of a purchaser. *Archer* v. *Snapp*, Andr. 342. Even as against the heir of a mortgagor, tacking a bond of the ancestor's to the mortgage is allowed only in order to avoid circuity of action : see the note to *Hamerton* v. *Rogers*, 1 V. 513. If the heir sell the equity of redemption, his vendee may redeem the land without paying the money lent on bond to the mortgagor ; *Bayley* v. *Robson*, Prec. in Cha. 89 : but a devisee of the equity of redemption, since the Statute of Fraudulent Devises, would be bound to discharge both demands. *Challis* v. *Casborne*, Prec. in Cha. 407 ; *Price* v. *Fastnedge*, Ambl. 686. So, if the mortgage were for a *term* of years, the executors of the mortgagor could not redeem it without discharging any bond debt due by the testator to the mortgagee ; though an assignee of the equity of redemption, or a creditor of the testator, might come for redemption upon payment of the mortgage debt only. *Coleman* v. *Winch*, 1 P. Wms. 776 ; *Demandry* v. *Metcalf*, Prec. in Cha. 419 ; and see the note to *Hamerton* v. *Rogers, ubi supra.*

3. The rule laid down in the principal case, that where the whole matter appears on the face of the report, a party who has not taken exceptions to the report may bring forward his objections at the hearing, was recognized in *Brodie* v. *Barry*, 1 Jac. & Walk. 471 ; (see, however, *Brown* v. *Sansome*, M'Clel. & Younge, 434 ;) and, upon a similar principle, errors of figures may be corrected, even after enrolment of a decree, provided the errors are apparent on the face of

the decree, but if any extrinsic fact is to be inquired into, the cause must be re-heard. *Weston* v. *Haggerston*, Coop. 135; *Brookfield* v. *Bradley*, 2 Sim. & Stu. 65.

4. That, where personalty is so "ear-marked" as to be capable of being clearly distinguished, Courts of Equity will be disposed to consider it as appropriated in favor of *cestuis que trust*, see *Vulliamy* v. *Noble*, 3 Meriv. 616.

[* 232]   MOORE *v.* FOLEY.

[ROLLS.—1801, JULY 2, 6.]

CONSTRUCTION of a covenant for renewal under the like covenants, &c.; that it was not for perpetual renewal: the Courts leaning against that construction, unless clearly intended (a).
Legal instruments not to be construed by the acts of the parties (b), [p. 238.]

By indentures of lease, dated the 12th of November, 1759, Lord Foley granted certain premises to Robert Moore, his executors, administrators, and assigns, for the lives of his three children, Robert, James, and Mary, Moore, and of the longest liver of them : in trust for them successively, at the yearly rent of 60*l*. 3*s*. 4*d*.; and also. paying at the decease of every of them, the said Robert, James, and Mary, 40*l*. as a heriot.

The lease contained a covenant, that, when any one of them, the said Robert, James, and Mary, Moore, should happen to die, then the survivors of them, the said Robert, James, and Mary, Moore, their heirs and assigns, should within one year next after the death of such one of Robert, James, and Mary, Moore, as should first happen to die, pay to Lord Foley, his heirs or assigns, the sum of 42*l*. 6*s*.; and that Lord Foley should upon receipt of that sum and request and surrendering the said grant at the cost of Robert Moore, the elder, his heirs or assigns, grant unto the survivors of them the said Robert, James, and Mary, Moore, and to such other person as the said survivors should nominate, the premises; to hold to the survivors of them, the said Robert, James, and Mary, Moore, and such other person as the said survivors should nominate, for and during the natural lives of such two of them, the said Robert, James, and Mary, Moore, as should happen to survive, and for the life of such third person as the said survivors of them, the said Robert, James, and Mary, Moore, should nominate ; and for the life of the longest liver of them, for their natural and respective lives successively, and not jointly, at, for, and under the like rent, covenants and conditions, as were therein contained and reserved ; and moreover it was mutually granted and agreed, that in such grant to be made by Lord Foley, his heirs or assigns, unto Robert Moore, the elder, his heirs, or assigns, (in trust, as aforesaid) it should be covenanted and

---

(a) *Abeel* v. *Radcliff*, 13 Johns. 297.
(b) Whether this principle can be maintained, see note (b), *Baynham* v. *Guy's Hospital*, 3 V. 294.

agreed, that when and as often as any one of the said three persons,
for whose lives the said grant should be made, should happen to die, then the * survivors of them should within one   [* 233]
year after the death of such one person pay to Lord Foley,
his heirs or assigns, the sum of 42*l.* 6*s.* ; and surrender the grant
then in being; and Lord Foley, his heirs and assigns, should upon
the payment of the said money and surrendering up of such grant
at the request and charges of the said survivors of such lessees execute another grant unto the said survivors of such lessees for and
during the lives of such two of the said persons as should be then
living and for the life of such other person as the said survivors of
the said lessees should nominate under the like rent, covenants, provisoes, and conditions as were therein contained; provided, that,
when any two of such persons, for whose lives such grant should
happen to be made, should happen to die within one year, and before such new grant ought to be made according to the true meaning of the said lease, then the survivor of such lessees should within
one year next after the death of such second person of the said three
persons, for whose lives such grant should be made, pay to Lord
Foley, his heirs or assigns, the sum of 102*l.* 6*s.* ; and that Lord
Foley, his heirs or assigns, should upon receipt of the said money
and surrendering up of the grant then in being at the request and
charges of such surviving lessee execute another grant unto such
surviving lessee for the lives of such surviving lessee and of such two
other persons as such surviving lessee should nominate, at, for, and
under, the like rents, covenants, and conditions, as were therein
mentioned and contained : Provided, that, if at any time Robert
Moore, the elder, his heirs or assigns, should upon the death of any
one or more of them, the said Robert, James, and Mary Moore,
neglect or refuse to pay to Lord Foley, his heirs or assigns, the said
respective sums, or to surrender the grant then in being, and accept
a new grant, it might be lawful for Lord Foley, his heirs and assigns,
to enter, and hold, until he and they should have received the said
several and respective sums with interest ; and then he and they
should make such grants, &c. as he and they ought to have made,
if the money had been paid at the time : Provided, that, if the heir
of Lord Foley should be within age at the time, when the new grant
should be made, no entry should take place till a month after he
should have attained his age.

Lord Foley died in 1766. Robert Moore, the younger, one of
the lives, died upon the 7th of July, 1793. Upon his decease James
Moore applied for a renewal according to the covenants to
* Andrew Foley, devisee in trust of the last Thomas, Lord   [* 234]
Foley. No renewal could then be made : the present Lord
Foley being under twenty-one ; but an act of Parliament was passed
enabling Andrew Foley to grant and renew leases. In April, 1796,
before any renewal Mary Moore, another of the lives, died. Upon
her death James Moore applied to have two new lives added ; offering to pay two fines of 42*l.* 6*s.* each. The parties differing as to the

proper covenants to be inserted in the new lease, the bill was filed by James Moore ; and a decree was made ; referring it to the Master to settle a lease.

An Exception was taken by the Defendant to the Master's report, approving a lease containing a covenant for perpetual renewal : viz.

When and as often as any one of the said three persons, for whose lives the said grant shall be made, shall die, Lord Foley, his heirs or assigns, shall within one year upon payment of 42*l.* 6*s.* and surrender of the grant then in being execute another grant to James Moore, his heirs or assigns, for the lives of the two survivors and such other person as James Moore, his heirs or assigns, shall nominate, under the like rents, covenants, provisoes, and conditions, as are herein contained ; and in case two such persons die within one year, before such grant, then within one year after the death of the second of the three persons, for whose lives the said grant shall be made, Lord Foley, &c. shall on payment of 102*l.* 6*s.* and surrender, execute a new grant for the lives of the survivor and such two other persons, as should be nominated, at, for, and under, the like rents, covenants, and conditions, &c.

Mr. *Lloyd* and Mr. *Lewis* in support of the Exception, insisted, the rule is now established, that a general covenant for renewal, subject to the like covenants, &c. is exclusive of the general covenant for renewal : and the Court will not without the strongest words insert so unreasonable a covenant. They relied on *Tritton* v. *Foote* (1) and the note there, *Russell* v. *Darwin* (2).

[* 235]   * Mr. *Richards* and Mr. *Cooke,* for the report.—These cases do not apply to this. The general principle until the decision of *Tritton* v. *Foote* and the case before Lord Camden was to make these leases perpetually renewable. But there are two covenants in this grant which distinguish this case. The second covenant puts it out of all doubt. The covenant now proposed is the very covenant for which they have stipulated. This lease has been always considered as perpetually renewable from the very first grant ; which was in 1662; and several instances have been found.

Mr. *Lloyd,* in reply.—The practice is not material; this construction upon these covenants being very modern. Upon what ground were these cases determined, except this; that such a covenant is unreasonable. The covenant for renewal was included under the general words in those cases. It is very difficult to collect the intention from these words ; and the Court will require the clearest intention for this purpose ; which is in effect giving away the estate.

July 6th. The MASTER OF THE ROLLS [Sir WILLIAM GRANT].—In the first part of this lease nothing is stated but the premises, the lives, for which they are granted, and the rent payable. If it rested there, the lease would be at an end, when those lives dropped. Then

(1) 2 Bro. C. C. 636.
(2) 2 Bro. C. C. 639, note.

comes the first provision for renewal. If it rested upon that, it would be a covenant for renewal upon the dropping of the first life only; and the moment they had got a new life in the place of that one that covenant would have been completely satisfied; unless they could insist, that the words "under the like rent, covenants and conditions," were meant to include that covenant for renewal; and that in the second lease a farther covenant for renewal should be inserted. But it does not stop there. They go on to make this stipulation with regard to the covenant to be inserted in that new lease, to supply the first life, that should drop; that "in such grant," (that is, the grant to fill up a new life in the room of that first dropping) it should be covenanted and agreed, that when and as often as any one of the said three persons, for whose lives the said grant should be made, should happen to die, another grant should be made for the lives of the survivors and such other person as should * be nominated, under the like rent, covenants, pro-   [* 236] visoes and conditions, as were therein contained. The mode adopted is not by providing directly, how long these renewals should go on, but by a covenant with regard to the renewal, to be introduced into the second lease. Then follows the provision for the case of two of them dying within a year.

This is all, that relates to the farther renewal. The first agreement is, that this stipulation shall be inserted in such grant; that is, the grant, that was to be made upon the dropping of the first life; and consequently the introduction of this stipulation into that would have the effect of entitling the lessee to a renewal upon the death of every one of the three persons comprised in the second grant. I lay out of consideration the first lease. The second will become in the nature of an original lease; when there is a grant for three lives, with this stipulation to be introduced into it; that when any one of the three dies, a new lease shall be granted for the lives of the survivors and a new life. Does that carry it farther than the lives of the three persons; whose names shall be contained in that second grant? I am of opinion it does not. There is no stipulation for any ulterior event; and there are no general words. The words are not "from time to time" as in *Furnival* v. *Crew* (1); upon which words Lord Hardwicke laid great stress; as amounting to an obligation to fill up lives upon the dropping at any time: but this covenant extends no farther than to introduce this very stipulation into this one new grant; and as to the lives only, to be contained in that grant. But the Plaintiff wants, not to have it introduced into this first grant, after the original one, but to have a stipulation for the same proviso in the subsequent grant; and if it is necessary to introduce it in the next, it must be *in infinitum*, upon this principle; that I can find out in the first a clear intention for a perpetual renewal. Otherwise I cannot carry it farther than the dropping of the three lives introduced into the second grant. So the Plaintiff

---

(1) 3 Atk. 83.

upon the whole would have the benefit of four renewals: one under
the covenant in the original grant; then having got his three lives
again he has that stipulation, when any one of them die.   There
                 are no general words of any kind.   They stop short at
[* 237]   that clause.   * The covenant is specific, to introduce it in-
                 to such grant only.   It is indentified and ascertained by
what is stipulated immediately before, that it is the grant upon the
dropping of the first life; and farther that it extends to the three
lives to be filled up, and no others.   There is not a word expressing,
that it was the intention of the parties, that it should be renewable
for ever.   I am perfectly at a loss to discover a ground for that intention; as they have expressed it.   Possibly their intention was for
a perpetual renewal: but it is not expressed: nor are there any general words: from which such intention can be collected.

I agree with the late *Master of the Rolls in Baynham* v. *Guy's
Hospital* (1); who says (2), " I collect therefore from these cases
this; that the Courts, in England at least, lean against construing a
covenant to be for a perpetual renewal; unless it is perfectly clear,
that the covenant does mean it.   *Farnival* v. *Crew*, 3 Atk. 83,
which is relied on in *Cooke* v. *Booth* (3), had clear words for a perpetual renewal; which made it impossible to construe it otherwise."

There being no clear words in this case, nor any words relative to
perpetual renewal, but the parties themselves having limited it, the
question is, whether the proviso, that the renewal shall be under the
same rents, covenants, and conditions as the first lease shall in the
absence of more positive stipulation amount to a perpetual renewal.
Upon *Tritton* v. *Foote* and *Russell* v. *Darwin* I am bound to hold,
that a covenant for renewal under the same covenants does not include the covenant to renew, but that it means only a second lease,
not a perpetuity of leases (4).   As to *Cooke* v. *Booth*, that was not
determined upon the ground, that a covenant for renewal did operate inclusively of that covenant: but Lord Mansfield goes almost
entirely upon the conduct of the parties: repeated renewals having
been made.   With regard to that mode of construing an instru-   ·
ment I refer to *Baynham* v. *Guy's Hospital;* where the Master of
the Rolls strongly protests against it.   I cannot hold, that it is perfectly clear, this covenant means a perpetual renewal; on the con-
                 trary the parties, if they meant to rest upon any thing as
[* 238]   a covenant for perpetual renewal, must * have rested upon
                 the words "under the like rents, covenants, and condi-
tions;" and probably they did; for the original lease was in 1759;
at which period these determinations had not taken place; and it
might have occurred to those, who prepared the lease, that it would
be sufficient.   For the reasons I have given, even if the acts of the

(1) *Ante,* vol. iii. 295; *Bayley* v. *The Corporation of Leominster,* i. 476, and the
note; 3 Bro. C. C. 529.
(2) *Ante,* vol. iii. 398.
(3) Cowp. 819.
(4) *Post, Iggulden* v. *May,* vol. ix. 325; *Dowling* v. *Mill,* 1 Madd. 541.

parties, which are said to have been upon this foundation of a perpetual renewal, were in evidence before me, I should not act upon them, for certainly that is not a very legal mode of construction; that a man having done an act without being bound to do it, or from mistake, shall therefore be bound for ever without the power of retracting (1).

I think, this Plaintiff is entitled to word one of his covenants a little differently from what he would, if he had not conceived he had this right. He is entitled to have a renewal as often as any of the lives drop; not merely the first. He is entitled to have the two new lives put in, and to have a renewal upon every one of them; not merely upon the first; as he has now shaped his covenant.

The exception was allowed. ____

THAT a covenant for renewal of a lease will never receive such a construction as would, virtually, lead to a perpetuity, if the language of the covenant be not perfectly unambiguous, see, *ante*, note 4 to *Taylor* v. *Stibbert*, 2 V. 437; and that legal instruments are not to be construed by the equivocal acts of the parties thereto, or by their understanding as to the effect of such instruments, see note 1 to *Eaton* v. *Lyon*, 3 V. 690.

GREGG, *Ex parte.*

[1801, JULY 4.]

UPON a second bankruptcy no allowance to the bankrupt: the estate not paying 15s. in the pound.

THE petitioner became a bankrupt in 1793; and a dividend of 10s. in the pound, was paid under the Commission. In 1799 he again became a bankrupt; and in December 1800 a dividend of 10s. in the pound was paid under that Commission; and in March following at a meeting for the purpose of making a final dividend the effects in hand appeared to be sufficient for a farther dividend of 2s. 6d.; upon which the petitioner claimed an allowance of 7l. 10s. per cent. (2). The assignee opposing the claim, and contending, that, as the petitioner had before been a bankrupt, the certificate under the second Commission protected only his person; but the allowance was the property of the creditors under the second Commission, the Petition was presented: *praying   [*239] an order for the allowance and the costs of the Petition out of the estate.

In opposition to the Petition an affidavit was made, that the de-

----

(1) *Baynham* v. *Guy's Hospital, ante,* vol. iii. 295.
(2) Stat. 5 Geo. II. c. 30, s. 7, repealed by Stat. 6 Geo. IV. c. 16; which gives an increased allowance. See s. 128.

ficiency in the bankrupt's accounts did not appear to arise from bad debts or losses; but the deponent believes, it arose from extravagance; and that his effects will not be sufficient to pay more than 13*s.* 6*d.* in the pound.

Mr. *Pemberton,* in support of the Petition.

The Petition was dismissed. ___

SEE the 127th section of the consolidated Bankrupt Act, statute 6 Geo. IV. c. 16.

HANSON *v.* GRAHAM.

[ROLLS.—1801, JULY 2, 8.]

THE word " when" in a will, alone and unqualified, is conditional: but it may be controlled by expressions and circumstances: so as to postpone payment or possession only, and not the vesting: as, where the interest of the legacy in the interval was directed to be laid out at the discretion of the executors for the benefit of the legatees, it vested immediately (a).

In the Civil Law the words " *cum* " and " *si*," as referred to legacies, are equivalent; and from that law this rule and most of our other rules upon legacies are borrowed (b), [p. 243.]

Distinction between a legacy at twenty-one and payable at twenty-one, borrowed from the Civil Law, but disapproved, [p. 245.]

A direction for maintenance has not the same effect in favor of vesting as giving interest (c), [p. 249.]

JAMES GRAHAM by his will, dated the 18th of March, 1771, gave to Mary Hanson, Thomas Hanson, and Rebecca Graham Hanson, the three children of his daughter Mary Hanson, 500*l.* a-piece of 4 per cent. Consolidated Bank Annuities, when they should respectively attain their ages of twenty-one years or day or days of marriage, which should first happen, provided, it was with such consent of his executors and trustees as therein mentioned; and he declared, his

---

(a) If the words " payable " or " to be paid" are omitted, and the legacy is given *at* 21, or *if, when, in case,* or *provided,* the legatee attains 21, or any other future definite period, this confers on him a contingent interest, which depends for its vesting, and its transmissibility to his executors or representatives, on his being alive at the period specified. 2 Williams, Executors, 886. See *Bunch* v. *Hurst,* 3 Desauss. 286; *Perry* v. *Rhodes,* 2 Murph. 140; *Marsh* v. *Wheeler,* 2 Edw. Ch. 156; *Rope* v. *Sowerby,* Taml. 376; *Howe* v. *Pillans,* 2 Mylne & K. 15; *Caldwell* v. *Kinkead,* 1 B. Monroe, 231; *Lister* v. *Bradley,* 1 Hare, 10; *Watson* v. *Hayes,* 9 Sim. 500; *Chesnut* v. *Strong,* 1 Hill, Ch. 123; *Kihler* v. *Whiteman,* 2 Har. 401; *Clapp* v. *Stoughton,* 10 Pick. 463. See, also, note (a), *Booth* v. *Booth,* 4 V. 399; note (a), *Mackell* v. *Winter,* 3 V. 236; note (b), *Batsford* v. *Kebbell,* 3 V. 363.

As a general rule, legacies are payable in one year. See note (d), *Hill* v. *Chapman,* 1 V. 405; note (a), *Crickett* v. *Dolby,* 3 V. 10.

(b) 2 Williams, Executors, 887.

(c) Where *interim* interest is given, it is presumed that the testator meant an immediate gift, because, for the purpose of interest, the particular legacy is to be immediately separated from the bulk of the property. *Vawdry* v. *Geddes,* 1 Russ. & M. 208. See, also, *Vize* v. *Stoney,* 2 Dru. & Walsh, 659; *Breedon* v. *Tugman,* 3 Mylne & K. 257: *Watkins* v. *Cheek,* 2 Sim. & Stu. 199; *Thackeray* v. *Hampson,* Ib. 214.

mind and will was, that the interest of said several 500*l.* amounting in the whole to 1500*l.* 4 per cent. Consolidated Bank Annuities, so given to his three grand-children, as aforesaid, as often as the same should become due and payable, should be laid out at the discretion of his executors and trustees in such manner as they or the survivor of them should think proper for the benefit of his said grand-children, till they should attain their respective ages of twenty-one years or day or days of marriage, and to and for no other use, intent, or purpose whatsoever; and after devising his real and leasehold estates, and giving two legacies of 10*l* each, he gave all the residue of his personal estate to his son Isaac Graham; and appointed him sole executor.

The testator died soon after the execution of his will. Afterwards, in 1774, Rebecca Graham Hanson died intestate at the age * of nine years; leaving her mother and her   [* 240] brother Thomas Hanson and her sister Mary Coates surviving. The mother died; and bequeathed all her personal estate to her son Thomas Hanson; and appointed him executor.

The bill was filed by Thomas Hanson and Mary Coates against Isaac Graham for an account of what was due in respect of Rebecca Graham Hanson's legacy of 500*l.* &c.

Mr. *Richards* and Mr. *W. Agar,* for the Plaintiffs.—The Plaintiffs insist, that though Rebecca Graham Hanson died under the age of twenty-one and unmarried, she took a vested interest in this legacy. Upon the first part of the bequest there would be a vested interest immediately on attaining the age of twenty-one or marriage: the word "when" not making a condition precedent, but only postponing the payment; according to a great number of cases: the last are *Doe* v. *Lea* (1), *May* v. *Wood* (2), and *Booth* v. *Booth* (3); in which all the others are noticed. *Booth* v. *Booth* was the case of a residue; upon which certainly some distinctions have been taken: and Lord Alvanley in that case acknowledges, that there is some distinction, notwithstanding what he says with reference to *Love* v. *L'Estrange* (4) in *May* v. *Wood*; which was the case of a particular legacy. In this case however, the rest of the will puts the case beyond all argument: the interest being given to the children; which will raise a vested interest: even though the capital should be given in words importing a contingency, *Stapleton* v. *Cheales* (5) is the leading case upon that point; which was acted upon in a great number of cases: *Fonnereau* v. *Fonnereau* (6), *Heath* v. *Heath* (7), *Walcot* v. *Hall* (8), *Lampen* v. *Clowbery* (9), or *Clobberie's Case* (10).

(1) 3 Term Rep. B. R. 41.
(2) 3 Bro. C. C. 471.
(3) *Ante,* vol. iv. 399. See the note, iii. 364, to *Batsford* v. *Kebbell.*
(4) 3 Bro. P. C. 337.
(5) Pre. Ch. 317; 2 Vern. 673.
(6) 3 Atk. 645; 1 Ves. 118.
(7) 2 Bro. C. C. 3.
(8) 2 Bro. C. C. 305.
(9) 2 Ch. Ca. 155.
(10) 2 Ventr. 342.

In this case the time is pointed out on account of the person, to whom the legacy is given.

Mr. *Romilly* and Mr. *Martin*, for the Defendant.—This question, like all others upon wills, is a mere question of intention. The rules that have been established, must be admitted; that, for [* 241] *instance, mentioned in *Stapleton* v. *Cheales* ; where the legacy is given at a certain period, and, where the period is pointed out only as the time, when the benefit intended is to come into enjoyment: or, as it is better expressed in modern times, where the time is annexed to the substance of the gift, and where to the payment only. There never was a case, in which the time was more clearly annexed to the substance of the gift; where it has been more clearly expressed to be given at the time mentioned, and not merely to be paid at the time. *May* v. *Wood*, and *Booth* v. *Booth* are not in the least applicable : the time being immediately connected with the payment. The Master of the Rolls in *May* v. *Wood* professing to lay out of his consideration the words "equally to be divided," overturns the whole class of cases. In the same case the Master of the Rolls also professed not to distinguish between a residue and a particular legacy: but in *Booth* v. *Booth* that is retracted. No case has determined, that the words, "when, if, at," alone will vest. Two periods are here mentioned; the age of twenty-one, or marriage with consent. Suppose, any of them had married without consent: would it have been vested ?

Upon the particular intention in this case there can be no doubt. The whole residue is given by the testator to his son. The reason for fixing these periods in giving the legacies to his grand-children is, that those were the times, when it would be necessary for them to receive their portions or advancements ; before which they were not likely to have occasion for them. If he had foreseen the event, that one would die at the age of nine years, he could not have intended the mother to take what he gave in the nature of a portion ; placing himself *in loco parentis*. That circumstance leads to the conclusion, that he did not intend the legacy to vest, if the legatee did not live to the time pointed out. In many cases the Court has gone expressly upon that ground ; holding, that a portion from a person *in loco parentis* would not vest ; though one from a stranger would. I admit, a legacy given at the age of twenty-one with interest in the mean time will be vested. The reason is, that when the testator directs interest to be paid out of that legacy in the mean time, he means to separate that legacy from the bulk of the estate immediately: though it is not to vest in actual enjoyment until the future time. A considerable distinction arises upon the [* 242] circumstance, that this is a *legacy of stock. The dividends are something actually existing ; and a distribution is necessary. They are not like interest of a legacy to arise at a future time ; which would not exist unless particularly given. The direction therefore, that interest is to be paid in the mean time, is separating that from the rest of the property. The dividends must arise; whether any disposition is made of them, or not. The early authorities proceed upon technical reasoning, and not so much upon the intention as the subsequent cases. Upon the argument from the gift of the dividends the words of contingency are nugatory. Though, generally speaking, a gift of the interest vests the legacy, a direction for maintenance is not equivalent to a gift of the interest : *Pulsford* v. *Hunter* (1). A gift of the dividends for maintenance is not equivalent to a gift of the interest ; and that is the object here.

Mr. *Richards*, in reply.—The judgment of Lord Alvanley in *May* v. *Wood* certainly applies to the first part of this will ; if it stood alone. His Lordship certainly put out of his consideration the words "equally to be divided." Without those words this is in the same terms, upon an uncertain event. *Booth* v. *Booth*, though a case of a residue, is applicable. But upon the latter part of the will it is impossible to doubt. All the cases agree, that, generally speaking, a gift of the interest vests the legacy. There may be cases, I admit, where the interest may be separated from the body ; but in this will it is given in respect of the body of the legacy. There is no distinction as to stock ; that in the one case it is separated more than in the other. *Pulsford* v. *Hunter* does not apply. The maintenance may not be equal to the interest of the legacy. A part only may be given for maintenance. In this will certainly the intention appears to vest the interest, as it should accrue from time to time. It is not given for maintenance ; as it was specifically in *Heath* v. *Heath*. But the interest is given ; and upon the general rule that draws the substance with it.

July 8th. The MASTER OF THE ROLLS.—The question is, whether this legacy vested. It is contended for the Plaintiffs, that it did vest, upon *two grounds; 1st, they say, it would have   [* 243] been vested ; supposing, there was nothing more than the words, with which the clause begins ; and that if it rested upon a legacy, when the legatee should attain the age of twenty-one or marriage, it is now settled, that these words give a vested interest ; and that is established by *May* v. *Wood ;* and undoubtedly a proposition is there laid down ; which would have the effect of making this a vested legacy ; if it is true in the extent there stated. The proposition is there laid down very broadly and generally by the late Master of the Rolls ; that all the cases for half a century upon pecuniary legacies have determined the word " when," not as denoting a condition precedent, but as only marking the period, when the party shall have the full benefit of the gift ; except something appears upon the face of the will to show, that his bounty shall not take place, unless the time actually arrived.

This proposition is stated so broadly and generally, that I rather doubt the correctness of the Report. Considering the well known

(1) 4 Bro. C. C. 416.

diligence of the late Master of the Rolls in examining cases, and his uncommon accuracy in stating the result of them, he would hardly have drawn this conclusion from an examination of the cases; for no case has determined, that the word "when," as referred to a period of life, standing by itself, and unqualified by any words or circumstances, has been ever held to denote merely the time, at which it is to take effect in possession; but standing so unqualified and uncontrolled it is a word of condition: denoting the time, when then gift is to take effect in substance. That this is so, is evident upon mere general principles; for it is just the same, speaking of an uncertain event, whether you say "when" or "if" it shall happen. Until it happens, that, which is grounded upon it, cannot take place. In the Civil Law the words "*Cum*" and "*Si*," as referred to this subject, are precisely equivalent; and from that law we borrow all, or at least the greatest part, of our rules upon legacies; and particularly the rule upon the subject immediately under consideration in that case, with reference to the words, by which a testator denotes his intention as to the gift taking effect, or taking effect in possession. In the Digest (1) it is thus laid down:

[* 244]   * "Si Titio, cum is annorum quatuordecim esset factus, legatus fuerit, et is ante quatuordecimum annum decesserit, verum est, ad hæredem ejus legatum non transire: quoniam non solum diem, sed et conditionem hoc legatum in se continet; si effectus esset annorum quatuordecim. Qui autem in rerum natura non esset, annorum quatuordecim non esse non intellegeretur. Nec interest utrum scribatur, si annorum quatuordecium factus erit, an ita: cum priore scriptura per conditionem tempus demonstratur; sequenti per tempus conditio: utrobique tamen eadem conditio est."

It is very true: the word "when," not so standing by itself, but coupled with other expressions or circumstances, that have a reference to the time, at which the possession of the thing is to take place, has been held by the Civil Law not to have so absolute a sense that it cannot possibly be controlled. Another passage in the Digest (2) is thus expressed:

"*Seius Saturninus* Archigubernus ex classe *Britanica* testamento fiduciarium reliquit heredem *Valerium Maximum* trierarchum: a quo petiit ut filio suo *Seio Oceano*, cum ad annos sedecium pervenisset, hereditatem restitueret. *Seius Oceanus*, antequam impleret annos, defunctus est."

Then it states, that a claim was made by the uncle of *Seius*, as next of kin, which was resisted by the fiduciary heir, who contended, that, as *Seius* had not lived to the age of sixteen, it was not vested. The opinion is this:

"Si *Seius Oceanus*, cui fideicommissa hereditas ex testamento *Seii Saturnini*, cum annos sedecim haberet, a *Valerio Maximo* fiduciario herede restitui debet, priusquam præfinitum tempus ætatis impleret, decessit: fiduciaria hereditas ad eum pertinet, ad quem cætera bona

(1) Lib. 36, tit. 2, s. 22.
(2) Lib. 36, tit. 1, s. 46.

Oceani pertinuerint: quoniam dies fideicommissi vivo *Oceano* cessit: scilicet si prorogando tempus solutionis, tutelâm magis heredi fiduciario permisisse, quam incertum diem fideicommissi constituisse, videatur."

* This distinction was transferred from the Civil Law   [* 245] to ours; at least so far clearly as regards pecuniary legacies.   In the case cited, *Stapleton* v. *Cheales*, it was clearly held, that the expressions "at twenty-one," or "if," or "when," he shall attain twenty-one, were all one and the same; and in each of those cases if the legatee died before that time, the legacy lapsed.   I do not find any case, in which this position has been ever contradicted. In *Fonnereau* v. *Fonnereau* (1) it was clear, if it had stood upon the first part of that bequest, it would have been held not vested.   Lord Hardwicke rests entirely upon the subsequent words, as controlling the word "when;" as it would have operated, standing alone. That will sets out precisely as this does; but when it went on with words, making the intention clear, giving interest for his education, with a power to the trustees to lay out any part of the principal to put him out apprentice, and the remainder to be paid to him, when he should attain the age of twenty-five, it was clear, upon the whole nothing but the payment was postponed.

A distinction has been introduced between the effect of giving a legacy at twenty-one and a legacy payable at twenty-one.   That is also borrowed from the Civil Law.   The Code (2) thus states it:

"Ex his verbis, do lego Æliæ Severinæ filiæ meæ, et Secundæ decem: quæ legata accipere debebit, cum ad legitimum statum pervenerit: non conditio fideicommisso vel legato inserta: sed petitio in tempus legitimæ ætatis dilata videtur:"

For there the words were, that the time of payment was to be at her legitimate age:

"Et ideo si Ælia Severina filia testatoris, cui legatum relictum est, die legati cedente, via functa est: ad heredem suum actionem transmisit; scilicet ut eo tempore solutio fiat, quo Severina, si rebus humanis subtracta non fuisset, vicessimum quintum annum ætatis implesset."

This distinction however has been held by some Equity Judges altogether without foundation; and by others it has been treated * as too refined.   Lord Keeper Wright, in *Yates* v.   [* 246] *Fettiplace* (3), alluding to the distinction in Godolphin and Swinburne from the Civil Law, declared it altogether without foundation.   Lord Cowper acknowledged, that it was at least a refinement: but he thought, it was now well established.   Lord Hardwicke likewise said, it was originally a refinement (4).   But in what did that refinement consist?   It was not in holding, that it should not vest before the age of twenty-one, but in holding, that it should vest,

(1) 3 Atk. 645; 1 Ves. 118.
(2) Cod. lib. 6, tit. 53, s. 5.
(3) Pre. Ch. 140; 2 Vern. 416.
(4) See *ante, Mackell* v. *Winter*, vol. iii. 536; *Bolger* v. *Mackell*, v. 509.

account of the infant Plaintiff; with liberty to him to apply at the age of twenty-one, that the Bank annuities purchased for his benefit and the cash placed to his account may be transferred and paid to him.   Several orders were made for laying out the residue accordingly.

[* 251]   * A petition, presented by the Defendant, the father and administrator of the late Plaintiff, prayed, that the Accountant General may transfer and pay to the petitioner several funds and cash standing in his name in trust in the cause to the separate account of the late Plaintiff.

Mr. *Wooddeson*, in support of the Petition, stated, that the object was to obtain this money out of Court ; the right being clear, and these funds detached from the rest of the cause.   The cause had abated by the death of the Plaintiff; and the Defendant could not revive ; being a necessary Defendant, as the only surviving executor and trustee under the will.

Lord CHANCELLOR [ELDON] asked, if he could make an order in a cause, that had abated.

Mr. *Lloyd (Amicus Curiæ)* said, it might be done in the case of an abatement by the death of one Defendant ; not, if there was an entire abatement by the death of the Plaintiff.

Mr. *Hollist (Amicus Curiæ)* said, where the right was clear by former orders and reports, and the application was only to get the money out of Court upon the clear right, so established, the Court would make the order without regarding the abatement.

Lord CHANCELLOR said, he would think of it ; and afterwards made the Order according to the Petition (1).

AFTER a decree, the defendant has a right to move in prosecution of such decree: *Bracey* v. *Sandiford*, 3 Mad. 468: and that money, which has been paid into Court in the course of a cause, may, on the abatement of the suit, be ordered to be paid out to the parties who appear to be entitled thereto, see *Barlee* v. *Barlee*, 1 Sim. & Stu. 100.

---

(1) This has been done even after the bill dismissed : *Wright* v. *Mitchell, post,* vol. xviii. 293 ; Beames on Costs, 206, n. 10.

LORD DURSLEY *v.* FITZHARDINGE BERKELEY.

[1801, JULY 7, 9.]

BILL to perpetuate testimony of the legitimacy of the Plaintiffs, entitled in remainder in tail after an estate for life: Demurrer by the seventh and eighth in remainder after the Plaintiffs and the other Defendants, all infants, overruled: any interest, however slight, being sufficient (a).

The next of kin of a lunatic, however hopeless his condition, have no interest whatever in the property (b); and therefore cannot sustain a bill to perpetuate testimony. So an heir apparent cannot have a writ *de ventre inspiciendo.* But they may contract upon their expectations; and may perpetuate testimony with reference to the interest so created, [p. 260.]

The Court will not perpetuate testimony of a right, which may be immediately barred by the Defendant (c), [p. 262.]

THE bill, filed by four infant sons of Earl Berkeley against his two other infant sons and against Admiral Berkeley and his infant son, stated, that Earl Berkeley under the will of Lord Berkeley of Stratton is seised for life of estates in the county of Dorset; with remainders to his first and other sons in tail male; remainder * to Admiral Berkeley for life, and to his first   [* 252] and other sons in tail male; remainder to the testator's right heirs. Earl Berkeley has six sons living: viz. the four infant Plaintiffs and two infant Defendants: the eldest, Lord Dursley, born in 1786; the second in 1788; the third in 1789; the fourth in 1795; the fifth in October 1796; and the sixth in February 1800.

The bill proceeded to state pretences, that the Plaintiffs are not the lawful issue of the Earl and Countess of Berkeley; alleging, that they were not lawfully married until the 16th of May, 1776, after the birth of the Plaintiffs; when the Earl was married to the Countess at Lambeth church by her maiden name of Mary Cole, spinster; and charged, that they were married on the 30th of March, 1785, at the parish church of Berkeley in the county of Gloucester by banns; which were published, and the ceremony performed, by the Reverend Augustus Thomas Hupsman, deceased; who was curate of that parish at the time of the publication of banns, and vicar of the parish at the time of the marriage. The second marriage was solemnized only as an act of caution and prudence in respect to any children that might be afterwards born: the first marriage having

---

(a) If the interest be a present vested one, it is immaterial how minute that interest may be, or how distant the possibility of its coming into actual possession and enjoyment may be. A present interest, the enjoyment of which may depend upon the most remote and improbable contingency, is a present estate: although with reference to chances, it may be worth little or nothing. 2 Story, Eq. Jur. § 1511; *Belfast* v. *Chichester,* 2 Jac. & Walk. 451.

As to bills to perpetuate testimony, see Story, Eq. Pl. § 299 to 307; 2 Story, Eq. Jur. § 1505 to 1513.

(b) Story, Eq. Pl. § 301; 2 Story, Eq. Jur. § 1511.

(c) It would be a fruitless act of power. Story, Eq. Pl. § 301; 2 Story, Eq. Jur. § 1511.

been a considerable time concealed at the request of the Earl; and there being great reason at the time the said marriage was made public, and the second marriage had, to apprehend, that the registry of the first marriage had been lost, and that a difficulty might occur in proving such marriage satisfactorily; particularly, as Hupsman was dead, and the person, who officiated as clerk at the ceremony, and who was one of the subscribing witnesses to the marriage, was also dead, or not to be found; but which registry and the entry of the publication of banns have lately been found; and as evidence the Plaintiffs charge, that the Earl being desirous, that his marriage should be kept secret for some time, consulted Hupsman as to the best manner of celebrating it so as that it should not be known to his friends.   Hupsman recommended him to be married at the parish church of Berkeley by banns; which were accordingly published, and the marriage had, in the presence of William Tudor and Richard Browne; and the entry was duly made of the publication and the due registry of the marriage, signed by the parties and the witnesses.   The bill farther charged, that Hupsman several times afterwards and prior to the birth of the [* 253]   Plaintiff Lord Dursley, * informed several persons of the marriage; and many persons in the neighborhood believed it; and the Countess herself soon afterwards mentioned it to the Earl in the presence of others; and he did not contradict her.   The prayer of the bill was, that the testimony might be perpetuated. .

To this bill the Defendants Admiral Berkeley and his son put in a demurrer; stating, that the Plaintiffs have not by their bill made a case to entitle them to have their witnesses examined, and their testimony perpetuated against the Defendants; that it appears by the bill, that the two other Defendants are the natural and lawful sons, born in lawful wedlock; and that they are tenants in tail male; and the limitations to Admiral Berkeley and his first and other sons in tail male are posterior to the estates in tail male given to the other Defendants; and therefore these Defendants are not necessary parties to the bill, nor ought to have been made Defendants; and the putting them to answer the bill and to be parties to the examination of the witnesses tends to create expense upon the part of the Defendants.

The other Defendants waited the result of this demurrer.

Mr. *Richards* and Mr. *Hollist* for the Demurrer.—There are now parties upon the record, who are tenants in tail in remainder anterior to any interest in Admiral Berkeley and his son.   How the Plaintiffs can. sustain the bill against those parties is not now the question: but these Defendants, who have demurred, are not bound to answer; nor are the Plaintiffs entitled to perpetuate testimony against them. The habit of this Court is not to bring before it in any discussion as to real estate any person standing in interest behind a clear tenant in tail.   In selling an estate for the payment of debts the familiar practice is not to call upon any person as a Defendant, who is posterior to an actual tenant in tail in existence; upon the principle, that formerly the tenant in tail had to a certain extent and in certain, cases the absolute interest in him; and now such an interest as this Court considers capable of being made absolute. He is always treated as having the whole and complete interest; and though he is only an infant, whose acts will not bind him, and this Court does not require, that the infant should have a Privy Seal for the purpose of suffering *a recovery, yet it will   [* 254] act upon the estate of the infant tenant in tail, as if he was an adult tenant in fee; directing a sale, &c. This sort of case cannot be distinguished from that of a bill for payment of debts and other familiar cases; but must be governed by the same principle. In the one case as well as the other all the interest is before the Court; when the tenant in tail is before the Court. Suppose, Lord Berkeley was tenant for life, with remainder to his eldest son in fee; and the bill was filed by the eldest son against Admiral Berkeley; who, if the eldest son was not legitimate, would be the heir; the bill could not be maintained; for clearly the Defendant would háve no interest; the law not considering such a possibility. There is no case upon this point; though there are some bearing an analogy to it. In Mitford (1) cases are put, in which the Plaintiffs had no certain interest. In this instance the Defendants in the contemplation of the Court have only an expectancy and possibility; which the Court will not acknowledge. In the case of the next of kin of a lunatic they are always considered as having more than merely an expectancy; for the Court calls upon them in the application of the personal property to object or consent. They have therefore an inchoate interest; and yet they have no right to file a bill; having only that sort of expectancy, of which the law cannot lay hold. These Defendants are in the same condition. There is a distinction between a bill to examine witnesses *de bene esse* and this bill; the former is generally brought by a person out of possession, and having witnesses infirm or aged, or a single witness and in aid of his trial at law, This sort of bill is directly the contrary; a bill brought by a person in possession; having no opportunity to examine his witnesses at law; the party meaning in future to resist. *Phillips* v. *Carew* (2), though in appearance a bill to perpetuate testimony, was in fact a bill to examine *de bene esse*. In opposition to this are *Parry* v. *Rogers* (3), and a dictum by Lord Hardwicke in *Brandlyn* v. *Ord* (4). *Shirley* v. *Earl Ferrers* (5), was also a case of examination *de bene esse*; and by a manuscript note, it appears that the order was made upon the Defendant's refusing to go to issue in the manner proposed; and upon that Lord Camden refused a similar application upon an affidavit, * that the witness was sixty-three and impaired in his   [* 255]

---

(1) Mitf. 138.
(2) 1 P. Will. 116.
(3) 1 Vern. 441.
(4) 1 Atk. 571.
(5) 3 P. Will. 77.

health: May 8th, 1769 (1).   In *The Duke of Dorset* v. *Gird-ler* (2), respecting a right of fishery, it was held, that the Plaintiff was entitled to examine his witnesses; as he was in possession; and there was no disturbance. These cases really do not apply to the subject. In *Smith* v. *The Attorney General* (3), before Lord Bathurst, assisted by Lords Chief Justice De Grey and Chief Baron Skynner, it was laid down that any person having a real interest in reversion or remainder may file such a bill; and the Lord Chancellor referred to something of the same kind laid down by Lord Hardwicke. In *Lord Suffolk* v. *Green* (4), which is similar to the case of a person not disturbed, but liable to be disturbed, Lord Hardwicke said, though it is not noticed in the report, that he did not know, in what case a party has not a right to perpetuate testimony; but that he must have a right present or future. The position laid down in that way is not supported by decision; and is much too large. There are but two cases on the subject: *Tyrell* v. *Co* (5), and *Seabourn* v. *Chilston*, or *Seybourne* v. *Clifton* (6). The former is rather against this demurrer. The Defendant to such a bill might have demurred; unless it was alleged that the marriage had actually taken place. The other case appears in the Register's Book (7) by the name of *Seabourne* v. *Cliston*. It appears from the Register's Book, that the bill was filed by the son and heir of Seabourne against a purchaser under a forged deed. Mr. Justice Archer was desired by the Lord Keeper to talk to the Judges upon it; and in 1670 the bill was dismissed upon the Plaintiff's motion, with 40s. costs: the Defendant's Counsel stating, that she had taken advantage of a slip to put in a demurrer. It is easy therefore to conjecture what was the opinion of the Judges. The bill might have been amended.

Upon the second point, a bill of foreclosure is never filed against any one except the tenant for life and the first tenant in tail; *Reynoldson* v. *Perkins* (8) The depositions taken in one cause may be read in another, upon the same question, against parties claiming under the same title. *Terwit* v. *Gresham* (9).   The
[*256]   * *Corporation of London* v. *Perkins* (10).   *Nevil* v. *Johnson* (11).   *Earl of Bath* v. *Bathersea* (12).

All these parties are equally purchasers under the same will. It

---

(1) But in *Pearson* v. *Ward*, 2 Dick. 648, Lord Thurlow granted a similar application; saying, he would have made a precedent, had there not been one. See *Shelley* v. ——, *post*, vol. xiii. 56.
(2) Pre. Ch. 531.
(3) In Chancery, 1777, cited *post*, vol. xv. 133, 6.
(4) 1 Atk. 450.
(5) 1 Roll. Abr. 383.
(6) Nels. 125, cited 2 Vern. 159; 1 Eq. Ca. Ab. 354.
(7) Reg. Book, 1669, B. fol. 520; 1670, B. fol. 499.
(8) Amb. 564.
(9) 1 Ch. Ca. 73.
(10) 4 Bro. P. C. 157.
(11) 2 Vern. 447.
(12) 5 Mod. 9.

is very extraordinary, that this bill should not have been filed till after the death of Hupsman.   There is no allegation, that Tudor is aged or infirm.

Mr. *Mansfield*, Mr. *Romilly*, and Mr. *Stanley*, in support of the bill.—It is perfectly established, that this bill lies for every person having a legal right; which he cannot bring into immediate discus- sion; however it arises.   It is so described in Mitford (1); and the instance of a person in possession without disturbance is put only as one case, to illustrate the general doctrine; and in a subsequent part (2) it is stated, that a demurrer to this bill will seldom hold; excepting, where the subject can be immediately investigated at law. In the only two cases, mentioned as applicable, there was an imme- diate right, though not immediately vested.   *Seabourne* v. *Cliston* is the only case, in which it is said, such a bill could not be support- ed upon a reversion; but the nature of the case shows, no bill could be supported.   First, the Plaintiff was a volunteer: 2dly, the De- fendant was a purchaser under a forged deed; which he believed good.   That ground appearing on the bill was sufficient to prevent Equity from giving any relief or aid against him.   The other cases cited have no application.   The decisions in these cases are consid- ered as decisions against the estate; to which the party succeeds with all the obligations put upon it by this Court.   *The Corporation of London* v. *Perkins* was upon tolls; as to which reputation is evidence.   In *Smith* v. *The Attorney General* this point was treated as perfectly clear; and it was expressly stated, that a bill by a Plain- tiff in such a situation will lie.   Chief Baron Skynner says it is not necessary, that the parties should have a present interest; that it is more likely to be future; certain, though future.   Lord Chief Jus- tice De Grey says, there are cases, in which there is a present right, but not possession; as a remainder upon an estate for life in posses- sion; and contingent, executory, interests; which are rights in property; though not in possession.   That case proceeded upon *the want of interest present or future.   The cases   [* 257] of bills to examine witnesses *de bene esse* proceed exactly upon the same ground; for the Plaintiff cannot on account of the circumstances have the benefit of that testimony immediately at law. The principle is the same.   There is an immediate interest: which cannot be immediately tried at law.

Upon the circumstances of this case, the second marriage itself naturally excites doubts as to any prior marriage.   There is a clear vested interest in the Plaintiffs.   They cannot bring the matter into immediate litigation, having no present interest.   None of them are purchasers; they are all volunteers under the same will.   The ob- ject of the bill is merely to perpetuate testimony, not to execute a trust, or for any other relief.   It is much to be lamented, that the difficulty of perpetuating testimony is so great; and that from the

---

(1) Mitf. 51.
(2) Mitf. 131.

strictness of the law in rejecting hearsay evidence, admitted in the law of many countries, rights are lost by the death of witnesses. For such a bill nothing more is necessary than that the Plaintiff and Defendant have an interest; but no authority requires that interest to be immediate and in possession. A contingent remainder I should have thought a sufficient interest in the Plaintiff: but these are vested remainders.

Next as to the remoteness of the interest of these Defendants. They complain, that the evidence may be used against them, and yet they are put in a situation to cross-examine. There is no decision, that a bill of this sort will not lie against a party having a certain, though remote interest. They have a clear interest, capable of fine and conveyance. In consequence of death they may be the only persons, with whom the Plaintiffs or their issue may have the contest. The ground is, that there is a right, which cannot immediately be brought into dispute. Parties having trusts to execute, &c. certainly need not go farther than the first tenant in tail: though I do not know, that it has been decided, that they may not, to meet the accident of death, and avoid bills of revivor. But the present subject of consideration is not what is to be done, where the estate is to be acted upon. The inconvenience, mischief, and failure of justice, are all on one side: if there are no means of preserving the testimony between persons, having a right in an estate, [*258] and others, having a future right, naturally *leading a contest. In such a bill as this the Plaintiff is bound to pay the costs. The evidence taken against a first tenant in tail could not be used at law against a remote tenant; and I should have thought it also clear in this Court: there being no privity between them; but clearly not at law; and the only object of the bill is to preserve evidence to be used at law. All, that has been decided is, that it is not necessary to make more than the first tenant in tail parties: 2 Eq. Ca. Ab. 166, pl. 8. The ground is the inconvenience; upon which a positive rule has been established, that, where the first tenant in tail is before the Court, no person more remote shall dispute that decree; but that is only a positive rule of equity: a very wise rule, from the great inconvenience, expense, and delay, by making so many parties. That cannot apply, where nothing is desired but to preserve evidence for a Court of Law: and it is impossible to draw any inference from the cases requiring relief. The principle of this bill is to guard against the inconvenience, that may happen at some future time by the loss of the evidence: an inconvenience much more likely to happen with regard to a remote title. This very case was put by Lord Chief Justice De Grey; who says, perhaps such a bill may be filed by a person entitled in remainder in tail under a strict settlement, suspecting a person prior to him to have been born before marriage; and he observes, that the interest may never take effect; as the estate tail may continue for ever. No instance has been produced of a demurrer by a subsequent remainder-man, because not made a party. In *Mildmay* v.

Mildmay, a bill as to timber, Lord Redesdale was of opinion, that all the remainder-men *in esse* should be made parties.

Mr. *Richards*, in reply.—No instance is produced of perpetuating testimony against an interest behind a tenant in tail. It is no answer, that the Defendants are entitled to their costs; and that practice itself shows, that it is improper to bring any person but the first tenant in tail before the Court. Where the Court is called upon to execute a trust, the rule is general; that if a Defendant is not a necessary party, he may demur. In *Mildmay* v. *Mildmay* the persons standing behind the tenant in tail did not object: 2dly, the question was as to cutting timber; and in whom was the property of the timber cut; whether it ought not to be secured in Court for the first tenant in tail attaining twenty-one, capable
* of alienating. If this devise had been to the use of   [*259] trustees, in trust for Lord Berkeley for life, with remainder to his first and other sons in tail, remainder over, and the first son filed a bill, calling on the trustees to execute any prior trust, and then to convey, suggesting a doubt, whether he was legitimate, and wishing to establish his right against the trustees, he must have made the next brother a party; having the question to litigate with him. Can it be necessary to bring all the remainder-men before the Court? It may be so, for the purpose of acting upon the estate, *sub modo*; but not in such a case as this; and where there are six other remainders in tail, before these Defendants can be introduced. Their interest is of no value whatsoever. It is very inconvenient therefore, that they should be put to the expense of this suit. Lord Chief Justice De Grey in the passage referred to expresses that opinion with a degree of caution; and the case he puts is not of a tenant in tail after six others. Suppose the number greater: it would be extremely harassing to hold, that they may all be made parties, merely because hereafter they are to have their costs; which is no sort of remuneration.

Lord CHANCELLOR [ELDON].—Before I decide this case, which is very singular, I shall look into all the authorities cited; not on account of the singularity of the case, but as to the general doctrine. No difficulty is alleged as to examining Tudor. In arguing this demurrer the fact as to the first marriage must for the present be taken to be true. The question therefore is, whether according to the rules of this Court the Plaintiff has a right to perpetuate the testimony of that circumstance, taken for the present as a fact? It is going beside the fact to examine the probability, or the reason of not bringing forward the alleged illegitimacy in the life of the clergyman; who it is alleged, celebrated the marriage. The story does not hang very well together, as to the publication of banns in the parish church, recommended by him as the best mode of keeping the marriage secret. There might be a marriage *de facto*, and a colorable publication of banns; and it might be convenient to him, that the real circumstances, by which he had contrived a marriage *de facto*, should not come out. His greater or less degree of criminality however certainly cannot affect these children. I must also lay out of the question, whether there could be a more convenient, just, or effectual mode of ascertaining the fact of the [*260]   *marriage at present ; or, whether it could be ascertained. The bill does not seek to ascertain it; but to preserve the means of duly trying the fact ; when an opportunity shall arise of conveniently and usefully trying it. This Plaintiff comes, stating himself not to have the means by any gift of property by his father or otherwise of trying the question at present : his father not having furnished those means by a conveyance or surrender of his estate. The question therefore is, whether a tenant in tail in remainder, without the means of provoking a trial at present, can file such a bill. . It appears to me very difficult to conceive, that he has not that right.

The case of *Smith* v. *The Attorney General* went upon this; that the next of kin of the lunatic had no interest whatever in the property. Put the case as high as possible ; that the lunatic is intestate ; that he is in the most hopeless state, a moral and physical impossibility, though the Law would not so regard it, that he should ever recover, even, if he was *in articulo mortis*, and the bill was filed at that instant, the Plaintiff could not qualify himself as having any interest in the subject of the suit. The case of an heir apparent was very properly put by Lord Chief Justice De Grey in his most luminous judgment. Upon that occasion he said, he never liked Equity so well as when it was like Law. The day before I heard Lord Mansfield say, he never liked Law so well as when it was like Equity ; remarkable sayings of those two great men, which made a strong impression on my memory. Lord Chief Justice De Grey said, that at law the heir apparent cannot have the writ *de ventre inspiciendo* in the life of his ancestor ; as for that purpose he must be *verus hæres*. If the ancestor was in a fever, a delirium, having made no will, and it was not possible for him to recover, still the law would look upon him as mere heir apparent, having nothing but an expectation, which is different from an expectancy in the legal sense, and as having no interest whatever upon that ground. In *Smith* v. *The Attorney General* it was held, that the bill would not lie. It is not to be taken upon the single *dictum* of any of the learned Judges, who assisted upon that occasion : but the whole judgment went upon distinguishing between that expectation, which the next of kin have in that case, and any sort of right, which the law allows to be an interest. A contingent interest is not the less a present interest.

It was not doubted in that judgment, that a vested [*261]   interest, *though in possibility the least valuable, that could be conceived, is yet of some value in consideration of Law ; and gives a right to preserve testimony. In the course of that cause cases were cited ; which go to this ; that though the next of kin could not file a bill, or the heir apparent (1) in the case put, yet

_____

(1) Nor the issue in tail during the life of the tenant in tail: *Allan* v. *Allan, post,* vol. xv. 180 ; *The Earl of Belfast* v. *Chichester,* 2 Jac. & Walk. 439.

they might respectively enter into contracts with respect to their expectations and possibilities; the evidence upon which they might perpetuate (a).   The Law would frame an interest in respect to the contract; and with reference to that they would have a right to perpetuate testimony; though they could not qualify themselves as to any interest in the subject itself.

It appears therefore, that unless there are grounds for entertaining doubt, with which at present I am not impressed, the Plaintiff has a sufficient interest to support this bill; if these Defendants are proper parties.   As to that, independent of the intermediate estates tail, upon the principles I have already stated there can be no doubt; for their interest is exactly of the same species; though less valuable, because posterior.   Next, does the intervention of the other estates tail prevent their being proper Defendants?   If so, the converse must certainly be maintained; for if these estates tail intervening could prevent their being Defendants, the consequence would follow, that if these Defendants contended upon the strongest evidence of circumstances, that the elder children were illegitimate, and were able to represent this case, that the two youngest children were of very tender years, and of such puny constitutions, that there was no moral probability, that either of them would attain the age of twenty-one, it must be admitted upon these principles, that these Defendants could not as Plaintiffs sustain a bill of this sort.   That would not be very convenient to justice.   I can conceive a power in a tenant in tail to say, a remainder-man should not file such a bill.   Suppose an eldest son illegitimate: and the father expressly devised to him in tail; leaving the reversion to descend; and that he also had a son by marriage: and a dispute had arisen; the eldest insisting, he was not illegitimate; and the younger, that the first marriage was to his mother; and he, as reversioner, should file a bill to perpetuate testimony.   I am not quite sure, that in such a case the elder might not say, he being in possession as a tenant in tail might .
suffer * a recovery, and destroy the reversion; and there-   [* 262]
fore equity could not interfere.   That might perhaps be
sustained by analogy to other cases: as, where there was a tenant of a lease for lives to him and the heirs of his body; and the lease was renewed to him and his heirs: according to the ordinary doctrine the equitable title would attach upon the legal estate; and upon a bill by a person entitled in remainder, for the purpose of attaching the equities of the old lease upon the new one, the Court said, it was nugatory; for by a deed he might bar them all; and say, he did not choose, the equities of the old lease should attach upon the new one. That might possibly apply to the case I have just put, and support a demurrer by the elder son to the bill of the younger, upon the ground, that a recovery would bar him(b).

But that is very different from this case; for no one can at present

---

(a) Story, Eq. Pl. § 301.
(b) Story, Eq. Pl. § 145, note.

bar the estate tail.   The argument cannot vary from the number of
estates tail.   These Defendants at the utmost can only contend, that
there are two remainder-men in tail, infants; neither of whom may
ever be able to bar them.   As to the consequence in point of convenience, I am much struck with the argument in support of the
bill.   Is it inconvenient to general justice, or to these Defendants,
that they should be parties?   First, the question imports all the persons to take an estate; all the interests making up the fee: and it is
as necessary in the view of what general justice requires, that the
testimony should be perpetuated against these Defendants as that
they should perpetuate the non-existence of the Plaintiff's title; and
with regard to the individuals it cannot be unjust to secure to these
Defendants the opportunity of cross-examining now to the extent, in
which there must be a cross-examination.   They must decide for
themselves as to the prudence of leaving the story with all the doubt,
that hangs about it, or of cross-examining: but if it is fit to cross-
examine, justice requires, that the Defendants, who may be affected
by the evidence, (for it is admitted in the argument for the demurrer, that the evidence will bind them) should have the opportunity
of deciding for themselves, whether it is prudent, and whether they
will now have the cross-examination.   I express it thus; for it may
be, that now only they will have the opportunity.   I agree to the answer to the objection as to the costs.   It is a sufficient ground
for protecting a Defendant from a suit, that he may
[* 263]   * be vexed by it, independent of any pecuniary consideration; and if he can defend himself against the demand, it
is not an answer, that he will some time or other have his costs.

In my present view of this case the demurrer must be overruled;
unless I should alter that opinion upon looking at these cases.

July 9th.   Lord CHANCELLOR [ELDON].—I have looked through all
the cases upon this subject; and I cannot find any case having a tendency to affect· the opinion I intimated, except that case stated in
Eq. Ca. Ab. and also in Vernon, under the name of *Seaborne* v. *Clifton* (a);' which in both books stands thus; a bill by a person, claiming a reversion, to perpetuate testimony against a purchaser for valuable consideration.   The books treat the demurrer as having been
allowed upon that ground; and in Vernon it is stated, that the bill
was dismissed; and the party lost the estate for the want of examining the witnesses.   I am much obliged to Mr. Hollist; who has furnished me with an extract from that case in the Register's Book; from
which it appears, that the case amounts to no decision at all.   The
son filed the bill upon this point; that his deed was genuine; and
the other forged.   The causes of demurrer were, 1st, that this was
a strange Court to prove a forgery in: 2dly, a purchase for valuable
consideration.   The Judge presiding here gave no opinion; but desired Mr. Justice Archer to talk with the Judges upon it.   The re-

(a) "Lord Eldon has manifestly doubted this case."   2 Story, Eq. Jur. § 1503,
note.

sult does not appear. Unquestionably the bill was not dismissed upon any of the grounds stated in the printed books: but under a suggestion, that the Defendant had taken advantage of a slip to put in a demurrer, leave was given to the Plaintiff to withdraw his bill on payment of very moderate costs. That is by no means an authority, that, if two persons are claiming a reversion, where one only can be entitled to it, a bill to perpetuate testimony will not lie. Nor did it establish a principle, which I think very difficult to maintain, that, if one of them had sold his title to a third person,-a bill to perpetuate testimony could not be maintained; for such a bill calls for no discovery from the Defendant; but merely prays to secure that testimony; which might be had at that time, if the circumstances called for it. If therefore that case had only this distinc- tion, of a *purchase for valuable consideration, it would   [*264]· require a good deal of consideration, before it should be disposed of, as turning upon a principle not applicable to this case (a). But, taking that not to be an authority upon this case, and particularly not to be an authority upon the reasons given in the printed books, it seems to me, that, independent of the circumstance of there being four Plaintiffs here and six tenants in tail, the whole reasoning in *Smith* v. *The Attorney General* goes to this point; that a remainder-man has a present interest, future in enjoyment, but as real in the contemplation of the law as if he was then seised in fee; and as against another person having a real interest of the same nature that case has gone the length deciding, that a bill to perpetuate testimony is capable of being supported, and a demurrer to it could not be allowed.

The specialties of the case are, that there are four Plaintiffs, all tenants in tail, and two Defendants, tenants in tail, standing at all events with priority of interest and priority of title to Admiral Berkeley and his son: but upon the principles I before stated it seems to me, that those specialties will not take this case out of the rule; particularly where the two tenants in tail are infants, and never may have the enjoyment; and where upon the single fact of a legal marriage in 1785 the title of all these children will be to be decided. I am much struck with the circumstance (though it may have been unavoidable) that the bill states a case clear of doubt; and then clothes it with infinite doubt; for it states this case; that there was a marriage in fact in 1785; that there is a living witness of that marriage; that there is a register; that there was a due publication of banns, and that there is now an entry of the marriage producible, signed by the parties and by the witnesses to that marriage. If these circumstances stood alone, the bill would not state a case of any doubt, or a case of perishable testimony, if I may so express myself; but upon the whole enough has been stated of the circumstances upon this bill to raise as questionable a case in fact as could be put upon a record; for it states, that the marriage was for certain reasons

(a) Story, Eq. Pl. § 809, note.

intended to be kept secret for some time ; and the means of accomplishing that object are certainly very singular : the marriage being attended with as much publicity and notoriety as could [* 265] be given to it : a *marriage in the parish church of Berkeley ; and according to this bill, attended with a due publication of banns ; with all the circumstances that belong to a marriage ; a due registry and signing by all the parties present ; and it alleges, that the thing was quite. notorious ; that the clergyman and parties were constantly talking about it ; and it became the habit and repute of the place.   The bill alleges, that because apprehensions were entertained, upon what foundation does not appear, that the registry was lost, and because the clergyman was dead, and one of the witnesses was either dead or not to be found, under these circumstances it was thought prudent to have another marriage.   As a circumstance of evidence for the consideration of a Jury that is pregnant with a great deal of observation ; for however prudent it might be as to the future issue, it was not marked with singular prudence to marry again under the maiden name of the lady, in order to prove the legitimacy of four children born antecedent to the second marriage.   A great deal of consideration ought to be had, if this should come before a Jury, which course it probably must take at last, as to the actual treatment of the children, born before and after this marriage, in the family.

But whatever difficulties arise in my mind upon this, the Plaintiff has stated upon his bill a case of an actual legal marriage, to be proved under all the difficulties, that belong to it ; with respect to which I think upon the principles I stated before he has a right to perpetuate testimony.   Independent of the consideration of general justice, and the particular ground in this case, cases might be put, and none can warrant the observation more than this cause, in which a bill to perpetuate testimony may be an excessively dangerous proceeding ; and upon that ground it is handsomely done towards justice by the Plaintiff to make Admiral Berkeley and his son parties.   He must be well acquainted, or at least has a better chance than others of being acquainted, with all, that has passed in the family ; and therefore he will have the opportunity, if he chooses to make use of it, to take a complete view of all the circumstances, to decide upon the condition of these children, and to bring out all the known facts ; that it may be determined for the sake of those, who are infants, what it may be proper to do with regard to the cross-examination ; whether there should be any cross-examination ; or, if any, to what extent.

[* 266]   * I do not know, who is the next friend of the children claiming under the second marriage : but I must say, that, whoever he is, no man ever took upon himself a more solemn and more delicate duty.   If he for any reasons of connection with any part of the family does not exert himself for those children as zealously as if he was supporting his own claim to the dearest interest in life, he does not do his duty to those children.   I say this ; because.

though this bill may be as properly conducted, as it may be most essential to the justice due to the children claiming under the first marriage that it should be conducted, yet if it should not be so conducted, it may be an instrument of mischief and oppression, or what would even require a harsher name, to the children claiming under the second marriage. It is some consolation to the Court, that the bill can be maintained against persons, who have an interest of a pecuniary value; which will enable them to aid those, who stood in the sacred relation of next friend to the children claiming under the second marriage (1).

The demurrer was overruled.

In order to support a bill to perpetuate testimony, the plaintiff must at the time have an actual interest: it is immaterial how minute that interest may be, or how distant the probability, or even the possibility, that such interest should come into his possession; provided it be a present interest, it is, in contemplation of law, an estate upon which such an application may be sustained: but a party cannot be heard who has not a present estate and interest, however proximate and valuable his contingent interest may be. *Allan* v. *Allan*, 15 Ves. 135. Thus, the next of kin of a lunatic cannot support a bill even to perpetuate testimony, with respect to the lunatic's affairs, however desperate his state may be; (*Sackville* v. *Ayleworth*, 1 Vern. 105;) for the law always recognizes a possibility at least, of his recovery; upon which event restitution of his property is to be made, and an account rendered, to himself alone. *Sheldon* v. *Fortescue Aland*, 3 P. Wms. 109; *Ex parte Whitbread*, 2 Meriv. 102; and see, *ante*, note 5 *Ex parte Bromfield*, 1 V. 453. Thus, also, an heir apparent cannot obtain the writ *de ventre inspiciendo*, though, unquestionably, this writ lies in behalf *veri hæredis* : *Ex parte Ayscoughe*, Mosely, 392: and the remedy is not confined to heirs by descent; a devisee, or *hæres factus*, is equally entitled thereto, in order to prevent his rights from being defeated by the introduction of a supposititious child. *Ex parte Belle*, 1 Cox, 299. As to the distinction between examination *in perpetuam rei memoriam*, and examination *de bene esse*, see *Morrison* v. *Arnold*, 19 Ves. 671.

---

(1) The result of the investigation in the House of Lords upon the right to the title established the marriage in 1796, as the only marriage. See the case of the *Berkeley Peerage*. As to bills to perpetuate testimony, see *Harris* v. *Cotterell*, 3 Mer. 678; *Angell* v. *Angell*, 1 Sim. & Stu. 83, and the authorities collected in the note, p. 93.

GIBSON *v.* JEYES.

[1801, JULY 8, 9.]

SALE of an annuity by an attorney to his client set aside under the circumstances.
To support a commission in nature of a writ *de lunatico inquirendo* it is sufficient,
　　that the party is incapable of managing his own affairs (*a*), [p. 273.]
Rule as to an attorney contracting with his client, or a trustee with his *cestuy que*
　　trust (*b*), [p. 277.]
General rule, that he, who bargains in matter of advantage with a person placing
　　confidence in him is bound to show, that a reasonable use has been made of
　　that confidence (*c*), [p. 278.]

THE bill was filed by the administrator of Ann Kerby to set aside
the sale of an annuity by the Defendant John Jeyes to Ann Kirby
for her life under the following circumstances.

Mrs. Kirby, a widow, above the age of seventy, residing at Northampton, employed Jeyes, an attorney of the same place, as her
agent. The transaction, which produced this suit, took place in
1798. Mrs. Kerby, being possessed of 900*l.* 4 per cent. Bank Consolidated Annuities, 100*l.* of which the Defendant had sold out for
her under a letter of attorney, in May 1798, executed a letter of
attorney dated the 21st of November 1798, empowering Theophilus
Jeyes, the son of the Defendant, to sell out the remaining 800*l,* ;
which he accordingly did, for the sum of 514*l.* 17*s.* 6*d.* Soon
afterwards the Defendant received 400*l.*, as the consideration agreed
　　　　　　upon for an annuity of 50*l.* a-year to Mrs. Kerby for her
[* 267]　life ; for securing which he gave her his bond, * dated the
　　　　　　26th of December, 1798, in the penalty of 800*l.* Jeyes at
that time was at the age of eighty. Mrs. Kerby died upon the 28th
of March, 1799 about three days after the first quarter became due,
but not having received any part of it except two guineas from young
Jeyes. Her death was in consequence of a paralytic stroke. Before this transaction she had attempted to sell a house, with a view
to purchase an annuity ; which project failed from a difficulty in the
title.

The bill prayed, that the stock might be replaced ; and charged,
that this transaction was a fraud ; that from the age as well as state
of health of Mrs. Kerby the price was much more than the annuity
was worth, and might have been purchased for according to the office
calculation ; that at the times of executing the two powers of attorney and the bond she was so debilitated in her mind as to be inca-

---

(*a*) *In the matter of Barker,* 2 Johns. Ch. 235.

(*b*) As to contracts between an attorney and client, see *ante,* note (*a*), *Newman*
v. *Payne,* 2 V. 199 ; as to purchases by an agent, note (*a*), *Massey* v. *Davis,* 2 V.
317 ; as to purchases by a trustee of a *cestui que trust,* note (*a*), *Whichcote* v. *Lawrence,* 3 V. 740 ; note (*a*), *Campbell* v. *Walker,* 5 V. 678.

(*c*) See 1 Story, Eq. Jur. § 311. It has been held that, where an account is
decreed to be taken between an attorney and his client, in the course of which the
attorney has taken securities from the client, the attorney must not only prove the
securities, but the consideration, for which they were given. *Jones* v. *Thomas,*
2 Y. & C. 498.

pable of forming any judgment for herself upon the transaction or of transacting business ; and that Theophilus Jeyes was obliged to point out to her the letters of her name ; which fact was not denied.

It appeared by the evidence of the apothecary, who had attended her many years, that from the 26th of October, to the 2d of November, 1798, she was very much indisposed by a violent bilious complaint ; from which she soon recovered ; and it did not appear to him to have effected her mind.   But by the other evidence produced by the Plaintiff, consisting of servants, who were constantly with her, and friends and others, who saw her frequently, imbecility of mind in a considerable degree, increasing for three or four years previous to her death, was established ; and it appeared, that she did not understand the nature of the transaction with Jeyes ; having a notion, that he was to keep her money for her, and let her have it, as she wanted it.   This was opposed on the part of the Defendant by the evidence of persons, who saw her occasionally, in favor of her general capacity, and her health, considering her time of life.   Theophilus Jeyes by his depositions in support of the answer of his father represented, that Mrs. Kerby had been very anxious to increase her income by the purchase of an annuity for her life ; for which she had made applications to different persons ; but refused an offer from William Gibson, the father of the Plaintiff; who said, he would give more than any *one else ; and actually offered   [*268] an annuity of 60*l.*, secured upon land ; declaring her reason, that she would have no concern or business with him.   The deponent advised her to defer her purpose; the stocks being then low ; and after some delay upon her still persisting recommended her to accept the offer of Gibson ; to which she positively objected ; saying she would have nothing to do with him, and complaining, that he had not behaved well to her.   After some days she expressed a wish, that the deponent would ask the Defendant to grant her an annuity for her life; which the Defendant at first refused ; but being repeatedly pressed at length complied with reluctance.   The deponent had procured for her the table of the terms of the Royal Exchange Assurance Office ; and she declared she would much rather purchase an annuity from the Defendant ; but would from the office, if he refused.   She strictly enjoined the deponent not to mention that this business had been so settled, to any person, and particularly to William Gibson ; with whom she was then on tolerable terms, and did not wish to fall out with him ; but was determined to have no dealings with him, &c.   She afterwards upon receiving the bond registered expressed her satisfaction.   On the 22d of March, 1799, she sent for the money, that would be due to her on Lady-day ; and the deponent sent her two guineas on account of the first quarterly payment of the annuity.

Other witnesses also stated, that previously to Christmas 1798 she had expressed uneasiness, that she could not prevail upon Mr. Jeyes to take her money upon the terms she wished, viz. to allow her a yearly sum in lieu thereof; and afterwards, she expressed her satisfaction at having prevailed upon him to do so.

The Actuary of an Assurance Office, examined on behalf of the Plaintiff, stated, that a person of the age of seventy years and a half in as good a state of health as persons generally enjoy at that age ought for a sum of 400l. to receive an annuity, payable quarterly, of 64l. 3s. during the term of such person's natural life : but a person of that age in an infirm state of health ought to receive more. The Actuary of another Office on the other side deposed, that, supposing Mrs. Kerby to have been of the age of seventy years and a half, and not laboring under any particular complaint or infirmity of [* 269] body, but enjoying a good state of * health, and living a regular life, and not given to any kind of excess, the value of an annuity of 50l. a year for her life, payable quarterly, was 438l. 10s. ; which is eight years and about three quarters of a year's purchase ; which was the fair price of the said annuity on the 26th of December, 1798, under the circumstances aforesaid.

The Defendant stated, that previously to this transaction the partnership between him and his son had ceased : but the weight of evidence was the other way ; and an advertisement of a subsequent date in their joint names as partners was produced.

The *Solicitor General* [Mr. *Spencer Perceval*], Mr. *Sutton*, and Mr. *Stratford*, for the Plaintiff.—The evidence in this case does not amount to this ; that Jeyes, the father, suggested the idea of the sale of an annuity : but it proves, that, however that was suggested, he took advantage of this old lady. The grounds upon which this relief is sought, are inadequacy of consideration, the circumstances of imbecility, under which she engaged in this transaction, and principally the situation of the Defendant as an attorney. It is in evidence, that upon executing the power of attorney to sell out the stock Jeyes the younger was under the necessity of pointing out to her the letters of her name. It is not probable, that at that time the Defendant did not know what was to follow. The principle, upon which these cases turn, is stated by Mr. Mansfield in *Fox* v. *Mackreth* (1) ; that where one person takes an unfair advantage of another, it is the peculiar province of equity to give relief.

Upon the third ground, attorneys are not to be permitted to deal with their clients upon the same terms as other persons ; and every sort of discouragement ought to be thrown in the way of such transactions : *Wamsley* v. *Booth* (2) : *Newman* v. *Payne* (3). Every principle applying to trustees applies equally to attorneys. This case illustrates the principle, that it is necessary to hold a strong hand over dealings between attorneys and their clients. If this was not the case of an attorney, it affords the strongest suspicion of imposture, from the circumstance, that no attorney was present at the [* 270] transaction, connected with age, infirmity, and * exorbi-

(1) 2 Bro. C. C. 400.
(2) 2 Atk. 25.
(3) *Ante*, vol. ii. 199. See the cases in the note, p. 204.

tant terms; especially, when compared with the terms offered
by Gibson, a relation of the family; who offered 60*l.* and landed
security. The scruples, which it is said she had, might have been
easily overcome by the Defendant.

Mr. *Mansfield,* Mr. *Lloyd,* and Mr. *Fonblanque,* for the Defendant.—This Defendant had ceased to be attorney to Mrs. Kerby;
and was succeeded in that character by his son. The rules as to
attorneys therefore have no application. But there is no rule that
an attorney may not deal with his client, if he deals upon fair terms.
Certainly the Court cannot watch the transaction too narrowly. In
Swayne's Case (1), determined by Lord Northington, he was trustee
as well as attorney; yet the transaction was established. It is now
fully settled, that a trustee, whether attorney, or not, may, if the
agreement is fair, buy of his *Cestui que trust.* In many cases the
Court has relieved upon collateral circumstances; but never upon
the single circumstance, that one party was the attorney. As to the
circumstances attending this transaction, the price is fair; and Mrs.
Kerby does not appear to have been more infirm than is usual at her
time of life; and her disorder according to the evidence of a medi-
cal man was not of a·nature to affect her mind; and she soon recovered. The evidence for the Plaintiff would be very dangerous to
found a decree upon. The rule as to weakness is stated by Sir
Joseph Jekyll (2): where a weak man gives a bond, if there be no
fraud or breach of trust in obtaining it, equity will not set it aside
only for the weakness of the obligor, if *compos mentis:* neither will
this Court measure the size of people's understandings: there being
no such thing as equitable incapacity, where there is legal capacity;
but if a bond be insisted to have been given for a consideration,
where it appears there was none, or not near so much as is pretended, equity will relieve against it. The real question between these
parties is, whether the price was fair. The Defendant adopted the
scheme of the Insurance Office; and has taken less than they would
have required.

Lord CHANCELLOR [ELDON].—I do not mean to contradict the
cases of trustees buying from their *Cestuys que trust:* but
the relation * between the parties must be changed: that   [* 271]
is, the confidence in the party, the trustee or attorney,
must be withdrawn. That is the principle of the cases of a trustee
buying for himself. There is evidence enough in this case, that
Mrs. Kerby knew what she was about; though the younger Jeyes
has not denied the very serious charge against him, that he was
obliged to point out the letters of her name, when executing the
power of attorney. The evidence of incapacity relates to the state
of her body: but it is clear, her mind had suffered by the shock
her health had received. An attorney buying from his client can
never support it; unless he can prove, that his diligence to do the

---

(1) Cited 2 Bro. C. C. in *Fox* v. *Mackreth.*
(2) 3 P. Will. 129, in *Osmond* v. *Fitzroy.*

best for the vendor has been as great, as if he was only an attorney, dealing for that vendor with a stranger. That must be the rule. If it appears, that in that bargain he has got an advantage by his diligence being surprised, putting fraud and incapacity out of the question, which advantage with due diligence he would have prevented another person from getting, a contract under such circumstances shall not stand. The principle, so stated, may bear hard in a particular case: but I must lay down a general principle, that will apply to all cases; and I know none short of that, if the attorney of the vendor is to be admitted to bargain for his own interest; where it is his duty to advise the vendor against himself. The younger Jeyes did not do his duty; as the Court would expect it. I put the question thus, without adverting to his taking the power of attorney, and selling the stock, before any specific treaty for an annuity was entered into. It was his duty to have duly informed himself of the state of her health and the other circumstances; with reference to which perhaps many persons would have dealt upon much more liberal terms than either an office or the Defendant. I cannot consider personal security as sufficient. But, from the general danger the Court must hold, that if the attorney does mix himself with the character of vendor he must show to demonstration, for that must not be left in doubt, that no industry he was bound to exert would have got a better bargain. Therefore, without imputing fraud, a general principle of public policy makes it impossible, that this bargain can stand.

For the Defendant.—The difficulty upon *Heathcote* v. *Paignon* (1) is, that it is impossible to find the exact market [* 272] price of an annuity * on account of the difference as to age, health and circumstances. The difference of value upon this evidence is not that great difference, to which Lord Thurlow alludes. With respect to the rule as to an attorney dealing with his client, it is of great importance to define it with exactness. So far as he is contracting with his client upon any matter, that might be the subject of his professional skill, there can be no better rule than that, which requires him to employ the extraordinary degree of diligence, that he would employ, if contracting on behalf of his client with a third person. But is it to be applied to every other transaction; for instance the purchase of a horse, or any other subject, not involving that confidence in his judgment which introduces the rule, and upon which it is founded? In *Newman* v. *Payne* the Lord Chancellor with every disposition to raise the rule as high as possible left the transaction as to the horse, where he found it; and did not bring that within the general principle.

The *Solicitor General*, in reply.—The circumstance, that the Defendant was the attorney, is sufficiently brought in issue to put it upon him to get rid of it. Almost all the witnesses speak to his being the attorney, and his son in partnership with him. With res-

---

(1) 2 Bro. C. C. 167.

pect to the objection, that the rule cannot extend to a purchase, which is not the subject of professional skill, as a horse, the knowledge of the circumstance, that the client wants a sum of money, may be very convenient; and is therefore by no means immaterial even upon such a purchase. But this purchase was connected with the duty of an attorney to watch over the interest of the client, and warn her against an improvident bargain. The sale of the stock was with a view to the purchase of some annuity; and it is all one transaction.

Lord CHANCELLOR [ELDON].—This case is put first upon incompetency to make such a contract: 2dly, Upon the insufficiency of the consideration; and the last ground is, that, if upon the mere incompetency or deficiency of the consideration there is no ground for relief, yet in the relation of the parties contracting the Court can find a principle, upon which they will rescind the contract; though between parties not so connected they might have permitted it to stand. Attending to the third ground, there is enough in this case to authorize the Court to say, there is probable evidence * of incompetency; the evidence of some degree of insuf- [* 273] ficiency of consideration, that can be felt, not as Lord Thurlow said in the case referred to, but as extremely material evidence, where it is to be connected with the third ground; whether that reasonable attention has been given to the interest of the purchaser, which under all the circumstances Jeyes was bound to give that interest. But I go a great deal farther; for upon the transactions disclosed by the evidence it is fairly questionable, whether this case might not support a Commission, not of lunacy, but in the nature of a writ *de lunatico inquirendo*; in which it must be remembered, it is not necessary to establish lunacy; but it is sufficient, that the party is incapable of managing his own affairs (1). I do not say, all this fell under the view of Jeyes; if it can be established with regard to the acts of this lady; but it is not sufficient to protect a party against the effect of such a proceeding, if it could be made out, that in visits such passages in her conduct did not fall under the observation of those, who visited her; for the proceeding would be to protect her against what her acts might be, when such acts did fall under the observation of third persons. Taking into consideration the circumstance of the execution of the power of attorney, and the folly of what she did, grounded upon the apprehension, that her income must be raised by any means, imbecility of mind and great improvidence are in this respect established; and upon a trial, whether she was to be trusted with the general management of her affairs, which would take in the periods, when she was in that situation, the probable result would be incapacity to that extent.

With regard to the insufficiency of value, where the case is put upon mere inadequacy (2), no relation whatsoever subsisting be-

(1) *Post, Ridgeway* v. *Darwin*, vol. viii. 65; *Ex parte Cranmer*, xii. 445.
(2) *Moth* v. *Atwood, ante,* vol. v. 845, and the note.

tween the parties, inducing one to repose confidence, and putting the other under the obligation of all the duty that situation requires, it was stated by Lord Thurlow in those cases, that you cannot affect the bargain upon mere inadequacy; unless it is so gross as to shock the conscience of any man, who heard the terms. That principle is loose enough: but it is one, by which Judges in Equity have felt themselves bound, and to act upon occasionally for the safety of mankind. There is no pretence for saying, * the in-adequacy in this case is gross in that degree. If it stood therefore upon that ground merely, it would be very hazardous to rescind this transaction. But the result is, that there is at least a most high moral probability, that with that diligence, which I will not say deserves a higher character than that of reasonable diligence, better terms might have been obtained for this lady.

[* 274]

I do not enter into the propriety of what was or was not done in former cases with reference to the market price of an annuity. If such a case should arise before me, my mind will be distressed by a number of considerations, that have hung upon it for many years as to that class of cases. To say, in the case of a grantor of the age of thirty, who has been covered with disease, probably affecting the duration of life, for many years, and in a greater or less degree, that is not to be considered with reference to the fairness of the bargain, is not easily reconcilable to reason. I am sure, it is not reconcilable to fact, even upon the Court's own principle; for when Lord Thurlow got the length of thinking it fit with regard to insur-ance to consider that circumstance, it seems equally reasonable, that in determining upon the adequacy of value he must look at the na-ture of the life itself; upon the nature and circumstances of which the insurance turns. Another circumstance is to be attended to. What an annuity is worth depends upon the circumstances of the party and the security. But it depends upon much nicer points: the prudence of the grantor; who may be in circumstances at the time quite unexceptionable. I cannot see, upon what principle it is said, the market price is to determine (1). In *Heathcote* v. *Paig-non* the market price was reported to be six years' purchase; and it was asserted in the report, which made no sort of distinction upon the circumstances of the grantor, the nature of the security, the state of health, or any one fact, that would enter into the considera-tion of a prudent purchaser, and even of an honest seller. The grantor was a young man, about thirty; but he had had two or three smart fits of the gout; and he was a young man, whose state of life as to the duration of it, with reference to that circumstance, was one, at which no prudent man could shut his eyes, nor any honest man desire it. Therefore upon the ordinary cases of annui-ties I must enter into the circumstances; or say, that not-

---

(1) See *post*, vol. viii. 137; x. 220. As to the rule for valuing annuities in bankruptcy, generally, or under special circumstances, see *post*, *Ex parte Thistle-wood*, *Ex parte Whitehead*, vol. xix. 236, 557; 1 Rose, Bank. Cases, 290; vol. ii. 358; 1 Mer. 10, 127.

withstanding all, that prudent and honest individuals would do out of Court, I must determine upon the market price in all cases.

But it is not upon the adequacy or inadequacy of value that it appears to me, this bargain cannot be held by Mr. Jeyes. To state it not too high, I will state, that this lady had lived to a very advanced period of life: a period, at which the Court does not strain much in saying, the client is entitled to all the providence and care the attorney's best and most active care can throw round her. Her affairs and those of her husband had been under the care of the Defendant. This Court cannot proceed upon those nice and delicate considerations in matters of property, that would suggest to him, that as matter of moral, and therefore imperfect, obligation, arising from that connection, there ought to have been upon his part a tendency not to discover that degree of tediousness and caprice, that made him weary of the connection: but if he did discover it in that degree, he ought to have dissolved the relation between them. At her age, of itself entitling her to the protection and providence I have stated, she had suffered in her health to a degree established by the evidence. That that was known to the Defendant is a fact too much in doubt to be asserted: but that her health was not very good at her years is obvious upon the whole of the evidence. Under these circumstances she had some improvidence about her affairs; or, as the Defendant will say, an inclination to augment her comforts. The mode she had adopted was selling a house for an annuity. That transaction went off upon some difficulty as to the title. If the Defendant, who certainly did not mingle himself in that transaction, had bought that house, and taken a conveyance of it, and being her attorney in the article of selling the house had permitted her to take nothing but a bond for an annuity, I could not well permit that species of dealing. That treaty going off, another plan was thought of. I now give credit to this; that it was her real purpose to bring the money produced by the sale of her stock to Northampton for the purchase of an annuity; though the evidence puts it in great doubt, whether she did not bring it for the purpose of spending it, as she wanted it. The younger Jeyes was employed to go to London to sell out the stock. I do not examine, why he did not state to her, that that was very imprudent: * no   [* 276] treaty for an annuity being entered into: nothing appearing to show, it was a prudent act to permit him to bring it home, to lie dead in a chest, and to be acted upon by her improvidence. It is not to be forgotten certainly, that he was obliged to point out to her how to spell her name, when executing the power of attorney. It is necessary to say broadly, that those, who meddle with such transactions, take upon themselves the whole proof, that the thing is righteous. The circumstances, that pass upon such transactions, may be consistent with honest intentions: but they are so delicate in their nature, that parties must not complain of being called on to prove, they are so. It appears upon the account, that this money was duly rendered to her; and all the items of charge are not only unexceptionable, but very reasonable. Her purpose of buying an annuity, it seems, had taken vast hold upon her mind. It was part of the moral and imperfect obligation upon Jeyes to contend against her purpose as much as possible: this however is in some degree excusable: as persons do not choose to advise against the inclinations of those they are advising. The conduct of King and Gibson, the one endeavoring to purchase her property, the other persuading her to sell, is in a degree inconsistent with their imputation of imbecility. But there is a wide difference between that transaction and that with Jeyes. It is very difficult for persons, in a moral and reasonable view having fair expectations of property, to determine how to act. In the case of a person liable to a commission of lunacy the feeling of a relation unwilling to take out a commission is not to be disapproved. The proposition of Gibson at the least was to give 60*l.* a year with landed security; and also to give 5*l.* or 10*l.* more than any one else would give; and if that was the purpose, with a view to bring home that property into the pockets of those, who had the natural claim to it, it cannot be said, that transaction stands under the same circumstances, as if a stranger was to take that to himself. But it is very different, when it is the case, not of a stranger, but of the attorney, acting under the confidence placed in an attorney, in an instance, in which the principles of this Court entitle me to say, he ought to have acted with more providence and attention than are required even in the case of parent and child.

[* 277]   * It has been truly said, an attorney is not incapable of contracting with his client. He may for a horse, an estate, &c. A trustee also may deal with his *Cestuy que trust;* but the relation must be in some way dissolved: or, if not, the parties must be put so much at arm's length, that they agree to take the characters of purchaser and vendor; and you must examine, whether all the duties of those characters have been performed (1). In the late case of *Fox* v. *Mackreth* it was never denied, that Mackreth might have purchased Fox's estate. When that cause was in this Court, I said, there never was an order more liable to objection than the order dissolving the injunction; for independent of all the circumstances in that cause this was proved upon the motion; that, giving the Defendant credit for every thing he insisted he was entitled to, the Court overlooked the circumstance, that he had money in his hands due to the Plaintiff beyond that, for which he was suing at law. That case was decided upon these grounds; that though he might have discharged himself from the relation, as trustee, he had not done so: on the contrary he distinctly stated, he would not conclude any thing as to the character of trustee with regard to third persons; carrying on the treaty as to Page's estate by surveyors paid by Fox;

(1) *Ante, Whichcote* v. *Lawrence,* vol. iii. 740, and the note, 752; *Campbell* v. *Walker, Ex parte Reynolds,* v. 678, 707; *Ex parte Hughes, Ex parte Lyon, post,* 617.

and gaining intelligence at the expense of the *Cestuy que trust.* An issue was pressed, whether Fox had not received enough for the estate ; though Mackreth had sold it for more : but the question was not upon the fact, whether the price paid to Fox was sufficient, but upon the principle, whether under the circumstances, if Mackreth had made more, he had disentangled himself from that situation, in which every benefit made by him was to result to the *Cestuy que trust.* The only fact was, whether he was disentangled from that situation. The moment it was decided, that he was not, it did not signify, whether the estate was sold upon fair terms between him and Fox ; for even a benefit arising by accident upon the principles of this Court should accrue to the Plaintiff. The argument for an issue therefore went quite beyond the question ; and the case might have been decided upon that principle in a great measure free from the implication of fraud.

* With respect to the case of the attorney, I have no   [* 278] difficulty in saying, Jeyes might have dealt for this annuity : but he had two ways of proceeding ; which this Court must have held it quite incumbent upon him, dealing with this lady, to attend to. If she proposed to him to buy it, he would have done well to have said to her, that Gibson would give more than any one else ; that it was his interest to do so ; that he would secure it upon real estate ; that it was more fit for her to deal with her relation than her attorney ; and the transaction would have a better appearance in the world. It was natural enough, that she should answer, she would not deal with Gibson, but would consider herself only and her own comforts, according to Benyon's advice to her. Then it would have been right for the Defendant to have declined it. Suppose, she had insisted, that he should be the person : it would be too much for the Court to proceed upon delicacies, such as these, and to say, he should not permit himself to contract with her. Therefore I say, he might contract : but then he should have said, if he was to deal with her for this, she must get another attorney to advise her as to the value : or, if she would not, then out of that state of circumstances this clear duty results from the rule of this Court, and throws upon him the whole *onus* of the case ; that, if he will mix with the character of attorney that of vendor, he shall, if the propriety of the contract comes in question, manifest, that he has given her all that reasonable advice against himself, that he would have given her against a third person. It is asked, where is that rule to be found ? I answer, in that great rule of the Court, that he, who bargains in matter of advantage with a person placing confidence in him is bound to show, that a reasonable use has been made of that confidence ; a rule applying to trustees, attorneys, or any one else.

If that is the rule, see, how this transaction proceeds. First, with regard to the security. This lady, at the age of seventy-one, in possession of stock, which had produced this money, and which therefore might have been in a certain way made a security *pro tanto* for the payment of the annuity, deals with a person stated to

be in very good circumstances, but of the age of eighty, with a large
family ; among whom that property will probably be parcelled out'
by distribution.   He proposes a bond as a security for her daily
          bread.   Is that what a Court of Justice can approve?
[* 279]   * It would have been his duty, advising her as against a
          third person, to have said, that in the natural course of
things that person of the age of eighty, nine or ten years older than
herself, might die in her life ; and she, surviving perhaps several
years, would have to go, not to any specific fund, the stock or the
money, not even to Gibson's public-houses, to which as a security
she had objected, but to get administration as a creditor, or to follow
the representatives.   It was his duty to say that as against himself.
But in other respects he did not exert reasonable diligence ; for there
was an absolute duty upon him to have made the most, not only of
the circumstance of age, but also of the actual state, in which she
was.   If he had been dealing to the best advantage with a stranger,
it would have been his duty to make accurate inquiries as to her
state of health ; and when proposing the purchase to a public office,
but more especially to individuals, he should have gone on behalf of
his client with all the information, that would have given her any
advantage.   If he had made inquiry of those living with her, he
must have learned the probability, that there was something more
than a bilious disorder, and of a kind, that might most materially
affect the consideration.   But the only inquiry was that, which the
circulation of the office paper produced.   Is that reasonable and
due diligence in such a case?   It appears to me a better bargain in
the general case to have taken the lower terms from the office than
these upon personal security ; for, in whatever way their liability is
formed, there is a regularity in their transactions, which is the foundation of their credit, and gives a value to their security, which that
of individuals will not fetch in the market ; if the market price
is to determine.   The opinions in evidence as to the value are worth
nothing in this sense ; that they only calculate upon mere age ; and
take all lives of the same age to be of equal value.   I will not say,
whether upon the difference in the evidence as to the value it is
grossly inadequate within Lord Thurlow's meaning : but it was the
duty of the attorney of this lady to get that 14*l.* a year for her, if
he could ; and it was negligence not to make that inquiry, which
any man buying an annuity would have made.   If the witnesses
agreed, that 50*l.* was enough, that would not be conclusive in
favor of the Defendant ; for the substance of their evidence is, that
the life was taken to be good ; and the Defendant would have fail-
          ed in this article ; that he had not made advantage
[* 280]   enough in the article * of her health ; as to which he must
          have been informed.   In that respect also there is a failure
of due diligence.   By that negligence a stranger, if the transaction
had been with a stranger, would have profited ; and it follows in
this Court, that, when you can characterize the conduct as negligence towards a stranger, by which he obtains an advantage, the

attorney becoming purchaser shall not hold that advantage, gained by his negligence. That is the principle, upon which I decide this cause as to Jeyes the younger ; and I am satisfied by this evidence upon the question, whether the Defendant is affected by the conduct of Jeyes the younger, that there is no distinction between them ; and the weight of evidence is against the alleged dissolution of partnership. It does appear, that the Defendant was unwilling to contract for this annuity. That circumstance disconnects the transaction of December from the sale of the stock in November ; and gets rid of a great deal of imputation.

As to the relief, it cannot go quite to the extent of the prayer. It must be only a decree, that the 400*l.* must be repaid with interest. If I am to conjecture, I do not go the length of saying, this money was brought from London for the purpose of the sale of this annuity. It may be so ; but if it is possible it may not be so, I must consider it as converted into an annuity in December 1798. I cannot therefore charge the Defendant to the extent of making him replace the stock ; which would make some difference. The principle, upon which I make the decree, carries the costs with it (1).

---

1. As to the scrupulous examination which transactions between solicitor and client undergo in Equity in order to prevent that confidential relation from being converted into the means of oppression ; see, *ante*, notes 2 and 3 to *Newman* v. *Payne*, 2 V. 199 ; and as to the difficulty of supporting a purchase by a trustee from his *cestui que trust* ; see the notes to *Whichcote* v. *Lawrence*, 3 V. 740.

2. Imbecility of mind, short of actual insanity, *may* support a commission in the nature of a writ *de lunatico inquirendo* ; but whether such commission shall or shall not issue, will be determined by the Court according to a sound discretion ; see the note to *Eyre* v. *Wake*, 4 V. 795.

3. That inadequacy of consideration (unless it be so great as to amount in itself, to evidence of fraud,) will not vitiate a contract between parties standing unconnected with each other : but that a purchase at an undervalue, by an agent, from his employer, can hardly ever be sustained ; see the notes to *Crowe* v. *Ballard*, 1 V. 215.

4. The real value of an annuity may depend upon many considerations, which the general principles of calculation, as made by the actuaries of insurance offices, cannot take into account, and the market price of an annuity may be so affected by the extrinsic circumstances of the times, and temporary public distress or scarcity of money, that the market price may be a very indifferent criterion for enabling a Court to determine as to the real adequacy or inadequacy of the price agreed to be given for an annuity. *Low* v. *Barchard*, 8 Ves. 137 ; *Underhill* v. *Horwood*, 10 Ves. 220. As to the principle upon which the value of an annuity is, usually, to be calculated, at any time subsequent to the purchase thereof, see note 2 to *Franks* v. *Cooper*, 4 V. 763.

---

(1) *Post, Alsager* v. *Rowley*, 748 ; *Detillin* v. *Gale*, vol. vii. 583 ; ix. 296 ; *Harris* v. *Tremenheere*, xv. 34 ; *Wood* v. *Downes, Montesquieu* v. *Sandys*, xviii. 120, 302 ; and the note, *ante*, vol. ii. 204 ; *Cane* v. *Lord Allen*, 2 Dow, 289.

WRIGHT *v.* MAYER.

[1801, JULY 10.]

MOTION to compel an attorney to produce papers of his client refused with costs (a).

A party might be compelled to produce papers connected with the relief (b), [p. 281.]

No *subpœna duces tecum* upon an attorney to produce papers of his client. It has been sometimes seen in a criminal case but is not to be followed (c), [p. 282.]

MR. MANSFIELD, Mr. *Richards,* and Mr. *Stanley,* for the Plaintiff, in a bill of discovery moved, that an attorney may produce certain cases and opinions of Counsel and other papers in his possession, belonging to his client.

Mr. *Lloyd* and Mr. *Pemberton, contra.*—This motion is perfectly new. It is not an application, that the party may produce [*281] *these papers; but that these persons, confidential agents, may produce these papers, delivered to them as attorneys; and state confidential communications. They have answered all collateral facts: but they refuse without the direction of the Court to produce any papers held by them as attorneys, or to answer the interrogatories as to any thing communicated to them in confidence.

(a) Communications with a counsel, attorney or solicitor, acting for the time being in the character of legal adviser, are privileged. See 1 Greenleaf, Evid. § 239, 240. An attorney is not bound to produce title-deeds, or other documents left with him by his client for professional advice; though he may be examined to the fact of their existence, in order to let in secondary evidence of their contents, which must be from some other source than himself. Ibid, § 241; *Brard* v. *Ackerman,* 5 Esp. 119; *Doe* v. *Harris,* 5 C. & P. 592; *Jackson* v. *Burtis,* 14 Johns. 391; *Dale* v. *Livingston,* 4 Wend. 558; *Brandt* v. *Klein,* 17 Johns. 335; *Jackson* v. *McVey,* 18 Johns. 320; *Bevan* v. *Waters,* 1 M. & M. 235; *Eicke* v. *Nokes,* Ib. 303; *Mills* v. *Oddy,* 6 C. & P. 728; *Marston* v. *Downes,* Ib. 381; *Bate* v. *Kinsey,* 1 C. M. & R. 38; *Doe* v. *Gilbert,* 7 M. & W. 102: *Nixon* v. *Mayoh,* 1 M. & Rob. 76; *Davies* v. *Waters,* 9 M. & W. 608; *Coates* v. *Birch,* 1 G. & D. 474; 1 Dowl. P. C. 540.

The rule does not require any regular retainer, as counsel, nor any particular form of application or engagement, nor the payment of fees. It is enough that he was applied to for advice or aid in his professional character. *Foster* v. *Hall,* 12 Pick. 89; *Bean* v. *Quimby,* 5 N. Hamp. 94.

(b) Whether the party himself can be compelled, by a Bill in Chancery, to produce a case, which he has laid before counsel, with the opinion given thereon, is not perfectly agreed. At one time it was held by the House of Lords that he might be compelled to produce the case, which he had sent, but not the opinion, which he had received. *Radcliffe* v. *Fursman,* 2 Bro. P. & C. 514. This decision was not satisfactory; and though it was silently followed in one case; *Preston* v. *Carr,* 1 Y. & Jer. 175; and reluctantly submitted to in another; *Newton* v. *Beresford,* 1 You. 376; yet its principle has since been ably controverted and refuted. *Bolton* v. *Corp. of Liverpool,* 1 My. & K. 88. See Greenleaf, Evidence, § 240.

It has been held that the privilege of a client, as to discovery, is not co-extensive with that of his solicitor, and, therefore, the son and heir was compelled to discover a case, which had been submitted to counsel by his father, and had come, with the estate, to his hands. *Greenlaw* v. *King,* 1 Beavan, 137.

(c) Where an attorney held a paper, delivered to him by his client, which the grand jury were desirous of seeing, the Court held him not bound to produce it. *Anonymous,* 8 Mass. 370.

The King v. *Dixon* (1) is decisive against this application. *Wilson* v. *Rastall* (2) turned upon the delivery being in confidence as a friend. The privilege is that of the client, not the attorney.

Lord CHANCELLOR [ELDON].—This motion is perfectly new. It does not follow, that it can succeed, even if the party could be compelled to produce these papers ; as I should think, without prejudice to argument upon it, she could. I recollect many cases, in which as part of the conduct, upon which the relief was to be asked, it was alleged, that the Defendant had taken opinions, and they were in his possession ; and that was charged as a fact, connected with other circumstances of conduct, from which an inference could be drawn as .to the relief to be given. In many cases the Defendant may deny, that the papers, the production of which is called for by the bill, (in this instance papers showing, she meant to evade this covenant), are in her custody or power: but they are in her power, if in the custody of her attorney. I am not sure however, that the mischief is not less than that which would be the consequence of a practice of drawing out of the hands of attorneys papers which are in their hands always in confidence. It is said in this case, you want only to produce the cases and opinions. It is not quite clear, whether that is not more mischievous than addressing to them all these interrogatories ; for the motives, and the purposes, for which they are put into the hands of the attorney, connected with the fact, that the opinions were taken, might make out, that the party did not mean to evade the covenant: but that would introduce a right to cross-examine as to facts certainly communicated in confidence. I am also struck with its being after publication ; though honestly accounted for. But upon the other principle, that it is the privilege of the client and the public, and that in this Court another mode is open, if it is not the fault of the party, I am of opinion, it would be too * dangerous to call for papers put into the [* 282] hands of an attorney confidentially. I never heard at law of a *subpœna duces tecum* upon an attorney, to produce the papers of his client. I remember in a case of forgery at Durham a man served with a *subpœna* to produce a forged deed. It has been sometimes seen in a criminal case : but that is not a precedent to be followed.

The motion was refused with costs (3).

As against his *quondam* client, a solicitor who refuses to proceed in a suit, retains only a qualified *lien* on the papers left in his hands, which will be so far controlled as not to prevent the hearing of the cause, (*Mereweather* v. *Mellish*, 13 Ves. 162 ; *Mayne* v. *Watts*, 3 Swanst. 95 ; *O'Dea* v. *O'Dea*, 1 Sch. & Lef. 316,) he will not be permitted by the exercise of his *lien*, to prevent his client from receiving justice; *Commerell* v. *Poynton*, 1 Swanst. 2 ; *Moir* v. *Mudie*, 1 Sim. & Stu. 282 ;

(1) 3 Bur. 1687.
(2) 4 Term Rep. B. R. 753.
(3) *Post*, vol. xix. 272 ; *Bligh* v. *Benson*, 7 Price, 205 ; *Fenwick* v. *Reed*, 1 Mer. 114 ; *Bush* v. *Lewis*, *Walker* v. *Wildman*, 6 Madd. 29, 47.

but the question becomes a very different one when (as in the principal case) an attorney is called upon by his client's opponent to produce the papers with which he has been confidentially entrusted, and which the client himself could not have been compelled to produce, the attorney, in such case, is not entitled to produce the documents, or disclose the communications, which he has received solely in consequence of his confidential situation; the privilege of refusing to make such disclosure is the privilege of the client and of the public, not of the attorney: *Parkhurst* v. *Lowten*, 2 Swanst. 216; *Stratford* v. *Hogan*, 2 Ball & Bea. 166: the question might assume a different complexion if the documents were such as the client was bound to produce: see, *post*, note 4 to *Taylor* v. *Popham*, 13 V. 59.

CHING *v.* CHING.

[1801, July 10.]

An award cannot be disturbed for mistake upon a question of Law referred (a).

UNDER a general reference of all matters in dispute the arbitrator, a clergyman, had made an award, deciding all the questions.

Mr. *Richards* moved to rectify an error in law; alleging no other ground, but that the arbitrator had made a wrong decision upon a question of law.

Lord CHANCELLOR [ELDON].—If a question of law is referred to an arbitrator, he must decide upon it; and, though he decides wrong, you cannot help it, In a case before Lord Rosslyn [Loughborough], Mr. *Mansfield* and I endeavored to open an award on the ground of mistake of the arbitrator; the question referred being as to the vesting of a legacy: but it was held, it would not do.

The motion was refused (1). ____

THAT where an arbitrator has professed to decide according to law, but mistook what the law really was, a Court may interfere to set that right; see, *ante*, the note to *Price* v. *Williams*, 1 V. 365, and note 5 to *Knox* v. *Symmonds*, 1 V. 369.

, (a) *Chase* v. *Westmore*, 13 East, 358; *Campbell* v. *Twemlow*, 1 Price, 81; *Steff* v. *Andrews*, 2 Madd. 6; *Wood* v. *Griffith*, 1 Swanst. 55; *Underhill* v. *Van Cortlandt*, 2 Johns. Ch. 339; *Roosevelt* v. *Thurman*, 1 Johns. Ch. 220; *Richardson* v. *Nourse*, 3 B. & Ald. 237; *Sharman* v. *Bell*, 5 M. & Selwyn, 504. See, also, 2 Story, Eq. Jur. § 1455.
(1) *Price* v. *Williams*, 3 Bro. C. 163; *ante*, vol. i. 365; *Knox* v. *Simmonds*, i. 369; *Morgan* v. *Mather*, *Dick* v. *Milligan*, ii. 15, 23; *Emery* v. *Wase*, v. 846; *post*, *Anderson* v. *Darcy*, xviii. 447, and the references. In *Kent* v. *Elstob*, 3 East, 18, some doubt was expressed as to the authority of this case, not perhaps with sufficient consideration; which called forth a confirmation of the doctrine, with a more detailed explanation of the principle, from the Lord Chancellor, in *Young* v. *Walter*, *post*, vol. ix. 364. See xiv. 271; *Steff* v. *Andrews*, 2 Madd. 6; *Campbell* v. *Twemlow*, 1 Price, 81; *Wohlenberg* v. *Lageman*, 6 Taunt. 254; *Wood* v. *Griffith*, 1 Swanst. 43, and the references in the note, 55. The result of the authorities seems to be, that under a general reference the arbitrator, taking all moral considerations into his view, may go beyond the law, with the view of dispensing what appears to him to be substantial justice: but if, meaning to declare the law, he misses his object, the Court will correct his error; and, if he perversely or wan-

COCK v. RAVIE.

[1801, July 10.]

A writ of *Ne exeat Regno* refused upon an undertaking for an indemnity: To obtain it there must be an equitable demand in the nature of a debt actually due (a).

The Plaintiff moved for a writ of *Ne exeat regno* against the Defendant Ravie under the following circumstances, proved by affidavit.

Ravie, living at Birmingham, was owner of goods, shipped on board the Jane, bound from Hull to Embden, which sailed from Hull; was captured by a King's ship; and was libelled in the Court of Admiralty. Ravie, proposing to give security applied to the Plaintiff and the other Defendant Smith to become sureties; offering to give them an indemnity. They accordingly became his sureties to the amount of 12,000l. They applied for the indemnity; and by a letter, dated the 2d of May, he proposes to give an indemnity, either by purchasing stock and lodging a security with them, or by leaving the writings of freehold property, stated to be subject to a mortgage. Another letter dated the 9th of May, written by his partner, likewise speaks of the security the Plaintiff had entered into, and proposes, that Ravie's brother at Hamburg shall give security; but in the mean time proposes to send the deeds. Another letter of the 19th of May says generally, that he will furnish the deeds to his attorney, for the purpose of making the security.

The affidavit then stated, that he is now about to leave the kingdom to go to Hamburg.

Mr. *Romilly* and Mr. *Cooke*, in support of the motion.—There is no case exactly like this: but the ground of these cases is, that there is an equitable demand. The Plaintiff has unquestionably a certain demand in equity. It does not rest merely upon their being sureties; though that would be sufficient: but there is an express undertaking to deposit these deeds; which would give an equitable mortgage. The estate being in mortgage, he could not give the legal estate. The only case, that has gone beyond a positive debt,

tonly makes an illegal award, will control an excess of power, amounting at least to misconduct. In *Chace* v. *Westmore*, 13 East, 357, and *Sharman* v. *Bell*, 5 Maul. & Selw. 504, the Court of King's Bench, refusing to interpose upon the suggestion of mistake not apparent, rely on the character of the individual arbitrator, as a barrister: a distinction, that has not received attention in any of the cases in Equity. The Lord Chancellor in *Young* v. *Walter*, alluding to the acknowledged competence of the arbitrator in that instance, as the motive to his appointment, applies his observations on the jurisdiction to arbitrators generally, as judges chosen by the parties to declare what shall be justice between them, instead of the strict law, to be obtained by suit in the King's Courts.

(a) As to the general nature of the writ *Ne exeat Regno*, see *ante*, note (a), *Carriere* v. *De Calonne*, 4 V. 577. As to the demands on which the writ is granted, see note (a), *Coglar* v. *Coglar*, 1 V. 94; note (a), *Russell* v. *Asby*, 5 V. 96.

is, where there are unliquidated accounts, and the Plaintiff states, that he believes, the balance will be in his favor.

[* 284]   * Lord CHANCELLOR [ELDON].—Has it not always been a money demand? Do you recollect an instance of a writ being applied to this sort of case?

For the Motion.—Russell v. *Asby* (1). The performance of an undertaking is as much a duty; giving a cause of suit: Prac. Reg. 289. The case of alimony is analogous. In *Parker* v. *Appleton* (2) the bill, though not stated very accurately, must have been for a specific performance.

Lord CHANCELLOR.—*Russell* v. *Asby* was a clear money demand. If, wherever the Plaintiff has a cause of suit, that is taken to be a cause of equitable suit, and in that case merely you may have the writ, there is no distinction. In the case of Alimony there is the decree for Alimony; and therefore it is a debt by law due to the wife (3). In what sum am I to mark this writ?

For the Motion.—In the value of the indemnity; which is stated to be 4000*l*. In *Russell* v. *Asby* there was no contract between the Plaintiff and the Defendant.

Lord CHANCELLOR.—I remember a bill filed to make the principal in a bond pay the debt. The party was going to America upon the 1st of June; and the bond would have been due on the 1st of July. That was very strong; yet Lord Thurlow refused the writ (4). Suppose, the next of kin file a bill against the administrator, praying this writ: though the whole property may be in the dominion of the administrator, you never mark the writ for more than has been actually converted; which shows it to be in the nature of a bill for a debt actually due. *Parker* v. *Appleton* seems to amount to no more than that they were partners in a joint adventure; and it was part of the project, that, when sold, the produce should be invested in American stock. Then the Defendant was trustee of one moiety for the Plaintiff; and the writ was marked for that. Suppose, this was an agreement for sale of an estate; and the Plaintiff had advanced 500*l*., part of the purchase money: could he have the writ marked for the value of the estate? I am sorry for it: but I cannot grant the writ.

The motion was refused.

As to the general principles, according to which an application for a writ *ne exeat regno* is either granted or refused; see, *ante*, the notes to *De Carriere* v. *De Calonne*, 4 V. 577.

---

(1) *Ante*, vol. v. 96.

(2) 3 Bro. C. C. 427.

(3) *Ante, Coglar* v. *Coglar*, vol. i. 94; *post, Shaftoe* v. *Shaftoe, Dawson* v. *Dawson, Oldham* v. *Oldham*, vii. 171, 173, 410; *Haffey* v. *Haffey*, xiv. 261. Upon this writ generally see the notes, *ante*, vol. i. 95; iv. 592; and Mr. Beames's Brief View of the Writ.

(4) *Post*, vol. vii. 173.

—— v. GWILLIM.

[1801, JULY 11.]

ORDER, that the Six Clerk may receive the answer without signature: the Defendant having gone abroad, and forgot to sign it: the motion being consented to (a).

MR. HART moved, that the answer of Sir Henry Gwillim may be taken without oath; and that the Six Clerk may be ordered to receive it without his signature; on the ground that the Defendant (1) in the hurry of going abroad, had forgot to sign his answer.

The motion was consented to; and the order was made (2).

SEE the note to —— v. *Lake*, 6 V. 171.

MATTHEWS, *Ex parte.*

[1801, JULY 11.]

A. TO discharge a debt due from him to B. procures his banker C. to direct his correspondent and partner D. to accept a bill drawn by B. Before the bill was due, C. and D. became bankrupt; C. being indebted to A. more than the amount of the bill, B. proved against the estate of D.; but afterwards received the whole from A. A. not having proved against the estate of C. in respect of the bill is entitled to stand in the place of B. against the estate of D.; whose proof, having been expunged, was re-instated for the benefit of A.

THE petitioner, of Liverpool, kept a banking account with Caldwell and Co. of Liverpool; and in the latter end of the year 1792 being indebted to Garland and Co. of Pool 1368*l.* 2*s.* 2*d.* for corn sold to him by them; for the purpose of discharging that debt directed Caldwell and Co. to give an order upon Burton, Forbes, and Gregory, in London, upon whom they drew, and with whom they were engaged in partnership, to accept a bill to that amount drawn by Garland and Co. A bill was drawn accordingly by Garland and Co. dated the 1st of January, 1793, by the direction of the petitioner; and by the direction of Caldwell and Co. was accepted by Burton, Forbes, and Gregory. In March 1793, before the bill became due, Burton, Forbes, and Gregory, became Bankrupt; and also Caldwell and Co. The bill was not taken up. Caldwell and Co. were indebted to the petitioner to an amount

(a) See note (a), *ante*, p. 171.
(1) Sir Henry Gwillim was appointed one of the Judges of the Supreme Court at Bengal.
(2) —— v. *Lake*, *ante*, 171; see the note, 172.

above 2000*l.* Garland and Co. proved the amount of the bill under the Commission against Burton, Forbes, and Gregory. Afterwards in 1796 upon an inquiry previous to a dividend, as to [* 286] what Garland and Co. had received upon their * securities since the proof, they stated, that since the proof they had received the whole debt from the petitioner; upon which the proof was expunged.

Under these circumstances the petition alleging, that the petitioner was deprived of receiving a dividend through Garland and Co. prayed that the proof might be reinstated ; and that an order should be made for a dividend of 2*s.* 6*d.* in the pound upon the debt of 1358*l.* 2*s.* 2*d.* to put him upon a footing with the other creditors.

Mr. *Pemberton,* in support of the Petition.—Mr. *Romilly,* for the Assignees. An order, *Ex parte Puller,* 22d December, 1800, was cited.

The petition stood for judgment.

Lord CHANCELLOR [ELDON].—The question upon this petition seems to be, whether under the circumstances the petitioner paying that demand of Garland and Co., in respect of which they had drawn upon Burton, Forbes, and Gregory, which bill they had accepted, and in respect of which Garland and Co. proved against their estate, had a right to say, Garland and Co. being paid by his money instead of the security he gave them should stand as trustees of the proof for his benefit ; and upon the best consideration I can give it I think, he has that right. It is necessary to consider it as to the situation of the petitioner with regard to Caldwell and Co., of Caldwell and Co. with regard to Burton, Forbes, and Gregory, and of Burton, Forbes, and Gregory, with regard to Garland and Co. The petitioner, being a creditor of Caldwell and Co. procures them to furnish Garland and Co. with the means of drawing upon Burton, Forbes and Gregory. They drew accordingly; and the moment Burton, Forbes, and Gregory, had given their acceptance to Garland and Co. the necessary effect was, that Burton, Forbes, and Gregory, in account against Caldwell and Co. had a right to consider themselves as having a demand against Caldwell and Co. to the amount of their acceptance ; and the effect of that was, that Caldwell and Co. had also a right to consider themselves debtors to the petitioner less than what they owed him by the amount of this sum ; for in effect they were bound to indemnify Burton, Forbes, and [* 287] Gregory to the extent of their acceptance. * Therefore if the petitioner in proving against Caldwell and Co. has carried to his debit the amount of this bill, then the petition is right. If on the other hand he has proved the whole debt against Caldwell and Co., not deducting that sum, then he will not have a .right to stand in their situation against the estate of Burton, Forbes, and Gregory.

Upon inquiry it appeared, that the petitioner had not proved in respect of this bill against Caldwell and Co. ; and the order was made according to the prayer of the petition.

---

1. THAT where there have been cross-paper transactions between the parties, one of them cannot be called upon to discharge a balance which may appear against him when the call is made, unless he is disentangled from all responsibilities in respect of outstanding bills, which have been put into circulation for the accommodation of the other party ; see, *ante*, note 1 to *Ex parte Walker*, 4 V. 373.

2. A person who has paid the original creditors of a bankrupt, is entitled to call upon them to exercise, for his benefit, the right they had to prove; substantially, he is to be considered as having purchased all their remedies. *Ex parte Lloyd,* 17 Ves. 246; *Ex parte Yonge,* 3 V. & B. 38; *Ex parte Lobbon,* 17 Ves. 335; and see also the 52d and the 55th sections of the consolidated Bankrupt Act, stat. 6 Geo. IV. c. 16.

ANONYMOUS.

[1801, JULY 11, 13.]

UPON a motion, that a Receiver may be at liberty to defend an ejectment, the parties interested being adult and consenting, a reference was made, whether it was for their benefit (a).

Upon a sequestration a mortgagee must come to be examined *pro interesse suo,* [p. 288.]

MR. OWEN moved, that the Receiver should be at liberty to defend an ejectment ; and to charge the expense in his accounts.

The Lord CHANCELLOR [ELDON] expressed doubt upon it ; and asked, why this person would not come, desiring to be examined *pro interesse suo.*

For the Motion.—Except in the case of a sequestration that has been done only in one instance, *Angel v. Smith ;* where, infants being concerned, the Lord Chancellor took that course : but it was thought very novel. The common course is to refer it to the Master ; but not, where it is clear. In this case the estate is devised to trustees, upon trust to receive the rents and profits, and to pay to a nephew 120l. a-year, until he marries with consent of the trustees ; then to him for life ; with remainder to the issue of the marriage ; and if he should marry without consent, or die without issue, then to the right heirs of the testator : this person being the heir. A decree was made for carrying the will into execution ; and a direction was given to take an account of the premises, of which he was seised. In 1794 the Report was made ; stating, that the testator died seised of the very tenement, which *is the subject of　[*288] this motion. The Receiver has been in possession from 1793 : the possession of the Court by its officer. If he defends any premises, of which he is not in possession as Receiver, this order

---

(a) A special order of Court seems necessary to authorize a person, in the character of receiver, to institute actions of ejectment. *Green v. Winter,* 1 Johns. Ch. 61.

will not protect him.   Notice of trial is given for the ensuing Assizes at Hereford.   All the parties really interested are adult ; and consent.

Mr. *Lloyd (Amicus Curiæ)* said, the understanding was, that, where there was a Receiver, no person would be permitted to bring an ejectment, or take any other proceeding, without the leave of the Court ; whoever did would be committed (1).

Lord CHANCELLOR said, he could not distinguish the case of a Receiver from that of a sequestration : why in the latter case a mortgagee, for instance, with a clear title to take possession must come to be examined *pro interesse suo* (2), and not in the other.

Lord CHANCELLOR said, he would give the Receiver leave to defend this ejectment ; but would reserve the consideration of the costs till after the trial : not approving a Receiver coming just before the trial, when it is impossible to have a reference to the Master whether it is for the benefit of the parties, that he should be at liberty to defend the ejectment.

Mr. *Owen*, saying they could get the Report in time, and offering to go before the Master, the order was made accordingly.

On the 1st of August, the Order was made upon the Report, that it would be for the benefit of the parties.

1. SEE, *ante*, the note to *Wynne* v. *Lord Newborough*, 1 V. 164, as to the necessity of the previous sanction of the Court to authorize a receiver to bring, or to defend, an ejectment.

2. It is a contempt of Court to disturb sequestrators ; if the sequestration be executed, the rule is settled, (as was intimated in the principal case,) that a party cannot claim, though by adverse title, in any other way than by coming to be examined *pro interesse suo ;* he must not attempt to bring an ejectment.   *Angel* v. *Smith*, 9 Ves. 336; *Kaye* v. *Cunningham*, 5 Mad. 406; *Gresley* v. *Adderley*, 1 Swanst. 579; *Dunne* v. *Farrell*, 1 Ball & Bea. 124; *Copeland* v. *Mape*, 2 Ball & Bea. 67; *Hamlyn* v. *Lee*, 1 Dick. 94; *Bowles* v. *Parsons*, 1 Dick. 142; *Hunt* v. *Priest*, 2 Dick. 540.   With respect to the general doctrine as to process of sequestration; see the notes to *Hales* v. *Shaftoe*, 1 V. 86.

(1) *Angel* v. *Smith*, *post*, vol. ix. 335.
(2) *Hamlyn* v. *Lee*, 1 Dick. 94.

ASTON *v*. LORD EXETER.

[1801, July 11, 13.]

Where the bill seeks relief as well as discovery, the Court will not upon motion aid the Plaintiff in proceeding at Law without the authority and control of the Court: any such proceeding must be under a decree. Therefore in such a case a motion, that the Defendant should produce deeds, &c. at the trial of an ejectment, was refused (a).

Duty of the tenant to keep the boundaries; and the Court will aid the reversioner to distinguish them; and, if they cannot be distinguished, will give him as much land (b), [p. 293.]

Mr. Benyon for the Plaintiff moved, that the Defendant may be ordered to produce and leave with his clerk in Court several deeds, dated in 1690, 1701, and 1702, set forth in the answers, and all other deeds relating to the premises, in aid of an ejectment brought ; and that copies may be produced at the * trial ;   [* 289] if the originals should not be produced.   The bill prayed a discovery and a commission to ascertain boundaries.

The Lord Chancellor [Eldon] expressing doubt upon this motion,

Mr. *Bell (Amicus Curiæ)* mentioned *Worsley* v. *Watson ;* in which the bill stated a settlement, and proceedings at Law ; and desired a discovery of that deed.   The answer denied the pedigree ; but admitted, they had the settlement.   A motion was made, that they should produce that deed.   Lord Rosslyn made the order ; and the cause was tried.   That was decided upon the general principle ; that if the party entered into a discovery of his title, he would in all probability be forced to go to Law ; and it answered the purposes of justice.   If he went to Law without that deed, he must have been nonsuited.

Lord Chancellor inclined against the motion ; alluding to the case of *Lady Shaftesbury* v. *Arrowsmith* (1) ; deciding, that the party was only entitled to the production of the deed, under which he claimed ; distinguishing between a mere bill of discovery in aid of an ejectment and a bill also praying relief in this way, followed up by a motion for a production in aid of an ejectment, not under the control of the Court; proceeding in Equity and at Law for the same thing.

July 13th.   Lord Chancellor.—I have looked into the order in the case of *Worsley* v. *Watson*, the 20th of November, 1800.   The

---

(a) See 2 Story, Eq. Jur. § 1493, note.   What may be effected by motion, see 1 Barb. Pr. 577, 578, b. 3, ch. 1, § 4 ; *Kershaw* v. *Thompson*, 4 Johns. Ch. 609 ; *Paff* v. *Paff*, Hopk. 584.

(b) It will be a sufficient ground for the exercise of the jurisdiction of Equity, that there is a relation between the parties, which makes it the duty of one of them to preserve and protect the boundaries ; and that by his negligence or misconduct, the confusion of boundaries has arisen.   1 Story, Eq. Jur. § 620.

(1) *Ante*, vol. iv. 66.

of that order I question ; because I cannot find any case to that extent ; and because it goes a length, to which Lord Rosslyn refused
to act in the case of *Lady Shaftesbury,* Lord Thurlow in *Burton* v.
Neville, and the Court of Exchequer in a case cited (1) in that of
Lady Shaftesbury. My doubts therefore as to granting these motions remain.

As to the motion in this particular case, there are other reasons
against it. This is not a motion for the purpose of having deeds, a
discovery of which is sought by the bill, produced in the Master's
office ; and where the order for the production is made upon the
ground, that it is only to complete the answer: but it is in a case,
where there is a bill and an answer, a motion to produce them to
the intent, that they may be made evidence upon an ejectment
brought, not under the view or control of the Court. The case is a
limitation of various estates to various uses ; and among them the
Plaintiff claiming by descent, finds a title, that was never barred by
intermediate acts. A term of ninety-nine years was created in
1690 ; and was therefore run out, before the bill was filed. That
term, the object of which was to raise portions for younger children,
was sold for 2000*l.* It appears by the answer of Lord Exeter, that
a fine was levied ; and under that the ancestor of Lady Exeter supposed, he had become entitled to an estate in fee ; and all the other
uses were barred. The Plaintiff contends, that the fine gave no
title ; and therefore claims the possession of this land from Lord
Exeter in consequence of the effluxion of time, during which the
title subsisted. They state, that Vernon being seised in
[* 293]   fee of a great number of premises has * so destroyed the
boundaries, that it is impossible to ascertain them without the assistance of a Court of Equity. Their bill is upon this
ground ; that they want discovery, to decide, whether there must
not be a Commission to ascertain the boundaries. Certainly it is a
duty upon the tenant to keep the boundaries ; and this Court will
aid the reversioner to distinguish them : and even will give him as
much land, if they cannot be distinguished (2). Lord Exeter, being
only seised of the freehold in right of his wife, from whom he was
divorced, is made the sole Defendant. He states, that he is in possession ; that the family, taking themselves to be entitled, have sold
to, and exchanged with, other persons : so that the premises are
partly in his possession, partly in that of others. Under these circumstances they bring an ejectment; and say, it is ready for trial
at Worcester ; and upon motion they desire, that that ejectment,
not under the control or view of·the Court, and in a case, in which
the bill asserts, that the Sheriff cannot deliver possession, if the
Plaintiffs recover, the deed of 1690 may be produced, and all the
subsequent deeds, and that they may be carried down to Worcester;
and this under an order of this Court; and where the Defendant
does not represent the inheritance of the estate. I doubt it; first,

(1) Cited *ante,* vol. iv. 69.
(2) *The Duke of Leeds* v. *The Earl of Strafford, ante,* vol. iv. 180.

upon what I have said; 2dly, because this case under the circumstances differs totally from that, in which Lord Rosslyn [Loughborough] made the order I have stated.

The motion was refused (1).

1. As to the cases in which a Court of Equity will interfere, by directing a production and inspection of deeds; see, *ante*, the note to the *Anonymous case*, 1 Ves. 29, and note 1 to *Lady Shaftesbury* v. *Arrowsmith*, 4 V. 66.
2. With respect to the only grounds upon which Courts of Equity interfere to give relief in cases of confusion of boundaries; see note 2 to *Strode* v. *Blackburne*, 3 V. 222.

HYLTON *v.* MORGAN.

[1801, JULY 11, 13.]

WHERE the bill seeks relief as well as discovery, the Court will not upon motion aid the Plaintiff in proceeding at Law without the authority and control of the Court: any such proceeding must be under the authority and control of the Court. Therefore in such a case the Court would not on motion order, that an outstanding term should not be set up by the Defendant against an ejectment brought by the Plaintiff (*a*).

MR. THOMSON, for the Plaintiff, moved upon the answer for an injunction to restrain the Defendant from setting up any outstanding term by way of defence to the ejectment brought by the Plaintiff, or any other ejectment he may be advised to bring for recovery of the premises. Notice of trial had been given.

Lord CHANCELLOR [ELDON].—The doubt I have is,   [294] whether the regular course of the practice of this Court is to be broken in upon; and that, which would be done all at once under a decretal order, is to be made the subject of several motions. In proceedings under the control of this Court a production is ordered on both sides; and from that production a benefit may arise to the party, with whom you are contending at Law; as in the last motion, there might be papers in the possession of the party applying, from which the identity of the premises would appear. This is quite new practice.

Mr. *Thomson*, in support of the motion, said, there was no such question in this case; which was merely a question of title. The bill is filed on the ground of illegitimacy. This application is not for any thing, that can prejudice the Defendant's title, or aid the Plaintiff's; but is merely to have a fair trial of the Plaintiff's right. The whole object of the bill is reducible to setting aside the outstanding term, which the Defendant admits, in order to have a fair trial. That may be done in any stage of the cause.

(1) See the next case.
(*a*) See 2 Story, Eq. Jur. § 1493, note. What may be effected by motion, 1 Barb. Pr. 577, 578, b. 3, ch. 1, § 4; *Kershaw* v. *Thompson*, 4 Johns. Ch. 609; *Paff* v. *Paff*, Hopk. 584.

Lord CHANCELLOR.—This happens to be a clear case: but in many instances there must be vast inquiry and expense ; and where the Defendant has a right to be protected by the decree, is it not bad practice to let a party coming for relief, with regard to which he is to proceed at law, proceed at law, before he entitles himself to that relief ? It is deciding the whole equity of the case before the decree. Is the Plaintiff to pick out his own mode of proceeding at law ; or, is not the principle of such a bill, that the Court directs the mode of proceeding at law under a decree ? In general till the decree the Court must suppose the parties to be litigating upon questionable rights.. Put the case, that at the hearing the Court may find it necessary to direct an issue ; or, if the trial should be by ejectment, to give special directions as to admissions, &c. Can it be right, that previously to the decree an ejectment is to go on at the hazard of proceeding in the very manner the Court would have prohibited? I will not act in particular cases against the practice. There are two ways of proceeding. You may get a discovery in aid of an ejectment : but if you will have equitable relief to aid the trial of your title at law, you must have that relief upon [* 295]   a decretal order prior to the trial at law. * Suppose, in the case in Atkins (1), upon this head of equity, that, when the decree was made, and a production by both parties ordered, the person presumed to be heir-at-law turned out not to be heir from papers in his own possession : would not the whole expense of the ejectment be thrown away ? It will be found, that what has been the constant practice of the Court is founded in a great deal of wisdom, when it is examined. The question now is, whether I should not stay the ejectment till the decree ; and then give such directions for a trial at law as may be necessary.

Mr. *Lloyd (Amicus Curiæ)* said, that certainly was the practice ; and this sort of relief never used to be given upon a motion prior to the decree.

July 13*th.* Lord CHANCELLOR [ELDON].—This case is similar to the last (2). The bill is filed for an account of all sums of money received by the Defendant or for her use on account of the rents and profits from the death of William Morgan. It states the will, made in 1788 ; and the death of the testator and the possession since. The motion is for an injunction to restrain the Defendant from setting up any outstanding term by way of defence to the ejectment brought by the Plaintiff, or any other ejectment he may be advised to bring for recovery of the premises. This is also therefore a bill for relief; which relief must be grounded upon some proceeding at law. The party without the control of the Court chooses, what his proceeding shall be ; and then he will probably

---

(1) 2 Atk. 282; 3 Atk. 124.
(2) *Aston* v. *Lord Exeter, ante,* 288.

drop the bill ; and it will have the effect of a mere bill of discovery. If the party chooses to file a bill of discovery, be it so ; but if he chooses to file a bill for relief, and take his chance of obtaining it, it is very difficult to make out, that the Court is to aid him in any step, meaning to drop the relief, and to make it a mere bill of discovery ; but not apprising the Court of that purpose. In this instance it is a question of legitimacy. The fact is, he was a Fellow of a College ; and it is stated that he married ; and his marriage was kept secret, till he removed to a College living ; and
* that there is no pretence for illegitimacy. The Plaintiff   [* 296] is a near relation of the family. If as to the pedigree, as to which, I apprehend, a production would be ordered, it should happen, that any thing in the possession of this relation of the family confirmed the allegation, that this son was legitimate, is it the same thing to send the party to try the question without any of those provisions, which would be secured upon an issue, ordering a production on both sides, &c. ? The very thing he is doing is part of the relief ; and he takes his relief piece-meal, part by motion, part by decree. The only cases like it are *Bettison* v. *Farringdon* (1), and *The Earl of Suffolk* v. *Howard* (2). It is impossible to follow that last' case in some points. The Defendant made the deeds part of his answer ; and upon that the Court seems to have ordered the production, and upon principle : but they did that, I apprehend, upon the ground, that the answer offered it ; and therefore it is not within *Burton* v. *Neville* (3) and *Lady Shaftesbury's Case* (4). Then as to the annuity, the Court seems to have thought, there was something very pitiable in it ; and the cause does not go on, till a decree can be regularly obtained : but the arrears are ordered to be paid in that stage. It is impossible to follow so irregular a proceeding as that. In *Bettison* v. *Farringdon,* whether the bill was for discovery or relief, the answer put an end to all possible claim ; referring to a recovery ; and the answer tendering to the Court a case, upon which they could determine, that the Defendant's legal title did not require trying, the Court upon motion gave leave to look into that. But the object in both those cases was, not to aid a proceeding at law brought without the view of the Court, but to prevent a proceeding at law upon the Defendant's insisting, it was unnecessary. That is very different. A discovery and production in the Master's office with that view is very different from a discovery and production upon a trial, not directed by the Court, and not under its control. So is a discovery in the Master's office with a view to see, what in the course of the cause, retained in equity, is fit to be done.

I am of opinion therefore, that it is not fit to aid these experiments at law, after a bill filed, without the authority of the

(1) 3 P. Will. 363.
(2) 2 P. Will. 176.
(3) Cited *ante,* vol. iv. 67.
(4) *Lady Shaftesbury* v. *Arrowsmith, ante,* vol. iv. 66.

Court, and not under its view (1). Setting aside this outstanding term is relief, and relief enough for you afterwards to go on for
an account of rents and profits.

The motion stood over, to give farther opportunity of looking
into it; and it was not brought on again.

1. IT is a mistaken notion to suppose, that as soon as a bill is filed to prevent
the defendants from setting up an outstanding term, to defeat an ejectment, the
plaintiff may bring an ejectment, not under the direction of the Court of Chancery, yet come to that Court, by motion, to prevent the term from being set up.
No ejectment must be brought by the plaintiff, in such a case, before the hearing
in Equity, unless by permission of the Court; for at the hearing, circumstances
might possibly appear entitling the defendants to equitable assistance in the trials
at law. *Byrne* v. *Byrne*, 2 Sch. & Lef. 537; *Beer* v. *Ward*, 1 Jacob's Rep. 196;
Barney v. *Luckett*, 1 Sim. & Stu. 419; *Northey* v. *Pearce*, 1 Sim. & Stu. 421.
And see the references given in note 1 to the last preceding case.

2. It appears to be now settled, that mere reference to documents by a defendant's answer, does not make those documents part of the answer so as to entitle
the plaintiff to their production. *The Princess of Wales* v. *The Earl of Liverpool*,
1 Swanst. 121; and see the note to *Richards* v. *Jackson*, 18 Ves. 422. It would
be different if the defendant not only referred to the documents but admitted they
were in his possession; and by the nature of his reference, incorporated them into
his answer; *Evans* v. *Richardson*, 1 Swanst. 7; *Gardiner* v. *Mason*, 4 Brown,
480; *Erskine* v. *Bize*, 2 Cox, 226; and see the note to *Darwin* v. *Clarke*, 8 V.
158.

DANIELL *v.* DANIELL.

[ROLLS.—1801, JULY 14.]

LEGACY after limitations for life and in default of children to be paid equally between two persons or the whole to the survivor of them, held not vested till the
time of division (*a*).

WILLIAM MANTELL by his will, dated the 2d of October, 1761,
reciting his marriage settlement, in pursuance of the power therein
gave the whole share and parts of such stock, which he had power
to dispose of, to trustees and their heirs, in trust after the decease
of his wife, dying without issue by him, to pay his sister Jane Daniell the interest of 1000*l.* out of the stock during her natural life;
and after her decease the principal or produce of the said 1000*l.* to
be paid to her two sons James Daniell and Francis Daniell, share
and share alike, to their own proper use for ever; in case they
should be living at the time of their mother's decease: but, in case
either of them should die before their said mother, then the whole
principal or produce of the said 1000*l.* to be paid to the survivor of
them for his own proper use and behoof for ever; and also to pay

(1) *Angel* v. *Smith*, *post*, vol. ix. 335; *Byrne* v. *Byrne*, 2 Sch. & Lef. 537;
Barney v. *Luckett*, *Northey* v. *Pearce*, 1 Sim. & Stu. 419, 420; *Beer* v. *Ward*,
1 Jac. 194.

(*a*) 2 Roper, Legacies, by White, 275, ch. 21, § 2.

his sister Margaret Sunderland the interest of 300*l.* out of the said stock during her natural life; and her receipt to be a discharge for the same, without the control of her husband; and the principal or produce thereof .after her decease to be paid to her child or children, if more than one, share and share alike; and also to pay his brother Henry Mantell the interest of 200*l.* for life, and the principal to his children in the same manner; but in case Margaret Sunderland and Henry Mantell should die leaving no issue, then to pay the interest of the 300*l.* and 200*l.* to his sister Jane Daniell for life; and after her decease the principal or produce of the said 300*l.* and 200*l.* to her children share and share alike for their own use for ever: if only one, to that one; and farther reciting, that he was possessed of * 2100*l.* Bank Stock 4 per cents.   [* 298] 1760, he gave to one of his trustees 100*l.* part thereof, and the residue of the said stock he gave to his said trustees and their heirs; in trust to pay his mother Jane Mantell the interest of 600*l.* stock, part of the said stock, during her natural life; and after her decease to pay the said 600*l.* to his said sister Jane Daniell; and as to the rest of his said stock, in trust for his trustees to pay the interest, dividends, or produce, to his wife Mary Mantell during her life; and after her decease to his children, to be equally divided between them: but if only one child, then the whole to such child, or to such child or children as she may be with child of, and born after his decease; but in case his wife shall leave no child or children of his at her decease living, then to pay the interest of 400*l.* part of the said stock, to his sister Margaret Sunderland during her life; and after her decease the said 400*l.* to be paid to her child or children, share and share alike, if more than one; and to pay the interest of 1000*l.* other part of the said stock, to his sister Jane Daniell during her life; and after her decease the said 1000*l.* to be paid equally between her said two sons James and Francis Daniell, or the whole to the survivor of them; declaring his will, that as the said moneys are in the East India Stock or Bank Stock, and to avoid dispute, those legacies and trust of payments on the division are to be paid in such proportion more or less in the hundred pounds as the said stocks shall at that time produce.   He appointed the trustees and his sister Jane Daniell executors.

By a codicil, dated the 26th of January, 1762, the testator gave his sister Jane Daniell 200*l.* to be paid out of his 4 per cent. annuities of 1760 upon the condition following; that his intent and meaning was, that the said 200*l.* should be appropriated to the use of her youngest son Francis, to put him apprentice to such trade as his mother should judge proper; and directed, that his said money should not be paid till the time of his being put out apprentice or to a clerkship: but should he die before being put out apprentice, in that case the testator gave the said sum of 200*l.* in equal shares to his said sisters Jane Daniell and Margaret Sunderland for their use for ever.

The testator died in 1766.   His wife had no children by him.

She married Thomas Colby, one of the trustees; and died in 1799. Margaret Sunderland died in the life of Mary Colby; having never had any issue. ·Jane Daniell also died in the life of Mary Colby. James Daniell and Francis Daniell were her two only children. Francis died in 1793 intestate, after the death of his mother; leaving Anne Daniell, his widow and administratrix.

The bill was filed by James Daniell, and Robert Hubble, executor of Mary Colby, against the representatives of Thomas Colby, the surviving trustee, and Anne Daniell; praying a transfer to Hubble, as executor of Mary Colby, of 400*l.* 3 per cent. Reduced Annuities, (the stock having been reduced by Act of Parliament) part of the said 1400*l.* stock, and the dividends accrued since the death of Mary Colby; a transfer of the 1000*l.* 3 per cent. Reduced Annuities to the Plaintiff Daniell, and the dividends since the death of Mary Colby; or, in case Francis Daniell took a vested interest in one moiety, then a transfer of one moiety to the Defendant Anne Daniell; who insisting, that her husband took a vested interest, claimed 500*l.* of the stock.

A question suggested, that the 400*l.* did not fall into the residue, was given up by the Defendants.

Mr. *Romilly* and Mr. *Phillimore*, for the Plaintiffs.—The only meaning of the words " or the whole to the survivor of them," under which the Plaintiff Daniell claims, is the survivor at the death. The testator speaks of the death of Jane Daniell as happening after the death of his wife; and if both are not living, then he gives it to the survivor of them at that time, at which it was to vest in possession. The 400*l.* not being given after the disposition to the children of Margaret Sunderland must be considered in the event undisposed of.

Mr. *Sutton* and Mr. *Roper*, for the Defendants.—As to the 1000*l.* stock, Francis Daniell having survived his mother was equally entitled with his brother. The best mode of construing that part of the will is to look to other parts, to see what was meant by the word "survivor." He meant, that, if neither should die in the life of the mother, both should be equally entitled: if one should die in the life of the mother, his representative would not be entitled.

[* 300]   The Plaintiff's construction, taking any other period, * must stand upon conjecture. There is no reason, why this sum should go to these young men in any other way than the prior sum of 1000*l.*

The MASTER OF THE ROLLS [Sir WILLIAM GRANT].—There is no doubt upon either question. First the 400*l.* is clearly undisposed of. As to the 1000*l.* the only question is, to what period the survivorship relates. There can be no doubt upon that; when we see the limitations, first to the widow for life, then to the children: if no child, then to Mrs. Daniell for life; then equally between her two sons, or the whole to the survivor of them. It is clear, he meant, the survivor at the time of the division. He did not conceive, that would take place, till both his wife and Mrs. Daniell were dead. He conceived, the deaths would happen in the order of the limitations. The mode, in which he disposes of the other sum confirms, instead of opposing, this construction; showing, that the period of division was the period, at which he intended it to vest. He had the same meaning as to this fund. He, who is alive, when the division is to take place, takes the whole of the capital; which must be transferred accordingly to the Plaintiff Daniell; and the 400*l.* Bank Annuities must be transferred to Hubble (1).

SEE, *ante*, note 2 to *Roebuck* v. *Dean*, 2 V. 265, and the farther references there given.

MAWSON *v.* STOCK.

[1801, JULY 7, 13, 15.]

A SEPARATE agreement, securing to some creditors, who had executed a deed of composition, a greater advantage than the other creditors would have under the deed, and without their knowledge, cannot be enforced (*a*).

Held in bankruptcy, that after voluntary discharge by agreement the creditor cannot make use of a security against third persons; where the effect would be to make the party discharged again liable, though in another form and in the shape of the demand of another person (*b*), [p. 305.]

IN February 1796, a Commission of bankruptcy issued against William Stock. Afterwards a proposal being made for a composition at 8*s.* in the pound, by a deed, dated the 30th of April, 1796, reciting the bankruptcy, and that Stock had proposed, and his creditors had agreed to accept, a composition of 8*s.* in the pound in full discharge of their said respective debts, and in consideration thereof had agreed to release and discharge Stock, his heirs, executors, and administrators, estate, and effects, of and from the debts so to them due and owing from him, and also to join in a petition for superseding the Commission, and that Stock had upon the date of the deed delivered to his creditors three promisory notes, signed by his sureties, Sabine, Newby, and Norton, for * 8*s.* in the pound,   [* 301]

it was witnessed, that in consideration of the premises the said creditors for themselves and partners did release to Stock, his heirs, executors, and administrators, all actions or causes of action they ever had, or could or might thereafter have, for any cause or thing previous to the date of the said Commission; and for the considerations aforesaid the said creditors relinquished and gave up to Stock, his executors, administrators, and assigns, all and singular the stock in trade, household goods, &c. book debts, and other debts and

(1) See *Roebuck* v. *Dean*, *ante*, vol. ii. 265, and the note, 267.
(*a*) See *ante*, note (*a*), *Eastabrook* v. *Scott*, 3 V. 456.
(*b*) See *ante*, note (*a*), *Rees* v. *Berrington*, 2 V. 540.

sums of money, due, owing or belonging,. to him from any person or persons whomsoever, and all bonds, bills, notes, and other securities, for the same, and all other the estate and effects whatsoever, of Stock, whereof or wherein he or any person or persons in trust for him or for his use was or were seised, possessed, or interested, on the day of the date of the Commission, or upon any day since, and, all benefit and advantage whatsoever, to be made, had, or derived, thereby and therefrom; with a covenant to join in a petition to supersede the Commission ; and a proviso, that Stock would indemnify the assignees and his creditors from all charges, &c. respecting the deed of composition.

At the date of the deed of composition the bankrupt was indebted to Mawson to the amount of 2221*l.* 4*s.* 10*d.*; and had given him bills and notes for securing part, viz. 1107*l.* 5*s.* 5*d.* Mawson proved and received a dividend of 8*s.* under the deed upon the whole sum of 2221*l.* 4*s.* 10*d.* Afterwards he received 20*s.* in the pound upon one of the bills, and different sums upon the others ; and as he insisted upon retaining to the extent of 12*s.* in the pound, the Commission having been superseded, Stock brought an action against him for the amount of that dividend; which he recovered; and a motion for a new trial was refused (1).

The bill was filed by Mawson; praying an injunction to stay proceedings in that action; and that an agreement mentioned in the bill might be declared binding, and be carried into execution. The bill stated the agreement, dated the 23d of May, 1796, and signed by Mawson and four other creditors; reciting the deed of composition, as bearing even date therewith; and that [*302] previous * to the delivery of the notes for the composition it was agreed, that the holders of such bills and notes as were then become due, and were fully paid, should deduct the amount of such bills and notes from their respective debts, and receive the composition only upon the residue ; and that the holders of such bills and notes as were not then due, or not then fully paid, should give an undertaking to refund 8*s.* in the pound upon the amount of such bills and notes as should be afterwards respectively paid in full, so soon as the same should be received; and that no bills or notes should be compounded without the consent of two of the sureties.

For the Plaintiff it was proved, that, though Stock was not a party to the agreement, the instructions were given in his presence and hearing; and with his consent and approbation. The agreement was prepared by the attorney, who sued out the Commission, and prepared the deed, and was signed by the Plaintiff and four other creditors, upon the proposition of one of the sureties. It was intended to bear even date with the deed; and a blank left for the date was afterwards, but before the signing, filled up, but by mistake dated in May, instead of April, 1796: but it was understood, that

(1) *Stock* v. *Mawson*, 1 Bos. & Pul. 286.

the whole constituted but one transaction; and the agreement was considered as incorporated in, and explanatory of, the deed. The Plaintiff compounded one of the bills with the consent of two of the sureties and of Stock. The sureties withheld the notes for the composition for several months in consequence of the bill holders refusing to sign such agreement. The Plaintiff received the amount of some of the bills; and paid according to the agreement the 8*s.* in the pound to Stock's shopman; who gave a receipt.

Henry Hogarth proved the agreement, &c.; and stated, that in May 1796 William Wallis came with Stock to the Plaintiff; and produced some deeds and papers. The Plaintiff said, it would take a long time to read them; and would *not* sign them without reading; though pressed; but Wallis saying, he would not call again, and the Commission must be proceeded in, and Stock saying, he and his family would be ruined, if the Plaintiff did *not* sign, the Plaintiff asked Wallis, whether, in case he should sign, he would stand exactly in the same situation as if the Commission had gone on. Wallis answered, "Yes, most assuredly," upon * which the Plaintiff signed; expressing, that he did so, [* 303] relying upon that. Stock frequently applied to the deponent to prevail upon the Plaintiff to sign the deed and the agreement.

The Defendant by his answer denied to the best of his knowledge and belief, that any such bills, notes, &c. particularly of the Plaintiffs, were not due at the date of the bankruptcy; and believes, they were due at the date of the deed; though some were not fully paid. He has heard, that the agreement of the 23d of May was entered into; but denies, that such agreement was prepared, or entered into, or signed; at the instance or request of the Defendant; or, that he was privy to such agreement. He denies, that it was the general intention, that the bill holders should retain the bills, and pay the 8*s.*, &c.; and that it was understood by him or his sureties, or, as he knows, by his attorney; stating, that the other bill holders delivered up their bills, &c. He admits the receipt of one of the bills by the Plaintiff, the payment of 8*s.* in the pound, and the receipt given by his shopman; and that it was with his privity, but not with any intention of ratifying the agreement; but by the advice of the attorney; who desired the Defendant to take any thing he could get as an acknowledgment. He denied, that it was the intention of the deed, that the bill holder should be in the same situation as if the commission had gone on; or that the agreement was incorporated in or explanatory of the deed.

Some of the bill holders, who upon executing the deed of composition gave up their bills, were examined by the Defendant.

This cause, having been fully argued by Mr. *Romilly* and Mr. *Heald*, for the Plaintiff, and Mr. *Mansfield* and Mr. *Leach*, for the Defendant, stood for judgment.

July 18. Lord CHANCELLOR [ELDON].—Upon the decision between these parties at law I formerly had some doubt, whether the case was properly decided : but that opinion was hastily formed : for upon the best consideration I am clearly of opinion, that under the circumstances disclosed to the Court of Law that judgment was right. The case did not bring before that Court a great variety of circumstances, that have appeared in this cause. The existence [*304] of * the agreement, the circumstances of the conduct of Stock, alleged by this bill to have taken place, which could have raised in the contemplation of that Court any question upon the equity, which in an action for money had and received might have formed a ground of defence, were not disclosed : but the simple question was, whether the effect of the deed of composition was such, that Stock had a right after the execution of that deed to recover. This bill does not proceed upon any ground alleging, that that decision was wrong. I think, it was right, upon the following grounds ; 1st, that there was a commission of bankrupt taken out against Stock, that produced proof of debts for creditors of different descriptions : creditors, who held no bills : creditors, who held bills ; and creditors of the description of Mawson, holding bills for part of their demands, and not for the residue. Under those circumstances the bankrupt seems to have been anxious to have the commission superseded ; and he proposes, according to the case in the Court of Common Pleas, and without reference to the additional circumstances before this Court, a deed of composition. The creditors sign the deed ; and give him a full discharge from all their demands ; releasing him and his estate entirely as against all their demands ; and they agree to assign all his estate to him, and to assign over all their securities ; and I mention it, because I do not think, the word " bills," as it stands in that part of the deed, has the sense the Court of Common Pleas put upon it ; for the words are " due and owing to him ; " and these bills are for money due and owing from him.

It is impossible to say, the bill holders, both with regard to the bankrupt himself and the other creditors, could have a right to receive more than 8s. in the pound. The bill holders are of two descriptions : 1st, holders of bills, upon which the bankrupt would be primarily liable, and bound to indemnify the other persons ; whose names are upon the bills ; and others holding bills, under which, though he is liable, other persons are primarily liable, and bound to indemnify him. As to the first class, where bills drawn for the accommodation of the bankrupt were accepted, or, where he was the acceptor with effects, and liable to indemnify all the other persons, the necessary consequence of this operating as a release would be, that, when the bankrupt paid 8s. in the pound, if the holders [*305] went to the acceptor for the bankrupt's accommodation * for the remaining 12s., though the holders had given him a discharge in full, and so as to make him a new man, that acceptor paying the 12s. in the pound would have had an unanswerable demand against the bankrupt for that 12s. Therefore against the faith of that transaction that demand is brought down upon the bankrupt; when the discharge was given for 20s. It has been held in bankruptcy, that after a voluntary discharge from the whole debt by agreement, (I do not mean by an Insolvent Debtor's Act), the creditor cannot make use of a security he has against third persons; where the effect would be to set up again, though in another form, and in the shape of the demand of another person, the bankrupt's liability. This would not hold, where the bankrupt was not primarily liable. Where the bankrupt is drawer, and the acceptance is upon the credit of effects in the hands of the acceptor, the general effect of a release of the drawer would not release the acceptor; for it would be *pro tanto* relieving the acceptor, and no prejudice to him whatsoever. The question then would be, not, whether the acceptor might say, the holder should not recover against him, but, whether the drawer having paid 8s. might not say to the acceptor, "you shall not pay except for my benefit." Upon that view the observation is just: when it is said, they assigned all his estate to him. Then it comes to this question: Can you in an action so mixed, containing so many different equities, say, one thing was meant as to one bill holder, and something very different as to another? There is nothing in the instrument, showing, such a distinction was intended: and I think, it was not. That is one of the inconveniences arising from the doctrine, that you may set up in answer to the objection for want, of notice to the drawer, that there were no effects in the hands of the acceptor. There never was a decision, with a view to public policy, more mischievous. Upon that doctrine a great part, if not the whole, of the mischief of accommodation paper, short in its consequences only of the mischief, that would follow any attempt at this day to cure it, is founded.

Under these circumstances; I think, the decision at law is right. It was objected, that, if so, there is no ground for relief in this Court; because the case stated by the bill would have formed a defence at law. If the case made by the bill could be made out in point of fact, I think, it would be a defence at law. The action *was for money had and received, founded upon [*306] the equitable title to receive; and therefore defeated by the equitable title to retain. If this case had been proved at law, I do not see, how the Plaintiff could have recovered. The case insisted upon at law was, that the intention of all parties was, that, let the consequence to the bankrupt and the other creditors be what it might, the bill holders should be left in possession of a right to work out payment of 20s. in the pound; that it was generally understood by all the creditors; and therefore a fraud upon none; and, if not generally known, the Plaintiff at law had stated to Mawson what was tantamount to a declaration, that such was the intention; and that he executed the instruments under the confidence created by the assertion, that the consequence of his executing them at the desire of Stock would be, that he would be able to recover against all the bill holders, until he should be satisfied 20s. in the pound; therefore in equity Stock is bound to make good that representation; and the deed in equity should be read accordingly; and therefore it was against conscience, that he should recover contrary to that; and that he should be heard to say, the deed had a different effect from his representation. But the proposition, so stated, embraces two facts: 1st, Whether Stock made any representation, upon which Mawson proceeded: 2dly, Whether it was a representation, that entitles Mawson to say all he has now suggested; not only, that it was intended by Stock and Mawson; but that Stock undertook to assure Mawson, he might act upon it, as i all the creditors knew it. I express it so: for it is impossible to deny, that, where a large body of creditors, partly consisting of bill holders, having a right to apply, not only to the common debtor, but also to others, all enter into a deed of composition, by which all on the face of it accept 8s. in the pound in absolute discharge of their demands, it is not competent to a particular description of creditors to go into another room, and say, that with the debtor they make a fresh agreement for their benefit; that, though they have absolutely discharged him in the presence of the others, yet by the separate agreement they will hold him so engaged to them, that they shall receive 20s. in the pound : and so to bring upon him the claims of others; from whom they receive that; though the other creditors thin him absolutely discharged. That is a fraud upon·th [* 307]   policy of the law, and *upon the other creditors; a frau upon third persons, of which it has been uniformly held that the debtor may take advantage.

If it stands upon the deed, and it does not appear, that other cred itors knew of it, it is very difficult either in law or equity to sustai the case of the Plaintiff. It is to be observed, this is not a deed, at taching upon a man untouched by any process at law, but upon man at that moment under a commission of bankrupt. The case must be considered with regard to all the circumstances attachin upon that situation. Upon the answer it appears, the transactio was in April and May; and the commission was not superseded til November. The petitioning creditor was one of these bill holders That creditor could not possibly agree to supersede the commission taking more upon his debt than any other creditor; whatever hi security was. Also, if a creditor, a bill holder, had been paid part o his demand by any person, whose name was upon the bill, and wh would have a right to say, he had paid as surety of the bankrupt that creditor might come at any time; desiring, that the proof shoul not be struck out, but should remain in trust for his benefit. The circumstances were not sufficiently attended to. It was absolutel incumbent upon the bill holder to make out, that there was such a agreement, not only between him and the bankrupt, but betwee the bankrupt and all the creditors; and all the Judges go upon this that unless all the other creditors knew of it, it would be a fraud and then Mawson could not retain what he had received upon thes bills.

The fact, charged in the bill, that the intention of the parties t the deed was, that such of the creditors, who were bill holders, should be put in the same situation, as if the commission had proceeded, is a fact, of which the deed is so far from being evidence, that it is evidence to the contrary ; and there is no evidence connecting the transactions with the bill holders with the knowledge of the other creditors; much less, connecting it as the effect of their intention, that the bill holders should have that advantage. Stock by his answer says, it was not the intention; and he carries his denial to a length, that surprises me, considering the evidence. He must have known, as I am satisfied his sureties knew, that there was an agreement with the bill holders to that effect. If * the agreement was prepared without his knowledge, and   [* 308] thereby a demand was raised against him, which the bill holders would not have had under the release itself, that was an act, that could not be done without a special authority from him or subsequent approbation. But still if the general creditors did not know that transaction, and did not mean, that the deed should operate one way as to them, and another way as to the other creditors, the policy of the law will reach the transaction ; whatever the intention of Stock might be ; unless there was a distinct undertaking, if such a thing could be, that no question upon the policy of the law could ever arise; and there might be, I think, that distinct undertaking ; which would have bound him so that he should not say, the other creditors did not know the transaction, and had not such intention. But the evidence does not amount to that by any means. It is incumbent upon the Plaintiff distinctly to prove, that such was the intention of the other creditors ; when it is distinctly denied by the answer. It is clear, the deed and the agreement were intended to bear even date. and were prepared together: a circumstance, that induces me to believe, the creditors did not know this; for then the transaction, if fair, ought to be by one deed; and it could not be fair to leave these creditors the chance of getting 20s. in the pound; the consequence of which would be, that Stock would not be discharged. Suppose, the Plaintiff had read the instruments, and had collected an assurance from them, that he was to stand in the same situation as if the commission was to go on ; still, if he acted upon that assurance, so collected by himself, he could not have held the benefit of that bargain ; unless the other creditors knew he had acquired it. Upon Hogarth's evidence it may be asked, how could Stock be totally ruined, if Mawson did not sign the writing upon that day; unless there was something more in it than what Stock says? It is impossible, that the question he states afterwards could have been asked, unless consequential upon previous communication ; and it is singular, when the act to be done was to have the effect of superseding the commission. The evidence, state it as high as you will, comes only to this; that Mawson wished to have an assurance, that the deed would place him in the same situation, as if the commission was not superseded. I am willing to go the length, though there is but one witness against the answer, of saying, that there is evidence enough in the circumstances to authorise me not to believe the Defendant, and to take it, that Wallis did with his privity give the assurance to the extent mentioned in the deposition: but the question results, whether these creditors can take the benefit of a separate. agreement; the Plaintiff not proving, though loudly called upon by what is put in issue and what passed in the Court of Common Pleas to prove, that he was acquiring these benefits for himself with the knowledge of the other creditors.   In that he has totally failed.

With this view of the case I am of opinion, that upon the policy of the law this bill cannot succeed.   I have gone fully into it; that the ground of my judgment may be understood.   The Defendant upon the equity arising out of the situation of the other creditors, not founded upon anything righteous as between him and the Plaintiff, has a right to say, the Plaintiff cannot succeed in this bill. Though I dismiss the bill, yet upon the answer, connected with all the evidence, I do not dismiss it with costs (1).

1. ANY secret agreement, securing to one creditor a greater benefit than to the rest, is a fraud upon a *general composition*, and renders the whole transaction void; see, *ante*, the note to *Eastabrook* v. *Scott*, 3 V. 456.

2. That the discharge of the principal debtor, reserving all remedies against his sureties, would, in almost all cases, be nugatory; as the sureties, when they were sued, would immediately seek relief over against their principal; see note 2 to *Rees* v. *Berrington*, 2 V. 540.

3. The rule, that where the drawer of a bill of exchange has no effects in the hands of the drawee, nor any right upon any other ground to expect the bill will be paid, he is not entitled to notice of its dishonor; knowledge being, in such case, substituted for notice; is a decision which has been regretted, not only in the principal case, but in many other cases, both at Law and in Equity, as tending to introduce nice distinctions, instead of adhering to a plain and intelligible rule. *Cory* v. *Scott*, 3 Barn. & Ald. 622; *Claridge* v. *Dalton*, 4 Mau. & Sel. 231; *Wallwyn* v. *St. Quinten*, 1 Bos. & Pull. 655; *Ex parte Wilson*, 11 Ves. 411; *Ex parte Heath*, 2 V. & B. 240.

4. As to the rights of sureties, who have paid the demand against their principal, to come in under a commission of bankrupt against him; see note 2 to *Ex parte Matthews*, 6 V. 285.

5. That a decree may be made upon the testimony of a single witness, if supported by circumstances, against the positive denial contained in the defendant's answer; see note 2 to *Mortimer* v. *Orchard*, 2 V. 243.

(1) *Ante, Eastabrook* v. *Scott*, vol. iii. 456; *post, Palmer* v. *Neave*, xi. 165, 235, 6, and the note; *Ex parte Sadler*, xv. 54.

POLE *v.* LORD SOMERS.

[1801, July 14, 16.]

In a case both of election and satisfaction by the will of a parent as to two subjects of claim by his younger children under a settlement a case of election
was raised as to a third subject, stock vested in trustees, upon the construction of the will (*a*).

The question, whether evidence, viz. a schedule written by the testator subsequent
to the will, could be admitted; was not decided (*b*).

Upon a presumption of satisfaction by will evidence admissible: 1st, to constitute
the fact, that the testator was debtor: 2dly, to meet or fortify the presumption,
[p. 321.]

Evidence admitted upon equities arising out of presumptions; and in the case of
the next of kin and executor evidence between the will and the death of the
testator, but as to his intention at the death of the will, [p. 324.]

By indentures of settlement, previous to the marriage of Reginald
Pole and Ann Buller, dated the 26th of April, 1751, the fortune of
Ann Buller; consisting of several funds, amounting in the whole to
3500*l.* was directed to be paid to trustees; and Reginald Pole covenanted with the trustees to do all acts for empowering them to receive the said moneys; upon trust to invest the same in lands of inheritance, to be settled to the use of Reginald Pole for life, without
impeachment of waste; remainder to Ann Buller for life; and after their deceases to the use of all and every such child or children
as they should have, in such shares and proportions, and at such
times, and under such restrictions as Reginald Pole should appoint
by deed or will; and for want of his appointment, according to the
appointment of Ann Buller, surviving him; and in default of appointment, then to and among all and every such child and
children and their heirs, * equally between them, share and   [*310]
share alike, as tenants in common, and not as joint tenants; in case there should be more than one; and in case there
should be no such child, upon other trusts.

   The sum of 950*l.*, part of 1071*l.*, 8*s.* 7*d.*, one of the trust funds,
which was paid to the trustees, was laid out in the purchase of the
manor of Cotleigh; which was conveyed to the uses of the settlement; and the remainder of that sum, after defraying the expenses,
was received by Reginald Pole. Ann Pole died in 1758. The
issue of the marriage was five children. Another part of the funds,
to the amount of 1000*l.* was paid to the trustees upon the 24th of
March, 1761, and was invested in their names in 1025*l.* 12*s.* 10*d.*
4 per cent. Consolidated Annuities. The sum of 1385*l.* 14*s.* 3 1-2*d.*,

---

   (*a*) For the recent cases on the subject of election and satisfaction, see *ante*,
note (*a*), *Hinchcliffe* v. *Hinchcliffe*, 3 V. 516, and notes to *Butricke* v. *Broadhurst*,
1 V. 171; *Baugh* v. *Read*, 1 V. 257, and *Blake* v. *Bunbury*, 1 V. 514.

   (*b*) See 2 Starkie, Evid. 569 (5th Amer. from last London edit.); *Shelton* v.
Shelton, 1 Wash. 56; *Dewit* v. *Yates*, 10 Johns. 156. Parol evidence is admissible
to show the state of his property when the testator made his will. *Hyde* v. *Price*,
1 Coop. 208; *Webley* v. *Langstaff*, 3 Desaus. 509.

all, that was received upon the remaining trust funds, was received in 1764 by Reginald Pole, and was mixed with his own money.

Reginald Pole by his will, dated the 19th of March, 1767, after several specific legacies, and giving his chambers in the Temple to his eldest son Reginald, gave Mary Collins an annuity of 6l. for life; for the payment of which he charged all his estate and effects both real and personal. Then reciting, that his aunt Hawkins had promised to give him 2000l., of which sum she had already advanced him 1000l., in assured confidence, that she would fulfil the said promise, he gave his daughter Ann 2000l. and to his daughter Sarah 2000l., to be paid at the age of twenty-one, or marriage, provided with the consent of his executors and their aunts; if without consent, he revoked the legacy; and gave the same equally among all his other children, share and share alike. He gave his son Charles Morice 2000l., when twenty-one; and to his son Edward 1000l., when twenty-one; assigning the reason of the difference, that his aunt Hawkins had lately assured him, that the 1000l. remaining, before mentioned as unpaid, she had by will given to Edward; and had also obliged him (the testator) to promise in writing to give the said 1000l., if it came into his possession, to his said son: directing it accordingly to be paid in that event to his said son. The maintenance and education of his children during their minority he directed to be taken from the whole produce of his real and personal estate; always taking care, that the expenses did not ex-

[*311]   ceed the growing profits. *He also empowered his exec-
          utors to sell, if they think proper, his chambers in the
Temple, and also, if necessary, the manor of Cotleigh; and to apply the produce during his son Reginald's minority to any use or purpose they should judge would be for his benefit and advantage; and he empowered them to lay out any part of his said younger sons' respective fortunes during their respective minorities to any use or purpose for their respective benefit and advantage. All the residue of his estate and effects both real and personal not before devised, after payment of his debts and legacies, he gave and bequeathed to Reginal, his eldest son.

At the bottom of the will was a memorandum, dated the 20th of September, 1767, that one of the sums of 1000l. before mentioned, given to his daughter Sarah, was the 1000l. formerly received of his aunt Hawkins, at her request given by him to his daughter Sarah.

The sum of 1000l., mentioned in the will to have been promised by the testator's aunt, was paid to him in his life. He died in November 1769, not having made any appointment. The bill was filed by Edward Pole; praying, that the Plaintiff may be declared entitled to one fifth part of the said estate and effects, and an account of the rents and profits received by the Defendant Reginald Pole Carew, the eldest son, &c.

The answer, which was not replied to, stated, that at the death of the testator the sum of 1025l. 12s. 10d. 4 per cent. Annuities was standing in the names of the trustees: but except that fund and the manor of Cotleigh they had no other part of the trust property: the rest having been received by the testator, and mixed with his own property. Among the papers of the testator, was found a schedule or estimate of the state of his personal property down to the 4th of September, 1769, written by the testator. The only part of his personal property not mentioned in that schedule was the furniture of his house. ,Besides the estates mentioned in his will he had a tenement for the lives of himself and the Plaintiff, producing something less than 29*l.* a-year; and three farms were settled after the marriage upon him and his wife and their issue, in the same manner as by the other settlement; and for want of such issue, or an appointment by the testator, to him and his *heirs. The answer [*312] insisted, that the testator meant to dispose of all the trust property; as the manor of Cotleigh was by the will specifically given to the Defendant; and as he had not assets to answer the legacies of 2000*l.* each to his four younger children without the application of his trust funds; and the said legacies appear calculated upon the property in the schedule, which comprised the stock and the sum of 1385*l.* 14*s.* 3 1-2*d.*

The schedule referred to by the answer began thus:

" This is not to be annexed to my will; being only intended for giving in one view to my executors the state of my securities."

Then after stating several securities, bonds, notes, mortgages, &c. came this entry: " Stock in my trustees' names, Philip Rashleigh and John Buller in 4 per cent. Consols, cost 1000*l.* at 97 three-eights one eight brokerage 1025*l.* 12*s.* 10*d.*" .

Afterwards under the date 24th June, 1769, were the following entries:

" Deduct	. . . .	£2020	0 0
" Do. O. S. S. Annuities	.	1119	0 0
" Do. Llanrath	. . .	1385	14 3 1-2

Other entries followed; and the last .date was the 4th of September, 1769.

Mr. *Mansfield*, Mr. *Alexander*, and Mr. *Stanley*, for the Plaintiff.— Under the effect of this paper, found among the testator's papers, but not proved as part of his will, it is contended, that the testator meant to dispose of the whole of the trust property. The testator gives his executors power to sell the manor of Cotleigh; and it cannot be disputed, that he acted upon that as his own; and a distinct intention appears in the will, that his eldest son should have the benefit of that. With respect to the 4 per cent. Annuities, standing in the names of his trustees at his death, it does not appear, that he had that fund in contemplation. There is no case of election, where it does not appear upon the face of *the will, [*313] that the testator meant to dispose of that property, out of which the claim was made, as his own. There is nothing of that sort in this will.

If this schedule is to be taken into consideration, he does
consider that fund as part of his property: but the schedule cannot be looked at.   It could not be proved as testamentary; for at the beginning he directs, that it shall not be annexed to his will.   It cannot be read as any evidence by way of
addition to the will, and to show the effect of it, so as to raise a
case of election as to this part of the trust fund.   The claim of the
Defendant must be under the residuary bequest.   The natural import of the words is only what was his property.   It has been decided, that mere general words, without reference to a power, cannot apply to the subject of that power (1).   To take this paper into
consideration would be introducing evidence in a way, in which it
never has been permitted, and, contrary to all the rules, construing
a written instrument by collateral evidence.   The question is,
whether under the words "my estate and effects" he meant to include this particular fund.   The great distinction between *Hinchcliffe* v. *Hinchcliffe* (2) and many other cases there noticed is, that
in all of them the books and papers were produced to show the
fact, that from the situation of the property it naturally fell within
the description of the will; that the property said to be claimed
against the will, was actually within·it; that the testator had dealt
in such a way as to make it his estate.   Lord Alvanley in *Hinchcliffe* v. *Hinchcliffe* states distinctly, that he would not suffer the evidence to construe the will.   In this instance it is applied to show,
he meant this subject; though it was not his.   Upon the will the
only argument is, that having given his eldest son the manor of Cotleigh, that being a part of the trust property, though not in the
hands of the trustees, he meant to give him the whole.   That is
much too strong an inference.   If he forgot the settlement, that
cannot avail the Defendant.   An intention for election is not to be
inferred from loose words.   This would be a bad appointment; the
words of the power being "all and every."   With respect to that
part of the fund which was received by the testator in his life, the
case is more favorable for the Defendant: but there is as express
an intention, that it should be subject to the debts.

[* 314]   * Mr. *Richards*, Mr. *Romilly*, and Mr. *Leach*, for the Defendant.—The question applies only to the stock : the rest
of the fund, except that and the manor of Cotleigh, being admitted
to have been in the testator's hands; and therefore being a debt
from him to his children; and then there is no doubt, that giving
them a greater sum will be a satisfaction.   This is a demand of a
portion: between which and other debts there is a distinction.   This
is the case, not of a person exercising a power under the settlement,
but rather of one, who had forgotten the settlement.   He treated
the manor of Cotleigh as subject, not to his appointment, but to his
dominion;   and, if that should not be exercised, as what would

---

(1) *Andrews* v. *Emmott*, 2 Bro. C. C. 297.   See *ante*, vol. ii. 592.
(2) *Ante*, vol. iii. 516; see the note. 530.

descend to his heir. Having certainly forgotten the settlement as to the manor of Cotleigh, it is very difficult to say, he remembered it for any purpose. This paper is admissible upon principle and authority; not to construe the will, but to show what the testator himself thought of his property; what he conceived to be his property. You may give in evidence an account of the actual property of the testator; that he had made a particular subject his own. It is impossible, that the proposition can rest there. It must go farther, to this extent, that he treated property, which was not his own, as his own. If he treated the trust fund as his own, it is as much his for the purpose of this argument as what he mixed with his own money; and then the election is a consequence. Upon a devise of Blackacre with its appurtenances evidence is always admitted to show what the devisor held with it. In *Pulteney* v. *Lord Darlington* (1), upon the question of election the rent-rolls of General Pulteney were given in evidence, to show, he treated the estate tail as his own. In *Wright* v. *Rutter* (2) and *Rutter* v. *M'Lean* (3) there was a circumstance clearly *dehors* the will, as much as in this case; viz. the deed, under which the will was made; the testator thinking the property his own; and the wife was put to her election. There are a great many other cases of this kind; where the testator conceived property not his to be his; and evidence of this kind has been admitted. *Eden* v. *Smith* (4) certainly is not a case of this sort. For some time the Lord Chancellor doubted very much the propriety of admitting that evidence; but at last admitted it; and principally upon the authority of *Hinchcliffe* v. *Hinchcliffe*. Evidence has constantly * been admitted to   [* 315] show, who is the person described, and what is the subject described. The objection is, that, where there is something to answer the description, evidence of any thing farther shall not be given. There is no authority for such a distinction; and cases are to be found, which could not have been so decided, if such a distinction exists. Upon that supposition in the case of a legatee described by both a different christian and surname there ought to have been an inquiry, whether there was any one to be found, having both these names. In *Smith* v. *Coney* (5) a legacy was given to a person by the description of the Reverend Charles Smith of Stapleford Tawney in the county of Essex. There were two persons; Richard Smith, incumbent of Stapleford Tawney at the date of the will; and Charles Smith, an officer in the army; and evidence was admitted. In a case heard yesterday your Lordship referred it to the Master to see, whom the testator meant by his sister Jane. In the cases of satisfaction, by an advancement subsequent to the will, evi-

(1) Reg. Lib. A. 1773, fol. 710; cited *ante*, vol. iii. 521, in *Hinchcliffe* v. *Hinchcliffe*; *post*, in *Druce* v. *Denison*, 385.
(2) *Ante*, vol. ii. 673.
(3) *Ante*, vol. iv. 531.
(4) *Ante*, vol. v. 341.
(5) *Ante*, 42.

dence of that fact being received, evidence must be received of all
facts of the testator's conduct subsequent to the will to show what
he intended; and in those cases the evidence is not applied as an
explanation of the will. The other case of satisfaction, where a
portion was originally provided by contract, and then a will gives a
portion to the same amount, arises upon the same presumption.
The Court is bound to admit evidence upon the same principle;
and the will is not affected. The meaning of the will in such cases
is plain: but the question is, whether the testator meant, that something collateral to the will should also take place; and the evidence
is introduced to rebut a presumption; and it is to be received
whether applying to the period before or after the will, the question
being, not as to the intention upon the will, but as to an intention
collateral to the will. Whether the declarations are before or after
the will is perfectly immaterial; if they are evidence of the intention at the time. The opinion expressed by Mr. Justice Buller (1)
in *Nourse* v. *Finch,* that declarations subsequent ought not to be received, was not approved by Lord Rosslyn [Loughborough]. *Gul-
liver* v. *Poyntz* (2). As the Court raises the presumption as matter
of evidence, they are bound to admit evidence against it. That is
the ordinary case of admitting evidence to rebut a pre-
[*316] sumption; which is only a rule * of evidence. In *Hinchcliffe* v. *Hinchcliffe* the evidence was introduced in aid of
the presumption; to confirm the rule of the Court; to show an intention, that the provisions given by the will should stand in the
place of the prior provision by settlement. That was a case of the
same nature as this; a claim under a settlement of the mother's
fortune, previous to the marriage. The only difference is the power
of appointment in this case.

If the evidence cannot be received, there is enough in this will
to show, the testator did not intend, that these children should have
more than he gave them by the will; and that construction is supported by the leaning of the Court against a double provision, and
the favorable consideration for the heir, appearing in all the cases of
portions.

Reply.—All the cases of election are, where settled property has
been devised; as if it was not settled. The money the testator
mixed with his own certainly raises a demand against his assets; and
it is certainly very difficult to argue, that the demand in respect of
that is not satisfied. But the stock vested in trustees stands upon a
very different ground. No act has been done to alter the property;
and no notice is taken of it in the will; nor does any inference
arise upon it, except from the disposition as to the manor of Cotleigh; which, I admit, does afford some; that, as he supposed,
that, which was purchased with part of the trust fund was his
own, so he thought the rest of the trust fund his own. But
that inference is not strong enough to raise a case of election. It

(1) *Ante,* vol. i. 359.
(2) 2 Black. 736.

does not follow, that he made the same mistake as to that fund that he did as to the estate.   There is nothing in the will showing, he did not mean the children to have any thing more.   There can be no inconsistency in each of them taking one fifth of the trust fund remaining unaltered.   This distribution will not occasion any inequality.   This is not a claim to take from the eldest son as a debt, any thing in his hands, that passed to him by the will.   How can the testator be said to have dealt with this property ?   He never altered it.   He suffered it to remain with the trustee ; receiving nothing but the interest ; which by the settlement he was entitled to receive for life.

*As to the paper, there is no difference in this respect   [*317] between that and a parol declaration ; and the real question is, whether any parol declaration at any distance of time, twenty or forty years, after the will, can be admitted to show, that when he made his will, he had that subject in contemplation.   In *Lord Darlington* v. *Pulteney* the will itself contained a sufficient indication of the intention.   *Hinchcliffe* v. *Hinchcliffe* does not affect this case.   In that there did not exist, as in this, any trust property, the subject of the settlement, in the state, in which it had been since the marriage, vested in trustees : but all the subject of the settlement was gone ; and it was the ordinary case of satisfaction.   *Wright* v. *Rutter* and *Rutter* v. *M'Lean* are not applicable.   There the property was the testator's, when he made his will ; and it would have been very strong to say, the wife should undo that in opposition to his will ; taking benefits under it.   *Eden* v. *Smith* is so singular a case, that it must be considered as an exception to all rules, and not applicable to any other case.   Some distinction seems to have been there suggested between parol declarations and writing: but there cannot be such a distinction.   That decision stands upon the singular circumstances of the case.   The papers might have been burnt at any time.   They were all in the testator's possession.   The arguments from other cases, in which evidence has been admitted to explain a will, have no relation to this.   They are all cases of latent ambiguity ; where the will cannot operate, unless other evidence is called in.   This case has no ambiguity latent or patent.   In the cases of the mistake of the name the inquiry must be confined to the family or acquaintance of the testator.   I admit, upon questions of satisfaction evidence must be admitted, and on both sides, to destroy or confirm the presumption, which the Court raises for want of a better ground.   From the nature of a presumption evidence must be admitted to destroy it, and therefore to confirm it ; either written or parol ; as in the case of the executor and next of kin ; in which it is now determined, with reluctance certainly, that it is admissible on both sides.   Here there can be no question of satisfaction as to the stock ; unless it is previously assumed, that the testator considered it his property ; and meant to give it.

Lord CHANCELLOR [ELDON].—If by taking farther time, I could hope to give a judgment, that would be more satisfac-

tory either to myself or the parties, I should reserve an opportunity of farther considering this case: but I am perfectly
satisfied, that, whether I have drawn a right conclusion, or not,
upon the whole case, I shall not be able by any farther discussion with myself to alter that opinion. The case is not precisely
like any former case. It is not purely a case of either satisfaction,
or election. As to the manor of Cotleigh it is a case of election.
As to the sum mixéd with the property of the testator, it is a case of
satisfaction; and the question is, how the third subject, the stock
actually vested in trustees, is to be treated; regard being had to the
fact, that as to the two other subjects involved in the same trust it
is a case both of election and satisfaction. The right of the Plaintiff
rests upon the effect of settlement, the transactions prior to the will,
as far as they can be looked at in the way, in which the Court can
look at them, according to the rules of evidence, upon the will, and
upon that paper: if the Court under all the circumstances is authorised to read it. The settlement from the frame of it would have
left no doubt as to this sum; if in fact it had not been laid out in
stock; but had been received by the father; for upon the marriage
he would have become entitled to these funds *jure mariti:* but the
form, in which the trust for the children attaches upon it, is a covenant by the father, that he will do all acts empowering the trustees
to receive the money. If therefore he had received it, and it was
in his hands at his death, it would be like *Hinchcliffe* v. *Hinchcliffe.*
The money being to be laid out in land, when received, is in this
Court to be considered as land; and the limitation in default of appointment is, as I understand it, to the children as tenants in common in fee; and they had a right to say, that, wherever the money
was found, it was to be laid out in land upon those trusts. The
manor of Cotleigh having been conveyed to the uses of the settlement, the children are at law tenants in common in fee of that.
The sum of 1385*l.* 14*s.* 3*d.* having been received by him, and being
in his hands, bound by his covenant, he was debtor to his children
for that sum, considered here as land; of which they were tenants
in common in fee; and the 1000*l.* paid by his permission to the
trustees, and invested in stock, must also be considered in this Court
as land, of which also they were tenants in common in fee. This
was the state of affairs at the date of the will. He had it in his
            power unquestionably upon the principles of this Court, as
[* 319]   applied to * cases of election, to purchase either for him-
            self or others the interests of his children in both those
articles; by tendering to them by his will a consideration, which
they should think more eligible for them than insisting upon their
rights under the settlement in the land, and the money, considered
as land. As to the sum in his hands, for which he was debtor to
his children, he might, as a debtor of any description, by his will
satisfy that debt. As a parent, he must be taken to have intended
to satisfy the claim of his children, to whom he was indebted, if the

will contains such provisions as this Court will hold a satisfaction of a debt from a parent to his children.

In the bequest of the annuity he first uses the words "all my estate and effects both real and personal;" upon which he charges that annuity. It would be strong to say, he meant by those words in that part of the will to charge with that annuity of 6*l.* the manor of Cotleigh, and the stock standing in the names of trustees for his children; and yet I do not know, how it can be said, that by the same words in any other part of his will he did mean to embrace those parts of his property, unless those words in this part have the same meaning. Then he proceeds to provide what he calls, or what upon a fair construction I am entitled to say he meant to call, the fortunes of his younger children. In the manner, in which these gifts are conceived, with respect to being more or less beneficially given, there are circumstances of difference between the provision by the settlement and that by the will: but it has long been settled, that slight circumstances will not alter the doctrine of satisfaction in this Court between parent and children. The circumstance of his assigning the reason of the difference as to his són Edward shows, he meant equality. He seems to have had a perfect reliance on Mrs. Hawkins; that if she should survive him, she would give Edward the 1000*l.* He seems to have intended, if he should survive her, to give this sum to his son in discharge of his duty to her and to him; and he remarks in the memorandum made some time after the will, that 1000*l.* of the 2000*l.* given to his daughter Sarah he had received upon the like condition from Mrs. Hawkins. Certainly events might happen, in which Edward would receive only 1000*l.*: viz. if Mrs. Hawkins had withdrawn her intention of kindness: but that would only have raised a case of election or of
satisfaction; if the will taken altogether raised such a   [320]
case. I agree, the observation, that he meant, they should
be all equally provided for, does not go for much; for if there was no more, this is only an equal addition to their fortunes. Upon the clause directing maintenance it is to be observed, that, if the words "my real and personal estate," as there used, comprehend nothing more than what in a strict sense was his real and personal estate, this direction for maintenance operates in fact as a direction, that the rents of the manor of Cotleigh, the dividends of the stock vested in the trustees, and, if the money in his ,hands could be claimed as a debt, the interest of that also, should accumulate; and then it is to be taken as a direction, that the children are to be maintained out of the produce of the real and personal estate, considered as exclusive of these three subjects. The question then breaks out strongly upon the will, what did the testator mean by his real and personal property? This is the case of a testator making the ordinary and usual provision for the maintenance and education of his children out of the rents, profits, and produce of his real and personal estate; and looking to the case ordinarily looked to in settlements and by provident testators, he provides for their advancement in the world

by giving powers to his executors to break in upon the funds respectively given to his children; and he expressly gives a power of selling the manor of Cotleigh. How could he give that power to his executors, unless he thought, he had a disposing power over that property, or meant to assume that power, or thought he did make a devise of it, taking all his will together, under the devise of his real and his personal estate? That construction is strengthened, when you advert to this; that he actually received part of the trust money; and had that in his hands; a debtor, it may be admitted, for that sum: but the money received by him was his: the fund, out of which that debt must be paid, was his. The fund including it therefore would pass under the words "my personal estate:" whether subject to debts is another question; but this being the case of parent and children, and a provision made by the will beyond the amount of the debt; it is disposed of among his personal estate, not subject to the payment of this as a debt; for the provisions of the will raise a case, not of election, but of satisfaction as to this demand. By his will he has taken upon himself to dispose, or thought he had power to dispose, of the manor of Cotleigh and the money re-
[* 321]   ceived *by him as his estate, or at least he intended to make it pass under those words by giving his children a consideration, raising a case of satisfaction. As to those two subjects therefore the Plaintiff cannot succeed (1).

The next question is one, which, I own, has embarrassed me very much: whether under all the circumstances the Plaintiff can succeed as to the stock. Upon the best judgment I can form upon this case, considered as a very particular case, standing almost by itself, a case upon the head both of election and satisfaction, I am of opinion, the Plaintiff cannot succeed. The question, that has been discussed, is of very great importance, as to the admission of evidence, in order, as it is said on the one hand, to explain the will, and on the other, not to explain the will, but to show, either, what ought to be the effect of two instruments upon each other, or, what the testator meant with regard to the will as to this sum of stock; and whether he meant to consider it his own, or, whether what he did by the will manifests his intention to purchase it for his own estate. Upon looking through the cases, of which there are a great many, to which it is not necessary to resort, the effect being extremely well collected in some of them, I think *Hinchcliffe* v. *Hinchcliffe* perfectly well decided. It is no more than this. The testator was entitled to an annuity and other property, settled, or under covenant to be settled, so that the children would have had vested interests. At his death no one subject of the settlement was existing, either in him or any party claiming under him, for the benefit of the objects of the settlement. The 6000l. was otherwise disposed of: the leasehold house was sold: the person, for whose life the annuity was held, was dead. The will being made, it was absolutely

_____

(1) *Ante, Ellison* v. *Cookson*, vol. i. 100, and the notes, 112, 259.

necessary for the Court to know what had become of the property settled ; and the result of the inquiry was only, that the testator had so dealt with it, that he was debtor for the whole to his children. Then it raised the ordinary question ; whether the will, being the will of a parent, was meant to be a satisfaction of the debt, whether by covenant or otherwise, to his children ; and therefore it is agreed, that such a will being upon the doctrine of this Court presumed a satisfaction, evidence was properly admissible * upon two   [*322] grounds: first to constitute the fact, that he was debtor: 2dly, either to meet or to fortify the presumption, founded upon the doctrine of the Court. There is no difficulty therefore in that case. The question is exactly the same as to the money received by the testator ; if this schedule was made either before or after the wi l: with regard to that sum, his will in this Court affording a presumption of satisfaction, it would be competent to meet that presumption by evidence, and to admit evidence to confirm it ; and as to that this schedule undoubtedly would be evidence. I agree also to *Wright* v. *Rutter* and *Rutter* v. *McLean* ; where an assignment was made of a wife's chose in action under circumstances, which would not make it a valid and effectual instrument in this Court as between the husband and wife : but it made that his property, till it was undone ; and being so, *prima facie* the will disposing of his property affected it ; and therefore in that instance also a case of election was very properly raised.

With respect to the case of *Pulteney* v. *Lord Darlington*, it is hardly proper at this day to observe upon it : as far as it is, I am not unwilling to give my assent to the inclination of opinion expressed by Lord Rosslyn (1), that it was carrying it a great way to say, that because General Pulteney in his accounts had dealt with an estate tail, which in a very ordinary sense he might think his, therefore in a will disposing of his property he intended to include it, having property to an immense amount to answer the words. That case is a strong one in that respect. If the decision turned upon that point, I must regard it as something very like a determination, that parol evidence may be received to prove, that that is the testator's property which in the sense of the law is not his. I agree to it, if it goes upon a manifestation in the will itself, that he means to call that his own, which in a legal sense is not his own. The will then manifests the intention : and then it endangers the administration of justice not to put the case upon that ground, and say, that is sufficient, but to go out of the will, appreciating the effect of parol evidence ; which, first, does not by any means amount to a manifestation of that it is supposed to manifest, and, next, the admission of which perhaps is not to be vindicated upon any principle that can be readily stated.

As to the case of *Eden* v. *Smyth*, I am not sufficiently informed upon it to state, whether the evidence is admissible, or not. If what

(1) *Ante,* vol. iv. 537.

is stated in the report as to the bond from Sir Frederick Eden to Mr. Smyth, that the paper produced would operate as a release, is to be taken as Lord Rosslyn's opinion, and if that opinion is right, then certainly it was properly received in evidence ; and the question then is only whether that opinion is well founded.   As the bond, in which Sir Frederick Eden and Mr. Smyth were both bound, and which being paid by the father would give him an equity to call upon his son, the claim being only an equity, I do not know, that the evidence was not admissible to meet it.   But as to bonds due to the testator from his son, it is very difficult to say, evidence is admissible to prove, the testator did not mean to make a demand upon those bonds.   If the evidence goes to this, that he had done any act amounting to a release, then it was improper to call them bonds.   But the case is infinitely too complicated for me to presume to say, it was not rightly decided.

In this case, if the whole trust property was in the same state as the sum of 1385l. 14s. 3 1-2d. remaining in the hands of the original debtor under the settlement, perhaps *Hinchcliffe* v. *Hinchcliffe* would be an authority in point for receiving the evidence ; for that money in the hands of the testator would be expressly in the same situation as the money in the hands of the Bishop of Peterborough ; a fund to come to the hands of the trustees by the effect of the covenant and acts of the father.   But the case is not so circumstanced ; and it differs from all the cases in these respects ; that as to the manor of Cotleigh the legal estate was actually vested by acts done in pursuance of the covenant in the children.   So the money laid out in stock, being actually vested in the trustees by acts done in pursuance of the covenant was vested in them for corresponding equitable estates.   The question then is, whether upon the circumstances I can from this will and the schedule, if it is evidence, infer, that the testator meant to purchase for his eldest son the manor of Cotleigh, the trust money in his own possession, and also this trust stock.   Upon the head of satisfaction he has clearly purchased for his eldest son the money in his possession ; upon the head of election he has proposed to his younger children the purchase of the manor of Cotleigh for his eldest son ; and the question [*324] *is, whether the will taken altogether, attending to those two circumstances, affords such a probability or presumption, that by the words " my estate and effects both real and personal," he meant to describe also this trust stock, that upon the will itself, or upon this paper, taken together with what arises out of the will, I can say, he did mean to purchase this for the benefit of his eldest son.   The schedule is very particular.   Of necessity it must have been written after the 4th of September, 1769: for that date appears on the face of it ; and the question is, if the will contains no manifest purpose to purchase this property by describing it as his real and personal estate, whether that purpose can be made manifest in such a case by a paper, that could not be written for above two years after the will.   I was very much struck with that, as applied to the ordinary case: but upon equities arising out of presumptions I find the Court has admitted such evidence. In the case of the executor and next of kin the presumption is met by evidence ; and it has been met by such evidence as makes the observation in the argument satisfactory ; that you must see, whether the testator says any thing upon the subject between his will and his death ; for in *Clennell* v. *Lewthwaite* (1) there is not a single declaration, upon which the executor was held not to be a trustee, but declarations, of which the first was made rather more than a year after the date of the will. In one of these cases some of the authorities are stated, to meet what Mr. Justice Buller intimated (2), that if he should sit longer in this Court, he would not permit the evidence to be read. Certainly those are cases of declaration subsequent to the will ; but, as I read the cases, they are cases, in which the parol evidence of declarations or transactions subsequent to the will was parol evidence pregnant with testimony as to what the testator meant at the time he made his will. They are also cases different from this in some respects. They would apply to this, if the question was merely with regard to the money in the hands of the testator himself: because the doctrine, that the will satisfies the debt, being founded upon a presumption of intention, if you find a paper like this, subsequent to the will, expressive of that presumption, it is evidence, not against the will, but in support of it ; and would be evidence to encounter the presumption. But as to the manor of Cotleigh, which was actually purchased, and conveyed to the uses of the settlement, and the trust money, actually *in   [*325] the hands of the trustees upon the trusts of the settlement, it is not a question of presumption, but of election. This therefore is not evidence applying merely to a question of presumption ; and it is to be considered, whether such evidence is admissible with regard to the question of election. The case of *Hinchcliffe* v. *Hinchcliffe* does not appear to apply to it with regard to that ; for the evidence was there admitted to prove, what had become of the property ; and that what had been done would make it necessary for the Court to construe the will as affording a presumption, that the settlement was not to be acted upon. That was a question of satisfaction. I observe, at the end of the Report the Master of the Rolls says, he desires to be understood, that the books are admitted upon the question of election ; upon which question he takes them to be admissible: but not to explain the will ; and he grounds himself in that upon what Lord Chief Justice De Grey and Baron Eyre are represented to have said in *Pulteney* v. *Lord Darlington*. If the evidence was admitted to prove, as Baron Eyre says, that what he thinks his must be taken to be his, the evidence in that way is to all intents and purposes admitted to explain the will (3).

(1) *Ante*, vol. ii. 465, 644.
(2) *Ante*, vol. i. 357, in *Nourse* v. *Finch*.
(3) During the argument the Lord Chancellor, with reference to the concluding passage of the judgment in *Hinchcliffe* v. *Hinchcliffe*, stated the distinction thus :

If therefore this case is to stand upon this schedule only, and the will itself is not pregnant with the conclusion, that the testator meant, that this trust property should pass to his eldest son, I should have great difficulty in admitting the evidence, in the first instance, and considerable, I do not say invincible, difficulty in holding, that, if admitted, it does evince, what was the intention at the time of mak-
. ing the will.   The observation applies equally to the cases of pre-sumption rebutted by evidence.   In *Clennell* v. *Lewthwaite*, for in-stance, it proceeded from the accident, that the testator lived long enough to hold those gossiping conversations, that the executor held the property.   The answer to that is, that in cases of presump-tion, that being against the legal title, evidence has been admitted against the presumption ; and the executor and next of kin run
          the risk of his speaking or remaining silent till his death.
[*326]   *If that has been applied to cases of election, it seems to
          me to be applied upon a principle not exactly the same ;
and upon a principle, which perhaps is not very accurately applied to wills devising real estate.   I now allude to *Brady* v. *Cubitt* (1) and those cases upon an implied revocation of a will ; in which it was said, evidence of declarations was admitted, because it is to re-but an equity.   If they meant to say, that parol evidence is admitted, to get the better of a presumption, that is accurate : but it is perfect-ly inaccurate to say, that any thing like an equity is to be rebutted. The expression therefore in some of the Reports is not so accurate, as it should be.   It is, not rebutting an equity, but answering a pre-sumption.

Upon the question, whether that species of evidence, that is ad-missible to bar a presumption, is admissible to raise a case of elec-tion, the authorities in the affirmative have not presented themselves to me; unless the cases, that have been alluded to, are to be taken to be authorities.   Suppose then this paper admitted, the question is, does it speak the intention at the date of the will?   Even the cases, to which I have now alluded, require that.   Upon that I incline to think, that fairly taken it may be considered a declaration by the testator as to what he meant at the date of the will.   This paper seems to demonstrate, that he meant as to his general personal estate, what the law would say he meant, not only what was his per-sonal estate at the date of the will, but what should afterwards become so.   This property was his in a certain extent.   He was receiving the interest.   Therefore upon the paper and the title of it, it is reasonable evidence, that he would speak of it as his personal estate, in the same manner as he spoke of his securities as his.   But if the case stood on this alone, I do not mean to say, whether I

that evidence is not received to give a different construction to the words of the will ; but is received to determine, whether the Court will say, the meaning of that will was, that the covenant should be satisfied by the provision of the will.
(1) Dougl. 30. See *Gibbons* v. *Caunt, ante,* vol. iv. 840; and the note, 848; *Kenebel* v. *Scrafton,* stated *ante,* vol. v. 663 ; 2 East, 530.

should admit the evidence, or how I should decide it.   I should
have great difficulty upon it unquestionably.   But upon the whole
of the will taken together, though the construction is not free from
risk, there is very strong reason to say, the will itself manifests, that
he meant, this property should pass as his personal estate.   There
is demonstration upon the will, that he meant, the estate of Cotleigh,
of which in point of law he was only tenant for life, with
interests in remainder *in fee vested in his children,   [* 327]
should pass as real estate.   The observation is just, that
in most cases of election there is an express devise of the estate;
but if that part of the will relating to the estate of Cotleigh is pregnant with inference, that he thought that his real estate, which was
not strictly his, having exactly correspondent interests in the other
subjects, and if he has effectually devised to his eldest son two of
those subjects as his real and personal estate under the head either
of election or satisfaction, is it the better construction, that by those
words he meant to comprehend a subject, in which his interest was
precisely the same, or, that he meant to exclude that?   I cannot say,
he meant to exclude it; unless I say, he meant to distinguish the
third subject of the trust, where there is no reason to make the distinction; and unless I say that in a case, in which he was providing
portions and fortunes for his children; where he must be taken to
mean to devest estates at law vested in them, and to satisfy the debt
he owed them; meaning to dispose of what they could claim under
the settlement; and unless I say, that the maintenance is to come ı
out of the residue, in an aggregate sum, including the manor of Cotleigh, and the money in his own possession; but that the dividends
of the stock should not be touched for that purpose; that it should
be contra-distinguished from the mass of his personal estate; and
accumulate; neither disposable for maintenance or education; and
also, that the power of advancing the children would include the
two former subjects, but not the last; and that he had a purpose to
keep that entire, until they should attain the age of twenty-one.   I
do not think that the true meaning of this will.   I construe it in the
same way, as Mr. Alexander says the Court construed the will in
Pulteney v. *Lord Darlington;* that there is sufficient in the will
itself, to infer, that the intention of the testator was to dispose of the
whole as his own.   If that is to be stated as presumption, and not
construction, then this evidence might be admitted; and would very
much fortify the construction.   It clearly may be admitted as to the
money in his hands.   But the question turns upon construction, as
distinguished from presumption, as to the third subject.   I have
therefore so much doubt, whether the evidence can be admitted,
that, without saying, whether it can, or not, I decide this upon the
will; that by the will, taking the whole together, the testator has
manifested, that he meant to pass the whole of this property to his
eldest son.

Under these circumstances the Plaintiff must elect; and if

he elects to take under the will, the bill must be dismissed, but without costs (1).

———

1. WITH respect to the general principle upon which the doctrine of election is founded, and the possible difference in the extent of the application of that doctrine to cases of deeds, and cases of wills ; see, *ante*, note 3 to *Blake* v. *Bunbury*, 1 V. 194, and note 1 to *Lady Cavan* v. *Pulteney*, 2 V. 544, with the farther references there given. As to the admissibility of parol evidence to raise a case of election ; see note 2 to *Stratton* v. *Best*, 1 V. 285.

2. For the authorities that intended satisfaction of a debt, and *a fortiori* of a portion, by a legacy of equal or greater amount, is to be presumed ; see the notes to *Ellison* v. *Cookson*, 1 V. 100; note 2 to *Barclay* v. *Wainwright*, 3 V. 462; note 6 to *Blake* v. *Bunbury*, 1 V. 194; note 2 to *Wilson* v. *Piggott*, 2 V. 351; and note 2 to *Sparks* v. *Cator*, 3 V. 530.

3. The propriety of admitting evidence, *dehors* the will, to show, that a testator intended the gift of a legacy, or of a bond, as a release of a demand, is questionable; see note 1 to *Maitland* v. *Adair*, 3 V. 231, and note 2 to *Eden* v. *Smyth*, 5 V. 341.

4. How far parol declarations of a testator are admissible to rebut legal presumptions, as to the respective claims of his executors, or of his next of kin; see note 3 to *Clennell* v. *Lewthwaite*, 2 V. 465, and note 3 to *Nourse* v. *Finch*, 1 V. 344 : see also *Matthews* v. *Warner*, 4 V. 208. And with respect to implied revocations of wills, which, like all other *prima facie* presumptions, may be rebutted, see note 3 to *Gibbons* v. *Caunt*, 4 V. 840, and note 2 to *Baxter* v. *Dyer*, 5 V. 650.

———

DRURY *v.* MOLINS.

[1801, JULY 20.]

INJUNCTION against ploughing up pasture upon a covenant to manage in a husband-like manner (*a*).

MR. AINGE moved for an injunction to restrain a tenant from committing waste by ploughing up pasture land. The lease contained no express covenant not to convert pasture to arable ; but there was a covenant to manage pasture in a husband-like manner.

The Lord CHANCELLOR [ELDON] said, he thought that equivalent ; and granted the injunction till answer and farther order.

———

SEE note 2 to *Pulteney* v. *Shelton*, 5 V. 147.

———

(1) *Druce* v. *Denison, post*, 385. See as to election, the notes, *ante*, vol. i. 523, 527.

(*a*) See *ante*, note (*a*), p. 106; *Lord Grey de Wilton* v. *Saron*.

THE MARQUIS TOWNSHEND v. STANGROOM. ·
STANGROOM v. THE MARQUIS TOWNSHEND.

[1801, JULY 17, 21.]

PAROL evidence admissible in opposition to a specific performance of a written agreement upon the heads of mistake or surprise as well as of fraud; and upon such evidence the bill was dismissed. Another bill for a specific performance of the agreement, corrected according to the same evidence, contradicted by the answer, was also dismissed (a).

(a) As to the meaning of the word *surprise*, as used by Courts of Equity; see 1 Story, Eq. Jur. § 120, note, 134. Jeremy seems to suppose that there is something technical in its meaning; Jeremy, Eq. Jur. 366; Eden on Injunction, (2d Am. ed.) 21, 27, notes.

If a mistake is clearly made out by proofs entirely satisfactory, equity will reform the contract so as to make it conformable to the intent of the parties. But if the proofs are doubtful and unsatisfactory, and the mistake is not made entirely plain, equity will withhold relief; upon the ground, that the written paper ought to be treated as a full and correct expression of the intent, until the contrary is established beyond reasonable controversy; 1 Story, Eq. Jur. § 152; *Gillespie* v. *Moor*, 2 Johns. Ch. 585; *Lyman* v. *U. Ins. Co.*, 2 Johns. Ch. 630; *Middleton* v. *Perry*, 2 Bay, 539; *White* v. *Egan*, 1 Bay, 247; *Graves* v. *Boston Marine Ins. Co.*; *Barndollar* v. *Yate*, 1 S. & R. 160; *Smith* v. *Williams*, 1 Murphy, 426; 2 Cranch, 442; *Geer* v. *Ward*, 4 Desaus. 85; *Washburn* v. *Merrill*, 1 Day, 139; *Peters* v. *Goodrich*, 2 Conn. 146; *Mead* v. *Johnson*, 2 Conn. 592; *Argenbright* v. *Campbell*, 3 Hen. & M. 144; *Christ* v. *Diffebach*, 1 S. & R. 465; 1 Sugden, Vendors and Purchasers, (6th Am. ed.) 257–271, where the different ways are shown, by which the mistake may be established by parol evidence, Ib.; *Wiser* v. *Blachley*, 1 Johns. Ch. 607. In admitting parol evidence for this purpose, Courts of Equity establish an exception to the general rule excluding parol evidence to vary a written contract. 1 Story, Eq. Jur. § 156; 2 Ib. § 767; 1 Greenleaf, Ev. 296a. This exception to the rule has been equally applied to written instruments within and without the Statute of Frauds. 1 Story, Eq. Jur. § 158; *Andrews* v. *Essex Fire & Mar. Ins. Co.*; 3 Mason, 10; *Delaware Ins. Co.* v. *Hogan*, 2 Wash. Cir. 5; *Finley* v. *Lynn*, 6 Cranch, 238.

Whether Courts of Equity will sustain a claim to reform a writing, or to establish a mistake in it by parol evidence, and for specific performance of it when corrected, in one and the same bill, is a point on which there are opposite authorities. The English are against it. 1 Story, Eq. Jur. 161; *Attorney General* v. *Sitwell*, 1 Younge & Coll. 559–582, 583. But Mr. Chancellor Kent has decreed relief to a plaintiff, standing in this predicament; *Gillespie* v. *Moor*, 2 Johns. Ch. 585; *Keisselbrock* v. *Livingston*, 4 Johns. Ch. 144. See also *The Hiram*, 1 Wheaton, 444; *Hunt* v. *Rousmaniere*, 8 Wheaton, 211; *S. C.* 1 Peters, Sup. C. 13; *Hogan* v. *Delaware Ins. Co.*, 1 Wash. C. C. R. 422. In *Tilton* v. *Tilton*, 9 N. H. 385, tenants in common agreed to make partition pursuant to the award of referees, and executed deeds for that purpose. In the deed to the plaintiff, a tract of land, assigned to him, was omitted by mistake. The parties took possession according to their deeds. The Court held, that the mistake should be rectified, and that a specific performance of the contract, as to the tract omitted, should be decreed. The mistake in this case was denied in the answer; see the learned notes of Mr. Perkins, note (a); *Pember* v. *Mathers*, 1 Bro. C. C. 54, and note (a); *Jordan* v. *Sawkins*, 4 Bro. C. C. 354; also *Langdon* v. *Keith*, 9 Vermont, 299; *Westbrook* v. *Harbeson*, 2 McCord, Ch. 115; *Wesley* v. *Thomas*, 6 Harr. & John. 24; *Newson* v. *Buffalow*, 1 Dev. Eq. 379; *Gower* v. *Sterner*, 2 Wheat. 74–79; *Abbe* v. *Goodwin*, 7 Conn. 373.

It seems that the power of rectifying written contracts by parol proof is not

Parol evidence admissible to rebut an equity (a), [p. 336, note.]
The rule, that a written agreement within the statute of Frauds cannot be varied
by parol, does not affect a subsequent, distinct, collateral, agreement, [p. 338,
note.]

CHRISTOPHER STANGROOM was in possession by lease from the
Marquis Townshend of a farm in the parish of Langham, consisting
of 446 acres, 3 roods, and 23 perches, at an annual rent of 290*l.*
Jane Garrett was tenant of another farm under the Marquis; and
those two farms comprised all the lands belonging to the Marquis in
that parish. About the end of the year 1796, a treaty commenced
between Spearing, agent to the Marquis, and Stangroom, for a renewal of Stangroom's lease; and an agreement, dated the 4th of
May, 1797, was signed by Spearing and Stangroom, entitled, "A
statement of the quantity of land and annual value of the farm belonging to the Marquis Townshend in Langham, in the occupation
         of Christopher Stangroom, as proposed to be let upon a
[* 329]   lease for twenty-one years from * Michaelmas 1797." This
         agreement then stated the arable and pasture land particu-
larly, by acres, roods, and perches; in all 425 A. 1 R. and 26 P. " be
the same more or less;" that the rent was to be 270*l.* a-year; and
expressed some other terms.

The first bill prayed a specific performance of that agreement;
charging, that about the same time an agreement took place with
Mrs. Garrett for a renewal of her lease, comprising also a part of
Stangroom's farm, about 24 acres; that the Defendant Stangroom
was aware of that agreement, and of the terms, upon which he was
to have his own lease; and that the agreement with Stangroom
contains the same quantity of land as a schedule, made out in the
presence of Stangroom, and with his assistance from a general map:
about 24 acres being deducted from his farm, to be added to Mrs.
Garrett's; and 2 A. 3 R. 80 P. being taken from her's to be added
to his. Notice to quit was given to both tenants on the 3d of April,
1797.

Stangroom by his answer denied, that he assisted Spearing in
making out the schedule from the map; or, that he knew of it. He
admitted a proposal, made to him by Spearing about the 29th or
30th of March, or the 1st of April, to take from his farm about 25
acres; and that the rent for the farm he was to have should be
290*l.*; which proposal he refused. He denied any knowledge of

within the limited equity jurisdiction of Massachusetts; *Leach* v. *Leach,* 18 Pick.
68–73; *Dwight* v. *Pomroy,* 17 Mass. 303–325–329; *Babcock* v. *Smith,* 22 Pick. 61.
The correction of a mistake in a deed is within the equity powers of the Court of
Maine; *Peterson* v. *Grover,* 20 Maine, 363.

(a) The meaning of this is, that when a certain presumption would in general be
deduced from the nature of an act, such presumption may be repelled by extrinsic
evidence, showing the intention to be otherwise. 1 Greenleaf, § 296; *Mann* v.
Mann, 1 Johns. Ch. 231; Gresley, Evid. 210; 1 Sugden, Vendors & Purchasers,
233, (6th Am. ed.)

Mrs. Garrett's agreement for any part of his farm, or any knowledge of any such intention, except for the exchange of about eight acres; which was proposed by Spearing; and to which the Defendant did not object.

Spearing and another witness, Hammond, proved, that the map was the general standard of the quantity of lands; and was referred to as such by Stangroom and the other tenants; that Stangroom's and Mrs. Garrett's lands were then mixed; and about 24 acres of Stangroom's were convenient for Mrs. Garrett. Spearing also proved an exhibit, the schedule of the farms, referred to by the bill, in his hand-writing, entitled, "The farm in the occupation of Christopher Stangroom at Langham:" the two first sides were written in December, 1796, at Stangroom's house: the third side written afterwards; where, the deponent does not know; but the whole written to ascertain the quantity of land proposed * to be   [* 330] let to Mrs. Garrett; and taken from the map: the two first sides made out with the privity and assistance and in the presence of Stangroom; and the whole communicated to him previously to or at the time of the proposal to her. The third side contained the 24 A. 3 R. and 7 P. proposed to be taken from Stangroom, and 2 A. 3 R. 33 P. to be taken from Mrs. Garrett, and added to Stangroom's farm. Mrs. Garrett's agreement in writing was proved, according to a verbal agreement, stated by Spearing, on the 13th of April, 1797, for a lease for 14 years of 14 score acres, at a rent of 170l. He stated, that Stangroom had notice of the verbal agreement. Hammond also proved, that he informed Stangroom of her verbal proposal; and that her written proposals were shown to him: and a paper was produced in the hand-writing of Stangroom, and delivered by him to Hammond, at the end of March 1797, to be delivered to Mrs Garrett; stating loosely the extent of Mrs. Garrett's farm; and that she was to have about 20 acres more, and calculating the rent she was to pay upon the footing of her verbal agreement. Spearing on his cross examination denied; that he proposed an exchange of eight acres only; as stated by the answer.

The cross bill prayed a specific performance of the written agreement.

Mr. *Lloyd*, Mr. *Romilly*, and Mr. *Johnson*, for Stangroom, objected to the admission of evidence.—There is no instance, in which an agreement has been varied by parol evidence of conversations. This is not put upon the ground of fraud or misrepresentation. *Lord Irnham* v. *Child* (1), *Hare* v. *Shearwood* (2), *Lord Portmore* v. *Morris* (3), *Rich* v. *Jackson* (4), *Gunnis* v. *Erhart* (5), *Meres* v. *Ansell* (6).

(1) 1 Bro. C. C. 92.
(2) *Ante*, vol. i. 241; 3 Bro. C. C. 168.
(3) 2 Bro. C. C. 219.
(4) 4 Bro. C. C. 514.
(5) 1 H. Black. 289; *Higginson* v. *Clowes, post*, vol. xv. 516.
(6) 3 Wils. 275.

In *Jenkinson* v. *Pepys* (1), in the Exchequer, upon the sale of an estate by auction, the particular was equivocal as to the woods : but it was clear, the purchaser was to pay for timber and timber-like trees. There was a large underwoood upon the estate. At the sale, the article being ambiguous, the auctioneer declared, he was only to sell the [* 331] land, and every thing growing upon the * land must be paid for. The Defendant, the purchaser, insisted he was only to pay for timber and timber-like trees, not for plantation and underwood. The declaration at the sale was distinctly proved : but it was determined, that the parol evidence was not admissible. In this case all this was treaty antecedent to the execution. To proceed upon the evidence would put an end to the statute (2).

Mr. *Mansfield*, Mr. *Richards*, Mr. *Fonblanque*, Mr. *Horne*, for the Marquis Townshend.

This is the case of a latent ambiguity, requiring explanation *aliunde.* Each party desires the assistance of the Court. In *Baker* v. *Paine* (3) the evidence was admitted ; certainly in a case of mistake. Surprise and mistake come very near fraud. If Stangroom is permitted to hold this land, intended to form part of Mrs. Garrett's farm, and made so by the agreement with her, the effect will be fraud. *Joynes* v. *Statham* (4) is decisive ; and according to the established doctrine, that if the Court can be satisfatorily informed, that the agreement is not such as the party thought it was, it shall not be enforced.

The evidence was read without prejudice. The case was then argued upon the effect of the agreement and the evidence ; the Plaintiff in the original cause contending, that the agreement clearly referred to the quantity of land by acres, roods, and perches ; and the words, " be the same more or less " meant only, that they did not warrant the measure ; and the description of lands in the occupation or Stangroom was satisfied, with that restriction ; and did not necessarily mean all the lands in his occupation ; and that it would be impossible to enforce Stangroom's agreement literally, particularly against Mrs. Garrett.

For the Plaintiff in the cross bill it was insisted, that there was no ambiguity in the agreement. The farm in the occupation of Stangroom was intended to be let. The words " be the same more or less " showed, the parties meant to be bound by the des- [* 332] cription of the person, not of the quantity of * land.

Those words must refer to all the preceding items : and might answer twenty acres ; as they would without doubt a less quantity ; though not, if it was considerable. Upon the other construction those words are useless. The treaty was completely at an end by the notice to quit. The evidence does not amount to the

(1) Stated by the Master of the Rolls in *Higginson* v. *Clowes, post,* vol. xv. 516. See 1 Ves. & Bea. 528.
(2) 29 Cha. II. b. 3.
(3) 1 Ves. 456.
(4) 3 Atk. 388.

assertion that Stangroom ever agreed; and all the conversations were antecedent to the date of the agreement.

Lord CHANCELLOR [ELDON].—The argument of these causes certainly furnishes questions of great importance, as well as some difficulty. It is contended by the original bill, that it is competent to the Court to make a decree against Stangroom upon all the circumstances and the written paper. He insists by his cross bill, that he is not bound to execute such an agreement: or rather, that it is not the true sense of the agreement; that he has an agreement in his possession, entitling him to a lease for twenty-one years of all the lands in his occupation ; stating the true meaning to be a lease of his old farm; and, that agreement being obtained without fraud, no evidence is to be admitted to vary the sense of it; and that upon no other principle than that founded upon the rules of evidence in this Court, as applying to the circumstances and his conduct, can the Court look at the parol evidence, even for the purpose of refusing him a specific performance of his contract: much more strongly contending, that the Court cannot enforce against him a contract, the subject of which will not correspond with the description, being only a part of it; and attempting to add another property; which upon no practicable construction of any words in the written agreement can be said to be comprehended in it.

Upon the question as to admitting parol evidence, it is perhaps impossible to reconcile all the cases. *Lord Irnham* v. *Child* went upon an indisputably clear principle ; that the parties did not mean to insert in the agreement a provision for redemption ; because they were all of one mind, that it would be usurious; and they desired the Court, not to do what they intended, for the insertion of that provision was directly contrary to their intention, but they desired to be put in the same situation, as if they had been better informed, and consequently had a contrary intention (a). The answer is, they admit, it was not to be in the deed : *and   [*333] why was the Court to insert it; where two risks had occurred to the parties : the danger of usury, and the danger of trusting to the honor of the party. The same doctrine was laid down in *Lord Portmore* v. *Morris*, and in *Hare* v. *Shearwood* by Mr. Justice Buller; and, speaking with all the veneration and respect due to so great a judicial character, the point, in which it seems to have failed, is, that he thought too confidently, that he understood all the doctrine of a Court of Equity. It cannot be said, that because the legal import of a written agreement cannot be varied by parol evidence, intended to give it another sense, therefore in Equity, when once the Court is in possession of the legal sense, there is nothing more to inquire into. Fraud is a distinct case, and perhaps more examinable at law ; but all the doctrine of the Court as to cases of unconscionable agreements, hard agreements, agreements entered into by mistake or surprise, which therefore the Court will not exe-

---

(a) 1 Story, Eq. Jur. § 113; *Hunt* v. *Rousmaniere*, 1 Peters, S. C. 16.

cute, must be struck out, if it is true, that, because parol evidence should not be admitted at Law, therefore it shall not be admitted in Equity, upon the question, whether, admitting the agreement to be such as at Law it is said to be, the party shall have a specific execution, or be left to that Court, in which, it is admitted, parol evidence cannot be introduced. A very small research into the cases will show general indications by Judges in Equity, that that has not been supposed to be the Law of this Court. In *Henkle* v. *The Royal Exchange Assurance Company* (1), the Court did not rectify the policy of insurance ; but they did not refuse to do so upon a notion, that, such being the legal effect of it, therefore this Court could not interfere ; and Lord Hardwicke says expressly, there is no doubt, the Court has jurisdiction to relieve in respect of a plain mistake in contracts in writing as well as against frauds in contracts : so that, if reduced into writing contrary to the intent of the parties, on proper proof that would be rectified. This is loose in one sense ; leaving it to every Judge to say, whether the proof is that proper proof, that ought to satisfy him ; and every Judge, who sits here any time, must miscarry in some of the cases, when acting upon such a principle. Lord Hardwicke saying, the proof ought to be the strongest possible, leaves a weighty caution to future Judges. This inconvenience belongs to the administration of justice ;

[*334]   that the *minds of different men will differ upon the result of the evidence ; which may lead to different decisions upon the same case. In *Lady Shelburne* v. *Lord Inchiquin* (2) it is clear, Lord Thurlow was influenced by this, as the doctrine of the Court ; saying (3), it was impossible to refuse, as incompetent, parol evidence, which goes to prove, that the words taken down in writing were contrary to the concurrent intention of all parties : but he also thought, it was to be of the highest nature ; for he adds, that it must be irrefragible evidence. He therefore seems to say, that the proof must satisfy the Court, what was the concurrent intention of all parties ; and it must never be forgot, to what extent the Defendant, one of the parties, admits or denies the intention. Lord Thurlow saying, the evidence must be strong, and admitting the difficulty of finding such evidence, says, he does not think, it can be rejected as incompetent (4).

I do not go through all the cases ; as they are all referred to in one or two of the last. In *Rich* v. *Jackson* (5) there is a reference

---

(1) 1 Ves. 317.
(2) 1 Bro. C. C. 338.
(3) 1 Bro. C. C. 341.
(4) *Ante, Doran* v. *Ross,* vol. i. 57, and the note, 60.
(5) The Lord Chancellor referred to the following note of the judgment in that cause; which is rather more full than the Report; 4 Bro. C. C. 514.

1794. *Feb.* 26th. Lord CHANCELLOR [LOUGHBOROUGH]. In this case I have found myself upon two different occasions, where it has come before me, in that difficulty, into which a Judge will always bring himself, when his curiosity or some better motive disposes him to know more of a cause, than judicially he ought. Upon the evidence, which I took at the trial in order to bring this case to *Joynes* v. *Statham*, and a note of that case preserved in Lord Hardwicke's manuscript.   He states the proposition in the very terms ; that he shall not confine the evidence to fraud ; that it is admissible to mistake and surprise ; and it is very singular ; if the Court

---

before the Court of Law, I gave credit to the veracity of the witnesses ; and, believing them, it is impossible to doubt, that the state of the transaction is, as the Plaintiff has represented it; that in the agreement the terms, upon which they treated, in the understanding and reasoning of the parties were, that the rent should be a net rent without any deduction.   But the parties, whatever their communication had been, had executed the matter by signing a written agreement. The construction of that agreement it is impossible to doubt.   It is a lease for twenty-one years at a rent of eighty guineas, to be paid twenty guineas quarterly. The execution of that undoubtedly is, that the tenant paying the rent pays twenty guineas, so much in money, and his land-tax receipt making up the twenty guineas. That being the certain, clear, effect of the instrument, makes the whole of the contract upon the condition of that letting.   The prior conversations and the manner of drawing it up by one party and signing it by another can have no influence. The real question is, whether in this Court any more than at Law, where the Judges have said, I ought not to have admitted the evidence, and I approve their determination, it ought to be admitted ; whether there is any distinction in a Court of Equity, where a party comes to enforce a written agreement by obtaining a more formal instrument, and to add in doing that a term not expressed in the written agreement, * and of such a nature, as to bear against the   [* 335] written agreement.   I have looked into all the cases; and I cannot find, that this Court has ever taken upon itself in executing a written agreement by a specific performance to add to it by any circumstance, that parol evidence could introduce: but it has often with great propriety, where an attempt has been made to obtain by a decree of this Court a farther security or more ample interest, than the party was in possession of by the paper itself, refused, if it appeared, the demand was fraudulent or unfair.   The case of *Joynes* v. *Statham* was relied on. That was a case, where parol evidence was admitted on behalf of the Defendant ; who by that evidence showed, that the Plaintiff had taken an unfair advantage of the evident ignorance of the Defendant, and drawn an agreement for him in terms similar to that in this case, in which the same circumstances occurred.   The Defendant set out, that his rent was to be a clear rent without any deduction. Lord Hardwicke admitted him to rebut the equity, and specifically to show that case by parol evidence.   I looked into Lord Hardwicke's own note book upon it. It is very short: not above two or three lines.   He mentions *Walker* v. *Walker*,* that was cited to him: a decision of his own; and then he makes this entry: "Decree specific performance upon the terms submitted to by the answer; the Plaintiff rather choosing this than to have his bill dismissed with costs."   The result of his opinion therefore was to have dismissed the bill with costs.   Giving the Plaintiff a decree for a specific performance was not making a decree upon the evidence, but upon the submission of the Plaintiff and of the Defendant in his answer to execute a lease upon the fair terms.   In *Walker* v. *Walker* the point was exactly the same.   The bill was to substantiate a charge upon a copyhold estate surrendered by John Walker, the eldest brother of both parties, to Ralph Walker. It was an absolute surrender, upon condition, that he should pay out of the estate annuities of 5*l.* to a brother and of 40*s.* to a sister.   The charge was ineffectual at law.   They attempted to recover the annuities there, and could not.   Then they came into equity to make good these charges, which they could not at law.   Two defences were set up.   One is not mentioned in Atkyns, and was not material. The other was, that John Walker was dying at the time; that in the communication, he had with the family, he made this arrangement; that he would surrender that copyhold to Ralph, who would be his heir; and that he should pay these annuities to Thomas Walker the brother and to the sister: and Thomas was to surrender to Ralph subject to his own life another copyhold, which he had.   The

* 2 Atk. 98.

will take a moral jurisdiction at all, that it should not be capable of being applied to those cases ; for in a moral view there is very little difference between calling for the execution of an agreement obtained by fraud, which creates a surprise upon the other party, and desiring the execution of an agreement, which can be demonstrated to

evidence proved it to demonstration : and that it was a promise, when the instructions were given for surrendering the first copyhold, that Thomas would surrender his. The surrender of the other was first perfected ; and then Thomas said, " I admit, I promised : but I have got John fast ; and am not bound." Then he applied for the annuity. They said, he should have the annuity, when he would perform the condition. The cases quoted were from Vernon, where a testator had been prevented from altering his will by the undertaking of the party to do what the testator would have compelled him to do but for that undertaking. In the [*336] objection taken I observe (you do not often find great reasoning in *Lord Hardwicke's notes, but generally a short answer) the counsel says, it was to establish an agreement: " no," says Lord Hardwicke, " it was to rebut an equity." The other defence set up was dishonest. The result was, Lord Hardwicke dismissed the bill, praying the establishment of the equitable charge, but without costs, upon the special ground, that the Defendant had set up another defence in his answer, which he knew to be perfectly false.

Legal v. *Millar* * is not the same sort of case : but it runs upon the same ground. There the bill was dismissed. It was brought to establish an agreement for a lease of a house. The agreement was in writing ; that in consideration of the Defendant's repairing the house, which by the paper he agreed to do, the Plaintiff should take a lease at a rent of 30*l.* a year. After execution it turned out, that the house could not be repaired ; and that it would be better to rebuild it ; and a fact took place, that as between the parties destroyed the agreement ; for it was rebuilt by mutual consent ; and a new agreement was made by parol for a rent of 40*l.* The Plaintiff afterwards thought proper to bring the bill to have the lease at the rent first agreed on in consideration of repairing. Sir John Strange had no difficulty to admit the evidence of the latter agreement ; for it was an independent, substantive, collateral, agreement after the original agreement was *rebus ipsis et factis* totally at an end : but he dismissed the bill : because it was a bill without any equity or good conscience.

Pitcairn v. *Ogbourne* † is not applicable. The objection there was taken to the competency of the evidence. I wonder at it ; for the real objection was to the relevancy. It was a secret, fraudulent, and collateral, agreement, that a bond, which appeared to be for the payment of 150*l.* should be but for 100*l.* The other sum was held out as a blind to the uncle of the lady ; from whom she had great expectations. Sir John Strange read the evidence ; and then he found, he was doing nothing ; for after reading it, it proved only a fraudulent agreement, which could not prevail : but the objection points not to the competency of the evidence, explanatory of the agreement : but it was a defeazance collateral, and independent, and made at another time. *Baker* v. *Paine* ‡ has no reference to this question. There was a great deal of evidence ; which was properly admitted ; because the bill was upon this ground. The parties had entered into a minute of an agreement between them. After execution of it they had given it to an attorney to be drawn up ; and the agreement, he drew up, varied from the minute, and most materially, in consequence of his ignorance of the transaction between the parties. It was between the captain of an India ship, entitled to his privilege to the amount of 1500*l.* and the Defendant. He sold his goods in a lump to the Defendant ; and in the transaction they made a computation of what the amount of his privilege might be, and what would be the amount of the deductions, in the whole 46 1-2 per cent. upon the supposed price. Annexed to this computation they made a minute of the agreement ; and in that it was mentioned, that the 46 1-2 per cent. was to be deducted on the above mentioned account. They gave this minute to the attorney ;

* 2 Ves. 299.
† 2 Ves. 375.
‡ 1 Ves. 456.

have been obtained by surprise. It is impossible to read the report of *Joynes* v. *Statham*, and conceive Lord Hardwicke to have been of opinion, that evidence is not *admissible in   [* 338] such cases; though I agree with Lord Rosslyn [Loughborough], that the report is inaccurate. Lord Rosslyn expressly takes the distinction between a person coming into this Court, desiring, that a new term shall be introduced into an agreement, and a person admitting the agreement, but resisting the execution of it by making out a case of surprise (1). If that is made out, the Court will not say, the agreement has a different meaning from that, which is put upon it; but supposing it to have that meaning, under all the circumstances it is not so much of course, that this Court will specifically execute it. The Court must be satisfied, that under all the circumstances it is equitable to give more relief than the Plaintiff can

---

and he made the deduction of 46 1-2 per cent. to be upon the amount of the *bargained premises*; using a phrase, that did not apply to it at all. The goods consisted of China ware. It happened by the China ships missing their voyage, that the captain's goods sold for 4000*l*.; * upon which the purchaser [* 337] said, "I have overpaid you; you are my debtor in respect of the deduction of 46 1-2 per cent. which you are to answer." The obvious consequence was, that it was an impossible transaction; for the more the goods sold for, the less the seller was to get. The evidence was that of India captains and brokers as to the usage of the trade. Lord Hardwicke heard it all, very properly. The minute of the agreement was very short; and referred to accounts; and related to transactions in trade. It was to be explained by the course of that trade and the manner of dealing; and the final result was to rectify the blunder by the minute. Lord Hardwicke's note adds, the parties afterwards settled it by consent.

Filmer v. *Gott* * is referred to in the case in the Term Reports †. That last case does not refer to this in the least. There the Quarter Sessions held the four guineas paid towards the expense of the fine to be part of the consideration of the conveyance; and the Court of King's Bench affirmed their order. In *Filmer* v. *Gott* the evidence was not to contradict the deed; but to show, that it was obtained by fraud and upon a false consideration; which is one of the ingredients of the fraud.

It would be difficult to find more cases than those cited, that are strictly applicable. None go farther than this in the decisions and rules laid down; that parol evidence of the conduct of the parties, the manner of conducting the transaction, the unfairness and hardship, may afford a good ground to leave the party in the condition, in which he put himself at law, to make what he chooses to make of it; but ought not to make this Court give him any aid. If the Defendant had not got by this paper what would be a security at law, and had applied to me, and the case was reversed as to the situation of the parties, I would not put the Defendant in a better condition, than that paper had put her in. It is impossible to admit any deviation from the rule at law. That confines the whole to the written agreement; and does not admit that to be varied by any evidence of the conversation or conduct of the parties.   That rule will not affect the case of a subsequent, distinct, collateral, agreement; but the evidence, which I have heard, and ought not to have heard in this case, is evidence of what passed at the time of, and prior to, the written agreement. The lease must be according to the written agreement. I suppose the Plaintiff would not wish for a lease according to that.

(The Plaintiff declined to execute such a lease.)

Lord CHANCELLOR, [LOUGHBOROUGH.] I must therefore dismiss the bill; but I will not dismiss it with costs.

(1) *Post*, *Mortlock* v. *Buller*, vol x. 292; and the note, 305, xiii. 135.

* 7 Bro. P. C. 70.
† *The King* v. *The Inhabitants of Scammonden*, 3 Term. Rep. B. R. 474.

have at law; and that was carried to a great extent in *Twining* v. *Morrice* (1). In that case it was impossible to impute fraud, mistake, or negligence: but Lord Kenyon was satisfied, the agreement was obtained by surprise upon third persons; which therefore it was unconscientious to execute against the other party interested in the question. It had been decided frequently at law, that there could be no such thing as a puffer at an auction. That, whether right or wrong, has been much disputed here (2). In that case we contended, that all the parties in the room ought to know the law. Lord Kenyon would not hear us upon that; and I do not much wonder at it; but Blake being the common acquaintance of both parties, and having no purpose to bid for the vendor, unfortunately was employed to bid for the vendee; and others, knowing, that he was generally employed for the vendor, thought, the bidding was for him. Lord Kenyon said, that was such a surprise upon the transaction of the sale, that he would 'leave the parties to law; and yet it was impossible to say, that the vendee appointing his friend, without the least notion, much less intention, that the sale should be prejudiced, was fraud, surprise, or any thing, that could be characterized as morally wrong. That case illustrates the principles, that circumstances of that sort would prevent a specific performance; and that it is competent to this Court, at least for the purpose of enabling it to determine, whether it will specifically execute an agreement, 'to receive evidence of the circumstances, under which it was obtained; and I will not say, there are not cases, in which it may be received, to enable the Court to rectify a written agreement,

[* 339]   * upon surprise and mistake, as well as fraud : proper, irrefragable, evidence, as clearly satisfactory, that there has been mistake or surprise, as in the other case, that there has been fraud. I agree, those producing evidence of mistake or surprise, either to rectify an agreement, or calling upon the Court to refuse a specific performance, undertake a case of great difficulty : but it does not follow, that it is therefore incompetent to prove the actual existence of it by evidence.

The conclusion upon this case is, .that I can give relief upon neither bill. I will not say, that upon the evidence without the answer I should not have had so much doubt, whether I ought not to rectify the agreement, upon which Stangroom relies, as to take more time to consider, whether the bill should be dismissed. But the evidence must be taken, due regard being had to the answer; and the Court is not to decide upon the allegation as to the probability against the answer, not only to take out of his contract part of the land he held, but to insert land, which he never did hold, and of which he states he never did agree to become the occupier. Though I admit all the observation upon the depositions, stating the communication to Stangroom by Spearing of the third side of the paper,

---

(1) 2 Bro. C. C. 326.
(2) *Conolly* v. *Parsons, ante*, vol. iii. 625, note.

produced in evidence, it is clear upon all the other circumstances, that Stangroom knew prior to that agreement, that there had been treaty with Mrs. Garrett to let her have the land described in the third side of that paper. A most material fact is, that Stangroom admits, that upon the 29th or 30th of March, or the 1st of April, Spearing proposed to him, that his farm should be varied. It is said, he objected to that proposition : but he admits, that at that time Spearing delivered to him a paper, which corresponds in most if not all, its parts with the agreement of the 4th of May. If that paper amounts to a proposition, that he was not to have his old farm, and it corresponds with the paper of the 4th of May, and Spearing executed that paper with the notion, that it demised, what he proposed to demise upon the 29th or 30th of March, or the 1st of April, the other taking it as not demising what was proposed at the prior time, there cannot be a stronger case of surprise ; with this additional fact, that before the execution of the agreement Mrs. Garrett represented, that the bargain proposed to her was hard. She was to have more lands in this parish. Where was *she   [* 340] to get more, but out of the occupation of Stangroom ; all the lands in that parish being let between them ? He sends her word, that she is to have the additional quantity. What is that but saying, that he was to give up so much ; for it could be procured from no other quarter ? Recollecting also, that the map was in his possession, was referred to, and was something to amend by, that it gave map quantities, and the papers were reformed as to their quantities by that map, furnishing 446 acres, as the quantity in the possession of Stangroom, and 425, as the quantity proposed to be in his possession, the latter made up by reduction of 24 acres and the addition of three, it is impossible, taking all this together, to prove, that it was the intention of the parties, that if those two treaties were carried into effect, he should have the whole. It appears, that Spearing managing for his landlord, and these tenants doing the best for themselves, had not come to an agreement up to the 1st of April. Then notice to quit was given to both. That is said to be a determination of all treaty. It is put on the other side as speeding the business. Steps are taken directly ; and Mrs. Garrett makes her agreement by parol upon the 13th of April ; the effect of which is to give her the benefit of that part of the treaty, which was to take from Stangroom that part of his farm. That agreement was communicated to Stangroom. He knew, she had a parol agreement, perhaps not strictly one, that, even if confessed, would have bound, but an agreement, that in all honor, conscience, and fair dealing, ought to bind ; she relying upon the honor of her landlord, that she was to have that property in her occupation, which Stangroom himself had advised her to take. The subsequent agreement with Stangroom does away the effect of the notice to quit.

The question therefore is, whether upon the face of the agreement connected with a latent circumstance, now disclosed, you are now at liberty upon the latent fact disclosed to inquire into the nature of

the agreement itself; if there is something upon the face of it inconsistent with that fact disclosed : whether evidence can be admitted
upon the ground of that fact disclosed; one part of the agreement importing what the other part does not import: next, whether if Stangroom really understood, he was to have the whole of his old farm,
he shall have a specific execution ; if the other party could
[* 341]   not so understand it. As to the expression * "more or
less," I do not say, those words in a contract will not include a few additional acres: but if the parties are contending
about three acres, it would be very singular upon those words to
add twenty-four map acres ; which he knew were already demised,
as far as parol could demise them, to Mrs. Garrett. It is almost
impossible that he could mean to include them. Therefore upon
the head of the true meaning of the agreement, I think the parol
evidence may be introduced: but, without determining that, the
evidence is so complete to show, Spearing did not mean it at the
time of the agreement, and that Stangroom must have known, that
he could not mean it, that he is therefore to be left to law.

As to the other part of the case, I cannot possibly execute an
agreement so perfectly different from that Stangroom has signed. I
am to consider it with reference to his answer; by which he has
positively denied it. The whole agreement is to be taken together;
and the whole must be executed or abandoned. I cannot find out,
what was the parcel of land in the possession of Mrs. Garrett, that
he was to have. It is not distinctly stated : nor is it admitted. I
cannot therefore give a specific performance upon that bill ; and
under all the circumstances with regard to the admission of evidence,
attending to the purpose and the view, with which it is to be admitted in this Court, both bills must be dismissed, without costs, on
account of the inaccuracy of all the transactions (1).

----

1. THAT, as a general proposition, parol evidence ought not to be received, to
add a new term to an agreement, in order to have the agreement, when so added
to, or qualified, specifically performed; see, *ante*, the note to *Hare* v. *Shearwood*,
1 V. 241; but that an agreement which does not actually embody all the terms
may be enforced, provided it contain a reference to other documents, by which the
particulars may be unequivocally established; and also, that upon questions of
specific performance, evidence may be received in Equity, which could not be listened to at Law : see notes 2 and 3 to *Brodie* v. *St. Paul*, 1 V. 326: the attempt
to act in Courts of Common Law upon supposed analogy to the practice and principles of Courts of Equity, has been declared to be very dangerous, not only in the
principal case, but on many other occasions: see note 8 to *Cooth* v. *Jackson*, 6 V.
12, and the farther references there given.

2. Unless part performance has taken the case out of the statute, specific performance of an agreement different from that set up by the plaintiff's bill will not
be decreed, notwithstanding such different agreement may be established by
proofs, in the progress of the cause; see note 3 to *Mortimer* v. *Orchard*, 2 V. 243.

3. Though parol evidence can never entitle a plaintiff to call upon a Court of
Equity to execute, in his favor, a written agreement, with an addition, or variation,
introduced by such parol testimony; still, a defendant may, in many cases, be en-

----

(1) See *ante*, the note, vol. iii. 38; *Post, Mortlock* v. *Buller*, x. 292; xvi. 83;
Cadman v. *Horner*; *Savage* v. *Brocksopp*, xviii. 10, 335; *Ogilvie* v. *Foljambe*, 3
Mer. 53; *Hitchcock* v. *Giddings*, 4 Pri 135.

abled to resist performance of a written agreement, by means of parol evidence: see the notes to *Calverley* v. *Williams*, 1 V. 210. Fraud is not the only head upon which parol evidence may be received, and upon which if satisfactorily made out, specific performance may be refused: the propriety of letting in evidence of mistake or surprise, stands upon precisely the same ground. *Ramsbottom* v. *Gosden*, 1 V. & B. 168; *Clowes* v. *Higginson*, 1 V. & B. 527; *Lord W. Gordon* v. *The Marquis of Hertford*, 2 Mad. 120; *Garrard* v. *Grinling*, 2 Swanst. 248; *Flood* v. *Finlay*, 2 Ball & Bea. 15; *Willan* v. *Willan*, 16 Ves. 82; *Mortlock* v. *Buller*, 10 Ves. 305.

4. In what cases a vendor, by auction, may properly employ a bidder on his behalf, to prevent an unreasonable sacrifice of his property; see the note to *Bramley* v. *Alt*, 3 V. 620.

5. Of course, where a variation of the terms first arranged has been reduced into writing, such variation, if fairly agreed for, forms part of the contract to be executed. *Robson* v. *Collins*, 7 Ves. 133.

6. The right of Courts of Equity to enforce, or to refuse enforcing, specific performance of contracts, is a discretionary jurisdiction, though not to be exercised arbitrarily or capriciously; see note 1 to *Brodie* v. *St. Paul*, 1 V. 326.

7. Lord Thurlow, (like Lord Eldon, in the principal case, and in *Beaumont* v. *Bramley*, 1 Turn. 50, 55,) thought "strong, irrefragible" evidence. necessary, to prove mistake or surprise, in order to authorize relief. Lord Hardwicke appears to have considered "reasonable presumption" sufficient. *Simpson* v. *Vaughan*, 2 Atk. 33.

8. There are many cases in which a Court of Equity will neither enforce specific performance of an agreement, nor decree the agreement to be delivered up; but will leave each party thereto to make the best of his case at law. *Willan* v. *Willan*, 16 Ves. 83; *Mortlock* v. *Buller*, 10 Ves. 306.

WEDDELL *v.* MUNDY.

[ROLLS.—1801, JULY 21.]

BEQUEST to A., her executors, &c., provided, that in case she shall die under twenty-one or without leaving any husband living at her death, it shall go over, vested at twenty-one upon the intention: the word "or" being construed "and," (*a*).

WILLIAM HOOPER by his will, after giving some annuities, gave to trustees 1000*l.*; upon trust to place that sum out at interest, and the dividends and interest to pay towards the support, and maintenance, and education, of his daughter Mary Hooper for and during the term of her natural life; as the trustees should think proper; and after her decease to pay and transfer the principal to the lawful husband of his said daughter, if she shall * hap- [* 342] pen to leave any behind her at the time of her decease; which said sum of 1000*l.* together with the said securities she thereby gave and bequeathed to him accordingly; provided his said daughter shall not leave any lawful issue of her body living at the time: but if she shall happen to leave any such, then he declared his will, and gave and bequeathed the said principal sum of 1000*l.* to and among all and every such his grand-children equally be-

---

(*a*) See note (*a*), *Maberly* v. *Strode*, 3 V. 450.

tween them share and share alike, to be paid to them respectively
upon their respectively attaining their ages of twenty-one years ; and
if any or either die under that age, he gave the share or shares of
him, her, or them, so dying equally between the survivors ; and if
there should be only one, to that one.   He also gave and bequeathed
to his said daughter all the rest, residue, and remainder of his personal estate, of what kind soever, to hold to her, her executors, administrators, and assigns, for ever : provided always, and he declared, his will was, that in case his said daughter shall happen to
die under the age of twenty-one years, or without leaving any lawful husband living at the time of her death, then he gave to his
father-in-law and several other persons several legacies ; all which
he directs to be paid within twelve calendar months next after his
decease in case of the death of his said daughter under age, as
aforesaid ; and in such case he did thereby give and bequeath all
the rest, residue, and remainder, of his personal estate and effects,
whatsoever and wheresoever unto his two nephews equally ; and he
appointed his trustees executors ; and gave them legacies.

After the death of the testator Mary Weddell, his only child,
having attained the age of twenty-one, and married, filed the bill
with her husband ; and the question was upon the right of the
Plaintiffs under the residuary clause.

The *Solicitor General* and Mr. *Leach*, for the Plaintiffs.—The
question is, whether this interest is vested, the Plaintiff having attained the age of twenty-one, or still contingent, depending on
another event, whether she shall leave a husband living at the time
of her death.   The testator intended only one event, consisting of
two circumstances ; and the word " or " must be construed " and."
The subsequent clause, directing payment of the legacies within
[* 343]   twelve months after the testator's decease in case of the
                  * death of his said daughter under age, as aforesaid, and
                  in such case giving the residue to his nephews, shows that
intention ; not referring to either of two events.   This makes the
case infinitely stronger than the former cases, in which the word
" and " had been substituted for " or."   Upon the other construction, if she should leave children, but no husband, this property
would go over.

Mr. *Richards* and Mr. *Raynsford*, for the Defendants.—This
will, though very inaccurate, expresses two contingencies.   The disposition of the 1000*l.* must be coupled with that of the residue.   In
the event of her death without husband or children, that sum of
1000*l.* would fall into the residue ; and the Defendants would take
it as part of the residue ; which she never could.

The MASTER OF THE ROLLS [Sir WILLIAM GRANT].—After the
testator has given the residue of his personal estate to his daughter
in words, that would vest it absolutely in her, he is supposed to take
it away from her by words, which would prevent it from ever vesting
in her.   The Plaintiff's construction is the only one ; and makes the
two parts consistent.   The expression " under age, as aforesaid "

means, not leaving a husband; and in that passage he seems to have contemplated her death in his life. There can be no doubt he meant "and" by "or;" and cases are not necessary for that construction; if you can make out the intention (1). Decree according to the prayer of the bill.

SEE note 1 to *Maberly* v. *Strode*, 3 V. 450.

ABBOTT *v.* ABBOTT.

[ROLLS.—1801, JULY 21.]

EXECUTOR held a trustee for the next of kin of the residue undisposed of upon a legacy, against an argument upon the will opposing the presumption, (a).

JAMES ABBOTT by his will disposed in the following manner.

"To William Abbott my eldest brother I give 10*l.* as a legacy, and to his four children 10*l.* each; and to Stephen Abbott 10*l.* to him as a legacy; and to his three sons 10*l.* each; and to John Abbot deceased his four children, three sons, 10*l.* each, and to his daughter Hannah Lumley 20*l.*; and to my sister * Sarah   [* 344] Nickles, only daughter of Elizabeth Nickles, 20*l.*; and to my brother Thomas Abbott 10*l.*; and to his only daughter 20*l.*; and the annuity of the three Miss Vaughans of Suffolk Street, Middlesex Hospital, to my sister Mary Ellington: she to have it for her natural life; and her husband William Ellington not to have any thing to do with it: but to be at her disposal; and after her death to be divided among the survivors and added to the annuity 130*l.* during her natural life; and the said William Ellington to have 5*l.* for mourning; and to my brother Samuel Abbott 20*l.*; and to my brother Joseph Abbott of Froom 10*l.*; and" to five persons by name "one guinea each for a ring; and to my nephew James Abbott whole and sole executor."

The only question was, whether the Defendant James Abbott, the executor, who was one of the children of William Abbott, was entitled to the residue beneficially, or was a trustee for the next of kin.

Mr. *Richards* and Mr. *Stanley*, for the Plaintiffs. Mr. *Romilly* and Mr. *Hall*, for the Defendant, contended, that this amounted to giving him the executorship.

The MASTER OF THE ROLLS [Sir WILLIAM GRANT], suggested, that the construction of the last clause might be to give him a guinea for a ring.

Mr. *Romilly* said, that construction would not be consistent with

(1) *Maberley* v. *Strode*, *ante*, vol. iii. 450, and the references in the note, 452.

(a) In most, if not all of the States, the executor is a trustee for the residue undisposed of in all cases. See *ante*, note (a), *Nisbett* v. *Murray*, 5 V. 158; note (a), *Nourse* v. *Finch*, 1 V. 344.

the manner, in which all the other legacies were given ; in which the person preceded the sum.

The MASTER OF THE ROLLS (after some farther discussion at the bar) said, it would be too much in such a case to give the Defendant the residue beneficially ; and declared him a trustee for the next of kin (1).

SEE the notes to *Nourse* v. *Finch*, 1 V. 344.

[* 345]   BARRINGTON *v.* TRISTRAM.

[1801, JULY 17, 22.]

A BEQUEST for all and every the child and children of A. includes every child born before the period of distribution ; which in this case was the attainment of the age of twenty-one by the eldest, the marriage of a daughter, or the death of a child under twenty-one, leaving issue. Upon the general rule a child by a subsequent marriage was included, notwithstanding a strong implication in favor of children by the prior marriage (a).

Dividends on specific legacy of stock from the death of the testator.

Costs of a doubt upon the meaning of the will out of the general property.

ADMIRAL BARRINGTON by his will, dated the 22d of February, 1797, after devising his real ·estate, and disposing of a leasehold house, and the furniture, &c., gave and bequeathed to his nephew Barrington Price 10,000*l.* 3 per cent Consolidated Bank Annuities, part of his stock in that fund ; which he directed to be transferred to his said nephew for his own use and benefit within one month after the testator's decease : but if his said nephew should happen to die in his life-time, then the testator directed, that his executor should stand possessed of the said 10,000*l.* 3 per cent. Bank Annuities upon trust for all the children of his said nephew Barrington Price lawfully begotten, which shall be living at his decease, or born in due time afterwards, in equal shares, if more than· one ; to be transferred to a son or sons at the age of twenty-one, and to a daughter or daughters at the like age, or marriage with consent of the executor ; the dividends to be in the mean time applied for maintenance and education ; with survivorship in case of the death of any one or more dying before twenty-one or marriage without leaving any child or children ; if leaving any, upon trust for the child or children, in the same manner ; and if Barrington Price should die in the testator's life, leaving only one child living at his decease, or born in due time afterwards, or if more, all but one should die before becoming entitled to any share, and without leaving issue, upon trust for such

(1) *Nisbett* v. *Murray*, *ante*, vol. v. 149 ; and the references in the notes, 158 ; and vol. i. 362.

(a) See *ante*, note (a), *Middleton* v. *Messer*, 5 V. 136 ; *Hill* v. *Chapman*, 1 V. 405, note (a).

one ; and if Barrington Price should die in the testator's life without leaving any child or children living at his decease or born in due
time afterwards, or if any, they, their child, children or issue, should
die before coming entitled to the said stock as a vested interest,
then the same to fall into the residue, and go to his nephew George
Barrington, residuary legatee and executor.

After several other legacies the testator gave to the Plaintiffs the
sum of 5000*l.* part of his stock of and in the 3 per cent. Bank Annuities ; upon trust for and for the benefit of all and every the child
and children of his niece Mrs. Tristram, the wife of the Reverend
Thomas Tristram, if more than one, in and by equal parts or
shares ; and to be vested interests in, and transferred to,
* such of them as should be a son or sons, as or when he   [* 346]
or they should attain his or their age or ages of twenty-one
years respectively, and in and to such of them as should be a daughter or daughters at the like ages, or upon his or their marriage or
marriages before such age with consent of the Plaintiff, or the survivor, his executors, &c. ; and he directed, that the dividends thereof, or such part or parts thereof, and so much as the Plaintiff should
think fit, should be in the mean time applied for the maintenance
and education of the children of his said niece Mrs. Tristram during
their respective minorities, without any regard to the ability of their
father, or his situation or circumstances in life ; but if any of the
children of the said Mrs. Tristram, being a son or sons, should die
before the age of twenty-one, or, being a daughter or daughters, before that age, not having been married with such consent, and without leaving any issue then living, then the expectant parts or shares
of such children so dying before being vested of and in the said
5000*l.* 3 per cent. Annuities should go or accrue to, and be upon
trust for the benefit of, the surviving children of his said niece Mrs.
Tristram, if, more than one, in equal shares ; and should be vested
interests in, and transferred to, each of them respectively at the like
ages or times as the original shares ; and the dividends of such surviving shares should be in the mean time applied for the maintenance and education of such surviving children during minority :
but if any of the children of his said niece Mrs. Tristram, son or
daughter, sons or daughters, should die before twenty-one, leaving
any child or children, the share of every such child so dying under
age, and leaving issue, should be upon trust for the benefit of his,
her, or their child or children, if more than one, in equal shares ;
and should be vested interests in, and transferred to, each of them
respectively at the like ages or times, or upon the marriage of such
of them as should be a daughter or daughters, with like consent as
before directed respecting the shares of the child or children of his
said niece Mrs. Tristram, and with the same survivorship as before,
in case of such child dying under twenty-one and without issue, as
aforesaid ; and that the dividends, &c. of the last-mentioned shares
should be applied for the maintenance and education of such last-
mentioned child, &c. during minority ; and if all the children of his

said niece Mrs. Tristram, except one, should die, before he, she, or
      they, should become entitled to any part of the said 5000*l.*
[* 347]   * annuities by virtue of that his will, and without leaving
      any issue, as aforesaid, then and in that event he gave the
whole upon trust for such only surviving child; and directed, that
it should be transferred to such child, if a son at twenty-one, if a
daughter, at that age, or marriage with such consent, as before: but
if all and every the child and children of his said niece Mrs.
Tristram should die, before they or any of them should become entitled to the said 5000*l.* 3 per cent. Bank Annuities as a vested interest, and without leaving any child or children, which should live
to become entitled thereto, as a vested interest, then and in that
event he gave the said 5000*l.* Bank Annuities upon trust for all the
children of the said Barrington Price, which shall be living at the
decease of the surviving child of his said niece Mrs. Tristram, in the
same manner as directed concerning the said 10,000*l.* Bank Annuities; and if none of the children of Barrington Price or their
issue should live to become entitled, the said 5000*l.* stock to fall into
the residue.

The testator died soon after the execution of his will. Thomas
Tristram died, according to one witness, in 1796; leaving six children by his wife. She married again; and by that marriage had
one child, Louisa Jane Cooke. That child claiming a share, and
the Tristrams claiming the whole, as the only children living at the
death of the testator, the bill was filed by the trustees to have the
different rights ascertained.

Mr. *Alexander,* for the family of Tristram.—It was originally held
in the cases, that a general bequest of this sort applied only to the description of persons at the death of the testator at farthest: but some
late cases have let in persons answering the description before the
distribution, That construction, which would let in the child by the
second marriage, would make a considerable part of this disposition
impossible. The question is, whom the testator meant by the child
or children of his niece Tristram. If the construction is extended to
a child coming *in esse* after the death of the testator, you may extend it under this will, so as to give to the children of that child
a proportion of the fund at the age of twenty-one; which is extending the vesting beyond the period allowed by law: a difficulty, that
      cannot occur if it is understood children born at the death
[* 348]   of the testator. The * Court will incline to that meaning,
      that will meet all the events, that can happen.

Mr. *Sutton* and Mr. *Owen,* for the Defendant Cooke.—This is
merely a question of intention. The rule, that all children are let in,
until there must be a distributive share given to one, must govern
this case: *Andrews* v. *Partington* (1), *Hoste* v. *Pratt* (2), *Middleton*

---

(1) 3 Bro. C. C. 401.
(2) *Ante,* vol. iii. 730; see the notes, 732, i. 408.

v. *Messenger* (1).   Suppose, all the children by the first husband
died, before the money was distributable : is the bounty, evidently
intended as a provision for the children of his niece, to lapse?   The
Court will not incline to such a construction.   The difficulty suggested must be considered, when the case arises : but one eventually
bad limitation in a will does not of necessity govern the construction.
Tristram, the father, appears to have been dead when the will was
made.

The Lord CHANCELLOR [ELDON.]—The rule of the Court now being to let in all children, until there must be a distributive share given
to one, the construction upon the whole of this will seems to be, that
every child must be let in, until some child attains twenty-one, or
dies, leaving issue.   The first attaining twenty-one must be paid his
• share, and then it must be apportioned ; unless some other prior
event would compel you to fix the shares.   The rule of the Court
has gone upon the anxiety to provide for as many children as possible with convenience.   Therefore any coming *in esse*, before a de-
terminate share becomes distributable to any one, is included.   My
private opinion is, he never thought of his niece marrying again ; but
the object was the children of Mr. Tristram.   The words " the wife
of the Reverend Thomas Tristram " are merely words of description.
In the direction for maintenance, without regard to the ability of
their father, I should suppose, he thought Mr. Tristram was alive,
and that he meant him : but the words are not so ; and if the rule is
to include all children coming *in esse*, before there must be a distributive share given to one, the words " their father" in that passage are
not sufficient to support my private opinion against the rule.   In the
gift over he excludes children of Barrington Price, that
should not be living *at the death of the surviving child of   [*349]
Mrs. Tristram.   There too, I think, he meant children by
Mr. Tristram : but it would be very difficult to make out the title of
the children of Barrington Price against her children by any other
husband.   The difficulty put by Mr. Alexander confirms my private
opinion : but the rule requiring, that all children shall take, who
come *in esse*, before there is a necessity for determining the share of
any child, it only comes to this ; that the testator has given to persons, whom the law makes certain, property, with a limitation over,
which cannot take effect ; which happens every day.   Notwithstanding a strong conjecture against my judicial opinion, I am bound to
declare, that every child of Mrs. Tristram shall take, who will come
into existence before any son of Mrs. Tristram attains the age of
twenty-one, or any daughter attains that age, or marries, or any child
marries, and dies, leaving issue : for a child may marry, and die
under twenty-one, leaving issue.   Decree, that the stock shall be
transferred to the Accountant-General, and the costs of all parties
paid out of the residue.   Wherever a testator by his will raises a
doubt upon the meaning of it, his general property pays for settling

(1) *Ante*, vol. v. 136; *Prescott* v. *Long*, ii. 690; *Godfrey* v. *Davies*, *ante*, 43.

that doubt (1). This being a specific legacy of stock, the dividends are due for maintenance from the death of the testator (2).

———

1. WHEN a testamentary bounty is bequeathed to a class, such individuals of that class as are *in esse* at the time appointed for distribution of the gift must take the whole, notwithstanding others may possibly afterwards come *in esse*, who, if they had been born in due time, would have participated; see, *ante*, note 3 to *Hill* v. *Chapman*, 1 V. 405.

2. Whenever a suit is occasioned by a difficulty arising out of the will of a testator, the costs are to be borne by the general fund of the property. *Pearson* v. *Pearson*, 1 Sch. & Lef. 12; *Jolliffe* v. *East*, 3 Brown, 27; *Studholme* v. *Hodgson*, 3 P. Wms. 302.

3. A specific legacy is a gift, not only of the thing or fund itself, but of all its produce, from the time of the testator's death; see note 2 to *Kirby* v. *Potter*, 4 V. 748.

———

PAINE *v.* MELLER.

[1801, JULY 22.]

CONTRACT for the sale of houses; which from defects in the title could not be completed on the day. The treaty however proceeded upon a proposal to waive the objections upon certain terms. The houses being burnt before a conveyance, the purchaser is bound, if he accepted the title; and the circumstance, that the vendor suffered the insurance to expire at the day, on which the contract was originally to have been completed, without notice, makes no difference. A reference to the Master was therefore directed to inquire, whether the proposal was accepted, or acquiesced in, on behalf of the purchaser, (a).

UPON the first of September, 1796, the Plaintiffs sold to the Defendant by auction some houses in Ratcliffe Highway, upon the

———

(1) Beames on Costs, 13, 14.
(2) *Webster* v. *Hale, post,* vol. viii. 410.
(a) As to the extension of time for completing the title, see *Hepburn* v. *Dunlop,* 1 Wheat. 179, 196; *Hepburn* v. *Auld,* 5 Cranch, 262; *Ramsay* v. *Brailsford,* 2 Desaus. 583. Time may be of the essence of a contract; but it is not generally so treated. See note (a), *Harrington* v. *Wheeler,* 4 V. 686. As to laches in completing a purchase, see note (a), to *Marquis of Hertford* v. *Boore,* 5 V. 719; note (b) and (d), to *Omerod* v. *Hardman,* 5 V. 722.

A vendee, being equitable owner of the estate from the time of the contract for sale, must pay the consideration for it, although the estate itself be destroyed between the agreement and the conveyance; and on the other hand he will be entitled to any benefit which may accrue to the estate in the interim. 1 Sugden, Vendors & Purchasers, 468, (6th Amer. ed.) where are cited two Scotch cases which sustain this ground. The Roman law is also in accordance with it. Institutes, iii. 24, § 3.

In matters of positive contract, it is no ground for the interference of equity, that the party has been prevented from fulfilling it by accident; or that he has been prevented by accident from deriving the full benefit of the contract on his own side. 1 Story, Eq. Jur. § 101. Where there is an express covenant, rént must be paid, notwithstanding the premises are accidentally burned down during the term; Ibid, § 102; *Balfour* v. *Weston,* 1 T. R. 310; *Fowler* v. *Bott,* 6 Mass. 63; *Hallett* v. *Wylic,* 3 Johns. 44; *Pollard* v. *Shaeffer,* 1 Dallas, 210; *Wagner* v. *White,* 4 Harr. & Johns. 564; *Ripley* v. *Wightman,* 4 McCord, 447; *Gates* v. *Green,* 4 Paige, 355; *Linn* v. *Ross,* 10 Ohio, 412; 3 Kent, Com. 465–468.

usual terms, a deposit of 25*l.* per cent. and a proper conveyance to
be executed upon payment of the remainder of the purchase-money
at Michaelmas next. The premises were with others subject to
certain annuities: but a trust of stock was declared for the payment
of these annuities. The first abstract delivered was clearly defective: so that the purchase could not be completed at
* the time. A farther abstract was delivered to the solici-   [* 350]
tor for the Defendant at the end of September or the beginning of October. He insisted upon having a release from the
annuitants. The treaty continued through October; and about the
end of that month the Defendant's solicitor agreed to waive all
objections, if the Plaintiff would allow him eleven guineas, and if
the trustees of the stock would join in the conveyance; and refused
a proposal to give up the purchase. The Plaintiff agreed to make
the allowance desired. On the 4th or 5th of November the Defendant's solicitor sent a draft of a conveyance. The trustees of the
stock were prevailed upon to join in the conveyance by a new
declaration of trust. The draft was returned to the Defendant's
solicitor: the deeds were engrossed; and upon the 16th or 17th of
December he declared himself satisfied with the title; and said, the
deeds would be ready in two or three days; and that he should
complete the purchase under the promise of the eleven guineas.
Upon the 18th of December, the houses were burnt: the insurance
having been suffered to expire at Michaelmas 1796. On the 20th
of December the Defendant's solicitor wrote a letter; observing,
that he had taken an objection to the freehold title; and should not
have thought any thing more of the purchase but for the covenant
of indemnity from the trustees, inserted in the draft by him, and approved by one of the trustees of the stock: but as that had been
struck out by another trustee, he could not advise his client to accept
the title; and he should call for the deposit.

The bill was then filed; praying a specific performance of the
contract; and a decree was made by the late Lord Chancellor, simply referring it to the Master, to see, whether a good title could be
made. This decree was dissatisfactory to both parties, as not deciding the question; and a petition of re-hearing was presented by the
Plaintiff.

Mr. *Mansfield* and Mr. *Cox,* for the Plaintiff, insisted, that the
objection to the title from the charge of the annuities was frivolous:
there being a fund of stock with a trust declared upon it.

Mr. *Sutton* and Mr. *Lewis* for the Defendant.—The delay in performing this contract arose from the defect of the title; and the
Plaintiff ought to have acquainted the Defendant with the
* circumstance of the insurance expiring. In *Stent* v.   [* 351]
Baylis (1), referred to in *Mortimer* v. *Capper* (2), Sir

(1) 2 P. Will. 217.
(2) 1 Bro. C. C. 156.

Joseph Jekyll expresses a clear opinion upon this case (1). *Pope*
v. *Roots* (2).

Mr. *Mansfield*, in Reply.—All the cases referred to are got rid of
by *Jackson* v. *Lever* (3).   The former cases proceeded upon this
fallacy, that the party could not have the thing bought; for chance
had decided against him : but he had the chance; and he must take
it each way.   In the case of a life it might last fifty years, and might
drop the next day.   But this is not a purchase of property depending upon the contingency of life, like an annuity.   A man purchasing a house is to consider with himself, whether he will insure, or
not.   Not a word was said about insurance : therefore notice was
not incumbent on the Plaintiffs ; and there was as much negligence
in the Defendant in not inquiring about that.   Such an accident did
not occur to either of them.   If in the sale of a house nothing is
said about insurance, it could not enter into the bargain.

The Lord CHANCELLOR [ELDON].—The abstract first delivered
was undoubtedly imperfect in certain respects.   It did not go back
farther than forty-three years ; and there was no specific mention of
the property in Ratcliffe Highway in the abstract.   There was also
the objection upon the annuities.   Unquestionably that abstract was
not satisfactory ; and the express condition of the sale could not be
complied with (4).   Of course the Defendant could not be called
on to pay his purchase money.   Then it was with the vendee to
choose to go on with the bargain or to put an end to the contract.
The agent however chose not to put an end to it ; and though a circumstance took place at Michaelmas sufficient to put an end to any
action of law, the contract was kept alive, at least to the 10th of
December.   It is clear, the objection was given up as to the freehold
title ; and the only difference was as to the indemnity against the
annuities, affecting these with other premises.   I do not consider,
whether this objection is of form or substance : but leave it to be
determined, when it may be necessary, whether the pur-
[* 352]   chaser under such circumstances has not a right * to insist,
that the annuitants shall release the premises ; or, whether
this Court will say, under all the circumstances the purchasers shall
take the premises burthened with the annuities with a great number
of others ; and seek their indemnity against the trust property and
the trustees ; if they preferred a personal covenant by the trustees.
If in equity these premises belonged to the vendee, he would have a
title to the rents and profits at Michaelmas by relation ; and he must
pay the purchase money with interest from that time.   First, it is
said, the title was never accepted in fact : 2dly, if not, under these
circumstances a Court of Equity will not compel a specific performance.   As to the second point the objection is grounded upon two
circumstances : 1st, the simple fact of the fire ; 2dly, that the prem-

(1) 2 P. Will. 220.
(2) 7 Bro. P. C. 184.
(3) 3 Bro. C. C. 605.
(4) *Harrington* v. *Wheeler, ante,* vol. iv. 686 ; and the note. 691.

ises had been insured prior to the contract; that that fact and the fact, that the insurance expired at Michaelmas 1796, were not disclosed; and that the premises afterwards remained uncovered by any insurance. The authority of Sir Joseph Jekyll has been mentioned: but no case has been cited in support of that *dictum;* and it is in a degree suggested, not admitted at the Bar, that it may be considered over-ruled by subsequent cases. As to the mere effect of the accident itself no solid objection can be founded upon that simply; for if the party by the contract has become in equity the owner of the premises, they are his to 'all intents and purposes (1). They are vendible as his, chargeable as his, capable of being incumbered as his; they may be devised as his; they may be assets; and they would descend to his heir. If a man had signed a contract for a house upon that land, which is now appropriated to the London Docks, and that house was burnt, it would be impossible to say to the purchaser, willing to take the land without the house, because much more valuable on account of this project, that he should not have it. As to the annuity cases and all the others, the true answer has been given; that the party has the thing he bought; though no payment may have been made; for he bought subject to contingency. If it is a real estate, he of course has it.

Then as to the non-communication, I cannot say, that in my judgment forms an objection; for I do not see, how I can allow it, unless I say, this Court warrants to every buyer of a house, that the house is insured, and not only insured, but to the full extent of the value. The house is bought, not the benefit of any existing policy. However general the practice of insuring from fire is, it is not universal; and it is yet * less general that houses are insured to their   [* 353] full value, or near it. The question, whether insured or not, is with the vendor solely, not with the vendee; unless he proposes something upon that; and makes it matter of contract with the vendor, that the vendee shall buy according to that fact, that the house is insured. I am therefore of opinion, that if the agent on behalf of this purchaser did accept this title previously to the destruction of the premises, the vendors are in the situation, in which they would have been, if the title and the conveyance were ready at Michaelmas 1796, but by the default of the vendee were not executed, but the title was accepted, and the premises were burnt down on the quarter day. As to the fact, where there has been a great deal of treaty, and a considerable hardship must fall upon one party, if the case is to be put entirely upon the fact, the Court must guard against surprise; and I am not sure, even the Plaintiff's witnesses accurately understand the nature of the facts

---

(1) 2 Ves. & Bea. 387; *Harford* v. *Purrier*, 1 Madd. 532; *Acland* v. *Cuming*, 2 Madd. 28. See the note, *post*, vol. xiii. 563; *Akhurst* v. *Jackson*, 1 Swanst. 85. As to a sale before the Master, the property is not changed, so as to throw the loss upon the purchaser, until the report is confirmed; *Post, Ex parte Minor*, vol. xi. 559; xiii. 518. Nor is he then considered as owner, unless he has accepted the title, and paid in his money; *Mackrell* v. *Hunt*, 2 Madd. 34, n.

they depose to. It is to be observed, they are all the Plaintiff's
agents, subject to the influence necessarily belonging to that situation. The case is therefore not sufficiently clear upon the fact; and
there ought to be some reference to the Master or an inquiry before
a jury: but that must not be upon the validity of the title; for it is
clear, the objection to the freehold title, that it was not old enough,
and the other objection, that the purchaser had a right to insist upon
a release of the annuities, were waived. The question between
them is, whether the parties agreed, that an indemnity should be
given in any form; and if so, in what form. The inquiry must be,
whether the title had been accepted by the agent on behalf of
the Defendant on or before the 18th of December, 1796. That inquiry will miscarry, unless the Master or the Jury, if satisfied, that
there was an acquiescence in the proposal, shall be of opinion, that
is an acceptance of the proposal. I should think, a Court of Law
would hold that: but if there is any doubt of it, I would rather refer it to the Master to inquire, whether the agent on behalf of the
Defendant had accepted or acquiesced in the proposal; with a direction, that he should be examined: and they will appreciate the
credit due to him; and will not forget, that he was bartering for
himself for eleven guineas; if that appears.

The decree was reversed; and the reference to the Master directed accordingly.

1. THAT time may be made of the essence of a contract, see note 2 to *Eaton* v.
Lyon, 3 V. 690; but that the right to object on that ground should be promptly
urged, if at all, see the note to *The Marquis of Hertford* v. *Boore*, 5 V. 719.
2. Where there has been no stipulation as to interest, the general rule of the
Court is, that a purchaser who completes his contract after the time mentioned in
the agreement, or particular, of sale, must be considered as if he had been in possession at the regular time, and must pay interest on his purchase money, and
take the rents and profits, from that time: *Esdaile* v. *Stephenson*, 1 Sim. & Stu.
123: for it is the established doctrine of Equity, that if a contract for purchase be
finally completed, the estate is considered as belonging to the purchaser, by relation, from the date agreed on by the contract; notwithstanding the title may not
have been made out at the time appointed: *Seton* v. *Slade*, 7 Ves. 274; *Rose* v.
Cunynghame, 11 Ves. 554; *Rawlins* v. *Burgess*, 2 Ves. & Bea. 387: the consequence is, that whether the estate be improved, or lessened in value, after the contract, (and no blame be imputable to either party,) the vendee takes the benefit, or
bears the loss: *Harford* v. *Purrier*, 1 Mad. 538; *Revell* v. *Hussey*, 2 Ball & Beat.
287: and that the rule applies to contracts for annuities, reversions, or leases for
lives; which contracts must be performed, though, before the money is paid, the
lives on which the contingencies depended, have fallen in; see *Twigg* v. *Fyfield*,
13 Ves. 517; *Gowland* v. *De Faria*, 17 Ves. 25; *Coles* v. *Trecothick*, 9 Ves. 246;
Jackson v. *Lever*, 3 Brown, 613; *Pritchard* v. *Ovey*, 1 Jac. & Walk. 403; *Lord
Kensington* v. *Phillips*, 5 Dow, 72. It seems, however, that there may be cases
in which specific performance will not be decreed, when the subject of an executory contract has become reduced in value: see, *post*, the note to *Ex parte Minor*,
11 V. 559.

GOUGH v. THE WORCESTER AND BIRMINGHAM CANAL COMPANY.

[1801, July 24, 25.]

CONSTRUCTION of a covenant in a lease, that if the lessor shall be minded to set out any part of the premises for a street or streets, or to sell any part to build upon, he may resume upon certain terms. If he resumed, having a *bona fide* intention to build, though that cannot be acted upon, there is no Equity for the tenant. 2dly, The generality of the latter words are not restrained by the former to buildings of any particular species: therefore a contract with a Canal Company for the lands resumed was enforced: warehouses being within the meaning of the lease; and wharfs, at least as appurtenant, and wanted for the enjoyment of the warehouses. A compensation was decreed for the land covered with water; and as to towing paths, and the banks of basons, though strictly subjects of compensation, yet upon a rehearing and after great litigation the Court would not reverse the decree, and direct another reference to the Master, merely on that account.

HARRY GOUGH by indentures of lease, dated the 26th of May, 1749, demised some lands in the neighborhood of Birmingham to Joseph Richards for a term of ninety-nine years at the annual rent of 47l. and the farther yearly rent of 8l. for every acre of meadow or pasture, which had not been in tillage for ten years last, that Richards should at any time during the term plough up. The lessee covenanted within three years to lay out 350l. at least in new building two messuages, and in erecting dwelling-houses upon part of the * premises then marked or staked out for   [* 354] that purpose, 30 yards by 120. He also covenanted to occupy in a husband-like manner, and not to demise or grant over the lease to any person except his wife, children, or grand-children, for any term exceeding a year without license; with the usual proviso for re-entry.

The lease also contained this covenant; that if the said Harry Gough, his heirs or assigns, shall be minded to set out any part of the ground hereby demised (except the piece of land above mentioned to be marked or staked out for the said lessee, his executors, administrators, and assigns, to be built upon) for a street or streets, or to set or sell any part or parts thereof to build upon, and shall at any time during the said term give to the said lessee, his executors or assigns, two months' notice in writing of such intention, then it shall be lawful for the lessor and his heirs to enter upon such ground, to be set out for a street or streets, or to be set or sold, as aforesaid, to build upon, and to dispose thereof for the purposes aforesaid, as he or they shall think fit; and that from and after such entry or entries the said lessor, his heirs or assigns, shall discount and allow, or otherwise it shall be lawful for the said lessee, his executors and assigns, to retain yearly out of the rents reserved, as much money for all such ground of the said demised premises, as shall be set out for a street or streets, to be set or sold to be built upon, as shall be proportionable to the reserved rent for the whole; which is to be taken by the said lessee, his executors or assigns, in full satisfaction for all such ground as shall be set out for a street or streets, or set or sold for the purposes aforesaid; and that no greater or other satisfaction or detainer shall be made by or to the said lessee, his executors or assigns, on account thereof: but it is farther agreed, that all such ground as shall be set out for a street or streets, or to be set or sold to build upon pursuant to the said agreement, shall, as soon after the same shall be set out for the purposes aforesaid as may be, well and sufficiently be hedged and fenced from the ground thereby leased adjoining thereto, at the expense of the lessor, his heirs, and assigns.

The lessor died several years ago; having devised all the premises comprised in the lease to his wife and her heirs. She died; leaving an only son, her heir at law and devisee. The town of Birmingham increasing rapidly, the widow and her son gave several notices of resumption under the covenant; and the tenants delivered up the land accordingly. The lease by mesne assignments became vested in John Guest. Most part of the premises resumed was let upon building leases: but some pieces, one particularly, consisting of 3 roods and 20 perch, remained in the possession of the son.

In the 31st year of King George 3d, 1790, an Act of Parliament passed, incorporating the Worcester and Birmingham Canal Company. Upon the 9th of July, 1792, Guest was in possession of 13 or 14 acres; and Gough was in possession of the said piece of 3 roods and 20 perch. An agreement took place between Gough and the Canal Company; by which he was to demise to them all his lands in the occupation of Guest or his under-tenants, and two messuages, and two small tenements thereon, with the appurtenances; they paying for all such part as he has a right to take from Guest, pursuant to the provision in his lease, at the rate of 25*l.* per acre per annum, from the time they take possession: and paying to Gough for such part as he has not a right to take from Guest, pursuant to such proviso, the rent Guest pays during his lease and afterwards at the rent of 25*l.* per acre: the Company to hold the said land in perpetuity under the rents above specified; without paying any consideration for the buildings erected thereon. Upon [*356] *the 18th of September, 1792, notice was served upon Guest under the clause of presumption to quit the land, except the piece staked out to be built upon at the granting of the lease. Possession was delivered accordingly by Guest; and the Company took possession of that land, and also of the 3 roods and 20 perch, of which Gough was in possession; and dug brick earth; and exercised other acts of ownership.

Guest afterwards set up claims; and in July, 1793, called a meeting of the commissioners under the act; who made their award on the 9th of August; by which reciting, that it appeared to them, that the Company had caused all the land in the occupation of Guest or his under-tenants and the appurtenances, to be marked

out, as wanted by them for the purposes of the navigation; and farther, reciting the agreement between Gough and the Company, they
determined that the Company should pay the said rent of 25*l.* per
annum an acre for all and every the said lands as should be so taken
and used by them, and so proportionable for a greater or less quantity than an acre, to Guest, his executors, &c. for such part of the
lands as at the time of making the agreement was in his occupation,
for the rest of the term of ninety-nine years and to Brother and
Lynden, his under-tenants for their terms, and from the expiration
thereof to Guest during the remainder of the term. The Act gave
no appeal.

The Company refusing to pay Gough, a notice was served by him
on the 21st of May, 1795, requiring them to attorn to him under the
agreement; and no answer being returned he brought an ejectment
in the Court of King's Bench; which was tried at the Summer Assizes for the county of Warwick in 1795; when the jury found,
that six acres, part of the land, were taken for the use and purpose
of the navigation; and the remainder for the purpose of building
streets; and that such six acres were sufficient for the building of
wharfs and warehouses. That was upon evidence to that fact taken
by agreement. A verdict was then taken for the Plaintiff, subject
to the opinion of the Court upon a case reserved; stating all the
facts, and, among them, that the Company had dug and used a quantity of brick earth, and exercised other acts of ownership; and also
stating the above finding of the jury upon parol evidence.
Upon the 2d of June, * 1796, judgment was given for the   [* 357]
Plaintiff for all the premises, except the six acres.

Gough offered the Company a lease at a rent of 25*l.* an acre per
annum, and upon being paid the arrears; and in the same letter his
agent observed, that though by this decision he was not entitled to
the whole of the six acres, yet he was by no means precluded from
obtaining a compensation for his right of building upon this land,
and other rights attached to him as landlord; and proposing a reference to individuals or a jury under the act, to determine, what the
compensation should be. Upon the 3d of June, 1796, a bill was
filed by the Canal Company against Gough; praying a specific performance of the agreement, and an Injunction to restrain him from
proceeding at law to obtain judgment or execution. Gough by his
answer stated, that the conveyance they tendered reserved only the
rent reserved in the lease; and also comprised the 3 roods and 20
perch. Upon the 12th of July, 1796, the Company offered by a
letter from the Solicitor for them and Guest to take the whole of
Gough's land at 25*l.* an acre per annum, as formerly agreed upon.
A correspondence followed between the agents: and a letter, dated
the 11th of January, 1797, stated, that the Company had at length
determined upon the quantity of land to be taken for the canal;
which was 9 acres and 38 perch; that that was all the land they
conceived they should have occasion for; and that what remained
was all compact, and the most eligible part for building on.

The bill, upon which this cause was instituted, was filed by Gough upon the 27th of May, 1797 ; praying, that his rights and interests in the premises may be ascertained ; that he may be quieted in the enjoyment ; that the agreement may be specifically performed, so far as it can be performed ; that the Company may accept a lease accordingly, except the six acres; that the compensation to be paid by them to the Plaintiff for the six acres may be ascertained ; that an account may be taken of the rents of the premises, except the six acres, since the Company had possession ; and an account of what is due to the Plaintiff in respect of the six acres during the possession of the Company, and of the compensation, which ought to be paid to him, and for payment upon such accounts ; and that the [* 358] Plaintiff's rights under the clause in * the lease and the several contracts and agreements may be settled ; and that an Injunction may be granted to restrain Guest and his undertenants from proceeding in ejectment against the Plaintiff and the Company, and from all proceedings at law against the Plaintiff.

The bill charged, that the price was agreed upon on account of the situation of the premises, and their value to be let or sold for building, and the probability, that an opportunity would soon offer to the Plaintiff of letting or selling the premises for that purpose. The Company never agreed to pay so high a price for land for the purposes of the Canal ; which could not be let or sold for building ; and if the land could have been used only for the purposes of husbandry, for which alone Guest could use it, they never would have given near so high a price.

The Canal Company by their 'answer stated, that it was understood upon the treaty, that the Plaintiff had a right under the covenant in the lease to take from Guest for the purpose of building upon all the land, except as in the bill mentioned, but not to sell or demise to them for the purpose of the navigation ; and therefore they applied to Guest to deliver them possession ; which he promised, if they could agree with the Plaintiff for the purchase of his interest; and in confidence of such promise the agreement with the Plaintiff took place. The price was in consideration of the situation of the premises, as convenient and necessary for the use of the navigation, and of the value the premises were worth to be let or sold for building. They admitted, that they have not paid, or offered, near so high for any other land, purchased for the purpose of the canal ; which is not in a situation, where it might be let for the purpose of building upon ; and if the land could have been used only for husbandry, they would not have given the same price. They never entered upon the 3 roods and 20 perch. They made 1,500,000 bricks. Under the award of the Commissioners Guest demised the land to them: namely, 13 acres 12 perch (including 1 rood 39 1-2 perch of the land staked out for building at the date of the lease) at 25l. an acre for all, except the 1 rood 39 1-2 perch. They were advised, the award of the Commissioners controlled the agreement. They want no more than 9 acres and 38 perch for the purpose of the canal ;

and are not warranted by the Act to take more; and are prohibited by the Statute of Mortmain from taking more. They insisted, that their agreement with the Plaintiff was annulled, not only by the award, but by the judgment in the ejectment; and Guest's demise to them of the 13 acres 12 perch, was also become of no effect. They stated, that they are willing to pay a rent of 25*l.* an acre per annum for the 9 acres 38 perch, to whomsoever is entitled: but it was claimed both by the Plaintiff and Guest. They admitted, that at the time they took possession it was understood, that the Plaintiff had a right to resume all the land, except what was mentioned in the bill to be marked and staked out for the lessees to build upon.

Guest by his answer insisted, that part of the land resumed having remained in the Plaintiff's hands, and not being let or sold to build upon, was contrary to the clause in the lease. He stated, that evidence was given before the Commissioners, and it was understood then, that the Company would want the whole of the land for the purposes of the navigation; and they have declared so. He also stated, that the land was not of any considerable value on account of the prospect of being built upon. In that respect he was contradicted by the Company and the under-tenants.

Of the Defendants the Canal Company only entered into evidence. Several witnesses stated, that 9 acres 38 perch were wanted for the purposes of the navigation: *i. e.* for making a bason, erecting sluices, wharfs, and places for landing goods, cranes, weight-booms, and other engines, to be used for the canal. One witness stated, that what he thought necessary to be applied to the purposes of the navigation was not sufficient with regard to the traffic expected: the Company having taken other lands of Sir Thomas Gooch. Another witness stated, that part of the land was necessary for the purpose of the navigation; the whole was not. Three acres one rood are at present unnecessary for the navigation.

By the decree, pronounced upon the 9th of December, 1799, it was declared, that the Plaintiff at the date of the agreement was entitled to the whole of the land in question for the purpose of building, except the land in the original lease mentioned to have *been staked and marked out for building; and a   [* 360] reference to the Master was directed, to ascertain the quantity, &c.; and to distinguish the excepted land, and to ascertain the quantity of such part of the rest as was covered with water for the use of the canal navigation; and how much of the land covered with water was, when the Company took possession, in the occupation of Guest and the under-tenants; and it was declared, that the Company should accept a demise in perpetuity of all the lands, subject to the interest of Guest in the piece of land in the original lease mentioned to have been staked and marked out; reserving a rent of 25*l.* an acre per annum for the whole, except the last-mentioned piece, and for that a proportion of the rent reserved by the original lease during the remainder of the term thereby granted; and after the expiration of that term 25*l.* an acre, to the Plaintiff, his heirs and assigns, from the time the Company took possession. An account of the rents was directed; and an inquiry, what compensation by a sum in gross or an annual rent ought to be made to Guest and the under-tenants for their respective interests in such parts as were covered with water: if a sum in gross, to be paid by the Plaintiff, if an annual rent, by the Company, to Guest and the under-tenants. An account was directed of the rents paid already by the Company to Guest and the under-tenants in respect of the lands, except those marked out for building in the original lease; and in case the compensation to Guest and the under-tenants shall be by a sum in gross, it was directed, that they repay to the Company what shall appear upon such account to have been received by them: but if by a rent, that they deduct and retain the amount of such rent as shall at the time of taking said account be due to them respectively, out of the moneys received by them respectively; and pay the overplus, if any, to the Company. The Master was directed to settle the proportion of rent, which by the original lease ought to be abated by the Plaintiff in respect of the lands to be demised to the Company, exclusive of the land marked out, as aforesaid. An injunction was directed to restrain Guest and the under-tenants from disturbing the possession of the Company under the demise. The Plaintiff was directed to pay the costs of the Defendants, except the Company and Guest, and the Company to repay to the Plaintiff the costs he was directed to pay, together with his own costs.

[*361]   * A petition of rehearing was presented by Guest upon the following grounds: 1st, that the decree is erroneous in giving the Plaintiff any present right or interest in any part of the premises; upon which the Plaintiff had not at the time he served the notice or at the filing of the bill a *bonâ fide* intention of building streets or houses: the building streets or houses being the only purpose, for which the Plaintiff was authorized by the clause of resumption to call for the land; and the Plaintiff has proved, that he had no such intention having stated by his bill the agreement with the Company; and he must have known, they could not take lands for the purpose of building streets or houses, or any other purpose than those of the canal only; therefore the notice was fraudulent, to deprive the Defendant Guest of the benefit he might derive by means of the canal:

Secondly; that the verdict was proceeded upon as conclusive evidence against the Defendant Guest, as to the quantity of land intended to be applied by the Company for the purposes of the navigation: notwithstanding the Company by their answer stated, that they should want a larger quantity for such purposes: therefore the Defendant was not concluded by such verdict; but was entitled to an issue or some other mode of inquiry:

Thirdly; that the decree refers it to the Master to settle the compensation, if any should be made to Guest, for his right and interest in so much land as was covered with water : whereas the Act directs all compensation to be assessed by a jury :

Lastly; that the decree has not directed the costs of the suit to be paid to Guest; as it has directed with regard to the other Defendants, the under-tenants.

Mr. *Richards* and Mr. *Horne,* in support of the petition of rehearing. Mr. *Mansfield* and Mr. *Thomson,* for the Canal Company. Mr. *Romilly* and Mr. *Toller,* for the Plaintiff, in support of the decree.

The Lord CHANCELLOR [ELDON], stating the case   [362] very particularly, delivered his judgment (1).

It must be upon the conviction of the Legislature, that some very considerable public benefit will arise from such an undertaking, that they give such large powers of breaking in upon private property by these Acts of Parliament; and it has happened in this, as in most other instances, that the Commissioners were not satisfied with the very large powers they had. Their award was at least very absurd.

The generality of the latter words of this covenant is not to be confined to streets, nor even to building houses; and the observation is well founded : that the former words being so confined, the generality of the latter shows a different intention. The Company by their answer say, they want only 9 acres 38 perch for the purpose of the canal; and are not warranted to take more : but I am clearly of opinion, that having made the agreement with the Plaintiff for the greater quantity they could not retract. With respect to the 3 roods 20 perch, that were not actually built upon, my opinion, if that had been brought distinctly before the Court, would have been, that if the jury could have been satisfied, that the landlord had an intention *bonâ fide* at the time of building upon them, and afterwards found, he could not, there was no ground for this Court to say, that because that intention was not finally acted upon, therefore the tenant had an equity. There is great difficulty as to frauds upon covenants; and it is much safer to go by the literal construction. Upon that the Plaintiff had a right to resume any part for the purpose of building upon, and for no other purpose. The verdict, that the six acres were taken for the use and purpose of the navigation, is very loose. If five of those acres were taken for the purpose of building ware-houses, that would have been for the purpose of the covenant; the terms of which are not restrained to buildings of any particular * species. Upon the evidence all   [* 363] the six acres were taken for the purpose of building : for their situation, close to the town, at the end of the canal, was most

---

(1) The Lord Chancellor remarked with disapprobation the unusual length of the petion of rehearing; and inclined to make the petitioner pay the expense occasioned by so unnecessarily loading the record, as it appeared, against the advice of his Counsel: but afterwards his Lordship said, that, as this was a very complicated case, and allowing for the apprehension and anxiety of the party, that in bringing it before the Court nothing material should be omitted, he should simply affirm the decree.

gave and devised the capital messuage, called Great Witley, and
all other the messuages, manors, lands, tenements, and hereditaments
late belonging to Thomas, Lord Foley, deceased, which he (the testator) was entitled to under his Lordship's will, or otherwise, in the
counties of Worcester, Stafford, Middlesex, Salop, and Hereford,
(except the manor of Malvern, and certain other premises therein
after otherwise devised), whether freehold, leasehold, or copyhold,
subject nevertheless to the charge thereinafter mentioned for making
up the deficiency, if any should arise in paying his legacies therein
mentioned, to and to the use of his brother Robert Foley and
Abram Turner, their executors, &c. for the term of ninety-nine years,
to commence from the testator's decease, without impeachment of
waste: and from and after the end, expiration, or other sooner
determination, of the said term, to the use of his eldest son Thomas
Foley for life: remainder to trustees to preserve contingent remainders; and from and after his decease to the use of other trustees
for 100 years, to commence from his decease; in trust for raising a
jointure for any wife or wives he should marry, out of any part of
the annual rents, issues, and profits, of the said manors, &c. not
exceeding the yearly value of 2000*l.*, or an annuity or rent-charge,
not exceeding the yearly value of 1500*l.* clear of all deductions;
and to pay the same half yearly on the 25th of March and 29th of
September: the first payment to be made on which of those days
shall first happen next after the decease of Thomas Foley; and from
and after the end, expiration, or other sooner determination, of the
said term of 100 years, and subject thereto, to the use of other
trustees, their executors &c. for a term of 1000 years to commence
from the day of the decease of his said son Thomas Foley; in trust
by and out of the rents, issues and profits, of the same manors, messuages, lands, tenements, and hereditaments, or by sale or
[* 365]   mortgage * thereof, or of a competent part thereof, or by
other ways and means, to levy and raise any sum or sums
of money not exceeding in the whole the sum of 30,000*l.* for and
towards the portion and provision of all and every the younger
child and children of the said Thomas Foley, for such estates, in such
proportions, under such restrictions, and to be paid to him, her, or
them, at such time and times, and with such interest or maintenance,
as the said Thomas Foley should by any deed, will, or appointment,
by him to be executed in the presence of two or more witnesses,
limit, declare, or appoint; and for want of such limitation, declaration, or appointment, to be equally divided between them, if more
than one, share and share alike; and from and after the end, expiration, or other sooner determination, of the said term of 1000
years, and subject thereto, to the use of the first and other sons of
the said Thomas Foley in tail male; with remainders to the use of
Edward Foley, the testator's second son, and his first and other sons,
and Andrew Foley, his third son, and his first and other sons, in
strict settlement; with the like powers to his said sons of making
jointures and charging portions: with similar remainders to the

daughters of the testator and their sons successively ; and then to
the daughters of his sons and daughters respectively, as tenants in
common ; remainder to his brother in tail ; remainder to his sister
in fee.

The testator then declared his will to be, that all the messuages or
tenements, which he held by lease from the trustees or devisees of
the late Countess Dowager of Oxford in the county of Middlesex,
should go and be enjoyed by his said trustees and such person and
persons, upon such conditions, uses, trusts, intents, and purposes, as
the said manor of Witley and other the estates of the said Thomas
Lord Foley deceased therein before limited, as far as the nature
thereof would admit ; and he gave all other the leasehold estates,
late of the said Thomas Lord Foley, which he (the testator) was
entitled unto by virtue of his Lordship's will, to Robert Foley and
Abram Turner, their executors, &c. for and upon the same uses
and purposes as the manor of Witley and other the estates of the
said Thomas Lord Foley, as therein before limited, or as near as by
the tenure thereof the same could be limited ; with the power of
renewing such of the said leases as were renewable.

* The testator then devised other estates in the county of   [* 366]
Hereford, to Robert Foley and Abraham Turner, their executors, &c. for a term of 101 years, to commence from the day of his
decease, without impeachment of waste ; and after the end, expiration, or other sooner determination, of that term, and subject thereto,
to Edward Foley for life ; remainder to trustees to preserve contingent
remainders ; remainder to trustees for 102 years, to commence from his
decease, without impeachment of waste, in trust for raising a jointure
of 1200*l.* a-year out of the annual rents, issues, and profits, &c. (as
expressed in the limitations of the other estates to the eldest son) ;
and from and immediately after the end, &c. of that term, to trustees for 500 years, to commence from the death of Edward ; in
trust by the ways and means aforesaid, or by any other ways and
means to levy and raise portions, not exceeding 10,000*l.*, for his
younger children, for such estates, in such portions, under such restrictions, and to be paid at such times, as Edward Foley should by
deed or will appoint ; and for want of appointment equally ; and
from and after the end or other determination, of that term to his
first and other sons in tail male ; with similar remainders to Andrew
and his sons and Thomas and his sons successively ; and then to the
daughters of the testator, &c.

The testator devised other estates to the use of his son Andrew
for life ; remainder to trustees to preserve contingent remainders ;
remainder to trustees for 98 years, to commence from his decease,
without impeachment of waste ; in trust for raising an additional increase of jointure for his present or any after-taken wife, out of all
or any part of the annual rents, issues, and profits, &c. (as in the
other limitations) not exceeding 400*l.* a year ; and from and immediately after the end or other sooner determination of that term,
and subject thereto, to trustees for 999 years, to commence from the

decease of Andrew Foley; in trust by the ways and means aforesaid, or by any other ways or means to levy and raise any sum, not
exceeding 10,000l. for and towards the additional portion of his
younger children, for such estates, &c. (as in the limitations to Edward); and with similar remainders to his first and other sons, and
Edward and Thomas and the testator's daughters, and their sons
respectively, &c.

[* 367]   *The trusts of the terms of 99 years and 101 years
were declared to be, that the said Robert Foley and Abraham Turner, and the survivor, &c. should take the rents, issues, and
profits, of all the manors, &c. and cut timber and underwood as
they shall think proper, not exceeding 3000l. in one year; and out
of those funds and the rents, &c. in the first place according to
.their will and pleasure, and not otherwise, allow yearly or oftener to
or for the use of his sons Thomas and Edward Foley any sum or
sums of money, not exceeding in the whole in any one year 6000l.,
until such of their debts as were then provided for and should be
due at his decease should be discharged; and in the next place to
pay and discharge a mortgage, and all such of the debts of his said
two eldest sons and the interest due thereon respectively as in any
schedule or schedules annexed to his said will, or in any other schedule or schedules by him hereafter to be made and subscribed, should
be contained; or as they, his said trustees, in their judgment and
discretion should think fit and expedient; but so as that neither his
said sons nor their creditors should have any interest in or power
over the estates; and after the decease of his said sons, and payment of the debts, &c. the terms to attend the inheritance.

The will then contained provisions, that in case of the death of
his eldest son without issue male, Edward and his sons should take
the estates devised to him; and Andrew and his sons all the other
estates, except some devised to be sold; and that the portions, legacies, &c. under the will should be in satisfaction for all portions,
&c. under the marriage settlement of the testator.   Then after
some directions as to legacies and an annuity, he charged all the estates devised to him by Thomas Lord Foley, and not herein devised
to be sold, with so much as his personal estate should be deficient to
answer the legacies herein-before given, or to be given by any codicil; and he devised other estates in trust to be sold; and the money
to be applied in payment of his legacies and annuity, as aforesaid,
and afterwards of the schedule debts, as the money under the terms
of 99 years and 101 years.   He then gave several legacies, and
among them to his grand-daughter Caroline Georgiana Harriet,
daughter of Thomas Foley, 5000l.

[* 368]   The testator by a codicil, taking notice * of the death of
Abraham Turner, appointed his son Andrew Foley a trustee in his stead.

The testator died some time afterwards; leaving Thomas Lord
Foley his eldest son and heir, a tenant for life under the will; who
died in 1793; leaving Thomas Lord Foley, his only son, and one

daughter Caroline Georgiana Harriet, his only younger child; who in 1796 married Christopher Codrington, Esquire; and by the settlement previous to that marriage, dated the 8th of August, 1796, reciting, that the last Lord Foley had died without having executed any appointment respecting the said sum of 30,000l. and that Miss Foley was become entitled to the whole of that sum; and that it had been agreed, that the said sum should immediately after the intended marriage become the absolute property of Mr. Codrington, and that the surviving trustee of the term of 1000 years should covenant to assign the residue of the said term to him, as soon after the marriage as it could conveniently be done by way of mortgage for securing the said sum of 30,000l. with interest from the 5th of July, 1795, to which time all interest on the said sum had been paid, it was witnessed, and the trustee covenanted accordingly.

By other indentures of the same date, reciting, that Mr. Codrington was desirous of making the said 30,000l. a provision for his daughters and younger sons by the said marriage, he covenanted, that he would, after the said mortgage to be made to him, assign the same, upon trust to permit him to receive the interest of the said 30,000l. for his life; and after his decease to pay the said sum of 30,000l. amongst all his younger children by the said marriage, in such shares and proportions as he and Mrs. Codrington should appoint, as therein mentioned; with various provisions in default of appointment; and in case there should be no younger child, who should become entitled to the said sum of 30,000l. upon trust for Mr. Codrington, his executors, &c.; with a power to the trustees with the consent of Mr. and Mrs. Codrington to call in the 30,000l. and invest it in the funds in the names of the trustees.

By indentures, dated the 1st of September, 1796, the surviving trustee of the term of 1000 years assigned to Mr. Codrington; to hold for the residue of the term, * subject to redemp-   [*369] tion; if Lord Foley or the person, who for the time being should be entitled to the premises comprised in the term immediately expectant on the determination thereof, should pay to Mr. Codrington the sum of 30,000l. with the interest due thereon from the 5th of July, 1795, on the 1st of March next; and by indentures, dated the 2d of September, 1796, Mr. Codrington assigned and transferred the said sum of 30,000l. and the interest to become due from the marriage and all his interest in the term of 1000 years; to hold for the residue of the term, subject to redemption, as aforesaid; to have and receive the said sum of 30,000l. and the interest thereof to become due from the marriage upon the trusts and for the intents and purposes expressed concerning the said sum and interest in the settlement, dated the 8th of August, 1796. The trusts of the term of 100 years were satisfied.

The bill in the first cause was filed by Mr. and Mrs. Codrington, and their children, four infant daughters, against Lord Foley, who was under the age of twenty-one, about eighteen, and the trustees of the term of 1000 years; praying an account of the principal and

interest due on the security of the premises comprised in the term of
1000 years; that what shall be found due may be paid by the Defendant Lord Foley to the other Defendants upon the trusts of the
settlement; or that Lord. Foley and all other persons entitled to
redeem may be foreclosed; and that what shall be coming from
the said account may be raised by sale of a sufficient part of the
premises comprised in the term of 1000 years; and that the trustees
may be directed to pay the Plaintiff Christopher Codrington what
shall appear to be due for arrears of interest of the said sum of
30,000*l.*

The trustees of the term by their answer admitted that the interest made payable upon the sum of 30,000*l.* is at the rate of 4 per
cent. only; that no payment had been made on that account; and
that the Plaintiffs had applied to them to raise that sum and the interest due, or at least to procure the interest to be raised to 5 per
cent.

The Defendant Andrew Foley, the surviving trustee in the terms
of 98 years and 101 years, and also one of the trustees in
[* 370]   the *marriage settlement of the Plaintiffs, by his answer
stated, that under the trusts of these terms the yearly sum
of 6000*l.* was paid in the proportion of 4000*l.* to the testator's son
Thomas Foley during his life, and 2000*l.* to his son Edward Foley;
which latter payment still continues; that their debts upon bonds
and notes and by simple contract at the testator's death amounted
to 87,800*l.*; great part of which has been since paid under the trusts
of those terms; all, that remains unpaid, amounting only to about
12,112*l.*; which the Defendant believes will be wholly satisfied by
Midsummer 1802. He farther stated, that at the testator's death
several other sums were due from his sons Thomas and Edward
Foley for principal moneys advanced to them in the purchase of annuities granted by them to the amount of 120,454*l.*, exclusive of a
large sum due for arrears; and the annuity creditors in 1792 agreed
to release all claims for arrears of their respective annuities, and to
accept their principal money originally advanced by them, on having
the said principal secured by annual instalments of 8000*l.*, but without interest, out of the trust estates comprised in the terms of 99
years and 101 years. That object was carried into effect by indentures, dated the 1st of March, 1793; under which the sum of
56,000*l.* has been paid by instalments in part discharge of the principal sum; in respect of which 64,454*l.* remains a charge on the
trust estates.

The answer suggested, that the Defendant cannot concur in raising the principal sum of 30,000*l.* or increasing the interest on account of the infancy of the Defendant Lord Foley, and the trusts of
the term of 99 years not being fully performed. The Defendant
farther insisted, that in case these impediments should not be considered sufficient; yet as the Plaintiff Mr. Codrington previously to
the execution of the settlement expressly promised and agreed to
wait for the principal and interest, until Lord Foley should attain

the age of twenty-one, and the assignment of the term to the Plaintiff being made under a persuasion, that he would not attempt to make the same available to enforce payments prejudicial to Lord Foley, until the trusts of the prior term of 99 years were satisfied, or, at least, until Lord Foley attained the age of twenty-one, the Plaintiffs are not entitled to the relief prayed.

The agreement of Mr. Codrington to wait, till Lord   [371]
Foley should attain the age of twenty-one, was also set up
by the answer of Edward Foley; and according to the answers and the evidence of an agent the circumstances were these.   The agent being in July 1796 sent to London to take instructions for the settlement informed Mr. Codrington of the situation of Miss Foley's fortune; explaining the trusts of the will; and particularly, that she was entitled to 5000*l.*, a legacy from her grand-father, and also to the said sum of 30,000*l.*, as the only younger child of her father, carrying interest from his death in 1793, charged on all the estates of Lord Foley comprised in the term of 99 years.   The deponent then stated the trusts of the terms of 99 years and 101 years, the amount of the debts, with which the estates were charged, and the progress that had been made in reducing them; and Mr. Codrington having heard the statement said, as that was the situation of Miss Foley's fortune, he would wait till Lord Foley came of age; but wished to have the 5000*l.* as soon as it could be got in.   The answers and evidence represented the general understanding of all persons concerned in the settlement to have been, that Mr. Codrington must wait, till the trusts of the terms of 99 years and 101 years were satisfied, or till Lord Foley should be of age; and stated, that the interest upon the sum of 30,000*l.* was made to commence from the 5th of July, 1795; as Mr. Andrew Foley had advanced money for Miss Foley's education; and it was agreed, the sums advanced for that purpose, which amounted to two years' interest, should be deducted from the interest of the 30,000*l.*

The Cross Bill prayed, that the trusts of the terms of 99 years and 101 years should be fully satisfied, before those of the term of 1000 years should be executed.

An objection was taken on the part of the Plaintiffs to the admission of evidence, as being in contradiction to the deed.   That objection was over-ruled, and the evidence read: the Lord Chancellor declaring it admissible to the point, that having it distinctly before him he understood his right; and gave it up.

Mr. *Sutton* and Mr. *Romilly*, for the Plaintiffs.—The objections against raising this portion are, first, that as it is to be
raised out of a *reversionary term it cannot be made avail-   [* 372]
able, until the trusts of the preceding term are satisfied:
2dly, that the Plaintiff has waived his right.

Upon the first objection, there is no such absolute rule; though the Court leans against that construction, if they can discover any circumstances, affording an inference, that the portion was not to be raised, till the term came into possession.   None of the reasons

usually assigned, for the sake of the reversioner, &c. apply to this
case. This is no more in the direction of the Court than in the
option of the trustees; as Lord Macclesfield says in *Sandys* v.
Sandys (1). How could this power be executed, so long as the
trusts of the preceding term remained unsatisfied; but by the trusts
of the reversionary term. It is true, the children of Lord Foley, the
son, could not have their portions raised in the life of their father.
That the children may not be independent of their father, and many
other reasons, operate to that: but after the death of the father the
natural time for raising the portions arrives. No argument arises
from the legacy of 5000*l.* to Mrs. Codrington. Only one child was
born at the date of the will; and the testator could not know, what
number of children there might be. It cannot therefore be contended, that his bounty to her was to be a satisfaction, till the other provision could be conveniently paid.

The cases upon this subject are very numerous. *Greaves* v. *Mattison* (2), *Corbett* v. *Maidwell* (3). Certainly the former of these
cases has been much observed upon; and was not approved in
Reresby v. *Newland* (4): but the latter has been followed. *Gerard*
v. *Gerard* (5), *Staniforth* v. *Staniforth* (6). In *Butler* v. *Duncomb* (7) there was an express provision for raising the portion after
the commencement of the term. Those cases were very strong.
In *Pierpoint* v. *Lord Cheney* (8) the question was, whether interest
should be raised by mortgaging a reversionary term. The principle
to be extracted from all the cases is, that unless something appears
upon the face of the instrument to postpone the raising of the portion, it is to be raised, though out of the reversionary
[*373]   *term. *Ravenhill* v. *Dansey* (9). *Brome* v. *Berkeley* (10);
in which case it was refused; because the maintenance,
which was to precede the portion, was not to commence, until the
estate of the trustees should take effect in possession. *Hebblethwaite*
v. *Cartwright* (11) before Lord Talbot; who was Counsel in most of
the preceding cases before Lord Macclesfield. *Stanley* v. *Stanley* (12), *Hall* v. *Carter* (13). *Stevens* v. *Dethick* (14) turned upon
the distinction taken in *Brome* v. *Berkeley*. *Lyon* v. *The Duke of
Chandos* (15). In *Smith* v. *Evans* (16) Lord Northington adopted

(1) 1 P. Will. 707; see 709.
(2) Sir T. Jones, 201.
(3) 1 Salk. 159.
(4) 2 P. Will. 93.
(5) 2 Vern. 458.
(6) 2 Vern. 460.
(7) 1 P. Will. 448.
(8) 1 P. Will. 488.
(9) 2 P. Will. 179.
(10) 2 P. Will. 484.
(11) For. 31.
(12) 1 Atk. 549.
(13) 2 Atk. 354.
(14) 3 Atk. 39.
(15) 3 Atk. 416.
(16) Amb. 633.

the ideas of those Chancellors, who had refused it, and of those, who had done it; and observed, that the inconvenience of a younger child starving for want of his portion is as great as the injuring the estate of the eldest son by raising the portion out of the reversion. The last case is *Lady Clinton* v. *Lord Robert Seymour* (1); in which the Master of the Rolls observes, that Lord Macclesfield in *Pierpoint* v. *Lord Cheney* thought himself bound to raise the maintenance, if the infant wanted it; and only directed the inquiry to see, whether it would be for her benefit, and would leave sufficient for her portion. It is plain therefore, that with all this reluctance the Court has considered itself bound; where it could be seen, that the payment was not to be postponed. The result is, that the Court must find something to resist the application of this doctrine. The objection upon which the Court have hesitated, the father having been tenant for life in most of the cases, does not exist in this. No time being limited for payment of the portion, and the term commencing upon the father's death, it would carry interest from that time. The question in all the cases has been with the person entitled to the estate, contending, that raising it by anticipation would be an injury to him. Those cases have no analogy to this; in which the Defendant is entitled to an estate tail, not to commence, till this portion is paid. What principle of equity is there for postponing the raising of this portion to his estate tail? It appears by the answer that all the incumbrances, the subject of the prior trusts, have been paid, except 12,500*l.*: and that might have been paid long ago by the rents and profits; and then this sum of 30,000*l.* would have been the first charge. The Plaintiff only * de-   [* 374] sires the arrears of interest from 1795; to which time it was paid; and that the interest may be raised from four to five per cent.

Upon the second point, there is nothing amounting to a waiver of the right. The Plaintiff acquiesces in the representation, that he can have neither principal nor interest, till the prior trusts are satisfied; but that representation is founded in mistake; and therefore cannot affect the right. A waiver presupposes an admission of the right; but it was represented to him, and understood by all parties, that he had no such right. Afterwards, when his right was discovered, he calls upon them. It ought to be shown, that being aware of his right he contracted to give it up; but the evidence amounts only to this, that he acquiesced in that untrue statement without inquiry.

Mr. *Mansfield* and Mr. *Lewis*, for the Defendant.—Upon the first question, with respect to the inconvenience, there is no fund for the interest; and as to the principal, nothing could be more ruinous than raising this portion by this reversionary term. It is to be postponed, not to the end of the term of 99 years, but to the period, when the prior trusts shall be satisfied; which trust are very pecu-

(1) *Ante*, vol. iv. 440.

liar. This portion is to be raised by sale or mortgage, by the common words: but it is impossible to obtain a mortgage, and a sale must be extremely disadvantageous. Nothing could be raised during Lord Foley's life; and till those trusts are satisfied, he could not be entitled to any thing. There is no more difficulty in supposing, the testator would shut out his grand-daughter, than his son, till those debts should be paid. In the course of the next year all the debts remaining will be paid; and then Lord Foley suffering a recovery can pay the portion without embarrassment. All the questions in those cases arose upon the circumstance, that the parent was living; and it is curious to observe, upon what circumstances they turned: every Lord Chancellor regretting, when considering himself bound to raise the portion. Great discretion is reposed in the trustees as to all except the scheduled debts. After those are paid, the incumbrances will be no more than the instalments of 8000*l.* a-year for a few years, and a clear fund will remain beyond that of several thousands. The intention was, that, whenever the condi-
[* 375] tion of the * fund was such as to leave sufficient disencumbered for payment of this portion, then the portion should be raised; and it could not be intended to be raised, until the fund should be sufficiently disencumbered.

Upon the question of waiver the Plaintiff agreed to wait, at least till Lord Foley should be of age: his solicitor and conveyancer having the will before them. Under these circumstances will the Court do this contrary to that agreement; when Lord Foley will be of age in a few months: no fund now existing: every guinea of the rents and profits, except what is absolutely necessary for maintenance, being appropriated to the debts? The legacy of 5000*l.* is evidence against this attempt.

July 27*th.* The Lord CHANCELLOR [ELDON] (after stating the case very particularly).—Under these circumstances the Plaintiffs say, they are entitled to have this sum of 30,000*l.* raised, with 5 per cent. interest. If they can succeed in having it raised, by the effect of raising it they will of course receive 5 per cent.; for at present money cannot be got at 4 per cent., the ordinary interest of the Court. The claim is resisted upon two grounds: first, that under the effect of the will they are not entitled at present to have this sum raised, nor to have the interest either at 4 or 5 per cent. paid; founded upon this farther objection, that the trusts of the terms of 99 years and 101 years are not yet satisfied; and though the interest will run on, while those trusts are unsatisfied, yet that neither principal nor interest can be raised, till those trust are satisfied.

The second objection is, that if according to the rules of the Court, independent of the circumstances of the Plaintiff's conduct, he is entitled to have that sum raised and the interest paid, yet, attending to the circumstances of his conduct prior to and during the treaty of marriage, one part of the terms of the contract is,

that this sum should not be raised; and with a view to the convenience of the estate under all the circumstances at the 'time of the
marriage he entered into a contract, bargaining not to have that
sum raised nor the interest paid, till the trusts of those terms are
satisfied.

* As to the latter ground, I am perfectly satisfied upon   [* 376]
the answers and the evidence, that it is impossible to sustain that ground of defence. The whole of the case upon that
amounts simply to this; that every party in that treaty took it for
granted, that the effect of the will was, that this money could not
be raised; and the Plaintiff's conduct comes to no more than this;
that such a representation being made to him, and those, who advised him, understanding it so, he expressed his willingness to marry,
notwithstanding that part of Mrs. Codrington's fortune could not
come into possession, till the trusts of those terms should be satisfied. There is no ground to impute a breach of contract to the
Plaintiff in filing this bill. It will be more accurately represented by
putting it thus; that if he was entitled to it, no one asked him to
give it up; if it was matter of doubt, it was not the intention of the
parties to contract upon it as matter of doubt, and to decide in the
contract the doubt as against Mr. Codrington: but they all took it
for granted, there was no power in the trustees to raise this; and
therefore there could be no title in him to call for it. The proposal
was made on the one hand under that persuasion; and under that
persuasion, as matter of persuasion and not of contract, the marriage was had.

The cause was argued, and very ably, with reference to a great
number of cases, which have not a very direct application to the
question furnished by this particular will. Most of those cases, I
may say, all of them, were cases, in which the question was, whether
the portion was to be raised without prejudice to some life estate
antecedently limited and then existing. Previously to the case of
Corbett v. *Maidwell* (1) there had been some cases, which have been
treated in subsequent cases as very strong: particularly *Greaves* v.
Mattison (2); with regard to which I observe in *Corbett* v. *Maidwell*, Lord Cooper does not seem in any degree to disapprove of it.
He lays down the rule thus:

" 1st. That though a term is limited in remainder to commence
after the death of the father, yet if the trust is to raise
a portion payable at the age of eighteen or a day of * mar-   [* 377]
riage, without question the daughter shall not wait the
death of her father; but at the age of eighteen or marriage may
compel a sale of the term."

" 2dly, So it is, if the trust of a term for raising daughters' portions
be limited to take effect, in case the father dies without issue male

(1) 1 Salk. 159.
(2) T. Jones, 201. See Mr. Cox's note to *Butler* v. *Duncomb*, 1 P. Will. 453;
and the note, *ante*, vol. ii. 481; *Lady Clinton* v. *Lord Robert Seymour*, iv. 440;
post, vol. xix. 528.

by his wife, and the wife die without issue male leaving a daughter, in such case the term is saleable in the life of the father."

Lord Cowper doubted, whether he could have gone so far, in case the matter were *res integra.* He then states the reasoning, upon which that was founded; that by the death of the mother the possibility of issue male was extinct; that all, that was contingent, had happened; and then states *Greaves* v. *Mattison*; in which case, I take it to be clear from the context, the remainder to the first son in tail male was to the first son by that marriage.

But in *Corbett* v. *Maidwell* the portions were to be raised for daughters, who should be unmarried or not provided for at the death of their father. Lord Cowper says, they could not be raised; for all the contingency had not happened; and it could not be determined till the death of the father, who was entitled. He makes no remark in disapprobation of *Greaves* v. *Mattison*; which is very strongly observed upon in subsequent cases by Lord Macclesfield. In one case, I think, he ascribes to it the term "nonsense." In another he speaks of the convenience and inconvenience. Lord Cowper's observation as to that is, that it would be to no purpose for any one to make deeds, if the argument of convenience or inconvenience should prevail to over-rule them. Several decisions were made afterwards by Lord Macclesfield; who seems to disapprove any inclination but a leaning to lay hold of any circumstances to disappoint the claim to have the portion raised in the life of the father. He appears to have been much influenced by arguments of policy as to convenience and inconvenience; and he states conversations, impertinent enough, which he supposes young ladies to hold with their fathers. Lord Hardwicke follows him to the full extent; if he does not go beyond it; and both of them seem to [* 378] depart from Lord Cowper's concluding observation * by giving great effect to arguments of convenience and inconvenience. Lord Hardwicke however in *Stanley* v. *Stanley* (1) lays down the rule thus:

"If there be a term for years, or other estate, limited to trustees for raising portions for daughters, payable at a certain time, which is become a vested interest, they shall not stay till the death of the father and mother, unless some intention appears to postpone it; and if there does, the Court will always take notice of such intention, and postpone it accordingly; and the latter cases, as *Brome* v. *Berkeley*, 2 P. Wms. 484, and others, show, the Court will lay hold of very small grounds, that speak the intent of the parties to hinder the raising the portions in the life of the father and mother."

Lord Hardwicke seems to have adopted very much Lord Macclesfield's opinions, or rather those of Lord Trevor; who, it seems from the conversation between him and Lord Macclesfield, stated 3 Atk. 42, thought, Lord Macclesfield went too far. Lord Hardwicke felt

(1) 1 Atk. 549.

all the inclination to narrow the rule ; as Lord Trevor expressed it :
but with that inclination he lays down the rule in *Stanley* v. *Stanley* ;
as I have stated it.

According to Forester, 32, Lord Talbot thought this the true
rule ; that it depends upon the particular penning of the trust ; and
he agrees with Lord Cowper; that if all the contingencies had happened, the portion must be raised, notwithstanding the inconvenience, or there would be an end of deeds. Lord Northington follows him ; and expresses his approbation of all, that the Court had
done in all times; for in *Smith* v. *Evans* (1) he expresses in a degree an approbation of the general rule, and of the decisions, which
upon small circumstances have formed departures from it. He ad-
vises that the Court should adhere to both ; doubting, whether those
latter decisions should have been made.

In *Conway* v. *Conway* (2) Lord Thurlow is made to say this :
" Where a man gives portions, charged on a term to arise upon
the death of a party, it shows, that they are not to be paid
* till after the death of that party ; and that though it be   [* 379]
upon attaining twenty-one or marriage, yet that it can
only be, where the term shall come into existence."

Upon looking at my own brief in that cause and to other cases I
am satisfied, Lord Thurlow never did express himself in the words
there attributed to him ; which appear to contradict all the authorities. That doctrine is directly contrary to that of Lord Cowper,
Lord Hardwicke, and what all the cases, whether proceeding upon
sufficient circumstances denoting intention, or not, do in effect say,
that there must be some circumstances in the will or settlement denoting the intention to take the case out of the general rule ; which
is, that the portions shall be raised at the days or times limited, unless the will or settlement contain circumstances indicating an intention, that they are not to be raised at those days or times.

In *Lady Clinton's Case* (3) Lord Alvanley expresses himself
thus (4) :

" But notwithstanding the numerous cases upon this point, in
most of which the party contending for the portion or maintenance
has succeeded, it is now perfectly settled, and the more modern
cases have clearly established, and it appears to have been the opinion of Lord Macclesfield, who always found fault with what his predecessors had done, but always went as far as they did, that the
Court will lay hold of any words, from which it can be fairly inferred, that it was not the intention to charge a reversionary term with
raising portions in that manner, which must bring infinite inconvenience upon the reversioner ; and if upon the context of the settlement any thing can be collected, by which it may appear, that it
could not be the intention of the parties to raise them in that way,

(1) Amb. 633.
(2) 3 Bro. C. C. 267.
(3) *Lady Clinton* v. *Lord Robert Seymour, ante,* vol. iv. 440.
(4) *Ante,* vol. iv. 460.

the Court is extremely eager to lay hold of that. That has been uniformly laid down by Lord Cowper, Lord Macclesfield, and all their successors."

Upon this general state of the doctrine of the Court it appears to me, that the proper rule is that Lord Talbot states; that [* 380] the * raising or not raising must depend upon the particular penning of the trust and the intention of the instrument. I do not think, the Court ought to be eager to lay hold of circumstances. The Court ought to hold an equal mind, while construing the instrument; and I cannot agree with what is said in *Stanley* v. *Stanley*, that very small grounds are sufficient. If they are sufficient to denote the intention, they are not small grounds: if they are not sufficient to denote the intention, the Court does not act according to its duty by treating them as sufficient; thereby disappointing the true intention of the instrument.

The rule upon the whole depends upon this; whether it was the intention of the parties to the instrument, attending to the whole of it, that the portion should or should not be raised in this manner; taking it *primâ facie* to be the intention upon the general rule, if there is nothing more than a limitation to the parent for life, with a term to raise portions at the age of twenty-one or marriage, if there is nothing more, and the interests are vested, and the contingencies have happened, at which the portions are to be paid, the interest is payable, and the portions must be raised in the only manner, in which they can be raised: that is, by mortgage or sale of the reversionary term. It appears to me, that this case is distinguishable from all these cases in this circumstance; that this is not attempted to be raised with any prejudice to the life estate of the parent. Therefore if the policy of a provident or improvident marriage would apply in other cases, it would not here; for it is clear as to the children of all the sons none of them can call for their portions in the lives of their fathers; the sum depending upon the appointment of the father by deed or will; which therefore might not become effectual till his death; and the proportions and restrictions, in and under which they are to take the same, and the times, must also depend upon the will of the father. Therefore, if the trusts of these terms were satisfied, still the portions could not be raised. There is no pretence of inconvenience as to the policy of marriage, or with regard to the enjoyment of the life estate, or the estate tail; for that must also have commenced in possession, before any child could claim the portion.

[* 381] * This will does not provide for a great many cases, that might, and some of which did, happen. The person, who drew the will, undertook a task so difficult, that it was hardly possible sufficiently to execute it. The testator meant to give to the trustees of the terms of 99 years and 101 years a power of providing for the creditors of his two sons; excluding from all interest in the premises comprised in those terms the creditors and his eldest and second sons. Whether he meant, that creditors of every description

should have the benefit of it, that annuity creditors by liquidating
their demands into a principal sum should have the benefit of it, it is
not useful now to consider ; for the words are sufficient to enable
the trustees to provide for such creditors. But he forgot, that his
first named devisee was his eldest son and heir at law ; and if the
eldest and second sons and the creditors were to have no interest, it
was not adverted to, that the law would create an interest somewhere. Notwithstanding this therefore, the creditors found, they
could either compel the trustees to provide for them, or there was a
resulting trust for the eldest son ; and if he did not take under the
devise, he would take in that way ; and so they might come at their
debts, whether the trustees chose they should be paid, or not. That
raised some suits very embarrassing in expense, that led to the arrangement made by the trustees. The testator also forgot another
case, that might happen ; that Lord Foley, Edward Foley, and Andrew Foley, might all of them die within two or three years after
the testator ; leaving a great number of younger children. Certainly it was not adverted to, if that case had happened, how they were
to be provided with their portions ; regard being had to the powers
of the trustees of the terms of 99 years and 101 years to provide
for all these creditors. Whether it was thought, that if Lord Foley
and Edward Foley should die, the trustees would do well to make
no provision for creditors, or, whether they calculated upon their
living, until the creditors should be satisfied by the application of the
rents, in which case there would be no embarrassment, because the
children could claim no portion in the life of either of them, does
not appear. Edward Foley is still living. Lord Foley is dead ; and
an arrangement has taken place with the annuity creditors ; turning
their demand into a capital sum, to a very large amount, about
80,000*l.* The demands of the other creditors were reduced to
13,000*l.*, and the annuity creditors were reduced to about
60,000*l.*: *and these sums were to be payable by in- [*382]
stalments of 8000*l* a year.

It does not appear in the cause, whether as against the tenant in
tail Lord Foley the mode of paying the annuity creditors and the
other creditors by these instalments does or does not exhaust the
whole rents and profits ; whether the tenant in tail notwithstanding
this arrangement does or does not receive any income from his
estate tail : but it is clear, the term for raising the portion over-
rides the estate tail ; and if the intention of the settlement is, that
the tenant in tail should receive any thing, before the trusts of these
terms are satisfied, *a fortiori* those, who take paramount, must.
Therefore if Mr. Codrington could now be answered, that he should
not receive the interest of the 30,000*l.* till those trusts are satisfied,
and he should say to the trustees, that they had applied some of the
rents and profits to the maintenance or to any other purpose for the
tenant in tail, he might say, that if they were right in asserting, that
he could not claim either the interest or the principal of the portion,
until the trusts of these terms are satisfied, they were wrong in that

application; and he might call that back, and apply what had been
so paid to the trusts of those terms; to the intent, that those terms
might be cleared of those trusts as expeditiously as possible for the
benefit of him, entitled at all events to have the portion raised
against the estate tail. It is clear therefore, if the bargain with the
creditors has not exhausted the whole rents and profits, the trustees
have a fund, that he has a right to have applied to his principal and
interest, and which upon the principle of the trustees themselves he
might have applied to the benefit of the creditors to discharge the
trusts of the terms for his benefit. If the trustees say, the creditors
have no right but what depends upon their will and pleasure, he
might say, their will and pleasure has determined, that he must have
it, by saying, the creditors shall not; for it is clear, the trustees
cannot keep it; and it remains to be disposed of, as if there was no
direction. It is clear therefore, they are wrong in their own principle: but they have dealt rightly as to the tenant in tail; the will
giving these respective estates for life to the three sons; giving powers in their lives to provide for their younger children at their deaths
a fund, that according to the express terms of the will in the case of
Lord Foley would carry interest, and upon the rules of the Court
would carry interest as to the children of the other tenants
[*383]   for life, having become vested, when they had * occasion
for them, viz. upon attaining twenty-one or marriage, and
which by the rules of the Court would sink, if they did not attain
those periods (1); and providing in the case of Andrew Foley in
the same manner as with respect to the others; and as to him, it is
clear, there is no term over-riding his life estate, and no power for
jointuring, &c. interposing. It is clear, the testator meant the portions to vest immediately upon the death of Andrew, if the children
had occasion for them. A strong inference arises from that, that he
did not mean to postpone the portions of the children of the two
eldest sons, till the trusts of those terms were satisfied: the management being committed to the trustees; who might by an arrangement, that would not defeat the purpose, provide for those creditors,
if they thought proper. There is also a strong inference from this;
that in a given event Andrew Foley was to come into the situation
of Edward as to the estates devised to Edward, and as to his powers
of jointuring, raising portions, &c. It is true, he is not by that de-
vested of his original estates. He remains owner of them with the
powers originally given to him. But the testator never meant, that
if Andrew came into Edward's situation, he should not have those
powers as to those estates, till after these trusts are satisfied, but with
regard to his original estates he should have those powers.

Upon the whole, the intention was, that these portions should be
payable at such ages, days, and times, as Lord Foley should appoint;
and that power precludes all arguments of inconvenience and impol-

_____

(1) *Pearce* v. *Loman, ante,* vol. iii. 135. Mr. Cox's note to *The Duke of Chandos* v. *Talbot,* 2 P. Will. 612.

icy, and the possibility of its interfering with his life estate. But his giving that power to Lord' Foley, and directing interest till that time, at which Lord Foley should fix the principal to be paid, and the thing being a portion, is demonstrative of his intention that, notwithstanding the trusts of those terms are not satisfied, the portion was vested at such time as Lord Foley should appoint after the decease of Lord Foley, carrying interest in the mean time.

There is much less inconvenience in this case than in holding the doctrine in *Corbett* v. *Maidwell* and *Stanley* v. *Stanley ;* for *there the rule was laid down, as applying to a life estate;   [*384] out of the rents and profits of which the interest of the portion could not be satisfied, but must accumulate against the reversion.   That is not the case here; for the testator has given 6000l. a-year to Lord Foley and Edward Foley.   The rest of the rents and profits of their life estates are left, as far as he could as to the disposal of them, to the absolute discretion of the trustees; and they might collect, that it was possible, that Lord Foley and Edward Foley might die, before any arrangement could be complete; and therefore as to the powers under these terms they had to manage an arrangement, which ought to provide for the younger children and the eldest equally of Lord Foley and Edward Foley; and it was in their power to make an arrangement with the creditors, that would leave them the means of providing for these portions in events, that might have happened; without which some of these children must have starved; and others have been doomed to that pittance, which was never intended to be all they should take.

The case is within the rule, as laid down in the books; and also the payment prayed by the bill is directed by the express letter of the trust; and in a case, in which it is not owing to the effect of the will, but to something done by virtue of it, if there shall be heaped upon the reversioner, accumulated interest, and there are no circumstances, (small circumstances and small grounds are words I do not like to hear in any Court) denoting, that it was the intention, not only, that the Plaintiff should wait for her portion to the last hour of her life; but also, in a case, in which I am bound to say, if that was the intention, the testator must also have intended to starve the representatives of the two first branches of his family in a case, that might have happened.   Therefore according to all the cases and all the distinctions the Plaintiff is entitled to interest, to the time, at which it is paid (1); that is, to 1795, and to have this portion raised.

Declare, that the Plaintiff is entitled to have the portion raised, with interest at 4 per cent. before the filing of the bill and interest at 5 per cent. from the filing of the bill.   I give no costs upon this bill.   The bill to restrain the raising of the money must of course be dismissed with costs. '

*I have found a note in a book I happen to have,   [*385]

(1) *Post, Lyddon* v. *Lyddon*, xol. xiv. 558.

1 Eq. Cas. Abr., that belonged to Mr. Brown, who was a great practitioner in this Court, in the margin in his hand-writing, upon the report of *Butler* v. *Duncomb*. I observe it the rather, because Mr. Cox in his note upon that case, having used the industry of examining the Register's Book, says, it appears, the sum of 3000*l.* was divided by agreement. Mr. Brown says, he had heard Lord Talbot say often, that upon the rehearing of *Butler* v. *Duncomb* the portion was directed to be raised; but he had heard Lord Hardwicke say as often, that though upon the rehearing it was directed to be raised, that was by an agreement for the purpose; and it was so directed by consent.

———

See the notes to *Willis* v. *Willis*, 3 V. 51.

DRUCE *v.* DENISON.

[1801, JULY 29, 30.]⁻

A STATEMENT of property written by the testator, and his books of accounts, admitted as evidence, that he considered as his property, and meant to dispose of, property, not strictly, though in some sense, his : viz. mortgages and leases, the property of his wife under a Will, by which he was executor with her before marriage (*a*).

Provisions by a marriage settlement not held a purchase of all the property of the wife ; unless that purpose is expressed, or clearly imported (*b*).

A provision by marriage settlement in lieu, bar and satisfaction, of all dower or thirds, which the wife might otherwise be entitled to out of all the real and personal estate, held to bar her interest in what was not disposed of by the Will of her husband (*c*).

Whether an agreement by a husband for a lease of part of his wife's term will bind her after his death, as an actual lease does, and if so, whether the rent is his property, or survives to her with the reversion, *Quære* (*d*).

If a testator by a paper, subsequent to his will, says, he has bequeathed, that which he has not bequeathed, that paper may be proved as testamentary ; and the property will pass (*e*), [p. 397.]

Parol evidence admissible upon a latent, not upon a patent ambiguity ; to rebut equities, grounded upon presumption ; and perhaps to support the presumption ; to oust an implication ; and to explain, what is parcel of the premises granted or conveyed (*f*), [p. 397.]

SAMUEL DENISON by his will, dated the 26th of November, 1792, reciting, that by settlement previous to his marriage with Lucy Denison 4000*l*. 4 per cent. Bank Annuities, 3000*l*. Reduced Annuities, and 3000*l*. India Annuities, were settled, so that Lucy Denison in case of surviving her said husband would be entitled to the whole, and that he had covenanted to secure to her the farther sum of 160*l*. per annum for life out of such other real and personal estate as he should die possessed of, confirmed the settlement, except as to that covenant ; in lieu of which he directed his executors to purchase

---

(*a*) See 2 Starkie, Evid. 569 (5th Amer. ed.); *Shelton* v. *Shelton*, 1 Wash. 56 ; *Webley* v. *Langstaff*, 3 Desauss. 504 ; *Dewit* v. *Yates*, 10 Johns. 156. Parol evidence is admissible to show the state of his property, when the testator made his will. *Hyde* v. *Price*, 1 Coop. 208 ; *Webley* v. *Langstaff*, 3 Desauss. 509.

(*b*) The executors of the husband may be entitled, to the exclusion of the widow, to her choses in action, although not reduced by him into possession, by reason of an ante-nuptial settlement on the wife ; for the husband may entitle himself to all his intended wife's personal estate, whether in possession or in action, or which she may afterwards acquire, by becoming a purchaser of it previously to and in contemplation of marriage. But a mere *settlement* will not entitle the husband, or his executors, to the whole of the wife's fortune. There must be an agreement for the purpose, either express or implied ; for if the stipulation be for a part only of her property, that necessarily excludes the residue. 1 Williams, Exec. 620 ; 1 Roper, Husband and Wife, 289, (2d edit.) See *Tabb* v. *Archer*, 3 Hen. & M. 399.

(*c*) See *ante*, note (*a*), *Pickering* v. *Stamford*, 3 V. 332.

(*d*) See *Tucker* v. *Stevens*, 4 Desauss. 532.

(*e*) See 1 Williams, Exec. 60. But since the Stat. 1 Victoria, c. 26, § 39, all wills of personal estate must be signed *at the foot thereof*, and in presence of two witnesses. See *ante*, note (*a*), *Ellis* v. *Smith*, 1 V. 12.

(*f*) See note (*a*), *Hare* v. *Shearwood*, 1 V. 243 ; note (*b*), *Baugh* v. *Read*, 1 V. 257.

Bowzer.—Upon the question as to the mortgages, the testator having done no act to reduce the *choses in action* of his wife into possession, this private memorandum can have no effect.   What equitable circumstances are there, to which the report alludes?   His wife
being beneficially interested, his being executor with her can make
no difference.   If he had made a settlement in consideration of what
she brought to him, or with a view to his becoming entitled, then he
would be in equity entitled as a purchaser; but it is impossible to
contend, that any such intention can be collected from this settlement.   Therefore to these mortgages of 2600*l.* and 200*l.* Mrs. Bowzer having survived her first husband is entitled.

It is impossible for her certainly to avoid taking upon herself the
bond debt.   The bond was given by the two executors:
[* 389]   but the testator taking no beneficial * interest must be
considered as giving it for the benefit of the other executor.   She must therefore pay that debt.

Next, as to the leasehold estates: the Report is right, that the reversion, under-leases having been granted, survived to the wife.   Lord
Coke states (1), that if a man be possessed of a term of forty years
in the right of his wife, and maketh a lease for twenty years, reserving a rent, and die, the wife shall have the residue of the term : but
the executors of the husband shall have the rent ; for it was not incident to the reversion ; for that the wife was not a party to the
lease.   A question perhaps may be made, whether she was not entitled to the rent.   Lord Coke there states, that the rent would belong
to the husband: but there is a note of Lord Hale against that.   The
case there referred to is reported in Popham : but the passage, to
which Lord Hale refers, does not appear.   It is clear however, she
will be entitled to the reversion of the leasehold property after the
expiration of these leases; unless her husband can be considered as a
purchaser.   The Master has considered an agreement for a lease as
a lease : but that is only a declaration of an intention ; which he has
never actually executed.   That, which is intended to be done, is
not to be considered as done between husband and wife, under these
circumstances.   For that there must be some equitable circumstances ; making it incumbent upon the person claiming the property to
give effect to the intention.   No case has occurred between husband
and wife upon the intention to reduce her *chose in action* into possession.   If therefore, as far as actual leases were made by the husband, reserving rent to him, the property was so far made his, those
resting only in agreement belong to her.   The principle is, that the
husband has a right to dispose of the chattel real of his wife, and to
reduce her *chose in action* into possession : but he must do the act :
he must assign : contract will not do.   If he had sued for her *chose*
in action, and died pending the action, even after judgment, the action
or judgment would survive to her.   The entries in the testator's books
can have no effect to reduce these *choses in action* into possession.   The

_____

(1) Co. Lit. 46, *b.*

reduction into possession must be during his life. Even a disposition by will cannot have that effect : much less a paper not testamentary. The material question is, whether the wife is precluded by the settlement from taking her share of the residue ; into which the specific bequest to Samuel Price Denison must fall. The settlement states, that the provision of 160*l.* a year, in the place of which the will substitutes an interest in 10,000*l.* stock for her life, is to be in lieu, bar and satisfaction, of all dower or thirds out of his real and personal estate. It will be said upon this, she could not take any thing in case of intestacy out of his personal estate. That provision was made with a view to children, to bar her claim upon the personal estate in the case of an intestacy, there being children ; for a third of the personal estate is not the portion, to which she is entitled in the event, that has happened : there being no children. In that case she is entitled to a larger portion. The settlement, being made upon marriage, looked to the other event. The expression " dower or thirds " is considered applicable to real estate. If the intention had extended farther, he would have said " any distributive share." *Cleland* v. *Cleland* (1). *Garforth* v. *Bradley* (2). *Salway* v. *Salway* (3).

Mr. *Mansfield*, Mr. *Piggott*, Mr. *Richards*, Mr. *Alexander*, Mr. *Stanley*, Mr. *Steele*, and Mr. *Pemberton*, for the next of Kin.—The Plaintiff Mrs. Bowzer takes a very large bounty by this will ; and must elect. The paper produced in this case is clearly contemporary with the will ; in which respect it is distinguished from the late case of *Pole* v. *Lord Somers* (4). This testator speaks of the paper as the statement of his property at the time of his will ; and it is very emphatical. With respect to the under-leases there is no doubt, they operate as an assignment of so much ; and the husband is entitled to the rent. That is the clear doctrine from Lord Coke ; and notwithstanding the note of Lord Hale there is no doubt as to the reason of it. It is a sale of part ; and he might have sold the whole. As to an agreement for a lease, an agreement in this Court is a lease. A mere agreement to be executed for valuable consideration would be enforced against remainder-men behind, though deriving nothing from him. As against himself his agreement is as good as his lease, and even, as against her surviving, both would be bound to perform the agreement ; which is an act, to which he was competent during the coverture. Then * taking a share of   [* 391] the assets she shall not say, they shall be diminished by her refusing to perform the agreement. If the husband agreed to pledge her *chose in action* for his debt, or otherwise dealt with it, could she insist upon her rights, merely because a legal conveyance was not executed ? If this Court would enforce such a contract, they will consider such an exercise of substantial dominion over the property,

---

(1) Pre. Ch. 63.
(2) 2 Ves. 675.
(3) Amb. 692.
(4) *Ante*, 309.

such a dealing with it, as putting her right out of the question.   He
might have assigned it without consideration.   In Comyn's Digest (1)
it is laid down, that if a husband possessed of a term for years in
right of his wife leases for a less term, and for the security of money
borrowed of his lessee covenants to make him another lease after
the end of the former, the wife shall be bound thereby; for this
covenant amounts to a disposition of the estate in equity pursuant
to the power in her husband.   *Steed* v. *Cragh* (2), *Bates* v.
Dandy (3).

As to the paper, we must refer to the argument of *Pole* v. *Lord
Somers*.   In *Pulteney* v. *Lord Darlington* (4) upon the question as
to the 20,000*l.*, whether to be considered real or personal estate,
Lord Thurlow received in evidence the accounts of the steward of
General Pulteney; in which that sum was mentioned as part of the
personal estate.   Lord Thurlow's decision was, that that sum was at
home; and there was no purpose to be answered by laying it out in
land.   That account having been received in evidence *a fortiori*
must this paper; for nothing can apply more to the purpose at the
time of making the will: the testator putting in what is his personal
estate; affording the most distinct evidence, that he considered this
his property, when he made his will.   This case, which is very singular, is not exactly like *Hinchcliffe* v. *Hinchcliffe* (5): which is a
case of satisfaction; and therefore, as your Lordship observed in *Pole*
v. *Lord Somers*, there could be no doubt, that the evidence was admissible.   But this case is much more like *Pulteney* v. *Lord Darlington*.
The paper in that case was under much less favorable circumstances.
It was not signed by the testator at the date of his will and with a
view to it.   The paper was written by his steward: but it
[* 392]   was in his custody; and * it appeared, that he some way
acted upon it in making his will; and the question was,
whether a sum of money, which he had the power of making real or
personal estate, should be considered real or personal upon that
evidence.   In this case the testator had it in his power to make
this property his or her's.   This is a much more favorable case than
Pole v. *Lord Somers*.   The testator there had no power to make
the property his own; as this testator and General Pulteney had.'
This paper shows the clear intention at the date of the will.   It appears from the indorsement, that the paper and the will were written
upon the same day.

As to the right of the Plaintiff to the personal estate, she is deprived of dower and all right to any share of the personal estate in
all events.   The word "thirds" is only the common expression used
in such settlements, generally applied to real estate, rarely to per-

(1) 2 Com. Dig. 150, tit. Chancery, 2 M. 5.
(2) 9 Mod. 42.
(3) 2 Atk. 207.
(4) Reg. Lib. A. 1773, fol. 710; cited *ante*, 314, in *Pole* v. *Lord Somers*, vol. iii.
521, in *Hinchcliffe* v. *Hinchcliffe*.
(5) *Ante*, vol. iii. 516; see the note, 530.

sonal; where the object is to make a complete bar of any right in the wife by marriage out of the estate of her husband. No distinction, whether there shall be children or not, is intended. Some expressions in the clause settling the 160*l.* a-year show, that was all she was to take. It is declared to be the meaning, that at all events, if she survives him, she shall have that sum of 160*l.* a-year. The argument as to the event supposed to have been in contemplation, whether there should be children or not, cannot apply as to the dower. In either event she will be barred as to the real estate; and though loosely expressed, this must be as much a bar as to the personal estate. The settlement is in satisfaction of all her rights as a widow. *Walker* v. *Walker* (1).

Mr. *Romilly*, in reply.—The question as to the paper is the same as that in *Pole* v. *Lord Somers*. It is perfectly clear, this paper was written after the will: how long after, does not appear. If this is relied on, as declaratory of his intention, it ought to be proved as testamentary. That could not be in *Pole* v. *Lord Somers*; that paper being written after the will, and directed not to be annexed to it. Then it must be only evidence; and parol evidence might as well be received. It is said, independent of that paper, he acted upon the property as his own: but it appears only, that he meant to consider it as his own as far as it was his * in right   [* 393] of his wife, not his to all intents and purposes. His receipt of the rent is consistent with that limited interest. He had a beneficial interest in it, and power to dispose of it, if he chose, during the coverture; and it is to be remembered, that he was himself a lawyer. It is necessary to show by clear, unequivocal, acts, that he meant it to be his, and to go to his representatives.

The question as to the agreements is very difficult. The passage in Comyn's Digest cites the very worst authority. The agreement is enforced against the heir in cases of dower; because the heir represents the ancestor: but that doctrine is never applied to the case of husband and wife. Many analogous cases show, that such an intention will not do. If a husband sues for his wife's *chose in action* a much stronger indication of intention, and obtains judgment, but dies before execution, it will survive. So it will in the case of an arbitration, and death before award. This bears a much stronger resemblance to the execution of powers. Will the Court aid a defective execution of a power against a wife for the benefit of a stranger? She does not represent him in this respect. It is a right to dispose of her property: he attempts to dispose of it by an ineffectual act. Upon what principle is a Court of Equity to execute it? The execution of a power by a tenant for life would perhaps be enforced against the reversioner in favor of a purchaser for valuable consideration. That is the only case, that bears any analogy to this: but would it, if defectively executed? Has the Court ever

---

(1) 1 Ves. 54. See *Pickering* v. *Lord Stamford, ante,* vol. ii. 272, 581; iii. 332, 492, and the note, 338

enforced an agreement for a lease against the remainder-man? It is supposed, an agreement for a lease would of itself make a case of election: but there is no instance of carrying the doctrine of election so far.

As to the other question, the Plaintiff's right to a distributive share, the ground is, that it appears, the parties were very anxious to make a provision for children of the marriage; and they seem not to have had in contemplation any other event.

Lord CHANCELLOR [ELDON].—The question whether such a paper can be admitted in evidence, which I studiously avoided in *Pole* v. *Lord Somers*, must now be decided. This case is more favorable for admitting it; the paper in that case being drawn up long after the will. It is also less liable to objection than the ac-
[* 394]   count * in *Pulteney* v. *Lord Darlington;* this paper being written by the testator himself.

As to the actual leases, at this day there is no doubt, that to the extent of the terms the husband actually granted he became owner (*a*). As to the agreements for leases my apprehension at present is, that in this Court he is also to be considered owner of those interests. If he assigns his wife's *chose in action*, he gives no legal title to it. It is by agreement in most cases of *choses in action* that the assignee takes it. His covenant is in this Court a disposition of it, that could be enforced against him; and as against him at least would go to the representative of the person agreeing with him. If it cannot be enforced against his wife, he will be answerable upon his covenant; and then the question is, whether the wife can claim. Upon the head of election that fact of the agreement shows, he treated the property as his.

As to the word " thirds," the clear intention must be taken to mean her interest in case of intestacy. If that word did not occur, I doubt, whether the personal estate would not have been included under the word " dower." The word "thirds," is never used accurately. It is a sort of expression in common parlance, descriptive of the interest upon an intestacy. It must depend upon the domicil. The Plaintiff's argument is too ingenious upon the construction of a settlement; and cannot apply, where that word is connected with "dower;" which would apply to both events, whether there are children, or not.

July 30*th*. Lord CHANCELLOR.—I am at present disposed to decide this cause upon a ground, that does not make it necessary to determine the points as to an agreement for a lease by the husband; and if the cause should be re-heard upon the point, on which I decide it, I shall wish, that a search should be made upon the point, whether it ever has been decided, that an agreement will or will not bind the wife; and, if it will, whether the rent is to be paid to her or the husband. If that is untouched by decision, I think, it will

---

(*a*) 1 Williams, Exec. 478.

be found, the analogy to other cases will make out, that an assignment in equity is to this purpose as good as an assignment at law. But I say that without prejudice. The principle is stated, without saying any thing as to the authority of the case, towards the conclusion of *Steed* v. *Cragh.*

As to the other points, first, whether the settlement was a purchase of the wife's fortune, upon so much of the case as appears to me I do not think it was. According to the modern cases it is established, that the settlement for that purpose must either express it to be in consideration of the wife's fortune; or the contents of it altogether must import that; and plainly import it, as much as if it was expressed. That is the result of the cases upon the subject; and it is not worth while to consider in what respect the older cases are unsatisfactory; involving inquiries not very easy to execute (a).

As to the actual leases, I adhere to the opinion, that they were an alienation by the husband. As to the question, whether the settlement was a bar of the wife's interest in any undisposed residue, I abide by my opinion, given yesterday, that it was the intention of the parties, and that is sufficiently manifested by the language of the settlement, though inaccurately expressed, in the events that have happened, to purchase out the wife's interest in the undisposed residue. The question then is, whether the leasehold interests passed by the will; and the 600l. remaining of the mortgage for 2600l. after clearing the legacy of 2000l.; which unquestionably was the primary charge upon it, and the bond of the executor and executrix only a collateral security. If therefore the mortgage has become the husband's he must exonerate her from that engagement: so, if it became the wife's, she must exonerate him from the bond. Then the question is, whether under the circumstances the 200l. mortgage and the leases are to be considered as passing under the effect of the residuary clause of his will. The settlement not being to be considered a purchase of her fortune, the testator must be considered entitled in right of his wife to the possession of these leases and mortgages; entitled to the possession not only as husband, but also, as he and she were executor and executrix, to such possession, as he would have in that character. In a certain sense therefore this property was his, in right of his wife, and as far as it was capable of being considered his as executor with her; and if she had
died first, independent of the effect of the survivorship　[396]
to him as husband, supposing, any other person had been
entitled to this property in remainder after her life, it would have been his as trustee for that person, in the sense, in which a trustee can call the trust property his. If he had paid the bond, which he and his co-executrix, whom he afterwards married, entered into for the payment of the legacy of 2000l., the mortgage of 2600l. would have been his to the extent of making good the demand by virtue

(a) 1 Williams, Exec. 621.

. of that payment against the assets of the testatrix. After the marriage by his books, which must be evidence, if the paper is evidence; he treats the mortgages of 2600*l.* and 200*l.* as his, but as his in right of his wife. With respect to the leasehold estates the testator had with regard to those premises, of which he had made actual leases, acquired considerable interests in the strictest sense his. As to those premises, to which the agreements apply, he had attempted at least to acquire interests in the strictest sense *his;* and as to the residue of the interests he retained them in the sense, in which I have represented him to have had interests previously to those leases and agreements, as husband and as executor with his wife. At his death those interests would cease; and all not effectually disposed of would survive to his wife. His will therefore is certainly to be construed with regard to this circumstance; that it begins to speak at the moment, when those residuary interests were no longer his in any sense : but it is to be remembered, that at the date of the will they were his in a strict sense to the extent of his own acts, and in some sense beyond that. It would be difficult to say, the persuasion one has as an individual, that he was providing by express acts in his will for all his wife should have, would be sufficient to bar her from taking, not under his acts and provisions, but by virtue of her own title. If therefore she is to be barred from claiming the residue of these terms and the mortgage interests, it must be, not by the effect of the express provisions for her, but by the dispositions in favor of other persons; and that cannot be, unless under all the circumstances by the words " my personal estate" he can be held to mean to pass that, which was his in some sense, but not in a strict sense. If that can be done, it will of course raise a case of election.

[* 397]   *I had great difficulty upon this question in *Pole* v. Lord Somers;* and I make this decision, as bowing to authorities, which it is my duty to follow, rather than as being satisfied, that upon the rules of evidence, as they were formerly understood, this paper can be admitted in evidence. If it could not, there would not be much injustice; for I am upon reflection strongly disposed to hold, that, if the construction of the words " my personal estate" will not pass the property, and the paper cannot be let in, the Ecclesiastical Court would be inclined to receive it as testamentary, notwithstanding some of the contents; for their principle seems to be, that if the testator by a subsequent paper says, he has bequeathed by a former instrument, that, which he has not bequeathed, they will hold that subsequent paper a dispositon, as being a declaration of his will at the time he made it to dispose by the will; not in terms expressing, that it is then his will, but that he has disposed of it before. · If therefore the paper could not be received as evidence in this Court, they ought to have an opportunity of propounding it to the Ecclesiastical Court as a testamentary paper.

Upon the question of evidence, this, though written, is in a sense parol; and it seems, as far as *dicta* go, that parol evidence ought

to be received upon a latent ambiguity, not upon a patent ambiguity (1); that it ought to be received to rebut equities founded
upon presumption, and perhaps to support the presumption; to oust
an implication; and to explain, what is parcel of the premises
granted or conveyed. As to a patent ambiguity, I do not see, how
you can easily apply those cases to a case proposing to show, that
the words "my personal estate," which have in them no patent ambiguity, have in this sense a latent ambiguity; that he meant that,
which is in no sense his personal estate. When a man devises to
his son John, and happens to have two sons of that name, supposing
one to be dead, there is a latent ambiguity, letting in parol evidence,
but parol evidence perfectly consistent with the description in the
instrument. From those cases therefore it cannot be collected, that
by a devise of his estate, parol evidence may be admitted to show,
that he was devising another man's estate.

 * As to the cases upon presumption of satisfaction of [*398]
portions, if a testator means to satisfy a debt by covenant
or otherwise, the instrument creating the debt is not construed
against the import of it, nor the instrument satisfying it: but a presumption of law is raised from the connection between the parties,
that he means to satisfy the debt. In *Hinchcliffe* v. *Hinchcliffe* the
parol evidence was let in with great propriety, to show, that the testator by acts done had disposed of all the property settled, and by the
effect of the disposition had made himself a debtor to his children.
Then this Court would construe the will precisely as if he had been
originally a debtor. He had disposed of the property and received
the money; and had got in his pocket that money, which was in a
sense his. The debt affected all his estate; and therefore the
Court held upon the presumption arising between father and child,
when the parol evidence had proved the circumstances of the property, constituting the child a creditor upon the father, that the father
was upon the principles of this Court understood to mean to satisfy
the debt. So, in the case of portions, where the father is not strictly
debtor; where, for instance, he is tenant for life, and the portions
attach upon the family estate, upon principles a little difficult perhaps to sustain at first, but now established perfectly, it was held,
that the father was purchasing for the family estate; and giving the
portion, intending to satisfy the debt of the family, as in the other
case intending to satisfy the debt from himself. Therefore evidence
is let in to meet the presumption; and then evidence must be let in
to fortify the presumption. But I am apprehensive, that the Court
did this in old cases with much more jealousy than in later cases.
There was a time when the Court was very jealous of admitting parol declarations, except those, that passed about the time of the will;
and it appears from what Lord Hardwicke says in *Blinkhorn* v.
Feast (2) and what is stated in *Mascal* v. *Mascal* (3) with regard to

(1) *Ante*, vol. i. 259; *Parsons* v. *Parsons*, 266, and the note, 267.
(2) 2 Ves. 27.
(3) 1 Ves. 323.

the case there cited, that the time of making the declarations is very material (1).   There are strong traces of a disposition in these and other cases not to lean with all the attention, that has been given in late cases, to declarations before or after, and particularly at a great distance after, the will.

[* 399]   * Then are the cases of election (2) to be governed by the same principles as cases of satisfaction?   Most of the latter go upon this principle; that where a father or any one else is in the character of a debtor, attending to this, that in some circumstances the Court will presume an intention in a father (3), which they would not in the case of another person, the Court says, the disposition of what is strictly his property shall satisfy the debt; and no violence is done by that.   But upon election all the cases say, you must make out, that he describes the subjects, of which he means to dispose.   The question then is, whether the testator has so described the subject; and if not, whether you can let in parol evidence, *prima facie* applicable, to prove, though he has used words not so descriptive, they shall be taken to be descriptive.   That there is authority for that at this day, whatever difficulties occur upon it, as an hypothetical proposition, I dare not deny.   The difficulties upon it are great.   In *Pulteney* v. *Lord Darlington* the testator had 20,000*l.* in his hands; for which he was debtor to the trusts of the settlement.   That sum was *prima facie* real estate in his hands.   He was tenant for life; and all the real uses of a strict settlement attached upon it.   His steward put down upon paper, that this sum of 20,000*l.* was part of his estate.   Suppose the case to stand nakedly upon that, and he makes his will the same week, and, *a fortiori* if four or five years after receiving that account, it would be very strong, to say, that because the steward apprehends that to be his master's property, the master knows nothing to the contrary; and his ideas must be the same; and he must use the terms in his will in the same sense as the steward used them.   But to say that, not only to make that construction against the persons interested in the money upon the will, but also to hold, that the testator never corrected his idea between the time, when he saw the paper, and the time of executing the will, and against those, who have interests to be displaced by proof, is very strong.   If there is in the will an indication, that some part of that property was meant to be disposed of *eo nomine* by the will, that is strong to show, he did mean to dispose of some property in a strict sense not his own; and it may be argued upon that, that he meant to dispose of the whole property subject to the same uses.   But even that presses a great deal against those, who have interests, to be displaced by proof; and it is competent at least to say, that having shown an intention

[* 400]   to * dispose of part he does not necessarily mean to dispose

---

(1) See *ante*, vol. i. 359, in *Nourse* v. *Finch*, and *Hornsby* v. *Finch*, ii. 72; *Clennell* v. *Lewthwaite*, ii. 465, 644.

(2) See the notes, *ante*, vol. i. 523, 527.

(3) See *Hope* v. *Lord Clifden*, *post*, 499.

of the rest.   But the circumstance to which I advert, is, that *de facto* that paper was admitted as evidence; and that is a judgment of this Court upon the admissibility of evidence, and that judgment recognized in the highest place.

It is impossible also not to admit, that Lord Alvanley, has in the strongest words said (1), that evidence of this sort is to be admitted, and upon the authority of that very case; and there is nothing, that abates from the authority of that *dictum*, except that, as I understand the case, that *dictum* does not belong to it.   Lord Alvanley refers to what Lord Chief Justice De Grey said in *Pulteney* v. *Lord Darlington*.   If the circumstances were evidence, that they made an impression upon the mind of that learned Judge, is very considerable.   But the difficulty I have is, upon what principle he suffered those circumstances to make an impression upon his mind.   Baron Eyre goes a great deal farther; saying, he does not agree to the position laid down in the general sense of it; that, where a man gives all his estate, he does not mean to give what is not his; what he thinks his, is, in the sense he uses the word, his.

These principles being so laid down in *Pulteney* v. *Lord Darlington*, and *Hinchcliffe* v. *Hinchcliffe*, it is not for any one sitting here upon any embarrassment arising in his own mind to deny their application : but I repeat, that I do not understand these *dicta;* as far as they say, upon cases of election evidence is admissible, but not to explain the will.   If they mean, that it is admissible only to explain the subjects of bequest ambiguously described, and then not to explain the will, but to make you understand what subjects the testator meant to describe, which upon the face of the will you cannot understand, that is intelligible : but, if they mean, that it is admissible to prove, what the testator meant by the words " my personal estate," and that he meant a great deal more than those words would carry by their natural or legal import, and if a case of election is raised upon that, in fact and substance evidence is admitted to raise a case of election, thereby explaining the will.   It is not enough for me to say, that * is the effect of it; for   [* 401] upon reasoning of a contrary tendency the Court has established, that this sort of evidence has been admitted.

The other cases cited in *Hinchcliffe* v. *Hinchcliffe* have no relation to it : *Ellison* v. *Cookson* (2), and all the others upon presumption and satisfaction, for the reasons I have stated; and all I can find is one or two *dicta* of Lord Thurlow in *Jeacock* v. *Falkener* (3) and *Fonnereau* v. *Poyntz* (4).   The former, it is to be observed, is a case of satisfaction.   Lord Thurlow is there made to say, " evidence cannot be read to prove, what the testator meant by the words used in his will : but it may as to facts, upon which the testator made his will."   Mr. Lloyd upon that cited the case of *Broughton*

(1) *Ante*, vol. iii. 530.
(2) 3 Bro. C. C. 61; *ante*, vol. i. 100.   See the notes, 112, 259.
(3) 1 Bro. C. C. 295.
(4) 1 Bro. C. C. 472.

v. *Errington* (1) ; and, I believe, it was upon the argument of that
case that my mind was impressed with the distinction.   That case is
intelligible: but the words attributed to Lord Thurlow are not.   The
declarations were let in upon the old ground: but what is meant by
the latter part of that proposition, I do not understand.   If I am to
collèct it from what Lord Thurlow says in *Fonnereau* v. *Poyntz*,
which is subsequent to his own decision in *Pulteney* v. *Lord Darlington*, Lord Thurlow there (2) says, he lays out of the case all
declarations of the testatrix of what she really meant to give at the
time of making her will, and all statement of her property, from
whence it might be ihferred, what she meant.   Upon what ground
then did he admit the evidence?   As I have always understood,
and now understand it from this Report, upon this ground ; that
the testatrix having given, as a species of stock, that, which was of
no known denomination of stock, the will showed, she meant to give
something ; but did not ascertain the subject she meant to give.
Therefore Lord Thurlow looked at the property, in order to prove,
what she meant ; the will proving, that she meant to give something ; but the description of the subject not being intelligible.
That was not contradicting any description in the will.   It was nòt
saying, that was the personal estate of the testatrix, which was not
her personal estate ; but that she meant by these words what she
         might be taken to mean ; because upon the words, attend-
[* 402]   * ing to the different species of stock, at the bank, it could
         not be ascertained, what species she did mean : it being
clear, that she meant some.   That case therefore in no degree supports *Pulteney* v. *Lord Darlington*, nor the *dictum* at the conclusion
of *Hinchcliffe* v. *Hinchcliffe:* nor does it carry the old cases upon
parol evidence one tittle farther than they had gone.

Then the question is, can I admit this paper as evidence ?   That
question arises in a case, in which this property was more or less
strictly the personal estate of the testator in all the senses I have
represented, independent of evidence ; the testator having by actual
leases acquired out of his wife's property personal estate of his own,
having by agreements for leases acquired such interests as those
agreements would give him, having constituted himself, if he ever
should pay the bond debt, a creditor upon his wife's *chose in action*,
and in that respect made that his own, and, beyond those interests,
acquired by his own acts, having his wife's personal estate in this
sense his, in right of his wife, whether in such a complicated situation it is possible to admit parol evidence, that by the words " my
personal estate " he meant, not only his strictly, but also that, which
in a sense must be admitted to be his personal estate ; attending to
the fact, that a great portion of this property he must be entitled to
dispose of ; because he had made it in a strict sense his.   If the
question was new, I should doubt, whether in a case so circum-

_____

(1) 7 Bro. P. C. 461.
(2) 1 Bro. C. C. 477.

stanced it would be a violation of the rule to admit evidence ; for it is not a contradiction of the will ; but only goes to this ; that, as he might mean the words in the one sense or the other, he did mean that property, which in both senses was his.　But it is not necessary to decide upon that ground ; for after the case of *Pulteney* v. *Lord Darlington,* and what Lord Chief Justice De Grey, Baron Eyre, and Lord Alvanley, have said, whatever my own opinion might have been prior to *Pulteney* v. *Lord Darlington,* (and I agree with Lord Rosslyn [Loughborough], that I cannot see, upon what principle the evidence was admitted in that case) after all this authority, I do not think myself at liberty to reject this paper as evidence.　It is with great satisfaction, that receiving it I find, it is evidence contemporary with the will : for it leaves as little to hazard as can be in such a sort of case.　It may be stated as a fact, that the moment the testator had made his will he sat down to state the effect of it.　This paper has the *same date.　He calls it a state-　[* 403] ment of his property.　He correctly abstracts the will ; including all the leasehold estates, as his own, the mortgage for 2600*l.* ; estimating it at only 600*l.* the residue beyond the legacy charged upon it ; the 200*l.* ; and, what is very remarkable, leaving out the contingent legacy ; which never produced any thing to him. That, from which he derived actual benefit, he takes as his own ; and what was contingent, whether to be received by his wife, or not, he leaves out.

Under these circumstances, and subject to any review, if it can be found fit to attempt to shake these authorities, I am of opinion, the testator did bequeath all this as his own personal estate.　If so, the other points will not arise ; and I am the more satisfied upon the justice of the decision ; because, though I do not think, Lord Chief Justice De Grey was correct in allowing circumstances to make an impression upon his mind, if they never ought to have found their way to his mind, this paper must either be looked at as evidence, or the party ought to have the opportunity of propounding it as a testamentary paper to the Ecclesiastical Court.

This cause was not re-heard.　Before the decree was drawn up, it appeared that the mortgage for 200*l.* was not contained in the paper.　The sum of that amount was another sum belonging to the testator.　That mortgage was therefore excepted.

It was said at the Bar, that there was no trace of *Steed* v. *Cragh* in the Register's Book ; and that it appeared from the Register's Book, that in *Pulteney* v. *Lord Darlington* all sorts of papers were read : agreements of solicitors ; cases and opinions of Counsel, &c.

---

1. THAT there are authorities for enforcing virtually the covenant of the husband against his wife, and that, at all events, even when this course has not been followed, still, if the husband has entered into a covenant respecting his wife's interests, should she refuse to assist in carrying it into effect, the husband will be answerable in respect of such covenant, see *Innes* v. *Jackson,* 16 Ves. 367, and note 4 to *Emery* v. *Wase,* 5 V. 846.

2. Where a husband makes a settlement, in consideration of the wife's whole fortune, that fortune, notwithstanding it may consist entirely of *choses en action*, is looked on, without any more particular agreement for that purpose, as purchased by the husband, and it will go to his executors: but, if the settlement was made in consideration of a part only of the wife's fortune, then the remaining part, if not reduced by the husband in possession during his life, will survive to the wife, in the absence of an express agreement to the contrary: *Cleland* v. *Cleland*, Prec. in Cha. 63 : for the mere fact of his having made a settlement upon his wife at the time of marriage, is not sufficient to entitle the husband to the wife's *choses en action*, or chattels ; to constitute him a purchaser thereof, there must be an agreement, either express or implied: *Salwey* v. *Salwey*, Ambl. 693: and, according to the principal case, the implication must be as plain as if the matter were actually expressed. It is also well settled, that a settlement, in consideration of the fortune of the wife, will be understood to have been intended to apply only to her fortune at the time; unless the settlement expressly, or by clear import, comprehended all future property which might devolve upon the wife. Where no distinct agreement to that effect appears, should any subsequent accession of *choses en action* accrue to the wife, in such a shape that the husband cannot lay hold of it without the assistance of a Court of Equity, the wife will, according to the established rule of such Courts, be entitled to an additional provision out of that additional fortune, as against either the husband or his assignee; and if the husband die first, not having reduced the property into possession, nor having assigned it for valuable consideration, the whole will survive to the wife. *Milford* v. *Mitford*, 9 Ves. 95, 96; *Carr* v. *Taylor*, 10 Ves. 579. And see note 3 to *Norbone's case*, 2 Freem. 282, (2d edit.) See also, *post*, note 1 to *Scawen* v. *Blunt*, 7 V. 294.

3. As to the doctrine of election, see the references given, *ante*, in note 1 to *Pole* v. *Lord Somers*, 6 V. 309.

4. That a recital of a previous devise of real estate will not amount to a devise, though a recital of a previous bequest may possibly amount to a gift of personalty, see the note to *Frederick* v. *Hall*, 1 V. 396.

5. With respect to the admissibility of parol evidence, in order to explain latent ambiguities in testamentary instruments, see the notes to *Baugh* v. *Read*, 1 V. 257, and the notes to *Parsons* v. *Parsons*, 1 V. 266. That such evidence may be given to raise a presumption of trust, in exclusion of an executor's legal title to the residue of his testator's property undisposed of, or, on the other hand, to repel such presumption, see note 3 to *Nourse* v. *Finch*, 1 V. 344, and note 3 to *Clennell* v. *Lewthwaite*, 2 V. 465; and where the subject of devise is described by reference to some extrinsic fact, it has been held that it may, not merely be competent to the Court to admit extrinsic evidence, but it may be absolutely necessary to let in such evidence, in order to ascertain the fact referred to, as the only mode of ascertaining the real subject of devise: *Sanford* v. *Raikes*, 1 Meriv. 653: it has been said also repeatedly, that circumstances *dehors* the will may be evidence to show what is the property intended to be disposed of, though such evidence may not be admissible to show how, or in whose favor, that disposition was intended to be made; (*Judd* v. *Pratt*, 13 Ves. 174 ; *Attorney General* v. *Grote*, 3 Meriv. 320 ; *Penticost* v. *Ley*, 2 Jac. & Walk. 210 ; *Hewson* v. *Reed*, 5 Mad. 451 ;) but upon principle, (see note 2 to *Stratton* v. *Best*, 1 V. 285,) at least as a general rule, (see note 1 to *Baugh* v. *Read*, 1 V. 257,) it is only when ambiguity is introduced by such extrinsic circumstances, that extrinsic evidence may, from the necessity of the case, be admitted to explain that ambiguity. *Loe* v. *Chichester*, 4 Dow, 93. And see note 4 to *Standen* v. *Standen*, 2 V. 589.

6. As to presumed satisfaction of a portion, or even of a debt, by a legacy of equal, or greater, amount than such portion or debt, see the notes to *Ellison* v. *Cookson*, 1 V. 100, and the farther references given in the note to *Tolson* v. *Collins*, 4 V. 483.

7. With respect to the different degrees of credit and weight to be attached to declaration of a testator, according to the time at which such declarations were uttered; whether at the time of making his will, or subsequently, or previously thereto: see note 3 to *Clennell* v. *Lewthwaite*, 2 V. 465.

8. That the admissibility of parol evidence in order thereby to raise a case of election, is a doctrine resting rather upon authority than upon sound principle, see note 2 to *Stratton* v. *Best*, 1 V. 285.

CHAPMAN v. BROWN.

[ROLLS.—1801, JULY 8, 30.]　·

TRUST by will for building or purchasing a chapel, where it may appear to the exec utors to be most wanted : if any overplus, to go towards the support of a faithful gospel minister, not exceeding 20l. a-year ; and if any farther surplus, for such charitable uses as the executors should think proper. The whole trust void, not only as to the real estate and a mortgage, but also as to all the personal estate ; and the real estate went to the heir at law ; and the personal to the next of kin.

ELIZABETH BROOKS by her will, dated the 21st of June, 1776, after giving, among several other legacies, if there should be any poor relations of her's at the time of her decease, as far as the second, that can be said to be in want, 5l. to each, and directing all her wearing apparel to be distributed among her poor relations at the discretion of her executors, gave all the rest and residue of her estate and effects whatsoever, freehold and otherwise, to her executors, after payment of the above legacies and her funeral expenses, for the purpose of building or purchasing a chapel for the service of Almighty God ; and gave her two small silver waiters, her large silver cup, and her best damask table cloth and two damask napkins, for the use of the Communion table of the same ; and requested, that her bureau-book-case with all her books may be deposited in the said chapel ; and desired, that the chapel may be, where it may appear to her executors to be most wanted; and if any overplus should remain from the purchasing or building the same, she requested, that it might go towards the support of a faithful gospel minister, not to exceed the sum of 20l. a-year ; and if after that any farther overplus should remain, she desired, that the same may be laid out in such charitable uses as her executors shall think proper ; and she appointed the Reverend Richard Hill and Thomas Chapman her executors. The latter was one of five legatees of 20l. ; and to the former she gave 10l. for his trouble.

The testatrix died upon the 12th of June, 1800. Hill having renounced, Chapman proved the will; and filed the bill; praying an execution of the trusts of the will.

The heir at law by his answer claimed the real estate ; and the next of kin claimed the personal estate.

Mr. Richards and Mr. Hart, for the heir at law, and next of kin.— This is such a devise and bequest, as the Court will not execute. It is clear as to the land. As to the personal estate,
* it is given so, that an investment in land must necessari- [* 405]
ly have been in the contemplation of the testatrix. If the words are to be confined to building a chapel, supposing the ground to be already furnished, a case upon that point is now depending before the Lord Chancellor. In the argument of that case The Attorney General v. Tyndall (1) was cited ; in which Lord Northington

_____

(1) Amb. 614 ; 2 Eden, 207.

against the general course of preceding cases held, that the application of personal estate to buildings already in mortmain still is amortising.   A proposition directly contrary to that is broadly laid down in *Corbyn* v. *French* (1) ; viz. that it may be applied for the purpose of ameliorating, beautifying, sustaining or repairing, buildings upon land already in mortmain.   The Lord Chancellor wished to have the point more considered, than it could have been as a short cause.   But in this case it is clear, the testatrix intended land to be procured.   Land already in mortmain cannot meet her idea of purchasing.   She had no idea of land under such circumstances ; intending a distinct charity of her own.

The distinction of Lord Hardwicke is stated in *The Attorney General* v. *Nash* (2) and many other cases, collected in Highmore ; that erecting a chapel is considered as founding the thing ; building, otherwise.   But it is always considered a question of construction.   *Foy* v. *Foy* (3) had two bequests in it ; of which one was considered good : the other, not.   Lord Kenyon said, he would have declared both void ; if there had not been an hospital existing.   Here is no chapel existing.   Then as to the disposition of the surplus, the Court cannot take notice of that ; because the first disposition cannot take effect.   *The Attorney General* v. *Goulding* (4).   This gospel minister must according to her intention be attached in some way to this chapel.   The first purpose not being warranted, the second must fail with it.   If the chapel cannot be purchased, you cannot fix upon any surplus to apply to any minister : the residue being the surplus upon an account, to ascertain the sum necessary for the purchase of the chapel ; which account cannot be taken.   How can it be described to the Master, how much will be wanted for the building : a building of what value ?   The whole [*406] fund cannot be applied to the minister : for * that is not the intention.   It is acknowledged in all the authorities, that if the first object fails, that, which is dependent upon it, must fail.   *Moggridge* v. *Thackwell* (5) is a very strong case : but is now to be re-heard (6).   The Master must then say, who is the minister to have the 20*l.* a year for ever.   The additional bequest is not distinct, but connected with the general design of charity.   By establishing the stipend alone the Court will go against the intention ; which was, that a minister of her own should have it : that not being the main object : but only for the purpose of providing a minister to do the duty of the chapel.   There is a mixture of vanity in this, as in all these cases.

Then, as to the point, whether the Crown will be entitled to apply the residue to any charitable purpose, this will does not afford a

(1) *Ante*, vol. iv. 418.   See page 427, 428.
(2) 3 Bro. C. C. 588.
(3) Cited 3 Bro. C. C. 591.
(4) 2 Bro. C. C. 428.
(5) 3 Bro. C. C. 517 ; *ante*, vol. i. 464.
(6) Upon the rehearing the decree was affirmed ; *post*, vol. vii. 36.

sufficient ground for that. In *Moggridge* v. *Thackwell* the particular object was pointed out by the will.

Mr. *Nolan* for the Attorney General in support of the Charity.— This disposition is not void, except as to the real estate and the mortgage (1). All these objects are legal. It must be admitted, that it would be void, if the trust was merely to purchase a chapel: but being for the purpose of either building or purchasing, in the alternative, if the purpose of building can be supported, the Court will give effect to that mode, which may be established. If therefore this can be sustained as a bequest for the purpose of building upon land already in mortmain, or if land should be given, it may be established. The discretion given to the trustees as to the situation of the chapel, where it may appear to them to be most wanted, is strong in support of this charity. *The Attorney General* v. *Nash* and all the other cases establish this; that where that discretion is given, if the trustees can exercise it in a legal manner, the Court will carry it into effect; where it is possible to apply it upon land already in mortmain.

But if that is void, the other disposition is valid. If the minister was to exercise his function in the chapel, according to *The Attorney General* v. *Whitchurch* (2) and other cases, the principal
* failing, the adjunct must also fail. But in this instance [* 407]
there is nothing to connect them. Her bounty to the
minister is limited to 20*l.* a year; importing clearly, that he must be supported by other means. The appointment should be by the executors, or by reference to a Master. As to the surplus, this is a condition precedent. A bequest may be void in one part, and good in the limitation over: *The Attorney General* v. *Hartley* (3). All the cases upon the doctrine of *cy pres* go upon this principle; that, where it is evident, some distinct object of charity should take place, before the legacy should lapse, the Court will fulfil that intention. In this will the intention is clear, that the representatives shall take nothing, but the whole shall go to charity, from the legacies to the relations.

July 30th. The MASTER OF THE ROLLS [Sir WILLIAM GRANT], (after stating the case).—The only question is with regard to the validity of the bequest for charitable purposes. It is contended for the heir at law, that as to the real estate the devise is void; and that unquestionably is so. It is also clearly void as to the mortgage. By the next of kin it is contended, that the disposition is void, so far as it directs the residue to be laid out in building or purchasing a chapel; and it is contended by the Attorney General on behalf of the charity, that being in the alternative, to build or purchase, if either of those purposes could legally be effected, the trust ought to be carried into execution; and that undoubtedly would be so. It is

(1) *House* v. *Chapman, ante,* vol. iv. 542.
(2) *Ante,* vol. iii. 141.
(3) 4 Bro. C. C. 412.

insisted, that the purpose to build a chapel upon ground already in mortmain is legal ; though to purchase ground for the purpose of building a chapel is not legal. *The Attorney General* v. *Bowles* (1) was referred to, as an authority, that, if there is a bequest of money to be laid out in building a chapel or school, the intention is to be taken to be, to build, in case a piece of ground already [* 408] in * mortmain could be found for that purpose ; and that case undoubtedly is an authority for that.

But this case appears to have been over-ruled by a great number of subsequent decisions. Upon the principle established by the case itself it seems a little extraordinary, that a testator having made no reference whatsoever to the case of land being already in mortmain, the Court should suppose an intention, that he has not in the most remote degree pointed to. But Lord Hardwicke in favor of a charity held, that such an intention might be presumed.

The first case, in which that authority was impeached, is *The Attorney General* v. *Tyndall* (2) before Lord Henley. In a subsequent case, *The Attorney General* v. *Hutchinson* (2), Lord Bathurst takes Lord Henley to have there decidedly over-ruled the other case. In argument he certainly did over-rule it ; for he disapproved of the ground, upon which that was decided ; but the case immediately before him did not call for that decision ; for it was not a case of the same kind. In that case the direction was expressly to purchase : and there was no option. But all the reasoning of Lord Henley went in direct contradiction to the former case. He held that the statute had two objects ; first, that you shall not give land for the benefit of a charity ; 2dly, that you shall not realize for the benefit of a charity ; that the mischief is the same ; for, if that precedent was to prevail, a piece of ground, that was only worth 50*l.* might be made worth 20,000*l.* ; which undoubtedly is putting it in mortmain.

But a case directly in point occurred before Lord Northington in 1764, *Pelham* v. *Anderson* (4) ; for there 2000*l.* was given to build or erect an hospital. That was determined by him to be void. That case did directly over-rule *The Attorney General* v. *Bowles,* the purpose being precisely the same. Then came the case of *The Attorney General* v. *Hutchinson* ; to which I have before alluded, in 1775 ; where the bequest was, according to the report in [* 409] Ambler, for the purpose of erecting, and, according * to a note in Brown, for erecting and building a free school. A

(1) 2 Ves. 547. Lord Hardwicke's opinion upon this subject, as expressed in that case, *Vaughan* v. *Farrer,* and *Cantwell* v. *Baker,* there cited as *Gastril* v. *Baker,* comes to this ; that, if the object can be attained by any other means than a purchase of land, as by an application of the fund upon land already in mortmain, or by a gift of land, or hiring a house, it shall have effect; and in *The Attorney General* v. *Tyndall,* Amb. 614, 2 Eden, 207, the Master of the Rolls, following Lord Hardwicke's authority allowed the trustees two years to procure, if they could, a gift of land. See *Grieves* v. *Case, ante,* vol. i. 548, and the note, 554 ; *Henshaw* v. *Atkinson, Johnston* v. *Swan,* 3 Madd. 306, 457.
(2) Amb. 614.
(3) Amb. 751 ; 1 Bro. C. C. 444, in a note.
(4) 1 Bro. C. C. 444, in a note.

strong circumstance there was, that there was in the parish a piece of ground in mortmain; upon which a school had formerly been erected; and it was contended, that the fact was in the testator's contemplation; and the intention was to re-erect the school upon that foundation: but Lord Bathurst thought, that, as the testator had not himself pointed to that intention, it was not to be presumed by the Court. Therefore it was not to be taken as a mere bequest for the purpose of erecting or building a school; and it had been determined in *Pelham* v. *Anderson* and the other cases, that such a bequest was void.

Then the case of *Foy* v. *Foy* (1) occurred; which went much farther than either of these cases. There the legacy was given towards the erection and endowment of an hospital. Lord Hardwicke in *Vaughan* v. *Farrer* (2), and *Gastril* v. *Baker* (3) held, that to erect does not necessarily imply to build, much less a purchase of ground for building. He held, it might mean merely an endowment: but Lord Kenyon in *Foy* v. *Foy* held, that, if there was no hospital already existing, that would be void.

Then came the *Attorney General* v. *Nash* (4); in which the words "erect and build" occurred. The former undoubtedly is not so strong as the other, from what Lord Hardwicke had held, that it might mean an endowment. Therefore in that case the word "build" was the operative word. But Lord Thurlow held the bequest altogether void, and allowed the demurrer.

In this case the alternative is to build or purchase. It is admitted, a bequest to purchase would be void; and it is determined by all those cases, that a bequest for the purpose of building a chapel is equally void. That bequest therefore falls to the ground.

The next question arises upon the direction; that if any overplus remains after the purchasing or building the chapel, it shall go towards the support of a faithful gospel minister, not exceeding *20l. a-year. It is contended by the next of kin,   [* 410] that this is a bequest dependent upon the former; and, that failing, this must likewise fail, upon the authority of the *Attorney General* v. *Goulding* (5). The late Master of the Rolls seemed (6) to doubt a little the doctrine of that case in the *Attorney General* v. *The Earl of Winchelsea* (7): but afterwards in the *Attorney General* v. *Boultbee* (8) he approved of that doctrine; and acted upon it. It is then contended, that this is not dependent upon the other purpose; but is for the support of a minister generally, not at that chapel. I am clearly of opinion, she must have meant a minister in

(1) At the Rolls, 1st February, 1785; cited 3 Bro. C. C. 591.
(2) 2 Ves. 182.
(3) The name of the Plaintiff in that cause was Cantwell.
(4) 3 Bro. C. C. 588.
(5) 2 Bro. C. C. 428.
(6) 3 Bro. C. C. 379.
(7) 3 Bro. C. C. 373.
(8) *Ante,* vol. ii. 380; iii. 220· See also iii. 145; *Attorney General* v. *Hinxman,* 2 Jac. & Walk. 270.

that chapel, which she meant to be purchased.   It would be quite absurd to suppose, she intended no provision for the minister of her own chapel; but that a provision should be made for the minister at some other chapel, to be built by a stranger.   Therefore upon the authority of the *Attorney General* v. *Goulding* and the *Attorney General* v. *Boultbee* that bequest must fail; as the chapel is not to have existence.

Upon these two parts of the case I have had very little difficulty: but I have been a good deal embarrassed as to the ultimate bequest of the residue, to be applied by the executors in general charitable purposes.   Standing by itself, a bequest of a residue to be employed in such charitable purposes as the executors shall think proper is a good bequest; supposing it legal to do as the testatrix had directed, and a residue had been left, after those purposes were answered, there would have been a good bequest of it; and therefore the question is, whether that ulterior bequest is to fail, because the prior bequest cannot take effect.   If it could be reduced to any certainty, how much would have been employed by the executors for the other purposes, the residue ought to be employed under this last direction, namely, for charitable purposes generally.   I have considered, whether that can be ascertained by a reference to the Master, to see, how much would have been sufficient for this chapel: but upon consideration it is quite impossible to give any direction, that would not be vague and indefinite, to a degree almost ridiculous: an inquiry, what they might have employed for building a chapel, with-

[* 411]   out knowing what kind of chapel: the *testatrix having given no grounds to ascertain, what kind of chapel: no locality.   It is utterly impossible to frame any direction, that would enable the Master to form any idea upon it.   If she had even pointed out any particular place, that might have furnished some ground of inquiry as to what size would be sufficient for the congregation to be expected there: but this is so entirely indefinite, that it is quite uncertain, what the residue would have been; and therefore it is void for that uncertainty.   She had no view to any residue but a residue to be constituted by actually building a chapel.   She contemplated no residue but with reference to that.   It is impossible to ascertain it in the only manner, in which she meant it to be ascertained.   It is impossible for the Court to apply it.   Therefore the whole of this disposition is void.

Declare the devise and bequest for these charitable purposes void; and that the real estate belongs to the heir at law; the personal to the next of kin.   ____

WHERE a bequest which if it stood alone would be valid, is merely an accessory to a devise which is void, and from which it cannot be clearly separated, the whole must fail together: see note 6 to *Moggridge* v. *Thackwell*, 1 V. 464.   As to the Statute of Mortmain, see the notes to *Grieves* v. *Case*, 1 V. 548.

CLARKE v. SETON.

[Rolls.—1801, July 10, 30.]

No interest beyond the penalty of a bond; except under special circumstances (a).

In 1798 Thomas Clarke contracted with the trustees under an Act of Parliament for the sale of certain estates to purchase an estate called Peplow Hall for 39,500*l.*   Thomas Williams claiming against the estate under judgments to an amount above 1500*l.*, the purchaser desired, that before the whole purchase-money should be paid, those·debts should be discharged : but the trustees having some doubt as to the fairness of the demand of Williams, thought it necessary, that it should be investigated.   This produced a deed, dated the 4th of August, 1798 ; under which 3000*l.* part of the purchase-money, was invested in stock in the names of trustees; upon trust, in case those judgment debts should upon the 4th of August 1779 remain unsatisfied, to sell the stock, and satisfy the debt out of the produce.   The debt not being discharged in January 1800, the bill was filed by Clarke and one of the trustees of the stock *against the trustees for the sale of the estate, the other   [*412] trustee of the stock, and Williams : praying, that the rights of the trustees and of Williams in the stock may be ascertained ; and that an account may be taken of what is due to Williams for principal and interest upon his judgments ; and that he may be paid out of the stock.

The debt appeared upon Williams's answer thus :

A bond, dated the 3d of January, 1775, for 500*l.* with a penalty of 1000*l.*

Interest to the 10th of May, 1779, 608*l.* 14*s.*

A bond, dated the 12th of September, 1782, for 112*l.* 16*s.* with interest ; with a penalty of 305*l.* 12*s.*   Upon that bond 185*l*, 8*s.* 3*d.* was due for principal and interest at the time of filing the bill ! Upon the former bond judgment was entered up in Michaelmas Term 1781.   No judgment was entered upon the other bond.   All claims were settled, except as to the bond for 500*l.*, upon which the obligee insisting upon the whole arrear of interest beyond the penalty, it became necessary to file the bill : the purchaser pressing to have the business concluded.

Mr. *Richards* and Mr. *Bell*, for the Plaintiffs. — In *Creuze* v. *Hunter* (1) the late Lord Chancellor was clearly of opinion, that a judgment does· not carry interest, if the debt in its nature does not carry interest ; and said, *Bickham* v. *Cross* (2) turned upon the particular circumstances.   The same point was determined in *Des-*

(a) See *ante*, note (a), *Mackworth* v. *Thomas*, 5 V. 331 ; note (a) and (c), *Creuze* v. *Hunter*, 1 V. 157.
(1) 4 Bro. C. C. 157, 316 ; *ante*, vol. ii. 157.
(2) 2 Ves. 471.

champs v. *Vanneck* (1). Interest was not given beyond the penalty . in *Sharpe* v. *The Earl of Scarborough* (2) and *Mackworth* v. *Thomas* (3). Without going into the former cases a series of late decisions has settled this point. The last, *M' Clure* v. *Dunkin* (4), upon which alone any doubt could arise, was determined upon the distinction, that the action was brought on the judgment; and Lord

Kenyon admits, that if the action had been upon the bond,
[* 413]   the objection would have held. That brings it back to
     all the other cases; the result of which is, that there shall be no interest upon a judgment; unless the debt in its nature carries interest; upon which it is expressly put in all these . cases. It never carries interest in the Masters's office. If it is said, the fund was producing interest: so was the land producing rent before. Perhaps the ground of refusing to go beyond the penalty is laches. *M' Clure* v. *Dunkin* does not appear to have been much argued. There are many debts, in which damages would be given, but upon which a Court of Equity would not allow interest. *Lord Dunsany* v. *Plunkett* (5), *Audely* v. ———— (6), *Duvall* v. *Terry* (7); which was put upon delay. *Elliott* v. *Davis* (8). All these are done away in the late cases. The distinction is, where a Court of Law gives interest as matter of contract, and as matter of damage. To that is to be referred the direction to compute interest upon such debts as carry interest.

Mr. *Romilly* and Mr. *W. Agar*, for the Defendant Williams. — The cases cited do not bear in the least upon this: this question being, whether parties bringing this creditor here can take securities from him upon any other terms than doing him complete justice. In the cases cited the creditors were either Plaintiffs, or persons coming voluntarily into the Master's office upon a bill of creditors. In *Hale* v. *Thomas* (9) the distinction is taken; that, where the party is coming for relief, desiring an injunction to prevent the creditor from using the securities he has at law, the terms are paying what in natural equity he is bound to pay. The same distinction is also clearly stated in Equity Cases Abridged (10). Cases of that nature are perfectly established; and are consistent with the modern cases. If this creditor had taken possession by *elegit*, they must have come as mortgagors paying the interest. In *Deschamps* v. *Vanneck*, which decision was certainly a surprise upon persons of great experience, the late Lord Chancellor must have been mistaken as to an action upon a judgment at law; and was misled by the prothonotary,

---

(1) *Ante*, vol. ii. 716.
(2) *Ante*, vol. iii. 557.
(3) *Ante*, vol. v. 329. See the note, i. 452.
(4) 1 East, 436.
(5) 2 Bro. P. C. 251.
(6) Hardr. 136.
(7) Show. P. C. 15. See the note, *ante*, 79.
(8) Bunb. 23.
(9) 1 Vern. 349; 2 Ch. Ca. 182, 186.
(10) 1 Eq. Ca. Ab. 92, pl. 7.

from whom he inquired ; for that is the case of *M'Clure* v. *Dunkin* (1).   In *Deschamps* v. *Vanneck*, the debt was not upon a bond, but a judgment.   It would be very strict to say a debt upon a bond carrying interest in its *nature should cease to   [*414] carry interest, because a judgment has been recovered upon the bond.   *Godfrey* v. *Watson* (2) is decisive upon this, as to the judgment.   But besides this, this creditor is entitled by virtue of interest being made of this fund.   From the time this bill was filed he would be entitled : the object of the bill being to prevent him from proceeding at law ; there being a fund for paying him in equity.   The fund cannot be producing interest for one of the parties, and not for the other.   If there is any difference, the legal rule ought to be applied in this case ; this creditor not coming with any claim upon assets, but being brought here for the purpose of preventing him from using his legal remedy; and therefore being entitled to every thing he could have at law.

The MASTER OF THE ROLLS [Sir WILLIAM GRANT].—The only question is, how much is really due to the Defendant Williams.   For that purpose he is made a party to this suit ; and he claims payment out of this fund ; contending for interest beyond the penalty of the bond.   On the other hand it is contended, that he is not entitled to any thing beyond the penalty.   Upon that point I take it to be perfectly ascertained at this day, that the penalty of the bond is the debt.   I always understood it to be so at Law ; and should have thought, the question would have been, whether it was so in Equity.   Certainly for many purposes the penalty is not held to be the debt in Equity ; and therefore it might have been thought, that it was not so in all cases ; but that the principal was the debt ; and the interest was to be calculated upon that beyond the penalty.   But the contrary is established in Equity ; and the uniform rule in Equity is never to go beyond the penalty.   But, what would not have been expected, it has been doubted whether that is so at Law; where the penalty is considered the only debt ; and originally the party could not have been relieved against it at Law ; but must have gone into Equity for relief upon payment of principal, interest, and costs.   In *Lord Lonsdale* v. *Church* (3) however, Mr. Justice Buller doubted that doctrine ; and said, the old cases were not founded upon principle ; and that at law the *penalty is not to be   [*415] considered the debt ; but interest in the shape of damages may be recovered beyond the penalty.   If it could, it ought always to be so recovered : for it proceeded upon the ground, that the principal is the debt, and the penalty only a security for it.   If that was established to be so at law, I should think, it would almost have followed, that in Equity interest should be calculated in the same manner ; for upon an account of the demand of a creditor, having a

(1) In that case the judgment was upon a bond.
(2) 3 Atk. 517.
(3) 2 Term Rep. B. R. 388.

legal demand, a Court of Equity can have no right to cut off any part of his demand : the only object of the account being to determine, how much he is to receive from the assets ;* and accordingly, Mr. Justice Buller did not conceive, that there would be any difference in that respect at Law and in Equity ; for in *Knight* v. *Maclean* (1), sitting in this Court, he held, that in Equity the interest ought to go beyond the penalty. Lord Thurlow dissented from that ; not upon the ground, that, if it was true at Law, it would not be so in Equity, but because he thought the penalty the debt both at Law and in Equity : and he stated considerable difficulties : what was that interest beyond the penalty : was it a debt by specialty or simple contract ? It was wholly out of the bond. Therefore Lord Thurlow conceived, that at Law the penalty was the debt, and likewise in Equity ; and decided accordingly both in *Tew* v. *Lord Winterton* (2) and *Knight* v. *Maclean* (3). In *Wilde* v. *Clarkson* (4) the Court of King's Bench dissented entirely from *Lord Lonsdale v. Church* ; and in the late case, *M'Clure* v. *Dunkin*, Lord Kenyon was quite clear, that if the action had been upon the bond, nothing more could have been recovered than the penalty : but the action being upon the judgment, it was determined, that the Plaintiff might go beyond the penalty.

It is clear therefore, that both at Law and in Equity, the penalty is the debt. The consequence is, this Defendant is wrong altogether in this claim of interest beyond the penalty. But it was farther contended for him, that there are equitable circumstances, that entitle him to have interest beyond the penalty ; admitting the general rule to be as I have stated it; and they cite cases, *Duvall* v. *Terry*, and *Lord Dunsany* v. *Plunkett*, to show, that,
[* 416]   * where the party comes to be relieved, the terms may be imposed upon him of paying interest beyond the penalty. In the former of these cases the Plaintiff came upon the ground of fraud ; and the Court refused to relieve him, except as to the penalty. The relief was whimsical : for they relieved him against the penalty, but the consequence was, that he was obliged to pay a great deal more ; for then they made him pay the original debt with the interest ; which was much beyond the penalty.

But it is unnecessary to examine that doctrine, or that of *Lord Dunsany* v. *Plunkett* ; for in this case no relief is sought against the Defendant Williams. He has not sued out an *elegit*, or got an execution, which they seek to set aside. They only desire him to inform them, what the debt is; there being a fund, out of which they offer to pay it. That is not seeking relief against him. Nothing could possibly be due to him but the penalty ; upon the supposition, that it was the case of a bond. He never insisted upon more by his answer. He does not insist, as it was thrown out that he might be

(1) 3 Bro. C. C. 496.
(2) 3 Bro. C. C. 489.
(3) 3 Bro. C. C. 496.
(4) 6 Term Rep. B. R. 303.

entitled, upon interest on his judgment.   With respect to that, waiving the consideration, that the claim is not set up by him, I do not
say, there are not cases, in which interest may be allowed upon a
judgment, though a judgment upon the bond, and beyond the penalty.   Such cases have occurred ; where there has been great delay
by writs of error, &c. as in *Bodily* v. *Bellamy* (1).   But it is not of
course in every case.   Williams, if he had brought an action, would
not have had any claim to interest.   He does not state any delay in
his way, or any reason to prevent him from suing upon the judgment
at any time, since it was entered up.   It was entirely his own fault;
not like a case, in which there is no fee-simple estate to resort to,
and he was reduced to the necessity of bringing an action against the
party.   In such a case it would be very fair to allow interest.   But
there is no ground here.   In no way could he have recovered any
more than the sum, for which he obtained his judgment, viz. the
1000*l.* ; and he ought to have taken that sum ; which I take it from
the correspondence he might have had.   Consequently upon payment of that sum to him he shall acknowledge satisfaction upon the
judgment.

SEE note 3 to *Ex parte Mills*, 2 V. 295, the note to *Mackworth* v. *Thomas*, 5 V.
329, and note 4 to *Lady Cavan* v. *Pulteney*, 2 V. 544.

HOLBECKE *v.* SYLVESTER.   [*417]

[1801, JULY 30.]

PRACTICE as to excepting for costs (*a*).

THE Plaintiffs filed their bill as mortgagees, and also for the purpose of having contracts carried into execution ; in which latter
object they failed.   The usual decree was made with respect to the
mortgages, for an account of the principal, interest, and costs.

An exception was taken by the Plaintiffs to the Master's Report;
that in taxing the costs of the Plaintiffs, relating to their mortgages,
he had disallowed so much as were incurred by making the Defendants, who had entered into the contracts, parties ; whereas he ought
to have allowed them : they being necessary parties.

Mr. *Mansfield*, for the Defendants, objected, that there cannot be
an exception for costs ; it must be by petition.

Lord CHANCELLOR [ELDON].—I understand the practice to be,
that if the decree has directed costs, and the Master has not taxed
'them, you may except : but if he has proceeded upon the costs, but

(1) 2 Bur. 1094 ; *Clarke* v. *Lord Abingdon*, *post*, vol. xvii. 106 ; *Atkinson* v.
Atkinson, 1 Ball. & Beat. 238.
(*a*) See 2 Smith, Ch. Pr. (Am. ed.) 368, 369 ; 2 Madd. Ch. Pr. (4th Am. ed.)
510.

has not allowed several items, which are claimed, there must be a petition.

Mr. *Romilly* and Mr. *Stratford*, in support of the Exception, stated the practice to be, though there cannot be an exception for costs only, yet if the party excepts upon any other ground, he may add an exception for costs; as upon a re-hearing or appeal upon other grounds you may enter into the question of costs; though you cannot rehear or appeal for costs only.

The exception was allowed; and it was referred back to the Master to review his Report, as far as it related to the costs respecting what was due upon the mortgages to the Plaintiffs; with a direction not to allow costs occasioned by any other demand except as mortgagees (1).

GENERALLY speaking, the Master's report is final as to costs; and exceptions do not lie to it. *Lucas* v. *Temple*, 9 Ves. 300; *Pitt* v. *Mackreth*, 3 Brown, 321. However, the Master might, possibly, in a particular instance, deviate so far from the established rules as to costs, that it would be hard to exclude the party aggrieved from bringing the question before the Court; the proper means of doing which would be by petition: *Purcell* v. *M'Namara*, 12 Ves. 171; *Hunt* v. *Fownes*, 9 Ves. 70: for, although there can be no re-taxation of a bill in respect of mere *quantum*, yet, upon a special case, made by petition, either of irregularity in the proceedings, or that the Master has acted upon a mistaken principle, the Court will interfere. *Fenton* v. *Crickett*, 3 Mad. 497.

[* 418] ALDRIDGE *v.* MESNER.

[1801, JULY 21, 31.]

UPON a bill of interpleader the Defendant, who made it necessary, was ordered to pay all the costs; and the Plaintiff has a lien for his costs upon the fund paid into Court (a).

THE Plaintiff filed a bill of interpleader against Mesner and Whitchurch; the former of whom bought a horse from the latter by auction for seventy-nine guineas. The Plaintiff was the auctioneer. The horse was warranted sound. He was returned as unsound the day after by the terms of the sale the purchaser was to be at liberty to return him, but before the Plaintiff had paid over the money. The Defendant Whitchurch demurred to the bill; and both parties bringing actions for the money against the Plaintiff, he moved for an

(1) *Post*, vol. ix, in 299, the Lord Chancellor expressed doubts as to the distinction taken in this case; and in *Hunt* v. *Fownes*, ix. 70, the claim of costs was allowed on petition. Lord Thurlow's rule in *Pitt* v. *Mackreth*, 3 Bro. C. C. 321, requiring a petition, praying leave to except, has been since followed. See *post*, vol. xii. 170; *Fenton* v. *Crickett*, 3 Madd. 496; *Ex parte Leigh*, 4 Madd. 394; and Mr. Beames's observations on Costs in Equity, 238, 9. See *Hughes* v. *Williams*, *post*, 459, and the note, as to Exceptions to Interrogatories settled by the Master.

(a) See *ante*, note (a), *Dowson* v. *Hardcastle*, 1 V. 368.

injunction. The late Lord Chancellor being of opinion, that the action brought by Mesner against Aldridge would try the merits, made an order upon that motion, that the action of Mesner should proceed ; that Whitchurch should be restrained from proceeding in his action : and should undertake the defence of the other action for Aldridge. That action ended in a nonsuit. The demurrer was not argued.

Mr. *Grimwood*, for the Plaintiff, moved, that his costs may be paid out of the fund, which he had paid into Court, without going on with the cause ; observing, that he was a mere stake-holder; and citing *Aldrich* v. *Thompson* (1).

Mr. *Stanley* and Mr. *W. Agar*, for the Defendants, insisted, that this was not an interpleading bill ; and the Plaintiff was not a mere stake-holder ; that he ought to have paid over the money immediately, when the horse was not returned at the time specified ; that he was not entitled to any costs; and the bill ought to be dismissed.

Lord CHANCELLOR [ELDON].—Under the circumstances, that have taken place, to all substantial purposes the Defendant Whitchurch has waived his demurrer. Both the Defendants have waived all objection, and decided the cause by submitting to that order. Besides, I am not ready to admit, that this is not an interpleading bill ; for I have tried actions more than once in which it appeared clearly, that the condition to return a horse by a certain
day was inserted on purpose, because the defect would   [419]
not appear till a day or two after that day. The justice of the case is, that the Plaintiff should have his costs ; and he has a lien for them upon the fund.

July 31st. An order was made on motion that Mesner should pay all the costs. The Lord Chancellor said, he considered the bill as in the nature of an interpleading bill at least; and upon an interpleader, if there was no fund in Court, costs would be given against the party, who occasioned it (2).

As to the general doctrines with respect to bills of interpleader, see, *ante*, the notes to *Dungey* v. *Angove*, 2 V. 304 ; and, that costs may be given to a defendant in a suit, which, though not strictly one of interpleader, is in the nature of an interpleading bill, see *Dunlop* v. *Hubbard*, 19 Ves. 205.

(1) 2 Bro. C. C. 149.
(2) *Ante, Dowson* v. *Hardcastle*, vol. i. 368, and the note, 369.

PRIESTLEY *v.* LAMB.

[1801, August 1, 5, 12.]

Upon a marriage of a ward of the Court under flagrant circumstances, the clergy-man and clerk were ordered to attend: the husband was committed; and the Lord Chancellor directed the proceedings to be laid before the Attorney General; expressing his opinion, that contriving a marriage without a due publication of banns is a conspiracy at common law.

By the Canon Law, which is binding on the clergy, it is highly criminal to cele-brate marriage without a due publication of banns; which must suppose information as to the residence, [p. 423.]

Penalties by that law and the statute law upon the clergyman, [p. 423.]

Ann Lamb, entitled to a fortune of between 2000*l.* and 3000*l.* was placed by her uncles, living in Lincolnshire, at a boarding-school at Camberwell kept by three sisters. In January 1801, when she was about the age of seventeen, Timothy Priestley, the brother of the governesses, and employed there in the capacity of writing-mas-ter, being a widower, paid his addresses to her; and in February they were married. Ann Lamb being a ward of the Court, a peti-tion was presented to the Lord Chancellor, and the following cir-cumstances appeared upon the affidavits.

The marriage took place at the parish church of St. Andrew's, Holborn, by banns, in the presence of Elizabeth Priestley, one of the sisters of Timothy Priestley, and another person. Elizabeth Priest-ley had quitted the partnership with her sisters at Christmas 1800: but it did not appear, that she had quitted the house. The parties left Camberwell on the morning the marriage took place; and it did not appear, whether the lady had actually resided in the parish. Timothy Priestley stated by his affidavit, that he consulted with the parish clerk of St. Andrew's, how he could be married; and the clerk told him, that the marriage, if with the consent of the friends of the lady, might be by license: if without their consent, [* 422] it must be by banns; and he must take a lodging * for her in the parish: he himself having chambers in Furnival's Inn. This affidavit was in some respects contradicted by the clerk. They were afterwards again married at the parish church of Lam-beth; and the clerk of that parish by his affidavit stated, that it is not customary to make any inquiry as to the residence of parties ap-plying to be married. The two sisters, who remained mistresses of the school, denied any knowledge of the fact of the marriage.

The Lord Chancellor [Eldon] immediately committed the hus-band; and observed, that this was a very flagrant case, from the sit-uation of the mistresses of the school, *in loco parentis;* and *Thomp-son's Case* (1) being mentioned by Mr. Pemberton, his Lordship or-

---

(1) The marriage in that case was by license: Thompson the husband having made the necessary affidavit for that purpose. The wife upon inspection being evidently under age, Lord Rosslyn ordered the clergyman to attend; and se-verely reprimanded him; and, having immediately committed Thompson, directed the Attorney General to indict him. He was accordingly indicted; and convicted.

dered not only Elizabeth Priestley, but the two ministers, who celebrated the marriages, and the clerks, to attend.

Aug. 5*th.*   The parties attended in Court accordingly.

Lord CHANCELLOR.—I cannot consistently with my ideas of justice call upon any of the parties now present for any explanation.
Upon the circumstances disclosed it is just to say, I hold in such ab-
horrence the robbery, that has been committed by this man of the
fortune of this young lady, that I will not believe upon his affidavit
the account he gives of what passed between him and the clerk of
St. Andrew's.   If she did go from the school to this residence, it
must have been an evasive residence.   It could not have been more
than a week.   With respect to Elizabeth Priestley, it would not be
out of the practice of the Court to commit her for the contempt.   As
to the other sisters, it is a miserable explanation of their conduct to
say, only, that they did not know of the fact of the marriage.   It will
rest with them to explain farther, or not, whether they knew of the
treaty.

By the affidavit of the clerk of the parish of Lambeth it is disclosed, that they conceive in that parish, that they do their
duty * to the public, and to the individuals, whom they   [* 423]
are to marry, never making any inquiry as to the residence
of the parties.   In the Canon Law, which binds the clergy of this
country (1), from 1328 to 1603, it is laid down, that it is highly
criminal to celebrate marriage without a due publication of banns ;
which must be interpreted a publication of banns by persons having
to the best of their power informed themselves, that they publish
banns between persons resident in the parish ; and very heavy penalties are by that law inflicted upon clergymen celebrating marriage
without license or a due publication of banns.   It does not rest there ;
for by the Statute Law it would be very difficult for the clergyman
to protect himself against express penalties by more than one act.
Then the Marriage Act (2) expressly provides (3), that no parson,
vicar, minister, or curate, shall be obliged to publish banns between
any persons, unless they shall seven days at least before the time required for the first publication, deliver to such parson, &c. a notice
in writing of their true christian and sirnames, and of the house or
houses of their respective abodes, within such parish, &c. and of the
time, during which they have dwelt in such house or houses respectively.   A subsequent clause (4) makes it felony in a clergyman
to celebrate marriage without license or publication of banns.   I do

---

Millet v. *Rowse, post,* vol. vii. 419.   See the note, *ante,* vol. i. 155 ; *More* v. *More,*
2 Atk. 157 ; *Ex parte Ashton,* 1 Dick. 23.

(1) 2 Atk. 157.   The canons do not bind the laity, unless confirmed by Parliament.   See *Middleton* v. *Crofts,* 2 Atk. 650, 2 Str. 1056, where the subject is fully
discussed.

(2) 26 Geo. II. c. 33,   See the new Marriage Act, 4 Geo. IV.

(3) Sect. 2.

(4) Sect. 8.

not mean to intimate, that a clergyman believing, there was a residence, would be guilty within that clause. But upon the principles of the Common Law, as well as the Statute Law, laying penalties upon marriage without license or a due publication of banns, though such a fact should not be within the meaning of that clause, it has the character of an offence within the law of this country. What other sense can be given to the 10th section of the Act: which looking at the person ruined, as this girl is, enacts, that, after there has been a marriage *de facto* with publication of banns, no evidence shall be given to disprove the fact of residence in any suit, in which the validity of marriage comes in question. But for all other purposes it may be the subject of inquiry ; and the law of the country would reach it by a Criminal Information. It is a more difficult question, whether it can be considered a conspiracy.

From what I have seen in this Court, alluding to the
[* 424] * cases, in which Lord Thurlow and Lord Rosslyn [Lough-
borough] ordered the attendance of the clergymen, I know, that this subject is carried on with a negligence and carelessness, that draws in gentlemen of good intentions ; and I feel, that it may be very difficult in this great town with all possible diligence to execute this duty as effectually as the law seems to require, that they should execute it : but, where a case has occurred, in which it is clear, that if any one of the parties had done what the law required from all of them, this marriage could not have taken place, I must say, it amounted to a criminality, which I hope will not occur in future. This is so base and wicked a transaction, that treating it merely as a contempt will not satisfy the ends of justice. Following the case, in which the marriage was had upon a license unduly obtained, I will have the point examined for the sake of the public, whether obtaining a marriage without a due publication of banns is not an offence at common law.

Without asking an explanation of any of the parties for obvious reasons, I shall order the proceedings to be laid before the Attorney General, to sift the transaction, and to see, whether any of the parties cannot be convicted of a conspiracy at common law. As to the fortune, it must be referred to the Master to receive a proposal ; and upon the circumstances the Master will, I am persuaded, take care, that neither Priestley nor any one belonging to him shall ever touch a shilling of that property, real or personal.

Aug. 12th. Priestley afterwards presented a petition to be discharged out of custody on executing a conveyance according to a proposal approved by the Master : but the Lord Chancellor would not make the order ; observing, that, what remained was with the Attorney General : his Lordship expressing his opinion, that, exclusive of the contempt, contriving a marriage by an undue publication of banns is a conspiracy ; for which he may, and ought to be, indicted.

The two sisters, the mistresses of the school, made an affidavit, of their total want of knowledge or suspicion of the treaty ; upon which the Lord Chancellor observed, it was with regard to them reduced to a case of negligence, different from positive conni-vance.

THE Marriage Act, 4 Geo. IV. c. 76, prescribes the rules by which the publica-tion of banns is to be regulated: the statutes 5 Geo. IV. c. 32, and 6 Geo. IV. c. 92, have made some amendments to the previous act. The 21st section of the statute 4 Geo. IV. c. 76, declares any person who shall solemnize a marriage un-duly, guilty of felony, and liable to be transported for fourteen years, provided the prosecution shall be commenced within three years after the offence commit-ted. And the 23d section of the same act declares that, when a marriage is sol-emnized between parties under age contrary to the act, by false oath or fraud, the guilty party shall forfeit all property accruing from the marriage; and empowers the Court of Chancery, (although the parties may not be wards of the Court,) to declare such forfeiture; and to order and direct that all such estate, titles, or in-terest, in any property which may at the time have accrued, or shall thereafter accrue, to such offending party, by force of such marriage, shall be secured under the direction of the Court, for the benefit of the innocent party, or of the issue of the marriage, or any of them, in such manner as the Court shall think fit: and if both the parties so contracting marriage shall, in the judgment of the Court, be guilty, the Court may settle and secure such property, or any part thereof, imme-diately, for the benefit of the issue of the marriage. When the party is a ward of Court, and has been married without its sanction, the general jurisdiction, without any aid from the act of Parliament, enables the Court to direct such settlement of the property of the ward, which is under its control, as may seem to be called for by the circumstances of each particular case. See, *ante*, note 1 to *Stevens* v. *Sav-age*, 1 V. 154, and note 1 to *Stackpole* v. *Beaumont*, 3 V. 89.

REEVES *v.* BRYMER.

[1801, August 5.]

Maintenance allowed for the time past (*a*).

A PETITION was presented for an allowance for the maintenance of the infant daughter of the petitioner according to the Master's Report; and claiming two sums, which the petitioner had paid and made himself liable to for her maintenance previously to the Report.

The Lord Chancellor [Eldon] observed, that the old practice was, that if the father had by any means maintained his children, the Court would not reimburse him.

Mr. *Hart,* in support of the petition, and Mr. *Richards (Amicus Curiæ)* said, the practice had been altered very soon after Lord Rosslyn [Loughborough] came into the Court; and the late Master of the Rolls [Sir R. P. Arden] had made several orders of this sort; which had been found necessary.

The Lord Chancellor expressed his approbation of the practice, as altered; and made the order (1).

THAT, in proper cases, an allowance for the maintenance of infants may be made retrospectively, as well as for the time to come, is well settled; not only by the principal case, but by *Sherwood* v. *Smith,* 6 Ves. 454; *Greenwell* v. *Greenwell,* 5 Ves. 199, and other authorities stated in note 2 to the last cited case.

THE EARL OF UXBRIDGE, *Ex parte.*

[1801, August 5, 6.]

Order, without a cause in Court, upon the general jurisdiction over a solicitor, that he shall deliver his bill; for the purpose of getting from him title-deeds deposited with him for suffering recoveries, &c.

The object of this petition, presented without any cause in Court, was to get title-deeds out of the hands of a solicitor, with whom they had been deposited for the purpose of suffering recoveries in the Court of Great Sessions in Wales and drawing deeds, [*426] upon paying him his bill; and the petition * prayed, that he might deliver his bill; but did not desire to restrain him from proceeding at law.

Mr. *Hart,* in support of the petition.—This petition is presented upon the general jurisdiction of the Court over solicitors.   In a

---

(*a*) See *ante,* note (*a*), *Greenwell* v. *Greenwell,* 5 V. 199.
(1) *Post, Sherwood* v. *Smith,* 454; *Sisson* v. *Shaw, Collis* v. *Blackburn,* vol. ix. 285, 470; *Maberley* v. *Turton,* xiv. 499. See *Hosle* v. *Pratt, ante,* vol. iii. 730, and the note, 733.

case (1) before Lord Rosslyn a solicitor had merely prepared an affidavit to found a docket for a Commission of Bankruptcy : and the business ended there ; the Commission never having been taken out. The solicitor brought an action against his client ; and Lord Rosslyn upon the general control of the Court over a Solicitor directed the bill to be taxed ; and restrained him from proceeding at law. That is not desired by this petition ; though the petitioner offers to pay the bill. No other course can be adopted but this or a bill in Equity ; as the deeds cannot be described sufficiently for an action of trover.

The solicitor did not appear.

The Lord CHANCELLOR [ELDON] said, there was no doubt, the Court exercised this jurisdiction long before the Statute (2) ; which did little more than introduce the regulations, under which the jurisdiction should be exercised ; and, as the solicitor did not appear, granted the order ; but afterwards his Lordship directed it to be stopped ; expressing some doubt upon it.

The next day the Lord CHANCELLOR said, he had looked into the cases ; and was satisfied by a case in the Term Reports (3), and another in Strange and Modern (4), that the application might be made ; and made the order.

SEE note 3 to *Ex parte Smith*, 5 V. 706.

FLETCHER, *Ex parte.* [* 427]

[1801, AUGUST 6.]

THE Court will not appoint a Master in Chancery to an office, in respect of which he will be liable to account; as committee of a lunatic's estate. The Court refused to appoint a person committee of a lunatic, upon the circumstances ; particularly, that he had agreed to give part of the profits to another (a).

THE prayer of this petition was, that Fletcher may be appointed committee of the person of a lunatic ; and that another gentleman, who was one of the Masters of the Court, may be appointed committee of the estate. Objections were taken to both appointments : as to the latter, on grounds of public policy, with the additional circumstance, that the appointment of any one of the profession of the law would have a tendency to irritate the lunatic. As to Fletcher,

---

(1) *Ex parte Smith, ante*, vol. v. 706 ; *Ex parte Arrowsmith, post*, vol. xiii. 124. In the Matter of *Aitkin*, 4 Barn. & Ald. 47. See the distinction in *Ex parte Wheeler*, 3 Ves. & Bea. 21 ; *Ex parte Partridge*, 2 Mer. 500 ; and Beames on Costs, 272 to 277.

(2) 2 Geo. II. c. 23.

(3) *Hughes* v. *Mayre*, 3 Term Rep. B. R. 275.

(4) *Strong* v. *Howe*, 1 Str. 621 ; 8 Mod. 339.

(a) The heirs and next of kin of a lunatic may be the committee. *Matter of Persse*, 1 Moll. 439 ; *Matter of Lord Bangor*, 2 Moll. 518. But even the eldest son and heir must give security. *Matter of Frank*, 2 Russ. 450. See, also, *Ex parte Fermor*, Jac. 404 ; 2 Barbour, Ch. Pr. 236.

LEICESTER, *Ex parte.*

[1801, August 8.]

A COMMISSION of bankruptcy supersedeable under Lord Loughborough's order, dated the 26th of June, 1793, is not actually superseded, till the writ of supersedeas issues; and therefore having been opened, and the bankruptcy adjudged, after the order made for the supersedeas, but before the writ sealed, notice of the application having been according to the practice in the office sent to the solicitor, the commission was supported, *Quære.*

Whether the order of Lord Apsley, dated the 12th of February, 1774, that a docket struck, and no commission issued thereon, shall in no case prevent a commission by another creditor upon an application not made in less than four days, can be strictly acted upon: the established practice in the office being at variance with it; and there being danger of fraud.

The rule of Courts of law, that all affidavits shall be filed a certain time before the discussion: the practice of this Court otherwise; and preferred notwithstanding the inconvenience. (See note (1),) [p. 432.]

THE petition stated, that upon application at the Bankrupt Office upon the 10th of July by the agent of an attorney at Liverpool for the purpose of striking a docket against Marsden and Tonge, of Liverpool, it was found, that seven dockets were struck, and some commissions issued, against them under various firms; but none of them interfering with his application, except one docket, struck on the 25th of June preceding at the instance of Layton, a merchant in London. No commission had issued upon that docket: but the solicitor was informed, that the solicitor, who bespoke the commission, must be sent to and his answer received, before the other documents could be received. The next day he was informed, that the former commission would be sealed: in consequence of which he withdrew his application. On Saturday, the 25th of July, the time for opening the former commission expired; and it became supersedeable under the order (2) of the late Lord Chancellor, dated the 26th of June, 1793; and the petitioner became entitled to a supersedeas and a new commission. A petition was presented; and upon the 27th of July an order was made by the Lord Chancellor, that the former commission should be superseded; and 10*l.* 18*s.* 2*d.* was paid for the supersedeas and for a new commission; which was directed to be sealed at the next seal. Upon the 29th the former commission was opened; and Marsden and Tonge were declared bankrupt. Notice of the adjudication was given at the Bankrupt Office; and notice to the petitioner's agent, that his application must be considered void.

[* 430]   * The prayer of the petition was, that the supersedeas may be sealed, the proceedings under the former commission stayed; and that a new commission may issue: or if the Lord Chancellor should be of opinion, that the former commission ought

---

(1) See the General Order in Bankruptcy, 16th Nov. 1805. 2 Cooke's Bank. Law, 8th ed. 273.

(2) 2 Cooke's Bank. Law, 372, 264, 8th ed. by Mr. Roots.

not to be superseded, then, that the choice of assignees may be adjourned; in order to give the country creditors an opportunity of voting.

It was stated by the affidavits, that the commission was ordered by a creditor in London without any knowledge, that an act of bankruptcy had been committed; and he afterwards wrote to Lancashire for the purpose of procuring witnesses to prove an act of bankruptcy. Some delay was occasioned by endeavors to procure a deed of trust; in which object the solicitor at Liverpool, who applied for the second commission, joined.

Mr. *Mansfield* and Mr. *Pemberton*, in support of the petition.—This commission is irregular, first, upon the order of Lord Apsley (1): no commission having issued on the docket struck at the time of the application by this petitioner. Also under Lord Loughborough's order the new commission ought to have been immediately sealed, without any notice to the solicitor, who struck the first docket. The order for the supersedeas signed by the Lord Chancellor, put an end to the commission; though the seal was not put to the writ. If this practice prevails, it will counteract Lord Loughborough's order; for still the attorney, who struck the first docket, has the preference. A case in the bankruptcy of Jenkins and Reddily will probably be cited in support of this practice; a case, in which Lord Rosslyn directed, that the commission that had issued, should be prosecuted: but his Lordship had considerable doubt upon it; and said, he should prevent that practice in future.

Next upon the particular circumstances, disclosed by the affidavits, this practice of striking a docket immediately, (and there are seven in this instance) without any evidence of an act of bankruptcy, is very improper (2).

* Mr. *Piggott* and Mr. *Cooke* in support of the Com-   [* 431] mission.—The practice is perfectly settled; and your Lordship will not overset it in a particular instance. Upon the ground now taken there never would be occasion to take out the writ of *supersedeas :* but that is the authority, which supersedes the Commission; the order is not the operative act. There are several other instances, besides that, which has been mentioned. In the bankruptcy of *Higgs* (3), in the bankruptcy of *Frith* (4), and in the bankruptcy of *Kirkpatrick* (5), all subsequent to the last order, this practice prevailed: and it was held, that the order is not infringed,

---

(1) 12th February, 1774. 2 Cooke's Bank. Law, 369. (See page 371), 8th ed. by Mr. Roots, 263.

(2) The Lord Chancellor said, he had often been surprised at this mode of swearing to an act of bankruptcy first, and inquiring afterwards, whether there was an act of bankruptcy. On this ground a charge usually made in the bill of costs for procuring this evidence is, if after striking the docket, always disallowed by the commissioners.

(3) In 1797.

(4) In 1800.

(5) December, 1800.

if the Commission is in process; though, from unavoidable circumstances, as in some cases, the absence of Commissioners, &c., the adjudication cannot be obtained within the fourteen days.   The object of the order was to prevent Commissions being sealed, that are never intended to be opened, in order to prevent others being taken out.   But that is very different from this case.   This Commission was intended to be opened as soon as it could be.   In *Ex parte H——* (1) the Commission was sealed upon the 19th of November. A meeting of creditors was called, for the purpose of an arrangement; and it was agreed to endeavor to get a deed of trust.   That delayed the opening of the Commission until the 8th of August following; when the Commission was opened at Exeter: but that could not be known in London; and a *supersedeas* was obtained. Upon a petition to annul that *supersedeas*, Lord Thurlow did annul it; and ordered a *procedendo* upon the first Commission.

Upon the particular circumstances of this case, here also there was a fruitless attempt to get a deed of trust; and this country solicitor was present upon all occasions.   There was a notorious act of bankruptcy: Marsden and Tonge having notoriously absconded at the time the docket was struck; their creditors being thereby delayed.   That was ground enough for striking a docket: but it was necessary to find out persons who could swear to the fact, and to send to Lancashire for witnesses.   When the solicitor wrote to Lancashire, the answer was, that they could obtain no information; the servants were all tutored.   At last the clerk was found in London; who proved the act of bankruptcy upon the 29th of July.

[* 432]   Lord CHANCELLOR [ELDON].—I have often * thought of a rule, that all affidavits should be filed a certain time before the discussion, according to the rule of the Courts of Law: but in opposition to that there has been the uniform practice of this Court; where the mischief has been daily felt, and complained of, without an attempt to remedy it; and by my own experience at Common Law I am convinced, that though that rule is very convenient for the despatch of business, he, who is heard last, frequently introduces a state of transactions, which governs the judgment; and which, if explained, would satisfy the Court, that it is made ancillary to the greatest injustice.   We must therefore, I think, submit to the inconvenience of the practice of this Court (2).

With respect to the first ground, upon which this petition is presented, the effect of the order for a *supersedeas*, I have no doubt, that an order for a *supersedeas* is not a *supersedeas*.   It is a declaration of the Court, that it is fit under the circumstances, that the writ of *supersedeas* should issue.   Many circumstances may arise between the date of the order and the sealing of the writ, that would prevail upon the Court to recal the order; and there might be many cases, in which the Court would think, the writ improvidently issued; and

---

(1) Before Lord Thurlow, 1791.
(2) See the General Order in Bankruptcy, 16th Nov. 1805.   2 Cooke's Bank. Law, 8th ed. 273.

would supersede it. But with regard to the order of 1793, supposing, there was no practice upon it, it says only, that the Commission shall be supersedeable: but it is not superseded, till some step is taken to produce that effect. The person applying for the order may calculate, within what time he can get the writ. By a regulation, now founded upon the express approbation of the Legislature, if he chooses to have the writ privately sealed, there ·is a larger fee ; and he chooses for himself, whether he will have it more or less speedily. He knows, that under the order the Commission being only supersedeable still remains an operative process, till he does a farther act. If by the effect of the order it remains a process, upon which a proceeding can be had, and proceedings are had, the same as would have been, if the writ issued in a later stage, where is the inconvenience in letting the former Commission go on? There may be many cases, in which it would be gross injustice to construe the order otherwise ; as if the evidence, upon which the solicitor taking out the Commission thought he was to proceed, was fraudulently kept back (1), until an application could be made for a
* *supersedeas*, with a view to have the gain of the Com-   [* 433]
mission, and to cover the frauds of the bankrupt. If
therefore the Commission has got to that extent of efficacy, before it is actually superseded, the progress to which it was the object of the order of 1793 to secure, it is not unwholesome to say, that order has been rightly construed according to the practice, that has obtained. At all events, if I thought the construction of the order wrong, I should not alter the practice in this instance ; for it must always be a rule to use the information gained in any particular case for the purpose of regulating the practice in future, but not to alter it in that instance.

As to the other point, upon Lord Apsley's order, it is more difficult to reconcile that with the practice. The words are very strong ; that a docket struck and no Commission issued thereon shall in no case prevent the issuing a Commission by another creditor, so as the application be not made in less than four days after the docket struck. But that order was made in 1774 ; upon 'which a practice has obtained, contrary, I admit, to the very terms of the order. As to this particular case, if the Solicitor had not submitted to the practice of sending to the other party, I should have been in a situation, in which I have found myself in a Court of Law : a practice having prevailed for a series of years contrary to the terms of an order of the Court, and sometimes contrary to an act of Parliament, it is more consistent to suppose, some ground appeared to former Judges, upon which it might be rendered consistent with the practice ; and therefore, that it would be better to correct it in future, not in that particular instance. Upon the question, whether that order is to be altered or to be acted upon according to its terms, which are at variance with the practice, I am not now prepared to deliver a decisive

(1) *Ex parte Freeman*, 1 Ves. & Bea. 34.

opinion; for this practice having been ever since permitted to grow
up as expository of the order, if my opinion was different from w_ha_t
it is as to the policy of the order according to its terms, I must collect,
that there is in that practice testimony given, that according to the
terms it would be an inconvenient-order. According to the best of my
judgment at present that order, if acted upon with the strictness its
terms would warrant, would open a door to fraudulent prac-
[* 434] tices in bankruptcy wider * than what now exist to such an
extent that nothing but the efforts of the Legislature can
close it.

Upon the whole there is no ground for granting this application
farther than for the purpose of letting the country creditors vote in
the choice of assignees (1).

1. Though Lord Rosslyn's General Order in Bankruptcy, dated 26th June,
1793, and cited in the principal case, has been since repeatedly declared to be a
most wholesome one, in general cases, (*Ex parte Mavor*, 19 Ves. 540; *Ex parte
Luke*, 1 Glyn & Jameson, 363,) still it has been decided that its application is discretionary; and thnt, if it were inflexible, a regulation, intended to prevent fraud,
might frequently be made an instrument to extend it. *Ex parte Freeman*, 1 Rose,
384; *Ex parte Sanden*, 1 Rose, 86. If, therefore, there has been always a *bona
fide* intention to prosecute the commission, though some delay have arisen, yet,
when that delay is satisfactorily accounted for, the commission will not be superseded. *Ex parte Soppitt*, Buck, 82; *Ex parte Knight*, 2 Rose, 322. When a
commission has been opened, and an adjudication thereunder obtained, it has been
held that Lord Rosslyn's order is satisfied, notwithstanding publication has not
been made in the Gazette within the number of days limited for proceeding under
the commission by that order. *Ex parte Ellis*, 7 Ves. 136. The case just cited,
however, has been declared to stand alone, and to have been decided upon its
own very particular circumstances. *Ex parte Handerson*, Coop. 228.
2. As to the authority which long uninterrupted practice gives to any course of
proceeding, see, *ante*, note 4 to *Ellis* v. *Smith*, 1 V. 11.

(1) See the next case. *Ex parte Ellis, post,* vol. vii. 135.

LAYTON, *Ex parte.*
HARDWICKE, *Ex parte.*

[1801, AUGUST 11, 12.]

AN order for a *supersedeas* has no effect, until the writ issues.

A joint commission against two partners in England, another partner residing abroad, superseded.

Where two Commissions are taken out against the same party, the Court will exercise a discretion, controlling the strict right; and support that, which is most convenient; if the objections to it can be removed by superseding the other.

Abuse of a Commission by delaying the execution of it with a view to another arrangement.

Whether, and under what circumstances, a trader can plead in abatement a partner abroad, *Qu.* [p. 438.]

Where one partner is an infant, or lunatic, there cannot be a joint commission of bankruptcy against the others: separate commissions must be taken out. Altered by st. 6 Geo. IV. c. 16, s. 16, [p. 440.]

THE petition of Layton stated, that a docket was struck by the petitioner upon the 25th of June against William Marsden and Christopher Tonge, of Liverpool, in the county of Lancaster, merchants, dealers, chapmen, and co-partners, carrying on trade under the firm of William Marsden and Company. Upon the 29th of July they were found and declared bankrupts under that Commission. The debt due to the petitioner was 2000*l.* Another Commission was issued against William Marsden and Christopher Tonge, of Liverpool, in the county of Lancaster, described as partners with John Anthony Frasche, of the city of Leghorn in Tuscany, and Thomas Martorelli, of the kingdom of Naples, merchants, partners, dealers, and chapmen, trading in England under the firm, William Marsden and Company. The docket, upon which that Commission issued, was struck upon the 29th of June upon the petition of Hardwicke and Cavendish of Manchester.

The petition farther stating, that the latter Commission is unnecessary, and cannot be supported, not only on account of the prior Commission, but also as being a Commission against two of four partners, prayed, that the latter Commission may be superseded.

The petition of Hardwicke and Cavendish stated, that the Commission taken out by them was sealed upon the 1st of July, the first general seal after the docket struck; and was received at Manchester * on the 4th. The petitioners thought it their [* 435] duty out of respect to the other creditors to call a meeting; especially as three fourths in number and six eighths in value of the creditors were at Manchester; and on account of a negotiation for an arrangement upon another plan the Commission was not open until the 18th; and then the Commissioners wishing for farther proof of the act of bankruptcy by Tonge adjourned to the 25th; when they were declared bankrupts. Upon the 28th notice of the adjudication of the bankruptcy appeared in the Gazette.

This petition then stated, that Layton's Commission, sealed on the 11th of July, was upon the 27th ordered to be superseded on the application of Leicester (1) ; that upon the 29th that Commission was opened ; and they were found bankrupt ; suggesting, that that Commission was virtually and effectually superseded by that order.   The petition farther stated, that the business had been hitherto carried on at Manchester under the firm of Marsden and Frasche, and at Liverpool under the firm of Marsden and Company.   At Manchester the creditors were in number 103, and to the value of 66,000l.: at Liverpool 65, in value 9000l. ; and in other places 18, in value 16,000l.   The prayer of this petition was that the other Commission may be superseded.

In support of Layton's Commission the affidavit of a clerk to Marsden and Frasche stated, that they carried on business as merchants at Liverpool under the firm of Marsden and Company.   That partnership expired on the 1st of February last ; and Marsden took Tonge in ; and from that time the business was carried on at Liverpool and Manchester under the firm of Marsden and Company; and the deponent believes, that there was no other partner; and that Martorelli was only a clerk.

The affidavits in support of the other petition stated, that all the four were partners.   Francis Hardwicke swore, that Marsden informed him, a new partnership was about to take place between him, Tonge, Frasche, and Martorelli; and that part of the goods were looked out by Martorelli; and the deponent understood him to be a principal.   William Hardwicke swore, that in April or May Marsden, in order that a consignment of goods might [* 436]   *be made, gave the firm thus, "Frasche, Martorelli and Company at Naples."

The *Solicitor General* [Hon. *Spencer Perceval*], Mr. *Piggott*, and Mr. *Cooke*, in support of Layton's Commission.—The case of *Marlar* and *Pell* (2), and many others have determined, that a commission against two of four partners cannot be supported.   That principle is recognised in *Streatfield* v. *Halliday* (3).   The point has never been ruled in the case of a partner resident abroad ; but the principle is, that there is no joint debt from Marsden and Tonge; for it is the joint debt of the four.   Two of them being out of the kingdom, amounts only to this; that two of them have not committed an act of bankruptcy.   There can be no distinction in principle from that circumstance.   It would be the same, if they lived at Liverpool. They ought therefore to have had two separate commissions.   This is often the case of great banking houses.   In the case of *Lane, Frazer*, and *Boylston*, no commission could be taken out against the last, till he had committed an act of bankruptcy by lying two months in prison.   In *Ex parte Henderson* (4) it was decided, that one of

(1) *Ex parte Leicester*, the preceding case.
(2) *Allan* v. *Hartley*, Mich. 25 Geo. III.; 1 Cooke's Bank. Law, 5.
(3) 3 Term Rep. B. R. 779.
(4) *Ante*, vol. 183.

the partners being an infant, a joint commission against the others
could not be supported. It is a very serious question, which the
petitioner has a right to have tried, whether persons dealing with
the world as partners can defeat their creditors by setting up a sleep-
ing partner. The affidavits state, that Martorelli was in this country, acting in the business, choosing the goods: therefore the
ground from his being abroad fails: the fact being false. A plea
in abatement would hold at law; whether the course is to outlaw
the person out of the jurisdiction, and then proceed against the
other.

Another ground, upon which the second commission is irregular,
is, that the docket was struck too soon: the four days not being
complete under Lord Apsley's Order (1). It ought not to have been
struck before the 30th of June. It would not have been received at
the office, but that from the difference of the description it was
thought, they were different persons; and the consequence of that is
the party, who took out the other commission, had not
* the notice, to which under the practice of the office upon   [* 437]
Lord Apsley's order he was entitled.

Mr. *Richards*, Mr. *Romilly*, and Mr. *Wetherell*, in support of
Hardwicke's petition.—In fact the Commission taken out by Hardwicke was first used; and they never took any step in the other, till
it appeared in the Gazette, that this had been executed. Almost
all the property and creditors are at Manchester and Liverpool.
There is infinite inconvenience in laying by so long after the docket
struck. If these four persons are partners, their Commission is
equally open to objection, being against two only; which the other
discloses. The principle as to partners living here must be admitted: but it never has been decided, that, because there are partners
living abroad, a Commission cannot be supported against the partners living here. Upon principle such a decision would be very
inconvenient; and ought, if possible, to be avoided. There is no
instance of a plea in abatement at law upon this point. *Darwent* v.
Walton (2). Every thing can be done under the Commission, that
could be done under a Commission against all the partners. The
description of these persons as partners is mere surplusage; and can
have no effect. In *Ex parte Law* a Commission had issued against
Smith, describing him as partner with Clayton. Another Commission issued against Smith as trading alone. An attempt was made
to supersede the first; and Lord Thurlow said, the description of
him as partner with another has no meaning: but the practice prevailed before his time; that in truth it was only a separate Commission:
that description not having any effect to make it a joint Commission.

Lord CHANCELLOR [ELDON].—The general orders in bankruptcy
must be applied with regard to cases, in which from the difficulties,
that may occur, fourteen days and sometimes more, may be neces-

(1) 12th February, 1774; 2 Cooke's Bank. Law, 869, 8th edit. by Mr. Roots,
263. See the preceding case.
(2) 2 Atk. 510.

sary for opening a Commission : but I am not at present disposed to
say, that in all cases the solicitor taking out the Commission has a
right to hold the other creditors at arm's length : not proposing an
arrangement, while the parties stand merely in the relation of debtor
and creditor ; but taking out a Commission, and holding it
[* 438]   over the bankrupt : sealing up his mouth ; and, * instead
of executing the Commission with all due diligence, as directed by the Great Seal, making it the means of bartering for
some other arrangement.   Such a use of a Commission, though it
may be expedient in some cases, will be grossly enormous in many ;
and is an abuse of the authority of the Great Seal ; upon which I
should be disposed to say, a Commission so conducted should not
be executed.   The consequence is, that under a notion of convenience the effect of the bankrupt laws is destroyed.

It did not occur in this bankruptcy, that a very grave question
might arise upon the point, whether persons living here, and trading
openly as partners, could plead in abatement, that there was a partner abroad.   There may be circumstances, upon which a great deal
of argument would be necessary to convince me, that such a plea
would do.   Suppose, they had carried on business only as Marsden
and Tonge, and the creditor did not know, that there was a dormant partner : he would have his option ; for he is not bound to
consider the dormant partner as his debtor.   But this business was
carried on under the firm, not of Marsden and Tonge, but of Marsden and Company ; and if persons will deal without inquiring of
whom the firm consists, it does not follow necessarily, that in that
case a plea in abatement would not do.   In Lord Chief Justice
Willes's report of *Crispe* v. *Perrit* (1) he states, that it was very
familiar at that day, notwithstanding what appears in Atkyns, for
joint creditors to prove under a separate Commission.   But the discussion of this question is not very useful in bankruptcy ; for if in
fact the effects were those of the three, the creditors of the three
might insist upon a distribution among them.

This is therefore not to be embarrassed with the question upon the
plea in abatement ; with respect to which the question is, not upon
the matter in the declaration, taken with the plea, but upon the declaration itself ; how it would be, if the fact, that there were partners
abroad, appeared upon the declaration ; and I remember, when that
notion of being bound to plead in abatement, was new in Westminster Hall.

[* 439]   * The point upon the *Supersedeas* I have already determined (2) ; and I am still of the same opinion.   The next
question is, independent of the effect of that order, does the proceeding in this Commission upon the 25th of July under the circumstances preclude what was done under the former Commission ?   Whatever may be the inconvenience upon the former, I should be obliged

---

(1) Willes's Rep. by Durnford, 467 ; 1 Atk. 133.
(2) *Ex parte Leicester*, the preceding case.

to say, it does not, upon the principle I stated the other day ; that the practice cannot be reformed in the present instance ; though it may be fit to reform it in future.   The practice of the office is, that if a docket is struck under one description, and another application comes with another description, the latter is received ; as, though it is against the same person, that cannot be known : otherwise notice would be sent to the other party, according to the practice in the office.   These jarring proceedings arise out of the accidental circumstance of the different description in the second docket ; which leading to this embarrassment must therefore prejudice him, who has given a different description, though by accident.   If therefore this case is to be determined upon the question of form, supposing both Commissions proper as to the trading, &c. that question must be decided with the first Commission.   But if that is so, notwithstanding a clear right to take out a Commission, yet, if there are two Commissions, and the Court sees, that by superseding one, the other may be made good, and will answer the purpose of convenience to the creditors and the bankrupt himself, the Court will supersede the one, if the objections to the other would thereby be removed.   There is therefore no doubt of the authority of the Court to overturn the London Commission, if it should think fit to do so.   But I do not see, how the Lancashire Commission could stand if I should overturn the other.   That is founded upon the debt of persons, who have erroneously represented themselves to be creditors of the four (1).   If he is creditor of the three, the same objection arises ; and it is impossible to support his Commission : at least it is so doubtful, that if I can support the other, I would not put it in peril by superseding that and leaving this.   It is very material, if the person resident abroad has been in England.   But it is very difficult to discriminate this from the case of * partners, where one is   [* 440] an infant or a lunatic ; in which cases it is clear, you cannot have a joint Commission against the others ; but separate Commissions must be taken out (2).   I do not see the convenience of saying, the affairs of the three shall be arranged under a joint Commission against two rather than under separate Commissions: the process under such a joint Commission no more attaching upon the effects of the three than under a separate Commission.   But there is a fundamental objection in the petitioning creditor's debt ; for the reasoning in *Crispe* v. *Perritt*, as reported by Lord Chief Justice Willes, went upon this ; that a Commission of bankruptcy is an action and execution in the first instance : but it must be according to the nature of the debt ; and the execution is the several fruit of the action joint.

---

(1) The fact proved to be, that Frasche was not a partner; but it was not discovered until the hearing.

(2) *Ante, Ex parte Henderson*, vol. iv. 163 ; *post, Ex parte Martin*, vol. xv. 114. By the statute 6 Geo. iv. c. 16, s. 16, a Commission may be issued against some partners, not including all of the firm ; and may be superseded as to one or more without affecting its validity as to the others.

Then upon the question, whether this can be reformed, I feel no inclination for that: nor would it be desired, if the creditors of the three are to run away with all the effects. In that case it would not be worth while to ask the matter of this petition. If under these circumstances I cannot support the Lancashire Commission, I am relieved from the consideration of the comparative number of creditors in one part of the country and another: and therefore do not state, what weight I should give to those circumstances, farther than, as a general proposition, that they do not make much impression on my mind. Upon the affidavits I am not satisfied, that there ever was such a partnership as that of the two alone. It was pressed, that Layton has a right to try, whether the two are not to be considered with respect to his debt as the only partners. If I was satisfied, that in fact the effects belong to the three, I am not sure, that I should permit a Commission to stand, merely to determine that point of law, which would not attach upon the administration of the effects. The Solicitor therefore must inform himself of that fact.

After some inquiry from the Solicitor the petition *Ex parte Hardwicke* was dismissed; and the order was made according to the prayer of the other petition. ____

1. THAT a commission of bankruptcy ought, in general cases, to be proceeded with as directed by the General Order of Lord Rosslyn; but that, under peculiar circumstances, it may be only reasonable to allow a longer time for the opening a commission; see the notes to the last preceding case.

2. It is no longer necessary to include a dormant, or even an avowed, partner in a commission against other members of the same firm; see note 3 to *Langston* v. *Boylston*, 2 V. 101, and note 2 to *Ex parte Hamper*, 17 V. 403.

3. As to the incapacity of an infant to sue out a commission against another party, or to be made a bankrupt himself; see the note to *Ex parte Barrow*, 3 V. 554; but that Equity will give no summary relief, by superseding a commission issued against an infant, who has fraudulently held himself out as an adult; see note 1 to *Ex parte Henderson*, 4 V. 163.

4. That it is inaccurate, though not uncommon, to speak of a commission of bankruptcy as "an action and execution in the first instance;" see note 4 to *Hankey* v. *Garrett*, 1 V. 236, and note 3 to *Ex parte Brown*, 2 V. 67.

ASHLEY, *Ex parte.*
CORSER, *Ex parte.*

[1801, Feb. 7; August 8.]

A PERSON, in the habit of receiving the money of a Friendly Society, having no treasurer appointed, upon notes carrying interest, payable a month after demand, is not an officer of the Society, so as to entitle them to a preference under the statute 33 Geo. III. c. 54. s. 10.

RICHARD SMITH and George Watson, Attorneys, in partnership at Whitchurch in Shropshire, were from the commencement of the establishment of a Friendly Society in the habit of receiving from the Stewards the money of the Society, whenever it amounted to a sum, which they considered worth placing out at interest; giving their promissory notes from time to time carrying interest. Watson died; and Smith became bankrupt in 1795. At the time of his bankruptcy he was indebted to the stewards of the Society to the amount of 145*l.* upon his promissory notes, payable on one month's notice; which sum was composed of principal and interest due on several promissory notes of Watson and Smith. No person had been appointed treasurer of the Society.

The first of these petitions was presented by the Steward of the Society under the Act (1) for the encouragement of Friendly Societies, to have the money due from the bankrupt paid by the assignees.

The petition came on before Lord Rosslyn (*a*) [Loughborough].

Mr. *Benyon*, in support of the Petition.—Though there is no appointment of the bankrupt as treasurer in the books of the Society, he was in the habit of receiving the money of the Society from time to time; in which case your Lordship has held, that a person receiving the money from time to time is in the nature of a treasurer; and it is not necessary under the Act, that he should be appointed. That is the only ingredient wanting in this case.

Mr. *Pemberton*, for the Assignees.—It is not pretended, that this bankrupt was either trustee or treasurer, or that he held any office. He was an attorney in the neighborhood; in whose hands the stewards from time to time placed the money of the Society; for which he gave them security. A prior clause (2) in this * Act authorizes the treasurers or trustees to place out the   [* 442] money on private or government securities. The clause, upon which this petition is presented, is expressly confined to money received by virtue of his office; and the intention clearly was, that only debts due by officers of the Society should be preferred; not debts from people entrusted by them with the money.

---

(1) Stat. 33 Geo. III. c. 54. The clause (sect. 10,) is stated *ante*, 99, *Ex parte The Amicable Society of Lancaster*; see the note, 100.

(*a*) Anterior to his resignation of the great seal, which took place April 14th, 1801. See *ante*, 5 V. 880; note (*a*); 2 V. 61.

(2) Sect. 6.

Mr. *Cooke (Amicus Curiæ)* said, in the case alluded to the party, though not formally named treasurer or trustee, was in fact executing the office.

The Lord CHANCELLOR [ELDON].—I have a recollection of it; and take it so. I determined upon his being in fact treasurer. He had been so, I think, from the commencement of the Society, before the Act. But this is no more than the case of any banker.

. Mr. *Benyon*, in reply.—This is not one act, but a constant habit, when any money was received, of paying it to these persons; and when it amounted to this sum of 145*l.* a note was given.

Lord CHANCELLOR.—It was not a deposit of money, and one note given: but it is admitted, that it was regularly paid to them upon interest; they giving their notes. In order to make interest of the money, they paid it to an attorney of character; taking interest notes upon it. I think the petition right.

Upon this judgment the order was made accordingly, that the assignees should pay to the Stewards of the Society the sum of 145*l.* The other petition was afterwards presented; praying, that the order might be discharged. That petition came before Lord Eldon.

Mr. *Romilly* and Mr. *Pemberton*, in support of the Petition.—The words of the Act are very plain. In the matter of *Spendlow* (1), a case, upon which this order was made, the party was appointed treasurer. Another case, *Ex parte Askwith* (2) certainly [* 443] is against * this petition. The objection was made, that the party was not appointed treasurer; but the Society had lent the money to him at interest. The Lord Chancellor said, there being no other treasurer, his having the money in his hands was equivalent. But the particular circumstances of that case do not appear. This bankrupt upon the affidavits in support of the other petition could not possibly be considered treasurer.

Mr. *Benyon*, for the Society.—The late Lord Chancellor thought this case the same as *Ex parte Askwith*; and there have been several orders of the same kind; in which this has been considered equivalent to an appointment. Any person appointed to receive the money from time to time is treasurer for the time being.

Lord CHANCELLOR [ELDON].—The question is a dry question of fact; whether the bankrupt was or was not the treasurer of this Society. If he was not, it is clear, the Society had not against individuals, with whom their officers chose to deal, the extensive remedies given by this Act against persons holding offices under them. I do not recollect enough of the cases cited to be able to state the particular circumstances: but I apprehend from the order in *Ex parte Askwith*, and what is now stated, those decisions went upon this, as a fact proved to the satisfaction of the Court, that they were to be considered as treasurers; that they were in fact treasurers;

(1) 21st December, 1798.
(2) 6th June, 1795.

and in the order *Ex parte Askwith* there is an allegation, that the
bankrupt entered into the Society as an honorary member; served
the office of president; and accepted that of treasurer, under what
circumstances does not appear.   No particular mode of election is
pointed out by the Act: but he is in fact to be elected; and you
must collect from the circumstances, whether he is constituted treasurer or other officer.   Suppose, the Steward had distributed the
money among all the bankers of this city; taking notes, payable at
a month's notice with interest: no doubt the Legislature did not
mean, that there should be 1500 treasurers; and yet the same argument would prove them all so.   This is therefore not a question at
law; but, whether under the circumstances of putting the money
into the hands of the bankrupt, payable by note at a month with interest, he is to be considered treasurer; where there is no other.
Upon my view of the Act it does not occur to me, that this
bankrupt either received or * retained this money by virtue   [* 444]
of any office; or, that the circumstance of this loan, payable at a month with interest, will make him a treasurer, merely because no other treasurer was appointed; or that you shall imply
upon the mere receipt of the money with such security, that he is a
treasurer, either self-elected, or with the approbation of the Society;
for it would go this length; that every one receiving the money
would be treasurer; if no other was elected.   The treasurer is to be
the creature of election.   A preceding clause (1) of the Act has
clearly contemplated this case.   Under that clause if there was a
treasurer, or, if not, a trustee, who laid out money upon private security of this sort, the persons would have the money in their hands;
but the Legislature confines the special remedy to the case of those,
who have it, not as debtors merely, but in that character, and also
as having charged upon them duties and trusts; for the clause giving this special and extensive remedy does not give it to those, to
whom the officers of the Society have lent the money; but stops
short.   The eighth section is also material.   If the relation, in which
this person stood to the Society, was formed by a security, in which
they expressly stipulate, that he shall not pay over the money upon
demand, can the intention of the transaction be to place him in an
office, the person exercising which the Legislature has said shall pay
it over on demand; upon whom therefore the Society might contrary
to the stipulation of the note call to have it paid over at a moment's
notice?   Observe the consequence in another respect.   If benev-
olent persons should give these Societies property, or, if persons
should withhold money, which they had a right to demand, the Society would under this construction of the Act be enabled to call
upon this person as treasurer; and would file their bills, and defend their suits, in his name.   He must therefore be a person elected, and accepting the office; and it is too much to say, a person,
to whom their money is lent upon this sort of security, is *ipso facto*

---

(1) Sect. 6.

to become the treasurer by the fact of .that loan, liable to the duties, inconveniences, and obligations, imposed by the Act upon the officers.

Therefore, not meaning to say, the cases referred to are not rightly decided, if the Lord Chancellor [Loughborough] collected, that the parties had accepted the office, however elected [* 445] into it, it does not appear * to me, that it ever was the intention to constitute in this person the character of treasurer; and it is impossible to argue it so high from the mere fact of his becoming a debtor to the Society, that he became an officer of the Society; and then it is clear, they have not this remedy against him. Reverse the order; and let them prove the debt under the commission.

See the note to *Ex parte The Amicable Society of Lancaster*, 6 V. 98.

RICKETTS, *Ex parte.*

[1801, August 10.]

The time enlarged for a bankrupt, who had omitted to finish his examination; but the order would not discharge a prosecution for the felony.

The petition stated, that the petitioner, a bankrupt, had surrendered; and attended upon his examination. On the last day, the 25th of April, the examination not being finished, the meeting was at his request adjourned to the 21st of May. On the 20th he attended the assignees at Bristol; and returned to Charlcombe near Bath to search for more vouchers: but not being able to find any he did not attend again; being ill, and almost in a state of mental derangement from the threats of the assignees, that he would be committed. The assignees denied, that they had threatened him. The petition also stated, that they would not let his clerk attend with him.

The prayer of the petition was, that a meeting may be appointed to finish the bankrupt's examination.

The Lord Chancellor [Eldon] made the order; observing, that this order would not discharge him from a prosecution for felony: Lord Thurlow had determined that.

Mr. *Mansfield*, for the petition.

Mr. *Romilly* and Mr. *Bell*, for the assignees, mentioned *Ex parte Grey* (1).

Although the punishment to which non-surrender may subject a bankrupt is mitigated, by the 112th section of the statute 6 Geo. IV. c. 16, still the penalty is

(1) *Ante*, vol. i. 195; *post, Ex parte Higginson*, xii. 496; *Ex parte Johnson*, xiv. 36; *Anon.*; *Ex parte Jackson*, xv. 1, 116; *Ex parte Berryman*, 1 Glyn. & Jam. 223.

more severe than would be merited by a party who has not delayed to make his surrender from fraudulent motives, but solely in consequence of mistaken advice; in such cases, it has long been the practice of the Court, at its discretion, to order the commissioners to accept the surrender of the bankrupt, after the usual time for surrendering has elapsed; such an order, however, did not prevent a prosecution, and operated only as an intimation of the Chancellor's opinion, that the bankrupt did not keep out of the way fraudulently, and that if prosecuted, he would not be convicted, or if convicted, would receive a pardon: *Ex parte Shiles,* 1 Mad. 249; *Ex parte Lavender,* 18 Ves. 19: but now, the 113th section of the statute above cited enacts, that the Lord Chancellor shall have power, as often as he shall think fit, from time to time, to enlarge the time for a bankrupt's surrender, provided an order to that effect be made six days at least before the day on which such bankrupt was to have surrendered himself.

CUNDALL, *Ex parte.*   [* 446]

[1801, August 10.]

BANKRUPT surrendered in discharge of his bail, and discharged by the creditor; having never been charged in execution; this is no election; and the creditor was admitted to prove, (a).

Debtor two Terms in prison without being charged in execution is entitled to his discharge.

A COMMISSION of bankruptcy issued on the 9th of October. In the vacation after Trinity Term the petitioner had sued out a writ of *Fieri Facias* against the bankrupt, returnable in Michaelmas Term. After the bankruptcy a writ of *Capias ad Satisfaciendum* was lodged with the sheriff, for the purpose of fixing the bail. The bankrupt surrendered in discharge of his bail; but was never charged in execution; and was discharged by the petitioner, before he had been in prison two months. Under these circumstances the petitioner prayed, that he might be admitted to prove his debt under the commission.

Mr. *Richards,* in support of the petition.

Mr. *Johnson, contra.*—If the bankrupt had been taken, that would have been clearly an election by the creditor; and he could not have resorted to the commission. There is no distinction from the object to fix the bail. In both cases the question is, whether the creditor has had a satisfaction for his debt. Though not taken by the sheriff, he was by the bail in consequence of that writ; and was surrendered by them. The bankrupt was in substance, though not in form, charged in execution. Unless the creditor had a right to resort to the effects at the time of the surrender, he cannot now.

Lord CHANCELLOR [ELDON].—There is this difference; if he had

This indulgence is given to the bankrupt at his own expense; *Ex parte Carter,* 4 Madd. 394. Consent of the assignees not necessary; *Ex parte Shiles,* 1 Madd. 248.

(a) See *Beaty* v. *Beaty,* 2 Johns. Ch. 430.

stayed two Terms in prison without being charged in execution, he
would have been entitled to his discharge.   The creditor might have
resorted to his effects; declaring, that he would not charge him in
execution.   Until he charges him in execution, he is not barred.
If once he proceeds against the effects, a Judge at Chambers would
say, he has consented to elect.   This turns out to be a voluntary act
by him surrendering himself in discharge of his bail.   Issuing the
writ is not enough.   If he had been taken under the writ, that
would be another thing.   It is impossible to say, the mere surrender
of a man in discharge of his bail amounts to charging him
[* 447]   in execution by the creditor, an act, done by *him, ascertaining, what his election is; for it is upon the ground of
the act of the creditor, that an execution by him after the bankruptcy
is an election.

The Order was made (1).   ____

THE rule laid down in the principal case has been since repeatedly recognized,
namely, that a debtor's surrender in discharge of his bail cannot be deemed an
election on the part of his creditor to proceed at law, so as to bar the creditor from
coming in under a commission, more especially when he has not proceeded to
charge the debtor in execution; and when the body of the debtor has been taken
in execution, the case is only so far varied, that the creditor, if a subsequent commission issue, must elect whether he will continue to hold the bankrupt in execution, or to prove under the commission: *Ex parte Arundel*, 18 Ves. 231; *Ex parte
Knowell*, 13 Ves. 193; *Ex parte Parquet*, 14 Ves. 495: if the bankrupt be in prison, or custody, at the suit of, or detained by, a creditor, such creditor cannot prove
or claim under a commission against the debtor, without giving a sufficient
authority in writing for the discharge of the bankrupt: should the commission,
however, be afterwards superseded, the creditor may proceed in his action *de novo*,
as if he had never elected to take the benefit of such commission; see the 59th
section of the statute 6 Geo. IV. c. 16.

SMITH, *Ex parte.*

IN THE MATTER OF HARTSINK AND CO.

[1801, AUGUST 8, 11.]

LIEN.

THE petition was presented; claiming a lien upon a quantity of
platina, deposited with the bankrupts, who were engaged in a concern, called "The Original Security Bank of Hartsink and Co."
formed upon the plan of issuing notes upon the security of deposits.
These notes were in this form: promising upon the 5th of December
next and after that date upon demand to pay to James Cantfort or
order 200*l.*, "being a portion of a value as under deposited in

security for the payment hereof, according to a receipt in our hands;" and marked with letters with reference to the property.

The property was assigned to Hartsink and Co., their executors, administrators, and assigns, to and for their own use and benefit absolutely for ever; and the owner did for himself, his executors and administrators, warrant and defend the said platina unto the said Hartsink and Co., their executors, &c. against him, the said owner, and against all and every other person and persons whatsoever.

A memorandum was indorsed, that they would permit the owner to show the platina to any person for the purpose of buying or cheapening the same; and in case of any contract for the purchase thereof or of any part, then that Hartsink and Co. will deliver the same to such buyer or buyers, if they approve the price agreed upon; and that Hartsink and Co. will not sell, unless the owner shall fail to provide for and make good the payment of the notes, when due: if they fail in that, then Hartsink and Co. may sell; and first pay the notes outstanding, interest, &c., and if the owner shall provide for and take up the notes, and indemnify *Hartsink   [* 448] and Co. then they shall re-sell and re-deliver to the owner all such parts remaining.

The petition was presented by the indorsee of three notes issued upon the deposit of the platina. The affidavit of Hartsink stated, that a lien was intended.

The *Solicitor General* [Hon. *Spencer Perceval*], in support of the Petition.—In addition to the affidavit of Hartsink, that a lien was intended, the circumstance, that the property was marked, and the terms of the notes, imply a lien; and the other construction will operate a gross fraud.

Mr. *Richards, contra,* insisted, this was only a deposit of value, not a lien.

The Lord CHANCELLOR [ELDON] said, this was a question of a good deal of difficulty upon the demand arising out of these instruments; and suggested, that a bill ought to be filed.

Aug. 11*th.*—The parties consented to take the directions in bankruptcy; and came to an agreement as to all except as to the excess of the bills issued beyond the value of the platina.

Lord CHANCELLOR.—If the bankrupts issued bills to the amount of 1500*l.*, when the security was worth only 1000*l.*, that is a fraud by them as to the 500*l.* excess. If they take out bills to the amount of 500*l.*, they put it then, as it ought to be; and redeem themselves from the fraud. Consequently the platina is liable to the first bills for 1000*l.* then out; and the assignees can be in no better situation than the bankrupts. They state upon the face of the bills, that they are for value received in the article deposited as a security. It is an assertion therefore upon every bill, that they have full value in that article for that bill; and they cannot as against third persons allege.

that they have not platina to that value.   If they cannot as against
         third persons allege that, it necessarily drives them out
[* 449]   of the account.   The fundamental * vice of this bank
         was issuing bills far exceeding the value of the property
deposited.

The order was made by consent according to the minutes agreed
upon ; with a previous declaration, that the holders of the bills have
a right to have the platina applied in discharge of them.

BLOXHAM, *Ex parte.*

[1801, AUGUST 11.]

CREDITOR having securities of third persons to a greater amount than the debt
   may prove and receive dividends upon the full amount of the securities to the
   extent of 20*s.* in the pound upon the actual debt.

KIRKPATRICK, of Liverpool, having an account with the petitioners as his bankers, from time to time remitted bills to answer his
drafts, and among others six bills drawn by him and accepted by the
bankrupts Young and Glennie.   Kirkpatrick also becoming bankrupt, the petitioners proved under his Commission the sum of 3234*l.*
12*s.* 11*d*, due to them upon a balance of accounts.   They also
proved under the Commission against Young and Glennie the sum of
3869*l.* 10*s.* 3*d.* the amount of the six bills accepted by them.   A
dividend of 2*s.* in the pound was declared under the Commission
against Young and Glennie ; which dividend was paid to the petitioners upon the sum of 3234*l.* 12*s.* 11*d.* only, without prejudice :
the assignees refusing to pay the dividend upon the residue of the
amount of those acceptances ; suggesting, that the petitioners were
entitled to receive a dividend only upon the actual balance due to
them from Kirkpatrick.   No dividend had been declared under the
Commission against Kirkpatrick.   •
   The prayer of the petition was, that the assignees under the Commission against Young and Glennie may pay.to the petitioners the
dividend of 2*s.* in the pound upon the residue of the sum of 3869*l.*
10*s* 3*d.* proved by them ; and that they may receive upon the whole
of the said sum future dividends, not exceeding 20*s.* in the pound,
upon the debt to them from Kirkpatrick : the petitioners insisting,
         the bills accepted by Young and Glennie are to be con-
[* 450]   sidered collateral securities, to be retained, until * the
         whole of the debt due to them from Kirkpatrick shall be
fully satisfied.
   Mr. *Mansfield* and Mr. *Cooke,* in support of the petition insisted, that the decision upon the petition *Ex parte Bloxham* in the

bankruptcy of *Purdy* (1) was against all the former orders ; *Ex parte Crossley* (2) : *Ex parte King* (3) ; and others before Lord Thurlow and Lord Rosslyn [Loughborough].

Mr. *Richards* for the assignees insisted, that they were right in confining the dividend to the actual debt; and said, Kirkpatrick was indebted to these bankrupts.

Lord CHANCELLOR [ELDON].—I looked upon it as settled, that you cannot hold the paper of the bankrupt, and prove beyond your actual debt upon it ; but that you may have the paper of third persons, those persons being indebted to your debtor in more, and you may prove to the whole amount, not exceeding 20*s.* in the pound upon the original debt. Suppose, you owe 1000*l.* and as a security assign a bond for 2000*l.* ; cannot the creditor prove the 2000*l.* till he gets the 1000*l.* ? The petitioners are creditors of Young and Glennie for the whole amount of their acceptances : they are creditors of Kirkpatrick for less : in this situation they have a right to apply their legal demand against Young and Glennie to the extent of obtaining the full amount of their actual debt. The case is no more than this : Kirkpatrick had an account with the petitioners ; and sent them bills accepted by this bankrupt from time to time to cover that account. If the petitioners can only prove the amount of their debt, they have not the full benefit of the security. It is not material, that Kirkpatrick was indebted to Young and Glennie ; for you cannot attach equities upon bills of exchange. The petitioners therefore must prove the amount of that paper, given to them to secure that debt.

The order was made.

SEE, *ante*, the notes to *S. C.* 5 Ves. 448.

BAINBRIDGE, *Ex parte.*   [* 451]

[1801, AUGUST 10, 12.]

ORDER under st. 5 Geo. II. c. 30, s. 31, that new assignees may be chosen, and that the commissioners may execute a new bargain and sale and assignment, the former being vacated: all the assignees being dead; and the heir at law of the survivor an infant.

ALL the assignees under a Commission of bankruptcy being dead, and the survivor having left an infant heir at law, this petition was presented ; praying, that two new assignees may be chosen ; and

(1) *Ante*, vol. v. 447. Reversed, *Ex parte Bloxham*, *post*, 600. See the note, *ante*, vol. v. 449.

(2) 1 Cooke's Bank. Law, 158, 8th edit. by Mr. Roots, 177 ; 3 Bro. C. C. 237.

(3) 1 Cooke's Bank. Law, 157, 8th edit. 177.

that the Commissioners may execute a new bargain and sale and assignment; the former being vacated.

The Lord CHANCELLOR.said, it was very right, if it ever had been done : but the difficulty was to find a precedent.

Mr. *Piggott*, in support of the Petition, produced an order for that purpose ; *Ex parte Bury;* the assignee being dead; and there being a representative.

Lord CHANCELLOR [ELDON].—That was the case of a provisional assignee; which makes all the difference; for the full assignment devests his estate; but nothing can take it out of this infant heir of the surviving assignee.

Mr. *Piggott* said, there was no difference in that case; as they always make the provisional assignee join.

Mr. *Cooke (Amicus Curiæ)* said, Lord Rosslyn [Loughborough] had made an order of this sort under the authority of the statute (1).

Lord CHANCELLOR.—I think, this may be done.   The Act of Parliament gives the authority (2).

The Petition was ordered.   ____

THE 56th section of the statute 6 Geo. IV. c. 16, expressly removes all difficulties as to directing a new bargain and sale and assignment of a bankrupt's real and personal effects.

---

(1) Statute 5 Geo. II. c. 30. s. 31.   The statute 3 Geo. IV. c. 81, s. 5, declares, that this clause extends to deeds of bargain and sale.

(2) *Ex parte Leman, Ex parte Cooke, post,* vol. xiii. 271 ; Buck, 319 ; see the note, 322, and the General Order of Lord Loughborough, 8th March, 1794; *Ex parte Harris,* 3 Madd. 473.

THE ATTORNEY GENERAL *v.* GREEN.

[1801, July 17, 24; August 12.]

A LONG lease of a charity estate in 1715 at a great undervalue decreed to be delivered up; and an account directed with just allowances.

In 1715 the charity estate, the subject of this information, then let at 31*l.* a year, having upon it some buildings considerably out of repair, was demised by the trustees to the grandfather of the Defendant for the term of 999 years in consideration of an . additional rent of 4*l.* a year, and the sum of 500*l.* at least to be laid out in repairs. The annual value at present is between 90*l.* and 100*l.*

Mr. *Richards* and Mr. *Johnson*, for the Relators. Mr. *Romilly*, for the Defendant.

This was considered a new case ;. and stood for judgment.

Lord CHANCELLOR [ELDON].—I can find no precedent for the regulation of the judgment of the Court in such a case. I take the Defendant to be the personal representative of his grandfather ; to whom this charity estate was demised by this lease; which is in effect a purchase of the perpetuity for that increased rent of 4*l.* a year and the sum to be laid out; making the fund, that was to produce the old rent and that additional rent, so much better security as an expenditure not to be short of 500*l.* would make it. It is impossible, that a person taking in good faith would take such a lease as that. The difficulty is how to give a person not taking in good faith the benefit of that situation, that I would give a trustee laying out money for the benefit of the charity, and desiring for his own benefit that sort of interest in the charity fund, that would secure him the re-payment. I am in a good deal of difficulty how to deal with the case. I apprehend, the result of an inquiry, having the object of securing the lessee that benefit, would be, that he is already paid. He must have credit for having paid the original and additional rent. He cannot have credit against the charity for having expended more than 500*l.*; for it would be much too dangerous to inquire by the evidence of persons making valuations now, and speculating upon the price of buildings in 1715 and the possible value of what they conceive, for they cannot know any thing, as to the value of the old materials upon the premises. It is safer therefore to proceed * upon the evidence the deed   [* 453] furnishes ; concluding, that the trustees called upon him to lay out not less than 500*l.*, and to say, that is all he ought to be taken under these circumstances to have laid out. If so, he must have 25*l.* a year interest upon that 500*l.* since the expenditure; which with the rent would be 59*l.* a year. Then, this interest being satisfied by that rent, the question upon the inquiry would be, whether the 500*l.* must not be satisfied now by the excess of the rent beyond the 59*l.* a year, about 30*l.* a year, going to sink the

SITTINGS BEFORE MICHAELMAS TERM.

[42 Geo. III. 1801.]

THE DUCHESS OF NEWCASTLE, *Ex parte.*

[1801, Oct. 30.]

THE Court refused to make an order under an Act of Parliament for the sale of estates upon the opinion of a conveyancer, approving a conveyance, without a reference to the Master.

UNDER an Act of Parliament for the sale of estates of the Duke of Newcastle, directing the conveyance to be such as the Court should think proper, a motion was made by Mr. Sutton upon the opinion of a conveyancer, that a deed of appointment would be the proper conveyance.

The Lord CHANCELLOR [ELDON] disapproved the practice of coming upon the opinion of a conveyancer; and referred it to the Master.

SHERWOOD *v.* SMITH.

[1801, Nov 5.]

MAINTENANCE allowed for the time past as well as the time to come (*a*).

LEGACIES of 500*l.* each were given to grand-children by the will of their grand-father. Some of them presented a petition, praying an inquiry, whether their father has been and is of ability to maintain and educate them; by whom they have been maintained and educated since the death of the testator; whether any and what allowance hath been made; and what will be the proper allowance for maintenance and education for the time past from the death of the testator, and for the time to come, until their ages of twenty-one, or farther order. The father had only an income of 120*l.* per annum, and a large family.

[*455]   *Mr. *Richards*, in support of the petition, said, the practice now is to inquire as to the time past as well as the time to come.

The Lord CHANCELLOR [ELDON] said, he understood the practice

(*a*) On the subject of maintenance, see *ante*, note (*a*), *Greenwell* v. *Greenwell*, 5 V. 199; *The matter of Bostwick*, 4 Johns. Ch. 100.

to have been altered in that particular ; and made the order accordingly (1).

SEE, *ante,* the note to *Reeves* v. *Brymer,* 4 V. 692, and the farther references there given.

——— *v.* OSBORNE.

[1801, Nov. 6, 13.]

ON motion a reference directed to inquire, whether the Defendant, a trustee, remains accountable for any acts done by him as trustee, and, if not, to settle a release (*a*).

THE bill was filed by creditors against the executors and devisees in trust, subject to the.payment of debts. All the estates were sold under the decree.

Mr. *Wooddeson,* for the Defendant Osborne moved for a reference to the Master to appoint a new trustee in his room, and to settle the form of a release, and discharge him from the trust, on the ground, that he had never acted, or received any part of the purchase-money ; and that he was of a very advanced age.

The motion was made on the first day of Term before the Master of the Rolls, sitting for the Lord Chancellor, who expressed doubts, whether it could be done without a suit ; and directed the motion to be made before the Lord Chancellor.

The Lord CHANCELLOR [ELDON].—It would be a dangerous proceeding upon a mere statement at the bar to order a trustee to convey, and so dismiss him ; as if there was no demand against him. It is not the course of the Court to look through all the proceedings. Refer it to the Master to look through the proceedings, and to see, whether this Defendant remains accountable for any acts done by him as trustee; and in case he does not, then to settle a release.

TRUSTEES are not to be changed, and new ones appointed, without the authority of the Court; unless a special provision to that effect is contained in the instrument by which the trust is created. *Buchanan* v. *Hamilton,* 5 Ves. 722; *Webb* v. *The Earl of Shaftesbury,* 7 Ves. 487; *Millard* v. *Eyre,* 2 Ves. Jun. 94.

---

(1) *Reeves* v. *Brymer, ante,* 425, and the note.
(*a*) As to the appointment of new trustees; see *ante,* note (*a*), *Millard* v. *Eyre,* 2 V. 94.

PELLEW *v.* ————.

[1801, JULY 20; AUGUST 12; Nov. 13.]

A REFERENCE of an answer for impertinence is waived by a subsequent reference
for insufficiency (a).
After a reference for insufficiency the answer cannot be referred for impertinence (b), [p. 458.]

THE Plaintiff on the 25th of June, obtained an order referring the
answer for impertinence. On the 2d of July he obtained another
order, referring the answer for insufficiency. These references were
made to different Masters. Warrants were taken out upon both;
but no farther proceedings took place under the reference for impertinence. Under the reference for insufficiency a report was obtained; establishing four exceptions, and over-ruling two. A motion
was made for the Defendant to discharge the order of reference for
impertinence.

Mr. *Hall,* in support of the motion.—The subsequent order of
reference for insufficiency was a waiver of the former order. There
is a distinction between scandal and impertinence : as to the former,
the Court takes care to keep its records pure : but taking any step
in pleading is a waiver of a reference as to impertinence. *Lady
Abergavenny* v. *Lady Abergavenny* (1). *Anon.* 2 Ves. 631 (2).
The judgment of the Master upon the insufficiency does not weigh
upon this point: for the mere act of the second reference, no proceedings being had upon the former, is a waiver. Lord Rosslyn
according to a note of a case on the 19th of January, 1796, seemed
to consider this point clear ; though it was not in judgment before
him. The note says, that an order referring exceptions, after the
eight days had expired, was discharged. There had also been an
order referring the answer for impertinence ; and it was held, that
the exceptions taken to the answer waive the impertinence ; though
you may certainly refer for impertinence, and afterwards take exceptions too.

According to this note it is laid down as clear, that after an order
of reference for impertinence you may refer for insufficiency. But
if no proceedings are had upon the reference for impertinence, and

(a) If exceptions are taken for both insufficiency and impertinence, they must be
taken and referred at the same time. *Woods* v. *Morrell,* 1 Johns. Ch. 103; *Hart* v.
Small, 4 Paige, 333. As to exceptions for impertinence, see 1 Barb. Ch. Pr.
202–205 ; *Van Rensselaer* v. *Brice,* 4 Paige, 174; *Bally* v. *Williams,* M'Cle. &
Young, 334; *Desplaces* v. *Goris,* 1 Edw. 350; *Scudder* v. *Bogert,* 1 Edw. 372;
Jolly v. *Carter,* 2 Edw. 209; *Wagstaff* v. *Bryan,* 1 Russ. & M. 28; *Spencer* v.
Van Duzen, 1 Paige, 555; *Livingston* v. *Livingston,* 4 Paige, 111.; *Franklin* v.
Keeler, 4 Paige, 382; *Whitmarsh* v. *Campbell,* 1 Paige, 645.
(b) The complainant is not precluded in New York, from excepting to the farther
answer of a Defendant, for impertinence, although it purports to be an answer to
the old exceptions for insufficiency only; *Hart* v. *Small,* 4 Paige, 333.
(1) 2 P. Will. 311.
(2) *Anon. ante,* vol. v. 656.

you have had the effect of the other reference, that is a waiver of the former. In *Dixon* v. *Olmius* a plea of a fine and recovery of prodigious length was put in. After a reference for impertinence the anxiety of the parties led them to set down the plea for argument: and that was held clearly to destroy the reference for impertinence. Any step taken after such a reference, and that reference not proceeded in, is a waiver of it; particularly in a case of double dilatories. The reason of the thing requires, and therefore it ought to be the practice, that the report upon the impertinence ought first to be obtained; for passages may be struck out upon the reference for impertinence, that would be an answer to the exceptions.

Mr. *Romilly* and Mr. *Thomson*, for the Plaintiff.—It is certainly decided, that if a party takes a proceeding in the cause, he cannot refer for impertinence: but it does not follow, that an order referring exceptions is a discharge of a prior order of reference for impertinence. That has been never decided. Upon principle can it be? The questions of impertinence and insufficiency are quite distinct. Upon the objection, that passages may be struck out as impertinent, that would be an answer to the bill, the answer ought in all cases to be first referred for insufficiency: and then the whole practice of the Court is wrong. What possible inconvenience can there be? In the instance, upon which that objection is made, the inconvenience is to the Plaintiff; who must then take an insufficient answer. On the other hand it would be very inconvenient, if the report upon the impertinence must be obtained before a reference for insufficiency.

Mr. *Hollist* (*Amicus Curiæ*) said, nothing could be found exactly in point; but that a reference for impertinence cannot be obtained after an order for time to answer; nor by a Plaintiff after reply: it must be the first step: in this case, until the result of the reference for impertinence appears, the Court cannot say, whether the answer is insufficient.

Mr. *Hollist* also cited an order to show, that a reference for impertinence stops the proceedings.

Mr. *Richards* (*Amicus Curiæ*) said, Lord Chief Justice Eyre thought, the reference for impertinence must be first disposed of.

* *Nov.* 13*th*.   Lord CHANCELLOR.—Upon the best con-   [* 458]
sideration of this point I think, the reference for insufficiency before the result of the reference as to the impertinence is a waiver of the latter reference: for there is abundance of cases both in print and manuscript, proving, that if you refer for insufficiency, you cannot afterwards refer for impertinence; and I have always understood the practice to be so. This is just the converse of that: but it is very difficult to say, what principle sustains the one, that will not sustain the other. I should think, upon a mere order of reference for impertinence, and nothing done upon it, and then an order of reference for insufficiency, which order was first, and which last, would make no great difference; for the good sense is, that the re-

sult of the reference for impertinence should be known, before you
refer for insufficiency ; that the Master, to whom that is referred,
should have the purified record, if I may so express it, before him.
Therefore what I understood Lord Rosslyn [Loughborough] to have
said in the note, that has been cited, is, that if the reference for impertinence has been gone through, then, the record being, as it
ought to be, you may refer for insufficiency.   To examine the two
points together would be very inconvenient for this reason ; that if
the reference for impertinence is in one Master's office, and the
other reference in another, one Master, considering, whether the answer is sufficient, may say, it is, because a passage is in it, which
very passage may be by the other Master struck out, as impertinent :
and the former might think it not impertinent.   At all events it is
impossible, that these two orders can be executed by two different Masters ; as I cannot expect that two Masters will agree as
to what is or is not impertinent ; feeling, how difficult it is in the
case of *Hughes* v. *Williams* (1) to say, what is impertinent.

In this case what I have been considering is, whether, there being
clearly a want of accurate knowledge as to the practice, I may not
in this particular instance stay the proceedings upon the reference
for insufficiency, that I may know the result of the reference as to
the impertinence ; and then send the purified record to the Master
          upon the insufficiency ; declaring the practice for the fu-
[* 459]   * ture.   I think, therefore, the best way is to let the ref-
          erence for impertinence go on ; declaring, that this is not
to operate as a precedent in future (2).

SEE the notes to the *Anonymous case*, 5 V. 656.

HUGHES v. WILLIAMS.

[1801, AUGUST 1, 12; Nov. 13.]

OBJECTIONS to interrogatories settled by the Master for impertinence must be
taken by exceptions, not by petition, as an objection to the appointment of a
receiver, (a).

UPON a bill of foreclosure the usual accounts were decreed ; and
the Plaintiff having been in possession, it was directed, that he
should be examined upon interrogatories ; which were settled by

(1) The next case.
(2) See *Lacy* v. *Hornby*, 2 Ves. & Bea. 291; *Raphael* v. *Birdwood*, 1 Swanst.
228.   Reference for impertinence good cause against dissolving an injunction;
Fisher v. *Bayley*, *post*, vol. xii. 18; *Goodinge* v. *Woodhams*, xiv. 534.   In the latter
case, Lord Eldon imposed the condition of procuring the report in a week; *Dansey*
v. *Browne*, 4 Madd. 237.
(a) See *Remsen* v. *Remsen*, 2 Johns. Ch. 499.

the Master. The Plaintiff presented a petition; praying, that certain parts of the interrogatories may be expunged, as impertinent.

Upon a doubt suggested, whether the objections ought to be made by petition or exceptions, Mr. *Thomson* for the Defendant said, that, where the report does not require confirmation, the course is to petition against it: but in the case of a report of the insufficiency or impertinence of an answer the proper mode is by exception; which must be filed in a limited time, and with a deposit.

Mr. *Richards*, in support of the Petition.

Lord CHANCELLOR [ELDON].—I have no doubt, that exceptions will do: but it is very questionable, whether this can be done by petition. I think, it is quite out of the reach of the principle, that this can come on in this way; for then the party will have a right to 'petition without calling upon the Master to consider the objection. That is not the case upon exceptions. The objection to the appointment of a receiver is a question upon a dry, simple fact; that the Master has approved a particular person.

Nov. 13*th.* The Lord CHANCELLOR said, he was satisfied, the proceedings upon the impertinence of the interrogatories may be by exceptions; which were filed accordingly (1).

———

Lord ELDON's determination of the question in the principal case, was in conformity with the opinion delivered by Sir Thomas Sewell, M. R. in *Stanyford* v. *Taylor*, 2 Dick. 548, though Lord Thurlow, in the case cited, came to a different conclusion. That an objection to the Master's appointment of a receiver may properly be made by petition, see *Wynne* v. *Lord Newborough*, 15 Ves. 283; though the Master's selection is never disturbed on light grounds; see *ante*, the note to *Thomas* v. *Dauskin*, 1 Ves. 452.

———

DARE *v.* TUCKER.　　　[* 460]

[1801, Nov. 13.]

A PURCHASER, who cannot have the original title-deeds, the estate being sold in a great number of lots, is entitled to attested copies at the expense of the vendor, notwithstanding the inconvenience and expense (a).

MR. HART on behalf of a purchaser moved for an order, that attested copies of title-deeds should be delivered ât the expense of the vendors; insisting upon the ordinary rule, that a purchaser has a right to attested copies of deeds relating to his estate with

———

(1) In *Stanyford* v. *Tudor*, 2 Dick. 548; and *Paxton* v. *Douglas, post*, vol. xvi. 239, it was held, that the exceptions should be taken, not to the Master's allowance of the interrogatories, but to the Report, whether the examination is sufficient, or not. *Ante, Holbecke* v. *Sylvester*, 417, as to excepting for costs.

(a) As to the importance of the original title-deeds in England, see *ante*, note (*a*), *Ford* v. *Peering*, 1 V. 72.

others; where, his estate being of inferior value, he cannot have the originals.

Mr. *Romilly,* for the Trustees, opposed the motion upon the authority of a case before Lord Rosslyn [Loughborough], and the great inconvenience, the estate having been sold in 144 lots, and upon an undertaking, that there should be a covenant for the production of the deeds, but no attested copies; which was denied by the purchaser.

Lord CHANCELLOR [ELDON].—This is of great consequence. There being 144 lots in the sale of this estate, what an infinite number of attested copies may be necessary. The old practice was precisely according to the motion. The case before Lord Rosslyn, I apprehend, went upon a covenant, as matter of agreement upon the sale, that the vendor should produce the original title-deeds (1); and Lord Rosslyn construed it, not only, that he engaged to produce the title-deeds, but as a negative stipulation, that he should not give attested copies. The pressure of the Stamp Duties, I believe, led to that determination. Purchasers have set a value upon these attested copies, which does not belong to them. They are waste paper upon ejectment, unless between the parties themselves. It has struck me as very convenient, that a short Act of Parliament should be passed, declaring, that a copy certified by the Master to be a true copy should be evidence. I think, you must give them attested copies, unless you leave the originals, or make some other proposal in the Master's Office. It will throw a prodigious expense upon the trust, if all the purchasers are to have attested copies; and yet I rather think, they are entitled. What is now required is reasonable enough; not copies of all the deeds, but only so far back as to make a title: that is, an estate tail, that has been barred (2).

_____

IT is quite settled, that a purchaser of small lots, part of an estate sold before the Master, is entitled to have, at the expense of the vendor, attested copies of the title deeds which are to accompany the principal purchase, when no stipulation on the subject has been made: *Boughton* v. *Jewell,* 15 Ves. 176; *Berry* v. *Young,* 2 Espin. 640, n.: as to the value of an enrolled deed, or the copy of such deed, by way of evidence; and the difference taken where the estate passes by the enrolment, as in a bargain and sale; or where it is only enrolled for safe custody; see *Lady Holcroft* v. *Smith,* 2 Freem. 259, (2d edit.) and the notes thereto; as also *Harvey* v. *Philipps,* 2 Atk. 541, and *Stillingfleet* v. *Parker,* 6 Mad. 248; *S. C.* Colles, P. C. 337.

_____

(1) *Barclay* v *Raine,* 1 Sim & Stu. 449.
(2) Mr. Hart said, that in *Bird* v. *Le Fevre* the lots were more than 200; and the copies came to 1000l.; *Boughton* v. *Jewell, post,* vol. xv. 176.

INNES *v.* MITCHELL.

[Rolls.—1801, June 9, 11, 15.]

Bequest of the debt, which shall be owing on a particular day, taken, as it stood on that day; and not affected by consignments from the West Indies on account since the death of the testator, which happened previous to the day specified.

William Innes by a codicil, dated the 20th of June, 1790, after several legacies, proceeded thus:

" Tenthly, I give to the eldest son of my late nephew Alexander Innes and of Janet Sharpe the mother all the debt which shall or may be owing to me by the late John Crawfurd of Bellfield estate in Jamaica on the 1st day of January 1794 say 1794 whether by bond mortgage or open account to the sole use of my said grand-nephew subject to his paying to his brothers I think there are two of them one hundred pounds each during their lives or only fifty pounds I mean yearly in case such debt does not exceed eight thousand pounds sterling or that his two brothers shall be entitled to one fourth part of the yearly interest at 5 per cent. on whatever the sum or debt may be owing by Bellfield estate."

By another codicil, dated the 23d of March, 1793, the testator taking notice of the above bequest goes on as folllows:

" 3d, In page 7th I give all the debt which shall be owing by the late John Crawfurd of Bellfield estate at the 1st of January 1794 which I now alter to the 1st of January 1796 subject to the said eldest son of the said Alexander Innes now Thomas Innes to whom that debt is given on his paying to his two brothers one fourth part of the interest of the sum such debt may happen to be at my death at the rate of 5 per cent. during the lives of both or only one of such brothers."

The testator died on the 14th of January, 1795.

Upon the bill of Thomas Innes against the executors two points were made; first, that the Plaintiff became entitled to the debt bequeathed to him upon the testator's death: 2dly, that, if the Court should be of opinion, he was not entitled to the debt until the 1st of January, 1796, the executors had by undue management with the executor of Crawfurd, who was the brother of * one   [* 462] of them, for the purpose of disappointing the Plaintiff's legacy in favor of the residuary legatees, diminished the debt at the 1st of January, 1796. By a decree made at the Rolls in June, 1799, various inquiries were directed as to the amount of the debt at the death of the testator, and what had been remitted on account between that period and the 1st of January, 1796.

The Master's report stated, that the debt at the death of the testator was 15,405*l*. 2*s*. 4*d*. exclusive of judgments, to the amount of 3855*l*. 8*s*. 10*d*. According to the usual course of dealing the balance upon the 1st of January, 1796, would have been 14,517*l*. 16*s*. 3*d*. besides judgments: and no part of the sum of 3000*l*. which the

executors upon the 31st of December, 1795, carried to the credit of
the debt, would have been so carried, if the testator had lived to
1796.   The report then stated a correspondence between the executor of Innes and the executor of Crawfurd ; in which the latter was
directed to consign over to the former the whole crop within the year
1795, and to avoid drawing bills until after the 1st of January, 1796 ;
stating the purpose to be to vary the amount of the debt by an ac-
celeration of payment on account of the difference it will make in
favor of the residuary legatees.   In consequence of those directions
credit was taken for the 3000*l.* the net proceeds of the crop of 1794,
on account of the Bellfield estate.   The report then stated the accounts, the state of the debt, and the application of the produce of
the estate for several years.

Exceptions were taken by the Defendant to the report.

Mr. *Piggott*, Mr. *Romilly*, and Mr. *W. Agar*, for the exceptions.

Mr. *Alexander* and Mr. *Cullen* for the report, upon the first point
insisted upon the case of *Hutcheon* v. *Mannington* (1), and the wisdom of the rule established in that case, confining the time to the
death of the testator ; and for that purpose even rejecting positive
words, rather than leave it to the management of executors to ascertain the amount.

[* 463]   * *June* 15*th.*   The MASTER OF THE ROLLS.—[Sir WM.
GRANT] — The words of the first codicil create no doubt
as to the time, at which the principal legatee should take his legacy :
the period, at which it was intended, that he should take the debt,
being evidently the 1st of January, 1794; which by the subsequent
codicil is altered to the 1st of January, 1796.   That is all, that can
properly be said to be a question of construction.   It is contended,
that no payment was made from August to the 1st of January, 1796.
On the other hand it is insisted, that a diminution took place in
that interval : the executors contending, that the consignment of
sugars made in the intermediate time by the managers to the executors is to be taken as a diminution of the debt over and above all the
charges. • The Plaintiff contends, that no part of that was to be carried over, until the actual balance was ascertained.   If the receipt
of a consignment has never been considered as a payment, how can
it be so considered in this case?   The question is, I admit, whether
there was an actual payment.   Clearly there was no actual payment
There was no sum upon the 1st of January, or at any other time,
which could have been handed over.   The executor, if he had been
called on for that purpose, would have refused to hand over the
money ; and would have said, he was under acceptances for more
than that.   It is said, that, if a bankruptcy had happened, the property could not have been got out of the hands of the consignee:
no ; for there would have been a lien.   Upon the whole the
testator must be taken to have intended the debt, as it stood

---

(1) *Ante*, vol. i. 366, and the note, 367 ; *Gaskell* v. *Harman*, *ante*, 159, and the
note, 165 ; *post*, vol. xi. 489 ; *Sitwell* v. *Bernard*, *post*, 520.

upon the 1st of January, 1796, and the amount to be ascertained without any regard to the amount of the consignments in 1795; and therefore it is to be taken, as it stood upon the 10th of August, 1795.

1. THAT a Court of Equity must not be induced to put a forced construction on the words of a will, merely because the obvious meaning of the words is a strange one; but that when the language of a will is not so explicit as to exclude all extrinsic considerations, the inconsistencies which might arise out of one construction, or be avoided by another, are constantly attended to; and that in order to collect the intention of the testator, every part of his will must be considered; see, *ante,* note 4 to *Blake* v. *Bunbury,* 1 V. 194.

2. Although, in the principal case, it was held, that the language of the will confined the Court to consider the bequest as an annuity only, and not as a legacy; yet it has been frequently determined, that a sum bequeathed for the purchase of an annuity is a vested interest in the annuitant, who may elect to take the money, without having it laid out in the purchase of an annuity; see the authorities cited in the note to *Barnes* v. *Rowley,* 3 V. 305.

INNES *v.* MITCHELL.　　　[* 464]

[ROLLS.—1801, Nov. 12, 16.]

BEQUEST of an annuity of 200*l.* for the use of A. and her children, to be paid out of the general effects until it is convenient to the executors to invest 5000*l.* in the funds in lieu thereof for her and their use, and to the longest liver, subject to an equal division of the interest, while more than one alive; held an annuity, not an absolute legacy, (*a*).

WILLIAM INNES, having by his will given several annuities, and directed the mode of payment by investing a convenient sum, by a codicil, dated the 20th of June, 1790, made the following bequest:

" I give to Mrs. Janet Innes relict of my late nephew Alexander Innes two hundred pounds per annum for the use of herself and children which annuity is to be paid out of my general effects until it is convenient to my executrix and executors to invest five thousand pounds in the funds in lieu thereof for her and their use and to the longest liver of her and her children subject to an equal division of the interest while more than one of them alive."

(a) Where the interest or produce of a legacy is given to, or in trust for a legatee, or for the separate use of such legatee, without limitation as to continuance, the *principal* will be considered as bequeathed also. 2 Roper, Legacies, by White, 331, ch. 21 § 9. If, however, from the nature of the subject, or the context of the will, it appears that the produce or interest of the fund was only intended for the legatee, the gift of the interest will not pass the principal. Ibid, 333.

If the annuity be given to a man and the heirs of his body, it is in the nature of an estate tail; and to prevent a perpetuity, the common law gives him an absolute interest in the annuity; *Bradhurst* v. *Bradhurst,* 1 Paige, 331. See also, *Charstie* v. *Vause,* 1 Sim. 153; *Dawson* v. *Hearn,* 1 Russ. & M. 606; *Wergall* v. *Brome,* 6 Sim. 99; *Robinson* v. *Townsend,* 3 Gill. & J. 413; *Paterson* v. *Leith,* 2 Hill. Ch. 16; Hovenden's note to the preceding case, *ante,* p. 463.

The testator died in January 1795. The bill was filed in January 1799 by Janet Innes and her three children against the executors; praying, that the Defendants may be decreed to invest the said sum of 5000*l*. in satisfaction of the bequest, and to pay the Plaintiff interest thereon since the time they have had assets in their hands sufficient to satisfy the same; the Plaintiff Janet Innes submitting to allow what she had received in respect of the annuity of 200*l*.; that an inquiry may be directed, to ascertain, when they received such assets; and an account of the personal estate: and in case the Court shall be of opinion, that the Plaintiffs are not absolutely entitled to the said 5000*l*., that they may be declared entitled to the interest thereof during their lives and the life of the survivor of them, &c.

The Defendant, the acting executor, by his answer stated, that he is unable to set forth, whether the personal estate will be sufficient to pay the legacy claimed by the bill; unless it is to be preferred to common pecuniary legacies.

Mr. *Alexander* and Mr. *Cullen*, for the Plaintiffs.—The first consideration is, whether this is an absolute legacy of 5000*l*. The expression, "until it is convenient" in this codicil can
[* 465]   receive no * other construction than this: as soon as the executors have received clear assets applicable to the discharge of the legacy. The second point is, whether this continues to be a mere annuity, or, whether the legatees are not entitled to the interest of the 5000*l*. during their joint lives: and the survivor to take the capital of the whole. The latter part of the clause "subject to an equal division of the interest, while more than one of them alive," upon which it will be contended, that they are not to have any interest in the principal, will not detract from the prior absolute gift.

Mr. *Romilly*, and Mr. *Leach* for the Defendant.—The question is, whether the principal or the interest only of 5000*l*. is given. The use is clearly applied only to the interest; to an annuity, as long as it is in the shape of annuity, without a capital, and the interest of the capital, when that capital is invested. The same direction is given as to the annuity to his wife and the other annuities; that a particular part of his property shall be set apart for the payment of that particular annuity. If these Plaintiffs were entitled to the 5000*l*. immediately, of what use is the direction, that it shall go to the longest liver of them? The annuity of 200*l*. is the substantive gift; the will then directs, out what fund that is to come: the subsequent words are mere limitations of the gift. That construction is sensible and consistent: the other supposes a second substantive gift. Then suppose the mother had died the day after the testator, the consequence would have been, that the children would have had nothing till the 5000*l*. was invested.

Mr. *Alexander*, in reply.—The other parts of the will as to the other annuities do not apply: the continuance of those annuities being distinctly expressed, and the words of this bequest having a contrary import, the inference is directly the reverse. How can this be a continuance of the same annuity? The case put of the death of the mother, before the 5000*l.* should be produced, and the conse-quence, that the children would be unprovided for, are not material. These dispositions are in a very inaccurate instrument: but I do not conceive, that consequence would follow. The children would not-withstanding her death be entitled to the annuity, until the other provision should be made.

* *Nov.* 16*th.* The MASTER OF THE ROLLS [Sir WIL-   [* 466] LIAM GRANT].—It is very difficult to form any decisive opinion upon a codicil so very obscurely penned; but I am inclined to think it was not the intention of the testator to give a principal sum, but only to secure an annuity. It is a mode taken by the tes-tator in many parts of his will; giving annuities; and directing the mode, in which they shall be paid. The difference here is, that 5000*l.* is directed to be invested in lieu thereof; but still for the same purpose, I apprehend; and the only difference between this and the other bequests is, that in the others the expression is a con-venient sum; in this a specific sum is mentioned: but it is evident upon the whole, the testator did not mean to convert the annuity at a given period into a legacy of a specific sum; but intended, that it should continue as annuity during the lives of the legatees; and the survivor of them should receive the whole interest; and, till there is a survivor, all the legatees shall receive the whole annuity among them (1).

RIGBY *v.* M'NAMARA.

[1801, Nov. 19.]

A PERSON, who by opening the biddings has occasioned a resale at a considerable advance, though not himself the purchaser, is not entitled to costs, (a).

UNDER a decree for the sale of estates Charles Mills purchased for 2200*l.* Thomas Ellis obtained an order to open the biddings upon the usual terms, paying the costs and making a deposit of 500*l.* Upon the resale Mills was again declared the best purchaser for 3200*l.* A motion was made by Ellis, that the deposit of 500*l.* might be repaid to him, and, on the ground of the benefit to the estate from his bidding, that he might be allowed his costs of the order of resale and paying in the deposit.

Mr. *Stratford* for the parties entitled to the money opposed this as to the costs on the ground, that this was a speculation, which

----

(1) This decree affirmed on appeal by the Lord Chancellor, *post*, vol. ix. 212.
(a) As to opening biddings and the practice thereon in the United States, see *ante*, note (a), *Anonymous*, 1 V. 453; note (a), *Chetham* v. *Grugeon*, 5 V. 86.

failed; that he opened the biddings for the benefit of himself, not of the estate; and the failure of that speculation did not entitle him to the costs.

The Lord CHANCELLOR [ELDON] refused the motion as to the costs; observing, that the costs were in the nature of a premium paid by him for the opportunity of bidding (1).

SEE, *ante*, the notes to *S. C.* 6 V. 117.

[* 467]   BOARDMAN *v.* MOSTYN.

[1801, Nov. 19.]

BILL for specific performance of a parol agreement to grant a farm lease with the usual and customary covenants of the neighborhood and an injunction to prevent an ejectment; the Plaintiff having taken possession. Upon the answer, stating the insolvency of the Plaintiff and various breaches of the agreement during five years' possession, to the ruin of the estate, the injunction was continued on an undertaking to give judgment in ejectment, go to commission, and set down the cause for next term, paying the rent into Court. Defendant also insisted on a covenant not to assign, that is the subject of inquiry as to the custom of the neighborhood (a).

WHETHER the answer admitting possession taken under the agreement takes the case out of the statute of Frauds, where it is not clear, what the agreement was, *Quære*, (b), [p. 470.]

The Court endeavors to collect, what are the terms [p. 471.]

THE bill prayed a specific performance of a parol agreement made in October 1796, to grant a lease for twenty-one years of premises in Wales to the Plaintiff, with the usual and customary covenants of the neighborhood, and an injunction to restrain the Defendant from bringing an ejectment: the Plaintiff having taken possession under the agreement. On the answer coming in the Defendant obtained an order to dissolve the injunction, unless cause.

The Defendant by his answer stated, that he never meant or promised to grant a lease without a covenant to prevent assigning without license. He does not believe, the Plaintiff laid out any money farther than a tenant would be obliged to do for raising crops, and which must have been repaid. The Plaintiff committed wilful, extravagant, waste upon the premises; permitting them to become impoverished for want of expending the produce and manure; having

(1) *Post, Earl of Macclesfield* v. *Blake*, vol. viii. 214; *Trefusis* v. *Clinton*, 1 Ves. & Bea. 361. Beames on Costs, 239; *Post, Owen* v. *Foulks*, vol. ix. 348; *West* v. *Vincent*, xii. 6, the case of exception, noticed in *Earl of Macclesfield* v. *Blake*, where the object in bidding was the benefit of the family. As to opening biddings generally, see the note, *ante*, vol. ii. 55.

(a) Equity will not decree a specific performance where such a decree would be inequitable under all the circumstances. See *ante*, note (a), *Willingham* v. *Joyce*, 3 V. 168.

(b) See *ante*, note (a), *Hare* v. *Shearwood*, 1 V. 241; note (a), *Brodie* v. *St. Paul*, 1 V. 326.

sold all the hay and corn; and having during his occupation, without consent, cut timber, grubbed up hedges, and laid fields, before separated, together, and taken down out-houses, and sold the lead. About Michaelmas 1799 he sold off his cattle and stock; discharged his servants; and left nothing upon the premises. He was arrested for 128*l.* arrears of rent due at Lady Day 1800; and the Defendant from compassion liberated him upon giving a promisory note for part; upon which note he was again arrested; and he afterwards discharged the debt.

The answer farther stated, that the Defendant neglected to sow barley from inability to buy seed; that great part of the cattle in the farm-yard was not his own; that he has set the premises; and a few months ago he left his residence; and his gone with his family to reside at Liverpool; trying to get into some sort of business; and is supported in the litigation by his brother; and that the premises are going to decay. The answer farther suggested the Defendant's belief, that the Plaintiff is in insolvent * circum- [* 468] stances; and stated several circumstances in support of that allegation, showing, that he was in great distress.

Mr. *Romilly* and Mr. *Benyon* for the Plaintiff showed cause against dissolving the injunction.—The whole contest is, whether this covenant ought to be inserted as a usual covenant; for it is admitted, that an agreement partly executed has taken place: the answer stating, that the Plaintiff entered into possession in pursuance of it. Independent of the breaches of covenant, if the cause was at hearing, there would be no difficulty in decreeing a specific performance. Without contending, after the doubt expressed by your Lordship upon that point (1), that the mere admission of the agreement by the answer takes the case out of the statute (2), this case is clearly out of it, the agreement being part performed by taking possession; which is not an equivocal act. The question then is, whether the possession shall be changed, before the subject comes to be finally sifted upon evidence. As in *Williams* v. *Cheney* (3), if the Plaintiff should be willing to take a lease with the covenant, a specific performance would be decreed.

With respect to the breaches of covenant, stated by the answer, the time is not specified; though it is generally intimated, that they took place prior to 1799; and then they were afterwards waived; for the answer states, that the Plaintiff was arrested for rent due at Lady Day, 1800. If the Defendant knowing, that these acts had been committed, waived them by receipt of rent, he cannot afterwards say, they were a forfeiture in Equity. The rule is the same in Equity as at Law.

Mr. *Lloyd,* Mr. *Richards,* and Mr. *Pemberton,* for the Defendant.—The injunction ought to be dissolved. This is entirely in the sound discretion of the Court. If upon the answer, which must be

(1) *Ante,* 37, in *Cooth* v. *Jackson;* see the note, vol. iii. 38.
(2) 29 Char. II. c. 3.
(3) *Ante,* vol. iii. 59.

taken to be true, the Court finds, that continuing the tenant in possession will ruin the estate, and that he is quite incompetent to perform the covenants, under the circumstances, the change
[* 469]   of possession cannot be a real injury to the Plaintiff. * It
has never been determined, that the mere entry in pursuance of a parol agreement is sufficient without something else; as
money laid out.   The contest is now merely, whether there is to be
a covenant not to assign.   With respect to that the later decisions
in the Exchequer and before Lord Rosslyn in opposition to *Henderson* v. *Hay* (1), before Lord Thurlow, are, that such a covenant
is a usual covenant: *Folkingham* v. *Croft* (2).   The Defendant
swears, he never intended or promised to grant a lease without such
a covenant.   Thought it is admitted, that the Plaintiff took possession under an agreement for a lease for twenty-one years, if any
circumstance happens, that renders him incapable of fulfilling his
part of the contract, or, that would be a sufficient ground for an
ejectment, the other party cannot be compelled to grant a lease.   In
Willingham v. *Joyce* (3) it was held upon great consideration, that
if a man after entering into a contract of this nature committed a
felony, or became manifestly insolvent, the Court would not enforce
the contract; and that is a very sound determination.   The same
doctrine was held in *Brooke* v. *Hewitt* (4).   In granting a term for
so long a time the Court will, as matter of sound discretion, see,
whether the tenant is in a situation to perform his engagements.
Granting a lease or continuing the Plaintiff in possession of the
premises under the circumstances disclosed by the answer will produce irreparable injury.   On the other hand how can he be injured
by changing the possession: neither he nor his family being in the
actual occupation?   He has abandoned the possession; and underlet; which with notice of the dispute as to the covenant he ought
not to have done: but it was from mere necessity.   Several other
circumstances show complete insolvency.   Will the Court give such
a tenant to any man?   Enough appears to show, that the bill must
be dismissed; and if so, for what purpose is the possession to be continued except to give him an opportunity of totally dismantling the
premises?   The inconvenience would not be near so considerable,
if, the possession being now given to the Plaintiff, a specific performance should be afterwards decreed.

[* 470]   * Mr. *Romilly* in Reply.—The question now is as to
continuing the Plaintiff in possession.   In *Willingham* v.
Joyce notwithstanding the facts, that were stated, Lord Rosslyn continued the injunction.   The Defendant knew, the Plaintiff had been
a trader at Manchester, and had become a bankrupt; which is no

_____

(1) 3 Bro. C. C. 632.
(2) 3 Anst. 700.   That case is over ruled, and the authority of *Henderson* v.
Hay established in *Church* v. *Brown, post*, vol. xv. 258.   See *Vere* v. *Loveden*, and
Jones v. *Jones*, xii. 179, 186.
(3) *Ante*, vol. iii. 168; see the note, 169.
(4) *Ante*, vol. iii. 253.

reason. The facts stated by the answer are inconsistent; and the Court cannot say, the Plaintiff is incapable of disproving it. In many cases mere possession in pursuance of the agreement has been held sufficient. *Wills* v. *Stradling* (1). No ejectment has been yet brought. Though changing the possession will not be an injury personally to the Plaintiff, it will to the under-tenant; who will have his remedy against the Plaintiff.

Lord CHANCELLOR [ELDON].—The length, to which the Court has in fact dispensed with the statute, makes it very difficult to be sure of deciding correctly upon these motions for injunctions; for it is exceedingly difficult in this stage of the cause to collect, what of necessity the Court will do, when the proofs come before it; giving due attention to the decisions, that have been made in equity upon the statute. It is clear upon the Plaintiff's statement, that the lease must have been in the nature of a husbandry lease; under which the land was to be fairly dealt with. He does not bring forward a dispute upon that: but he says, that under this agreement he was to be at liberty to assign; and that in pursuance of the agreement he entered into possession. The Defendant states a perfectly different agreement; that the tenant was not to be at liberty to assign; that the agreement was for a lease for twenty-one years, with the usual and customary covenants of the neighborhood; and he contends, that a covenant not to assign, and, I apprehend, he means under-letting also, is a usual and customary covenant of the neighborhood. It is said, that if the Defendant admits, that possession was taken in pursuance of the agreement, that takes it out of the statute. That it may have that effect in cases, where it appears, what the agreement was, may be clear; but *non constat*, that it has, where that does not appear. At the same time unquestionably the Court has gone a great way upon that. In a case, that came from Malton in Yorkshire, possession having been delivered in pursuance of a parol agreement, and a dispute arising upon the terms of the agreement, Lord Thurlow * thought proper to send it to   [* 471] the Master, upon the ground of the possession being delivered to inquire, what the agreement was. The difficulty there was in ascertaining that. The Master decided, as well as he could; and then the cause came before Lord Rosslyn [Loughborough] upon farther directions; who certainly seemed to think, Lord Thurlow had gone a great way; and either drove them to a compromise; or refused to go on with the decree upon the principle, on which it was made.

The great difficulty in this case will be upon the admissibility of evidence; for a parol agreement with liberty to assign is perfectly different from the agreement admitted by the Defendant; which is an agreement under the covenants for the management and enjoyment, which the usage of that neighborhood would infuse into such a lease; and when the Defendant admits, that in pursuance of the

(1) *Ante*, vol. iii. 378; see the note, 38.

agreement, meaning that in his answer, possession was taken, he does not admit, that it was taken in pursuance of the agreement stated by the bill: nor do I know, that the Plaintiff has tendered a case, upon which, attending to what is denied by the answer, consistently with the provisions of the statute it is competent to introduce the proofs: but it is not inconsistent, that, if the Court has the means of finding out the customary covenants, they may not prohibit assigning; and if they do, that they may not prohibit underletting. Perhaps, if it was *res integra*, the soundest rule would be, that, if the party leaves it so uncertain, the agreement is not taken out of the statute sufficiently to admit of being enforced: but in all the cases in Equity, the Court has at least endeavored to collect, if they could, what were the terms the parties have referred to. Upon the nature of the agreement therefore it is impossible in this stage of the cause, to dissolve the injunction. *Williams* v. *Cheney* does not amount to much; for adverting to the terms of the contract the Master of the Rolls said, it was only an agreement, that if the party could grant a lease, he would; and he does not say, what he would have done, if it had been an absolute covenant. But I do not go upon the point as to assigning or under-letting; which must be the subject of inquiry as to the usual and customary covenants of the neighborhood. Upon the other part of the case, taking the agreement to be such as the Plaintiff says it is, and looking to the De-

[* 472]   fendant's account of the Plaintiff's conduct, recollecting, also, that * his conduct is now only to be collected from the answer, certainly in this stage I do not think it right to dissolve the injunction. On the other hand the answer must be taken to be true upon this application: particularly regarding the consequence of changing the possession; and looking accurately to the mischief the Defendant may sustain from not changing it. The article having provided, that the estate should be possessed in a husbandlike manner, under covenants calculated to give it its proper value during the whole lease, if after five years, from 1796 to 1801, the tenant has so misused the land, that it may be difficult to recover the value it would have had, if properly possessed, during the remainder of the term, it would be extraordinary to say, it is fit to give the tenant the execution of the contract, merely to give him the chance of trying to restore it; and if he has plainly violated his contract, it will be very difficult to persuade me at the end of five years to grant him a lease, the covenants of which it is demonstrable he would have broken, if it had been granted to him before. I do not think, the waiver by receipt of the rent prevents the Defendant from desiring the Court not to put him in the power of such a tenant hereafter. Without going through all the circumstances, which are certainly very strongly stated in the answer, it is impossible not to say, this is not a very favorable case for the tenant *prima facie*. I do not say, he is to be bound by the answer: but it is wholesome to take care not to uphold the injunction but upon terms, which will secure to the Defendant the whole benefit he could have, if the in-

junction was not sustained. An ejectment has not been brought. The Grand Sessions will not be till Easter. If therefore the Plaintiff will undertake to give judgment in the ejectment, without putting the Defendant to expense, and go to commission, and set down the cause for hearing next Term, then if the bill shall be dismissed, possession will be given without a trial; and if the bill should be sustained, no execution shall issue.

Liberty was given to amend the bill by stating an offer by the Defendant in November 1800, just before the bill was filed, to execute a lease. The rent was ordered to be paid into Court. The injunction was afterwards dissolved without opposition.

---

1. A COVENANT in a lease against alienation without license, is at least as old as *Dumpor's case*, 4 Rep. 119; but this by no means proves such a covenant to be an usual one: and though in *Folkingham* v. *Croft*, 3 Anstr. 701, the Court of Exchequer held, that on an agreement for a lease "with all usual and *reasonable* covenants," a covenant not to underlease or assign is implied: and Lord Kenyon determined, in *Morgan* v. *Slaughter*, 1 Espin. N. P. C. 8: that an agreement for a lease with "*fair* and usual covenants," implied a covenant not to assign, or underlet, without leave of the landlord in writing; still it has been decided, both by Lord Thurlow, in *Henderson* v. *Hay*, 3 Brown, 632, and by Lord Eldon, in *Church* v. *Brown*, 15 Ves. 271; that a covenant not to assign without license, does not come within the meaning of a contract to grant a lease with "common and usual covenants," without some more express stipulation. In this conclusion Sir William Grant finally concurred in *Browne* v. *Raban*, 15 Ves. 531; it was, in fact, a conclusion in perfect conformity with his honor's own reasoning, in the previous cases of *Vere* v. *Loveden*, 12 Ves. 184, and *Jones* v. *Jones*, 12 Ves. 189; though he then felt himself hampered by the decisions of the Court of Exchequer, and of Lord Kenyon.

2. That where the rights of creditors under a commission (who may have been induced to give credit to the bankrupt on the faith of his known agreement for a lease) do not interfere; the insolvency of a proposed tenant would be a weighty objection to a specific performance of an agreement for a lease; see, *ante*, the note to *Willingham* v. *Joyce*, 3 V. 168.

3. In order to obtain a decree for specific performance, the subject and terms of the agreement must distinctly appear; and (unless in cases of part performance, perhaps, which may sometimes justify a distinction as to this matter,) the weight of authority seems to be in favor of holding, that those points must be stated in the plaintiff's bill, and proved as stated. *Savage* v. *Carroll*, 2 Ball and Bea. 453; *Daniels* v. *Davison*, 16 Ves. 256, and see, *ante*, note 3 to *Mortimer* v. *Orchard*, 2 V. 243.

4. Part performance, no doubt, in Equity, takes an agreement out of the Statute of Frauds, when the terms of the agreement are clear; but nothing is to be considered as a part performance, which does not put the party seeking a specific execution into a situation which is a fraud upon him, unless the agreement be performed; see note 3 to *Brodie* v. *St. Paul*, 1 V. 326; thus, when possession is delivered, according to agreement, the bargain is in part executed. *Butcher* v. *Stapley*, 1 Vern. 365; *Pile* v. *Williams*, 2 Vern. 455; *Wheeler* v. *Newton*, Prec. in Cha. 16. If it were held otherwise, a party let into possession, on a parol agreement, would be liable as a wrong-doer, and trespasser; see note 1 to *Wills* v. *Stradling*, 3 V. 378. And it is not necessary that a written agreement should embody all the terms; it may be enforced, provided it contain such a reference as may enable the particulars to be unequivocally established *aliunde*; see note 2 to *Brodie* v. *St. Paul, ubi supra.*

5. The peculiar nature of the subject demised, may make it impracticable to determine, by reference to *local* usage, what covenants ought to be introduced into a lease, in execution of an agreement in general terms; and in such cases, of

course, *general* usage alone must be looked to; *Church* v. *Brown*, 15 Ves. 267, and see *Garrard* v. *Grinling*, 2 Swanst. 249.

6. A covenant against assignment of a lease will not restrain the tenant from underletting; *Crusoe* v. *Bugby*, 2 Wm. Bla. 767; but a covenant against underletting will preclude the more complete alienation of an assignment. *Greenaway* v. *Adams*, 12 Ves. 400.

7. That a Court of Equity will not decree specific performance, at the suit of a tenant in possession under an agreement for a lease, when such lease, if perfected, must contain a covenant which the tenant has already broken, and which covenant is of such a nature as not to make the breach thereof relievable in Equity; see the note to *Williams* v. *Cheney*, 3 V. 59.

[* 473]   WALKER *v.* WETHERELL.

[ROLLS.—1801, Nov. 19.]

GENERAL rule, that a trustee shall not of his own authority break in upon the capital of an infant's fortune (*a*).

The Court very rarely has broken in upon the capital for the mere purpose of maintenance, though frequently for advancement (*b*).

THE decree made in this cause, upon a bill for an account against executors, directed the usual reference to the Master, to imquire, what was proper to be allowed for the infants during their minority, and, who had maintained them.

Upon the Master's report it appeared, that the fortunes of the children did not amount to more than 300*l.* each. Their mother after the father's death married one of the executors; who claimed before the Master sums considerably exceeding the interest of their respective fortunes for their maintenance, education, and advancement. The Master having allowed the claim, exceptions were taken to the report by the Plaintiffs, the surviving children.

Mr. *Lloyd*, Mr. *Richards*, Mr. *Sutton*, and Mr. *Raynsford*, in support of the Exceptions.—There is no case, in which an executor has been allowed to go beyond the interest of an infant's fortune in maintenance. In *Davies* v. *Austen* (1), a very favorable case, the rule of the Court prevailed against it. The executor ought to apply to the Court for the purpose of any advance beyond the interest. These allowances are very unequal: to one only 70*l.*: to another 241*l.*

Mr. *Romilly* and Mr. *Hart*, for the Defendant.—This Defendant married the mother of the Plaintiffs, when they were very young; took them into his family; and placed them out in the world; taking one into his business; and they now complain, that he has not maintained them as paupers in a workhouse. There is no such

(*a*) See *ante*, note (*a*), *Lee* v. *Brown*, 4 V. 362; 2 Williams, Exec. 1012; *Kingsland* v. *Betts*, 1 Edw. 596.
(*b*) See 2 Williams, Exc. 1014.
(1) *Ante*, vol. i. 247, and the note, 249; *Lee* v. *Brown*, vol. iv. 362.

strict rule upon this subject. In general certainly the income only is to be applied for maintenance : but, where more has been necessarily paid, as in this instance, the Court has never said, the executor has done wrong, and shall lose the whole. It would be a mischievous rule, that in no case a guardian shall allow more than the interest for 'maintenance ; and that the moment the parent dies the children are to be reduced to perhaps 10*l.* a year for *maintenance and education. In this case there has   [* 474] been no extravagance. The sum of 241*l.* allowed for one of the children was the amount of the fee upon placing him with a surgeon, and the other expenses incident to that situation. The child, for whom 70*l.* only was allowed, died an infant ; and the Plaintiffs representing her have the benefit of all the savings.

The MASTER OF THE ROLLS [Sir WILLIAM GRANT]. — This objection on the part of the Plaintiffs is rather ungracious ; for from the sums stated by the Master there is no reason to apprehend great waste or negligence ; and there would be more solid reason for complaint, if he had kept them in that situation, in which they must have been, if maintained upon the interest of their fortune only. But my impression is, that the rule has been never to permit trustees of their own authority to break in upon the capital. I am not aware, that the Court has ever sanctioned that conduct in a trustee. It very rarely has occurred, that the Court itself has broke in upon the capital for the mere purpose of maintenance (1) ; though frequently for the purpose of putting the child out in life ; but as to mere maintenance, I doubt it, even upon a petition presented. It is a great misfortune, if the capital is so small as not to leave a comfortable maintenance and education ; but what can the Court do ?

But, whatever might be done upon particular circumstances, it is impossible to sanction a trustee in breaking in upon the capital. There are no particular circumstances in this instance upon the one side or the other. It is not shown, that there were expectations of fortune, which made it necessary to provide a suitable education. The capital might be exhausted in a few years. On the other hand no particular extravagance upon the part of the executor appears. On the contrary, applications were made to him by some of the executors, stating, that the children could not live upon the interest. This claim is therefore ungracious : but it is better, that an individual should suffer a hardship, than that a general rule of the Court should be broken through in a point, that would endanger the interests of all children. The Report therefore must be reviewed in that part, which allows the Defendant these sums.

The Exceptions were allowed.

———

SEE the note to *Davies* v. *Austen,* 1 V. 247.

_____

(1) See an instance, the infant's property being very small ; *Ex parte Green,* 1 Jac. & Walk. 253.

AUSTEN *v.* HALSEY.

[1801, Nov. 2, 20.]

CHARGE of legacies by implication upon a fund arising from the accumulation of rents and profits, dividends and interest (*a*).

The other questions were not determined: 1st, whether the real estate was charged by implication from words, which could be otherwise satisfied; and, if not, whether the will, directing an estate to be purchased and settled upon the testator's son with remainders over, for which the testator afterwards contracted, and the purchase-money having been paid out of the personal estate under a power in the will for that purpose, the legatees by marshalling could have the benefit of the vendor's lien upon the estate for the purchase-money.

ROBERT AUSTEN being seised and possessed of freehold, copyhold, leasehold, and personal estates, and having surrendered the copyhold estates to the use of his will, by his will, dated the 26th of December, 1796, and duly executed to pass real estates, after directions for erecting a monument and some small legacies for charitable purposes and to servants, gave to his dear children Frances and Elizabeth the sum of 3000*l.* a-piece, in case they attained the respective ages of twenty-one years: but if either should die, before she should attain her age of twenty-one years, then he directed, that the legacy of her so dying should go to the survivor; but if both should die before that age, then the whole should lapse, and be wholly void.

He gave to Elizabeth Franklin the sum of 1000*l.*; and he desired his trustees to pay and allow such sums as they in their discretion should think proper or necessary for and towards the maintenance and education of his children out of the rents and profits, interest and dividends, of his real and personal estate. Then, after giving his trustees 100*l.* each, he gave, devised, and bequeathed, all and every his manors, messuages, lands, tenements, tithes, and hereditaments, freehold, copyold, and leasehold, (not in settlement) and over which he had any power of disposition, and not therein before disposed of, and also the reversion in fee of his real estates in the county of Surrey which are in settlement, and also all and every part of his personal estate of what nature or kind soever, not thereby before disposed of, (except his large diamond ring, his books, manuscripts, pictures, drawings, medals, and coins,) unto Henry Halsey Lannoy Richard Coussmaker, and William Bray, their heirs, executors, and administrators, according to the different nature and quality of his said estates respectively, in trust to convey and assign the same real and personal estates respectively and all the savings and increase thereof, unto his son Henry Edward Austin, his heirs, executors, and administrators, for ever, when and so soon as he should attain his age of twenty-one years, or marry before that age with the previous consent and approbation of his guardian or guardians, or the major

(*a*) See 2 Williams, Exec. 1222. As to the distinction between the real estate and personalty, as funds for the payment of debts and legacies, and as to charges on the real estate, see *ante*, note (*a*), *Kidney* v. *Coussmaker,* 1 V. 436; note (*a*), *Hamilton* v. *Worley.* 2 V. 62.

part of them then living: but in case he should marry before
that age without such consent, the testator directed his said trustees. immediately on such marriage to convey, settle, and assure,
all and every part of his said freehold and copyhold estates
to the use of his said son for his life; remainder to trustees
to preserve contingent remainders; remainder to the first and every
other son of the body of his said son successively in tail general;
and, in default of such issue, to the use of the first and every other
daughter of the body of his said son successively in tail general; and
in default of such issue, or if his said son should die under the age
of twenty-one, without having been married, then in trust to convey,
settle, and assure, all his said freehold and copyhold estates to his
(the testator's) daughter Frances, her heirs and assigns for ever, in
case she should attain the age of twenty-three years, or marry before
that time with such consent, as aforesaid: but if she should marry
before that time without such consent, then he directed his said trustees immediately on such marriage to convey, settle, and assure, his
said freehold and copyhold estates to the use of said daughter Frances for her life, with similar remainders in strict settlement to her sons
and daughters successively in tail general, as before limited with respect to his son; and in default of such issue, or in case Frances should
die under the age of twenty-three without having been married, then
with similar remainders in favor of his other daughter Elizabeth
and her children; and if she should die under the age of twenty-three
without having been married, then to the use of his said trustee
William Bray, his heirs and assigns for ever; and in case his said son
should not attain the age of twenty-one, or marry before that age with
such consent and approbation, as aforesaid, then he directed his
said trustees to convey and make over his said leasehold estates
and all and every other part of his personal estate above devised to them, together with all the savings and accumulations,
that should be made from the produce of his real and personal
estate, as aforesaid, after payment of legacies and the purchase-money
therein after directed, unto his said daughters in equal shares and
proportions; each such share to be an interest vested in and divided
and delivered to them respectively, when and so soon as they should
respectively attain the age of twenty-three years or marry before that
time with the previous consent of their guardians, as aforesaid: but
if either of them die before the age of twenty-three, or marry before
that age without such consent, then he gave her part or
share to her sister * if she attain the age of twenty-three   [*477]
years, or marry under that age with such consent; and if
neither of them attain the age of twenty-three, or marry under that
age with such consent, then he gave both such parts or shares to
such grand-child of him (the testator) by either of his aforesaid
daughters as should at the death of the survivor of them be entitled
to the possesion of his aforesaid real estates under and by virtue of
that his will; and if there should be no such grand-child, then he
gave both such shares to the person or persons, who at the death of

fendants shall be authorized to pay for the maintenance out of the
rents and profits of the freehold and copyhold estates, and to apply
the surplus of the rents and profits thereof with the rents of a leasehold house and the interest and produce of the other parts of the
personal estate and the accumulations thereof in payment of the
        legacies.

[* 480]   * The cause came on for farther directions. By the
        Master's Report it appeared, that the personal estate was
deficient, in consequence of the circumstances stated by the answer:
but that the accumulations of the rents and profits, interest and dividends, would be sufficient to answer the legacies.

Mr. *Mansfield* and Mr. *Hall*, for the Plaintiffs.—Upon the question, out of what fund the deficiency of the personal estate is to be
answered, first as to the general charge, every thing contained in the
previous part of the will may be considered a disposition both of the
real and the personal estate to the amount of the charge ; and the devisee takes only the residue. That construction is not too great a
strain. If a legacy was given, and then all the residue not before
disposed of, and nothing but that legacy was before disposed of, and
there was no personal estate : that would be held a real devise of so
much of the estate as would answer the amount of that legacy. By
this will both real and personal estates are given in the same sentence ; and the accumulation from the real and personal estates is
given over in one event expressly subject to legacies.

Upon the other question, there is a great difference in marshalling
against an estate descended and an estate devised. This is the case
of an estate descended. A devise can operate only upon the estates
the testator actually has at the date of the will ; and in this instance
the testator according to the words of the statute (1) *had* not the
land either by a legal or an equitable title. In *Langford* v. *Pitt* (2)
it was decided, that an estate contracted for after the date of the
will cannot pass by the will. Then, where one party has a right to
resort to two funds, and the other has one only, the Court marshals ;
making an arrangement, that will provide for the payment of every
claimant. The vendor of this estate had a right in equity to resort to
the estate sold for the payment of his purchase-money. If any difference arises from taking a security for his money, none was taken
in this case. That the vendor has such right is proved by *Chapman*
v. *Tanner* (3) ; and even the circumstance of taking a security
has been held not to destroy the right. Lord Hardwicke did the
same thing in effect in *Pollexfen* v. *Moore* (4), a perplexed case;

---

(1) 32 Hen. VIII. c. 1 ; 34 Hen. VIII. c. 5.
(2) 2 P. Will. 629.
(3) 1 Vern. 267; *Post*, 752, in *Nairn* v. *Prowse*, the lien was lost by taking
stock by way of pledge; but without determining the general question, whether
any security would have that effect. See *Mackreth* v. *Symmons*, *post*, vol. xv. 329,
and the references.
(4) 3 Atk. 272. See Mr. Sugden's observations on that case, Law of Vend. &
Purch. 5th edit. 468.

and in *Walker* v. *Preswick* (1), the case of a ship, his Lordship lays down the same doctrine as to land; which is followed
by Lord Loughborough in *Blackburn* v. *Gregson* (2); where
bonds were taken, and part of the money was paid. At the
death of this testator no part of the purchase-money was paid; and
no security whatsoever was taken. Unless a republication took place
after the contract, the will could not dispose of this estate. Therefore this is a descended estate; and the claim of marshalling is made
against the heir. If there is a right to resort to two funds, there is
no difference, by what title, whether legal or equitable; and there
are cases of legacies charged upon land, which being paid out of the
personal estate gave the common legatees a right upon the real estate: *Masters* v. *Masters* (3). The Court will struggle against such
an accident as this. This testator had as much intention, that the
legacies should be paid, as to give the devised estates.

Mr. *Romilly* and Mr. *Newbolt*, for the Defendant the son.—As to
a general charge, it is impossible to imply such an intention upon
this will. Besides, there is something to satisfy the words "not
therein disposed of:" viz. the direction, that the maintenance and
education shall come out of the rents and profits, &c. The words
relied on occur only upon the disposition in the event of the son
dying under twenty-one, and not having married before that age
with consent; and then the word "legacies" may be referred to the
personal estate. But it might be the intention, that in that event
these legacies should be paid out of the accumulation: an intention
not improbable, upon the supposition, that the real estate was to go
to other persons than his son: but it does not follow, that the testator intended that charge against his son.

The other question is the only one of any difficulty. It is said,
this is a case of marshalling against an heir, because the contract for
the purchase of this estate was made after the will: but can there
be a doubt, that the codicil directing his executors to apply his personal estate in that purchase and to settle the purchased estate upon
his heir at law is a disposition to take effect? A testator
may direct, that a thing may be purchased and given * to   [* 482]
a legatee: as in all cases, where a legacy is said to be of
quantity, and not specific. So he may direct stock to be purchased.
This must therefore be considered marshalling against a devisee;
and it is settled by many decisions, that there can be no marshalling
as between a legatee and a specific devisee: *Clifton* v. *Burt* (4).
Forrester v. *Lord Leigh* (5). Both are equally objects of bounty.
This testator has expressly directed his personal estate to be applied
in purchasing this real estate, to be settled on his son. I do not
know, that the doctrine of marshalling has ever been applied against

----

(1) 2 Ves. 622.
(2) 1 Bro. C. C. 420.
(3) 1 P. Will. 421.
(4) 1 P. Will. 678.
(5) Amb. 171.

an heir in a case of this kind. There is a material distinction between the common cases of marshalling by the equity of this Court
and a case of this species: the testator looking forward to his situation of purchaser of this estate, and directing the application between those, who are to take. *Pollexfen* v. *Moore* is a very complicated case, and difficult to follow : but Lord Hardwicke seems to
say, that equity subsists only between the vendor and vendee ; and
does not extend to a third person. The decision does not quite
agree with that. The disappointment of a legatee is a case, that
always happens, where there is a disposition of property without ascertaining, what it is. It is impossible for the Court to go upon such
a ground.

Upon the face of the will there is no intention to charge the real
estate with the legacies ; and it is impossible to give the legatees a
right to have this estate, specifically directed to be purchased and
settled, sold again.

Mr. *Mansfield,* in reply.—It is objected, that the provision for the
payment of the legacies out of any fund arising from the real estate
is to be found only in one part of this will: but that shows, the testator thought, he had charged both funds. The expression "after
payment of legacies" supposes a precedent charge ; and shows, the
testator thought that fund liable to pay the legacies, though not
expressly charged by him. Though this direction as to the accumulation is expressed only in the event of the death of the son and
the daughters taking the estate, the testator must be supposed to
have the same intention as to all of them, that the accumulation should be laid out in the same manner: that is, minus the
legacies.

[* 483]   * As to the other question, it is said, such an equity has
never been raised between a devisee and a legatee. That
is not the law of this Court. Where a mortgagee upon a devised
estate has been satisfied out of the personal estate, that shall not
defeat a legacy (1). A mortgage constitutes a lien : a bond does
not ; and therefore there is a distinction. But there is no difference
as to marshalling between legal and equitable liens.

May 20*th.* Lord CHANCELLOR [ELDON] stating the will, delivered
his opinion. There are three points: 1st, Whether the deficiency
of the personal estate to answer the legacies is to be made good out
of the fund arising from the accumulation of the real and personal
estate : 2dly, Whether the legacies are charged upon the real estate :
3dly, If not, whether the legatees can stand in the place of the
vendor of the estate, directed by the codicil to be purchased, in respect of his lien upon the estate for his purchase-money.

Upon the question, whether the legacies are charged upon the
bulk of the real estate, it would be going farther than any of the

---

(1) *Oneal* v. *Mead,* 1 P. Will. 693. See 1 P Will. 680; other cases collected in
Mr. Cox's note to *Clifton* v. *Burt*; *Hamilton* v. *Worley, ante,* vol. ii, 62; 3 Bro. C.
C. 199.

cases has yet gone, to say, that they are charged. Where a child would be unprovided for, one is afraid of the inclination to struggle for that construction; for it is struggle: but no case has gone the length of determining, that words, which are capable of being otherwise satisfied, as these are, would amount to such a charge by implication. I have a private persuasion, that the testator thought, these legacies were charged: but I cannot act upon it.

Upon the next question, whether, supposing, the legacies are not charged upon the real estate, this purchased estate may by circuity be made answerable to the legacies, *Pollexfen* v. *Moore* is the only case cited: but without that authority I consider it clearly settled, that the vendor has a lien for the purchase-money, while the estate is in the hands of the vendee: I except the case, where upon the contract evidently that lien by implication was not intended to be reserved (1). That is in equity very like a charge; and
the cases of marshalling seem to have gone this length;   [484]
that, where there is a charge upon an estate descended, a
legatee shall stand in the place of the person having that charge, resorting to the personal estate (2); and I do not think a power to apply the personal estate, which is all that is given by this codicil, amounts to a command, leaving no discretion to the trustees. There is a difficulty here from the circumstance, that the estate purchased has not descended, but is devised; and there is a difference in marshalling as to that. In this instance it is devised to the heir with many remainders over. It may be found difficult for the legatees by means of this circuity to find a fund for payment.

But I shall give no opinion upon that; for the savings being sufficient with the bulk of the personal estate to pay the legacies, according to the true meaning of this will those savings are the fund. In a case, that has not happened, it is quite clear, they are the fund: namely, the case of the son dying, before he takes the bulk of the savings. As to the daughters, one might live to take the fund two years after the death of the other, who might have attained the age of twenty-one, and have become entitled to the legacy. So both the daughters might die, before either became entitled to that fund of the savings; which in that case is given over to others. Upon the whole will I am of opinion, the testator meant the same in the case, that has happened, as in that clause; that whoever takes that fund shall take it subject to the legacies. The rents, and profits, interest and dividends, are made one joint fund for the maintenance; and if it is taken out of the personal estate, I must suppose, he meant, that if his daughters should die, having attained the age of twenty-one, and received maintenance out of the personal estate, there must have been an account against the accumulation of the real estate, to apportion it; to the intent of reserving the interest of the personal estate for the capital of the legacies.

---

(1) *Post, Nairn* v. *Prowse*, 752; *Mackreth* v. *Symmons*, vol. xv. 329.
(2) *Post, Trimmer* v. *Bayne*, vol. ix. 209.

Though the same words "after payment of legacies" are not in the clause giving the savings to the son, as they are in those giving them to the daughters, yet, attending to the other clause, and taking the three passages together, the legacies are to come out of that fund of the savings, if they are sufficient; as they are.

[* 485]   * Therefore declare accordingly: but I give no opinion, whether the legacies are a charge upon the real estate, or could be worked up to that effect by marshalling.

[THIS note relates also to *Austen* v. *Halsey*, *Bedford* v. *Halsey*, 13 V. 125.]

1. That neither the heir nor devisee can claim to have incumbrances attaching upon real estate discharged out of the ancestor's or testator's personal estate, to the disappointment of specific or even general legatees; and that, as against real estate descended, if specialty creditors of the ancestor exhaust his personal estate, his legatees may stand in the place of such creditors; which equity they will also have as against a *residuary*, though not against a specific devisee; see, *ante*, note 2 to *Hamilton* v. *Worley*, 2 V. 62. Assets, however, cannot be marshalled unless where the legatee, at the time when the legacy becomes due, has a distinctly established claim upon the personal estate, and upon that solely; it will not be done in order to let in a legatee against the personal estate, where the legacy was charged upon the real estate exclusively, but fails to affect it, as a continuing charge, in consequence of accidental events arising subsequently to the death of the testator; *Pearce* v. *Loman*, 3 Ves. 139; *Prowse* v. *Abingdon*, 1 Atk. 486. Lord Thurlow, in *Kidney* v. *Coussmaker*, 1 Ves. Jun. 440, declared "a very little" would suffice to subject a testator's real estates to payment of his debts: and to this doctrine Lord Alvanley assented in *Shallcross* v. *Finden*, 3 Ves. 739; but with respect to legacies, a mere implication is not sufficient; there must be a clear intention manifested in the will that the devisee shall take subject to legacies, in order to charge real estate therewith: *Keeling* v. *Brown*, 5 Ves. 362; still where the testator is making a provision in the same clause, for the payment of both debts and legacies, the natural inference is, that he intended both to be paid in the same way; (*Bootle* v. *Blundell*, 1 Meriv. 233;) and where the testator has blended his real and personal estate into one fund, which aggregate fund he has charged generally with all legacies, the produce of the real estate will be liable, not only to debts, but to all legacies well given. *Currie* v. *Pye*, 17 Ves. 468; *Bench* v. *Biles*, 4 Mad. 188.

2. As to the *lien* which every vendor retains upon the estate he has sold, for the amount of the purchase money; unless he has waived such *lien*, by accepting a totally distinct and independent security; see note 2 to *Ex parte Hunter*, 6 V. 94.

3. The case of *Pollexfen* v. *Moore*, (which was cited in the principal case,) Sir William Grant, in *Trimmer* v. *Bayne*, 9 Ves. 211, said, was reported in a very obscure and perplexing manner; adding, that the decision was directly against the *dictum* ascribed to Lord Hardwicke, by whom that decision was made. That *dictum* intimated, that the *lien* of a vendor upon the estate he had sold, was personal between himself and the vendee, and could not be extended to third persons; but this doctrine was expressly repudiated in *Trimmer* v. *Bayne*, just cited; and Lord Eldon, in *Mackreth* v. *Symmons*, 15 Ves. 349, has subsequently determined, that where there would be a *lien* as between vendor and vendee, the vendor will have the *lien* against a third person, who had notice that the money was not paid. In *Headley* v. *Redhead*, Coop. 51, where the vendor of an estate would, as a creditor for his purchase money, have absorbed the assets of the deceased vendee, a rateable contribution was decreed, as between the *devisee* of the estate and the legatees under the purchaser's will.

4. When a period for payment of a legacy is appointed, subsequent failure in performing, or even positive acts in breach of, an express condition annexed to the legacy, cannot affect the right to receive it. *Brydges* v. *Wotton*, 1 V. & B. 138; *Osborn* v. *Brown*, 5 Ves. 529; *King* v. *Withers*, Finch. 27; *Knight* v. *Cameron*, 14 Ves. 393; *Pullen* v. *Ready*, 2 Atk. 587; *Desbody* v. *Boyville*, 2 P. Wms. 547.

TWOGOOD v. SWANSTON.

[1801, Nov. 21.]

A BANKRUPT pending a commission has a right to an inspection in respect of the surplus; and the Lord Chancellor will take care, that at the close of it he shall have justice: but in this case the bankrupt was not permitted to surcharge and falsify in the Master's office the accounts settled by the commissioners long ago: though palpable errors specifically pointed out by a short petition would be rectified.

THIS cause arose out of the bankruptcy of Mills, Warrington, and Swanston; the accounts in which were extremely complicated: but the result was a surplus after paying 20s. in the pound (1).   Swanston, the surviving bankrupt, being dissatisfied, presented a petition in the cause; the object of which was to be at liberty to surcharge and falsify the accounts; including those settled by the Commissioners, before the bill was filed.   The petition stated some errors; which were admitted.

Mr. Mansfield and Mr. Cox in support of the Petition said, that the common practice of passing accounts before the Commissioners is for the assignees to prove them upon their oath merely: but the Commissioners do not examine into them, unless particular objections are pointed out.

Lord CHANCELLOR [ELDON].—In this case, as it frequently happens, it was necessary for the Lord Chancellor, sitting in bankruptcy, to call in aid his general jurisdiction.   There is no doubt, that under the general direction of the statutes relative to bankruptcy to take due order of the bankrupt's estate a duty arises to the bankrupt as well as to the creditors; not for the purpose of enabling him to harass them, but for the purpose of doing him justice, and particularly of informing him, what creditors have demands upon his estate; and the Chancellor must give him the benefit of an inspection, and at his instance as well as that of the assignees.   The interest of the creditors makes the account settled by the Commissioners an account of very high character; for they have *an interest to shut out every one they can.   But it does   [* 486] sometimes happen, that there is a surplus to come to the bankrupt; and if that is foreseen by the creditors, it is well known, they are quite indifferent beyond the 20s. in the pound; and to say, the bankrupt is not to have an opportunity of examining into such questions, would be great injustice.   Therefore pending the Commission there might be many applications, that ought to be complied with by the Commissioners; and at the conclusion 'the Chancellor will fail in taking due order as to the bankrupt's estate, unless he has

(1) In consequence of that interest was given upon such debts as either upon the face of the security or by force of the contract carried interest.   See *Ex parte Morris*, ante, vol. i. 132; *Ex parte Champion*, *Ex parte Hankey*, 3 Bro. C. C. 436, 504.   In *Ex parte Mills*, ante, ii. 295, those orders by Lord Thurlow were upon a rehearing affirmed by Lord Rosslyn.

pending that administration secured at the close of it the means of
doing full justice to the bankrupt.   If the bankrupt is not pending
the Commission to have an inspection, that he may know, who is,
and who is not, to be admitted a creditor, how is it possible, that he
should not at the close of the concern ?   Otherwise it follows of necessity, that the assignees must pay dividends according to the order of the Commissioners, whether right or improvidently made.   If
the bankrupt can at the close of the Commission show, they were
improvident, what is the Court to do ?   Is the assignee to be personally answerable, having paid under the order of the Commissioners ?
If such a case could be raised against assignees, is it possible to raise
such a case against a surviving assignee ?   He represents the estate
in all points, to which justice requires that he should represent it :
but if all of them paid these dividends wrongfully, is the bankrupt,
or are the creditors, by a short petition to establish that equity only
against the surviving assignee, and to make him pay all ; taking his
remedy, as he can, against the representatives of those, who are
dead ?   As to errors in the account, the question is not to be discussed against the surviving assignee alone, but in a case bringing
all parties forward, and furnishing questions of equity to be decided
upon all the circumstances.   It cannot be got at in this way.

Then as to surcharging and falsifying, there is a clear distinction
between the accounts previous and subsequent to 1789.   The rule
of the Court as to surcharging and falsifying certainly is to state
error enough upon the bill to show, there is reason for it.   He
proves some of those errors ; and gets a decree.   It is said here,
they have proved an error of 150*l.*, another of 100*l.* ; and are likely
to prove another as to 260*l.*   I pass over another error ;
[* 487]   * as it is matter of the subsequent account, and matter of
exception.   That is the rule : but I must recollect this
case ; and looking at it as at the time of the bill filed, it was an
account settled in the administration of bankruptcy, as to dividends
paid ; with regard to which it would be monstrous to permit the
bankrupt under these circumstances to surcharge and falsify, or to
charge the assignees.   It is an account settled under the authority of the Chancellor, and in view of the Commissioners ; and it is
proved by affidavit, that to a certain degree Swanston had an in-
tercourse with the estate during the Commission.   I do not say, palpable errors are not to be set right : but for the benefit of all parties
I will not let them go into the Master's Office for the chance of
finding errors.   The Master would be trying questions upon a great
number of items, which he would not be intended by the Chancellor to
try.   Therefore, the party undertaking, that Swanston shall have
credit for these sums, there is no reason to send it to the Master at
all ; for all the rest is open to exception : but if Swanston can by a
short petition state, what items ought to be expunged upon clear
grounds, I do not say, I would not hear him : but it is not right
with regard to his assignee, if after having passed his accounts in
this way before the Commissioners, I should send him to an account

to the extent, to which that obtains in the Master's Office. I shall give no costs in such a case. I think it quite enough merely to give permission to make an application to the Court, as to such items as he can specifically point out.

The petition was dismissed upon an undertaking to give up the sum of 105*l.* &c. admitted to be errors, and subject to exceptions as to the subsequent account.

THERE are many cases in which, from the magnitude of the subject, or other circumstances, a bill has been directed; although in most respects, the questions might have been proper for the jurisdiction, by petition, in bankruptcy. *Ex parte Barfit*, 12 Ves. 16; *Saxton* v. *Davis*, 18 Ves. 82. And it is unquestionable, that a bankrupt's interest is to be considered, as well as that of his creditors, in determining whether proceedings under a commission have been properly conducted. *Ex parte Hughes*, 6 Ves. 623. The right of a bankrupt to inspection of his books and papers, is expressly allowed by the 116th section of the statute 1 Geo. IV. c. 16; indeed it would be obviously unjust to impose upon a bankrupt the almost impracticable duty of putting in his examination, at a risk which, though no longer extending to loss of life, is still highly penal, yet, upon an apprehension that he may abuse the indulgence, refuse him the means of inspection, by which alone he can reasonably hope to render his examination correct. *Ex parte Ross*, 17 Ves. 378.

ANGERSTEIN *v.* HUNT. [* 488]

[1801, Nov. 21.]

UPON breach of an injunction, restraining an act, the proper course is personal service of notice of motion, that the Defendant shall stand committed: not the practice to move, that he shall show cause, why he shall not stand committed (a).

Where the injunction is to do a thing, the course is to move, that he shall do it by a particular day, or stand committed, [p. 488.]

PREVIOUSLY to the vacation an injunction had been granted to restrain the Defendant from ploughing up a rabbit-warren farther than was necessary for the sustenance of the rabbits.

Mr. *Romilly* for the Plaintiff moved, that the Defendant should show cause, why he should not stand committed for breach of the injunction: upon affidavits, that he had ploughed up thirty acres; and was proceeding farther.

Lord CHANCELLOR [ELDON].—It is not the practice in this Court for a man to show cause, why he should not stand committed. The motion ought to be, that he shall stand committed for breach of the injunction; and it ought to be made upon personal (1) service upon him, that the Court will be moved for that purpose. Where the injunction is to do a thing, the course is to move for an order, that he shall do it by a particular day, or stand committed. But this is not

---

(a) See *Schoonmaker* v. *Gillett*, 3 Johns. Ch. 311.
(1) *Ellerton* v. *Thirsk*, 1 Jac. & Walk. 376.

to do a thing.   The proper mode therefore will be, to serve him
with notice, that the Court will be moved, that he shall stand committed.

THE rule laid down in the principal case, requiring *personal* notice of a motion
to commit a party for breach of an injunction, was followed in *Ellerton* v. *Thirsk*,
1 Jac. & Walk. 376.

CAFFREY *v.* DARBY.

[ROLLS.—1801, Nov. 11, 17, 23.]

TRUSTEES charged with a loss occasioned by their negligence, though without any
    corrupt motive (a).
The costs followed of course.
Property possessed by a bankrupt in *auter droit* is not within the st. 21 Jam. I. c.
    19, s. 11, [p. 496.]

JAMES CAFFREY, being possessed of a public-house in St. Giles's,
as assignee of a lease for twenty-five years from Lady Day 1786
at the yearly rent of 60*l.* died; having by his will bequeathed to
his wife all and every thing he was then possessed of, and all moneys
due to him for the sole use of his wife and children.   Administration with the will annexed was granted to his widow; who took
possession of the stock in trade, and carried on the business.

By indentures, dated the 11th of July, 1789, reciting, that Ann
              Caffrey was desirous of making a provision for her four
[* 489]   children * to the extent of the property, which her late
              husband died possessed of; that a marriage was agreed on
between her and Peter Priest: and in order to secure the provision
intended it was agreed, that the lease, the stock in trade, and effects
and household goods, which Ann Caffrey was then in possession of,
and which were the property of her late husband, should be assigned and made over to John Darby and William Bedells; Ann Caffrey
with the consent of Priest assigned all her estate in the premises,
with the lease, and all the stock in trade, household goods, and all
other goods and chattels, the property of her late husband, to Darby
and Bedells, their executors, &c.; upon trust, that they should
stand possessed thereof as a security for raising the sum of 800*l.*;
to be applied and disposed of, as after mentioned: that is to say;
as soon as said 800*l.* or any part thereof should be raised by sale of
said premises or some part thereof, or by the payment of Priest to
·the trustees, the same were to be from time to time invested in the
public funds or upon mortgage, the security to be approved by the
trustees, or the survivor, his executors, &c. in their names: upon
trust, that they, Darby and Bedells, and the survivor, &c. should re-

(a) See *ante*, note (a), *Rowth* v. *Howell*, 3 V. 565; note (a), *Powell* v. *Evans*, 5
V. 839.

ceive the dividends or interest arising from said 800l. or so much thereof as should from time to time be invested, as aforesaid: and after the receipt thereof pay the same into the hands of the said Ann for and during her natural life, to and for her sole use and benefit; whose receipts alone notwithstanding her coverture should from time to time be good and sufficient discharges: to the intent, that the same should not be at the disposal of or subject or liable to the control, debts, forfeitures, or engagements, of said Peter Priest or any aftertaken husband, but only at her own separate disposal: and from and after the raising and investing said 800l., as aforesaid, then upon trust to transfer said premises unto Peter Priest, his executors, &c., for his own benefit; and as to the said 800l. so to be raised and invested, as aforesaid, from and after the decease of said Ann upon farther trust, that the trustees should pay the interest and produce of said 800l. or such part thereof as should be invested, as aforesaid, in and about the maintenance and education of her said children in such manner as the trustees should think most proper, until James Caffrey should attain the age of twenty-one, and Ann, Catherine, and Elizabeth, Caffrey, should attain that age, or be married; and then that they, the trustees, should pay and transfer * said 800l. or so much thereof as should be so   [* 490] invested, as aforesaid, to and among the said children in equal shares and proportions, to the sons at the age of twenty-one, and to the daughters at that age or marriage, which should first happen; with a provision for survivorship among them in the event specified; and if all of them should die in the life-time of their mother without leaving issue, then upon trust to pay or transfer the same unto Peter Priest, his executors, &c.: Provided, that so long as Peter Priest or his assigns should pay into the hands of the trustees not less than 100l. a-year, which was to be invested in Government or other good securities upon the trusts aforesaid in part of said 800l. so agreed to be invested, until the whole of said 800l. should be invested upon the trusts and for the purposes aforesaid, it should be lawful for said Peter Priest to possess, occupy and enjoy, said premises thereby assigned, and to make use of the stock in trade, household goods, and effects; so that a stock of equal worth of said Peter Priest was kept up; which together with the other estate would be sufficient to answer said 800l. or such part thereof as might not be invested upon the trusts aforesaid.

The marriage took place soon afterwards; and Priest took possession of the house, stock in trade, furniture, and effects, mentioned in the indentures; and continued to carry on the business from July 1789 till the 11th of July, 1797. Darby had received from him on the 28th of June, 1791, on account of the trusts of the settlement 100l. by different payments; and on the 19th of May, 1792, the farther sum of 100l. also by different payments; and on the 30th of July, 1793, 50l. more; which sum of 250l. was the whole that was received on account of the trust. In 1797 Priest became insolvent; and on the 9th of July, 1797, being two days before the last instalment ought to have been paid, the trustees took possession ; and on the next day Priest absconded ; and a commission of bankruptcy soon afterwards issued against him. The assignee under the commission disputing the right of the trustees, it was agreed, that the premises should be sold without prejudice. The trustees accordingly proceeded to a sale of the house ; which produced 405*l*. The assignee under the commission received 445*l*. 18*s*. by the sale of the household goods, fixtures, and stock in trade ; and the [* 491] household goods and fixtures having been valued * at 276*l*. 12*s*. 6*d*., the trustees brought an action against the assignee for so much of that sum as would with the other sums received by them on account of the trust make up the sum of 800*l*. Under that action all matters in question between the parties were referred to arbitration ; and the arbitrator by his award, dated the 1st of November, 1798, decided, that the Plaintiffs at law had no cause of action. On the 3d of November the first and final dividend of 8*s*. in the pound was made under the Commission ; but the trustees made no claim. The bankrupt obtained his certificate.

In Michaelmas Term the trustees applied to the Court of King's Bench by motion to set aside the award ; which motion was refused (1).

The bill was filed on behalf of the children ; praying, that the trustees may be decreed to transfer the stock purchased with the trust fund to the Accountant General, an account of what they had received under the trust ; and that they may be charged with the deficiency.

The trustees, by their answer stated, that between July 1793 and July 1797 they at various times applied to Priest and his wife to make farther payments : but they alleged, that from the pressure of the times, which had considerably decreased their business, they were not able from their profits to make the payments according to the settlement ; but that although they were not making a profit so as to make farther payments, yet they maintained, clothed, and educated, the Plaintiffs ; and were not incurring any debt; nor taking any other than the usual credit to carry on their business ; and the Defendants always understood from them, that the persons they dealt with were acquainted with the settlement ; and the Defendant Ann Priest frequently desired the Defendants, the trustees, not to pursue any adverse measures; for it would be the ruin of herself and her children, were they compelled to quit the house and business ; as the Plaintiffs were maintained and educated out of the profits of the business.

The answer farther stated, that Peter Priest assigned as a farther reason for not being able to make farther payments, that [* 492] * he had been imposed upon by his wife as to the property ; being obliged to pay a debt of 145*l*. with which he was unacquainted at the date of the settlement.

(1) *Darby* v. *Smith*, 8 Term. Rep. B. R. 82.

The Defendants submitted, that the legality of the award still remains open: and that it is bad upon the face of it; proceeding upon the ground of the statute 21st Jan. I. c. 19. s. 10 & 11. operating upon the property; and that being advised, that the award had proceeded upon a mistake of the law, and was therefore illegal, they did not conceive themselves entitled to prove any debt under the Commission; and therefore did not apply; and between the date of the award and the dividend they had no opportunity of applying to set aside the award. They stated, that they had no fraudulent intention; and acted to the best of their judgment; and they claimed to be allowed the costs they paid under the award, the expenses of the sale; and Darby, who was the attorney, who had advised and prepared the settlement, claimed the amount of his bill on that account.

Mr. *Piggott*, Mr. *Romilly*. and Mr. *Wynne*, for the Plaintiffs, and Mr. *Wingfield*, for the Assignees of the Bankrupt, Defendants, in the same interest, admitted, that the trustees had no bad motive; but insisted, that they must be answerable for the loss to the trust fund.

Mr. *Richards* and Mr. *Cooke*, for the Defendants, the Trustees.— The fair intention of these trustees is admitted; that they were not influenced by any corruption or motive of gain to themselves. The Court will therefore feel satisfaction, if they can avoid making a decree against them. It would be a decision of great importance; that trustees without any benefit are to be made answerable, when they have conducted themselves to the best of their judgment in the fair execution of their trust. The nature of the subject of this trust, the business of a public-house, must be considered. It would have been a breach of trust in them to have sold the property upon failure of payment of the instalments. This was in the nature of a mortgage certainly. Is the trustee of a mortgage, neglecting to enter upon a failure of paying the interest, to be liable, merely because by an accident the property is destroyed, as by a superior title? These trustees acted *bonâ fide*: * having   [* 493] nothing in view but the good of the family; and during part of the time it was for the good of the family; and the loss arose by act of law, a bankruptcy. In such a case trustees have never been charged as for wilful default. Supposing the point of law was doubtful, they cannot be charged for not knowing it. Opinions were given in their favor upon that point. It was certainly a question of considerable doubt. If they had not permitted the husband to use the property, they would have acted directly against the spirit, though according to the letter, of their trust. This case is analogous to that of trustees putting money in the hands of a banker. A fair and honorable discretion was exercised according to the very spirit of the deed. The decision of the arbitrators and of the Court of King's Bench is very capable· of being resisted; and it may very well be argued, that this case does not fall within the stat-

ute of James 1st (1). The case in the King's Bench met with little
argument; and may be considered a hasty decision. *Ex parte
Marsh* (2) and *Viner* v. *Cadell* (3) are against it. They had no
time between the date of the award and the dividend to make a
claim under the Commission; and their claim, if they had made it,
could not have been admitted; for claiming the goods themselves
they could not have been admitted to prove a debt. The Plaintiffs
are still entitled to follow the property in the hands of the assignees;
who must stand in the situation of the bankrupt. But they were in
fact aware of the settlement and the claims under it.

As to the deductions claimed by the trustees, they are clearly entitled to their expenses, the costs of the action, though unsuccess-
ful; unless it could be shown that it was wantonly brought. If the
Court goes the length now desired, it will add another difficulty to
those, which make it almost impossible to procure trustees to act.

Mr. *Piggott*, in Reply.—*Viner* v. *Cadell* is unquestionably right;
and clearly distinguishable from the determination in the court of
King's Bench upon this case. There was no transaction changing
the property. These arrears were very considerable in so short a
time. I admit, there was no corrupt motive: but are trus-
[* 494] tees * for infants to permit arrears to accrue for a length
of time? Can it grow better? What is called an accident must have been foreseen as an inevitable consequence of permitting him to be in arrear, and that arrear increasing. I admit,
when the event, the bankruptcy, happened, they· did the best they
could in the situation, in which they had placed the property.

Nov. 23d. THE MASTER OF THE ROLLS [Sir WILLIAM GRANT.]
— The question is, whether the loss arising from the deficiency of
this trust fund is to be borne by the infants, or to be made good by
the trustees. The case arises upon a conveyance from Ann Caffrey
to the trustees: but the real transaction was a sale of this property
to the husband for 800*l.*, payable by instalments; the last instalment payable in 1797. It appears, the whole of the property sold
for more than 800*l.*: but as it was found, the trustees were not entitled to the sum, for which the furniture and other effects sold, the
deficiency is considerable. It is contended for the trustees, that
though undoubtedly there was originally property sufficient to answer the 800*l.*, and though a loss has now taken place, so that they
cannot receive the amount in value of that property, it was lost by
means, for which under the circumstances they are not responsible.
First, it is obvious, they say, it could not be intended, they should
proceed rigorously to enforce payment of each sum of 100*l.*, as it
became due; for so long as the security they had taken remained

(1) 21 Jam. I. c. 19, s. 11.   See statute 6 Geo. IV. c. 16, s. 72; *Post, Ex parte
Martin,* vol. xix. 491, and the note, 494.
(2) 1 Atk. 158.
(3) 3 Esp. 88.

good the 800*l.* would be forthcoming; and they had only to look to that; the wife was to look to the interest.   It was therefore in nature of a mortgage; and, as in the common case, it is not to be expected, that they were to have enforced it at the precise day; that it would have been disadvantageous to the children themselves to have proceeded rigorously year by year to enforce payment of the instalments; for the children were maintained by him.   There is also some evidence of entreaties by the wife, that her husband might not be pressed.   Then they say, it appears, that by their delay in getting in the money no loss has been sustained; for the loss was not occasioned by that; and but for the decision in the Court of King's Bench the property would have been ultimately sufficient for the purposes of the trust; and the *loss   [*495] was occasioned by the decision of a very doubtful question of law: as it is hard to make them responsible for that.

On the other hand it is to be considered, that this was money payable by instalments; not a sum to be paid at once, as a mortgage is; and secured too, partly, upon an estate daily diminishing in value: a short lease, for twenty-five years, commencing in 1786; also upon a sort of property very uncertain in its nature; for it must be entirely in the custody of the person having the possession of the house, furniture, &c.   From these two considerations, the diminishing value of the property, and the mode of payment by instalments, I am of opinion, the trustees were not justified in any great indulgence: the person, if not positively bound, holding the property under a condition; for it was evident, that his inability would be constantly augmenting.   If he was unable to pay the first instalment, he must be still less able to pay the sums accumulated from permitting them to run together.   The cases of payment by instalments and at once are quite different.   In the latter the debtor may be able to pay that sum to-morrow, or next year: but the chance of receiving money by instalments depends upon its being regularly received.   Therefore, even though the trustees might not have been under the necessity of exacting from the husband the money on the precise day, yet they ought not to have given great latitude.   They were hardly justifiable in permitting two instalments to become due; still less three; still less four.   But here they permit him to remain four years in possession without receiving a shilling.   That is evidence, that he was not prosperous.   It did not turn out as well as he expected.   It might be supposed, that he was running in debt with other people.   The trustees might have expected a controversy with the creditors.   They ought therefore to have taken some step for the security of the infants; particularly when that is combined with the other circumstance, that the property was diminishing in value.   Notwithstanding the lease sold at last for not much less than he was to pay, it was property naturally diminishing in value; and as to the rest of the trust property the security was of very little value.

It would be very dangerous. though no fraud could be imputed to the trustees, and no kind of interest or benefit to themselves was looked to, to lay down this principle; that trustees might without any responsibility act, as these did: in eight years, within which time the whole money ought to have been paid, receiving only 250*l.*; and taking no step as to the remainder. It would be an encouragement to bad motives; and it may be impossible to detect undue motives. If we get the length of neglect in not recovering this money by taking possession of the property, will they be relieved from that by the circumstance, that the loss has ultimately happened by something, that is not a direct and immediate consequence of their negligence: viz. the decision of a doubtful question of law? Even supposing, they are right in saying, this was a very doubtful question, and they could not look to the possibility of its being so decided, yet, if they have been already guilty of negligence, they must be responsible for any loss in any way to that property: for whatever may be the immediate cause, the property would not have been in a situation to sustain that loss, if it had not been for their negligence. If they had taken possession of the property, it would not have been in his possession. If the loss had happened by fire, lightning, or any other accident, that would not be an excuse for them, if guilty of previous negligence. That was their fault.

The question at law was treated as an extremely nice question at the bar; and the case as an unlooked for decision. I do not see, how the question could have received a different decision. The case is very different from those, which were cited: *Ex parte Marsh* and *Viner* v. *Cadell*. In each of those cases the widow having the husband's property in her possession, the second husband as such fell into the possession of that property, of which the wife had the possession. That is a possession in *auter droit* merely. There was no room for a contrary decision without holding, that there can be no such thing as a possession in *auter droit* without making the property liable under the statute. There was no fault in any person in leaving the property in that possession, in which it ought not to be. But in this case there is an assignment by the administratrix to the trustees; vesting in them the legal property. The trustees give the possession to Priest. He was entitled to the possession by the terms of the trust deed, under the proviso, so long as he continued to pay the 100*l.* a year. He possessed not in [*497] *auter droit*, but in his own * right, under, and according to, this deed. The instant he failed to pay the 100*l.* a year regularly they were entitled that instant to take the possession from him. They leave it with him, just as if he had made those payments. As to all the rest of the world the trustees took upon them the responsibility: dealing, as if he had paid them. It is directly within the act; leaving in his possession goods, which they might have taken any day out of his possession. The decision in the Court of King's Bench is perfectly right; and it is impossible, that there could be any other decision: but if it was wrong, that would not have altered the determination here; for, as between the trustees and the bankrupt's estate the question is decided and at rest; and is not to be overhauled here.

The decree therefore must be for an account according to the prayer of the bill; and if there is any deficiency, the trustees must make it good.

As to the allowances claimed by the trustees, even if they are compelled to make good the loss, particularly the costs of the suit with the assignees, it is a necessary consequence of the decision, that no costs can be given to them; for the suit was made necessary by their laches; and therefore cannot possibly be at the expense of the fund. They were taking the chance of escaping from the effect of their own negligence. They must bear the whole expense of that suit. As to the expense of the sale of the lease, which it is alleged, must have been incurred at all events, that depends upon the result of the account; for if they neglect to sell, till the property is diminished in value, and if otherwise it would have produced enough both for the 800*l.* and the expenses of the sale, then they are not entitled; for the deficiency was the consequence of their laches. If any expense was incurred in the execution of their trust, they will be entitled to that. The costs of the cause must of course be given against them (1).

1. As a general rule, executors must get in the property of their testator by all possible remedies: if in any case this should appear to be a disadvantageous mode of proceeding, the executors should not take the decision of that question upon themselves, but refer it to the judgment of the Court; see, *ante*, the note to *Powell* v. *Evans*, 5 V. 839; and it must be at the risk of executors or trustees, who leave the money of the *cestuis que trusts* in a state of insecurity, though they may have been induced to permit this without any personally corrupt motives. *Brice* v. *Stokes*, 11 Ves. 319; *Lord Shipbrook* v. *Lord Hinchinbrook*, 16 Ves. 480; *Walker* v. *Symonds*, 3 Swanst. 42.

2. That property held by a bankrupt *en autre droit*, is not within the statute of 21 Jac. 1, was held, long before the decision of the present case, though more doubtfully, by Lord Hardwicke, in *Ex parte Marsh*, 1 Atk. 159.

3. That trustees, although they are generally entitled to their costs, may not only lose them, but be obliged to pay the costs of other parties, when the suit has been rendered necessary by the negligence or misconduct of the trustees themselves; see note 2 to *The Attorney General* v. *The City of London*, 1 V. 243.

(1) See Beames on Costs, 154, 5, 6; *ante*, *Powlett* v. *Herbert*, vol. i. 297; *post*, *Raphael* v. *Boehm*, *Sanderson* v. *Walker*, xiii. 590, 601.

WILLS v. SLADE.

[1801, Nov. 27.]

No objection to a partition, that other persons may come in *esse* and be entitled (a).

Elizabeth Wills being entitled to the reversion or remainder in fee of an undivided moiety of a capital messuage and four small messuages, subject to the life estates of herself and her husband, and son-in-law Richard Wills, and having a power to devise notwithstanding coverture, by her will devised all the messuages, tenements, moieties, lands, hereditaments, and premises, with their appurtenances, so limited, from and after the decease of Richard Wills unto all and every the child and children of the body of Richard Wills, lawfully to be begotten, equally to be divided between them, part and share alike, as tenants in common, and not as joint tenants, and to the several and respective heirs of the body and bodies of all such child and children respectively lawfully issuing ; and if there should be more such children than one, and one or more should die without issue of his, her, or their, body or bodies, then and so often as to the part or parts of such child or children so dying without issue she willed, that the same should remain to the use of the survivors or survivor of them as tenants in common, and to the heirs of the body of such survivors or survivor ; with a devise over in default of such issue to a nephew in fee.

After the death of Elizabeth Wills the bill was filed for a partition by Richard Wills and his four infant children against the devisees of the person entitled to the other undivided moiety ; who had been in possession of the mansion house ; and also upon the death of their devisor entered into possession of all the rest.

Mr. *Sutton* and Mr. *Steele*, for the Plaintiffs, said, an objection had been taken from the possibility of other children.

Mr. *Richards*, for the Defendant, said, all parties were willing to have a partition, if it could be made.

Lord Chancellor [Eldon].—At all events you are entitled to a partition during the life of the tenant for life (1). But I think, this is no objection ; for, if so, in every case, where there is a [* 499] settled estate * with remainders to persons, who may come *in esse*, there never can be a partition.

(a) It does not constitute any objection in Equity, that the partition may not finally conclude the interests of all persons ; as where the partition is asked only by or against a tenant for life, or where there are contingent interests to vest in persons *in esse*. 1 Story, Eq. Jur. § 656; *Gaskell* v. *Gaskell*, 6 Sim. 643; *Striker* v. *Mott*, 2 Paige, 387 ; *Woodworth* v. *Campbell*, 5 Paige, 518; Jeremy, Eq. Jur. 304.
(1) So tenant for years may have a partition, *Baring* v. *Nash*, 1 Ves. & Bea. 551.

The decree was made for an account and a Commission for partition between the Plaintiffs and Defendants according to the prayer of the bill.

SEE note 3 to *Mundy* v. *Mundy*, 2 V. 122.

HOPE *v.* LORD CLIFDEN.

[1801, Nov. 27.]

PORTION vested in the case of parent and child by implication from the whole settlement, against express words (*a*); and a clause of survivorship upon the death of a child, before the portion should become payable, was upon the authorities construed, before it should be vested (*b*).
Posthumous child to be considered as living (*c*), [p. 510.]

BY indentures of lease and release, dated the 3d and 4th of March, 1739, previous to the marriage of Eliab Breton and Elizabeth Wolstoneholme, in consideration of the marriage and of a settlement of the same date by Elizabeth Wolstoneholme of her estate of inheritance for the benefit of Eliab Breton and the issue of the marriage, and for other considerations, certain real estates in the county of Northampton were conveyed to trustees and their heirs; to the intent, that Mary Breton, the mother of Eliab Breton, should receive a rent charge of 400*l.*, secured by a term of 99 years upon part of the said premises; and, subject thereto, to the use of Eliab Breton for life; remainder to trustees to preserve contingent remainders; remainder to trustees for 150 years for securing a jointure of 300*l.* a year to Elizabeth Wolstoneholme in bar of dower; and subject thereto to the use of trustees, their executors, &c. for a term of 500 years; remainder to the first and other sons of the marriage in tail male; remainder to Eliab Breton, his heirs and assigns for ever.

The trusts of the term of 500 years were declared to be, in case there shall be any child or children of the said Eliab Breton on the body of the said Elizabeth Wolstoneholme his intended wife to be begotten living at the time of the decease of the said Eliab Breton or afterwards born alive other than such as shall be heir male of his body for the time being, then the said trustees, their executors, &c. shall and do after the decease of the said Eliab Breton, but subject nevertheless and without prejudice to the said several annuities or yearly rent charge of 400*l.* and *300*l.* by sale   [*500] or mortgage of the said premises comprised in the said

---

(*a*) As to the construction of marriage settlements, particularly according to the recital, see note (*a*), *Doran* v. *Ross*, 1 V. 59.
    (*b*) See *ante*, note (*a*), *Willis* v. *Willis*, 3 V. 51.
    (*c*) See *ante*, note (*a*), *Clarke* v. *Blake*, 2 V. 673; note (*a*), *Thelluson* v. *Woodford*, 4 V. 227.

term of 500 years or of a competent part thereof for all or any part of the said term, or by or out of the rents, issues and profits, thereof in the mean time until such sale or mortgage can be made, or by all or any the ways and means aforesaid, raise and levy the sum of 5000*l.* of lawful money of Great Britain for the portion and portions of all and every the child and children of the said intended marriage other than and except an eldest or only son; to be applied and disposed of in manner following: in case there shall be but one such child, then such child shall have the whole sum of 5000*l.* for his or her portion: and in case there shall be two or more such children, then the said sum of 5000*l.* to be equally divided between or amongst them share and share alike: the portion or portions of such of them as shall be a son or sons to be paid to him or them at his or their respective age or ages of twenty-one years; and the portion and portions of such of them as shall be a daughter or daughters to, be paid to her or them at her or their respective age or ages of twenty-one years or day or days of her or their respective marriages which shall first and next happen after the decease of the said Eliab Breton; and if any of the said younger sons shall attain the age of twenty-one years, or any of the said daughters shall attain the age of twenty-one years or be married in the life-time of the said Eliab Breton, then the portion and portions of such of them as shall be a daughter or daughters, younger son or younger sons, shall be paid to him, her, or them, within three months next after the decease of the said Eliab Breton, unless the said Eliab Breton shall by any writing or writings under his hand and seal direct the same to be raised in his life, which it is hereby agreed and declared it shall and may be lawful for him to direct or appoint accordingly; so as the same be no prejudice to the said several rent-charge of 400*l.* and 300*l.* so limited to the said Mary Breton and Elizabeth Wolstoneholme, as aforesaid, or either of them. And also upon this farther trust; that in the mean time from and after the decease of the said Eliab Breton, until the same portion or portions shall become payable, they the said trustees, their executors, &c. shall and do by and out of the rents, issues and profits, of the premises so limited to them for the said term of 500 years, as aforesaid, but subject nevertheless and without prejudice to the said [* 501] several rent-charge of 400*l.* and 300*l.* * raise, levy, and pay, such yearly sum and sums of money for the maintenance and education of the child and children of the said intended marriage entitled to portions under the trusts of the said term, until their said portion or portions shall become payable, as are herein after mentioned (that is to say): in case there be but one such child, the yearly sum of fifty pounds, till he or she shall attain the age of twelve years; and from and after that age, and until his or her portion shall become payable, the yearly sum of one hundred pounds; and if there shall be two such children, the yearly sum of forty pounds for each of them, till they shall respectively attain their respective ages of twelve years; and from and after their respective ages of twelve years the yearly sum of 80*l.* a piece; and if there shall be three or more of such children, such yearly sum for each of them, until their respective portions shall become payable, as will amount unto and be equal with the interest of their respective portions after the rate of four pounds per centum per annum; the said yearly sum or sums for maintenance to be paid at or on the feasts of Saint Michael the archangel, and the annunciation of the blessed Virgin Mary in every year by even and equal portions; the first payment thereof to begin and be made at or on such of the said feasts as shall first and next happen after the decease of the said Eliab Breton: Provided nevertheless, and it is hereby agreed and declared, that if any of the said children of the said intended marriage entitled to the portions under the trusts of the said term of five hundred years shall happen to die, or become an eldest or only son, before his, her, or their portion or portions shall become payable, then the portion and portions of him, her, or them, so dying or becoming an eldest or only son, shall go, accrue and be paid, unto the survivors and survivor and others and other of them, when his, her or their, original portion or portions shall become payable by virtue of these presents: Provided also, that in case all the children of the said marriage entitled to portions under the trust of the said term of five hundred years shall die, before any of their said portions shall become payable, then the said sum and sums of money so to be raised for such child and children, or so much thereof as shall not then be raised, shall not be raised, but shall cease for the benefit of the person and persons entitled to the reversion or remainder of the premises immediately expectant on the determination of the said term of five hundred years; and then also such sum and sums of * money as shall be then raised for or towards   [* 502] such portion or portions, as aforesaid, shall be paid unto the same person and persons so next in reversion or remainder as aforesaid.

The indentures also contained a proviso, that, if Eliab Breton should in his life-time settle, give or advance, unto. for, or upon, any of the children entitled to portions any sum or sums of money, lands, tenements, goods, or chattels, for and towards their advancement, preferment in marriage or otherwise, then such sums of money, or the value of such lands, tenements, goods, and chattels, to be received by, given to, or settled upon, such children, should be accounted as part, if less, or, if as much or more, for the whole, of the portions provided for them, as aforesaid; unless the said Eliab Breton should by writing under his hand and seal signify the contrary.

The issue of this marriage was four children: three sons; Michael Harvey, William, and Eliab, and one daughter, Mary. The daughter attained the age of twenty-one in the life of her father; and married John Hope; by whom she had three sons. Mary Hope died in the life of her father; who died in December 1785; leaving his wife and three sons surviving. Michael Harvey Breton, who had

different from this; for there it is, in case any should die "before
his, her, or their, portions should become due or payable." Upon
any construction of this settlement there are events, in which the
grand-children would not have been entitled to the benefit of it. If
in these cases there should be no children living, but all had left
children, the term in that case would be determined: and there
would be no right to raise any portion. If that was the meaning, is
it very absurd to go a little farther; and provide, that the children
surviving should take the whole, not the representatives of a deceased child? *Wingrave* v. *Palgrave* (1) is very material in this
view. The proviso there only repeats at the end what was in effect
expressed in the beginning of the settlement; that if no child should
be living at the death of the parent, nothing should be done under
the term. The Defendant's construction is perfectly consistent with
the whole settlement. If all the children die, leaving children, nothing is to be done under the trust: if some die, then all shall accrue
to those living at the death of the father. So, if a younger son becomes the eldest, his portion is to go to the others. The same construction must be put upon that as upon the clause devesting the
interest by death; and the Plaintiff must in the same way contend
against that: but the provision is express; and the intention must
be admitted, that, if he became the eldest son, his interest as a
younger son should go to the others. The words "entitled to portions" in the clause respecting advancements by the father do not
vary the construction; for it cannot be denied, that a power was
given to him to advance the portions in his life; and if he had, that
would be a vested interest, and also put in possession; and that
clause extends to an advancement at any time of the child's life.
In *Willis* v. *Willis* the Lord Chancellor thought it very material in
these cases to ascertain, what would be the decision in certain
events. The Plaintiff's construction is impossible; unless the introductory words are expunged; and is quite inconsistent with the
provision, under which, if there had been ten children, who
[* 506] all died in the life of the father, this sum could not * have
been raised. If one of ten children had survived, could
the Court say, the representatives of the other nine would be entitled? Such a construction, making it depend upon the event,
would be preposterous. The circumstance of there being a child
living, &c. is a condition precedent to raising the portion. Whether the father would leave a child was in uncertainty during his life.
Therefore during his life the whole 5000*l.* was in contingency; and
if so, no part could during his life be vested in any child. The
power given to him to direct the 5000*l.* to be raised during his life
was for the purpose of enabling him to make that a vested interest,
which otherwise would during his life be a contingent interest: but
that power was never executed. This event of a younger child attaining twenty-one and dying in the life of the father probably did

(1) 1 P. Will. 401.

not occur to the drawers of the settlement; and therefore was not provided for; as, upon wills particularly, there are many events of which the parties had no foresight. The introductory words are the first thing; upon which the whole proceeds; and must prevail, unless afterwards explained. In *Wingrave* v. *Palgrave* the Lord Chancellor goes much upon the proviso as to the term ceasing: but the words in this settlement as to that leave the question just as it was; and the contingency, upon which the term was to arise, has happened.

Mr. *Mansfield*, in reply.—According to the letter the event, in which this sum is not to be raised, has not happened. There is the strongest implication upon the whole of this settlement, that the children might become entitled to portions in the life of their father. If ever latitude is to be allowed to words, it ought upon a marriage settlement; the object of which is to provide for the issue. Upon the whole of this settlement taken together it is a provision for the issue of the marriage. No argument arises from what is thrown in with respect to a younger son becoming the eldest; for the law of this Court would have produced that effect, whether expressed, or not; and that is not determined by the time of vesting; for if he became the eldest son before the day of payment, he would lose his portion. *Chadwick* v. *Doleman* (1), and other cases.

Lord CHANCELLOR [ELDON].—Though I agree with   [507] Lord Thurlow's expression in *Woodcock* v. *The Duke of Dorset*, that the words are strong, and difficult to manage, and notwithstanding the strength of opinion expressed by the Counsel against this claim, I feel a strong inclination at this moment in favor of it. It is quite clear upon all the cases, that, to get rid of the difficulty, the Court looking upon it as a hard thing to impute to a father, that he should mean, a child having attained twenty-one, or come to marriageable years, and formed a family, yet, because that child dies in his life, the descendants should have nothing, and feeling that not to be a probable intention in a parent, have thought themselves at liberty to manage the construction of the words, as they would not in the case of a stranger, or upon a matter of contract, without any mixture of parental feeling. In *Wingrave* v. *Palgrave* it is obvious, if a son had lived to the age of twenty-one, he might have destroyed the trust term. Of necessity therefore a circumstance existed, that is relied upon for the Defendants in this case, that the claim of the daughter must have been contingent during the whole life of the father; as he might have a son. Two contingencies are expressed in that case: dying without an heir male, and leaving a daughter or daughters; and that from the context, which gives a clear exposition, that it was not meant having had a daughter, must mean at his death. In *Woodcock* v. *The Duke of Dorset* also the expression is "leave." In the former case it was held a condition precedent; because the word "leaving" meant

_____

(1) 2 Vern. 528.

upon the context at his death; and secondly, because the term at
law was gone; and it must have been considered by the Court, as
if never in the settlement. It was impossible therefore, that there
could be any doubt upon that case.

The case of *Emperor* v. *Rolfe*, the date of which I mark, in 1748,
was very like a new decision. It seems therefore to have been a
long time, before the Court could get over the natural effect of words
so strong and so difficult to manage. The construction in that case
was, that the words "grow due and payable" were, for the benefit of the estate, and attending to the motives of parental feeling,
with reference to the age of twenty-one or marriage in the life of
the parent, to secure the portion. There was a contingency there;
at least a contingency to devest what was vested under
[* 508] the former words. That is certainly different * from this
case; in which it is contended, that the contingency is
one, that prevents the vesting, not merely to devest. *Cholmondeley*
v. *Meyrick*, which in the subsequent case of *Willis* v. *Willis* the
Lord Chancellor cites from an accurate note of the settlement, was
decided in 1758. A very material circumstance in that case is,
that the father might have appointed by will. It might have been
argued, that those, who were to take for want of appointment, were
the objects of appointment. The difficulty was, that as he had the
power of appointing by will, the children to take could not be determined, till he was dead. It might therefore have been contended, that it did mean children, unless they survived; so as to be the
objects of such an appointment. But the case in default of appointment having actually happened, and a child having attained the age
of twenty-one in the life of the parent, though the words were "due
or payable," which have the same meaning as "due and payable"
in *Emperor* v. *Rolfe*, the Court would not be entangled with the
other question; but said, they were glad, the case had not arisen, in
which that argument could be pressed; and as there was no appointment, *Emperor* v. *Rolfe* might be followed, though the child died
in the life of the parent; and died, not before one contingency, before the portion became due, though before the other, its becoming
payable.

A great many cases have followed in this Court; proceeding upon
the authority of these two. The next, that was cited, is *Woodcock*
v. *The Duke of Dorset*; which is stronger than any other: for,
if the word "leaving" is construed in the context with "survivor,"
it is impossible to deny, that there was a contingency existing during
the lives of the parents; as it is contended that there is here. The
recital is a circumstance in the deed, upon which you can argue to
the intention: but it is not that sort of circumstance, that the Court
would, except between parent and child, lay hold of to destroy by
the recital the obvious and clear effect of the words in the other
parts of the deed. The words in this case are much stronger than
those in *Wingrave* v. *Palgrave*. The words "if there should be but
one such child," upon the natural construction must mean one child

left at the death of the survivor. It would be impossible to raise an ambiguity upon that in any other case than that of parent and child. In any other case the answer would be, that the Court had no * right to say otherwise; for the money would have been   [* 509] in the hands of Lord Gower; and no trust upon it. But Lord Thurlow went this length; that in the case of parent and child a child having attained the age of twenty-one, and having occasion for a portion, though dying in the lives of the parents, is a child living at the death of the survivor. He certainly goes that length upon the intention; observing, that the words were very strong and difficult to manage. *Willis* v. *Willis* is also a very strong case; though distinguishable in some circumstances: but if that had been matter of contract, where the relation was not considered, the decision could not have been as it was upon those words.

I agree, in this case there are words difficult to manage: but the intention of the settlement, I mean the natural intention, regarding it as the case of father and child, must direct me, and these cases authorise me to struggle with language; for it is struggling with language; and it does not follow, that because cases are put, in which I could not struggle effectually, that I cannot prevail in the case, that has happened; if the words will bear me out in that according to the rules and authorities. Upon the true intention of this settlement, in possession upon these cases of this rule, that *prima facie* a child having attained twenty-one or marriage is to be considered a child entitled to a portion, upon the ground, that I shall not impute to a father the intention to leave a child, having occasion for a portion, without one, it is upon those, who say, the child is not entitled, to show that from the tenor and words of the settlement; and it is not enough for them to argue, that they have manifested that, because they have pointed out another case, in which it would have been impossible for the Court to have said, that child was entitled. If upon the words she is entitled in the case, that does exist, the Court would rather give the portion than struggle to oust her of it, because in another case they would have struggled ineffectually. In this settlement the trust is prior to the estate tail. In that respect it is not like *Wingrave* v. *Palgrave.* But unquestionably it is a legal estate in remainder during the life of the father; and if there is a contingency, it is not in the creation of the term, but in the expression of the trusts. As to that the words are exceedingly difficult to manage; and I cannot go the length of Mr. Mansfield, that the words "living at his decease" mean "born in his life." The words *immediately following, "or afterwards   {* 510] born alive," give a clear meaning to that; for though modern decisions (1) have held, that a posthumous child is to be considered a child living, that was not clear in 1739; when this settlement was made; and therefore these words are thrown in. I

---

(1) See *ante,* vol. iv. 321, 322, 334, 341, 342, in *Thellusson* v. *Woodford,* and the references.

upon the context at his death; and secondly, because the term at
law was gone; and it must have been considered by the Court, as
if never in the settlement. It was impossible therefore, that there
could be any doubt upon that case.

The case of *Emperor* v. *Rolfe*, the date of which I mark, in 1748,
was very like a new decision. It seems therefore to have been a
long time, before the Court could get over the natural effect of words
so strong and so difficult to manage. The construction in that case
was, that the words "grow due and payable" were, for the benefit of the estate, and attending to the motives of parental feeling,
with reference to the age of twenty-one or marriage in the life of
the parent, to secure the portion. There was a contingency there;
at least a contingency to devest what was vested under
[* 508] the former words. That is certainly different * from this
case; in which it is contended, that the contingency is
one, that prevents the vesting, not merely to devest. *Cholmondeley*
v. *Meyrick*, which in the subsequent case of *Willis* v. *Willis* the
Lord Chancellor cites from an accurate note of the settlement, was
decided in 1758. A very material circumstance in that case is,
that the father might have appointed by will. It might have been
argued, that those, who were to take for want of appointment, were
the objects of appointment. The difficulty was, that as he had the
power of appointing by will, the children to take could not be determined, till he was dead. It might therefore have been contended, that it did mean children, unless they survived; so as to be the
objects of such an appointment. But the case in default of appointment having actually happened, and a child having attained the age
of twenty-one in the life of the parent, though the words were "due
or payable," which have the same meaning as "due and payable"
in *Emperor* v. *Rolfe*, the Court would not be entangled with the
other question; but said, they were glad, the case had not arisen, in
which that argument could be pressed; and as there was no appointment, *Emperor* v. *Rolfe* might be followed, though the child died
in the life of the parent; and died, not before one contingency, before the portion became due, though before the other, its becoming
payable.

A great many cases have followed in this Court; proceeding upon
the authority of these two. The next, that was cited, is *Woodcock*
v. *The Duke of Dorset*; which is stronger than any other: for,
if the word "leaving" is construed in the context with "survivor,"
it is impossible to deny, that there was a contingency existing during
the lives of the parents; as it is contended that there is here. The
recital is a circumstance in the deed, upon which you can argue to
the intention: but it is not that sort of circumstance, that the Court
would, except between parent and child, lay hold of to destroy by
the recital the obvious and clear effect of the words in the other
parts of the deed. The words in this case are much stronger than
those in *Wingrave* v. *Palgrave*. The words " if there should be but
one such child," upon the natural construction must mean one child

left at the death of the survivor. It would be impossible to raise an ambiguity upon that in any other case than that of parent and child. In any other case the answer would be, that the Court had no * right to say otherwise; for the money would have been   [* 509] in the hands of Lord Gower; and no trust upon it. But Lord Thurlow went this length; that in the case of parent and child a child having attained the age of twenty-one, and having occasion for a portion, though dying in the lives of the parents, is a child living at the death of the survivor. He certainly goes that length upon the intention; observing, that the words were very strong and difficult to manage. *Willis* v. *Willis* is also a very strong case; though distinguishable in some circumstances: but if that had been matter of contract, where the relation was not considered, the decision could not have been as it was upon those words.

I agree, in this case there are words difficult to manage: but the intention of the settlement, I mean the natural intention, regarding it as the case of father and child, must direct me, and these cases authorise me to struggle with language; for it is struggling with language; and it does not follow, that because cases are put, in which I could not struggle effectually, that I cannot prevail in the case, that has happened; if the words will bear me out in that according to the rules and authorities. Upon the true intention of this settlement, in possession upon these cases of this rule, that *prima facie* a child having attained twenty-one or marriage is to be considered a child entitled to a portion, upon the ground, that I shall not impute to a father the intention to leave a child, having occasion for a portion, without one, it is upon those, who say, the child is not entitled, to show that from the tenor and words of the settlement; and it is not enough for them to argue, that they have manifested that, because they have pointed out another case, in which it would have been impossible for the Court to have said, that child was entitled. If upon the words she is entitled in the case, that does exist, the Court would rather give the portion than struggle to oust her of it, because in another case they would have struggled ineffectually. In this settlement the trust is prior to the estate tail. In that respect it is not like *Wingrave* v. *Palgrave*. But unquestionably it is a legal estate in remainder during the life of the father; and if there is a contingency, it is not in the creation of the term, but in the expression of the trusts. As to that the words are exceedingly difficult to manage; and I cannot go the length of Mr. Mansfield, that the words "living at his decease" mean "born in his life." The words *immediately following, "or afterwards   {* 510] born alive," give a clear meaning to that; for though modern decisions (1) have held, that a posthumous child is to be considered a child living, that was not clear in 1739; when this settlement was made; and therefore these words are thrown in. I

_____

(1) See *ante*, vol. iv. 321, 322, 334, 341, 342, in *Thellusson* v. *Woodford*, and the references.

am therefore not authorised to say, there is not a contingency,
properly expounded for the Defendants.   But the case of *Woodcock*
v. *The Duke of Dorset* is a direct answer to that ; establishing
expressly, that notwithstanding the contingency the portion is vested
according to the natural meaning of the words.

It is said, if there was no younger child at the death of the father,
none of these younger children could have had their portions.   I do
not conceive that.   It might have been as well argued in *Woodcock* v. *The Duke of Dorset ;* in which case it is clear, that in that
event Lord Thurlow must have held, that they would have had it ;
and in fact has held, that if they married or attained twenty-one,
though they died in the life of both parents, they would have been
entitled.   There is not a word in the context to sustain that opinion
in that case.   There is considerable context to support it in this.
The legal term existing, if it could be said to exist at law, though
all died in the life of the father, they should take (1).

But it is not necessary to decide that here ; for, if they could not
have taken in that event, does it follow, that a child is not to take,
when, there being some children surviving, the term not only exists,
but the trusts are to be executed for some children ?   Consider the
words, and the question ; which is, whether, in case there is any
child living at the death of the father, for whom the trusts ought to
be executed, a child, who attained twenty-one or married, but died
in the life of the father, is one of the objects of the trust, that is to
be executed for somebody.   In this case and upon these authorities
I should say, the words "such child" must refer to the immediate
antecedent "all and every the child and children," except an eldest
or only son, not qualified by the contingency.   Upon the clause as
to what is to be raised in the life of the father, if the words
[* 511]   introducing the *contingency are to determine the character of the child, and no child but one living at the
decease of the father is entitled, how is the power to be exercised,
and the proviso to have effect ?   It may be said, the father may
direct such a child to take, even though the contingency should not
happen, upon which the trusts of the term were to be exercised.
There is not a word in the settlement in support of that ; and that
would be as strong a construction to support the act of the father as
I am making to support this according to former cases.   The other
clauses relied on for the Plaintiff do not afford all the argument, that
has been attributed to them.   The expression as to survivorship still
includes the question, who are entitled to portions.

Upon the whole I have a strong inclination, if I can, to construe
this in such a manner as to hold the daughter entitled.   The authorities go full as far : many of them a great deal farther.   With that
inclination I do not hesitate to say, it would be better to construe all
instruments according to their terms, and not to spell out what they
might have meant.   I should have had great difficulty in going the

---

(1) *Powis* v. *Burdett, post,* vol. ix. 428.

length of prior authorities: but as they have gone so far, it is my inclination, and I think, my duty to follow them. I should have no objection to have this case spoken to again : but if that course should not be taken, and I should not mention it before the first day of causes, you will understand it is my opinion, that this may be supported.

No farther argument was offered at the Bar, and the Lord Chancellor not having expressed any change of opinion, the decree was made ; declaring, that Mary Hope had a vested interest in one third of the sum of 5000*l.* and that the same with interest at the rate of 4 per cent. from the death of Eliab Breton ought to be raised by sale or mortgage.

1. As to the leaning of Courts of Equity, when the language of a settlement is at all ambiguous, in favor of such a construction as would give vested interests to the children of the settlor at the time when they stand in need of a provision; see, *ante*, notes 1 and 3 to *Willis* v. *Willis*, 3 V. 51; and to the authorities there cited, add *Bradish* v. *Bradish*, 2 Ball & Bea. 487, and *Driver* v. *Frank*, 3 Mau. & Sel. 32.

2. That the operative part of a settlement may be reformed, so as to accord with the intention declared in the recital ; see the note to *Doran* v. *Ross*, 1 V. 57 ; and see farther as to the effect of a recital in a settlement, note 4 to *Dundas* v. *Dutens*, 1 V. 196.

3. A child *en ventre sa mere*, is considered in existence as much as if it were actually born ; see note 2 to *Clarke* v. *Blake*, 2 V. 673.

GRANT, *Ex parte.*   [* 512]

[1801, Nov. 28.]

TENANT for ninety-nine years, if she shall so long live; remainder to trustees to preserve contingent remainders; remainder to the heirs of her body ; remainder over to the same trustees upon trust for other persons. Upon the application of those persons and the trustees under the statute 6 Anne, c. 18, the husband of the tenant for life was ordered to produce her.

MR. ROMILLY moved under the statute of Queen Anne (1), that —— Woodroffe may be ordered to produce the body of Mary Woodroffe, his wife ; to whom the estate in question was limited for ninety-nine years, if she should so long live ; remainder to trustees to preserve contingent remainders ; .remainder to the heirs of the body of Mary Woodroffe : and for default of such issue to the same trustees upon trust to sell, and divide the produce among certain persons.

The motion was made on behalf of the trustees and the *cestuys que trust* in default of issue of Mary Woodroffe, upon affidavits, stating, that she left her husband nine years ago ; and had not been since

---

(1) Stat. 6 Anne, c. 18.

heard of; and that, while she was known to be living, she never
had any child. The husband continued to hold the estate in her
right.

A doubt was suggested, whether this case was within the statute;
the application being made by persons not immediately entitled upon
the death of the party.

The Lord CHANCELLOR [ELDON] requiring evidence, that Mary
Woodroffe was not pregnant whèn she left her husband, an affidavit
was made: stating, that she was not then pregnant to the best of the
knowledge and belief of the deponents.

The Lord CHANCELLOR under these circumstances made the order.

A SIMILAR order to that made in the principal case, for the production of the
cestui que vie, according to the provisions of the statute of Anne, was granted in
Ex parte St. Aubyn, 2 Cox, 373. And according to the statute 19 Car. 2, c. 6,
with respect to leases dependant on lives, the *presumption* of the duration of life
with respect to persons of whom no account can be given, ends at the expiration
of seven years from the time when they were last known to be living: the same
rule is adopted in the statute 1 Jac. I, c. 11, against bigamy. *Doe* v. *Jesson*, 6
East, 85; *Doe* v. *Deakin*, 4 Barn. & Ald. 434; *The King* v. *Inhabitants of Twining*, 2 Barn. & Ald. 389; *Holman* v. *Exton*, Carth. 246. But where proceedings
are commenced under the above cited statute of Car. 2, for the recovery of tenements upon the presumed death of the *cestuis que vie*, the party entitled for the
lives of such absent persons may, in order to give proof of their existence, obtain
a commission for the examination of witnesses beyond the seas. *Brown* v. *Petre*,
2 Swanst. 237. See, as not irrelevant to this subject, the note to *Lee v. Willock*,
6 V. 605.

ANONYMOUS.

[1801, Nòv. 28.]

UPON opening biddings the Court refused to dispense with a deposit, or to order a
trifling one, upon particular circumstances (*a*).

MR. STANLEY moved to open biddings without making any deposit, or at least upon a very small one, under these circumstances;
that the purposes, for which the sale was directed, would be answered by the produce of the other lots, exclusive of that, which was the
subject of the application: which was made by the tenant for life
with remainder to his children; and the tenant for life meant to buy
in that lot. It was also stated, that he was in distressed circumstances.

Mr. *Richards*, for the purchaser insisted, that he had a right to
retain his purchase, unless got rid of by another purchaser in the
regular course.

Lord CHANCELLOR [ELDON].—The mischief is, that I should discharge a purchaser, who has made a deposit, for one, who will not

---

(*a*) As to opening biddings and the practice thereon in the United States, see
ante, note (*a*), *Anonymous*, 1 V. 453; note (*a*), *Chetham* v. *Grugeon*, 5 V. 86.

make one.   The deposit is the only hold the Court has upon the purchaser.   I recollect, when the manor of Great Thurlow in Norfolk was sold, while Lord Thurlow was Chancellor; on whose behalf I moved to open the biddings before Sir Thomas Sewell upon an advance from 5700*l.* to 6700*l.*   The Master of the Rolls inquiring, what deposit would be made, I answered, that all the parties were satisfied with the purchaser: the Master of the Rolls replied, not knowing the circumstance, that if the Lord Chancellor was the bidder, he should make a large deposit; the deposit being the only hold the Court has on a purchaser; and ordered a deposit of the whole advance.

This application desires indirectly what could not be asked directly.   If an estate was directed to be sold in ten lots upon a calculation, and nine having been sold had produced so much more than was calculated, that there was no occasion to sell the tenth, and an application was made, stating, that the tenth was ordered improvidently to be sold, and praying, that it might not, I do not know, that such a motion would not succeed.   But this lot has been sold with the others.   This therefore is desiring me to do indirectly what could not be desired directly, in this * instance, the   [*514] lot having been actually sold; viz. that there shall not be a deposit.   There must be a deposit; and it must be upon all the usual terms (1).

A deposit of 600*l.* was ordered.

See the note to the *Anonymous case,* 1 V. 453, and the notes to *Rigby* v. *M'Namara,* 6 V. 117.

COFFIN *v.* COOPER.

[1801, Nov. 28.]

Answer referred for scandal on the motion of another Defendant (*a*).
Reference for scandal upon the application of any one, not a party, or even without a motion.
What is material or relevant not to be considered scandal (*b*).
Principle of referring scandal to the Master in the first instance, [p. 515.]
Difference between Plaintiff and Defendant, referring for impertinence, not applicable to scandal, [p. 515.]

Mr. Newbolt for one Defendant moved, that the answer of another should be referred for scandal; observing, that there was no precedent of such a motion by a Defendant; though by a Plaintiff

(1) *Rigby* v. *Macnamara, post,* 515; *ante,* vol. ii. 55, the note to *Watson* v. *Birch.*
(*a*) Exceptions for scandal may be taken by a co-defendant; but not for impertinence.   1 Barb. Ch. Pr. 203.   See also, 1 Smith, Ch. Pr. (Am. ed.) 158, 159, 569, 570; 2 Madd. Ch. Pr. 201, 202; 1 Hoff. Ch. Pr. ch. 4, § 1, p. 170, 171.
(*b*) Any unnecessary allegation bearing cruelly upon the moral character of an individual, is scandalous, 1 Barb. Ch. Pr. 41.

it is of course. If this cannot be done, the Plaintiff and one Defendant may combine to reflect upon the character of another. The principle as to scandal is to keep the records pure.

Mr. *Hall*, for the other Defendants.—The matter is relevant; and therefore not scandalous. It consists of facts introduced to show, that a will and codicil ought to be set aside, as improperly obtained.

In all cases of fraud it is necessary to put in issue the material facts. *Fenhoulet* v. *Passavant* (1), before Lord Hardwicke. If relevant in any way, being material it can be neither scandal nor impertinence.

Lord CHANCELLOR.—I do not recollect an instance of an application by a Defendant: but I cannot conceive, that the Court would not do it even without a motion; and that it is not competent to any one to apply; and I would not lay down, that a person, not a party to the record, could not (2). It is the duty of the Court to the public to take care, that its records shall be kept pure. I agree, that, because an answer strongly reflects, it is not to be called scandal, if material, and relevant to the justice of the case. But the [*515] suggestion is enough to put it upon the Court to * examine, whether it is scandalous; and whether, if it is, it is not to be considered so, because material or relevant.

Therefore refer it to the Master to see, whether this is scandal. With respect to the principle of sending it to the Master in the first instance, whether upon the impossibility for the Court to inquire itself in the first instance, or whether it is partly upon delicacy as to character, I think there is enough in the latter ground for thinking it better to send it there than inquire into it here in the first instance. I think, there may be a difference between a Plaintiff and a Defendant referring for impertinence : but the ground of that difference does not apply to scandal (3).

---

1. .WITH respect to references of pleadings for scandal or impertinence, see the notes to the *Anonymous case*, 5 V. 656; the application for this purpose is a motion, of course, requiring no notice: *Eastham* v. *Liddell*, 12 Ves. 201 : and there can be no proceeding before a Court of Equity, which, if made the vehicle of scandal, the Court will not examine, with a view to reform it : depositions, or a statement of facts, carried in before the Master, and affidavits in bankruptcy or lunacy, all come within the same rule in this respect: *Cocks* v. *Worthington*, 2 Atk. 236; *Erskine* v. *Garthshore*, 18 Ves. 115; *Ex parte Le Heup*, 18 Ves. 223; *Ex parte Simpson*, 15 Ves. 477; *Anonymous case*, 3 V. & B. 93: but nothing that is relevant to the matter in issue is scandalous. *Lord St. John* v. *Lady St. John*, 11 Ves. 539; *Fenhoulet* v. *Passavant*, 2 Ves. Sen. 24; *Earl of Portsmouth* v. *Fellows*, 5 Mad. 450.

2. As to the practice of decreeing a specific performance, when it appears that a good title to an estate, which has been the subject of contract, is capable of being made good within a reasonable time; see note 6 to *Cooper* v. *Denne*, 1 V. 565.

---

(1) 2 Ves. 24; *post*, *Lord St. John* v. *Lady St. John*, vol xi. 526.

(2) See Lord Bacon's orders, Mr. Beames's edit. 25. In 1819, 4 Madd. 252. The Vice Chancellor decides the contrary; and as it is represented, with his Lordship's concurrence : but by a manuscript note of Mr. Beames it appears, that his Lordship has since decided according to *Coffin* v. *Cooper*, and Lord Bacon's orders.

(3) For other distinctions in practice as to scandal and impertinence, see *ante*, *Pellew* v. ———, 456, vol. v. 656, and the note. *Anon.* 2 Ves. 681.

RIGBY *v.* MACNAMARA.

[1801, Nov. 27, 28.]

THE Court will not discharge a purchaser and substitute another even upon paying in the money without an affidavit, that there is no under-bargain (*a*).

MR. WETHERELL moved, that one person might be substituted for another; who was a purchaser under the decree.

The purchaser appeared by Counsel; and consented.

The Lord CHANCELLOR refused the motion; saying, this was one of the mischiefs of consent: the effect would be discharging a purchaser, who had made a deposit, for one, who might be worth nothing: but he should be discharged whenever the new purchaser paid in the money (1).

The next day Mr. *Wetherell* moved on behalf of the new purchaser, that on his paying the money he might be substituted, and the other discharged.

The Lord CHANCELLOR said, this might be an ingenious device, with a view not to come to the Court to open the biddings; * and he would have an affidavit, that there is no   [*516] under-bargain; for the new purchaser may give the other a sum of money to stand in his place, and so deceive the Court (2).

SEE, *ante*, the notes to *S. C.* 6 V. 117.

REEVES *v.* BRYMER.
BRYMER *v.* REEVES.

[ROLLS.—1801, DEC. 1, 2.]

CIRCUMSTANCES not sufficient evidence of a release of a bond debt (*b*).
Upon a question of presumption of satisfaction in a hard case the Court gave the executors leave to bring an action upon the bond; but would not direct it.

THESE causes (3) came on for farther directions after the Master's report; which among other things stated, that the executors had not

---

(*a*) As to opening biddings in the United States, and the practice thereon, see *ante*, note (*a*), *Anonymous*, I V. 453; note (*a*), *Chetham* v. *Grugeon*, 5 V. 86.

(1) *Post, Vale* v. *Davenport*, 615. As to opening biddings, see *ante, Anon.* 513; vol. ii. 55, the note to *Watson* v. *Birch.*

(2) *Vale* v. *Davenport, post*, 615.

(*b*) Cases may occur where a deed or the instrument originally valid, has by subsequent events, legal or equitable, because *functus officio.* 2 Story, Eq. Jur, § 705; *Flower* v. *Martyn*, 2 M. & C. 459; note (*a*), *Eden* v. *Smyth*, 5 V. 341. A release may be established by circumstantial evidence. 2 Starkie, Evid. 712, (5th Am. ed.); *Washington* v. *Brymer*, ibid, note: Peake, Evid. Appendix.

(3) Reported, *ante*, vol. iv. 692.

possessed any part of the testator's estate since the 16th of May, 1791, when the residue was distributed according to the decree, except a bond dated the 27th of September, 1766, from William Brymer, the Defendant in the first cause, in the penal sum of 800*l.*, with condition for payment of 400*l.* with interest at the rate of 5 per. cent. on the 27th of September next, and except certain leasehold estates.

With respect to the bond the Master stated, that he found by the affidavit of William Brymer, that in 1766 he borrowed the sum of 400*l.* from the testator; and thereupon executed the aforesaid bond. About five or six years afterwards the deponent's affairs became embarrassed: and he applied again to the testator; who refused to advance him any more money; and alleged as a reason, that the deponent had already had 900*l.* of him: meaning 500*l.*, which the testator paid him as a marriage portion with his daughter, and the 400*l.* secured by the aforesaid bond; and that the deponent might do as he pleased with the sum he then owed him; as he should never ask him for it, or require him to pay it; but that he would not advance him any thing more, or to that effect. Upon other occasions, and many years after the execution of the said bond, when the deponent had solicited the loan of money of the testator, he reminded the deponent of his having given him what he owed him on the aforesaid bond: and assigned that as a reason for his refusing to comply with the deponent's request; and in consequence of the testator's having repeatedly declared to the deponent, that [*517] he never meant to call *upon him for payment of the aforesaid bond, and the deponent never having been asked or required by the testator to pay the same or any part thereof, the deponent conceived and verily believed, that the testator had many years since cancelled or destroyed the said bond. The deponent farther stated in 1778 he took the benefit of an Insolvent Act. By that act (1) it is enacted, that the future real estates as well freehold as copyhold, salaries of officers under government, money, or money in the funds, or lent upon real security only, of every person or persons, taking the benefit of the act, which after the time of his, her, or their, total surrender of his, her, or their, estate and effects under such act, he, she, or they shall or may be seised of in his, her, or their, own right or use, by grant, demise, or purchase, shall remain and be liable to his, her, or their, respective creditors, &c.

Mr. *Piggott*, Mr. *Richards*, and Mr. *W. Agar*, for the Plaintiffs; Mr. *Romilly*, and Mr. *Steele*, for parties in the same interest, insisted, that the bond ought to be enforced.

Mr. *Sutton* and Mr. *Hart*, for William Brymer.—Either what is stated in the report is evidence of a release, according to *Eden* v. *Smyth* (2) and *Aston* v. *Pye* (3); or from the length of time a presumption of payment or satisfaction arises.

---

(1) Stat. 18 Geo. III. c. 52.
(2) *Ante*, vol. v. 341.
(3) Stated *ante*, vol. v. 350, 354.

Reply.—Clearly there is neither payment nor satisfaction. The only question is as to the release. In *Eden* v. *Smyth* (1) there were many circumstances: but the Lord Chancellor did not consider it as a release; though under all the circumstances he thought, Sir Frederick Eden ought not to be sued at law. In this case there are no circumstances: there is nothing but this conversation between the testator and Brymer himself; which cannot be considered a release of this bond either at law or in equity.

The circumstance of taking the benefit of the act of insolvency is sufficient to rebut the presumption. The Court will at least send this to a jury.

* The MASTER OF THE ROLLS.—What was it consid-   [* 518]
ered to be in *Eden* v. *Smyth?* It must be something.

You say, it was not a release: but it had an effect equally beneficial to the obligor. However numerous the circumstances, all that goes only to the weight and amount of the evidence.

Dec. 2d. The MASTER OF THE ROLLS [Sir WILLIAM GRANT].—This objection to the right of Brymer to receive in right of his wife her proportion of the residue is, that he is debtor by this bond to the estate; and that proportion therefore ought to be applied to that debt in the first place. The bond is as old as 1766. He objects, that he ought not to be charged with it for two reasons: 1st, On account of the intention of the testator to forgive him the debt: 2dly, That the presumptive bar from length of time ought to operate against any demand upon it. These two grounds are certainly inconsistent. The one supposes, the bond never has been paid, from the intention of the obligee never to demand payment of it: the other desires the Court to presume it satisfied. I should not have been sorry to have found any specific ground, upon which I could have exempted this poor old man from this charge; for there is every reason to suppose, it was not the intention of the testator to exact it; and the Defendant had from the lapse of time and what passed between him and the testator no reason to believe, he did intend it. It is said, there is evidence of a release from what passed between them; and *Eden* v. *Smyth* is cited to show, that such circumstances may amount to evidence of a release. First, Brymer does not state, that he has any evidence, that he can produce, of what passed between him and the testator. Therefore in an action he could not avail himself of such a defence. He does not state, that any thing passed, except with himself, no other person being present. In *Eden* v. *Smyth* there was a letter of Mr. Smyth: in which he declared, he had released. That was good evidence, from which it might be inferred, that an actual release was executed. But, independent of that, I much doubt, whether, if all he states to have passed with the testator could be proved, it

(1) As to that case, see *Pole* v. *Lord Somers*, and *Druce* v. *Denison*, *ante*, 309, 385.

would amount to evidence of a release. It is very different from
the assertion of Mr. Smyth. This is nothing more than
[* 519] that he never meant * to demand payment. He says, he
had given him the 400*l.* he owed him upon his bond ; that
he might make what use he pleased of it ; and he never meant to
require payment, &c. All that is nothing more than a declaration
by the testator, that he never would sue for this money ; which
certainly is not sufficient to operate as a release ; though if declarations of this kind are put in writing, if by a testamentary paper, it might operate as a gift to him of the money due upon the
bond.

As to the other ground, of presumption of satisfaction, if there was
any probability of benefit to the obligor, I would certainly in such a
case put them to recover at law. But I fear, that would put him to
a useless expense ; for from the circumstances I apprehend, they
would succeed ; and the bar would not operate. They would be
able to show from his own declarations, that he had not paid the
bond ; and that he proceeded upon quite a different ground, the for-
giveness of the debt. It is only a presumption ; which may be rebutted by showing, it was not paid ; and that for many reasons the
presumption from the length of time does not arise. The testator
might have abstained from suing him, because it would have been to
no purpose.

The Plaintiff's Counsel then stating, that Brymer's share of the
residue did not amount to what was due upon the bond, applied for
a direction to the executors to bring an action.

The MASTER OF THE ROLLS said, he would not direct them to bring
an action ; but declared, that the executors should be at liberty to
bring an action upon that bond ; that the other shares of the residue
should be paid ; and Brymer's reserved till the event of the action ;
with liberty to apply.

————

SEE, *ante,* the notes to *S. C.* 4 V. 692.

SITWELL *v.* BERNARD.

[1801, July 27; Dec. 5.]

Testator directed the residue of his personal estate, subject to the payment of legacies, annuities, debts and funeral expenses, with all convenient speed to be laid out in real estates, to be settled in strict settlement; and that the interest of such residue should accumulate, and be laid out in lands to be settled in like manner. Various circumstances having delayed the collection and investment of the personal estate, the tenant for life was held entitled to the interest from the end of a year after the death of the testator (*a*).

General rule, that legacies, where no interest is given by the will, shall carry interest at 4 per cent. only, and from the end of a year after death of the testator; except where it is given by way of maintenance; though the fund produces more; and the interest shall not be increased by the effect of appropriation (*b*).

A legatee having taken a mortgage in part payment, subject to an agreement for payment out of the other assets and a resumption of the mortgage, was held entitled to the benefit of that agreement; accounting for the difference of interest.

The Court will look at principles of convenience; as in the rule, that legacies shall be payable at the end of a year, [p. 539.]

Francis Sitwell by his will, dated the 5th of February 1792, gave to his wife 1000*l.* a-year during her life, as a jointure and in lieu of dower; and directed the same and all other annuities given by his will to be paid half yearly clear of all deductions; the first payment of them to be at the expiration of six months after his decease; and he also gave to his said wife his house near Sheffield, called Mount Pleasant, with the appurtenances, together with the use of the furniture belonging to the house for her life; and after her death he gave the furniture belonging to the said house to his executors, to be sold and go as part of his personal estate, and he gave to his wife his town house in Audley Square with its appurtenances, together with the use of the furniture belonging thereto for her life; and after her decease he gave the same to his executors, upon trust to sell his said town house, and to divide the net money arising from the sale thereof equally between his two sons Francis Sitwell and Hurt Sitwell.

The testator then reciting, that Samuel Phipps under the trusts and powers in his (the testator's) late uncle's will had devised the real estates in the county of Northumberland, which were devised to the said Samuel Phipps by the testator's uncle, in trust to be settled

---

(*a*) As to the duty of executors to call in debts due the testator, see *ante,* note (*a*), *Powell* v. *Evans,* 5 V. 839.

It seems to be established that the person taking the residue for life is entitled to the proceeds from the death of the testator. 2 Williams, Exec. 997; *Stair* v. *Macgill,* 1 Bligh, N. S. 662; *S. C.* 1 Dow, N. S. 24. See also *Parry* v. *Warrington,* Madd. & Geld. 155.

Legacies are payable at the end of a year from the testator's death. See *ante,* note (*a*), *Crickett* v. *Dolby,* 3 V. 10.

From what time the conversion should be supposed. 2 Story, Eq. Jur. § 790, note.

(*b*) As to the rate of interest allowed in Equity, and particularly on legacies, see *ante,* note (*b*), *Lewis* v. *Freke,* 2 V. 507; 2 Williams, Exec. 1027.

on the testator for life, with remainder to his son Francis Sitwell for
life, with remainder to trustees to preserve contingent remainders,
with remainder to his (Francis Sitwell's) first and other sons successively in tail male, with divers remainders over, gave to his said son
Francis Sitwell, considering, he would be entitled to the said Northumberland estates on his death, the sum of 20,000*l.* ; and he gave
to his son Hurt Sitwell 30,000*l.* ; which sums he directed to be paid
to them respectively on their attaining their respective ages of 21 ;
the interest of which said respective sums was (after applying thereout respectively what his executors should think reasonable for their
respective maintenance and education) to accumulate from the time
     of his decease at the rate of 4*l.* per cent. per annum, for
[* 521] the benefit of his said two sons * respectively, to be added
     to· the principal, until the said principal sums should be-
come payable ; and it was his will, that his executors or the survivor
of them should have power at his or their discretion to advance any
part of the said sum of 20,000*l.* and 30,000*l.* respectively for the
purpose of placing out or advancing his said sons Francis and Hurt
or either of them in life, before such son should attain the age of
twenty-one years ; and in case his said son Francis should die under
the age of twenty-one years, then the testator directed, that his said
legacy of 20,000*l.*, or so much thereof as should not have been applied
or advanced, as aforesaid, should sink into the residue of his personal
estate. The testator gave a similar direction with respect to the legacy
of 30,000*l.* given to his son Hurt.

The testator then gave to his grandson Charles Wake 5000*l.*, to
be paid him on his attaining the age of twenty-one, if he should
live to attain that age; but not to carry any interest in the mean
time; and if he died under that age, then to sink into the residue of
his personal estate. He gave to his sister-in-law Catherine Warne-
ford an annuity of 400*l.* for her life and 500*l.* ; to each .of the children of his late niece Catherine Slater 400*l.*, to be paid to sons at
twenty-one, or to be sooner applied for their benefit, if his executors
should see fit, and to daughters at twenty-one or days of marriage,
which should first happen ; to Richard Slater 200*l.* ; to his niece
Jane Heaton an annuity of 100*l.* during her life for her separate
use and 100*l.* ; and in case she should marry and leave issue, to
each of her children 200*l.*, to be paid to sons at twenty-one, or to
be sooner applied for their benefit, if his executors should see fit,
and to daughters at twenty-one or days of marriage ; and he directed, that interest at 4 per cent. should be paid in respect of the legacies given to the children of his late niece Catherine Slater from
his decease, until their respective legacies should become payable, as
aforesaid, and also in respect of the legacies given to the children
(if any) of his said niece Jane from her decease, until the said
legacies should become payable. He then gave several annuities
and legacies, some to servants; and directed, that the several
legacies and annuities before given should be paid without prejudice to any sums, which should be due from him to any of the

legatees or annuitants ; and he directed his executors to continue
some weekly and other allowances to some poor persons at Renishaw in Yorkshire during their lives ; and he gave the furniture, plate, books, linen, china, wines, carriages, horses, and
effects, whatsoever, which should belong to, or be in or about
his house, offices, and grounds, at Renishaw at the time of his
decease to his eldest son Sitwell Sitwell for his own use and benefit ; and directed his executors to pay any annuities or legacies,
which by any writing under his hand or signed by him at any time
thereafter he should direct or appoint to be paid.

He then gave all his personal estate unto his executors for the
purpose of paying his said legacies and annuities and his debts and
funeral expenses, and such other legacies and annuities as he might
thereafter give ; and subject and without prejudice to the payment
of any legacies, annuities, debts, and funeral expenses, he directed
his executors or the survivor of them with all convenient speed to
lay out and dispose of the rest and residue of his personal estate in
the purchase of manors, lands, tenements, or hereditaments, in
England, of inheritance in fee-simple in possession, to be settled,
as thereinafter mentioned ; and directed, that the interest of such
residue of his personal estate should accumulate and be laid out in
lands to be settled in like manner as he had directed the residuum
of his personal estate.

The will then directed the limitations of the estates, so to be purchased, in strict settlement to the testator's eldest son Sitwell Sitwell
for life, without impeachment of waste, with remainders to his first
and other sons successively in tail male, then to Francis Sitwell and
his sons, Hurt Sitwell and his sons, Charles Wake and his sons, respectively, in the same manner ; and the ultimate remainder to the
testator's right heirs ; with powers for his son and grandson, when
in possession, to grant leases, not exceeding twenty-one years ; and
he declared, that the legacies and estates therein before given and
limited to his said three sons Sitwell, Francis, and Hurt, by that his
will, were on condition of their joining, as to his son Sitwell as soon
as might be after his decease, and as to his sons Francis and Hurt
as soon as might be after they should respectively come of age, in
such acts, deeds fines, recoveries, and assurances, as his executors
should require to confirm Phipps's disposition of his (the
testator's) uncle's estates in the county of * Northumber-   [* 523]
land ; and in case any of his said sons should within
twelve months after such respective times, as aforesaid, refuse so to
do, they should forfeit the legacies and estates thereby given to
them ; and the benefit of such legacies and estates so forfeited
should go as part of the residuum of his personal estate.   He appointed Thomas Bernard and Richard Huddleston executors, and
guardians of his sons Francis and Hurt, until they should attain
their respective ages of twenty-one ; empowering them to place out
any moneys, part of, or arising from, his personal estate, which
should come to their hands by virtue of his will, or any moneys, part

of his personal estate, which they should retain as a fund to answer the payment of his legacies and annuities, on real or Government securities, and to change the securities. Then, after the usual clause of indemnity, he requested his son Sitwell Sitwell would settle his house, called Mount Pleasant, after the decease of his wife, with the grounds, &c. in such manner that it should be enjoyed as an hospital for the benefit of the town of Sheffield and neighborhood.

By a codicil, dated the 13th of December, 1792, stating among other things, that his wife had died since his will, he gave to his son Sitwell Sitwell all his plate, linen, and china, which was given to his wife; and directed, that the diamonds and jewels should be valued, and made into three separate lots of equal value, to be divided between his three sons; and he gave to his said sons Francis Sitwell and Hurt Sitwell 10,000*l.* each in addition to the said sums of 20,000*l.* and 30,000*l.* given them respectively by his said will; the said sums of 10,000*l.* each to be paid to them at the same times and upon the like events and with the like interest as directed concerning the said sums of 20,000*l.* and 30,000*l.* by his said will. He gave to his daughter-in-law Mrs. Sitwell Sitwell, in case she should survive her husband, an annuity of 400*l.* for her life, in addition to her jointure, to be paid half-yearly: the first payment to be made at the end of six calendar months after the death of his son Sitwell Sitwell; to his grand-daughter Many Alice Sitwell 2000*l.* to be paid on her attaining twenty-one, but not to carry interest in the mean time; and if she should die under that age, then to sink into the residue of his personal estate. Then, after some farther pecuniary legacies, specific legacies of linen and furniture, and

[* 524]   some annuities, * the first payment to be at the end of six months after his decease, he gave to the Lying-in-Hospital, to which his wife was a subscriber, 200*l.* to be paid out of his personal estate; and reciting, that since the making of his will the trustees of the Sheffield Infirmary had fixed upon a site for building an infirmary, towards which he had subscribed 500*l*, he gave to the trustees of the said infirmary the farther sum of 500*l.* to be paid out of his personal estate towards the building of the said infirmary. He revoked the request in his will respecting his house and grounds at Little Sheffield being settled by his eldest son to be enjoyed as an hospital; and gave the said house and grounds to his said son Sitwell Sitwell, his heirs and assigns for ever. He empowered and directed his executors in the settlement directed of the manors, lands, &c. to be purchased with the residue of his personal estate, to secure, charge, and make payable, out of such manors, &c. to be purchased with the residue of his personal estate, the sums given or directed to be paid by his will and codicil for the benefit of the several annuitants and other persons; and he gave Thomas Bernard the annual sum of 200*l.* during the first seven years after his decease, as a compensation for his loss of time, but not as a satisfaction for his expenses in the execution of the will; and he directed all the legacies and annuities by the codicil to be in addition to those by the will.

By another codicil, dated the 28th of July, 1793, the testator gave a legacy of 100*l*. He died in September, 1793 ; leaving a personal estate amounting to upwards of 150,000*l*. ; a considerable part of which being outstanding on large mortgages could not be got in ; and in Michaelmas Term, 1797, the bill was filed by Sitwell Sitwell; praying the necessary accounts ; and that it may be de-clared, that the Plaintiff is entitled to the interest of the clear resi-due of the personal estate, not specifically bequeathed, so far as such residue had not been laid out in the purchase of land under the will, from the end of one year after the testator's death, or such other period as the Court should be of opinion the Plaintiff was entitled thereto ; that such interest might be paid to the Plaintiff ; that such parts of the residue as had not been laid out in the purchase of lands might be so laid out according to the will, and subject to the payment of the said legacies to the Defendants Hurt Sit-well, Charles Wake, and Mary Alice *Sitwell ; that the [* 525] Plaintiff may be let into possession of the estates, when purchased, subject to the annuities, &c.; and that in case the Court should be of opinion, that the legacies given to Hurt Sitwell ought then to be provided for out of the personal estate not specifically be-queathed, then that a sufficient fund might be set apart out of such personal estate to answer the same, in case he should become en-titled thereto ; and all necessary directions, &c.

The decree, pronounced in 1798, directed the usual accounts and payment of the legacies and the arrears of the annuities ; and an appropriation to answer the legacies to infants and the annuities : an inquiry, what steps had been taken to get in the personal estate out-standing upon securities ; that the Master should state the clear resi-due, and how it had been disposed of, and distinguish what part con-sisted of principal, and what part had arisen from interest from the end of twelve months after the testator's death.

The Master by his Report, made in November 1800, stated the accounts ; and that all the legacies had been paid except the lega-cies of 30,000*l*. and 10,000*l*. to Hurt Sitwell and the 5000*l*. to Charles Wake, and 2000*l*. to Mary Alice Sitwell. Hurt Sitwell attained twenty-one on the 26th of June, 1799. Francis Sitwell at-tained twenty-one in October, 1796 ; and soon afterwards applied to the executors for payment of his legacies ; when they informed him, that having contracted for the purchase of an estate, which would require great part of the money then in their hands, they could not without great inconvenience to the trust pay him the whole in cash ; but they were willing to pay him in the following manner ; in cash 12,500*l*., and the remaining sum of 17,500*l*. part of a mortgage debt of 33,000*l*. due to the testator, secured upon the estates of the late Saville Finch, Esquire. Francis Sitwell in answer stated, that in order to benefit his brother he was willing to receive his legacies in the manner proposed, upon condition, that the executors should out of the first moneys, which should come to their hands, pay him the said sum of 17,500*l*. and resume the mortgage ; which they agreed to.

In consequence of that he accepted the 12,500*l.* and a transfer
of the mortgage : and in April 1798 on his application to the
executors to resume the mortgage a memorandum, dated the 16th
of April, 1798, was signed by Francis Sitwell and the executors ; stating, that it was understood and agreed, that the mortgage of 17,500*l.* shall be taken back ; and the mortgage money
paid to Francis Sitwell out of the moneys expected to be
shortly paid in part of a mortgage of 51,000*l.* due to the testator's
estate ; part of which had been lately paid to the executors, and
applied by them, except, 1500*l.* lent to Francis Sitwell on his bond ;
and the residue is in a course of payment ; and this is agreed to by
the executors, as far as they can consistently with their duty and the
due execution of their trust.

The Report farther stated, that accordingly on the 16th of April,
1798, the Defendants advanced to Francis Sitwell 1500*l.* upon his
bond. He therefore claimed 16,000*l.* : offering to re-transfer the
mortgage ; and the executors also claimed to have that sum paid to
him in part resumption of the mortgage ; which claims the Master
submitted to the Court.

The Report stated, that the only sums remaining due on mortgage exclusive of the said 17,500*l.* are 20,000*l.*, the balance of the said
mortgage for 51,000*l.*, and another mortgage of 17,500*l.* ; that soon
after the testator's death notices were given to pay the said mortgage debts ; but the heir of the mortgagor for 51,000*l.* being a minor,
no proceedings could be had with effect, until he attained twenty-
one in June 1796. The Defendants were induced to delay filing a
bill by a proposal to pay the mortgage by a sale : which took place
accordingly : but many of the purchasers not being able to complete
their purchases, the Defendants had been compelled to receive the
money by instalments ; conceiving that more for the benefit of the
testator's estate than to file bills : but from the difficulty in raising money in the present times and other circumstances 20,000*l.*
still remained due.

With respect to the other mortgage of 17,500*l.* the Report stated,
that the executors in Easter Term 1796 filed a bill ; and upon the
23d of May, 1798, obtained a decree for a foreclosure :
[* 527]   * but several orders for time had been obtained : the last
upon the 20th of January, 1800, for six months.

The Report then stated, that the executors had laid out part of
the personal estate in the purchase of real estates ; one of which
they purchased from the Plaintiff.

The questions were, 1st, Upon the Plaintiff's claim to the interest of
the personal estate from the end of a year after the testator's death.

2dly, As to the right claimed by Francis Sitwell to have the mortgage resumed by the executors, and the remainder of his legacy paid
in money.

3dly, Upon the claim of the legatees to interest at 5 per cent.

Mr. *Romilly*, Mr. *Hollist*, and Mr. *Cox*, for the Plaintiff.—Upon
the first question, there is no case precisely like this : but *Hutcheon*

v. *Mannington* (1) bears a strong analogy. That was the case of a legacy, given over, if the legatee should die, before he might have received the legacy. This residuary disposition would be very clear, except for the latter part ; for the persons beneficially entitled could not be prejudiced by the negligence of the trustees ; who would have been bound to lay out the fund at the end of a year after the death of the testator. The latter part of the clause would be satisfied by the interest accumulating within the year, the usual time allowed for the executor to collect the property. Another way of satisfying those words is by referring them to the legacies to his grandson and grand-daughter, directed not to be paid till the age of twenty-one, and not to carry interest in the mean time. This is to be considered, as if the Plaintiff had no other provision under the will. He could not mean, that the executors should have the power of delaying the investing of his personal estate in land, as long as they thought proper. They delayed three years, before they even took steps to call in the mortgages. They might have had a decree *nisi* against the infant * mortgagor. But the　[* 528] other mortgagor was of age. In *Hollingsworth* v. *Hollingsworth* (2) there was a devise in trust to sell, and divide the produce among brothers and sisters, or their children in case any should be dead, before the estates should be sold. The bill was filed by some children, upon the ground, that the estates were not sold during the lives of the parent : but the Lord Chancellor held decidedly, that it made no difference ; for the estates were to be taken to have been sold at the death of the testator. The case of *Entwistle* v. *Markland* (3) is a direct authority for giving the tenant for life the inter-

---

(1) *Ante*, vol. i. 366, and the note, 367 ; 4 Bro. C. C. 491, note ; *Gaskell* v. *Harman*, *ante*, 159, and the note, 165 ; *post*, vol. xi. 489.

(2) Stated from the Register's Book, *post*, vol. viii. 558, in the judgment of *Elwin* v. *Elwin*.

(3) *Bertie Entwistle* v. *Markland*. In CHANCERY, 24th July, 1795.

Henry Entwistle, Esq. by his will, dated the 10th of August, 1775, after directing his legacies, debts, &c. to be paid out of his personal estate, as to, all his money and securities for money, and all his estate and interest in such securities by mortgage or otherwise, and all his plate, jewels, goods, and personal estate, whatsoever, gave and bequeathed to the Defendant Markland and others ; upon trust as soon as might be after his death to call in and receive all the money due to him on the said securities or otherwise with the interest thereof, and to convert all his other personal estate into money ; and without delay and with all convenient speed to lay out and apply the whole of such moneys and the interest thereof to accrue and accumulate in the mean time in and for the purchase of freehold lands and tenements of inheritance in England, to be conveyed on such purchases thereof from time to time to the trustees and the survivor and his heirs and assigns, upon trust to and for the use of such persons and for such estates and with such limitations and in such manner as therein after declared as to such purchased lands and tenements ; and immediately after the purchase thereof, as also as to all the messuages, &c. whereof he should be seised at his decease, he devised the same to the trustees and the survivor and his heirs ; to the use of his brother Robert Entwistle for life without impeachment of waste ; with remainder to his trustees to preserve contingent remainders ; remainder to his first and other sons in tail male ; remainder to the Plaintiff for life without impeachment of waste ; with life remainest, not only of the money not laid out in land, but of what had not been collected. The late Lord Chancellor directed the interest to be computed from the end of a year, as a reasonable time. Some such line must be drawn. The Court must solve the difficulty. It cannot rest with the discretion of the executors; or depend upon the greater or less degree of diligence exerted in getting in the estate. The fair time is the end of a year from the testator's death; according to the common rule as to legacies; which is established for convenience; to avoid the difficulty of inquiring in all cases, where the funds were actually got in. Some other period more satisfactory must be found: or that rule must prevail. With great industry perhaps the executors might have got in this property within the year: under some circumstances it could not be done in several years. *Stuart* v. *Bruere* (1) is another strong authority for this claim.

---

ders to the trustees and to his sons: and with other remainders over. The trustees were appointed executors.

By a codicil the testator for the better collecting and getting in his personal estate gave his executors full power to settle all accounts; and he also gave them like power either to continue or to call in and lay out again, until proper purchases could be found, all or any part of his money at interest on such security real or personal or funds as they should think proper.

The testator died upon the 25th of January, 1784. Robert Entwistle died on the 30th of April, 1787. The Plaintiff by his bill prayed (*inter alia*), that he might be declared entitled to the interest of the residue of the testator Henry Entwistle's personal estate from the death of Robert.

Upon the Master's Report it appeared, that the first tenant for life had possessed a considerable part of the personal estate; and agreed to sell real estates of his own to the executors to the will. It appeared also, that there had been opportunity of laying out part of the personal estate; which had not been so laid [* 529] out; and that several * parts of the personal estate were out upon mortgages; on which it had become impossible for want of heirs and persons abroad to get in the money: the Report stating the evidence of an attorney as to what he had done for that purpose.

The cause coming on for farther directions, it was declared, that the personal estate of the testator Henry Entwistle not having been applied, as the same was got in and received, in the purchase of real estates, pursuant to the directions of the will, the Plaintiff Bertie Entwistle was entitled and ought to receive the interest of such personal estate or of such part thereof, which had been got in and received, and not so applied, from the death of the testator Robert Entwistle; and it was ordered, that the several sums of interest appearing by the Master's Report, dated the 30th of December, 1794, to have been paid into the hands of Jones and Company at 2 and 3 per cent. per ann. amounting to 425l. 4s. 10d., and the sums of 597l. 2s. 8 1-4d. and 295l. 17s. 6d. in the Report mentioned to have been received by Markland and Chadwick on account of such interest, be paid by the said Defendants to the Plaintiff Bertie Entwistle out of 3405l. 17s. 10d., cash paid into the bank of Jones and Company; and that the remaining sum of 4140l. 15s. 4d., the balance of 5543l. 12s. 3 3-4d., being the total amount of such interest, reported to have accrued from the death of Robert Entwistle, and which is still outstanding, together with the future interest of the outstanding personal estate of the said testator Henry Entwistle, until the same shall be got in and laid out in the purchase of lands, be paid to the Plaintiff Bertie Entwistle, when and as the same shall be got in and received. (See *post,* 537.)

(1) *Stuart* v. *Bruere* — At the ROLLS, 2d December, 1785. Before the Lord Chancellor, 29th July, 1793, 1st April, 1794.

E. E. Hewer by will, dated the 28th of March, 1782, devised to the Defendants Bruere and Spooner and the survivor of them, his heirs and assigns, an undivided

Upon the second question, Francis Sitwell having taken this mortgage·is now bound ; and cannot insist on having his whole legacy out of the personal estate, a deficient fund.   He would have been entitled to interest upon his legacy at 4 per cent. only ; and upon the mortgage he has received 5 per cent.

---

fourth part of a freehold estate at Clapham, Surrey ; upon trust, that they should as soon as conveniently might be after her decease sell the same ; and out of the money arising thereby * and the rents and profits accruing before [* 530] such sale she directed her said trustees to pay and discharge all incumbrances, which at the time of her decease might be on her part or share of any money in the public funds ; and the remainder of such profits of the said premises till such sale, she directed her said trustees to place out on government securities ; upon trust to pay the interest and dividends of such government securities unto the Plaintiff, her nephew, for his life ; and after his decease to pay the interest and dividends to his son or sons, (if more than one,) equally for life ; and after the decease of the son or sons of the Plaintiff to transfer one moiety of the government securities to the Defendant Abraham Blackborne, his executors, or administrators, and the other moiety to the Defendant Charles Cockrell, his executors or administrators.   She then devised to the same Defendants her undivided fourth part of a freehold estate at Fotheringay (Northamptonshire) ; upon trust, that they should as soon as conveniently might be after her decease sell the same ; and out of the money arising thereby and the rents and profits accruing due before such sale she directed, that all principal and interest, which should be then due on a mortgage of the said premises, should be in the first place paid and satisfied ; and she devised to the same Defendants other freehold estates in Norfolk and at Portsmouth, some fee-farm rents in Derbyshire and Yorkshire, freeholds in Burlington Street, &c., together with all her moneys in the public funds, (not therein-before disposed of), upon trust, that they should as soon as conveniently might be after her decease sell the said premises and money in the public funds ; and out of the money arising thereby and the rents and profits accruing due before 'such sale she directed her debts and funeral expenses and her legacies to be paid.   She gave the Plaintiff 100*l.* and other legacies ; and after payment of all her debts, funeral expenses, and legacies, declared a trust to pay and apply the remainder of what should arise by sale of her share of the estate at Fotheringay and of her other premises, together with her money in the public funds, for the same uses and upon the same trusts as what should arise by the sale of her share of the estate at Clapham, after payment of all incumbrances.   She then devised to the same Defendants her freehold and copyhold estates at Warfield Villa (Berks) and her furniture therein, and other specific effects ; upon trust, that they should as soon as conveniently might be after her decease sell the said premises and effects and all the residue of her personal estate : and place out the money arising thereby and the rents and profits accruing before such sale on government securities ; and pay the interest and dividends thereof to the Plaintiff for his life, and after his decease to his eldest son for his life, and after his death to other persons.

The testatrix died on the 10th of January, 1785.   The Plaintiff, Sir Simeon Stuart, who was her heir at law, by his bill insisted, that he was entitled to receive the rents and profits of the real estates and the dividends of the money in the funds from a reasonable time after the testatrix's decease ; and that they ought not, till all the estates were sold, to be considered as part of the principal, to be laid out upon the trusts of the will.

The decree, made at the Rolls on the 2d of December, 1785, after directing the general account of the testatrix's personal estate and its application, and the payment into the bank, it being admitted, that some part of the testatrix's real estate had been sold, directed an account of the money ; and the rest of the estates to be sold in the usual manner, and the money to be carried to the account of each estate ; and then directed * an account of the rents and profits of [* 531] the said real estates ; distinguishing the rents of each of the said estates respectively accrued since her death to the time of the sale or sales thereof respectively, received and to be received by the said Defendants, the trustees ; and what should be coming on that account to be paid into the bank ; to be placed to

Mr. *Mansfield* and Mr. *Hart*, for the Infant Tenant in Tail in remainder, Defendant.—In this case the will is to guide the Court. The residue is never supposed to exist till the end of a year; upon the supposition, that by that time the executors will have collected assets enough to pay the debts and legacies, and that previously to that period they are employed in getting in the assets. In this case the interest is to be calculated upon the residue; and that does not exist legally before that period. The inter-

---

the credit of the cause to the like accounts as the money to arise by the sale of the estates respectively.

The decree made by the Lord Chancellor on the 29th of July, 1793, directed the Defendant Charlotte Bruere, as administratrix of her father Goulstone Bruere, to retain 206*l*. 0*s*. 8*d*., the balance due to her on the account of the personal estate, the sum of 660*l*. 0*s*. 9*d*., due to her for principal and interest of her legacy, and what shall be taxed for her costs of the suit, out of 2088*l*. 8*s*., the balance reported due on account of the rents and profits, and pay the residue out of the assets of her father; and to transfer 9965*l*. 7*s*. 4*d*. and 966*l*. 6*s*. 3*d*. 3 per cent. Reduced Annuities, and 7403*l*. 1*s*. 7*d*. and 1273*l*. 5*s*. 7*d*. 3 per cent. Consolidated Bank Annuities, standing in the names of the executors; of whom G. B. was the survivor, to the Accountant-General; and pay the interest now due thereon to the Plaintiff: 7205*l*. 19*s*., part of the Reduced Annuities, to be carried to the account of the Warfield estate, subject to farther order; 986*l*. to the account of the personal estate; the residue of those annuities to the account of the rents of the real estate; 7684*l*. 12*s*. 4*d*., part of the Consols, to be transferred to the account of the personal estate; the residue of the Consols (991*l*. 14*s*. 10*d*.) to be carried to the account of the rents of the real estate; all the said Bank Annuities to be subject to the contingencies in the testatrix's will, and subject to farther order; the interest to accrue on all the said Bank Annuities before mentioned to be paid to the Plaintiff until farther order. The sum of 3430*l*. 0*s*. 2*d*. cash to be paid to the Plaintiff: 7456*l*. 16*s*. 5*d*. (part of 43,082*l*. 7*s*. 6*d*. 3 per cent. Annuities in the name of the Accountant General in trust in the cause) to be carried over to the account of the personal estate: 10,096*l*. 17*s*. 6*d*. other part, to be carried over to the account of money raised by sale of the Clapham estate: so much of the residue of this stock (which consists of the money raised by the sale of the Fotheringay, Norfolk, London, and Portsmouth, estates, and the fee-farm rents,) to be sold, as will raise 3573*l*. 10*s*. 6*d*., due to Elizabeth Stuart for principal and interest of her legacy; and 5413*l*. 2*s*. 3*d*. due to Abraham Blackborne for his debt, and costs not before provided for, be sold and those sums paid: the residue of those Bank Annuities to be carried to the account of money arisen by sale of the estates at Fotheringay, Norfolk, London, and Portsmouth, and of the fee-farm, subject to the contingencies in the will; and the interest of these annuities to be paid to the Plaintiff till farther order. An inquiry was directed, how much of the said Bank Annuities arose from the rents and profits of those estates accrued since the death of the testatrix, and previous to the sale of those estates; and as to those rents and profits the parties were to be at liberty to apply.

By an order made upon the 1st of April, 1794, it was directed, that so much of the sum of 1795*l*. 7*s*. 10*d*. 3 per cent. Annuities in trust in the cause as will be sufficient to raise 414*l*. 14*s*. 4*d*. being interest accrued since the 10th of January, 1785, the day of the death of the testatrix, of 219*l*. 5*s*. 6*d*., part of the money received by the Defendant Abraham Blackborne, and by him paid into the bank, and laid out in the purchase of the said Bank Annuities, be sold, and the sum of 414*l*. 14*s*. 4*d*. paid to the Plaintiff: the residue of the said Bank Annuities to be carried over to the account of the testatrix's Warfield estate and general personal estate; and the dividends due and to become due upon the said Bank Annuities until such sale and carrying over, and the future dividends of the residue of the said Bank Annuities after such sale be paid to the Plaintiff during his life in like manner as the interest and dividends of the other Bank Annuities standing in the name of the Accountant General to the several accounts in trust in this cause are directed to be paid by the former orders of the Court. (See *post*, 536.)

est therefore cannot stop then. It is impossible to refer these words to the interest of the two legacies. That is not the interest of the personal estate. It probably occurred to the testator, that the mortgages could not be got in till after a period much longer than a year. One mortgage is for 50,000*l.* Knowing that, he might mean the interest to accumulate, and become a fund for the purchase of real estates as well as the principal. The Plaintiff might have filed a bill, and compelled the executors to call in the money as soon as possible. *Hutcheon* v. *Mannington* is a very singular case. *Hollingsworth* v. *Hollingsworth,* as it is now stated, seems an extraordinary decision. Different objects were in view. It was a considerable stretch under those circumstances to say, the time of the sale was not material. In *Entwistle* v. *Markland* the first taker lived between two and three years; and he must have had it: yet there is nothing in the decree giving any interest to him. The words of the will here are indefinite: but the direction is very specific, with all convenient speed to lay out the residue of his personal estate and all the accumulation, as an aggregate fund; and, till laid out in land, no person is to have any usufruct. The Plaintiff might lie by in collusion with the executors, and take a larger income in this way.

The *Solicitor General* [Mr. *Spencer Perceval*] and Mr. *Huddleston,* for the Defendant Hurt Sitwell.—Notwithstanding the words of the will, the legacy ought to * carry interest at   [* 533] the rate of 5 per cent. instead of 4; being given out of a fund bearing 5 per cent. In *Lewis* v. *Freke* (1) this point of interest was much considered. Lord Hardwicke was in favor of the higher rate of interest: *Beckford* v. *Tobin* (2), *Denton* v. *Shellard* (3); saying, the nature of the fund is to be considered. In 1799, when this legatee was of age, it was impossible to raise the money even at 5 per cent.

Mr. *Murray,* for the Defendant Francis Sitwell, the second son, insisted, that he was entitled to his legacy out of the first assets, that come in; stating, that he was not dissatisfied with the agreement; but that it was not carried into execution according to the purport of it; and the executors had a sufficient sum to answer his legacy, if they had not engaged in the purchase.

Mr. *Romilly,* in Reply.—They do not argue, that the executors might take as much time as they please; and prevent the tenant for life from having any benefit: but they must make out that proposition. It is clear, the testator was not speaking of the residue after all the debts and legacies paid; for he directs it without prejudice to the payment of the legacies, annuities, and debts. Upon the other construction the words " with all convenient speed " must be struck out. There was no laches in the Plaintiff. The circumstance, whether a bill is filed, or not, cannot alter the duty of the executors: but suppose, it was the case of an infant, what good reason can be

---

(1) *Ante,* vol. ii. 507.
(2) 1 Ves. 308.
(3) 2 Ves. 239.

assigned for not filing a bill of foreclosure for three years? The indulgence to the mortgagor by enlarging the time ought not to prejudice the rights of others. In *Stapleton* v. *Palmer* (1) the same question occurred.

The question attempted as to the interest is perfectly new.

Dec. 5*th.* The Lord CHANCELLOR [ELDON], having stated the case, delivered the following judgment:—Under the cir-
[* 534]   cumstances appearing in the Master's * Report it was im-
possible for the trustees to call in a very considerable part of the personal estate; attending to those obstructions, which perhaps a wholesome attention to the convenience of those, who are debtors, throws in the way. This testator had a very large personal estate out upon security; partly upon a mortgage affecting the estate of an infant, under that species of embarrassment, that it was very material for him, when of age, that a considerable part of his property should be sold; and the arrangement for payment to the estate of the testator took this course; that the purchasers should from time to time pay to the trustees of this will the purchase-money in part discharge of that debt; and perhaps that was as convenient and as expeditious a mode as any, that could be adopted; without prejudice undoubtedly to their personal remedies, if they had any; for the infant was not an obligor in the bond made upon the mortgage. It appears also, that a considerable part of the personal estate was secured upon a mortgage by Lord Mulgrave; and the executors, as far as they had it in their power to take remedies against the real estate charged with that debt, took those steps certainly not so speedily, as they might. Few steps were taken to call in a considerable part of the personal estate for four years; for, after they did begin, they found, they were embarrassed by the circumstances of the times; which produced from this Court an enlargement of the time of foreclosure; carrying it over a considerable period: an Equity, which binding the testator also bound his devisees. The estate obviously consisted of a great variety of securities, which, to render them productive, would occasion great expense and delay; and it might have consisted of securities hardly saleable, much less of such, upon which the money was capable of being collected.

The case was reasoned for the tenant for life in this way; that under such circumstances, and in all cases of personal estate directed to be so laid out, considering, what it might be, it is incumbent upon the Court to adopt a period, at which it should be considered as laid out with regard to the interests of the tenant for life and those in remainder. The case afforded great difficulty in the terms of the will; providing for an accumulation of interest; and directing the
interest accumulated to be laid out upon the same trusts in
[* 535]   the purchase of land as the bulk of the property * producing the accumulation. In answer to the suggestion,

that an application should have been made by the tenant for life to
have the trusts executed, the case of an infant was put strongly and
fairly. The Plaintiff happened to be of age ; but if he had died,
leaving an infant son, in which case the trustees ought to have acted,
as if a bill had been filed, the question would have arisen, what the
Court ought to do upon a bill filed by the infant, when adult. It
was also very strongly said for the Plaintiff, that the case ought to be
considered, as if he had no other provision under this will. It is
true, he has real estates under it : but put the case, that he had not ;
and that he was to derive an interest, and that a life interest only,
in the investment of the personal estate in land : what ought to be
the construction as between him and the persons in remainder ; if it
happened, that a great part or the whole was subject to difficulties
and embarrassments in the collection, which the testator could not
have foreseen ? It may be asked, are the trustees immediately to
file bills of foreclosure, whether prudently, or not ; to admit no arrangement; to bring actions upon the bonds, and the covenants ; to
file bills for the purpose of following the assets of the original mortgagors ; to institute every species of legal diligence in every case,
in which it might be wholesome, and might perhaps be as prejudicial
to the interests of those in remainder by bringing into hazard the
bulk of the personal estate, in order to forward the perception of interest by the tenant for life ?

In this view of the case a very considerable question arises upon
the construction of the will, addressed to the discretion of the Court.
The first consideration with reference to that is, how far the Court
had in other cases construed instruments somewhat similar in their
terms : and in effect how far the Court had assumed such discretion,
as enabling them upon the whole to make a useful and wholesome
construction of such a will between particular interests and those
entitled to the bulk of the property. However difficult in the first
instance to adopt such a construction, if in different instances such
wills have been so construed, it would be very hazardous upon this
will, almost in terms affording such a construction, not to adopt it :
not only with reference to the case itself, but because the refusal to
adopt it, even against strong words, incurs the hazard of
bringing into question those decisions. *The first case   [* 536]
upon words similar, but very far from the same, is *Hutcheon*
v. *Mannington*, before Lord Thurlow. The construction Lord
Thurlow thought himself of necessity obliged to put upon the words
I thought then was too bold, if I may presume to say so. His
Lordship thought, there was an indication of a purpose, such as was
contended for by the Plaintiff : but that it was impossible to inquire,
when each and every part of the estate could have been received,
collected, and got in; and seems to admit, that he was driven
by the impossibility of measuring that purpose of the testator
to consider it vested at his death ; and he held all the legatees
entitled to their legacies, though none had received them. That

case (1) is a strong authority, particularly in the passage as to the direction to sell real estate, to show the length the Court will go upon general grounds of convenience in the construction of a will, indicating a purpose, which it is almost impossible to execute consistently with the other purpose, that the party, in whose behalf it is to be executed, shall beneficially enjoy the interest intended by the testator.

The case of *Stuart* v. *Bruere* was upon a will, which applies not only to the bulk of the property directed to be sold, but goes the length of embracing also the intermediate rents and profits, before the estate should be sold; and though estates were not sold, and the intermediate rents and profits are subjected to the same trusts, the Court thought themselves at liberty under the circumstances to give to the tenant for life the beneficial interest of the money; though the sale was not actually made. The words in that will "as soon as conveniently may be after my decease" are in effect the same as those in this will.

The first decree, upon the 2d of December, 1785, somewhat more than a month prior to the end of a year from the death of the testatrix, ordered all the sales to be made, and the money to be laid out according to the will; and declared the title of Sir Simeon Stuart to the interest of the fund to be constituted by the decree. The sales being delayed, Sir Simeon Stuart presented a petition to the late Lord Chancellor; insisting, that under the circum-
[* 537]   stances, the general * intention being, that he should have the beneficial interest of the fund for his life, he ought not to be delayed in the perception of that benefit by the non-execution of the trusts; and the rents and profits of the real estate ought not to go to the capital, the sales having been delayed, when that intention was clear. The principle, upon which Lord Rosslyn [Loughborough] decreed, was, not taking the period of a year from the death of the testatrix as the period, from which the petitioner was to receive the rents and profits, making the necessary abatements for the interest of debts, &c., but taking the period of the decree in 1785. The difference in time was not much: but the difference in the principle is something. Lord Rosslyn by his order, made upon the petition and a report of the state of the funds, notwithstanding the language of the decree was, that the rents and profits till the sale and the interest and dividends of the stock, till converted into money, should go to form one fund, the interest of which the Plaintiff was to take, considers the sales as made in the view of this Court by the decree, which ordered them to be made; and taking care to reserve a sufficient fund for debts and legacies, gave him the rents and profits and the interest of the fund unconverted from that period.

(1) The Lord Chancellor having observed, that the case ending by agreement could not be stated as a decision upon the subject, Mr. Romilly said, the agreement was not with respect to that point: as to that they took the decision of Lord Thurlow: upon which the Lord Chancellor admitted, that the case had all the authority of a decision.

Lord Rosslyn seems to think, there is a principle in the justice of the Court requiring him to consider that as done, when it was ordered to be done; differing from Lord Thurlow, who considered it as ordered to be done from the death of the testator. Lord Rosslyn considering it as done from the date of the decree, procured by the providence of the party himself.

From these decisions therefore it is uncertain, what is the true period in the case of a person having discretion enough to file a bill, and the case of an infant: whether the death of the testator, or the decree, if a suit was instituted: or, whether the Court would say, that was a convenient period for this purpose, which for other purposes is determined to be convenient; though it does not often hit the real justice of the case, namely, a year from the death of the testator.*

The next case is *Entwistle* v. *Markland;* as to which I am clear, the register has not correctly taken the declaration of the principle of the Court as to the interest of the tenant for life. That declaration ˙is not very consistent; arïd it goes beyond the *declaration of the Court. It is quite clear from　　[* 538] ' the proceedings and the report, that the person, who got the rents and profits, though tenant for life in remainder, got the produce of property, that no diligence of the executors would have enabled them to collect and get in. The words of that will are nearly the same as in this. The codicil also brings it very near this case. It appeáred, that several parts of the persona estate were out upon securities, such in their nature, that though at first probably very convenient securities, upon mortgage, they had become otherwise; and it was quite impossible that they could be got in. The terms of the will therefore connected with the evidence adverted to personal estate, directed to be got in with all convenient speed, which could not possibly be got in; and was not left outstanding from negligence and dilatoriness of the executors. The principle of Lord Rosslyn upon that must have been mistaken in the decree upon my own recollection and a comparison of the ordering part of the decree with the declaration as to the principle. The principle of the first part of the declaration is obviously right; for if the personal estate was got in, and not applied, it was dilatoriness; which should not prejudice any one. It is inaccurate in first supposing all the personal estate got in, and in the latter part supposing, that only part had been got in. But upon the report it appears, not only, that great part had not been got in, but, that with no diligence it could have been got in. The claim therefore of Robert Entwistle, the first taker for life, was left out. But the decree afterwards goes on to order, that the Plaintiff shall have the interest of that part of the personal estate. Lord Rosslyn's opinion must have been, that the embarrassments the state of the property created made impracticable the general purpose, that the tenant for life should have the enjoyment of the interest of the property; and he seems to have been of opinion, that he had no option. But it amounts nearly to destroying the natural effect of the one or the other part of the will. Lord Rosslyn thought, the best construction was to further the enjoyment of the property, as the testator meant it.

This case then does not come on unprejudiced by decision; for under the circumstances upon the report, the delay in receiving the money, certainly occasioned in part by the trustees delaying, (I desire not to be understood to say, culpably) for three years, [* 539] perhaps * very wisely, and in all instances forbearing to sue upon the personal remedies, as well as the remedies attaching upon real estate, perhaps most wisely for those in remainder by not destroying the means of the debtors to pay, agreeing to take payment by sale of the mortgagor's estates, and in parcels, instead of foreclosures, which the Court has not disapproved, considering the great expense and delay of proceeding in that way, with no dilatoriness, but upon circumstances, which the law of this Court considers reasonable grounds for delay, under all these circumstances, the cases, to which I have alluded, have not left me to struggle with the difficulties, that would have occurred, if this had been an original case, untouched by prior decisions. Without saying, what my opinion would have been upon the question originally, I cannot say, I will give the tenant for life no relief, without saying, the decree in *Entwistle* v. *Markland*, a case nearly in *ipsissimis terminis*, is wrong; that *Stuart* v. *Bruere*, which, though not so precisely, is very nearly, this case, is wrong; and that what Lord Thurlow hinted to be a provident and due construction of the will before him was wrong. But I think, those cases are founded upon a principle, which if the terms of the will allow you to make such a construction, is bottomed in evident convenience; and I lay great stress upon this; that it is the very best construction for those, who are to object to the claim of the tenant for life. This Court will look at principles of convenience. Where an estate is given in various legacies, and the residue is given, it is a rule of convenience, that authorises this Court to say, for there is no language in the will for it, that those legacies shall be payable at the end of a year from the death of the testator; because, as a general rule it may be taken, that the personal estate may be collected within a year; though in many instances that falls enormously to the prejudice of the residuary legatee. The same convenience has made the Court say, the residuary legatee shall not claim till the end of the year (1). In many cases the Court supposes the residue to carry interest: though in many cases the residue does not carry interest; but the Court takes the interest for a particular legatee from the residue, as a general rule of justice and convenience; though in many instances falling out against an individual. There are other cases before Lord Hardwicke upon the point, whether interest at 4 or 5 per cent. shall be paid upon legacies; and prior cases in Peere Wil-

---

(1) *Stott* v. *Hollingworth*, 3 Madd. 161.

liams: the Court attending to the productiveness of the fund, or the contrary.   But now it is a general rule, that where no interest is given by the will, except where it is given by way of maintenance, it is only to be allowed at 4 per cent. from the end of the year; though it may appear to have produced in the period interest at 5 per cent.   Particular justice is disappointed in particular cases: but upon this principle, alluded to by Lord Thurlow in *Hutcheon* v. *Mannington*, that the inquiry as to the state of the personal estate, when each and every part could be got in and made productive, is endless and immeasurable, the Court cuts the knot by doing what in general cases is convenient; though in particular cases both convenience and justice may be disappointed (1).

In this case the property is large; and that circumstance as well as the consideration of justice and convenience made me hesitate : but the principle cannot be different on account of the amount of the property.   The question is, whether there is too much in this will to prevent me from adopting that rule of convenience, that has been adopted in the other cases.   *Entwistle* v. *Markland* disposes of the objection from the clause as to accumulation of interest of the residue.   That case also answers the objection from the power given to the trustees to call in money, and lay it out upon interest, before it should be laid out in land.   The case must be considered, as if this was the only provision for the Plaintiff; and it is to be considered, not only as a case, in which part might be got in, and part not, but as if all the personal estate was subject to the same embarrassment; and the question then is, attending to the accumulation, whether upon the whole will, considered upon the principles of the Court and the decisions, the testator could mean, that if the property could not be cleared in the whole life of the tenant for life, the interest of the tenant for life was to be wholly disappointed.   We are apt to lay hold of circumstances, though too critical, if they will assist in collecting the general purpose.   Without straining the construction of the word " residue," though, I admit, in general it is such as is contended for the Defendant, there are circumstances, which may produce accumulation, that may be taken to answer the direction as to that.   Annuities are directed by the will to be paid out of the personal estate.   By the codicil they are charged upon the land, when the personal estate shall be invested in land.   It would * be singular, that the testa-   [* 541] tor should mean the annuitants to receive their annuities before investment, and that the tenant for life should remain in a situation to get nothing.   As to the legacies, some carrying no interest, others carrying interest, less perhaps than the fund might produce, there would be an accumulation of interest upon those; and though in a sense that would fall within the reach of the word " residue" yet he might have meant to apply the direction of the

---

(1) *Fearns* v. *Young, post.* vol. ix. 549.

will as to accumulation more strictly ; and I would struggle for any construction rather than adopt a construction, which, not from dilatoriness of the trustees, but only from circumstances, to which probably the testator did not look, has a tendency wholly to disappoint the intention as to the beneficial enjoyment. If the words of the will allow me, I ought to follow these decisions ; and the necessity of not following them is very much weakened by the words of those wills. They have left in uncertainty the period, from which the tenant for life of the land, when purchased, was to commence with regard to the enjoyment of the interest of the personal estate, in the contemplation of this Court real estate, but not actually become so; which imposes upon the Court considerable difficulty. Lord Thurlow's rule is put upon the naked case of an estate directed to be sold, no burthens upon it, &c. Lord Rosslyn in the first case takes the decree within the year. *Entwistle* v. *Markland* goes upon a rule like neither of the preceding cases. It is not the right rule to say, that, where a decree is obtained, directing a trustee to do some act, the time is that of the decree ; for the language of the decree is no more than the language of the will. The Court orders it to be done only because the testator has ordered it to be done.

The Court cannot mean, that the decree, because the money was not laid out in convenient time, is to give date to the enjoyment of the property ; as if it had been laid out in convenient time. If the trustees have not done what they ought, the Court orders it without prejudice to the interests of the persons entitled, as if it had been done. In *Stuart* v. *Bruere* Lord Rosslyn gave the interest prior to the end of the year, probably, because he saw in the report, that he could have provided for the interest of the debts and legacies at the time of the decree. Upon the dry case put in *Hutcheon* v. *Mannington* the Court had not to encumber itself with the payment of debts out of the produce of the estate, or the time neces- [* 542] sary for inquiring, what debts there *were. That case therefore does not apply to this ; and upon the whole, if the Court can adopt a general rule of convenience, it must be, that it will act upon the enjoyment of the tenant for life at that period, when upon its own rule it supposes the purposes to be answered, before the fund can be cleared, can be answered : and that here it is impossible to say, the tenant for life can have the interest of the residue before the time, when the fund can be constituted by an investment in land clear of debts, legacies, and annuities ; when all those can be provided for. The Plaintiff therefore must wait one year.

The question then will be, whether he is to wait longer ; and if so, whether he must not of necessity wait, till the personal estate can be actually collected. Part may be collected from time to time in his life ; and he might enjoy the rents and profits of the estates purchased with those parts. But it might happen, that no part might be got in in his life. Suppose, these debts on mortgage were the only part of the personal estate : it is impossible to say, when either

of those funds could be realized. The Court is therefore driven
either to take the end of the year upon the principle of general convenience, or to examine in each particular case, what convenient
speed and reasonable diligence would have done : what negligence
or the law of the country or other circumstances have prevented ;
and make those inquiries at the hazard of obtaining no clear result. I
am therefore disposed to say, justice requires, that the Plaintiff should
have the interest from the end of the year ; and the more so, because I am clear, that distributing that justice to him is consulting
the essential interests of the persons in remainder ; for then from his
death they will have the benefit of that, whether the fund is converted into land, or not ; and if that is not done, the rule may press
as hard upon them ; and some of them may have no actual enjoyment of the money. Suppose the tenant for life should call upon
the trustee to get in the money with all possible diligence : it would
be very difficult for the trustee in many cases at his own risk to determine, that he would not take all the remedies competent to him ;
and unless by this sort of equalizing rule, if I may call it so, we give
a discretion to the trustees to make a husband-like management, the
tenant for life might insist upon a bill being filed ; or enter
upon the estate ; or he might arrest the * mortgagor ; or   [* 543]
bring actions of covenant. The trustees might say to the
tenant for life, he would not put the property in risk ; but he would
be bound upon an inquiry in this Court to show a solid reason for
objecting to the proceeding. The consequence would be in every
instance an inquiry, whether the trustee acted reasonably, or not.
What a waste of property disputes arising out of such circumstances
would occasion ; even if the property should be eventually got in :
but we know, securities are put in great hazard by too much pressure ; and these considerations lead me to think, there is a strong
analogy in the general rule ; which in many instances is not applicable to particular circumstances : and I am justified upon the whole,
though I have had great difficulty upon it, in saying, the construction ought to be that, which will give the tenant for life the interest
from the period, at which in the contemplation of this Court the
residue would be formed as residue ; viz. the end of the year, conceiving it hard upon him to take the time of the decree : recollecting, that the former decree directs an inquiry, as to what had been
done, without directing the money to be called in ; which certainly
it ought upon that principle (1).

The directions must be such as to provide for an appropriation as
to legacies and annuities ; as to legacies, both such as carry interest
less than 5 per cent., and such as carry no interest till the time of
payment. In the appropriation as to legacies it would be fit to consider, whether the necessity of appropriating may not give the
legatees a larger interest than is given by the will, upon *Green* v.
Pigot (2) : but there have been other cases since, in which it has

(1) See 1 Turn. 238, *Angerstein* v. *Martin*, 244: *Hewett* v. *Morris*.
(2) 1 Bro. C. C. 103.

been held not to be the legitimate effect of appropriation to give a larger interest, than if there was no appropriation.

The second point is, whether the legatees are entitled to more than 4 per cent.; and particularly one, who had taken a mortgage for his legacy. As to the general point I have taken it to be clearly settled, that, where no rate of interest is given by the will, the Court gives 4 per cent.; and where any rate of interest is directed by the will, the Court gives that; and there is no reason from par-

[* 544] ticular circumstances to depart from the general rule as * to legatees. The cases cited from Vesey show, that it was not at that time a settled rule, whether there should be 4 or 5 per cent.; but that it was rather the inclination of the Court to give 5, as to personal estate, particularly if producing interest. But that rule, I take it, has been altered; and the general rule is, as I have stated. One case (1), that was cited, does not bear upon it: a person charging under a power had given 5 per cent.; and the Court said, he might, if he did not give more than legal interest.

As to the transaction of the mortgage, there is no doubt, Francis Sitwell, when of age, might take payment of his legacy by a mortgage, if he thought proper; and feeling, that it would be attended with inconvenience, might make a bargain, that, when the estate should produce money enough to pay him, they should take it back again. That seems to be the agreement. I understand, he will not take finally to the mortgage; and, if not, the transaction is undone; and he puts himself back to the situation of legatee; and then in the account he must give credit for the difference between 4 and 5 per cent. received in the mean time. If he holds to the mortgage, it is so much payment; and he will keep the 5 per cent.

---

1. THAT as a general rule, at all events, trustees and executors are bound to press on all their remedies for the recovery of debts due to the trust estate; and that if any securities shall seem proper to be continued, the point should be left to the judgment of the Court, not decided by the personal discretion of the trustees and executors themselves, unless that discretionary power has been expressly, or by clear implication, given to them: see, *ante*, the note to *Powell* v. *Evans*, 5 V. 839; it is not, however, to be understood universally, that trustees and executors are bound immediately to call in money, which they find placed out on good security: *Orr* v. *Newton*, 2 Cox, 277; *Sadler* v. *Turner*, 8 Ves. 621; *Angerstein* v. *Martin*, Turn. 241; on the contrary, a Court of Equity will not permit a real security to be called in, without an inquiry whether it would be for the benefit of all parties interested: and in some instances, it may be equally for the benefit of the tenant for life, and of those in remainder, that the property should not be shifted from a good real security. *Howe* v. *Earl Dartmouth*, 7 Ves. 150.

2. In *Angerstein* v. *Martin*, (cited above,) Lord Eldon declared that case to be the very reverse of the principal case, in which, his Lordship added, he did not mean to lay down any general rule that the tenant for life of a residue, directed to be laid out in the purchase of real estate, is entitled to the interest only from the end of a year after the death of the testator: the hesitation was, whether, under the circumstances interest could be claimed at the expiration of that period, by the party who was to be tenant for life of the estate when purchased; and it was not without difficulty the Court held, that the direction in the principal case, for accu-

---

(1) *Lewis* v. *Freke, ante,* vol. ii. 507.

mulation, should operate only for one year, and then, notwithstanding the conversion directed by the will was not completed, that the beneficial enjoyment should be the same as if the conversion had been actually made. But where a testator, after giving an immediate interest in his real estates to a tenant for life, has directed the residue of his personalty, subject to payment of debts and legacies, to be laid out with all convenient speed in the purchase of lands, to be settled forthwith to the same uses as his previously given real estates; with a proviso, that the trust moneys, until they should be so laid out, might be invested on government or real securities, the dividends and interests of which were to go and be paid as the rents of the lands to be purchased would go and be payable; the tenant for life is entitled to the interest of so much of the personal estate as is not necessary to be applied for the payment of debts and legacies from the death of the testator; see *Kilvington* v. *Gray*, 2 Sim. & Stu. 400: see also, as relevant to this matter, *Fitzgerald* v. *Jervoise*, 5 Mad. 30; *Hewitt* v. *Morris*, 1 Turner, 244.

3. That a Court of Equity, on grounds of general convenience, will go great lengths in the construction of a will not easily rendered consistent, but of which the general intent seems to be not to postpone the beneficial enjoyment; see notes 2 and 3 to *Hutcheon* v. *Mannington*, 1 V. 366; and that legacies given in general terms out of personal estate, are due at the end of a year from the testator's death, from which period they will carry interest, although it may have been impossible, by any diligence, to get in the outstanding effects and securities by that time; see note 4 to the same case.

4. No unnecessary delay on the part of trustees will be allowed, to benefit themselves, or to affect the interests of third persons; see note 6 to *Hutcheon* v. *Mannington, ubi supra.*

5. That, in endeavoring to ascertain the doubtful meaning of a testator, the inconsistencies which might arise out of one construction, or be avoided by another, are constantly attended to; see note 4 to *Blake* v. *Bunbury*, 1 V. 194.

6. In *Webb* v. *Webb*, 2 Dick. 746, Lord Thurlow appeared to be of opinion, that where money was appropriated by investment in the public funds, for payment of a contingent legacy, the legatee would be liable for any loss which might arise from a fall in the funds, and be entitled to any benefit if the price of stock should improve; but in *Alcock* v. *Eames*, 2 Dick, 578, his Lordship made a totally opposite decision.

7. As to the rate of interest allowed by Courts of Equity, see the note to *Lewis* v. *Freke*, 2 V. 507.

PERRY *v.* WHITEHEAD.

[1801, Dec. 5.]

THE want of a surrender of copyhold estate cannot be supplied for grandchildren (*a*).

No interest by way of maintenance upon a legacy simply to a grandchild or a natural child (*b*), [p. 546.]

CATHERINE WHITEHEAD by her will, dated the 3d of June, 1798, made the following disposition:

"I give, devise and bequeath, all my freehold and copyhold houses, messuages, lands, tenements and hereditaments, whatsoever in London and wheresoever situate and being with their and every of their appurtenances unto my two executors hereinafter named, to be by them sold and disposed of or divided at their own will and discre-

---

(*a*) See *ante*, note (*a*), *Hills* v. *Downton*, 5 V. 557.
(*b*) See *ante*, note (*a*), *Crickett* v. *Dolby*, 3 V. 10.

tion ; after which I give one share or third part of the same unto my five nieces, Catherine, Ann, Fanny, Charlotte, and Harriet, the children of my late daughter Perry of Newport, share and
[* 545]   share alike, their heirs, executors, * and assigns ; and if any
of the said nieces should happen to die before the day of marriage and before they arrive at the age of twenty-one years, then I will and desire, that such fifth part bequeathed to her so dying shall be equally divided among the surviving nieces share and share alike."

The testatrix appointed her daughters Constantia Skynner White-head and Fanny Whitehead, her executrixes. She died in May, 1799 ; leaving her five grand-daughters by her deceased daughter, described in the will as her nieces, and their two brothers John Perry and James Perry, surviving ; her co-heirs at law, viz. her two sur-viving daughters and her two grandsons being also heirs according to the custom of the manor ; and the copyhold premises not having been surrendered to the use of the will.

The bill was filed by the five grand-daughters ; charging, that the copyhold premises having been surrendered by the testatrix upon mortgage, no surrender was necessary to the use of her will ; the legal estate not being in her ; and that if a surrender was necessary, the want of it ought to be supplied in Equity.   The bill therefore prayed, that the Plaintiffs may be declared entitled to one third part of the copyhold premises ; and that if the Court should be of opin-ion, that a surrender was necessary to give effect to the devise, the want of the surrender may be supplied.

The Defendants, the daughters and grandsons of the testatrix, by their answer stated, that the mortgage had been paid off by the tes-tatrix ; that the premises were surrendered to the use of the mort-gagee and his heirs, subject to redemption ; and at the same Court, subject to the said mortgage surrender, they were surrendered to the use of the testatrix and her husband during their lives and the life of the survivor ; and after the decease of the survivor to the use of the heirs and assigns of the survivor ; and the testatrix survived her husband.   They farther stated, that the mortgagee never was ad-mitted ; and the legal estate was vested in the testatrix until her death ; and descended.   They insisted, that a surrender to the use of the will was necessary to effectuate the devise : and that the Plaintiffs, being merely the grand-children of the testatrix, are not
entitled to have the defect of surrender supplied to the
[* 546]   prejudice of the Defendants, as heirs at law ; * especially
as two of the Defendants are the daughters of the testatrix,
·and the other Defendants are totally unprovided for, except that John Perry is entitled to the fee-simple of two small houses, which descended to him as heir at law of his father, and a moiety of a free-hold messuage, left to him by the will of his grandfather, of the an-nual value of 19*l.* in the whole, and also, that James Perry is entitled to the fee-simple of the other moiety of the last mentioned messuage, but to no other real or personal estate.

Mr. *Mansfield*, Mr. *Richards*, and Mr. *Fonblanque*, for the Plaintiffs.—The relief sought by this bill is certainly contrary to what has been considered a general rule of the Court since the final decision of *Kettle* v. *Townsend* (1), in the time of King William: Lord Somer's decree in favor of a grandson being reversed by the House of Lords. But in later cases different Judges have expressed an opinion, that the point deserved to be re-considered. In *Chapman* v. *Gibson* (2) Lord Alvanley went much at large into the subject; and said, he did not see, why a grand-child should not have the same equity: for the statute of Elizabeth (3) has made it compulsory on a grandfather to provide for him. Lord Rosslyn also in *Hill* v. *Downton* (4) expressed a strong opinion against the decision of the House of Lords. The ground, that a grandfather is not bound to provide for his grand-child, as a father is for his child, and the former therefore is not under the same moral obligation, would sound extraordinary out of a Court of Judicature; and certainly affords no reason. The statute of Elizabeth imposes the same obligation upon a grandfather and grand-mother as upon the parents; which is the sense of the Legislature and of mankind. There is no other decision against a grand-child. There is a case the other way (5) prior to that in the House of Lords. The opinion of the Master of the Rolls in *Watts* v. *Bullas* (6) is decisive in favor of grand-children; and in *Fursaker* v. *Robinson* (7) Lord Cowper doubted the case of *Kettle* v. *Townsend*.

Lord CHANCELLOR [ELDON].—Where a legacy is given to a grand-child, without more, would that grand-child take interest, as a child *would? In the case of a grand-child must [* 547] there not be something more (8) than merely giving a legacy; something, showing, that the testator put himself *in loco parentis?* Is there any case for that in favor of a natural child, simply upon a legacy, without any thing to show, the testator put himself *in loco parentis?* In *Grave* v. *Lord Salisbury* (9) Lord Thurlow would not in the case of a natural child say, a legacy was redeemed by an advancement (10). The difficulty with me is this; can I sitting here contradict a decision of the House of Lords?

For the Plaintiffs.—*Fursaker* v. *Robinson* was the case of a natural child: but the point as to maintenance has since been considered in *Crickett* v. *Dolby* (11), and an opinion expressed by Lord Alvanley in favor of the natural child. This testatrix certainly meant to put

(1) 1 Salk. 187.
(2) 3 Bro. C. C. 229.
(3) Stat. 43 Eliz. c. 2, s. 7.
(4) *Ante*, vol. v. 557; see page 565.
(5) *Anon.* 2 Freem. 197.
(6) 1 P. Will. 60.
(7) Pre. Ch. 475; 1 Eq. Ca. Ab. 123, pl. 9.
(8) *Hill* v. *Hill*, 3 Ves. & Bea. 183.
(9) 1 Bro. C. C. 425.
(10) *Ante*, vol. iii. 12, and the note; *post*, xii. 23.
(11) *Ante*, vol. iii. 10.

herself *in loco parentis*. As to the question, whether the children
are provided for, that underwent great consideration in *Hills* v.
Downton; and Lord Rosslyn thought, as Lord Hardwicke thought
before, that circumstance ought not to weigh. In many instances
the Courts below have considered themselves at liberty to depart
from a decision of the House of Lords upon very minute circumstances. Lord Thurlow did so in *Tweddell* v. *Tweddell* (1) ; and so
are all the cases upon general bonds of resignation (2).

Mr. *Romilly*, for the Defendants, was stopped by the Court.

Lord CHANCELLOR.—I feel great difficulty in hearing this cause.
The question with me, adopting all the sentiments of the great persons named, as far as they go, with due submission to that Court,
which has a right to bind me and them, is, whether I can set up my
judgment against a judgment of the House of Lords. A rule of
Law laid down by the House of Lords cannot be reversed by the
Chancellor; though if there is any difference from a circumstance,
that was not before the House of Lords, the cause may be decided
upon that.

[* 548]   * It is said the grandmother put herself *in loco parentis*.
But it appears, there are other grand-children, to whom
she forgot her duty; and who are unprovided for. The case of
a grand-child, where the father is alive, and abundantly providing
for it, is very different from the case, where the father is dead. As
to the statute of Elizabeth, if the father is living, the grandfather is
under no legal obligation. The rule of law must remain, till altered
by the House of Lords. Therefore dismiss the bill: but it is impossible to give costs; where the Plaintiffs have had so much encouragement from *dicta*.

1. THE statute 55 Geo. III. c. 192, renders a previous surrender to the use of a
testator's will no longer necessary, to give validity to his disposition of copyhold
tenements.

2. In order to entitle an infant grandchild to interest upon a legacy, by way of
maintenance, when no express provision to that effect is to be found in the testator's will; there must at least be some indication that the testator intended to put
himself *in loco parentis*: see, *ante*, note 2 to *Crickett* v. *Dolby*, 3 V. 10; and also
note 1 to *Godfrey* v. *Davis*, 6 V. 43.

(1) 2 Bro. C. C. 101, 152.
(2) See *The Bishop of London* v. *Fytche*, 1 Bro. C. C. 96.

SPURRIER *v.* FITZGERALD.

[ROLLS.—1801, DEC. 1, 2, 7.]

A BILL alleging a written agreement may be sustained by evidence of a parol
agreement (a).
After answer admitting an agreement, and submitting to perform it, the bill being
amended as to other circumstances, the Defendant was not permitted to take
advantage of the Statute of Frauds by the answer to the amended bill; and a
specific performance was' decreed (b).

THE bill stated, that the Plaintiff was possessed of a messuage,
coach-house, stables, and buildings, situate at the' corner of Lower
Seymour Street and Orchard Street, and in Calmel's Mews, in the
parish of St. Mary-le-bone, for two several terms of years; and being desirous to sell the same for the remainder of the said terms
respectively, the Defendant contracted with him for the same: and
she the Defendant by writing under her own hand agreed to give
the Plaintiff the sum of 1800*l.* for the said messuage, coach-house,
stables, &c. for the residue of the said terms respectively, and the
fixtures; and the Plaintiff agreed to sell the said messuage, coach-
house, stables, &c. and fixtures at and for that sum; and which said
sum of 1800*l.* the said Defendant agreed to pay the Plaintiff, as follows: that is to say; the sum of 900*l.* down, and the remainder
thereof in two years, and to give the Plaintiff her bond for securing
the payment thereof: and the Plaintiff refers to the agreement or
writing in the Plaintiff's custody. The prayer of the bill was, that
the said agreement, so as aforesaid made by the said Defendant
with the Plaintiff, may be specifically performed, &c.

The Defendant by her answer, stating the Plaintiff's interest in
the premises for two several terms of 85 years and 75 years and a
half, admitted, that she contracted for the same with Mr.
Phipps; to whom the Plaintiff by a letter dated * the 30th   [* 549]
of April, 1800, referred her, as his agent, to treat on his
part for the sale thereof. She stated, that she contracted respecting the same verbally, but not in writing under her own hand or
signed by her. She verbally agreed to give the Plaintiff the sum of
1800*l.* for the said premises for the residue of the terms and for the
fixtures; and admits, the Plaintiff, or Phipps as his agent, agreed
to sell the same to her for that sum, payable by instalments, as
stated in the bill.

(a) In strictness of law, and independent of the Statute of Frauds, a mere written agreement not under seal and a verbal agreement are regarded as of the same
nature. The leading distinction is between contracts by specialty, and those by
parol. See Greenleaf, Evid. § 275; *Stackpole* v. *Arnold,* 11 Mass. 30; *Bayard* v.
Malcolm, 1 Johns. 467; *Sinclair* v. *Stevenson,* 1 C. & P. 582; *Hunt* v. *Adams,*
7 Mass. 522. Proof of a sale of goods or payment of money, may be made by
parol, though there be a receipt, without accounting for its absence; parol proof
being of as high a nature as the receipt. *Southwick* v. *Heyden,* 7 Cowen, 334.
  If a party admits that there was some agreement, parol evidence of it is admissible in Equity. See *ante,* note (a), *Hare* v. *Shearwood,* 1 V. 241.
  (b) As to the effect of amendments of a bill, see *ante,* note (b), *Lord Abingdon*
v. *Butler,* 1 V. 210.

upon any other.   In the passage referring to the agreement *or* writing in the Plaintiff's custody it is impossible to separate the sentence, or to take advantage of the word "or;" for he cannot refer
to a verbal agreement in his possession.   The Plaintiff now desires the Court to perform, not the agreement he states, but a verbal agreement stated by the answer.

With respect to the point upon the Statute of Frauds, though
there is no case, in which it has been precisely settled, it is now understood upon the strong opinion of. Lord Chief Justice Eyre and
Lord Rosslyn, and of the present Lord Chancellor in the late case
of *Cooth* v. *Jackson* (1), that a Defendant admitting an agreement,
but insisting upon the benefit of the Statute by his answer, shall not
be compelled to perform it.   If the terms of the agreement are admitted, whether the Defendant submits to perform it, or not, all danger of perjury is out of the question.   The submission to perform
the agreement therefore does not vary the case.   It was at a certain
time; and when the Plaintiff stated certain terms, with which he
said, he would be satisfied.   When the Defendant said, she was
ready to perform that agreement, seeing what the Plaintiff prayed,
he ought to have closed with that; and to have replied to the answer, and set down the cause.   Instead of that, amending the bill,
making a new case, and requiring another answer, he has entirely
waived that submission; which was made upon a case different
from that now stated.   This would be manifest injustice.   The
Plaintiff now claims a compensation for the delay and the expense
of repairing the injury to the house: upon the ground, that she
bound herself to perform the agreement.   If that had been stated
originally, would she have submitted to perform the agreement?
The time is also material.   This Defendant has lost her object of a
residence in town for one winter.   Though at that time she was
ready to take the house, yet now, nine months afterward, when it is
deteriorated, and a bill filed, she insists, she shall not be compelled.
The whole answer is to be taken together, as one record.   She takes
the defence the law gives her; and of which she has a right to avail
herself against a new case.   The amended bill is entirely a new bill;
and the answer is considered an answer to a new bill.   In
[* 553]   * *Moore* v. *Edwards* (2) there were two answers; but
Lord Rosslyn was of opinion, that the Defendant might
have the benefit of the Statute, if insisted upon by the second
answer.

Mr. *Piggott*, in Reply.—This is not a case of different agreements: nor is the agreement originally stated in any degree varied
by the amendments.   The Court is left in no doubt as to the nature,
effect, or terms, of the agreement.   The opinion expressed by the
Lord Chancellor has not been acted upon; and the point cannot be
considered as decided.   But, supposing that to be so, the benefit of
the Statute must be taken at the time the agreement is confessed;

(1) *Ante*, 12; where the subject is fully discussed, and the authorities referred
to.   See also the note, *ante*, vol. iii. 38, 39, 40, to *Pym* v. *Blackburn.*
(2) *Ante*, vol. iv. 23.

for if the party submits to perform it, upon the same authority there is an end of the Statute. The agreement, of which the Plaintiff asks the performance, is that, which the Defendant admits, and submits to perform : no other. The bill was filed on the 2d of July, 1800. On the 17th of November, 1805, the Defendant put in that answer, admitting the agreement, as stated by the Plaintiff; denying only the form of it; namely, that it was evidenced by ʻwriting; and she submits to perform it. If she was then at liberty to object to the form of the agreement, namely, by parol, as a reason, why she was not bound to perform it, it was incumbent upon her then to claim the benefit of the Statute : but she does not. On the contrary she submits to perform it; and insists, that it was owing to the Plaintiff, that it was not performed without the bill. The amendments had nothing to do with the agreement. They were made necessary by the Defendant's stating circumstances to show, that it was the Plaintiff's fault, that the agreement was not performed by her. By the answer to those amendments, put in not till March 1801, she for the first time claimed the benefit of the Statute. This was a fraud on the Plaintiff : for up to that time the Plaintiff could not but consider the agreement as a subsisting agreement, binding him, and binding the premises. At any rate it was entirely misleading him; for if the Defendant had, when she confessed the agreement, insisted on the Statute, the Plaintiff would have been at liberty to consider his bill as at an end, and himself and the premises contracted for as discharged from the agreement. On the contrary the first answer leads him to conclude, that it is a subsisting agreement; and reduces the cause to a mere question, by whose fault the agreement * had not been performed; and the   [* 554] authority of the Court to enforce it had been rendered necessary. The Plaintiff proceeded in his cause to clear that question : and till almost a year after the agreement was entered into, and the bill filed, the Plaintiff is led by the pleadings, to treat it as a subsisting agreement; and is never told by the Defendant, that it was an agreement, as to which, though she admitted the substance of it in all particulars, she nevertheless meant to avail herself of the form as a reason for refusing to execute.

Dec. 7th. The MASTER OF THE ROLLS [Sir WILLIAM GRANT].— This bill is filed for the specific performance of an agreement. The Defendant by her answer admits a parol agreement; and submits to have it carried into execution : but she now contends, that a specific performance of that agreement ought not to be decreed : 1st, because the Plaintiff having by his bill stated an agreement in writing ought not to be permitted either by reading the answer or by other evidence to prove a parol agreement: 2dly, if he should be permitted to prove a parol agreement, yet the Defendant is at liberty to insist upon the benefit of the Statute of Frauds ; as she has by her answer to the amended bill, notwithstanding her submission to perform it by the answer to the original bill. As to the first point, it is a little ambiguous upon the face of the bill, whether the Plaintiff did or did

not mean to state this to be a written agreement. It seems, he meant in the first place to represent a contract, without saying, whether it was in writing, or not ; and then, that some of the terms were expressed in writing, signed by the Defendant. But taking it, that he meant to represent the whole to have been in writing, I take it not to have been ever established, that a Plaintiff is bound to prove all the allegations of his bill with so much strictness and precision as a Plaintiff at law is obliged to prove his declaration : it is sufficient, if a Plaintiff here proves the substance of his bill. He cannot certainly have a decree for the execution of a different sort of agreement from that laid ; an agreement of a different import or tendency ; for then the evidence would not support the bill. But the difference between a written and a parol agreement consists in the mode, in which they are evidenced. This objection does not at all depend upon the Statute of Frauds. The objection, provided it is an objection at all, would have been equally
[* 555]   *good, if no such statute had been made ; that the Plaintiff ought to prove the allegation, not only in substance, but all its circumstances ; that evidence of a written agreement will not support the allegation of a parol agreement ; or evidence of a parol agreement the allegation of a written agreement. No such rule was ever established. At law it is even now sufficient, as it was before the Statute, to allege an agreement generally ; which throws it upon the Defendant to allege that it is not in writing. In *Whitchurch* v. *Bevis* (1) Lord Thurlow stating the case of *Child* v. *Lord Godolphin* considers the allegation of the agreement being in writing to be thrown into the bill for the mere purpose of forcing the Defendant to plead the Statute instead of demurring ; and it seems, there the allegation was of a written agreement ; to which the Defendant pleaded, that there was no written agreement.. Lord Thurlow says, " That plea was ordered to stand for an answer, with liberty to except ; and upon a rehearing obtained by the Defendant the order was confirmed ; and Lord Macclesfield said, the plea of the Statute was right ; but that she ought to have denied the agreement by answer ; for if she confessed it, the Court would enforce it ; that if the bill had stated the agreement generally, a demurrer might have been allowed ; but where the agreement is stated to be in writing, the plea must be supported by the answer (2)."

That shows, that, if the Plaintiff alleges a written agreement, the Defendant will be reduced to the necessity of pleading, and supporting the plea by an answer ; which would not be necessary, if this objection would hold ; for the Defendant would run no risk ; as according to this the Plaintiff could not have performance of the agreement in any way ; having alleged it to be in writing.

The next head of defence, that the Defendant, having by the answer to the amended bill claimed the benefit of the Statute, is in the same condition, as if she had originally insisted upon the Statute,

(1) 2 Bro. C. C. 559.
(2) 2 Bro. C. C. 566. See the note, *ante*, vol. iii. 38, 39, 40.

raises the question so often agitated ; whether, if the Defendant confesses the agreement, but at the same time insists upon the Statute,
he shall be compelled to perform it. But this Defendant does
not bring it to that question ; for having once * submitted   [*556]
to perform the agreement, it is impossible for her afterwards
to insist upon the Statute. At the time she confessed the agreement she ought to have interposed that guard. At that time it was
incumbent upon her to say, whether she would avail herself of it.
The reason she alleges, that the Plaintiff did not think fit to be satisfied with her answer, but amended his bill, and required a farther
answer as to the details and circumstances, is no reason for withdrawing her submission. It is well known, that it is with great difficulty permitted to a Defendant to make any alteration in his answer,
even upon a mistake ; as where an executor by mistake submitted to
account for the residue of the next of kin ; and afterwards discovering his right upon some late cases to insist upon having it beneficially applied : yet the Court refused to permit him to withdraw that
submission. What ground is there here for withdrawing a submission deliberately made ? The Plaintiff did not amend his bill for
the purpose of obliging her to confess a new or a different agreement.
He was contented with her answer as to that; but wished to put
himself in a better plight as to her allegation of non-performance
upon his part; and that it was his own fault, that the agreement was
not performed without the necessity of a suit. The agreement was
out of the question. It was at rest between them. There was an
agreement, and a submission to perform it ; and the only question
between them was as to the costs of this suit, whether it was necessary.

The Defendant having therefore submitted to perform the agreement confessed by her, it is of course to decree her to perform it ;
and all the other circumstances are merely as to the costs, such as
may influence the Court as to the payment of them, upon the point,
whether it was necessary for the Plaintiff to institute this suit; or,
whether it was his fault, that the agreement was not performed. But
it is a mere matter of course to decree a performance.

At the Defendant's desire a reference to the Master was directed
as to the title; and whether the proper consents were obtained as to
the erection of the balcony.   ___

1. To what extent a defendant is bound by submissions, in his answer to an
original bill, after the plaintiff has amended; see, *ante,* note 3 to *Lord Abingdon*
v. *Butler and Benson,* 1 V. 206.
2. That admission of a verbal agreement respecting lands does not preclude a
defendant from insisting, even at the hearing of the cause, on the Statute of
Frauds ; see note 3 to *Moore* v. *Edwards,* 4 V. 23.
3. Unless part performance has taken the case out of the statute, Courts of
Equity will not decree specific execution of an agreement different from that
which the plaintiff has alleged by his bill ; notwithstanding such different agreement may be established by proofs, in the progress of the suit; see note 3 to
Mortimer v. *Orchard,* 2 V. 243.

TURNER *v.* MOOR.

[ROLLS.—1801, DEC. 7.]

LEGACY to A. or in case of his death to his issue, absolute in the parent (*a*).
"Or" construed "and:" the intention requiring it (*b*), [p. 560.]

JOHN CANTLEY by his will, dated the 2d of April, 1796, gave and bequeathed to John Turner and Robert Turner all his leasehold messuages, lands, tenements, and premises, in the county of Cornwall, to hold to them, their executors &c. as tenants in common and not as joint tenants, for the residue of the respective terms. The will then proceeded thus:

"Being possessed at this present time of property in the national funds, to wit, to the amount of 15,000*l.* of stock in the 3 per cent. Consolidated Annuities, I hereby leave and bequeath the said 15,000*l.* of said stock to my nephew Mr. Robert Dalrymple now or lately residing in India, or in case of his death to his lawful issue: but if my said nephew should be deceased at the time of my death without leaving any lawful issue, then and in that case I leave and bequeath to the aforesaid John Turner of Turner-hall, or in case of his decease to his lawful issue 3000*l.* of the said stock. Also in like manner I leave and bequeath 3000*l.* of said stock to the aforesaid Robert Turner of Menie or his lawful issue. Also in like manner I leave and bequeath 6000*l.* of the said stock to my cousin Captain M'Naughtane Ramsay, mariner, now or lately residing in the town of Leith near Edinburgh, or in case of his death to his lawful issue."

Upon the bill of John and Robert Turner and Ramsay against the executors the decree directed an inquiry, whether Robert Dalrymple or any of his issue were living at the death of the testator.

The Master by his report stated his opinion that Dalrymple not having been heard of since the time of his sailing on a voyage to India on the 22d of December, 1785, must in all human probability have perished in the prosecution of that voyage, being many years before the death of the testator; and no evidence having been proved to show, that he ever was married, but the contrary appearing by the evidence, he conceived, he never was married.

[* 558]   * The cause coming on for farther directions, the Master of the Rolls directed a petition to be presented on behalf of the children of the Plaintiffs, some of whom had attained the age of twenty-one. The petition suggesting, that the Plaintiffs are entitled only to the interest of the legacies respectively, and that the principal of such legacies upon their respective deaths became distributable among the issue of the Plaintiffs respectively, who may be

---

(*a*) In cases like the present, Courts have endeavored, from the nature and circumstances of the bequest, or the context of the will, to determine the signification of the limitation "in case of his death," &c. See *ante*, note (*a*), *Lord Douglas v. Chalmer*, 2 V. 501.

(*b*) See *ante*, note (*a*), *Maberly v. Strode*, 3 V. 450.

living at the time they may respectively die, prayed, that the legacies
may be secured.

Mr. *Martin*, in support of the Petition.—Upon the wording of
this will and the circumstances a life interest only was intended for
the persons named in the will. That construction also must prevail
upon the legal import of the words according to the decisions. If
the will had stopped after the disposition to Robert Dalrymple, he
could have had no more than a life interest : but knowing the circumstances as to that nephew, the will being made eleven years after
he had sailed on a voyage, in which in all probability he perished,
the testator adds words, showing, he meant to guard against the
event of the decease of his nephew in his life. He was clearly
aware of the import of the words he was using. If he had the same
event in his view as to the other persons, he would have inserted
similar words after each particular bequest: but that being omitted,
the will stands, as if the words applied to Robert Dalrymple had
never been introduced.

There have been various cases, upon words, in some precisely
similar, in others nearly so ; which have been considered as curtail-
ing the interest of the first taker to a mere interest for life : *Billings*
v. *Sandom* (1) ; which from a fuller manuscript note appears to be
accurately reported, as far as it goes : *Nowlan* v. *Nelligan* (2) ; *Lord
Douglas* v. *Chalmer* (3), determined in a great measure upon the
authority of *Billings* v. *Sandom*. The Court has uniformly held it a
life interest only upon such words. The words used in this will are
words of purchase ; and if this had been a devise of land, the parent
would have had an estate for life only, not an estate tail ;
which has afforded the ground, upon * which the Court has   [* 559]
gone in these cases. Upon the other construction the
Court must supply words ; which is never done without a manifest
intention. Supposing, the intention was to give the parent an absolute interest, the rule " *Quod voluit non dixit*," applies.

Mr. *Romilly*, for the Plaintiffs, was stopped by the Court.

The MASTER OF THE ROLLS [Sir WILLIAM GRANT].—My recollection of the case of *Lord Douglas* v. *Chalmer* induced me to express
a wish, that the construction of this will should be a little farther
considered. But that case is very clearly different. First, it is quite
clear here, the intention was, that if the testator's nephew Robert
Dalrymple should be living at his death, he should take absolutely,
and his children should take nothing. The reason assigned for the
testator expressing himself with more particularity as to him, his absence in India, and the uncertainty, whether he was not dead, furnishes no reason for giving him upon the supposition, that he was
alive, a larger interest than any other legatee ; and it is clear, that,
if he was alive, the testator intended him to take the whole, and that

(1) 1 Bro. C. C. 393.
(2) 1 Bro. C. C. 489.
(3) *Ante*, vol. ii. 501, and the note, 507 ; *Hinckley* v. *Symmonds*, iv. 160 ; *King*
v. *Taylor*, v. 806.

the children should take nothing. That gives the rule for the construction of the same words, when occurring again in other parts of the will. The same phrase is repeated after the bequest to each of the other legatees; and having himself clearly expounded his meaning in one instance he must be supposed to have the same meaning by the same words in the other parts. The case I have mentioned is different from this in another respect. That was a bequest to a married woman. The mention of the issue clearly implied, that he did not intend an absolute legacy to her; which in effect would ·have been a legacy to her husband. The Lord Chancellor therefore proceeded a good deal upon the apparent intention of the testatrix; not meaning an absolute gift to the husband, but a provision for the wife and children. There also the word was "and;" which was relied on in *Billings* v. *Sandom*; as showing, that both parties are to take a benefit, the parent and the children. The words cannot be fully satisfied without giving each some interests which can be only by giving an estate for life to the parent and the capital to the children after the death of the parent. Here the word is "or."

[* 560]   Both are not to take: but either the parent or the children in the alternative; *and though in many cases "or," has been construed "and," you must show an intention requiring that (1). The natural import is to exclude the one from any participation of that, which is given to the other.

I have not the least doubt therefore upon this will, though I wished it to undergo a little farther consideration, that it was not necessary to make the children parties. The prayer of the petition being refused, the directions are of course.

---

1. WORDS, which, in their ordinary sense, are sufficient to convey an absolute gift of a legacy, must not be cut down by introducing a qualification not necessary to make the whole will consistent; see, *ante*, the note to *Lord Douglas* v. *Chalmer*, 2 V. 501, and, *post*, the notes to *Stanley* v. *Stanley*, 16 V. 491.

2. Where the same words occur in different parts of the same will, it is a sound general rule to give them the same meaning throughout; (*Goodwright* v. *Dunham*, 1 Doug. 267; *Doe* v. *Jesson*, 5 Mau. & Sel. 99; *Hawe* v. *Hawe*, 3 Atk. 526;) and one doubtfully expressed bequest may be explained by the testator's own exposition as to another bequest of a similar nature; (*Stenhouse* v. *Mitchell*, 11 Ves. 357;) but the very same words may be differently construed, and have different operations, when applied, in the same will, to different descriptions of property, governed by different rules: *Forth* v. *Chapman*, 1 P. Wms. 667; *Keiley* v. *Fowler*, Wilmot's Notes, 313; *Elton* v. *Eason*, 19 Ves. 77: thus, the same words of limitation, which will give an estate tail in freehold property, will carry the absolute interest in leasehold: *Exell* v. *Wallace*, 2 Ves. Sen. 325; *Crooke* v. *De Vandes*, 9 Ves. 203; *Green* v. *Stephens*, 17 Ves. 73.

3. As to the admissibility of construing the word "and," in testamentary instruments, as if it were "or," see note 1 to *Maberley* v. *Strode*, 3 V. 450.

---

(1) *Ante, Weddell* v. *Mundy*, 341; *Maberly* v. *Strode*, vol. iii. 450, and the references in the note, 452.

SMART v. PRUJEAN.

[1801, Dec. 11.]

LEGACIES out of real estate, given by an unattested paper, cannot stand, unless that paper is clearly referred to by a Will duly executed; so as to be incorporated with it: in this instance there being no such clear reference upon the contents of the instrument, the legacies failed: the circumstance, that a paper was found inclosed in the same cover with the Will, indorsed as his Will, not being sufficient (a).

Legacy to such purposes as the superior of a convent or her successor may judge most expedient, void as a superstitious use, [p. 567.]

ANTHONY LOWE, a Roman Catholic priest of Gravelines in Flanders, being seised in fee of some real estates in England, by his will, dated the 5th of December, 1789, duly attested according to the Statute of Frauds (1), gave and devised to John Prujean and his son, their heirs, and assigns, his real estates, describing them; upon trust, that immediately and as soon as conveniently might be after his decease they should sell the same; and in the mean time and until the sale apply the rents and profits, after deducting their costs, unto such person or persons, and for such ends, intents and purposes as he, the testator, should by a private letter or paper of instructions, which he in his will mentioned he intended to leave with Mrs. Johnson, then residing at Gravelines, or with her successor for the time being, direct or appoint; and from and immediately after the sale he directed his trustees to pay the money, which should arise therefrom, and the interest, until the principal should be paid, unto and for the benefit of such person, and in such manner, as he the testator should by the like private letter or paper of instructions direct and appoint. He gave to each of his trustees twenty guineas for their trouble; and he gave and bequeathed all the residue of his estate, both real and personal, unto the same trustees, their heirs, executors, and administrators, for the use and benefit of such person as should be *named in the said private letter or paper [*561] of instructions; and he appointed his trustees executors.

The testator died at Gravelines in December 1794. Immediately after his death, in his bureau in the room, in which he had resided, belonging and adjoining to the monastery of English nuns at Gravelines, of which Clementina Johnson, referred to in the will, was superior, two paper-writings were found in the same envelope with the will; which envelope was sealed up, and indorsed in the hand of the testator, " The will of Anthony Lowe."

(a) According to a recent English statute (1 Vic. c. 26, § 9), and the legislation of several of the United States, the same form is prescribed for the execution of a will of personal property, as in that of a will of land. See *ante*, note (a), *Mathews* v. *Warner*, 4 V. 186; note (d), *Habergham* v. *Vincent*, 2 V. 204.

Several instruments of different natures may constitute a will. See 1 Williams, Exec. 61; *Sandford* v. *Vaughan*, 1 Phillim. 39, 128; *Harley* v. *Bagshaw*, 2 Phillim. 48; *Masterman* v. *Maberly*, 2 Hagg. 235. See, also, *Milledge* v. *Lamar*, 4 Desauss. 623; *Smith* v. *Attersoll*, 1 Russ. 266.

(1) 29 Char. II. c. 3.

These papers were, as follows; both in the hand-writing of the testator.

"John Prujean, Esqr. and his son John trustees and executors of my will—Gentlemen, I desire, that immediately after my decease you will (previously deducting your charges and expenses in the execution of your trust) pay the rent of my houses, in case they shall not then be sold, or if sold, pay the monies, that shall arise by such sale, and the interest thereof, and transfer and make over the securities for the same, unto Mrs Clementina Johnson now residing at Gravelines in Flanders, or to her successor then in being, or to such other person or persons as they or either of them shall appoint. By this you will much oblige, Gentlemen, your most affectionate friend and humble servant, Anthony Lowe. Gravelines, April the 17th, 1789."

The other paper was directed thus: " Reverend Mother Abbess ;". and was in the following words:

" Dear Madam—As to the worldly estate or effects I may die possessed of or entitled to in England, I have devised them by will to John Prujean, Esqr. and his son, upon trust nevertheless that the said gentlemen shall after my decease as soon as conveniently may be sell and dispose of my messuages or tenements situate in St. John's Street in Carlow Court, &c.; and in confidence moreover that they will after deducting their charges and expenses in the execution of their [*562] trust pay the rent of my houses, if they shall not then be sold, or if sold, pay the money, * that shall accrue by such sale, and the interest thereof, and transfer and make over the securities for the same, unto your Reverence or your successors then in being, or to such other person or persons as you or your successor shall think proper to appoint. As on the one hand I stand indebted to 40l. sterling to Mr. Errington, and on the other hand bequeathed two legacies of twenty guineas to my executors, I am inclined to think the sum you will receive in consequence of the sale of my property, Mr. Errington being paid, and the just mentioned legacies discharged, may amount to about 300l. or 400l. sterling. The first hundred pounds I desire Sister Winifred Clare's acceptance of as a compensation for the loss she heretofore unfortunately sustained in her fortune. A second similar sum I beg may be placed out to interest towards the entertainment of church linen; and third hundred to be applicable to the purpose or purposes, which you or your successor may judge to be most expedient. Should the sum you receive exceed 300l., the overplus I entreat you to remit to Miss Catherine Mackey, provided it does not surpass 50l. In case it does, what may remain in your hands after you have given her the 50l. you'll be pleased to accept for your own particular uses. As nothing more occurs to mind that I could wish to add, except that I earnestly recommend myself to your's and your community's pious prayers, and beg you will be so kind as to get fifty masses discharged for the repose of my poor soul, and one low mass yearly to the same end, I shall therefore conclude with the unfeigned assurance of how much and sincerely I am, Dear Madam, your and your community's most truly wellwisher and devoted humble servant, Anthony Lowe. Gravelines, April 17th 1789.

" N. B.—The legacy projected in favor of Miss Catherine Mackey, which I confidently trust will fall to her share in consequence of the sale of my little property proceeds partly from the real esteem and regard I have for her, and more particularly from the knowledge I have of her indigent circumstances."

Clementina Johnson, the abbess, died in the life of the testator. Immediately on his death the cover containing all these papers was delivered to the lady, who * succeeded Mrs. [* 563] Johnson, as abbess. Prujean the elder died in the life of the testator : but his son took possession of the real and personal estate and the title-deeds. A *caveat* was entered by two cousins of the testator, claiming as his heirs at law and next of kin, against the probate of any of these papers ; and they filed the bill against Prujean, and against Winifred Clare and Catherine Mackey ; praying, that Prujean may be declared a trustee for the Plaintiffs as to the real and the residue of the personal estates, and deliver up the possession and the title-deeds, and account for the rents and profits, and the personal estate, &c. ; insisting, that the papers found with the will could not be considered as the papers intended by the testator.

Mr. *Mansfield* and Mr. *Johnson,* for the Plaintiffs.—Upon the whole of the will and the circumstances there is no disposition whatsoever of this estate. It is admitted, that there was no paper in the hands of Mrs. Johnson at her death ; and there is no proof, that the testator ever did deliver to her any paper, expressing the purposes to which his property should be applied. There is therefore no disposition of either the real or personal estate. As to the papers set up by the Defendants as a disposition, they bear date several months prior to the date of the will ; and the expression in one of them is " *I have devised by will ;* " referring to a will previously made. That paper cannot possibly operate upon the beneficial interest of property given by a will made months before. The objects of that paper also are clearly superstitious. The legacy to Sister Winifred Clare is given to her as a nun ; and the overplus is given to the abbess in that character ; and, it must be supposed, for superstitious uses : part being directly so appropriated. The other two legacies perhaps might be good, if the will could have any operation : but it cannot. There is however no personal estate, and then these papers being unattested can have no effect upon the produce of the sale of the real estate. Can they be so connected with the will as to form part of it? It was originally doubted, whether debts incurred after a charge of debts upon real estate would be charged : but that is now settled ; and in *Habergham* v. *Vincent* (1) it was determined farther, that under a charge of legacies upon real estate legacies given by a * subsequent unattested paper would [* 564] be charged, by analogy to the case of debts. But all those

_____

(1) *Ante,* vol. ii. 204 ; 4 Bro. C. C. 353.

instances were cases of auxiliary charge in aid of the personal estate;
and in *Habergham* v. *Vincent* the Lord Chancellor expressly confines
his opinion to that; excluding a primary charge; as this is. The
money produced by the sale of land is considered as land: *The Attorney General* v. *Lord Weymouth* (1). So, the rents, are part of
the land. A rent is within the Statute of Frauds as a tenement.
The heir at law then must take, however strong the intention against
him, unless the real estate is disposed of.

Mr. *Romilly* and Mr. *Jordan*, for the Defendants.—It cannot be
denied, that a considerable part of the disposition by this paper is to
a superstitious use; and so far without doubt the Defendant is a
trustee for the heir. The legacies to Winifred Clare and Catherine
Mackey are mere personal legacies; and the only question is as to
the legacy of 100*l*. to the Superior of this convent for the purposes,
which she or her successor may judge most expedient; whether the'
character, in which it is given to her, is sufficient to show, it is for a
superstitious use.

As to the objections to the other legacies, first, that no paper was
left in the hands of Mrs. Johnson, and that the date of these papers
is anterior to that of the will, it refers to a paper left with her or her
successor for the time being. These papers were found sealed up
with the will in a room in a house belonging and adjoining to the
convent. They are therefore, though not literally in the possession
of the Superior, in a house belonging to, and a part of, the convent.
That qualification is only as evidence of the identity; and under the
circumstances this paper was sufficiently left with the Superior.
They were sealed up with the will by the testator himself; though
dated before. The indorsement in his handwriting is sufficient evidence of that; and that at that time he sealed them up and published them as testamentary papers, stating his intention as to his
property. Then what objection can be made to the legacies to
Winifred Clare and Catherine Mackey, clearly given for their private
benefit; the reason expressed; and not having any view to the community or the purposes of the society?

[* 565]   *As to the objection for want of witnesses it is now
            clearly settled, that a testator may dispose of real estate by
a paper unattested, but sufficiently referred to by a will attested by
three witnesses. This paper, though written before the date of the
will, was recognized and published afterwards. The paper referred
to by the will is as much a part of the will as if contained in it.

The reply was stopped by the Court.

Lord CHANCELLOR [ELDON].—I am very strongly of opinion,
thinking, these two legacies would be good, if the fund was well
given, that there is not sufficient legal certainty, to be collected from
the instrument signed by three witnesses, that the testator has disposed of his real estate. The rule goes no farther than this: (I except charges for debts and legacies): that if the produce of real
estate is to be disposed of, you must show an instrument in effect
executed by the testator in the presence of three witnesses; and

(1) Amb. 20.

evidencing from its own contents, that it is so, in a sense; even if no attestation is annexed to it. The rule of law is, that an instrument properly attested, in order to incorporate another instrument not attested, must describe it so as to be a manifestation of what the paper is, which is meant to be incorporated; in such a way, that the Court can be under no mistake (1). In that way of putting the case it is not necessary to decide, whether the testator's intention before making the will, was, if these papers are incorporated, that his will should not be consummate, till they were delivered to the Superior; though, if the cause was decided upon that ground, I am not sure, it would be wrong; for I can imagine, that he might have conceived a purpose of piety; and, taking it to be the most rational purpose of piety, he might consider, that notwithstanding his purpose at that time he might have more favor to his relations afterwards; and they might become as proper objects of his piety as any other; and therefore he might intend to dispose of the money for such purpose as should be expressed in a paper he intended to leave with the Superior. I always thought the construction of *Heylin* v. *Heylin* (2) rather critical. That case, however, was decided by high authority. But I take all these papers to have been prepared on the *same day. It is a more seri-   [* 566] ous thing to execute a will than to sign a letter: therefore, I apprehend, he signed the letters then; but hesitated about executing the will till December. Judging as a private individual, there can be no doubt, that, when he executed the will, he meant that instrument and these two letters should have their effect; but unless the rule of law allows me, I cannot establish the letters; and I am not satisfied, he meant them to have their effect, unless delivered to the Superior; as he might mean that to be a part of the act to make the will complete. The intention of leaving them with her can never under the circumstances, in which he lived, be satisfied by the circumstance of finding them in the convent. He was living, and had his bureau, in that room, belonging to the convent; and it is impossible upon that circumstance to say, that according to his intention he had left them with her. From his residence he could not avoid leaving them there. This is fortified by what follows. Mrs. Johnson lived some time; and he never left any paper with her; or delivered any to her successor. Certainly at his death the abbess had no notion they were left with her; for she desires the will to be brought to her; and gets possession of it. In favor of an heir at law, whom I must see disinherited by nothing but a clear manifestation of intention, it would not be too strong to say, the testator did not mean his will to be consummate, unless he should do that act of leaving it with the Superior, which he never did.

But there is another ground: not whether the same envelope or superscription is evidence, that the testator meant, these should be the papers referred to; but whether I must of necessity collect from the contents of the will, that they should be considered the same.

(1) See *Wilkinson* v. *Adam*, 1 Ves. & Bea. 422.
(2) Cowp. 130.

The same cover is nothing with reference to the statute; and the superscription has not three witnesses. The true question is, if these papers were found in the bureau with the will, can I say from the contents of the will, these two papers are the papers referred to? Suppose, several other papers were found with them: could I say, this will would have enabled me to select these two as the only papers referred to? The rule and my opinion are, that the will has not by its contents sufficiently identified these papers to enable me to say, they are necessarily incorporated: if not, they are [*567] not attested by three witnesses; and it is admitted on *all hands, that this sort of disposition, unless the antecedent paper is incorporated, cannot be brought within the rule as to debts and legacies charged on real estate by an unattested paper. I cannot therefore give these parties their legacies; though I regret it.

During the argument the Lord Chancellor expressed his opinion, that the legacy of 100*l.* for such purposes as the Superior of the convent or her successor should judge most expedient, being given in that character, was sufficient to show, it was for a superstitious use (1).

1. THAT no unattested codicil can have any operation upon land, or the produce of land; though a duly attested will may, by a reference distinctly identifying a previously written document, make the dispositions therein contained a part of his will; as, also, that the donee of a power affecting lands may, by virtue of a special reservation to that effect, execute the same, by a will not attested according to the Statute of Frauds; see, *ante,* note 2 to *Fettiplace* v. *Gorges,* 1 V. 46.

2. Plain words of gift, to some person capable of taking, or words of necessary implication, are required to disinherit an heir at law. See note 6 to *Pickering* v. *Lord Stamford,* 2 V. 72.

BRYDGES *v.* PHILLIPS.

[ROLLS.—1801, Nov. 23.]

To exempt the personal estate from the debts the Will must show that intention by indication plain: a provision for the debts out of the real estate is not sufficient (*a*).

FRANCIS WILLIAM THOMAS BRYDGES by his will, dated the 1st of March, 1788, after the usual introduction, as to being of sound mind, &c. appointed his wife Ann guardian to his only daughter, an infant about four months old; and confirmed the settlement made upon their marriage in all respects. The will then proceeded thus:

---

(1) *De Garcin* v. *Lawson, ante,* vol. iv. 433, note; *Cary* v. *Abbot, post,* vii. 490; 3 Mer. 399; *Attorney General* v. *Power,* 1 Ball. & Bea. 145.

(*a*) See *ante,* note (*a*), *Kidney* v. *Coussmaker,* 1 V. 436; note (*a*), *Gray* v. *Minnethorpe,* 3 V. 103; note (*a*), *Hartley* v. *Hurle,* 5 V. 540.

"But should I die soon, in which case there may be long minority of my daughter, and to obviate any difficulty, that may arise in my affairs upon that account, I give and devise to my worthy friends and trustees Robert Phillips and Francis Woodhouse, Esq. all and singular my manors, messuages, tithes, lands, and hereditaments, within the said county of Hereford, which are not included in my said settlement, or have not since been purchased by me, and the equity of redemption of and in the same respectively, to hold to the use and behoof of them, their heirs and assigns; in trust nevertheless to sell and absolutely dispose of the same or such part and parts thereof as they shall judge most convenient to part with; (with power in the mean time to pay off the mortgage now affecting the same; and for that purpose to take up money; and confine or restrain such * new mortgage to such parts of the   [* 568] premises, which are not intended to be disposed of; and which will be very ample to answer both purposes); and by and with the money arising thereby in the first place to pay off and discharge all my just debts (except the said mortgage of my said estates, and a charge of 4000*l.* to my two sisters Ann and Catherine; which by my said settlement are provided for, and directed to be paid out of another fund): and in the next place to raise and pay to my half-sister Elizabeth Creighton Brydges, now living with my father at Madley, the sum of 1000*l.* to carry lawful interest from the day of the death of my said father; unless I shall in my life-time (and which I fully intend doing) make as large and ample a provision for her in some other way; and in the last place to raise and pay to my said dear wife the sum of 4000*l.* for her own use and benefit; and the rest and residue of my said unsettled estates, as also all other my manors, messuages, lands, tithes, and hereditaments, whatsoever, both freehold, leasehold, and copyhold, which were so settled upon my marriage, in case I shall die without issue male either born in my life-time or after my decease I give, devise, and bequeath to my said dear wife for the term of her natural life; and from and immediately after her decease to the use of my said dear daughter Ann and the heirs of her body lawfully to be begotten; and in default of such issue to the use of my said two sisters Ann and Catherine, and their respective heirs, as coparceners, and not as joint-tenants."

The testator then directs and earnestly requests, that, in case he shall die without issue male, as before mentioned, and his said daughter shall succeed to and inherit his said estates, any husband she may marry, shall take the surname of Brydges, and transmit the same to his posterity, being the issue or descendants of his said daughter Ann; and then proceeded, as follows:

"And I farther direct, that all the plate, linen, china ware, books, household goods, and other furniture and effects, at Tiberton aforesaid shall remain there as and in the nature of heir-looms, for the use of my said daughter, or such other person and persons, who may take or inherit my said estates under and by virtue of the said settlement, this my will, or either of them. I give and continue to my said father for his life the possession of the house he now inhabits at Madley aforesaid, and of the several lands thereto belonging, and now in his possession, together with the annuity or allowance of 80*l.* a year, which I have hitherto made him ; which I desire he may enjoy, and have the same paid him regularly, as usual, during his life ; and which I hereby charge upon all and every part of my said unsettled estates."

Then, after giving legacies to his servants, and 100*l.* to each of his trustees Phillips and Woodhouse for their trouble, the testator concluded thus:

" All which said last mentioned legacies I desire may be paid out of my personal estate (except that part given as aforesaid for heirlooms); and all the rest and residue of my said personal estate (except as aforesaid) I give and bequeath to my said dear wife, whom together with the said Robert Phillips and Francis Woodhouse I constitute and appoint executrix and executors of this my will."

The testator died in 1793 ; leaving two daughters co-heiresses ; one of whom is since dead. The bill was filed by Elizabeth Creighton Brydges and Joshua Scrope and Ann, his wife, who was the testator's widow, to have the will established, &c. Upon an issue directed, *Devisavit vel non*, the will was established.

The cause coming on upon the Equity reserved, the only question was, whether the personal estate was exempt from the debts.

Mr. *Richards* and Mr. *Alexander*, for the Plaintiffs.—The general principle is certainly, that the personal estate is the fund naturally applicable to debts ; and therefore there must be something to show the intention, that it shall be exempted. This is a devise of particular, excepted, estates, not by way of charge, but to be sold and absolutely disposed of. Simple contract debts are in this respect legacies ; a bounty to the creditors ; who had not before the means of coming at the real estate. Here is a bequest to the wife as residuary legatee ; and not in the character of executrix, for the [* 570] * purpose of distributing in the course of that duty. The words " except as aforesaid " in the residuary disposition are material ; showing, that the residue intended is the residue subject only to a deduction in respect of the legacies given out of the personal estate ; affording an irresistible inference, that the personal estate was to go to her subject to no other charge; and that the debts were to go out of the real estate. Certainly in *Burton* v. *Knowlton* (1) some stress was laid on the direction to pay the funeral expenses ; and Lord Rosslyn laid stress upon the omission of that in *Tait* v. *Lord Northwick* (2) : wishing to distinguish that case from the other. Lord Hardwicke in *Walker* v. *Jackson* (3) considers the insertion of those words as of no weight.

---

(1) *Ante*, vol. iii. 107. See the references to that case, the note, 106; and *Hartley* v. *Hurle*, vol. v. 540.
(2) *Ante*, vol. iv. 816.
(3) 2 Atk. 624.

Mr. *Piggott*, for the Defendant, was stopped by the Court.

The MASTER OF THE ROLLS [Sir WILLIAM GRANT].—There is certainly room for conjecture, that this testator did mean to throw the whole of the debts upon his real estate. But it is only a probable conjecture; there is no certainty, no clear, unambiguous, intention to be collected from the whole will, that he meant that; and there is no distinct difference between this case and *Tait* v. *Lord Northwick*. Very small differences may be pointed out; but such as would form no guide for other cases; and leading to puzzle and confuse, rather than to give assistance to those, who may be called upon to advise as to the construction or frame of wills. There is in this, as in many cases, a very distinct provision for the payment of all the testator's debts by the sale of real estates. There is no provision for the payment of the funeral expenses. I think, the omission of that has had full as much weight in some of the late cases as is due to it. Perhaps it is true, as has been stated from Lord Hardwicke, that it is more a phrase of form than indicating a settled intention; and that either the insertion or omission of it means little. But it is argued, that wherever the personal estate is taken to be exempted, either the whole personal estate, or the residue after charges, it is taken as a specific legacy; and if it is once broken in upon, how is it liable to one charge and not to another? You oppose the construction, that it is subject only to particular legacies, by showing, there is * something else,   [* 571] that must come out of it. In that way the argument is applied from the omission to provide for funeral expenses; and that is the only way, in which it has application; for I do not think, there is much inference from it as to the intention.

This testator then proceeds to give particular legacies out of the real estate; and it is said, it is clear, those legacies must come out of that, and no other, fund. True; for they have no existence but by the Will; and must come out of the fund the testator points out. But the debts have a separate and independent existence. He then disposes of some part of his personal estate as heir-looms; and gives certain legacies, directed to be paid out of the personal estate. It is said, that shows, the debts are to be paid out of the real estate. That intention appears with no degree of certainty. He might have meant only to distinguish those legacies from the other legacies, to be paid out of the real estate. No clear intention appears to make a distinction between debts and legacies; and that the latter only shall come out of the personal estate. It is said, the words " except as aforesaid " refer to those few legacies immediately before given. That is clear misconstruction. They refer to what is immediately before mentioned, viz. what is excepted for heir-looms. In *Tait* v. *Lord Northwick* there was more room for arguing, that the residuary clause had reference to the two legacies immediately before given: but it was held to mean the general residue; that it must be taken as such; and must be subject to every thing naturally a charge upon the fund, of which it is the residue; though the testator does not

distinctly enumerate every thing payable out of it. The residuary
legatee cannot take the fund except after discharging every thing
payable out of it.

Upon the whole of this will there is no indication plain of an intention to exonerate the personal estate from the omission to provide
for the funeral expenses. I rather conjecture, that the testator did
intend, that the real estate he had set apart should be devoted to the
payment of his debts. I could not be certain, that I might not be
mistaken even in privately supposing that: but there is no ground
            upon which I can judicially collect a settled intention.

[* 572]   * The trustees and executors are not in this case wholly
            the same persons. Where they were the same, that has
been used as an argument against the exoneration. In this will two
of the executors are trustees: but then the wife is added.

S̲e̲e̲, *ante*, the notes to *S. C.* 3 V. 123.

SALLES *v.* SAVIGNON.

[1801, Nov. 16; Dec. 8.]

In the case of a ward of the Court a marriage in fact is sufficient to ground the '
    contempt.
Upon the marriage of a ward of the Court, both parties being foreigners, and the
    property abroad, and the marriage in Scotland on the day the bill was filed, the
    Court took jurisdiction; but did not commit the husband; ordering him to
    attend from time to time, and to be at liberty to make a proposal.

Upon a petition presented on the marriage of a young lady, a
ward of the Court, the circumstances appeared to be these.

Both the parties were foreigners, natives of the Island of Martinique; and all the lady's property was in that island; except the consignments made to this country, since that island had been reduced
by his Majesty's forces. The marriage took place in Scotland upon
the same day that the bill was filed. The husband had previously
written to the guardian and mother of the lady in Martinique, offering any settlement they should approve. The young lady by affidavit stated her apprehension of the petitioner's purpose to take her
to Hamburgh and marry her to his son. Some doubt was also suggested as to the validity of the marriage.

The parties attended in Court under an order for that purpose.

Mr. *Bell*, in support of the petition.

Mr. *Cox* for the husband suggested a doubt, whether the Court
would assume jurisdiction under such circumstances; observing, that
the whole of this proceeding is founded in fiction; and that any
order in this instance would carry the principle a great way.

The Lord Chancellor [Eldon] held, that a marriage in fact
was sufficient to ground a contempt of the Court. His Lordship

expressed some displeasure at the husband's not attending upon the first notice: but observing, that his being a foreigner might be some excuse, would not commit him; but ordered [* 573] him to attend from time to time, when required, and forthwith to lay a proposal before the Master. An inquiry into the circumstances of the marriage, and as to the circumstances of the parties, were also directed.

Upon a subsequent attendance an order was made, that the husband should be at liberty to go before the Master; and execute such settlement as should be agreed upon, with the approbation of the Court (1).

_____

ACTUAL notice that an infant has been made a ward of Court, is not necessary to be established, in order to constitute a marriage with such a party, without the license of the Court, a contempt. *Herbert's case*, 3 P. Wms. 116. As to the general course of proceeding, when such a marriage has taken place, see, *ante*, the note to *Stevens* v. *Savage*, 1 V. 154, and note 1 to *Stackpole* v. *Beaumont*, 3 V. 89.

_____

ANONYMOUS.

[1801, DEC. 12.]

ORDER, after verdict upon an issue to examine *de bene esse* a witness above seventy; suggesting an intention to move for a new trial (a).

AFTER trial of an issue directed in this cause, Mr. *Bell* for the Plaintiff moved, that he might be at liberty to examine a witness *de bene esse*, for the purpose of securing his testimony in case of his death, upon the ground, that it was intended to move for a new trial; and the witness was above seventy years old.

The order was made.

_____

WHEN a witness is seventy years of age, an order for his examination *de bene esse*, with a view to secure his testimony in case of his death, is never refused: *Rowe* v. ——, 8 Ves. 262; *Pritchard* v. *Gee*, 5 Mad. 364: and where matters of importance in a cause, with respect to which an issue is directed, lie within the knowledge of one person only, it is not necessary to show that he is either old or infirm, to ground an application for his examination *de bene esse*. *Pearson* v. *Ward*, 2 Dick. 648; *S. C.* 1 Cox, 177; *Shirley* v. *Earl Ferrers*, 3 P. Wms. 77; *Hankin* v. *Middleditch*, 2 Brown, 640; *Brydges* v. *Hatch*, 1 Cox, 423. The order will also be made when a witness is quitting the realm, or when he is going out of the jurisdiction, though only to a different part of the kingdom; as, for instance, to Scotland; where the process of the Court of Chancery could not reach him to compel his attendance at the trial of an issue. *Botts* v. *Verelst*, 2 Dick. 454. But though the three cases above specified are those in which it is most usual to

(1) *Ante*, *Stackpole* v. *Beaumont*, vol. iii. 89; *Stevens* v. *Savage*, i. 154, and the note, 155.

(a) Courts of Equity will entertain a bill to preserve the testimony of aged and infirm witnesses, resident at home, and of witnesses about to depart from the country, to be used in a trial at law, in a suit then pending, if they are likely to die before the time of trial may arrive. 2 Story, Eq. Jur. § 1514.

make an order for examination *de bene esse*, yet Lord Eldon has declared, that he should have no hesitation in granting such an application in other cases, upon reasonable and just grounds shown; and that, where there were more witnesses than one, yet, if the peculiar circumstances were such, that the death of one witness might have the same effect as the death of all, great indulgence would be properly applied. *Shelley* v. ———, 13 Ves. 57. It was, perhaps, on this principle, that two persons were examined *de bene esse*, without stating their age, in *Lord Cholmondeley* v. *The Earl of Oxford*, 4 Brown, 156. So, the illness of a witness, if it be properly certified that his state is dangerous, will justify an application of this nature ; which, however, when made on this ground, will be looked at with jealousy. *Bellamy* v. *Jones*, 8 Ves. 32. Though a witness may not be quite seventy years of age, at the time when an order for his examination *de bene esse* is applied for, yet the impossibility of bringing the question, as to which his evidence would be material, to an early trial, might be a ground for dispensing with the general rule ; (*Fitzhugh* v. *Lee*, Ambl. 65;) but Lord Eldon has intimated, that this ought never to be done without extreme caution. *Anonymous case*, 19 Ves. 321 ; *Palmer* v. *Lord Aylesbury*, 15 Ves. 301, the note to which case see, *post*. Where a bill has been filed to perpetuate testimony, if a *subpœna* has been served, and the defendants (whether they be adult or infants) have not entered an appearance in due time, but, being in contempt, a messenger has gone, and on his return states that the defendants have absconded and are not to be found, the plaintiff will be allowed to examine his witnesses *de bene esse*, upon terms, to be prescribed by the Court as the circumstances of the cases may require. *Frere* v. *Green*, 19 Ves. 320. As to the distinction between examination to perpetuate testimony, and examination *de bene esse*, see *Morrison* v. *Arnold*, 19 Ves. 671 ; see also, *ante*, the note to *Lord Dursley* v. *Fitzharding*, 6 V. 251.

TROUGHTON *v.* BINKES.

[1801, Dec. 15, 17.]

CREDITORS under a deed of trust cannot have a decree for redemption against a mortgagee ; unless a special case ; as collusion (*a*); that the trustee refuses, &c. In this case the bill by the creditors prayed, not a redemption but a sale (*b*); to which the mortgagee would not consent ; but submitted to be redeemed ; and the bill was dismissed.

THE bill was filed by four persons, claiming as creditors of Henry Evans Holder, on behalf of themselves and all other creditors, who shall come in and contribute to the expense of the suit, against the

---

(*a*) Where a mortgagor has conveyed his Equity of redemption to trustees for the benefit of his other creditors, the trustees alone are generally the proper parties to a bill to redeem, and not any of the creditors entitled under the trust. Story, Eq. Pl. § 184. Unless where there is some special cause, as collusion. Ib. § 516; *Holland* v. *Baker*, 3 Hare, 68. Hence it is, that a mere annuitant of the mortgagor (who has no interest in the land) has no title to redeem. 2 Story, Eq. Jur. § 1023; *White* v. *Parnther*, 1 Knapp, 229. See, also, the cases cited in note (*a*) to Eden on Injunctions, (2d ed.) 354; *Holland* v. *Prior*, 1 Mylne & K. 240; *Long* v. *Majestre*, 1 Johns. Ch. 305; *ante*, note (*a*), *Utterson* v. *Mair*, 2 V. 95.

(*b*) A sale will be ordered in many of the American Courts of Equity ; and it is the prevailing practice in Ireland. It is done without any distinction, whether there is a power to sell contained in the mortgage, or not. 2 Story, Eq. Jur. § 1025; 4 Kent, Com. 181, 182; *Brinckerhoff* v. *Thalhimer*, 2 Johns. Ch. 486 ; *Mills* v. *Dennis*, 3 Johns. Ch. 369.

trustees under a general deed of trust for the creditor (1), the Daniels, claiming under a prior mortgage, and being consignees of the estate in Barbadoes, Norton a judgment creditor, Spragg, the assignee of Holder, and against Holder himself; who died before the hearing.

The Plaintiffs Kidd and Kennett were at the date of the trust deed creditors of Holder to the amount of 42*l.* for goods sold. Subsequent to the deed of trust Holder contracted another debt with them to the amount of 136*l.*; for which he executed a mortgage to them of the same estate in Barbadoes, with the stock for ninety-nine years, and warrants of attorney to confess judgment. By indentures, dated the 23d of December 1796, Kennett and Kidd assigned their debts and securities to the Plaintiff Troughton. The fourth Plaintiff Boxham was a creditor, as indorsee of a bill of exchange drawn by Holder, and dishonored.

The bill prayed an account of the profits and produce of the plantation, &c. received by the Daniels, and of the application, and of what is due to them and to Norton on their securities; and that the premises may be sold; and that the money produced may be applied in the first place in payment of what shall be found due to the Daniels and Norton. The bill also prayed an account against the trustees, and an application according to the trusts of the deed for the benefit of the creditors.

The Defendants, the Daniels, who claimed under their mortgage a debt of above 7500*l.*, by their answer refused to consent to a sale; and they stated, that they are ready and willing on being paid the whole of what is due to them on their mortgage and their costs to convey, as the Court shall direct; but submit, the Plaintiffs are not entitled to have the accounts prayed taken as against them, unless the Plaintiffs will undertake to redeem said premises and to pay to the Defendants the whole of what now remains due to them on said mortgage.

Mr. *Piggott*, Mr. *Romilly*, and Mr. *Jordan*, for the Defendants, the Daniels, insisted, that the Plaintiffs had no right to redeem them, notwithstanding the submission in their answer; that the bill * did not seek a redemption; and the submission to   [* 575] do that, which the Plaintiffs do not seek, cannot supply the want of proper allegations in the bill and the prayer of that relief; and that the Plaintiffs ought to have amended the bill and to have shown a right to redeem.

The MASTER OF THE ROLLS (2) [Sir WILLIAM GRANT].—Most of the relief sought by this bill is of course. But it prays an account against the Daniels: and that the estate may be sold; and the money applied in the first place in payment of what shall be due to them. It is admitted, there could be no sale; the mortgagees not consenting to a sale. The Plaintiffs are creditors under the trust

(1) See *Spragg* v. *Binkes*, *ante*, vol. v. 583.
(2) *Ex relatione.*

deed. The trustees could come for a redemption: but I doubted, whether two or three creditors could come in their own names to redeem for their own benefit. It struck me as extraordinary, that they should file a bill to redeem for themselves, and so gain a preference; for then they must be redeemed. But it is now admitted, that they cannot claim to redeem to that extent; but if any creditors choose to come in and contribute, then all are to have the benefit. I should have thought, the trustees should have come, and have claimed the benefit for them (1); not, that the creditors themselves should come in the first instance, and as a matter of course. For that a case must be made; that the trustees were called upon to redeem; and they refused. A case of that kind, *Franklyn* v. *Ferne*, was stated; in which the general principle was recognized; but it was decided that the Plaintiff had made a case. Lord Chief Baron Parker stated the established principle, that he, who has the legal estate, must redeem; unless a special case is made; as, that trustees or executors are colluding (2); or, if they are unsafe. I am therefore confirmed in my opinion, by the authority of that case as well as by analogy, that the Court cannot in this short way decree redemption. In *Utterson* v. *Mair* (3) it was alleged, that the executor was an insolvent person. The assignees demurred; as the executor was the person to make the demand; and the demurrer was allowed. The Lord Chancellor was of opinion, that a case might be made: but that was not done. In this case I [*576] am of opinion, *that, though a ground is made for redemption, this bill is not framed for that relief.

Dismiss the bill against the mortgagees.

See, *ante*, the notes to S. C. 5 V. 583.

‌ HODGES, *Ex parte*.

[1801, Dec. 22.]

No order can be made under Lord Eldon's Act, 39 and 40 Geo. III. c. 56, authorising the payment of money, in trust to be laid out in land, to be settled, to the tenant in tail, without a previous inquiry as to incumbrances.

This petition was presented under the late Act of Parliament (4), for the purpose of having money, in trust to be invested in land, to be settled, paid to the person, who would be tenant in tail.

The Lord Chancellor [Eldon] said, that Lord Rosslyn [Loughborough] had settled, that there must always be a reference to the

(1) *Post, Benfield* v. *Solomons*, vol. ix. 77; *Saxton* v. *Davis*, xviii. 72; 1 Rose, 79.
(2) *Doran* v. *Simpson, ante*, vol. iv. 651; *Alsager* v. *Rowley, post*, 748.
(3) *Ante*, vol. ii. 95; 4 Bro. C. C. 270. See the note, *ante*, vol. ii. 96.
(4) Statute 39 & 40 Geo. III. c. 56; *ante*, vol. v. 12, n.

Master, to inquire, whether the parties had in any manner incumbered their interests in the money.

Mr. *Alexander*, in support of the petition suggested, that in a plain case that reference might be dispensed with.

The Lord CHANCELLOR said, he never would dispense with it; observing, that in the plainest case it cannot without that inquiry appear, whether the parties have incumbered their interests.

The order accordingly directed an inquiry, whether the parties are entitled, and under and subject to what charges and incumbrances (1).

SEE the note to *Binford* v. *Bawden*, 1 V. 512.

BRETTELL, *Ex parte.*

[1801, DEC. 22.]

UNDER a general residuary disposition by will to a natural son, his heirs, executors, administrators, and assigns, for ever, to and for his and their own proper use and behoof, a trust estate did not pass (a).

By an order, dated the 18th of November, 1801, the Master was directed to inquire, how certain real estates were vested in George Brettell, an infant; and whether he was an infant trustee or mortgagee within the statute (2).

* The Master's Report stated a mortgage in fee in   [* 577] 1775 of gravel-kind lands in Kent to Thomas Brettell, as trustee for John Brettell. Thomas Brettell died in 1795; having, by his will, dated the 15th of January, 1791, duly executed according to the Statute of Frauds (3), made the following residuary disposition:

"All the rest, residue, and remainder of my estate and effects whatsoever and wheresoever and of what nature or kind soever, I give and bequeath the same unto my natural son George Hall, now a midshipman belonging to my ship the Canton, his heirs, executors, administrators, and assigns, for ever, to and for his and their own proper use and behoof."

The testator appointed William Lushington and the said John Brettell his executors. George Hall afterwards assumed the name of Brettell; and in 1800 died, a widower and intestate, leaving a

---

(1) *Ante, Ex parte Bennet, Ex parte Dolman*, 116. See the note, vol. i. 512.

(a) Notwithstanding this case, it seems to be received that lands held by a testator, as mortgagee or trustee, will pass by the general words in a will, unless it can be collected from the language of the will, or the purposes and objects of the testator, that the intention was otherwise. See *ante*, note (a), *Leeds* v. *Munday*, 3 V. 348.

(2) 7 Anne, c. 19.

(3) 29 Char. II. c. 3.

daughter, named Ann, and a son, named George, his only children, both now infants under the age of four years; and administration was granted to John Brettell and James Farrer, the guardians of the infants, until one of them should attain the age of twenty-one. John Brettell died on the 21st of May, 1801, intestate; and administration of his personal estate was granted to his widow, Ann Brettell; who was entitled to the equity of redemption previously to her marriage.

The Master stated, that he was of opinion, that the said real estates passed by the said devise in the will of Thomas Brettell; and were then vested in George Brettell; the infant, as the [* 578] only *son and heir of George Hall, otherwise Brettell; and that the said George Brettell was an infant mortgagee within the Statute.

The petition was presented by Ann Brettell; praying, that the Report may be confirmed; and that the infant may be directed to convey.

Mr. *Romilly*, in support of the Petition.—The last case, *The Attorney General* v. *Buller* (1), contradicts the former, *Ex parte Sergison* (2). The Lord Chancellor there understands the rule to be, that an intention to pass the trust estate must be shown. In this will no such intention appears. The most general words are used: and this also is a disposition to a natural child; and it will be very inconvenient, if the trust estate goes to him. As there is no inference of intention, upon the authority of that case the Master's Report is wrong. The words in that will "all my real and personal estate, not before hereby given," &c., might be supposed to refer to trust estates.

Lord CHANCELLOR [ELDON].—When the rule comes to be put upon the intention appearing in the will, it raises a class of cases, which it is very difficult to dispose of. With respect to the convenience, I rather agree with what the Attorney General says in the case referred to; for, besides an estate tail, you cannot tell, how many contingent remainders and executory devises there may be. When the testator speaks of estates in trust for him, and says nothing about estates in him in trust for other persons, the inference is, that he did not mean them. In this instance it is very strong from the circumstance, that the person, to whom the testator gives the residue of his estate, is a natural son; and if he should die without children and without a will, the legal estate might go to the Crown. On the other hand, the testator meaning to give every thing he had to the natural son might very probably mean to give every thing, that would fall within those general words. This discussion began with Sir Thomas Sewell; and his idea was, that the word "my" would not refer to what was not beneficially his. In this will there are the words "to and for his and their own

---

(1) *Ante*, vol. v. 339; see the notes, 341; and vol. iii. 349.
(2) *Ante*, vol. iv. 147.

proper use and behoof." Probably the testator meant nothing by that: but a meaning must be attributed to every word. I rather think, there is not enough here to make the infant a trustee.

Declare, the infant is not a trustee within the statute; and therefore dismiss the petition (1).

THAT, under a general devise, estates held by the devisor on mortgage, or in trust, will pass, unless from the context of the will, or from a disposition not consistent with a limited right, it can be collected, that he did not mean to pass such estates; see, *ante*, note 7 to *The Attorney General* v. *Bowyer*, 3 V. 714.

• WARD, *Ex parte.*

[1801, DEC. 22.]

ANY fair and reasonably provident application as to the execution of a Commission of lunacy is not discouraged: but in this instance the petition being wholly groundless was dismissed with costs (a).
Whether a mere stranger having no interest would be permitted to traverse an Inquisition of lunacy, *Quære.*
Right to traverse an Inquisition of lunacy under the statute 2 Edw. VI. c. 8, s. 6, [p. 580.]

THIS petition, praying leave to traverse an Inquisition of lunacy, was presented by an entire stranger without any interest. An objection was taken upon that ground; and upon the affidavits it was clear, there was no ground for impeaching the Commission.

Mr. *Romilly* and Mr. *Thompson*, in support of the petition. Mr. *Mansfield*, for the committee.

Lord CHANCELLOR [ELDON].—This petitioner does not qualify in himself any interest; and I do not recollect any instance, in which the Court has permitted a mere stranger to traverse the inquisition (2). I will not say without farther consideration, when it may be necessary to decide the point, whether the Court would permit it or not. Whatever may be the rule as to that, I should hope, the wisdom, policy, and humanity, of the law with regard to these unhappy persons would never be disappointed: for my own experience enables me to say, the Court has not been in the habit of discouraging any

---

(1) In *Lord Braybroke* v. *Inskip, post,* vol. viii. 417, upon consideration of all the cases it was decided, that a general devise will pass a trust estate; unless the contrary intention can be collected from expressions in the will, or purposes or objects of the testator: and the Lord Chancellor disclaims any conclusion in this case from the expression, that it was given to the use and behoof of the party farther than as he could collect the intention to give a property, which he could enjoy as beneficially as his own.

(a) As to commissions of lunacy, see 2 Story, Eq. Jur. § 1365; 2 Barb. Ch. Pr. 227, 228; *Wendell's Case,* 1 Johns. Ch. 600; *Hawk's Case,* 3 Johns. Ch. 567; *M'Clean's Case,* 6 Johns. Ch. 440.

(2) See Amb. 112; *Fust's Case,* 1 Cox, 418.

fair and reasonably provident application with regard to the situation of a person, allowed to be a lunatic (1), if he is more pressed in the execution of the commission than a tender and humane consideration of his circumstances would authorise, or of a person not allowed to be a lunatic, but made the object of a commission. The law has provided, that no person shall be put in such a situation, deprived of his liberty and the administration of his affairs, until the

[* 580]   fact is ascertained by a proceeding, that I must admit to be *ex parte:* a proceeding, which the law * supposes may collect mistake; and therefore has given a positive right to certain persons to traverse the inquisition (2).

This is the petition of a person, who, as far as I can perceive upon the affidavits, lays no foundation whatever for impeaching the Commission in any one circumstance at the same period as the finding of the Jury; but certainly not in any one circumstance of conduct or misconduct, that has happened since the finding. The petition therefore must be dismissed. As to the costs, though I do not think, the true interest of lunatics is consulted by persons, who act upon their own views of the sanity or insanity, formed upon occasional conversations, and come too rashly to this Court without sufficient inquiry, yet it is the duty of the Court not to censure too hastily any application upon a subject so very important as this. In this particular case I do not think, that censure would be too hasty; and therefore the petitioner must pay the costs: the petition being ill founded, and most rashly presented: but if the parties on the other side will act so far upon the general principle, inclining the Court not to discourage applications of this nature, they will sacrifice to general humanity by not calling for the costs. If however they do call for them, I am of opinion upon the whole, I cannot very well refuse them.

The Petition was dismissed with costs.

As to the general doctrine with respect to traverses of inquisitions of lunacy, see, *ante,* the notes to *Ex parte Wragg,* 5 V. 450. The recent statute of 6 Geo. IV. c. 53, allows *any* person, giving the requisite security, to traverse an inquisition.

---

(1) *Ex parte Ogle, post,* vol. xv. 112.
(2) Stat. 2 Edw. VI. c. 8, s. 6; *Ex parte Wragg, Ex parte Ferne, ante,* vol. v. 450, 832; see the note, 452; and as to a traverse to a Commission of Escheat, *Ex parte Webster, post,* 809.

JONES *v.* PENGREE.

[1801, Dec. 21, 26.]

PLEA, covering too much, ordered to stand for an answer, with liberty to except (*a*).
Whether transactions between principal and agent are within the Exception in
the Statute of Limitations as to merchants' accounts, *Quære* (*b*).
Whether, in order to have the benefit of the Exception in the Statute of Limitations as to merchants' accounts, some transaction must have passed within six
years, *Quære* (*c*).

THE bill stated, that the Defendant George Pengree carried on
business in partnership with several persons, among other things
in large copper works and concerns in the county of Glamorgan;
and Benjamin Jones was employed by the Company as their
agent; and they were indebted to Jones at his death in
*May 1787. Jones during his agency made remittances [*581]
by bills, &c. to the Defendant and Company and others
to the amount of 5912*l*. 14*s*. 5*d*. and upwards; and he also lent and
advanced to the Defendant 500*l*.; for which the Defendant gave
Jones his promisory note, payable with interest: but such note is
lost; and was never satisfied. The Defendant is the surviving partner, or if the other partners are not dead, the Defendant by virtue of
some arrangement with him is become solely liable to the partnership debts; and there are mutual accounts unliquidated between
the Plaintiff, as administratrix of Benjamin Jones, and the Defendant. The bill charged, that the accounts of dealings and transactions between the parties in 1785 and 1786 were never settled, by
the negligence of the Defendant; that if any accounts were settled,

(*a*) When a plea is ordered to stand for an answer, it is merely determined, that
it contains matter, which may be a defence, or part of a defence; but that it is
not a full defence; or that it has been informally offered by way of plea; or that
it has not been properly supported by an answer, so that the truth of it is doubtful.
Story, Eq. Pl. § 699; Mitford, Eq. Pl. by Jeremy, 303; *Orcutt* v. *Orms*, 3 Paige,
459. It is allowed to be a sufficient answer to so much of the bill as it covers,
unless, by the order, liberty is given to except. Ib. *Leacroft* v. *Dempsey*,
4 Paige, 124.

(*b*) The accounts must be "such as concern the trade of merchandise," "between merchant and merchant, their factors, or servants." See W. W. Story,
Contracts, § 702; *Blair* v. *Drew*, 6 N. H. 235; *Codman* v. *Rogers*, 10 Pick. 118;
Spring v. *Gray*, 6 Peters, 151; *S. C.* 5 Mason, 528. In the latter case Mr. Justice Story has discussed all the cases on the exception of merchants' accounts
with his accustomed accuracy and learning. Unliquidated accounts between
merchants, in the capacity of principal and factor, have been held to be within
the exception. *Stiles* v. *Donaldson*, 2 Dall. 264; *S. C.* 2 Yeates, 105.

(*c*) The Exception does not apply to *stated* accounts. *Webber* v. *Tivill*,
2 Saund. 125; *Toland* v. *Sprague*, 12 Peters, 300. It has been held to apply in
the following cases to *closed* accounts. *Mandeville* v. *Wilson*, 5 Cranch, 15; *Bass*
v. *Bass*, 6 Pick. 362; *Davis* v. *Smith*, 4 Greenl. 339; *Sherman* v. *Sherman*, 2 Vern.
276; *S. C.* Eq. Cas. Abr. 12; *Catling* v. *Skoulding*, 6 T. R. 193; contra *Union
Bank* v. *Knapp*, 3 Pick. 96. But the great weight of authority constrains its
application to accounts running within the space of six years. *Spring* v. *Gray*,
5 Mason, 528; *S. C.* 6 Peters, 151; *Union Bank* v. *Knapp*, 3 Pick. 96; *Coster* v.
Murray, 5 Johns. Ch. 522. In the last case the authorities on this point are ably
collected and considered by Mr. Chancellor Kent.

they are erroneous : stating various remittances in 1783 by Jones;
and that the Defendant has frequently within the last six years admitted, that he was indebted to Benjamin Jones, as aforesaid, and
promised to account; but pretends, Jones was indebted to him;
and refuses to render an account, &c. ; and prayed an account, &c.

As to so much of the bill as seeks an account of any dealings
and transactions between Benjamin Jones and the Defendant in his
separate capacity, or the Defendant and his partners, and a discovery touching such account, and to compel the Defendant to pay
any balance, &c., and as to any relief prayed upon the foundation
of any such accounts, the Defendant pleaded in bar, that if the
Plaintiff had any cause of suit, concerning the matters in the bill
mentioned, the same arose above six years before filing the bill and
serving the Defendant with process; averring, that within six years
he did not admit, that he was indebted to the Plaintiff in any manner whatsoever; and did not promise or agree to account, &c.; and
therefore pleaded the Statute of Limitations (1).

And as to so much of the bill as the Defendant had not pleaded
to, he answered, admitting the trading, &c., the employment of
Jones, as agent, and that in the course of such employment he paid
and received large sums belonging to the partnership, but not any
other sums, as the Defendant knows or believes, on ac-
[* 582]   count of * the partnership. He denied, that Jones lent
money to the partners, or that the Defendant received
money to the use of Jones, or that the Defendant and his partners
were indebted to Jones, &c. He also denied, that he lent Jones
500l. or any other sum upon his promisory note, or otherwise. He
stated, that he believes, Jones died, as mentioned in the bill; and
the Plaintiff is his administratrix; that Lawrence Bond was a partner with the Defendant : and does not know, whether he is living,
or not: if dead, admits, he (the Defendant) is solely liable, as sole
surviving partner : if living, denies, that he (the Defendant) is solely
liable. He denies any application till shortly before the bill; that
any accounts were unsettled through his negligence; that he made
any admission within six years, that he was indebted to Jones; or
promised to account, &c. (as charged by the bill). He stated his
belief, that Jones died insolvent; and the Plaintiff lay in gaol for a
small sum; therefore submits, if she had any demand, she would
not have permitted it to lie so long dormant.

Mr. *Romilly* and Mr. *Heald*, in support of the plea.—One objection, that will be made to this plea, is, that these are merchants' accounts; and therefore the Statute of Limitations does not apply.
These are not merchants' accounts : but, if they were, the exception (2) in the Statute extends only to cases, in which there has
been some transaction within six years; and then the effect is to

(1) Stat. 21 James I. c. 16, s. 3.
(2) It does not extend to the case of a tradesman and his customers : *Coles* v.
Harris, 1 Esp. Dig. 151; *Wace* v. *Wyburn*, Bul. N. P. 149.

take the whole out of the Statute: *Welford* v. *Liddel* (1). In
Crawfurd v. *Liddel* (2) the bill prayed an account of transactions
under a patent for extracting oil from tar. A plea of the statute
was put in; with an averment, that these were not merchants' accounts. For the Plaintiff *Catling* v. *Skoulding* (3) was cited: but
Lord Rosslyn was of opinion, that the meaning of the exception in
the statute was, that if any transaction between the parties took
place within six years, none of the transactions shall be barred; but
that, where all the transactions were over more than six years, the
statute might be pleaded as well to merchants' accounts as others;
and the plea was allowed.

* The jurisdiction of this Court as to putting limits to   [* 583]
suits does not depend upon the Statute; but is much older.
Smith v. *Clay* (4).

Mr. *Owen*, for the Plaintiff.—The object of this bill is an account
of transactions unliquidated, that took place in the life of Benjamin
Jones; and the charge is, that there were mutual accounts between
the parties. Anticipating a supposed defence, that accounts were
settled every year, the bill states, that in 1785 and 1786 no accounts
whatsoever were settled, by the default and negligence of the Defendant; and suggests a variety of errors in the accounts supposed
to be settled in 1783. Another charge is the admission of the debt
within the last six years, and the pretence of cross demands; which
he refuses to discover.

The defence against this bill is a plea of the Statute of Limitations and an answer. The objection now urged from the length of
time and inconvenience of unravelling accounts, &c. may be material at the hearing; but cannot avail upon the argument of the plea.
To the plea there are various objections. The introductory part
goes, not only to the dealings and transactions allowed by the bill to
have passed more than six years ago, but to any discovery relating
to them; which goes even to those charges introduced for the purpose of taking the case out of the Statute; covering therefore that
part, to which the Plaintiff is entitled to an answer, and to which
the Defendant has given an answer. The next part is an evasive
plea of *Non assumpsit infra sex annos:* a sort of answer; that he
has not admitted within six years, that he is indebted to the Plaintiff in any manner whatsoever, and did not promise or agree within
six years to come to an account; and this is followed by an answer
in the very same words. In that respect it is very multifarious.
All this part of the plea may be true, that he did not within six

---

(1) 2 Ves. 400. That question, discussed at the bar in *Duff* v. *East India
Company*, *post*, vol. xv. 198, was decided, as here stated, in *Barber* v. *Barber*,
xviii. 286. See xix. 185; *Foster* v. *Hodgson*, and Mr. Beames's Elements of Pleas
in Equity, 163.

(2) Before Lord Rosslyn, 15th Nov. 1796.

(3) 6 Term Rep. B. R. 189.

(4) Amb. 645; the note to *Lord Deloraine* v. *Browne*, 3 Bro. C. C. 633; *Hercy*
v. *Dinwoody*, 4 Bro. C. C. 257; *ante*, vol. ii. 87; *Jones* v. *Turberville*, ii. 11, and
the note, 15.

years admit, that he was indebted, or promise to account; and yet
it may be true, that he had not paid the Plaintiff; pretending a great
counter-demand.

Next; this is within the exception of the Statute. It does not
appear, that the case before Lord Hardwicke was a case
[* 584] of merchants' * accounts. The exception in the Statute
is general. In *Catlin* v. *Skoulding* Lord Kenyon says (1)
distinctly, that merchants' accounts are out of the Statute. There
was an item within six years; upon which they let it go to a Jury:
but it was decidedly held, that if it appears upon the plea or replication, that they were merchants' accounts, no length of time is a
bar. The words " factor or servant " are nugatory; unless the exception applies to a transaction between a merchant and his servant.

A plea also may be bad, as not covering enough : *Blacket* v. *Longlands* (2). This plea is also defective in that respect. It ought to
go to every thing, except the charges introduced into the bill for the
purpose of taking the case out of the Statute ; which it is necessary
to answer. A plea of the Statute of Limitations is a plea in bar;
which admits the title of the Plaintiff to sue the Defendant. This
plea consequently admits, that the Plaintiff as administratrix has a
right to sue the Defendant in respect of these transactions. Then
the Defendant has over-ruled his plea by answering to the very parts,
to which the plea goes : *Pope* v. *Bish* (3). The answer goes on to
state, what is in the nature of a dilatory plea, that Bond is a necessary party. He has not answered the material charge ; which if ad-
itted, is sufficient of itself to take the case out of the Statute.

Mr. *Romilly*, in reply.—In *Catling* v. *Skoulding* there is only a
ictum. Merchants' accounts, if no transaction has passed within six
ears, are not taken out of the Statute by the exception. It is very
doubtful, whether this can be considered a case of merchants' accounts : a gentleman possessing copper works; and employing an
agent on them.

Lord CHANCELLOR [ELDON].—The Plaintiff states, that the other
partners are dead ; but not as an absolute fact; but, that if they are
not dead, the Defendant by virtue of some arrangement is become
solely liable to the partnership debts. That is denied by the answer.
Then, will the plea, that he, who says he is not solely answerable,
has not promised within six years, sufficiently nega-
[* 585] tive, that some of the other persons have not promised?
Will that answer support the plea ?

Reply.—It is only necessary to meet by averments those allegations, that take the case out of the Statute; and the allegation is,
that only the Defendant promised. In *Blacket* v. *Longlands* any answer must have over-ruled the plea ; as the plea was to all the relief
and discovery : but this Defendant must put in an answer. " In all
these cases if any matter is charged by the bill, which may avoid the

(1) 6 Term Rep. B. R. 193.
(2) 1 Anst. 14.
(3) 1 Anst. 59. See *Bayley* v. *Adams*, *post*, 576.

bar created by the Statute, that matter must be denied, generally, by way of averment in the plea; and it must be denied particularly and precisely by way of answer to support the plea (1)." The reason is, that the Plaintiff is entitled by Exceptions to compel the Defendant to answer precisely to all the cases put, in this bill for instance, as exceptions to the Statute. It is not necessary in the plea to give the reason for saying, he is not indebted; and that is the reason, that there must be an answer; that the Plaintiff may have the opportunity of excepting. In the averments of the plea it is only necessary to state the fact generally, without descending to all the particulars. The allegation of this bill is merely, that the Defendant admitted within six years, that he was indebted; not stating an admission, that there were unsettled accounts.

Upon the objection, that the plea is over-ruled by the answer, the Defendant has pleaded to the account and discovery of these partnership dealings and transactions. But a distinct transaction is stated in the bill; that Jones lent the Defendant 500l.; and the note given for that sum is lost. That is stated as quite a distinct transaction. The Defendant has not pleaded to the discovery of that; though above six years ago. It was never held, that, where a Plaintiff states two demands, to each of which a plea of the Statute lies, he cannot use it as to one, and not as to the other. As to that distinct demand the Defendant has not availed himself of the Statute; but has given the discovery. Upon this argument it must be taken, that the answer is sufficient; as by excepting it may be made so; but that objection never can be used upon the argument of a plea.

*As to the objection, that this is multifarious, the De-   [*586 fendant must of necessity state, that the cause of action did not arise within six years; and the *assumpsit* within six years, if charged, must be denied.

Mr. *Owen* observed, that the plea certainly extended to the transaction as to the 504l. by the words in the introduction "in his separate capacity."

Lord CHANCELLOR.—My present opinion is, that this plea is not good. I think, the answer covers a great deal too much (2).

Dec. 26th. The plea was ordered to stand for an answer with liberty to except (3).

___

1. THERE having been conflicting decisions on the question, whether the exception in the Statute of Limitations, (21 Jac. 1, c. 16, s. 3,) in favor of accounts between merchants, applies, where there has been no dealing whatever between the parties within six years, or whether it is necessary that the last *item* of the account, at least, should have occurred within that time: *Foster* v. *Hodgson*, 19 Ves. 185: but the last express decision upon the subject establishes the rule, that the statute will be a bar, where all accounts have ceased for more than six years. *Barber* v. *Barber*, 18 Ves. 286.

___

(1) Mitf. 212.
(2) See Mr. Beames's Elements of Pleas in Equity, 37, 9.
(3) See *Bayley* v. *Adams, infra.*

2. A plea, which, even if its statement were admitted, alleges nothing that would be a good defence to the bill brought against the defendant, must, of course, be overruled; but a more frequent ground of objection to a plea is, that it covers too much; in which case, it is usually ordered to stand for an answer, with liberty to except: *Maitland* v. *Wilson*, 3 Atk. 814: if the last-intimated condition were not added to the order, and the plea (not being coupled with, or supported by, an answer) went to the whole bill, the plaintiff could not except; for the Court by saying, without more, that the plea should stand for an answer, must be intended to have meant a *sufficient* answer: *Sellon* v. *Lewen*, 3 P. Wms. 239 : but, wh're an answer in support of the plea has been put in, and any material allegation in the bill is untouched by such answer, there, although the plea may be ordered to stand for an answer, without liberty to except, as far as relates to the plea; yet exceptions may be taken to the answer by which it is supported. *Coke* v. *Wilcocks*, Mosely, 73; see the note to the next following case but one.

---

(1) DOWNES *v.* THE EAST INDIA COMPANY.

[1802, JAN. 16.]

ORDER for Defendants to be at liberty to withdraw a demurrer set down to be argued, on payment of costs to be taxed.

A MOTION was made on behalf of the Defendants for liberty to withdraw a demurrer ; which was set down to be argued.

Lord CHANCELLOR [ELDON] made the order on payment of costs to be taxed.

WHEN a fair case is made out, and the application comes in good time, it is in the discretion of the Court to give a defendant leave to amend his demurrer, upon proper terms. *Baker* v. *Mellish*, 11 Ves. 70, 76.

---

(1) *Ex relatione.*

BAYLEY. v. ADAMS.

[1802, JAN. 19.]

PLEA of the Statute of Limitations, supported by an answer, ordered to stand for an answer, with liberty to except: the charges of the bill not being sufficiently answered (a).
Whether the charges of the bill must be met by way of averment in the plea, as well as by the answer, Quære (b).
Office of a plea in bar at law to confess the right to sue, and avoid it by matter dehors : so in this Court in general cases, [p. 594.]
The excepted cases; where the plea must be supported by an answer (c), [p. 594.]

THE bill which was filed by the executors of Joseph Winder on the 20th of February, 1801, stated, that the Defendant from June, 1771, till November, 1775, employed Winder as his stock-broker and also as his agent or banker in London; during which time the Defendant transmitted Navy Bills to be sold ; for the produce of which as well as other remittances the De-   [* 587] fendant drew upon Winder from time to time : or otherwise such produce was paid by Winder to him when he came to London.   On the 3d of October, 1771, an account was settled ; upon which a balance of 899l. 16s. 4d. was due to the Defendant. On the 17th of January, 1772, they settled another account, which was signed by the Defendant; upon which a balance of 90l. was due to the Defendant.   From that time, though Winder sent accounts from time to time, no farther account was settled between them until the 17th of August, 1783 ; on which day another account was settled ; upon which the balance due to the Defendant was 168l. 18s. 11d.

The bill farther stated, that though the last account was not signed by the Defendant, it was admitted to be correct in various letters written by him and by Anthony Adams, his nephew, by his direction ; particularly by a letter, dated the 27th of November, 1775;

_____

(a) As to the effect of ordering a plea to stand for an answer with liberty to except, see ante, p. 580, note (a), Jones v. Pengree.

(b) It is now firmly established, that the plea, as well as the answer, must contain averments, negativing the circumstances set up in the bill in avoidance of the defence.   Story, Eq. Pl. § 680, 754; Mitford, Eq. Pl. by Jeremy, 239–241, 298, 299 ; Heath v. Corning, 3 Paige, 566 ; Foley v. Hill, 3 Mylne & C. 475.   Thus, a plea of the Statute of Limitations should contain averments, denying the charges of the bill ; and it should also be accompanied by an answer in support of the plea, answering and denying the circumstances of fraud, and the other circumstances, which go to avoid the bar.   Story, Eq. Pl. § 754 ; Hovenden v. Annesley, 2 Sch. & Lef. 635 ; Goodrich v. Pendleton, 3 Johns. Ch. 384 ; Kane v. Bloodgood, 7 Johns. Ch. 134 ; S. C. 2 Cowen, 360.

(c) Pleas are divided into two sorts; one commonly called pure pleas, which rely wholly on matters dehors the bill, such as a release, or a settled account.   Story, Eq. Pl. § 651, 667.   The others are called, in contradistinction, pleas not pure, or anomalous pleas, and sometimes negative pleas.   They rely wholly on matters stated in the bill negativing such facts as are material to the rights of the plaintiff ; and they require an answer to be filed which is subsidiary to the purposes of the plea.   Ib. § 670; Mitford, Eq. Pl. by Jeremy, 244, note (f); Foley v. Hill, 3 Mylne & C. 475.

wherein the nephew desired Winder to send down his account from the 17th of August, 1773, to that time, and his uncle would make remittances. Winder accordingly sent the Defendant an account up to the 13th of November, 1775 ; by which a balance of 1002*l.* 9*s.* 1*d.* appeared due to Winder.

The bill then stated, that, after the aforesaid account had been so delivered to the Defendant, Winder made repeated application for payment of the balance by letters and otherwise ; and the letters, which he wrote to the Defendant from the end of November 1775, are now in the Defendant's possession or power : but the Defendant, though he at times admitted, that the last mentioned account was correct, and that the balance of 1002*l.* 9*s* 1*d.* was due from him to Winder, yet under various pretences evaded the payment thereof ; and he and Benjamin Adams, his son, by his advice, wrote several letters to Winder, in which they made the aforesaid admission ; and fixed several different times from the Defendant's coming to London and settling the said account, and paying the balance ; and the Defendant was in London in September 1790 ; and he then under pretences, that there was some difference between his account and Winder's, or some other pretences, prevailed on Winder to entrust him with the vouchers for the payments, [* 588] amounting to 14,313*l.* 13*s* 7*d.*, to examine ; and * he gave Winder a receipt for them, dated the 25th of September, 1790 ; which is now in the Plaintiff's possession. Winder afterwards made repeated attempts to have the account settled and the balance paid to him by the Defendant ; but he was not able to accomplish it ; and particularly in his last illness, and a few days previous to his death, he caused the last mentioned account to be transcribed ; and struck the balance in his own hand ; and it was his intention to have taken legal measures to enforce the payment ; but he died before he had an opportunity, on the 23d of March, 1795.

The bill then stating, that the Plaintiffs had several times applied to the Defendant to settle the account, and pay the balance, and that he refused, sometimes pretending, that no such transactions had taken place, at other times, that he had paid the balance to Winder, charged the contrary ; and that though the Defendant frequently promised to pay the aforesaid balance of 1002*l.* 9*s.* 1*d.*, yet he never did in fact pay any part thereof to Winder in his life, but that the whole (with the exception of an error to the amount of 1*l.* 7*s.* 8*d.*, charged to the Defendant twice) was due to Winder at his death. The bill farther stated, that the Defendant will at times admit that ; but then pretends, that the Plaintiffs are barred by the Statute of Limitations from recovering any part of the aforesaid balance from him ; whereas the Plaintiffs charge the contrary ; and that after the death of Winder the Plaintiffs applied to John Adams, the son of the Defendant who resides in London, for a settlement of the aforesaid account ; and the said John Adams, who acted in that behalf as the agent of the said Defendant, informed the Plaintiffs, that the said Defendant was equally desirous with the Plaintiffs to have the account settled ; but, that the vouchers, relating to it, and which had been delivered to the said Defendant by Winder, had been lost ; and he desired to have a copy of the account, as made out and balanced by Winder, delivered to him ; and he promised, it should be examined and settled ; and the Plaintiffs farther charge, that they did cause a copy of the said account to be made out and delivered to him ; and he agreed to refer the said account to arbitration, but afterwards receded from such agreement; and refused to do so.

*The bill then stating other pretences of errors, par-   [*589] ticularly an error of 1000*l.* in the account settled and signed by the Defendant on the 17th of January, 1772, Winder not having given credit for the sum produced by the sale of a Navy Bill for 1000*l.*, charged the contrary ; and that the accounts were correct in every item ; that the Defendant was in London, when the said Navy Bill was sold : and the produce thereof was paid to him by Winder, and in support of that charging, that it appears from the account settled on the 17th of January, 1772, and the fact is, that Winder received from the Defendant on the 8th of January, 1772, the day, on which the said Navy Bill was sold, 81*l.* 3*s.* ; for which as well as a smaller sum received from him on the day the account was settled, Winder gave the Defendant credit in the account; and therefore the Defendant would have discovered the omission of 1000*l.*, and would not have signed that account, or settled and allowed the account of the 13th of August, 1773, in which the sum of 1*l.* 7*s.* 8*d.* is again by mistake charged for commission on sale of the same Navy Bill, had not the produce thereof been previously paid to him ; and the Plaintiffs farther charge, that the Defendant never applied to Winder or made any demand for the produce of the said Navy Bill ; and that the Defendant has made some entry in some of his books of account or memorandums of the receipt of the produce of the said Navy Bill, amounting to 980*l.* or thereabouts ; and such books, &c. are now in his custody or power : but he refuses to produce the same; and he has also in his custody or power all the vouchers relating to the payment of the aforesaid 14,318*l.* 13*s.* 7*d.*, which were delivered to him by Winder.

The bill prayed an account of all the aforesaid dealings, &c. and payment of what shall appear due ; and that the said vouchers may be delivered up.

The Defendant put in a plea and answer. As to so much of the bill as states, alleges, or charges, any accounts, dealings, or transactions, to have subsisted, passed, or taken place, between the Defendant and Winder, and seeks to have any answer or discovery from the Defendant touching all or any such accounts, &c., and as to the whole of the relief sought or prayed by the bill, * the   [*590] Defendant pleads the Statute of Limitations (1) ; and the Defendant avers, that the causes of action or suit against the Defend-

---

(1) 21 James I. c. 16, s. 3.

ant in the said bill `stated, alleged, or mentioned, or any of such causes, did not arise or accrue at any time within six years next before the day of filing the said bill.

And the Defendant not waiving his said plea, &c. for answer to the residue of the said bill, &c. saith, he hath been informed, and believes it to be true, that his son John Adams, in the bill named, who resides in London, and hath for some time occasionally acted as the Defendant's agent in London, was applied to by the complainants after the death of Winder for some such purpose as in the bill mentioned : but this Defendant doth not know, nor hath been informed save by the bill, nor doth believe, that the said John Adams on that or any occasion informed the complainants or any of them, that this Defendant was desirous to have the account in the bill mentioned settled ; or that the vouchers relating thereto, and which are in the bill alleged to have been delivered to the Defendant by the said Joseph Winder, had been lost, or to that or any such effect: nor doth the Defendant know, nor hath been informed, save by the bill, nor doth he believe, that the said John Adams on being so applied to or on any occasion promised, that the account in the bill mentioned should be examined and settled, or to that or any such effect.

Saith, he does not know, nor hath been informed, save by the bill, nor doth believe, that the said John Adams at any time or upon any occasion agreed with the complainants to refer the accounts in the bill mentioned to arbitration.   `

Saith, that he never directed, empowered, or authorised, the said John Adams to make any such promise or request as in the bill mentioned to the complainants, or to refer or agree to refer the accounts in the bill mentioned to arbitration ; and the Defendant denies all unlawful combination and confederacy in and by the said bill charged.

Mr. *Romilly* and Mr. *Johnson*, in support of the plea.—The object of this bill is an account of transactions, which [* 591]   ended * twenty-six years before the bill was filed ; which was only a month within the six years.   The principal objection will be, that the facts stated in the answer ought also to be inserted by way of averment in the plea.   But why should they be repeated ?   In *Pope* v. *Bish* (1) and *Edmundson* v. *Hartley* (2) it was on that ground held, that the answer overruled the plea.   The first consideration is, whether the bill contains any allegation of fact, that takes the case out of the Statute.   Upon the bill there is no promise by the Defendant or any person authorised for that purpose by him ; the allegation is only, that the son of the Defendant, acting without his authority as his agent, made the promise.   The bill does not state, that he had authority: or, that he had acted upon any other occasion as agent of the Defendant.   As there is no allegation of that nature, no averment upon that subject is necessary in the plea.

If however that statement in the bill is considered as taking the case out of the Statute, then upon the authority of the cases in the Exchequer the denial by the answer is sufficient, without also a denial by way of averment in the plea. The case (1) referred to in the passage in Mitford (2) against this does not contain any decision of the point, for which it is referred to. Since that case the general form of pleading this Statute has been, that the cause of action hath not accrued within six years; and that is correct; for it follows the Statute. There are certainly *dicta* in support of the general proposition stated by Mitford, that there must be denials by averment in the plea and also by an answer: but there is no authority for that; and it is inconsistent with the office of a plea, to reduce the cause to a single point. Instead of shortening the cause a plea would have the effect of creating a necessity for double averments, by the plea and the answer. The case, in which it is necessary to have averments by the plea also, is, where those facts make part of the equitable bar; as in the case of a purchase for valuable consideration notice must be denied; for the purchase without that is not a bar. But there is nothing in this bill calling for any averment beyond the general one introducing the plea of the Statute.

No special promise is * alleged. As to *Edmundson* v. [* 592] *Hartley*, many cases, in which the party has been permitted to plead the thing, which the bill seeks to set aside, are stated by Mitford (3); as an award, a release, &c.; but there is no authority for the position, that the circumstances must be denied both by plea and answer.

Mr. *Alexander* and Mr. *Pemberton*, for the Plaintiff.—The reason of the rule, upon which the first objection rests, is, that the plea should constitute a complete bar to the suit. Therefore the plea must by averment answer the charges, which, if true, would avoid the plea. That is the reason stated in Mitford. If the Plaintiff takes issue upon the plea, and it does not contain a complete answer to the bill, the plea may be proved; and yet the case stated by the bill may entitle the Plaintiff to succeed. The reason, upon which a denial by answer is also necessary, is, that the averments of the plea need not follow the charge particularly. That must therefore be done by answer; in order that the Plaintiff may have an opportunity of excepting. It is assumed, that the son acted as agent of his own authority: but it must be intended, that he acted as an agent properly constituted. The allegation is sufficient to call for answer; and therefore according to the rules of pleading it is sufficient to call for averments by the plea. Another objection is, that there never was a plea of this kind without a denial of a promise within the six years, as at law, *non assumpsit infra sex annos*, as

(1) 3 Atk. 70.
(2) Mitf. 212, 13.
(3) Mitf. 209.

well as, that the cause of action accrued within six years. All pleas
of this sort also contain an averment, not only, that there was no
promise or cause of action within six years before the bill filed, but
also, before any process issued; and though the act of Parliament (1) certainly requires the bill to be filed, before process
issues, the constant practice is otherwise; and the irregularity is
cured by appearance. Some charges of this bill are not noticed
either by the plea or the answer: one allegation, which by fair construction may be supposed to include promises to Winder; that he
made repeated applications for payment of the balance. It was
necessary to aver by this plea, that the Defendant had made no such
promise as is stated, and that his son was not authorised to settle
the business. *Davie* v. *Chester* (2) and *Hoare* v. *Par-*
[* 593]   *ker* (3) are express authorities in support of the * position
in Mitford. The object of a plea is to bring a single point
in issue; and upon this plea these facts would not be in issue. The
plea is also bad, as being both to discovery and relief. The Statute
of Limitations clearly cannot be pleaded to the discovery of the time,
when the cause of action accrued.

Mr. *Romilly*, in Reply.—As to the discovery wanted, they may
except to the answer. The constant practice is to plead the Statute
to a bill for discovery merely. The last plea of this sort (4) was
both to discovery and relief; and no such objection was taken.

The great objection is to the necessity of averments in the plea.
There is no judicial authority, that distinctly proves that, except
Davie v. *Chester*. In the case in Atkyns (5) the objection was, that
the Defendant had not answered the circumstances; not that he had
not answered them by the plea; for which point it is referred to in
Mitford (6). The same book refers to *Lingood* v. *Croucher* (7)
and *Lingood* v. *Eade* (8). *Hoare* v. *Parker* does not in the least
apply. The plea was as to particular pieces of plate: but there was
no general averment, that the Defendant had not any other plate deposited with him; though by his answer he denied, that he had any
other. Consequently the plea was not alone an answer to the bill;
and the Plaintiff was under the necessity of replying to both the
plea and the answer. According to this argument issue must be
taken upon a great number of points instead of one. Certainly a
plea must be a complete answer to the bill; and therefore a plea of
purchase for valuable consideration must aver, that it was without
notice: so the plea of an award to a bill to set it aside for fraud
must deny fraud: but the question is, whether it must deny all the
circumstances, from which the Plaintiff infers fraud. That is a very

---

(1) Stat. 3 & 4 Ann. c. 16.
(2) Mitf. 217.
(3) Mitf. 217; 1 Bro. C. C. 578.
(4) *Jones* v. *Pengree, ante,* 580.
(5) 3 Atk. 70.
(6) Mitf. 213.
(7) 2 Atk. 395.
(8) 2 Atk. 501.

different question.   The plea of *non assumpsit infra sex annos* at law must in substance be the same as, that the cause of action did not accrue within six years: otherwise, unless a cause of action arose upon the promise, it would not be a case within the statute.   The allegation of this bill as to the promise is not of a promise within six years.   It is only necessary to meet allegations that would take the case out of the Statute, not those, that might by possibility have that *effect.   What principle can there be for   [*594] the distinction taken by the Court of Exchequer upon a plea of an award?   All these pleas of award, releases, &c. have been put upon the same ground.   The objection to the allegation of the son's agency is, that the statement, that he acted as agent, is not stating, that he was agent.   If this plea is wrong, the Defendant will have leave to amend.

Lord CHANCELLOR [ELDON].—With regard to the merits, I should feel a strong inclination to let you amend this plea; for upon the statement of the Plaintiff nothing more is really in dispute than whether credit was given in an account produced a great many years ago for the produce of a Navy Bill.   The question, whether the amendment is necessary, has introduced a great variety of very important considerations.   If the result of the opinion stated in Mitford is accurate, it is very difficult to reconcile the two cases in the Court of Exchequer with that result from the former cases.   Those two cases in the Exchequer seem to import, that this is the rule of pleading in equity; that, if a bill is brought to set aside an award upon grounds admitting the award made, but seeking to cut down the effect of it by alleging grounds of partiality, and corruption, the Defendant may plead the thing, the dissolution of which is sought by the bill; putting it in this form; that the plea shall merely aver the existence of it, and contain no allegation in the body of the plea as to the circumstances, upon which the award is impeached; but the Defendant may express what his conscience suggests as to those circumstances, not in the body of the plea, but in an answer.   The first difficulty upon that is how to consider that record filed by the Defendant, consisting partly of what is called plea, partly of what is called answer, as in a correct sense either a plea or an answer.   The office of a plea in bar at law is to confess the right to sue; avoiding that by matter *dehors*; and giving the Plaintiff an acknowledgment of his right, independent of the matter alleged by the plea.   The plea alleges some short point; upon which, if issue is joined, there is an end of the dispute.   In this Court, in general cases, not classed among those, where certain averments seem to have been required both by the plea and the answer, but, where the Defendant *pro hâc vice* for the sake of the argument, admits the whole bill, I have understood the rule to be the same here as at law, that the plea admitting the bill interposes matter, which, if true, *destroys it; and upon the truth of which the   [*595] Plaintiff is at liberty to take issue.   Cases have arisen, in which it has been thought necessary both to plead, and to repeat the

assertions of the plea in an answer : that is, as it is technically expressed, the plea is supported by an answer.   Those cases are very
various ; and I own, I should have entertained an idea, before I
heard of those cases in the Court of Exchequer, that, if a bill was
filed to set aside an award upon special circumstances, the first difficulty would be upon the maxim referred to by the Report : " *Excep-
tio ejusdem rei, cujus petitur dissolutio.*"

But it is true, that, not only upon awards, but releases, judgments,
&c. the Court had admitted a plea, called a plea, though in its nature
very different from the character of a plea in general cases ; for it is
not, strictly speaking, admitting the fact stated, and by the effect of
new matter, introduced by the Defendant, getting rid of it, but admitting one fact in the bill, and either by plea, or by answer, or by
both, setting up again that, which the bill seeks to impeach, by denying either in the plea, or the answer, or both, all the circumstances, which the Plaintiff admits, if truly denied, are sufficient to bar
the relief.   The cases in the Exchequer are confined to the plain
case of an award ; in which case, it is said, you are at liberty to
plead the award ; in that sense alleging something, that meets the
effect of the bill by the plea.   But can that be said, if you only admit the existence of the instrument stated by the bill ; which by the
effect of the other circumstances stated by the bill is impeached ? If
this were *res integra*, I should have thought it more difficult to say,
the Defendant was bound to set out all the circumstances by averment in the plea ; and could fortify it by an answer denying those
circumstances.   Such a record is neither plea nor answer, but something like a mixture of both, and very inaccurate.   That this was the
general idea is evident from the book, that has been referred to ;
which is the production of a very diligent and learned man, not once
given to the world, or hastily, but after search and research into every
Record, and again given to the world by him.   There is hardly one
point of equitable proceeding with regard to pleas, with which it is
not exceedingly difficult to reconcile those two cases in the Exchequer : for instance, what is said in Mitford (1) as to a
[*596] bill brought to impeach a decree on the * ground of fraud
used in obtaining it ; that " the decree may be pleaded in
bar of the suit, with averments " (in the plea, it appears by the context) " negativing the charges of fraud, supported by an answer fully
denying them."   So of a judgment (2) : "If there is any charge
of fraud, or other circumstance shown as a ground for relief, the
judgment or sentence cannot be pleaded, unless the fraud or other
circumstance, the ground, upon which the judgment or sentence is
sought to be impeached, be denied, and this put in issue by the plea,
and the plea supported by a full answer to the charge in the bill."

In the case of a stated account also (3) " If error or fraud are
charged, they must be denied by the plea as well as by way of

(1) Mitf. 197.
(2) Mitf. 205.
(3) Mitf. 208.

answer." So with regard to an award (1); which is the subject these cases in the Exchequer more particularly allude to: " if fraud or partiality is charged against the arbitrators, those charges must not only be denied by way of averment in the plea, but the plea must be supported by an answer, showing the arbitrators to have been incorrupt and impartial." Upon the Statute of Limitations (2) : " where a particular special promise is charged, to avoid the opera- tion of the Statute, the Plaintiff must deny the promise charged by averment in the plea, as well as by answer to support the plea." So as to a purchase for valuable consideration (3): "The special and particular denial of notice or fraud must be by way of answer ; that the Plaintiff may be at liberty to except to its sufficiency. But notice and fraud must also be denied generally by way of averment in the plea ; otherwise the fact of notice or of fraud will not be in issue (4)."

This is laid down here distinctly, and in many other books ; for I have lately looked into the point for another purpose; and I think, I may say, whatever doubt may be expressed as to the necessity of denying by plea and answer, that there is no countenance for that upon the old authorities. Sir John Mitford's idea is, that if you are to call this defence a plea, it must be such that issue may be taken upon it as a plea ; and if it is substantiated by evidence as a plea, there is an end of the cause. Where the * Defend- [* 597] ant not stating merely matter *dehors,* but admitting part of the charge, gets rid of it by circumstances, I do not know, that it might not be called a plea and answer ; but that is a record of a character very distinct from that, which is usually called a plea.

With respect to the first of the cases in the Court of Exchequer, I wished to know, what was the event of it, after leave was given to strike out the averments. If the plea had no part of that, which was contained in the answer, how could the Plaintiff proceed upon that, so amended, as a plea ? It admits the award, the very fact stated in the bill. Must it not be complete as a plea ; and contain in itself all the allegations, which being proved are necessary to authorise a judgment for the Defendant ? To the record so purged the character of a plea, technically speaking, does not belong : neither can it technically be called an answer: but it is something called a plea and answer; being in substance the same, as if the Defendant had answered. It is impossible not to feel the authority belonging to these cases. The point was decided upon reconsider- ation in the second case : and therefore the question, if this record

---

(1) Mitf. 209.
(2) Mitf. 212.
(3) Mitf. 216.
(4) *Post, Jones* v. *Davis*, vol. xvi. 262; xviii. 182, *Morison* v. *Tournour ; Evans* v. *Harris*, 2 Ves. & Bea. 361. In *Dodd* v. *Worrall*, in Chancery, 20th November, 1805, Lord Eldon ordered a plea to stand for an answer, with liberty to except; holding clearly upon *Davie* v. *Chester*, that fraud must be denied by averment in the plea as well as by answer. *Roche* v. *Morgell*, 2 Sch. & Lef. 721 ; *Cork* v. *Wilcock*, 5 Madd. 328. Mr. Beames's Elements of Pleas in Equity, 23.

necessarily furnished it, would make it proper to consider, whether
the principles, upon which I have argued, are right or wrong; and
whether the conclusion drawn in Mitford, not only as to one point,
but upon every point, which analogy brings within the reach of argument, has been ill collected.   In supporting this plea the Counsel
have felt the difficulty of contending, that there must not be averments both by the plea and by answer.

As to amending the plea, if the averments in the plea were the
same as the answer, and if the Defendant cannot say a great deal
more, I much doubt, whether the averments in the bill are sufficiently
denied.   The allegations of applications to settle are certainly put
very loosely in the bill: but I would take it to be a bill distinctly
stating in effect, that the cause of action was gone much more than
six years.   The allegation as to the authority of the son I understand
to mean this in legal construction; that he acted at the time of the
application as agent in the article of the settlement of accounts; and
if so, it cannot be doubted, that the Defendant authorising him
within six years to act as his agent for the settlement of the accounts,
                  would amount to a new Assumpsit; and take it out of the
[* 598]   Statute.   This therefore is a very material * charge.   Ob-
          serve, how the Defendant answers.   He does not state,
what sort of agent his son was.   As I conceive, he was bound to .
state, whether he was the agent in the article of the settlement of
accounts.   There is no distinct answer to that.

The concluding statement, that he never authorised John Adams
to make any such promise or request, or to agree to refer the accounts to arbitration, may be answered honestly, as he conceives
the fact; but it may be false both in law and fact; for if he had
admitted, that the other was agent for the settlement of accounts,
what was the power of an agent so constituted is the construction of
law upon the fact; and that mere appointment, if distinctly admitted, would take it out of the Statute; importing, that there were accounts to settle; and the direction and power, which the Defendant
supposes himself not to have given, would be implied in law in that
character.   I have a strong doubt therefore, whether the plea, if to
be amended, must not be amended in substance, beyond merely
throwing into it the allegations of the answer.   But in such a case
I would not preclude the Defendant from amending as to the averments in the plea; if any averments are necessary.   The objection
goes to this; that the plea would be good almost without averments
in the plea or the answer; for if the plea is, that the cause of action
did not arise within six years, and if a new Assumpsit should be
proved, then it does not contain that, upon which the party must go
to issue effectually, and proving his case would be entitled to dismiss
the bill.   But that will not do; for this is a bill stating, that the
cause of action arose a great while beyond six years; admitting,
that, if that was all, the Statute would be an answer: but it states
also, that the reply to that is, that within six years a new transaction
has taken place; which forms a new Assumpsit; upon which the

Plaintiffs say they are entitled to the relief. It would be quite anomalous to go to issue upon a plea, the issue upon which must be quite unnecessary, unless other circumstances are brought forward, or to proceed in the suit without knowing by plea or by answer, whether the circumstance to take the case out of the operation of the Statute has or has not existence.

The case therefore must not be reduced to a decision upon the point, whether the averments must be both in the plea and the answer; as I think, if the averments were in both, they are not *sufficiently averred. Upon that point I will not say [*599] more than that it seems difficult to support the two cases in the Exchequer. If the Defendant chooses to amend the plea, or both the plea and the answer, I will not object to it; but he must answer much more fully, before I shall consider it sufficient.

The plea was ordered to stand for an answer, with liberty to except, except as to setting forth the accounts (1).

---

1. WHERE the plaintiff's bill contains charges which, if true, would in Equity avoid the defendant's plea, those charges must be denied, both by averments in the plea, and also, (in order that the plaintiff may have an opportunity of excepting,) by an answer in support of the plea. *Anonymous case*, 3 Atk. 70; *Lingood* v. *Croucher*, 2 Atk. 396; *Moreson* v. *Turnour*, 18 Ves. 182; *Roche* v. *Morell*, 12 Sch. & Lef. 727; see the note to the last preceding case but one. Upon the same principle, where a bill not only impeaches an account, but also charges that the plaintiff has no counterpart; if the defendant plead *a stated account*, he must annex it; otherwise, although there might be errors on the face thereof, the plaintiff could have no opportunity of pointing them out; and, in such case, the plea would only be admitted to stand for an answer, with liberty to except. *Hankey* v. *Simpson*, 3 Atk. 303. And although it seems to be now understood, that a *negative plea* may be good, and that the defendant need not answer to *every* circumstance tending to that point as to which *he tenders an issue* by his plea; (*Drew* v. *Drew*, 2 V. & B. 161, 162;) still, it is quite clear, a defendant cannot protect himself, by a negative plea, from the discovery of a variety of circumstances charged in the plaintiff's bill, which, if disclosed, would establish the fact in issue. *Evans* v. *Harris*, 2 V. & B. 364. A plaintiff is entitled to an answer, upon oath, to every *material* collateral circumstance, well charged as evidence of the general fact; (*Jones* v. *Davis*, 16 Ves. 265; *Arnold* v. *Harford*, 1 M'Clel. & Younge, 334;) a plea which negatives the plaintiff's title, may protect a defendant from answer and discovery as to the subject of the suit, but will not protect him from answer and discovery with respect to such matters as are specially charged as evidence of the plaintiff's title. *Sanders* v. *King*, 6 Mad. 63, 85: see note 2 to *Jerrard* v. *Saunders*, 2 V. 187, and note 1 to *Renison* v. *Ashley*, 2 V. 459.

2. Although, as already has been intimated, a party who pleads must also, in very many cases, answer in support of his plea: *Leonard* v. *Leonard*, 1 Ball & Bea. 324; *Hildyard* v. *Cressy*, 3 Atk. 304: still, there are pleas of such a nature as obviously not to require the support of an answer; for instance, a plea that the discovery sought would subject the defendant to penalties. *Claridge* v. *Hoare*, 14 Ves. 66.

3. Lord Eldon, in *Dolder* v. *Lord Huntingfield*, 11 Ves. 293, again adverted, as he did in the principal case, to the inaccuracy of admitting on the record a species of plea, which is not strictly either a plea, answer, or demurrer, but a little of each.

4. To plead "to such part of the bill as is not answered," is a bad form of pleading, because it puts the Court to the trouble of seeing what is, and what is

---

(1) *Ante, Bowers* v. *Cator*, vol. iv. 91, and the note.

not, answered; and deprives the plaintiff of the benefit of taking exceptions to the answer; (*Broom* v. *Horsley*, Mosely, 40;) but a plea with an exception, not requiring a reference to the answer, is not necessarily bad, either in substance or form. *Howe* v. *Duppa*, 1 V. & B. 516.

HOOPS, *Ex parte.*

[1802, Jan. 22.]

ENROLMENT of a Patent cannot be dispensed with for the purpose of preventing the specification being made public.
After a Patent has passed, the time for enrolment cannot be enlarged without an Act of Parliament.

THE petition was presented by the Patentee of an invention for making paper from straw; and the object of it was that the Lord Chancellor would dispense with the enrolment, or, that some provision should be made to prevent the specification from being made public; suggesting the danger, that foreigners might obtain copies of the specification in consequence of the enrolment.

Mr. *Sutton* and Mr. *Roupel*, in support of the petition.

Lord CHANCELLOR [ELDON].—How can I do this? Either upon this or some other case in the last Session a clause for this purpose was inserted in an Act of Parliament; and upon the motion of Lord Thurlow, upon reasons applying not only to that but to all cases, and seconded by Lord Rosslyn, the clause was universally rejected; and rejected, as it appeared to me, upon very substantial grounds; in which I readily concur. As to the worth of the apprehension suggested, a man has nothing more to do than to pirate your invention in a single instance; and he will then force you to bring an action; and then the specification must be produced.

But with regard to the King's subjects a very strong objection occurs; which makes it necessary, that the specification should be capable of being produced. They have a right to apply to the Patent Office to see the specification: that they may not throw [600*] *away their time and labor, perhaps at a great expense, upon an invention upon which the Patentee might afterwards come with his specification, alleging an infringement of his Patent; when if those persons had seen the specification, they never would have engaged in their projects. The enrolment is therefore for the benefit of the public.

It was then desired, that the time, which would expire on the 17th of the next month, might be enlarged; in order that the petitioner might apply to Parliament.

Lord CHANCELLOR.—I cannot do that, if the Patent has passed; for the Patent is void, if the proviso is not complied with. You should have applied to the Attorney General, before the Patent

passed, for a longer time upon the special circumstances.   I cannot
take the Great Seal from a patent, and repeal it in the most essential point.   It is a legal grant, with a proviso for the benefit of all
the King's subjects.   You can do nothing, except by an Act of
Parliament to enlarge the time mentioned in the proviso.

The Petition was dismissed. ___

In *Ex parte Beck*, which was a case calling for every proper indulgence, Lord
Thurlow held, (as Lord Eldon did in the principal case,) that it would be an abuse
of power in the holder of the Great Seal to alter the date of a patent.   See farther, as to the doctrines with respect to patent rights, note 1 to *Ex parte O'Reily*,
1 V. 112.

BLOXHAM, *Ex parte.*

[1802, JAN. 27.]

CREDITOR having securities of third persons to a greater amount than the debt
may prove and receive dividends upon the full amount of the securities to the
extent of 20s. in the pound upon the actual debt.

THE object of this petition was to have the order made by Lord
Rosslyn [LOUGHBOROUGH] dismissing a former petition (1), discharged ; and that the petitioner may be permitted to prove and receive dividends under the Commission against Purdy, in respect of
the residue of the amount of the bill accepted by him, and indorsed to them by Almond as a collateral security for his debt, according to the prayer of that petition, undertaking to refund, in case
the dividends under both Commissions should exceed 20s. in the
pound upon Almond's debt.

This petition was presented in consequence of the order   [601]
(2) made upon the petition by the same parties in the
bankruptcy of Young and Glennie.

The *Solicitor General* and Mr. *Cox,* in support of the Petition, insisted upon the last order, setting up the older cases ; observing,
that this bill was the inducement of the petitioners to discount the
other.

Mr. *Mansfield,* for the Assignees, being called upon by the Lord
Chancellor, referred to Lord Rosslyn's order.

Lord CHANCELLOR [Eldon].—There must have been some misunderstanding upon it ; for the case is only this.   A party wants to
have a bill discounted.   The banker refuses to discount upon
the credit of that bill only.   The other says, he has in his hands
another bill ; and offers that as a security for the former.   What is

---

(1) *Ante, Ex parte Bloxham,* vol. v. 448.
(2) *Ex parte Bloxham, ante,* 449 ; and the note, vol. v. 449.   See *Ex parte Leers,
post,* 644.

that but a right to prove against both estates, until 20*s.* in the pound has been obtained ?

Ordered according to the prayer.

———

Sɛɛ, *ante,* the notes to *S. C.* 5 V. 448.

———

BARWIS, *Ex parte.*

[1802, Jan. 27.]

Joint Commission of bankruptcy superseded on the ground of the infancy of one partner on the petition of the assignees under a separate commission.

THE petition was presented by the assignees under a separate Commission of Bankruptcy against one of two partners ; praying, that a joint Commission should be superseded on the ground of the infancy of the other partner.

Mr. *Cullen,* for the Assignees under the joint Commission, admitting, that upon the application of the infant himself the Commission must be superseded, suggested a doubt, whether it could upon the application of a third person.

Lord CHANCELLOR [ELDON] said, he had no doubt of the authority of the Court to supersede the Commission (1).

———

SEE the note to *Ex parte Barrow,* 3 V. 554.

———

[* 602]   PEELE, *Ex parte.*

[1802, Jan. 29.]

To make a partnership liable to a demand in respect of a separate transaction an agreement must appear (*a*).
No action of covenant but between parties, [p. 604.]

KIRK, a warehouseman, carrying on business under the firm of Kirk and Company, being indebted to Sir Robert Peele for goods sold, after that debt was contracted, entered into a treaty with Ford,

———

(1) *Ante,* 440 ; *Ex parte Henderson,* vol. iv. 163 ; *post, Ex parte Watson,* xvi. 265 ; 1 Ves. & Bea. 494 ; 2 Christian's Bank. Law, 17, 18. A commission cannot be supported by trading during infancy : *post,* vol. xiv. 603.

(*a*) In cases of this nature the primary consideration is, not so much to ascertain between what parties the original contract was made, as to whether there has subsequently been, with the consent of all the parties, any change or extinguishment of that contract. Story, Partnership, § 153 ; Collyer, Partn. 364, 365 ; *Vere* v. *Ashby,* 10 B. & C. 288 ; *Lloyd* v. *Ashby,* 2 B. & Adolph. 23 ; *Hovey* v. *Roebuck,*

a breeches maker, for forming a partnership. About four months afterwards a Commission of Bankruptcy issued against them. No articles having been executed, Ford disputed the point of partnership; which was tried at law; and the partnership was established upon the evidence of acts done.

The object of this petition by Sir Robert Peele was to prove his debt, as a joint debt, carried into the partnership accounts. In support of the petition the affidavit of Copeland stated, that it was agreed that the separate debts of Kirk should be assumed by the partnership; that entries were made in the books with the knowledge of Ford, and particularly, that the goods furnished by the petitioner were entered at a reduced price. This was opposed by the affidavit of Ford, denying the agreement or even knowledge of these circumstances.

Mr. *Mansfield* and Mr. *Thomson*, in support of the Petition.— This debt may be proved as a joint debt upon the authority of *Ex parte Clowes* (1) and *Ex parte Bingham* (2). Otherwise the effect would be a gross fraud.

Mr. *Romilly*, for the Assignees.—The circumstances, under which this partnership took place, are, that Ford having saved 5000*l.* by his business was applied to by Kirk to become a partner with him. The latter was to give a statement of the business; but, before that statement was given, Ford found himself by law a partner, and soon afterwards in consequence bankrupt: Kirk being clearly a bankrupt at that time. The point, upon which this claim is resisted, is, that Ford never consented to take upon himself the debts of the old house; which upon the evidence he never did. It is not disputed, that there were some entries in the * books; but   [* 603] the question is, whether Ford knew of any such entries or such books. It is admitted, that these goods were sold long before this partnership was in contemplation: and therefore upon the credit of Kirk alone. This debt clearly cannot be proved; unless the evidence goes a great deal farther, showing an agreement to take to the debts or privity. It is not disputed, that by agreement the debts of the former partnership may be brought into the new partnership: but there must be an express agreement for it: and it is not of course. That has been decided in many cases: of which the last is *Shirreff* v. *Wilks* (3). In that case there was no evidence, that Robson, the new partner, did not know the transaction, nor on the other hand. Therefore, it was presumed, that he did not know it.

---

7 Taunt. 157; *Ketchum* v. *Durkee*, 1 Hoffm. 528. If the original debt is exclusively contracted by one partner on his own account, but has been assumed by the partnership, with the consent of the creditor, as a partnership debt, it will henceforth be treated in his favor as a joint debt. Story, Partner. § 368, 370. See, also, 3 Kent, Comm. 41–44.

(1) 2 Bro. C. C. 595; 1 Cooke's Bank. Law, 258, 551; 8th edit. 274, 534.
(2) 1 Cooke's Bank. Law, 551; 8th edit. 534.
(3) 1 East, 48; *post, Jervis* v. *White*, vol. vii. 413; *Ex parte Bonbonus*, viii. 540; *Willet* v. *Chambers*, Cowp. 814; *Shirreff* v. *Wilks*, 1 East, 48; *Hope* v. *Cust*, stated 1 East, 53; *Sandilands* v. *Marsh*, 2 Barn. & Ald. 673.

In this case, though it is sworn by Copeland, that Ford knew it, that under the circumstances is not to be credited. Joint debts unimpeached have been proved against Ford to the amount of 3000*l*. He cannot therefore have any interest.

Mr. *Mansfield*, in reply.—This is a question of fact upon the contradictory evidence of Copeland and Ford ; the latter of whom is interested in respect of the surplus and the bankrupt's allowance ; and the former unimpeached. There is no doubt, that the price of these goods stands in these books as a debt. The case cited was upon the naked circumstances. The question is, whether this is a debt so carried into the partnership as to become a joint debt. The result of the evidence is, that the goods were transferred into the partnership stock ; and the price became a partnership debt. It is not explained, how the capital of these partners was to be formed. It seems as if Ford was to bring in money. He advanced 1500*l*. to Kirk ; who must bring in that value in some way.

Lord CHANCELLOR [ELDON].—From this petition I could not collect the nature of the question, that was to be argued. The goods were supplied upon the credit of Kirk, for any use he pleased, however improper. If he chose to sell or to give them to a person insolvent the day afterwards, the petitioner could not have followed the goods ; but must be contented with his action against [* 604]   *Kirk. The *prima facie* effect of carrying the goods into the partnership at a different price would be a sale by Kirk to the partnership. It is not easy to conceive, why selling the goods to a partnership, of which he was one member, should alter the case ; and it is admitted by all the cases, that if the goods were sold to the new partnership for a farthing advance, if not a fraud, but taking it as a sale, the goods could not be followed. It is said, in these cases if the partners agree, that the separate debts due to each should become the joint property in consideration of both taking upon them the debts of both, .that is an agreement between the partners, and binds the creditors ; not at law clearly ; for the agreement of the two would not give a right of action to one ; unless some old cases could be supported ; in which it was held, that an action of covenant might be brought by him, for whose benefit the covenant was made, as well as him, in whose name it was made: but those cases, I think, are not now law. Though it is not argued, that such an agreement binds the creditors at law, it is said, it binds all creditors, and gives benefits to some creditors, in bankruptcy. As to the fraud, he, who sells upon credit, puts himself upon the *bona fides* of him, to whom he sells ; and there may be cases, where the fraud is as great upon the separate creditors as in a supposed case upon the joint creditors. It is mere accident, how the hardship falls. I agree, it is settled, that, if a man gives a partnership engagement in the partnership name with regard to a transaction, not in its nature a partnership transaction, he, who seeks the benefit of that engagement, must be able to say, that, though in its nature not a partnership transaction. yet there was some authority beyond the mere circumstance of partnership to enter into that contract, so as to bind the partnership; and then it depends upon the degree of evidence. In *Shirreff* v. *Wilks* very slight evidence possibly might have been sufficient to show, that the partner knew, the stock had been sold, and the benefit taken into the stock, in which he was partner, and therefore it was conscientious, that he should become liable for that. Slight circumstances might be sufficient, where in the original transaction the party to be bound was not a partner, but at the subsequent time had acquired all the benefit, as if he had been a partner in the original transaction: and it would not be unwholesome for a Jury to infer largely, that that obligation, clearly according to conscience, had been given upon an implied authority. *So here, if this was a case, in which it was   [*605] found upon the trial, that this man was a partner upon a long existing partnership, with a regular series of transactions, books, &c. a knowledge of what his partner had been doing might be inferred against him; that, which in common prudence he ought to have known. But that is not the case of this partnership. It was a treaty. It is not even yet agreed, how the stock and partnership were to be formed. In the course of that treaty Ford, ignorant of law, permits acts to be done, which the law holds to be partnership acts. It is a very different consideration, whether this man, so trepanned into a partnership, had got regular books, &c.; and it is difficult to say, not only, that knowing this he had agreed to it, but that he knew it; in which case I am afraid he must be bound. That fact has not been sufficiently inquired into. In a sense the bankrupt certainly is an interested witness. It is also to be observed, that the joint creditors are also interested, thus. Here are joint creditors; who deal upon the supposition, that the stock in hand is acquired by these two persons. Then separate debts might have been assumed, which would have sunk the dividend of the persons dealing with them both to nothing.

The order directed a reference to the Commissioners to inquire, whether at the commencement of the partnership any debts due from Kirk on account of his stock in trade were assumed, and any debts due to him carried into the partnership, with the knowledge and assent of Ford. The Petition was afterwards dismissed, without prejudice to filing a bill; the Lord Chancellor thinking the questions too considerable to be decided on petition.

---

1. As to the right application of joint and separate estate, under a commission of bankruptcy, see, *ante*, notes 3 and 4 to *Hankey* v. *Garrett*, 1 V. 236, see also note 5 to *Lyster* v. *Dolland*, 1 V. 431.

2. That an agreement between partners as to their debts, for the conversion of separate debts into joint debts, or *vice versa*, will be invalid, without the accession of the creditors, see *Ex parte Williams*, Buck, 15; *Ex parte Freeman*, Buck, 472: see also the note to *Ex parte Bonbonus*, 8 V. 540.

LEE v. .WILLOCK.

[1802, Jan. 21; Feb. 1.]

Upon a reference to the Master as to the fact of a person's death, the report only stating the circumstances, viz. absence abroad fourteen years (a) without any account of him, but not drawing the conclusion, it was referred back to the Master to state, whether he was dead at the time, when administration was granted; especially as two years more had elapsed since the report.

A PETITION was presented by the plaintiff Mrs. Lee; claiming under a will two shares of a fund; one in her own right; the other as administratrix of her son Charles Lee, upon the presumption of his death.

[* 606]　　*By a decree pronounced at the Rolls an inquiry was directed as to the fact of the death of Charles Lee. Upon that question the Master did not draw any conclusion: but the report stated the circumstances; that Charles Lee went to America; that upon his arrival there a letter was received from him: and that since that period, which was fourteen years before the date of the report, he had not been heard of. Since the date of the report two years more had elapsed. No reason appeared, why he should not have been heard of, if living.

Mr. *Romilly* and Mr. *Steele*, in support of the Petition.—Under the statute of Charles II (1), seven years are sufficient to raise a presumption, that a person, upon whose life a copyhold is held, is dead. The Court may proceed by analogy to that; and accordingly in

---

(a) By the early law of England, *seven* years were the term of an apprentice. Stat. 5 Eliz. cap. 4, § 31. In the Statute of Bigamy, (Jac. I. c. 11, § 2), it was provided that, "it shall not extend to any person whose husband or wife shall be continually remaining beyond the seas by the space of *seven* years together, or whose husband or wife shall absent himself or herself, the one from the other, by the space of *seven* years together within the king's dominions, the one of them not knowing the other to be living within that time." In the statute concerning leases determinable on lives (19 Car. II. c. 6), it was provided, if any person for whose life any estate has been granted, remain beyond sea, or is otherwise absent *seven* years, and no proof made of his being living, such person shall be accounted naturally dead. Afterwards in the case of *Doe* v. *Jesson*, 6 East, 83, it was declared by Lord Ellenborough, that in accordance with these statutes, the presumption of the duration of life, with respect to persons of whom no account can be given, ceases at the expiration of *seven* years. This principle was again recognised by the same Court in *Lloyd* v. *Deacon*, 4 B. & Ald. 433, and has been adopted in the jurisprudence of the United States. See Tomlins's Law Dict. art. *Death*; 2 Stephens, N. P. 1555, 1556; 1 Greenl. Evid. § 41; 1 Phil. Ev. 197; Cowen's Notes, No. 381; *King* v. *Paddock*, 18 Johns. 141; *In re Hutton*, 1 Curt. 595; *M'Comb* v. *Wright*, 5 Johns. Ch. 263; *Doe* v. *Nepean*, 5 B. & Adolph. 86; *Battin* v. *Bigelow*, Peters, C. C. 452; *Miller* v. *Beates*, 3 S. & R. 490.

It is not necessary that the party be proved to be absent from the United States; it is sufficient, if it appear that he has been absent for *seven* years, from the particular state of his residence, without having been heard from. *Newman* v. *Jenkins*, 10 Pick. 515; *Innis* v. *Campbell*, 1 Rawle, 373; *Spurr* v. *Trimble*, 1 A. K. Marsh. 278; *Wambough* v. *Shenk*, 1 Penning. 167; *Woods* v. *Woods*, 2 Bay, 476.

For the origin of the rule establishing *seven* years as the period at the expiration of which the presumption of human life ceases, see 6 Law Reporter, 529–541.

(1) 19 Cha. II. c. 6.

Thorn v. *Rolfe* (1) a person was presumed dead, because not heard of for seven years. In *Dixon* v. *Dixon* (2) the Court also acted upon such a presumption; and though the time in that instance was twenty-five years, no time has been fixed.

Mr. *Lloyd* and Mr. *Hart*, for the Defendants.—In *Dixon* v. *Dixon* the Master, as in this case, not having drawn a conclusion, the Master of the Rolls sent it back to him to draw a conclusion; which being, that the person was dead, the decree was made upon that.

Lord CHANCELLOR [ELDON].—The evidence is strong in favor of this presumption. But I approve what I understand to have been always Lord Alvanley's course, to make the Master draw the conclusion. It is singular, that the Court should send such a question to the Master, and that he should send it back to the Court. But in this instance if I should determine it, it would be rash; for above two years more have elapsed since the report; and how can I know, that in that time some information might not have been obtained; which if it was now before the Master, might induce him to form a conclusion one way or the other. At least the addition of two years would make the presumption stronger.

1802, *Feb.* 1.   Lord CHANCELLOR.—I am quite satisfied,   [* 607] I cannot grant the prayer of this petition in the full extent, upon considering such circumstances as are stated to me. First, the Master has not executed the order. He ought to have drawn the conclusion. Next, the order is not quite right; for the issue of fact to be tried, before this petition can succeed, is, whether Charles Lee died before the letters of administration were taken; for if he cannot be presumed dead before that, I shall not have a proper representative before the Court. It must therefore go back to the Master to say, whether Charles Lee was dead, when the petitioner became his personal representative.   ____

WHEN a legatee has not been heard of for twenty years, payment of the legacy to those next entitled will be ordered, they entering into a recognizance to refund, in case he should afterwards appear, and claim: *Bailey* v. *Hammond*, 7 Ves. 590; and the presumption of death from length of time goes back to the first moment of uncertainty as to the party's existence. *Webster* v. *Birchmore*, 13 Ves. 362; see, *ante*, the note to *Ex parte Grant*, 6 V. 512.

(1) Dy. 185, *a.*; Moor. 14; Anders. 20.
(2) 2 Bro. C. C. 510.

SINCLAIR v. HONE.

[Rolls.—1802, Feb. 1.]

A codicil expressed in the event of the testator's death, before he joins his wife, was executed after their separation in the West Indies upon his voyage for England. That voyage being prevented by accident, he joined her: they lived together there and in England, having returned together; and the testator having afterwards gone to Corsica, and thence to Lisbon, died there. The Codicil was held to be contingent, and did not take effect under the circumstances. Probate not conclusive; not being refused except in a plain case.

William Sinclair, by his will, dated the 30th of January, 1795, after directing his funeral expenses and debts to be paid with all convenient speed after his decease, gave, devised and bequeathed to his wife Augusta Sinclair one moiety of all the real and personal estate he should die possessed of, to hold to her and her own use, subject in the event of her marrying to the payment of 1000l., for the benefit of the children he might have, as therein mentioned. Then, after a farther provision for children, in case he should not have a child living by his said wife at the time of his decease, or to be born after his decease, or having issue by her they shall all happen to die before any of them shall attain twenty-one, or be married with consent, as aforesaid, then and in such case he directed, that upon the decease of the survivor of his children 500l. of the last bequest (the 1000l. charged for his children in the event of his widow's marriage) should be paid to his wife for her own use; and the other 500l. among the children of his brothers John and Duncan Sinclair, living at the death of the survivor of his children. Then after some other legacies he gave all such property as he might die possessed of over and above all that is hereby disposed of unto and amongst all the children,

[* 608] which he might have living by his said wife at the time of his * decease, together with his said wife, the same to be divided amongst his said wife and children in equal proportions share and share alike; and he directed, that in case of his death during his residence in the West Indies, and it should be the will of his wife to remain there, his household furniture should be reserved to her for her sole use and benefit for her life, and after her decease be disposed of. He directed his freehold and leasehold lands and property in Dominica to be sold; and made some farther dispositions in favor of his wife and his children in the event of his having children.

The testator afterwards made the following codicil:

" In case I die before I join my beloved wife Augusta Sinclair I leave to her all my property 500l. to my brother Duncan excepted to be paid to him when my beloved wife can spare it. In witness my hand in presence of Captain John Hall and Alexander Hall, this 16th May 1795. William Sinclair."

The testator died in 1798; having never had any issue; and in Michaelmas Term 1799, the bill was filed by John Sinclair and his children, and the children of Duncan Sinclair, claiming their legacies, against the testator's widow and her second husband, and Duncan Sinclair, and the executors and trustees.

The Defendant Hone and his wife, the testator's widow, insisted on the codicil as a revocation of the will.

By a decree at the Rolls an inquiry was directed, whether it was the intention of the testator at the date of the codicil to go to England, and for what purpose, and to return to Dominica at any and what time, and under what circumstances; or whether it was his intention, that his wife should follow and join him in England, or elsewhere under any and what circumstances.

The Report stated, that the testator at the time of making his will and for many years preceding was storekeeper to his Majesty's Board of Ordnance in the island of Dominica; where he had fixed his residence. At the date of the codicil it was his intention
*to leave his wife at Dominica, and go to England for the [*609] purpose of obtaining promotion in the Ordnance Department, and also with a view to recover or secure the payment of a debt of 2000*l.* and upwards; and it was his intention to return to Dominica and join his wife at his residence there, when he had finished his business in England, unless his promotion had been elsewhere than at Dominica or in the West Indies; in which case it is thought, the testator would not have gone back to Dominica; but would have required his wife to follow and join him in England, or, wherever else he had obtained promotion and a permanent situation.

With the aforesaid intention he took leave of his wife and family; and proceeded to the place, whence the packets sailed for England; and while there and in hourly expectation of embarking he made the codicil. The packet by accident sailing without him, he endeavored to overtake her; but could not; in consequence of which he returned to his house; where he lived with his wife and family during his subsequent residence in the island. In the course of the ensuing year the testator and his wife went together to England, and took a house and lived at Shooter's Hill some time; when the testator getting the appointment of Ordnance Storekeeper in Corsica repaired to that island about April 1796; leaving his wife resident at his dwelling-house at Shooter's Hill. On the evacuation of Corsica he was ordered to Lisbon with the troops; whither he went; and was at length appointed Commissary and Paymaster to the Artillery serving with the army in Portugal; and shortly after obtaining such promotion died suddenly at Lisbon.

The cause coming on for farther directions upon this Report, the only question was upon the construction of the codicil; whether under the circumstances disclosed by the Report it revoked the will.

The codicil was proved in the Ecclesiastical Court.

Mr. *Piggott* and Mr. *Alexander*, for the Plaintiffs.—The codicil from the time the testator joined his wife became totally ineffectual. The Defendants must contend, that the words "in case I die before

I join my beloved wife " mean, in case he dies absent from his
              wife.   It is impossible to resist these plain, direct, words,
[* 610]   in * effect a condition precedent.   Suppose, he had died,
              while they were living at Shooter's Hill.

Mr. *Richards*, Mr. *Romilly*, Mr. *Greenwood*, and Mr. *Hubbersty*,
for the Defendants.—This case is not like *Parsons* v. *Lanoe* (1) in
which Lord Hardwicke considered the will as merely a provisional,
contingent, disposition.   This testator was about to undertake a
voyage for the purpose of soliciting promotion ; which was prevented by an accident.   He had not departed from her for England at
that time.   He had not therefore left her.   They came together to
England.   They lived here together.   Then he goes to Corsica;
then to Lisbon ; and there he dies.   It is not to be contended, that
the words mean in case of any absence: but the object was his
death in the first absence, that should take place after the execution
of that codicil.   The words import present gift.   The rational construction is, that this is, not a contingent, but an absolute, disposition by a man foreseeing the event of not joining his wife again ;
and the construction may be, lest he should never join her.   It is
not immaterial, that the Ecclesiastical Court have granted probate of
this instrument.

Mr. *Piggott*, in Reply, was stopped by the Court.

The MASTER OF THE ROLLS [Sir WILLIAM GRANT].—There is
nothing in the objection upon the probate of this codicil granted by
the Ecclesiastical Court.   That it is evident from the inquiry, that
was directed.   I do not say, there may not be a case, in which it
would be the duty of that Court to refuse probate ; where the objection was so plain, that there could be no doubt ; as in the case of
Parsons v. *Lanoe* ; where it was clear, that he had returned.   In
such a case the Ecclesiastical Court might refuse probate : the paper
being clearly not intended to have effect in the event, that happened.   But, where there is a doubt, to say, they may refuse probate, merely because in one possible event the instrument may be
left inoperative, cannot be maintained.   Upon that ground they
would try every case upon the effect of a codicil.   In the case of
double legacies the second may be only repetition.   If that is de-
              termined, the codicil operates nothing.   The Ecclesiasti-
[* 611]   cal Court are not to * take upon themselves the decision
              of that question, before they grant probate.   This there-
fore is totally different from the case supposed by Lord Hardwicke,
in *Parsons* v. *Lanoe*.   But if I had more doubt upon it, after this
decree, when it is stated, that the objection was made, and over-
ruled, I would let the party take some other course, of appealing
against this decree, as containing a nugatory reference.

Then, as to the construction of this codicil, one view, that has
been taken at the bar, would dispose of it at once ; that it contains
no condition ; but is an absolute and immediate bequest ; that the

---

(1) 1 Ves. 189.

meaning is, that the testator now being about to proceed upon the voyage now gives his wife the whole of his fortune.   That would be infinitely too violent a construction.   The words are words of as positive and express condition as can be.   The question is only, whether a contingency exists or not ; and I am of opinion, there was condition and contingency.   Then has it happened ?   I wished to have heard distinctly stated, by what motives the testator is supposed to have been actuated ; for, if a clear and distinct intention appears, the Court would go a great way to carry it into effect, though perhaps not in words very accurately expressed.   But if the Court is left at a loss for the intention, there is a necessity for abiding by the words : for there is no motive for departing from them. This is an absurd condition on the face of it ; and no satisfactory reason has been assigned by any one for giving his wife the whole of his fortune, if he dies absent from her, and only a part, if he lives to join her.   But he chose, and had a right, to make that condition, however absurd.   If no motive can be discovered, I must abide by the letter of the condition.   This is supposed to be the same as if the testator had sat down by his wife to make this codicil ; but it appears from the Report, he had left her, and for a continuance, as he supposed ; and a voyage was to intervene.   Separated from her under those circumstances he makes this codicil.   But he does join her, it is true, in the same island.   It is true, that voyage, in contemplation of which he makes this codicil, never took place.   But then what is the case I am to represent to myself, in which he would have said, the contingency had happened ; for if it has not happened by his joining her, could this have become ever contingent ?   It is supposed to mean the first separation,
* that may take place : but it is clear, he had not in con-   [*612] templation any future separation.   He was not thinking of a voyage to Corsica, or a voyage to be made twenty years afterwards.   The argument would be just as good, if he had given up his intention of going to England altogether ; and had lived twenty years with her upon the island ; and had then made a voyage. That would have been in some respects a stronger case than this ; for it would have been leaving her upon the island, and a recurrence to the same circumstances.   But this is totally different. He joins her ; lives with her ; and then takes a new voyage.   Can I apply the codicil to that new voyage ; taking it upon the strict words ?   at least it must have been upon the same sort of case. This is a case he never thought of.   Not knowing, what he meant, I must abide by the words ; and then the condition has happened ; and the codicil therefore does not take effect.

Consequently the account must be taken according to the prayer of the bill.

_____

1. A WILL or codicil may be made, in such terms as to render it totally dependent on a contingency whether the paper writing containing the conditional disposition shall ever become a testamentary instrument ; and unless the specified contingency which is to make it to make it take effect as such should happen, the

writing ought not to be proved in the Ecclesiastical Court. But when the disposition only, and not the instrument, is made' contingent, the latter ought to be proved in the· Ecclesiastical Court as a will, leaving the determination, as to the validity of the disposition, to the proper Courts. *Parsons* v. *Lanoe,* 1 Ves. Sen. 109 ; *S. C.* Ambl. 559, and cited in *Johnston* v. *Johnston,* 1 Phillim. 485.

2. That no implied case must be added to that which is expressed in a will, where such implication is not necessary to render the whole consistent; and that, when the meaning of a will is plain, it would be in vain to urge that such meaning is a "strange" or "absurd" one, see note 4 to *Blake* v.·*Bunbury,* 1 V. 194.

WALKER *v.* EASTERBY.

[1802, JAN. 29; FEB. 5.]

No order, that a Plaintiff residing abroad shall give security for costs, where there are co-plaintiffs residing in England (a).

AN' order was obtained by the Defendant, as of course by petition at the Rolls, that the Plaintiff Walker, who resided in Guernsey, should give security for costs, and that in the mean time the proceedings should be stayed.

The Defendant was proceeding by attachment to the Mayor's Court according to the custom of London, for a balance of 180*l.* in the hands of the other two co-plaintiffs, Le Mesuriers, belonging to Walker. The bill prayed an injunction.

Mr. *Steele,* for the Plaintiffs, moved, that the order should be discharged ; insisting, that this was never done in such a case ; where there were more Plaintiffs than one, and the others resided in England, and in this instance in London.

[* 613]   *Mr. *Wetherell,* in support of the order, said, the Le Mesuriers, being merely the Garnishees, were only nominal Plaintiffs.

There was a difference of opinion in the Register's Office as to the practice. One of the Registers said, there was no instance of an order upon one of the Plaintiffs only to give security for costs.

Lord CHANCELLOR [ELDON] observed, that the Defendant has security for his costs against each of the Plaintiffs (1).

Feb. 5th. The motion having stood over, that the practice might be ascertained, the Lord Chancellor, referring to an instance (2), in which Lord Hardwicke in 1755 under similar circumstances discharged the order without costs, made the same order in this case.

SEE the notes to *Green* v. *Charnock,* 1 V. 396.

(a) See *ante,* note (a), *Green* v. *Charnock,* 1 V. 396.
(1) *Lloyd* v. *Makeam, ante,* 145.
(2) *Winthorp* v. *Royal Exchange Assurance Company,* 1 Dick. 282; 7 Taunt. 307. See the note, 1 Ball. & Beat. 566, and Beames on Costs, 178, as to Security for Costs.

HEATH, *Ex parte.*

[1802, Feb. 5, 6.]

BANKRUPT's certificate shall not be stayed, in order to give a person, insisting on a right to stop *in transitu*, an opportunity of proving, in case he should fail in his action.

A PARCEL of cheese, to the amount of about 400*l.*, was supplied by the petitioner on account of the bankrupt. The bankruptcy taking place soon afterwards, the petitioner got possession of the cheese, before it reached the bankrupt; and insisted upon a right to stop it *in transitu* (1). The assignees contended, that under the circumstances it could not be stopped *in transitu*; and offered to let him prove under the Commission; which he refused. An action was brought; which was likely to be tried in about three weeks.

Under these circumstances the petition prayed, that the bankrupt's certificate may be stayed; in order that, if the petitioner should fail in the action, he may have an opportunity of proving his debt.

The Lord CHANCELLOR [ELDON] doubting, whether the certificate could be stayed at the instance of a person, who according to the right he now insists upon is no creditor, [*614] the petition stood over for the purpose of endeavoring to find an instance.

Mr. *Cox*, in support of the petition, not being able to produce an instance, the Lord Chancellor refused to make the order.

THE Court is always humanely cautious not to *delay* a bankrupt's certificate on questionable grounds: *Ex parte Fydell* 1 Atk. 75. *Ex parte Williamson* 1 Atk. 82; and a certificate is not to be finally granted or refused by the Lord Chancellor, *ex arbitrio*; *Ex parte Gardner* 1 Ves. & Bea. 47. *Ex parte Joseph* 18 Ves. 342. A certificate will not be stayed, merely because a creditor has presented a petition for an order to be permitted to prove his debt, after the commissioners' certificate of conformity has been laid before the Lord Chancellor: *Ex parte Curtis* 1 Rose, 274. *Ex parte Smith*, 1 Glyn & Jameson, 196: but, unless a satisfactory reason is given why the application was not made earlier, (*Ex parte Dyson*, 1 Rose, 67, n.; *Ex parte Adams*, 2 Brown, 48; *Ex parte Birch*, 1 Mad. 603,) the only indulgence to which a party who has been wanting in reasonable diligence can be entitled, will be permission to prove; letting the certificate go on. *Ex parte Cundall*, 1 Glyn & Jameson, 38. In order to stay a certificate, the party applying must come in time, and *serve his petition* in time; otherwise the certificate will go, and the petition to stay it will be dismissed with costs: *Ex parte Hopley*, 2 Jac. & Walk. 222: and see *Ex parte Ewart*, 1 Glyn & Jameson, 196, n.

---

(1) *Lickbarrow* v. *Mason*, 2 Term Rep. 63.

MAWSON, *Ex parte.*

[1802, Feb. 6.]

GENERAL inspection of a bankrupt's books, for the purpose of getting rid of the certificate by proving gambling transactions, refused.

THE object of this petition was to get rid of a bankrupt's certificate; suggesting gambling transactions; and for this purpose praying an inspection of all the bankrupt's books. The Lord Chancellor had ordered the Secretary for bankrupts to look into the books for a particular instance suggested: but it was not found.

Mr. *Johnson*, in support of the petition, pressed for farther inquiry, or at least an affidavit, that the books contained nothing of that kind.

Lord CHANCELLOR.—This is a point of great delicacy. A man gets his certificate; and a creditor, who will have nothing to do with the Commission, desires to see all the books, in order to defeat the certificate in this way.

Another point is, whether you have not slipped your time. I doubt very much, when the certificate has been allowed, and has its legal effect, whether a person, no creditor under the Commission, can come in this way for a discovery, to obtain which he may file a bill. I do not think, you can get rid of a certificate, that has been obtained, in every case, in which you can stay (1) a certificate.

THE reluctance of the Court to assist in defeating a certificate actually granted to a bankrupt, will naturally be still stronger than the disinclination to *stay* a certificate, before it is granted; yet, authorities are cited, in the last preceding note, to show that a certificate is never delayed without much caution; no doubt, a certificate will not be granted, or if it has been granted, may be avoided, when the gambling transactions prohibited by the 130th section of the stat. 6 Geo. IV. c. 16, are proved against a bankrupt; *Ex parte Kennet*, 1 Rose, 194; *Hughes v. Morley*, 1 Barn. & Ald. 26; but the principal case has determined that the Court will not aid a speculative inquiry, after certificate granted, upon a bare suggestion that gambling transactions may possibly be brought to light: and see, *post*, note 3 to *Ex parte Hall*, 17 V. 62.

(1) *Ex parte Henderson*, Buck, 557.

VALE *v.* DAVENPORT.

[1802, FEB. 6.]

ONE purchaser not substituted for another without affidavit, that there is no underhand bargain (*a*).

UPON a sale before the Master, —— Walter was reported the best
bidder at 1050*l.*

Mr. *Westcote*, on behalf of the Purchaser, and —— Griffith, moved, that Griffith may stand in the place of Walter; and that Walter
may be at liberty to pay the money into Court in the name of Griffith, and may be let into possession from Christmas last.

The motion was made on affidavit of service of notice upon the
Plaintiff and Defendant.

The Lord CHANCELLOR [ELDON] said, that would not do without
an affidavit, that there is no underhand bargain between them (1).

SEE note 3 to *Rigby* v. *M'Namara*, 6 V. 117.

GREATOREX *v.* CARY.

[ROLLS.—1802, FEB. 8.]

A WIDOW not put to election between her dower and an annuity by the Will of
her husband.
For that the claim of dower must be inconsistent with the Will (*b*).

SAMUEL GREATOREX by his will, duly executed to pass real estate,
gave and bequeathed to his wife the sum of 150*l.* per annum so long
as she should continue his widow and unmarried; and which said
annual sum he desired his said executors would pay her half yearly
out of the produce of his real and personal estate; which personal
estate he desired might be placed out at interest to assist his real
estate in the payment of such annuity, or so much of his personal
estate as should be necessary for that purpose; and he desired, that
the first payment of the said annuity should be made six months after his decease.

The testator also gave and bequeathed to his wife all his household goods and furniture, with all his plate, linen, and china, to and
for her own use and benefit; and in the event of his dying without

---

(*a*) See *ante*, p. 515, note (*a*), *Rigby* v. *M'Namara*.
(1) *Rigby* v. *M'Namara*, *ante*, 515.
(*b*) In order to exclude dower, the instrument containing the bequest ought to
contain some provision inconsistent with the claim to it. See *ante*, note (*a*), *Wake*
v. *Wake*, 1 V. 335; *Foster* v. *Cook*, 3 Bro. C. C. 351, (Am. ed. 1844), and Mr. Perkins's note (*b*).

leaving any child he gave, devised, and bequeathed, all the residue of his real and personal estates unto his sister Ann Baker, her heirs, and assigns for ever.

[* 616]   * The bill was filed by the testator's widow; claiming the annuity under the will and also her dower and freebench; and the accounts having been directed, the point came on upon farther directions.

The Report ascertained the rental of the testator's freehold lands, at 100*l.* a year; and that by the custom of the manors, of which the copyhold estates were held, there was no freebench.

(1) Mr. *Lloyd* and Mr. *Thomson*, for the Plaintiff, insisted upon .the cases of *French* v. *Davies* (2), *Strahan* v. *Sutton* (3), and particularly *Forster* v. *Cook* (4).

The MASTER OF THE ROLLS [Sir WILLIAM GRANT].—I do not see, how this case can be distinguished from *Forster* v. *Cook*. The estate in that case was given to trustees upon trust to pay the annuity to the wife: in this it is given directly to her. The question in all these cases is, whether the testator meant to give away his wife's dower; which he could not do directly. For that it must be seen clearly, that he meant to dispose so, that, if she should claim dower, it would disappoint the will. It must appear, that there is a repugnancy. Upon the whole I am clearly of opinion, that the Plaintiff is entitled to dower (5).

THAT a widow can never be put to her election, between her paramount right to dower, and a bequest of something else, unless the intention of the testator to confine her to one of the provisions is clearly demonstrated; see, *ante*, notes 2 and 3 to *Wake* v. *Wake*, 1 V. 335.

At the end of Hilary Term, in consequence of the death of Lord CLARE, Sir JOHN MITFORD, having resigned the Chair of the House of Commons, succeeded Lord CLARE as Lord Chancellor of Ireland; and was created a Peer of the United Kingdoms by the title of Baron REDESDALE, of Redesdale, in the County of Northumberland (a).

(1) *Ex relatione.*
(2) *Ante*, vol. ii. 572.
(3) *Ante*, vol. iii. 249.
(4) 3 Bro. C. C. 347.
(5) *Couch* v. *Stratton, ante*, vol. iv. 391; *Boynton* v. *Boynton*, 1 Bro. C. C. 445; and other cases collected in Mr. Sanders's note, 2 Atk. 426; and the notes, *ante*, vol. i. 259, 337.
(a) For a sketch of the career of Lord Redesdale, see *ante*, note (b), 1 V. 21.

HUGHES, *Ex parte.*
LYON, *Ex parte.*

In the Matter of Dumbell.

[1802, June 6, 8.]

Sale by assignees under a bankruptcy by auction to one of the creditors, previously consulted as to the mode of the sale, and contrary to an order, that a Receiver should be appointed to sell: another sale was directed: the estate to be put up at the aggregate amount of the purchase-money and the sum laid out in substantial improvements and repairs; which were to be allowed in case of a sale at an advance: but, if no farther bidding, the purchaser to be held to his purchase.

Assignee of a bankrupt, instead of selling the estate taking a lease himself, is answerable for profit or loss (a).

Assignee of a bankrupt not justified in deferring a sale; and in such a case, if called upon to sell, will incur the peril of answering any depreciation, [p. 622.]

John Dumbell was concerned with several other persons in a bank at Stockport; and was also a separate trader. In 1793 a separate Commission of Bankruptcy issued against him; and the petitioner Thomas Lyon and Crossfield were chosen assignees.

The Stockport bank being insolvent, in 1794 an agreement took place between the creditors of the bank, the partners in the bank, and the assignees of the bankrupt Dumbell; and it was agreed among other things, that the joint property should be conveyed to trustees for the benefit of the joint creditors; and the assignees under the Commission against Dumbell should out of his separate estate in the first place pay the sum of 15,009l. for the use of the joint creditors: then they were to pay Dumbell's separate creditors 20s. in the pound and interest; and to apply the surplus in payment of the partnership debts. Deeds were executed accordingly. The assignees of Dumbell neglected to pay the 15,009l.; and in other respects misconducted themselves; and the joint creditors being dissatisfied with them, and also with the conduct of the trustees, to whom the joint property had been conveyed, filed a bill to have the trusts carried into execution. In 1799, no decree having been made, Mangles was by consent appointed receiver of the joint property; with power to sell.

The separate property of Dumbell consisted partly of the reversion of some corn mills at Warrington, and of some leasehold cotton mills. At the date of the bankruptcy the cotton mills were of great value: and might have been sold for a considerable sum: but the assignees neglecting their duty, the mills were greatly diminished in value; and were daily growing worse. After various applications both in the cause and the bankruptcy an order was in April 1800 made in the bankruptcy, upon the petition of the bankrupt,

---

(a) The rules and recent cases with regard to dealings by trustees with the trust property, will be found, *ante*, note (a), *Whichcote* v. *Laurence*, 3 V. 740; note (a), *Campbell* v. *Walker*, 5 V. 678.

appointing a receiver of Dumbell's separate property; with directions to sell, and to bring the produce into the bank.   This
order was not pursued : but it was agreed between the solicitor
for the joint creditors and Mayer, the solicitor for Dumbell's assignees, with the privity of the assignees, that the cotton and corn
mills should be sold immediately by Skynner and Dyke by auction;
and they were accordingly advertised for the 5th of August, 1800.
On that day Lyon, the assignee, and Mayer, the solicitor, came from
Warrington ; and attended; but as the sale of the corn mills was
put off in opposition to their wishes, they were desirous of preventing the sale of the cotton mills ; and with that view proposed, that
they should be put up at 3000*l.*, a sum far exceeding the value.
The solicitor and those concerned for the joint creditors, and also for
several of the separate creditors of Dumbell, were satisfied, that they
were not worth much, if any thing, more than 2000*l.* ; and proposed
that they should be put up at that sum.   Pending this discussion in
a private room, a little previous to the hour of sale, Mr. Hughes, the
principal joint creditor of the Stockport bank, viz. to the amount of
above 19,000*l.*, went into the room ; and being informed of the difference, and asked his opinion, said, he would abide by what Mr.
Dyke thought right; who having heard both sides was of opinion,
that the premises ought to be put up at 2000*l.* ; and Hughes assented.

The cotton mills were accordingly put up at 2000*l.* ; with a declaration, that, if any one advanced upon that sum, they would be
'knocked down to him.   Several persons were in the room; and
Lyon and Mayer among them.   After a considerable time, no one
bidding, Hughes advanced 10*l.*, and was declared the purchaser.
No objection was then taken by Lyon and Mayer: but they afterwards signified, that they should not acquiesce in the sale. . Though
they both live at Warrington, they permitted Hughes to take possession of the mills without interruption, and to lay out large sums
in repairs and lasting improvements.   In September following Mangles was appointed receiver of Dumbell's separate property ; and
he approved the sale to Hughes; and was satisfied, that 2000*l.*
was as much as the property was worth.   The assignees refusing
to deliver an abstract to Hughes, to enable him to complete his
purchase, he in December 1800 applied in the cause for an abstract.

[* 619]   * The Lord Chancellor [Loughborough] directed that motion to stand over ; in order that the assignees might present
a petition in the bankruptcy.   A petition was accordingly presented by
Lyon, the acting assignee ; the object of which was to set aside the
sale and to have the cotton mills re-sold before a Master ; suggesting
collusion between Hughes and the Solicitor for the joint creditors;
who were concerned in the sale.   Another petition was presented
by the separate creditors of Dumbell ; praying, that other mills, his
property, may be sold.

The Lord Chancellor [Loughborough] ordered, that the sale

should be set aside ; and that a re-sale should take place before the Master; and made no order upon an application of the Counsel for Hughes for an allowance for repairs and improvements.

The other petition was presented by Hughes to set aside that order; or otherwise to be allowed for repairs and lasting improvements.

Mr. *Richards*, Mr. *Alexander*, and Mr. *Owen*, in support of the petition of Hughes.—Upon the general point, whether a person, who has advised the mode of sale, and acted as agent, can be the purchaser, when this sort of question arose upon the purchase of a trustee for creditors, Lord Hardwicke in *Whelpdale* v. *Cookson* (1) was of opinion, that the sale should stand, if affirmed by the majority of the creditors. That was recognised in the late case of *Campbell* v. *Walker* (2) ; in which case the rule was laid down by Lord Alvanley only to this extent; that *prima facie* the thing was at an end : not, that an end might be put to it at any time. If the general proposition is pushed to the extent now desired, it would go infinitely beyond any thing, that has ever been done. In *M'Enzie's* case the person employed to sell and to conduct the sale was the purchaser. If all the creditors must consent, the consequence would be very unfortunate. Suppose out of these seventy creditors sixty-five were in favor of the sale: the other * five [* 620] might very absurdly oppose it, or from some improper motive. Upon the circumstances of this case it is very different from that of a trustee ; and here was acquiescence. There is no pretence, that Hughes was acting in concert with the Solicitor, who was entrusted to sell. Hughes is a private gentleman of fortune, residing in Surrey. These mills were no object to him; but he was a large creditor, tired with the delays; and anxious that the business should be closed. When he entered the auction room he had not the most distant idea of bidding. The sale was set aside principally upon this; that the slight part he had taken in the private room clothed him with the character of agent, or a person employed in selling. At all events he must be allowed the money laid out in repairs and improvements.

Mr. *Pemberton*, for the creditors of the Stockport Bank, expressed their wish, that the sale should be confirmed.

Mr. *Mansfield*, Mr. *Lloyd*, and Mr. *Benyon*, in support of Lyon's petition.

In *Hall* v. *Noyes* the sale was set aside upon the mere dry point, that the trustee could not buy ; though the sale was clearly advantageous. At this sale there was no other bidder than Hughes. He had notice, that evening, that the sale could not stand. Having notice, that it would be impeached, it was his own folly to lay out money. The late Lord Chancellor was struck with the circumstance

(1) 1 Ves. 9. Stated from the Register's Book, *ante*, vol. v. 682, in *Campbell* v. *Walker*.
(2) *Ante*, vol. v. 678.

of his being in consultation with these persons before the sale; and also, that he acted in concert with the Receiver; under whom by the authority of the Court the sale ought to have taken place. Hughes appears a person consulted, and advising as to the mode of the sale. The sale also, as conducted, was a violation of the order of the Court. Lord Rosslyn proceeded upon no other ground than the situation, in which Hughes stood: his own Solicitor present, and the parties contriving the manner of selling the estate; not upon the ground of undervalue, or, that the assignees did not concur. The reason of the general rule, that such a sale shall not stand, is the improper use, that might be made of a rule less strict. The Court never can know the value. Upon the objection as to the Receiver, there may be a great deal of management to prevent a sale by the Receiver.

[*621]   Mr. *Richards*, in Reply.—*This purchaser is not tenacious of his contract; being anxious only, that he may not be out of pocket: but the creditors are in favor of the contract; and have a right to retain it. To consider this question fairly, it must be supposed, that the creditors complain. Hughes was capable of being the purchaser. He was not a trustee. There is a manifest distinction between a trustee to sell, and agents, servants, surveyors, &c. A trustee is incapable of purchasing, unless for the *cestuy que trust*, not only upon considerations of general policy, but from the nature of the thing. In the common case of a trust to sell for the payment of debts, or for a distribution among infants, he must continue a trustee for those purposes. He cannot discharge himself by his own act. In that case it would be absurd to suppose, he could sell to himself. While the estate is in him, his character of trustee continues. In point of law therefore it is impossible for him to purchase; and the consideration he gives is not material. But the case of an agent is very different; and if the transaction is fair, no advantage taken, and he has given more than any other man will give, the Court, though looking at it with jealous eyes, will not set it aside. The question must always be, whether he has dealt fairly with his employer. The ground against him must be abuse of confidence. He cannot say, as a stranger may, *caveant emptor et vendor.*

No concealed knowledge is imputed to this purchaser. Every thing was communicated by the assignee. There was no possibility of misrepresentation by him and his solicitor in the conversation between them, who residing at a distance could know nothing accurately of the property, and the others distinctly acquainted with it. Suppose, the sale to Hughes had taken place in the private room, without going to the auction. It may be prudent, but there is no rule making it imperative upon a trustee to sell by auction. In many instances the mode of selling by auction would be mischievous. Many people will not buy by auction; and property frequently will produce more by private contract; and even will not sell by auction. In this sort of case the question must always turn upon the value;

and upon the evidence this sale was at a fair value. If a great majority of the creditors are in favor of the sale, great attention ought to be *paid to them; and they ought to be   [*622]
permitted to keep it notwithstanding the opposition of one
or two, perhaps very unreasonable, and from malice. The alleged
notice by the assignees was no more than refusing at night to perform a contract executed in the morning. They are the persons
now applying. Shall they be heard, the creditors not moving?
The assignees even took no step, till forced on by an application
for the abstract. It is impossible, that Hughes should not be repaid
the money expended; by which alone the property is now of any
value to the creditors.

Lord CHANCELLOR [ELDON].—With respect to the application of
the separate creditors for a sale of that property, with which Hughes
has no concern, the bankruptcy happened so long ago as 1793.
There seems to have been a speculation upon the part of the bankrupts to save the wreck of their fortune, and upon the part of the
assignees to promote their own interest; and with that view they
seem to have laid aside the law, and to have acted just as they
thought proper; entering into contracts singular enough in their
arrangement. One of the first transactions, instead of a sale under the Act of Parliament, was a demise of these mills for nine-
teen years in consideration of 16,000l. : one of these lessees, being
one of the assignees under the Commission, was incapable of that
character; and if any benefit has been made by him from that situation, it will follow, that he must account for it; and if he has sustained a loss, he must take the consequence of having done an act
the Court cannot approve. The lessees subdivided the premises at
an annual rent; making a profit out of the bankrupt's estate by
these transactions. The bankruptcy goes on through a vast mass
of irregular transaction to 1801 : and then the creditors and the
bankrupts begin naturally enough to complain, and state, thus, as it
generally turns out, the management of the estate in this way is
likely to end ruinously to all the parties. In Sir George Cole-
brooke's case the assignees thought proper to husband the estate;
in hopes, that by the event of war or peace it might be brought to
a better market : a considerable number of creditors assenting : but
Lord Thurlow said, it was not competent to any body of creditors
to assent against individual creditors, however few in number; and ordered the estate to be brought to sale * forth-   [*623]
with; and, as was intimated in that case, I wish to intimate in this, that if any individual creditor stated distinctly to this
assignee, that he was dissatisfied with his conduct, and called upon
him to execute his trust from time to time, and if the estate sold
for 2000l.; and might, when the assignee was so called upon,
have sold for 7000l. he would be in the peril of answering the difference.

Upon the other part of the case, I do not impute fraud to Hughes,
even in the view of this Court : but it is impossible to permit him

LACEY, *Ex parte.*

[1802, FEB. 3, 5.]

As to a purchase by a trustee of the trust property the rule is, that it shall not prevail under any circumstances, unless the ʹconnection appears satisfactorily to have been dissolved (a transaction to be viewed) with great jealousy from the opportunity of acquiring knowledge as trustee), or by universal consent. But as against him it shall stand ; as, if more cannot be obtained. The rule applies to all agents, and most strictly to assignees in bankruptcy from their great power (*a*).

In this instance, that of an assignee, another sale was directed : the premises to be put up at the price he gave ; and, if no more bid, his purchase to stand. As he had bought them in at a former sale at a higher price, when there was another bidder to a greater amount than the final purchase, *Quære,* how the assignee is to be charged as to that difference.

Assignee of a bankrupt, purchasing dividends, is a trustee for the creditors or bankrupt according to the circumstances.

A banker, receiving the money under a bankruptcy, ought not to be an assignee. Executor cannot buy the debts for his own benefit, [p. 628.]

THE subject of this petition was strong charges of misconduct by assignees under a Commission of Bankruptcy executed in the country ; one of whom was a banker ; into whose bank the [*626] money was paid. Another of the assignees * was himself the purchaser of part of the bankrupt's estate, sold under the Commission ; and he also purchased from some of the creditors their dividends. The estates in question, consisting of three lots, were twice put up to sale. At the first sale the assignee was the purchaser at 420*l.* : another person, bidding *bona fide,* having gone to 415*l.* The assignee having them again put up some time afterwards was at the subsequent sale again the purchaser at 375*l.* The Solicitor for the Commission appeared at the sale bidding for the assignee.

Mr. *Romilly,* in support of the petition.

Mr. *Richards* and Mr. *Stratford* for the assignees said, persons were misled by the rule, as laid down in *Whichcote* v. *Lawrence* (1) ; not, that a trustee cannot buy from the *Cestuy que trust* ; but, that he, who undertakes to act for another in any matter, shall not in the same matter act for himself ; and therefore a trustee to sell shall not gain any advantage by being himself the person to buy.

Lord CHANCELLOR [ELDON].—The rule I take to be this ; not, that a trustee cannot buy from his *Cestuy que trust,* but, that he shall not buy from himself. If a trustee will so deal with his *Cestuy que trust,* that the amount of the transaction shakes off the obligation, that attaches upon him as trustee, then he may buy. If that case is rightly understood, it cannot lead to much mistake. The true interpretation of what is there reported does not break in upon the Law as to trustees. The rule is this. A trustee, who is entrusted to sell

---

(*a*) The rules and recent cases with regard to dealings by trustees with the trust property, will be found, *ante,* note (*a*), *Whichcote* v. *Lawrence,* 3 V. 740 ; note (*a*), *Campbell* v. *Walker,* 5 V. 678.

(1) *Ante,* vol. iii. 740 ; see page 750.

and manage for others, undertakes in the same moment, in which
he becomes a trustee, not to manage for the benefit and advantage
of himself. It does not preclude a new contract with those, who
have entrusted him. It does not preclude him from bargaining,
that he will no longer act as a trustee. The *Cestuys que trust*
may by a new contract dismiss him from that character; but
even then that transaction, by which they dismiss him, must according to the rules of this Court be watched with infinite and the most
guarded jealousy; and for this reason; that the Law supposes him
to have acquired all the knowledge a trustee may acquire;
which may be very useful to him; but the *communica-   [*627]
tion of which to the *Cestuy que trust* the Court can never
- be sure he has made, when entering into the new contract, by which
·he is discharged. I disavow that interpretation of Lord Rosslyn's
doctrine, that the trustee must make advantage. I say, whether he
makes advantage, or not, if the connection does not satisfactorily
appear to have been dissolved, it is in the choice of the *Cestuys que
trust*, whether they will take back the property, or not; if the
trustee has made no advantage. It is founded upon this; that
though you may see in a particular case, that he has not made advantage, it is utterly impossible to examine upon satisfactory evidence in the power of the Court, by which I mean, in the power of
the parties, in ninety-nine cases out of an hundred, whether he has
made advantage, or not. Suppose, a trustee buys any estate; and
by the knowledge acquired in that character discovers a valuable
coal-mine under it; and locking that up in his own breast enters
into a contract with the *Cestuy que trust*; if he chooses to deny it,
how can the Court try that against that denial? The probability is,
that a trustee, who has once conceived such a purpose, will never
disclose it; and the *Cestuy que trust* will be effectually defrauded.
In the case of *Fox* v. *Mackreth* (1), so much referred to upon this
subject, and now become a leading authority, in which I have now
Lord Thurlow's own authority for saying, he went upon a clear mistake in dissolving the Injunction, it was never contended, that if Fox
in a transaction clear of suspicion, but which, as I have stated, must
be looked at with the most attentive jealousy, had discharged Mackreth from the office of trustee, he would not have been able to hold
the purchase. Why? Because, being no longer a trustee, he was
not under an obligation not to purchase. But we contended, that it
was not in the power of Fox to dismiss him; that the trust was accepted under an express undertaking to the friends of Fox, that the
trustee should not be dismissed without their privity; that Fox himself had too much imbecility of mind as to these transactions; and
we contended, that between the dates of Mackreth's taking upon
himself the character of trustee and purchasing he had acquired a
knowledge of the value of the estate by sending down a surveyor at

(1) 2 Bro. C. C. 400 ; 2 Cox, 320.

up at the sum of 375*l.* ; if any one bids more, the assignee shall not have them ; and if not, he shall take them; reserving my opinion upon the question, how he is to be charged as to the difference in the amount of the two sales; and declaring him a trustee as to the dividends purchased; being clearly of opinion, that an assignee cannot under any circumstances buy a debt for his own benefit (1).

Upon the other circumstances appearing in this petition the Lord Chancellor alluded to the case (2) from Worcester, and another from Bristol ; observing, that the mischief is enormous; and some means must be found to prevent bankers from having concern with the legal part of the execution of a Commission of Bankruptcy.

---

1. As to the general doctrine of the principal case ; see the reference given in the last preceding note.
2. The rule laid down in the principal case, that an executor must not buy, for his own benefit, debts due from his testator's estate: was again stated in *Ex parte James,* 8 Ves. 336.
3. When an estate is sold by auction, the certain effect of a bidding by a person known, or even supposed, to be interested in raising the price, is to chill the sale, and restrain the free biddings of others: *Downes* v. *Grazebrook,* 3 Meriv. 209 ; *The Marquis Townsend* v. *Slangroom,* 6 Ves. 338 : and therefore if the solicitor in the cause has bought in any lots, merely with a view to benefit the estate, and prevent a sale at what he thought an undervalue, he will not be discharged as the purchaser. *Nelthorpe* v. *Pennyman,* 14 Ves. 517.
4. By the 102d section of the statute 6 Geo. IV. c. 16, it is enacted that no money belonging to a bankrupt estate shall be paid into any banking house, or other house of trade, in which any commissioner, assignee or solicitor, engaged. in the commission, is interested.

---

(1) Other cases of the same nature, that occurred about this time, *Ex parte Tanner, Ex parte Attwood,* and *Owen* v. *Foulkes,* received the same determination : the Lord Chancellor repeating these principles ; and declaring the general rule, that no trustee shall buy the trust property, until he strips himself of that character, or by *universal* consent has acquired a ground for becoming the purchaser; and that the rule is to be more peculiarly applied with unrelenting jealousy in the case of an assignee of a bankrupt; adding, that it must be understood, that, whenever assignees purchase, they must expect an inquiry into the circumstances.

Owen v. *Foulkes* was upon a purchase by the solicitor in the cause, a bill by creditors ; the purchase perfectly fair ; the solicitor bidding openly in the presence of very respectable persons concerned for mortgagees and creditors ; and declaring, it was for himself; the sale at that time also being necessary : but the general rule prevailed.

The Lord Chancellor observed upon *M'Enzie's case,* that the course of sale under an order of the Court of Session in Scotland is this. They set [* 631] a value upon the property ; * which they call the upset price; which is obtained by a person, called a common agent; who by evidence procures all the information he can ; upon which a judgment is formed as to the real value. In *M'Enzie's case,* the ground, upon which the House of Lords after a great number of years set aside a purchase by the agent, was, that he, who was to instruct the Court how to sell, should not buy under the authority of the Court.

His Lordship added, that he always thought what Lord Thurlow said was very wise ; that there is no case, in which it is useful upon general principles, that the same Solicitor should be employed on all sides: in many cases it is a great saving of expense certainly: but, where property is to be brought to sale, to pay creditors, &c., great mischief is occasioned by it.

(2) *Ex parte Edwards, ante,* 3.

LISTER *v.* LISTER.

[ROLLS.—1802, FEB. 17, 24.]

GENERAL rule upon a purchase of trust property by the trustees on their own account, that at the option of the *cestuy que trust* it shall be resold; being put up at the price, at which the trustees purchased: who, if there is no advance, shall be held to their purchase (*a*).

THE subject of this bill was a purchase by trustees for infants of some lots, part of the trust property. The sale was by auction. The trustees bid on their own account; and were declared the purchasers. The bill prayed, that the sales may be declared void; and that the estate may be re-sold.

The trustees by their answer insisted, that they had given the best price for the lots they purchased, that could be obtained.

Mr. *Richards* and Mr. *Johnson*, for the Plaintiffs, referred to the late cases (1) before the Lord Chancellor; in all which his Lordship took the same course, as a general rule; that the estate should be put up again at the price, at which the trustee purchased; and if no more was bid, he should be held to his purchase.

Mr. *Cox*, for the Defendants.—There *ought to be an   [* 632] inquiry, whether the lots were sold fairly and at the utmost value. It certainly must now be admitted, that they cannot hold a beneficial purchase: but they may hold it, if no better price could be got at the time. The reason of the resistance is, that in consequence of this sale the estate has been much benefited by paying off mortgages and bonds, carrying interest at 5 per cent. No fraud is proved. It would be a strong thing in such a case to hold, that the estate should keep the benefit arising from paying off these debts, and then undo the transaction from the beginning.

Mr. *Richards*, in reply.— Some expressions in Lord Rosslyn's judgment in *Whichcote* v. *Lawrence* (2) led to some doubt as to the universality of the rule. But in *Ex parte Lacey* (3) the Lord Chancellor said, that part of the case was misunderstood by us; and upon looking into the words accurately I think so. In *Campbell* v. *Walker* (4) the rule is laid down by Lord Alvanley, that a trustee purchasing the trust property is liable to have the purchase set aside, if in any reasonable time the *Cestuy que trust* chooses to say, he is not satisfied with it. In a subsequent case, before the Court of Exchequer, a case of creditors, the bill was delayed twelve years; but the Court made the decree; holding, that the laches could not apply to a body of creditors. In all the late cases the Lord Chancellor took

(*a*) The rules and recent cases with regard to dealings by trustees with the trust property, will be found, *ante*, note (*a*), *Whichcote* v. *Lawrence*, 3 V. 740; note (*a*), *Campbell* v. *Walker*, 5 . 678.
(1) See *Ex parte Hughes, Ex parte Lyon, Ex parte Lacey*, *ante*, 617, 625.
(2) *Ante*, vol. iii. 740; see page 750, and the note, 752.
(3) The preceding case.
(4) *Ante*, vol. v. 678.

the same course, as a general rule, in opposition to *Whelpdale* v. *Cookson* (1).

The MASTER OF THE ROLLS [Sir WILLIAM GRANT].— Such an inquiry as is prayed by the Defendants was never directed. The Court has never gone so far by implication to countenance the transaction. ' The very circumstance, that the lot is knocked down to the trustees, proves, that no better price could be got at the time. That therefore, if it is to prevail, would make every sale to a trustee good.

The rule is a rule of general policy, to prevent the possibility of fraud and abuse; for it may not always be possible to [* 633]   know, * whether the property was undersold. I was not aware, that the Lord Chancellor had laid down a general rule as to the terms; that the property should be set up again at the risk of the trustee. It is a very important consideration, whether that is to be taken as a general rule. If it is, I must adhere to it : but if it turns upon special circumstances, I see no special circumstances in this case. These lots must be resold at all events. The only question is, whether they shall be put up at the price, at which the trustees purchased.

Feb. 24*th.* The cause having stood over, the Master of the Rolls said, he had mentioned it to the Lord Chancellor; and his Lordship said, he meant to lay down a general rule; and understood, it had been so established, in Lord Thurlow's time.

The decree was therefore made in conformity to the preceding cases.

1. As to purchases of trust property by the trustees; see the note to the last case but one; and note 2 to the last preceding case.

2. Lord Eldon, in *Sanderson* v. *Sanderson*, 13 Ves. 603, declared that he had frequently laid it down, as a principle in bankruptcy, that where trustees for infants had purchased the trust property the Court would not disturb the sale, if it appeared to be beneficial to the infants; and would disturb it, if it did not appear to be for their benefit. That principle, his lordship added, though open to objection, must be adhered to, until a better could be found; and see the note to *Earl Powlett* v. *Herbert*, 1 V. 297.

(1) 1 Ves. 9. Stated from the Register's Book, *ante*, 682, in *Campbell* v. *Walker.*

WATKINS *v.* LEA.

An estate held by copy of Court Roll, according to the custom of the manor, but in case of intestacy distributable as personal estate, and in other respects differing from copyhold, passed under a residuary bequest of the personal estate, not with copyhold estates under a general devise of all freehold and copyhold messuages, lands, &c. with limitations in strict settlement, upon the whole Will and the circumstances.
Devise of all freehold lands would include leases for lives (a); though the limitations are inapplicable, [p. 642.]

By the custom of the manor of Broadwas and Doddenham, in the county of Worcester, the estates situate within the manor are held of the lords by copy of Court Roll; and according to the custom are granted by copies of Court Roll for two lives in possession and two in reversion upon trust for the persons beneficially interested; and are devisable by the persons beneficially interested without any surrender to the use of the will; but in case of intestacy are not descendible to the heirs: but are distributable as personal estate; and on the death of any life and surrender of the other lives then in being and payment of the customary fines, the lords of the manor have made new grants by copies of Court Roll * for   [* 634] two lives in possession and two in reversion for the benefit of the persons beneficially interested.

At a Court Baron, held for the said manor on the 23d of October, 1775, Gregory Watkins, a customary tenant of the manor, being then the only life in possession, surrendered; and Josiah Lea and Thomas Smith surrendered the reversion of the same estates; and the lords of the manor granted to the said Gregory Watkins and to the said Josiah Lea, in trust for Gregory Watkins, to surrender, when by him, his executors, administrators, or assigns, required, the said premises; to hold the same unto Gregory Watkins and Josiah Lea upon trust as aforesaid for the term of their lives and the life of the longest liver successively according to the custom of the manor; and Gregory Watkins gave to the lords certain fines; and was admitted tenant; and at the same Court the lords granted to Thomas Smith and John Smith, in trust for Gregory Watkins, to surrender, when by him, his executors, administrators, or assigns, required, the reversion of the same premises; to hold upon trust as aforesaid for the term of their lives and the longer liver successively according to the custom, immediately after the decease, surrender, or forfeiture, of Watkins and Lea; and Watkins gave other fines on that occasion.

Gregory Watkins being so seised, and being also seised in fee simple of freehold estates in the counties of Worcester, Stafford, and Somerset, and of copyhold estates of inheritance in the county of Stafford, and a small copyhold estate of inheritance in the manor of

---

(a) *Aylett* v. *Aylett*, 1 Wash. 300.

Hagley in the county of Worcester, and possessed of leasehold and
personal estates, and having duly surrendered all his copyhold estates of inheritance, except the said estate within the manor of
Hagley, to the use of his will, by his will, dated the 31st of October,
1787, and duly executed to pass real estates, directed, that all his
debts should be fully paid ; and subject thereto, after giving several
annuities and legacies, gave to Joseph Lea and Gregory Watkins
100*l.* a-piece, to be paid at the end of twelve months after his decease, if they were then capable to give a release, or otherwise,
when they should become capable thereof : to the payment of all
which legacies and annuities he subjected as well his personal as
real estates, if his personal estate should be insufficient to
[* 635]   * discharge the same. He gave and devised to his kinsman John Watkins all and singular his freehold and
copyhold messuages, lands, tenements, and hereditaments, whatsoever, situate in the several counties of Worcester, Stafford, and
Somerset, or elsewhere within the kingdom of Great Britain ; to
hold to him and his assigns for the term of his natural life without
impeachment of waste ; remainder to trustees to preserve contingent
remainders ; remainder to the first and other sons of John Watkins
in tail male ; with several remainders over in the same manner in
strict settlement, and the ultimate limitation to the right heirs and
assigns of the testator for ever.

The testator then, after giving several specific legacies to William
and Josiah Lea, gave the several sums of 100*l.* and 50*l.* upon trust
to pay the former sum to the Treasurer or the Governors of the
Worcester Infirmary and the latter to the Treasurer of the Charity
School in Kidderminster ; which said sums of 100*l.* and 50*l.* he
thereby charged upon his personal estate, and willed the same to be
paid thereout, and applied towards carrying on the charitable designs
of the said societies ; and he gave and bequeathed all the rest, residue, and remainder, of his personal estate and effects whatsoever
after payment of his just debts, legacies, and funeral expenses, to
William and Josiah Lea, share and share alike ; and he appointed
them executors.

The testator died in 1789. The bill was filed by John Watkins,
the first devisee for life, claiming under the will, and particularly
praying, that the grants of the copyhold estates within the manors
of Broadwas and Doddenham might be declared to have been in
trust for the benefit of the Plaintiff and the other persons entitled to
the freehold and copyhold estates under the will ; which was the
only question.

The Defendants, the residuary legatees, by their answer suggested,
that when a *feme covert* becomes beneficially interested in such
copyhold premises, the husband may sell the same without the concurrence of the wife, unless she happens to be one of the persons,
for whose lives the said premises are granted ; and that,
[* 636]   although such premises are held by copy of * Court Roll,

yet the persons beneficially interested therein may dispose of such interest by deed and without any surrender in Court.

Mr. *Mansfield*, Mr. *Alexander*, Mr. *Romilly*, and Mr. *Horne*, for the Plaintiff, and Mr. *Richards*, for a Defendant in the same interest.—These estates, notwithstanding the peculiarities of their tenure, are clearly copyhold; passing by surrender, though it is supposed not usual to surrender them, and held by copy of Court Roll, according to the custom of the manor. The testator devises all his copyhold estates. There is no doubt, that under a devise of all the devisor's freehold estates, or a general devise of lands, &c. an estate held for lives would pass; and why should not copyhold estates so held pass under a general devise of copyhold estates? This is not like the cases, in which it has been contended, that leaseholds for years would pass under a general devise of all lands, &c. Here certainly is a variety of limitations, which properly apply only to estates of inheritance: but that is not an uncommon circumstance: testators not adverting to it. There are many cases of leasehold estates in consequence of clear unequivocal words coupled with real estates for the purpose of being carried on as far as the rules of law and equity will permit, notwithstanding words of limitation not strictly applicable to such estates. This is as like a perpetual estate as can be from the number of lives and the habit of renewal. The circumstance, that the charitable legacies are charged upon the personal estate, shows, that the testator considered this as real estate. The residue of the personal estate given to the Leas must be such personal estate as he had charged with those legacies; that could not be charged upon real estate; and which therefore must not be taken to be included. The Defendants must contend, that this estate, though held by copy of Court Roll according to the custom, is not copyhold, merely because in case of intestacy it is divisible as personal estate. An estate held for lives, though by the Act (1) distributable as personal estate, does not on that account lose its description. This is a mere question of intention. The case of *Rose* v. *Bartlett* (2), and those, which have followed it, will be relied on, from the circumstance, that the limitations are inapplicable. But this testator has devised a great number of real estates,
* freehold and copyhold, not distinguishing any of them; [* 637] meaning the limitations therefore to apply to those estates
only, to which they are applicable. But it has been decided, that this circumstance alone will not do: *Addis* v. *Clement* (3), *Lane* v. *Lord Stanhope* (4). This estate is always renewable; like that in *Addis* v. *Clement.* Though there never has been a decision against *Rose* v. *Bartlett*, the Courts of late have not been disposed to favor it: *Lowther* v. *Cavendish* (5), *Turner* v. *Husler* (6); in both of

(1) Stat. 14 Geo. II. c. 20.
(2) Cro. Char. 293.
(3) 2 P. Will. 456.
(4) 6 Term Rep. B. R. 315.
(5) Amb. 356.
(6) 1 Bro. C. C. 78.

which *Rose* v. *Bartlett* was not treated with much respect. *The Attorney General* v. *Andrews* (1) is very applicable. This testator had no copyhold estate in Worcestershire, that could pass by the will, except this: the only other copyhold he had in that county not being surrendered to the use of the will. The Defendants attempt to take under this will, not as customary heirs; insisting, that the testator intended to give his copyhold estates by a bequest of his personal estate, not by the devise of his copyhold estate.

Mr. *Lloyd* and Mr. *Cox*, for the Defendants, the residuary legatees.—The case was fully argued before the late Lord Chancellor: who considered it so doubtful, that he never came to a conclusion upon it. This estate is nominally copyhold: but substantially it is only a freehold lease to a person, his executors, administrators, and assigns, for the lives of others. It has no quality applicable to copyhold estate. It is liable to debts; and passes without surrender; and has never been the subject of recovery. If a man is possessed in right of his wife, it passes by the husband's conveyance without any examination of the wife. The expression of the trust is to surrender, when by him, his executors, administrators, or assigns, required. The legal estate could not pass to the tenant for life; but must remain in the trustees. In *Addis* v. *Clement* and *Turner* v. *Husler* the estate was occupied with others: and the latter was upon a demise of tithes out of that very estate. Lord Rosslyn threw out an opinion, that *Addis* v. *Clement* might be right upon that ground; that the estates had been occupied together; an inference arising from that sort sort of union, that the testator [* 638] might have intended them to go * together. This case does not afford the least circumstance of that kind. These estates were never occupied with the copyholds of inheritance or the freehold. There is no contiguity, and no reason to imagine, he meant these estates to be enjoyed together. The limitations are perfectly inapplicable. If a son of the tenant for life should live an instant, his father would take this estate absolutely as his administrator: it never could go with the estates of inheritance; and the will would be disappointed. The last limitation in this will is to the right heirs of the testator. That would be the old interest of the testator in so much of the property as is undisposed of; and that would not have gone to the heir: this property being limited to him and his executors. The argument is fair, that, where he meant a strict settlement, he meant those capable of being so limited: but as to the personal property an absolute gift was intended; and no limitation. If this had been a leasehold estate, and the devise general of all lands, &c. the same argument would have applied; and according to the last case, *Thompson* v. *Lawley* (2), which seems full as well considered as any of the others, it would have gone into the personal estate. That would do no vio-

---

(1) 1 Ves. 225.
(2) *Ante*, vol. v. 476, and the note, 478; 2 Bos. & Pul. 303.

lence to the intention. The words are sufficiently satisfied. Upon such an estate as this it is absurd to speak of impeachment of waste, trusts to preserve contingent remainders, &c. The will is satisfied by his having freehold estates in one county and copyhold in another, copyhold of inheritance, which may be supposed intended to pass. It has always been held a considerable argument, that the copyhold estate was surrendered to the use of the will. *The Attorney General* v. *Andrews* is not applicable; amounting only to this; that the Court would get rid of the want of surrender in the case of a younger child. *Rose* v. *Bartlett* and all the other cases contained words, that looked like an intention to pass all the testator had : but the limitations being inapplicable, the Court thought, it could not be intended, if there was sufficient to satisfy the will without that estate. This will has nothing more special in it showing an intention to pass this, than in the wills in *Thomson* v. *Lawley* and *Sheffield* v. *Lord Mulgrave* (1). Here is copyhold estate, in its nature devisable, and which he has shown he meant to devise; having surrendered it to the use of his will. This is a copyhold * estate, but of a personal nature. The strong ground   [* 639] is, that the limitations are wholly incapable, an argument, upon which *Sheffield* v. *Lord Mulgrave, Doe* v. *Buckner* (2) and many other cases turned; admitting, that the estate might pass under circumstances. Another head of cases has been treated in the same manner; upon the question, whether under the general words "all my estate" an estate held by the testator as a bare trustee passed (3). The late Lord Chancellor looked at the limitations; and where the subject was real estate, hampered with limitations, which could not be supposed applicable to a trust estate, held, that it could not be included; and that seems also to be Lord Alvanley's opinion (4).

Mr. *Mansfield*, in reply.—This testator meaning to give every copyhold estate he had in any part of the kingdom could not have used words more appropriate. The argument, that the limitations are inapplicable, a circumstance common in dispositions of freehold and leasehold estates, is too slight to defeat the general intention, expressed in the plainest words. What reason could he have as to the charitable legacies, but that he knew, they could not be charged on his real estate ? *Rose* v. *Bartlet, Thompson* v. *Lawley,* and the other cases of that class, do not apply here. It is very different to decide, that a general devise of all lands, with a description applicable to estates of inheritance, will not include leasehold estates, and that a devise of all and singular his copyhold estates will not include copyhold estates. Land and leasehold are frequently contradistinguished in the western part of the kingdom. When the case

(1) *Ante,* vol. ii. 526; 5 Term. Rep. B. R. 571.
(2) 6 Term Rep. B. R. 610.
(3) *Ante, Ex parte Brettell,* 577 ; *Attorney General* v. *Buller,* vol. v. 339, and the references.
(4) *Ante, The Duke of Leeds* v. *Munday,* vol. iii. 348, and the notes, 349; v. 341.

of *Sheffield* v. *Lord Mulgrave* came back, considerable doubt was
entertained as to the decision of the Court of King's Bench; and
Lord Rosslyn would not act upon it.   Certainly there was something
very particular in that case with regard to the renewal of the lease,
directed only in a particular event.   The decision at law went merely
upon this ; that the particular direction as to the renewal might be
           what was meant by the words "hereinafter mentioned and
[* 640]   devised." In *this case there is no one circumstance
           against the Plaintiff, except the limitations ; and there is
nothing to restrain the general words.   The words cannot be satisfied by the copyhold estates in other counties, if any one copyhold
in any county is left out ; and there are none in Worcestershire, that
pass by the will.

   Lord CHANCELLOR [ELDON].—If I had been aware of the nature
of this case, I would have taken a mode of having it decided, that
would in effect have given me the opinion of a Court of Law.   I
have been struggling to frame a case : but it is infinitely difficult to
do that.   If I had been aware of that difficulty, I would have desired
the assistance of some of the Judges ; and am still disposed to take
that method ; for this is a case of considerable difficulty and consequence ; and if it involves the consideration of *Rose* v. *Bartlet*,
Thompson v. *Lawley*, and the other cases upon that subject, it is peculiarly fit, that it should be argued with that assistance.   My own
opinion upon the principles, that ought to regulate the Court with regard to those cases, I formed with great labor ; and came to this conclusion ; that *Rose* v. *Bartlet* afforded a clear, intelligible, rule ; by
which you might judge ; applying a doctrine of law, familiar and
easily understood as to legal instruments.   It is impossible to deny,
that Lord Hardwicke in *Chapman* v. *Hart* (1) and *Knotsford* v.
Gardiner (2) held, that *Rose* v. *Bartlet* was sacred ; that it was not
to be touched ; and he must have been informed of *Addis* v. *Clement*,
before his immediate predecessor : but he held that rule clear doctrine, a land-mark in the law.   If any fault is to be found in what
he says, it is a fault on the other side ; that perhaps according to the
note he carries his idea farther than a strict attention to the rule
could justify.

   As to *Lowther* v. *Cavendish*, it is difficult to believe, Lord Northington said what is reported.   He was a great lawyer and very firm
in delivering his opinion ; and if he dissented from *Rose* v. *Bartlet*, I
rather think, he would in a firm and manly way have denied that case
to be law, rather than have thrown out such an observation.   With
           respect to *Lane* v. *Lord Stanhope*, when the general rule
[* 641]   is *understood to be according to *Rose* v. *Bartlet*, and a
           question arises as to an exception out of that rule, there
will be a difference of opinion upon the intention arising from the
circumstances ; as those circumstances operate upon different minds.

---

(1) 1 Ves. 271.
(2) 2 Atk. 450.

But there is no great mischief in that : so long as the general rule is acknowledged, and the difference arises only from the views of different minds, construing the same circumstances.   As to what Lord Kenyon says (1) in that case upon *Pistol* v. *Riccardson* (2), supposing, that Lord Mansfield's opinion would have been different if *Addis* v. *Clement* had been adverted to, I am not quite sure of that. In that case I should not have followed *Addis* v. *Clement*.   Some of the distinctions in that case appear to me, not only not solid, but incapable of being reconciled to legal doctrine.   I am also of opinion, that, instead of struggling by little circumstances to take cases out of a general rule, it is more wholesome to struggle not to let little circumstances prevent the application of the general rule.   There is hardly one of those cases, in which it is not said, that the general intention was to make the leasehold estate go with the real estate as far as by the rules of Law and Equity it can.   Such an intention is very familiar in fact (3) : but no conveyancer would have attempted to execute such intention in the way, from which in any of those cases that imputed intention has been held a ground for passing the leasehold estate.   The mode of doing it is plain ; either by very special limitations as to the leasehold estate, as there were in *Pelham* v. *Gregory* (4) ; technical limitations, to prevent it from vesting, and to carry it as far as the rules of Law and Equity will admit ; or, if general words are preferred, you state, that it shall go as long as the rules of Law and Equity will permit it to be enjoyed with real estate : that is, nearly till a recovery can be suffered ; viz. till the age of twenty-one of the tenant in tail.   Then the rule of law will not let it go farther : whereas the other will go, till a recovery is suffered. In all these cases that intention might have been frustrated immediately after the testator's death ; as where the limitation is to the father for life ; with remainder to the son in tail ; and a son had lived a minute : the whole effect would be, that the father would have taken the whole leasehold estate.

I never could see the policy of taking cases out of a   [642] general rule of law, which all may understand, upon the ground of intention, which the testator has taken no one of the ordinary means to express. This case will not turn upon that. The circumstance, that the limitations are inapplicable, is very strong for inferring the intention, if the words leave it ambiguous, whether leasehold estates are meant, or not : but if the testator has expressly said, he meant leasehold estate, however ignorantly, idly, or ineffectually, he has described the subject, it is in vain to resort to that circumstance ; for you cannot strike out the description.   There are frequent instances both of deeds and wills, in which leasehold estates are given and settled with freehold estates ; sometimes even a lease for ten years ; with all these limitations in strict settlement, trustees to preserve con-

(1) 6 Term Rep. B. R. 353.
(2) Stated 2 P. Will. 459, in Mr. Cox's note to *Addis* v. *Clement*.
(3) *Ante, The Duke of Newcastle* v. *The Countess of Lincoln*, vol. iii. 387.
(4) 5 Bro. P. C. 435.

lease was always considered as personal estate, at least to the extent of being assets : *Ripley* v. *Waterworth*, 7 Ves. 438 ; *Duke of Devonshire* v. *Kinton*, 2 Vern. 719 : though, in other respects, it was formerly held to retain the character of freehold ; and not to be distributable under the intestacy of the deceased tenant *pur autre vie : Oldham* v. *Pickering*, Carthew, 376 : but this is now settled definitively to the contrary, by the statute 14 Geo. II. cap. 20, sect. 9 ; see note 4 to *Ripley* v. *Waterworth*, 7 V. 425.

4. Every devise of land, whether in particular or general terms, must of necessity be specific : *Howe* v. *Earl Dartmouth*, 7 Ves. 147 ; *Nannock* v. *Horton*, 7 Ves. 399 ; *Milner* v. *Slater*, 8 Ves. 305 ; *Hill* v. *Cock*, 1 Ves. & Bea. 175. See note 2 to *Brydges* v. *The Duchess of Chandos*, 2 V. 417.

5. Whether a residuary gift of the testator's personal estate, shall, or shall not, be understood a gift of his copyholds, seems to be a question which must be determined upon the intention, if that can be distinctly collected. ` *Rumboll* v. *Rumboll*, 2 Eden, 19.

LEERS, *Ex parte.*

[1802, FEB. 6, 11.]

DIVIDENDS declared upon a bill of exchange, though not received, must be deducted from the proof by the endorsee under another Commission of Bankruptcy.

Proof by obligee under a Commission against the principal, at the request of the surety, securing the obligee by paying the amount of the bond into a banker's, [p. 646.]

POURTALIS and Company, of London, drew a bill of exchange, dated the 23d of July, 1799, on Cloessen, Kieckhoefer, and Company, of Hamburgh, for 750*l.*, payable three months after date, to the order of Mendez Pereira and Castellain ; which was accepted ; and endorsed by Mendez Pereira and Castellain, to the order of Pierre Boursier de Ruesnas, a merchant at Hamburgh, and afterwards endorsed by him to Leers and Company.

The bill was protested for non-payment. In January 1800, a Commission of Bankruptcy under the Great Seal of Great Britain issued against Mendez Pereira and Castellain. Cloessen, Kieckhoefer, and Company, and Pierre Boursier de Ruesnas [* 645] also were *made bankrupts. Leers and Company caused the bill to be claimed against both their estates according to the due course of such proceedings at Hamburgh ; and a dividend of 6*s.* in the pound was declared of the estate of Cloessen, Kieckhoefer, and Company ; and a dividend was also declared of the estate of Pierre Boursier de Ruesnas.

Leers and Company not having received any part of those dividends applied to be admitted to prove under the Commission against Mendez Pereira and Castellain for the amount of the bill of 750*l.* and the charges : but the Commissioners refused to admit the proof for the whole sum ; alleging that they ought to deduct the amount of the dividends reserved from the estates of Cloessen, Kieckhoefer, and Company, and Pierre Boursier de Ruesnas ; upon which the petition was presented by Leers and Company; insisting, that not having yet received any part of the said reserved dividends they are entitled to prove the whole amount of the bill and charges against the estate of Mendez Pereira and Castellain; and praying accordingly, that they may be admitted to prove the full amount, and receive dividends *pari passu* with the other creditors, until they are fully paid the amount of the bill and charges.

This petition was mentioned on several days: the Lord Chancellor expressing considerable doubt, whether a man having a bill, by virtue of which he has three debtors, is not entitled to prove the whole against each estate, until he has received 20s. in the pound (1).

Mr. *Cooke*, being applied to by the Lord Chancellor as to the practice at Guildhall, stated, that a dividend declared was constantly deducted; observing, that in *Brown* v. *Bullen* (2) it was decided, that an action for money had and received lies for the amount of the dividend the moment it is declared: and it would be singular, if the creditor could arrest in that action, and yet go before the Commissioners, swearing, he had received no security or satisfaction whatsoever.

*Mr. *Romilly* and Mr. *Leach* in support of the petition,   [*646] put the case of a dividend declared immediately; the party at Hamburgh, and knowing nothing of it: whether it would be payment in that case.

Lord CHANCELLOR made the order, that the dividends should be deducted according to the practice, as stated by Mr. *Cooke;* still expressing doubt as to the principle of it: and, in answer to the objection from the difficulty put as to the creditor taking the usual oath, referring to the case of principal and surety in a bond: the principal being a bankrupt, and the obligee insisting on payment from the surety is desired by him to prove under the Commission, and he will pay the amount into a bankers (3).

1. As to a creditor's right to prove his whole demand against the estate of each of the parties, whose bills or securities he holds; and not only to prove in respect of any collateral securities, against the estates of all those who entered into such securities, but also to take dividends upon each of such proofs, to the extent, in the whole, of twenty shillings in the pound upon his actual debt; though all payments previously received, and (generally speaking,) all dividends *declared* from the estate of another party, must be deducted from the proof he tenders under a different commission; see *ante*, note 1 to *Ex parte Bloxham*, 5 V. 448.

2. That dividends under a commission of bankruptcy are to be recovered by petition to the Lord Chancellor, only; and not by action; is now established by legislative enactment; see stat. 6 Geo. 4 c. 16, s. 111.

3. As to the right of sureties, or parties otherwise liable for the debts of a

(1) See *Ex parte Bloxham, ante,* 449, 600; vol. v. 448, and the note, 449.
(2) Doug. 392. This was altered by Statute 49 Geo. III. c. 21, s. 12, directing, that no action shall be brought for a dividend; and authorising the Lord Chancellor on petition to order payment, with interest and costs; and that is adopted by the Statute 6 Geo. IV. c. 16.
(3) *Ex parte Todd,* 2 Rose Bank. Cas. 202, note; *Ex parte Atkinson,* 1 Cooke's Bank. Law, 210, 8th edit. by Mr. Roots, 232; *Ex parte The Royal Bank of Scotland, post,* vol. xix. 310; 2 Rose, 197.

bankrupt, to prove against his estate, after they have discharged the debt; see the 52d and 55th section of the statute just cited; see, also, note 2 to *Ex parte Matthews*, 6 V. 285.

JENKINS v. HILES.

[1802, Feb. 20, 22, 23.]

General rule, that the Court will not decide upon a title without a reference to the Master; unless unequivocally, and without fraud or surprise, waived: a Plaintiff seeking a specific performance of a contract being entitled to the opportunity of making out a better title before the Master; and the Defendant having a right to farther inquiry, beyond the objections arising on the abstract, upon the principle, that the bill seeks relief beyond the law.

Charge or direction by deed or will for payment of debts generally, followed by specific dispositions: the purchaser is not bound to see to the application (a), [p. 654.]

By indentures, dated the 5th of April, 1761, Edward Cludd demised to Joseph Hiles certain estates and premises; to hold to Joseph Hiles, his executors, administrators, and assigns, for the term of 99 years, if Hiles and his wife and their daughter, or any or either of them, should so long live, at the yearly rent of 63*l.* 3*s.* 4*d.*; with a proviso for re-entry, if Hiles, his executors, &c. should lease or assign the premises or any part without the license of Cludd, his heirs or assigns, in writing first had; except such disposal as Joseph Hiles should make of the premises entire for the benefit of his wife or any child or children without parting the same.

By indentures, dated the 4th of February, 1763, Joseph Hiles in consideration of 200*l.* paid to him by Cludd assigned the premises to John Stamer for the residue of the term under the yearly rents, covenants, provisoes, conditions, and agreements, in the [* 647]   * original lease, in trust for Cludd, his executors, &c. subject to redemption.

By indentures, dated the 20th of January, 1766, in consideration of 283*l.* 12*s.* 3*d.* paid by John Windsor to Cludd, and 216*l.* 7*s.* 9*d.* paid by him to Hiles, the premises were assigned to Windsor, his executors, &c. for the residue of the term, subject to the rents, cov-

---

(a) Wherever the trust or charge is of a defined and limited nature, the purchaser must himself see, that the purchase-money is applied to the proper discharge of the trust; but wherever the trust is of a general and unlimited nature, he need not see to it. 2 Story, Eq. Jur. § 1127; 1 Madd. Ch. Pr. 352, 496; Madd. Ch. Pr. 103; 1 Powell, Mortgages, ch. 9, p. 214-250, Coventry & Rand's edit.; *Shaw* v. *Bower*, 1 Keen, 574; *Braithwaite* v. *Britain*, 1 Keen, 206, 222.

Where a testator, by his will, charged his real estate with the payment of debts generally, and afterwards devised his real estate to a trustee upon certain trusts for other persons, it was held, that the trustee had a right to sell or mortgage the estate so charged for the payment of the debts; and that, upon such sale or mortgage, the purchaser or mortgagee was not bound to look to the application of the purchase or mortgage money; *Ball* v. *Harris*, 4 Mylne & C. 264; *Eland* v. *Eland*, 4 Ibid, 420. See also *Lining* v. *Peyton*, 2 Desaus. 375; *Taliaferro* v. *Minor*, 1 Call, 524.

enants, provisoes, reservations, conditions, and agreements, mentioned and comprised in the original lease, subject to redemption by
'Joseph Hiles, his heirs, executors, and administrators.

By indentures, dated the 25th July, 1767, Joseph Hiles in consideration of 100*l.* paid to him by John Hammonds, assigned the
premises to Hammonds, his executors, &c. for the residue of the
term, and also during all the other estate, term and interest, which
Joseph Hiles, his executors, &c. might have under the said lease,
subject to the rents, provisoes, covenants, and agreements, contained in the original lease : and . subject to the mortgage vested in
Windsor.

By indentures, dated the 20th of January, 1769, Windsor in
consideration of 500*l.* paid to him by James Hiles assigned and
Joseph Hiles ratified and confirmed, to James Hiles the premises
for the residue of the term, at and under the yearly rents, covenants,
provisoes, conditions, and agreements, contained in the original
lease, subject to redemption by Joseph Hiles, his heirs, executors,
and administrators.

James Hiles having filed a bill of foreclosure against Hammonds,
in February 1771 an agreement took place ; by which the account
of the interest was settled ; and it was declared, that the principal
should carry interest at 4*l.* 10*s.* from Lady Day next ; and Hammonds agreed to make a lease to James Hiles for seven years at a
rent of 105*l.* 10*s.* ; out of which the original rent to Cludd was to
be paid, and the interest of the mortgage to be retained ; and the
remainder to be paid to Hammonds.

In September 1775 Hammonds died ; having by his will given
all his personal estate to his two daughters Anna, the wife
of * John Jenkins, and Sarah Breach. Samuel Breach,   [* 648]
the husband of the latter, died intestate in January 1791 ;
and administration was granted to his widow.   -

James Hiles having been in possession under the agreement of
1771 without paying any rent, except the original rent to Cludd,
Jenkins and Breach served him on the 26th of September, 1786,
with notice to quit, and on the 24th of March following tendered
him 111*l.* 19*s* 6*d.* for principal and interest remaining due on his
mortgage, and 25*l.* for repairs and improvements ; which he refused ; and also refusing to deliver up possession, they threatened
to file a bill ; which led to articles of agreement, dated the 18th of
February, 1790 ; by which Jenkins and Breach in consideration of
300*l.* agreed to assign to James Hiles the lease of 1761 and the
premises for the residue of the term ;' and Hiles agreed, that he
would on the execution of such assignment, which it was agreed
should be executed before the 3d 'of May next, pay the said 300*l.*
At the same time the assignment of July 1767 of the equity of redemption by Joseph Hiles to Hammonds, and the articles of 1790,
so executed by Jenkins and Breach, were delivered to James Hiles :
who was also in possession of the original lease.

The bill was filed by Jenkins. and his wife and Sarah Breach

against James Hiles; praying, that the Defendant may be decreed
either to accept a proper assignment of the equity of redemption,
and to pay the consideration, with interest from the time mentioned
in the said articles for payment; or that he may account for the
rents and profits; and that on payment of what shall be found due
for principal and interest on his mortgage the Plaintiffs may be let
into a redemption, &c.

The Defendant by his answer stated, that he believed no consideration whatever was paid by Hammonds for the assignment from
Joseph Hiles; who having married one of the daughters of Hammonds, and being imprisoned for debt, and intending to take the
benefit of the Lords' Act or some other Insolvent Act, executed the
assignment to Hammonds voluntarily without any consideration for
the sole purpose of defrauding his creditors; and he stated declarations of Hammonds and Joseph Hiles to that effect. He
[*649]   *farther stated, that he was willing to carry into execution the articles of agreement on having a good title made;
. but the Plaintiffs are not capable of making a valid disposition of
the equity of redemption without the license of Cludd; and, suggesting the bankruptcy of Samuel Breach, submitted, that the Plaintiffs
ought to have delivered an abstract of their title, or at least of so
much as commences with, and is derivative under, the Commission
of Bankruptcy against Breach; that his interest is in his assignees;
and the Plaintiffs had not explained, how they claim title under the
assignees; nor do they take notice of it by the bill.

Upon that answer coming in the bill was amended; stating the
bankruptcy of Breach; and that having obtained his certificate he
purchased from his assignees one moiety of the premises, subject to
the mortgage, for 10*l.* 10*s.*; which by deed of assignment, dated
the 8th of July, 1784, was assigned to him accordingly for the residue of the term.

The Defendant went into evidence, that the objections were taken
by his attorney; and that no abstract was delivered. The answer
was replied to: but the Plaintiffs did not go into evidence.

Mr. *Romilly* and Mr. *Hollist* for the Plaintiffs, in answer to the
objection to the title for want of a license from the original lessor
insisted, that the condition was determined by the license given,
when the mortgage was made in trust for him in 1763; according
to *Dumper's Case* (1).

Upon the other objections they contended, that the Defendant had
dealt with Hammonds, as being entitled; and the delivery of the
abstract was unnecessary: the Defendant being in possession of all
the deeds. They farther urged, that, all the objections appearing
upon the pleadings, the Court would decide upon them without a
reference to the Master.

[*650]   *Mr. *Lloyd* and Mr. *Stratford*, for the Defendant.
The license in this case might be special, and under re-

---

(1) 4 Co. 119.

strictions; not like that in *Dumper's Case,* which was general, and certainly destroys the condition. This transaction was nothing more than a license to mortgage in trust for the owner of the estate. In Equity there may be some difference between a license to alien generally and a license to enable the lessee to make a mortgage. A Court of Law does not look at the proviso for redemption : but this Court only considers it a pledge for payment of the money. Such a license could not in Equity be considered a forfeiture of the lease : for he cannot be considered as parting with his property. The redemption is given to Hiles, his heirs, executors, and administrators, not assigns ; and the assignment is expressly subject to the covenants, provisoes, conditions, and agreements, in the original lease.

But it is now insisted, that the Court in a case of this kind can upon the bill and answer decide a question of title without a reference to the Master. That is perfectly new. The only authorities for such a proposition are two late cases, *Rose* v. *Calland* (1) and *Omerod* v. *Hardman* (2). No authority is to be met with previous to the former of these cases; and it may reasonably be doubted, whether those decisions are correct. The reason for having a Report and proceeding by Exceptions is, that the ground upon which the Court proceeds, may appear upon the Record. This is analogous to the rule at law, that a writ of error cannot be brought upon an interlocutory judgment. It is often said, that the Master's Report is the same as a final judgment at law. If this can be done upon one or two objections, why not upon any number, if appearing upon the pleadings? In *Marlow* v. *Smith* (3), the title was referred to the Master; though the only point was, whether a trust estate passed by a general devise (4). In *Roake* v. *Kidd* (5), though mere questions of Law were to be decided, Lord Alvanley would not decide them *without a reference to the Master. The   [* 651] same course was taken in *Cooper* v. *Denne* (6) and *Abel* v. *Heathcote* (7). In the latter there could not have been a more naked question. Nothing could have sent that to the Master but the form of the Court, requiring the title to be stated. Upon this subject it is very important, that there should be some known, general, rule. The decision in *Omerod* v. *Hardman* was given in opposition to a deliberate opinion of Lord Redesdale and others. A reference is more necessary upon facts; where facts may come out before the Master. In this case every suspicion is thrown upon the title by the conduct of the Plaintiffs.

---

(1) *Ante,* vol. v. 186.
(2) *Ante,* vol. v. 722.
(3) 2 P. Will. 198.
(4) See *ante, Ex parte Brettell,* 577, and the note, 579; *The Duke of Leeds* v. *Munday,* vol. iii. 348, and the note, 349; *Ex parte Sergeson,* iv. 147; *The Attorney General* v. *Buller,* v. 339, and the note, 341.
(5) *Ante,* vol. v. 647.
(6) *Ante,* vol. i. 565.
(7) *Ante,* vol. ii. 98 ; 4 Bro. C. C. 278.

Mr. *Romilly*, in reply.—In this case certainly there cannot be a decree in the first instance without consent; as it does not appear, that there was an assignment by the assignees of the bankrupt; without which a good title cannot be made. But the inquiry ought to be confined to that point; and is not to be a general reference to inquire, whether a good title can be made.

Upon the point now urged, that there is an invariable rule, no matter what may be the state of the pleadings, that a reference to the Master may be insisted on, no such .rule appears in any of the cases, that have been referred to. In *Marlow* v. *Smith* the bill was not for a specific performance; and the question as to the title could not come on except upon the Master's report. In *Cooper* v. *Denne*, *Abel* v. *Heathcote*, and *Roake* v. *Kidd*, no question was made, whether the points might not have been decided at the original hearing, if upon the state of the pleadings they could have been decided. There is no decision against the two last cases. But there is a great difference between the general proposition, that upon a bill by a vendor the purchaser shall be compelled to take the title stated without a reference, and such a case as this: the Defendant submitting to have the agreement carried into execution; and stating the points, upon which he objects. What can be the reason of a rule creating great additional expense? What advantage is there in having the opinion of a Master upon the very points now before the Court ? If the Defendant chooses to state his [* 652] objections upon the answer, the Court may * decide upon them.   There is great objection to this; for the ground may not appear in this way; as it is not necessary, that the exception should state the point ; •which in *Abel* v. *Heathcote* was said to be modern practice ; and that the usual way was to take the exception generally, that the Master has stated, that a good title cannot be made.   There is more advantage therefore in having the point clearly stated upon the record.

Upon the first objection it is said, there is something peculiar in this case ; and the assignment is not absolute, but by way of mortgage.   These covenants are always held to great strictness ; *Crusoe* v. *Bugby* (1).   *Roe* v. *Galliers* (2).   A mortgage is an absolute assignment at law.   There is the same objection to that ; for the only object to the covenant is, that the lessor shall not have a tenant he does not approve of.   Upon the objection, that the assignment is subject to the covenants, conditions, and provisoes of the original lease, there is nothing special in the assignment.   Every assignment must be subject to all the covenants ; and these words being tacitly included have no operation.   But if there was any ambiguity, it is removed by the conduct of the lessor ; who has accepted a tenant and received rent under this assignment for thirty-three years.   It would be impossible for him now to bring an ejectment.   As to the

(1) 3 Wils. 234 ; *ante, Seers* v. *Hinde*, vol. i. 294.
(2) 2 Term. Rep. B. R. 133.

objection, that the assignment to Hammonds by Joseph Hiles was fraudulent, it has stood unimpeached for thirty-five years; and the Defendant himself filed a bill of foreclosure against Hammonds; and afterwards entered into this agreement with him; considering him as mortgagor.   Under these circumstances they cannot have an inquiry, whether that consideration was paid upon a deed executed so long ago; and then there is nothing to refer as to that.

Lord CHANCELLOR [ELDON].—I feel very great disinclination to make the decree, which under all the circumstances I think myself required to make.   That disinclination is diminished by the consideration, that though the decree in form cannot be what I wish, it will in substance and the execution of it not operate otherwise than if I could make the decree I wish to make.   But I am of opinion, I am bound to refer this to the Master; to see, whether a
* good title can be made to the equity of redemption,   [* 653] which is the subject of this contract.

It is admitted, that, where a bill is filed for specific performance of a contract for the purchase of real estate, in ordinary cases the Defendant may have a reference upon the title for asking for.   I always conceived, that was not a rule founded merely in. practice, and not in any assignable principle; but that it is really founded in principle, and a principle somewhat of this nature; that if, instead of bringing an action of damages for breach of covenant, the Plaintiff comes here for a specific performance, the Defendant has a right, not only to have such a title as the Plaintiff offers upon the abstract unauthenticated, but, in consideration of the relief sought here beyond the law, to have an assurance about the nature of his title, such as he cannot have elsewhere.   Therefore the Court never acts upon the fact, that a satisfactory abstract was delivered; unless the party has clearly bound himself to accept the title upon the abstract: but though the abstract is in the hands of the party, who says, he cannot object to it, yet he may insist upon a reference.   Why? Because the decree compels the other party to produce all the deeds, papers, &c. in his custody or power; from which reasonable and solid objections to the title may be furnished; which would never have fallen under the view of the purchaser, unless the Court wrung from the conscience of the vendor that sort of information, which a purchaser could by no other means acquire.   Inquiries and examinations also may be directed; by which the title may be shifted in a way, in which it never could upon a mere abstract, authenticated as the vendor thought proper.   The rule therefore is founded upon a right, that gives specifically all the assurance, which in the nature of things the party can have from sifting the conscience of the party, who sues him in this Court as to the matter of title   I have never understood, that the rule has gone this length; that the Defendant against whom a specific performance is sought, may not by an answer unequivocal, to which he was not drawn by surprise, the propriety of which is not rendered disputable by any subsequent discovery, waive the benefit of this principle; and come here, saying in effect, he trusts the representation of the Plaintiff without the obligation of an oath upon his conscience; offering in the first instance to the decision of the Court one neat dry point; upon which alone his objection rests. The rule has not been considered so absolute. But such instances, if they have occurred in practice, will not shake the rule; but forming an exception would confirm the general rule.

On the other hand *Rose* v. *Calland* and the case in the Duchy Court are not cases of this class; the vendor in those cases coming for a specific performance: the vendee calling for a decision; and objecting, if that is his title, and he puts himself upon it, and chooses to abide by that, and admits, that nothing he can do will heal the deficiencies appearing upon the title. I should there also be disposed to think, that, if the general rule is, that the vendor is entitled to clear away all difficulties by what he can do between the hearing and the Report, it would be difficult to say, there could not be a case, in which the Plaintiff might not have stated himself so conclusively, that the Court should hesitate in the first instance to decide. If I am to state a doubt upon the case in the Duchy Court, it would be a doubt, whether it could be collected from what was stated by the Plaintiff, that, if the title was imperfect, it was stated conclusively, or, whether, if stated conclusively. it was doubtful. Upon that case I shall only say, that passages have crept into the Report, which it is very difficult to reconcile with the ordinary practice of this Court and some of the doctrine very familiarly applied here. I allude to some passages as to what trustees for payment of debts and legacies can do, stated with a degree of doubt, which it is not wholesome should remain as an authority (1).

[*655]　　　　* As to *Rose* v. *Calland*, I consider it only as a case, in which the Plaintiff did state himself as not being able to state a better title; not as an authority, that, if he had said he could make a better title between the hearing and the Report, the Court would have bound him to what he had stated in his bill; and that on account of that statement he had given up the right to a specific performance. It is impossible to deny, that upon the old authorities a specific performance might be obtained, if the title could be made

---

(1) The Lord CHANCELLOR during the argument observed upon that case, that the Court were mistaken in supposing, the purchaser had any thing to do with the annuity to the lunatic, the legacy of 400*l.* &c. If that was so, his Lordship said, he should agree with the judgment; but it was long settled, that where a man by deed or will charges or orders an estate to be sold for payment of debts generally, and then makes specific dispositions, the purchaser is not bound to see to the application: it is just the same as if the specific bequests were out of the Will. The case under consideration would shake that rule. The trustees had the legal estate under the deed: and the trust was to sell for payment of debts generally. They were therefore enabled to make a title to the purchaser; who was not bound to see to the payment of the legacy, the annuity, &c.

See the authorities collected by Mr. Fonblanque, 2 Treat. Eq. 148, 149. As to an executor pledging the assets as a security for his own debt, see *post, Hill* v. *Sampson*, vol. vii. 152; *Taylor* v. *Hawkins*, viii. 209; *M'Leod* v. *Drummond*, xiv. 353: xvii. 152.

good before the Report (1). The Court would execute the contract then ; regard being had to the justice due to particular cases. Where the vendor is Plaintiff, if the rule is founded in a principle of conscience, and requiring all possible security to be given to the purchaser, the Court will at least take care, that, where it is contended that the Defendant has waived his right to a reference, it shall be clear that there was no surprise upon him, and that there has been a full and fair representation as to the title on the part of the Plaintiff ; not merely that representation, which a conscientious man would make, after due diligence, but that which a conscientiously diligent man would make. But, where from fraud or surprise on the part of the Plaintiff there has been deficient information, the Court will take care, that a Defendant shall never be surprised by the effect of a submission made upon want of full information. In the ordinary case of purchase, if any thing is discovered afterwards, the Court acts upon the conscience of all parties, while it has its finger upon the money ; and after any submission ; provided the discovery is made before the money is gone out of Court.

In this case there is no intention on the part of the Plaintiff to sink any circumstances as to the title ; and I go upon the application of a general principle in a case, in which individually out of Court I should think myself hardly bound to apply it ; alluding to the length of possession and other circumstances. The Defendant states certain objections. Suppose, the answer says, those objections being removed, he will take the title: am I to bind him by that ? The answer intimates the circumstance of Breach's bankruptcy ; and that produces from the Plaintiffs a perfectly different representation of their title. Can it be said, that a Defendant is bound by a submission, the answer stating a fact, which alters the title ; and makes it necessary to amend the bill, and introduce * a fact, which ought, and which must have been [* 656] in the Plaintiff's knowledge ; and in that representation laying a ground for considerable examination ? It is admitted, that the Defendant is not bound upon that point. But why is he bound upon the others ? Am I to presume, that those points are right, and that there is no other ; and in the case of parties, admitting themselves wrong in a material instance ? Upon this ground I am compelled with great reluctance to refer this title. I have an opinion upon the objection as to the license, and as to the transaction with Hammonds ; considering the length of time, and from whom the objection comes : but referring the title generally I shall say no more upon those questions. I am not justified, considering the general rule, in saying, there can be no objection to the title of a Plaintiff, stating in his original bill, that it is free from objections, to which by his amended bill he admits it to be open.

---

(1) *Post, Wynn v. Morgan,* vol. vii. 202; x. 315; xvi. 275. Farther evidence may be produced before the Master on both sides : *Vancouver v. Bliss,* xi. 458. But this rule, that a purchaser may be compelled to take a title, not made until after the contract, is not to be extended ; 2 Jac. & Walk. 289.

The decree accordingly directed a general reference as to the title ; and an inquiry, whether any abstract was required; and whether any and what application was made by the Plaintiffs to the Defendant, before the bill was filed ; and what was the result.

---

1. WITH respect to the practice of directing a reference to the master, when upon a bill brought for specific performance, the single question is, whether the vendor can make a good title; see *ante,* note 6 to *Cooper v. Denne,* 1 V. 565. But that a purchaser by taking possession of, and exercising acts of ownership over, the estate he has contracted for, may be held to have waived his ordinary right of examining the title; see note 2 to *Calcraft* v. *Roebuck,* 1 V. 221.

2. Trustees for payment of debts generally, and not merely of specified or scheduled debts, can make a good title to the property devised to them for such general purposes, and a purchaser from them is not bound to see to the application of the money; *Rogers* v. *Skillicorne,* Ambl. 189; *Smith* v. *Guyon,* 1 Brown, 185; *Williamson* v. *Curtis,* 3 Brown, 95.

3. As to the effect of even an innocent misrepresentation, in precluding a vendor from insisting on a specific performance; and that, wilful misrepresentation may possibly be such as to afford grounds for rescinding a contract, after it has been completely executed; see the note to *Wakeman* v. *The Duchess of Rutland,* 3 V. 233; and notes 2 and 3 to *Oldfield* v. *Round,* 5 V. 508.

ELLISON *v.* ELLISON.

[1802, Fɛʙ. 24.]

Distinction as to volunteers. The assistance of the Court cannot be had without
consideration to constitute a party *cestuy que trust* ; as upon a voluntary covenant to transfer stock, &c. (*a*). But if the legal conveyance is actually made,
constituting the relation of trustee and *cestuy que trust*, as if the stock is actually
transferred, &c., though without consideration, the equitable interest will be
enforced.

Settlement of leasehold estates not revoked by a subsequent assignment by the
trustee to the settlor, entitled for life, or by the will of the latter: no intention
to revoke appearing : and the terms of a power of revocation not being complied
with.

In general cases trusts will not fail by the failure of the trustee (*b*), [p. 663.]

By indentures, dated the 1st of July, 1791, reciting a lease, dated
the 6th of June preceding, of collieries at Hebburn and Jarrowwood,
in the county of Durham, for thirty-one years to Charles Wren
and others ; and that the name of Wren was used in trust for
Nathaniel Ellison and Wren in equal shares, it was declared,
that Wren, his executors and administrators, would stand possessed of the lease in trust as to one moiety for Ellision, his execu- *
tors, &c.

* By another indenture, dated the 18th of June 1796,   [* 657]
reciting, that Ellison was interested in and entitled to one
undivided eighth part of certain collieries at Hebburn and Jarrow,
held by two several leases for terms of thirty-one years ; and that.
he was desirous of settling his interest, he assigned and transferred
all his interest in the said collieries and all the stock, &c. to Wren,
his executors, administrators, and assigns, in trust for Nathaniel Ellison and his assigns during his life ; and after his decease in trust
to manage and carry on the same in like manner as Wren should

---

(*a*) Courts of Equity will not enforce a mere gratuitous gift, or moral obligation.
2 Story, Eq. Jur. § 973 ; *Tufnell* v. *Constable*, 8 Sim. 69 ; *Flower* v. *Master*, 2
Mylne & Craig, 459 ; *Baun* v. *Winthrop*, 1 Johns. Ch. 336 ; *Edwards* v. *Jones*, 1
Mylne & C. 226, 237 ; *Duffield* v. *Elwes*, 1 Bligh, N. S. 529–531 ; *Jefferys* v.
Jefferys, 1 Craig & Phillips, 138 ; *Black* v. *Cord*, 2 Har. & Gill, 100 ; *Groves* v.
Groves, 3 Young & J. 163 ; *Banks* v. *May*, 3 A. K. Marsh. 436 ; *Wycherley* v.
Wycherley, 2 Eden, 177 ; *Hale* v. *Lamb*, Ib. 294. Unless the gift is perfected and
complete, so that nothing farther remains to consummate the title of the donee.
2 Story, Eq. Jur. § 706*a*, 787, 793*a*, 973, 987, 1040*b* ; *Minturn* v. *Seymour*, 4 Johns.
Ch. 498 ; *Fortescue* v. *Barnett*, 1 Mylne & K. 36 ; *Sloane* v. *Cadogan*, Sugden on
Vendors, Appx. No. 26.

It is no matter, if the consideration be meritorious, or if the parties, seeking the
intervention of the Court, stand in the relation of a wife or child. 2 Story, Eq.
Jur. § 987 ; *Holloway* v. *Headington*, 8 Simons, 325 ; *Jefferys* v. *Jefferys*, 1 Craig
& Phillips, 138. See also *McInhire* v. *Hughes*, 4 Bibb, 187 ; *White* v. *Thompson*,
1 Dev. & Bat. 493.

(*b*) The appointment of new trustees is an ordinary remedy, enforced by Courts
of Equity, where there is a failure of suitable trustees to perform the trust, either
from accident, or from the refusal of the old trustees to act, or from the original or
supervenient incapacity to act, or from any other cause. See 2 Story, Eq. Jur.
§ 1287 ; *ante*, note (*a*), *Brown* v. *Higgs*, 5 V. 504 ; note (*a*), *S. C.* 1 V. 707.

carry on his own share; and upon farther trust out of the profits to pay to Margaret Clavering during the remainder of the term, in case she should so long live, the yearly sum of 103*l*. 2*s*. 8*d*.; which sum is thereby mentioned to be secured to her by an indenture, dated the 14th of May last; and subject thereto in trust to pay thereout to Jane Ellison, in case she should survive Nathaniel Ellison, during the remainder of the term, during the joint lives of Jane Ellison and Anne Furye, the clear yearly sum of 180*l*.; and after the decease of Anne Furye then the yearly sum of 90*l*. during the remainder of the term, in case Jane Ellison should so long live; and subject, as aforesaid, upon trust to pay thereout to each of the children of Nathaniel Ellison, that should be living at his decease, during the remainder of the term, during the joint lives of Jane Ellison and Anne Furye, and the life of the survivor, the yearly sum of 30*l*. a piece, and after the decease of the survivor the yearly sum of 15*l*.; and upon farther trust to pay the residue of the profits arising from the collieries to the eldest son of Nathaniel Ellison, who should attain the age of twenty-one; and upon the death of Margaret Clavering then upon trust to pay to each of the children of Nathaniel Ellison the farther yearly sum of 10*l*.; with survivorship, in case any of the children should die before twenty-one, or marriage of daughters, provided none except the eldest should be entitled to a greater annuity than 50*l*.; and upon farther trust to pay the residue to the eldest son: provided farther, in case all the children die before twenty-one or the marriage of daughters, upon trust to pay the whole to such only child at twenty-one, or marriage of a daughter: provided farther, in case the profits to arise from the colliery should not be sufficient to pay all the annuities, the annuitants except Margaret Clavering should abate; to be made up, whenever the profits should be sufficient; and upon farther trust, in [* 658] case Wren, his * executors, or administrators, should think it more beneficial for the family to sell and dispose of the collieries, upon trust to sell and dispose of the same for the most money, that could reasonably be got, and to apply the money in the first place in payment of all debts due from the colliery in respect of the share of Ellison; and subject thereto to place out the residue on real securities and apply the interest in the first place in payment of the annuity of 103*l*. 2*s*. 8*d*. to Margaret Clavering, then to the annuities of 180*l*. or 90*l*.; then to pay all the children of Ellison during the life of Margaret Clavering the yearly sum of 22*l*. 10*s*., and to pay the residue of the dividends and interest to the eldest son of Ellison in manner aforesaid; and if the dividends, &c. should not be sufficient for the annuities, the two annuitants except Margaret Clavering to abate; and after her death to pay to each of the children of Nathaniel Ellison the farther yearly sum of 2*l*. 10*s*. for their lives; and after the decease of Margaret Clavering and Jane Ellison upon trust to pay to each of the children of Nathaniel Ellison the sum of 500*l*., in case the money arising from the sale should be sufficient; then upon trust to divide the same equally

among all the children, share and share alike; and subject, as aforesaid, to pay over the residue to the eldest son on his attaining twenty-one; and it was declared, that the portions of the children should
be paid to the sons at twenty-one, to the daughters at twenty-one
or marriage; and in case of the death of any before such period to
pay that share to the eldest son at twenty-one; and if only one
child should survive, to pay the whole to such one at twenty-one,
or marriage, if a daughter; and in case all die before twenty-one,
&c. then the said Charles Wren, his executors and administrators,
shall stand possessed of the said collieries and the money to arise by
sale .thereof, subject as aforesaid, in trust for Nathaniel Ellison, his
executors, administrators, and assigns.   It was farther declared,
that the annuities should be paid half yearly; and that upon any
such sale the receipt of Wren, his executors or administrators,
should be a sufficient discharge to purchasers.   Then followed this
proviso.

"Provided always and it is hereby farther declared that it shall
and may be lawful for the said Nathaniel Ellison by any deed or
deeds writing or writings to be by him signed sealed and delivered in
the presence of and attested by two or more credible
* witnesses, to revoke determine and make void all and   [* 659]
every the uses trusts limitations and powers herein before
limited and created of and concerning the said collieries and coal
mines, and by the same deed or deeds or by any deed to be by him
executed in like manner to limit any new or other uses of the said
collieries and coal mines as he the said Nathaniel Ellison shall think
fit."

By another indenture, dated the 3d of July, 1797, but not attested
by two witnesses, reciting the leases of the collieries, and that the
name of Charles Wren was used in trust for Nathaniel Ellison and
himself in equal shares; and that Ellison had advanced an equal
share of the moneys supplied for carrying on the collieries, amounting to 9037l. 10s., it was witnessed, that in consideration of 4518l.
15s. Wren assigned to Nathaniel Ellison one undivided moiety or
half part of all the said collieries demised to him by the said several
leases, with a like share of the stock; to have and to hold the said
collieries to Ellison, his executors, administrators, and assigns, for the
residue of the said terms, subject to the rents, covenants, and agreements, in the said leases; and to have and to hold the stock unto
Ellison, his executors, administrators, and assigns, to and for his and
their own proper use for ever; with the usual covenants from Wren
as to his title to assign, &c. and from Ellison to indemnify Wren, his
executors, &c.

Nathaniel Ellison by his will, dated the 22d of June, 1796, after
several specific and pecuniary legacies, gave all the rest and residue
of his personal estate and effects of what nature or kind soever not
before disposed of, to his wife and Wren and the survivor and the
executors and administrators of such survivor; upon trust to call in
and place the same out in the funds or on real securities; and he di-

taken in *Colman* v. *Sarrel,* independent of the vicious consideration.
I stated the objection, that the deed was voluntary: and the Lord
Chancellor went with me so far as to consider it a good objection to
executing what remained in covenant.   But if the actual transfer
is made, that constitutes the relation between trustee and *cestuy que
trust,* though voluntary, and without good or meritorious consideration; and it is clear in that case, that if the stock had been actually
transferred, unless the transaction was affected by the turpitude of
the consideration, the Court would have executed it against the trustee and the author of the trust.

In this case therefore the person claiming under the settlement
might maintain a suit, notwithstanding any objection made to it, as
being voluntary; if that could apply to the case of a wife and
children; considering also, that Mrs. Clavering was an annuitant,
and not a mere volunteer.   But it was put for the Defendants thus;
that though the instrument would have been executed originally, if
the subject got back by accident into the author of the trust, and
was vested in him, then the objection will lie in the same manner,
as if the instrument was voluntary.   I doubt that for many reasons:
the trust being once well created; and whether it would
[* 663] apply at all, where the trust was originally * well created;
and did not rest merely in engagement to create it.   Suppose, Wren had died; and had made Ellison his executor: it would
be extraordinary to hold, that, though an execution would be decreed against him as executor, yet, happening to be also author of
the trust, therefore an end was to be put to the interest of the *cestuy que trust.*   But it does not rest there; for Ellison clothes the
legal estate remaining in Wren with the equitable interests declared
by the first deed; making him therefore a trustee for Ellison himself
first, and after his death for several other persons; and he has said,
he puts that restraint upon his own power: not only, that he shall
not have a power of revocation, whenever he changes his intention,
but that he shall not execute that power, nor be supposed to have
that change of intention, unless manifested by an instrument, executed with certain given ceremonies.   My opinion is, that, if there
is nothing more in this transaction than taking out of Wren the estate clothed with a trust for others, with present interests, though
future in enjoyment, and that was done by an instrument with no
witness, or only one witness, it is hardly possible to contend, that
such an instrument would be a revocation according to the intention
of the party, the evidence of whose intention is made subject to restrictions, that are not complied with.   The only difficulty is, that
the declaration of the trusts in the first instrument could not be executed, the second instrument being allowed to have effect.   It is
said, a power was placed in Wren, his executors and administrators,
not his assigns, if in sound discretion thought fit, to sell, and to give
a larger interest to the younger children than they otherwise would
take.   If Wren had not after the re-assignment that discretion still
vested in him, I think, it would not be in the executors of Ellison,

and it could not be exercised by the Court ; though in general cases trusts will not fail by the failure of the trustee (1). But though the effect would be to destroy the power of Wren, which I strongly doubt, attending to the requisition of two witnesses, I do not know, that it would destroy the other interests. I think therefore, upon the whole this trust does remain notwithstanding this re-assignment of the legal estate to Ellison. I do not think, consistently with the intention *expressed in the first instrument, and   [*664] the necessity imposed upon himself of declaring a different intention under certain restrictions, that if a different intention appeared clearly upon the face of the instrument, the latter would have controlled the former. But I do not think, his acts do manifest a different intention. Supposing one witness sufficient, the second deed does not sufficiently manifest an intention to revoke all the benefits given by the first deed to the children ; and it is not inconsistent, that he might intend to revoke some and not all.

As to the will, it is impossible to maintain, that the will is a writing within the meaning of the power : considering, how the subject is described. The word "residue" there means that estate, of which he had the power of disposing, not engaged by contracts, declarations of trusts, &c. It was necessary for him to describe the subject in such a way, that there could be no doubt, he meant to embrace that property.

Upon the whole therefore this relief must be granted ; though I agree, that, if it rested in covenant, the personal representative might have put them to their legal remedies, he cannot, where the character of trust attached upon the estate, while in Wren ; which character of trust therefore should adhere to the estate in Ellison ; unless a contrary intention was declared ; and the circumstance of one witness only, when the power reserved required two witnesses, is also a circumstance of evidence, that he had not the intention of destroying those trusts, which had attached : and were then vested in the person of Wren.

_____

1. THAT Courts of Equity, although they take no notice of a contract merely voluntary, while such contract remains *in fieri* will enforce it, as between the parties, when the act, though voluntary, has been completed, see, *ante*, note 2 to *Colman* v. *Sarrell*, 1 V. 50.

2. The Court of Chancery will not, in general cases, permit a trust, or a power coupled with a trust, to be disappointed by the failure or negligence of the trustee: see note 4 to *Moggridge* v. *Thackwell*, 1 V. 464, and note 2 to *Bull* v. *Vardy*, 1 V. 270.

_____

(1) *Ante, Brown* v. *Higgs*, vol. iv. 708 ; v. 495 ; *post*, viii. 561.

O'CONNOR *v.* COOK.

[1802, Feb. 24, 25.]

Issue directed on a Modus for certain lands, amounting to 1*s.* per acre for all tithes, notwithstanding the apparent rankness.
Courts of Equity formerly more in the habit of deciding questions of fact than lately, [p. 671.]
Rankness of a modus is only evidence; not an objection in point of law, [p. 672.]
Distinction as to rankness between a modus for tithe of particular things and a farm modus, [p. 672.]

THE bill was filed by the lessee under a lease for twenty years granted by Trinity College, Cambridge, of all the tithes both great and small of the hamlet or district of Streetfields, in the parish of Monkskirby, against an occupier of the lands for an account of the tithes of milk and agistment subtracted since Michaelmas 1797.

The Defendant by his answer set up a modus of 20*l.* a-year, payable half yearly, for the lands called Streetfields in lieu and satisfaction of all tithes; and suggested, that such modus had been payable long before time of memory, and does not exceed the value of the tithes, for which it hath been payable; which he represented to be about 50*l.* a year.

The effect of the depositions was, that Streetfields was one entire farm of near 400 acres. Within the rectory are Cestersover and several other hamlets. Streetfields in its present state of cultivation is worth 30*s.* an acre; and if in tillage would be worth 40*s.* The yearly value of the great and small tithes in the present state of cultivation is from 3*s.* to 5*s.* an acre (according to the different witnesses); and if in tillage, would be 15*s.*, computed from the present high price of every article and the present high cultivation of the land. The sum of 20*l.* was immemorially paid as a modus or rate-tithe in lieu and satisfaction of all tithes; which modus or rate-tithe was also supported by general reputation.

The other evidence consisted of extents and inquisitions *post mortem*: an extent in the third year of Richard II. 1380, of the alien priory of Monkskirby, in which the jury found 384 acres in Monkskirby; of which 192 were arable, worth 3*d.* an acre, and 192 uncultivated, worth 1*d.* an acre per annum; total value 60*s.*; and *decimæ gabarum* in the whole hamlet of Monkskirby were worth per annum 60*s.*; also, that Thestrewaver was parcel of the priory; and there was there of rent 9*s.*; and that *decimæ gabarum* there were [* 666] eight marks, 5*l.* 6*s.* 8*d.* The tithes of wool and lamb * belonging to the priory in all the twenty hamlets were worth per annum 27*l.*; and the other small tithes, mortuaries, and oblations, ten marks; 6*l.* 13*s.* 4*d.*

Upon an inquisition *post mortem*, 19 Ed. IV. A. D. 1480, it was found, that the manor of Thestrewaver with the appurtenances was of the annual value of 20*l.* beyond repairs; and by another in 1546, the 39th of Hen. VIII. it was found, that Thestrewaver and Coxford with the appurtenances and twenty messuages, comprised 500 acres; 200 meadow, and 300 pasture; and the said manor and all the said lands were of the annual value of 60l. beyond repairs (1).

The *Solicitor General* and Mr. *Bell*, for the Plaintiff.—The modus set up, a shilling an acre, is too rank. *Troutbeck* v. *Lawson* (2). *Startup* v. *Doddridge* (3). Where the rankness is so plain, the Court will not send it to a jury: otherwise it must be carried to this extent; that the Court can in no case decide without an issue. *Moore* v. *Beckford* (4). *Ekin* v. *Pigot* (5). From Acts of Parliament and many other things, of which the Court can take notice judicially, they can judge of the rankness; and, where it most clearly appears, they may determine upon it. The Statute of Edw. III. and others fix the average price of the quarter of wheat at 6s. 8d. That was in the fourteenth century. But carrying it back 300 years farther, it will be found, that the quarter of wheat was at 2s. only, which would make this modus much more than the value of the land. Whether these tithes were formerly payable upon arable land, or not, depends upon the meaning of the word "*gabarum*" (6), occurring in this extent; whether it includes every thing bound up *in fasces*, sheafs or bundles; as corn and hay.

Mr. *Romilly* and Mr. *Martin*, for the Defendant.—There must be an issue. From the length of time this must be presumed an immemorial payment; unless it contains something in itself * destructive of itself. This is a question of fact certainly;   [* 667] but notwithstanding that, if it is so clear, that the Court cannot have the least doubt, an issue will not be directed. But by refusing an issue in such a case as this numerous decisions will be overturned. The consideration of the rankness of a modus is very different, when it is applied to a parochial modus for any particular article, even throughout a parish, and, when it is payable for any particular district. It is very easy to see the price of any particular article at the time of memory, the expedition of Richard I. to the Holy Land. But it is very different as to land; for one acre of land is not of the same value as another, though separated only by a hedge. It is extremely difficult to ascertain the value of land at any particular time; not only of particular land, but of land throughout the kingdom. That proceeds only upon conjecture as to the value of corn at particular times. There may be a variety of circumstances, that may have depreciated the value of land. The evidence, that has been read, because no objection was taken, does not show, that Streetfields is within the hamlet of Cestersover; of which there is no evidence. The bill states Streetfields as a distinct hamlet: but no

---

(1) The Lord Chancellor observed, that the instruments made the value of the tithes unaccountably large in proportion to the value of the land.
(2) 1 Wood's Exch. 223.
(3) Salk. 657; 2 Lord Raym. 1158.
(4) Cited in *Pyke* v. *Dowling*, 2 Black. 1257; 3 Gwill. Tith. 1166.
(5) 3 Atk. 298.
(6) For the meaning of the word "*garba*" see *Sims* v. *Bennet*, 3 Gwill. Tith. 874.

evidence of that being found, the Plaintiff now endeavors to have it considered as part of the other; in which he fails. But taking it so, and admitting 20*l.* to have been three times the value in the time of Henry VI. or Edward IV. that is not conclusive. The depreciation in those times of civil commotion does not determine the value at another time. At this time there has not been an enemy in the country for a century and a half. The argument from the present rent, to get at the value of the tithe, is very fallacious. It is never assessed at that value. The value of the land is a very complicated question of fact; not like the question upon a single article. The present rule seems to be to send this sort of modus to an issue; which only revives the former practice. In *Sansom* v. *Shaw* (1) this doctrine of a rank modus was considered a sort of innovation. That it is a question of fact appears from the certificate in *Pye* v. *Dowling* (2). In many other cases, upon smaller or greater payments, the Court has considered some of them good, and some fit for a jury. *Bedford* v. *Sambell* (3). *Ekins* v. *Dormer* (4). In *Hardcastle* v. *Slater* (5) the objection of value was considerably greater [*668] * than in this instance. In a late case in the Court of Exchequer, *Fermor* v. *Lorraine,* evidence of the value of the rectory very ancient was not considered sufficient to prevent it from going to a jury. The argument for the Plaintiff proves too much; applying to all the cases, in which issues have been directed upon a modus of 1*s.* an acre. The inquisitions *post mortem,* it is well known, are very inaccurate. Favor is shown to the family; and the estate is taken at a nominal value. But this is not evidence applying to the land in question; and it is not competent to prove the value of other land, though contiguous. How can the Defendant meet the evidence? How can he cross-examine? The Defendant has a right to assume, that at the time of the composition it was for the most valuable tithe, corn and grain. He may go farther; he may assume, that the composition might from the piety of the person be higher, and intended to be beneficial, with a view to the future increase as well as the present value of the tithes (6).

In *Chapman* v. *Smith* (7) the argument now used would have applied; and would have been sufficient to prove it 1500*l.* a-year. All the arguments applicable to this case were used in *Grascomb* v. *Jeffries,* cited by Lord Hardwicke (8). Nothing is produced in this case, but that the tithes are 50*l.* a-year; and therefore, it is contended, this modus is too large. In *Ekin* v. *Pigot* there is a circumstance distinguishing it entirely; and that case certainly was not followed by the Court of Exchequer in *Fermor* v. *Lorraine.* The

(1) 2 Gwill. Tith. 806.
(2) 2 Black. 1257; 3 Gwill. Tith 1166.
(3) 3 Gwill. Tith. 1058.
(4) 2 Gwill. Tith. 800.
(5) Amb. 41.
(6) See the case of an inclosure put by Lord Hardwicke, 2 Ves. 516.
(7) 2 Ves. 506.
(8) 2 Ves. 515.

modus appeared to have been 30*l.* a-year.   Afterwards an agreement took place to give the clergyman a piece of land, of 6*l.* a-year;
and therefore the modus should be 24*l.* a-year.   Pope Nicholas's
taxation showed, the whole value of the living was not more than
——.   But the acknowledged inaccuracy of that taxation was what
the Court of Exchequer went upon.   *Twells* v. *Welby* (1) was much
stronger; for the modus of a shilling per acre for all tithes was only
when the land was used for meadow and pasture; which is generally
the least productive to the rector.   The decision undoubtedly proceeded principally upon the circumstance, that the Jury had not found
the fact, as they ought; but still it proves, that an issue was directed
upon a much higher modus.   *Ashby* v. *Power* (2) applies
to the representation attempted of * this case.   If they had   [* 669]
shown, what the value of the land and the living formerly
was, yet, being only matter of inference, as is said in that case, it
ought to be sent to a Jury.   The moduses in that case were higher
or equal to this.   Few were less than 1*s.*: many higher.   In *Bishop* v.
Chichester (3) the modus of 2*s.* 6*d.* for every acre of corn and grain
was enormous.   It does not appear, that any issue was directed:
but it was objected to as being rank; and the expression is, that so
the Lord Chancellor inclined to think.   According to the calculation now made the value must have been 5000*l.* a-year.   I believe,
an account of tithes was decreed as to that: but the Lord Chancellor did not form a decisive opinion upon it.   *Edge* v. *Oglander* (4)
is certainly a very strong case; but has been often cited.   In *Atkyns* v. *Lord Willoughby de Broke* (5) the Court was disposed to
decide against the rector, if he had not insisted upon an issue.   The
Chief Baron there made the distinction as to a farm modus and one
for a particular species of produce.   But there is a much stronger
distinction between a parochial modus and one for any particular
district of land.

As to the receipts for the rate-tithe, that expression is often used;
though it is not clear, what it means: but it is never applied to a
temporary, varying, composition; and is always understood to be
some ancient payment; the origin of which is not known.   It is in
some receipts called a rate-tithe; in others a modus; and it cannot
be inferred, that it is not a modus, because the clergyman chooses to
call it a rate-tithe.   Lord Hardwicke says (6), the Rector does not
often choose to give the receipt *qua* modus; that he may not injure
his successor; and the occupier must take such receipt as the parson thinks fit to give him; but Lord Hardwicke also says, that an-
ciently those payments were not called by the term "modus;"
Richards v. *Evans* (7).   It is not necessary even in pleading to call

(1) 3 Gwill. Tith. 1192.
(2) 3 Gwill. Tith. 1238.
(3) 2 Bro. C. C. 161; more full, 4 Gwill. Tith. 1316.
(4) Cited Bunb. 391.
(5) 2 Anstr. 397; 4 Gwill. Tith. 1412.
(6) 2 Ves. 512.
(7) 2 Gwill. Tith. 802; 1 Ves. 39.

But what is the value of land in a particular parish, and what therefore it is proper to give per acre, is a very complicated question.
The owner might have been in possession of land of very different
values; and might commute upon the whole; though, if not an
average commutation, it would be a very improvident commutation
for a distinct part. The ownership might have been severed; and
then it would be very rash to conclude against a modus, admitted
to be too great for any particular part; when the very foundation is,
that he thereby got the liberty of compensation for the tithes in the
other lands. So upon a farm modus: I cannot weigh the propriety
of it: but I cannot forget, that great Judges have said in Equity,
and put it to Juries, that there may be a convenience in having a
farm modus; which may induce an individual to give more in that
way than he would as a modus for particular titheable produce, or,
per acre of arable land, and not including hay, &c.; and they have
stated, that piety might induce them to give rather more than less
than the value to the clergyman.

With regard to the cases, I never could persuade myself, that 1s.
per acre upon the principal of rankness was not in all probability a
monstrous payment; and that the payments sent to be tried at law
were not monstrous. But still the judges have thought,
[* 673]   *even such payments ought to go to trial; and verdicts,
under which in many cases even more than 1s. an acre has
been claimed, have been confirmed. What is this more than 1s. an
acre for all tithes of this farm, in whatever form cultivated or occupied; not for agistment, milk, lamb, or any other particular tithe?
It is said in the argument, this land has formerly been arable.
There is very little evidence upon that. I cannot conclude, that it
was not; and there is no evidence authorising me to say, this modus may not be shown by some evidence to be as reasonable a commutation for tithes, even put so distributively, and not as a farm
modus, as in some of those cases, where 1s. an acre has been given
even for tithe of hay alone. The cases certainly are very strong.
But when I find issues directed in cases full as strong, and Judges
acting upon them afterwards, it would be too bold in me to refuse
the Defendant an opportunity of submitting to a Jury questions not
more improbable than occurred in those cases; which in the result
were supported by evidence; and were thought to be satisfactorily
supported by the Courts, who sent those questions. Upon this subject I distrust myself, when I observe the comparative value of the
tithes; and am struck with the large value of the tithes, compared
with the estimated value of the land at that day. In this case it is
enough for me, that I cannot unravel the difficulty, so as to satisfy
myself, it was not a great deal more than a tenth of the value of the
land. The case tried by Mr. Justice Buller seems very strong. It
was sent to be tried under circumstances sufficient to make them
pause. One circumstance was very strong, as to the value of the
whole rectory at the time. No Judge felt more than Mr. Justice
Buller the extent, to which he thought the Law authorised Juries to

presume facts. I remember a case of presumption upon the advowson of Chester le Street (1). The manor was granted to the Milbanke family with an express exemption of the advowson. They had presented in one or two instances; and the Jury was directed by Lord Mansfield to presume, that the Crown had made a grant; which grant was not producible; and Mr. Justice Buller held that direction of Lord Mansfield perfectly right. Lord Chief Justice Eyre was no friend to that doctrine of presumption; and yet, hostile as he was to strong presumptions, he sent that case back to be tried upon the presumption, whether 1*s.* an acre was a good modus upon land, proved worth 16*s.* an acre, and * four   [* 674] years before worth 13*s.* an acre. Attending to Mr. Bell's calculation upon the naked question, can it doubted, looking back to the time of Richard I. whether it was a fair commutation? No one could hesitate upon it: but still the Court of Exchequer said, it was a question of fact: and they sent it back to be tried; and the conclusion was perfectly right. It might have been said, as Lord Kenyon said, will you send it to the prejudices of a Jury, not to their judgment? I cannot talk about that. I send it to their judgment; and ask them, what they think upon their conscience, directed by their oath.

I am not at liberty therefore, after what has passed in former cases, and whatever may be my persuasion as to the truth of this case, to say, this must not be tried. In *Fermor* v. *Lorraine* I never had the least doubt, that the modus was too rank: but the Court sent it to an issue.

An issue was directed, which was tried at the assizes for the county of Warwick; and a verdict was found for the Plaintiff in the issue, the Defendant in Equity, establishing the modus. A motion was made for a new trial on the grounds of misdirection of the Judge, and new evidence since discovered. The former ground referred principally to the observations of the Judge on Pope Nicholas's survey, as entitled to little weight; that in the ministers' accounts in the time of Hen. VIII. Streetfields was not mentioned; that it did not appear to be part of Cestersover; and it might be presumed, that there was another bailiff and another minister's accounts as to Streetfields. The new evidence was a deed of partition, in consequence of which a fine was levied, expressly comprising Streetfields as part of Cestersover (2).

————

1. IT is discretional in a Court of Equity, whether it will, or will not, take upon itself the decision of all questions of fact, introduced in a tithe cause; and, when an issue has been directed to a Court of Law, whether a second or third trial shall, or shall not, be ordered: see, *ante*, note 1 to *Canons of St. Paul's* v. *Crickett*, 2 V. 563, and the farther references there given.

————

(1) *Powell* v. *Milbanke*, stated Cowp. 103, in *The Mayor of Hull* v. *Horner; post*, vol. viii. 130, n. *Harmood* v. *Oglander.*
(2) A new trial was granted; in which the Plaintiff in Equity obtained a verdict; and the account was directed. *Post*, vol. viii. 535.

2. A Defendant to a bill brought for tithes in kind, may, no doubt, have the benefit of a composition real, if he can show it to have had existence, and to have been entered into with the concurrence of all proper parties; provided, also, he put this defence properly on the record: see the concluding passage of note 1 to *Strutt* v. *Baker*, 2 V. 625; but, as there is a clear distinction with respect to the evidence by which a modus and a composition real may be supported, the occupier of land must not lull the tithe-owner into security, by giving him reason to suppose no other defence than that of modus will be set up: see note 2 to *The Canons of St. Paul's* v. *Crickett, ubi supra.* It is true that a modus may have originated, it is even probable that most moduses did originate, in a composition; *Chapman* v. *Monson*, 2 P. Wms. 573; but then, a modus must be proved to have had existence from the remotest time of legal memory; whilst a real composition, insisted on as such, must have commenced within time of memory, and its commencement must be proved: it is not, indeed, absolutely necessary to produce the deed of composition, when it can be inferred, from satisfactory evidence, that it did once exist: *Hawes* v. *Swaine*, 2 Cox, 179; *Chatfield* v. *Fryer*, 1 Price, 256; *Heathcote* v. *Mainwaring*, 3 Brown, 217: but still, a Defendant who insists on a real composition cannot allege mere non-payment as evidence that such a deed once existed; *White* v. *Lisle*, 3 Swanst. 346, citing *Bullen* v. *Michell* 2 Price, 399; *Bolton* v. *The Bishop of Carlisle*, 2 Hen. Black. 263; *Chatfield* v. *Fryer*, 1 Price, 260. And see note 1 to *Rose* v. *Calland*, 5 V. 186. If this were permitted, and if a defence of composition real might be supported by evidence of usage, so as to give it the character of a modus, no one would ever be advised to plead a modus; when, by pleading at once a composition real, he could have the advantage of non-usage, and would also get rid of any objection on the score of rankness: *Ward* v. *Shepherd*, 3 Price, 625: but this is not permitted; there is an established barrier, separating modus from composition real; the two defences differ, both as to their nature, and as to the proof by which they must be supported; and an issue will not be directed to try a composition real, when the Defendant has by his answer only alleged a modus; *Bennett* v. *Neale*, Wightwicke, 361.

3. A modus is termed *rank*, when its amount is so large as to have greatly exceeded the value of the tithes at the period when Richard I. departed on his crusade; from which date the time of legal memory is held to commence: the question of rankness then, is one of fact, rather than of law; and is usually sent to a jury, when the least doubt arises: indeed, a modus is never established against a parson, without a trial at law, if he desire an issue: *Short* v. *Lee*, 2 Jac. & Walk. 497; *Bullen* v. *Michell*, 2 Price, 423; *Williams* v. *Price*, 4 Price, 156: but where the rankness of a modus is palpable, it would only cause the parties needless expense, were a Court of Equity to direct an issue for trial of a fact, as to which it felt perfectly satisfied. See note 1 to *The Canons of St. Paul's* v. *Crickett*, 2 V. 562.

4. Upon the principle of quieting possession, and not disturbing titles long acted upon, grants are frequently presumed; *Hillary* v. *Waller*, 12 V. 242, 267. And see note 2 to *Pickering* v. *Lord Stamford*, 2 V. 272.

DREWE *v.* HANSON.

[1802, Feb. 27.]

In enforcing contracts upon the principle of compensation for a variance from the description the Court has gone so far, to the extent even of wholly defeating the object of the purchaser, that, where the principal subject of the contract was all the corn and hay tithes of a parish, and of the hay tithe half was allotted to the Vicar, and the other half commuted for a customary payment, the nature of that payment, the extent of meadow, and the possible conversion from arable, not distinctly appearing, the injunction against recovering the deposit was continued after answer (a).

An injunction having been obtained, restraining the Defendant from proceeding at law to recover his deposit, the usual order was made for dissolving the injunction, unless cause, upon the answer coming in ; by which the following circumstances appeared.

In August the Defendant purchased from the Plaintiff by private contract an estate, consisting of some farms, and the tithes of the parish of Bishop's Lincomb in Devonshire, for the sum of 11,000*l.* the purchase to be completed on the 25th of December. The description in the particular as to the tithes was this : "Also the valuable corn and hay tithes of the whole parish of Bishop's Lincomb." An abstract was soon afterwards delivered ; and a rental : containing the general description of the garb (1), otherwise the tithe, of hay and corn : the latter expressing nothing relative to tithe of hay ; but containing these entries :

"Custom pay about 2*l.*"

"Farms out of tillage this year and not in composition 5."

"Estates occasionally in tillage but not in composition 20."

In September the Defendant went into Devonshire to see the estate ; and employed a surveyor to look over it. Upon the 14th of December he wrote to the Plaintiff, refusing to complete his purchase ; and calling for his deposit.

The corn tithes arose from about 8000 acres ; and were paid by annual composition. The tithe of hay was from so much of about 2000 additional acres, as was meadow (how much did not appear) : one half of the tithe of hay contained in the allotment belonging to the vicar : the other half commuted for by a payment of 2*l.* per annum ; the nature of which did not appear : the conversations upon the subject not carrying it farther than belief, that it was a modus. The answer also stated, that the tenants had converted arable to meadow, and threatened to convert more.

** Mr. *Romilly* and Mr. *Cox*, for the Plaintiff, showed   [* 676] cause against dissolving the injunction.—This is a subject

---

(a) Courts of Equity look to the substance of the contract, and do not allow small matters of variance to interfere with the manifest intention of the parties. See *ante*, note (a), *Craven v. Tickell*, 1 V. 60; note (a), *Calverley v. Williams*, 1 V. 210; note (a), *Calcraft v. Roebuck*, 1 V. 221; note (a), *Bowles v. Round*, 5 V. 508.

(1) As to the meaning of the word "*garba*," see the preceding case.

of compensation. The objection also is waived; not having been taken by the purchaser from August till December: *Fordyce* v. *Ford* (1). In *Lowndes* v. *Lane*, as to compensation, the estate not being tithe-free, as represented, Lord Thurlow went much into the application of the principle of " *Caveat emptor* " (2) ; and no doubt was entertained, that it was a subject of compensation ; and as there was a direct warranty, that it was tithe-free, compensation was given as to that ; but not as to the wood; with respect to which there was enough to put the purchaser upon inquiry. In *Poole* v. *Shergold* (3) also Lord Kenyon gave compensation for some part ; to which no title could be made. In that case was cited the case of a contract for a house and a wharf; and though no title could be made to the wharf, the purchaser was compelled to take the house.

Mr. *Mansfield* and Mr. *Heald*, for the Defendant.—There is no instance, in which a person contracting for all the tithes of a parish has been compelled to take half, or to take it subject to a modus, purchasing tithe in kind. *Pincke* v. *Curteis* (4) came at last to this question : the estate having been sold as tithe-free, whether the exemption extended to after purchased lands, recovered from the sea. The subject of the purchase was an estate at Gillingham, part stated in the particular to be tithe-free. It turned out, that the land paid no great rectorial tithes under a title derived by grant from the Crown of the tithes with the land: but the vicar was entitled to the small tithes. Subsequent to the grant the land was recovered from the sea. Upon exceptions to the Report it came before Lord Loughborough, and for farther directions ; who was finally of opinion upon great consideration, that the purchaser should not be held to that purchase: certainly against the decisions upon estates sold tithe-free, which turned out to be subject to tithe. The same doctrine has prevailed in subsequent cases ; that if the man cannot have substantially the thing for which he contracted, he shall not [* 677] be bound, though small * matters are the subject of compensation. *Calcraft* v. *Roebuck* (5) went upon the misconduct of the Defendant: otherwise that contract could never have been performed.

Upon the circumstances, there is nothing like a waiver. All that passed was a delivery of the abstract in August. There was no negotiation about the title : nor was the Defendant called upon to say, whether he would take it. The Plaintiff acquiesced, till the Defendant should determine, whether he would take it, or not. He went down with a surveyor to make inquiries ; the result of which appears in October. The principal of several objections was the modus for tithe of hay. That necessarily would compel him to

(1) 4 Bro. C. C. 494.
(2) *Ante, Bowles* v. *Round,* vol. v. 508.
(3) 2 Bro. C. C. 118.
(4) 4 Bro. C. C. 329.
(5) *Ante,* vol. i. 221; see the note, 226.

agree with the tenants as to the tithe of corn. In *Fordyce* v. *Ford* the parties went on disputing about the title ; and it appeared clear, that the objection was waived. In *Lowndes* v. *Lane* the party only wanted compensation ; not objecting to his purchase.

Mr. *Romilly*, in reply.—There certainly have been instances of compensation for tithes, as part of a large contract; when the vendor could make a title to every thing else ; as in the case put of a contract for the purchase of land tithe-free ; which is nothing but a contract for the land and the tithe. In all those cases the party has contracted for something, which it is not possible to give him : but as that is not the great object of his contract, it is a subject of compensation. The same argument applies, where the estate contains a less number of acres than represented. But this is a contract for tithes with other property ; and the tithe of hay is of very inconsiderable value (1). The Defendant certainly could not take till the day, on which the purchase was to be completed, to say, whether he would take it. He was bound to take the objection, as soon as it was known. What applications was the Plaintiff to make? The moment the rental was put into the Defendant's hand he knew the state of the objection. All this time he was speculating, whether he should carry the contract into execution.

* Lord CHANCELLOR [ELDON].—Without meaning to   [* 678] say, what may be the final decision, I am of opinion, attending to all the circumstances, it is too hazardous to say, there is not a fair and reasonable question, whether this contract may not be specifically executed. It is certainly to be observed, that under the head of specific performance contracts substantially different from those entered into have been enforced. In the case of a contract for a house and a wharf, the object of the purchaser being to carry on his business at the wharf, it was considered, that this Court was specifically performing that man's contract by giving him the house without the wharf. So in *Shirley* v. *Davis*, in the Court of Exchequer, the subject of the contract was a house on the north side of the river Thames. supposed to be in the county of Essex ; but which turned out to be in Kent ; a small part of which county happens to be on the other side of the river. The purchaser was told, he would be made a church-warden of Greenwich ; and though his object was to be a freeholder of Essex, he was compelled to take it. So in *Lord Stanhope's Case* the object was to get an estate tithe-free ; and yet Lord Thurlow obliged him to take it subject to tithes (2).

In this case the hay-tithes were represented to be of so much of about 2000 acres as happened to be employed in meadow : how

---

(1) This was denied by the Defendant.

(2) *Howland* v. *Norris*, 1 Cox, 59; *post*, vol. vii. 270; xvii. 280; 1 Mer. 23, 104. See the strong opinion of Lord Erskine upon these cases in *Halsey* v. *Grant*, *post*, vol. xiii. 73. In 2 Swanst. 225, *Binks* v. *Lord Rokeby*, Lord Eldon declares, that he would not follow those cases. *Ker* v. *Clobery*, stated by Mr. Sugden, Vend. & Par. 251, 5th edit. where the authorities are collected.

much is not at all distinctly in proof.   There is something like a distinct representation as to the arable land, but not amounting to a warranty.   It appears also, that the corn tithe was really the principal part of the estate ; that the farms were purchased for the purpose of enjoying the corn tithe estate.   The aspect of the particular is a farm in hand, rendered beneficial by the circumstance, that the purchaser would have the whole tithes of the parish of corn and hay ; which is also some· representation, that the tithes are to be taken in kind ; and I take it so as to the corn tithe ; being paid for by annual composition.   As to the nature of the payment for the moiety of the tithe of hay, it is not understood, whether it is a modus, or a payment capable of being shaken in Law.   It is impossible to deny, that the purchaser under such a particular is put in a situation of great hardship.   The abstract does not correct the representation ; as the rental in a degree does.   If this case [* 679] stands simply upon the representation in the * particular, the abstract, and the rental, it would be within the authorities.   That they are extremely strong cannot be denied ; and upon a motion for an injunction a precedent cannot be established, to affect the vast class of authorities upon a point of such importance, turning upon all their particularities.   In the case of an estate sold tithe-free it is a prodigiously strong measure in a Court of Equity to say, as a discreet exercise of its jurisdiction, that the contract shall be performed ; the Defendant swearing positively, and proving, that he would have nothing to do with the estate, if not tithe-free.   That, though a very strong proposition, does not come up to this case ; for in those cases the Court probably speculates, that tithes and lands are the subjects of separate and accurate valuation ; and the value of the one does not affect the other ; and therefore, though there is a failure as to the tithes, a part only of the subject of the contract, the whole is not affected ; as it would be, if the contract was for tithes only.   Suppose it proved, that this farm was taken for the purpose of enjoying the corn tithe principally ; that the hay tithe was a very small object ; great part of that capable of being taken in kind ; but a small part, not much affecting the bargain, liable to an exemption or modus : the Court in such a case might decree upon the doctrine of compensation.   But it will be very different, if it turns out upon examination, that 1 or 2000 acres are capable of being converted to the purpose of producing hay ; or, that a part or the whole may be converted from arable to meadow.   All those considerations are very material upon the question of compensation ; and it is impossible to determine now, that this will not be within the reach of some of the authorities a case for compensation.

Upon the conduct of the party this may differ materially from *Fordyce* v. *Ford*.   In that case, only seven acres were freehold ; and all the rest leasehold : but the abstract distinctly stated what was freehold, and what leasehold.   From the delivery of the abstract it was perfectly understood beyond dispute, without any ground for inquiry, that it was leasehold unquestionably and irrevocably.   The purchaser receives the abstract; treats upon it with full knowledge up to, and long after, the day, on which the contract was to be performed, not upon the nature of the property, *but   [* 680] the title; and the Master of the Rolls thought, there was a clear waiver. I doubt extremely, whether that will turn out to be the case here. Taking the representation in the conversation to be, that they believe it to be a modus, and supposing the purchaser could have been off the bargain at that ·moment, which is very questionable, can it be said from what passed afterwards, that he cannot now; having contracted under this representation, and learning no more afterwards than that they conceive it to be a modus? That is not like the representation as to the leasehold property, but one requiring a reasonable time for inquiry. Suppose, he had said, he would take it notwithstanding, if the quantity of land likely to produce hay was small, or, provided it would not effect the value of the other part of the purchase: some time was necessary to inquire into that; to know, whether the tenants mean to convert the arable land into meadow, and can by that force him to an agreement as to his corn tithe. The answer swears, they threaten this; that they have done it in some instances; and mean it in more. The inference will depend a great deal upon the extent, to which the fact may exist; and till that is determined, I cannot say, whether this can lie in compensation. If it goes to the destruction of the corn tithe, he not only loses the hay tithe, but he does not get the thing, which is the principal object of the contract. It is not merely a small abatement.

I cannot therefore decide this cause upon the grounds now before me. There is question enough, independent of the conduct of the Defendant, to lay a fair ground for litigation. The injunction must therefore be continued (1).

----

1. TRIFLING inaccuracies of description will not vitiate a sale where full compensation can be made to the purchaser; and the incorrect description of the subject of sale was not intentionally made, with a purpose to mislead: see, ante, note 2 to *Calverley* v. *Williams*, 1 V. 210: but this doctrine has been carried too far, and certainly ought not to be extended: see note 1 to *Calcraft* v. *Roebuck*, 1 V. 221. And a purchaser is never held to his bargain, and obliged to accept compensation for a difference between the representation made to him and the actual subject of sale, when such difference extends to the quality of the whole estate: *Drewe* v. *Corp*, 9 Ves. 368: nor is a purchaser ever compelled to take an indemnity against a contingency which may, if it should occur, shake the title offered to him: *Balmanno* v. *Lumley*, 1 Ves. & Bea. 225; *Paton* v. *Rogers*, ibid, p. 353; *Halsey* v. *Grant*, 13 Ves. 79: though, possibly, if the question of indemnity arose only as to a small incumbrance upon a considerable estate, this might admit a different consideration; provided the estate would, notwithstanding the incumbrance, be still perfectly marketable; *Wood* v. *Bernal*, 19 Ves. 221. So, if it appear that the title to a very small part of a considerable estate cannot be made good; this, if not essential to the full enjoyment of the remainder, may, perhaps, be a fair subject of compensation; but, in many cases, the objection may be a complete answer to a bill for a specific performance; *Knatchbull* v. *Grueber*, 1 Mad. 167; *S. C.* on appeal, 3 Meriv. 145.

----

(1) The parties had pressed for the opinion of the Lord Chancellor upon the question; and the cause was afterwards settled.

2. It was the observation of Lord Thurlow, that the principle upon which the jurisdiction of Courts of Equity to enforce specific performance, was originally founded, had been enlarged, till a specific performance in Equity had become, not unfrequently, a performance of any thing else rather than the real contract. *Stewart* v. *Alliston*, 1 Meriv. 32. And though the very able judge, just named, was considered, in the principal case, to have decided inconsistently with his own sense of justice in *Lord Stanhope's case*, where the object of the purchaser was to get an estate that was tithe free, but it was intimated he was compelled to take it subject to tithe; this supposed inconsistency has been cleared up, since the decision of the principal case, by a publication of a full report of the case alluded to, the real title of which is *Howland* v. *Norris*, and which may now be found in 1 Cox, 59; from that report it appears that the estate in question was not subject to tithes in kind, but only to a small money payment in lieu of tithes; a very different objection, which came fairly within the principle of compensation. Lord Kenyon was as decidedly hostile as Lord Thurlow, to compelling a party to go on with a purchase contrary to the object of the original agreement; *Poole* v. *Shergold*, 1 Cox, 274. And Lord Erskine distinctly said, he would never exercise such a jurisdiction; *Halsey* v. *Grant*, 13 Ves. 78. Lord Eldon, not only in the principal case, pointed out the hardship of enforcing contracts different from those really entered into, but in *Ker* v. *Cloberry*, (stated in Sugden's Law of Vendors, p. 251, fifth edit.) applied the remedy; deciding that the purchaser of an estate sold as tithe free, cannot be compelled to take it, if subject to tithe. The old class of cases, on this head, may therefore safely be considered as entirely overruled. It is true, Lord Eldon, in a case subsequent to that last cited, where the particular of sale stated that "*about* thirty-three acres, of the estate to be sold, were tithe free;" held that the same principle did not apply; *Binks* v. *Lord Rokeby*, 2 Swanst. 223. But the cases are clearly distinguishable; for, in the latter, the purchaser had sufficient notice to put him on his guard; and if he neglected inquiry into the precise state of the case, all he could fairly claim was compensation; *Hill* v. *Bulkley*, 17 Ves. 401; *Fenton* v. *Browne*, 14 Ves. 149; *Trower* v. *Newcome*, 3 Meriv. 704. When a purchaser omits to use reasonable diligence, he must not complain if the maxim *caveat emptor* is applied to him; *Lowndes* v. *Lane*, 2 Cox, 563.

3. Quit rents and rent charges are fair subjects of compensation; *Esdaile* v. *Stevenson*, 1 Sim. & Stu. 124; *Horniblow* v. *Shirley*, 13 Ves. 83; *Halsey* v. *Grant*, 13 Ves. 80; but where the rent charge is only a portion of a rent charge issuing out of an entire estate, of which the premises offered for sale are only part, the vendee will not be compelled to accept compensation, and complete the contract, unless the vendor can procure an apportionment of the rent charge to be properly made; *Barnwell* v. *Harris*, 1 Taunt. 431; and where this is impracticable, specific performance cannot be had, if the nature of the charge was concealed; but when, at the time of sale, bidders are informed of a charge overruling the whole estate, and that, as amongst the tenants of the several parts of an estate, a particular part is to exonerate the rest, a bidder for other parts cannot insist on any better exoneration, although the indemnity agreed on may appear open to possible objections. *Casamajor* v. *Strode*, 2 Swanst. 353, 355; *Walter* v. *Maunde*, 1 Jac. & Walk. 182, 188. Specific performance cannot, however, be enforced, where a leasehold, offered for sale, has been represented to be subject to an apportioned rent, but it turns out that the apportionment has not been regularly made, with the concurrence of all proper parties; the privity of the lessee is requisite in order that the vendee may have a complete remedy against him for the apportionment. *Bliss* v. *Collins*, 5 Barn. & Ald. 884.

4. The principal case was not brought before the Court again, after the decision on the motion for an injunction: see Mr. Vesey's note to *Halsey* v. *Grant*, 13 Ves. 79.

BARKER *v.* DACIE.

[1801, Nov. 2, 18, 23; Dec. 5, 15. 1802, March 3.]

Bill by a Clerk in Court against a Solicitor for payment of a certain sum, stated as the amount of the Plaintiff's bill for fees and disbursements. Demurrer to the relief overruled.

No decree, where the Defendant might have demurred, [p. 686.]

General demurrer lies, the Plaintiff being entitled to discovery, but not to the relief (*a*), [p. 686.]

Solicitors modern officers of the Court, compared with Clerks in Court, [p. 687.]

Account consequential upon discovery; though there may be a proceeding at law (*b*), [p. 688.]

THE bill, filed on the 24th of June, 1801, stated, that in 1780 the Defendant, an attorney and solicitor, first began to employ the Plaintiff as his clerk in Court in such Chancery suits as he was concerned in; and the Plaintiff having done business for the Defendant for many years without receiving any money on account, in October 1796 delivered a bill; and wrote a letter desiring to have it discharged. The bill amounted to 46*l*. 11*s*. 8*d*. The Defendant sent no answer to the letter; and concealed himself: but accidentally meeting the Plaintiff assured him, that on the first day of the present Trinity Term he would call and discharge the account, and finally settle with the Plaintiff.

The bill farther stated, that the Defendant had no intention of satisfying the Plaintiff's demand; but removed from place to place to avoid him and his other creditors; and that the sum of 46*l*. 11*s*. 8*d*. is now justly due to the Plaintiff; and has been so for many years antecedent to the delivery of the bill; and in answer to the pretences, upon which it suggested, that the Plaintiff refused to satisfy the demand, charged, that the Defendant never paid Plaintiff any money on account of his bill, and that he has no receipt or discharge, &c.; and prayed, that the Defendant may be decreed to pay to the Plaintiff the sum of 46*l*. 11*s*. 8*d*., the amount of his aforesaid bill of fees and disbursements.

The Defendant demurred to the relief for want of equity, and the Plaintiff's remedy, if he is entitled to any relief, being at law; and as to the discovery answered; admitting, that he employed the Plaintiff, and that a bill was delivered, but to what amount he is un-

---

(*a*) The rule seems to be different in England and America. See *ante*, note (*b*), *Brandon* v. *Sands*, 2 V. 514; note (*a*), *Renison* v. *Ashley*, 1 V. 459; Story, Eq. Pl. § 312; *Livingston* v. *Story*, 9 Peters, 632, 658.

(*b*) The Court having acquired cognizance of the suit for the purpose of discovery will entertain it, for the purpose of relief, in most cases of fraud, account, accident, and mistake. 1 Fonblanque, Eq. b. 1, ch. 1, § 3, note (*f*); *Middletown Bank* v. *Russ*, 3 Conn. 135; *Ryle* v. *Haggie*, 1 Jac. & W. 234; 1 Story, Eq. Jur. § 64–69. There are authorities in the English Courts which conflict with this doctrine. 1 Story, Eq. Jur. § 455. It seems to be generally adopted in the United States, Ibid, § 456; *Armstrong* v. *Gilchrist*, 2 Johns. Cas. 424; *Rathbone* v. *Warren*, 10 Johns. 587; *King* v. *Baldwin*, 17 Johns. 384; *Ludlow* v. *Simond*, 2 Cain. Cas. Err. 1, 38, 39, 51, 52; *Stanley* v. *Cramer*, 4 Cowen, 727.

able to set forth; and stated, that in 1790 he ceased to employ the Plaintiff. He denied the promise to pay the bill, or settle the account; and though he admitted having changed his residence, denied, that he did so to avoid payment of his creditors.

Mr. *Roupel,* in support of the Demurrer.—The demur-
[* 682] rer is put in upon the ground, that this bill * is merely an attempt to give a jurisdiction to this Court in a case admitting full and effectual relief at law. The relief is merely payment of a sum of money. No equitable circumstances are alleged. The only pretence is, that the Plaintiff is an officer of this Court. The privilege in general holds; but applies only to suits, in respect of which the Court has jurisdiction; as, where there is a concurrent jurisdiction: but where, as in this instance, this Court has not the natural jurisdiction, the privilege cannot hold. If the Clerk in Court is to be considered as an attorney or solicitor, the authorities are against such a bill. There is an old case, *Lord Ranelegh* v. *Thornhill* (1) in support of such a suit: but subsequent cases have established the practice: *Parry* v. *Owen* (2); which, it is remarkable, is the case referred to in Mitford (3) as an authority, that this Court will not entertain a suit, where relief may be had at law. The case of *Fell* v. *Christ Church College, Oxford* (4), ended in a compromise. The circumstance, that this Plaintiff is a Clerk in Court, cannot change the jurisdiction from law to equity. If he has the privilege of suing at law, it must be in the Petty Bag.

Mr. *Richards* and Mr. *Romilly,* in support of the bill.—The general doctrine, that, a bill does not lie, where relief may be had in an action, is not disputed; but this is not within that principle. This bill is not filed by an executor, but by the officer himself; whose duty calls him to attend the Court; and who is to be resident in the Court and the offices belonging to it. Thence the privilege arises. The Defendant is not a stranger, having no connection with the duties of the Court, as in *Perry* v. *Owen*; but is a Solicitor. This demand arises from business done in this Court in the Course of the Plaintiff's duty, as Clerk in Court, and the Defendant's as a Solicitor. It would certainly be inconvenient to refer such a subject to any other jurisdiction. Can the Master of the Court of King's Bench determine upon fees arising in this Court for business done here; receiving evidence, as he must, of the business in this Court? Clearly such a demand can here only
[* 683   *be determined with convenience, by analogy to those cases at law, where an attorney is privileged to sue and be sued in the Court, in which he practices, upon the principle, of his necessary attendance. Though upon a legal demand, there is a concurrent jurisdiction. Upon a bill of costs in a Court of Law, the principal

---

(1) 1 Vern. 203.
(2) Amb. 109; 3 Atk. 740.
(3) Mitf. 111.
(4) Before Lord Thurlow.

being there gives the jurisdiction; and, if necessary, the Master or other officer will take to his assistance a person out of this Court.

The authorities are in favor of this bill; and there is no authority against it.   The case cited from Vernon brought the merits distinctly before the Court upon a bill of review.   In *Norris* v. *Bacon* (1) a plea of the Statute (2) was put in, on the ground, that Plaintiff had not signed his bill: and that plea was allowed: which admits the jurisdiction.   *Moor* v. *Row* (3) was the case of a bill by a barrister; to which a demurrer was allowed, on the ground, that his fees were honorary; and therefore there was no remedy: but it seems to have been conceived, that if there was any remedy, it would be by bill in this Court.   *Parry* v. *Owen* was the case of an executrix; and the report in Ambler must be erroneous (4).   Clearly there could not have been a summary application; which can be made only by the client, not the attorney; and an executor is not within the Statute (5).   The ground of the decision does not appear in Atkyns.   In Mitford the case is only cited for the general proposition.   *Fell* v. *Christ Church College* was the case, not merely of fees, as Clerk in Court, but of a bill of costs as Solicitor. The Plaintiff put in a schedule of the bill of costs.   Lord Thurlow was much dissatisfied; but did not allow the demurrer.   It came frequently before the Court: but there was no decision; and it ended in the Defendant's paying the demand to a degree.   That case is therefore a clear authority, that Lord Thurlow could not allow the demurrer.   The argument upon it goes a great way in favor of this bill, merely for fees due to the Plaintiff, as Clerk in Court.   *Tancred* v. *Cheater* (6) was a mixed case, between precisely the same parties, but not wholly upon a bill of costs.   A great part of the demand however was a bill of costs.   The Defendant insisted, the costs ought * not to be inserted.   Lord Alvan-   [*684] ley decreed an account generally; not conceiving, that the Plaintiff was bound to go to law for the costs; both parties being officers of this Court; and the business in this Court.

Such being the state of the authorities, your Lordship will have to decide this case upon general principles.   Those being cases of solicitors, this is much stronger; the case of a Clerk in Court, suing merely for fees, to which he is entitled only under the Lord Chancellor's orders.

Mr. *Roupel*, in Reply.—This is admitted to be a clear legal debt. The privilege, I admit, is in a degree personal, and in general cases the officer is not to be drawn into another Court: but that is only in cases of concurrent jurisdiction; where a remedy may be given here according to the ordinary principles, upon which this Court

(1) 1 Vern. 312.
(2) Stat. 3 James, I. c. 6.
(3) 1 Rep. Ch. 21.
(4) See the note, 94. Beames on Costs, 288, 9, and Appendix, No. 20. Mr. Beames, stating this case from the Reg. Book, finds the report in Ambler correct.
(5) Stat. 2 Geo. II. c. 23, s. 22.
(6) At the Rolls, before Lord Alvanley.

gives the remedy: not, where the remedy is completely at law.
The inconvenience does not apply; as the Plaintiff may sue in the
Petty Bag. The objection of this demurrer is, that he comes on the
wrong side of the Court. It is not necessary, that the bill should
undergo taxation. It is said, a Clerk in Court is not entitled to fees,
except under the order of the Lord Chancellor. That order would
be evidence of his right; and then he may prove the items. It
must be admitted, the party was not entitled to the remedy stated
in Ambler's report of *Parry* v. *Owen:* but it is clear, if the demurrer was wrong in that case, the decision must have been upon the
general principle, that such a bill does not lie for a solicitor's fees.

The judgment upon this demurrer was several times postponed,
to give an opportunity for farther inquiry; and additional authorities
were cited. 1 Prax. Alm. 306, a demurrer to such a bill was over-
ruled. A plea of the Statute of Limitations to such a bill: 2 Prax.
Alm. 283. Bill by a solicitor: to which an answer was put in, not
a demurrer: Cursus Cancell. 41. *Hamilton* v. *Hodgson*, 26th April,
1746. *Langstaffe* v. ———, 16th April, 1774. A great many
instances were produced of bills filed by solicitors and clerks in
Court, signed by persons of great character. *Colman* v.
[*685] *Highmore,* *a bill by a clerk in Court, demanding a specific sum, 64*l.* *Powell* v. *Edwards,* also a bill by a clerk
in Court. *Hutton* v. *Marnon,* a bill by a clerk in Court, filed the
1st of July 1756. *Mears* v. *Mears,* 12th of May, 1761: a bill by a
clerk in Court against a solicitor for fees. A bill filed in 1711 by
R. W., against M. D.; to which an answer was put in: but the
record was not found. *Robinson* v. *Ellis,* another instance. The
result is a clear course of practice, though not verified by decrees.
It was said there were several other instances of bills by clerks in
Court against solicitors for fees; but they were all settled without
any answer put in.

On the other side it was said, that three only of the bills appeared
to have been actually filed: one was *Powel* v. *Edwards:* a bill by a
clerk in Court; not against the debtor himself, but his executors, for
an account of his personal estate and satisfaction out of his assets,
involving a variety of other things: a bill, that might have been filed
by any creditor; and it stated several difficulties in prosecuting the
claim at law; alleging, that the witnesses were all dead.

The bill in *Mears* v. *Mears* was filed: but no appearance was entered; and it does not appear, whether a subpœna issued. That
bill alleges various sums received from the Defendant on account of
the Plaintiff's bill; that the vouchers had been delivered up; and
no evidence could be produced at law; but that upon an account a
balance would appear due to the Plaintiff. In such a case, an account and mutual credit, exclusive of any other circumstance the
jurisdiction was clear.

Colman v. *Seymour* comes nearer this point than any other case;
containing none of those other equitable circumstances, exclusive of

that of privilege. A copy of the bill is produced: but it is not known, whether any appearance was put in, or any thing was done under it.

In the instance cited from Prax. Alm. published among a variety of precedents, the Plaintiff introduced charges to give the Court jurisdiction; that he was at a great charge in suing out several *writs, &c.: instead of relying upon a broad prin- [* 686] ciple or known practice, laboring to protect himself against a demurrer by those allegations. The prayer was, that the Defendant should show cause, why he should not come to an account. The demurrer to that bill cannot be found. The case in Cursus Cancell. was a bill for an account: the Defendant had arrested the Plaintiff; and the bill also prayed an injunction. These instances do not establish such a clear course of practice as to enable your Lordship to support this bill either upon practice or any known principle.

Lord CHANCELLOR [ELDON].—I have been furnished with what appears in the Register's Book as to the case in Vernon; which being upon a bill of review is a decision of great importance. But it does not quite satisfy me. The reason given is, that the party should have demurred, and not have permitted it to go to a hearing. The rule now is, that if you could have demurred to the bill, the Court will not make a decree at the hearing.

In *Mears* v. *Mears* there is a very material charge; that the clerk ' in Court had delivered his vouchers to the Defendant. Consequently he could not possibly go on at Law; and then the observation applies, that wanting discovery, the Court gives relief, particularly in matters of account.

Mar. 3. Lord CHANCELLOR.—In this cause the Plaintiff and the Defendant are both officers of this Court. The Defendant has not availed himself of the rule, that has lately obtained; that if the Plaintiff is not entitled to the relief, he shall not have the discovery (1); but has adopted a course, that prevailed in times, not very remote, by demurring to the relief and answering to the discovery. The question is, whether a Clerk in Court, dealing in that character with a Solicitor, as such, can file a bill for an account and payment of the balance: or, to put it more pointedly to the circumstances, whether the Clerk in Court stating this case, and that a sum is due, can maintain the suit: the Defendant resisting the demand, as not due in the whole or in part; but not showing, what part has been paid, and how the account stands. * It is ob- [* 687] jected, that the bill cannot be sustained for several reasons. First, it is said, the demand is purely at Law; that if the bill pointed to a proper subject of this jurisdiction, it ought to have been merely for discovery, to enable the Plaintiff to get evidence in support of an action; and farther, that if there is any thing in the

_____
(1) See *ante*, the references, vol. iii. 347; and in the note, ii. 461.

character of the Plaintiff, giving him a personal right of suing here, he ought not in a matter of this sort to sue in this Court, as a Court of Equity, farther than to have a discovery ; and having had that he ought to bring an action in the Petty Bag.

I do not at present go, for it is unnecessary, into any detailed observation upon the passages in the books of practice as to the right of a Clerk in Court to sue, not any body, but a Solicitor, by bill. Such passages are to be found certainly. Nor shall I go into any particular observation upon the forms of pleading in such cases, which are also to be found there, nor into observation upon the various cases, many of which were cited, proving, that such bills have been entertained, and acted on, perhaps a little diversified in their circumstances. I barely state the inference arising from the fact, that many instances are cited of bills by Clerks in Court against Solicitors for fees ; which have been signed by the most respectable persons ; and which, though not matured into decrees, are so far authority, that the Defendants submitted. These proceedings satisfy me (and fully to this extent, that I ought not to allow the demurrer) that the practice has been understood to be, that a Clerk in Court may sue a Solicitor for an account of their dealings and transactions in that relation ; and may sue him by bill in Equity. I believe, it will be found, that the Solicitors are very modern officers of the Court, compared with the Clerks in Court (1) ; and in the nature of the business and the manner of transacting it that it will rest frequently more in the knowledge of the Solicitor, what he is indebted to the Clerk in Court, than in the knowledge of the Clerk in Court, what demand he has ; and there may be an account, which is to be settled by a production of papers furnished to the Solicitor by the Clerk in Court ; which will regulate the demand upon the Solicitor. This Court therefore, as it decrees and deals in matters of account

[* 688] from the inconvenience at law, assuming the credit of taking the account * with regard to proceedings in the Court and the fees upon them better than, or at least as well as, a Court of Law, has been in the habit of conceiving and expressing a strong inclination to entertain jurisdiction in matters of this sort ; and where discovery is wanted, we know, it will be followed up by taking an account ; even where there may be a proceeding at law. I am of opinion, this Plaintiff might bring an action at law ; provided he had the evidence ; and we remember, the case of Mr. Hill and the Six Clerks went to law (2).

I was surprised to hear, that Lord Rosslyn [Loughborough] expressed a doubt, whether any Judge would try a cause between officers of this Court(3). If the officer had a legal right, the Judge could not refuse to try it. But it does not follow, that, because he has a legal right, he may not sue here. It depends in some degree

---

(1) See the partition, *Ex parte The Six Clerks, ante,* vol. iii. 589. *Post, Ward v. Hepple,* xv. 297.

(2) *Ante,* vol. iii. 596, 597.

(3) That was intimated at the Bar.

upon the usage and the inherent jurisdiction of the Court to compel its officers to do justice to each other, particularly in the matter of fees. As this bill is framed, it is as bold an experiment as the Plaintiff could make; and perhaps the Defendant might have put upon the Record a defence, that might have made it difficult to sustain the bill, unless upon such inherent jurisdiction, to be exercised not only by petition but by bill. The Plaintiff takes upon himself to state, what is the result of the account, and therefore to remove all difficulty; reducing himself to the situation of a person having a clear liquidated sum, incapable of being entangled. But upon the true nature of the bill I rather think, what he meant was to state, that there was an account; that he had collected the result of it at this sum; and I rather think, this mode of stating the bill, alleging, that this sum is due, and a promise to pay it, was meant to take it out of the Statute of Limitations, rather than with reference to what was conceived to be the jurisdiction of the Court. The bill is capable of being so understood; and if not, rather than shake what seems a privilege of the officers of the Court, I would allow the Plaintiff to amend.

I do not think upon consideration, any of the cases cited on the other side distinctly apply as authorities against this bill; for the Court is to deal very differently, when dealing with the executor of an officer of this Court, contending against an officer, and between two officers of the Court. There is a distinction in the *relation of the parties; which may perhaps account for   [* 689] some of the cases referred to; which are very shortly reported; and of which I have not been able to procure farther information. Under all the circumstances the habit of the Court gives so much of negative authority, that this demurrer ought to be overruled. I do not know, that there is great inconvenience even in filing a bill. With an inclination, that a motion might be made, or a petition presented, I also am of opinion the Defendant might relieve himself from the bill; admitting, that he was a Solicitor; and desiring upon motion a reference to the Master to take the account: the suit would be ended; and the Court as to costs would have an opportunity of finally doing justice. Upon the whole there is authority enough for over-ruling the demurrer; whatever may be the decree at the hearing.

The Demurrer was over-ruled (1).

1. WITH respect to the general doctrine, that a Plaintiff who asks relief to which he is not entitled, cannot insist on a discovery to which, if he had asked no more, he would have been entitled, see, *ante*, note 1 to *Renison* v. *Ashley*, 2 V. 459.

2. In many cases, although the Plaintiff might maintain an action at law, a Court of Equity will take jurisdiction; the general rule, however, laid down in the principal case, that an account in Equity is consequential upon discovery, even where there may be proceedings at law, may admit occasional exceptions, when

(1) The Defendant paid the demand.

the subject is mixed up with a question which can be best determined at law: see note 2 to *Toulmin* v. *Price*, 5 Ves. 235.

3. As to the remedy of a clerk in court for his fees, see note 10 to *Ex parte Smith*, 5 V. 706; and that formerly the whole of the duties now performed by solicitors in the Court of Chancery, rested with the clerks in Court, see *Cowell* v. *Simpson*, 16 Ves. 280; *Gardner* v. ———, 17 Ves. 387.

THE UNIVERSITIES OF OXFORD AND CAMBRIDGE v. RICHARDSON.

[1802, March 1, 2, 3.]

Upon the Answer to a bill by the Universities of Oxford and Cambridge, the King's Printer not joining, but being made a Defendant, an Injunction, restraining the sale in England of Bibles, prayer-books, &c. printed by the King's Printer in Scotland, was continued to the hearing.
Injunction, where there can be no account, [p. 705.]
Injunction to prevent that, which is unjustly done, or threatened, [p. 706.]
Injunction granted or continued to the hearing, though the legal title doubtful; as upon Patent rights (a), [p. 707.]
Since the Union of Great Britain and Ireland the Great Seals are distinct for Patents among other purposes, [p. 708.]
Whether the Patents granted to the King's Printer vest the copyright, or are merely authorities, *Quære*, [p. 713.]

The bill stated, that by several Letters Patent before and since the 13th year of Queen Elizabeth the Plaintiffs are entrusted with the especial privilege and authority of printing within their respective Universities, and of selling or causing to be sold throughout his Majesty's dominions or elsewhere all manner of books and works of whatever description, not prohibited by public authority, and whether the same may be or not contained or mentioned in any other Royal Charter or Grant to any other Printer; and that under their said res-

(a) If the patent has been granted for some length of time, and the patentee has put the invention into public use, and has had an exclusive possession of it under his patent for a period of time, which may fairly create the presumption of an exclusive right, the Court will, in such case, ordinarily interfere by way of preliminary injunction, pending the proceedings; reserving of course, unto the ultimate decision of the cause, its own final judgment on the merits. 2 Story, Eq. Jur. § 934, 935; *Hill* v. *Thompson*, 3 Meriv. 622; Eden, Injunc. Ch. 12 P. 260; 1 Madd. Ch. Pr. 113; Jeremy, Eq. Juris. 316; Cooper, Eq. Pl. 154, 155, 156; *Bacon* v. *Jones*, 4 M. & Craig, 433, 436; *Ogle* v. *Ege*, 4 Wash. C. C. 534; *Isaacs* v. *Cooper*; Coxe's Digest, 533; 4 Wash. C. C. 259; *Rogers* v. *Abbot*, 4 Wash. C. C. 514; *Livingston* v. *Van Ingen*, 9 Johns. 570; Phillips on Patents, 451, 469; *Sullivan* v. *Redfield*, 1 Paine, 441.
If the thing sought to be prohibited, is in itself a nuisance, the Court will interfere to stay irreparable mischief without waiting for the result of a trial; and will, according to the circumstances, direct an issue, or allow an action, and, if need be, expedite the proceedings, the injunction being in the mean time continued. But, where the thing sought to be restrained is not unavoidably and in itself noxious, but only something, which may according to circumstances prove so, then the Court will refuse to interfere, until the matter has been tried at law, generally by an action, though in particular cases an issue may be directed for the satisfaction of the Court, where an action could not be framed so as to meet the question. Per. Brougham, Chanc.; *Ripon* v. *Hobart*, 1 Cooper, Sel. Cas. 333; *S. C.* 3 Mylne & K. 169.

pective grants and privileges they are entitled to print within their
said respective Universities, and to sell within the same and elsewhere, all editions or copies of the Holy Bible, New Testament, and
Book of the Common Prayer, Administration of the Sacrament, and
other rites and ceremonies of the Church of England, in concurrence
with such person or persons, who for the time being may be his
Majesty's Printer ; and that no other person or persons or body corporate whatever besides the Plaintiffs and his Majesty's Printers for
the time being or their assigns are entitled to print or publish within * England any editions or copies of the Holy   [*690]
Bible, &c. ; or to sell within England any other edition
or copies of the said books than such as have been printed and published by or for the Plaintiffs and the King's Printers for the time being or their assigns or one of them ; and that the Plaintiffs together
with the King's Printers for the time being have respectively from
time to time printed and published and sold for a reasonable price a
considerable number of editions and copies of all the said books fully
adequate to the necessary use of and actual demand from time to
time made for them by all his said Majesty's subjects within England,
and adapted in size, number, execution and price, for the accomoda-
tion of all ranks and descriptions of his said Majesty's subjects ; and
that they have respectively been at great pains and expense in preserving the text of the said books pure and correct, and of furnishing
a sufficient supply of all the said books for the use of his Majesty's
said subjects, and more especially of late years have respectively
printed and published so great a number of editions and copies of all
the said books, that for several years last past his Majesty's Printers
have not found it necessary to print any new editions or copies of the
said books, but have left the due supply thereof wholly to the Plaintiffs ; who have respectively employed a very large capital in such
printing and publishing.

The bill farther stated, that by Letters Patent, dated the 8th of
July in the 39th year of his reign, his present Majesty granted to
John Reeves, George Eyre, and Andrew Strahan, to each of them,
and each of their executors, administrators and assigns, for a term of
years therein mentioned, and not yet expired, the office of Printer to
his Majesty amongst other things of all bibles, &c. thereby forbid-
ding all other persons whatsoever within England from printing any
of the said books, or from importing and selling any of the said books
printed out of England during the time in the Patent mentioned ;
and that the interest of John Reeves in the same has by mesne assignment become vested in Eyre and Strahan ; and the Plaintiffs
and Eyre and Strahan having lately discovered, that some attempts
have been made to invade their said privileges, Eyre and Strahan
joined with the Plaintiffs in publishing an advertisement, that they
will take such measures against all printers and vendors of
the same as they are * warranted to do for the protection   [*691]
of their rights, and preventing the publishing and vending
the Holy Scriptures and Liturgy of the Church by any other than

those, who have just license and authority for the same; and the Plaintiffs in September last finding, that the same illegal practices were persisted in by many Printers and Booksellers throughout England caused a hand-bill to be circulated among the trade in general giving them notice of the Plaintiffs' intention of immediately instituting a suit in this Court against the invaders of said privilege.

The bill then stated, that William Richardson and John and James Richardson of London have taken upon themselves to print and publish within England divers copies or impressions of the English Bible, New Testament, and Book of Common Prayer, without the privity, consent or authority, of Eyre and Strahan, or of the Plaintiffs; or the said Defendants have imported and sold, or exposed for sale, within England, divers copies or impressions of the said books printed out of the said realm or within the said realm without the privity or consent of Eyre and Strahan, or the Plaintiffs; and that the said Defendants have lately imported from Scotland or elsewhere, not within England, divers copies of the English translations of the Bible in quarto, and printed respectively in Scotland or elsewhere, not within England; and have in London or elsewhere within England sold or exposed for sale divers copies or impressions of the said books respectively. The bill then charging, that the Plaintiffs have suffered considerable loss; and have already been considerably impeded, and are daily suffering more serious interruptions, in being enabled to furnish his Majesty's subjects within this realm with a proper supply of the said books from the unjustifiable practices, as hereinbefore charged, of said Defendants; and that the Defendants Eyre and Strahan have refused to join in this suit, prayed an injunction and account.

The Defendants, the Richardsons, by their answer submitted, that they are entitled to sell in England editions and copies of the said books, which have been printed and published by his Majesty's Printers. They stated, that they believe, it may be true, that the Plaintiffs or the persons delegated by them have from time to time printed and published a considerable number of editions [* 692]   *and copies fully adequate to the necessary use of, and actual demand by all his Majesty's subjects in England, and adapted in size and number (but not in execution or price, as the Defendants believe) for the accommodation of all ranks and descriptions of his Majesty's subjects, and have been at great or some pains and expense in preserving the text pure and correct, and in furnishing a sufficient supply; and have employed a very large or some capital in printing and publishing the said books; that an advertisement of such tenor as in the bill, was published; and that a hand-bill of such purport was generally circulated throughout the trade. They believe, that the said delegates and not the Plaintiffs published said advertisement; and circulated the said hand-bill. They deny, that they have printed and published within England any copies or impressions, or any of the books, in the bill mentioned; but admit, that as partners in trade, and in exercise of their

privileges as British subjects and Freemen of the City of London,
they have imported from Scotland, and no where else, and sold in
London, but not elsewhere within England, divers numbers of one
edition of the said books, of which they have set forth an account; and
say, that all the copies and impressions, so imported and sold by Defendants, were printed and published by and for the King's Printers in
Scotland; and were sold by the Defendants on their own account;
and they insist, that the King's Printers in Scotland for the time being are duly authorised and privileged to print and publish the said
books in Scotland; and that these Defendants are authorised to sell
the same in England; for by Letters Patent under the Seal by the
Treaty of Union of England and Scotland to be kept and used in
Scotland in lieu of the Great Seal of that kingdom, dated the 2d of
November in the 26th year of his present Majesty, reciting Letters
Patent, dated the 21st of June, 1749, during forty-one years from
the expiration of the Patent granted by King George the First,
dated the 6th of July, 1716, for forty-one years, his Majesty nominated James Hunter Blair and John Bruce their heirs, substitutes, or
assigns, his sole Master Printers in Scotland for forty-one years from
the expiration of the Patent then existing, with full power to use,
exercise, and enjoy, the said gift and office during the space before
mentioned, with all the profits, emoluments, immunities,
exemptions, and privileges, to the same belonging, as * far   [* 693]
as agreed with the articles of the Union and the existing
laws of Great Britain, and especially the sole and exclusive privilege
of printing in Scotland Holy Bibles, New Testaments, Books of
Psalms, Books of Common Prayer, Confessions of Faith, and the
larger and Shorter Catechisms in the English language.

The answer farther stated, that the Letters Patent granted to
Kincarde, and Letters Patent to other persons prior thereto, contained, as Defendants believe, the like privileges and authority; and
insisted, that such books as have been, and may be, printed under
the exclusive authority and privilege given by said Letters Patent to
the King's Printers in Scotland, did become a subject of property or
article of trade within the act hereinafter mentioned, in the same
manner as books printed under the exclusive authority granted to the
King's Printer in England; and that in consequence of the Act of
Union the persons authorised by the said Letters Patent to print the
said books in Scotland have a right to send such books into England,
and there to sell the same; and in like manner the persons authorised to print the said books in England have a right to send such
books into Scotland, and there to sell the same; and for forty years
past, and, as Defendants believe, for many years previous, such practice hath not been considered illegal or contrary to the Letters Patent.

The answer then stated, that the Defendants admit, they did sell
the said books so printed in Scotland under the said authority, and
imported, without the privity of Plaintiffs and the King's Printers in
England; and insist, that it was not necessary to obtain the consent
or authority of Plaintiffs and the King's Printers in England.   They

deny, that they have imported or sold, or exposed to sale, any edition, copies, or impressions, printed out of Great Britain ; and say, the copies printed by the Plaintiffs are selling in London at 17s. 3d. ; and the copies printed by the King's Printers in Scotland sold in London at 11s. 2d. only : and the quality of the paper, and the type, printing, and execution, of copies printed in Scotland are very superior to, and better adapted for the use of the public than, the copies printed by the Plaintiffs or their delegates ; and that the text is equally pure and correct ; and the Defendants have frequently heard complaints from the booksellers and others, not only [* 694] of the prices, * but also of the quality, printing, and execution, of the copies printed by the Plaintiffs or their delegates, which they believe well founded. They believe, his Majesty's Printers in England have not given to the Plaintiffs or their delegates any privilege or authority whatsoever either for printing or publishing the said books in England, or for preventing the Defendants from selling in London copies printed and published in Scotland ; and his Majesty's Printers in England do not directly interfere with that part of the trade ; and say, Defendants and other persons have for many years past carried on a very extensive and valuable trade with foreign countries, and particularly with the United States of America, by exporting copies of said books, published in Scotland, and brought into England ; and unless permitted to be sold, as heretofore, they believe, not only such valuable branch of trade will be destroyed, or very greatly diminished, but a considerable revenue arising from the duties on the paper and leather will also be lost to Great Britain.

A motion was made for dissolving the injunction upon the answer put in.

Mr. *Plumer*, Mr. *Alexander*, and Mr. *Thomson*, in support of the motion.—This is a question of considerable importance. To sustain an injunction under the notion of irreparable waste the Plaintiffs ought either to have established their title at law, or to have been in actual possession of the exclusive privilege. The general question is, whether the subjects of this kingdom may not buy and sell what by the King's authority is printed within the realm. The prerogative even does not go so far ; being confined to the printing and publishing : the reason of the prerogative ceasing there. The Plaintiffs claim a monopoly injurious to the great interests of the public. The Attorney General is not a party. The claim is not made on behalf of the King's Printer ; who is made a Defendant ; declining to assert the claim made by these Plaintiffs. The bill seeks, not only an injunction to restrain the sale of these books, (the prayer being confined to the sale, though the charges go also to the printing,) but also an account of the profits already made. The injunction prayed is to restrain them from selling these books any where. An injunction is not granted, unless the legal right is established at law by decision or by long usage : if not, the Court will have the right established : *Hills* v. *The University*

of Oxford (1); in which cause the Plaintiff was the King's
Printer; and an injunction till the trial was refused. In *Millar* v. *Taylor* (2) all the Judges express themselves in the same
way as to injunctions in the Court of Chancery; that such injunction never is granted on motion, unless the legal property of the
Plaintiff be made out; nor continued after answer, unless it still remains clear: that the Court never grants injunctions in cases of this
kind, where there is any doubt: a doubtful legal title must be tried
at law, before it can be made the ground of an injunction, &c. (3).

In this bill they have not stated the instruments, upon which their
own title or that of the Defendants is founded; but the general result only of the instruments, under which they claim; and the import and effect only in general terms of letters patent and charters,
by which without doubt this among other privileges is granted to
them. They have set forth the Letters Patent 39th Geo. III. to the
King's Printer; which purport to impose a negative upon every other
person. Nothing in these letters Patent can strengthen the Plaintiffs' title. They attempt to unite themselves with the King's Printer; who singly possesses the right; stating also, that the King's
Printer has not for several years exercised the right: but has left it
entirely to the Plaintiffs. The bill contains no averment, that the
books sold by the Defendants are in any respect inferior in the execution, or in respect of the price calculated to impose upon the un-
wary. The answer swears, that the type, paper, and execution, are
in all respects superior, the text equally correct; and the price a third
less. The interest of the public is the main foundation of this prerogative. All, that respects the printing, is certainly the just subject
of monopoly; on account of the important duty upon his Majesty
to supply his subjects with these books: but, when they are printed,
every principle opposes a restraint of the sale on behalf of the King
or any claiming under him. That is the true principle, governing
the Law upon this subject, and recognised in a very important Act
of Parliament. According to Mr. Yorke's very elaborate argument (4) the prerogative is limited to printing and publishing or importing from * foreign countries; whether it is   [* 696]
considered on the ground of copyright or any other.
There can now be but two principles, upon which the prerogative
can be considered founded: copyright; or, as the King is head of
the church. The consequence, stated by the Plaintiffs, is the injury
to their private property, not to the public. The pecuniary loss is
the ground made; and the account is prayed in respect of that.
The object of the Letters Patent, generally referred to in the first
paragraph of the bill, is all manner of books, not prohibited by public authority; and is not confined to books of this description.

---

(1) 1 Vern. 275.
(2) 4 Burr. 2303.
(3) 4 Burr. 2377, 2400.
(4) 1 Burn's Eccl. Law, 353. In the quarto edition the substance of the Patents
is stated.

There is a broad distinction between the nature of this right and the right of a patentee. The Plaintiffs do not represent, that the Letters Patent have given them more than a privilege and authority. They speak of an exclusive right, only, when uniting themselves with the King's Printer. But these Defendants are not called upon to argue the question with the King's Printers or the King. The title, as stated, is nothing but a license to them with impunity from the penalties of the Star-Chamber to print and sell: but no right of property, no control over others, is given; which appears from the certificate (1) in *Baskett* v. *The University of Cambridge.* What right has a person purchasing a license from a patentee to call in question the exercise of the invention by another person; much less, to have an account? Where is the legal right, infringed by the publication of another? How would they declare upon their right? Must they not aver, that they are entitled to the exclusive right? Are the Defendants liable to account to more than one person? Suppose after the account granted to the person licensed the patentee should come for an account. There were five patents: two to the University of Cambridge: and three to Oxford. That granted in the 26th year of King Henry VIII. to Cambridge has no mention of bibles, prayer books, &c.; which were not the object of that patent, being previous to the translation of the bible. The others were in the 3d, 8th, and 13th Charles I. One was a confirmatory patent, giving particular rights over other books, long hid in the libraries, having no reference to these books; but as to those others, never before published, giving an exclusive right for twenty-five years and ten years.

The charter, 11th Charles II., was also merely confirmatory. [*697] All these amount to *nothing more than a license. The plain language is so; and more was never contended for than an exception in favor of the Universities of a right to print, unfettered by the exclusive right of the King's Printer.

In *Baskett* v. *The University of Cambridge* (2) this was so considered. They argued against the universality of the monopoly. In *Hills* v. *The University of Oxford* the Lord Keeper says, it was never meant, they should print more than for their own use, or a small number more to compensate their charge. The right, upon which these Defendants insist, the authority of the King's Printer in Scotland, giving an express power and exclusive right to print these books in that country, is as good as that of the King's Printer in England. The printing and publishing being legal, the only question is, whether the sale can be controlled by the Plaintiffs. Can this be called an unauthorized, pirated, edition? In *Eyre and Strahan* v. *Carnan* (3) the ground of the prerogative was laid down, not as property, but duty; to take care, that these books are correct. These books are properly printed under the King's authority: where, is of no consequence. This authority is recognized by Act of Par-

---

(1) 2 Burr. 664; 1 Burn's Eccl. Law, 373.
(2) 2 Burr. 661; 1 Burn's Eccl. Law, 347.
(3) In the Court of Exchequer, 1781.

liament allowing a drawback upon paper used for the purpose of printing bibles and prayer-books in Scotland, in the same manner as to the King's Printer and the Universities in England.   The sale is not a subject of restraint; unless when the books are not printed under proper authority; as where books of this kind are printed abroad.   The competition is of infinite benefit to the public; of which this case is an instance.   The danger of establishing such a monopoly in the sale would be very great: the object being to furnish the public upon easy terms; proper care being taken to preserve the text correct.   These books, when printed under proper authority, are as much a subject of sale as any other, under the fifth article of the Union.   This limitation would be contrary to all the Statutes giving an unlimited right of trade, and particularly the Act of Union; as a grant of the right of printing and publishing with the exception of a particular county in England would be illegal.   Upon the argument of the Plaintiffs, books of this kind, purchased in Scotland, and being part of the library of a gentleman, coming into
* this country, could not be sold.   The answer states the   [* 698]
usage for a great length of time, and the Plaintiffs state no
more; not pretending, that they have ever exercised control, or that books of this kind have not always been sold with impunity.   The control now set up is sustained neither by authority nor usage.   A very considerable export trade will be stopped by this monopoly. Every improper addition to the price of such books is a tax upon the peasantry of this country; and the mere reservation of a rent upon the lease of this privilege is a considerable and unnecessary addition.   Under this usage, the right never having been established at law, this cannot be stated as a clear case; and your Lordship will take the same course, that was adopted in *Hills* v. *The University of Oxford*; in which case the title was established by Acts of Parliament, &c.   A great loss has been already sustained by the restraint of this injunction.

The *Solicitor General* [Hon. *Spencer Perceval*], Mr. *Mansfield*, Mr. *Richards*, and Mr. *Romilly*, for the Plaintiffs, showed cause against dissolving the injunction.—The necessary consequence of the Defendants' success in this trade from the difference of the price of labor, &c. must be to beat down completely the interest of the Universities under their Patents, if the difference in the price that is represented, exists; and the Defendants will have a monopoly.   It will not however turn out, that there is that difference upon articles of equal value.   It has been decided, at least as between the King's Printers in England and Scotland, that the right now contended to be in the latter does not exist.   The argument upon the articles of Union proceeds upon mistake.   It might as well be contended, that after the Union a citizen of London might exercise the privileges of a citizen of Edinburgh there, and *vice versâ*.   The meaning of that clause is only, that the subjects of Scotland shall have the same privileges in England, that the subjects of England have, &c. not to enable them to do that in England, which the subjects of Eng-

land cannot do. The Patent to the King's Printers in both countries are evidently confined to each respectively. With respect to the passages (1) cited from *Millar* v. *Taylor*, the inter-
[* 699]   * mediate passage shows the origin of the doubt in *Tonson* v. *Collins*; which doubt is now fully removed by what passed in *Baskett* v. *Parsons* (2); when the very question was before the Master of the Rolls; and a perpetual injunction was decreed. Afterwards in 1720 or 1721 an application was made against the Defendant Parsons for breach of the injunction by having brought books of this sort into the kingdom; upon which application he was committed for a contempt. That decision received farther confirmation in the House of Lords upon an appeal from a decree of the Court of Session in Scotland; which was varied in favor of the right of the King's Printer in England, confining the right of the Scotch Printer to Scotland. That case was *Baskett* v. *Watson* (3). The Defendant was the King's Printer in Scotland. The interlocutor was, that the Defendant might print and sell bibles in any part of the United Kingdoms or elsewhere. It was ordered in the House of Lords, that the interlocutor should be varied by leaving out the words " in any part of the United Kingdoms, or elsewhere : " as to the rest it was affirmed. The right therefore upon these authorities cannot be considered doubtful.

The state of the two countries is assimilated to the case of two counties in England. It is not to be presumed, that the King would limit the sale of these books within his dominions : but by virtue of the prerogative he may subdivide and apportion the grant; and it would be extremely difficult for the grantee to sell or enable another to sell beyond those limits in direct opposition to that restraint. Notwithstanding the Union, for all the municipal jurisdiction of the Great Seal, for all the purposes of acquiring rights under the Great Seal, the countries remain as distinct, as formerly. What would be the privilege and advantage of the right to print only? The object is the publication and sale. If the sale cannot be restrained, the prerogative is fruitless.

As to the right of the Plaintiffs, it is a concurrent right with the right of the King's Printer; which is exclusive of every
[* 700]   one * else. The Attorney General was not a party in the case at the Rolls. This right certainly has not been taken as a mere license. In Mr. *Yorke's* argument it is called a privilege; as a grant operating upon the right of the Crown; and granting a right and interest in the thing; which was in the Crown to grant. There is no reason to apprehend, they would be liable again to account to the King's Printer. That must be arranged in this suit; in which, as he is before the Court, care will be taken of his interest. How can these Defendants argue against monopoly, claiming

---

(1) 4 Burr. 2400.
(2) Before Sir Joseph Jekyl, at the Rolls, 8th July, 1718; and upon appeal before Lord Chancellor Parker, 2d May, 1719; when the decree was affirmed.
(3) In the House of Lords, 16th of January, 1717.

under a monopolist? The only question is, who shall have it: all claiming under a grant from the Crown, an exclusive right against all persons, except those appointed by the Crown, like a license for a market. The exercise of this monopoly is granted to the Universities by way of trade. The object upon the charters appears to have been to grant all the advantage, that could be derived from carrying on the trade of printing and selling these books. Though the expression is general "all books," it must be understood to be restrained to what are called prerogative copies. The clear exclusive right in the King being admitted, how can it be disputed against his grantee: the King reserving the right of granting the same privilege to other persons; as was done afterwards to the Printer; in which grant there are exclusive words, preventing a farther grant to any other person. That grant necessarily makes the right of the Universities exclusive, with the exception of the right of the King's Printer. This cannot be compared to a license to use a patent invention, nor to a grant of the right of fishing in the water of another. There is no doubt, every person claiming under such a grant may bring an action for the invasion of the right, like the action of a commoner. A person having the grant of a market may bring an action against any one setting up another within the limits: *Yard* v. *Ford* (1). Grants of fairs, market, fisheries, &c, conveying very valuable rights to a subject, are mere authorities; and if those common law liberties and franchises are usurped, the remedy is by *quo warranto*. All those rights proceeding from the Crown, are mere authorities. There is no argument therefore against a right, that it is by license. It is not of course to direct an account, which is only adopted as a just and fair mode of estimating the damages. A discovery is necessary in those *cases; [*701] and then the habit of the Court is to direct an account, instead of sending it to law to estimate the damages; obliging the party to sue in two Courts. This injunction would not prevent exportation to foreign countries, perhaps even through this country: the object being only the sale in England. The word "importing" in the case at the Rolls must be understood to be for the purpose of sale in this country. The instance put of books in a private library could not come within the description of trading; unless made use of as a cover. The usage cannot be set up against these solemn decisions. This trade was probably carried on at first so as not to admit of detection: and was detected by degrees: so that it was not an object to apply until it grew to some magnitude. Those cases also have decided that it is not necessary, that all persons, having interests in the monopoly, should be parties; as in those neither the Crown nor the Universities were parties. The effect of that objection would be, that the King's Printer by refusing to be a co-plaintiff might put an end entirely to the right of the Universities.

(1) 2 Saund. 172.

As to the objection upon the account (1), those *dicta* that the account supports the injunction, began with the case of an injunction to restrain cutting timber. In the common case of waste there is no doubt, that the Court perpetually interposes, where there can be no account; as in the instance of a tenant digging clay for bricks, an injunction is obtained immediately: so in cases of copyright before publication: *Pope* v. *Curl* (2).   The principle is, that the Court will not suffer such rights to be invaded; and it is very convenient from the difficulty of getting at what ought to be the subject of the account.   In *Jesus College* v. *Bloom* (3) Lord Hardwicke says, the damage is the ground of the injunction, in direct opposition to that notion as to the account; which is there treated as following the jurisdiction to grant the injunction.   In *Selby* v. *Selby* there could be no account.   The intention to commit waste is alone sufficient; and the allegation always is of an intention to commit waste; also, that the Defendant has cut a tree, or put a plough in the ground, not for the *purpose of an account,* but as decisive evidence of his purpose.   The injunction is the relief, not any thing interlocutory.   In *Jackson* v. *Cator* (4) it was clear, there could be no account; the right to the trees being expressly reserved: yet the injunction was granted; and afterwards made perpetual (5).   The difficulty of ascertaining the proportions will not prevent the right of the Plaintiffs to an account in the first instance, upon the principle of copyright; as this is in effect.   The Court may reserve the right of deciding as to the proportions: but it is clear, the Defendants are not entitled to retain the profits.

[* 702]

Mr. *Plumer,* in reply.—The intermediate passage (6) in Lord Mansfield's judgment in *Millar* v. *Taylor* only refers to a particular case; going to obviate the idea of any doubt entertained upon the question of literary property; but that passage does not affect the result of what I cited for the general principle, that there must be a clear, plain, case; or the right must be established at Law.   Upon this question there is very considerable doubt, what will be your Lordship's opinion, or that of a Court of Law.   The supposition, that this usage commenced in wrong, assumes the question.   This is the first attempt against this usage; for *Baskett* v. *The University of Cambridge* was upon a new attempt to extend the right to printing Acts of Parliament.   Neither of those cases has decided this ques-

---

(1) A difficulty was suggested by the Lord Chancellor as to the way, in which the account should be taken, with reference to the King's Printer, upon the supposition, that the injunction is supported by the account: his Lordship expressing at the same time an opinion against the accuracy of the *dicta* to that effect. See *ante*, 89. *Post*, 705; vol. ix. 346.

(2) Before Lord Hardwicke, 5th June, 1741.

(3) 3 Atk. 262. See *The Marquis of Lansdown* v. *The Marchioness Dowager of Lansdown*, 1 Madd. 116.

(4) *Ante*, vol. v. 688.

(5) See also *Gibson* v. *Smith*, 2 Atk. 182; where a threat to open mines was held a sufficient ground for an Injunction.

(6) 4 Burr. 2400.

tion.   In that before the House of Lords the question did not arise ; and as it was not in issue, the interlocutor was properly corrected. The question was merely between persons claiming as proprietors of the patent, *inter se*, whether Watson was entitled to any participation in the patent, or not.   The certificate in *Baskett* v. *The University of Cambridge* goes a great way against the case at the Rolls. This question is perfectly distinct from all questions of property, private right, and pecuniary emolument.   This is a subject of public trust, not of private emolument.   It would be an abuse of the privilege, where it is found to interfere with the primary object, for which the privilege exists.   The private right, if it militates with the public object, must give way.   Upon private patent-rights the main object is the private advantage and emolument of
* the patentee, as a remuneration to him.   The interest   [* 703] of the public is to multiply the sellers.   The commodious supply of the public with these books is the main object ; and if the article is made by royal authority, it is immaterial, who sells, or, where it is sold.   The controlling principle is to facilitate the object and lessen the expense.   The Universities could not exclude each other, or the King's Printer, from selling, or even from printing in Oxford or Cambridge.   In *Baskett* v. *Parsons* there was evidence of fraud upon the patent by introducing books printed in Holland under the pretence, that they were printed in Scotland ; and that being the main object, the injunction was general, against importing contrary to the patent.   All the usage subsequent to *Baskett* v. *Parsons* is contrary to it.   That decision therefore cannot preclude the discussion.   An intention to grant a monopoly cannot be presumed ; and the words do not import it.   License and monopoly are perfectly distinct.   At the date of the charter of Hen. VIII. these prerogative copies did not exist.   That could only be effectual as a license ; for a monopoly extending to all manner of books could not be granted.   The Star-Chamber had a general power over the press at that time.   All these patents were existing before the abolition of that Court.   They were mere protections against the seizure of books and the interruption of printing by the Star-Chamber.   Mr. Yorke contended only for the right of doing the thing, not for an exclusion.   The instance of the grant of a market is not like this.   That in its nature is an exclusive right.

Lord CHANCELLOR [ELDON].—I am perfectly satisfied, that, if the King's Printer was a Plaintiff, these Defendants must be enjoined ; that what they are doing is not according to law.   The doubt I have is, whether these Plaintiffs are the persons to enjoin : but, notwithstanding that, as there is no doubt upon the illegality of what the Defendants are doing, I should not scruple to enjoin them till the hearing.

The construction put by Courts of Law upon these Letters Patent is, that notwithstanding the generality of the terms, giving that power or right, whatever it is, they give the Universities the faculty

of multiplying the copies belonging to the King; and no objection
as to the generality of the terms has been held to affect
[*704]   *the validity of those powers, which the King may lawfully grant.   The license or authority given by the Letters Patent confines them to the power of printing in the limits of
the Universities; not excluding the King's Printer or others; unless
they can upon their own statutes, confirmed perhaps by Act of Parliament.   The purpose of the power expressed in the Letters Patent
is the sale out of the Universities, and not only that, but any where
in the King's dominions; and certainly these words are very large:
but if the question arose with respect to Scotland also, the answer
would be the same, that is to be inferred from the certificate in *Baskett* v. *The University of Cambridge*; that the prior patent to the
Scotch printer would exclude them; and that upon the true construction of all the patents it was not intended, that the books they
should print within the University should be sold in Scotland.   It is
not however necessary to decide that.   Whether they and the King's
Printers have printed more or less, provided there is a sufficient supply for the subjects of this country, is immaterial; if they have a
concurrent authority.   The allegation, that they have employed a
large capital, is a material allegation; for the duty cannot be exercised without great expense; and then every infringement, having
a tendency to defeat the purposes of that expense incurred in the
necessary establishment for the execution of that duty, has a tendency, not only to the pecuniary damage of those entrusted to discharge it, but also to put an end to the regular supply by authorised
persons of books, which the constitution has supposed to be of such
a species, that the public ought to have a security, that the publication shall be such as it ought to be, not in subsequent inquiries, but
previous checks and regulations to this extent; that it shall be by
some persons, whom the law entrusts with it, as matter of duty.
With respect to the patent of the King's Printer, engaged in printing Acts of Parliament, Proclamations, and other Acts of State, and
possibly they may be entitled to print the Annals of Courts of Justice (the Year Books, I see, are mentioned), the establishment necessary for such a concern is of such extent, if the right is to be exercised according to the duty, that perhaps if the Crown had granted
a revocable patent, nothing could be found more contrary to the
interest of the public than to stop such an establishment at a moment's warning; nor any thing more detrimental to the prerogative;
as the establishment necessary for such a concern cannot be speedily
    .   provided.
[*705]   *I entertain a very strong doubt, whether if the Plaintiffs could not maintain the suit without making the King's
Printer a Defendant, they can do so, making him a Defendant;
for the suit proceeds upon a notion, that they have in themselves
a right to restrain; which will carry along with it a right to call
upon the Court to enjoin and for an account.   It does not necessarily follow, that, because the King's Printer has that right,

these Plaintiffs have it : nor, that if they have not that right without joining him, they will acquire it by joining him as a Plaintiff. In the nature of the Plaintiff's interest there must be a right to enjoin : or this suit would not be capable of being maintained, because the King's Printer is made a Defendant. If a duty is imposed upon the King's Printer in the nature of his right to prevent any person infringing it, and the consequence of his exercising his right according to his duty would be, that his right would generate a protection for the right of the Universities, whatever is the species of it, and that upon his public duty he can be called on to exercise that right, to the intent of giving that protection to these Plaintiffs, that is not the case this bill aims at, or the principle, upon which it is framed. The argument of reciprocity, that Scotch books may be sold here, and English books in Scotland, assumes the question ; for those, who contend, that books printed in Scotland cannot be sent to England, admit, that books printed in England cannot be sent to Scotland.

One question, which does not connect itself immediately with the nature of the title of the Plaintiffs, but would have had a place for discussion equally, if the bill had been filed by the King's Printer, is, whether, if the Court cannot find an accurate mode of estimating the profits, an injunction can be granted. Suppose it now admitted, that the King's Printer had, I do not say a concurrent authority (though it may be inferred, from some modes of reasoning upon the certificate in *Baskett* v. *The University of Cambridge* that the King's Printer had but an authority), but a concurrent copyright which Mr. Yorke supposes may exist in these matters, with the Universities, taking each of them to have a concurrent copyright with him : if the bill was filed by the King's Printer himself, the difficulty of saying, what share of the profits he was entitled to, would have been as great as the difficulty of estimating the profits in the case, as it is admitted to exist. The *King's Printer having by ad-   [*706] mission prohibitory clauses in his patent, and supposing for the argument the Plaintiffs had also, can it be contended, that on account of that difficulty they should not have that equity, which this Court administers as preventive justice for the very purpose of prohibiting others from making profit, and with the very intent perhaps, that the difficulty of estimating the profits shall not work an injustice to the Plaintiffs. I am of opinion, that, if it would be a due disposal of this case to send it to a Jury upon an issue, *quantum damnificatus*, as to each of the persons, which the Court often does, yet the right to the injunction, to prevent in future that, which is unjustly done or threatened, would be sufficient to support the bill (·1).

Cases may be put clearly illustrative of that. · Suppose, a tradesman going out of trade leaves three partners ; who give him a consideration for retiring ; the partnership between those remaining to exist for three years ; and afterwards it is understood, that the retir-

---

(1) See *ante*, 89, 701.

ing partner is to carry on the trade for his own benefit, covenanting not to carry it on within five miles of the others, which would be legal, either during or after the partnership about to take place; after that partnership ceased, and split either into two and one or three separate persons, if that covenant was with each and every of them, each would have a right to restrain him ; and yet the question, how much any one was damnified, or had lost, could never be duly decided without taking into consideration, what the respective profits would have been ; and the case would have every difficulty upon an issue.   Suppose, in the case of Lord Byron (1) there had been a variety of mills upon that stream : I do not say, they would have a concurrent right in the use of the water, though they would in this sense, that each was to have it : but the Court would have enjoined at the instance of any one ; as he would have a complete title in himself.   The cases as to waste, where it is threatened (2), and no account can therefore be due, also, where the waste is so insignificant, that even a Court of Law under an old statute would have a right to remit the damages, if minute, are all cases, where there can be no account ; and yet to prevent that mischief the party has a [*707]   right to an injunction, not only to the *hearing, but a perpetual injunction, if the circumstances warrant it.

It is then said, in cases of this sort the universal rule is, that, if the title is not clear at law, the Court will not grant or sustain an injunction, until it is made clear at law.   With all deference to Lord Mansfield, I cannot accede to that proposition so unqualified.   There are many instances in my own memory, in which this Court has granted or continued an injunction to the hearing under such circumstances.   In the case of patent rights, if the party gets his patent, and puts his invention in execution, and has proceeded to a sale, that may be called possession under it, however doubtful it may be, whether the patent can be sustained, this Court has lately said, possession under a color of title is ground enough to enjoin, and to continue the injunction, till it shall be proved at law, that it is only color and not real title.   There have been several instances of late. Can it be said, that the patent in the case of Boulton and Watt (3) was not doubtful?   The Court of Common Pleas were divided upon the validity of it.   Upon the first argument in the Court of King's Bench they were inclined to hold it bad : but they altered their opinion ; and decided in favor of it.   This Court enjoined them all the time during the pendency of the proceedings at law, upon the ground, that they had had possession of the invention under color of the title, which a patent, questionable in that degree, gave.   That declaration therefore is not to be understood in that unqualified manner.

Another case, without stating more, cited in the argument, is *Bas-*

---

(1) *Robinson* v. *Lord Byron*, 1 Bro. C. C. 588.
(2) *Gibson* v. *Smith*, 5 Atk. 182.
(3) *Boulton* v. *Bull*, 2 H. Black. 463, *ante*, vol. iii. 140; *Hornblower* v. *Boulton*, 8 Term Rep. 95. See *post*, *Harmer* v. *Blane*, vol. xiv. 130; *Hill* v. *Thompson*, 3 Mer. 622.

kett v. *Parsons*, before Sir Joseph Jekyll, an authority of a very high
nature.   From that authority, upon that very point, under the very circumstances existing in this cause, there was an appeal; and that decree was affirmed, and in a period, which directly connects itself
with the proceeding in the House of Lords in the other cause, whatever may be the precise nature of it.   This is the authority of Sir
Joseph Jekyll, confirmed by the Lord Chancellor; and pointedly
with regard to the question now addressed to the Court; and afterwards the Lord Chancellor explains the decree; which was
to restrain the King's Printers in Scotland.   * That is not   [* 708]
only an authority upon the point of the right of the King's
Printer in England to restrain the King's Printer in Scotland, but
also upon the point, whether the Court will enjoin, and continue the
injunction to the hearing, before any trial at law upon the point.
The same thing occurred in Lord Byron's case; who disputed the
right of the Plaintiffs: but an injunction was ordered, that he should
so manage his pond-head till the trial, as it had been managed previously to that day, upon which the complaint was made.   If therefore there was an absolute, invincible difficulty in taking the account,
the consequence would be only an issue *quantum damnificatus:* yet
if the right was in a due sense, sufficient for this bill, concurrent in
the Plaintiffs and the King's Printer, that right to restrain would be·
a sufficient ground to come for an injunction, in order to prevent the
species of mischief by infringement of the exclusive right; even if
under the circumstances according to the rules of this Court the
Plaintiff could only have brought an action; and the bill will not
necessarily finally fail, if it turns out, that they cannot have an account or an issue *quantum damnificatus;* and that the only relief
they can have is the injunction.

The next question is as to the right of the Defendants, stated by
their answer.   If it can be sustained, it must go to this; that the
King's subjects in Ireland have, notwithstanding any patent like this
granted to the King's Printer in Ireland, a right to introduce into
that country books printed by the King's Printer in Scotland; and
that the King's subjects in Scotland have a similar right to bring
into Scotland books printed in England or Ireland by the King's
Printer.   Independent therefore of authority, the proposition asserts
a right in the King's subjects to control his grant in a most material
and efficacious way.   It is familiar, that if a patent for an invention
is confined to England, it would not extend to Ireland.   If a distinct patent is granted for Ireland, the very circumstance of taking
them under the distinct Great Seals, which are still distinct for that
purpose, among others shows the reason; and time is always required with regard to the day, at which the enrolment of one patent is
to be made, on account of the purpose to get a patent elsewhere;
and it is always understood, that the right in a patent for one
country is confined to that; and would not enable the
party to bring the article for sale * into the other.   Yet   [* 709]
upon all those cases the argument is perplexing: but that

is in the nature of the thing. It might be asked, whether the King's subjects could not buy that article in Ireland, and bring it here ; and if any one did, whether it might not be sold as part of his effects. To that I do not know an answer. It is enough to say, if it is legal, that circumstance has not stood in the way of this proposition ; that you cannot bring those articles here for the purpose of trading. That circumstance belongs rather to the necessity of the habits of life ; and has never prevailed against the law, protecting the sole right of the party.

But it is said, this case differs from that of a patent invention for a watch, &c. : in such a case the Common Law right is not carried on by the King's authority ; and that authority gives the right to introduce it into this country. It is a strong proposition, that the King's authority is by implication to do that, which, giving the authority, he expresses it is not his intention to authorize ; for the Patent to the King's Printer not only does not contain any intention to give it for that purpose, but expresses a different intention, so strong, that implication to the contrary is impossible. Then what is the law upon the subject ? The language of the Patent, import-ing, that this is against the right, it must be proved ; not by any necessary effect of the King's grant ; considering that he granted particularly to Scotland, not as part of the same kingdom ; for he was not then King of both countries as one realm ; and his grant as King of Scotland could hardly be fairly taken into consideration in construing upon principles of English law his grant as King of England.

But it is much safer to apply to authority upon the direct point than to reason it eighty years after the decision upon speculation. This decision of *Baskett* v. *Parsons* was three times made in this Court at the suit of the King's Printer upon books, which he had the sole right to sell in England ; that a subject cannot buy under the authority of the patent for Scotland similar books printed there, for the purpose of importing them into England, in order to sell them there. It is said, you are to look at the *bona fides* of the thing ; and the truth was, that they were printed in Holland, and imported as if printed in Scotland. The Record is a complete answer to that argument ; for though the Plaintiff alleges, the De-
[*710]   * fendant bought elsewhere than in Scotland, the Defend-
ant avers, he had bought in Scotland ; and insists that as a subject and under the particular effect of the articles of Union he had a right to sell in England what he averred he had bought in Scotland.   Sir Joseph Jekyll restrained him upon the point. If he had made a case, that would have been only for the assist-ance of his judgment ; not sending it to a trial at law. But he takes upon himself, as he might, to decide the law ; and by the De-cree restrains the Defendant from selling all these books in the man-ner, in which he contended he was entitled to sell them. From that decree there was an appeal to the Lord Chancellor, who affirmed the decree ; and afterwards there was a subsequent application against the

Defendant for a contempt; and then he raised this point, that Scotland was not a foreign country; and the Lord Chancellor says, the decree meant to restrain him as to books printed by the King's Printer in Scotland ; deciding that to be an infringement of the right of the King's Printer here, against which the Court will enjoin.

The effect of usage and understanding, as amounting to that possession, which is so much regarded in granting or continuing injunctions, ought to be attended to. In *Baskett* v. *The University of Cambridge* the Universities had not been in the habit of printing Acts of Parliament; and the want of that habit was much regarded by the Court; who sent a case, even before they would grant the injunction upon a doubtful question in favor of those, who never had the possession. But in this case the usage and possession are affected by prior usage and possession, confirmed by judgment of law, the validity of the right under the other distinctly before a Court of Justice, and three times determined to be against law. If this usage was stronger than it appears in this answer, it would not authorize me to declare, that has ceased to be law, and given way to usage. Here there is no such thing as a law going into desuetude; and modern usage cannot be regarded as of equal authority with the judgment of this Court.

I do not state the judgment of the House of Lords as a direct judgment upon the question. But, attending to the grounds, upon which it is put, and the necessary connection with the judgment of this Court at that period, it cannot be represented as indifferent, * or destitute of all authority upon this point.   [* 711] I am of opinion, I am not at liberty to consider this upon the ground of such possession as is represented on the part of the Defendants as sufficient to prevent the continuance of this injunction; and I lay no stress upon the circumstance of having granted the injunction; which was upon general allegations, that books came from other parts as well as Scotland. But I cannot regard such possession as sufficient to prevail against a judgment of this Court unshaken and this acquiescence under it.

But the question so put is with regard to the King's Printer. It was decided at his suit; that he is entitled to say, it is illegal, as against him; and it is another question certainly, upon the point, whether the Universities have a right to restrain; and in that respect this case is very peculiar. If it should turn out finally, that they have not that right, there will be a miscarriage in restraining at their suit : but that will be in a case, in which these Defendants will have as little right to complain as can be imagined ; for the peculiar distinction of the case is, that the restraint will be upon a person, who, upon these authorities it must be admitted, has no right in law to what he is doing; and the complaint can only represent, that he may have a title to do what is unjust against the complaint of these parties, but not against another person, representing the Crown; from which these corporate persons derive their authority. If it can be represented to be doubtful in a degree, whether these Plaintiffs can restrain, my opinion is, that the public interest may be looked to, upon a subject, the communication of which to the public in an authentic shape, if a matter of right, is also matter of duty in the Crown; which are commensurate. The principle of the law is, that this duty and this right are better executed and protected by a publication of books of this species in England by persons confided in by Letters Patent under the Great Seal of England. If that is the principle, the question cannot be raised, whether a communication of the privilege by the introduction of Scotch and Irish books would be beneficial. Upon that supposition the law will rather interpose a guard against the consequences by previous restraint, than correct them afterwards; for another reason too; that, as the Scotch and Irish printers are not obliged to bring them here, the period may arrive, when having by the introduction of their editions [* 712]   * destroyed the English establishment, and, when no sufficient establishment is left here to supply these books according to the right and duty of the Crown, they may retire from it. It is not accurate to say, these privileges are not granted for the sake of unlimited sale, and for the benefit of the Universities, &c. They are to a certain degree, like all other offices, calculated for that sort of advantage, that will secure to the public the due execution of the duty; upon this principle, pervading all the branches of our constitution (which does not adopt the wild theories, that require the execution of a duty without a due compensation), that the duty is well secured in one way by giving a responsibility in point of means to the person to execute it. Where the fees are fixed, they are the due reward. Where they are not ascertained, the benefit shall be reasonable; and if an unreasonable price should be placed upon these works, these authorities and patents would be put in considerable hazard. The profit also ought to be calculated with a view, not only to secure present advantage, but, that the establishment may be continued in the country.

As to the argument upon the comparison of the text, the prices, &c. I have nothing to do with the monopoly, and the question, which edition is best; if it is matter of legal right, upon a confidence imposed by the law. But if the salesmen are driven out of the market, the price will be raised; and then all that advantage would vanish; as in the instance of a salmon fishery, that I remember. The reasoning, which affects to depreciate monopoly, will perhaps tend to create it; and it is impossible to forget the relative price of labor in these two countries upon such a question.

I do not now inquire, whether the King's Printer by not joining in this suit to restrain these Defendants is doing justice to his duty under this patent. But the next consideration is, whether there is in the authorities given to the Universities, attending to the true nature of the possession, which I say upon that authority has been in them, reason to think, that at their suit the injunction may be sustained at the hearing. This is said to be a mere license. There

is considerable doubt, whether it is not in its nature very like that to
the King's Printer; though he has it under the denomination of a grant of the office; which however as to * the   [* 713]
execution of the duty is nothing but an execution of authorities given to it.   I doubt, whether Mr. Yorke is correct in considering these patents as vesting the King's copyrights.   It may very
well be argued, that they remain still vested in the King; and the
grants are nothing more than authorities to exercise the right of
multiplying those copies, which, if not granted, remain vested in the
King, exercising them according to the public necessity, charging
reasonably.   It is true, there is a fee granted; and there are prohibitory clauses: but I doubt much, whether, if the grant purported
to be of the whole of his authority for such a period, that prohibitory
clause is really necessary; whether the grant of all his authority
would not as necessarily for the benefit of the patentee prohibit
others from printing as prohibitory clauses; for the nature of the
King's authority is exclusive.   There is also ground in the certificate
in *Baskett* v. *The University of Cambridge* for considering the grant
of the office as really nothing more than a grant of authorities.   The
expression is, that the Universities "are entrusted with a concurrent
authority."   Whether others have more authority must depend upon
the effect of the instruments.   But if the grant is nothing more than
of the King's authority, there is a necessary exclusion.   The officer
must of necessity have the duty as well as the right of exclusion,
from the duty of the Crown on behalf of the subject to exclude others.   The effect of that certificate is, that with respect to prior
patents to the King's Patentees, they had the effect of preventing
the King from granting concurrently to the Universities; which
could have no operation, till the prior patents ceased.   If the grant
to the Universities had been as universal in point of extent, instead
of being limited, upon the same principle it must have been held,
that the grant to the King's Printer subsequent to that to the University could have had no effect: but it was held a grant of part of
that interest, which had been granted by the prior grant; and which
would take effect, when the prior grants ceased to have effect; that
it has become split; this grant being only to print in the Universities,
and sell every where in England: the other, to print every where.
They are consistent in this sense.   The two Patents amount to an
apportionment into different proportions of the authority, carrying
along with it the duty, and therefore in some degree the right to exclude.   Mr. *Yorke* so considers it, and puts it strongly, as
a concurrent right * to print, and then it must be to ex-   [* 714]
clude.   It would be extraordinary, if it depends upon the
King's Printer, whether the Universities are to have that, which they
had in a manner to his prejudice, without the least benefit.

Under the circumstances therefore these Plaintiffs have that interest in them, which entitles them to have this injunction continued to
the hearing.   The injunction relates only to England.   I do not

apprehend it to mean, that these parties shall not sell Scotch books in foreign countries.

The Injunction was continued.

---

1. IT is now perfectly established, not only by the principal case, but by many others, that, although in cases of waste, the jurisdiction of Equity to give an account is grounded merely upon the obvious right to an injunction, and that, if an injunction be not prayed, an account will not be decreed, (*Grierson* v. *Eyre*, 9 Ves. 346; *Pulteney* v. *Warren*, 6 Ves. 89,) yet the converse by no means holds:—an injunction may, in very many cases, properly issue where there can be no account: for one great object of the jurisdiction is to prevent the commission of waste, in respect of which a subsequent decree for an account might be a very imperfect remedy; *Gibson* v. *Smith*, 2 Atk. 183, and see, *ante*, note 3 to *The Mayor of London* v. *Bolt*, 5 V. 129.

2. With respect to the doctrine of waste, as applied to the cutting of timber, by persons not authorized so to do, see notes 2 and 3 to *Lee* v. *Alston*, 1 V. 78, and notes 3, 4, 5 and 6 to *Pigot* v. *Bullock*, 1 V. 479.

3. That an injunction may be granted, in restraint of invasion upon alleged patent rights, though the legal title may be disputed, see the note to *Bolton* v. *Ball*, 1 V. 270: yet a positive legal or equitable title is necessary to sustain a motion against waste upon land: see the note to *Price* v. *Williams*, 1 V. 401.

4. As to the general doctrine with respects to the exercise of equitable jurisdiction in restraint of literary piracy, see the notes to *Cary* v. *Faden*, 5 V. 24.

WRIGHT *v.* SIMPSON.

[1802, March 4, 5, 6.]

Tʜᴇ property of an American loyalist having been confiscated during the American war, subject to the claims of such of his creditors as were friendly to American independence, to be made within a limited time, and in fact according to the evidence farther restrained to the inhabitants of the particular State, a bill to have bonds delivered up, or to compel the creditor to resort in the first instance to the fund arising from the confiscation, was dismissed; on the ground, that it did not appear, that the creditor had the·clear means of making his demand effectual against that fund: the Lord Chancellor also expressing an opinion in favor of the right to sue personally even in that case, against the authority of *Wright* v. *Nutt*, (3 Bro. C. C. 326; 1 Hen. Black. 136,) (a).
Presumption, that the Courts of foreign countries decide according to law; but open to evidence (b), [p. 730.]
A surety may be sued in the first instance: but, if the creditor sues the principal first, and gives time, the surety is discharged (c), [p. 734.]
Surety, depositing the money and indemnifying against expense, &c. may compel the creditor to go against the principal, and even to prove under a Commission of Bankruptcy, for the benefit of the surety (d), [p. 734.]

(a) As between the debtor himself and the creditor, where the latter has a formal obligation of the debtor, and also a security, or a fund, to which he may resort for payment, there seems no ground to say (at least, unless some other Equity intervenes,) that a Court of Equity ought to compel the creditor to resort to such fund, before he asserts his claim by a personal suit against his debtor. Why, in such case, should a Court of Equity interfere to stop the election of the creditor, as to any of the remedies, which he possesses under his contract? There is nothing in natural or conventional justice, which requires it. 1 Story, Eq. Jur. § 640; Eden, Injunc. ch. 2, p. 38, 39, 40; *Hayes* v. *Ward*, 4 Johns. Ch. 132.

(b) In *Alivan* v. *Furnival*, 1 Cromp. Mees. & Ros. 277, it seems to have been held, although not expressly so laid down by the Court, that the proceedings of foreign Courts must be presumed to be consistent with the foreign law, until the contrary is distinctly shown; and that, therefore, the principle adopted by a foreign Court in assessing damages cannot be impugned, unless contrary to natural justice, or proved not to be conformable to the foreign law. See also *Martin* v. *Nichols*, 3 Sim. 458; *Becquet* v. *McCarthy*, 2 B. & Adolp. 951; Story, Conflict of Laws, § 605, note.

Foreign judgments have been held conclusive by Lord Nottingham, Lord Hardwicke, and Lord Kenyon; *Kennedy* v. *Cassilis*, 2 Swanston, 326, note; *Boucher* v. *Lawson*, Cas. 7 Hard. 89; *Roach* v. *Garvan*. They were held examinable by Lord Mansfield, Lord Chief Baron Eyre, and Mr. Justice Buller; *Walker* v. *Witter*, Doug. 1; *Herbert* v. *Cooke*, Willes, 36, note; *Bayley* v. *Edwards*, 3 Swanst. 703; *Phillips* v. *Hunter*, 2 H. Black. 410; *Galbraith* v. *Neville*, cited Doug. 6, note 3; *Tarleton* v. *Tarleton*, 4 M. & S. 21. The present inclination of English Courts seems to be to sustain the conclusiveness of foreign judgments; *Guinness* v. *Carroll*, 1 B & Adolph. 459; *Becquet* v. *McCarthy*, 2 Ib. 951; *Contra* per Brougham, *Houlditch* v. *Donegal*, 8 Bligh, 301, 337 to 340.

The general doctrine of the American Courts is, that they are *prima facie* evidence, but that they are impeachable. 2 Kent, Comm. 118; 4 Cowen, 520, note 3; *Bissell* v. *Briggs*, 9 Mass. 462; *Borden* v. *Fitch*, 15 Johns. 121; *Green* v. *Sarmiento*, 1 Peters, C. R. 74; *Field* v. *Gibbs*, 1 Peters, C. R. 155; *Aldrich* v. *Kinney*, 4 Conn. 380; *Shumway* v. *Stillman*, 6 Wend. 447; *Hall* v. *Williams*, 6 Pick. 247; *Starbuck* v. *Murray*, 5 Wend. 148; *Davis* v. *Peckars*, 6 Wend. 327; *Buttrick* v. *Allen*, 8 Mass. 273; *Pawling* v. *Bird*, 13 Johns. 192; *Hitchcock* v. *Aicken*, 1 Cain. 460; *Hoxie* v. *Wright*, 2 Vermont, 263; *Bellows* v. *Ingraham*, 2 Ib. 575; *Barney* v. *Patterson*, 6 Harris & J. 182. The subject of Foreign Judgment is considered by Mr. Justice Story with great fulness and accuracy. Story, Conflict of Laws, § 584, 618.

(c) See *ante*, note (a), *Rees* v. *Berrington*, 2 V. 540.

(d) A surety has the right to call upon a creditor to do the most he can for his

The holder of a bill of exchange may be compelled to prove under the bankruptcy
of the acceptor for the benefit of the drawer, [p. 734.]
A person attainted may be charged in execution, [p. 734.]

THE object of this bill was the same as in the cause of *Wright* v.
Nutt (1), to compel creditors of the late Sir James Wright, who
was Governor of the Province of Georgia in North America at the
commencement of the American War, to deliver up their securities ;
or at least in the first instance to resort to the American Government for satisfaction out of the fund arising from his confiscated
property. The particular circumstances attending this debt were
these.

Sir James Wright executed two bonds, dated the 21st of September, 1768, and the 8th of March, 1769, each for 5000*l.* Carolina
currency, borrowed from the obligee Benjamin Smith of Charleston.
In August 1770 Smith died, leaving his brother Thomas Smith and
John Motte and others his executors. The Defendant John Simpson, of London, who was his limited administrator with the will
annexed under a power of attorney from Motte, the surviving executor, as to sums due to him, brought an action in Trinity Term
    1791.

[* 715] * Upon the disturbances breaking out in America, Sir
    James Wright having fled, in March 1776 an Act of As-
sembly passed in the State of Georgia ; enacting, that he and several other persons should be attainted, and adjudged guilty of high
treason, and should be liable to severe penalties ; and all their
estates and property, real and personal, were thereby confiscated,
and declared to be in the actual possession of the State ; and a
Board of Commissioners was appointed ; who were to sell all the
real and personal estates of the persons named in the Act ; and the
moneys arising by such sales were to be paid into the Treasury of
the State ; and all persons having any demand upon the forfeited
estates were to lay their claims before the Board ; and after liquidating all such claims on the forfeited estates the Board was to empower the Sheriff to sell the estates both real and personal by auction for the money of that State only, and to the inhabitants, being
actually citizens of and resident within the same ; and the persons
having any claims or demands on the estates of the attainted persons were to make the same before the expiration of sixty days after
the passing of that Act, or to lose their claims.

In 1778 the King's troops having taken possession of the Province
of Georgia, Sir James Wright returned, and resumed his government : but upon the evacuation of the Province by the King's
troops, he and the other persons, who had adhered to the British
interest, were again compelled to fly ; and by an Act passed by the

---

benefit; and if he will not, a Court of Equity will compel him; see *ante*, note (*a*), ·
Rees v. *Berrington*, 2 · V. 540; 1 Story, Eq. Jur. § 639; *Antrobus* v. *Davidson*, 3
Meriv, 579; *King* v. *Baldwin*, 2 Johns. Ch. 561; *S. C.* 17 Johns. 384; *Hayes* v.
Ward, 4 Johns. Ch. 432.

(1) 3 Bro. C. C. 326; 1 H. Black. 136.

House of Assembly*on the 4th of May, 1781, after the declaration of independence, reciting the former Act, it was enacted, that Sir James Wright and many other persons should be, and were thereby banished from that State for ever ; and, if they returned, should be guilty of felony without benefit of clergy ; and that all the estates both real and personal of all the said persons, with all debts, dues and demands, whatsoever due to them, should be confiscated to the use and benefit of that State ; and the moneys to arise from the sales, which should take place by virtue of that Act, should be applied to such uses as that Legislature should direct ; and that all debts, dues and demands, due to merchants or others residing in Great Britain, were thereby sequestered ; and the Commissioners appointed by the said Act were thereby empowered to recover, receive, and deposit, the same in the Treasury of the State in the same manner * as debts confiscated, there to remain   [* 716] for the use of the State ; and reciting, that there were several just claims and demands, which might be made by the good and faithful citizens of that State and others of the United States of America against the estates confiscated by that Act, it was enacted, that any persons well affected to the independence of the United States, having debts owing them from the persons named in that Act, or, who had any just claim in law or equity against any of such confiscated estates, should bring his claim or enter his action within the space of twelve months from the passing of that Act ; and in default thereof every such person should be for ever debarred from deriving any benefit from the same.

The Act then pointed out the mode of proceeding for such creditors : either by claim before the Commissioners, or by action at law ; in which case the sum recovered was to be paid by a certificate, to be issued by the Governor or Commander in Chief ; which certificates were to be taken in payment for any purchase at the sales of the confiscated estates.

By other acts of the State of Georgia and of Congress Sir James Wright was rendered incapable of suing any person in Georgia or any other of the United States.

The bill, which was filed in 1791, by the executors of Sir James Wright, stated, that upon his first flight from the province of Georgia he left there all his property to the amount of 90,000l. ; and all his plantations and property were finally seised, and sold ; that Motte and the other executors were well affected to the Americans ; and therefore they have, or might have, obtained payment ; that Sir James Wright's loss was under the commission for inquiring into the losses of loyalists ascertained at the sum of 30,000l. : but the Commissioners took into their consideration the amount of the debts due to persons friendly to America ; for the payment of whose debts provision was made by the American Government out of the confiscated property ; and that applications were made by Sir James Wright and by his executors to Motte and the other executors to re-

Ogden (1) expresses his perfect coincidence with the doctrine of
Wright v. *Nutt.* Again, upon the motion to dissolve the injunction
in this cause, after Motte's answer came in, Lord Loughborough
said, where a creditor has two funds, he shall not make an oppressive use of his power against one ; where he cannot give the debtor
the benefit of the other ; observing, that this was more than neglect;
it was oppressive in the creditor, and with a view to oppression ;
and upon that ground the injunction was continued to the hearing.
Upon these authorities, express decisions upon the very point, these
Plaintiffs are entitled to protection ; unless the creditor used due
diligence ; and upon the facts it appears he did not ; and your Lordship will prevent oppression by suing now, when he might have had
payment twenty years ago. Rules of law cannot meet every combination of circumstances : but the equitable jurisdiction is more enlarged ; proceeding upon principles of universal justice ; which must
not be defeated by slight obstacles ; as in the cases, in which equity
has interposed in respect of public policy or public justice. For-
[* 720]   merly Courts of Law would not advert to such considerations : of late * they have made some progress in that way :
but they have not gone the length of Courts of Equity.
The Legislature have gone some way to prevent the sale of offices (2) ; but still it is necessary in some cases to come here ; as in
Law v. *Law* (3) ; *Harrington* v. *Duchatel* (4) ; upon considerations of public policy, which, though they cannot influence a Court
of Law, impose a duty, and create a right. Can there be a higher
consideration, than that, which encourages the loyalty of the people
of this country? The proof is thrown upon the creditor, that he has
done all in his power to make his demand available, by a fund distinctly provided for him. It is not contended, that the jurisdiction
of this Court extends to enforcing the observance of every moral
duty : but though this subject is anomalous in its circumstances, the
equity is not new in its principle. The judgment in *Wright* v. *Nutt*
displays the principle of the rule ; and clearly establishes, that it
ought to prevail in a Court of conscience. It may be objected, that
this Court cannot interpose against a legal right : but the maxim,
" *Sic utere tuo ut alienum non lædas,*" is not only a maxim of law,
but a principle of equity. Before the rule as to marshalling assets
prevailed, the practice was to restrain a judgment creditor by injunction from going first against the personal estate: *Mills* v. *Eden* (5).
The principle of equity is so strong that it applies even against the
prerogative : *Sagitary* v. *Hyde* (6). *Porey* v. *Marsh* (7). *Lanoy*
v. *The Duke of Athol* (8). So, where a creditor having an inter-

(1) 1 Hen. Black. 123; 3 Term Rep. 726.
(2) Stat. 5 & 6 Edw. VI. c. 16.
(3) For. 140; 3 P. Will. 391.
(4) 1 Bro. C. C. 124.
(5) 10 Mod. 487.
(6) 1 Vern. 455.
(7) 2 Vern. 182.
(8) 2 Atk. 444.

est to get priority at law, a decree is obtained by another creditor: there this Court interposes against the legal right; and subjects it to considerable inconvenience.   The case of a man making over his property for the payment of his debts is very different.   That is his own act.   With respect to *M'Donald's Case* (1), and *Holditch* v. *Mist* (2), it would be strange, if, because a man had committed a felony, he should be protected from a civil right: that privilege should grow out of delinquency.   *Holditch* v. *Mist* was a case of fraud.   Formerly a bankrupt was regarded in that light.   Is that the case of Sir James Wright?   If he had gone back to Georgia, he would have been attainted of high treason: but in this country it must * be remembered, that his only crime was   [* 721] his loyalty and allegiance.   His disability was not merely in respect of the property withdrawn.   The recompense for the purpose of paying this debt would have been forfeited.   It will be said, the creditor would have been paid in depreciated money; and that ought to weigh now.   But, might not the debtor, if not deprived of his property, have discharged the debt there in such depreciated paper, which is proved to have been a legal tender?   A man acting with common good intentions would have attempted to make his demand available, as far as he could; giving his debtor to understand, that he must not be prejudiced by it.   They show an application; but not that they followed it up; and took the course prescribed. They ought at least to have gone as far as they could without incurring expense.   This is an attempt, as Lord Loughborough expressed it, to increase the effect of confiscation.   A deduction was made in the allowance from this country in respect of the debts to be paid out of this fund.   Till 1791, when that fund, which is so reduced upon the supposition that these debts were paid out of the fund in America, was provided by the bounty of Parliament, the action was not brought.

The *Solicitor General* [Hon. *Spencer Perceval*], Mr. *Mansfield*, and Mr. *Stanley*, for the Defendants.—This creditor could not be for ever be debarred from his legal demand, because he did not make his election in one year.   The Act of Assembly was a bar only to an application against the confiscated estates, not, as it is contended, to any other demand against the debtor.   The evidence does not state, that these certificates were a legal tender; but they were merely made receivable in payment of the purchases of the forfeited estates.   The proof lies upon the Plaintiffs.   There is no such principle of equity as is now set up: nor did this case ever furnish the facts, to which it would apply; and if it ever did, it does not at the present moment.   If this fund was, as it is supposed by the argument, money in the next room, and the creditor wilfully,. maliciously, and oppressively, would not take it, but would proceed against the debtor, the case would be very different.   Nothing like

(1) Fost. 59.
(2) 1 P. Will. 695.

that is in evidence.   Surely some time is necessary for an executor
to consider, what would be the effect of taking this depre-
[* 722]   ciated * paper in payment under this act.   He could not,
if he had taken it, afterwards go against the debtor, because the paper fell.   *Arnold* v. *Holker* (1) seems to the contrary :
but it does not appear, upon what principle ; for according to that
law it would have been a legal payment.   Suppose, the paper instead of falling had risen ; the surplus could not have been claimed
by the debtor.   The cases put by your Lordship (2) would fall
within the principle ; if it was recognized as a principle of this
Court.   In the case of a bankrupt before certificate, or, putting it
more strongly, before certificates were known, might not the creditor refuse to come in, and pursue him at law ?   Will not this Court
permit him to come in for the express purpose of defeating the certificate ?   Where a bill was put into the hands of a bankrupt before
his bankruptcy without indorsement, and discounted, it was held,
that either an action of trover might be brought, considering it as a
tort, or an action for money had and received ; and in the former
case it was no answer, that the bankrupt had obtained his certificate.
In the case of a person attainted suppose a pardon by Act of Parliament, reserving the forfeiture : he may be charged in execution.

The cases of marshalling assets, &c. do not apply.   All that arrangement is for the benefit, not of the debtor, but the creditor.
In the case of bankruptcy the creditor is permitted to elect, whether
he will come in under the Commission, or not; and he would not
even be put to his election, if there was any reasonable doubt,
which was for his advantage.   Certainly a bankrupt is not now
treated upon the whole principle of fraud.   Considering this as a
pledge it would be strange that it should be forced upon the creditor.   Can the debtor take advantage of this act, by a country not
his own, and not intended for his benefit?   *Holditch* v. *Mist* is in
point; and the fact in that case, that the fund was in the same
country, brought it much nearer the principle.   In *Hornby* v. *Houlditch* (3) Lord Hardwicke recognises that case.   Why may
[* 723]   not this creditor avail himself of two * remedies ?   A
mortgage has several.   He has a right to choose for himself.   At least it should be clearly made out, that they had called
upon him, and had undertaken to bear all the consequences, if the
application should prove fruitless.   It is not proved, that the representatives of Smith at the time were friends to American independence.   The answer says, Smith never was friendly to it; which is
also confirmed by Sir James Wright's letters ; and there is no proof
to the contrary.   M'Intosh's evidence is, that some claims by persons resident out of Georgia were referred to Sir James Wright's
estate in England; because he had carried away great personal

(1) In the Court of Exchequer.
(2) The observations, that fell from the Court during the argument, are stated
more at large in the judgment.
(3) And. 40 ; 1 Term Rep. 92.

property, and left nothing but his lands. They must therefore first
establish, that this claim could have been made available. Your
Lordship observed, that the strong ground is, that the creditor is to
be considered a subject of the country, and a party to the act. That
would apply equally to *Holditch* v. *Mist*. But this case does not
supply that fact. Smith, the creditor, was an inhabitant of Carolina. The different states are for the purpose of Legislation distinct.
The greatest hardship might follow to the family of this creditor
from such an injunction. Are the *Cestuis que trust* to be barred, as
well as the trustee, because in one year he has not taken this particular mode and novel process? Is he to be considered upon the
principle of a *devastavit?* It must be carried to that extent: or
how are the *Cestuy que trusts* to be protected? There can be no
doubt, that, if he could have obtained payment, he would. This
provision is confined to friends to American independence. As to
the mode, not a shilling was to be paid in cash. There is no evidence, that Sir James Wright had not the means of paying this or
any other debt. Hardship, though certainly entitled to some consideration, is not alone a ground for relief. In *Kempe* v. *Antill* (1)
Lord Thurlow appears to have entertained a very different opinion
from that, which he afterwards adopted.

Mr. *Richards*, in reply.—This Equity is certainly new in specie :
but the principle is not new. In *Kempe* v. *Antill* Lord Thurlow
seems of opinion, that, if the creditor had the fund in his
own * hands, he should be enjoined. This is not the case   [* 724]
of two subjects of the same country, though originally so.
Though the creditor died before the Rebellion, Motte, who now sues,
admits that he was friendly to it; and what he says as to Smith is
only, that he was of a quiet turn, and disposed to yield to the prevailing power. Motte, a member of an American state, though not
of Georgia, joined in this act; admitting himself a party, an active
member in that treason and rebellion. Though the states are distinct, yet they are members of the same great state; like different
jurisdictions in this country. By the rebellion the contract certainly
became different as between the parties. The alteration was not
made by any act or consent of the debtor, but by external force acting upon him, and with the assistance of every member of that state.
No case has been stated, in which by the act of the state, of which
the Defendant was a member, the contract has been varied. The
cases of marshalling are applicable to show, that a Court of Equity
does act upon a principle injurious to the creditor for the sake of doing
justice to all. What right has the Court in that instance to lessen
the security, or vary the nature of the contract; to make the obligee
wait till the value of the real estate is seen? There is no principle,
that will not equally apply to this case. The Court in these cases
drives the creditor from a fund, to which he chooses to go, and to
which he was entitled by his contract to go, to another, to which he

---

(1) 2 Bro. C. C. 11.

does not wish to go, for the sake of doing more general and ample justice.

With respect to the cases in bankruptcy, they are really within the principle, for which we contend. They are legislative declarations in favor of it. The instant it appears that the debtor acts fairly he gets his certificate; and then is he not discharged? All the previous steps, putting him in prison, election, &c. are only to attain the object of the legislature, the application of his property to his debts. The principle is, that the legislature taking from him all the means of paying his debts protects him. It does not follow, that if Motte does not succeed here, he will be charged with a *devastavit.* It is not necessary for the Plaintiff to consider that. It is the consequence of his own act. I deny, that under the particular circumstances of this case the debt follows the person: the nature of the contract being altered by the acts, to which Motte as a member of that state, which procured the property to [* 725] be * confiscated, was a party; receiving as such the advantage derived from the confiscation.

Holditch v. *Mist*, if not capable of being distinguished, was overruled by *Wright* v. *Nutt*. But it may be distinguished. Holditch was a member of this community; certainly a party to the Act of Parliament, passed for the purpose of doing justice to the objects of the South Sea bubble; and that case, it must be remembered, was decided at a time, when the passions of the country were very much inflamed by the circumstance of that affair. If a person places all his property in the hands of trustees, that is his own act, and he knows the consequences. Certainly therefore that will not protect him. With respect to the case of a person attainted, the law attending the contract is supposed to make part of it. The law of the land is, that the attainder shall not free him from his debts. Besides, the property being forfeited to the Crown, the creditor has no fund to go to. But in this instance the property is made amenable to the debt. Then as to the case of the bill of exchange, put by your Lordship, the nature of the contract is, that, the acceptor being a bankrupt, the holder giving notice may go against the drawer; who comes upon the bankrupt's estate to the extent of the dividend. The nature of this contract has no resemblance to that. Sir James Wright had no power to make his property available: but his creditors had that power. With respect to the case of the obligee and surety, that is a contract between the parties. The obligee is not bound to sue the obligor. With respect to him by the nature of the contract both are principals. The surety has a right to go in some way against the obligor; if not upon the bond, because it is paid, in an action for money had and received.

As to the necessity of making a request, in the case of the surety the obligee is not bound to make a request. But it was the duty of this creditor, involved in the act of the State, making the fund accessible to him, and depriving the debtor of it, to apply; and not having done so he is guilty of gross oppression. The Plaintiffs are not answerable for the shortness of the time. They do not mean, that they had no notice; and it would be difficult to say, they had not: but they say, they sent a memorial to the state; which they never followed up. How was a banished man to make *an application during the flagrancy of rebellion? As to   [* 726] the property left, even M'Intosh states, that he left his estate and plantations. There was therefore property, which they never attempted to make available, and which we could not: the amount, I admit, is not ascertained: but there is foundation for an inquiry as to that; and to what extent it might have been made available. Motte by his negligence may have suffered the opportunity to escape. The objection as to the certificates is stated very loosely. The Act of Assembly provides for the payment within a year; and gives the purchasers liberty to pay the certificates to the state. Be the depreciation what it may, still something might have been procured from this estate.

The Lord CHANCELLOR [ELDON] stated the case; and delivered his opinion.—This debt was contracted upon personal security; and the nature of the contract, if it does not necessarily imply, that the creditor did not mean to place himself in the circumstances, which belong to the nature of a pledge, and I do not mean to insinuate, that it does, admits, that he might have in his contemplation rather to accept a personal contract, and that only, than to entangle himself with any questions, in which he might be engaged, if in addition to the personal security he had constituted himself a creditor by a pledge, placed in his hands for a debt. It is admitted, these bonds were given for money actually advanced. It is also admitted by the proceeding in this Court, that in law notwithstanding the alteration of circumstances the debt is legally due by the contract; and this bill insists, that there is in the circumstances and facts, connected with the conduct of the Defendants, as to what they have done, or might have done without wilful default, a ground for saying, a Court of Equity ought to cut down the admitted legal effect, yet subsisting, of the legal contract. The creditor was a member of Carolina, not of Georgia; and, as far as there is any evidence as to his temper with regard to this country or that, it seems to import rather, that he was well affected to this country; though not very distinctly. One of the executors also upon the evidence, not very distinct as to that either, appears rather having an affection kind than hostile to this country. As to Motte the evidence is more distinct; representing him well affected to America. It does not appear, how far * the office of executor in this case carries with it the   [* 727] beneficial interest (1). If it does not, the question is, how far shall the equity affect those beneficially interested, if they were well affected to this country; regard being had to the circumstance, that one executor was well affected, the other ill affected, to

(1) In answer to a question from the Lord Chancellor upon this it was said at the Bar, that Motte, who had married a daughter of Smith, had some interest under the will; but was also a trustee for others.

America.   Such an hypothetical case must be looked to, before you
can collect the law upon principles applying to such cases as these.
No question arises upon the first act of confiscation : but Sir James
Wright was again obliged to fly ; and the property, which he had,
and could not remove, (for there is evidence, and strong evidence,
that he did remove some) fell under the grasp of another act of confiscation.   Upon the policy of that act I make no observation.   It
gives to the creditors well affected to America the means of applying to the confiscated property, as a fund for payment of their debts ;
and it must be admitted, the debtor himself was completely barred
from all possibility of recourse to that property ; and that he neither
had nor could aquire an interest in that fund so reserved, in the
mode, in which it was reserved, for the payment of certain debts.

Upon this case, notwithstanding all this argument, and an able
argument, that Motte must be considered himself an author of that
act, and that Smith, though, if it can be so put, with good affections
to this country, and the *cestuis que trust* also, are to be taken as the
authors of it, yet it is clearly the law of this country, that their own
act so expressed varies no one legal incident or quality of the contract.   The relief must therefore be in equity only.   With all deference I am disposed to think it very difficult to maintain that
equity ; having infinite difficulty in reconciling my mind to this
point ; that the act of the individual, if bound up to the act of the
state, shall be considered bound up with it to equitable, but not to
legal, principles ; and that the contract shall be affected in one
Court, and not in the other.   I feel the more difficulty upon this, as
neither Lord Thurlow, Lord Kenyon, nor Lord Loughborough, relied at all upon that way of putting the case.   They put the doctrine upon different grounds certainly.   This is a question of great
          importance ; and if I found myself bound to decide
[* 728]   * this cause, not upon the facts, but upon the principle laid
          down in the authorities, to which I am referred, admitting,
the facts formed a ground for the application of that principle, I
should have been obliged to express a different opinion from all
those authorities, much as I respect them.   I should certainly have
thought it my duty to consider the case very much, before I should
have permitted myself to express that contradiction of authority ; the
more peculiarly, as it was not till this argument that I could suggest
some color of answer to the difficulties, that my mind presented to
itself.

Upon this question Lord Thurlow, Lord Kenyon, and Lord Loughborough, the last certainly extra-judicially, but in a case, upon which
his consideration was much interested, and therefore carrying as
much authority as under any circumstances an extra-judicial opinion
can, proceeded upon principles, that are stated very distinctly and
very anxiously in this Report (1).   It appears by Lord Thurlow's
judgment, that the attention of the Legislature had been called to

_____

(1) 1 Hen. Black. 136.

the situation of these parties; and propositions had been made upon it in Parliament. Lord Thurlow's opinion was, and certainly that is very correct, that, let such events happen, as might, influencing or destroying the means of the debtor to make good the contract, if the duties which arise out of it, formed a legal and natural right of the creditor to sue the debtor under those circumstances, nothing could be more delicate than the interference of the Legislature, taking away from motives of compassion those stipulated rights, into which the debtor thought fit to enter. That led Lord Thurlow to form an opinion upon the right of the creditor very favorable to the debtor; and satisfied him not only, that it was too delicate to be meddled with, if it was necessary, but that, as it was not necessary, it was the more unfit to take that course. That idea was therefore dropped; and a bill was filed.

In this Report it is laid down as Lord Thurlow's clear opinion (1) that the principle is, " that, provided a case is made, by which it appears, that there is in the hands of a creditor either possession of the estate in fact, or the clear means of effecting that possession, * he ought to be called on so to do, or at least the　[* 729] Court should interpose."

If there is no risk, no delay necessary to recover possession of the fund, if no expense is necessary, no intermediate risk of losing, while you are looking to one fund, another, which is answerable, as in many instances, that is one sort of case; and you are paid without prejudice. With regard to the last part of that proposition I am ready to say, that if it is to be taken as between the creditor and the debtor only, that if the creditor has the clear means of effecting the possession, he ought to be called on so to do, or at least the Court should interpose, the equity is new. I do not say, because it is new in specie, it is not therefore to be administered, if there are analogies from other cases, out of which a principle may be extracted, sufficient to support that equity. The judgment is very correctly taken: but it is a little too short in this part; for it drops a circumstance, that is to be found in another part of the judgment, that the creditor has not the means of assigning to the debtor those means he had of affecting the property. Lord Thurlow then says, as to *Holditch* v. *Mist*, he does not profess to over-rule it; but professing not to over-rule that case, unless the circumstance, relied on by Mr. Richards, that the parties there were subjects of the same country, or other circumstances distinguish it, I say, Lord Thurlow has over-ruled it. He says, he does not know how to apply that case to the case then under consideration; but that he retains his opinion, that a creditor will be bound by an application to this Court to use fair *bonâ fide* diligence in order to make the most of his debtor's estate in the place, where the law of the country has applied that estate to the payment of his debts.

Here also Lord Thurlow does not notice the circumstance, that

---

(1) 1 Hen. Black. 151, 2, 3.

no assignment could be made; nor attend to a circumstance, deserv-
ing some attention, as connecting itself with the inference from all
the cases of non-application of the creditor to a pledge, taken even
in the original constitution of the contract, or another surety : the
cases stating a distinction between not acting, where no request has
been made, and a refusal to act, where there has been a request.

    Lord Thurlow then stating the circumstances, under
[* 730]   which that application was *made, proceeds, that " in
    order to make a good and effectual bar in equity to a de-
mand at law, it will be necessary to show, that the estate of Sir
James Wright confiscated in America was of greater value, not only
than the sum now in question, but than all sums claimed upon that
estate ; consequently, that there was a fund sufficient to have paid
the whole ; for if it should turn out to be a defective fund, and capable of satisfying the debt but in part, it can only operate as a discharge *pro tanto.*"

Upon the obvious meaning of the language of this part of the
judgment, the *onus probandi* is thrown upon Sir James Wright. I
do not say, that in other parts it is not put upon the other parties :
but I doubt, whether the language of every part is consistent upon
the point, on whom the proof lies. The passage immediately following states, that in the second place it must be shown, that by the
justice to be obtained in that country, this demand was competently
made. There the language throws the proof upon the others.
With the next passage, that the Courts of that country must be supposed to be deciding according to the laws of that country, I agree
to this extent ; that natural law requires the Courts of this country
to give credit to those of another for the inclination and power to do
justice (1) ; but not, if that presumption is proved to be ill founded
in that transaction, which is the subject of it ; and if it appears in
evidence, that persons suing under similar circumstances neither had
met, nor could meet, with justice, that fact cannot be immaterial as
an answer to the presumption, when we are dealing with such an
equity as this. So, understanding them to be deciding according to
the laws of that country, I should say under this Act, if this clause
means, they should let in all debts, I must suppose, they would let
in those from Carolina, as well as Georgia. But if the contrary is
proved, the principle obliges me to suppose, their decision upon that
is right ; and that is the true interpretation of the law, which they
themselves put upon it.

Lord Thurlow proceeds, that " therefore if a formal and final de-
    cision had been obtained, by which it became impossible
[* 731]   to * have obtained a shilling of the whole of that demand,
    that would likewise be a sufficient answer; for the bill pro-
ceeds upon the idea, that the fund was complete ; and that it is still
available ; or, if not so, that it has been owing to the conduct of the
other party."

(1) As to the plea of sentence of a foreign Court, see Mr. Beames's Elem. of
Pleas in Equity, 200.

I do not hesitate to declare, that it is not necessary, that a formal demand should be made in the individual case ; provided it is proved from what has been done in other cases, that the demand would have been useless.

These are the principles, coupled with the circumstance, that the creditor cannot assign the benefit of the fund to the debtor, that led Lord Thurlow, Lord Kenyon, and Lord Loughborough, to this decision. This is great authority; not only from the consideration given to it, but, as it was followed up by great consideration afterwards, and adhered to ; and there is the clearest concurrence of Lord Kenyon ; who, I admit, subscribes fully to the whole doctrine ; and there is the additional authority of Lord Loughborough in *Folliott* v. *Ogden ;* declaring his full and absolute concurrence in this doctrine. There is also Lord Thurlow's act subsequent, stating his mind as impressed with the verity of this doctrine to a great extent ; and I think, he has carried the principle farther than his own doctrine would require ; for when *Wright* v. *Nutt* came finally before the Court, when it was found necessary to deliver the fund to Nutt, I can see no ground requiring him to give security. Supposing the doctrine correct, that was pressing it beyond the principle.

It is impossible to deny, that I argued that case with a full persuasion in my own mind, that the case was in specie perfectly new ; and that there was difficulty in finding a principle quite satisfactory to support the equity. The first difficulty is this. Is it the law, that under such circumstances the personal liability of the debtor is taken away? That is not contended. It must be founded upon the law of nations, I presume. Is it the law, that under such circumstances the remedies resulting out of that liability shall be restrained by confining the remedies to particular funds, or by confining them altogether as to the person, till the *creditor   [* 732] has had recourse, not to all the funds of the debtor, but to some of his funds, which funds in the original constitution of the debt, and the transaction, forming the relation of debtor and creditor, the debtor did not propose, nor the creditor receive, as the funds to be charged by the contract with that debt? Suppose, Smith, adverting to the circumstances of that day, a probable revolution, or at least troubles in America, had said, he would have nothing to do with the estate ; but had so good an opinion of Sir James Wright's personal responsibility, that he would take a personal contract ; knowing, he had property here and in other countries ; and that responsibility would go with him, wherever he went: suppose him to stipulate expressly, that he shall not be implicated in the justice of the state, but shall have merely a personal contract. The very circumstance of the necessity of giving notice with respect to a bankrupt acceptor, the reasoning requiring that, is of this sort: it is not upon grounds of malice, oppression, &c. ; but, that you have no right to judge for the drawer what he can make out of the imprisonment of the acceptor, operating by way of duress upon the feelings and affections of third persons. This is the effect of the con-

tract they actually made.   Then why should not the terms and effect
of the contract determine their meaning rather than conjecture.
This is said to be oppression, wilful wrong and injury.   What right
is there to apply these terms to the effect of the contract?   The
maxim " *Sic utere tuo ut alienum non lædas,*" is mentioned.   That
assumes the question ; which is, what is *suum,* what, *alienum.*   The
right to sue is conceded.   Then how is it to be taken away without
the consent of the creditor?

Consider it as the case of a pledge.   If originally a pledge was
given in the terms of the contract, if the true effect is, that the
creditor should have all the remedies belonging to the nature of a
pledge, and also personal responsibility, following the person every
where, it is questionable at least and a great deal of argument
would be required to make out, that the revolution would have operated to drive the creditor to the pledge, and to compel him to give
up the other remedy at the instance of the debtor.   But the difficulty is much enhanced, when the pledge is not given to the creditor .
by the terms of the contract, but is thrown to him by an
[* 733]   * act, not his own ; unless it is so upon the ground of his
presumed consent as a member of the state ; to the
difficulty of which I have before alluded.   If it is not to be considered his own, and by the terms of the contract he has the personal
responsibility, what right has the debtor to say, he shall take the
pledge ; and with this effect, that, till he has endeavored to make
the most of it under circumstances more or less favorable as to the
result, he is, not to give up the personal responsibility, but to suspend
all the fruits to follow from it.   There is great difficulty in that ; and
if the principle is right, it establishes the equity, though the pledge
cannot be considered originally contracted for, or subsequently taken
with the consent of the creditor ; for there is no such qualification
upon their principle ; which must be right without that circumstance,
so much insisted on in the argument for the Plaintiffs upon the doctrine in this case, to which I am alluding.

I am not sure, that the case of bankruptcy does not admit an
answer.   I am unnecessarily going into the case ; as I shall decide it
upon the facts.   The case of bankruptcy had struck me as furnishing considerable difficulty ; and I cannot get rid of it upon the
ground of delinquency.   The law, to which every creditor is a party,
(which affords an answer to the Plaintiff's argument, except so far
as there may be a distinction upon the circumstance, that the individuals are of different countries) vests the whole of the bankrupt's
property in the assignees ; and leaves it purely to the creditors,
whether his future effects shall not also be brought within the reach
of the effect of the assignment.   Formerly, when the creditors could
not give a certificate, even the opportunity of getting a discharge
was taken away.   Yet under those circumstances the creditor was
allowed to lay hold of the person of the debtor, in order to squeeze
from third persons the means of getting his debt.   But this answer
to that case strikes me ; that the circumstance, that the creditor

cannot assign the fund, does not belong to it : or if it does, then you raise a case, in which the debtor has no right to complain. Suppose the bankrupt has ten creditors : nine come in under the Commission ; and one refusing to come in arrests him : if his estate is equal to paying 20s. in the pound to all, what would have gone to the tenth goes to the bankrupt as surplus, which operates as an assignment to the bankrupt of that * portion. If the   [* 734] effects are not sufficient to pay all, then the bankrupt has no right to complain ; for he cannot find an equity against one creditor not going in, if the fund has been applied in discharging the debts of other creditors.

As to the case of principal and surety, in general cases I never understood, that as between the obligee and the surety there was an obligation of active diligence against the principal. If the obligee begins to sue the principal, and afterwards gives time, there the surety has the benefit of it (1). But the surety is a guarantee ; and it is his business to see, whether the principal pays, and not that of the creditor. The holder of the security therefore in general cases may lay hold of the surety ; and till very lately even in circumstances, under which the surety would not have had the same benefit, that the creditor would have had. But in late cases, provided there was no risk, delay, or expense, as in the case put, of the money in the next room, indemnifying against the consequences of risk, delay, and expense, the surety has a right to call upon the creditor to do the most he can for his benefit ; and the latter cases have gone farther. It is now clear, that if the surety deposits the money, and agrees, that the creditor shall be at no expense, he may compel the creditor to prove under a Commission of Bankruptcy, and give the benefit of an assignment in that way (2). That case therefore perhaps does not bear much upon it.

So the case of a bankrupt acceptor, and the holder and drawer of a bill would admit the same answer as the case of the bankrupt ; for the holder may be compelled to prove for the benefit of the drawer ; if not, the drawer sues upon a contract, the terms of which flow out of the original contract, of the benefit of which he could not be deprived under those circumstances.

Upon the case of the attaint the contract is taken to mean, that if party becomes civilly dead for his crime, and that takes away all his property by forfeiture, yet the law implies out of that contract, that the creditor can charge his person in * execu-   [* 735] tion ; and even in circumstances, from which there is no ray of hope of getting any thing by it, the creditor has a right to take his chance of that. A case, that was put in the argument deserves attention. Suppose a pardon by Act of Parliament, reserving the benefit of the forfeiture : the creditor a party to that ; and consent-

(1) *Ante, Rees* v. *Berrington,* vol. ii. 540; and the note, 544.
(2) See *Beardmore* v. *Cruttenden,* 1 Cooke's Bank. Law, 211; 8th edit. by Mr. Roots, 233. *Post,* vol. x. 414, *Ex parte Rushforth;* xi. 22; 2 Swanst. 191, and the note; 1 Turn. 229, 231.

ing to the forfeiture therefore : the debtor must remain in gaol. The Court has no right to apply the terms "wilful, malicious, and oppressive," to what the law under those circumstances allows. But it may be objected, that the fund is not a fund for the payment of the debt. But put the case, as in ordinary cases, that the Crown would pay the debt ; and the creditor should refuse to go to that fund, and should insist upon his right to imprison the debtor. The right to go to the Crown is not a legal right ; which could be insisted on. It is too thin a claim, of imperfect and secondary obligation ; and it would be impossible therefore to discharge the debtor.

But the point is decided, if *Holditch* v. *Mist* stands. That case is directly in point. Can it be said, the Legislature intended to make a provision for the creditors, not requiring them to come in as against that provision ; and that they should retain the power of suing the debtor personally ? There was an absence of intention. Their inclination would rather have been to take away that power : but without adverting to that they did leave it. There was a creditor in possession of all the rights Lord Thurlow, Lord Kenyon, and Lord Loughborough, allude to, except the circumstance of not being able to assign the fund ; and he refuses to go in ; and proceeds personally. This Court then said, it was the natural, legal, genuine, fruit of the contract : and what Equity was there, independent of the incapacity to assign the fund ? That case is an authority directly in point ; and I must know satisfactorily, why it should be overruled.

The next consideration is, whether the want of power to assign the fund makes the whole difference : or the distinction, alluded to this day, connected with that ? As to the first, I have strong doubt, whether I can attach such an Equity, arising out of the circumstance, that a fund was prepared without the consent of the creditor (otherwise than by the act of the State, to which he belongs, which is disposed of by the very state of this case,) that under the [* 736] * disadvantage of having no fund pledged he shall be put under all the disadvantage, that would have followed from his seeking originally to have a pledge. The cases cited of double securities, marshalling assets, &c. are not wholly inapplicable ; in which this Equity has been administered, not at the suit of the debtor, but certainly arising out of his acts ; and he does indirectly receive benefit. But I doubt, whether they go the whole length of this ; and the principle obviously was not relied on in those judgments of Lord Thurlow, Lord Kenyon, and Lord Loughborough. In this case, if Smith had taken a note of hand, and had no other than personal security, is it clear, that, if an event happens afterwards, with reference to which it might be that he thought proper to take that very security, that Equity attaches upon his conscience to make him consider the debtor answerable otherwise than according to the nature and circumstances of the security? In many circumstances he might have suffered severely by taking that instead of a pledge. Then why in different circumstances should he not have the advantage ?

If therefore my decision was to depend upon my accession to these authorities, I am not prepared to say, I could agree to them. I am relieved in a great degree from the necessity of future consideration with respect to this case; for I am of opinion, that, if the principles laid down in that judgment were clearly right, the facts of this case do not bring it within the reach of those principles. They all concur, that the creditor must have the clear means, and it must be shown, that he has the clear means, of making his demand effectual. Has this creditor had such clear means? First, as to the creditor himself, it is at least not clear, that he was one of the well affected, that could have had recourse to this fund. One of the executors appears to have been friendly to this country; the other adverse. Next, it does not appear, whether the *cestuys que trust* were well or ill affected. But, whether they are, or not, am I to hold the creditor under this sort of equity, certainly if substantial, thin; is the creditor under these circumstances to have this decided at his risk? Suppose, this debt was the only debt Sir James Wright owed; that he had money in this country to pay it, and no other fund except the money arising out of the confiscated estate in America; are these creditors at their own risk under all the circumstances to seek to make the *demand effectual   [* 737] out of the confiscated estates; taking it also, that Sir James Wright was an expensive man; and that these creditors had not a shilling but this debt, not only for their subsistence generally, but for the means of support, while trying this question in America, or for effectually trying the question? Is there any justice in this equity, compelling them at such hazard to apply to a fund, seized on by an act of confiscation, interpreted by those, who are to administer it, and in fact applied, according to the evidence of M'Intosh, to the debts of citizens of Georgia, and not of Carolina creditors: but, if applicable to debts generally, to be satisfied by the certificates, under a great depreciation? The creditors take that paper at their own risk; and it is a grave question notwithstanding *Arnold* v. *Holker*, whether, if they take it without the consent of their debtor, it would not be accepted at law in full satisfaction of the debt; and whether without proof, that any Carolina creditor did, or could, make his demand effectual, and where there is evidence, that the confiscated property was made applicable only to the inhabitants of Georgia, and for the benefit of that state, I am to say, there was wilful default in not making the claim; and, that, if made, it would have been effectual: a great deal more than is to be inferred from this evidence, if it can be called so; for the whole case is proved in a way, that leaves it without the character of evidence.

Therefore from this non-claim under such peculiar circumstances of risk and difficulty, when it was no part of the original contract of the creditor, that he should act, I cannot impute wilful default; so as to charge the creditor as a trustee guilty of a breach of trust in not claiming; and I ought to hesitate, unless better satisfied than

I can be by this evidence, that, if the claim had been made, it would
have been followed by consequences as beneficial as are supposed.
Without prejudice therefore to the question of law, and without
intending to have so much, but under an apprehension, that this
cause may go farther, and that it may be useful, that all the difficulties, by which my mind is pressed, may be made known, I am of
opinion, that whatever may be done with a case clearly within the
range and reach of that authority, this case is not within it; therefore the bill must be dismissed. Under all the circumstances, and
particularly with respect to that authority, it would be infinitely too
much to dismiss it with costs.

1. THE ground upon which the drawer of a bill of exchange is discharged from
liability to the holder in respect thereof, if he has not received due notice of its
dishonor, is, that the holder, omitting to send such notice to the drawer, must be
presumed to have given credit to some person liable as between him and the
drawer: and it has been held, in *Ex parte Barclay*, 7 Ves. 598, as well as in *Staples*
v. *Okines*, 1 Esp. N. P. C. 333, and in *Stewart* v. *Kennett*, 2 Campb. 177, that
notice of the dishonor of a bill must be given to the drawer and indorser by the
holder himself or his authorized agent, otherwise that the drawer will be discharged; but in later cases, at law, it has been decided, that it is sufficient for an
indorsee to prove that the drawer of a bill had notice of its dishonor from the
acceptor or any party to the bill: *Rosher* v. *Kiernan*, 4 Campb. 87; *Wilson* v.
Swabey, 1 Starkie, 34: and also, that if the endorser of a bill receive due notice of
its dishonor from any person who is a party to the bill, he is directly liable upon it
to a subsequent indorser, although he had no notice of the dishonor from such subsequent indorser; *Jameson* v. *Swinton*, 2 Campb. 373. It seems, also, that want
of notice to a drawer of the dishonor of one of his bills of exchange may be supplied by evidence of his acknowledgment to the holder, when asked if the bill
would be paid, that "it would not:" *Brett* v. *Levett*, 13 East, 214: but such an
acknowledgment, made by the drawer after he has committed an act of bankruptcy,
is inadmissible as evidence, in an action by his assignees, to prove the petitioning
creditor's debt, in order to support the commission; *Smallcombe* v. *Bruges*, 1
M'Clel. 60. And the necessity of notice is not dispensed with by any understanding which existed between the parties; for evidence of such an understanding can
never be admitted to vary the legal operation of an instrument: *Free* v. *Hawkins*,
8 Taunt. 97: nor, in any case, will mere knowledge of the dishonor of a bill, however distinctly it may appear a party liable to be charged had such knowledge, be
equivalent to due notice given to him from the holder; for unless such notice be
given, it may be supposed that the holder intends to give credit to some other
party; *Esdaile* v. *Sowerby*, 11 East, 116; *Tindel* v. *Brown*, 1 T. R. 169. Even
when the drawer of a bill of exchange has become bankrupt, and absconded
before it was due, and the acceptor also has become bankrupt before the bill was
due, the holder will not be entitled to prove the bill under the commission against
the drawer, if he has failed to give notice of the dishonor of the bill to the
assignees of the said drawer; at all events when the bankrupt drawer's house was
open, and a notice left there would have reached his assignees; *Rhode* v. *Proctor*,
4 Barn. & Cress. 524. If, indeed, the bill was dishonored before assignees of the
bankrupt drawer's estate were chosen, notice to the bankrupt himself will be
sufficient; *Ex parte Moline*, 19 Ves. 217.

2. In general cases, giving time to a principal debtor is a discharge of his sureties: see, *ante*, note 2 to *Rees* v. *Berrington*, 2 V. 540. As to the rights of sureties, or other parties liable for the debts of a bankrupt, to prove, after they have
paid such debts, against his estate, should he become a bankrupt, see the 52d and
55th sections of the consolidated Bankrupt Act; (stat. 6 Geo. IV. c. 16;) and that
any person, who has paid the original creditors of a bankrupt, is entitled to call
upon them to exercise, for his benefit, the right they had to prove under his commission, see note 2 to *Ex parte Mathews*, 6 V. 285.

3. The rule, that where a creditor has a clear remedy for his debt as against

two funds, Equity will not allow his option to be exercised so as to disappoint another creditor who has an interest in one fund only, is well settled: *Aldrich* v. *Cooper*, 8 Ves. 388; *Trimmer* v. *Bayne*, 9 Ves. 211; and a similar equity is, under certain circumstances, exercised in favor of legatees, by marshalling their testator's assets: see note 2 to *Kightley* v. *Kightley*, 2 V. 328, and note 1 to *Austen* v. *Halsey*, 6 V. 475. But the rule adverted to can have no fair application where the original contract of a creditor was for an interest only in one fund, in such case, although the form in which he took his security was by bond, yet if it was stipulated that he should only act upon it as a personal security, for his own benefit, there would be no ground for compelling him to go against the real estate of the debtor for the benefit of other creditors; and this would be more palpably inequitable where, as in the principal case, it did not appear that the creditor had the clear means of making his demand effectual against any other fund than that which he originally looked to.

HILL *v.* BINNEY.   [* 738]

[1802, March 8.]

THE answer of an administrator to a creditor's bill, stating, that he believes, the debt is due, whether that is sufficient foundation for a decree, *Quære.*

THE bill was filed by a creditor against an administrator; who, by his answer stated, that he believed, the debt was due.

Mr. *Fonblanque* for the Plaintiff, expressed a doubt whether that was a sufficient foundation for a decree.

The Lord CHANCELLOR [ELDON] inclined to think it sufficient: but Mr. *Richards* (*Amicus Curiæ*) suggesting, that it was doubtful, Mr. *Fonblanque* consented to exhibit an interrogatory.

JERVIS *v.* WHITE.

[1802, March 10.]

DEFENDANT ordered to pay money into Court before answer in a case of gross fraud, appearing upon affidavit by the Plaintiff and by the Defendant in answer (*a*).

THE object of this bill was to dissolve the partnership between the Plaintiff and the Defendant, and an Injunction against issuing securities in the name of the partnership. Before the answer came in, a motion was made, that the Defendant should pay money into Court; upon affidavits by the Plaintiff and by the Defendant in answer,

---

(*a*) The application for payment of money into Court may be made, either upon an admission in the Defendant's answer, or, under special circumstances, upon affidavit before answer. 1 Barbour, Ch. Pr. 236. See the subject of motions for the payment of money into Court. Ibid, Book I. ch. 7, § 5.

disclosing a case of gross fraud upon the Plaintiff, a young officer;
who seeing an advertisement in a newspaper for a partner in a
liquor-trade, represented as producing 7000*l.* a-year, answered it;
and was induced to pay 850*l.* in cash, to transfer stock, and to give
a promisory note; in all which he had advanced above 1800*l.* The
whole turned out a mere bubble: the partnership effects not exceed-
i ng the value of 150*l.* The Plaintiff had received back 267*l.*; and
500*l.* had been applied to the partnership debts.

Mr. *Romilly* and Mr. *Ainge,* for the Defendant, objected, that
there was no instance of compelling the payment of money into
Court before answer.

Mr. *Mansfield,* Mr. *Lloyd,* and Mr. *Pemberton,* in support of the
        motion, admitted that in the case of an account, where it
[* 739]   was * uncertain, whether there would be a balance; distin-
        guishing this as a gross fraud; and comparing it to the
case of waste in which the Court interferes upon the ground of irreparable mischief to secure the fund.

Lord CHANCELLOR [ELDON].—I think, I am at liberty in this case
to fasten upon the affidavit of the Defendant in answer; as Lord
Kenyon did in *Vann* v. *Barnett* (1); where though it was held,
that in general in such cases the Court will not deal effectively between the parties, till the answer comes in, yet if the Defendant
answers the affidavits, the Court will look at the affidavit as if it
was the answer. This is not a distinct admission of a sum of money
in the Defendant's hands: but upon the two affidavits, and the Defendant's having undertaken to give an explanation, he is in the
situation, in which an executor very often is. The Defendant must
therefore on or before the last Seal pay this money into Court, deducting what the Plaintiff has received, and what he admits has
been applied in the partnership debts, subject to an application for
the whole or any part to be applied in discharge of the partnership
debts, as the Court shall think proper

I go this length upon the ground of gross fraud (2).

[THIS note relates also to S. C. 7 V. 413, and 8 V. 313.]
1. Formerly, for the purpose of getting money paid into Court by a defendant,
it must have appeared upon his *answer* that the money was due; it was next determined, that if the debt appeared clearly to be due by the *examination* of the defendant in the Master's office, that was a sufficient ground for the order; and subsequently it was resolved, that although the defendant had not cast up the schedule he carried in before the Master, (thereby avoiding the admission of any certain
debt,) there the result of the schedule may be verified by *affidavit,*—furnishing the
sum which one party has a right to demand, and the other is bound to pay.
Quarrell v. *Beckford,* 14 Ves. 178. But the only ground upon which, in general
cases, payment of money can be ordered into Court, is admission, in some shape
or other, by the defendant: the Court will not try the *items* of an account, or order

(1) 2 Bro. C. C. 158. *Post, Huguenin* v. *Baseley,* vol. xiii. 105. In the case of
an executor, *Middleton* v. *Dodswell,* xiii. 266.
(2) *Post, Jervis* v. *White,* vol. vii. 413. Receiver on affidavit, before answer,
Lloyd v. *Passingham,* xvi. 59; *Duckworth* v. *Trafford,* xviii. 283; *Metcalfe* v.
Pulvertoft, 1 Ves. & Bea. 180; *Brodie* v. *Barry,* 3 Mer. 695; *Scott* v. *Becher,* 4
Price, 346. See the note, 2 Swanst. 138

a balance to be paid in, as such balance may be collected from books in the Master's office: *Rae* v. *Gudgeon*, Coop. 305: if, indeed, such books were so referred to as to make them part of the defendant's *answer* or *examination*, that might be held a sufficient admission, upon the strength of which the money appearing to be due might be ordered into Court. *Mills* v. *Hanson*, 8 Ves. 69 and 91.

2. In *Dixon* v. *Astley*, 3 Meriv. 135, (and cited, as to this point, ibid. 379,) Lord Eldon again acted upon the doctrine, that counter affidavits of a defendant were tantamount to an answer from him, for the purpose of founding on his own admissions an order for payment of money into Court. And a vendee may, by taking possession and exercising acts of ownership over the estate he has contracted for, render himself liable to be called upon to pay the purchase money into Court, before he has either answered or been in contempt, or has put in any examination or affidavit; (*Cutler* v. *Simons*, 2 Meriv. 103; *Blackburne* v. *Stace*, 6 Mad. 69;) though, of course, when by the terms of the contract the purchaser was to have possession before the title was cleared, the vendor cannot move to have the purchase money paid into Court on the mere fact of possession being taken. *Dixon* v. *Astley*, *ubi supra*; *Gell* v. *Watson*, 3 Mad. 227.

3. It has been stated above that admission of the demand, in some shape or other, must be made by the defendant before, in general cases, money can be ordered into Court: an analogous doctrine was formerly held as to granting a receiver, which Lord Kenyon, in *Van* v. *Barnett*, 2 Brown, 158, (cited in the principal case,) said was not usually done before answer: but Lord Thurlow had, several years previously, appointed a receiver of an infant's estate upon the filing of the bill, and before a *subpœna* even to appear had been served. *Pitcher* v. *Helliar*, 2 Dick. 580. And Lord Bathurst had, in the still earlier case of *Compton* v. *Bearcroft*, (as stated in note to 2 Brown, 158,) granted a motion for a receiver before answer. In modern times, the order is made whenever the merits appear by affidavit, and justice requires it. *Duckworth* v. *Trafford*, 18 Ves. 283. And although it is with reluctance that a Court of Equity interposes against the legal title by appointing a receiver, (*Berney* v. *Sewell*, 1 Jac. & Walk. 649,) yet in cases of fraud, clearly proved, or of imminent danger to property if the intermediate possession should not be taken under the care of the Court, a receiver will be appointed on motion, grounded on affidavit. *Lloyd* v. *Passingham*, 16 Ves. 70; *Huguenin* v. *Baseley*, 13 Ves. 107; *Stilwell* v. *Wilkins*, Jacob's Rep. 283. So, if a defendant has got out of the way, to avoid being served with a *subpœna*, a receiver may be appointed against him, upon the plaintiff's affidavit. *Maguire* v. *Allen*, 1 Ball & Bea. 75. And though a strong case is required against an executor before the administration of his testator's assets can be taken from him, yet, upon affidavit of danger to the property and misapplication thereof by the executor, the Court would interfere, by appointing a receiver, before answer. *Anonymous case*, 12 Ves. 5; *Middleton* v. *Dodswell*, 13 Ves. 269. Where a trustee, also, has refused to act, the Court will, on the application of all parties beneficially interested, appoint a receiver before answer: *Brodie* v. *Barry*, 3 Meriv. 696: but where there is a trustee sufficiently empowered, and willing, to act for the plaintiff's security, it would be improper to grant a receiver of the trust property upon an *ex parte* application. *Buxton and Parnham* v. *Monkhouse*, Coop. 42. The cases in which a motion, in behalf of a purchaser, for a receiver before answer, has been refused, have turned upon the fact, that the party making the application could not state that he had, strictly speaking, an equitable title; but where the purchaser can compel execution of the contract, he is held to be entitled to a receiver. *Metcalfe* v. *Pulvertoft*, 1 Ves. & Bea. 184.

4. That it may be a very salutary exercise of equitable jurisdiction to order the instruments to be delivered up, even in cases where they may be void at law, see, *ante*, note 1 to *Colman* v. *Sarrell*, 1 V. 50, and note 2 to *Toulmin* v. *Price*, 5 V. 235: and that although the invalidity of an impeached instrument might be the subject of an action, yet if the jurisdiction of Equity has once attached, it will be matter of discretion whether an issue or action shall be directed or permitted, see note 2 to *Newman* v. *Milner*, 2 V. 483.

5. As to suffering a record to be delivered out of the Court of Chancery, see the note to the *Anonymous case*, 1 V. 152.

CURTIS *v.* PERRY.

[1802, March 8, 10.]

Ships purchased by one partner held separate property as between the creditors after his bankruptcy and the death of the other, upon the circumstances; particularly the Registry being made in the name of the one partner only (*a*); and being afterwards continued for a purpose, that would have prevented any claim of the other: viz. a fraud upon an Act of Parliament.

In the case of a bargain and sale without enrolment the vendor will be compelled to make a title, [p. 745.]

Where the interest in a ship is derived under the party's own act and contract, not executed according to the Registry Act, it cannot be reformed in equity any more than an annuity deed, not according to the Annuity Act (*b*), [p. 745.]

Whether the Ship Registry Acts, 26 Geo. III. and 34 Geo. III. have any effect upon trusts implied or arising by operation of law, *Quære* (*c*), [p. 746.]

Bill for a reconveyance of a qualification to sit in Parliament given by a father to his son dismissed with costs (*d*), [p. 747.]

Partnership of three manufacturers in Lancashire sold their goods in London in the names of two only: upon their bankruptcy as among their creditors the property was held to be, where the order and disposition was at the time of the bankruptcy, according to Statute of 21 James I. c. 19, s. 11, [p. 747.]

Henry Nantes and Richard Muilman French Chiswell carried on business in London in partnership as merchants, under the firm of Richard Muilman and Company. In 1796 Nantes purchased several ships; the sales of which were duly registered under the Act of Parliament (1) as the sole property of Nantes. On the 3d of February, 1797, Chiswell died; and on the 11th of the [* 740] same month a Commission of Bankruptcy issued * against Nantes, as the surviving partner. The Plaintiffs Curtis and Clarke had in 1796 supplied some of the ships, purchased by Nantes, with biscuit; other Plaintiffs had supplied other sea stores; and some as ship builders had become creditors in respect of the ships.

Under an order made in the bankruptcy the Plaintiffs proved their

---

(*a*) See Abbott, Shipping, 34, Story's note; *Lamb* v. *Durant*, 12 Mass. 55; *The King* v. *Collector of Customs*, 2 M. & C. 223; *Micoll* v. *Mumford*, 4 Johns. Ch. 522; *S. C.* 20 Johns. 611.

(*b*) The remedial power of Courts of Equity does not extend to the supplying of any circumstance, for the want of which the the legislature has declared the instrument void; for, otherwise, Equity would, in effect, defeat the very policy of the legislative enactment. 1 Story, Eq. Jur. § 177.

(*c*) There is nothing in the Registry acts of the United States, which prevents *one* citizen from being the legal owner, and taking the usual oath, and there being a good subsisting equitable title in *another citizen*. A mortgagee may take out a register in his own name, notwithstanding the Equity of the mortgagor; *Weston* v. *Penniman*, 1 Mason, 360. In causes of possession Courts of Admiralty will look to the legal title, and who is the legal owner in possession of the bill of sale, in opposition to any asserted *equitable* interest in other persons; *The Sisters*, 5 Rob. 155; *S. C.* 4 Rob. 275; *The New Draper*, 4 Rob. 287; see also *Robinson* v. *McDonnell*, 5 M. & S. 228; Abbott, Shipping, 34, Story's note; see 3 Kent, Com. 147, 148.

(*d*) 1 Story, Eq. Jur. § 296, 297.

(1) Stat. 26 Geo. III. c. 60, s. 17.

debts upon the separate estate of Nantes: but a claim being set up
by the joint creditors to the ships, as being the property of the partnership, the bill was filed ; praying, that they may be declared to be
part of the separate estate of Nantes, and applied in payment of the
Plaintiffs and the other separate creditors.

The Defendants, the assignees under the Commission, by their
answer admitting, that the contracts and engagements with respect
to these ships were in the single name of Nantes stated that Nantes
purchased the ships without the knowledge of his partner ; and being desirous of concealing the transaction from him registered them
in his own name ; except one, which was registered in the name of
Janson, a clerk of the partnership; but that the purchase and outfit,
though not entered in the books of the partnership, were taken out
of the partnership funds.   In January 1796 Nantes finding it impossible to conceal the transaction from his partner gave him a list of
the ships, in which he was engaged ; and in consequence of such
disclosure the ships were brought into the partnership account ; and
the disbursements on that account were paid out of the partnership money on the 13th and 14th of January, 1796 : but Mr. Chiswell being a Member of Parliament and liable to penalties, if the
ships were employed in the service of Government, as some of them
were, the registers were continued in the names, in which they had
been registered.   The earnings of the ships were afterwards received
by Muilman and Company ; and placed to the account of the ships
in the partnership books ; and the subsequent expenses were paid by
Muilman and Company, and placed to the debit of the same accounts.   They also stated bills drawn on, and paid by, the partnership in 1796 and the beginning of 1797, on account of supplies for
the ships by some of the Plaintiffs.

Evidence was produced by the Plaintiffs, that Nantes acted as
sole owner; that he was made debtor for the provision
supplied *by the Plaintiffs, Curtis, in 1796; that it is   [*741]
usual to debit the owners, if their names are known ; that
the captains are sometimes named; but generally not, where the
owners are known.

For the Defendants a clerk of the partnership proved, that he
gave all the orders for the ships to the tradesmen in the name of
Muilman and Company, as well prior to the 31st of January, 1796,
as afterwards.   It was also proved, that all the ships were in the beginning of 1796 entered in the partnership books as joint property,
and always considered so from that time.   Receipts given by some
of the Plaintiffs to the partnership were also produced.

The Plaintiffs' books were offered in evidence ; containing entries, sometimes making Nantes debtor; sometimes the ships and
owners, without names; sometimes the ships and captains; but that
evidence was rejected.

The Lord Chancellor [Eldon] directed an inquiry to be
made at the Custom House, to see, who were considered the owners there : but it proved fruitless: the owners not being named in

the entries or certificates granted ; and no oath being necessary except in the instance of a bounty or a drawback : and then it may be made by shippers of goods, agents or clerks.

The *Solicitor General* [Hon. *Spencer Perceval*], Mr. *Richards,* and Mr. *Martin,* for the Plaintiffs.—The register is conclusive as to the legal title. No difference arises from the circumstance, that the possession is in the Defendants ; which in substance will not be disturbed : their possession being referred to their respective titles, as assignees of the joint and separate estates. If Chiswell had claimed the property in these vessels, this Court would not have interfered ; nor any other. The answer would have been, that the possession was for the purpose of a fraud upon an Act of Parliament ; in which case the maxim "*portior est conditio defendentis*" prevails at law and in this Court. That fortifies the objection from the registry in the name of Nantes only. The same objection holds notwithstanding Chiswell's death. It is impossible to inquire into this transaction without discovering the illegal purpose : to which the Court will give no assistance. Whatever therefore is by legal evidence proved to be the separate property of Nantes must be considered
[* 742]   * and divided as such. The oath which must be made
by all the proprietors, was made by Nantes only. This Court will make the same construction upon the policy of the act ; and will not raise a trust in favor of a person, who within the intent of the act could not be the owner : *Hibbert* v. *Rolleston* (1). The two classes of creditors having equal equities, the Court will not deprive either of the legal preference. Chiswell not only did not comply with this Act of Parliament, but did every thing to evade it for the purpose of defeating another Act of Parliament, commonly called the Contractor's Bill. Since the case of *Rolleston* v. *Hibbert* another Act of Parliament (2) has been passed, to meet the doubts expressed in that case, whether parol contracts might be entered into ; which would in this Court effectually bind the property. That cannot now exist. *Camden* v. *Anderson* (3), in which Lord Kenyon alludes to the reason of Lord Thurlow's decree in *Hibbert* v. *Rolleston,* shows the strict construction put upon the act : for that was a case, not of fraud, but mistake. A corrupt consideration will not support a contract or a trust. The circumstance of hardship is not sufficient to prevail against these acts : *Westerdell* v. *Dale* (4). The mere act of a. partner drawing out more than his share of the profits, and investing it in property, gives no lien.

Mr. *Mansfield,* Mr. *Alexander,* and Mr. *Stanley,* for the Defendants.—Upon the circumstances these Plaintiffs are not separate creditors : if they are, they have no right against this, considered as joint property. There is evidence, that all orders for the repair and supplies of these ships were given in the name of the house. The

---

(1) 3 Bro. C. C. 571; 3 Term Rep. 406.
(2) Stat. 34 Geo. III. c 68, s. 14.
(3) 5 Term Rep. B. R. 709.
(4) 7 Term Rep. B. R. 306.

act has left open this question; and it was so considered by Mr. Justice Buller in *Rolleston* v. *Hibbert*; whether there may not be an implied trust by operation of law as to the ownership, where the purchase was made with joint property; like a trust by operation of law, notwithstanding the Statute of Frauds (1); as if the ship had been purchased with the money of another. No mischief intended to be provided for by the act can arise from this. If one partner chooses to employ the partnership fund in a certain branch of trade, there is certainly a strong * equity for the other   [* 743] to call on him to bring the whole into the partnership.

Chiswell therefore, if living, might succeed upon the ground, that these ships were purchased with the partnership fund. The argument from the contractor's bill might have been used, if Chiswell had called for the share of the profits; but has nothing to do with this question: neither has the case cited; the principle of which is, that the party had taken a bill of sale illegal within that act. How can these be considered as separate creditors, upon the evidence, that the orders were given in the name of the partnership, and the receipts given by these very plaintiffs to the partnership, and bills drawn and paid by the partnership on that account? With respect to the joint creditors the ships are joint property. They can know nothing of the registry, &c. They give credit according to the apparent property of the house; part of which these ships were.

In the bankruptcy of *Shakeshaft, Stirrup, and Salisbury* (2), it was decided, that wherever the property is in possession at the bankruptcy, it should be considered the property of the two, or the three, or the separate property, or that of the house. So, if there is a debt due by one partner only, yet if it has been transferred into the partnership debts, and the house has been in the habit of charging the partnership with interest, so as to show, that it was to be considered as due from the partnership, and not from the separate partner, in administering the affairs of the bankruptcy that shall be considered as due from all the partners. This is therefore to be determined upon the principles and rules usually prevailing in bankruptcy. Analogous cases may be put upon the Statute of James I. (3). It does not follow, that, though the property belongs to one, they can consider themselves separate creditors, when the interests of third persons come in question: the credit given being joint. The distribution ought to be among the joint creditors in respect of the visible ownership; the property upon the act of James I. being joint, as between the two classes of creditors; with reference to whom the question is very different from what it would have been between Chiswell and Nantes. Can this Navigation Act repeal that Statute? The object was to ascertain, who are the owners; while the ship is navigated as British. The policy of the act does not apply to the case of a * bankruptcy; making an immediate sale necessary; which   [* 744]

---

(1) 39 Char. II. c. 3.
(2) *Ante*, 123, *Post*, vol. xi. 414.
(3) Stat. 21 James I. c. 19, s. 11.

must be to British subjects.   The visible owner within the act of King James is he, who does public acts with respect to the property.

The *Solicitor General* [Hon. *Spencer Perceval*], in reply.—One joint receipt produced is not on account of any of these ships ; and there is no doubt, there were partnership transactions.   The answer admitting, that all the contracts and engagements were in the single name of Nantes, as sole owner, how could the Plaintiffs expect to be compelled at the hearing to prove their right as separate creditors, and to meet the evidence from these receipts ?   If by express contract credit is given to two, yet the creditor has a right to look to the legal title ; and has a right to sue the person, having the separate property ; according to what Lord Mansfield says in *Rich* v. *Coe* (1) as to the treble security ; one of which is in respect of the legal ownership, having the personal security ; which is not prevented by the express contract.   If an action had been brought against Nantes in the life of Chiswell, could a plea in abatement have been put in under these circumstances: Nantes having the registry in his own name, and all the legal documents of the property ?   The bankruptcy makes a very considerable question here: so also may the death of the party.   The law has not gone the length, that specific effects fraudulently purchased by one partner with the partnership property may be followed.   The visible ownership, as far as it goes, is upon the circumstances with Nantes.   After the discovery by Chiswell of the fraud committed by Nantes in this application of the partnership property the visible ownership remained precisely the same ; and farther, the registry was continued in the name of Nantes for the fraudulent purpose of defeating the Contract Act.   If Nantes had become a bankrupt, the answer to a claim by Chiswell would have been the Statute of James I. ; which, as far as it applies, is with the Plaintiffs.   The equities are equal : and then this Court will not interfere without some particular circumstances.

Lord CHANCELLOR [ELDON].—The first question, whether these Plaintiffs are separate creditors is easily disposed of.   It is not contended, that all the Plaintiffs are joint creditors : and one
[*745]   separate * creditor may maintain the bill in behalf of himself and all other separate creditors ; and there is one.

The principal question is, whether these ships are joint or separate property.   As to the former of these Acts of Parliament it is enough to say, the Legislature had in view a particular policy.   The Court is to collect, by what means they meant to enforce it ; and if that can be collected, the duty of the Court is to give that construction to the Act, that will enforce the means.   The Act is founded upon this ; that it is wise and politic, for the purpose of giving encouragement to British ownership and ships British built, that there shall be this registry ; and to effect that policy it has been thought necessary, that upon every transfer of the ship there should be some document

_____

(1) Cowp. 636.   See 7 Term Rep. 312.

of that transfer, to enable you to trace the ship through its ownership and connections from first to last ; to ascertain, whether she has
been ever wholly or partly owned by foreigners ; and her construction and repairs in a British or a foreign port. For this purpose the
Statute has prescribed the form ; and particularly, that the certificate
of the registry shall be recited in terms. Shortly afterwards the case
of *Hibbert* v. *Rolleston* occurred ; when it was conceived, that the
party taking the transfer had an equitable interest, though no legal
property, the directions of the Act not being pursued ; and that an
equity arose to have the title-deed reformed (1). It was compared
to the case of a bargain and sale without enrolment ; in which this
Court would compel the vendor to make a good title. On the other
hand it was contended, that the policy of the Act required, in a case,
where the title was to be acquired by the contract of the party, not
implied, which was not carried into execution precisely according to
the terms of the Act, that this Court should not interpose. This was
one of the cases, in which Lord Thurlow, when resigning the Great
Seal, sent his decree to the Register, without assigning any reasons :
but I know, his Lordship's opinion was, as Lord Kenyon has intimated, that he could no more reform the title, where the interest was
derived under the party's own act and contract, not executed in the
terms of the Statute, than he could reform an annuity deed, not according to the Annuity Act (2).

   * *Camden* v. *Anderson* followed that case ; and I was a   [* 746]
good deal struck with it ; for it went this length. The
declaration must necessarily aver, in whom the interest is ; and they
averred, it was in four ; and proved, that the registry was in the
name of two only ; and the Court of King's Bench, which has gone
to the thinnest interest to support a policy of insurance, held, that
the averment was not substantiated by the fact. That case therefore very strongly confirms *Hibbert* v. *Rolleston.* But it must be
remembered, the two parties claiming to be partners claimed by
their own act ; where their contract and title were not according
to the terms of the Act. The case then requires this ; that if a
man enters into a partnership, where one of the articles is a ship,
there must be a new registry. The occasion of the second Act (3)
was the doubts thrown out in *Rolleston* v. *Hibbert ;* and the policy
of the former Act was thought so material to the interests of this
country, that a declaratory clause (4) was put in the second Act in
direct opposition to those doubts.

   I desire it to be distinctly understood, that I give no opinion whatsoever upon the effect of those two Acts of Parliament in cases of

---

   (1) See *post, Mestaer* v. *Gillespie,* vol. xi. 621; *Speldt* v. *Lechmere,* xiii. 588; *Ex
parte Yallop,* xv. 60; *Ex parte Houghton,* xvii. 251; *Thompson* v. *Leake, Thompson* v. *Smith,* 1 Madd. 39, 395; *Brewster* v. *Clarke.* 2 Mer. 75; *Ex parte Burn,* 1
Jac. & Walk. 378; *Kirtley* v. *Hodgson,* 1 Barn. & Cress. 588.
   (2) Stat. 17 Geo. III. c. 26, repealed by stat. 53 Geo. III. c. 141. See the note,
ante, vol. ii. 36.
   (3) Stat. 34 Geo. III. c. 68.
   (4) Sect. 14.

trusts implied by law (1), and not arising out of an act, in which the contracting parties join. It is unnecessary to say any thing upon that farther than that in a great variety of cases the interests of mankind would require the Court to consider long, before they should say, those Statutes would prevent trusts implied or arising by operation of law. But in this instance I am relieved from any necessity of determining, either that the cases, that have been decided, are right, or of considering, what ought to be the decision upon that sort of case, which I have just noticed; for it is perfectly clear, that, if this is to be considered as a question between Chiswell and Nantes, the former could not be heard to say, he had any interest in these ships. I do not go upon the circumstance, how Nantes got the money, with which he purchased them; whether it was Chiswell's money, posssessed by contract with him, or by fraud; or whether he laid out that specific money in this purchase. He did acquire these ships in his own individual person; and Chiswell to effect the purpose he had must be understood to have agreed, that [* 747] Nantes should be apparently * the sole owner. The reason for waiving any right Chiswell had in consequence of the manner, in which Nantes made this purchase, the object of keeping the ships registered in the name of Nantes, was, that a profit might be made by the employment of them in contracts with Government; and Chiswell was a Member of Parliament; who, the law says, shall not be a contractor. The moment the purpose to defeat the policy of the law by fraudulently concealing, that this was his property, is admitted, it is 'very clear, he ought not to be heard in this Court to say, that is his property. In the case of a bill filed to have a reconveyance of a qualification given by the Plaintiff to his son to enable him to sit in Parliament, the purpose being answered (2), the bill was very properly dismissed by Lord Kenyon with costs.

Then shall the creditors of Chiswell claim the benefit? It is contended, that they shall, by the operation of the Statute of James I: these ships having been in the order and disposition of Chiswell and Nantes. For that purpose they must be so at the time of the bankruptcy. If that was true in fact, possibly the argument might be sustained (3). In the case of *Shakeshaft, Stirrup,* and *Salisbury,* all three, being manufacturers in Lancashire, sold their goods in London in the names of Shakeshaft and Stirrup only. A credit was therefore acquired by them as three in Lancashire and two in London, which affected the distribution of their property in bankruptcy (4). It might be therefore contended, that where the order and disposition was, there the property as among the creditors should

---

(1) See *post, Ex parte Yallop,* vol. xv. 60, and the note, 71.
(2) See *Platamore* v. *Staple,* Coop. 250; *Brakenbury* v. *Brakenbury,* 2 Jac. & Walk. 391, 395.
(3) *Ex parte Burn,* 1 Jac. & Walk. 378; *Kirkley* v. *Hodgson,* 1 Barn. & Cress. 588.
(4) *Post, Ex parte, St. Barbe,* vol. xi. 413; see the note, 415.

be taken to reside at the bankruptcy. But in this instance it is not true in fact; and it is hardly possible it should; for the circumstance, that the bankruptcy happened so soon after the death of Chiswell, does not vary the case. The creditors thought proper to carry in the bills for furnishing the ships in the name of both. But that is not decisive: the house being in great repute; and the bills being so carried in to them rather as living together. As to the books, no evidence can be received by them. As to the visible property and ownership, the purpose of Chiswell required it to be in Nantes alone. The registry was in his single name; and he alone made the agreements with the masters and sailors; and though the inquiry I directed has not produced all the effect, it has established, that nothing can be produced, attributing the ownership of these vessels to Chiswell. The persons, * on whose be-   [* 748] half the contracts were made, are described generally as owners; and Nantes acting solely, the weight of the evidence is, that the ownership and disposition with the world was in Nantes only. Another circumstance is, that in fact the ownership must by the previous death of Chiswell be with Nantes only at the time of the bankruptcy. Nothing of trust for himself and Chiswell occurs in this case.

Therefore without carrying the authorities farther, or farther confirming them, or inquiring into the effect of any trust arising by operation of law as to these acts, I am of opinion, that the legal property is in Nantes; and there was no visible ownership in any one else, making it just, that this, which was separate property between the partners, shall not be separate property between their creditors. This therefore is separate property; and to be distributed as such.

---

1. THE due registration of British vessels has been secured by new enactments; the numerous former acts of Parliament on the subject have been repealed, and the whole consolidated into one code, by the statute of 6 Geo. IV. c. 110: the provisions of that statute must be complied with, or no effectual transfer or mortgage can be made of any vessel, or share thereof. See, *ante*, the note to *Ex parte Stangroom*, 1 V. 163.

2. Relief is given upon a bargain and sale, though not inrolled; it is treated as evidence of an agreement to convey, and the conscience of the party is held bound to the completion of a farther assurance,—that obligation arising from the payment of the money: *Mestaer* v. *Gillespie*, 11 Ves. 625: for the want of inrolment deprives a deed of bargain and sale of its *legal* effect only; but the policy of the Ship Registry Acts would be defeated if, in such cases, non-observance of the forms thereby prescribed did not render instruments affecting such property void to all intents and purposes; *Davis* v. *The Earl of Strathmore*, 16 Ves. 428; *Ex parte Yallop*, 15 Ves. 67.

3. As to the possible distinction, intimated in the principal case, when trusts affecting interests in shipping arise by operation of law upon bankruptcy or death, and are not created by the acts of the parties, with respect to the conclusive evidence of property which the registry of the vessel affords, see *Ex parte Houghton*, 17 Ves. 254. Indeed it has been often decided that the old Ship Register Acts did not repeal the statute of James I. c. 19; but that, notwithstanding a ship may have been registered in the name of one partner only, yet if the apparent ownership and disposition thereof were left in the hands of the whole partnership, it must, under a commission against them, be treated as joint property. *Ex parte*

Burn, 1 Jac. & Walk. 378; *Monkhouse* v. *Hay,* 2 Br. & Bing. 114; *Mair* v. *Glennie,* 4 Mau. & Sel. 244; *Robinson* v. *Macdonnell,* 5 Mau. & Sel. 237. It is provided, however, by the 72d section of the stat. 6 Geo. IV. c. 16, that the doctrine held, in bankruptcy, as to reputed ownership, and its consequences, shall not invalidate or affect any transfer of a vessel, or a share thereof, made as a security for any debt by mortgage or assignment duly registered: and although, by the 45th section of the general Register Act, (6 Geo. IV. c. 110,) it is enacted, that the mortgagee of a vessel, or a share thereof, is not to be deemed an owner, and that the mortgagor shall not be deemed to have ceased to be owner, except so far as may be necessary to make the vessel, or share, available for the payment of the debt which the mortgage was intended to secure, yet the 46th section enacts, that if transfers of ships, or shares thereof, by way of mortgage or assignment in trust, for security of debts, are duly registered, the right of the mortgagee, or assignee for the purpose aforesaid, shall not be in any manner affected by any subsequent act of bankruptcy committed by the mortgagor or assignor, notwithstanding such mortgagor or assignor, at the time he becomes bankrupt, shall have in his possession, order and disposition, and shall be the reputed owner of the vessel, or share, mortgaged or assigned as aforesaid, but that such mortgage or assignment shall take place of, and be preferred to, any claim on the part of the assignees under the bankruptcy of the mortgagor or assignor.

4. With the exception just stated, in favor of duly registered mortgages and assignments of shipping by way of security for just debts, it is well settled, both by the principal case and by *Smith* v. *Watson,* 2 Barn. & Cress. 408, that the policy of the statute of James I. c. 19, must not be contravened, but that the doctrine so long maintained in bankruptcy, with respect to the consequences of visible and reputed ownership, must be upheld, and take effect as against a party who allows such appearances to exist; he must not come in competition with the creditors of the man whom he has himself furnished with the means of obtaining fictitious credit.

5. Although a conveyance was executed with an intent to give the grantee a colorable qualification, yet, if the grantor obtain possession of the instrument, Equity will not interfere either to restrain him from making use thereof at law, or the *heir* of the grantor from setting up an outstanding term, to defeat the grant: if the question were between the grantor himself and the grantee, the latter part of the rule just stated might admit of doubt; (*Brackenbury* v. *Brackenbury,* 2 Jac. & Walk. 394;) for, provided a deed be *complete,* its alleged fraudulent purpose will not, necessarily, be allowed to confine its operation as against the grantor: *Cecil* v. *Butcher,* 2 Jac. & Walk. 572; *Birch* v. *Blagrave,* Ambl. 266; *Wildbore* v. *Parker,* Mosely, 125: though where no actual fraud, in contravention of positive law or of public policy, has been committed by means of a colorable deed, the grantee may be restrained from suing thereon, (*Platamore* v. *Staples,* Coop. 253,) provided the deed was executed for a particular purpose, which never took effect, (*Roberts* v. *Roberts,* 2 Barn. & Ald. 369; *Stratford* v. *Powell,* 1 Ball & Bea. 21,) and the instrument has always been kept in the hands of the grantor. *Antrobus* v. *Smith,* 12 Ves. 45. In such a case, a Court of Equity would certainly not call the grant into operation; the utmost extent of its interference would be to retain the plaintiff's bill, giving him leave to bring an action. *Cecil* v. *Butcher,* 2 Jac. & Walk. 578. The material question would be as to the *completeness* of the transaction; for although a deed be voluntary, and retained in the maker's own custody, yet if it be once perfected, and was not prepared with a view to being brought forward at a future time for a particular purpose, which fails, it cannot be revoked at the maker's pleasure. See, *ante,* note 2 to *Colman* v. *Sarrell,* 1 V. 50, and to the authorities, there cited, add *Sear* v. *Ashwell,* 3 Swanst. 411; *Bolton* v. *Bolton,* 3 Swanst. 414 and *Doe* v. *Knight,* 5 Barn. & Cress. 691. A deed may have been executed solely in contemplation of a particular purpose, which fails of taking effect, yet that circumstance may not be sufficient to prevent the operation of the instrument; for instance, if a man convey the whole of his estate in trust to certain uses until his intended marriage, and die before marriage, any previous testamentary disposition made by the conveying party will certainly be revoked by the conveyance: and, it should seem, his heir at law could not successfully contend that, for other purposes, the instrument was inofficious, supposing the uses thereby declared went to exclude him: if they were in his favor, his title would be good *quacunque via. Earl of Lincoln* v. *Roll,* Show. P. C. 155. It may be observed

that, in the case last cited, no circumstances are stated which can lead to a supposition that the transaction was *ex parte*, or that deed was not completed by delivery.

6. When the several partners in one firm have individually engaged in distinct trades, in case of the bankruptcy of any or all of the different concerns, proof of a debt due from one of the separate partnerships to another has been permitted, as between the different concerns; for although no demand could arise between partners in respect merely of different branches of a joint concern, yet the course of authorities has been, that a joint trade may prove against a separate trade, and *vice versa*, notwithstanding the individuals engaged in the separate trade may be members of the joint firm. *Ex parte St. Barbe*, 11 Ves. 414. But (except in cases where articles of one trade have been furnished to another trade) before a partner engaged in a distinct concern can, in his separate capacity, establish a demand against the partnership in which he is jointly concerned, the joint creditors must first be paid: it seems the advance of money to the partnership by one of the partners will raise no such equity. *Ex parte Sillitoe*, 1 Glyn & Jameson, 384. As between the partners themselves, no doubt the share of each in the joint fund must be subject to any demand of the other upon the partnership; (*Ex parte Harris*, 2 Ves. & Bea. 212;) but the whole fund, as it exists at the time of the bankruptcy, must be applied in payment of the joint debts, before any demands arising between the several partners can be attended to: *Ex parte Hargreaves*, 1 Cox, 440 (which is the authority alluded to in the principal case under the title of, "*Shakeshaft, Stirrup, and Salisbury*,"): for although joint creditors have no *lien* upon partnership effects, and the distribution of the joint estate in payment of the partnership debts, in the first place, is the equity of the, partners with regard to each other, and not that of the joint creditors, still, it is of necessity that the joint creditors should be first paid, in order to administer justice between the partners themselves. *Ex parte Ruffin*, 6 Ves. 127; and see, *ante*, note 1 to that case. And although, as has been already stated, a joint firm may go against the estate of one of the same firm, who is also engaged in a different concern, (*Ex parte Castell*, 2 Glyn & Jameson, 125; *Ex parte Yonge*, 3 Ves. & Bea. 34,) and a relaxation of the rule which prohibits one partner to prove in competition with the creditors of the firm of which he is a member has taken place, so far as to allow such proof in respect of demands arising out of dealing in a distinct trade, still, the question "what is a dealing in a distinct trade?" must always be looked at with great care: mere advances of money from one trading establishment to another, in which the lenders are partners, Lord Eldon has said, will not take the case out of the general rule. *Ex parte Sillitoe*, 1 Glyn and Jameson, 382.

7. In ordinary cases, a creditor who holds a joint and several security, must elect whether he will go against the joint or the separate estate of debtors; (*Ex parte Hay*, 15 Ves. 4; *Ex parte Bevan*, 10 Ves. 109;) and he is generally bound to make his election before the dividend is declared of the estate against which he has proved; by acting also as a creditor against one of the estates, so far as to be a party to proceedings affecting the same, his election is determined, and he cannot afterwards revert to the other estate; (*Ex parte Husband*, 5 Mad. 421;) unless peculiar circumstances call for an exception to this rule. *S. C.* on appeal, 2 Glyn & Jameson, 5. But this doctrine of election does not apply where the creditor has contracted for a double security against distinct firms; there, if bills be drawn by joint partners upon a distinct firm, though that firm may be constituted of some of the same individuals, proof may be made against both estates: *Ex parte Adam*, 1 V. & B. 496; *Ex parte Wenslay*, 2 V. & B. 254; and, not only will such proof be allowed, but the creditor, it seems, may take dividends out of both estates. *Ex parte Bonbonus*, 8 Ves. 546. This appears to be the necessary consequence of the two established rules, that the same persons may be both drawers and acceptors; and that, in bankruptcy, a creditor has a right to prove and avail himself of all collateral securities from third persons, to the extent of twenty shillings in the pound upon his actual debt. *Ex parte Parr*, 18 Ves. 69, and see, *ante*, note 1 to *Ex parte Bloxham*, 5 V. 448. It has also been decided, and that by the highest tribunal of the realm, that where the business of a number of firms has been carried on under the same general name, the holder of any of their bills may have recourse to every one of the firms for payment, unless he can be fixed with knowledge that the bills he holds were the bills of one of the separate firms only. *Fleming v. M'Nair*, cited in 3 Dow, 229.

ALSAGER v. ROWLEY.

[1802, March 12, 13, 16.]

THE general principle, on which a debtor to the estate cannot be made a Defendant to a bill by a creditor or residuary legatee against the executor, unless collusion, insolvency, or some special case, applies equally to the case of a creditor over-paid by the executor (a).

In a case of that sort upon the circumstances of suspicion, particularly attending to the character of the creditor, as attorney and confidential agent to the testatrix, an issue was directed.

THE cirumstances, under which this bill was filed, are stated in a former report (1).

The cause coming on for hearing was argued very fully upon the circumstances, as to the demand set up by the Defendant Johnson ; and a great deal of evidence was produced on both sides ; upon which it was contended for the Plaintiffs, that collusion between the executors and Johnson was established ; that the proceeding before the arbitrator, under which the sum of 1175*l.* 9*s.* 8 1-2*d.* was awarded as due to Johnson, was a mere pretence ; the charges being admitted without any investigation in consequence of the collusion of the parties ; and the attention of the arbitrator not being directed to the real object of the inquiry.

[* 749]   * Mr. *Mansfield*, Mr. *Richards*, and Mr. *Johnson*, for the Plaintiffs, also insisted strongly on the peculiar character and duty of Johnson, as attorney and confidential agent to the two Mrs. Alsagers.

Mr. *Romilly*, and Mr. *Fonblanque*, for the Defendant Johnson, insisting, that the collusion was not made out, and insolvency, in the executors not being suggested, relied on *Utterson* v. *Mair* (2) and the other cases of that class, as authorities, that the Defendant Johnson was improperly made a party to this bill ; that if the residuary legatee can file such a bill, every creditor and every pecuniary legatee may ; that this is by the circuity of a bill in equity getting a re-examination at law of that, which has finally failed at law : and the utmost amount of the case is a *devastavit* in the executors ; with which the Defendant Johnson has nothing to do.

Lord CHANCELLOR [ELDON].—The established rule of the Court is certainly, as it has been argued upon *Utterson* v. *Mair* and the other cases, that in ordinary cases a debtor to the estate cannot be

---

(a) See *ante*, p. 573, note (a); also note (a), *Alsager* v. *Johnson*, 4 V. 217 ; *Long* v. *Majestre*, 1 Johns. Ch. 305.

(1) Reported *ante*, vol. iv. 217, by the name of *Alsager* v. *Johnson*, upon an Exception to the Master's Report, that the Answer of the Defendant Johnson was impertinent.

(2) *Ante*, vol. ii. 95, and the note, 96 ; 4 Bro. C. C. 270 ; *Doran* v. *Simpson*, vol. iv. 651 ; *Troughton* v. *Binkes*, *ante*, 573 ; *Elmslie* v. *M'Aulay*, 3 Bro. C. C. 624 ; *Isaac* v. *Humpage*, 3 Bro. C. C. 463 ; *ante*, vol. i. 427 ; *Burroughs* v. *Elton*, *post*, vol. xi. 29.

made a party to a bill against the executor: but there must be, as the cases express it, collusion or insolvency. That very principle admits, that, if there is solvency, the executor must pay: if there is collusion both are liable. As to collusion, I have a manuscript case, a note of Mr. Brown, a considerable practiser in this Court formerly; and it is confirmed by Lord Hardwicke's note; which I also have. The case is *Beckley* v. *Dorrington*, the 12th of December, 1737; and is a material authority with reference to *Utterson* v. *Mair* and the other cases. The note is this:

"One of two residuary legatees brought his bill against the executor and the other residuary legatee and a debtor; suggesting no fraud; nor suggesting any negligence in the executor. The bill was dismissed as against the debtor at the Rolls. Upon appeal the Lord Chancellor said, there is no doubt, this is an improper bill as against the debtor. It cannot be without a *special   [*750] case: for there can be regularly no suit against the debtor, but by the executor; who has the right both in law and equity. If he even releases, and is solvent, neither a creditor of the testator nor a residuary legatee can bring any bill against that debtor. There must be collusion or insolvency, or some special case; otherwise it would overthrow all the law relating to *devastavits* and the rights and property of executors. The Court will interfere, if there is such special case; as collusion or insolvency; and then the bill may be brought against both the debtor and the executor. But here this bill is not founded upon any special case; and there must be a special case: or otherwise the bill is inconsistent with the general rules both of Law and Equity."

Lord Hardwicke there in the judgment does not state any thing as to negligence. That is in the argument by the counsel; and in *Newland* v. *Champion* (1) delay in the representative is also stated as one of the special cases, as well as collusion: but no notice is taken of the former in the judgment. If the general principle will not allow you to bring a bill against both the executor and a debtor in the given case, the same principle will apply to the case, where you bring a bill against the executor and a creditor improperly paid by the executor; that is, that, if there is no collusion, or special case, if the executor is not insolvent, he stands the middle man, responsible to the residuary legatee for the property, misapplied by paying a man as a creditor, who was not a creditor, as in the other case for the property outstanding in a debtor.

These principles, connected with the circumstances appearing in this case, would enable the Court to reach the executors, if it turns out, that no demand was due to Johnson, or a less demand than is established by the award. With respect to collusion, it is very difficult to define, what that is. I agree, it is not necessary, that the parties should talk over the matter in a room, as they appear to have done in this instance at Congleton, in order to settle, what demand

---

(1) 1 Ves. 105.

years old; who from that time until his marriage lived with Maurice Lloyd, as part of his family, except when at school; and was treated by him as his own child; and by a bond, dated the 10th of April, 1784, reciting a marriage intended between William Vaughan Palmer and Emily Warren Glubb, daughter of John Glubb, and that in consideration of the portion to be advanced by Glubb it was agreed, that Lloyd should become bound to Glubb, that the heirs, executors, or administrators, of Lloyd within six months after his decease pay to Glubb, his executors, &c. 3000*l.*, to be placed at interest for the purposes, and subject to the provisos expressed in an indenture of even date, Maurice Lloyd became bound accordingly.

By indentures of the same date, reciting the intended marriage and the said bond, Glubb accordingly covenanted with Lloyd, that he, his executors, &c. should, as soon as conveniently could be after Lloyd's death, and after he should have received the 3000*l.* lay it out; and pay the interest to William Vaughan Palmer for life, subject to a proviso, determining his interest upon the event of his surviving his intended wife, and having no issue by her then [* 753] living, or, having issue, the death of all under * twenty-one and unmarried; and after his decease, in case she should survive him, to pay the interest and dividends to her for life; and after the decease of the survivor to pay, &c. the principal unto and amongst all and every the child and children, equally; and in case there should be no child, or all should die under twenty-one and unmarried, in trust for the executors, &c. of Lloyd.

The marriage took place on the 20th of April, 1784, and there are three children; who, with their father, are living: but the mother is dead. It was admitted, that the 3000*l.* had not been paid. Maurice Lloyd died on the 2d of June, 1796.

434; *Wragg* v. *The Comptroller General*, 2 Desauss. 509; *contra, White* v. *Casanove*, 1 Hayw. & Johns. 106; *Cox* v. *Fenwick*, 2 Bibb, 183; *Gilman* v. *Brown*, 1 Mason, 214; *Kennedy* v. *Woolfolk*, 3 Hayw. 197; *Fish* v. *Howland*, 1 Paige, 20.

This lien cannot be retained against creditors, holding under a *bona fide* mortgage or conveyance from the vendee, nor against a subsequent purchaser without notice. *Bayley* v. *Greenleaf*, 7 Wheat. 46; *Roberts* v. *Salisbury*, 3 Gill & Johns. 425; *Gann* v. *Chester*, 5 Yerger, 205; *contra, Twelves* v. *Williams*, 3 Wharton, 493; *Shirley* v. *Sugar Refinery*, 2 Edwards, 511. See, also, 4 Kent, Comm. 154, (5t¹ ed.) note.

It is said that the assignee of a bond for the purchase-money has a lien on the land if the assignor had. *Kenny* v. *Collins*, 4 Litt. 289; *Ewbank* v. *Poston*, 5 Monro, 287; *Edwards* v. *Bohannan*, 2 Dana, 99; *Johnston* v. *Groathmey*, 4 Litt. 317. But see *Iglehart* v. *Armiger*, 1 Bland, 524. So, of a note. *Edwards* v. *Bohannan*, 2 Dana, 99. But not where the note is endorsed without recourse. *Schuebly* v. *Ragan*, 7 Gill & Johns. 120.

The cases and distinctions on the subject of equitable lien may be found in Mr. Perkins's learned notes; *Cator* v. *Bolingbroke*, 1 Bro. C. C. 303, note (4); *Beckett* v. *Cordley*, 1 Bro. C. C. 358, note (c); *Blackburn* v. *Greyson*, 1 Bro. C. C. 420, note (a).

The vendor of personal property has no lien for the purchase-money on the property, though it be still in the vendee's hands. His only lien is founded on possession. W. W. Story, Contracts, § 499, § 500; *Lickbarrow* v. *Mason*, 2 T. R. 63; *James* v. *Bird*, 8 Leigh, 510; *Warren* v. *Sproule*, 2 A. K. Marsh. 533.

By another bond, of the same date, reciting the intended marriage, and that on the treaty it was among other things agreed, that
Lloyd towards a provision for Palmer and his intended wife should
pay to Palmer an annuity of 130*l.* for his life, or until Lloyd should
`procure him an appointment, producing that income, Lloyd bound
himself to Glubb accordingly.   That annuity, it was admitted, was
paid up to the death of Lloyd, but no payment had been made since;
and no appointment had been procured for Palmer.

By indentures of the same date, reciting the intended marriage,
and, that it had been agreed, that Glubb should settle 1000*l.* upon
the trusts after expressed, he covenanted with Maurice Lloyd, that
he would place out that sum in their names, upon trust to pay the
interest, dividends, &c. to the intended wife for life for her separate
use; and after her decease to the husband for life, and after the decease of the survivor to pay the capital to the children (as in the
other indenture), and if there should be no child, or all should die
under twenty-one and unmarried, upon trust for the survivor of the
husband and wife.

That sum was accordingly invested in 1120*l.* 5 per cent. Navy
Annuities in the names of Lloyd and Glubb; and Lloyd paid the
dividends to Mrs. Palmer, until he sold out the stock on the 4th of
February, 1786, for 1150*l.*, having obtained a power of attorney
from Glubb; and Lloyd applied the money to his own
* use; but continued to pay the dividends to Mrs. Palmer   [* 754]
till his death.

The Report then stated affidavits to show, that Maurice Lloyd
was considerably indebted, and insolvent in April 1784.   It farther stated, that he had on his marriage with the mother of Palmer
covenanted to settle for the benefit of Palmer 1500*l.* 4 per cent.
Annuities; the value of which he paid to Palmer on his attaining
twenty-one; and received a release, dated the 20th of February,
1783.

The Report farther stated, that the Defendant Michell was seised
in fee of estates in Somersetshire, and possessed of leasehold premises for terms of ninety-nine years, determinable on lives; and by indentures, dated the 5th of June, 1795, Michell agreed to convey to
Maurice Lloyd, his heirs, executors, &c. the said estates on or before the 24th of June instant; and Lloyd agreed, that in consideration of such conveyance he would on or before the said 24th of June
transfer into the name of the said Defendant so much Long Annuities as would produce the sum of 100*l.* per annum, with the dividends due thereon; and in case the average selling price of Long
Annuities should not rise within two years, so that the stock so to be
transferred might be sold for 2200*l.*, Lloyd, his executors, &c.
would pay to the Defendant the sum of 2200*l.*' on receiving from
him a re-transfer of the said annuities: provided, it should be at the
option of Lloyd at any time within the two years to pay Defendant
so much money as with the then selling price of such Long Annuities would produce 2200*l.*

The Report stated, that the estates were conveyed and assigned accordingly; and a receipt for 2200l., the consideration of the purchase, was signed on the back of the conveyance of the freehold estates; and the title-deeds were delivered to Lloyd. By articles of agreement, dated the 31st of July, 1795, reciting the articles of the 5th of June, and the conveyance, and that Lloyd had transferred the Long Annuities, he covenanted according to the provisions of the former articles, that in case the average price of the [* 755]   Long Annuities should not rise within two * years, so that the stock so transferred might be sold for 2200l. he would pay the 2200l. on receiving a transfer of the annuities; subject nevertheless to a proviso, empowering Lloyd to demand from the Defendant a transfer of the said annuities on payment of 2200l. to him; and the Defendant covenanted to transfer on payment of that sum.

It then stated, that Lloyd did not during his life propose to pay the 2200l.; and that the stock did not rise within the two years, so that it could be sold for that sum; and after the decease of Lloyd on the 2d of June, 1796, viz. in July, 1797, the Defendant with the consent of the administratrix sold the Long Annuities for 1481l. 5s. The Defendant therefore claimed a lien on the estate for 718l. 15s., the residue of the purchase-money, with interest.

With respect to the debt of the Plaintiff Nairn the Report stated, that on the 15th of March, 1796, Maurice Lloyd borrowed from Nairn 2000l. on the deposit of a bill or note for that sum, and Lloyd agreed to pay interest at 5 per cent. On the 16th of April, 1796, some time before that bill became due, Nairn delivered up that bill to Lloyd; and received from him the conveyance by lease and release, dated the 13th and 14th of July, 1795, of the Somersetshire estates in consideration of 2200l. in trust for Lloyd, his heirs and assigns, and also his promisory note payable after the 25th of June next on three days' notice. A term of 1000 years, commencing in 1782, of part of the estate had been on the 14th of July, 1795, assigned to a trustee for Lloyd, his heirs or assigns, to attend the inheritance. That assignment was not delivered to Nairn.

The Master found therefore, that the said indentures of lease and release were deposited as a security for the 2000l. and interest.

The cause coming on for farther directions the questions were, first, upon the claim of Mrs. Glubb, as representative of her husband, against the estate of Lloyd in respect of the instruments executed upon the marriage of his son-in-law Palmer; whether that marriage was a sufficient consideration to support them [* 756]   *against the creditors of Lloyd, as to the provisions for Palmer, the husband, viz. the interest of the 3000l. for his life, and the annuity of 130l. 2dly, Whether the Defendant Michell under the circumstance, that he had taken a security for the purchase-money of the estate he sold to Lloyd, could have a lien on the estate, as vendor; and if he still retained the lien. 3dly, Whether he could insist upon it as against the Plaintiff Nairn.

Mr. *Romilly* and Mr. *Leach,* for the Plaintiff.—Upon the question of lien, there is no lien in this case. The circumstance of taking a security is a relinquishment of the lien of the vendor upon the estate : *Bond* v. *Kent* (1), *Fawell* v. *Heelis* (2). Those cases are questioned in *Blackburn* v. *Gregson* (3), but the doubt rests upon no authority but that opinion of Lord Loughborough. In *Chapman* v. *Tanner* (4) it appears from the Register's Book, as was observed by Lord Bathurst in *Fawell* v. *Heelis,* that the vendor had retained the deeds. It never can be said, that this Defendant did not mean to relinquish his right upon the estate ; for from the nature of the security he has expressly done so. If the vendor takes no security, he has a lien ; for he has not parted with the estate. But in this case he has not only relied upon a security, but a security postponed to a future time. He is in the situation of a mortgagee, who has postponed himself by negligence. The Plaintiff, as an equitable mortgagee, is a purchaser for valuable consideration without notice. Between equities that, which has the strongest right to call for the legal estate, is protected. Could this vendor have had an injunction ? A Court of Equity would at the suit of Nairn have compelled Lloyd to suffer Nairn to use his name to recover possession, or to have the legal estate conveyed.

Mr. *Alexander* and Mr. *Fonblanque,* for the Defendant Michell, contended, that there was an equitable lien in consideration of the money not being actually paid ; relying on the opinion expressed by Lord Loughborough in *Blackburn* v. *Gregson,* that the lien remains under such circumstances ; and insisted that there was no other criterion between these parties than the priority in point of time.

* Mr. *Hall* for Mrs. Glubb, insisted, that the marriage   [* 757] was a sufficient consideration to support all the uses of the settlement ; and cited *Newstead* v. *Searles* (5) ; in which it was held, that the marriage was a sufficient consideration for children by a former marriage.

Mr. *Romilly,* in reply.—The security is in effect a covenant to pay at the end of two years. Can it be contended, that the vendee was not owner during that time ? Could he not have contracted for the sale of the estate? Except the *dictum* of Lord Loughborough in *Blackburn* v. *Gregson* there is no authority for a lien, where the vendor has taken a security. According to a manuscript note of *Fawell* v. *Heelis* Lord Bathurst gives a much more full account of *Chapman* v. *Smith* upon examining the Register's Book than appears in the report ; stating, that there was a special agreement, that the vendor should keep the writings ; and he had not taken a security ; and therefore there was a lien. That case therefore is no authority

(1) 2 Vern. 281.
(2) Amb. 724 ; 1 Bro. C. C. 422, *n.* 3d edit ; 2 Dick. 485.
(3) 1 Bro. C. C. 420.
(4) 1 Vern. 267.
(5) 1 Atk. 265.

whatsoever upon this question. It does not appear in *Blackburn* v. *Gregson*, upon what ground Lord Camden proceeded in *Tardiff* v. *Scrughan*. It does not appear, that he went upon a lien. The security taken in this case, with the peculiar circumstance, that the payment is so distant, during which time the vendor deprived himself of all remedy, must have the effect of discharging the estate.

The next question is, whether a lien can be claimed as against the Plaintiff, an equitable mortgagee. In *Pollexfen* v. *Moore* (1) Lord Hardwicke says, this equity subsists only between vendor and vendee; and no third person can avail himself of it (2). Could the Defendant, having put it in the power of Lloyd to make such a security, have got the deeds from the plaintiff? A Court of Equity would have given no assistance for that purpose. The Plaintiff might have brought an ejectment in the name of Lloyd; and the Court would have compelled him to let his name be used. The Plaintiff might have got the legal estate. It is not pretended, that the Defendant set up any claim for part of the purchase-money unpaid. The Plaintiff therefore has a right to avail himself of his situation: having the deeds; and being in a situation to [*758] *file a bill and get the legal estate from Lloyd. There is no authority establishing, that where persons have different equities upon different grounds, the Court will only regard the time; and consider the person having priority in time to have priority in law. The Court will consider the circumstances; whether there has been laches, &c.; as in the familiar case of 1st, 2d, and 3d, mortgagees. The Plaintiff therefore is entitled to have the sum of 2000*l.* paid out of the produce of the estate sold before the Master; and the Defendant Michell can come in only with the other simple-contract creditors.

The MASTER OF THE ROLLS [Sir WILLIAM GRANT].—It is admitted, that Mrs. Palmer is to be considered a purchaser with respect to the provision made for her and her children by the deeds executed by Lloyd previously to the marriage of Mrs. Palmer; though he was under no obligation to make such provision : the marriage being a consideration for it. It is then contended, that with regard to the provision made for the husband Mr. Palmer this is to be considered merely a voluntary settlement; and therefore Glubb, the trustee, is not entitled to claim in respect of the annuity of 130*l.*, or the interest of the sum of 3000*l.* for the life of Palmer. There is no such distinction. The consideration runs through the whole settlement. It has been sometimes doubted, whether the consideration of marriage would extend to objects unconnected with the marriage, as remainders to collateral relations. But every provision with regard to the husband and wife falls directly within the

(1) 3 Atk. 272. See Mr. Sugden's observations on that case, Law of Vendor and Purchaser, 5th edit. 468, 470.

(2) See *Austen* v. *Halsey*, *ante*, 475. That *dictum* overruled by *Trimmer* v. *Bayne*, *post*, vol. ix. 209. See *Mackreth* v. *Symmons*, xv. 323, 339, and the references.

consideration; and the wife is interested in the provision for the husband as well as that for herself. The marriage is consented to, in consideration, not only of her interest in the event of survivorship, but of his income and the provision he is thereby enabled to make for her and her children during his life. It is not material, that, when the provision is made for the husband, it may be liable to his debts. She takes the chance of that; just as she does, if she marries a man of fortune; supposing, that in the event of debts contracted his creditors may take his fortune from him. But he has the means of providing for his family. When the provision is once made, as it has been by the marriage, no event afterwards can alter it. The question is, whether at the time it was voluntary, or upon good consideration. It is immaterial therefore, that in this instance * the wife is dead. If it was necessary, it might   [* 759] be said, the provision for the husband enables him to maintain the children. But the case would be the same, if there were no children; for if a settlement is made upon the marriage of a son upon the husband and wife for their lives, and afterwards upon the children, and the wife dies without any issue, and therefore the husband is the only object, it could not be contended, that the father's creditors could impeach that settlement; and take from the son the provision for his life; and if not in that case, it cannot be done in the case of a stranger; for it is not from the relation of father and son, that the creditors are debarred. If it was a mere voluntary settlement of that sort, it could not be protected from creditors. But the consideration of marriage protects it (1).

Upon the question as to the claim set up by Michell to a lien, it is now settled, that equity gives the vendor a lien for the price of the estate sold without any special agreement. But, supposing he does not trust to that, but carves out a security for himself, it still, remains matter of doubt, and has not received any positive decision, whether that does or does not amount to a waiver of the equitable lien; so as to preclude the vendor from resorting back to that lien, the security proving insufficient. Without entering into that question, whether every security (2) necessarily amounts to a waiver, it is impossible to contend, that there may not be a security, that will have that effect; that will be a waiver. By conveying the estate without obtaining payment a degree of credit is necessarily given to the vendee. That credit may be given upon the confidence of the existence of such a lien. The knowledge of that may be the motive for permitting the estate to pass without payment. Then it may be argued, that taking a note or a bond cannot materially vary the case. A credit is still given to him; and may be given from the same motive; not to supersede the lien, but for the purpose of ascertaining the debt, and countervailing the receipt indorsed upon the convey-

(1) As to the extent of the consideration of marriage, see *ante*, vol. ii. 410; *post*, vol. xviii. 92; and the references in Mr. Sanders's note, 3 Atk. 188, to *Goring* v. *Nash*; *Sutton* v. *Lord Chetwynd*, 3 Mer. 249.

(2) *Ex parte Peake*, 1 Madd. 346; *Grant* v. *Mills*. 2 Ves. & Bea. 306.

ance. But, if the security be totally distinct and independent, will it not then become a case of substitution for the lien, instead of a credit given because of the lien? Suppose, a mortgage was made upon another estate of the vendee: will equity at the same time give him what is in effect a mortgage upon the estate he sold: the obvious intention of burthening one estate being, that the other shall remain free and unincumbered? Though in that case the vendor would be a creditor, if the mortgage proved deficient, yet he would not be a creditor by lien upon the estate he had conveyed away. The same rule must hold with regard to any other pledge for the purchase-money. In this case the vendor trusts to no personal security of the vendee; but gets possession of a Long Annuity of 100*l.* a-year; which according to the rise or fall of stock might or might not be sufficient for the purchase-money. He has therefore an absolute security in his hands, not the personal security of the vendee. Could the vendee have any motive for parting with his stock but to have the absolute dominion over the land? It is impossible, it could be intended, that he should have this double security, an equitable mortgage, and a pledge, which latter, if the stock should rise a little, would be amply sufficient to answer the purchase money.

Therefore, without entering into the general question, whether every security taken necessarily amounts to a waiver of the lien of the vendor, I am clearly of opinion, that this vendor has by taking this pledge waived his equitable lien. Of course therefore he can have no precedency against the Plaintiff; and can only stand *pari passu* with the rest of the creditors; having no preference over them. It is therefore unnecessary to determine the remaining question.

———

1. UNDER settlements made before marriage, the parties married are purchasers, for the benefit of their children as well as themselves, but post-nuptial settlements, when made, not by the direction of a Court of Equity, or under other circumstances to be presently adverted to, but privately between the husband and wife themselves, cannot be sustained as against purchasers; for the tie of marriage, when the contract is completed, supplies no valuable consideration; (*Beaumont* v. *Thorp,* 1 Ves. Sen. 27; *Randall* v. *Morgan,* 12 Ves. 73;) and the statute of fraudulent conveyances, 27th Eliz. c. 4, renders all *voluntary* settlements void, as against purchasers; *Buckle* v. *Mitchell,* 18 Ves. 110; *Metcalfe* v. *Pulvertoft,* 1 V. & B. 183. But, when post-nuptial settlements are directed to be made by the Court of Chancery, the Court will, of course, support its own acts, even as against a subsequent purchaser of the settled property: (*Wheeler* v. *Caryl,* Ambl. 121;) by the approbation of the Court, such settlement will have ceased to be voluntary; *Ball* v. *Coutts,* 1 V. & B. 299. And a settlement made by a man, after marriage, on his wife, in consideration of an additional portion then received from her friends, (though such settlement was made without the intervention of a Court of Equity,) has been supported against a subsequent mortgagee of the estate in settlement, notwithstanding a mortgagee is, *pro tanto,* a purchaser: *Jones* v. *Marsh,* Ca. *temp.* Talb. 64: but the actual payment of the consideration for such settlement, (either at the time it was executed, or afterwards, in pursuance of the agreement to that effect, *Brown* v. *Jones,* 1 Atk. 190,) must be proved, in order to make such post-nuptial settlement good, as against mortgagors or purchasers: *Gardiner* v. *Painter,* Sel. Ca. in Cha. 65: such proof, however, being made, the settlement, it seems, will be good, not only as against subsequent mortgagees, who are considered in Equity as merely

qualified purchasers, but also as against absolute purchasers; *Colvile* v. *Parker*, Cro. Jac. 158; *Doe* v. *Routledge*, Cowp. 711.

2. The doctrine held in bankruptcy is analogous to that above stated: if a sum of money has been advanced to a woman by any of her friends, as a new portion, and, in consideration thereof, the husband made a new settlement, the property comprised in such settlement will not pass by the bargain and sale to the assignee under a commission against the husband; (*Ward* v. *Shallett*, 2 Ves. Sen. 16; *Ex parte Hall*, 1 V. & B. 114:) the assignee, in such case, could have no better claim than the husband himself; *Brown* v. *Jones*, 1 Atk. 191.

3. The adequacy of the consideration for a settlement, will not be very nicely scrutinized, (*Jones* v. *Marsh*, Ca. *temp.* Talb. 64,) if the transaction be an honest one; (*Nunn* v. *Wilsmore*, 8 T. R. 529;) but if it be colorable only, it cannot stand; *Doe* v. *Routledge*, Comp. 712; *Finch* v. *The Earl of Winchelsea*, 1 P. Wms. 283. In the case last cited it was clearly held, that articles of settlement, made for a valuable and adequate consideration, and the money paid, will, in Equity, bind the estate, not only as between relations in the same family, as mere volunteers, but will also prevail against any judgment *creditor, mesne* betwixt the articles and the conveyance : but *quære*, whether this was not meant to apply to a judgment creditor who had notice of the articles? Whether a settlement covenanted for on marriage, but resting in articles, will be decreed to be carried into execution against *purchasers*, is a point with respect to which lord Hardwicke appears to have entertained doubts; (*Ramsden* v. *Hylton*, 2 Ves. Sen. 309 ;) probably the transaction, if imperfect, would not be supported, as the statute of 27 Eliz. c. 4, has a stronger operation in favor of *purchasers*, than the statute of Eliz. c. 5, has in favor of *creditors ;* and, even as against creditors without notice, whose incumbrances give them a *lien* on the settled estate, the articles would not prevail, though they would against mere general creditors. *S. C.*

4. Limitations in a marriage settlement, extended to collateral relations, are, as far as relates to the collaterals, held, in general cases, to be voluntary, and therefore void, as against a subsequent *bona fide* purchaser for valuable consideration; (*Sutton* v. *Chetwynd*, 3 Meriv. 254; *Johnson* v. *Legard*, 3 Mad. 283;) but, where the settlement is made through the instrumentality of a party, without whose concurrence no valid settlement could have been made, that party has a right to make such conditions for his assistance as he pleases; (*Roe* v. *Mitton*, 2 Wils. 356; *Middleton* v. *Lord Kenyon*, 2 Ves. Jun. 410;) and if he insist on a provision, or a limitation in remainder, in favor of any persons who would not come within the consideration of marriage, they will yet come within the contract; though collaterals, their claims will not be those of mere volunteers, and consequently will not be within the statutes of either 13th or the 27th Eliz.; *Pulvertoft* v. *Pulvertoft*, 18 Ves. 92; *Goring* v. *Nash*, 3 Atk. 189; *Osgood* v. *Strode*, 2 P. Wms. 256. And though, as between the intended husband and wife, when there are no other parties to the contract, who had a right to make, and who have made, special stipulations, if the marriage only was the consideration for that settlement, the limitations thereof may be fairly and naturally restrained to objects within that consideration: yet, when either party has given up any interest, that will extend the consideration to all the limitations; *Jones* v. *Boulter*, 1 Cox, 296; *Vernon* v. *Vernon*, 2 P. Wms. 594; *Ithell* v. *Beane*, 1 Ves. Sen. 216; *Hale* v. *Lamb*, 2 Eden, 295.

5. As to the *lien*, which every vendor retains on the estate which he has sold, for the amount of his purchase money, see, *ante*, note 2 to *Ex parte Hunter*, 6 V. 94.

MILLES v. MILLES.

[ROLLS.—1802, MARCH 16.]

A LEASEHOLD estate renewable being bequeathed with limitations in the nature of a strict settlement, the habit being to renew annually and to underlet, the decree declared, that the fines upon renewal ought to be paid out of the rents and profits ; and that the person entitled for life undertaking to pay those fines out of the rents and profits was entitled to the fines on renewal of the under-leases ; and a renewal to such of the under-tenants as should be desirous of it was directed.

JEREMIAH MILLES by his will, dated the 29th of July, 1786, after bequeathing a leasehold estate in Harley Street to his wife Rose Milles for her life, together with the furniture, plate and effects, therein, and giving other specific and pecuniary legacies, gave and bequeathed all his freehold and copyhold or customary manors, messuages, farms, lands, tenements, and hereditaments whatsoever, and wheresoever, and whether in possession, reversion, or remainder, (reciting, that he had surrendered the copyhold part·thereof then in his possession to the use of his will,) with their and every of their rights, members, and appurtenances, to the several uses and under and subject to the several powers after limited and declared concerning the same : viz. to the use of the first son of his body begotten or to be begotten, and of the heirs of his body issuing ; and for default of such issue to the use of the second, third, fourth, and all and every other, the son or sons of his body to be begotten, severally, successively, and in remainder one after another as they and every of them shall be in seniority of age and priority of birth, and of the several and respective heirs of the body and bodies of all and every such son and sons issuing ; the elder of such sons and the heirs of his body issuing always to be preferred and to take before the younger of such sons and the heirs of his and their body or bodies issuing ; and for default of such issue to the use of the first daughter of his body begotten or to be begotten and of the heirs of her body issuing ; and for default of such issue, to the use of the second, third, fourth, and all and every other the daughter or daughters of his body to be begotten, severally, successively, and in remainder one after another as they and every of them shall be in seniority of age and priority of birth, and of the several and respective heirs of the body and bodies of all and every such daughter and daughters issuing, the elder of such daughters and the heirs of her body being always preferred and to take before the younger of such daughters and the heirs of her and their body and respective bodies issuing ; and for default of such issue to the use of his brother Thomas Milles and the heirs of his body ; and for default of such issue to the use of his brother Richard Milles and the heirs of his body ; [* 762]   *and for default of such issue to the use of his sister Hariet Milles and the heirs of her body ; and for default of such issue to his own right heirs.

The will then proceeded thus :

" And I give and bequeath all and singular my leasehold manors, towns, messuages, farms, lands, tenements, and hereditaments, situate in the kingdom of Ireland or elsewhere, which I hold under any leases for any term or terms of years (and which are not herein before devised), unto my dear wife Rose Milles and my said brother Thomas Milles, their executors, administrators, and assigns, for all my estate, terms, and interest, therein ; upon trust, that they the said Rose Milles and Thomas Milles, and the survivor of them, his or her executors, administrators, or assigns, shall and do by and out of the rents and profits of the same leasehold premises respectively pay the rents and annual sums reserved in and by the leases thereof ; and subject thereto do and shall renew the leases of the same premises from time to time, and as often as they respectively shall deem expedient, but not otherwise ; of which I leave them sole judges ; and for that purpose do and shall from time to time make such surrenders of the leases so to be renewed as shall be requisite and necessary in that behalf ; and do and shall by and out of the rents and profits of the same leasehold premises or by mortgage thereof, or of any part thereof raise so much money as shall be sufficient for paying the several fines and other necessary charges of such renewals, whatever they may choose to renew ; and subject thereto do and shall stand and be possessed of all the same leasehold premises, and subject to my wife's life estate my said brother Thomas Milles, his executors and administrators, shall stand and be possessed of my aforesaid leasehold messuage with the appurtenances in Harley Street aforesaid, together with the pictures, household goods and household furniture, linen, plate, china and glass ware and utensils, that shall be in or about my said leasehold messuage in Harley Street at my death, in trust for the only or eldest son for the time being of my body until such only or eldest son or some one such son shall first attain the age of twenty-one years or die leaving issue of his body living at the time of his death, * which shall first   [* 763] happen ; and then in trust for such son so attaining the age of twenty-one years or dying leaving issue as aforesaid, which shall first happen, his executors, administrators, and assigns ; and if there shall be no son of my body, who shall attain the age of twenty-one years or die under that age leaving issue of his body living at his death, then in trust for the only or eldest daughter for the time being of my body until such only or eldest daughter or some one such daughter shall first attain the age of twenty-one years, or die leaving issue of her body living at the time of her death, which shall first happen, and in trust for such daughter so attaining the age of twenty-one years or dying and leaving issue, as aforesaid, which shall first happen, her executors, administrators, and assigns ; and if there shall be no daughter of my body, who shall attain the age of twenty-one years or die under that age leaving issue of her body living at her death, then in trust for my said brother Thomas Milles, and his executors, administrators, and assigns, if he or any issue of his body

shall be living at the time of the failure of such issue of my body as
aforesaid ; but if the said Thomas Milles or any issue of his body
shall not be then living, then in trust for my said brother Richard
Milles, and his executors, administrators, and assigns, if he or any
issue of his body shall be living at the time of the failure of such
issue of my body, as aforesaid : but if the said Richard Milles or
any issue of his body shall not be then living, then in trust for my
said sister Harriet Milles and her executors, administrators, and assigns, in case she or any issue of her body shall be living at the time
of the failure of such issue of my body, as aforesaid : but if said
Harriet Milles or any issue of her body shall not be then living, then
in trust for such person or persons as shall at the time of the failure
of such issue of my body, as aforesaid, happen to be my heir or
heirs at law."

The testator then empowered his wife and brother Thomas and
the survivor, and his or her heirs, executors, and administrators respectively during the minority of such son or daughter of the testator's body as should for the time being be entitled under the limitations and trusts aforesaid of the possession of his aforesaid freehold,
copyhold, and leasehold, estates, from time to time by indenture
under their, his or her, respective hand and seal, to make
[* 764]   * any lease or leases of all or any of the same freehold,
copyhold, or leasehold, estates for any term or number of
years whatsoever, and either in possession or reversion, for such fines,
and under such rents, and upon such terms and conditions, as the said
trustees should respectively think fit; and also to sell and dispose of
all or any of the timber or underwood growing upon any of his said
freehold, copyhold, and leasehold, estates respectively, and which
he (the testator) might, if living, cut down ; with liberty to the purchaser of the timber, &c. to enter, and carry away the same, and do
all other necessary acts with respect to such timber as shall be from
time to time assigned or set out by the trustees respectively ; and
also out of the rents and profits of the same estates to repair and
keep in repair all the farms, buildings, hedges, ditches, and fences,
thereon, and generally to inspect, oversee, manage, and superintend,
all and singular his said freehold, copyhold, and leasehold, estates,
and transact and do any thing from time to time for the supporting,
letting, and improving the same, and the income thereof and the interest of the several persons entitled thereto in possession and remainder in every particular in the most beneficial manner, and to the
best advantage, as his said trustees respectively should according to
their uncontrolled direction and judgment think proper.

The testator then reciting, that he was fully sensible, how necessary it is for the true interest of the person in possession of his Irish
leases, that the manager of them for the time being should have the
fullest and amplest power to renew either with his landlord or his
several under-tenants, and should have power either to sell the interest remaining in the said leases, or to suffer them to expire and run
out by failure of such renewals, and that he had the most unbound-

ed confidence in the goodness and sound judgment of his dear wife
and brother Thomas, he thereby gave them the same discretion and
powers in the conduct of his Irish property, as if the same did absolutely belong to them ; and he thereby gave them full authority to
act in the said trust as may seem best to them, without thinking
themselves bound or called upon to act in any other manner than
their own good understanding and hearts shall dictate to them ; and
he thereby expressly authorised and empowered his said wife and
brother and the survivor of them at their, her or his, discretion during the continuance of *the trusts thereby re-   [* 765]
posed in them to sell and dispose of all or any of his said
leasehold estates in Ireland, either before or after the leases thereof
should be renewed, to any person or persons whatsoever for the best
price, that could be got ; and he empowered his said brother Thomas during the life of his wife at her desire and after her death at his
discretion, if he should deem it for the benefit of the person for the
time being entitled under the trusts aforesaid to the rents and profits
of his said leasehold house in Harley Street, to sell and dispose of
the same leasehold house with the appurtenances for all his estate
and interest therein ; and he directed, that the money arising from
his said leasehold estate in Ireland and in Harley Street should be
applied upon the trusts and for the purposes herein after mentioned ;
with the usual clause, that the receipt of the trustees should be a
discharge to the purchasers ; and that they should not be obliged to
see to the application of the money, &c.

The testator then gave all his moneys, securities for money, money in the funds, mortgages in fee and for years, and all his estate
and interest in the premises therein comprised, and all the residue
and remainder of his goods, chattels, and personal estate and effects whatsoever and wheresoever not herein before disposed of, to his
said wife and brother Thomas, and their heirs, executors, and administrators, respectively, upon trust to convert into money all his
said residuary personal estate ; and after payment of his debts and
funeral and testamentary expenses, to invest the clear surplus thereof, together with the clear moneys, if any, produced by sale of all
or any of his leasehold estates herein before authorised to be sold,
as aforesaid, in the purchase of manors, farms, messuages, lands,
and tenements or hereditaments, in fee simple in England ; whereof
not more than one sixth in the value of any one purchase shall be
copyhold ; and settle, convey, and assure, the estates so to be purchased to, for, and under, and subject to, the several uses, limitations, powers, and provisions, before declared concerning his freehold estates before devised, or such of them as shall be existing,
undetermined, and capable of taking effect ; but subject nevertheless to an estate for life to be limited to his said wife, if living, in
such of the said manors and messuages, lands, tenements, and hereditaments, as shall be purchased with the moneys arising
from the sale of his leasehold messuage * with appurte-   [* 766]
nances in Harley Street ; and he directed, that in the mean

time and until such purchase shall be made, the clear surplus of his residuary personal estate and from the sale of his said leasehold estates shall be laid out or continued at interest in or upon Government or real security in the names of his said trustees, with full power to vary the securities from time to time, as they shall see occasion; and that the dividends and interest of the same Government or real securities shall from time to time be paid to or received by such person or persons as would be entitled to the rents and profits of the said freehold and copyhold estates herein before directed to be purchased, in case such purchases were actually made. He appointed his wife and brother Thomas executrix and executors of his will.

By a codicil, dated the 28th of July, 1796, the testator after making some alterations in and additions to the pecuniary legacies bequeathed by the will proceeded thus:

"And whereas I have by my said will given and devised all my freehold and copyhold or customary, manors, messuages, farms, lands, tenements, and hereditaments, from and after my decease to the use of my first and other sons successively in tail, with divers remainders over; and have also given and bequeathed all my leasehold estates which I hold and am entitled to for any term of years in Ireland or elsewhere and which are not therein before devised to my said dear wife Rose Milles and my said brother Thomas Milles in trust from and immediately after my death for my eldest or only son for the time being, with divers remainders or limitations in the nature of remainders over in case I shall have no son that shall attain the age of twenty-one years or die under that age leaving issue, now I do by this my codicil give and devise all my said freehold and copyhold or customary manors, messuages, farms, lands, tenements, and hereditaments, other than and except my two freehold and copyhold estates at East and West Hannifield in Essex and Cockfield in Suffolk, from and immediately after my decease unto my said wife and her assigns during her widowhood; and I direct, that she .my said wife and my said brother shall stand possessed of all my said leasehold estates, in trust that the same may be held and en-
[* 767]   joyed, and that the rents and profits thereof * may be received and taken, by my said wife during her said widowhood for her own use and benefit."

And from and after the death or second marriage of his said wife then he gave and devised all his said freehold, copyhold, or customary manors, lands, &c., except as aforesaid, and from and immediately after his decease he gave and devised the said excepted freehold and copyhold estates, the copyhold part whereof he declared was surrendered to the use of his will; and he directed, that his said trustees of his said leasehold estates shall stand possessed thereof, to, for, upon, and under and subject to, such and the same uses, trusts, powers, and provisos, ends, intents, and purposes, as he had by his said will limited and expressed and declared of and concerning his said freehold, copyhold or customary and leasehold estates respectively ; and he thereby gave during the widowhood of his said wife unto her and his said brother, and in case of his death to his said wife alone the same power of leasing, ordering, and managing his said freehold, copyhold, or customary, and leasehold, estates, and of surrendering and renewing the leases of his said leasehold estates, and of raising and paying the fines and fees for renewing such leases, and of selling his said leasehold estates, and giving receipts for the purchase-money, and of investing such money in the purchase of other estates, and till such purchase of other estates in Government or real securities, as are in and by his said will given to his said wife and brother and the survivor of them during the minority of his children ; and in all other respects he ratified his will.

The testator died in 1797 ; having had no issue male ; and leaving three infant daughters ; his co-heiresses at law.

The bill was filed by the widow ; praying, that the Plaintiff as tenant for life of the testator's said leasehold estates may be declared to be entitled to receive and retain to her own use the fines to be paid by the under-tenants of the testator's leasehold estates upon renewing their respective terms therein; and that the Defendant Thomas Milles may be directed to concur with the Plaintiff in granting to such of the respective tenants of the said leasehold estates as should be desirous of renewing their terms therein, *leases of their respective tenements for the full   [* 768] term of twenty-one years upon their paying to the Plaintiff the proper fines for such renewed terms ; or in case the Court shall be of opinion, that the Plaintiff is not entitled to receive and retain to her own use the whole of such fines, then that it may be declared, in what proportion the fines ought to be divided and apportioned between Plaintiff as tenant for life and the persons entitled in remainder to the said leasehold estates.

Thomas Milles by his answer, admitted, that the leasehold estates of the testator were held by him under the Bishop of Waterford ; and that the Bishop for the time being hath been accustomed to grant leases to the testator and those, from whom he derived the said leasehold estates, for the term of twenty-one years ; and that such leases have been from time to time renewed at the old accustomed rents upon surrender of the existing leases and payment of fines ; and that the testator had been accustomed many years before his death to make annual surrenders of the said leases to the said Bishop, and to obtain from him new demises for the full term of twenty-one years ; and that at the time of his death he had a term of nearly twenty-one years unexpired in the said estates.

The testator underlet the said estates to various tenants for terms of twenty years ; and was accustomed from time to time to accept surrenders of the leases of his tenants, and to grant them new leases for the term of twenty years at the old rent, receiving from such tenants fines proportioned to the value of the renewed terms of years ; and that the under-tenants did not regularly apply for, and obtain such renewals from the said testator, as he renewed his own leases ;

but that occasionally they suffered many years to elapse, before they applied for and obtained renewals.

At the decease of the testator many of his tenants held for terms of twenty years commencing in 1788; and other for the like terms, commencing in 1792; but none of their leases had been renewed subsequent to the year 1792.

The Plaintiff and Defendant have annually surrendered the subsisting leases, and obtained renewals for the full term of [* 769]   * twenty-one years and the old accustomed rent: and the Plaintiff has paid the fines and fees of such renewals.

The Plaintiff and Defendant have not renewed the leases of any of the under-tenants since the testator's death: but many of them have applied for that purpose; and offered to surrender their existing leases, and pay fines proportioned to the value of the renewed terms to be granted.

The Defendant stated, that in his opinion it would be beneficial to the persons interested in the said leasehold estates, that such renewals should be granted; and prayed the directions of the Court.

The question was, how the fines to be paid upon the renewal of the under leases should be disposed of.

Mr. *Richards* and Mr. *Hart*, for the Plaintiff. Mr. *Sutton* and Mr. *Kenrick*, for the Defendants.—The decree declared, that the fines to be paid for renewals of the leases of the testator's leasehold estates ought to be paid out of the rents and profits thereof; and the Plaintiff Rose Milles undertaking to pay the fines to be paid on the renewals of such leases out of such rents and profits it was declared, that she as tenant for life of the said estates is entitled to her own use to the fines to be paid by the under-tenants of the said estates upon the renewal of their respective leases during her widowhood: and it was ordered, that the Defendant Thomas Milles should join with the Plaintiff in granting leases to such of the respective tenants of the said leasehold estates as shall be desirous of renewing their terms in the leases of their respective tenements (1).

As to the rate of contribution between tenants for life and remainder-men, towards renewal fines, see, *ante*, the note to *White* v. *White*, 4 V. 24.

_____

(1) *Lord Montford* v. *Lord Cadogan, post,* vol. xvii. 485; xix. 635; 2 Mer. 3.

TEMPLE *v.* THE BANK OF ENGLA |

[1802, MARCH 18.]

NOTWITHSTANDING the Act of Parliament 39 & 40 Geo. III. c.
England may still be made parties to a Bill to restrain a transf
since that Act.
A Demurrer by the Bank was over-ruled.
Injunction in Chancery in the Vacation: the Court being always
An application under the Act 39 and 40 Geo. III. c. 36, to restrai
making a transfer without making them parties, must be upo
Defendants, or on affidavit, as in cases of waste, [p. 773, note.]

THE bill stated, that Elizabeth M'Rae of Jamaica,
other personal estate entitled to a large sum in the 4
cent. Bank Annuities, by her Will, among other *legac
gave to Richard Henry Temple 2000*l.*: but in case of
decease in her life she gave the said legacy of 2000*l.*
and she directed, that the said legacy of 2000*l.* and
should be paid out of the moneys arising or to aris
due to her out of the said 4 per cent. Bank Annuiti
same was by the Will made chargeable therewith;
pointed two persons in London and two in Jamaica j
erally executors.

The testatrix died in 1799. Richard Henry Templ
life. The executors in England proved the will; ai
themselves of the 4 per cent. Bank Annuities and othei
tate. The latter was more than sufficient for the debt
penses and legacies, except those charged upon the Ban
and those Annuities were more than sufficient for the leg
upon them. The executors transferred the Bank Annuit
own names.

The Bill, which was filed on behalf of the infant siste
Henry Temple against the two executors, who had pro
and against the Bank of England, prayed, that the lega
may be raised by sale of the Bank Annuities, and paid in
&c.; and that the Defendants, the executors, may be res
transferring, and the Bank, from permitting them to transi
Annuities.

To this bill the Bank put in a general demurrer.

Mr. *Piggott* and Mr. *Wooddeson,* in support of the
The only question is, whether since the late Act of Par
the Bank can be made parties to a suit for this purpos
prevent a transfer of stock. The Act of Parliament h
made it *quite unnecessary, that they should be partie
A privilege was intended to the Bank as well as to tl
suitor. This case bears analogy to those, in which th
has demurred as to discovery, on the ground, that having

---

(1) Statute 39 & 40 Geo. III. c. 36. Costs to the Bank in cases w
Edridge v. *Edridge,* 3 Madd. 386.

he might be examined as a witness; or as to relief, that no decree
can be had against him.   The act has prescribed a mode of relief
without making the Bank parties.   But it is objected, that the words
of the act are optional and not imperative.   The words of the third
section are imperative; and as to the first the spirit of the law requires a similar construction.   The words there are not imperative;
because it was not supposed, that Plaintiffs would voluntarily incur
unnecessary trouble and expense.   It would be the height of inconsistency, that suits already commenced should be peremptorily dismissed, but that new suits might be commenced.   There are many
instances in the construction of Acts of Parliament in which words
of permission have been construed imperative.   There is an impropriety in making the Bank parties to such bills and upon common
occasions.   Such suits have been very numerous; and there may be
abatements; and then there cannot be a revivor for costs (1).

Mr. *Pemberton,* for the Plaintiff, observed, that unless the words
can be construed to be imperative there was an end of the cause.
The object of the Legislature was an accommodation to the public;
but this is no accommodation; for instance, if an executor was about
to transfer stock during the long vacation; as the application under
the act can only be made, when the Court is sitting.   Upon an application to the Court of Exchequer under this act so much difficulty
was found in proceeding under it, and so much expense likely to be
incurred, that leave was given to amend the bill and make the Bank
parties.

The Plaintiff's Counsel was then stopped by the Court.

Lord CHANCELLOR [ELDON].—I am of opinion with the Plaintiff;
though very reluctantly.   With respect to the objection, that has
just been made, the Lord Chancellor could give an injunction in the
Vacation.   The Court of Chancery is always open (2).

[* 772]   * But I am of opinion, that the Legislature has missed
this case.   The right of the subject before this act was
most clear, to file a bill to restrain a person from making a transfer
of stock, and the Bank from permitting a transfer; and Lord Kenyon was of opinion, that notice to the Bank without more would
operate as an injunction.   That however it is not necessary to consider: but the right to file a bill for this purpose before the act being clear, the question is, whether the act has made it unlawful to
make the Bank parties in that very case, in which it was before lawful.   Nothing could be more easy than to do that; and in the third
section the Legislature contemplate the causes then existing;
and put an end *brevi manu* to all causes then existing: but they
have not said so as to future suits: whatever the intention might
have been.   The word "depending" in the first clause I take to
mean "depending or that shall depend:" though that is not very
accurate.   The act looking prospectively seems to contemplate either
the cases, in which the Court would grant an injunction by their own

(1) See *ante, Morgan* v. *Scudamore,* vol. ii. 313; iii. 195.
(2) *Post,* vol. vii. 257; 2 Swanst. 11.

inherent powers, if the Bank was a party, or, if the Bank was not a party, by the powers given by this act.   In many cases words of this sort have been construed imperative, as has been urged.   But this act in its language contemplating both cases, where the Bank is a party, and where not, has not prohibited making them parties in future suits ; though in terms prohibiting, that they shall be kept before the Court in depending suits.   I may conjecture ; but I have no authority to interfere, to take away what was before that act the right of the subject.   At the same time I very much approve the demurrer put in by the Bank.   The object of the act being to save expense, they have acted very honorably and laudably in taking the opinion of the Court.

The Demurrer was overruled (1).

———

1. In what sense the Court of Chancery is always open, see, *ante*, note 1 to *The Mayor of London* v. *Bolt*, 5 V. 129).

2. That, when the legislature passes an act for the benefit of parties who may be plaintiffs under such circumstances as the act contemplates, the said act is not

———

(1) The *Attorney General* v. *Gale*, in CHANCERY, 23d June, 1802.
    The Bank being made parties under the decision of *Temple* v. *The Bank of England*, and the object, a discovery and to restrain a transfer, having been obtained, Mr. Owen moved to dismiss the Bank on payment of their costs.
    The Lord Chancellor [Eldon] said, he understood, doubts had been intimated as to the decision in *Temple* v. *The Bank of England* and the case in the Court of Exchequer ; but that having repeatedly thought of it since, he had not a particle of doubt in his mind of the propriety of that decision.
    * In *Hammond* v. *Maundrell*, 27th Nov. 1801, upon a bill by one   [* 773] residuary legatee and executor against the other, Mr. Owen made an application under the Act of Parliament, to restrain a transfer of the fund without making the Bank parties, as a motion of course, without notice or affidavit ; expressing at the same time a doubt, whether it should be so ; suggesting however the danger of notice, and that previously to the Act a subpœna had the effect of an injunction.
    Lord Chancellor [ELDON].—The Bank never would admit that, even upon a subpœna and a bill filed.   The doubt I have is upon the right of the Defendants to contend, that I ought not to make such an order ; whether that Act entitles me to make the order without hearing the Defendant interested in the fund ; whom before that Act passed, when the Bank were made parties to the suit, I must have heard. You must previously to the Act have given notice to that party, having an essential interest.   Then the meaning of the Act is, that you should discuss the point with the Defendant ; and then the order should be made upon the Bank ; though they are not parties.   The mischief you allude to is, that, unless you have a speedy order, and without giving the Defendant two days' notice, he may transfer in the meantime.   But that existed before the Act ; and the Court will apply the same remedy, if you come upon a special ground and affidavit, as upon a case in the nature of a bill to restrain waste ; lest the fund should be transferred in the meantime.   Suppose, the Plaintiff knew, that if the Defendant could not transfer 10,000l. next Monday, he would be ruined ; and had a malice or an interest in his ruin. That mischief is done by such an application upon a false Bill ; as it may be, if without affidavit.   It would therefore be a very dangerous precedent to restrain the Bank from transferring the money of a person, who is a party in the cause, without giving notice ; unless where from the necessity and urgency of the case you could not give notice : but then the application must be upon affidavit verifying, that such urgency and necessity exist.

    The motion was refused.
    See *Edridge* v. *Edridge*, 3 Madd. 386 ; and the note.

always necessarily to be construed as imperative on such parties, or as confining them to such statutable remedy; but that, if they had previously a different remedy at common law, they may, if they think it advisable, pursue that course, seems well settled; *Smith* v. *Doe, dem. Lord Jersey,* 2 Brod. & Bing. 494, 559, 609. When, however, an act of Parliament is made for the benefit of the defendants under the circumstances in contemplation, the plaintiffs will be bound down by the statute; *Drage* v. *Brand,* 2 Wils. 377. If the act, upon which the question arose in the principal case, was intended, as its preamble appears to imply, for the benefit of plaintiffs alone, then the first rule above stated would be applicable; but, if the third section of the statute could be construed as intended to give relief, farther than in respect of then existing suits, to the Governor and Company of the Bank of England, when made defendants to suits for transfers of stock, in which they claim no interest or *lien*; and, therefore, that the act was not intended solely, though it clearly was intended in part, for the benefit of suitors under it; then the question would assume a mixed character, to which neither of the rules stated would strictly apply. Lord Eldon, in the principal case, held the statute of 39 and 40 Geo. 3, c. 36, not to be imperative on suitors; and though Sir John Leach, from an earnest desire to save unnecessary expense, declared, in *Edridge* v. *Edridge,* 3 Mad. 386, that he would dismiss, with costs, any bill to which the Company of the Bank of England were made parties, if the relief prayed against them was obtainable by an application under the act; yet, in the later case of *Ross* v. *Shearer,* 5 Mad. 459, this course was not pursued. It may be observed, that in the case last cited the plaintiff, though he had served the Bank with a *subpœna,* and notice of the bill filed, which prevented the Company from assenting to a transfer of the stock in question, yet had neglected, after the answers came in, to move for an injunction; under these circumstances of *laches* on the plaintiff's part, the defendant obtained an order, on motion, that the Bank might be at liberty to transfer, unless, on or before a given day, the plaintiff should move for an injunction. But, except under such special circumstances, when the question is, whether the plaintiff has a title to, or *lien* upon stock, to suffer the defendant to move for an order on the Bank to permit a transfer, would be, in fact, allowing him to obtain a decree in the cause, by an interlocutory order; *Birch* v. *Corbyn,* 1 Brown, 572.

3. Previously to the passing of the statute already mentioned, it was decided, (and it should seem the principle would be the same since the statute,) that where the Governor and Company of the Bank of England are made defendants to a suit for the transfer of stock, in which they have no interest, the Court will not, on the application of the Bank in that suit, make an order on the litigating parties to restrain them from proceeding at law against the Bank to compel a transfer, though certainly the Bank may file a bill of interpleader for that purpose; *Birch* v. *Corbin,* 1 Cox, 145.

LLOYD *v.* LOARING.

[1802, MARCH 18, 19; MAY 13.]

DEMURRER to a bill by some members of a Lodge of Freemasons against others to have the dresses and decorations, books, papers, and other effects, of the Society delivered up, and an Injunction, was allowed, on the ground, that they affected to sue in a corporate character: but leave was given to amend: the Court holding jurisdiction for the delivery of a chattel; and, where there is a joint interest, permitting some to sue, as individuals, representing the rest, in other instances than those of creditors and legatees; if inconvenient to justice, that all should be parties (a).

THIS bill, filed by Evan Lloyd and two other persons on behalf of themselves and all other members of the Caledonian Lodge of Free Masons, except the Defendant Loaring, against Loaring and another person, stated, that Plaintiffs are members or companions of a certain ancient fraternity, society, or lodge of Free Masons, called or known by the name of the Caledonian Chapter, No. 2, and being No. 2 on the list of the societies of Royal Arch Free Masons, consisting of Plaintiffs and a number of other persons; and Plaintiff

---

(a) The defect of the title of the plaintiff to the character, in which he sues, is a good ground of demurrer. If a voluntary association of persons, not incorporated, should affect, by their bill, to sue in the style of a corporate body, the bill would be demurrable, if the objection appeared upon the face of it; for it is the exclusive prerogative of the government to create corporations, and invest them with the power of suing, as such, by their corporate name. Story, Eq. Pl. § 496, § 497.

The general rule is that all the parties in interest, although numerous, should be brought before the Court. An exception is allowed, founded on the fact of numerousness. Story, Eq. Pl. § 95. 1st. Where the question is one of common interest, and one or more sue, or defend for the benefit of the whole. Ib. § 97–106; *Hendrick* v. *Robinson*, 2 Johns. Ch. 296. As in the case of a few creditors maintaining a suit on behalf of themselves, and the other creditors of a deceased debtor. *Whitmore* v. *Oxborrow*, 2 Y. & Coll. New R. 13, 17; *May* v. *Selby*, 1 Y. & Coll. New R. 235; *Hallett* v. *Hallett*, 2 Paige, 18; *Ross* v. *Crary*, 1 Paige, 417, note. But the creditors who bring the bill, must allege that it is brought on behalf of themselves, and all the rest of the creditors. *Leigh* v. *Thomas*, 2 Ves. 313; *Brown* v. *Ricketts*, 3 Johns. Ch. 553. See, also, *Brinckerhoff* v. *Brown*, 6 Johns. Ch. 151; *Joy* v. *Wirtz*, 1 Wash. Circ. 417. By analogy to the case of creditors, one legatee may sue for himself and other legatees. Mitford, Eq. Pl. by Jeremy, 167; *Brown* v. *Ricketts*, 3 Johns. Ch. 553; *Pritchard* v. *Hicks*, 1 Paige, 273; *Fisk* v. *Howland*, 1 Paige, 23; *Caldecott* v. *Caldecott*, 1 Craig & P. 183; *Harvey* v. *Harvey*, 4 Beavan, 215, 220.

2d. The second exception is where the parties form a voluntary association for public or private purposes, and those, who sue or defend, may fairly be presumed to represent the rights and interests of the whole. *Mandeville* v. *Riggs*, 2 Peters, 487; *Baldwin* v. *Lawrence*, 2 Sim. & Stu. 18; *Hickens* v. *Congreve*, 4 Russ. 562; *Milligan* v. *Mitchell*, 3 M. & Craig, 72; *Small* v. *Atwood*, 1 Younge, 407.

3d. The third exception is where the parties are very numerous, and, although they have separate interests, it is impossible to bring them all before the Court. Story, Eq. Pl. § 120.

See *West* v. *Randall*, 2 Mason, 194, where the subject of parties in Equity is handled by Mr. Justice Story with great fullness and learning.

As to the jurisdiction of Equity for the specific delivery of a chattel, see *ante*, note (a), *Fells* v. *Read*, 3 V. 70.

Lloyd being the chief or principal officer, and the other two Plaintiffs secretaries or other officers of ·the said companion, chapter, or society: Plaintiffs as such three officers, as aforesaid, having the sole management and direction of the affairs of the said Caledonian Chapter; which said chapter has been duly certified, and the names of the members registered according to law.

The bill farther stated, that the said chapter or society held their meetings at the Horn Tavern; and the dresses and decorations, and the books and papers, tools and implements, and other goods and effects, of the said chapter or society were there kept in a chest; the key of which was kept by Lloyd, as principal officer. A union with another chapter, called the Prudence Lodge, having been proposed and assented to by the members then present, and that the future meetings should be held at the Free Masons Tavern, the Defendant Loaring and four other members then present authorised the janitor or servant of the said chapter to remove the said property to the Free Masons Tavern; the master of which was directed to deliver it to him on producing the written order and in the presence of Lloyd, and to no other person. The Defendants afterwards went there; pretending authority from Lloyd; and that by mistake he had sent the wrong key; and they broke open the chest; and took away all the said dresses, &c.

The bill farther stated, that by the rules and condition of the said society it is necessary, whenever any of the business or ceremonies are to be transacted or performed, that the Plaintiffs or one of them should be present; especially Lloyd as the president or principal officer; to whose care the key of the chest, and the effects, and the books, containing the laws and constitution and the accounts of the said society or chapter and the original warrant or charter are entrusted; and it is indispensable, that he should have possession of them; without which the society cannot properly be convened, or the business transacted; and the Defendant Loaring is interested in, or has a share in, the property vested in him as a joint tenant with the other members; and having got the exclusive possession of the said effects, is a trustee for the other members, and bound to restore them uninjured for the use of the society.

[* 775]   * The bill charged, that the Plaintiffs took a Bow-street officer to the house of the other Defendant Hannam; who acknowledged, that they had taken the property; and restored part of it, that was in his possession; but that Loaring has the greatest part, and in particular the books of the constitution, laws, and rules, of the said chapter or society, the books of account, names of the members, minutes of the proceedings, and the original warrant or charter, granted to them by the grand or head chapter of Royal Arch Masons; by which the Caledonian Chapter is constituted or authorised and continued, and without which original warrant or charter no meetings of the said chapter or society can be properly and regularly convened or held, or the business or ceremonies, or functions, of the said chapter or society performed; that the per

sons, by or from whom such constitution and warrant or charter
were granted, are all long since dead ; and no constitution or charter can now be had ; and if the said constitution or charter or warrant should be lost or destroyed, the said chapter or society would
either be wholly dissolved, and lose its rank and privileges among
the several different lodges or chapters, or be prejudiced or degraded ;
that the Defendant Loaring has threatened and intends to burn or
otherwise destroy the property, and in particular the books and the
original warrant or charter ; and that Plaintiffs are ignorant of the
particulars, of which the property consists ; and the Defendants refuse to discover, &c. ; whereby the Plaintiffs cannot take any effectual steps at law.

The bill prayed a discovery ; and that the Defendants may be
decreed to deliver up the said articles uninjured or undefaced ; and
in the meantime be restrained from disposing of, burning, or otherwise destroying, defacing, or injuring, them.

The Defendants demurred generally to this bill for want of Equity,
and also for want of parties.

Mr. *Piggott* and Mr. *Wooddeson*, in support of the Demurrer,
contending, upon the first ground of demurrer, that the transaction
stated by the bill was an indictable offence, and was so treated by
the Plaintiffs themselves, and secondly, that the interest stated by
the bill being joint, the Plaintiffs could not file a bill on behalf of
themselves and all others, as in the case of creditors, were
stopped * by the Lord Chancellor ; who asked, how the   [* 776]
Plaintiffs could come into Court, having no corporate
character.

Mr. *Romilly* and Mr. *Roupell*, for the Plaintiffs.—Societies of this
description are entitled to the protection of the Legislature, and are
recognised in the Act of Parliament against seditious meetings.
Fells v. *Read* (1) is an authority in all points for this bill. This is
no felony, as contended ; for there is a joint-tenancy. This is a
partnership.   As to the objection, that these persons have not a
legal, known, character, entitling them to sue, not being incorporated,
they do not sue as a corporation, or affect a corporate character.
They sue as a voluntary society, composed of individual members,
and in their individual capacity, on behalf of themselves and all the
other members.   What has that appearance is merely description ;
and to show, that they had complied with the Act of Parliament.
In *Chancey* v. *May* (2) the objection, that they had not defined the
purposes of their partnership, was not taken ; and in this case it was
unnecessary to do so.

As to the objection for want of parties, certainly with a few exceptions, as the cases of creditors and legatees, suing on behalf of
themselves and all others, all persons interested must be parties.

(1) *Ante*, vol. iii. 70 ; and the note, 73 ; *Lowther* v. *Lord Lowther, post*, vol. xiii.
95 ; *Earl of Macclesfield* v. *Davis*, 3 Ves. & Bea. 16.
(2) Finch's Pre. Ch. 592.

But that rule is not imperative, as if imposed by the Legislature: but it has been laid down by the Court, to prevent a multiplicity of suits, and do complete justice between all persons having any interest. The Court will not adhere to that rule or any other, if the consequence will be an absolute failure of justice. In *Chancey* v. *May* the rule was dispensed with upon the ground, that it would be impracticable to make them all parties by name. In *Pearson* v. *Belchier* (1) the objection would have applied just as in this case; for every person had a right to call for an account. The decision of that case certainly was on another ground, the delay. But no objection of that sort was taken; though certainly the Defendants threw every possible difficulty in the way; and that cause was a very long time depending in the Court.

Lord CHANCELLOR [ELDON].—If this is not a corporation, how could these five persons remove these articles? Loaring [* 777] himself had a * right to object to the proposed junction. If I consider them as individuals, the majority had no right to bind the minority. One individual has as good a right to possess the property as any other : unless he can be affected by some agreement. But how is this Court to take notice of these persons as a society? A bill might be filed for a chattel; the Plaintiffs stating themselves to be jointly interested in it with several other persons: but it would be very dangerous to take notice of them as a society, having any thing of constitution in it. As to the Statute referred to, the meaning was only to take them, provided they gave notice of their meetings, out of the operation of the Sedition Laws, not to acknowledge them. In this bill there is a great affectation of a corporate character. They speak of their laws and constitutions, and the original charter, by which they were constituted. In *Cullen* v. *The Duke of Queensberry* (2), Lord Thurlow said, he would convince the parties, that they had no laws and constitutions. But there was an allegation, that he was individually liable. It is the absolute duty of Courts of Justice not to permit persons, not incorporated, to affect to treat themselves as a corporation upon the Record. If the Plaintiffs had stated simply, that they and several persons were jointly interested, or even they on behalf of themselves and others, provided it was manifestly inconvenient to justice to make them all parties, and stating this case as individuals, upon the principle of *Fells* v. *Read* it might be very proper. That this Court will hold jurisdiction to have a chattel delivered up, I have no doubt: but I am alarmed at the notion, that these voluntary societies are to be permitted to state all their laws, forms, and constitutions, upon the Record, and then to tell the Court, they are individuals. Then what sort of a partnership is this; for it is now admitted to be a partnership? The bill states, that they subsist under a charter, granted by persons, who are now dead; and therefore, if

---

(1) *Ante*, vol. iv. 627 ; see the note, 628.
(2) The case of the Ladies' *Coterie*.

this charter cannot be produced, the society is gone.   U[
ples of policy the Courts of this country do not sit to
upon charters granted by persons, who have not the pre
grant charters.   I desire my ground to be understood di
do not think, the Court ought to permit persons, who c
as partners, to sue in a corporate character; and that i
of this bill.

The Demurrer was allowed.

May 13th. * The Lord CHANCELLOR, when the demur
rer was allowed, having thrown out an intimation, that th
Plaintiffs might amend, Mr. *Romilly* and Mr. *Roupell* move
to amend the bill.

Mr. *Piggott* and Mr. *Wooddeson*, for the Defendants, o
motion; insisting, that it would not be permitted in the c
partnership trade; that the decision in *Lord Coningsby* v.
Jekyll (1) was not considered regular (2): at least it
course, where the demurrer is not merely for want c
and that there is not a passage in this bill, in which the
taken by the Court does not occur.

Lord CHANCELLOR [ELDON].—If the Plaintiffs strike
present style as Plaintiffs, and sue as individuals, they wil
different persons.   I give them leave to amend, becaus
sure, I should not contradict some rule; having had gr
whether I should allow the demurrer.   That doubt is fou
this; that it has been decided, that individuals forming a
society may as individuals, not as a voluntary society, h
joint interest in a chattel, that this Court would take noti
interest, and of agreements upon it, not with reference to
voluntary society, but as individuals.   I allude to the
argued without success upon the tobacco-box.   With resp
decision I had considerable doubt, whether this very case
arise out of it.   I had great doubt, whether a voluntary a
for the best purpose is to meet without the authority of
tion, and make laws and statutes, which have no authority,
call upon this Court to administer all the moral justice,
arise upon the disputes among these, in a sense unauthorize
It is singular, that this Court should sit upon the conce
association, which in law has no existence; and in that
this Court should be ancillary to their agreements as to th
&c.   I was much disappointed with that case upon that p
though I never had a doubt as to the jurisdiction upon ch
tween man and man.   But it is too late to consider that now.

* In this case, though I cannot disguise from myself,
that the whole record attributed more of a corporate character than I ought to permit a voluntary society to put upo

(1) 2 P. Will. 300.
(2) See Mitf. 15, the note.
(3) *Ante, Fells* v. *Read*, vol. iii. 70.

ord, yet I could not devest myself of this notion altogether; that, though they had assumed that character, yet upon the whole bill there was a case represented fairly of individuals with a joint interest, absurdly representing themselves corporate; and I had doubt enough therefore, whether over-ruling the demurrer was absolutely right. By giving leave to amend I thought I might enable them to reduce the record to that, which, it is admitted, might be made by a new bill. Suppose, Mr. Worseley's silver cup was taken away from the Middle Temple: the society must some way or other be permitted to sue; and this is really the same; for it is not material, what it is. Upon the whole therefore I thought it fair to let them amend by striking out all that.

In the manuscript notes I have seen strong passages, as falling from Lord Hardwicke, that, where a great many individuals are jointly interested, there are more cases than those, which are familiar, of creditors and legatees, where the Court will let a few represent the whole. There is one case very familiar, in which the Court has allowed a very few to represent the whole world (1).

Leave was given to amend (2).

———

1. WHERE a number of persons have an interest in the same subject, if a Court cannot recognize them as a legally associated body, but is bound to consider them as individuals, Lord Eldon declared, not only in the principal case, but in *Ex parte Lacey*, 6 Ves. 628, that the majority have no right to bind the minority.

2. As to the jurisdiction which Courts of Equity exercise, for the delivery of specific chattels, and the permission granted to certain individuals to sue, as representing a joint interest, although they may not be a regularly incorporated society, provided they do not profess, by their bill, to sue as corporators; see, *ante*, the note to *Fells* v. *Read*, 3 V. 70.

3. A plaintiff, it has been said, is now frequently permitted, as in the principal case, to amend his bill, in order to avoid the effect of a demurrer, at any stage of the argument, before judgment is given thereon; (*Baker* v. *Mellish*, 11 Ves. 72;) and, before the demurrer is argued, it was long ago agreed, that the plaintiff may obtain leave to amend his bill, as of course. *Lord Coningsby* v. *Sir Joseph Jekyll*, 2 P. Wms. 300. Convenience, and the saving of both expense and time, have dictated a farther relaxation of practice in modern days; strictly speaking, after a demurrer is allowed, the bill is out of Court; and Lord Hardwicke said there was no instance of permission given to amend it; (*Smith* v. *Barnes*, 1 Dick. 67;) but Lord Eldon has declared, that he knew many cases in which, after a demurrer allowed, and the bill dismissed by order, it had been considered in the discretion of the Court to set the cause on foot again. And, as this indulgence is granted to a plaintiff, so, on the other hand, when, during the pendency of the argument of the demurrer, and before judgment, the Court sees the demurrer is too general; but that, if more confined, it would be good; permission will, for the sake of justice, be given to the defendant to amend the demurrer, at that stage of the proceedings. *Baker* v. *Mellish*, *ubi supra*.

4. As to the cases in which the general rule, requiring all parties interested in a suit to be before the Court, may be dispensed with, see, *post*, the note to *The Attorney General* v. *Jackson*, 11 V. 365.

———

(1) With reference to this the Lord Chancellor before alluded to the cases of *The Opera House, The Royal Circus*, and *Drury Lane Theatre*. See the note, *ante*, vol. i. 130.

(2) In *Smith* v. *Barnes*, 1 Dick. 67, after a demurrer allowed liberty to amend was refused. *Post*, vol. xi. 72, *Baker* v. *Mellish*.

PYLE v. PRICE.

[1802, March 19.]

BEQUEST to the testator's wife, if living at his decease, provided
widow: but if she should die before his decease, or afterw
then and in either of such cases to his father, "if he shall be
of my decease or of such marriage as aforesaid; and in cas
then living, I give and bequeath the same to my brother."
The father survived the testator: but died before the marriag
Upon her marriage the brother entitled.
Demurrer *ore tenus* (*a*).
No general rule, whether a demurrer for want of parties must st
[p. 781.]

THE bill stated, that John Pyle by his will, date
March, 1796, after directing the payment of his de
devised, and bequeathed, all his moneys, securitic
money, * stock in trade, household goods and furni
plate, linen, and china, and other effects whatsoever, an
what nature or kind soever, that should belong to him
his decease, unto his wife Ann Pyle if she should be liv
of his decease for her own use and to be entirely at I
sal, provided she continued his widow; but if his sa
happen to die before his decease or being then living
wards marry again, then and in either of such cases h
all his said money, securities, stock, household furnit
effects whatsoever as hereinbefore mentioned should g
ceived and enjoyed by his father Robert Pyle, "if he sh
the time of my decease or of such marriage as afore
case he shall not be then living I give and bequeath
my brother Robert Pyle," his executors, administrator

The bill farther stated, that the testator died soon
his will; and in July, 1800, his widow married t
William Price; and Robert Pyle the testator's fath
time after the death of the testator, and before the ma
Pyle; whereby the Plaintiff, Robert Pyle the younge

(*a*) A defendant may, at the hearing of his demurrer, orally assi
of demurrer, different from, or in addition to, those assigned
1 Barb. Ch. Pr. 108, 109. He cannot demur *ore tenus*, unless the
on the record. *Hook* v. *Dorman*, 1 Sim. & Stu. 227; *Metcalfe* v.
560. Under the general demurrer for want of Equity, a demu
parties may be made *ore tenus*. *Robinson* v. *Smith*, 3 Paige,
Strong, 3 Paige, 452. It must be made to the whole bill, and n
Shepherd v. *Lloyd*, 2 Y. & Jer. 490. After a demurrer to a par
been overruled, the defendant may demur *ore tenus* to the same
Hicken, 1 Keen, 385.

(*b*) The demurrer must show who are the proper parties, not i
for that might be impossible; but in such manner, as to point o
the objection to his bill, and to enable him to amend by makin
Story, Eq. Pl. § 543; Mitford, Eq. Pl. by Jeremy, 180; *Attorney*
4 Mylne & C. 17.

tled under the will to all the residue of the personal estate so forfeited by her marriage ; and prayed an account, &c. accordingly.

The Defendants Price and his wife put in a general demurrer to the discovery and relief.

Mr. *Lloyd* and Mr. *Stanley*, in support of the demurrer.—One cause of demurrer is, that the contingency has not happened upon the clause in this will. The word "then" may apply to either event.

Another cause, which, the demurrer being general, must be alleged *ore tenus* (1), is, that if that question is doubtful, there is a manifest want of parties: the personal representative of the father not being a Defendant. There is no authority requiring, that a demurrer for want of parties must state the parties; and that proposition is too general; for it may be out of the power of [* 781]   * the Defendant to name the party wanting ; and the case of *Tourton* v. *Flower* (2) shows the. contrary.

Mr. *Horne*, in support of the bill, was stopped by the Court.

Lord CHANCELLOR [ELDON].—With respect to the cause of demurrer for want of parties, besides the objection, that has been mentioned, to requiring the party to be stated, it may appear upon the bill, that the Plaintiff knows the party. Perhaps there is not a general rule either way (3).

But upon the construction of this will I am clearly and without any difficulty of opinion with the Plaintiff. The other construction makes great part of the will absolutely unnecessary : all, that follows the words " if he shall be living at the time of my decease " is absolute surplusage ; and means nothing. Upon that construction it was quite unnecessary to put both contingencies ; for if the father survived the testator, he or his representatives would have taken the whole, whether he survived the marriage, or not. It would therefore have been sufficient to have said, in case his wife should die before him, or afterwards marry again, it should go to his father ; and all the rest is surplusage. At the moment after the testator's decease she could not be married : and for that reason he there does not put the alternative.

The Demurrer was over-ruled.

___

1. THE doctrine laid down in the principal case, that a demurrer for want of parties need not always state the names of the requisite parties, was again recognized in *The Attorney General* v. *Jackson*, 11 Ves. 369: it is enough if the objection point out who the individuals are, by some description, enabling the plaintiff to make them parties.

2. A defendant may demur at the bar, *ore tenus; Tourton* v. *Flower*, 3 P. Wms. 370; if he cannot sustain the demurrer he has put on the record; *Attorney General* v. *Brown*, 11 Swanst. 288; and it has been said, the demurrer *ore tenus* may be upon another *ground* from that on the record; *Cartwright* v. *Green*, 8 Ves.

___

(1) *Post*, vol. viii. 408 ; *Pitts* v. *Short*, xvii. 213; and the note, 216.
(2) 3 P. Will. 369.
(3) See *Jackson* v. *Lee*, *Dalton* v. *Thomson*, 1 Dick. 92, 97. As to a plea see *Merreweather* v. *Mellish, post,* vol. xiii. 435.

408; but in a later case, it was laid down as a rule, by the s
judge to whom the former *dictum* is ascribed, that a demurrer
to that which the defendant has demurred to on the record. I
demurrer on the record is not good, he may, at the bar, assign
he cannot demur *ore tenus* upon a *ground* which he has not ma
demurrer on the record. *Pitts* v. *Short*, 17 Ves. 215. It may b
serve, that the words "cause" and "ground" are so freque
mously, (when applied to matter of discussion,) that particular c
sary to distinguish their different import in the passages just
cause to be here understood as the special reason, and the *grou*
principle? and ought it to be understood, that when the reason
not maintain the demurrer, *other reasons* may be shown to sustai
ple of objection, but that no new principle must be introduced,
rer, which is not assigned on the record? If this were so, the t
might still be reconciled, by considering the nature of the ques
v. *Green*. The Court by stopping that suit *in limine* upon a g
tenus, different from that put on the record, may have felt that
rule of practice, or form of pleading, which was then to be det
broad line of demarcation which separates Courts of Equity from
mon Law; and that where the question is shown to relate to a
Equity is bound, though that fact may not be shown with great
of form, instantly to withhold its interference, not for the sake
but for the preservation of the principles of the Court itself.

LUND, *Ex parte.*

[1802, MARCH 18, 20.]

WITNESSES to prove the act of bankruptcy not having obeyed th
    Commissioners an order was made, that they should attend th
    (See n. (1), p. 784.)
The jurisdiction of the Lord Chancellor in bankruptcy is distinc
    Court of Chancery, [p. 782.]
Commissioners of Lunacy have a power of summoning witnesse
    their office, [p. 784.]

THE witnesses summoned under a Commission of
prove the act of bankruptcy not having obeyed the
petition was presented : praying an order, that they sh
Commissioners.

* Mr. *Mansfield* and Mr. *Pemberton*, in support of
Petition.

This petition is new: but considering the nature o
there must be somewhere a power to compel the atten
nesses to prove those necessary circumstances, with
Commission cannot have effect. From the bond giver
tioning creditor it follows of course, that he must ha
some authority to call upon these persons to prove
stances. A strong implication also arises from the nat
mission of bankruptcy, requiring possession of the effec
as soon as possible ; a species of execution. The la
such a proceeding must authorise all the necessary
purpose. Under Commissions of lunacy without an

liament or express authority subpœnas, calling upon witnesses to attend, are issued of course by the Commissioners; whose authority comes in the room of the escheator or sheriff under the old writ (1). There is certainly this difference, that under that Commission a Jury is to inquire. But the power to summon witnesses is only by implication; and because without such a proceeding it would be quite impossible to execute the Commission.

This petition states, that the persons summoned at first took an objection by Council, that the Commissioners had not qualified; which shows the spirit of resistance and collusion. No such order as this petition prays can be found; but it stands upon analogy to what has been done in support of orders and summonses of the Commissioners. In *Ex parte Kerney* (2) no precedent was produced: but without any Lord Hardwicke took a strong measure in aid of the power of the Commissioners; for no Statute gives a power of committing for a contempt of the Commissioners' summons.

Lord CHANCELLOR.—There is great confusion in the language of every book relating to the subject, speaking of the Court of Chancery. The jurisdiction is not in that Court but in the individual, who happens to hold the Great Seal by a special authority [*783] *to issue Commissions of Bankruptcy (3); and there is not therefore a necessary consequence, that by that power the Lord Chancellor has in himself all compulsory powers of compelling all sorts of witnesses to attend. But very strong acts have been done. The case *Ex parte Kerney* and some others show, that the Lord Chancellor in bankruptcy has taken upon himself to do very strong acts; for according to the letters of the Acts of Parliament, for any thing expressed in them, when once he has granted a Commission, constituting the Commissioners the Court, he is *functus officio*. Yet in *Ex parte Kerney* Lord Hardwicke thought himself authorised, because the Commission issued under the Great Seal, to consider the act as a contempt of the Great Seal, as if sitting in the Court of Justice; and not only discharged the person arrested, but ordered the other under the penalty of commitment to give security to answer interrogatories; directing him to be examined; as would be done in the Court of King's Bench upon a contempt. I will look in Lord Hardwicke's notes for that case.

In 2 Black: 1142, Lord Northington speaking of this power is represented as using the same inaccurate language; speaking of the powers of the Court of Chancery; which has nothing to do with it. Lord Rosslyn also discharged a person returning from being examined before the Commissioners (4); which must be under a notion, that it is a contempt of the Great Seal. Whether that is right,

(1) The writ *De Idiota inquirendo et examinando.* See Fitzh. Nat. Brev. 530.
(2) 1 Atk. 54.
(3) *Post,* vol. viii. 250; xix. 473, 4, *Ex parte Smith; Ex parte Glandfield,* 1 Glyn & Jam. 387.
(4) *Ex parte Parker, ante,* vol. iii. 554; see the note. 351.

and the Great Seal having this special authority can c
contempt, as Courts do, strictly speaking, might have l
if there was not all this authority. I do not lay much s
bond; for in general the creditor is in possession of
if not, he ought not to make the oath; and he never co
the bond; for it will not be assigned; unless the Com
fully and maliciously taken out. The creditor taking
mission generally supposes himself able to bring witn
the act of bankruptcy; and it would be a sufficient an
to an application to have the bond assigned, that he
of the act of bankruptcy, &c. and could not get the
attend. It will turn out, I believe, that the Great Seal
exercised authority analogous to this; and if so, * I will
give up the authority. The Commissioners of Lun
came in the room of another authority; and were mea
the powers that authority had; and among those there
say, it must be incident to the office of Commissioner
summon witnesses. If a Commission of bankruptcy
executed without that power, it would be incident, I sh
the office of Commissioner; and if so, the question i
is in the person, who holds the Great Seal.

Some time afterwards the order was made for the
the witnesses (by name) before the Commissioners (1)

---

1. A PROCEEDING in bankruptcy is not a proceeding in Char
Thompson, 1 Glyn & Jameson, 308; nor would a judge empower
Lord Chancellor as Keeper of the Great Seal, be authorized, und
sion, to sit in bankruptcy; *Ford* v. *Webb,* 3 Brod. & Bing. 243.
tive to a question of bankruptcy, must not be headed " in Chanc
Glandfield, 1 Glyn & Jameson, 387; nor is it necessary that a con
be taken out by a solicitor; (*Ex parte Smith,* 19 Ves. 474:) a forti
of a common law court need not be admitted a solicitor in Chan
enable him to transact business in bankruptcy; *Wilkinson* v. *Di*
Cres. 160; though the bills of costs for such business are taxable
which extent only, the case *Collins* v: *Nicholson,* 2 Taunt. 322, mt
as an authority.
2. The power of commissioners of bankrupt to compel the att
nesses, is provided for by the 24th and 34th sections of the statute
3. As to the exemption from arrest of parties attending commiss
rupt; see, *ante,* the notes to *Ex parte Hawkins,* 4 V. 691.

---

(1) *Post, Ex parte Higgins,* vol. xi. 8; xiv. 450, 1; *Ex parte J*
Ex parte Chamberlain, xix. 481; *Commissioners of Charitable*
1 Dick. 61; *Ex parte Gardner,* 1 Ves. & Bea. 74. By Stat. 6 C
s. 24, the Commissioners are empowered, after they have qualifi
witnesses to trading and acts of bankruptcy, and to require the prodt
papers, &c.; and the person summoned shall incur such penalty f
or refusing to be sworn, &c. as after adjudication; for which see s

DAVIS v. LEO.

[1802, MARCH 11, 18, 20.]

INJUNCTION to restrain waste not granted without positive evidence of title (a).
Injunction against waste in favor of tenant for life; particularly as to ornamental
timber; not so much upon his interest as his enjoyment (b), [p. 787.]

MR. WHISHAW for the Plaintiff moved for an injunction to restrain the Defendant from cutting any timber or other trees on
the estates in the bill mentioned, planted or growing for ornament
or shelter of the mansion-house, park, and grounds, and any saplings, &c.

The affidavit of the Plaintiff stated, that he had been informed,
that Lætitia Leo, the late wife of the Defendant, Daniel Leo, of
Lannech in the county of Denbigh, was at her marriage seized in
fee simple of real estates in that county; which by a settlement previous to her marriage were limited to the use of Lætitia Leo for life;
remainder to the Defendant for life; remainder to the issue of the
marriage therein mentioned; and in default of such issue remainder
to such person or persons as Lætitia Leo should by deed or will
notwithstanding coverture direct or appoint; and in default of such
appointment with certain limitations over in favor of certain persons
therein named and their issue, and (amongst others) of the deponent
her first cousin, and his issue in manner therein mentioned; with
an ultimate limitation to the right heirs of Lætitia Leo.
[* 785]   The marriage took effect; and Lætitia Leo, * having a
*power reserved to her of executing a will as aforesaid, did
(as the deponent believes it is alleged by the Defendant Daniel
Leo), make and publish some writing or instrument purporting to
be her last will and testament; which, as it is alleged by Daniel
Leo, was duly executed; whereby she limited and appointed the
estates after the death of Daniel Leo in default of issue of the marriage unto and to the use of the Defendant Henry Leo, with remain-

---

(a) The Court will not entertain a motion for an injunction, in the nature of a
writ of estrepement, except where the title is clear. *Lowe* v. *Lucey*, 1 Irish Eq.
93; *S. C.* 1 Craw. & Dix. 634. See *Amelung* v. *Seekamp*, 9 Gill & J. 468;
Beatty v. *Beatty*, 2 Moll. 541; *Storm* v. *Mann*, 4 Johns. Ch. 21; 1 Bland, 576;
Joley v. *Stockley*, 1 Hogan, 247. There must be positive evidence of actual title.
2 Madd. Ch. (4th Am. ed.) 218; Jeremy, Eq. Jur. 335, 336; *Hough* v. *Martin*,
2 Dev. & Bat. 379. See 1 Smith, Ch. Pr. ch. 19, p. 596; *Read* v. *Dew*,
R. M. Charlton, 358; *Price* v. *Meth. Epis. Church*, 4 Ham. 547; Mr. Perkins's
note to *Whitelegg* v. *Whitelegg*, 1 Bro. C. C. 50.

(b) Where there is a tenant for life, remainder in fee, the tenant for life will be
restrained, by injunction, from committing waste, although if he did commit waste,
no action of waste would lie against him by the remainder-man for life, for he has
not the inheritance, or by the remainder-man in fee, by reason of the interposed
remainder for life. 2 Story, Eq. Jur. § 913; *Kane* v. *Vanderburgh*, 1 Johns. Ch.
11. So, an injunction may be obtained against a lessee, to prevent him from
making alterations in a dwelling-house; as by changing it into a shop or ware-
house. *Douglass* v. *Wiggins*, 1 Johns. Ch. 435. See, also, Eden on Injunc. 199,
(2d Amer. ed.)

der to his lawful issue in tail general; and, in default
with remainder to the issue of Daniel Leo by any su
riage in tail general; and, in default of such issue, ren
deponent for life; remainder to his issue in tail genen
remainders over.

The affidavit farther stated, that Lætitia Leo died
1801, without having revoked or altered her said alleç
ing her husband, and leaving no brother, but leaving t
Mary Puleston her only sister and heiress at law, su
there has been no issue of the marriage; that Daniel 1
ried; and that Henry Léo is an infant and unmarried
ponent believes, he has either under the said settleme
will and instrument a contingent interest expectant on
Daniel Leo and Henry Leo without issue: but nevei
able to procure a sight of the said instrument he cani
state his claim more particularly; that Daniel Leo h
the death of his wife been in possession; and the depoi
informed and believes, the said Defendant has in h
power the said settlement and the said will or instrur
has not proved the will; and he has not produced the
instrument, or furnished the deponent with any partici
ing the same; whereby he is prevented from stating
particularly.

The affidavit then suggested the intention to commi¹
that the Defendant had surveyed, valued, and mark :
sale; and advertised.

The Plaintiff by a farther affidavit stated, that Lætitii
the deponent believes, make and publish some instrume :
lowing the former affidavit); and that he grounds his
the following information: that a few days after the dec I
*of the testatrix the Reverend William Davies Shipl(;
whom the deponent believes to have been one of the tri
tees in the said marriage settlement and will, communica '
tents of the will to the Reverend Samuel Strong by let (
mission to make the same known to the deponent; whic I
forwarded to the deponent in London; and was to the ;i
fect; that by virtue of a power reserved in the said m
tlement Lætitia Leo had made a will; whereby she ¡
appointed according to the limitations stated in the form
and upon receipt of that letter the deponent applied f
copy of the will to Hughes, the Secretary of the Bishop of
who informed him, the will had never been proved; but.
as his memory served, he would state to the deponent th
of the said will, he himself having made a codicil there
and that the letter was to the same effect; except that I
did not well recollect, whether the said estates in defaul
Daniel Leo by a subsequent marriage were not limited t
vies, uncle of the deponent, and his issue, as tenants ¡
previous to the limitation to the deponent and his issue.

The motion was originally made upon the first of these affidavits.

Mr. *Whishaw*, in support of the motion.—The Master of the Rolls doubted, whether this sort of interest was sufficient to entitle the Plaintiff to an injunction of this sort: but the practice has been to grant injunctions upon very general allegation of interest, to prevent irreparable damage, till answer or farther order. The Plaintiff is the second tenant for life in remainder ; there being no tenant in tail *in esse.* Where the inheritance is to be affected, the general practice is to make all the tenants for life parties to a suit for any charge upon the estate. The Court will also attend to their interest for the purpose of protecting the estate from waste. An injunction is granted in favor of the person entitled in reversion or remainder generally: and formerly even without affidavits (1). That however is now over-ruled. The first tenant for life is entitled to [* 787] it: *Roswell's Case* (2); and *according to what is said in the note in Peere Williams, the heiress at law is made a party to this bill. The principle extends to the second tenant for life : *Perrot* v. *Perrot* (3).

Lord CHANCELLOR [ELDON].—There is no positive affidavit, that the will was made, under which the Plaintiff is next tenant for life to the Defendant Leo. This is a mere hypothetical title, upon the Plaintiff's information and belief, that a settlement was executed, under which Leo is tenant for life, and the Plaintiff remainder-man for life ; leaving it in that way. There is no instance of an injunction in such a case. Suppose, Leo was an old gentleman with five daughters ; and having this right intended by the exercise of it to provide for them ; and upon such an affidavit, merely to belief, he is restrained for a year ; and dies within that year ! An affidavit to information and belief is nothing in this sort of case. It must be irreparable mischief to a person, who swears to his title. I cannot grant the injunction ; unless a positive affidavit is produced.

Upon the other point, I have no doubt, a tenant for life may have an injunction, particularly as to ornamental timber ; for that is not so much upon his interest as his enjoyment.

March 18th. The motion was renewed upon the farther affidavit, above stated.

March 20th. Lord CHANCELLOR [ELDON].—I dare not grant an injunction in this case. The bill states a title sufficiently, if it was duly verified. But the affidavits disclose the case no farther than that it may or may not be true ; and I am of opinion, the Court ought not to grant an injunction, unless there is positive evidence of

(1) Prac. Reg. 243, 4.
(2) 3 P. Will. 268, n. ; 1 Roll. Abr. 377 ; 3 Atk. 210.
(3) 3 Atk. 94.

actual title. If those letters are true, they can swear to the truth of
them (1).

The Motion was refused. ____

SEE notes 3, 4, 5, to *Pigot v. Bullock,* 1 V. 479.

MOUNTFORD *v.* TAYLOR. [* 788]

[1802, MARCH 18, 19, 20.]

BILL by creditors by judgment, who had sued out *Elegits*, for a discovery of freehold estates; charging, that the Defendant upon his election as member of
Parliament, previously to the judgments, gave in his qualification; and if the
estates composing it were conveyed away since, it was without consideration.
Demurrer as to the qualification, &c.; and Answer to the rest, but not going to
the charge of conveyance without consideration: the Demurrer was overruled.
General denial not enough: there must be an answer to the sifting inquiries upon
the general question (*a*), [p. 792.]

THE bill stated, that John Mountford brought an action against
the Defendant upon a bond for 425*l.*; and obtained a judgment in
Hilary Term, 40 Geo. III.· Mountford died;· leaving the Plaintiff
Mary Mountford his executrix; who revived the judgment.

The Defendant being also indebted to the other Plaintiff Joseph
Sharp for work and labor and goods sold and delivered in the sum
of 85*l.* 10*s.* 3*d.*, Sharp brought an action; and obtained judgment
in Michaelmas Term, 41 Geo. III.

The bill farther stated, that, when the judgments were obtained,
the Defendant was, and ever since hath been, or now is, seised for
his own use of freehold estates for his life or some greater estate;
that the Plaintiffs sued out writs of *Elegit* upon these judgments:
but neither of them has been able to discover, where the estates of
the Defendant are situate; that they had frequently applied to the
Defendant, requesting payment; or that he would discover where
his estates are situate, and who are in the occupation of them: in
order that the Plaintiffs might obtain satisfaction of their judgments
by the *Elegits*; the Defendant not having to their knowledge any
personal property; and the Plaintiffs are prevented from taking his
person in execution by reason of his being a member of the House
of Commons, and having privilege of Parliament.

The Plaintiffs then in answer to a pretence suggested, that the

---

(1) *Pillsworth v. Hopton, ante,* 51; *post, Hanson v. Gardiner,* vol. vii. 305;
Smith v. Collyer, viii. 89.

(*a*) An answer must be full and perfect to all the material allegations in the bill.
It must confess, avoid, deny, or traverse all the material parts of the bill. Story,
Eq. Pl. § 852, § 855; Cooper, Eq. Pl. 313; 2 Daniell, Ch. Pr. 260, as quoted in the
note to Story, Eq. Pl. § 852; *Bally v. Kenrick,* 13 Price, 291; *Daniell v. Bishop,*
13 Price, 15.

Defendant was not at the time, when either of the judgments was obtained, nor hath been at any time since, nor is now, seised of or entitled to any freehold estates, charged, that the Defendant in or about 1795 on being elected a member of the House of Commons and on taking his seat took the oath as to his having the requisite qualification in point of property ; and that he then had such an estate in Law or Equity to or for his own use and benefit in lands, tenements, or hereditaments, clear of all incumbrances, as was of the annual value of 300*l.* above reprizes, and as qualified [* 789] * him to be elected and returned a Member of Parliament ; and he also delivered to the Clerk of the House of Commons or some other officer of the House a schedule, containing the particulars of the estate, whereby he made out his qualifications ; and the Plaintiffs are unable to obtain the said schedule : but the Defendant has or lately had some copy thereof, &c. ; and suggesting another pretence by the Defendant, that he has since conveyed the estates of which his qualification was composed, and a refusal to discover, when, to whom, or for what, charged, that, if the Defendant has since conveyed away the estates, which constituted his qualification, such conveyance was without consideration and in trust for himself.

The bill prayed a discovery.

The Defendant put in a demurrer and answer; stating, that as to so much of the bill as seeks a discovery from the Defendant, whether he did not, on the occasion of his being elected a Member of the House of Commons or taking his seat take the oath as to his having the requisite qualification, &c., or deliver to the Clerk or other officer of the House a schedule, &c., and whether such schedule was not signed by him, and whether the Plaintiffs are not unable to obtain that schedule, and whether the Defendant has not some copy thereof, &c. and as requires him to set forth such copy, &c. or to set forth in the best manner he is able the particulars of the estate, in respect of which he made out his qualification, where situate, in whose occupation, and what right or interest he had at the time of his said election in such estates, and to set forth when, and upon what occasion, to whom, and for what consideration, and with what view, and for what purpose he so conveyed the same, and the date &c. and material contents of the said conveyance or conveyances, the Defendant demurred ; for cause, that the complainants have not shown any right or title to have such discovery from the Defendant.

In answer to the rest of the bill the Defendant admitted the bond and judgment, the death of Mountford, and that the Plaintiff Mary Mountford, is his executrix ; that some debt is due to the Plaintiff Sharp ; and that he obtained judgment. The Defendant denied, that he was, at the respective times, when the judgments [* 790] * were obtained, or since, or is now, legally or in any other manner seised of, or legally or equitably or beneficially entitled for his own use and benefit to, any freehold messuages, lands, &c., for his life ; or that he or any person in trust for him hath any other estate or interest therein. He admitted the application and refusal; that he was elected a Member of the House of Commons in 1797; and that in consequence of his being a Member thereof and having privilege of Parliament the complainants are prevented from taking him in execution.

Mr. *Mansfield*, Mr. *Romilly*, and Mr. *Pemberton*, in support of the Demurrer. The object of this bill is idle curiosity. No creditor has a right to make these inquiries. The right of a creditor in the common case to a discovery of the real estate is admitted. But this Defendant has positively sworn, he has no real estate; and clearly is not bound to answer these impertinent questions. They ask, whether the Defendant had estates at a certain time, long before they recovered their judgments. They can have no interest in those estates. There is a positive and direct answer, that he was not seised of or entitled to any estate of freehold in Law or Equity at the time the Plaintiffs obtained their judgments, or since. No inference arises from the fact, that the Defendant was a Member of Parliament; for the Statute (1) says expressly, that the qualification may be copyhold estate; and it has been decided by the House of Commons, the only competent tribunal, that a rent charge would do. Neither of these could be touched by creditors.

Another objection is, that this discovery might subject the Defendant to an indictment for perjury; and avoid his seat under the Act of Parliament.

Mr. *Johnson*, in support of the Bill.—The answer to the last objection is, that is not the cause of demurrer assigned; which must be abandoned, before the Defendant can assign another *ore tenus*. But upon the nature of the case it is impossible for the Defendant to protect himself by that allegation, that he has sworn falsely; the bill charging, that he had taken the oath, and that it is true. * The general right of the creditor to come for a dis-   [* 791] covery of real estate in aid of his execution is admitted. The creditor then has a right to put any particular questions, the tendency of which may be to procure him that information. The general denial is not sufficient. If a bill was filed for a discovery of the consideration of a security and a variety of particulars with respect to that, the Defendant swearing broadly, that he paid full consideration, cannot protect himself from answering the particulars. The Plaintiffs have a right to ask as to the anterior time, to avail themselves, if they can, of that discovery against the persons, in whose possession the estates may now be. The fact of his election and taking the oath is produced as evidence, that he had freehold estates, and that he has not since parted with them, or has parted with them in such a manner, that the Plaintiffs are not deprived of their lien.

Mr. *Mansfield*, in reply.—The Plaintiffs might perhaps ask the Defendant, whether he had any estates, which he has conveyed in

---

(1) Stat. 9 Ann. c. 5.

trust for himself. This demurrer does not go to such an inquiry, but only to inquiries, which are wholly impertinent, as to the qualification, what passed in the House of Commons, and what he has done with the estate he gave in. Is he bound to set forth, what is become of any estate he had twenty years ago? It is enough in explicit terms positively to deny, that he ever executed any conveyance of such estates in trust for himself; and that he has any interest legal or equitable in any estate, upon which execution may be had by a creditor.

Lord CHANCELLOR [ELDON].—This is as important a case as ever came before the Court; not with regard to the particular circumstances belonging to it, but as to the general principle, which must govern all cases of the same kind, though not precisely of the same species. I must take it, that in 1797 the Defendant had an estate of 300l. a-year; subsequent to which time the judgments were obtained. It seems admitted that they have a right to come here for a discovery, where the property is, in order to make their judgments available. That certainly will not affect real property had, before the judgment was obtained, if no longer under such circumstances that the creditor can follow it: but it does not [* 792]   follow, * that he cannot, merely because it does not remain in the ownership of the debtor; for there may be many cases, in which he might. There is a material charge in this bill; that, if there was any conveyance, it was without considera- . tion. First, in the common case will a bill for a discovery lie, with all this particularity, to know every estate he has sold and disposed of for three years? If so, he may go back forty years. The very defence in this case supposes, the Plaintiffs have a right to call upon the Defendant at least to negative some general inquiries. The policy of the proceedings in this Court is, that a general denial is not enough; but there must be an answer to sifting inquiries upon the general question. There is a difficulty upon the objection, that this would extend to an estate parted with forty years ago without consideration; and I am not quite clear, that such a bill must not allege, that at a given time the Defendant was seised of given lands; (not simply suggesting as a fishing bill, that at some time or other he had some land); and that he conveyed those lands away fraudulently, to put them out the reach of this creditor.

March 20th.   Lord CHANCELLOR [ELDON].—This Demurrer must be over-ruled. The bill is met by a defence, admitting, that it is a proper bill; and the answer does not negative all, that is material to be answered. With respect to the nature of the qualification, if he had said, the property he gave into the House of Commons was not liable to execution, the Court ought to be content with that, without requiring from him more particularity. But the bill charges, that the Defendant delivered in a schedule of the particulars of the estates, whereby he made out his qualification, and that he has conveyed them without consideration, as evidence, that he has lands liable to execution; as they may be unquestionably. Upon that I think he must answer.

The Demurrer was over-ruled.

THE discovery which a Court of Equity gives upon a proper bill filed for that purpose, is not the mere oath of the party defendant to a general fact, but an answer upon oath, to every collateral circumstance charged as evidence of that fact; *Sanders* v. *King,* 6 Mad. 63; see also the notes to *Jerrard* v. *Saunders,* 2 V. 187, and the notes to *Bayley* v. *Adams,* 6 V. 586.

KENWORTHY *v.* BATE.   [* 793]

[ROLLS.—1802, MARCH 23.]

POWER of appointing real estate well executed by a devise to trustees to sell, and an appointment of the money produced by the sale (*a*).
Settlement upon such child or children as the father should appoint: appointment excluding one established (*b*).
Power to appoint land well executed by a charge (*c*), [p. 797.]
Power to charge includes a power to sell (*d*), [p. 797.]

By indentures of settlement, dated the 29th of September, 1753, in consideration of the marriage of Bartholomew and Ann Penny estates of Bartholomew Penny were conveyed to trustees and their heirs, to the use of Bartholomew Penny for life; remainder to the use of Ann Penny for life, for her jointure and in bar of dower; and immediately after the decease of the survivor of them then to the use of such child or children of said Bartholomew Penny on the body of said Ann his wife begotten or to be begotten as the said Bartholomew Penny should in and by his last will and testament in writing under his hand and seal duly executed give, direct, limit, and appoint: and, for want of such direction, limitation, and appointment to the use of the first son of the body of Bartholomew Penny on the body of said Ann, &c., and the heirs of the body of such first son; with similar remainders to the use of the second, third, fourth, and all and every other, son and sons successively, and remainders over; with the ultimate remainder to Bartholomew Penny and his heirs.

(*a*) A power to mortgage includes a power to execute a mortgage, with a power to sell. *Wilson* v. *Troup,* 7 Johns. Ch. 25. It is supposed that a power to sell for the purpose of raising money will imply a power to mortgage, which is a conditional sale, and within the object of the power. 4 Kent, Comm. 147, (5th ed.) Such powers are construed liberally, in furtherance of the beneficial object. A power to appoint land has been held to be well executed, by creating a charge upon it; and a power to charge will include a power to sell. Ib.
(*b*) If the interest be expressly indicated by the power, a different estate cannot be appointed under it; though, without positive words of restriction, a lesser estate than that authorized may be limited. 4 Kent, Com. 345, (5th ed.)
(*c*) 4 Kent, Com. 345, (5th ed.)
(*d*) 4 Kent. Com. 345, (5th ed.)

Bartholomew Penny, having survived his wife, died in 1798 ; having had by her, besides other children who died under age and unmarried, three sons and two daughters : viz. Thomas George Penny, William Theyer Penny, Elizabeth Mary Guillandeau, Ann Aubert, and Bartholomew Penny.   By his will, dated the 10th of December, 1795, reciting the settlement and the power therein contained, he gave, devised, and bequeathed, all the estates so settled and all the rest and residue of his estates real and personal to James Bate the elder and James Bate the younger, to sell and dispose of the estates above mentioned as soon as convenient after his decease ; and the net produce thereof together with the net produce of the remainder he should die possessed of he willed to be divided among his children ; and he thereby gave to his son Thomas George Penny one shilling, to be paid within twelve months after his decease ; to his son William Theyer Penny 500*l.* ; to his daughter Elizabeth Mary Guillandeau 500*l.* for her sole and separate use.   The rest and
[*794]   residue of all his effects he willed to be divided into four equal parts ; and he gave one fourth thereof to * William Theyer Penny, one fourth part thereof to Elizabeth Mary Guillandeau for her separate use ; one fourth part thereof to Ann Aubert for her sole and separate use ; and the remaining fourth part to Bartholomew Penny.

Bartholomew Penny, the youngest son, died in the life of his father.   In December 1799, William Theyer Penney became a bankrupt ; and the bill was filed by his assignees ; suggesting, that Thomas George Penney, the eldest son, went to the East Indies in 1772, and for upwards of twenty-seven years had not been heard of ; and praying, that if the Court shall be of opinion, that the estates are unappointed, the Defendant Bate may be decreed to deliver up the settlement ; and that a Receiver may be appointed, &c.

The Defendants insisted, that the will of 1795 was a good execution of the power ; and that by a prior will, dated the 1st of November, 1792, the testator gave, devised, and bequeathed, all the settled estates to Elizabeth Mary Guillandeau and her heirs for ever ; and she insisted, that if the will of 1795 was not a good execution of the power, the will of 1792 was not revoked thereby ; or, if revoked as a will, it was good as an instrument of appointment.

Upon an inquiry directed the Master's Report upon the circumstances stated, that Thomas George Penny died in 1775 without issue.

Mr. *Romilly* and Mr. *Roupell*, for the Plaintiffs.—The intention is plain, that this estate was to go as real property, as far as it could. There is no authority, that a power of appointing a real estate is well executed by selling it and disposing of the. money.   No case bears the least resemblance to this, except *Long* v. *Long* (1) ; which is very distinguishable in several circumstances.   *Thwaytes* v. *Dye* (2) will be cited.   But there is a material difference ; that there

(1) *Ante,* vol. v. 445.
(2) 2 Vern. 80.

the party did not devise the estate away from all his children; but
suffered it to go to the eldest in tail; giving rent-charges out of that
estate to the others.   Iu *Roberts* v. *Dixall* (1) also the estate went
to one of the children.

Mr. *Richards*, Mr. *Steele*, and Mr. *Stanley*, for the De-   [* 795]
fendants.—This was a power vested in the husband, to
enable him to provide for the children of the marriage; therefore to
be construed favorably.   In *Long* v. *Long* there was equally an intention to continue the estate real; the limitations being to the first
and other sons, &c.   But no intention was inferred from that circumstance; the father having a right to appoint to one in fee; and
the child might sell the estate.   In effect that, which arises from the
land, is equally the subject of appointment, as a rent-charge.   In
Thwaytes v. *Dye* there is no difference from the circumstance, that
the land is permitted to go to one of the sons.   That case is an
authority, that under a power of this kind the estate may be charged.
Is that an execution *modo & formâ* within the terms of the power?
In *Roberts* v. *Dixall*, which was the case of a mere naked power,
the language of the Court shows, that this. is a good execution.   In
Equity the intention is to be looked to.   The estate is all the beneficial interest in it.   Can the introduction of trustees vitiate the
whole?   Either this is a good appointment or not.   The father might
have given the estate or any portion of it to any one child immediately.   Where is the difference between giving the produce, and
giving the estate, to make produce of it?   *Long* v. *Long*, though
certainly differing in circumstances, in principle governs this case;
and was stronger; for the estate was to be limited to the eldest son
subject to a charge.   Suppose a mine had been discovered; he
might take the estate; paying the charge.   It was contended there,
that if for any reason he wished to keep the estate, he might have
done so, paying the charge: but the Lord Chancellor would not disturb it, the substance being executed.   In *Wilson* v. *Piggott* (2) the
principle is laid down correctly by Lord Alvanley; that where the
party has such a power, and demonstrates an intention to give a share
to any child, the Court will enforce it without attention to the mode,
in which it is given (3).   It is clear, that under such a power it is
not necessary to give a share to all: but it may be given to any one,
excluding the rest: *Swift* v. *Gregson* (4), *Spring* v. *Biles* (5).   The
Court will consider, whether the party has substantially executed.
The motive, providing for a family, ought to be liberally
* construed.   A division of a real estate into small portions   [* 796]
would be attended with great inconvenience.

But if this is not a valid execution of the power, then the former
will must stand.

(1) 2 Eq. Ca. Ab. 668.
(2) *Ante*, vol. ii. 351.
(3) *Ante*, vol. ii. 355.
(4) 1 Term Rep. 432.
(5) 1 Term Rep. 435, note.

Mr. *Romilly*, in reply.—The will of 1795 is certainly a revocation of every other execution of the power by will. It is impossible that this can be a good execution of the power at law. The utmost, that can be contended, is that the father having in substance done what he was entitled to do, the parties are entitled to the assistance of a Court of Equity. In the cases cited the legal estate was in the eldest son with the charges upon it. *Long* v. *Long* was thought a doubtful case; and there was no determination like it before. The Lord Chancellor went very much upon this; that the husband had a power to charge portions for the younger children to what extent he pleased, even to the value of the whole estate except the sum of 100*l.*; leaving no more than that for the eldest son; and therefore in substance he might have taken it from the eldest son. There was no limitation of the sum to be charged. A power of charging to any extent is the same as a power to give the whole. That power was so executed, that, if good at all, it was good at law: but this testator has attempted under the power to give to mere strangers.

The MASTER OF THE ROLLS [Sir WILLIAM GRANT].—It does not appear, that this case in specie has ever occurred; but in principle I cannot distinguish it from those, that have been cited. Three of those cases must have been ill decided, if it is true, that substantially a power to appoint land can be executed in no other way than by limiting the land itself.. In *Thwaytes* v. *Dye* the limitation was precisely the same as this: the power was to appoint the land itself; and the argument arose as much as it does here, that beyond that the party could not go; that there was no election, except to do nothing or to give the land. He had a power to give the land: but he gave them nothing in the land; but instead of that made the disposition stated in the Report. The objection was taken in the words, in which it was taken here. That was not a case in which he had directed a sale; but the effect of the decision, which was upon a plea, goes the length of showing, that a power to [* 797] appoint * land may in substance be executed without giving the land itself. If the heir's objection was a good one, it would have prevailed undoubtedly.

In *Roberts* v. *Dixall* also the power was to appoint land. The party did not appoint the land; but charged a sum of money upon the land; and it was held substantially an execution of the power. It was not contended to be so literally and formally. As an illustration of that Lord Hardwicke said, he might have directed a portion of the land to be sold, and the money to be paid to his daughters; and what he did was equivalent.

The case of *Long* v. *Long* determines this; and to enable a person to sell land it is not necessary to have that authority expressly given to him. There the party had no right to sell, but had a right to charge. There was a stronger case than this; for a power to charge is in its nature a more circumscribed power than a power to give land. In this case there is an absolute power to give the feesimple, the whole, out and out. to any one of the children, or to divide

'it among them. That is a more extensive power; for the implication from a charge is generally, that something is to be left. The
terms of the settlement in the other case gave room in a peculiar
degree for that implication; for it might be contended, that was
only a power to charge; and the estate was to be in the possession
of the eldest son. Of necessity it was to be implied, that the
estate was to be permitted to remain in the eldest son, to bear the
charge; and therefore nothing but a charge could be intended.
But it was held, that as there was nothing to restrain him in the
amount, and he might have charged the utmost value, he had done
only what was equivalent to that; and if the argument as to the
eldest son's receiving 100*l.*, that it amounted to the same as if the
charge had been to the full value except 100*l.*, is used, what is the
argument here? The conclusion there was, that therefore he might
sell the land; and give the son 100*l.*, instead of permitting land of
that value to continue in his possession. It was supposed, he had all
he was entitled to, if he had in money all he could have claimed in
land. That is therefore a direct determination, that a power to
charge includes a power to sell. Then, does not a power
to * give include a power to sell for the purpose of giving   [* 798]
the money instead of the land? It is impossible not to
collect from these cases a principle, that will bear out what is contended by the Defendants; though the case has not precisely occurred in terms.

' Declare the appointment well made, &c. (1).

---

1. THE decree made in the case of *Roberts* v. *Dixwell*, (cited in the principal
case,) is stated from Reg. Lib. B. 1738, fol. 119, 6, in No. 18, Appen. to Sugden
on Powers; and was recognised in *Palmer* v. *Wheeler*, 2 Ball & Bea. 28, as a clear
authority that a power to appoint land may be well executed by a charge of money.
2. The *dictum* ascribed to Sir William Grant in the report of the principal case,
that "the testator had an absolute power to give the *fee simple* to any one of the
children," has been, (apparently with good reason,) supposed by Sanders in the note
to p. 115, of his Treatise on Uses and Trusts, to have arisen from its not having
occurred to the very learned judge, that in the power in question, the usual words,
"for such estate or estates" as the donee of the power should appoint, were omitted.
This omission of words of limitation, Mr. Sanders contends, restrained the exercise
of the power to the appointment of *life estates* only.

---

(1) Upon the law of Appointment see *Boyle* v. *The Bishop of Peterborough, ante,*
vol. i. 299, and the note, 310.

LANE v. WILLIAMS.

The MASTER *of the* ROLLS *for the* LORD CHANCELLOR.

[1802, MARCH 24.]

MOTION under special circumstances upon Affidavit before Answer to restrain proceeding under a judgment refused.

MR. ROMILLY and Mr. *Thompson*, for the Plaintiff, moved for an injunction to restrain the Defendant from proceeding at law upon a judgment obtained twenty-four years ago, and that the bond, upon which it was obtained, should be deposited with the Master; upon affidavit, stating, that the Defendant, a tailor, was in¹ the habit of supplying young men with money, selling horses to them, and dealing in other transactions of a similar nature; that the Plaintiff had borrowed money from him; and incurred a debt of between 500*l.* and 600*l.*, for which the bond and judgment were given; part of the consideration being paid in clothes; and that the judgment had been long satisfied: another security being given.

For the Plaintiff *Patrick* v. *Harrison* (1) was mentioned; where the negotiation of a bill of exchange was restrained.

Mr. *Johnson*, for the Defendant.—Except in the case of waste and cases analogous there is no instance of restraining a proceeding at law before answer or until the Defendant is in contempt for not putting in an answer (2). *Patrick* v. *Harrison* was analogous to the case of waste. This is a very different case. What ground is there for depositing the bond with the Master. It is impossible to restrain the Defendant from proceeding to execution upon affidavit immediately on filing the bill. It is against all the course of the Court.

[* 799]   * Mr. *Romilly*, in reply.—Certainly this application is not made upon the general practice, but upon the particular circumstances, stated in the affidavit; to which no answer is made. The question is, whether under these circumstances, the judgment twenty-four years ago, and no proceeding since, this Court will just on the eve of the vacation, when there will be no opportunity to stay the proceeding, permit him to have the benefit of it.

The MASTER OF THE ROLLS [Sir WILLIAM GRANT].—Is there any instance, where the Court under any circumstances interfered upon affidavit to restrain a legal right?

Mr. *Romilly* mentioned *Isaac* v. *Humpage* (3).

Mr. *Johnson*.—That is a singular case; and the determination has been questioned. But it was upon the ground of fraud.

The MASTER OF THE ROLLS.—It was a case of collusion. I am

---

(1) 3 Bro. C. C. 476.
(2) *Post*, *Anderson* v. *Darcy*, *White* v. *Klevers*, *James* v. *Downes*, vol. xviii. 447 471, 522.
(3) *Ante*, vol. i. 427; 3 Bro. C. C. 463. See the note, *ante*, vol. i. 431.

afraid to make the precedent in such a case as this.   Here is a judgment; and *prima facie* every man, who has a judgment has a right to sue out execution.   It would be a very strong thing to interfere to prevent the legal consequences of a judgment.

The motion was refused.

Sᴇᴇ the notes to *Isaac* v. *Humpage*, 1 V. 427.

BLUNT *v.* CLITHEROW.

[Rᴏʟʟs.—1801, Nov. 30; Dᴇc. 21.   1802, Mᴀʀᴄʜ 25.]

A ʀᴇᴄᴇɪᴠᴇʀ is not to lay out money in repairs at his own discretion; but under circumstances an inquiry was directed; and the Report stating, that the expenditure was for the lasting benefit of the estate, and by the direction of the trustees, the Order for the allowance was made (*a*).

A ᴘᴇᴛɪᴛɪᴏɴ was presented by the Receiver appointed by the Court of the rents and profits of estates devised to the Plaintiff, an infant; praying, that the Master may be directed to allow the petitioner the following sums: 155*l.* 12*s.* 11*d.* for mason's and plaisterer's work; 165*l.* 11*s.* 10*d.* for carpenter's * work ; and   [*800] 140*l.* allowed to a tenant to complete other inside repairs, done to a house, the late residence of the testator, and part of the said estates: the Master having declined to allow these charges in passing the Receiver's accounts without the sanction of the Court.

The petition stated the following facts, verified by the affidavit of the petitioner; that these sums had been really and *bona fide* paid and allowed by the petitioner for the said repairs ; and that the same were in the opinion of the petitioner necessary and proper ; in order to render the house and premises tenantable; and a principal part of the repairs was made, or agreed to be made, previously to the appointment of the petitioner as.Receiver, by the direction and under the inspection of the trustees, to whom the estates were devised. .The petition farther stated, that the trustees had agreed to let the house to a respectable tenant during the infancy of the Plaintiff at a rent of 180*l.* per annum ; and that the tenant was induced to take the house by the said sums being agreed to be laid out in the repairs.

Mr. *Raynsford*, for the trustees, consented to the prayer of the petition.

The Mᴀsᴛᴇʀ ᴏғ ᴛʜᴇ Rᴏʟʟs [Sir Wɪʟʟɪᴀᴍ Gʀᴀɴᴛ] expressed a

(*a*) A receiver has very little discretion allowed him.   He must apply to the Court for liberty to bring or to defend actions.   Jeremy, Eq. Jur. 252; *Green* v. *Winter*, 1 Johns. Ch. 61.   So, also, to let the estate, and in most cases to be allowed to lay out money in repairs.   Ib.   2 Story, Eq. Jur. § 833*a.*   His possession is deemed the possession of the Court.   *Parker* v. *Browning*, 8 Paige, 388.

strong opinion, that he could not make such an order ; but permitted it to be mentioned again, if any precedent could be found.

Dec. 21*st.* Mr. *Kenrick*, in support of the petition.—An order was made upon the 17th of November, 1801, by the Master of the Rolls on the petition of a receiver in the case of *Cross* v. *Omerod ;* by which the Master was directed to inquire into a payment by the receiver of 2206*l.* in discharge of a mortgage, funeral expenses and legacies ; which the Master had declined to allow the receiver.

An order was also made by Lord Rosslyn [Loughborough] as of course, without even ordering the parties to attend him, referring it to the Master to inquire into sums expended by a committee in repairs of a lunatic's estates, and the propriety of future repairs. In *Garland* v. *Garland* a similar order was refused: the re-
[*801] ceiver * having persisted in expending large sums in repairs after prior sums had been allowed him in passing his accounts with a caution from the Master not to lay out any more. There is also an order in Mr. Newport's lunacy referred to by Lord Rosslyn (1). As to the repairs having been done by direction of the trustees, *Inwood* v. *Twine* (2). *Lord Winchelsea* v. *Norcliffe* (3), *Vernon* v. *Vernon* (4). The only authorities containing any thing in opposition to the prayer of this petition are *Fletcher* v. *Dodd* (5) and *Morris* v. *Elme* (6) ; amounting to nothing more than extra-judicial *dicta* as to this point. If the only object of the Court is to have a hold over the receivers, and to prevent a wanton, interested, or extravagant, expenditure, that object is more likely to be obtained, and with less expense, by a course necessarily bringing before the view of the Master such expenditure, than by putting the parties to the expense of a petition to obtain a previous order to consider of the propriety of the expenditure ; when even after that the accounts must again come before the Master.

Dec. 21*st.* The MASTER OF THE ROLLS [Sir WILLIAM GRANT] refused to make the order prayed ; but referred it to the Master to inquire into the circumstances of the expenditure of the said several sums ; and whether the same was for the lasting benefit of all the parties entitled to the said estates ; with liberty to state all special circumstances.

1802. *March* 25*th.* The Master by his Report stated the several facts contained in the petition to have been verified by affidavit; and that the trustees admitted, that the repairs were done by their directions ; that the mansion-house and land adjoining had been let,

(1) *Ante,* vol. ii. 72.
(2) Amb. 417.
(3) 1 Vern. 435.
(4) Before Lord Thurlow. Cited *ante,* vol. i. 456, in *Ex parte Bromfield.*
(5) *Ante,* vol. i. 85; see the note ; where it appears, that the strict rule on this subject has been relaxed.
(6) *Ante,* vol. i. 139.

as stated in the petition ; and that it probably would have remained untenanted, if such repairs had not been done ; and that in his opinion the expenditure was for the lasting benefit of the estate and the parties interested therein : and a petition was presented to confirm the Report.

* Mr. *Kenrick*, in support of the Petition to confirm the [* 802] Report, was stopped by the Court.

The MASTER OF THE ROLLS [Sir WILLIAM GRANT] said, as it was now ascertained, that the repairs were done by the direction of the trustees, he would make the order : but Receivers must understand, that they are not to be permitted to lay out money in repairs at their discretion.

1. THE rule formerly laid down, that neither receivers nor committees ought to be allowed for any expenditure incurred by them, without a previous application to the Court for its sanction ; (*Anonymous case*, 10 Ves. 104 ; *Ex parte Marton*, 11 Ves. 397 ; *Ex parte Hilbert, ibid* ;) at all events, where the expense has been at all considerable ; (*Attorney General* v. *Vigor*, 11 Ves. 563 ; *Waters* v. *Taylor*, 15 Ves. 26 :) has been, in later times, so far relaxed, that although a receiver has laid out money without a previous order of the Court, it is now usual to refer it to the master to see whether the transaction was for the benefit of the parties interested in the estate ; and if the Master make a favorable report, the receiver is allowed the money so laid out. *Tempest* v. *Ord*, 2 Meriv. 56.

2. Since the statute of 55 Geo. 3, c. 192, testamentary dispositions of copyhold are not invalidated for want of a previous surrender to the uses of the testator's will.

FORD *v.* ———.

[1802, APRIL 26.]

ORDER upon the Register of the Consistory Court to deliver original Wills, for the purpose of being produced at the hearing, on security.

MR. STANLEY moved, that the Register of the Consistory Court of Durham may be ordered to deliver several original Wills for the purpose of being produced at the hearing of the cause upon receiving security.

The Lord CHANCELLOR said, there was so much authority for the application, that he could not refuse it ; and that he had found a case among Lord Hardwicke's notes : but his Lordship expressed his surprise, that such a jurisdiction should have been exercised (1).

SEE the note to *Hodson* v. ———, 6 V. 135.

(1) *Hodson* v. ———, *ante*, 135 ; see *Fauquier* v. *Tynte*, *post*, vol. vii. 292, and the notes.

ROSS, *Ex parte.*

[1802, April 27.]

MONEY paid by order of a Friendly Society from time to time upon notes carrying interest, there being no treasurer appointed, is not money in the hands of the party by virtue of any office within the Act of Parliament, 33 Geo. III. c. 54, s. 10, entitling the Society to a preference in case of bankruptcy.

THE petition, presented by the president and stewards of a friendly society under the Act of Parliament (1), prayed that the assignees under a Commission of Bankruptcy may pay the sum of 334*l.* 4*s.* ; which the bankrupt Dawson had in his hands as treasurer at the time of his bankruptcy, either out of the joint or separate estate.

[* 803]   *Upon the affidavit it appeared, that no treasurer had been appointed by this Society. The president and steward were chosen annually. The bankrupt had served the offices of president and steward in different years. In the latter capacity he had received the money of the Society; but not in the former. The money, which was the subject of this petition, was from time to time paid to him by the stewards and clerks by the order of the Society upon promisory notes, bearing interest given by him in the name of the partnership to the president and stewards; and upon a change in the partnership by taking in his sons the security was changed.

The question was, whether under these circumstances this case was within the Act of Parliament.

Mr. *Cox,* in support of the petition.—Though by the rule of this Society no treasurer was formerly appointed, the bankrupt must be considered as coming under that description; and no person was in that situation, if he was not. Neither the president nor the stewards can be so considered. Certainly he was in the habit of giving a note for the money; and undoubtedly if these societies lend their money upon security, they must stand in the same situation as the other creditors. But the bankrupt in all other respects, except giving the note, acted as treasurer; and was considered as such by the Society: the money being from time to time paid to him, and to him only. This case is therefore within the spirit and meaning of the Act.

Mr. *Heald,* for the assignees, contended, that the bankrupt never received this money by virtue of any office; but merely as a banker, or a person, to whom it was paid under a resolution of the Society upon a security, bearing interest; and therefore not within the Act.

Lord CHANCELLOR [ELDON.]—In one case (2) Lord Rosslyn [Loughborough] held, that any man, who got the money of the So-

(1) Stat. 33 Geo. III. c. 54, s. 10.
(2) *Ex parte Ashley, ante,* 441.

ciety into his hands, was within the Act. Upon a subsequent petition (1) I could not agree to that. I had a most clear opinion, that it was impossible to *maintain the proposi- [* 804] tion, that a man, who by consent of the Society receives a sum of money, giving a promisory note for it as a debtor, is within the Act of Parliament an officer receiving it by virtue of his office. The case of another person receiving their money is the subject of another clause (2). If the bankrupt received as steward, president, as any officer of the Society, for what he received by virtue of his office you may make him accountable. But if the president received 300*l.*, and the Society afterwards authorised him to lend that out to a bank, in which he was a partner, they would not have it by virtue of his office. I have no conception upon the meaning of this Act of Parliament, that if they authorise him to lend it out upon security, the persons, to whom it is lent, can be said to have it by virtue of his office. By the consent of the Society it is taken out of that possession by virtue of his office.

I must observe, that, if these Friendly Societies expect the benefit of that very liberal, and perhaps more liberal than just, provision of the Legislature in their favor, that all creditors, however meritorious, shall be sacrificed to their demand, it is their business to take the protection given them in the mode, in which it is directed, by appointing a treasurer and making him give security according to the Act.

The affidavits being contradictory, I will order the Commissioners to inquire, whether any and what sums of money were in his hands at the date of the Commission by virtue of his office belonging to the Society. But let it be understood, my decided opinion is, that if the money was lent by the consent of the Society upon a promissory note, carrying interest, it is not money in his hands by virtue of his office.

You may bring an action, if you please, under this Act.

SEE the note to the case *Ex parte The Amicable Society of Lancaster*, 6 V. 98.

(1) *Ante, Ex parte Corser*, 441; *Ex parte The Amicable Society of Lancaster* 98; see the note, 100.
(2) Sect. 6.

GIFFORD, Ex parte.

[1802, APRIL 27.]

THE discharge of a surety by the creditor has not the effect of a discharge of the
principal without reserve; and therefore a co-surety is not discharged (a).
When it is ascertained, what each of the co-sureties has paid beyond his proportion, the equity as between them is arranged upon the principle of contribution
for the excess (b).
Grounds of the decision, that a discharge of the principal debtor, without a reserve
of the remedy against the surety, discharges the surety, [p. 807.]

MARSHALL and Haigh, creditors of Bedford upon a promissory
note, requiring farther security, Bedford, Niblock and Burgess, and
Baylis, joined in a promissory note, as a collateral security. Niblock
and Burgess and Bedford became bankrupts. Marshall and Haigh
proved the whole debt under each Commission; and afterwards
brought an action against Baylis; who entered into a composition
with his creditors; under which Marshall and Haigh received a div-

---

(a) As to the acts of a creditor which will discharge a surety, see *ante*, note (a),
Rees v. *Barrington*, 2 V. 540; Mr. Perkins's notes (a) and (b) to *Nisbet* v. *Smith*,
2 Bro. C. C. 582.
The principal case was considered by Lord Denman in *Nicholson* v. *Revell*,
4 Adolph. & E. 675; S. C. 6 Nev. & Mann. 200, and it was decided that the
creditor's discharge of one debtor on a joint and several note was *in law* a discharge of all the debtors. Lord Denman said that some of the expressions in *Ex
parte Gifford*, "would seem to lay it down that a joint debtee might release one of
his debtors, and yet, by using some language of reservation in the agreement between himself and such debtor, keep his remedy entire against the others, even
without consulting them. If Lord Eldon used any language which could be so
interpreted, we must conclude that he either did not guard himself so cautiously
as he intended, or that he did not lend that degree of attention to the legal doctrine connected with the case before him, which he was accustomed to afford."
It is said to be doubtful if this rule could be recognised universally in Equity.
1 Story, Eq. Jur. § 498a.
(b) Mr. Theobald in his Treatise on Principal and Surety, (ch. 11, § 283,
note (c), p. 267), thinks this decision could not have been made, and that it is mis-
reported. Mr. Justice Story says: " I see no reason to question either the accuracy of the Report, or the soundness of the doctrine. If the discharge of one
surety is not the discharge of another, it seems difficult to see, how the sum paid
by one surety shall take away the obligation of another to pay his proportion of
the original debt, if, upon the discharge, the right to proceed against such surety
for his proportion was expressly, or by implication reserved, to the extent of that
proportion." See 1 Story, Eq. Jur. § 498a, in the note where this topic is ably
discussed. Pothier adopts very much the same principles and reasoning as Lord
Eldon; asserting that the release by the creditor of one debtor would liberate all
the others, if the creditor meant thereby to extinguish the debt; but not if the
creditor meant to reserve his rights against the other co-debtors for their proportions. 1 Poth. Oblig. by Evans, n. 275, 278, 279, 280, 281, 521. He also holds -
that a discharge of one surety discharges the other sureties, for such proportion of
the debt, as, upon payment of the whole debt, they could have had recourse to
him for. Ibid, n. 275, 277, 280, 281, 428, 429, 445, 519, 520, 521, 523, [n. 556-560
of the French editions]. The rule of the Roman law is the same. See 1 Story,
Eq. Jur. § 498a, note.
Lord Redesdale has said; "If the creditor discharges one of the coparceners,
he cannot proceed for his whole debt against the others; at the most, they are only
bound for their proportions." *Stirling* v. *Forrester*, 3 Bligh. 591.

idend of 4s. in the pound ; the receipt for which was expressed to be for 191l. and two notes, which, when duly paid, will be in full of the said debt and all other demands from him. The dividend paid by the estate of Bedford was 4s. in the pound ; and that by the estate of Niblock and Burgess 5s.

The prayer of this petition was, that the proof against the estate of Niblock and Burgess may be expunged.

Mr. *Romilly* and Mr. *Whishaw*, in support of the petition.—There is no doubt upon the cases of *Rees* v. *Berrington* (1), *Nisbet* v. *Smith* (2), *Ex parte Smith* (3), *English* v. *Darley* (4), and *Law* v. *The East India Company* (5), that the creditor discharging the principal debtor discharges the surety. The question is, whether any difference arises from the circumstance, that this is the discharge of a co-surety. By settling in this manner with the co-surety Niblock and Burgess have every equity they could have had against him. They have put themselves in the situation of Baylis. The remedy then is, if it does not go to the extent of the prayer of the petition, to expunge the whole debt, that at least the estate of Niblock and Burgess is to be answerable only for so much as they are bound to pay, this transaction having taken place, and to stand in their place for a moiety of the dividends they may receive.

Mr. *Richards*, Mr. *Alexander*, and Mr. *Cooke*, *contra*.—This is not to be compared to the case of principal and surety. Bedford was *the original debtor. Other persons after-   [* 806] wards joined him in giving a security for the debt. The creditor may proceed against either. The only relief could have been a contribution among the sureties. If a surety offers to pay part of the debt, the creditor by receiving it does not affect his security : nor is the person discharged. No injury is done to any one. On the contrary the other persons liable are eased to the extent of the payment. It cannot affect the right to call upon the other debtors for the residue. So, if the creditor brings an action, and in the course of that action one of the sureties pays part of the debt, that can make no difference. That is no injury, but an ease, to the others. As to the form of the receipt, it is merely a discharge of that surety. There is no objection in the creditor saying, he will not call on that person for any more. No injury is done to any one by undertaking not to sue him. The creditor cannot be compelled to sue any one ; but may select any one. Baylis could not resist a bill for a contribution on the ground, that the creditor undertook to demand no more from him. The contribution must depend upon what they actually pay ; when that shall be ascertained. The ground of the cases cited is, that no step should be taken, which would have the immediate effect of throwing upon the party dis-

(1) *Ante*, vol. ii. 540 ; see the note, 544 ; *ante*, 734.
(2) 2 Bro. C. C. 579.
(3) 3 Bro. C. C. 1 ; 1 Cooke's Bank. Law, 168, 170, 4th edit ; 190, 8th edit.
(4) 2 Bos. & Pul. 61.
(5) *Ante*, vol. iv. 824.

Lord Thurlow, admitted, that, if there is a reserve of the remedies against the others, there is consent of the party, with whom the composition is made; and if out of that a demand arises against him, it is a demand, which began to exist with his consent expressed in the terms of the contract, and under some circumstances wisely and prudently given; for the party would not have entered into the contract, unless he was allowed to contract for that remedy over against the co-sureties. If Niblock and Burgess should not pay more than their moiety, the contract would be a beneficial contract for Baylis; for though paying more than Baylis they would not pay enough to bring an assumpsit against him. That would not therefore be an imprudent bargain for Baylis to make. It may however never be necessary to decide this; as it depends upon what dividends the estate of Bedford and of Niblock and Burgess pay. But I have a strong opinion, that under the circumstances the other persons liable upon this note are discharged, because Baylis was contented to make a bargain, the effect of which leaves him to his chance as to his ultimate liability between him and his co-surety; and therefore that relief cannot be given even to the extent, to which it is now modified.

The order was, that under the present circumstances the petition should be dismissed without costs, and without prejudice to presenting any other petition. ____

1. THAT a release to a principal debtor, (without special stipulations that the security for the debt shall not be liquidated, but that the remedy against the surety shall be preserved,) is a release to the surety; see, ante, note 2 to *Rees* v. *Berrington*, 2 V. 540; and although co-sureties do not stand in precisely the same relation to each other as principal and surety do, yet the principles are in a great measure the same: an arrangement between the creditor and the principal debtor may be of such a nature as to prevent the surety from enforcing that immediate payment over which is his right: and if such be the case, it is only reasonable that the creditor should be held to have discharged the surety, whom he has deprived of his remedy. So, although one surety has no remedy over against his co-surety, until he himself has actually paid more than his proportion of the demand, and when he has done this, and not before, his claim to contribution arises; yet if his means of enforcing this claim have been delayed by any arrangement between his co-surety and the creditor, it seems he will be discharged. *Mayhew* v. *Crickett*, 2 Swanst. 192.

2. Questions as to contribution, when a debt has been paid by one of several parties, all liable thereto, are proper for investigation and decision in Courts of Equity; *Rogers* v. *Mackenzie*, 4 Ves. 752; *Wright* v. *Hunter*, 5 Ves. 794; and more especially when the sureties are numerous, and there might be a multiplicity of actions at law upon the subject; *Craythorne* v. *Swinburne*, 14 Ves. 164. The right of contribution between sureties, (to the extent for which each has engaged himself,) will be just the same, whether they respectively became sureties by one, or by several instruments; *Cooke* v. ———, 2 Freem. 97; *Craythorne* v. *Swinburne, ubi supra*; *Mayhew* v. *Crickett*, 2 Swanst. 192; *Dering* v. *Earl of Winchelsea*, 1 Cox, 319; as to which last cited case, see Lord Eldon's observations in *Ex parte Hunter*, Buck. 556, and Lord Redesdale's remarks in *Stirling* v. *Forrester*, 4 Bligh, 590, 596.

WEBSTER, *Ex parte.*

The MASTER *of the* ROLLS *for the* LORD CHANCELLOR.

[1802, MARCH 26.]

ORDER upon petition for leave to traverse an Inquisition upon a Commission of Escheat, found in favor of the Crown.

THIS petition prayed leave to traverse the Inquisitions upon two Commissions of Escheat, found in favor of the Crown. The Commissions issued in 1798. The petitioner claimed as heir at * law of Mary Gardiner; stating, that she died, seised [* 810] in fee of the estates in question, in the counties of Northampton and Kent; and that her will was not executed according to the Statute of Frauds (1). In 1801 an ejectment was brought by the father and mother of the petitioner against the grantees of the Crown; in which the Plaintiffs were nonsuited, upon the return to the Commission.

Mr. *Romilly* and Mr. *Lewis*, in support of the Petition.—Of course the party is entitled to traverse the inquisition; if the Court is satisfied, there is reason to believe he is heir at law. It has been determined that the statute extended to Commissions of escheat as well as inquisitions by virtue of office. That is laid down in Stamford upon the prerogative; where a great deal is stated upon this. There is in this instance an affidavit of the pedigree; stating, that it was proved upon the trial of the ejectment: but it is not clear, that it is necessary, he should go into evidence of his pedigree, as upon an ejectment, or as he must upon traversing the inquisition; for this is a proceeding *ex parte;* and the jury must find, if there is no evidence to the contrary, that the party died without heirs. But though it is only necessary for the petitioner to state his belief of his being heir, he has gone into evidence of the pedigree.

Mr. *Richards* and Mr. *Cooke, contra.*—It is certainly necessary, that the person applying should make out a title, as much as upon an ejectment: Vaughan, 64: that is; he must show evidence, that would satisfy a Jury. Probable evidence, such as would be received in a Court of Law ought to be produced. The words of the Statute are "traverse that office or otherwise to show his right." Though the nonsuit in the ejectment was upon the production of the return to the Commission, the affidavits against the Commission state, that the Judge observed, the evidence was very loose. Upon such an application this Court will take care, that parties are not harassed, and put to an unnecessary expense. Therefore in lunacy a strong ground is always required upon the sanity and also upon the interest of the party applying (2). None of these affidavits show, that the registers have been searched as to marriage and

(1) Stat. 29 Ch. II. c. 3.
(2) See *Ex parte Ward, ante,* 579.

births, so as to produce evidence fit to be received in a Court of Law. At least security ought to be given for the costs; as has been done in lunacy.

Mr. *Romilly* in reply.—The party is entitled to traverse. The meaning of the words in the Statute referred to is, that it shall not prevent a petition of right; not to vest a discretion in the Court. The petitioner lays a *primâ facie* title; and it is not necessary here, upon an application *ex parte* in its nature to give all the evidence. Uncontradicted it is sufficient; and the Jury must find upon it. As to the costs there can be none. The king neither pays, nor receives costs. The Court is not at liberty to impose terms upon the party.

The MASTER OF THE ROLLS [Sir WILLIAM GRANT] took time to consider; and afterwards made the order.

The traverse was found in favor of the Crown.

It was agreed at the bar, that the application to the Court was proper; as in lunacy; though the words of that Statute (1) are full as strong; and the late cases *Ex parte Wragg, Ex parte Ferne* (2), were referred to (3).   ———

THE Statutes of Escheat are the 34th Edw. III. c. 14, the 36th Edw. III. c. 13, the 8th Hen. VI. c. 16, and the 1st Hen. VIII. c. 10: the provisions of these statutes, as to the qualifications of jurors upon escheats, have been altered by the 62d section of the stat. 6 Geo. IV. c. 50. The principal case was considered *in re Sadler*, 1 Mad. 582, as a binding decision, that the Court of Chancery has authority to allow a traverse to inquisitions of escheat, when a *prima facie* case is made out, to the satisfaction of the Court, that the petitioner is the heir at law of the party whose property the inquisition has found to be escheated; but a doubt was expressed, whether a party who, though alleging himself to be the heir at law, claims the escheated premises merely as a trustee, ought to be allowed to traverse. It has been determined, however, that the right of the subject to traverse inquisitions, by which property is found to be in the Crown, is not confined to cases in which the Crown claims the property by reason of the *incidents of tenure;* but is a general right, extending to every inquisition by which property is found to be in the Crown. *Ex parte Lord Guydir,* 4 Mad. 323. As to the right of traversing the proceedings under a commission of lunacy; see, *ante,* the notes to *Ex parte Wragg,* 5 V. 450.

———

EXLEIGH, Ex parte.

[1802, APRIL 28.]

PROOF under a Commission of Bankruptcy against an Overseer of the Poor in respect of money in his hands at the time of his bankruptcy before the period of accounting.

THE object of this petition was to prove under a Commission of Bankruptcy against one of the Overseers of the Poor in respect of money in his hands at the time of his bankruptcy.

---

(1) Stat. 2 Ed. VI. c. 8.
(2) *Ante,* vol. v. 450, 832.
(3) *Sadler's Case,* 1 Madd. 581; *Ex parte Lord Guydir,* 4 Madd. 361.

Mr. *Cooke* mentioned the case of *The King* v. *Egginton* (1), as unsatisfactory; observing upon the reason assigned by Mr. Justice Buller, that there could be no action, that still there might be a good equitable debt; which might be proved.

* The Lord CHANCELLOR disapproved that case: ob-   [* 812] serving, it was very dangerous to hold, that, because the time of accounting had not arrived, in case of the bankruptcy of the trustees there was not such an assumpsit as could enable them to prove. His Lordship said, that if there was no opposition, the order should be made.

IF a collector of taxes, who has received the taxes from the inhabitants of the parish or district, but who has not paid them over, become bankrupt, one of the inhabitants may prove for himself and the rest, against the bankrupt's estate. *Ex parte Child,* 1 Atk. 111.

GREENWAY, *Ex parte.*

[1802, APRIL 8.]

PROOF allowed under a Commission of Bankruptcy in respect of a bill alleged to be lost: but the most extensive indemnity to be given; and to be settled by the Commissioners (*a*).
Profert now dispensed with at law (*b*). The reason of that decision questionable, [p. 813.]

THE object of this petition was to be admitted to prove under a Commission of Bankruptcy in respect of a bill of exchange, alleged to be lost after indorsement. The affidavits stated, that the bill was returned from America protested; and the ship was captured in her return; and taken into the Isle of Rhe in Brittany.

Lord CHANCELLOR [ELDON].—To enable you to prove in respect of this bill, there must be a most extensive indemnity, even for the

(1) 1 Term Rep. B. R. 369.
(*a*) One ground of the peculiar jurisdiction of Equity in the cases of lost bonds and other instruments is in the incompetency of a Court of law to order a proper bond of indemnity to the defendant. 1 Story, Eq. Jur. § 82–86. See *Leroy* v. *Veedle,* 1 Johns. Cas. 417; *Pintard* v. *Tackington,* 10 Johns. 105; *Shields* v. *Commonwealth,* 4 Rand, 541; *Irwin* v. *Planters' Bank,* 1 Humph. 145. As to the proof of lost instruments, see 1 Greenleaf, Evid. § 558.
The Court in Massachusetts has no jurisdiction in cases of lost deeds, as an independent ground of Chancery jurisdiction. *Campbell* v. *Sheldon,* 13 Pick. 8. But the plaintiff may have a discovery in such case, as incidental to a question of trust. Ibid, 20.
(*b*) Until a recent period, there could be no remedy on a lost bond in a Court of Common Law, because there could be no *profert* of the instrument, without which the declaration would be defective. At present the Courts of law do entertain the jurisdiction, and dispense with the *profert*, if an allegation of loss by time and accident is stated in the declaration. 1 Story, Eq. Jur. § 81; *Read* v. *Brookman,* 3 T. R. 151; *Totty* v. *Nesbitt,* 3 T. R. 153; 1 Chitty, Pl. (9th Am. ed.) 365, 366; *Cutts* v. *United States,* 1 Gallis. 69; *Powers* v. *Ware,* 2 Pick. 451; *Smith* v. *Emery,* 7 Halst. 53; *Rees* v. *Overbaugh,* 6 Cowen, 748, 749; *Kelly* v. *Riggs,* 2 Root, 126; *Hinsdale* v. *Mills,* 5 Conn. 331.

sake of the bankrupt, who is interested in this; a complete indemnity, going to all the consequences against the holder, if the bill has not been paid, and against any demand, that may be made by future possible holders, if it should have been paid. When I was Chief Justice, I tried an action in the Common Pleas upon a bill, alleged to be lost: which had been previously endorsed by the payee. An indemnity was offered by bond: but I nonsuited the Plaintiff. The Counsel objected strongly upon the offer of indemnity; and it came before the Court upon a motion for a new trial; and there was a long discussion upon the nature of these indemnities in a Court of Law. The Court had not come to a decision upon it, when I left them; and I do not know the result. But I never could understand, by what authority Courts of Law compelled parties to take the indemnity.

Upon the new doctrine of dispensation with the *profert* of a bond that difficulty does not arise; for there is the finding of the Jury upon the evidence, that the instrument is lost; which is conclusive between those parties. That has been settled at law, certainly in opposition to the opinions of some of the greatest lawyers.
[* 813] * Since I have sat here, I have found in Lord Hardwicke's own hand (and he was one of the greatest lawyers, who ever sat in Westminster Hall) his most positive declarations, that upon such an instrument it is impossible to maintain an action without *Profert* (1). The law is however now settled otherwise (2). I do not presume to dispute it; for it may be settled upon grounds of pleading: it may proceed upon a supposed analogy to the proceedings in Courts of Equity; and it may proceed upon both. With regard to the supposed analogy to proceedings in Equity, it is questionable, whether sufficient attention was paid to the consideration, that in equity the conscience is ransacked; and the party alleging, that the instrument is lost, must make an affidavit, that it is not in his possession or power (3). The consequence is, that if a man having an annuity deed differing from the memorial is dishonest enough to put it in the fire, and then to say, it is lost, he is to prove the contents. The best mode of doing that seems to by producing the memorial; and yet that memorial, if the deed was produced, would have destroyed the deed (4).

The order was, that the petitioner should be admitted to prove upon giving an indemnity; the Commissioners to settle a proper indemnity (5).

1. SEE, *ante*, note 2 to *Toulmin* v. *Price.* 5 V. 235, and the farther references there given, as to the concurrent jurisdiction, at all events, of Courts of Equity, in many cases in which Courts of Law now profess to give relief.

(1) 1 Ves. 345, 393.
(2) *Read* v. *Brookman*, 3 Term Rep. B. R. 151. See the note, *ante*, vol. v. 236.
(3) See Mr. Fonblanque's note, Treatise of Equity, 16, 2d edit.
(4) For the alteration of the law upon annuities, see the note, *ante*, vol. ii. 36.
(5) *Walmsley* v. *Child*, 1 Ves. 341.

2. One strong argument for the *exclusive* jurisdiction of Equity in respect of lost securities, in all cases where complete justice to all parties cannot be done without securing indemnity to the payer, should the security be subsequently brought forward by a *bona fide* holder for valuable consideration, is the great difficulty of securing indemnity at law; *East India Company* v. *Boddam*, 9 Ves. 460; *Pierson* v. *Hutchinson*, 2 Swanst. 213; for a Court of Law cannot give a conditional judgment; *Mossop* v. *Eadon*, 16 Ves. 433; but where the lost instrument is not a negotiable one, as, for instance, where it is a promissory note, not payable to order, but only to the demand of the creditor; there, if the legal remedy can do justice to all parties, and no indemnity is necessary to be given, Equity, it seems, will not interfere. *S. C.* p. 434.

3. In *Davis* v. *Dodd*, 4 Taunt. 603, the Court of Common Pleas decided, that a plaintiff who has declared on a bill of exchange ought to produce it, and that, if he has lost it, the drawer is neither under legal or moral obligation to pay the amount to the party whose negligence has exposed him to the danger of being compelled to pay the bill when produced in the hands of another holder. The Court farther held that an express promise to pay the contents of a lost bill of exchange, which remains regularly negotiable, if given without some new consideration, could not be enforced. A suit in Equity was subsequently commenced, respecting the said bill of exchange, in the Court of Exchequer, and is reported in 4 Price, 176, and in Wils. Ex. Rep. 110, the bill being a negotiable one, the question was held proper for a Court of Equity to entertain, and it was referred to the proper officer to settle the indemnity requisite for the payer's security.

4. Though a promise to pay the amount of a lost bill of exchange, not overdue, and therefore freely negotiable, has been held to be (as above stated) a mere *nudum pactum;* yet when it is proved that the bill, subsequently lost, was not negotiated, at all events, till after the time of payment had arrived, there, as the bill, if it afterwards passed into other hands, would be subject to all the payer's equities in respect thereof; an agreement by the payee to discharge the payer from payment of the bill, on his engaging to pay, in a different mode, the money therein mentioned, is a sufficient consideration for such engagement. *Williamson* v. *Clement*, 1 Taunt. 523.

5. Where a vendor has received from the vendee in payment for goods sold, a bill of exchange, not due, drawn and accepted by two other persons, and the vendee has indorsed the bill in blank, should the vendor lose the bill before it is paid, he cannot sue the vendee, either for the price of the goods, or on the lost bill; having by his carelessness deprived the vendee of all means of recovering over, he must not turn round and sue the vendee for goods which have already cost him their full value. *Champion* v. *Terry*, 3 Brod. & Bing. 296; *Bevan* v. *Hill*, 2 Camp. 38˝.

6. If a security were proved to be *destroyed,* Lord Ellenborough declared he should have felt no difficulty on the receiving evidence of its contents, and directing a jury to find a verdict for the amount; but his Lordship added, that it is a very different case when a note is only stated to be lost; there, (as stated in the preceding notes,) if the bill was indorsed in blank, and was not overdue, it may have got into the hands of a *bona fide* indorsee for value, who might maintain an action upon it against a drawer. This brings the point to a question of indemnity, but whether an indemnity be sufficient or insufficient, his Lordship thought a Court of Law could not judge; he added, that there are *dicta,* to be sure, that upon the offer of an indemnity, the payee of a lost bill may recover at law; but those *dicta* are contrary to the principles upon which our judicial system rests; and if a plaintiff can neither produce a bill nor prove that it is destroyed, he ought to resort to a Court of Equity for relief: *Pierson* v. *Hutchinson*, 2 Camp. 212: much to the same effect are *Mayor* v. *Johnson and Eaton*, 3 Camp. 325; *Dangerfield* v. *Wilby*, 4 Espin. 159; *Poole* v. *Smith*, Holt's N. P. C. 145; *Powell* v. *Roach*, 6 Espin. 77. In opposition to the rule, that in order to recover upon a bill of exchange at law, the bill must be produced, or proofs given of its destruction; the case of *Brown* v. *Messiter*, 3 Mau. & Sel. 381 may be cited: in that case, upon the production of a copy of a bill which had been stolen, (the copy being verified by affidavit,) it was referred to the Master to see what was due for principal and interest upon the said bill. It should be observed, however, that no opposition was made to this proceeding, and even if the rule was not made by consent, still, as it was both obtained

and made absolute before a single judge, the precedent can hardly be esteemed of more weight than any one of the contrary decisions at *nisi prius.*

7. It should be observed, that although in ordinary cases, a plaintiff at law who declares upon a bill of exchange should produce it, yet where the party liable improperly detains the bill in his hands, he may nevertheless be sued thereon, notice being given to him to produce the bill; on his default to do which, parol evidence of the contents may be given. *Smith* v. *M'Clure,* 5 East, 476.

8. The maker of a promissory note cannot be liable in respect thereof to two parties at the same time; a holder, therefore, of one divided part of such an instrument, which part he produces, alleging the other to be lost, need not come into Equity to obtain payment, for no indemnity is in such case requisite for the security of the payer; and the holder of one half of such instrument, proving the other half to be lost, may sustain an action at law which, under those circumstances, is his proper remedy. *Mossop* v. *Eadon,* 16 Ves. 430. But the case would have been very different with respect to the half of a bank note, the holder thereof could only require payment upon giving an indemnity, a reasonable degree of relief, but one which we have seen in the preceding notes, is best fitted for the jurisdiction of Equity. At Law, payment of a bank note can only be enforced by production of the entire note; or by proof that the instrument, or the part of it which is wanting, has been actually destroyed: for the missing part may have got into the hands of a *bona fide* holder for value, who would have as good a right of suit upon that, as the holders of the other half would have in respect of the part produced by them. *Mayor* v. *Johnston and Eaton,* 3 Camp. 325.

CLAY, *Ex parte.*

[1802, April 28.]

Joint creditors admitted to prove under a separate Commission for the purpose of keeping separate accounts and assenting to or dissenting from the certificate, but not to receive dividends with the separate creditors.

This petition was presented by joint creditors; praying, that they may be admitted to prove and receive dividends under a separate commission.

[* 814]   *Mr. Johnson,* in support of the petition.

Lord Chancellor [Eldon].—The rule, that prevailed in Lord Hardwicke's time, and down to the time of Lord Thurlow was, that joint creditors should not be admitted to prove under a separate Commission for the purpose of receiving dividends with the separate creditors. Lord Thurlow altered that upon much consideration; thinking, the joint creditors ought to be admitted with the separate creditors; and left it so, when he left this Court. Lord Loughborough thought, that was not right; and got back again, not quite to the old rule; but he settled it, that they should prove only for the purpose of keeping separate accounts, but not to receive a dividend. I do not presume to say, which is the best rule; except, that the last is open to this difficulty; that the creditor is not a party to the proceedings under the Commission. But I think it better to follow the rule, that I find established, than to let it be continually changing, so that no one can tell, how it is. Therefore

unless some more prominent mischief can be pointed out, take the
order according to Lord Loughborough's rule (1).

See the note to *Ex parte Elton*, 3 V. 238.

STREET v. RIGBY.   [* 815]

[1802, APRIL 30.]

To a bill for discovery and relief Plea of an agreement to refer to arbitration over-
ruled.
Bill for specific performance of an agreement to refer to arbitration does not lie (*a*),
[p. 818.]
Variation as to a Plea : good to the Relief, but bad to the Discovery (*b*), [p. 819.]
Courts of Equity will not be ancillary to arbitrators by permitting the party to take
relief from them, coming to the Court for discovery (*c*), [p. 821.]
As to the effect of a covenant to forbear suit, *Quære* (*d*), [p. 821.]
Agreement to refer to arbitration does not bar an Action (*e*), [p. 822.]

THE bill stated articles of agreement between the Plaintiff and
Defendant, to become partners as attorneys and solicitors; by which

(1) *Ante, Ex parte Elton*, vol. iii. 238 ; *Ex parte Abell*, iv. 837. See the cases
collected, 1 Cooke's Bank. Law, 237, 4th edit. ; 8th edition, by Mr. Roots, 259,
and the note, *ante*, vol. iii. 243.
Ex parte Pinkerton, before Lord Eldon, 20th April, 1801 :—
The prayer of the petition was to be at liberty to prove under a separate commission the sum of 223*l*. 18*s*. 6*d*. upon a bill of exchange, drawn by two persons ; one
of whom was solvent, but abroad, and not likely to return ; and the other was the
bankrupt. They were connected only in this transaction. There was no joint
property.
The Lord Chancellor [ELDON] said, whatever he thought of a settled rule, he
should adhere to it, on account of the mischief arising from shaking settled rules ;
but observed, that it seemed very singular, that the nature of the debt should turn
upon the fact, whether there is joint property, or not.
His Lordship made the order, that the petitioner should be admitted to prove his
debt ; reciting, that it was admitted, there was no joint property.
In *Ex parte Nuttall*, 22d June, 1801, the Lord Chancellor also followed the
cases before Lord Loughborough ; observing, that he did so, that the rule should
not change with every new Judge, rather than from any other motive.
(*a*) This is not merely on the ground of public policy, but also upon the ground of
the utter inadequacy of arbitrators to administer entire justice between the parties,
from a defect of power in them to examine under oath and to compel the production of papers, as well as upon the ground of the utter impracticability of a Court
of Equity's compelling a suitable performance of such a stipulation between the
parties. Story, Partnership, § 215 ; 1 Story, Eq. Jur. § 670. See *ante*, note (*a*),
Mitchell v. *Harris*, 2 V. 129.
(*b*) See *ante*, note (*b*), *Brandon* v. *Sands*, 2 V. 514 ; note (*a*), *Renison* v. *Ashley*,
2 V. 459.
(*c*) Story, Eq. Pl. § 554, § 555 ; 2 Story, Eq. Jur. § 1495.
(*d*) A covenant not to sue operates as a release, to avoid circuity of actions.
See *ante*, note (*b*), *Mitchell* v. *Harris*, 2 V. 129.
(*e*) *Cartee* v. *Dawson*, 2 Bland, 264 ; 2 Madd. Ch. Pr. (4th Am. ed.) 318 ; *Allegre*
v. *Maryland Ins. Co.* 6 Harr. & J. 408 ; *Randal* v. *Chesapeake Canal Co.* 1 Har-
ring. 234 ; *Gray* v. *Wilson*, 4 Watts, 39 ; *Miles* v. *Stanley*, 1 Miles, 418 ; *Stone*
v. *Dennis*, 3 Porter, 231.

articles it was declared, that the partnership should be bound by all usual and customary conditions of partnership concerns, as fully as though the usual covenants, clauses and provisos, were inserted: and that either partner should have power to dissolve the partnership on giving two months' notice previous to the 1st of September, 1797, or any succeeding 1st of September: all disputes to be referred to arbitration ; and the arbitrators to have a power of dissolving the partnership, if they shall think proper.   The partnership was dissolved by consent upon the 1st of September, 1799.

The bill then stated that the Plaintiff made out the accounts; that several meetings took place for the purpose of examining them; at one of which meetings all the errors were finally settled and corrected, as far as the Plaintiff was then enabled to do so from the accounts rendered by the Defendant, and except as to a sum of 105l.; which had been received by the Defendant without the knowledge of the Plaintiff; but the Defendant, though requested, refused to settle or sign any account.   The Plaintiff afterwards sent the Defendant a draft of an agreement for arranging the outstanding debts : but no answer being returned, and the Plaintiff having found, that the Defendant had received 105l.; which had never been brought to account, Plaintiff claimed his share of that sum.   On the 1st of November, 1800, accounts were mutually delivered ; and there was only 4s. difference ; and the only sum in dispute was the said sum of 105l.; to which the Defendant claims to be entitled as separate money ; and the Defendant admitting, that the 105l. was the only question in dispute, that question alone was submitted to arbitration ; but the arbitrator declining to proceed on the reference, the Plaintiff sent the Defendant an account up to that time, and demanded payment.

[* 816]   * The bill farther stated, that without an account from the Defendant of his subsequent receipts on account of the partnership it will be impossible for any arbitrator to ascertain, what are the matters in difference between the parties; and charging, that the accounts stated to the Defendant were true, and that all the neccessary vouchers were communicated to him; and that the Defendant refused the account desired by the Plaintiff, prayed, that the Defendant may account for all sums received by him on the partnership account, not credited in the account rendered by him; and that the Plaintiff may be declared entitled to three fourths of the 105l.; an account of what is due to the Plaintiff on the accounts delivered ; with liberty to surcharge and falsify ; and that the Defendant may be decreed to pay the balance on the whole accounts aforesaid, with interest.

The Defendant pleaded in bar to the whole bill that the Plaintiff and Defendant by articles of partnership, dated the 27th of July, 1796, agreed to become partners from Christmas last to the 1st of September next, and from the 1st of September for one year, and so from year to year, subject to the provision for dissolution, &c. ; and it was thereby agreed, that all disputes relating to the said partnership, and the accounts, transactions and dealings, of the said parties in consequence thereof should be referred to arbitration.

The plea there referred to the articles; and averred, that all the discovery and relief sought by the bill relate to the partnership, and to the accounts, transactions, and dealings, of the parties, in conse- quence thereof only; and that the same have not, nor hath any part thereof, been referred to arbitration, except as to the sum of 105*l.* ; which alone was referred to arbitration: but as to that the arbitrator has declined to proceed; and such arbitration is determined without any award; and the Plaintiff did not even propose a reference, or nom- inate an arbitrator of the said matters and disputes, except as to that sum of 105*l.*; in respect whereof the arbitration is determined, as aforesaid; although the Defendant offered and was always ready and hereby offers to refer the same to arbitration.

* Mr. *Piggott* and Mr. *Hall* argued in support of the   [* 817] Plea; and cited the following cases: *Wellington* v. *M'In- tosh* (1). *Halfhide* v. *Fenning* (2). *Kill* v. *Hollister* (3). *Mit- chell* v. *Harris* (4). *Tattersall* v. *Groote* (5). *Astley* v. *Weldon* (6).

Mr. *Richards*, for the Plaintiff, was stopped by the Court.

Lord CHANCELLOR [ELDON].—This bill is produced upon a no- tion, that the matter averred in the plea in some way ousts the juris- diction of this Court; I do not know, whether the argument supposes it destroyed, but by putting it, as it were, in abeyance and suspension, till some proceeding is had before arbitrators. I give this Defendant the benefit of the construction put by him upon the articles: though it is fairly questionable, attending to the articles, whether the coven- ant extends to a settlement of all accounts posterior to the dissolu- tion. I will for the present purpose take that to be the meaning of the covenant. It has occured to me, that in almost every case of this sort the parties have adopted a fancy, that they can make any thing in the contemplation of the Court fit to be considered matter of dispute, upon which they think proper to dispute. That is not so. It must be that, which a Court will say, is fairly and reasonably made matter of dispute. Another circumstance is, that the parties do not frequently appreciate the effect of such a covenant. First, at Law, in the case in the Court of Common Pleas the Judges Heath and Rooke seemed to think it futile, and tantamount to a covenant to forbear suit. I take notice of the circumstance, as material with regard to *Halfhide* v. *Fenning*; for if the meaning of a covenant to refer is to forbear suit altogether, that covenant to refer, before you bring suit, and to suspend it in the mean time, would stand upon principles *pro tempore*, that it would be very difficult to say do not apply to both those covenants. Suppose an action brought. The

(1) 2 Atk. 569.
(2) 2 Bro. C. C. 336.
(3) 1 Wils. 129.
(4) 4 Bro. C. C. 411; *ante*, vol. ii. 129. See the note, 137, and Mr. Beames's Elements of Pleas in Equity, 232.
(5) 2 Bos. & Pul. 131.
(6) 2 Bos. & Pul. 346.

question would be, what the damages would have been, if the
Defendant had joined, and named an arbitrator, and evidence had
been produced (and what that would be could by no means be correctly proved) and an award had been made, giving some supposed
sum, which no proof could ascertain. The effect there-
[* 818]   fore of such a * covenant is, that as the damages are not
to be ascertained by evidence, nominal damages only can
be got. Whose fault is it? There are prudential ways of drawing
these articles. There might have been an agreement for liquidated
damages, to enforce a specific performance, if an action could not
produce sufficient damages, or Equity would not entertain a bill for
a specific performance. If they had enforced their legal remedy by
such a stipulated security, it would be very difficult to say, they
would also have a remedy in Equity. In the case from Astley's
Theatre (1) there was no dispute in the Court of Common Pleas, that
the actress might have agreed upon a liquidated sum to be forfeited
for non-attendance, &c. The Court were of opinion very properly,
that, where there was a stipulated sum in the covenant, that was the
stipulated damages; and the general sum of 200l. for breach of any
of the articles was a penalty: but it was not doubted, that sum might
have been made the liquidated damages, if they thought proper.
The party must put himself in a situation to have substantial damages.
In this case upon an action they could have only 1s.; for they could
not ascertain, what more they were to have.

Then what can they have in Equity? There is considerable
weight, as evidence of what the Law is, in the circumstance, that no
instance is to be found of a decree for specific performance of an
agreement to name arbitrators; or that any discussion upon it has taken
place in experience for the last twenty-five years. I was Counsel in
Price v. Williams (2): a case which justifies considerable doubts,
whether the eulogia upon the domestic forum of arbitrators are well
founded. That was a case before Lord Thurlow upon a bill for specific performance of such an agreement, sending parties to arbitrators, who might or might not be able to come to a decision; and
Lord Thurlow was of opinion, that the Court would not perform
such an agreement. The Court, if it is not part of the agreement,
cannot give them authority to examine upon oath; and the agreement itself cannot authorise any person to administer an oath. A
difficulty arises from the want of the conscience of the party.
This Court has given credit to itself, notwithstanding what
[* 819]   has passed in the Court of King's * Bench in their rules
upon Attachments, as likely to decide as well as arbitrators; and it requires a strong case to deprive a person of the right
to a decision here. In Price v. Williams the account came back
very favorable to my client: the result being, that a very small sum
was due from him. A vast number of exceptions were taken; and

(1) Astley v. Weldon, 2 Bos. & Pul. 346.
(2) 3 Bro. C. C. 163; ante, vol. i. 365.

the Court felt that sort of difficulty of dealing with the exceptions, that led to an arbitration ; though at first the Court would not hear of it ; and the party, who had not been able to establish any thing before the Master, in that mode gained several thousand pounds.— Then the difficulty occurred about the power of this Court to review the decision of arbitrators ; and in the end my client fared much worse than he would have done before the Master. That case and others led me to adopt a rule never to advise an arbitration afterwards.

If such a bill never has been usually filed in this Court, and if in that instance Lord Thurlow was of opinion it could not be maintained, the jurisdiction would stand upon principles not very intelligible, if a party, who by the imbecility belonging to the covenant could recover only 1s. damages in an action, coming to this Court for substantial justice, to have an account taken, that person, who could not file a bill for a specific execution of the agreement to refer, can say, that though he admits, neither of them could recover more than 1s. at law, and he cannot demand the relief by way of a specific performance, he can have it by pleading the covenant, if he is brought in the character of a Defendant ; and can compel the other to go to that tribunal, to which the Defendant coming in the character of Plaintiff could not oblige him to resort. It is very difficult to say, that should be the law of the Court. Then, is it so? I look upon the case of *Wellington* v. *M'Intosh* as an authority, that at that time it was not the law of the Court. At that period (1) the distinction, taken in later cases (2), had not obtained ; and the plea, though it might have been good as to the relief, was bad, if bad as to the discovery. As to that the course of the latter authorities seems to have altered the law of pleading (3). But *quoad* such a point as this the plea, if good to the relief, must be good to the discovery ; for this plea means this, if any thing ; that the parties will not harass * themselves by going to Courts   [* 820] of Justice ; but will state to each other what is in dispute, and refer that to arbitrators ; and entering into such a covenant they must be taken to mean, that they will be content with a decision upon such discovery as arbitrators can compel, without subjecting each other to the necessity for either to be examined upon oath, before arbitrators, who cannot examine them upon oath. They choose therefore that forum exclusive of the jurisdiction of the country to all intents and purposes ; meaning, that arbitrators shall from beginning to end do that, which they are enabled to do, viz. to decide between them as well as they can. It would be a breach of covenant, that would entitle them to nominal damages, to file a bill for discovery, as much as a bill for discovery and relief.

In *Halfhide* v. *Fenning* the whole of my argument according to

(1) *Ansty* v. *Dowsing*, 1 Dick. 95.
(2) See *Anth* v. *Sambourne*, 4 Bro. C. C. 498.
(3) See *Sutton* v. *The Earl of Scarborough*, *post*, vol. ix. 71, and, as to a Demurrer, the note, *ante*, vol. ii. 461.

the report amounts to taking the distinction between discovery and
relief, and putting the case upon that distinction; and if it was so
argued, I am not surprised, that Lord Kenyon should take it, that
the Counsel thought, if not upon that, it could not be supported.
But it is not to be put upon that distinction, but upon the ground I
have stated. It is said Courts of Law think these agreements very
wise. *Kill* v. *Hollister* however shows, that Courts of Law are
ready enough to say, the agreement of the parties shall not oust
their jurisdiction; though they permit it to oust the jurisdiction of
Courts of Equity. But they enforce the agreement, not as agreement, but by granting an attachment for breach of the rule. It is
dealing a little imperiously to say, that an agreement, which made
out of Court, would not bar an action, if made in Court, shall bar a
bill. It was justly observed upon the passage in Atkyns (1), that
arbitrators cannot administer an oath; and the agreement will not
enable them. We see in daily practice at Law, the Court administers the oath; and under that the parties go before the arbitrators.
It is said, the party must have discovery some way. But if the distinction cannot be maintained between a bill for discovery only and
for both discovery and relief, it must be said, they are bound to go
first before the arbitrators; and the party must be brought there;
and must refer: the parties to be examined upon honor;
[* 821]   for they cannot upon oath; and then it *is said, as in the
argument of these cases, if it so turns out, then they are
to come to this Court; saying, there is then a failure of the justice,
for which they covenanted; and therefore there is a jurisdiction in
this Court. Till *Halfhide* v. *Fenning* no such decree was ever
heard of.

Next, expressing it in terms of the highest respect and veneration
for that noble and learned person, now no more, I doubt, whether it
is a very wise exercise of the jurisdiction of this Court, recollecting,
that it is to give a relief beyond the law, not to order the parties to
go to law to take the effect of the stipulated remedy, but under a
positive covenant, not a negative covenant, that they will not sue,
(upon which there would be considerable difficulty) to send them by
way of experiment to that jurisdiction, so likely to miscarry, under
the circumstance, that it has not, unless received under the authority of the Court, a power to administer an oath, where the justice
that tribunal can render is so insufficient, though they have not expressly bound themselves by covenant; and, whether the Court
would not act more discreetly by saying, they are in a Court, where
justice can certainly be done; and as they have not stipulated to the
contrary, their fate shall be decided here, instead of sending them
to so improvident a tribunal. I recollect passages, in which Courts
of Justice, however full of eulogia upon these domestic forums, have
recollected their own dignity sufficiently to say, they would not be
ancillary to those forums; that the parties should not be permitted

---

(1) In *Wellington* v. *M'Intosh*, 2 Atk. 569.

to take their relief from them, coming here for discovery. It is
enough for me to say, it is not a necessary consequence of a covenant to refer, that the party thereby agreed to forbear to sue. I do
not enter into the question of the effect at law of a covenant to forbear to sue. But, supposing it good, in strict law it cannot be maintained, that having covenanted to refer the party has covenanted to
forbear to sue ; and if not, he has only left himself open to an action for damages, if he does not refer ; which the suit does not prevent, if thought advisable. It would be very strong to say, that,
where the legal remedy they have provided for themselves is utterly
incompetent to justice, this Court is precluded from granting its ordinary remedy, by a covenant, which does not in terms express an
undertaking not to resort to this Court: and must hold that doctrine
upon a plea ; in that shape permitting the Defendant to have in substance a specific performance, which would have been refused to him as a Plaintiff; at the hazard of * doing sub-   [* 822]
stantial injustice, of a delay of justice almost of necessity,
and, where the examination cannot be addressed to the conscience
of either the parties or the witnesses ; from which the subject cannot
be debarred unless by express terms, or necessary implication. That
this has not the effect of barring the legal remedy is clear from the
cases at law ; which agree, that it is still competent to him to take
the legal remedy (1). Then why not the equitable? The competency to take both stands upon the same principle.

But farther, those grounds are not necessary to the decision of this
cause. It is said to be natural and moral justice to give them this
benefit upon the plea. But what right has the Defendant to say that
upon this record ; which upon this argument must be taken to be
true? Then what right has he upon any principle of natural and
moral justice to call upon this Court to name arbitrators? Before
that he is bound to make a full and free disclosure as to what are the
matters in dispute. The bill states, that the Plaintiff has discovered,
that the Defendant received a sum of 105l. for a bill of costs, not
brought into the account. That was not a proper subject of dispute
before the arbitrator. When the Defendant has stated, whether he
has received that sum, in what manner, and under what circumstances, it may be proper matter of dispute, whether the Plaintiff is
entitled to any, and what part of it. But the fact, that this sum of
money is in these circumstances, leads to the allegation, that other
sums may have been received; and the Plaintiff may ask that question. He alleges, that the Defendant refused to answer that ; and
that no justice can be done, till it is answered. If there is nothing
to dispute about, plain dealing requires, they should not be driven to
go before arbitrators ; and that there should previously be a full discovery; and if these allegations are true, there is concealment,
which must disable the party from saying, he has a right under such
circumstances to go to arbitration under this covenant; and I have

(1) *Thompson* v. *Charnock*, 8 Term Rep. B. R. 139.

considerable doubt, to say no more of it, whether if they were before a Jury, and the party had refused to discover, it would not be very difficult to maintain an action; for he would not appear as having a right to an arbitration.

[* 823]   * Upon the special circumstances therefore this plea cannot be maintained; and it is not necessary to decide upon the general ground: but upon the point, whether that covenant, that would not prevent an action at law, would prevent a bill in equity upon such implication, no such thing being expressed in terms, I have an opinion; as to which I will not say more than that I do not think at present, this Court has upon such a covenant any right to say, the party has bound himself by any agreement not to resort to the equitable jurisdiction of the country.

The parties afterwards, when the cause came on to be heard, agreed to go to a general account.

1. That the jurisdiction of a Court is not ousted by an agreement of the parties to refer a question to arbitration; see, *ante,* the notes to *Mitchell* v. *Harris,* 2 V. 129.

2. In the principal case it was said, that the course of pleading was altered, and that, contrary to the earlier authorities, a plea, though good as to the relief, would be bad if the plaintiff were entitled to discovery; the wheel, however, has again turned, and the old rule of practice is re-established, at least with respect to those cases in which the discovery sought is incidental to the relief prayed; see the notes to *Renison* v. *Ashley,* 2 V. 459.

THOMAS *v.* LLEWELLYN.

[1802, MAY 1.]

THE time allowed for filing exceptions *nunc pro tunc* is two Terms and the following Vacation.

MR. HOLLIST for the Plaintiff moved to file exceptions *nunc pro tunc;* the answer having been filed in the Vacation after last Trinity Term.

Mr. *Hollist* said, some doubt had been entertained as to the time; but the practice was settled in the time of Lord Camden, that the party has two Terms, and the Vacation before the third (1).

The Order was made accordingly.

SEE the note to *Hewart* v. *Semple,* 5 V. 86.

(1) The first day of Easter Term was the 5th of May. *Dyer* v. *Dyer,* 1 Mer. 1. See the note, *ante,* vol. v. 87, to *Hewart* v. *Semple.*

HUTCHEON v. MANNINGTON.

[1802, May 1, 4.]

A NOTARY PUBLIC has credit everywhere (a); but the certificate of a Magistrate of a Colony abroad requires evidence to his character.

MR. LEACH moved, that a sum of 678l. 8s. 6d. Bank 3 per cent. Annuities, and 10l. 3s. 6d. cash, in the name of the Accountant General in trust in the cause, to the * account of   [* 824] Richard Mannington, may be transferred and paid under a power of attorney, executed in the Prince of Wales's Island in the East Indies, and attested by two witnesses.

The motion was made upon a certificate, signed and sealed by George Counter, Magistrate, and William Scott, Notary Public in that Island ; that the two subscribing witnesses to the power of attorney swore the affidavit produced ; that they were persons of credit ; and Scott was a Notary Public.

The affidavit was to the identity of Richard Mannington ; and stated, that the deponents witnessed the execution of the annexed Power of Attorney.

William Scott certified, as Notary Public, that the annexed writings were true copies.   Counter, it was suggested, was Governor of the Island.

The Lord CHANCELLOR [ELDON] thought the evidence not sufficient ; observing, that a Notary Public by the Law of Nations has credit every where : the Court therefore will give credit to him ; but that it was necessary to prove, that the other person was a Magistrate (1).

(a) A notary is described as a person who takes notes, or makes a short draught of contracts, obligations, or other writings and instruments. 27 Edw. III. st. 7, c. 7. At this time his chief duty is to attest deeds or writings, to make them authentic in another country ; but principally in business relating to merchants. Tomlins, Law Dict. art. Notary.   Notaries are of very ancient origin ; they were known among the Romans, and exist in every State of Europe, and particularly on the Continent.   Their acts have long been respected by the custom of merchants, and by the Courts of all nations. Bouvier, Law Dict, art. Notary ; 6 Toullier, Droit Civile, n. 211, note ; 2 Chitty, Pr. 36 ; Chitty, Bills of Exchange, Index, tit. Notaries ; Burn's Ecclesiast. Law, tit. Notaries.   In the play of Sir Giles Overreach, by Massinger, Sir Giles says :

        " ——————— I know thou art
        A public Notary, and *such stand in law
        For a dozen witnesses* ——————— "
                                        ACT V. Sc. 1.

The notarial protest of a bill of exchange receives credit in all Courts and places by the law and usage of merchants, without any auxiliary evidence. 3 Kent, Com. 93 ; Story, Bills, § 276.   It has been held that this protest is good without a seal, though it has been the practice to affix one. *Lambeth v. Caldwell*, 1 Robinson, Louis. 61.

(1) *Garvey v. Hibbert*, 1 Jac. & Walk. 180.   The authentication in that instance of the signature and seal of the Notary seems to have been unnecessary.

Upon inquiry at the India House it appeared from the proceedings of the Governor-General of Bengal, that George Counter was a Magistrate.

The Order was made.

[* 825]   * On the death of Lord KENYON in the vacation Sir EDWARD LAW, His Majesty's Attorney General, was called to the degree of Serjeant at Law ; and appointed Lord Chief Justice of the Court of King's Bench ; and was created a Peer of the United Kingdom by the title of Baron of ELLENBOROUGH in the County of Cumberland. His Lordship was sworn a Member of His Majesty's Most Honorable Privy Council (a).

The Honorable SPENCER PERCEVAL, His Majesty's Solicitor General, was appointed Attorney General to His Majesty.

THOMAS MANNERS SUTTON, Esq. Chief Justice of the North Wales Circuit, and Soliciter General to His Royal Highness the Prince of Wales, was appointed Solicitor General to His Majesty.

The Honorable THOMAS ERSKINE was appointed Chancellor to His Royal Highness the Prince of Wales.

. WILLIAM ADAM, Esq. one of His Majesty's Counsel, was appointed Solicitor General to His Royal Highness.

(a) For a sketch of Lord Ellenborough, see ante, note (a), 1 V. 24.

END OF THE SITTINGS BEFORE EASTER TERM.

TABLE OF CONTENTS.

BOSTON: L. H. BRIDGHAM, PRINTER.